A CATALOGUE OF THE FREDERICK R. KOCH COLLECTION

A CATALOGUE OF THE FREDERICK R. KOCH COLLECTION

AT THE BEINECKE LIBRARY
YALE UNIVERSITY

EDITED BY VINCENT GIROUD

IN COLLABORATION WITH

CHRISTA SAMMONS & KAREN SPICHER

NEW HAVEN

BEINECKE RARE BOOK & MANUSCRIPT LIBRARY

2006

Copyright © 2006 Yale University

Grateful acknowledgement is made to the following copyright holders:
Plate 20: By permission of the Association des Amis de Francis Poulenc (Benoît Seringe).
Plate 22: © 2006 Artists Rights Society (ARS), New York / ADAGP Paris.

LIBRARY OF CONGRESS CATALOGING-IN-PUBLICATION DATA

Beinecke Rare Book and Manuscript Library.
   A catalogue of the Frederick R. Koch collection at the Beinecke Library, Yale University / edited by Vincent Giroud in collaboration with Christa Sammons & Karen Spicher.
      p. cm.
   Includes bibliographical references (p.) and index.
   ISBN-13: 978-0-8457-3163-5 (alk. paper)
   ISBN-10: 0-8457-3163-7 (alk. paper)
  1. Koch, Frederick R. (Frederick Robinson) — Library — Catalogs.
  2. Music — Manuscripts — Connecticut — New Haven — Catalogs.
  I. Giroud, Vincent. II. Sammons, Christa. III. Spicher, Karen. IV. Title.

ML136.N48Y322 2006
016.78 — dc22

2006038843

Photographs by Robert Lisak: Plates 1–5, 7–9, 13, 14
Scanned by the Beinecke Library Digital Studio: Plates 6, 10–12, 15–22

CONTENTS

PREFACE *vii*

INTRODUCTION *ix*

PLATES *xi*

ABBREVIATIONS 2

CATALOGUE 3

WORKS CITED 345

INDEX 349

PREFACE

THE scholarly distinction of the collections in the Beinecke Rare Book and Manuscript Library of Yale University derives from generous philanthropy of collectors and donors that stretches over the centuries. The relationship to great collectors has been of special importance, for in addition to the material value of their gifts, they have donated the energy, time, expertise, and enthusiasm for the collecting enterprise that a library, even a great library, could not as an institution have summoned.

The Koch Collection constitutes a transforming gift. In one act of extraordinary generosity, the Frederick R. Koch Foundation made the Beinecke Library a major repository of modern musical manuscripts and related materials. The library has become a place to which scholars from around the world come to carry out research in music history and editing. Moreover, the gift has already enlivened and will continue to enrich the teaching of music, music history, and the life of modern musical culture within Yale University. Future courses and decades of scholarly work will be based on Koch Collection manuscripts by European composers of the nineteenth and twentieth centuries, a gathering that includes the score of Debussy's *Pelléas and Mélisande*, the finest group of Verdi letters outside Italy, a recently discovered manuscript of Offenbach's *Tales of Hoffmann*, and the vast musical archive of Sir William Walton. In addition to musical scores, the reader of this catalogue will encounter a significant array of literary and historical materials, including letters and manuscripts of Cocteau and Proust, letters of Henry James, and the archive of the Maugham family, to name but a few.

The collection as a whole reflects the extraordinary curiosity, imagination, and energy of Frederick R. Koch as a collector and as a connoisseur. Its catalogue stands as a monument to Mr. Koch's personal achievement and as a guide to future scholars, whose lives, work, writing, and teaching will benefit deeply from his generosity and erudition.

The catalogue also bears witness to the dedicated scholarship of Vincent Giroud, who for many years served the Beinecke Rare Book and Manuscript Library as curator of modern books and manuscripts, to the archival expertise of Karen Spicher, and to the editorial skills of Christa Sammons and James Mooney. Howard Gralla brought their work together in his masterful design.

FRANK M. TURNER
Director
Beinecke Rare Book &
Manuscript Library

INTRODUCTION

Some great collections are great because of their comprehensiveness. They are in-depth records of the production of one author or attempts to gather everything that has been published in a particular field: such are the Hyde-Eccles Samuel Johnson Collection at Harvard, or at Yale the J.M. Barrie collection of Walter Beinecke, Jr., or Betsy Beinecke Shirley's American children's literature collection, or Walter Pforzheimer's Molière collection. Other collections are great because of the extraordinary highlights they contain in a particular domain: thus (to limit ourselves to Yale) the Charles J. Rosenbloom's bequest, which included materials from the fifteenth century to modernism, or Chauncey Brewster Tinker's English literature collection. The Frederick R. Koch Collection has something in common with both types. It abounds in highlights: Brahms's *Alte Liebe*, Cocteau's *Mariés de la Tour Eiffel*, the short score of Debussy's *Pelléas et Mélisande*, the break-up letter sent by Dumas fils to the original "Dame aux camélias," Henry Miller's *Tropic of Cancer*, long-lost portions of the manuscript of Offenbach's *Tales of Hoffmann*, drafts for Proust's *A l'ombre des jeunes filles en fleurs*, sketches for Schubert's great *Fantasy in F minor*, the libretto of Verdi's *Ernani* in the composer's hand, and those for *Lohengrin* and *Siegfrieds Tod* (the Ur-*Götterdämmerung*) in Wagner's holograph; the list could go on and on. Yet describing the Koch Collection in terms of its highlights would not do it justice. Some of its subsets form large thematic units or indeed archives in the proper sense, acquired en bloc in the cases of William Walton (the near totality of his extant manuscripts) and Ermanno Wolf-Ferrari (half of his musical archive, the other half now in Munich), or assembled piecemeal, as those of Cocteau, Edward Lear, Massenet, Offenbach, and Proust, yet resulting for each in the finest assemblages on this side of the Atlantic.

As these examples make clear, the Frederick R. Koch Collection is gloriously eclectic. It features children's literature, German history, British and American caricature, music manuscripts, literary manuscripts, historical documents, and correspondences by artists, composers, critics, musicians, scholars, singers, and writers. In addition to manuscript material, it includes printed books, original drawings, photographs, and ephemera. It spans three and a half centuries, from the *liber amicorum* of a mid-seventeenth-century Nuremberg schoolteacher to James Merrill letters of the early 1980s. Among the countries represented are Austria, Belgium, Brazil, Britain, what is now the Czech Republic, Denmark, Finland, France, Germany, Hungary, Ireland, Italy, Mexico, Norway, Poland, Russia, Spain, and the United States. Areas of particular strength emerge from the variety: German Romantic and Post-Romantic music from Schubert to Richard Strauss, Italian opera from Verdi to Post-Verismo, French music from Berlioz to Poulenc, French literature from Hugo to Genet, British art, and British music. Should one search for a unifying factor, it can only be the collector's own taste, intellectual curiosity, and wide-ranging interests.

Accordingly, the present catalogue has not tried to impose on the collection an artificial classification, chronological or by genre, but seeks rather to emphasize and indeed celebrate the diversity of the collection in a single alphabetical list of its contents. Small items – at times single letters – will thus be found next to large ensembles.

Another remarkable aspect of the Frederick R. Koch Collection is that no collection of its size and caliber can ever have been assembled in so short a time. This will be apparent to any reader glancing at the provenance data listed, when available, at the end of each entry. While the dates span only a short eight years (1979–86), it will be clear that most items in the collection were in fact acquired, astonishingly, in an even briefer four years, between 1982 and 1985. Anyone who followed the auction scene at that time will recognize many of the treasures that became available in London, New York, and Paris: Ballets russes related items from the collection of Diaghilev's disciple Serge Lifar; the Halévy family papers offered at Drouot on 14 February 1985; nearly all the Leoncavallo scores that came up for sale in London on 17 November 1983; two of Verdi's most important correspondences, with Arrivabene and Piave, broken up and auctioned off over the course of several sales, and here substantially reassembled. This provenance history being in itself of more than purely anecdotal interest, we have included references to all published auction catalogues (especially Christie's, Sotheby's, Stargardt, and the various Drouot houses). We have not however attempted to trace provenance any farther, unless it was physically documented in the item described (bookplate, presentation inscription) or to identify a particularly illustrious former owner (Arturo Toscanini, Sacha Guitry).

A few explanations are necessary concerning the collection's history insofar as it has implications for this catalogue. The collection was originally deposited by its owner, the Frederick R. Koch Foundation, with the Pierpont Morgan Library, where it remained until its transfer to Yale in December 1996. Thus, the musical part of its contents will be found listed in J. Rigbie Turner's *Music manuscripts in the Pierpont Morgan Library: a catalogue* [New York: Morgan

Library], 1991. On 7 June 1990, a significant portion of the non-musical part of the collection was put up for sale in New York City, at a single Christie's auction, on the Foundation's behalf. Among the items that left the collection at that time were the manuscripts of Evelyn Waugh's *The vile bodies* and an exceptional series of letters by Frederick Rolfe, Baron Corvo to his publisher, John Lane. (For its part, the Beinecke acquired at that sale George Meredith's correspondence with Violet, Lady Milner.) Further items from the collection were offered at various Sotheby's sales in 1991 and 1992. Those that were bought in, both at the Christie's June 1990 auction and at these subsequent sales, were returned to the Foundation and were therefore included in the donation to Yale. Since these items are listed and described in widely available auction catalogues, these references are included in order to avoid any confusion.

A similar explanation is required concerning accession numbers, assigned by the Foundation's registrar to each unit at the time of acquisition and before deposit at the Morgan. These numbers reflect, more or less accurately, the order in which each item entered the collection. They were also used as provisional shelf marks, both at the Morgan and at the Beinecke. Now that the collection has been processed, they no longer serve this function for obvious reasons: while one number could be attached at times to an entire archive, itself comprising hundred of documents (thus the whole of Robin Maugham's papers were given the Foundation's number 191), at other times accession numbers would be assigned to a single Ravel or Verdi letter acquired individually. In the latter case, while it is essential that provenance information be retained for each item, researchers will be better served (and paging more efficient) if the material is regrouped and housed together in alphabetical order rather than dispersed in various boxes and folders. On the other hand, in the two decades during which the collection has been made available to scholars, first in New York, then in New Haven, the accession numbers have been cited in many publications and acquired, as it were, a life of their own. They have therefore been included in all cases at the end of the description, preceded by the acronym FRKF.

During those two decades, the collection has contributed in a major way to enriching scholarship on many of the artists, authors, and composers represented. In the case of manuscript material, we have tried to include references, especially to critical editions based on the material. Omissions, however, will be inevitable. In the few instances where we were aware of the material being exhibited, we have cited the exhibition catalogues. We also refer throughout to the catalogue of the exhibition *Heinrich Schütz to Henry Miller: Selections from the Frederick R. Koch Collection*, which was organized at the Beinecke Library in the spring of 2001, as part of Yale's tercentennial celebrations and to celebrate the presence of the Koch Collection at Yale.

The compiler of this catalogue has incurred a large debt of gratitude to the many people who have helped, in small or major ways, with its preparation in the course of more than four years and on two continents. Thanks must go in the first place to Frederick R. Koch himself for his constant encouragement and generous assistance with provenance information. The two Beinecke directors who served during that period, Barbara A. Shailor, now Yale's deputy provost for the arts, and Frank M. Turner, John Hay Whitney Professor of History, were equally generous and unwavering in their support at all stages of the project.

No words could adequately convey the gratitude due to Thierry and Pierrette Bodin for their inexhaustible kindness in answering queries about materials purchased in Paris and filling gaps in provenance records. Scholars and librarians who provided assistance on multiple occasions include Philippe Blay, Jean-Christophe Branger, Andrea Cawelti (Loeb Music Library, Harvard University), Damien Colas, Lisa Cox, Stuart Craggs, Fabrizio Della Seta, Alessandro di Profio, Nicolas Dufetel, Yves Gérard, Michele Girardi, Philip Gossett, Lorenza Guiot (Fondo Leoncavallo, Biblioteca cantonale di Locarno), Denis Herlin, Steven Huebner, Michael Kaye, Jean-Christophe Keck, Hervé Lacombe, David Lloyd-Jones, Richard McNutt, Jean-Michel Nectoux, Rita S. Patterson (Armstrong Browning Library), Robert Pounder, Michael Puri, Jeffrey Sammons, Dieter Schickling, J. Rigbie Turner (Morgan Library), Ransom Wilson, Richard Wilson, and Craig Wright. The list should no doubt be longer and any accidental omission would be deeply regretted.

At the Beinecke, Christa Sammons and Karen Spicher were not only of invaluable help as co-editors; they rectified many mistakes, the ones remaining being my sole responsibility. Precious assistance was also received from Ellen Doon; Diane Ducharme; Timothy G. Young, associate curator of modern books and manuscripts; and Stephen Parks, former curator of the James Marshall and Marie-Louise Osborn Collection, while Kate Lalli expertly managed the complex logistics needed to ensure the smooth circulation of proofs between a Beaujolais village and New Haven. Some of the illustrations are photographs made by Robert Lisak for the 2001 exhibition catalogue; others were scanned by the Beinecke Library digital studio. James Mooney displayed his usual flair and expertise as copy editor, while Howard Gralla, whose design of *Heinrich Schütz to Henry Miller* five years ago earned him praise and a prize, is no less entitled today to our gratitude and our admiration.

VINCENT GIROUD
October 2006

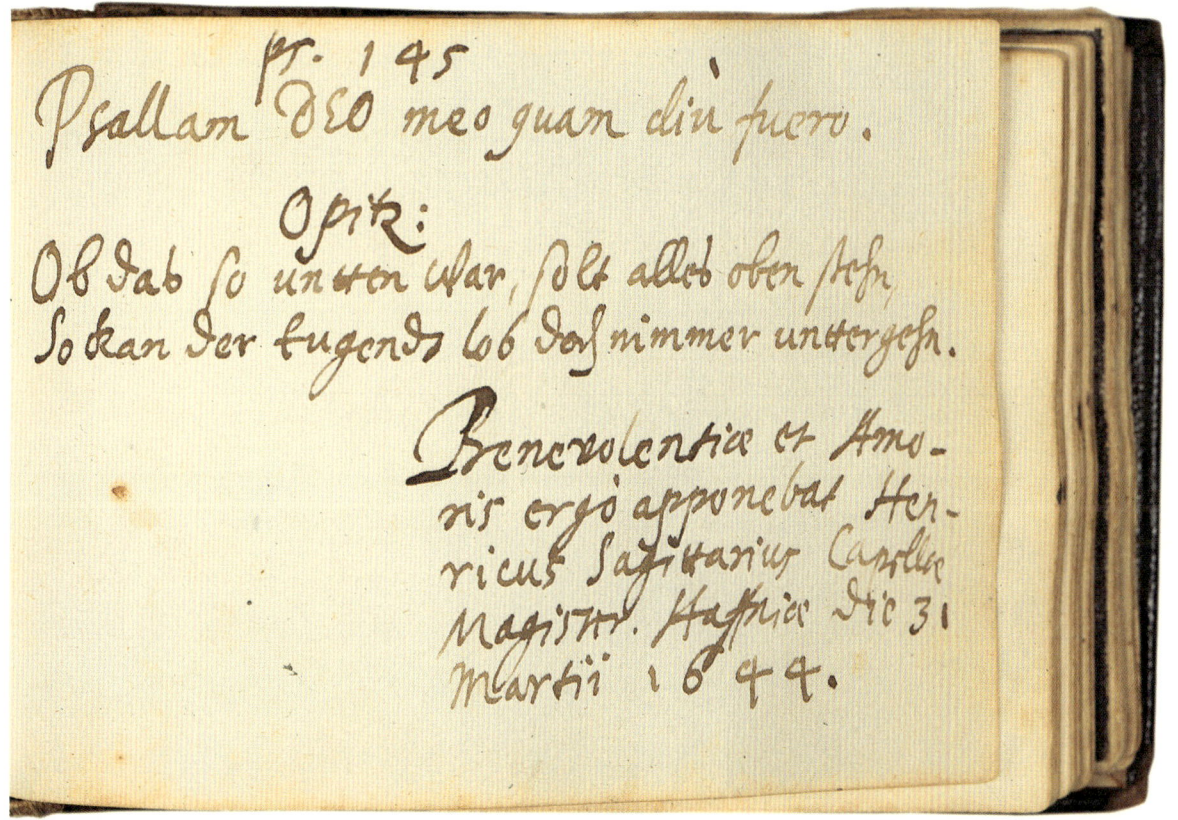

PLATE I   Heinrich Schütz, autograph inscription in the album amicorum of J. H. Augenstein, 1644. [Page 4]

PLATE 2 Handel, from the score of *Saeviat tellus inter rigores* in the hand of a copyist with the composer's annotations, 1707. [Page 93]

PLATE 3   Mozart, *Gavotte in B-flat major*, 1778. [Page 177]

PLATE 4   Schubert, from the *Fantasy in F minor for piano four-hands*, 1828. [Pages 274–75]

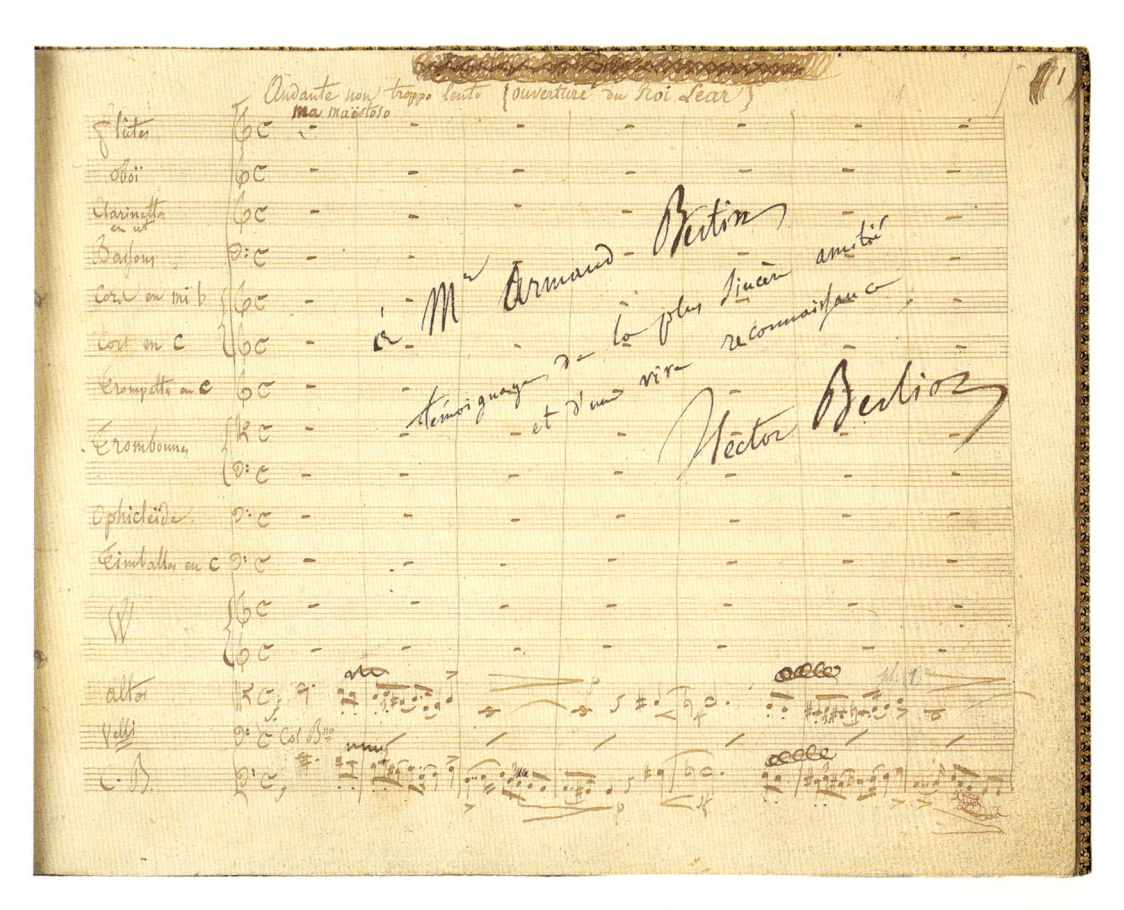

PLATE 5   Berlioz, from the full-score manuscript of *Grande ouverture du Roi Lear*, 1831. [Pages 12–13]

PLATE 6   Lear, "Man of New York," in a collection of limericks from the early 1840s. [Page 116]

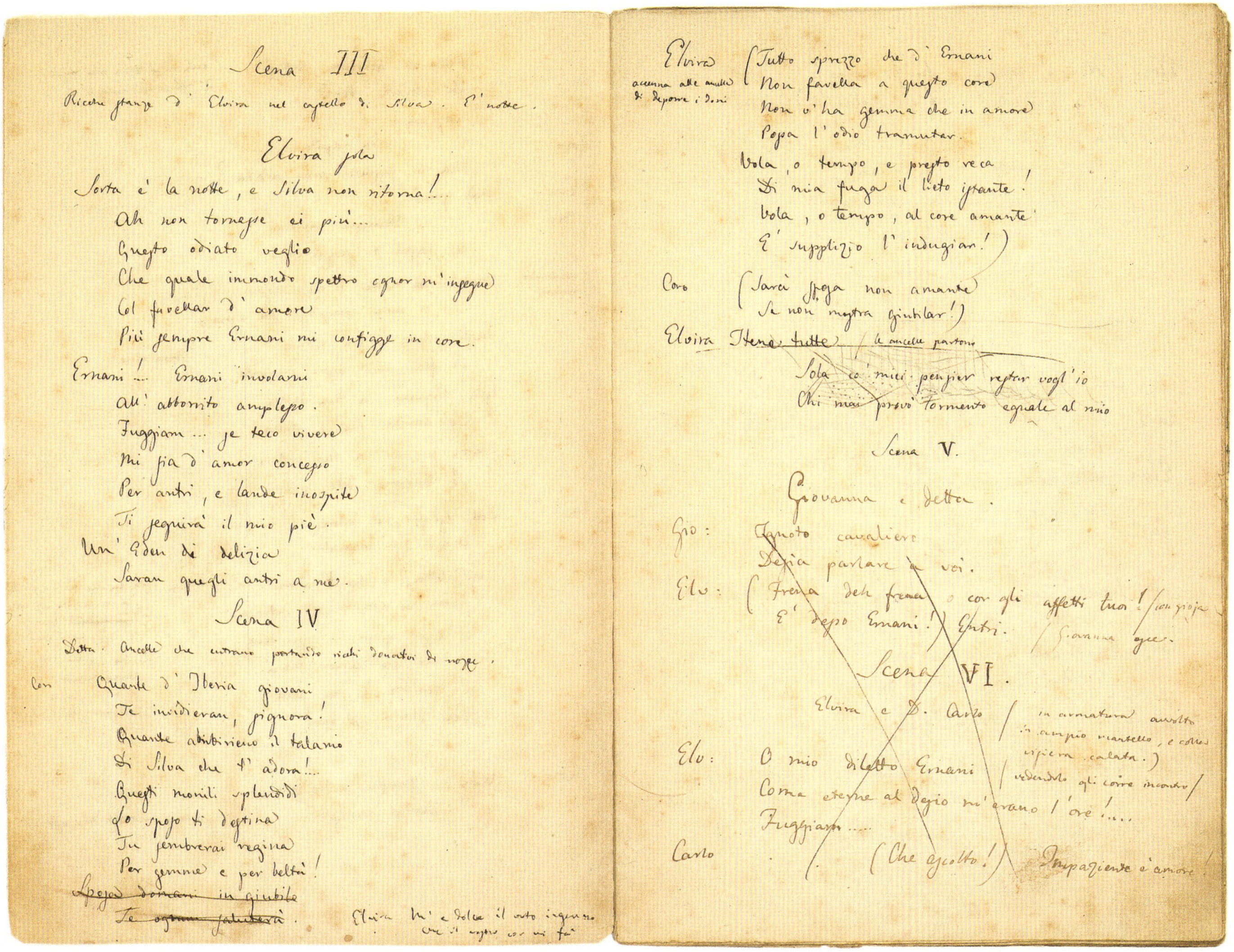

PLATE 7   Verdi, from Piave's libretto for *Ernani* in Verdi's hand, 1843. [Page 293]

PLATE 8   Mendelssohn, from the album of his 1829 tour of Scotland, 1847. [Page 167]

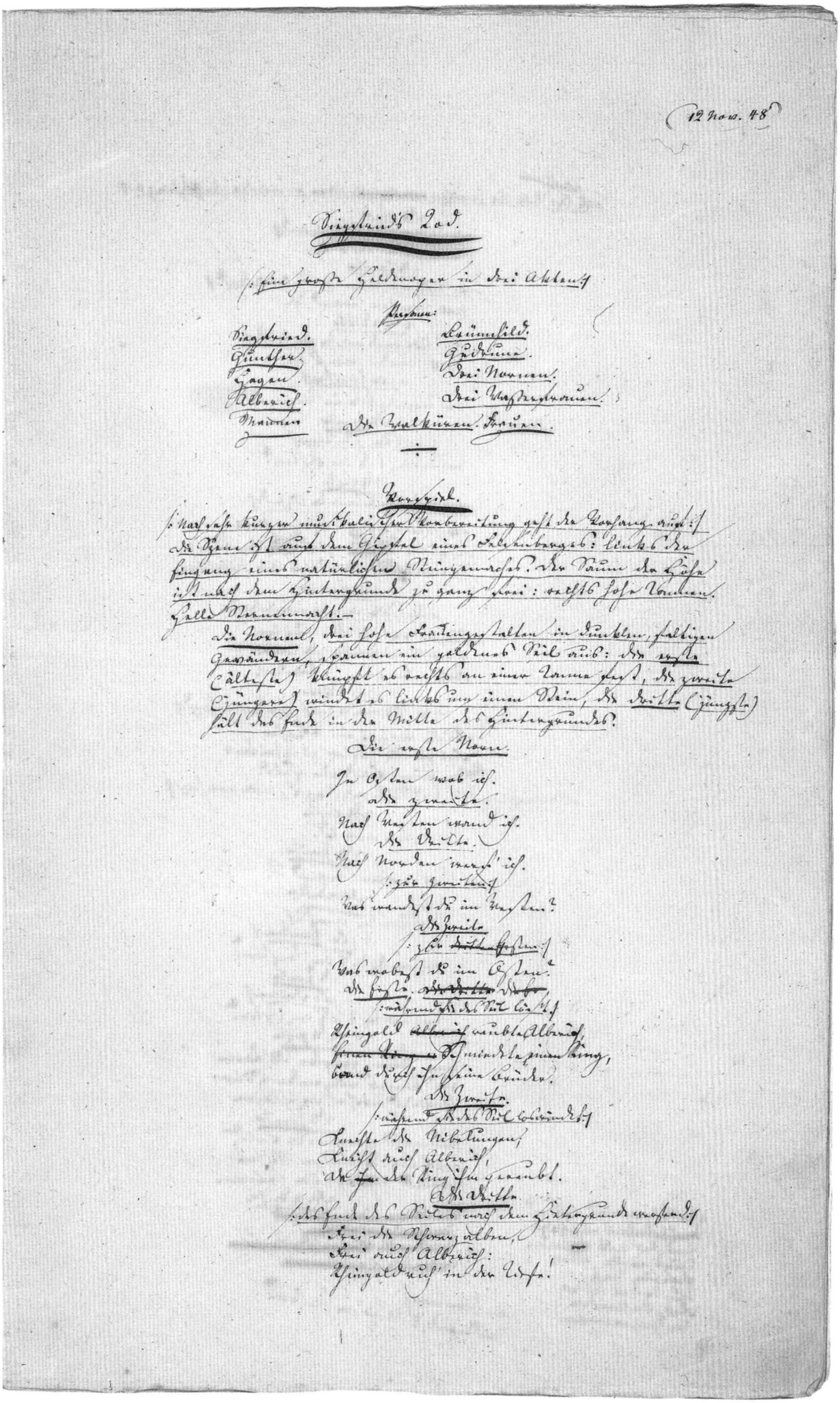

PLATE 9   Wagner, from the libretto of *Siegfrieds Tod*, the earliest version of *Götterdämmerung*, 1848.
[Page 306]

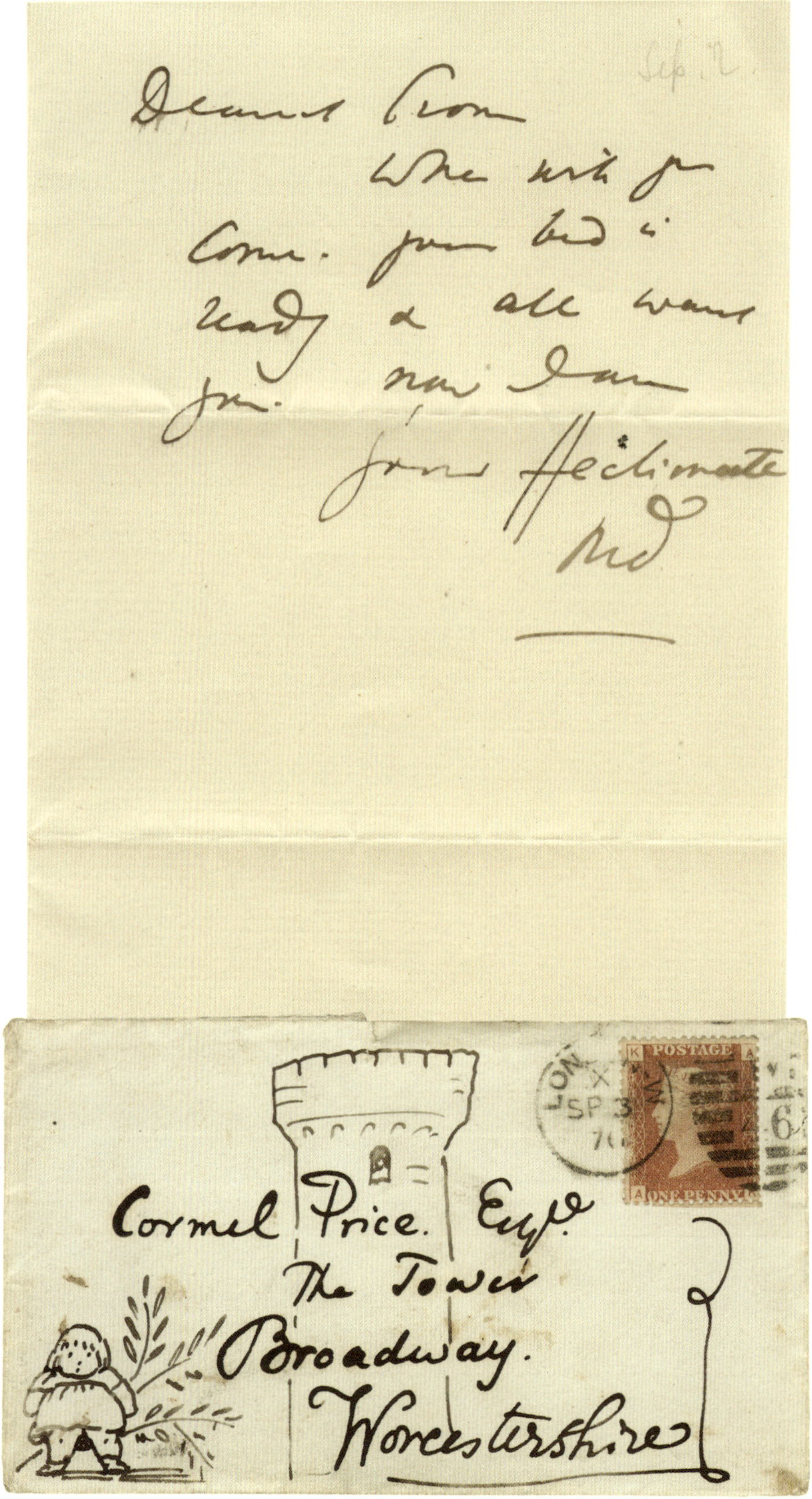
Dearest Crom
When wilt you
come. your bed is
ready & all wants
you. now I am
your affectionate
Ned

Cormel Price. Esqre
The Tower
Broadway.
Worcestershire

PLATE 10 Burne-Jones, letter to Cormell Price, postmarked 1870 Sept. 3. [Page 21]

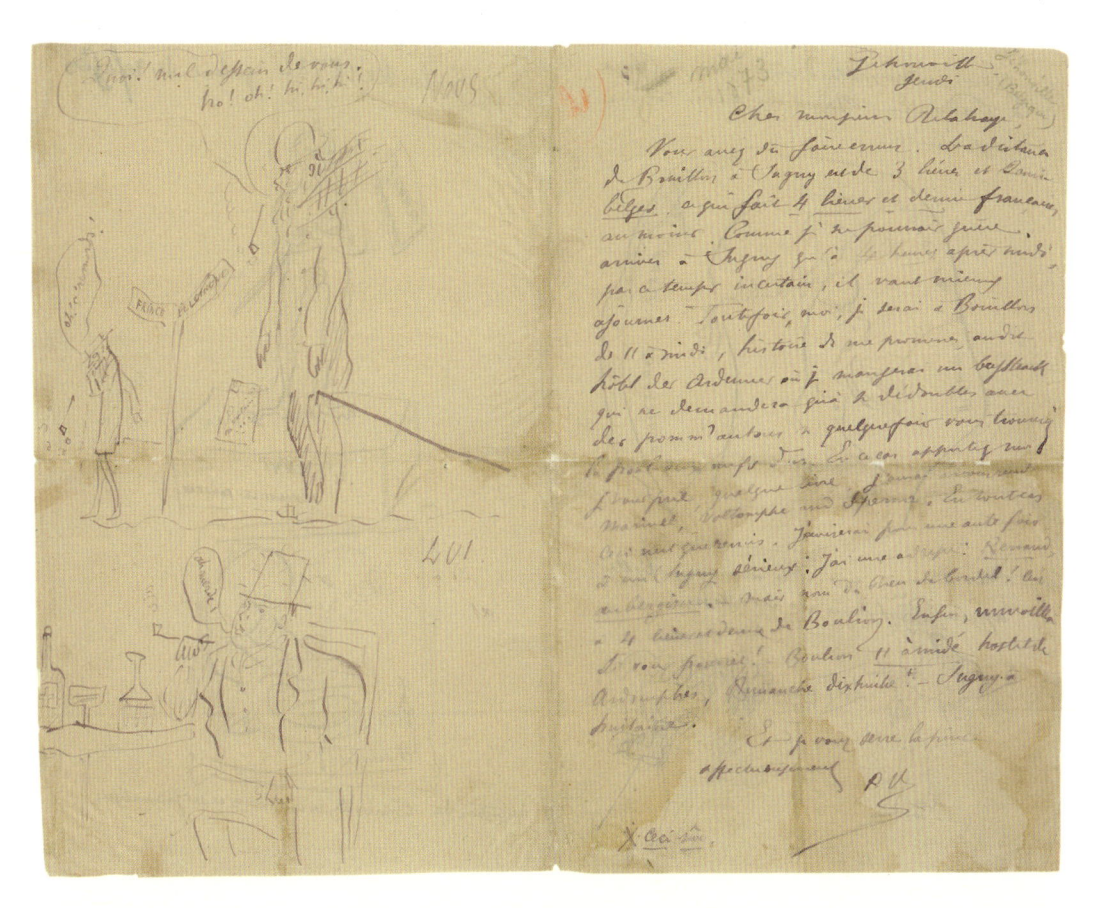

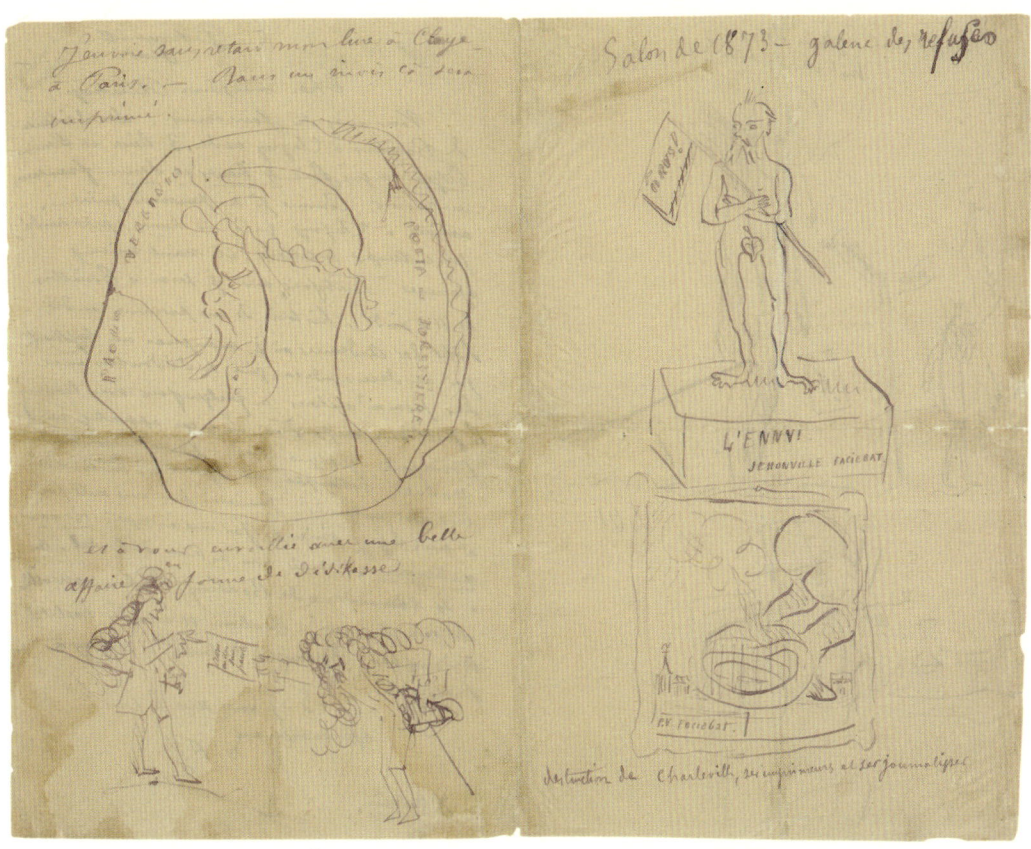

PLATE 11   Verlaine, illustrated letter to Ernest Delahaye, 1873 May 15. [Page 301]

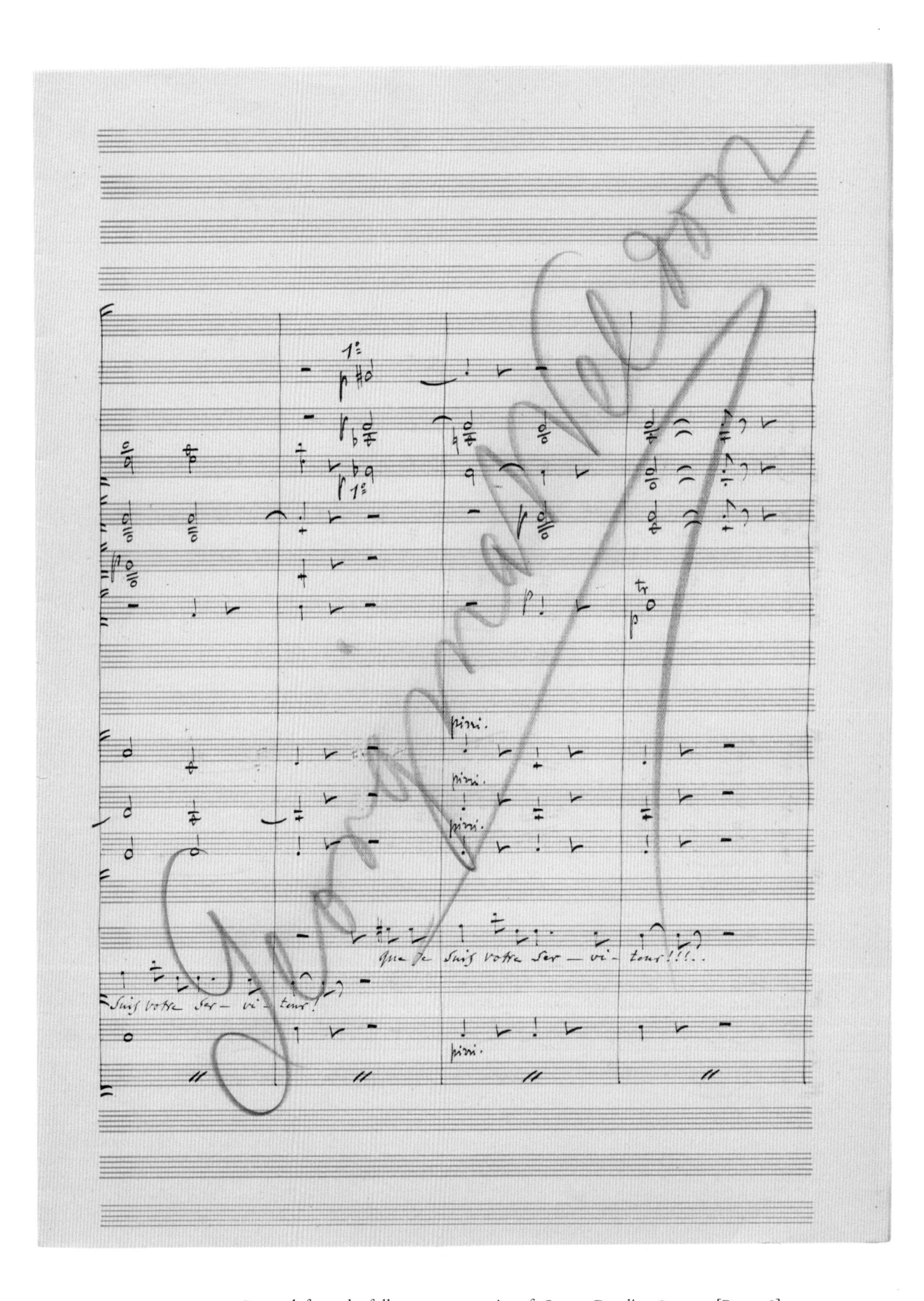

PLATE 12   Gounod, from the full-score manuscript of *George Dandin*, 1873–74. [Page 78]

PLATE 13   Offenbach, from the score of *Les contes d'Hoffmann*, ca. 1879–80. [Pages 185–88]

PLATE 14 Debussy, from the short-score manuscript of *Pelléas et Mélisande*, 1893–1901. [Pages 55–56]

PLATE 15   Mascagni in 1890. [Page 145]

Hotel National und Restaurant Rosmanith
am Bahnhof Friedrichstrasse.
Telephon: Amt I, 7156. Telegramm-Adresse: Nationalhotel Berlin.

BERLIN N.W.
Friedrichstr. 97.

den

Cher ami,

Je regrette beaucoup, mais aujourd'hui j'ai une invitation d'un ami que j'ai vu hier soir au Théâtre.
Comme je reste quelques jours ici si vous voulez bien vous arranger pour un autre jour. Présentez en attendant mes hommages à Madame Fürstner et agréez les meilleures amitiés de votre dévoué

R. Leoncavallo

20 juin 1897.

PLATE 16   Leoncavallo, letter to Adolph Fürstner, 1897 June 20. [Page 129]

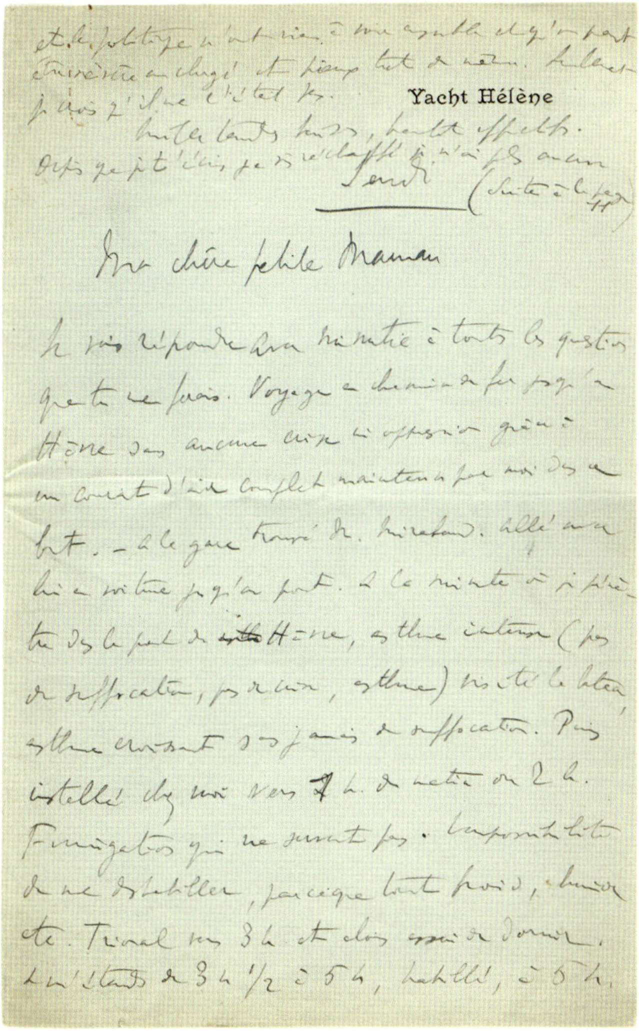

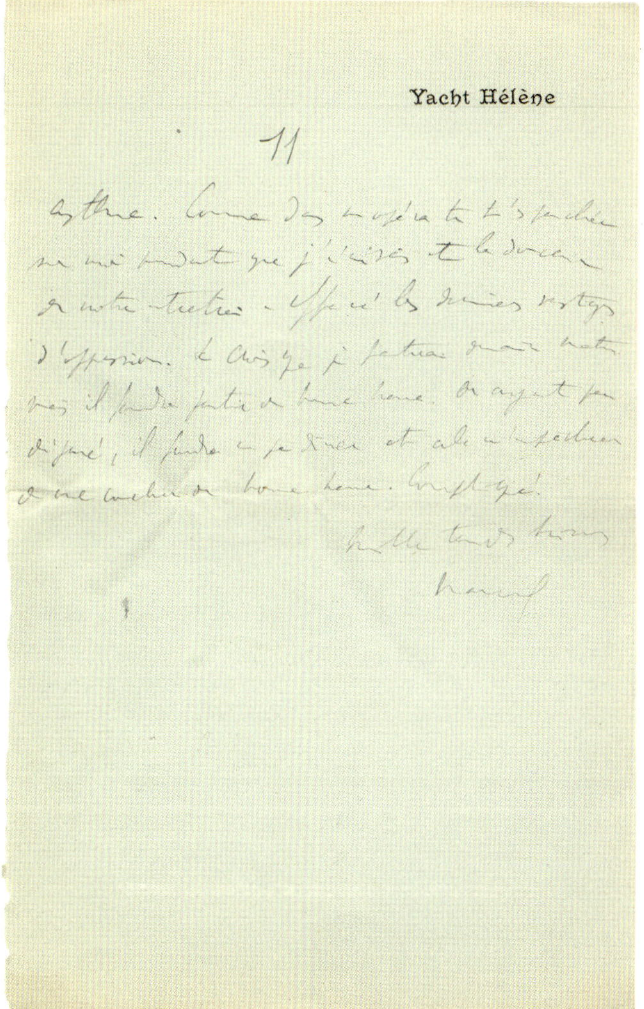

PLATE 17   Proust, from a letter to his mother, 1904 August 11. [Page 223]

PLATE 18   Massenet, from the orchestral score of *Roma*, 1909–10. [Page 148]

PLATE 19   Saint-Saëns, undated calligraphic note to Émile Renaud, before 1912. [Page 268]

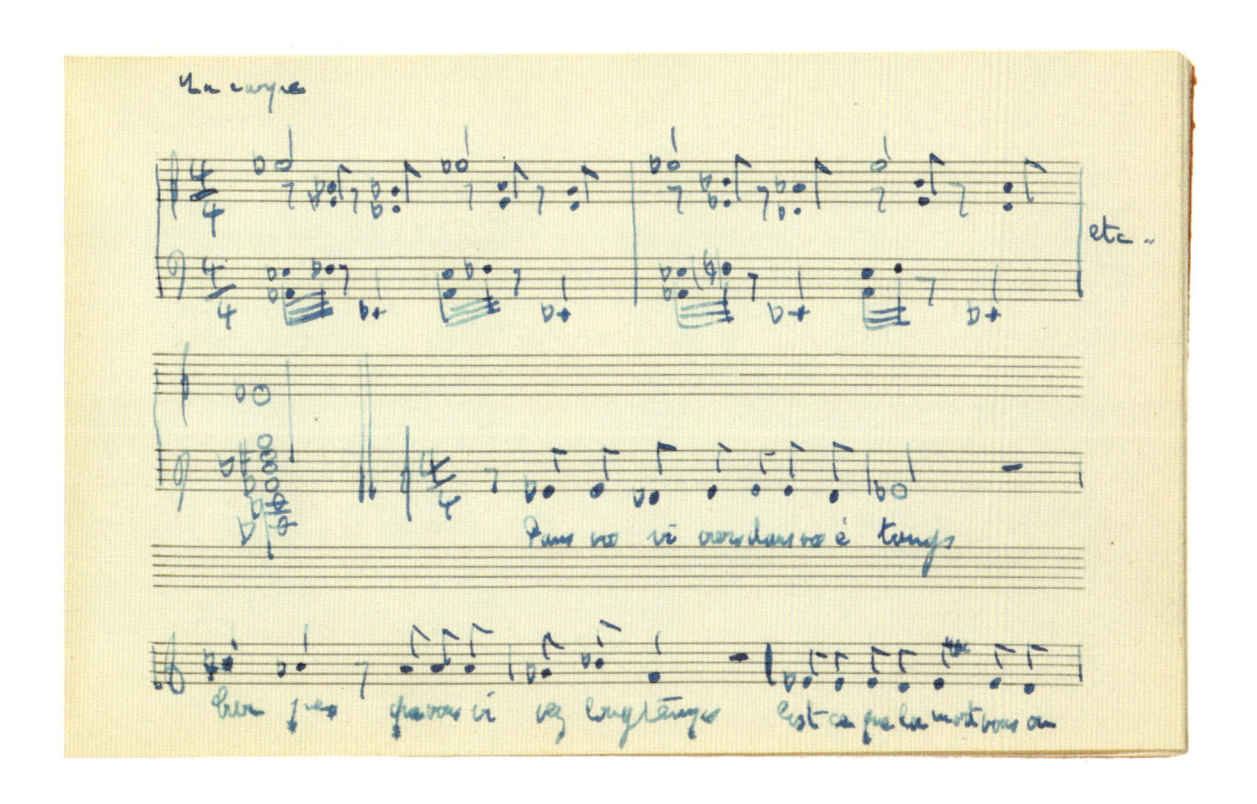

PLATE 20   Poulenc, undated musical quotation from *Le Bestiaire* ("La carpe"), in the album amicorum of Valentine Hugo. [Page 96]

PLATE 21   Puccini, postcard to Angelo Magrini, 1921 Feb. 24. [Page 233]

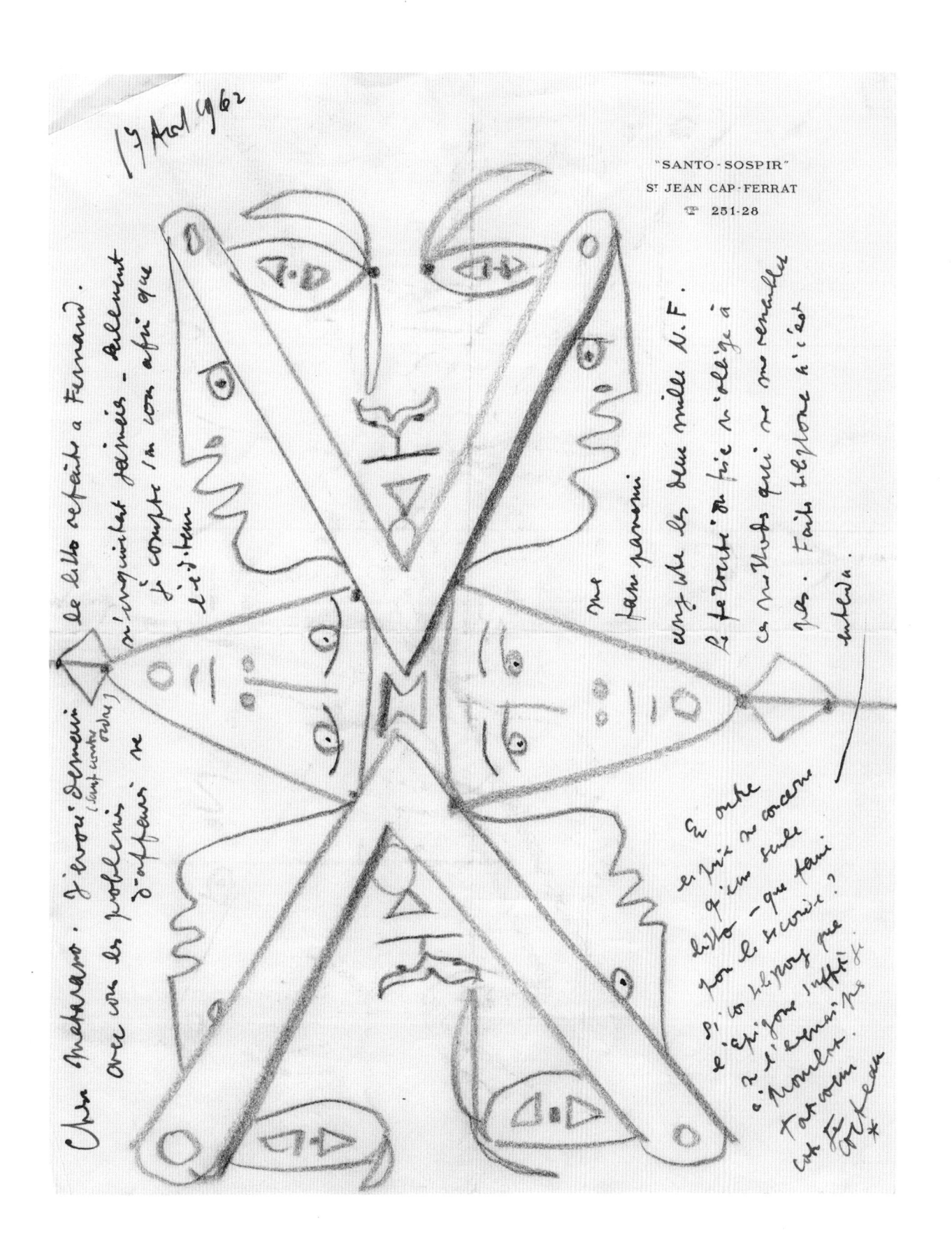

PLATE 22   Cocteau, illustrated letter to Henri Matarasso, 1962 August 17. [Page 39]

A CATALOGUE OF THE FREDERICK R. KOCH COLLECTION

ABBREVIATIONS

ALS   autograph letter, signed
ANS   autograph note, signed
APCS   autograph postcard, signed
env   accompanied by envelope
FRKF   Frederick R. Koch Foundation accession number
n.d.   undated
n.p.   no place
n.y.   without year
[s]   preceding indication taken from stationery
TLS   typed letter, signed
*   date and/or place taken from postmark

Measurements are given as width followed by height.

EUGEN D'ALBERT (1864–1932)

Letter to Julius Hertzka of Universal Editions

1927 Dec. 1, Berlin, ALS, 2 p., concerning *Die schwarze Orchidee*.

Marburg, Stargardt, 5–6 March 1985, lot 753.
FRKF 807

Letter to List und Francke

1890 Oct. 31, Berlin, ALS, 2 p., concerning an auction and accompanied by two lists of books in D'Albert's hand, marked up in ink and blue pencil.

Together with a photograph of D'Albert, signed by him, and identified on the back as having been taken in Lucerne in 1919, 9.5 × 13 cm.

Hamburg, Hauswedell und Nolte, 22 May 1984, lot 1580.
FRKF 316

RICHARD ALDINGTON (1892–1962)

Balls. Westport, Connecticut: privately printed, 1932.

1–10 [+ 4] p. One of an edition of 99 copies; printed by The Georgian Press in April 1932 according to the colophon and advertisement.

Kershaw 45.
New York, Swann Galleries, 11 Dec. 1986, lot 153.
FRKF 1261

W. H. AUDEN (1907–73)

Letters to Anne Bristow

Unless otherwise noted, all are autograph letters, signed, with envelopes, written from Larchfield Academy, Helensburgh, Dumbartonshire, where Auden taught from September 1930 until July 1932. See Humphrey Carpenter, *W. H. Auden: a biography* (Boston: Houghton Mifflin Company, 1981), p. 111–37. There is no mention of Anne Bristow in Carpenter or in Edward Mendelson, *Early Auden* (New York: The Viking Press, 1981).

1930
September: 5 (2 p., with a pencilled note to Anne Bristow, in a childish hand, on the verso of the envelope); [23*] (2 p.)
October: [14*] ("Thursday," 3 p. On p. [2] three 4-line stanzas from a "poem on Helensburgh"); 23 (2 p.)
November: [27*] (ANS, n.p., 1 p.)

1931
January: [12*] ("Monday," 2 p.); [16*] ("Friday," 2 p., discusses homosexuality)
February: [3*] ("Tuesday," 2 p., in pencil, mentions Christopher Isherwood's *The memorial*); [19*] (1 p.)
March: 9 (1 p., no envelope); [9*] ("Monday," 2 p.); [14*] ("Thursday," 1 p.); 20 (1 p.)
November: 6 (2 p., no envelope)

1932
January: 29 (dated 1931, 29 Jan. 1932* 2 p.)
June: 20 (1 p.)

Accompanied by a black-and-white photographic portrait of Auden as an adolescent (9 × 12 cm), inscribed along the right side: "The cerebral life would pay," and a sepia photographic portrait of Auden in profile (8.5 × 11.5 cm), inscribed on the photograph: "Utopian youth grown Old Italian / With love / from / Wystan."

London, Sotheby's, 23–24 July 1987, lot 128.
FRKF 1402

EDMOND AUDRAN (1842–1901)

Letter to Émile de Najac

1886 Jan. 1, Paris, ALS, 2 p., a dinner invitation; mentions Gustave Roger.

No work in collaboration between Audran and Émile de Najac (co-librettist of Emmanuel Chabrier's *Le roi malgré lui*) is listed in Grove or Grove Opera.

Paris, Laurin-Guilloux-Buffetaud-Tailleur (Drouot), 19 March 1986, lot 189.
FRKF 1124.5

JOHANN HULDREICH AUGENSTEIN

Album amicorum, ca. 1640–44

Oblong album (14 × 9.5 cm), 246 ff., comprising 24 gatherings of 5 or 6 bifolia of laid paper, unfoliated. Some pages were excised, while others are mounted on stubs. Most pages are blank, while ca. 80 contain inscriptions, generally in Latin, though some are in French, German, Greek, and Hebrew. A few include pen-and-ink or watercolor illustrations of religious or secular character, such as coats of arms, and there is one small pasted-on woodcut. Some notes at the bottom of the inscribed pages are evidently in Augenstein's hand.

On the verso of the first page, illustrated frontispiece in black ink, inscribed: "Iohan Huldericus Augenstein / Zeapoli Svevus. A⁰ 1644." Among the inscriptions are some from the poet Sigmund von Birken (1626–81), the theologians Jesper Rasmussen Brochmand, bishop of Zeeland (1585–1652), and Benedikt Carpzov (1595–1666) [this attribution is disputed in an unidentified note in pencil at the bottom of the page], the poet Johann Ludwig Faber, the satirist Johann Lauremberg (1590–1658), Magnus Daniel Omeis, the preacher Johann Reinboth, the composer Heinrich Schütz (1585–1672), and the theologians Johann Saubert (1592–1646) and Johannes Vogel (1589–1663).

The inscription by Schütz is a quotation from Psalms 146:2 ("Psallam Deo meo quandiu fuero") and two lines by Martin Opitz: "Ob das so untten war, solt alles oben stehn, / So kan der tugendt lob doch nimmer unttergehn." It is signed "Benevolentiae et amoris ergo apponebat Henricus Sagittarius Capellae Magister" and dated Copenhagen, 31 March 1644.

In contemporary dark brown morocco. On both boards, decorative monogram representing two wreaths, intertwined, with double gilt fillet along the edges. On the front board, gold-tooled above the monogram: I [erroneously blind-tooled as a B] H A Z, standing for "Iohannes Huldericus Augenstein [from] Zeapolis," and the date 1640. All edges gilt.

Augenstein, originally from Dinkelsbühl, Bavaria (Zeapolis), taught at the school of St. Sebald in Nuremberg.

Heinrich Schütz to Henry Miller, p. 14–15.
Marburg, Stargardt, 26 Nov. 1985, lot 915.
FRKF 1145

GEORGES AURIC (1899–1983)

Letters to Jean and Valentine Hugo

The letters mention *Les fâcheux*, *Paul et Virginie* (a collaboration planned between Raymond Radiguet and Erik Satie), as well as Milhaud's *Les euménides*, Radiguet, Proust, Paul Morand, and Satie. All are autograph and signed, all with envelopes except the last.

[1920 Oct.*] "Samedi 16," Paris, 2 p.

[1920] Dec. 19, [Paris*] 2 p., with a 4-measure musical quotation as postscript.

[1921]* Aug. 15, 4 p.

[1921 Nov. 21*] "Lundi," 36 bis rue Lamarck [Paris], 1 p.

FRKF 494

WILHELM BACKHAUS (1884–1969)

Photograph of the young Backhaus at the piano, taken in London in 1901 according to a note on the verso, 12 × 10 cm.

New York, Sotheby's, 22 May 1985, lot 431.
FRKF 744a

WILLIAM MICHAEL BALFE (1808–70)

Satanella

Holograph short-score manuscript, 1858, in black ink on unpaginated bifolia or single leaves of tall 14-, 20-, and 24-staff paper, usually on both sides. The pages are stitched in two gatherings, one of 15 leaves, the second of 23. Folio [11] of the first gathering is a sheet of oblong 18-staff paper with additional sketches for the passage entitled "Vision" on both sides. The manuscript is abundantly corrected and revised, with several passages present in at least two versions. The words are usually written out. There are also many indications of orchestration. The manuscript does not include the overture.

> On p. [1], perpendicular to the music, along the right edge of the page, dedication: "The final sketches of *Satanella* which I give to the darling child whom I adore - Feb. 1859." To the left of the inscription is another: "A mon petit Michel / de sa mère / 20 Dec /75 Fl. Culverwell."
>
> Centered at the top of p. [1], in Balfe's hand, "New Opera," and the date "August 24th 1858" in the upper left corner. At the top of folio [4] of the first gathering, the date "Sunday August 22 1858" is written in pencil, also in Balfe's hand. At the bottom of the final pages, following the words "So Hymen love crown," Balfe has written "with sometimes lightning thunder &c."

Satanella, or The power of love, romantic opera in four acts, libretto by Augustus Harris and Edmond Falconer after Alain-René Lesage's *Le diable boiteux*, was premiered at Covent Garden, London, on 20 Dec. 1858.

See William Alexander Barrett, *Balfe: his life and works* (London: William Reeves [1890?]), p. 230–32.
London, Sotheby's, 17 Nov. 1983, lot 80.
FRKF 227

SIR GRANVILLE BANTOCK (1868–1946)

I. MUSIC MANUSCRIPTS

Adrift

Holograph manuscript of this song for voice and piano, 1918, 6 p. Notated in dark blue ink, with markings in black, red, and blue pencil, on p. 1–6 of two nested bifolia of tall 18-staff paper (B. & H. Nr. 11 C / 7. 09).

> At the top of p. 1, in Bantock's hand: "Adrift. / from the Chinese Poet. Li Po. AD 702–762 / Rendered into English by / L. Cranmer-Byng. / Music by / Granville Bantock." Initialed and dated Abbots Norton, 12 Sept. 1918 at the end.
>
> Copyright statement (Copyright MCMXIX by Elkin & Co. Ltd.) and music publisher's number (E. & Co. 998) added in manuscript at the bottom of p. 1 in an unidentified hand.

Babyland

Holograph manuscript of this song for voice and piano, 1922, 4 p. Notated in black ink, with pencil markings, on p. 1–4 of a bifolium of tall 18-staff paper.

> At the top of p. 1, in Bantock's hand: "'Babyland' / [crossed out in blue pencil: Unison Song for Children] / Words by Graham Robertson. Music by Granville Bantock." Initialed and dated Birmingham, 11 Dec. 1922 at the end. Marked "very urgent" in pencil at the top of the first page.
>
> Copyright statement (Copyright MCMXXIII by Elkin & Co. Ltd.) and music publisher's number (E. & Co. 1352) added in manuscript at the bottom of p. 1 in an unidentified hand.

Boat song of the isles

Holograph manuscript of this song for voice and piano, 1928, 7 p. Notated in black ink, with corrections in black and red pencil, on two separate bifolia of tall 20-staff paper.

> On the front of the first bifolium, in Bantock's hand: "Boat Song of the Isles / Lyric by Sir Harold Boulton / Music by / Granville Bantock." Pencilled annotations for the engraver at the top of the title page. Initialed and dated at end Metchley Lodge, 7 Dec. 1928.

Dream merchandise

Holograph manuscript of this song for voice and piano, 1922, 7 p. Notated in black ink, with markings in black and blue pencil, on two nested bifolia of tall 18-staff paper.

> On the front of the first bifolium, in Bantock's hand: "'Dream Merchandise' / [crossed out in blue pencil: Unison Song for Children] / Words by Graham Robertson. Music by Granville

Bantock." Initialed and dated Birmingham, 7 Dec. 1922 at the end.

Copyright statement (Copyright MCMXXIII by Elkin & Co. Ltd.) and music publisher's number (E. & Co. 1350) added in manuscript at the bottom of p. 1 in an unidentified hand. Marked "Very urgent" in pencil at the top of p. 1.

The emperor

Holograph manuscript of this song for voice and piano, n.d. [1920?], 7 p. Notated in dark blue ink, with pencil corrections, on p. 1–7 of two nested bifolia of tall 18-staff paper (B. & H. Nr. 11 C / 7. 09).

At the top of p. 1, in Bantock's hand: "The Emperor / Text by Edward Powys Mathers / Music by Granville Bantock." Stamped 7 May 1920 at the top of p. 1.

Copyright statement (Copyright MCMXX by Elkin & Co. Ltd.) and music publisher's number (E. & Co. 1149) added in manuscript at the bottom of p. 1 in an unidentified hand.

The garden of bamboos

Three holograph manuscripts of this song for voice and piano, 1920.

Manuscript 1:

Notated in black ink, with pencil corrections, on p. 1–3 of a bifolium of tall 18-staff paper (B. & H. Nr. 11 C / 7. 09).

At the top of p. 1, in Bantock's hand: "'The Garden of Bamboos' / Text by Edward Powys Mathers / Music by Granville Bantock." Initialed and dated Birmingham, 17 Feb. 1920 at the end. Stamped 8 May 1920 at the top of p. 1; also, marked 29441 in pencil.

Copyright statement (Copyright MCMXX by Elkin & Co. Ltd.) and music publisher's number (E. & Co. 1151) added in manuscript at the bottom of p. 1 in an unidentified hand.

Manuscript 2:

Notated in black ink, with pencil corrections, on p. 1–3 of a bifolium of tall 18-staff paper (B. & H. Nr. 11 C / 7. 09).

At the top of p. 1, in Bantock's hand: "'The Garden of Bamboos' / Text by Edward Powys Mathers / Music by Granville Bantock." Initialed and dated Birmingham, 17 Feb. 1920 at the end. Stamped May 1920 at the top of p. 1.

Copyright statement (Copyright MCMXX by Elkin & Co. Ltd.) and music publisher's number (E. & Co. 1152) added in manuscript at the bottom of p. 1 in an unidentified hand.

Manuscript 3:

Notated in dark blue ink, with pencil corrections, on p. 1–3 of a bifolium of tall 18-staff paper.

At the top of p. 1, in Bantock's hand: "'The Garden of Bamboos' / Text by Edward Powys Mathers / Music by Granville Bantock." Stamped 20 July 1920 at the top of p. 1; also, marked 29441 in black ink. Note in red ink at the top, not in Bantock's hand: "Please add to Est: 754 & engrave as soon as possible. / E. & Co."

Copyright statement (Copyright MCMXX by Elkin & Co. Ltd.) and music publisher's number (E. & Co. 1151) added in manuscript at the bottom of p. 1 in an unidentified hand.

The golden nenuphar

Holograph manuscript of this song for voice and piano, 1918, 6 p. Notated in dark blue ink, with pencil corrections, on p. 1–6 of two nested bifolia of tall 18-staff paper (B. & H. Nr. 11 C / 7. 09).

At the top of p. 1, in Bantock's hand: "The Golden Nenuphar / from the Chinese Poet. Han Yu. A.D. 768–824. / Rendered into English by / L. Cranmer-Byng. / Music by / Granville Bantock." Initialed and dated at end Abbots Norton, 13 Sept. 1918.

Copyright statement (Copyright MCMXX by Elkin & Co. Ltd.) and music publisher's number (E. & Co. 1098) added in manuscript at the bottom of a page in an unidentified hand.

Heinrich Schütz to Henry Miller, p. 116–17.

The isles of the sea

Holograph manuscript of this song for voice and piano, 1928, 7 p. Notated in black ink, with corrections in black and red pencil, on two nested bifolia of tall 20-staff paper.

On the front of the outer bifolium, in Bantock's hand: "The Isles of the Sea / Lyric by Sir Harold Boulton / Music by / Granville Bantock." Initialed and dated Metchley Lodge, 17 Dec. 1928 at the end. Pencilled indications for the printer at the top of the title page.

Land of promise

Holograph manuscript of this song for voice and piano, 1930, 4 p. Notated in dark blue ink, with corrections and markings in pencil, on two nested bifolia of tall 20-staff paper.

On the front of the first bifolium, in Bantock's hand: "'Land of Promise' / Poem by Harold Boulton / Music by / Granville Bantock." Tipped-in revision of two bars of the accompaniment at the top of p. 2. Initialed and dated Metchley Lodge, 14 Feb. 1930 at the end. Marked "urgent" in pencil on the title page.

Copyright statement (Copyright MCMXXX by Elkin & Co. Ltd) and music publisher's number (E. & Co. 1761) added in manuscript at the bottom of page 1 in an unidentified hand.

Longing

Holograph manuscript of this song for voice and piano, 1929, 4 p. Notated in dark blue ink, with pencil corrections, on a bifolium of tall 18-staff paper.

At the top of p. 1, in Bantock's hand: "Longing / [cancelled: Text] Words by / Fiona Macleod / (William Sharp) / Music by / Granville Bantock." Initialed and dated Metchley Lodge, 25 April 1929 at the end.

Accompanied by a typescript of the text, 1 p., with manuscript annotations, possibly by Bantock, adding "William Sharp" in parentheses to the name of the author and the mention: "Reprinted by permission of Mrs. William Sharp."

Copyright statement (Copyright MCMXXIX by Elkin & Co. Ltd.) and music publisher's number (E. & Co. 1739) added in manuscript at the bottom of p. 1 in an unidentified hand.

Lullabye

Holograph manuscript of this song for voice and piano, n.d. [1922], 6 p. Notated in dark blue ink, with pencil corrections, on p. 1–6 of two nested bifolia of tall 18-staff paper.

At the top of p. 1, in Bantock's hand: "To an Aegipan ... / '[A cancelled] Lullabye' / [Cancelled in blue pencil: Unison Song for Children] / Words by Graham Robertson. Music by Granville Bantock." Initialed and dated at the end Birmingham, 10 Dec. 1922. Marked "very urgent" and "33371" in pencil at the top of p. 1.

Copyright statement (Copyright MCMXXIII by Elkin & Co. Ltd.) and music publisher's number (E. & Co. 1354) added in manuscript at the bottom of p. 1 in an unidentified hand.

The peach flower

Holograph manuscript of this song for voice and piano, 1920, 5 p. Notated in black ink, with markings in pencil, on p. 1–5 of two nested bifolia of tall 18-staff paper (B. & H. Nr. 11 C / 7. 09).

At the top of p. 1, in Bantock's hand: "The Peach Flower / Text by Edward Powys Mathers / Music by Granville Bantock." Initialed and dated Birmingham, 17 March 1920 at the end. Stamped 7 May 1920 and marked "29443" in pencil at the top of p. 1.

Copyright statement (Copyright MCMXX by Elkin & Co. Ltd.) and music publisher's number (E. & Co. 1155) added in manuscript at the bottom of p. 1 in an unidentified hand.

The red lotus

Holograph manuscript of this song for voice and piano, 1920, 6 p. Notated in black ink, with markings and corrections in black and red pencil and red ink, on p. 1–6 of two nested bifolia of tall 18-staff paper (B. & H. Nr. 11 C / 7. 09).

At the top of p. 1, in Bantock's hand: "The Red Lotus / Text by Edward Powys Mathers / Music by Granville Bantock." Initialed and dated Birmingham, 2 April 1920 at the end. Stamped 7 May 1920 and marked 294[33 cancelled]44 in pencil at the top of p. 1.

Copyright statement (Copyright MCMXX by Elkin & Co. Ltd.) and music publisher's number (E. & Co. 1153) added in manuscript at the bottom of p. 1 in an unidentified hand.

Reel "The Bobers of Brechin"

Holograph manuscript of this piano piece, 1917, 12 p. Notated in black ink, with markings in blue pencil, on a gathering of four nested, stitched bifolia of tall 12-staff paper (B. & H. Nr. 1 C.)

On the front of the outer bifolium, in Bantock's hand: "Reel. / 'The Bobers of Brechin' / for Pianoforte / by / Granville Bantock." Initialed and dated Birmingham, 9 June 1917 at the end.

Copyright statement (Copyright MCMXXIII by Elkin & Co. Ltd.) and music publisher's number (E. & Co. 957) added in manuscript at the bottom of p. 1 in an unidentified hand.

Waking song

Holograph manuscript of this song for voice and piano, 1930, 5 p. Notated in dark blue ink, with pencil markings, on p. 1–5 of two nested bifolia of tall 20-staff paper.

At the top of p. 1, in Bantock's hand: "Waking Song / Poem by / Harold Boulton. / Music by / Granville Bantock." Initialed and dated Metchley Lodge, 12 Feb. 1930 at the end.

Copyright statement (Copyright MCMXX by Elkin & Co. Ltd) and music publisher's number (E. & Co. 1762) added in manuscript at the bottom of p. 1 in an unidentified hand.

Yung-Yang

Holograph manuscript of this song for voice and piano, 1918, 7 p. Notated in black ink, with markings and corrections in pencil, on p. 1–7 of two nested bifolia of tall 18-staff paper (B. & H. Nr. 11 C / 7. 09).

At the top of p. 1, in Bantock's hand: "Yung-Yang / from the Chinese Poet Po-Chu-i. AD. 772–846. / Rendered into English by / L. Cranmer-Byng. / Music by / Granville Bantock." Initialed and dated Abbots Norton, 14 Sept. 1918 at the end.

Copyright statement (Copyright MCMXIX by Elkin & Co. Ltd.) and music publisher's number (E. & Co. 1001) added in manuscript at the bottom of p. 1 in an unidentified hand.

Accompanied by the optional violin solo parts for "Yung-Yang" and "From the Tomb of an Unknown Woman," written on p. [1] and [3] of a single bifolium of tall 18-staff paper, the first page torn at the top.

Music manuscripts accompanied by part of a wrapper with printed Elkin & Co. label, annotated in an unidentified hand "Sir Granville Bantock Compositions."

London, Phillips, 14 June 1989, lot 2.
FRKF 1362.01–.16

II. SIR GRANVILLE AND LADY BANTOCK'S GUEST BOOK, CA. 1908–48

Bound in red morocco, with double gold fillet along the edges; raised bands on spine, with double or single fillet decor; gold-tooled on spine: "Guest / Book / Sir / Granville / Bantock / 1908–1941." Top edge gilt.

The album includes the following:

"Hymn to Earth," holograph poem, initialed N.O.H. and dated 30 Oct. 1908.

Untitled haiku, in Japanese with English transliteration, signed Kajiro Watanabe and dated King's Norton, 15 Aug. 1910.

Untitled poem, in Greek, signed "Lycidas," with partial translation ("Begin, then, sisters of the sacred web …"), signed H.G[?] Cotham.

Hayes, Alfred. "November," autograph poem, signed and dated 2 Nov. 1909, 3 p.

Sharp, William. ALS, Argyll House, Kilcreggan, Argyll, n.d. Pencilled annotation by Bantock, with the indication that the letter was received on 17 Aug. 1898.

Autograph quotation from Verlaine's "Chanson d'automne," signed Iso Mutso and dated 10 Oct. 1925.

Autograph quotation, signed Hugh S. Robertson and T.H. Bisset, dated 16 May 1920.

Autograph quotation from Mallarmé's "L'après-midi d'un faune," signed T.E. Clark and dated Broad Meadow, 4 March 1911.

Autograph quotation, signed Marjory Kennedy-Fraser, n.d.

"Express: record of sensations," autograph poem [?] signed H. Wright [?] Henry and dated 19 Nov. 1921.

Autograph quotation from Sophocles' *Electra*, signed Ethel Strudwick and dated 12 Feb. 1911.

Autograph signature of William Arms Fisher, dated 13 Sept. 1912.

Photograph of Japanese figurines, with a red Japanese stamp and presentation inscription from Mr. and Mrs. Alvin Langdon Coburn, 28 Oct. 1916.

Cumberland, Gerald. "Day and Night," autograph poem, signed and dated 5 Feb. 1912.

Prokofiev, Sergei. Autograph musical quotation (identified as from the Second Piano Sonata), signed and dated 6 July 1914.

Young, Filson. "Jig," autograph poem, signed and dated 22 Feb. 1916.

Bantock, Raymond. "The old man," autograph poem, signed and dated 17 April 1918.

Bishop, T.H. Autograph inscription, signed and dated 14 Feb. 1937.

Russell, George [A.E.] "Be not so desolate," autograph poem, signed, n.d. [22 Oct. 1933] illustrated with a pen and blue ink and crayon drawing, signed A.E. The dating is provided in pencil at the bottom in Bantock's hand.

Janssen, Werner. Autograph musical quotation. Also, autograph inscription, signed, by Ann Narding Janssen, dated Feb. 1937.

Williams, Horace [?]. Autograph inscription, signed and dated 4 May 1934.

Carpenter, Edward. Autograph inscription, signed and dated 7–10 Nov. 1917.

Sibelius, Jean. Autograph musical quotation, with presentation inscription to Helen Bantock, signed and dated 19 Sept. 1912.

Newmarsh, Rosa. Autograph inscription, n.d.

Lenskii, Boris V. Autograph inscription in Russian, dated 27 Oct. 1916.

Raybould, Clarence. Autograph musical quotation, also signed Evelyn [Raybould] and dated 13 Jan. 1947.

Ashton, Algernon. Autograph musical quotation from his Quartet for Piano and Strings, no. 2 in C minor, with presentation inscription dated Birmingham, 23 June 1917.

Harris, William. Autograph musical quotation, signed and dated 22 July 1917.

Scott, J.R.U. Autograph musical quotation, signed and dated Nov. 1917.

"Old Tin Kap," autograph poem, dated "year of the horse."

Beecham, Sir Thomas. Jocular autograph musical quotation, with presentation inscription, signed, n.d.

Harty, Sir Hamilton. Autograph musical quotation, signed, n.d.

Tovey, Donald Francis. Autograph musical quotation, with presentation inscription, signed and dated 28 Nov. 1919.

Shaw, Geoffrey. Autograph musical quotation, with presentation inscription, signed and dated 11 Feb. 1920.

Autograph quotation, in Greek, signed W.H. Hadow, and dated 16 May 1920.

Korvalow [?] G. Autograph musical quotation, with presentation inscription to Helen Bantock, dated Birmingham, 1 May 1930.

Hart, Fritz, and Marvell Hart. Autograph inscriptions, dated 18 Aug. 1938.

Hougham, Arthur. "The Mountains of Eryri," autograph poem, calligraphed and illustrated, signed 11 Sept. 1934, 2 p.

Wood, Henry J. Autograph musical quotation, signed and dated Aug. 1941.

London, Sotheby's, 21 May 1987, lot 487.
FRKF 1390

CHARLES BAUDELAIRE (1821–67)

I. LETTERS

To Madame Aupick, his mother

1862 Aug. 11 [i.e. 10?] "Dimanche," n.p., ALS, 4 p. *Correspondance*, II:253–55.

See Christie's, London, 28 Nov. 1990, lot 150.
Paris, Laurin-Guilloux-Buffetaud-Tailleur (Drouot), 20 Nov. 1984, lot 193.
FRKF 666

To Victor de Mars

1855 April 7, n.p., ALS, 2 p., concerning *Les fleurs du mal*. *Correspondance*, I:312.

Victor de Mars, secretary of the *Revue des Deux Mondes*.

Paris, Drouot, 17 Oct. 1984, lot 18.
FRKF 495

To Auguste Poulet-Malassis

1860 Feb. 16, n.p., ALS, 6 p., concerning De Quincey; also mentions *Les fleurs du mal* and Constantin Guys. *Correspondance*, II:668–71.

Paris, Drouot, 29 March 1985, lot 44.
FRKF 956

II. PRINTED WORKS

Les épaves de Charles Baudelaire. Avec une eau-forte frontispice de Félicien Rops. Amsterdam: à l'enseigne du coq [i.e. Brussels: Poulet-Malassis], 1866.

[10] [I]–II, [1]–163 [+ 1] p. No. 5 of ten copies on China paper, from an edition of 260 copies. Untrimmed.

Five plates are bound in:

Félix Bracquemond's rejected frontispiece for the first edition of *Les fleurs du mal*, stamped in red in the upper left corner, and with the pencilled note at the bottom: "[one illegible word] inédit. Tiré à cinq épreuves."

Émile Roy's 1844 portrait of Baudelaire, with the pencilled note at the bottom: "1er état avant le fond et avant le cuivre coupé."

Baudelaire's 1848 self-portrait, with the pencilled note: "1 état avant le cuivre coupé."

Gustave Courbet's 1848 portrait of Baudelaire, marked "Gravé par B."

Bracquemond's 1861 frontispiece portrait of Baudelaire.

Bound in uniform black morocco, top edge gilt, raised bands on spine, with author, title, and year in gold lettering; gilt border on the verso of both boards, double sets of endpapers of purple marbled paper.

Heinrich Schütz to Henry Miller, p. 54–55.
Paris, Drouot, 20 March 1985, lot 23.
FRKF 567

III. MISCELLANEOUS

E. Durandeau

"Messieurs de la lyre. Les nuits de Monsieur Baudelaire." Lithograph on paper (21 × 27 cm), n.d.

Paris, Drouot, 18 Dec. 1984, lot 19.
FRKF 555

LEWIS CHRISTOPHER EDWARD BAUMER (1870–1963)

"Unhappily expressed"

Pen-and-ink drawing, lightly heightened with white, on paper mounted on heavy grey board (drawing: 29.5 × 24 cm) showing a couple in a salon, signed but undated.

The caption, written identically twice in pencil at the bottom of the sheet and on the board, reads: "She (who did not know they were to meet) 'Why, Mr. Brown, this is a pleasant surprise.' He (who did) 'I can't altogether say that it is so to me, Miss Jones.'"

London, Christie's, 21 July 1981, lot 251.
FRKF 105

AUBREY BEARDSLEY (1872–98)

The story of Venus and Tannhäuser: in which is set forth an exact account of the manner of State held by Madam Venus, Goddess and Meretrix, under the famous Hörselberg, and containing the Adventures of Tannhäuser in that Place, his Repentance, his Journeying to Rome and Return to the Loving Mountain. A romantic novel by Aubrey Beardsley. Now first printed from the Original Manuscript. London: For private circulation, 1907.

4to, [A4] B-L4. [1–13] 14–88 p. No. 2 of 50 on Japanese vellum, from a total edition of 300 copies.

Bound in vellum over boards. On the front board, in gold lettering: "The story of Venus and Tannhäuser by Aubrey Beardsley / Japanese Vellum Edition." Bookplate of John Quinn.

Gallatin, p. 107–08.
London, Christie's, 4 Feb. 1994, lot 133.
FRKF 1420

WILLIAM BECKFORD (1760–1844)

Letters to George Clarke

George Clarke became Beckford's bookseller and agent at the death of his father William on 3 August 1830. The letters document in great detail Beckford's collecting habits and contain references to sales and to rival collectors such as Richard Heber, usually designated as H.H.H. ("Hart Horn Heber"). The 1834 correspondence deals with the reception of Beckford's *Italy; with sketches of Spain and Portugal* and the new editions of *Vathek* and of *Biographical memoirs of extraordinary painters*. Clarke went bankrupt in 1835 and died of influenza in the same year.

Most letters are published in *The consummate collector: William Beckford's letters to his bookseller.* Edited with introduction and notes by Robert J. Gemmett (Wilby, Norwich: Michael Russell, 2000).

Unless otherwise noted, these autograph letters are unsigned, dated from Bath, and have one page.

1830

August: 4 (initialed); 5 (initialed); 8; 23; 27

September: 12 (3 p.); 19 (2 p., initialed); 20; 22; 26 (2 p., initialed)

October: 2 (Ashton Hall); 4 (Ashton Hall); 6 (Ashton Hall, 3 p., initialed); 11 (Ashton Hall); 18 (4 p.); 19; 24; 26 (2 p.); 28; 31

November: 2; 7 (3 p., initialed); 9 (2 p.); 11; [14?] (2 p. "Sunday," dated 21 Nov. 1830 in an unidentified hand; the date 14 Nov. is suggested by Gemmett); 16; 17; 21 (2 p.); 24; 25; 30 (initialed)

December: 2; 9 (2 p.); 17; 24 (3 p., initialed); 28 (3 p.)

1831

January: 2; 10; 18; 21; 30 (2 p.); [31] ("Monday")

February: 2; 3 (4 p., initialed); 6 (AN); 11; 15 (4 p.); 17; 20 (3 p.); 23 (4 p.); 27 (2 p.)

March: 2; 7 (3 p., initialed); 11; 15 (3 p., initialed); 16 (3 p.); 17 (2 p.); 18 (2 p., initialed); 22 (2 p.); [24] ("Thursday"); 29

April: 1; [4] (n.p., 2 p.); 5 (initialed); 12; 13; 17 (dated 24 April by Beckford but postmarked 17 April); 24; 27; 28 (3 p.); 30 (3 p.)

May: 4; 10; 14 (3 p.); 19 (2 p.); [20] ("Friday," postmarked 21 May)

June: 6

July: 1; 2 (3 p.); 10; 14 (2 p.); 17 (AN); 19 (3 p.); 24; 26 (initialed)

August: 2; 5; 9 (AN); 28 (4 p.)

September: 2; 4; 6; 9 (3 p.); 11 (3 p., initialed); 14; 28; 30 (2 p.)

October: 1 (2 p., initialed); 5 (4 p.); 8 (3 p.); 11 (2 p., initialed); 14 (3 p.); 19; 20 (4 p.); 25 (3 p.); 28; 30 (4 p.); 30 (a second letter, headed "2d Thoughts & 2d Edition")

November: 2; 4; 6; 11 (3 p.); 17; 20 (4 p.); 27 (3 p.)

December: 1 (4 p.); [1] (4 p., a second letter); 8 (4 p., initialed); 11 (3 p.); 16; 18; 19 (3 p.); 20 (3 p.); 21 (initialed)

1832

January: 2 (3 p.); 15; 20 (3 p.); 23

February: 1 (3 p.); 3; 4 (2 p.); 7; 12; 17 (4 p.); 21; 26

March: 2; 3 (3 p.); 6; 7 (n.p., 2 p.); 9 (initialed); 11; 13 (3 p.); 16; 20 (3 p., initialed); 22 (4 p.); 23 (3 p.); 25 (3 p.); 27 (3 p., initialed); 28; 29; 30 (initialed)

April: 1 (3 p.); 2 (3 p.); 3 (Gloucester); 4 (Gloucester); 6; 8 (initialed); 11 (3 p.); 13 (3 p.); 15; 20 (AN); 24; 27 (3 p.); 30

May: 24 (3 p.); 25; 27 (2 p.); 28; 29 (3 p.)

June: 5; 8; 12 (2 p.); 13 (3 p.); 17; 19 (2 p.); 22 (3 p., initialed); 24 (3 p.)

July: 5 (3 p.); 8 (AN); [10] ("Tuesday," 3 p.); 11; 25; 29; 31 (3 p.)

August: 1 (2 p.); 3 (3 p.); 9 (4 p.); 12 (3 p.); 16 (3 p.); 17; 19 (3 p., initialed); 23 (initialed); 26 (initialed); 29

September: 4 (3 p.); 12 (3 p.); 16; 24

October: 3 (3 p.); 4 (2 p.); 5 (3 p.); 9; 11 (3 p.); 15

November: 1; 2; 14 (3 p.); 23 (initialed); 25 (3 p.); 28; [29] ("Thursday")

December: 3 (initialed)

1833

February: 28

March: 6 (2 p.); 7 (2 p.); 10 (3 p.); 14 (3 p.); 18 (4 p.); 19; 20; 22 (3 p.); 24; 25 (3 p.); 28 (3 p.); 29 (3 p.); 31 (3 p.)

April: 2 (2 p.); 3 (4 p.); 4; 7 (3 p.); 9; 12 (3 p.); 14 (3 p.); 16; 19 (3 p.); 23 (3 p.); 25 (3 p.); 27 (n.p., 2 p.); 29 (3 p.) 30

May: 2; 3 (initialed); 19 (3 p.); 23 (3 p.); 26 (2 p.); 29; 31 (3 p.)

June: 3 (2 p.); 4 (4 p.); 5 (4 p.); 6 (3 p.); 7; 9 (4 p.); 12 (3 p.); 12 (p.m., Bath); 14 (2 p.); 17 (2 p., initialed); 18 (2 p.); 19 (3 p.); 21; 23; 25; 27 (3 p.); 30 (4 p.)

July: 2; 3; 5 (3 p.); 7 (2 p.); 12 (3 p.); 14 (4 p.); 15 (3 p.); 16 (3 p.); 17 (4 p.); 18 (4 p.); 19 (3 p.); 20 (3 p.); 21 (4 p.); 22 (4 p.); 23 (AN); 24 (3 p.); 25 (4 p.); 26 (3 p.); 27 (3 p.); 28 (3 p.); 29 (3 p.); 30 (3 p.); 31

August: 4 (2 p.); 6 (4 p.); 7 (2 p.); 8 (4 p.); 9 (4 p.); 10 (3 p.); 11 (3 p.); 12 (4 p.); 13 (4 p.); [14*] (3 p.); 15 (4 p.); 17 (4 p.); 28

September: 1 (3 p.); 10 (4 p.); 12 (3 p.); 17 (3 p.); 22; 26

October: 2; 6 (2 p.); 7; 13 (3 p.); 15; 19 (initialed, 3 p.)

November: 4; 5; 7 (3 p.); [8] ("Friday," n.p.); 10 (2 p.); 11; 12 (2 p.); 17; 24 (3 p.); 26; 28 (2 p.); 29

December: 1; 9 (n.p.)

1834

March: 3 (n.p., in pencil); 28 (signed in full, 3 p.); 29; 30; "Saturday Eve" (n.p., 3 p.)

April: 1 (3 p.); 2; 8; [14] (AN, n.p.)

July: 10 (4 p., also present in a secretarial hand); 13 (signed, 4 p., also present in a secretarial hand); 15 (2 p.); 20 (signed, 3 p., also present in a secretarial hand); 23 (3 p.); 27 (4 p.); 31 (3 p.)

August: 1 (4 p.); 3 (4 p.); 5 (3 p.); 10 (4 p.); 12 (4 p.); 15 (3 p.); 18 (4 p.); 31 (3 p.)

September: 3 (3 p.); 5 (3 p.); 9 (3 p.)

October: 8; 19

Undated

"Saturday" (n.p.)

From the collection of H. Bradley Martin. New York, Sotheby's, 1 May 1990, lot 2612.
FRKF 1357

FRANK BEECHING

An undated album of original drawings, mostly of scenes involving children. Unless otherwise noted, the drawings are pen-and-ink and watercolor on paper. Captions taken from the album are enclosed in quotation marks.

"A happy new year." Greeting card, collage and watercolor on board, gilt border, 4.8 × 8.5 cm

An angry little boy, 5.2 × 7.5 cm

"This is the way little boys go out riding in India," 10.5 × 7 cm

"Papa taking a quiet walk in the country," 12.2 × 8 cm

"Papa up a Gum-Tree," 7.2 × 10.5 cm

"This is a naughty boy who used to torment poor insects …," 9.3 × 9.3 cm

Man seated under a palm-tree, a giraffe eating out of his plate, 6.3 × 10.5 cm

"This is an old cat who thought he would look better without his whiskers …," 7 × 10.7 cm

"Papa out riding on a thorough-bred Elephant," 13 × 8.5 cm

"Papa on Outpost duty in the Burmese forests," 13 × 8.5 cm

"Oh Don't I Just Wish I Was A Nigger Like Him …," 11.5 × 10 cm

Man and wolf in a forest, 7.5 × 10 cm

Three children threatened by a snake, a lion, and a tiger, 6.5 × 10 cm

Tiger in front of a sign, 14.5 × 8.5 cm

"Papa finds a Cat in his Room!" 10.7 × 7.5 cm

"This is what master Tom did …," 14 × 11 cm

"A wicked clown …," 8 × 11 cm

"Policeman. 'Ha! thats the way you drink the beer …'," 8 × 11.8 cm

Baby being bathed, 9 × 7 cm

"I Wonder If This Is Like The New Baby …," 12 × 7.5 cm

"This stupid clumsy boy …," 7.5 × 9.7 cm

"A Happy night with the Mosquitoes," pen-and-ink on paper, 11 × 6.7 cm

"Papa 'at Home' …," 8 × 6.7 cm

"This is a naughty boy who has gone into the store-room …," 11.2 × 9.5 cm

"This is a man who wanted to have a goose …," 7.2 × 11.2 cm

"On The Chain Pier …," 12 × 8.5 cm

Landscape (possibly in India), watercolor and pencil, 13.7 × 9 cm

Boy teasing an old woman, 8.5 × 6 cm

"Crusty old Bachelor. 'Well Elly …'," 10.7 × 14 cm

Boy stealing handkerchief from a man, 6.8 × 9 cm

"This is a very naughty boy …," 11.3 × 7 cm

"Doctor. 'Well! and whats the matter …'," 11.2 × 10.5 cm

"Mama. 'Why Frank what is the matter …'," 13 × 10.5 cm

"This is a gentleman who thinks he is going to shoot a bear …," 7 × 11.5 cm

Elephant in landscape, watercolor and pencil, 11.2 × 7 cm

"This is a Camel on the banks of the Suez Canal," in pencil, caption in ink, 10.5 × 11.5 cm

Fountain, découpage in white paper pasted on brown paper, top angles cut, 7.5 × 7 cm

"This naughty boy has been chalking …," 7.2 × 11 cm

"Mama. 'Why, nurse!' …," 10 × 13 cm

"Soldier. 'Now then!' …," 10 × 12.5 cm

Boy being lifted in the air by his balloon, 7.2 × 11.3 cm

"This naughty boy has taken his fathers razors …," 7.2 × 11.2 cm

Boy being knocked from his horse, 9.7 × 6.5 cm

"I wish I was a pudding, Mama! …" 10.5 × 13 cm

Interior, 9.5 × 6 cm

"Street boy (to Policeman). 'Snowballs, Sir!' …" 9.7 × 11 cm

"Street boy. 'O! my eye!' …" 10.2 × 12.7 cm

"Rude boy. 'Ah! Here's the P'leece …'," 11.3 × 10.3 cm

"My eye, Tommy! …" 10.2 × 11 cm

"Don't baby! …" 11.3 × 9.2 cm

"I say Jessie do you understand French? …" 8 × 12 cm

Boy being chased by a gaggle of geese, 7 × 11.2 cm

Three street musicians, pen-and-ink and wash drawing with collage on paper, 10.2 × 13.3 cm

"Town boy to country boy. 'Who are they?' …" 10.2 × 13.5 cm

"Lizzy. 'Oh Papa!' …" 10 × 13.5 cm

"Small but brutal shoe-boy …," 9.6 × 10.5 cm

"Disgusting boy. 'I say Clara!' …" 7.5 × 12.3 cm

"A Christmas Box!" 7.2 × 12.5 cm

Boy on a pole marked "Dangerous," 7 × 9.3 cm

"Military man. 'Well!' …" 7 × 13 cm

"Ethel (sees a gentleman bathing …)," 7 × 11.2 cm

"This is a stupid old sailor …," 13 × 7.5 cm

"I say Arthur! …" 11.2 × 6.5 cm

Three men in a boat, one has just caught a fish, 7.5 × 11.2 cm

Original photograph with caption "Chemin de fer du Righi," 10.3 × 6.5 cm

Boy on a branch with tiger below, 11 × 7.2 cm

"Master is very sorry Mum …," 11.2 × 12.5 cm

Jockey being kicked over a barrier by his horse, 6.5 × 11.2 cm

"Honest sympathy, …" pen-and-ink and wash on paper, 12.7 × 7 cm

Man pouring water on an accordionist, 6.8 × 10.7 cm

Woman surrounded by dogs fighting, 6.2 × 10.7 cm

Explorer and native, 11.2 × 6.8 cm

"1st schoolboy. 'you're the new boy …'," 7.5 × 12 cm

Boys looking at guard on his horse, 10.2 × 6 cm

"Have you seen a deer …," 7.2 × 12.5 cm

"When a fat old gentleman …," pen-and-ink, 6.7 × 10.5 cm

"I pity this poor fellow when the Bees catch him!" 6.7 × 10.5 cm

"O! Yer don't want to go into Business …," 7.5 × 12.5 cm

"New governess. 'Come and rest a little …'," 7.3 × 12.5 cm

Two goblins, 6.7 × 10 cm

Colonial expedition, pen-and-ink, 11 × 9.4 cm

Pianist, pen-and-ink and wash and collage, 5.5 × 7.5 cm

"As you was!" pen-and-ink, 10 × 8 cm

"If you saw a poor man …," pen-and-ink and wash, 7.5 × 11 cm

"Kotah. Jan.y 6th. I try to shoot my dinner," pen-and-ink, 11 × 6.2 cm

Man on donkey, 10 × 7.4 cm

"Stop him Sir!," 7.5 × 8.2 cm

Boy kicking a nest from a branch, 7.2 × 10.2 cm

"What lots of energy …," pen-and-ink, 9.4 × 11.3 cm

Elephant carrying passengers, watercolor and pencil, 9.3 × 8.5 cm

There is no record of Frank Beeching in the DNB or the British Library on-line integrated catalogue.

London, Christie's, 1 July 1987, lot 83.
FRKF 1405

VINCENZO BELLINI (1801–35)

Letter to Count Giacomo Barbo di Castelnuovo in Berlin

[1832] March 22, Catania, ALS, 4 p., concerning *Norma*, Donizetti, and Giuditta Turina. Carmelo Neri, ed. *Lettere di Vincenzo Bellini (1819–1835)* (Palermo: Publisicula Editrice, 1991), p. 202–03.

London, Sotheby's, 9–10 May 1985, lot 9.
FRKF 756

HECTOR BERLIOZ (1803–69)

I. MUSIC MANUSCRIPTS

Grande ouverture du Roi Lear, H. 53

Holograph manuscript, in full score, 1831, 86 p. Notated in brown ink on bifolia of oblong 16-staff paper (28 × 21.5 cm), with subsequent corrections in black ink and later corrections in red ink, as well as occasional corrections (some apparently in the hand of the engraver) in pencil.

> The bifolia are numbered 1 to 17 in Berlioz's hand. The second page of a first bifolium numbered 4 was excised and is followed by a second bifolium also numbered 4. There are no nos. 6 or 7; in place of these missing bifolia are a single, substitute leaf and a bifolium numbered 7 bis. After bifolium 17, the remainder of the manuscript comprises a single leaf numbered 18 and single leaves paginated in pencil 20 to 31. There are cancels (with traces of wax seals), the first affecting the verso of leaf 18, the second the verso of page 28. The first cancel and pages 20–31 are in black ink throughout and appear to be a revision. The second cancel is written on a different paper (22 staves) and is a later revision, modifying both pages 28v and 30.

On title page, in Berlioz's hand: "Grande / ouverture / du / Roi Lear / Tragédie de Shakspeare / Dédié à Mr Armand Bertin / et composée / Par / Hector Berlioz / oeuvre 4ème / Nizza 7 mai 1831. / [in another hand:] Ade. C. (544) & Cie." Across the first page of the manuscript, autograph dedication: "à Mr Armand Bertin / témoignage de la plus sincère amitié / et d'une vive reconnaissance / Hector Berlioz."

Tipped in after the title page: ALS to Armand Bertin, n.p. [Paris] 12 Feb. 1840, 2 p., accompanying the gift of the manuscript. See *Correspondance générale*, II:629 (L702).

Bound in blue morocco with the same gilt-tooled decorative panel on both boards. Edges gilt. Spine gilt tooled: "Ouverture / du / Roi Lear / Nissa. / 1831."

First published by Ad. Catelin in 1840. See *New Berlioz Edition*, vol. 20.
Formerly in the collection of Léon Constantin. On verso of free front endpaper is a small red label with monogram "E.M.H.B."
Holoman, p. 104–07.
Heinrich Schütz to Henry Miller, p. 30–31.
FRKF 250

Le temple universel, op. 28, H. 137A

Fragments from the holograph manuscript of the original version for two double male choirs and organ of this chorus, n.d., 10 p.

The manuscript comprises three bifolia of 16-staff manuscript paper (blind stamp of Lard-Esnault), paginated 1 to 10 from the beginning of the music on the first page of the second bifolium. The manuscript comprises only the first 89 bars. Another leaf, corresponding to pages 13–14, was sold recently (Paris, Drouot, 17 Dec. 2001, lot 37) and is now at Yale. Other fragments are at Stanford (p. 11–12) and the National Library of Scotland (p. 15–18).

The first page of the first bifolium reads: "Le temple universel / Double choeur / [crossed out: Pour deux peuples / (Chacun chantant dans sa langue)] / Paroles de J F Vaudin / Musique de Mr Hector Berlioz."

Le temple universel is set to a text by Vaudin, a leader of the French male-voice amateur choral movement known as the Orphéon. It was originally to have been performed by forces of thousands at the Crystal Palace in London. Another large-scale performance planned at the Palais de l'Industrie in Oct. 1861 (the choristers, coming from 54 départements, were supposed to wear different colors) was rehearsed but the work was withdrawn.

Holoman, p. 399–401.
See *New Berlioz Edition*, vol. 14.
Paris, Drouot, 12 Dec. 1985, lot 12.
FRKF 913

II. OTHER MANUSCRIPTS

Speech given in Kehl, Germany

Draft, 20 June 1863, 2 p.

See *Correspondance générale*, VI:463–65.
FRKF 468

III. LETTERS

To Édouard Bouscatel

[1864] Dec. 12 [Paris] ALS, 1 p., concerning *Les Troyens*. *Correspondance générale*, VII:163–64.

FRKF 447

To Berthold and Louise Damcke

1864 Aug. 21, Paris, ALS, 4 p., concerning his promotion in the Legion of Honor and feelings of boredom. *Correspondance générale*, VII:94–95.

London, Sotheby's, 10 May 1984, lot 15.
FRKF 325

To Franz Dingelstedt

[1853] Aug. 16, Frankfurt, ALS, 2 p., concerning *La damnation de Faust*. *Correspondance générale*, IV:354.

Formerly in the Boston Public Library.
FRKF 446

To Alfred Dörffel

[1868] Feb. 22 [Paris] ALS, 1 p., on mourning stationery, concerning his poor state of health. *Correspondance générale*, VII:676.

Alfred Dörffel (1821–1905), German music critic and editor.

Marburg, Stargardt, 5–6 March 1985, lot 756.
FRKF 808

To M. Faivre

1841 Jan. 12 [Paris] ALS, 2 p., concerning the *Symphonie funèbre et triomphale*. *Correspondance générale*, VIII:189–90.

Paris, Laurin-Guilloux-Buffetaud-Tailleur (Drouot), 19 March 1986, lot 17.
FRKF 1115

To Humbert Ferrand

1865 Jan. 25 [Paris] ALS, 3 p. Mentions performances of the *Ouverture des Francs-Juges* at the Cirque Napoléon and the *Ouverture du Roi Lear* in New York. *Correspondance générale*, VII:209–10.

FRKF 1407

To Léon Halévy

1865 March 7, "Mardi soir," [Paris] ALS, 2 p. (env). Congratulates Halévy on his article in *Le journal des Débats* on the "Boeuf gras." *Correspondance générale*, VII:220.

Léon Halévy (1802–83), historian and playwright, was brother of Fromental and father of Ludovic and Élie Halévy.

Paris, Oger-Dumont (Drouot), 14 Feb. 1985, lot 4.

FRKF 689

To Richard Pohl

1863 May 16 [Paris] ALS, 3 p., concerning *Béatrice et Bénédict* and *Les Troyens*. *Correspondance générale*, VI:447.

Richard Pohl (1826–96) was the German translator of *Les soirées de l'orchestre* and the libretti of *Benvenuto Cellini* and *Béatrice et Bénédict*.

London, Sotheby's, 10 May 1984, lot 12.

FRKF 323

To Ferdinand Praeger

1856 Aug. 11, Baden-Baden, ALS, 3 p. (env), concerning his election to the Institut de France and *L'enfance du Christ*. *Correspondance générale*, V:349.

FRKF 1148

To Edouard Silas

[1855 June 13] "mercredi matin," [London*] ALS, 1 p., about *L'enfance du Christ*. *Correspondance générale*, V:105.

Edouard Silas (1827–1909), Dutch pianist and composer.

FRKF 445

To Gaspare Spontini

1832 March 29, Rome, ALS, 3 p., about the state of music in Italy and his hope to visit Spontini in Berlin. *Correspondance générale*, VIII:72–74.

FRKF 224

To Stephen de La Madelaine (i.e. Étienne Madelaine)

1861 June 25, Paris, ALS, 2 p., concerning embellishments he introduced to Agathe's act 2 aria in Weber's *Der Freischütz* in his treatise *Chant. Études pratiques de style. Leçon sur un air du Freyschütz*. *Correspondance générale*, VI:231.

London, Sotheby's, 10 May 1984, lot 10.

FRKF 322

[1862 April 12] "Samedi matin," n.p., ALS, 3 p., concerning *Les Troyens* and *Béatrice et Bénédict*. *Correspondance générale*, VI:291–92.

FRKF 448

Stephen de La Madelaine (1801–68) was a singer and a theoretician of singing.

IV. PRINTED WORKS

Mémoires … comprenant ses voyages en Italie / en Allemagne, en Russie et en Angleterre - 1803–1865. Quatrième édition. Paris: Calmann Lévy, éditeur, 1896–97.

2 volumes. 8vo, 4 p.l., [i]–[iv] 1–367 [+ 1] p.; 2 p.l., 1–430 p. Bound in half blue morocco; pale blue cloth boards; top edge gilt.

London, Sotheby's, 10 May 1984, lot 14.

FRKF 324.2–3

Les soirées de l'orchestre. Quatrième édition, entièrement revue et corrigée. Paris: Calmann Lévy, éditeur, 1884.

8vo, 2 p.l., 1–428 p. Bound in half blue morocco; blue and marbled paper boards; top edge gilt.

London, Sotheby's, 10 May 1984, lot 14.

FRKF 324.1

V. RELATED MATERIAL

Jullien, Adolphe (1803–73). *Hector Berlioz / sa vie et ses oeuvres. Ouvrage orné de quatorze lithographies originales par M. Fantin-Latour, de douze portraits de Hector Berlioz, de trois planches hors texte et de 122 gravures, scènes théâtrales, caricatures, portraits d'artistes, autographes, etc.* Paris: A la librairie de l'art, 1888.

4to, [i]–xvi, [1]–386 p., [1] leaf, 31.5 cm. Bound in quarter calf, light brown cloth boards, top edge gilt, gold-tooling on spine.

The Fantin-Latour plates are bound in as follows:

Verité (frontispiece)

Tuba mirum spargens sonum … (after p. xiv)

Symphonie fantastique / Un bal (after p. 50)

Lélio / La Harpe éolienne (after p. 82)

Harold en Italie / Dans les montagnes (after p. 104)

Benvenuto Cellini / Acte III / La fonte du Persée (after p. 122)

Roméo et Juliette / Confidence à la nuit (after p. 142)

La damnation de Faust / Apparition de Marguerite (after p. 186)

Sara la baigneuse (after p. 206)

L'enfance du Christ / Le Repos de la Sainte Famille (after p. 230)

Béatrice et Bénédict / Acte I / Nocturne (after p. 250)

La prise de Troie / Acte III / Apparition d'Hector (after p. 274)

Les Troyens à Carthage / Acte III / Duo d'amour (after p. 290)

Apothéose (after p. 366)

The portrait of Berlioz by Gustave Courbet, engraved by A. Gilbert, is bound after p. 326.

London, Sotheby's, 10 May 1984, lot 14.
FRKF 324.1

VI. LETTERS BY HARRIET SMITHSON BERLIOZ TO ANTHONY GALIGNANI

1831 Sept. 5, Spalding, ALS, 4 p., a request for financial help.

1831 Dec. 27, London, ALS, 6 p. Discusses her career and financial circumstances.

Paris, Laurin-Guilloux-Buffetaud-Tailleur (Drouot), 12 March 1984, lots 189–90.
FRKF 419–20

GERALD HUGH TYRWHITT-WILSON, BARON BERNERS (1883–1950)

Le triomphe de Neptune

Partly holograph short-score manuscript of this ballet, n.d., 48 p., in pencil or black ink, with additional markings in black ink and red or blue pencil, on a combination of nested bifolia and individual sheets of tall 12- or 16-staff paper.

The manuscript comprises the following sections:

"Entracte / Hornpipe," holograph, in pencil, 9 p., preceded by a title page marked, in Berners's hand: "Entracte / Hornpipe. / [in a different hand, possibly that of Serge Lifar:] Pour le / Ballet / 'Triomphe / de / Neptune' / [in Berners's hand] Lord Berners / 3 Chesham Place / S.W."; in the upper right corner of the first page, note, possibly in the hand of Serge Diaghilev: "Couper 40 mesures"; other indications in Russian, in an unidentified hand. Purple stamp of Serge Lifar on the cover.

"Acte I. Scène 6 Variazioni," 4 p., written in black ink in the hand of a copyist, with annotations in Berners's hand.

"Acte II. Scène [3 cancelled] 2. / La Grotte / (The Cavern)," 7 p., notated in black ink in a copyist's hand, with annotations in pencil by Berners and other annotations, in Russian, in an unidentified hand. At the end, note in Berners's hand: "2½ minutes."

"Gigue / Acte II. Scene 3," 8 p., notated in black ink in the hand of a copyist, with annotations by Berners in pencil, and other annotations in Russian, in an unidentified hand. On title page, in upper right corner, in Berners's hand: "Lord Berners / 3 Foro Romano / Rome."

"Finale. No 2 Danse de la Fée," 4 p., holograph, in pencil. Pasted-on revision at the bottom of p. [3].

"Acte 2. Finale. Nº 2. Danse des Quattre Harlequins," 8 p., notated in black ink in a copyist's hand, with annotations in Berners's hand.

"Schottische," holograph, in pencil, 1 p.

"Coupure de la dernière variation du 1er acte," holograph, in pencil, 1 p., with an annotation in Russian.

"Coupure dans la Matelotte," holograph, in pencil, 1 p.

"Introduction pour la Matelotte," holograph, in pencil, 1 p. Unidentified holograph sketches on the verso.

"Variation," holograph, in pencil, 3 p.; marked "3/4 minute" at the end. On the verso of p. [3] in Berners's hand: "Lord Berners / 3 Chesham Place / London."

Le triomphe de Neptune, on a libretto by Sacheverell Sitwell, was premiered by the Ballets russes, in a choreography by George Balanchine, at the London Lyceum on 3 Dec. 1926.

From the collection of Serge Lifar.
Heinrich Schütz to Henry Miller, p. 128–29.
London, Sotheby's, 9 May 1984, lot 146.
FRKF 300

GEORGES BIZET (1838–75)

Letter to Louis Gallet

[ca. 1873] ALS, 3 p., concerning the projected *Don Rodrigue*; mentions Edouard Lalo, Léon and Caroline Carvalho, and Jean-Baptiste Faure.

Marburg, Stargardt, 12 June 1986, lot 618.
FRKF 1328

Letter to Hector Gruyer

1858 Dec. 31, Rome, ALS, 6 p.

The tenor Hector Gruyer (stage name Guardi, 181?–98), pupil of Adolphe Bizet, the composer's father, was chosen to premiere the part of Faust in Gounod's opera. Having lost his voice at the dress rehearsal, he was forced to withdraw, to Bizet's bitter disappointment.

Quoted in Mina Curtiss, *Bizet and his world* (New York: Knopf, 1958), p. 78–80.
New York, Sotheby's, 15 Oct. 1982, lot 128.
FRKF 4

Letters to members of the Halévy family

All are autograph letters, signed, unless otherwise noted. In most cases, no date or place is given; supplied dates are bracketed.

> To Léon Halévy [1856 Sept. 23] "Mardi soir," Le Vésinet [but postmarked Paris] 3 p. (env)
>
> To Ludovic Halévy, 1860 Nov. 5, 1 p., concerning his mother's illness.
>
> [1867] 1 p., referring to a dress rehearsal on Monday, 23 Sept.
>
> To [Ludovic Halévy?] [1867] 1 p., concerning *La jolie fille de Perth*; mentions Henri Meilhac and Léon Carvalho.
>
> To Léon Halévy [1868] 1 p. Identified and dated by Ludovic Halévy.
>
> To Ludovic Halévy [before 1869] 1 p.
>
> To Léon Halévy [1869] 1 p. Identified and dated by Ludovic Halévy.
>
> To Ludovic Halévy [1869] Saint-Gratien, 1 p.
>
> To [Ludovic Halévy?] 1879 July 29, 1 p., on the death of Anatole Prévost-Paradol.
>
> To Ludovic Halévy [1870 Aug. 20] 1 p. Dated by Ludovic Halévy.
>
> To [Ludovic Halévy?] 1870 Nov. 18, Ambulances de la presse française, Mr Georges Bizet, membre protecteur[S], Paris, 1 p.
>
> To Ludovic Halévy, 1871 Feb. 24, Paris, 6 p.
>
> To Ludovic Halévy [1871 Dec.] 2 p. Dated by Ludovic Halévy.
>
> To Ludovic Halévy [1872 June] 1 p. Dated by Ludovic Halévy.
>
> To Ludovic Halévy [1872] 2 p. Dated by Ludovic Halévy.
>
> To Ludovic Halévy [1872–73] 1 p. Dated by Ludovic Halévy.
>
> [1873] July 7, 1 p.
>
> To [Léon Halévy?] "Vendredi soir" [after 1872] 3 p.
>
> To Léonie Halévy, 1 p.
>
> AL to Léonie Halévy, 2 p. Mentions Lamoureux; possibly incomplete.
>
> To [Ludovic Halévy?] 1 p.
>
> To Ludovic Halévy, 1 p.
>
> To [Ludovic Halévy?] 1 p.
>
> To Léon Halévy [after 1870] Conservatoire National de Musique et de Déclamation, Paris[S], 1 p., with an unidentified autograph note on p. [4].
>
> To Léon Halévy, 3 p.
>
> Also, ALS from Léon Halévy to Bizet, 30 Sept., n.y., n.p., 1 p.

Paris, Laurin-Guilloux-Buffetaud-Tailleur (Drouot), 12 Dec. 1985, lot 17.
FRKF 914, 914.5

Letter to "cher Monsieur"

[1872, late Oct. or early Nov., Paris?] ALS, 2 p., concerning *L'Arlésienne*; also mentions Gounod.

London, Sotheby's, 29 Nov. 1985, lot 18.
FRKF 1046

LUIGI BOCCHERINI (1743–1805)

I. MUSIC MANUSCRIPTS

Quintets for piano and strings, op. 57, G. 413–18

Holograph manuscript, in parts, of these quintets, 1799, 104, 88, and 75 p. Notated in black ink on both sides of sheets of oblong 8-staff paper.

> On the title page of the piano part, in black ink, in Boccherini's hand: "= Opera 57. = / Sei Quintetti Concertati tra due violini, Piano = Forte, viola, = / = e violoncello. = / = Composti, e Dedicati al [cancelled: Secrettario della Rep.ca Francese. = / = Da me Luigi Boccherini. Mano propria. = / = Parte del Forte-Piano. ="
>
> On the title page of the violin parts: "= Opera 57. = / Parte de due violini. / Boccherini."
>
> On the title page of the viola and cello parts: "= Opera 57. = / = Parte della viola, e del violoncello. = / = Boccherini. ="

Bound in three volumes in bright red glazed paper boards, with title gold-tooled on irregularly cut rectangles on the front boards: "Quintelti [sic] - / de / Boccherini - / piano [violons; alto & violoncelle]"; spines flat, decorated with seven single gold-tooled fillets.

Accompanied by an ALS from A. Desnoy to "Monsieur," 1881 Mar. 16, n.p., 3 p., concerning the Quintets. This letter came in an unstamped envelope marked: "Lettre incluse / Manuscrit / des trios [sic] de Boccherini / avec / l'édition appartenant / au B[ar]on Lagarde / Ces trios avaient été dédiés au Secrétaire Général du Directoire / le Citoyen

Lagarde / L'édition faite par le B[aro]n Lagarde / est dédiée à la Duchesse de Berry. / (Armoire murale de mon bureau) / HS."

Gérard, p. 461–68.
Heinrich Schütz to Henry Miller, p. 24–25.
London, Sotheby's, 29 Nov. 1985, lot 24.
FRKF 995

II. PRINTED MUSIC

Six Quintetti Spécialement composés pour le Piano-Forte avec accompagnemens obligés et concertans de Deux Violons, un Alto et un Violoncelle par Luigi Boccherini. Oeuvre posthume. Édition dédiée à S.A.R. Madame la Duchesse de Berri. Paris: Nouzou [1820].

Folio, unbound quires, in parts, each with the title page as above, and paginated [1]–57 (Piano); [1]–27 (Violino 1º); [1]–27 (Violini 2º); [1]–21, 11–12 being a single sheet inserted between 10 and 13 (Viola); [1]–21, 11–12 also a single-sheet insert (Basso). Op. 57, G. 413–18.

Gérard, p. 461–68.
London, Sotheby's, 29 Nov. 1985, lot 24.
FRKF 995.5

FRANÇOIS-ADRIEN BOIELDIEU (1775–1834)

Letter to Léon Halévy

1834, Jarcy, ALS, 1 p., concerning his son Adrien; also mentions Cherubini. Copy in Halévy's hand. In a folder labelled, in a secretarial hand: "Boieldieu. / 1826," and annotated by Ludovic Halévy: "et une lettre de 1834 / recopiée par mon père."

Letters to Mme Le Play

[1826 July 29, Paris*] ALS, 3 p., enquiring about the health of his "dear uncle."

1826 Nov. 6, Paris, ALS, 3 p., concerning a trip to Rouen.

n.y., Dec. 18, n.p., ALS, 3 p. In a folder marked in Ludovic Halévy's hand: "Boieldieu / 18 Xbre / Très curieuse lettre." Concerns his recipient's purchase of a piano and conveying the news of the death of his estranged wife and forthcoming remarriage.

Paris, Oger-Dumont (Drouot), 14 Feb. 1985, lot 45.
FRKF 691, 691.5

ALEKSANDR PORFIR'EVICH BORODIN (1833–87)

Letter to Marie Lynen

1886 Feb. 19, St. Petersburg, ALS, 3 p., a letter of thanks, in French. The enclosed photograph of the composer (11 × 17 cm, stamp of the photographic studio R. Sobolev, St. Petersburg, on the verso) is inscribed by him "A Madame Victor Lynen ... Hommage sincèrement affectueux," with a 4-measure musical quotation from his String Quartet no. 1, in A, dated 19 Feb. 1886. Not in S. A. Dianin, ed., *Pisma A.P. Borodina* (Moscow: Gosudarstvennoe izdatelstvo Muzykalnii Sektor, 1927–50).

Paris, Drouot, 12 June 1984, lots 197–98.
FRKF 469.1–2

JOHANNES BRAHMS (1833–97)

"Alte Liebe," op. 72, no. 1

Holograph manuscript of this song for voice and piano on a poem by Karl Candidus, 1876, 4 p. Notated in black ink on a bifolium of oblong 9-staff paper. At the top of the first page, "Alte Liebe. Karl Candidus." Signed at the end and dated 6 May 1876.

Published as the first of the *Five Songs*, op. 72.

McCorkle, p. 305–08.
Heinrich Schütz to Henry Miller, p. 66–67.
London, Christie's, 27 March 1985, lot 202.
FRKF 870

"Freiwillige her!" op. 41, no. 2

Holograph manuscript of this chorus for unaccompanied male voices on a text by Carl Lemcke, 1864, 4 p. Notated in black ink on a single bifolium of tall 12-staff paper. At the top of p. [1] in Brahms's hand: "Freiwillige her!" Signed and dated Jan. 1864 at the end.

Published in 1867 as part of *Fünf Lieder für vierstimmigen Männerchor*, op. 41. First performed in Vienna on 11 March 1893 according to Grove.

McCorkle, p. 147–50.
London, Sotheby's, 29 Nov. 1985, lot 30.
FRKF 1027

"Marschieren," op. 41, no. 4; "Gebt Acht," op. 41, no. 5

Holograph manuscript of these choruses for unaccompanied male voices on texts by Carl Lemcke, n.d., 4 p. "Marschieren" is written in black ink, with pencil corrections, on p. [1]–[3] of a single bifolium of tall 14-staff paper (blind stamp: PAPHDNL v NDDKOSTER HAMBURG); "Gebt Acht" is written on p. [4] of the same bifolium. Both published in 1867 as part of *Fünf Lieder für vierstimmigen Männerchor*, op. 41. According to Grove, "Marschieren" was first performed in Vienna on 27 Nov. 1867 and "Gebt Acht," also in Vienna, on 8 Dec. 1871.

McCorkle, p. 147–50.
London, Sotheby's, 29 Nov. 1985, lot 32.
FRKF 1028

FRIEDRICH WILHELM, KURFÜRST VON BRANDENBURG (1620–88)

Fragment of a manuscript document, signed, concerning Frederick William, margrave of Brandenburg. Margraviate of Brandenburg, 30 March 1659, 1 p.

Marburg, Stargardt, 5–6 March 1985, lot 1286.
FRKF 837

ELIZABETH BARRETT BROWNING (1806–81)

"Hugh Stuart Boyd. Legacies"

Autograph manuscript of this sonnet, n.d., 1 p., in black ink on the verso of a small sheet of paper (11 × 19 cm). Written ca. 1849 following the death of H.S. Boyd in 1848, and first published in *Poems* (1850).

From the collection of the Edward and Betty Marcus Foundation.
See Christie's, New York, 7 June 1990, lot 16; also Sotheby's, New York, 17 June 1992, lot 139.
New York, Christie's, 22 Nov. 1985, lot 9.
FRKF 1265

ROBERT BROWNING (1812–89)

"Life, we have long been friends together …"

Autograph manuscript of an 8-line poem, signed and dated 24 Nov. 1883, 1 p. Written in black ink, in microscopic characters, on stationery of Palazzino Alvisi, Venezia. The poem is a fragment from Barbauld, "Ode to Life." See Katharine C. de Kay Bronson, "Browning in Venice," *The Century Magazine* 63 (1902), p. 572.

The Brownings: A Research Guide [online resource], The Armstrong Browning Library of Baylor University, E0547.
London, Sotheby's, 16 July 1984, lot 62.
FRKF 507

MAX BRUCH (1838–1920)

Crux fidelis

Manuscript, in the hand of a copyist, of this duet for soprano and alto with piano accompaniment, 1907, 12 p.; also the vocal parts, in Bruch's hand, 1907, 6 p. The manuscript is written in black ink on three nested, stitched bifolia of 12-staff paper, paginated 1 through 12, and nested in a fourth bifolium (now detached) serving as wrappers.

> On the front wrapper, in Burch's hand: "Composed / for Carmela and Grazia Carbone / Crux fidelis. / (Hymn of Passion .3) / Duet / for Soprano and Alto / with Piano Accompaniment. / by / Max Bruch."

> The parts are written in black ink on the first three pages of two separate bifolia of 14-staff paper. They are both dated 17 March 1907 in pencil by the composer at the top of p. [1] and inscribed, the soprano part to Carmela, the alto part to Grazia. They are also signed in black ink and dated Berlin, 16 March 1907, on p. [3]. With a pencil note on p. [1] of a separate bifolium (now detached) of 10-staff paper with a pencil inscription by Grazia Carbone, indicating that the manuscript was given to her by Bruch.

> With a signed letter, partly autograph, to Carmela and Grazia Carbone, 1907 March 11, Berlin, 4 p., about *Crux fidelis*, accompanied by a small fragment of a music manuscript, with musical quotations described as being by Cherubini, Bruch, and Tchaikovsky on one side, and unidentified music on the other side, with a pencil attribution to [Anton?] Rubinstein.

Not listed in Grove.
London, Sotheby's, 10 May 1984, lot 25.
FRKF 326a–b

SIR EDWARD COLEY BURNE-JONES (1833–98)

I. DRAWINGS

"Mermaid on Brighton Beach"

Pen and brown ink drawing on paper (11 × 17.5 cm).

London, Christie's South Kensington, 16 Dec. 1985, lot 27.
FRKF 1256

Drawings for Archibald Maclaren's *The fairy family*, ca. 1854–56

"The Moss Family," pen-and-ink and graphite on paper, 10 × 14.5 cm.

Kneeling Youth, pen and black ink on paper, 6 × 14 cm, apparently intended as a tailpiece for the ballad "Fata Morgana" in the "Seas and Rivers" section.

"We the Orphan's head will shield," pen and black ink and graphite on paper, 9.5 × 14 cm, with the caption lettered in black ink at the top.

The three drawings above matted together.

"The Wee Fair Folk" and "Sun is setting, Silver moon Trembles in the skies …," graphite and pencil on paper, 17 × 14.5 cm, marked "unfinished" at the bottom.

"'Tis Hans the Miller, old Hans' heir," 6 pen-and-ink and pencil and graphite drawings on a single sheet, 21.5 × 17 cm.

"The Merman," pen and black ink and graphite on paper, 9.5 × 14.5 cm. The title is in pencil at the top; caption: "Within a little shelter'd bay" lettered on the right side.

See Archibald Maclaren, *The fairy family: a series of ballads and metrical tales illustrating the fairy faith of Europe*. Illustrated by Edward Burne-Jones, with an introduction by John Christian (London: Dalrymple Press, 1985. Published by the Dalrymple Press for Frederick R. Koch). The drawings are reproduced on p. 55 ("We the orphans"), 118–19 ("'Tis Hans the miller"), 164 (Kneeling youth), and 176 ("The merman"). The finished versions of "The wee fair folk" and "Two sisters dwell …" are on p. 58 and 135 respectively.

Heinrich Schütz to Henry Miller, p. 48–49.
FRKF 86

II. LETTERS

Many of the letters by Burne-Jones are on printed stationery, indicated as follows:

Grange^S = The Grange, West Kensington, W. [London]
Rottingdean^S = Rottingdean, Nr. Brighton

To the Rev. Stopford Brooke

Autograph letters, signed, all undated.

"Saturday," Grange^S, 3 p.

Grange^S, 4 p.

Grange^S, 4 p.

"Wednesday," Grange^S, 3 p. Mentions pictures of the Kings he has just finished.

Grange^S, 1 p. Illustrated with a self-caricature, showing him sitting on the floor with a collapsed partition next to him.

London, Sotheby's, 18 Dec. 1985, lot 259.
FRKF 1000

To W. H. Clabburn

1863 Jan. 20, "62 Gt Russell St" [London] ALS, 3 p. (env), concerning his "Theseus and Ariadne."

London, Phillips, 17 April 1986, lot 125.
FRKF 1257

To Canon Richard Watson Dixon

All are ALS, some from Georgiana Burne-Jones (GBJ).

[1856 Dec. 12*] 17 Red Lion Square, 1 p. (env)

[1873 Sept. 1, London*] 1 Poplar Place, Bristol Road, 4 p. (env). Illustrated with a self-portrait.

[1878 May 15*] The Grange, Northend, Fulham, 2 p. (env)

[1878 Dec. 11, London*] Grange^S, 1 p. (env)

1896 Oct. 3, from GBJ, Kelmscott House, 2 p. (env), reporting the death of William Morris.

1898 Dec. 2, from GBJ, The Grange, West Ken[sing]t[o]n, 2 p. (env)

1899 Apr. 4, from GBJ, 6 Pembroke Gardens, Kensington. W. [London]^S, 2 p. (env)

1899 July 5, from GBJ, Rottingdean^S, 4 p. (env)

1899 Aug. 6, from GBJ, Pembroke Gardens^S, 3 p. (env)

1899 Oct. 5, from GBJ, Pembroke Gardens^S, 3 p. (env)

1899 Oct. 31, from GBJ, Rottingdean^S, 3 p.

1899 Dec. 13. from GBJ, Rottingdean^S, 4 p. (env)

Undated

"Saturday morning," 17 Red Lion Square, 1 p.

Grange, 1 p.

Grange^S, 1 p.

n.p., 1 p.

Grange^S, 4 p.

62 Gt Russell St. Bloomsbury [London] 4 p. Illustrated at the end with a self-caricature.

Together with two loose, unassigned envelopes, postmarked 1 May 1880 and 17 Oct. 1896.

London, Sotheby's, 6 Dec. 1984, lot 416.
FRKF 872

To "Sir Edward"

n.d., Grange[S], ALS, 3 p.

n.d., Grange[S], ALS, 3 p., regretting not to be able to join his correspondent on a trip to Paris.

FRKF 975

To "Elsie"

These autograph letters, signed, are all undated.

Grange[S], 4 p. Written in pencil; illustrated with 6 pencil caricatures, some with captions, including a train.

Grange[S], 4 p. Illustrated with 4 pen-and-ink caricatures: a knight on a horse, a doctor and a patient, a blackbird, a self-caricature.

Grange[S], 3 p. Illustrated with 2 pen-and-ink caricatures: a rooster, a knight on a horse.

Grange[S], 3 p. Illustrated with 3 pen-and-ink caricatures: a cat, a self-caricature, a house.

Grange[S], 3 p.

n.p, 3 p. Illustrated with 3 pen-and-ink drawings: a cat, a woman reading a book, and a self-caricature.

n.p., 2 p. Illustrated with a pen-and-ink self-caricature. On paper, possibly for commercial use, with a wide red border with large white dots.

Rottingdean[S], 4 p. Illustrated with 2 pen-and-ink drawings: a rooster and a pig.

Grange[S], 4 p. Illustrated on all sides with pen-and-ink drawings of birds, also showing the face of Burne-Jones and a young woman, possibly Elsie herself.

Grange[S], 2 p.

Grange[S], "Monday," 4 p.

Grange[S], 2 p. Illustrated with a pen-and-ink drawing of two young children.

Grange[S], "Friday," 1 p. Illustrated with a pen-and-ink self-caricature.

Grange[S], 2 p. Illustrated with a pen-and-ink drawing showing Burne-Jones painting.

Grange[S], 4 p.

Grange[S], 1 p. Illustrated with "tears" in red gouache.

Grange[S], "Monday," 4 p. Illustrated with a pen-and-ink self-caricature.

Grange[S], "Monday," 3 p.

Grange[S], 2 p. Illustrated with a small pen-and-ink caricature: a flower with human face.

Grange[S], "Tuesday," 4 p.

Grange[S], 3 p.

Grange[S], 3 p.

Grange[S], 4 p.

Grange[S], 2 p.

n.p., 4 p.

"at a bookshop in town," 1 p. Illustrated with a self-caricature showing Burne-Jones painting.

n.p., 3 p.

Grange[S], "Sunday," 3 p. Illustrated with a pen-and-ink self-caricature.

Grange[S], 2 p. Illustrated with a pen-and-ink self-caricature: Burne-Jones with a cold.

Rottingdean[S], 4 p. Illustrated with a pen-and-ink drawing of a church.

With a pen-and-ink self-caricature on a small sheet of paper, 11.5 × 17.5 cm, inscribed "yours aff" and a pencil drawing of a chick next to a broken eggshell, on the verso of a small piece of stationery of West Hall, Byfleet, Weybridge, 9.5 × 15 cm, with pencil caption: "Is it time, he learnt."

The identity of the recipient, who lived in Kew, is not known. The correspondence, dating from the 1870s and 1880s, was evidently begun when Elsie was a young girl (the first five letters imitate the writing of a child) and continued through her engagement.

From the collection of Kenneth A. Lohf.
See Christie's, New York, 7 June 1990, lot 20; see also Sotheby's, New York, 17 June 1992, lot 141; and Sotheby's, New York, 17 Dec. 1992, lot 42.
FRKF 269

To Elizabeth Gaskell

Fragments of three letters to Elizabeth Gaskell, one of them on printed stationery of The Grange, the others with no place given; one dated "Thursday night" without year, the others undated, 6 p. On one side of each sheet are pen-and-ink caricatures of a majestic character identified in Burne-Jones's hand as "Julia Porkington."

Accompanied by an autograph note, signed [Amy?] Gaskell: "These letters from Sir Edward Burne-Jones to Mrs Gaskell are pure inventions of his fancy and fun. No Julia Porkington existed except in his imagination just for 'the fun of the thing.' He sometimes carried on imaginary stories for weeks, with illustrations, in his letters."

London, Christie's, 26 Feb. 1985, lot 158.
FRKF 892

To Luke Ionides

1889 May 14*, Rottingdean[S], ALS, 2 p. (env). Mentions Kate Vaughan.

n.d., Grange[S], ALS, 1 p. (env)

FRKF 311

To Miss Mackenzie

All are undated.

Grange[S], ALS, 4 p. Mentions Samuel Richardson; addressed to "My incomparable Miss Mackenzie."

Grange[S], ALS, 2 p.

Grange[S], ALS, 2 p.

n.p., ALS, 1 p.

FRKF 311

To Miss Macpherson

"Friday," Grange[S], ALS, 1 p., confirming an appointment.

FRKF 311

To Cormell Price

Most letters are undated.

1867
Sept., ALS, 2 p., annotated in ink [by Price?]: "fr: E. Burne Jones. Sep. /67."

1869
Aug., ALS, 1 p., dated in pencil.

1870
[Sept. 3*, London] ALS, 1 p. (env). The front of the envelope is embellished with drawings of a little girl and a tower.

1871
May 26, ALS, 2 p.

1872
Nov. 26, Grange[S], ALS, 2 p.
Dec., ALS, 1 p., dated in pencil.

1876
Aug., ALS, 1 p., dated in pencil.

1877
Aug., Tavistock Hotel [London?][S], ALS, 4 p., dated in pencil.

1878
Grange[S], ALS, 1 p., dated in pencil.

1881
Jan. 5, Brighton, ALS, 2 p., dated in pencil.
[April 16, Eastbourne*] APCS

1882
[April 12, London*] APCS
[April 15, London*] APCS
[July 30, Brighton*] APCS
[Aug. 15, London*] APCS
[Sept. 8*] Grange[S], ALS, 1 p. (env)

1883
[Sept. 17, Brighton*] ALS, 3 p. (env)
Oct. 4, Grange[S], ALS, 2 p., dated in pencil.
[Dec. 27, Brighton,*] ALS, 1 p. (env)

1885
Jan. 15, Grange[S], LS, 3 p. The date is not in Burne-Jones's hand. The opening salutation in a child's hand.
[March 23*] Grange[S], ALS, 3 p. (env)
[April 15, Hammersmith*] APCS
[April 20, Paddington*] Grange[S], ALS, 2 p. (env)
[April 20, London W.*] Grange[S], ALS, 3 p. (env)
Aug. [postmark illegible save for the year 1885] Grange[S], ALS, 2 p. (env), dated in ink.
[Aug. 6*] Grange[S], ALS, 1 p. (env)
Aug. 10, London, telegram
Sept. 2, Grange[S], ALS, 1 p.
[Oct. 27*] "Monday," Grange[S], ALS, 2 p. (env)
Oct. 28, Grange[S], ALS, 1 p. (env), dated in pencil. The envelope is elaborately calligraphic.

1886
[April 15*] Grange[S], ALS, 2 p. (env)
[May 8, Brighton*] ALS, 2 p. (env)
[May 24, Hammersmith*] APCS
June 28, ALS, 1 p., dated in pencil.
[Dec. 24*] Grange[S], ALS, 2 p. (env)
[Dec. 28*] Grange[S], ALS, 1 p. (env). The address on the envelope is calligraphic.

1887
[April 4*] Grange[S], ALS, 1 p. (env)
[July 21*] Grange[S], ALS, 2 p. (env)
[July 27*] "Monday," Grange[S], ALS, 2 p. (env). The letter is in pencil; elaborate calligraphy under the signature.
[Aug. 6*] "Sat:" Grange[S], ALS, 3 p. (env)
[Sept. 9*] Grange[S], ALS, 1 p. (env)
[Nov. 30*] Grange[S], ALS, 1 p. (env)

[Dec. 22*] Grange^S, ALS, 1 p. (env)
[Dec. 27*] Grange^S, ALS, 2 p. (env)

1888

March 1, Grange^S, ALS, 1 p. (env), with a caricature of a disappointed bearded character.
June 4, Grange^S, ALS, 3 p., dated in ink.
[July 28*] Rottingdean^S, ALS, 2 p. (env)
Aug. 2, Grange^S, ALS, 1 p. (env)
Aug., Grange^S, ALS, 2 p., dated in ink, with a drawing depicting rain.
[Oct. 9*] Grange^S, ALS, 3 p. (env)
[Oct. 19*] Grange^S, ALS, 1 p. (env), in pencil, enclosing a tally for a game between Burne-Jones and Price, 1 leaf.
[Dec. 21*] Grange^S, ALS, 1 p. (env)
Dec., Grange^S, ALS, 2 p., dated in pencil.

1889

[March 8*] 2 Mandeville Place W. [London]^S, ALS, 4 p.
April, Grange^S, ALS, 1 p., dated in pencil on envelope.
[April 19, Paddington*] APCS
Aug. [postmark illegible] Grange^S, ALS, 2 p. (env), dated in ink on envelope.
[Aug. 12*] "Sunday," Grange^S, ALS, 3 p. (env)
[Aug. 17*] "Saturday," Grange^S, ALS, 2 p. (env)
[Aug. 21*] Grange^S, ALS, 3 p. (env)
[Aug. 24, Brighton*] ALS, 1 p.
[Sept. 3, Brighton*] United Services College, Westward Ho: N. Devon^S, ALS, 2 p., a facetious letter, signed Colonel & Mrs. Tomquins.

1890

[Jan. 31*] "Friday," Grange^S, ALS, 1 p. (env)
[March 16*] "Wednesday," Rottingdean^S, ALS, 2 p. (env)
[April 7*] Grange^S, ALS, 1 p. (env)
[April 9*] Grange^S, ALS, 2 p. (env)
[April 12*] Grange^S, ALS, 1 p. (env)
[May 26*] Grange^S, ALS, 1 p. (env)
[June 9*] "Monday," Rottingdean^S, ALS, 1 p. (env)
[June 20*] Rottingdean^S, ALS, 3 p. (env)
June 22, Rottingdean^S, ALS, 1 p. (env)
Oct. 2, Grange^S, ALS, 2 p., dated in pencil.
[Dec. 15] Grange^S, ALS, 3 p. (env)

1891

[Jan. 2*] Grange^S, ALS, 2 p. (env)
[Feb. 23*] Grange^S, ALS, 1 p. (env)
[April 20*] Grange^S, ALS, 1 p. (env)
[April 22*] Grange^S, ALS, 1 p. (env)

[May 21*] Grange^S, ALS, 1 p. (env)
[June 2*] "Tuesday," Grange^S, ALS, 2 p. (env). Square cut out from front leaf.
[June 7*] Rottingdean^S, ALS, 3 p. (env)
[June 8*] "Sunday," Rottingdean^S, ALS, 2 p. (env)
[June 12*] "Friday," Rottingdean^S, ALS, 2 p. (env)
[June 13*] "Saturday," Rottingdean^S, ALS, 1 p. (env)
[July 22, Brighton*] "Tuesday," ALS, 1 p. (env)
[July 29*] "Tuesday," Rottingdean^S, ALS, 2 p. (env)
[Aug. 8, Brighton*] ALS, 2 p. (env)
[Aug. 10*] "Monday 2 o'clock," Rottingdean^S, ALS, 2 p. (env)
[Dec. 21*] "Sunday," Rottingdean (embossed)^S, ALS, 2 p. (env), illustrated with a drawing of 5 dominoes.
[Dec. 27*] "Sunday," Rottingdean^S, ALS, 2 p. (env)
Dec. 28, Brighton, telegram
[Dec. 29*] Rottingdean (embossed)^S, ALS, 3 p. (env)

1892

[Jan. 26, London*] APCS
[Feb. 27*] "Monday," Grange^S, ALS, 3 p. (env), written in pencil.
[April 7*] Rottingdean^S, ALS, 1 p. (env)
[April 16, London*] ALS, 1 p. (env)
[June 7*] "Tuesday," Grange^S, ALS, 3 p. (env)

1893

April 16, Grange^S, ALS, 1 p., dated in pencil.
[June 15, London*] ALS, 2 p. (env)
[Aug. 11, London*] ALS, 1 p. (env)
[Oct. 24, London*] ALS, 1 p. (env)

1894

[Jan. 10*] "Wednesday," Grange^S, ALS, 1 p. (env)
Feb. 14, Grange^S, ALS, 1 p. (env)
[June 10*] Rottingdean^S, ALS, 1 p. (env)
[Aug. 14*] Rottingdean (embossed)^S, ALS, 2 p. (env)
[Aug. 25*] Rottingdean (embossed)^S, ALS, 1 p. (env), written in pencil.
[Aug. 30*] Rottingdean (embossed)^S, ALS, 1 p. (env)
[Sept. 15*] "Saturday," Grange^S, ALS, 1 p. (env)
Oct. 26, "Saturday" [London*] ALS, 2 p. (env)

1895

[Jan. 12*] "Thursday," Grange^S, ALS, 2 p. (env)
[July 3*] Grange^S, ALS, 1 p. (env)
[July 27*] "Sat[urday]" Grange^S, ALS, 1 p. (env)
[Aug. 10*] "Sat[urday]" Grange^S, ALS, 1 p. (env)
[Sept. 6*] "Friday," Rottingdean^S, ALS, 2 p. (env)
[Sept. 28, Paddington*] APCS

1896

[March 3*] "Sat:," Grange^S, ALS, 1 p. (env)

[April 25*] Rottingdean, ALS, 1 p. (env)

[June?] "Sat:," Grange^S, ALS, 2 p.

[June?] Grange^S, ALS, 1 p. This and the preceding letter with an envelope postmarked 27 June 1896, with the note in pencil: "2 letters in same envelope."

[July 11*] Grange^S, ALS, 1 p. (env)

[July 29*] Grange^S, ALS, 1 p. (env)

[Aug. 26*] "Wednesday," Rottingdean^S, ALS, 3 p. (env)

[Aug. 28*] "Friday," Rottingdean^S, ALS, 1 p. (env)

[Sept. 5, Brighton*] ALS, 2 p. (env)

[Oct. 3*] "Sat. 1 o'clock," Grange^S, ALS, 1 p. (env)

[Oct. 12, London*] The Athenaeum (embossed)^S, ALS, 3 p. (env)

[Oct. 15*] Grange^S, ALS, 1 p. (env)

1897

[Jan 16*] "Sat:," Grange^S, ALS, 1 p. (env)

[Feb. 6*] "Sat.," Grange^S, ALS, 1 p. (env)

[April 3*] "Sat.," Grange^S, ALS, 1 p. (env)

[July 17*] "Sat.," Grange^S, ALS, 1 p. (env)

[July 31*] "Sat.y," Grange^S, ALS, 1 p. (env)

[Aug. 14*] "Sat[urday]" Grange^S, ALS, 1 p. (env)

[Sept. 4*] "Sat:," Grange^S, ALS, 1 p. (env). Elaborate flourish on the address side of the envelope.

[Dec. 18*] Grange^S, ALS, 1 p. (env)

1898

[Jan. 19*] Grange^S, ALS, 1 p. (env)

[Jan. 27*] "Thursday," Grange^S, ALS, 1 p. (env)

March 1, London, telegram

[April 30*] "Sat:," Grange^S, ALS, 1 p. (env)

[July 26*] Grange^S, ALS, 1 p. (env)

Undated letters:

ALS, Grange^S, 1 p.

ALS, Grange^S, "Thursday," 3 p.

ALS, Grange^S, 3 p.

ALS, Grange^S, "Sat[urday]," 1 p.

ALS, 1 p.

ALS, 1 p., written in pencil.

ALS, The Grange, North End S.W. [London] 1 p.

ALS, Grange^S, 1 p.

ALS, Grange^S, "Wednesday," 2 p.

ALS, "Satur[day]" 1 p.

ALS, 2 p., written in pencil.

ALS, Grange^S [Paddington, 30 Dec.* year illegible] 2 p. (env)

ALS, Grange^S, "Sat.," 2 p.

ALS, 1 p.

Also, an empty envelope, postmarked Paddington, 5 Oct. 1887.

Price, one of Burne-Jones's intimate friends, is addressed as "little Crom," "Kerhommy," "Krommie," "Koji," "Quodji," "Kew-v," and "Q." Most of the letters concern visits and appointments. They also convey personal and family news and one comments on the death of William Morris.

FRKF 215

To "My dear Shields"

"Wednesday," Grange^S, ALS, 2 p., concerning a visit.

FRKF 311

To "My dear Sir"

1864 Aug. 24, 62 Gt Russell Street [London] ALS, 1 p. Thank you note.

n.d., n.p., ALS, 2 p. Thanks for advice on "the little matter of speeches."

FRKF 311

To an unidentified correspondent

Rottingdean^S, ALS, 1 p. Arrangements for displaying pictures.

FRKF 311

Letter fragments

To an unidentified correspondent, Grange^S, 3 p., referring to having a cold. On p. [2] and [3] self-caricature showing Burne-Jones sick in a chair.

To an unidentified correspondent, 2 p. Signed "Ned." On the verso is a pen-and-ink portrait of two girls, captioned: "like this."

London, Phillips, 24 Oct. 1985, lot 580.

FRKF 1011

III. MISCELLANEOUS

"Burne-Jones' recipe for varnishing plaster casts." Manuscript in an unidentified hand, written on stationery of "Pen Pole, Shirehampton, Bristol," n.d., 2 p.

FRKF 311

"Score kept by Sir Edward Burne-Jones during a game played at Beaumont at a children's party." Note in an unidentified hand, n.d., n.p., 1 p.

FRKF 86

Philip Burne-Jones (1861–1926) Letters to Rennell Rodd

1884 Aug. 10, Arran, ALS, 8 p. Mentions Oscar Wilde.

1885 Feb. 22, Grange^S, ALS, 8 p. Mentions Oscar Wilde, William Morris, and Edward Burne-Jones. Illustrated with two pen-and-ink sketches, one showing a male model, the other a man and a clay figure posing for a painting in a churchyard.

FRKF 351a–b

ROBERT BURNS (1759–96)

Letter to "Clarinda" [Mrs. Agnes M'Lehose]

[1788 Jan. 10] "Thursday noon" [Edinburgh] ALS, 3 p., a love letter, signed "Sylvander," prompted by Clarinda's failure to nod to him when passing by his house. Tears in the second leaf caused by the removal (presumably by Mrs M'Lehose herself) of the recipient's name and address.

Ferguson 175.
See Christie's, London, 16 Dec. 1991, lot 280.
London, Sotheby's, 15 Dec. 1982, lot 99.
FRKF 116

GEORGE GORDON BYRON, BARON BYRON (1788–1824)

Letter to Stendhal

1823 May 29, Genoa, ALS, 3 p. Mentions *Rome, Naples, and Florence in 1817* as well as Walter Scott; accompanied by a contemporary translation and related notes.

Marchand, X:189–90.
Paris, Ader-Picard-Tajan (Drouot), 22 Nov. 1985, lot 14.
FRKF 1416

ENRICO CARUSO (1873–1921)

Letters to Emilia Tibaldi Niola

Both on the stationery of The Vanderbilt Hotel, New York, with envelopes.

> 1920 Sept. 22, ALS, 16 p., signed "E Carusiello."
>
> 1920 Nov. 23, ALS, 8 p.

London, Sotheby's, 9–10 May 1985, lots 45, 49.
FRKF 758.1, 758.3

Letter to Raffaele Niola

1920 Jan. 1, Hotel Knickerbocker, New York[S], ALS, 10 p. On the last page are two autograph self-caricatures of the singer, signed, showing him in 1888 and in 1920.

London, Sotheby's, 9–10 May 1985, lot 47.
FRKF 758.2

EMMANUEL CHABRIER (1841–94)

Letters to his wife, Marie Alice Dejean

> [1886 March 17, Brussels] ALS, 3 p., concerning the rehearsals of *Gwendoline*. *Correspondance*, p. 325–26.

Paris, Le Roux - Mathias (Drouot), 19 April 1985, lot 257.
FRKF 719.1

> [1888 July 2, Paris*] ALS, 1 p. (env), concerning *Briséïs*; mentions Catulle Mendès. *Correspondance*, p. 503.

Paris, Laurin-Guilloux-Buffetaud-Tailleur (Drouot), 12 Dec. 1985, lot 32.
FRKF 915.5

> 1891 June [i.e. Aug.] 3, Mt. Dore, ALS, 5 p., mostly concerning his health. *Correspondance*, p. 919–20.

Paris, Le Roux - Mathias (Drouot), 19 April 1985, lot 257.
FRKF 719.2

Letter to Georges Costallat

[1884 Sept. 7] "Dimanche," n.p., ALS, 3 p. Mentions *La Sulamite* and *Le roi malgré lui*, and Paul Burani (co-librettist for the latter). With several postscripts in pencil on the third page, with references to Paul Lacombe and Léon Carvalho. *Correspondance*, p. 246–47.

Paris, Laurin-Guilloux-Buffetaud-Tailleur (Drouot), 3 July 1985, lot 27.
FRKF 845a

Letter to Catulle Mendès

[ca. 1885 May 15] La Membrolle par Mettray (Indre et Loire), ALS, 3 p., concerning *Gwendoline*; also mentions Augusta Holmès and Vincent d'Indy. *Correspondance*, p. 273.

Paris, Laurin-Guilloux-Buffetaud-Tailleur (Drouot), 12 Dec. 1985, lot 31.
FRKF 915

CÉCILE CHAMINADE (1857–1944)

Chanson slave

Holograph manuscript of this song for voice and piano, 1879, 4 p. Notated in black ink on a single bifolium of tall 12-staff paper. At the top of p. [1], in Chaminade's hand: "Poésie de Paul Ginisty / Chanson Slave / C. Chaminade / A Mme Brunet-Lafleur." Signed and dated 25 Oct. 1879 at the end.

New York, Lion Heart Autographs catalogue, 1986.
FRKF 972

FREDERIC CHAPMAN (1823–95)

Yellow Book contract

Original manuscript contract for the *Yellow Book*, in the hand of Frederic Chapman, signed by Henry Harland and Aubrey Beardsley, [London] 19 April 1894, 1 p. The contract is between Elkin Mathews and John Lane, on the one hand, and Beardsley and Harland on the other.

London, Sotheby's, 18 Dec. 1985, lot 214.
FRKF 1007

CHARLOTTE OF BELGIUM, EMPRESS OF MEXICO (1840–1927)

Letters to Maximilian, emperor of Mexico

1866 Aug. 30, Miramar, ALS, 2 p. Mentions Prince Umberto of Italy.

1866 Sept. 9, Miramar, ALS, 11 p., on monogrammed stationery. Mentions Benito Juarez and Emperor Franz Joseph; accompanied by an enclosure, also in Charlotte's hand, entitled "Das Königreich Italien," 3 p.

1866 Sept. 19, Miramar[S] (mourning, monogrammed), ALS, 11 p. Mentions Osmont and Friant, General Castelnau, and Garibaldi.

Heinrich Schütz to Henry Miller, p. 56–57.

With an ALS, in Italian, to Charlotte from Maria Annunziata of Austria, 1866 Sept. 10, Vienna, 3 p., on monogrammed stationery, announcing the death of a friend, with a calling card printed "L'Impératrice du Mexique. / Grand Hôtel."

Once in the possession of Count Rudolf Rességuier. See Egon Caesar Corti, conte. *Maximilian und Charlotte von Mexiko, nach dem bisher unveröffentlichten Geheimarchive des Kaisers Maximilian und sonstigen unbekannten Quellen* (Zürich: Amaltheaverlag, 1924, vol. 2), p. 282–84 and 288.

Marburg, Stargardt, 22–23 March 1983, lot 1289.
FRKF 219

GUSTAVE CHARPENTIER (1860–1956)

I. MUSIC MANUSCRIPTS

Le couronnement de la muse

A 15-measure holograph fragment, in full score, written in black ink, with corrections in black and blue pencil, on the recto of a tall sheet of 24-staff paper. It begins with the tenor's words "Tendre muse sois toujours clémente." The rehearsal numbers 27 and 28 are noted. At the top of the page, in pencil: "Arrangement pour une exécution en plein air." Only the instrumentation, and a short draft in blue pencil, are present on the verso, which also includes a note of authentication ("Page autographe de Gustave Charpentier"), signed Claude Charpentier.

Le couronnement de la muse, spectacle in nine sections for solo voices, chorus, and orchestra, was premiered at the Nouveau Théâtre, in Paris, in June 1897; it was later incorporated into *Louise*, act 3, scene 3.

Paris, Hervé Poulain (Drouot), 5 April 1984, lot 7.
FRKF 441

Drafts

Two pages of unidentified drafts, written in black ink on both sides of a tall sheet of 24-staff paper. Note of authentication signed Claude Charpentier at the top of p. [1].

Paris, Laurin-Guilloux-Buffetaud-Tailleur (Drouot), 5 April 1984, lot 7.
FRKF 441.5

II. LETTERS

To Arthur Dandelot

[1900 Oct. 6, Paris*]. Note of thanks on visiting card, card and envelope with mourning border.

Arthur Dandelot (1864–1943) was a music critic, notably at *Le monde musical*, which he co-founded, and where the card is addressed.

Paris, Laurin-Guilloux-Buffetaud-Tailleur (Drouot), 3 July 1985, lot 27.
FRKF 845b

To an unidentified correspondent [Reynaldo Hahn?]

1894 Nov. 20, n.p., ALS, 1 p., concerning an unidentified score by Charpentier.

Paris, Laurin-Guilloux-Buffetaud-Tailleur (Drouot), 8 Feb. 1985, lot 115.
FRKF 658.1

FRÉDÉRIC CHOPIN (1810–49)

I. MUSIC MANUSCRIPT

Cantabile in B-flat major, WN 43

Autograph manuscript, in black ink on an oblong sheet of 8-staff paper, dated "Paris 1834" and signed by Chopin.

Accompanied by a Maggs Bros. invoice recording the sale of the manuscript on 23 June 1923 to Sigismund Goetze, Esq., in London, for the sum of £35. See Maggs catalogue 439, no. 485.

Unpublished during Chopin's lifetime, the *Cantabile in B-flat major* was first published in facsimile in 1925 in Basel and appeared in 1931 in Warsaw, edited by Ludwig Bronarski.

Kobylanska 1230.
Heinrich Schütz to Henry Miller, p. 34–35.
London, Bloomsbury Book Auctions, 30 Nov. 1983, lot 129.
FRKF 241

II. LETTERS

Note

Autograph note in black ink on a small oblong piece of paper with "FC" monogram embossed, listing four piano works by Hummel (2), Pixis, and Moscheles, and assigning them to his pupils, identified as C[omte]sse Juria [?] and C[omte]sse Anna.

FRKF 524

To George Sand

[1843 Oct. 29, Paris*] ALS, 1 p., reporting on his journey. The second half of the letter is from Sand's son Maurice Dudevant. Not in *Correspondance*.

FRKF 522

To an unidentified recipient

n.d., "Lundi matin," ANS, accepting an engagement in Kensington. Possibly written in London in 1848. Not in *Correspondance*.

FRKF 523

III. MISCELLANEOUS

Chopin's death and funeral

Wojciech Grzymala to Auguste Léo, 1849 Nov. 8, Paris, ALS, 3 p., in French, concerning the death of Chopin. *Correspondance*, III: 453–55.
Printed invitation to Chopin's funeral at the Église de La Madeleine in Paris on 1849 Oct. 30, 4 p., addressed on p. [4] to "Monsieur Bridgetown / à St. Cloud."

FRKF 525–26

PAUL CLAUDEL (1868–1955)

Letters to Daniel Halévy

1925 April 22, 80, rue de Passy [Paris] ALS, 1 p.

1925 May 30, 80, rue de Passy, ALS, 1 p.

1931 April 21, Ambassade de France aux États-Unis[S] [Washington, D.C.] ALS, 4 p.; comments on an article by Halévy on his work.

1932 Sept. 4, Château de Brangues, Morestel, Brangues[S], ALS, 2 p.

1932 Oct. 24, Ambassade de France aux États-Unis[S], ALS, 2 p., concerning Halévy's *Pays parisiens*.

Paris, Laurin-Guilloux-Buffetaud-Tailleur (Drouot), 12 Dec. 1985, lot 34.
FRKF 955

JEAN COCTEAU (1889–1963)

I. LITERARY MANUSCRIPTS: POEMS

Unless otherwise noted, the manuscripts are undated.

"A mon livre"

Autograph poem [ca. 1911–12], 4 p., in black ink on the recto sides of four oblong sheets. Signed "Jean Cocteau" on the last page, blank.

Published at the end of *La danse de Sophocle* (Paris: Mercure de France, 1912).

See *Oeuvres poétiques complètes*, p. 1450 and 1847–49.
Paris, Laurin-Guilloux-Buffetaud-Tailleur (Drouot), 19 March 1986, lot 50.
FRKF 950c

"Ascenceur"

Autograph poem, 1 p., in black ink on tracing paper.

Published in 1920 in *Poésies 1917–1920*. See *Oeuvres poétiques complètes*, p. 166–67 and 1598.
FRKF 1245.D05

"Avis"

Autograph poem, 1 p., in black ink on tracing paper.

Published in *Poésies 1917–1920*. See *Oeuvres poétiques complètes*, p. 208 and 1601.

Kenneth Rendell Catalogue 169.
FRKF 404

"Cadran solaire"

Autograph poem, 1 p., in black ink on tracing paper.

Published in 1920 in *Poésies 1917–1920*. See *Oeuvres poétiques complètes*, p. 209–10.
FRKF 1245.D05

Le Cap de Bonne Espérance

Holograph calligraphic manuscript of "L'invitation à la mort (Vol avec Garros)," 1918, 23 p., in purple ink, with some words underlined in green ink, on the recto sides of large sheets of thick tracing paper (40 × 60 cm). On p. 1, title: "L'invitation à la mort. / (vol avec Garros) -"
Also on p. 1, pencilled note in an unidentified hand: "Avant-dernière partie du poème / Le Cap de Bonne espérance / de Jean Cocteau / Ecrite pour Valentine Hugo / en 1918."

Oeuvres poétiques complètes, p. 61–67 and 1561–64.
FRKF 1245.B02

"Un cauchemar"

Autograph poem, 1 p., in black ink on one side of a single sheet, beginning "J'avais voulu monter aux tours de Notre Dame -"

Not located in *Oeuvres poétiques complètes*.
FRKF 1245.D04

"C'est en or précieux …"

Autograph manuscript, 1912 [for 1911?] on p. [1] of a bifolium, evidently torn from a book (or possibly an album), signed and dated "Jean Cocteau. / 1912 / (presque!)."
A quatrain in praise of Gabriel Astruc, beginning "C'est en or précieux, et non pas en vil stuc …" Possibly a book dedication. Astruc was at the time Diaghilev's impresario.

Not located in *Oeuvres poétiques complètes*.
FRKF 1245.D03

"Chanson pour elle"

Calligraphic poem, 1 p., in black ink on the recto of a single sheet. At the top of the page, in Cocteau's hand, the title "Hymne."

Published in 1909 in *La lampe d'Aladin*. See *Oeuvres poétiques complètes*, p. 1274–75 and 1837.
FRKF 1245.D01

"Compliment"

Manuscript poem, 1 p., in black ink, in capital letters, on a sheet of tracing paper.

Published in *Poésies 1917–1920*. See *Oeuvres poétiques complètes*, p. 194 and note p. 1598.
Kenneth Rendell Catalogue 169.
FRKF 401

"Conte"

Autograph manuscript of this prose poem, 2 p., in black ink on two sheets of tracing paper. Original title, cancelled: "La force de l'habitude."

Published in *Poésies 1917–1920*. See *Oeuvres poétiques complètes*, p. 228 and 1603.
FRKF 649.3

"Danseuse"

Autograph poem, 1 p., in black ink on the recto of a single sheet.

Published as: "Une danseuse" in 1920 in *Poésies 1917–1920*. See *Oeuvres poétiques complètes*, p. 173 and 1596.
London, Sotheby's, 29 Nov. 1985, lot 278.
FRKF 1047a

"Désir"

Calligraphic manuscript of the last two stanzas of this poem, 1906, 1 p., in black ink on the recto of a single sheet. Each stanza has 5 lines, with an additional stanza crossed out. One correction is in Cocteau's hand. Dated [1907 changed to] 1906, in Cocteau's hand, in the lower right corner.

Published in 1909 in *La lampe d'Aladin*. See *Oeuvres poétiques complètes*, p. 1316.
FRKF 1245.D01

"Deux faibles"

Calligraphic manuscript of this poetic tale, before 1914, 4 p., in black ink on p. [1], [3], [5], and [7] of a gathering of two nested, stitched bifolia. Incipit: "Prixus et Zariel marchaient côte à côte …"

Not located in *Oeuvres poétiques complètes*.
FRKF 1245.B01

"École de guerre"

Autograph poem, 1 p., in black ink on the recto of a single sheet of tracing paper.

Published in 1920 in *Poésies 1917–1920*. See *Oeuvres poétiques complètes*, p. 166.
London, Sotheby's, 29 Nov. 1985, lot 278.
FRKF 1047a

"Gaufres manèges tirs cirques feux d'artifice …"

Typescript poem with holograph corrections, 1 p., comprising four stanzas, each of four alexandrines with alternating rhymes. Accompanied by a white envelope marked, in Cocteau's hand: "Mon[sieur] Jean Guérin / à sa villa."

Not located in *Oeuvres poétiques complètes*.
Kenneth Rendell Catalogue 169.
FRKF 403

"Gravité du coeur"

Autograph manuscript, 1 p., in black ink on tracing paper.

Published in 1920 in *Poésies 1917–1920*. See *Oeuvres poétiques complètes*, p. 224 and 1602.
FRKF 1245.D05

"Hommage à Bernard Buffet: Gisant Debout"

Autograph poem, 1955, 1 p., in black ink on the verso of a large sheet torn from a spiral-bound notebook (32.5 × 41.5 cm). Signed and dated Sils-Maria, July 1955.

Oeuvres poétiques complètes, p. 959–60; see also p. 1781.
FRKF 450

"Mémoire"

Autograph poem, 1 p., in brown ink. Signed at the end and inscribed by Cocteau: "Très cher Enni, je retrouve ce poème inédit sous une pile de paperasse. S'il te plaît donne-le à notre Flouquet. Merci Jean."

Published in the Dec. 1958 issue of *Le journal des poètes*. See *Oeuvres poétiques complètes*, p. 1179 and 1819.
FRKF 354

"Mouchoir"

Autograph poem, 1 p., in black ink on tracing paper. Initial title, "Rimes d'Adieu," crossed out.

Published in 1920 in *Poésies 1917–1920*. See *Oeuvres poétiques complètes*, p. 230–31 and 1603.
FRKF 1245.D05

"Photographie"

Autograph poem, 1 p., in black ink on tracing paper.

Published in 1920 in *Poésies 1917–1920*. See *Oeuvres poétiques complètes*, p. 219.
FRKF 1245.D05

"Physique amusante"

Autograph manuscript, 1 p., in black ink on tracing paper. Two previous titles, "Catafalque" and "Phénomène," crossed out.

Published in 1920 in *Poésies 1917–1920*. See *Oeuvres poétiques complètes*, p. 226 and 1602.
FRKF 1245.D05

[Poem on a Stradivarius violin]

Autograph poem, 1 p., in black ink on a single sheet, beginning "Harmoniques n'importe où …"

Not located in *Oeuvres poétiques complètes*.
London, Sotheby's, 29 Nov. 1985, lot 276.
FRKF 1049a

"Portrait. Souvenir de Jules César"

Calligraphic manuscript of this prose poem, [before 1914], 2 p., in black ink on the recto sides of 2 single leaves.

Not located in *Oeuvres poétiques complètes*.
FRKF 1245.B01

"Les Primitifs"

Calligraphic manuscript of this prose poem, [before 1914], 1 p., in black ink on p. [1] of a single bifolium.

Not located in *Oeuvres poétiques complètes*.
FRKF 1245.B01

"Romance"

Autograph poem, 1 p., in black ink on a single sheet of tracing paper. Initial title, cancelled: "Un jeune homme vient de se pendre."

Published in 1920 in *Poésies 1917–1920*. See *Oeuvres poétiques complètes*, p. 191–92.
FRKF 649.1

"Le secret du bleu"

Autograph poem, 2 p., in black ink on tracing paper.

Published in 1920 in *Poésies 1917–1920*. See *Oeuvres poétiques complètes*, p. 220 and 1602.
FRKF 1245.D05

"Soir sympathique et inutile"

Autograph poem, 1 p., in black ink on one side of a sheet of heavy paper.

Published in 1910 in *Le prince frivole*. See *Oeuvres poétiques complètes*, p. 1351–52.

On the verso, autograph manuscript, partly calligraphic, of an unidentified poem or poetic fragment, beginning "Pauvre ami, c'étaient donc des cercueils les gondoles!," consisting of three stanzas of six lines each.

Not located in *Oeuvres poétiques complètes*.
FRKF 1245.D02

"Températures"

Autograph poem, 1 p., in black ink; only section 1 is present.

Published in 1920 in *Poésies 1917–1920*. See *Oeuvres poétiques complètes*, p. 159 and 1597.
FRKF 649.2

"Tout le diable et son train (ébauche d'un poème)"

Autograph poem, 1956, 1 p. Heavily revised draft, in blue ink on a single sheet, the upper right corner torn. Signed Jean Cocteau and dated Sils Maria, Feb. 1956.

On the verso, ANS to "cher Gabriel," mentioning that this is the second state of the poem.

Not located in *Oeuvres poétiques complètes*.
FRKF 1245.D07

"Le vase"

Calligraphic poem, 2 p., in black ink on p. [1] and [3] of a single bifolium. One correction on p. [1] is in Cocteau's hand.

Not located in *Oeuvres poétiques complètes*.
FRKF 1245.D01

"Vous caressez votre menton …"

Autograph poem in three stanzas, 1 p., in black ink on the recto of a single sheet.

Not located in *Oeuvres poétiques complètes*.
London, Sotheby's, 29 Nov. 1985, lot 278.
FRKF 1047a

II. OTHER LITERARY MANUSCRIPTS

"A Bréval"

Autograph manuscript notes, n.d. [but before 1914] 1 p. A list of names, including Adolphe Max, Catulle Mendès and his wife, and Laurent Tailhade and his wife. Illustrated with pen-and-ink drawings of faces, with various unidentified jottings in pencil on the verso.

FRKF 1245.C02

"L'acteur"

Autograph manuscript, n.d., 4 p., in dark blue ink on the verso sides of stationery of Maison du Bailli, rue du Lau, Milly. Incipit: "Diderot était fort habile à feindre dans la vie des émotions qu'il ne ressentait pas." Marked at the top, in Cocteau's hand: "Pour Festival Cannes." Signed "Jean Cocteau" at the end.

Paris, Laurin-Guilloux-Buffetaud-Tailleur (Drouot), 19 March 1986, lot 49.
FRKF 950a

[*L'aigle à deux têtes*]

"Costumes et décors de L'aigle à deux têtes"

Autograph manuscript, signed, n.d. [but ca. 1946] 1 p., in black ink on a verso of a tall sheet of folio-size paper. Incipit: "Puisque vous me demandez quelques lignes sur l'Aigle à deux têtes …"

Paris, Laurin-Guilloux-Buffetaud-Tailleur (Drouot), 19 March 1986, lot 28.
FRKF 1241

"L'alibi tragique"

Manuscript play in one act, n.d. [before 1914] 11 p., in black ink on the recto sides of ten individual sheets of paper; the title ("L'Alibi tragique / drame en un acte") and list of characters are on an additional half-sheet. The manuscript comprises an unnumbered scene between the Domino jaune and the Chef d'orchestre, and scenes numbered XXIII (Émilienne and the Chef d'orchestre), XXIV (la marquise, le duc), and [XXV?] (la marquise, le duc, le domino jaune).

No reference found in *Théâtre complet*.
FRKF 200

[Barbette]

Autograph manuscript of notes on Barbette, n.d. [1930?] 15 p. Hastily written in pencil on the recto sides or both sides of twelve loose pages of ruled paper. Incipit: "En 1930, Barbette se [met?] sur piste au cirque Médrano."

Barbette was the stage name of the androgynous American trapeze artist Vander Clyde (1904–73).

See Francis Steegmuller, *Cocteau: a biography*, new edition (Boston: Nonpareil Books, 1992), p. 522–29.
See *Le numéro Barbette* [1926], *Oeuvres complètes*, IX:257–63.
Paris, Couturier-Nicolaÿ (Drouot), 24 June 1987, lot 88.
FRKF 1311

[*La belle et la bête*]

Manuscript draft of a recorded presentation of the film, 1947, 7 p., in black ink, with corrections in black ballpoint pen, on the recto sides of seven loose leaves. Note at the top of p. [1]: "Enregistré pour La Belle et la Bête à Prague"; dated, also on p. [1], 17 Feb. 1947. Incipit: "C'est beaucoup plus qu'une voix qu'il faudrait vous faire entendre."

Paris, Laurin-Guilloux-Buffetaud-Tailleur (Drouot), 19 March 1986, lot 46.
FRKF 953b

Autograph manuscript draft of Cocteau's voice-over introduction to the film, in a paper folder labelled: "1er travail - pour le générique de la Belle et la Bête," 1 p., written in blue ink on the recto of a sheet of ruled paper. Incipit: "Avant de vous montrer notre travail, hommage à la grande mythologie française des contes de fées …"

Paris, Laurin-Guilloux-Buffetaud-Tailleur (Drouot), 19 March 1986, lot 29.
FRKF 1242

"Berthe Bovy, Marianne Oswald, mes interprètes"

Autograph manuscript of a talk on Berthe Bovy and Marianne Oswald, n.d., 3 p., in dark blue ink on the recto sides of three sheets of tracing paper. At the top of the first page, title, in Cocteau's hand: "Jean Cocteau parle de son interprète." Incipit: "Le public est une force de la nature."

See "Coupures de presse," *Oeuvres complètes*, X:334–35.
FRKF 1245.B07

"Le boeuf sur le toit"

Autograph manuscript, n.d., 3 p., in black ink on the recto sides of three individual leaves. On p. 1: "Le Boeuf sur le toit / Mime de Jean Cocteau / D. Milhaud / Dufy / interprété par les Fratellini / dans une soirée des / 6 musiciens." A recollection of the opening of the celebrated cabaret. Incipit: "En 22, au moment des Mariés - ouverture du Boeuf rue Boissy d'Anglas. / Milhaud me mène au bar Gaya près de Prunier …"

Accompanied by two photographs (9.5 × 13.5 cm) showing the Fratellini brothers in Cocteau's farce *Le boeuf sur le toit*, both initialled "JC" on the verso.

Le boeuf sur le toit, ou The Nothing Doing Bar, farce on music by Darius Milhaud, was premiered at the Comédie des Champs-Élysées on 21 Feb. 1920. See *Théâtre complet*, p. 25–29 and 1585–89.

Paris, Daniel Offret (Drouot), 16 April 1985, lot 23C.
FRKF 641

"Boutiques, conte"

Typescript, with autograph corrections, n.d., 18 p. Carbon copy with corrections in black ink and pencil, foliated 1–17. The title is handwritten on a separate sheet of laid paper. Incipit: "J'entre dans le magasin de nouveautés. Je me trouve au rayon du meuble."

FRKF 202

Bric-à-brac

Miscellaneous drafts for this play, n.d., 73 p., written in ink on 73 unpaginated single leaves, mostly folio size, usually on the recto sides but occasionally on both sides. It is a working, not a continuous draft, some passages present in multiple versions. There are numerous pen-and-ink illustrations and drawings, some embellished with blue pencil, notably two caricatures (on one page) of Catulle Mendès, the play's dedicatee.

Bric-à-brac, Fantaisie en un acte en vers, was published in *La lampe d'Aladin* (Cocteau's first book, later disavowed) in 1909, with a dedication to Mendès. See *Oeuvres poétiques complètes*, p. 1320–41.

Paris, Dominique Vincent (Drouot), 12 March 1984, lot 81.
FRKF 411

"Les cauchemars"

Autograph manuscript of a prose fragment, n.d. [but before 1914] 1 p., in black ink on the recto of a single leaf. Illustrated with pen-and-ink drawings of fantastic heads.

FRKF 1245.C01

[*Le coq et l'arlequin*]

Manuscript, in the form of a letter to André Gide, n.d. [1918?] 5 p., in black ink on the recto sides of five sheets of folio-size paper. A response to Gide's criticism, published by the Éditions de la Sirène in Paris in 1918.

Paris, Paul Renaud (Drouot), 12 June 1987, lot 168.
FRKF 1234

"Le critique et le théâtre"

Autograph manuscript, n.d. [1946] 8 p., in dark blue ballpoint on the recto sides of eight leaves. Signed "Jean Cocteau" at the end. Typed note tipped in on p. 1: "Pour Spectateur / Le critique et le théâtre / 30 Juillet 1946."

Oeuvres complètes, XI:445–51.
Paris, Laurin-Guilloux-Buffetaud-Tailleur (Drouot), 8 Feb. 1985, lot 15.
FRKF 661

"L'église de Chauvigny"

Autograph manuscript, n.d., 5 p., in blue ink on the verso sides of stationery of Maison du Bailli, Rue Du Lau Milly. Signed "Jean Cocteau" at the end.

Paris, Laurin-Guilloux-Buffetaud-Tailleur (Drouot), 8 Feb. 1985, lot 16.
FRKF 660

"En ce qui concerne les honneurs …"

Untitled manifesto, n.d., 1 p. Calligraphed in turquoise crayon on a large oblong sheet of paper (65 × 49.5 cm). Signed "Jean Cocteau" in the lower right corner.
FRKF 578

"En faveur du 16 millimètres"

Autograph manuscript, Jan. 1948, 9 p., in blue ink on nine leaves, foliated by Cocteau; signed and dated at the end. Accompanied by a postscript in a different hand.

Paris, Dominique Vincent (Drouot), 21 Dec., 1984, lot 77.
FRKF 735

"Hommage à Molière"

Autograph speech, 1946, 10 p., in blue ballpoint pen on the recto sides of ten individual leaves, foliated by Cocteau in blue pencil. Incipit: "Le roi vient de nouer ensemble …"

Oeuvres complètes, XI:462–64 ("texte lu pour l'inauguration de la Salle du Luxembourg, le 20 novembre 1946 par M. Julien Bertheau").
FRKF 239

"La jeune fille de Ver Meer"

Autograph manuscript of an essay on the Van Meegeren affair, n.d., 7 p., in blue ink on the recto sides of seven individual leaves. Signed "Jean Cocteau" at the end.
FRKF 1245.B08

"Les jeunes ont coutume de s'appuyer sur la présentation d'un aîné …"

Manuscript preface to a book by Georges Noel, n.d., 3 p., in blue ballpoint pen on stationery of "Santo-Sospir" at Saint-Jean-Cap-Ferrat. Signed at the end.

Georges Noel wrote the preface to *Images de Jean Cocteau* (Nice: Galerie Matarasso [1957]).

Kenneth Rendell Catalogue 169.
FRKF 406

"Jusqu'à nouvel ordre …"

Autograph manuscript draft of a preface to a book by [Fernand?] Imhauser, n.p., 1959, 2 p., in black ink on both sides of a sheet of paper; illustrated with a pen-and-ink drawing of a head. Incipit: "Jusqu'à nouvel ordre, et je recommande qu'on entende ce terme à la lettre, les jeunes avaient coutume de s'appuyer sur la présentation d'un aîné lorsqu'ils débutaient." Signed "Jean Cocteau * 1959" at the end.

Fernand Imhauser (1928–68), Belgian poet.
FRKF 974

Lettre à Jacques Maritain

Corrected typescript of this essay, on onionskin paper, with abundant manuscript deletions and corrections in ink and pencil, as well as printers' markings in several hands, 66 p. There are particularly long additions on p. 31, p. 32, p. 43, p. 45 (which was torn and taped back together), p. 48.

> The pagination is continuous from p. 1 to 37 and from 39 to 48 (there is no page 38). Page 49, headed "P.S." is renumbered in red pencil, replacing the original 3, typed. Page 50 was initially numbered 59; p. 51, 11; and p. 52, 12. Page 53 is entirely holograph; p. 54 was previously 14; p. 55–57 are holograph; p. 58 was previously 25; p. 59, 49; p. 60, 51; p. 61, 52; p. 62, 54; p. 63, 55; p. 64, 58; p. 65, 57; p. 66, 60; and p. 67, 49. Cancelled manuscript additions are found on the verso of p. 39.

Lettre à Jacques Maritain was first published in book form by Stock in Paris in 1926.

Oeuvres complètes, IX:265–306.

Paris, Laurin-Guilloux-Buffetaud-Tailleur (Drouot),
3 July 1985, lot 32.
FRKF 846

"Lettre au père Noël"

Autograph manuscript, Christmas 1955, 1 p. Pen-and-ink self-portrait and manuscript prose text, in black ink, on a sheet of tracing paper (25 × 32 cm). Incipit: "Je demande au père Noël de convaincre l'Eglise …" Signed Jean Cocteau and dated "Milly / Noël 1955."

FRKF 1245.C05

Les mariés de la Tour Eiffel

Autograph manuscript, 1923, 70 p., in black ink, with many corrections and deletions in pencil, in a 4to-size notebook of ruled paper, bound in boards decorated with floral motifs and beige spine, the front board and spine embellished with inscriptions in Cocteau's hand, repeating the names of the "Six" and the other contributors. The title on the spine is "La noce."

On folio 1r, manuscript half-title: "La noce massacrée / ou / [initial title, cancelled: La Tour Eiffel] / Les mariés de la Tour Eiffel / Tragi-comédie en un acte."

On folio 2r, manuscript title: "Jean Cocteau / "La Noce massacrée / ou / Les mariés de la Tour Eiffel / Musiques de Georges Auric - Louis Durey - - Arthur Honegger - Darius Milhaud - / Francis Poulenc - Germaine Tailleferre / Décor / d'Irène Lagut / Costumes / de Jean V. Hugo."

On folio 4r, another title page, cancelled throughout: "Jean Cocteau / La [Tour Eiffel cancelled] noce massacrée / tragi-comédie en un acte / avec ritournelle ouverture / marches, danses et chanson / populaires, parisiennes, orchestrées de / [cancelled: Georges Auric] / composées par / le groupe des Six / Décors et costumes de Jean Cocteau / et Jean Hugo / Décors d'Irène Lagut / Costumes de Jean V. Hugo."

On folio 9v, pen-and-ink drawing of the set in Cocteau's hand at the bottom of the page, and pencil drawing at the top of the page, showing one of the invisible actors in a box surmounted by a gramophone horn.

Inscribed in Cocteau's hand to Bolette Natanson on the front free endpaper: "Ma chère Bolette / Je ne sais pas quel cadeau / vous faire? vous aimez / Les Mariés. Ils représentent / pour moi une foule de / souvenirs du coeur. / Permettez moi de vous / les offrir en chair et en os. / Soyez heureuse / Jean / [drawing of a heart] / Décembre 1923."

First performed by the Ballets suédois of Rolf de Maré at the Théâtre des Champs-Elysées in Paris on 18 June 1920.

See *Théâtre complet*, p. 1599.
Heinrich Schütz to Henry Miller, p. 122–23.
Paris, Couturier-Nicolaÿ (Drouot), 5 June 1991, lot 29.
FRKF 1413

[Noailles, Anna de]

"Il y a quelque chose d'atroce dans cette habitude humaine …"

Holograph manuscript of an essay on the death of Anna de Noailles, dated 1 May 1933, in black ink on two pages of tracing paper. The date has been corrected from "avril."

Kenneth Rendell Catalogue 169.
FRKF 407

"Mais qui peut comprendre? Personne"

Holograph manuscript of an article on the death of Anna de Noailles, dated 1 May 1933, beginning with the words "Je viens de perdre une soeur …." It is written in black ink, with pencil corrections, on two pages of tracing paper, signed at the end. The date has been corrected from "avril."

Oeuvres complètes, X:329–30.
Kenneth Rendell Catalogue 169.
FRKF 405

"Les Noces de sable"

Two holograph manuscript drafts of an essay. One, untitled, on the recto (or, occasionally verso) sides of 22 unnumbered pages, is written in blue ballpoint on stationery printed 36, rue Montpensier, 1er; the other, also in blue ballpoint, is on the recto sides of 17 unnumbered leaves.

Paris, Laurin-Guilloux-Buffetaud-Tailleur (Drouot), 16 March 1984, lot 25.
FRKF 421

[*Orphée*]

"L'Orphée que vous allez entendre …"

Presentation of his play *Orphée* to the audience, n.d. [but 1926?] 4 p., in dark blue ink on both sides of two folio-size sheets torn from a spiral notebook.

Orphée was first performed at the Théâtre des Arts in Paris on 15 June 1926.

Paris, Laurin-Guilloux-Buffetaud-Tailleur (Drouot), 8 Feb. 1985, lot 17.
FRKF 659

[*Parade*]

Presentation of Erik Satie's *Parade*. Autograph manuscript, signed, of the 11-line text reproduced in facsimile on p. [4] of the program of the concert held on 6 June 1917, 1 p. Stamped and annotated by the printer. Incipit: "Satie se cache derrière son binocle …"

Accompanied by a copy of the printed program of the concert, held at 6, rue Huyghens, [Paris] XIVe, and including works by Georges Auric, Louis Durey, and Arthur Honegger in addition to *Parade*, [4] p. Also, short autograph note by Cocteau introducing Rimbaud's poem "Parade" (from *Les illuminations*), possibly for the same program. With a reference to Cendrars crossed out.

FRKF 916

[*Les parents terribles*]

Autograph draft of a presentation of *Les parents terribles*, n.d. [1938?] 5 p., in black ink on stationery of Théatre [sic] des Ambassadeurs, Paris. Incipit: "J'ai pris de longue date l'habitude, d'après l'accueil de la jeunesse …"

Les parents terribles was premiered at the Théâtre des Ambassadeurs, Paris, on 14 Nov. 1938.

Not located in *Théâtre complet*.
Paris, Laurin-Guilloux-Buffetaud-Tailleur (Drouot), 19 March 1986, lot 45.
FRKF 953a

"Un phénomène extraordinaire de notre époque …"

Autograph manuscript of an essay on modern art, n.p., n.d., 5 p., in black ballpoint pen on the recto sides of five individual oblong leaves. Incipit: "Un phénomène extraordinaire de notre époque, c'est que le rare a cessé de l'être …"

London, Sotheby's, 28 May 1986, lot 182.
FRKF 1237

"Préface"

Holograph manuscript, signed, of Cocteau's preface to Henri Matarasso's *Vie d'Arthur Rimbaud* [1959] 6 p., in brown ink, with corrections in blue ballpoint pen on versos of 6 leaves.

Published in Henri Matarasso and Pierre Petitfils, *Vie d'Arthur Rimbaud* (Paris: Hachette, 1962), p. [7]–9. See the letter to Henri Matarasso dated 29 May 1959.

FRKF 199

"Le premier verre de purge est bu …"

Autograph manuscript of Cocteau's response to an unidentified questionnaire, n.d. [ca. 1928?] 1 p., in brown ink on the recto of a single sheet. Signed at the end; also, autograph note at the bottom: "Cher Monsieur, Envoyez-moi une épreuve à l'hotel Wellcome Villefranche sur mer. A.M. Dans des violences la moindre faute ridiculise l'insolent. Votre JC."

Accompanied by "Réponse de M. Jean Cocteau," corrected proof of the same text (without the opening paragraph), n.d., 1 p., with the annotation "Merci. Votre / JC."

Paris, Laurin-Guilloux-Buffetaud-Tailleur (Drouot), 19 March 1986, lot 51.
FRKF 950b, 950d

"Reconnaiss[ance] au public d'Allemagne"

Autograph manuscript of a preface or dedication, n.d., 3 p., in black ballpoint pen on the recto sides of three individual leaves. Incipit: "Je n'aime ni les symboles ni les mystères …" Signed Jean Cocteau at the end.

FRKF 1245.B09

"Rien ne se croyait moins vu …"

Holograph manuscript of a preface to an unidentified publication by Germaine Everling Picabia on Picabia and the Dada movement, 1953, in blue ballpoint pen on the recto sides of three sheets of paper, foliated in Cocteau's hand; signed and dated 1953 at the end.

FRKF 203

"Roméo et Juliette"

Autograph manuscript of a public talk on his adaptation of the Shakespeare play, n.d., 11 p., in black ink on the recto sides of eleven individual leaves. Incipit: "Mesdames Messieurs / Il y a déjà bien des années que, pour les soirées de Paris du Comte Etienne de Beaumont …"

Cocteau's adaptation of *Romeo and Juliet* was premiered at the Théâtre de la Cigale in Paris in June 1924.

FRKF 1245.B06

"Les ruines de l'exposition"

Autograph manuscript of an essay or article, n.d., 6 p., in black ink on the recto sides of six sheets of stationery printed "37, rue Cambon." The last page is a half-page, torn. Title in Cocteau's hand at the top of p. [1]. In another hand, in pencil: "Ce Soir." Incipit: "Déjà la beauté se trouve embellie par les ruines."

FRKF 1245.B05

Le sang d'un poète - Préface de 1946

Autograph manuscript draft, signed, of the preface to a new edition of the scenario of the film *Le sang d'un poète*, [1946], 5 p., in black ink on the recto sides of five individual leaves of ruled paper; abundantly corrected.

Published in Jean Cocteau, *Le sang d'un poète: film. Photos de Sacha Masour* ([Paris]: R. Marin [1948]), p. 13–18.

Paris, Laurin-Guilloux-Buffetaud-Tailleur (Drouot), 19 March 1986, lot 30.

FRKF 1243

"Secrets de beauté"

Autograph manuscript of these aphorisms, n.d., 21 p., in dark blue ink on the recto sides of 21 leaves removed from a pad. The first 17 leaves are foliated in pencil in an unidentified hand; the next 3 are foliated by Cocteau 22 bis, 23, 24; the last page is unnumbered. Signed Jean Cocteau on p. 24 and [21]. At the bottom of p. 24, in Cocteau's hand: "notes prises pendant une panne d'automobile sur la route d'Orléans."

Largely published in the section "Secrets de beauté" in *Coupures de presse*, in *Oeuvres complètes*, X:345–71.

FRKF 1245.B10

Soignez la gloire de votre firme ...

Autograph manuscript of Cocteau's preface and captions for the illustrations by Jean Martin to this deluxe plaquette printed by Draeger frères, n.d. [ca. 1929] 12 p., in black ink on the recto sides of large folio sheets. The manuscript comprises a "Préface" (p. [2–9]) in the form of seven paragraphs, the lettered headings of which spell out Draeger's name, and eleven numbered "Légendes" (p. [10–12]). On the title page, the title "Draeger" is spelled in capitals, vertically, with a note to the printer on top.

Bound in half dark blue morocco and dark blue marbled paper boards; "Jean Cocteau-MS." gold-tooled on the spine.

Typed note bound in, on stationery of Robert Télin, "libraire 'Au lys rouge,'" together with a description clipped from a dealer's catalogue: "Manuscrit provenant de la bibliothèque de Walther Berry dont hérita feu le poète américain Harry Crosby. Ce dernier m'affirma que son oncle le reçut, avec d'autres manuscrits et livres, de Marcel Proust. Paris le 7 avril 1930 [manuscript signature:] Robert Télin."

Full title: "Soignez la gloire de votre firme et l'excellence de vos marchandises, car si vous les jugez bonnes, votre intérêt devient l'intérêt général."

See *Éloge de l'imprimerie*, *Oeuvres poétiques complètes*, p. 591–93 and 1709.

Paris, Boisgirard (Drouot), 28 May 1986, lot 102.

FRKF 1232

"Texte de la table tournante chez Jean Hugo"

Autograph manuscript, 1923, 1 p., in black ink on the verso of a sheet of stationery of Mas de Fourques, Lunel (Hérault). Title, in Cocteau's hand: "Texte de la / Table tournante / chez Jean Hugo - rue Chateaubriand. / (1923)."

FRKF 1245.D06

"Le théâtre est mort Vive le théâtre"

Autograph manuscript, 3 p., n.d., in brown ink on the verso sides of tall stationery of Hotel du Louvre, Paris. Incipit: "Je regrette que le théâtre et le cinématographe, au lieu de s'entr'aider ..." Signed at the end.

Paris, Couturier-Nicolaÿ (Drouot), 19 June 1985, lot 23.

FRKF 1086

Unidentified fragment of a dialogue or interview

Autograph manuscript, n.d., 2 p., on the recto sides of two loose leaves, unpaginated. The two questions, in Cocteau's hand, are "En somme, vous accusez Maritain, Claudel etc. d'aveuglement"; and "Vous m'avez dit qu'il vous était difficile de croire à l'église romaine."

Paris, Daniel Offret (Drouot), 18 Nov. 1985, lot 39.

FRKF 978

III. GRAPHIC WORK

Jean Genet

Pencil drawing of his head in profile on a sheet of tracing paper (21 × 27 cm). Inscribed "a Jean Genet" and signed "Jean Cocteau / 1947."

FRKF 1248E

Raymond Radiguet

Pencil sketch of Radiguet at a table in a café, drawn on the recto of a red envelope (19 × 12 cm). On the table in front of Radiguet is an issue of the journal *Le Coq*. In the right margin, pencilled inscription in an unidentified hand: "projet / de / Jean C / pour / un portrait / de RR / par moi / en relief / 1920."

FRKF 1245.A05

Raymond Radiguet and Georges Auric

Pen-and-ink sketches of their faces, drawn on a strip of blue paper (10 × 20 cm). Inscribed on the verso, in an unidentified hand: "Portrait de Radiguet and Auric."

FRKF 1245.A06

Erik Satie

Caricature, pencil on paper (25.5 × 20 cm), n.d., signed "Jean."

A similar drawing is reproduced in *Fanfare*, vol. 1, no. 2 (15 Oct. 1921), p. [27], with an inscription to Satie from Cocteau (not present here) dated 1920.

London, Phillips, 27 June 1985, lot 623.
FRKF 1419

Satyr

Drawing from the torso up, pencil on a single sheet of paper (21 × 27 cm); on the right side, also in pencil, a male profile; on the left side, head of a man.

FRKF 1245.C03

Self-portrait

Left side of Cocteau's face, charcoal on a 21 × 27 cm sheet of paper, n.d. [late 1950s or early 1960s?], signed Jean Cocteau at the bottom.

FRKF 1245.C06

Two hawks

Monogram-like drawing of two intertwined hawks, pencil on a sheet of thin 21 × 27 cm stationery printed: "36, rue de Montpensier. 1er" [Paris] n.d., but after 1940.

FRKF 1245.C04

Unidentified man

Drawing of a man at a desk, pen and black-brown ink on heavy paper, cut roughly in an oval pattern (ca. 16 × 28 cm). The book the man has in front of him is marked "Le bal du comte d'Orgel." Inscribed on the verso, in an unidentified hand: "J Cocteau / 1923."

FRKF 1245.A04

IV. LETTERS

To Georges Auric

[1943 spring] "Vendredi," 26, rue de Montpensier [Paris] ALS, 1 p.

1943 Aug. 25, n.p., ALS, 1 p.

1943 Dec. 22, n.p., ALS, 1 p.

Concerning *L'éternel retour* and *Renaud et Armide*, with mentions of Jean Marais and Pierre Drieu La Rochelle.

London, Sotheby's, 29 Nov. 1985, lot 277.
FRKF 1048

To Nora Auric

1940 July [14, Perpignan*] ALS, 2 p. (env). Mentions Christian Bérard, Boris Kochno, and the death of Édouard Vuillard; illustrated with a small drawing on the verso.

1940 July [22, Perpignan*] ALS, 1 p. (env). Mentions Sacha [Guitry?], Bérard, and Jean Hugo.

1954 Aug. 2, Saint-Jean-Cap-Ferrat, ALS, 1 p. (env)

London, Sotheby's, 29 Nov. 1985, lot 277.
FRKF 1048

[early 1940s] Roquebrune, APCS. Addressed to both Georges and Nora; also signed by Jean Desbordes.

London, Sotheby's, 29 Nov. 1985, lot 278.
FRKF 1047C

To Rolf Badenhausen

1952 Dec. 13, Milly-la-Forêt, ALS, 1 p. (env), concerning *Bacchus*.

1952 Dec. 20, telegram

Also, carbon copies of 2 TLS from Badenhausen to Cocteau, 1952 Dec. 17 and 31, n.p., 2 p. and 1 p.

Marburg, Stargardt, 26 Nov. 1985, lot 42.
FRKF 1230

To Paterne Berrichon

1922 Jan. 29 [Paris] ALS, 3 p., concerning Rimbaud.

Paris, Laurin-Guilloux-Buffetaud-Tailleur (Drouot), 16 Nov. 1983, lot 216.
FRKF 261

To "mon très cher Boulos"

1940 Sept. 15, Perpignan, ALS, 1 p., concerning *La machine à écrire*. Mentions Nora Auric.

FRKF 1245.E06

To Maurice Delamain

1923 April 14, n.p. [but England] ALS, 1 p.

[1923 July 23, receipt stamp date] n.p., ALS, 1 p. Mentions Henri Pourrat.

[1925 Oct. 15*] Villefranche-sur-Mer, ALS, 1 p.

[mid-1920s] n.p., ALS, 2 p.

[1926 Sept. 9, receipt stamp date] Villefranche-sur-Mer, ALS, 1 p., concerning the proofs of *Orphée*.

FRKF 1245.E05

[1926 Oct. 27, receipt stamp date] n.p., ALS, 2 p. Mentions Christian Bérard and Cocteau's forthcoming volume of verse (*Opéra*).

FRKF 649.5

[ca. 1926] n.p., ALS, 4 p., concerning *Le rappel à l'ordre*. Mentions Gide and Jacques Chardonne.

1930, 1, rue Tronchet [Paris] ALS, 2 p., evidently concerning his switching to Gallimard as publisher.

FRKF 1245.E05

Maurice Delamain, director of Stock, was Cocteau's principal publisher from 1923 until 1930.

To Jean Dongrie

1919 Dec. 28, "10 rue d'Anjou" [Paris] ALS, 2 p., (env). Mentions Paul Claudel.

London, Christie's, 29 May 1986, lot 249.

FRKF 1240

To Marie delle Donne

ALS, n.p, 2 p., addressed also to Robert [delle Donne] and Maurice [Sachs].

ALS, n.p., 2 p.

ALS, n.p., 2 p.

ALS, "Welcome Hotel" [Villefranche-sur-Mer] 1 p.

ALS, n.p., 2 p.

ALS, n.p., 2 p.

Though undated, the letters were all written during Cocteau's stay in Villefranche in the mid-1920s; they mention Valentine Gross (Hugo), Picasso, Proust, May Ray, Maurice Sachs, and Cocteau's play *La machine infernale*. Marie (later Baronne Wasmer) and her brother Robert delle Donne were the owners of the Hôtel Vouillemont, where Maurice Sachs worked as a receptionist; they are among the presumed models for *Les enfants terribles*. See Arnaud, p. 317 and 807 n. 75.

FRKF 204

To Willy Dortu

1923 Aug. 1, APCS, Le Piquey par Arès (Gironde). Mentions *Le grand écart*.

1923 Oct. 30, 10, rue d'Anjou [Paris] ALS, 1 p., sending him "un petit portrait de poche."

1923 Nov. 10, rue d'Anjou, ALS, 1 p.

[1928 March 13, Paris*] ALS, 1 p.

[1928 March 26, Paris*] ALS, 1 p. (env)

1951 Feb. 18, ALS, n.p., 1 p. (env)

1951 Sept. 23, n.p., ALS, 1 p.

1952 July 17 [Paris*] ALS, 1 p. (env)

1953 Nov. 30 [Saint-Jean-Cap-Ferrat*] ALS, 1 p. (env)

1954 Oct. 18 [Saint-Jean-Cap-Ferrat*] ALS, 1 p. (env), illustrated with a sketch of a stylized, reclining figure.

1956 Oct. 15, Saint-Jean-Cap-Ferrat, ALS, 1 p. (env)

1957 Oct. 20, n.p., ALS, 1 p., illustrated with a drawing of a head.

1959 March 20, n.p., ALS, 1 p.

1961 April 25, "Santo-Sospir," Saint-Jean-Cap-Ferrat[S], ALS, 1 p. (env)

1963 Aug. 6, Milly-la-Forêt, ALS, 1 p.

FRKF 1306.1

To Nino [Frank]

n.d., n.p., ALS, 1 p., concerning his health and a publication project by a certain T.; mentions Flechtlein and Vederkop.

Marburg, Stargardt, 5–6 March 1985, lot 50.

FRKF 799

To René Gaudier

1920 Aug. 10 [Paris*] APCS (env)

1920 Sept. 2, Le Piquey par Arès, Gironde, ALS, 2 p. (env). Mentions François Porché, Apollinaire, and Max Jacob.

1920 Oct. 4, Le Piquey par Arès, Gironde, ALS, 2 p. (env)

[1921 March 31, Var*] APCS, written on both sides (env), with a note from Pierre Bertin on the verso of the envelope.

1922 May 25, Le Lavandou, APCS. Quotes Montaigne and mentions Marie Laurencin.

1922 Aug. 18, Le Piquey par Arès, Gironde, APCS. Mentions Pierre and Marcelle Bertin.

1923 Sept., Le Piquey par Arès, Gironde, APCS (env). Mentions Radiguet and Picasso.

[1923 Dec. 27, Paris*] ALS, 1 p. (env), the first letter to use the "tu" form of address.

1926 Feb., Villefranche-sur-Mer, ALS, 1 p. Mentions the Bertins.

Accompanied by a loose envelope addressed by Cocteau to Gaudier [1921 Aug. 20, Arès*].

FRKF 1245.A08

To Jean Guérin

1958 Jan. 4, Santo-Sospir, Saint-Jean-Cap-Ferrat[S], ALS, 1 p. with a loose envelope addressed by Cocteau to Guérin, [1961 Jan. 27]

Marburg, Stargardt, 26 Nov. 1985, lot 43.
FRKF 1231

To Mary Hoeck

1949 June 27, Milly-la-Forêt, ALS, 1 p. Mentions the film of *Les enfants terribles* and *Orphée*.

Paris, Laurin-Guilloux-Buffetaud-Tailleur (Drouot), 19 March 1986, lot 31.
FRKF 1244

1963 March 3, Santo-Sospir, Saint-Jean-Cap-Ferrat[S], ALS, 1 p., concerning *La difficulté d'être* and the death of Poulenc (mentioning a projected collaboration on an opera based on *La machine infernale*).

Mary Hoeck was the English translator of *Maalesh* and other works by Cocteau.

London, Sotheby's, 28 May 1986, lot 519.
FRKF 1233

To Georges Hugnet

1950 Aug. 19 [Saint-Jean-Cap-Ferrat] ALS, 1 p. Mentions Picasso and "Le Catalan."

FRKF 1245.E08

1951 June 12 [Saint-Jean-Cap-Ferrat*] ALS, 1 p. (env), concerning the gift of a dessert spoon.

Marburg, Stargardt, 5 March 1985, lot 49.
FRKF 798

To Jean and Valentine Hugo

1943 May, Nice, ALS, 1 p.

FRKF 1245.E07

To Marcel Jallot

1951 Nov. 14, Milly-la-Forêt, ALS, 1 p.

FRKF 1245.E09

To Georges Kessel

[early 1920s] n.p., ALS, 1 p., concerning *Le Cap de Bonne Espérance* and Roland Garros.

[early 1920s] n.p., ALS, 1 p. Mentions Radiguet.

1926 Nov., Villefranche, ALS, 1 p.

1927 [Jan.?] Paris, telegram

London, Sotheby's, 29 Nov. 1985, lot 275.
FRKF 1050

1926 Dec., 10, rue d'Anjou [Paris] ALS, 1 p., on the verso of an invitation to a Cocteau exhibition opening.

London, Sotheby's, 28 May 1986, lot 184.
FRKF 1239

1927 [June or July] 10, rue d'Anjou, ALS, 1 p.

London, Sotheby's, 28 May 1986, lot 180.
FRKF 1235

1930 April 2, 9, rue Vignon [Paris] ALS, 1 p.

London, Sotheby's, 28 May 1986, lot 184.
FRKF 1239.

To Jean-Jacques Kihm

1959 Jan. 31, Santo-Sospir, Saint-Jean-Cap-Ferrat[S], ALS, 4 p. (env), concerning *Le Requiem* and *Le testament d'Orphée*.

Jean-Jacques Kihm (1923–70), philosophy teacher and poet, author of *Cocteau* (Paris: Gallimard, 1960, coll. "La bibliothèque idéale") and co-author with Elizabeth Sprigge of *Jean Cocteau: the man and the mirror* (London: Gollancz, 1968).

See Cocteau, *Lettres à Jean-Jacques Kihm*, texte établi et annoté par Françoise Bibolet et Pierre Chanel, avec cinq lettres de Jean-Jacques Kihm (n.p.: Rougerie, 1996), p. 54–55 ("lettre perdue").
FRKF 1245.E14

To Louis Laloy

[1927 Dec. 31, Chablis*] ALS, 1 p. (env), concerning Stravinsky.

Louis Laloy, music critic of *Comoedia*.

London, Sotheby's, 29 Nov. 1985, lot 278.
FRKF 1047b

To Daniel Lander

1955 Aug. 29 [Saint-Jean-Cap-Ferrat*] ALS, 1 p. (env), illustrated with a blue ballpoint pen drawing of two faces kissing.

FRKF 1245.E11

To Rolf Liebermann

1961 May 2, Marbella, ALS, 1 p. (env)

1961 Oct. 30, Paris, ALS, 1 p.

Concerning an invitation, declined by Cocteau, to stage Gluck's *Orphée et Eurydice* at the Hamburg Opera House during the 1962–63 season. Accompanied by carbons of two letters from Liebermann to Cocteau, both sent from Hamburg and dated 1961 April 17 and Oct. 23.

Hamburg, Hauswedell und Nolte, 22 May 1984, lot 1606.
FRKF 319

To Maurice Martin du Gard

[1922? May] Le Lavandou, ALS, 1 p., sending corrected proofs; mentions a reconciliation with Gide.

FRKF 1245.E03

1923 Aug. 5, Le Piquey par Arès (Gironde), ALS, 1 p. Reports on a trip to Greece and mentions *Plain-Chant*; Léon-Paul Fargue; Winaretta, princesse de Polignac; Léon Daudet; Maurice Barrès; and others.

FRKF 1245.E04

To Henri Matarasso

All are autograph letters, signed.

1957 Feb. 24, Suvretta House St. Moritz[S], 2 p.
[1957] April 6, n.p., 1 p.
1957 April 20, Académie française[S], 1 p.
1957 April 23, Santo Sospir, Saint-Jean-Cap-Ferrat[S], 2 p.
1957 April 27, Santo Sospir, Saint-Jean-Cap-Ferrat[S], 1 p.
1957 June 3, Santo Sospir, Saint-Jean-Cap-Ferrat[S], 2 p.
1957 June 28, n.p., 1 p.
1957 July 18, n.p., 1 p.
1957 July 23, Santo Sospir, Saint-Jean-Cap-Ferrat[S], 2 p.
1957 Sept. 5, n.p., 1 p.
1957 Oct. 21, n.p., 2 p.
1959 May 11, n.p., 1 p.
[1959?] "Lundi avant le depart," n.p., 1 p.
[1959] "Dimanche," Santo Sospir, Saint-Jean-Cap-Ferrat[S], 1 p.
1959 May 29, Santo Sospir, Saint-Jean-Cap-Ferrat[S], 1 p.
n.d., Milly-la-Forêt, 1 p.
1960 Jan. 9, Santo Sospir, Saint-Jean-Cap-Ferrat[S], 1 p.
[1960?] Jan.] "Lundi," Santo Sospir, Saint-Jean-Cap-Ferrat[S], 1 p.
1960 Jan. 20, n.p., 1 p.
1960 July 9, Santo Sospir, Saint-Jean-Cap-Ferrat[S], 1 p.
1960 Nov. 20, n.p., 1 p.
1961 Aug. 5, Santo Sospir, Saint-Jean-Cap-Ferrat[S], 1 p.
1962 Feb. 6, Santo Sospir, Saint-Jean-Cap-Ferrat[S], 1 p.
1962 Aug. 12, Santo Sospir, Saint-Jean-Cap-Ferrat[S], 1 p.
[1962] "Dimanche," Santo Sospir, Saint-Jean-Cap-Ferrat[S], 1 p.
1962 Aug. 17, Santo Sospir, Saint-Jean-Cap-Ferrat[S], 1 p., illustrated with a large pencil drawing.
1962 Dec. 1, n.p., 1 p.

The correspondence discusses mainly publication and exhibition projects, as well as Cocteau's preface to Matarasso's *Life of Rimbaud*. There are references to Louis Aragon, Pierre Bergé, Bernard Buffet, Lucien Clergue, and Pablo and Jacqueline Picasso.

FRKF 201

To Pierre Mortier

1909 Aug. 18, Paris, telegram
1909 Aug. 31, Paris, telegram
1909 Sept. 2, Paris, telegram
1909 Sept. 22, Paris, telegram
1909 Sept. 19, Paris, telegram
[1910 Jan. 27, Paris] ALS on one side of a card, "rue d'Anjou." Dated in an unidentified hand, possibly the recipient.
1910 July 31, Paris, telegram
1910 Oct. 14, n.p., ANS, 2 p. Dated in an unidentified hand, possibly by the recipient.
1910 Nov. 6 [Paris] ANS, 1 p. Dated in an unidentified hand, possibly by the recipient.
[1911 April 27, Paris*] APCS
1911 Oct. 16, Paris, telegram
1912 July 29, Paris, telegram
n.d., n.p., ANS, 1 p.
n.d., Paris, telegram

Accompanied by a printed invitation to attend an evening at the home of Jacques Doucet, Paris, 10 Feb., n.y., with the handwritten mentions of "Le costume antique grec ou romain est de rigueur," and "de la part de M. J. Cocteau." Also, a calling card ("Pierre Mortier") with a short handwritten message to Cocteau, [Paris], n.d., and an APCS to Cocteau, 1909 Sept. 3, Paris, sent c/o *Comoedia*.

Pierre Mortier, director of the periodical *Comoedia*.

Paris, Daniel Offret (Drouot), 18 Nov. 1985, lot 40.
FRKF 979

To Moyses at the Boeuf sur le toit

[ca.1922] Roquebrune, autograph draft, signed, of a telegram, 2 p., concerning Chanel; also mentions Jean Desbordes, Maurice Sachs, Gabriel Astruc, and Cocteau's *Le secret professionnel*.

Paris, Laurin-Guilloux-Buffetaud-Tailleur (Drouot), 12 June 1984, lot 30.
FRKF 456.

To Mila Niniteh

21 July 1951, n.p., ALS, 1 p., concerning Jean Genet's *Les bonnes*.

London, Sotheby's, 28 May 1986, lot 181.
FRKF 1236

To Marie-Laure de Noailles

1957 June 20 [Villefranche?] ALS, 1 p., concerning Cocteau's decorated chapel.

FRKF 1245.E12

To Léonce Peillard

1953 June 10, Milly-la-Forêt, ALS, 1 p.

1953 Oct. 13, 36, rue de Montpensier, Palais-Royal [Paris] ALS, 1 p.

1955 May 1, Saint-Jean-Cap-Ferrat, ALS, 1 p.

1955 May 26, Saint-Jean-Cap-Ferrat, ALS, 1 p.

1955 June 9, Milly-la-Forêt, ALS, 1 p.

1956 April 2, Saint-Jean-Cap-Ferrat, ALS, 1 p.

1958 July 5, n.p., ALS, 1 p., addressed to "Messieurs" and apologizing for not being able to decipher the signature of a letter.

1959 Nov. 29, n.p., ALS, 1 p.

1959, n.p., ALS, 1 p., concerning Roger Peyrefitte.

n.d., "Dimanche 13," Milly-la-Forêt, ALS, 1 p.

Also, envelope addressed by Cocteau to Peillard, postmarked 1955 May 18, Saint-Jean-Cap-Ferrat.

Léonce Peillard, writer and popular historian.

London, Sotheby's, 28 May 1986, lot 183.
FRKF 1238a

To Germaine Everling Picabia

Autograph letters, signed, concerning Cocteau's preface to a publication by Germaine Everling on the Dada movement (see above).

1953 Sept. 26, Santo-Sospir, Saint-Jean-Cap-Ferrat, 1 p.

n.d., "Lundi," Saint-Jean-Cap-Ferrat, 1 p.

n.d., "Vendredi," Saint-Jean-Cap-Ferrat, 1 p.

FRKF 203

To Robert de Saint-Jean

[1927 May 12, Paris*] ALS, 1 p. (env)

[1928 Feb., Paris*] ALS, 1 p.

[1928 July, Paris*] ALS, 1 p.

[1928 Aug. 7, Paris*] TLS, 1 p.

1930 March 31 [Paris, Revue hebdomadaire] ANS, 1 p.

1931 April [20*] 9, rue Vignon [Paris] ALS, 1 p. (env), suggesting a review for Jean Desbordes's book.

[1932 Oct. 22*] Saint-Mandrier (Var), ALS, 2 p. (env)

1932 Dec. 13, 9, rue Vignon, ALS, 1 p. (env)

[1935 March 19*] ALS, 2 p. (env)

[1947] n.p. [printed mention of 36, rue de Montpensier crossed out] 1 p.

[1950 April 17*] Milly-la-Forêt, ALS, 1 p. (env)

1951 Nov. 22 [Paris*] ALS, 1 p. (env)

n.d., ALS, 1 p.

Accompanied by the following:

Two printed cards, one thanking those who subscribed to Cocteau's sword as a newly elected member of the Académie française [1955], the other reproducing a drawing by Cocteau and a message in his hand: "merci de tout coeur pour mon épée" [1955]; an article by Cocteau on Al Brown, "Le poing final," corrected typescript, 8 March 1938, 2 p.; and a fragment of paper signed by Cocteau.

Paris, Laurin-Guilloux-Buffetaud-Tailleur (Drouot), 12 Dec. 1985, lots 43–44.
FRKF 954

To Jean-Paul Sartre

1958 May 5, Saint-Jean-Cap-Ferrat, ALS, 1 p.

1958 July 5, Saint-Jean-Cap-Ferrat, ALS, 1 p.

Paris, Laurin-Guilloux-Buffetaud-Tailleur (Drouot), 19 March 1986, lot 48.
FRKF 951

To Misia Sert

[1913 June, Venice*] ALS, 1 p.

[1913 Aug. 2, Maisons-Laffitte*] ALS, 1 p.

[1914 July 27, Maisons-Laffitte*] ALS, 1 p.

[1916 Nov. 29, Paris*] n.p., ALS, 1 p.

[1916 (month?) 25* postmark barely legible] ALS, 2 p.

[1916 June] n.p., ALS, 1 p. Dating is suggested by a pencilled note on an accompanying translation.

1917 Sept., Le Piquey par Arès, Gironde, ALS, 4 p.

1918 Sept. 6, Le Piquey par Arès, Gironde, ALS, 2 p.

1919 Aug. 24 [Husky par Mauléon (Basses-Pyrénées)] APCS

1922 Sept. 22, Pramousquier par Le Lavandou (Var), ALS, 2 p.

n.d., [ca. 1922] n.p., ALS, 1 p.

[1924 Aug. 28*] Villefranche-sur-Mer, ALS, 1 p.

[1930 Nov. 17, Paris*] ALS, 1 p.

1933 Feb. [Paris] ALS, 2 p.

1934 Dec., Cornier sur Vevey, Suisse, ALS, 1 p.

The following letters are undated; unless otherwise noted, no place is indicated.

ALS, 4 p.

ALS, 2 p.

ALS, 2 p.

ALS, 2 p., in the hand of Jean Desbordes, with a postscript by him

ALS, 4 p.

ALS [Paris] 1 p.

ALS, Hôtel Meurice, Paris[S], 1 p. Sent to Paris and forwarded first to Venice, then Bologna.

ANS, 1 p., on verso of a page from serial publication of Gaston Leroux's *Rouletabille chez le tsar*; at the top of the illustration, Cocteau has written: "Les Claude Anet"

ALS, "Mercredi," Le Piquey par Arès, Gironde, 4 p.

ALS, 6 p.

ALS, 1 p.

ALS [Boulogne?] 1 p.

Among the names mentioned in the correspondence are Gabriel Astruc, Georges Auric, Philippe Berthelot, Antoine Bibesco, Emmanuel Bibesco, Marthe Bibesco, Jacques-Émile Blanche, Georges Braque, Romaine Brooks, Blaise Cendrars, Serge Diaghilev, Léon-Paul Fargue, Henri Ghéon, Albert Gleizes, Valentine Gross (Hugo), Mireille Havet, André Lhote, Natalie Paley, Pablo Picasso, Raymond Radiguet, Erik Satie, José Maria Sert, Igor Stravinsky, Edgar Varèse, and Louise de Vilmorin. Cocteau's own works referred to include *Opéra*, *Le livre blanc*, *Le secret professionnel*. The letter of Feb. 1933 is a plea for help for Cocteau's friend "Marcel-pas-de-chance" [Marcel Servais] following his motorcycle accident (see Arnaud, p. 405 and 804, n. 94).

FRKF 198

To Valentine Tessier

1939 May, Versailles, 19, Place de la Madeleine (8e) / ANJou 06–80[S], ALS, 1 p.

n.d. [Clinique Lyautey] ALS, 1 p., in pencil.

Concerning *La machine à écrire*.

Paris, Laurin-Guilloux-Buffetaud-Tailleur (Drouot), 16 March 1984, lot 29.
FRKF 422

To Alice Turpin

[1925 March 27, Paris*] Thermes Urbains / 15, rue de Chateaubriand, ALS, 2 p. (env), concerning his drug rehabilitation; mentions André Maurois; with a postscript in pencil.

Paris, Laurin-Guilloux-Buffetaud-Tailleur (Drouot), 12 June 1984, lot 26.
FRKF 452

[1925 Aug. 10*] Villefranche, ALS, 1 p. (env), mentions Bernard Grasset and Jean Desbordes; with a postscript on the verso of the envelope.

Paris, Laurin-Guilloux-Buffetaud-Tailleur (Drouot), 12 June 1984, lot 31.
FRKF 457

[1925?] n.p., ALS, 1 p., concerning his drug rehabilitation; mentions Marie-Louise [Bousquet?].

Paris, Laurin-Guilloux-Buffetaud-Tailleur (Drouot), 12 June 1984, lot 28.
FRKF 454

[1926 Nov. 6*] ALS, 1 p., mentions Marie-Louise [Bousquet?] and Jean Desbordes.

Paris, Laurin-Guilloux-Buffetaud-Tailleur (Drouot), 12 June 1984, lot 31.
FRKF 457

[ca. 1928] "10 Rue d'Anjou" [Paris] LS, 1 p., dictated, in the hand of Jean Desbordes; mentions Desbordes's *J'adore*.

Paris, Laurin-Guilloux-Buffetaud-Tailleur (Drouot), 12 June 1984, lot 32.
FRKF 458

1929 March, Saint Cloud, ALS, 1 p., concerning negotiations with Bernard Grasset; illustrated with a large drawing of a hand holding a cigarette and a pencil.

Paris, Laurin-Guilloux-Buffetaud-Tailleur (Drouot), 12 June 1984, lot 27.
FRKF 453

1929 April 1, n.p., ALS, 1 p., concerning Bernard Grasset.

Paris, Laurin-Guilloux-Buffetaud-Tailleur (Drouot), 12 June 84, lot 31.
FRKF 457

1936 Oct., Mas de Fourques / Lunel (Hérault)^S, ALS, 1 p., responding to her letter from Calcutta.

Paris, Laurin-Guilloux-Buffetaud-Tailleur (Drouot), 12 June 84, lot 29.
FRKF 455

The following correspondence is all undated and without place; some dates and places have been supplied.

APCS [mid-1920s] postcard from a photograph of Cocteau.

APCS [mid-1920s] the postcard shows the "rue obscure" in Villefranche.

ANS, 4 p., a note in pencil beginning on the verso of an unstamped envelope marked "Mademoiselle Turpin" and continuing on the verso of three small printed receipts from Éditions Bernard Grasset. It mentions Chirico.

ALS [mid-1920s] [Villefranche?] 1 p. Mentions Bernard Grasset and André Maurois.

ALS [mid-1920s] Villefranche, 1 p. Mentions Maurice Sachs and Bernard Grasset.

ALS [mid-1920s?; Aug. 21, Villefranche*] 1 p.

ANS, requesting the return of a typescript.

ALS [mid-1920s?; Aug. 10, Villefranche*] 1 p. Mentions Marielle.

ALS [Paris?] 1 p. (env), requesting a visit; also mentions Bernard Grasset.

ALS, 1 p., concerning his friend Gills and Eugenio d'Ors; with a postscript in pencil mentioning Bernard Grasset.

ALS [May 9, Paris*] 1 p. Apologizes for lateness in proofreading for Bernard Grasset.

ALS [ca. 1925, Villefranche] 1 p. Mentions Radiguet's *Les joues en feu*.

ALS, 1 p. Mentions Philippe Berthelot, Marie-Louise [Bousquet?] and André Maurois.

Together with five loose envelopes, postmarked [illegible] 1925, 2 May 1925, 17 April 1928, 12 Oct. 1928, and 19 Oct. 1936.

Paris, Laurin-Guilloux-Buffetaud-Tailleur (Drouot), 12 June 84, lot 31.
FRKF 457

To Alfred Vallette

1921 July 17, Hotel de Paris, Besse-en-Chandesse, ALS, 2 p., concerning Paul Léautaud; also mentions Diaghilev and Germaine Tailleferre.

Paris, Ader-Picard-Tajan (Drouot), 2 Dec. 1986, lot 357.
FRKF 1409

To Albert Willemetz

1944 Dec. 5, 36, rue de Montpensier [Paris] ALS, 1 p.

Geneva, L'Autographe, catalogue 6, lot 103.
FRKF 563

1946 March 21, Paris, TLS, 1 p., concerning *Les parents terribles*; accompanied by "Avant la reprise de 'La machine infernale,'" typescript with autograph corrections, 1 p.

[1952 Dec.] ALS, 7 p., concerning the interruption of the performances of *Bacchus*; accompanied by a typewritten transcript of the letter, with a manuscript correction (by Cocteau?), 5 p.

Paris, Laurin-Guilloux-Buffetaud-Tailleur (Drouot), 20 Nov. 1984, lot 202.
FRKF 665

1954 Sept. 7 [Saint-Jean-Cap-Ferrat*] ALS, 2 p. (env), concerning *La machine infernale*.

[1954 Sept. 14, Saint-Jean-Cap-Ferrat*] Théâtre des Bouffes-Parisiens^S, ALS, 2 p. (env). Mentions Jean Marais and Elvire Popesco.

1957 Aug. 1 [Saint-Jean-Cap-Ferrat*] ALS, 1 p. (env). Mentions Sacha Guitry.

FRKF 1245.E10

1962 May 1, Milly-la-Forêt, ALS, 1 p.

Paris, Laurin-Guilloux-Buffetaud-Tailleur (Drouot), 20 Nov. 1984, lot 203.
FRKF 664

Accompanied by the following documents, part of FRKF 665:

"La Machine infernale / de Jean Cocteau," manuscript document, photostat, with manuscript corrections, concerning the recording of the play at the Studio des Buttes-Chaumont, 25 May 1954.

Jean Cocteau. "Le monde se tourne de plus en plus vers le passé." Autograph note, 1 p.

"Valse de Diane à la Houppe." Autograph manuscript in an unidentified hand, n.d., 1 p. No poem by Cocteau with this title is recorded in *Oeuvres poétiques complètes*.

Also, a clipping reproducing a drawing by Cocteau, showing an actor wearing a wig.

Albert Willemetz was director of the Théâtre des Bouffes-Parisiens.

Other letters

To "mon cher Festy"

1952 Aug. 29, n.p., ALS, 1 p., concerning a printing error in *Bacchus*.

Paris, Laurin-Guilloux-Buffetaud-Tailleur (Drouot), 19 March 1986, lot 47.
FRKF 952

To "Cher Louis"

1960 July 16, Saint-Jean-Cap-Ferrat, ALS, 2 p., concerning his election as "prince of poets"; mentions Jean Paulhan and Paul Fort.

FRKF 649.4

To "mon très cher Louis"

1961 Jan. 26, Santo-Sospir, Saint-Jean-Cap-Ferrat^S, ALS, 1 p. Mentions Radiguet.

FRKF 1245.A10

To "Mon Marcel"

1957 Aug. 8, Santo-Sospir, Saint-Jean-Cap-Ferrat^S, ALS, 1 p. "L'estrade d'actualité me dégoûte. […] Et comme il n'y a plus d'ordres on ne peut plus désobéir. C'était le seul luxe de la jeunesse."

FRKF 1245.E13

To "Mon cher Michel"

195[?] Oct. 18, 13 h, n.y., n.p., ALS, 1 p. Mentions flying saucers.

FRKF 355

To an unidentified German correspondent

1952 March 6, n.p., ALS to "Cher Monsieur," 1 p.

1952 July 4, Saint-Jean-Cap-Ferrat, ALS to "Cher ami," 1 p., concerning rights to *Orphée* in Germany; also mentions *Bacchus*.

Marburg, Stargardt, 19 June 1984, lot 56.
FRKF 479a–b

To "Mon cher ami"

n.d., n.p., ALS, 1 p. Mentions Darius Milhaud, a contract from the Société des Auteurs, and Desbordes, Paul Morand, and [Georges?] Kessel.

London, Sotheby's, 29 Nov. 1985, lot 276.
FRKF 1049b

To an unidentified female correspondent

[1912] Grand Hotel de Asis, Algiers^S, ALS, 2 p. Mentions Gide.

FRKF 1245.E01

To an unidentified friend

[1919?] May 10, Le Lavandou, ALS, 2 p., responding to Georges Gabory's attacks in the *NRF*; also mentions Radiguet.

FRKF 1245.A02

To an unidentified correspondent

[1924] n.p., ALS, 3 p. (env), possibly to a journalist or critic, sending information about his work up to 1923.

Kenneth Rendell Catalogue 169.
FRKF 402

To an unidentified friend

1931 Aug. [Toulon] ALS, 1 p., in pencil.

Marburg, Stargardt, 26 Nov. 1985, lot 41.
FRKF 1229

To an unidentified friend

[1920s?] n.p., ALS, 2 p., concerning Richard Strauss's ballet *La légende de Joseph*; mentions Hofmannsthal, Count Harry Kessler, Diaghilev, Nijinsky, and Fokine.

FRKF 1245.E02

To an unidentified British or American correspondent

1962 April 9, n.p., ALS, 1 p., illustrated with a profile of a young man, drawn in red pencil. Marked "answered 23/4/62."

FRKF 1245.A11

V. PRINTED WORKS

Cocteau. *Antigone; Les mariés de la Tour Eiffel.*
Paris: Librairie Gallimard, 1928.

8vo, [1–7], 8–152 [+ 10] p. First edition, *achevé d'imprimer* dated April 1928; in original paper wrappers. Profusely annotated by Cocteau on the verso of the front wrapper, p. [1]–[3], p. [162], the verso of the back wrapper; also, drawings by Cocteau on the back wrapper.

FRKF 1245.B03

Cocteau. *Drôle de ménage. Textes et dessins de Jean Cocteau.*
Paris: Paul Morihien, 1948.

Folio, [56] p. Number 164 of 720 on Vélin de Rives, from an edition of 2720 copies; signed by Cocteau in blue pencil on the page facing the colophon. Inscriptions in black ink; drawings in colored pencil, 1955.

FRKF 1245.C07

Cocteau. *Nouveau théâtre de poche: Parade; Le boeuf sur le toit; Le pauvre matelot; L'école des veuves; Le bel indifférent; Le fantôme de Marseille; Anna la bonne; La dame de Monte-*

Carlo; Le fils de l'air; Le menteur; Par la fenêtre; Je l'ai perdue; Lis ton journal; La farce du château; L'épouse injustement soupçonnée. Avec quinze dessins inédits de l'auteur. Monaco: Éditions du Rocher, 1960.

> 8vo, [1–10], 11–171 [+ 5] p. In original wrappers. Inscribed on the half title in blue ballpoint pen: "à Willy / Dortu / son vieil / ami / Jean Cocteau." The dedication is embellished with the drawing of a profile.

FRKF 1306.3

Fanfare. Vol. 1, no. 2 (15 Oct. 1921).

> Edited by Leigh Henry, published by Goodwin & Tabb, Ltd., London. Contains "Erik Satie," by Cocteau, p. [21]–25, and a drawing of Satie by Cocteau on p. [27].

London, Phillips, 27 June 1985, lot 623.
FRKF 1419

[Collaer, Paul] Arthur Honegger. *Antigone: tragédie lyrique en 3 actes, paroles de Jean Cocteau. Adaptation libre d'après Sophocle. Étude par Paul Collaer, suivie des principaux extraits de la presse française et étrangère concernant la création au Théâtre royal de la Monnaie de Bruxelles et au Stadttheater d'Essen.* Paris: Éditions Maurice Senart; Leipzig: Otto Junne G.m.b.H. [1928].

> 8vo, [1–5], 6–55 [+1] p. In original wrappers.

FRKF 1245.Supp.B

Romieu, Émilie et Georges. *La vie des soeurs Brontë.* Paris: NRF, Librairie Gallimard, 1929 (Vies des hommes illustres - N° 35).

> 8vo, [1–7], 8–288 [+ 2] p. "4e édition" printed on front wrapper and title page; no *achevé d'imprimer*. Profusely annotated by Cocteau on both the front and back wrappers, both recto and verso, and p. [1] and 225 on.

FRKF 1245.B04

VI. PHOTOGRAPHS

Berenice Abbott

Two photographs of Cocteau asleep, with a white mask next to him (18 × 13 cm) [early 1920s]. Annotation in his hand on one of the photographs: "Le chercheur dort."

Paris, Daniel Offret (Drouot), 16 April 1985, lot 23C.
FRKF 641

Silver-print photograph of Cocteau (17 × 23 cm) with a white mask in the lower right corner. Manuscript signature in capital letters: "Abbott - Paris" Inscribed by Cocteau: "à mon / cher / Willy Dortu, / coeur d'or - avec ma vieille amitié / Jean Cocteau / Bruxelles 1946."

FRKF 1306.2

Isabey

Photograph of Cocteau reading in one of the two gramophones of *Les mariés de la Tour Eiffel* (12.5 × 17 cm) [1920]. Blind stamp and stamp (on the verso) of Isabey, 23, Boulevard des Capucines, Paris.

Paris, Daniel Offret (Drouot), 16 April 1985, lot 23C.
FRKF 641

VII. MISCELLANEOUS MATERIAL

Petition for Jean Genet

Autograph draft of a petition to "Monsieur le Président," requesting a pardon for Jean Genet, n.d., 2 p. Written in blue ballpoint pen, with a few pencil corrections, on the recto sides of two 4to-size leaves.

Accompanied by 15 copies of the mimeographed petition with the mimeographed signatures, typed, of Cocteau and Jean-Paul Sartre, each copy signed respectively, in manuscript, by the following individuals: Gaston Gallimard, Armand Salacrou, Georges Auric and Marcel Achard, J.-C. Bernardet O.S.B., Georges Lacombe [film director], Francis Poulenc, Marcel Arland, Marcel Aymé, Charles Dullin, David Rousset, Jean Aurenche, and Pierre [Herbart?], enclosing an autograph note of support, signed, by Jacques Prévert, André Breton, and Benjamin Péret (a different text, printed on a half-sheet, though still with mimeographed signatures, typed, of Cocteau and Sartre), Jean Anouilh, Gabriel Marcel, Claude Autant-Lara (with attached autograph note, signed, on his stationery), and Thierry Maulnier.

FRKF 1248c

Notes from a séance

Autograph notes from a séance with Jean and Valentine Hugo, Georges Auric, Raymond Radiguet, and Cocteau in attendance, n.d. [but 21 April 1923] 4 p. Written in pencil, in various hands, on both sides of two 8vo-size leaves of paper. At the top of the first page, in an unidentified hand: "Valentine et Jean C. à la table"; at the top of the verso, in the same hand: "Auric et Radiguet à la table."

See Jean Hugo, *Le regard de la mémoire* (Arles: Actes Sud, 1983), p. 212–15.

FRKF 1245.A07

Letter to Valentine Hugo

From Mme Cocteau, 1921 Nov. 28 [Paris*] ALS, 4 p. (env)

FRKF 1245.A01

ALFRED CORTOT (1877–1962)

Letters to Pierre Bernac

1957 Oct. 14, Paris, Ecole normale de musique^S, ALS, 2 p., mentions the R.P. Ambroise-Marie Carré.

1958 June 21, n.p., ALS, 2 p.

1960 March 16, 5, av. de Jaman, Lausanne^S, ALS, 2 p., concerning École normale politics.

Paris, Oger-Dumont (Drouot), 14 Feb. 1985, lot 82.

FRKF 697

NOEL COWARD (1899–1973)

I. DIARIES

AUTOGRAPH DIARIES, 1941–70

1941, in ink and pencil in a W.C. Penfold Australian Diary for 1941, No. 22, One Day on a Page (20 × 32.5 cm).

1942, in pencil in a Ryman's Scribbling Diary for 1942, One Day to a Page (21 × 33 cm), bound in quarter brown morocco and black silk.

1943 Jan. to July 18, in pencil in a dark red buckram-bound Campbell's Rota Diary for 1943 (13 × 20.5 cm).

1943 July 19 through Nov., in pencil in a ruled notebook (13 × 20 cm), bound in moleskin and dark red cloth. On recto of the flyleaf, in Coward's hand: "Personal N.C. 1943 July 19th to November 30."

1943 Dec. to 1944 April 21, in pencil, with a few corrections in ink, in a ruled notebook (10.5 × 17.5 cm), stamped Webster's, 44 Dover Street, W.1., bound in bright red leather, with single gold fillet on front board, marked 1943 in Coward's hand. On free front marbled endpaper, in Coward's hand: "N.C. 1943 [November cancelled] December 1944 January & up to April 21st."

1944 April 23 to Sept. 6, in pencil, with a few corrections in ink, in a ruled notebook (11.5 × 18 cm), bound in blue moleskin. Marked 1944 twice, first on a label pasted on the front board (not in Coward's hand) and, in Coward's hand, on the verso of the front free endpaper.

1944 Sept. 7 through Dec., in pencil in a ruled notebook (10.5 × 16 cm), bound in dark green moleskin. Marked 1944 in Coward's hand on the verso of the front free endpaper and on the cover label, not in his hand.

1945 Jan. to July 6, in pencil, with a few corrections in ink, in a ruled notebook (12 × 18 cm), bound in brown moleskin. Marked 1945, not in Coward's hand, on a label pasted on the front board; and, in his hand, on the verso of the free front endpaper: "1945 January 1st July 6th."

1945 July 7 through Dec., in pencil, with a few corrections in ink, in a ruled Alwych Commercial Books notebook (11 × 17.5 cm), bound in black moleskin. On the verso of the flyleaf, in Coward's hand: "1945 July 7th December 31st."

1946 Jan. to March 12 and April 22 to July 14, in pencil in a ruled notebook (13 × 20 cm), bound in grey boards with green cloth spine. Marked 1946 on front board and, on the verso of the front board, in Coward's hand: "1946 January the 1st To July the 14th."

1946 March 13 to April 21, in pencil in a ruled notebook (13 × 20 cm), bound in grey boards with green cloth spine. Marked 1946 on front board and on the verso of the front board. On p. [1], above the opening entry: "Interlude in Paris."

1946 July 15 through Dec., in pencil in a ruled notebook (13 × 20 cm), bound in grey boards with green cloth spine. Marked 1946 on front board and "July 1946" on the verso of the front board.

1947 Jan. to July 24, in pencil and blue ballpoint pen in a ruled notebook (13 × 20 cm), bound in grey boards with green cloth spine. Marked "Jan 1947" on the front board and "January 1947" on the verso of the front board.

1947 July 25 through Dec., in blue ballpoint pen in a ruled notebook (11.5 × 18 cm), bound in grey cloth with brown moleskin spine. Marked 1947 on front board and "July 1947" on the recto of the flyleaf.

1948 Jan. to June 21, in blue ballpoint pen in a ruled notebook (11.5 × 18 cm), bound in grey cloth with brown moleskin spine. Marked 1948 on front board and "1948 January 1st until June 21st" on the recto of the flyleaf.

1948 June 22 through Dec. in blue ballpoint pen in a ruled notebook (13 × 20 cm), bound in grey boards with green cloth spine. Marked "1948" on the front board and "1948 June 22nd" on the verso of the flyleaf.

1949 Jan. to Sept. 30, in blue ballpoint pen in a ruled notebook (13 × 20.5 cm), bound in black moleskin. Most of the diary is written on the recto sides, with the Sept. entries continuing in reverse, on the verso sides, starting from the end of the notebook. Marked "1949" on the front board and on the recto side of the front free endpaper, and "January 1st 1949" on verso of front free endpaper.

1949 Oct. 1 to 1950 Feb. 28, in blue ballpoint pen in a ruled notebook (11 × 17.5 cm), bound in grey cloth and brown moleskin. Marked "1949 & 1950 to end of Feb" on the front board and "1949–1950," not in Coward's hand, on a pasted-on label, also on the front board, and "October 1949" on the front free endpaper.

1950 March 1 to June 19, in blue ballpoint pen in a ruled notebook (11 × 17.5 cm), bound in grey cloth and brown moleskin. Marked "1950 March–June" on the front board and "March 1950" on the front free endpaper.

1950 July 20 to Dec. 7, in blue ballpoint pen in a ruled notebook (11.5 × 17.5 cm), bound in blue boards with grey cloth spine. Marked "1950 July – December 8" on the front board and "1950" on the verso of the front board.

1950 Dec. 8 to 1951 July 13, in blue ballpoint pen in a ruled notebook (11.5 × 17.5 cm), bound in blue boards with grey cloth spine. Marked "Dec: 1950 to July 1951" on the front board and "1950" on p. [1] above the opening entry.

1951 July 14 to 1952 Jan. 30, in blue ballpoint pen in a ruled notebook (11.5 × 17.5 cm), bound in dark blue boards with dark blue cloth spine. Marked "1951" on the front board (and, not in Coward's hand, on a pasted-on label, also on the front board) as well as on the verso of the front board.

1952 Jan. 31 to Sept. 23, in blue ballpoint pen in a ruled notebook (11.5 × 17.5 cm), bound in dark blue boards with dark blue cloth spine. Marked "1952" on the front board (and, not in Coward's hand, on a pasted-on label, also on the front board) as well as on the verso of the front board.

1952 Sept. 25 to 1953 April 12, in blue ballpoint pen in a ruled notebook (11.5 × 17.5 cm), bound in dark blue boards with dark blue cloth spine. Marked "1952" on the front board and, not in Coward's hand, on a pasted-on label, also on the front board.

1953 April 22 to Dec. 1, in blue ballpoint pen in a ruled "Ideal" Series No. 4454/8½ notebook (17.5 × 22.5 cm), bound in burgundy cloth with a dark pink spine. Marked "Journal 1953" (not in Coward's hand) on a paper label pasted on the front board, and "Journal / 1953" on p. [1] above the opening entry.

1954 Jan. 1 to March 14, in blue ballpoint pen in a ruled notebook (16.5 × 20 cm), bound in black boards with bright red spine. Marked "Journal 1954," not in Coward's hand, on a pasted-on label on the front board.

1954 March 17 to April 15, in blue ballpoint pen in a ruled notebook (20 × 25 cm), bound in pink marbled boards with black cloth spine. Marked "March 1954 to April 1955" on the front board and "1954," in pencil, on p. [1] above the opening entry.

1955 April 24 to 1956 March 25, in blue ballpoint pen in a ruled notebook (20 × 25 cm), bound in pink marbled boards with black cloth spine. Marked "Journal 1955 56" (not in Coward's hand) on a paper label pasted on the front board and "1955," in pencil, on p. [1] above the opening entry.

1956 April 1 to Aug. 24, in blue ballpoint pen and dark blue ink in a brown spiral-bound The Wyring Line No. WB2363 exercise book (20 × 26.5 cm). Marked "April to August 1956" (not in Coward's hand) on a paper label pasted on the front board and "1956" on p. [1] above the opening entry.

1956 Sept. 2 to 1957 June 2, in black and blue ink and blue ballpoint pen in a spiral-bound Wyring Line No. WB2363 exercise book (20 × 26.5 cm). Marked "Sept. 1956 to June 1957" on the front board and "1956" on p. [1] above the first entry. Entries start on recto sides and continue in reverse on versos.

1957 June 5 to 1959 April 26, in blue ballpoint pen and dark blue ink, with a few corrections in pencil, in a ruled notebook (20 × 25 cm), bound in pink marbled boards with black cloth spine. Marked "1957 / 1958 / 1959" (not in Coward's hand) on a paper label pasted on the front board and "89 pages" (not in Coward's hand) on the verso of the front board.

1959 May 7 to 1960 March 20, in black and blue ballpoint pen in a ruled notebook (20 × 25.5 cm) bound in burgundy cloth with brown spine. Marked "1959/1960" (not in Coward's hand) on a paper label pasted on the front board, as well as on the recto and verso of the front board.

1960 March 29 to Nov. 20, in black and blue ballpoint pen in an Ideal Series No. 4457/8 ruled notebook (20 × 25.5 cm) bound in burgundy cloth with brown spine. Marked "1960" (not in Coward's hand) on a paper label pasted on the front board, as well as on the verso of the front board.

1960 Nov. 28 to 1961 April 9, in blue ballpoint pen in a ruled notebook (20 × 25.5 cm) bound in burgundy cloth with brown spine. Marked "1960/1961" (not in Coward's hand) on a paper label pasted on the front board, as well as on the recto and verso of the front board.

1961 May 5 to 1962 Feb. 19, in black and blue ballpoint pen in a ruled notebook (20 × 25.cm), bound in pink marbled boards with black cloth spine. Marked "May 5 - 1961 to Feb 19 - 1962" (not in Coward's hand) on the recto of the front board and on a paper label pasted on it.

1962 Feb. 22 through Dec., in black and blue ballpoint pen in a ruled notebook (20 × 25.5 cm) bound in burgundy cloth with brown spine. Marked "Feb–Dec 1962" on the front board and "Feb: – Dec: 1962" (not in Coward's hand) on a paper label pasted on the front board.

1963 Jan. 12 to 1964 May 16, in black and blue ballpoint pen in a ruled notebook (20 × 25.5 cm) bound in burgundy cloth with brown spine. Marked "1963/64" (not in Coward's hand) on a paper label pasted on the front board.

1964 June 6 through Dec. 27, in black and blue ballpoint pen on the recto sides of 29 unpaginated sheets of ruled paper (21 × 29.7 cm).

1965 Jan. 5 to Dec. 16, in black, blue, green, and purple ballpoint pen on the recto sides of 42 unpaginated sheets of ruled paper (21 × 29.7 cm). In a manila folder marked "Journal 1965."

1966 Aug. 8 to 1970 Jan. 25, in blue ballpoint pen on an unbound ruled ledger, stamped 1 to 50; an additional page, stamped 1, has been mounted in. Pages 34–42 are of the carbon copy. The pencilled note at the top of the last page, in the hand of Graham Payn, reads: "The last page of the Journals, typed put after the last previous entry, of Wed. Dec 31st 1969."

TYPED DIARIES, 1940–70

1940 Jan. 1 through Dec., on the recto sides of 80 leaves of onionskin paper, with occasional markings in red and green. Accompanied by a 3-page typed chronology of Coward's activities from 1 Sept. 1939 until 9 April 1941, carbon copy. Also a typed schedule, entitled "Visit of Noel Coward," prepared for his trip to Australia in Nov.–Dec. 1940, 4 p., carbon copy.

1941 Jan. 1 through Dec., carbon, on the recto sides of 181 numbered leaves, with deletions, corrections, and annotations in pencil, evidently in the hand of Graham Payn, some highlighted in red. On p. [1], above the opening entry: "N.C. Diary. (Australia)." Tied with a ribbon, in blue paper wrappers marked, in manuscript, "Diary," and in typescript, "1941."

1942 Jan. 1 through Dec., on the recto sides of 118 numbered leaves, with deletions, corrections, and annotations in pencil or ink. On p. [1], above the opening entry: "1942." Tied with a ribbon, in blue paper wrappers marked, in manuscript, "Top copy," and in typescript, "Diary 1942."

1943 Jan. 1 through Dec., on the recto sides of 136 numbered leaves, with deletions, corrections, and annotations in pencil and blue ballpoint pen, some possibly in Coward's hand. On p. [1], above the opening entry: "1943." Tied with a ribbon, in salmon paper wrappers marked, in manuscript, "Top copy / Diary," and in typescript, "1943."

1944 Jan. 1 through Dec., carbon, on the recto sides of 90 numbered leaves, with deletions, corrections, and annotations in blue and green ballpoint pen. On p. [1], above the opening entry: "1944." Tied with a ribbon, in blue paper wrappers marked, in manuscript, "Diary," and in typescript, "1944."

1945 Jan. 1 through Dec., on the recto sides of 78 numbered leaves, with deletions, corrections, and annotations in blue ballpoint pen and pencil. On p. [1], above the opening entry: "1945." Tied with a ribbon, in blue paper wrappers marked, in manuscript, "Top Copy," and in typescript, "Diary 1945."

1946 Jan. 1 through Dec., on the recto sides of 89 numbered leaves, with deletions, corrections, and annotations in blue ballpoint pen and pencil. On p. [1], above the opening entry: "1946." Tied with a ribbon, in blue paper wrappers marked, in manuscript, "Top Copy," and in typescript, "Diary 1946."

1947 Jan. 1 through Dec., on the recto sides of 90 numbered leaves, with deletions, corrections, and annotations in blue ballpoint pen and pencil. On title page: "Diary / 1947." Tied with a ribbon, in pink paper wrappers marked, in manuscript, "Top Copy / Diary," and in typescript, "Diary 1947."

1948 Jan. 1 through Dec., on the recto sides of 82 numbered leaves, with deletions, corrections, and annotations in pencil and blue ballpoint pen. On p. [1], above the opening entry: "1948." Tied with a ribbon, in blue paper wrappers marked, in manuscript, "Top Copy / Les Avants Copy / Diary," and, typed on a pasted-on label: "Diary 1948."

1949 Jan. 1 through Dec., on the recto sides of 80 numbered leaves, with deletions, corrections, and annotations in pencil and blue ballpoint pen. On title page: "Noel Coward / Diary for / 1949." Tied with a ribbon, in blue paper wrappers marked, in manuscript, "Top Copy / Les Avants Copy / Diary," and, typed on a pasted-on label: "Noel Coward / Diary for / 1949."

1950 Jan. 1 through Dec., on the recto sides of 93 numbered leaves, with deletions, corrections, and annotations in blue ballpoint pen and pencil. On p. [1], above the opening entry: "1950." Tied with a ribbon, in blue paper wrappers marked, in manuscript, "Top Copy / Diary," and, typed on a pasted-on label: "Diary / 1950." With two photocopies of corrected entries, from the same diary but a different typescript, laid in.

1951 Jan. 1 through Dec., on the recto sides of 95 numbered leaves, with deletions, corrections, and annotations in blue ballpoint pen and pencil. On p. [1], above the opening entry: "1951." Tied with a ribbon, in beige hard paper wrappers marked, in manuscript, "Diary 1950" on a pasted-on label.

1952 Jan. 1 through Dec., "Top copy," on the recto sides of 108 numbered leaves, with deletions, corrections, and annotations in blue ballpoint pen and pencil. On p. [1], above the opening entry: "1952." Tied with a ribbon, in blue hard paper wrappers marked, in manuscript, "Diary 1952" on a pasted-on label.

1953 Jan. 1 to April 12, "Top copy," on the recto sides of 20 loose, numbered leaves, with deletions, corrections, and annotations in blue ballpoint pen and pencil. On p. [1], above the opening entry: "1953." In a pink folder marked: "Diary an[d] Journal / 1953 to April 12."

1953 April 22 to 1956 Aug. 24, on the recto sides of 185 leaves, some carbon, with five consecutive paginations: [1] + [1]–16; [1] + [1]–10; [1] + 1–66; [1] + 1–68; [1] + 1–20. Deletions, corrections, and annotations in blue ballpoint pen and pencil. On the general title page: "Noel Coward / Journal / April 1953 / to / August 1956." The first section covers the period 22 April to 1 Dec. 1953. The second section covers the period 1 Jan. to 14 March 1954, with a title page: "Noel Coward / Journal / January to March 1954." The third section covers the period 17 March 1954 to 15 April 1955, with a title page: "Noel Coward / Journal / March 1954 to April 1955." The fourth section covers the period 24 April 1955 to 25 March 1956, with a title page: "Noel Coward / Journal / April 1955 to March 1956." The fifth section covers the period 1 April to 24 Aug. 1956, with a title page: "Noel Coward / Journal / April to August 1956." Bound with metal clasps within a burgundy folder, with a pasted-on paper label marked: "N.C. diary. April 1953. To August 1956."

1956 Sept. 2 to 1959 Dec. 27, on the recto sides of 175 leaves, with three consecutive paginations: [1] + [1]–89; 1–38; [1]–47. Deletions, corrections, and annotations in blue ballpoint pen and pencil. On the general title page: "Noel Coward / Journal / September 1956 / to / December 1959." The first section covers the period 2 Sept. 1956 to 29 Dec. 1957, the second the period 5 Jan. to 28 Dec. 1958, and the third the period 4 Jan. to 27 Dec. 1959. Bound with metal clasps within a burgundy folder, marked: "Noël Coward Diary / September 19-56. / To / December 19-59."

1960 Jan. 1 through Dec. 25, on the recto sides of 43 numbered leaves, with deletions, corrections, and annotations in blue ballpoint pen and pencil. On p. [1], above the opening entry: "1960." Tied with a ribbon, in grey hard paper wrappers with a paper label marked, in typescript, "Journal 1960."

1961 Jan. 1 through Dec. 26, on the recto sides of 49 numbered leaves, with deletions, corrections, and annotations in blue ballpoint pen and pencil. On p. [1], above the opening entry: "1961." Tied with a ribbon, in grey hard paper wrappers with a paper label marked, in typescript, "Journal 1961."

1962 Jan. 1 through Dec., on the recto sides of 45 numbered leaves, with deletions, corrections, and annotations in blue ballpoint pen and pencil. On p. [1], above the opening entry: "1962." Bound with metal clasps in burgundy wrappers with a paper label marked, in manuscript, "N.C. Diary January To December 1962."

1963 Jan. 12 through Dec. 29, on the recto sides of 48 numbered leaves, with deletions, corrections, and annotations in blue ballpoint pen and pencil. On p. [1], above the opening entry: "1963." Bound with metal clasps in burgundy wrappers with a paper label marked, in manuscript, "N.C. Diary January To December 1963."

1964 Jan. 13 to 1970 Jan. 25, on the recto sides of 188 leaves, with six consecutive paginations: [1]–46, [1]–60, [1]–61, [1]–27, [1]–22, [1]–10. Deletions, corrections, and annotations in blue ballpoint pen and pencil. The first section, headed "1964" above the opening entry, covers the period 13 Jan. to 27 Dec. 1964; the second the period 5 Jan. to 16 Dec. 1965; the third the period 2 Jan. to 16 Dec. 1966; the fourth the period 1 Jan. to 21 Dec. 1967; the fifth the period 23 Jan. to 29 Dec. 1968; and the sixth the period 26 Jan. to 31 Dec. 1969. The last two pages, unnumbered, are for the entry dated 25 Jan. 1970. They are almost entirely cancelled. Bound with metal clasps within a burgundy folder, marked on a pasted-in paper label: "N.C. Diary. January 1966 To December 1969."

See *The Noël Coward diaries*, ed. Graham Payn and Sheridan Morley (London: Macmillan, 1982).

FRKF 410e

II. WORKS BY NOEL COWARD

After the ball

Holograph drafts for Coward's lyrics to his adaptation of Oscar Wilde's *Lady Windermere's fan*. The manuscript comprises drafts for the following, written, unless otherwise specified, in blue ballpoint pen on tall leaves of ruled paper (20.5 × 33 cm).

7 pages of dialogue, under the heading "After buzz of conversation has died down a little," written on the recto sides of six numbered leaves, with a smaller additional sheet of unruled paper inserted between folios 5 and 6.

"Opening." 9 p. At the top of p. [1], in pencil, "Opening Chorus / [in a different hand] 'Oh What a Century.'" At the top of the last page, in Coward's hand: "Extra endings."

"I knew that you would be my love," 3 p.

"Oh what a season this has been," 1 p.

"Light is the heart," 4 p.

"Mr Hopper's chanty," 3 p.

"Sweet day," 3 p.

"Stay on the side of the angels," 1 p., with the heading "Lord Darlington / Act one."

"Crème de la crème," 3 p.

"May I have the pleasure," 1 p.

"Good evening, Lady Windermere …," 4 p.

"Who can she be," 2 p.

"All things, bright and beautiful," 3 p.

"I offer you my heart," 1 p.

"What can it mean, this desolate sense of dread?," 3 p.; at the top of p. [1]: "Aria / Mrs Erlynne / Act I."

"I feel so terribly alone," 2 p., headed in pencil, not in Coward's hand: "Lady Windermere's aria."

"So I beg you go" [Duet aria - Act II], 6 p.

"Accept dear Lady Windermere," 1 p., with the heading "Letter Song / Lord Darlington."

"Why is it the woman who pays / Trio," 5 p.

"All my life ago," 1 p., in pencil.

"Something on a tray," 2 p., headed "Something on a tray / Quartette / Act 2. / Scene 3."

"Faraway land," 4 p.

Drafts described as "Extras" on small accompanying pieces of paper, one for "Maudie Golightly," 2 p., one for "Now in the clear bright morning," 2 p.

Also, copyist's manuscripts, ozalid, each in beige wrappers, of the vocal scores for the following numbers:

"May I have the pleasure?" 7 p.

"Crème de la crème," 13 p.

"The woman who pays" (Trio), 8 p.

"Mr Hopper's chanty," 9 p.

"London at night" and "Men's goodnight song," 11 p.

"All my life ago," 5 p.

"I offer you my heart," [4] p.

"Letter song," 6 p.

"Stay on the side of the angels," 4 p.

"Something on a tray (Quartette)," 8 p.

"Farewell song (Lord Augustus)," 5 p.

"Mrs Erlynne's entrance," 10 p.

"Duet aria - Act II (Mrs Erlynne and Lady Windermere)," 18 p.

Accompanied by lists made by the former owner.

FRKF 410a

Conversation piece

Manuscript drafts, in pencil, comprising the following:

List of characters and synopsis, 5 p.

"Prologue / spoken by Sophie Orford and Martin James," 3 p.

"A cloud had passed across the sun," 3 p.

"Regency rakes," 3 p.

"Charming - charming - charming!" Written on stationery of 18, rue de la Ferme / Neuilly - Seine / Maillot 28–07, 1 p.

"Oh there's always something fishy about the French," 2 p.

Prologue to act 2, 2 p.

"The tree is in the garden," 1 p.

One page of dialogue between Melanie and Paul (not in Coward's hand), with a memo page "Keep with Conversation Piece."

"Quartette / There was once a little village by the sea," 2 p.

Accompanied by the original portfolio.

Conversation piece, a romantic comedy, was first performed in London in 1934.

FRKF 410b

Past conditional

Loose autobiographical notes, n.d., 8 p.

"General Events 1931–1939," in red ballpoint pen on the recto of a sheet of ruled paper, 1 p. Notes in blue ballpoint pen on verso.

"Notes / Past Conditional," in blue ballpoint pen on the recto sides of sheets of paper of various sizes (one consisting of two sheets taped together), 6 p. The journal-like entries are dated from every year between 1931 and 1939. Notes in pencil on the verso of one sheet.

"Tronda to Valparaiso," loose travel notes on a single sheet.

Preceded by a loose title page marked, in Coward's hand: "Notes / 'Past conditional.'"

The incomplete autobiography *Past conditional* was first published by Methuen in 1986 in a volume that also reprinted *Present indicative* and *Future indefinite*.

FRKF 410c

Present indicative

Partial holograph manuscript draft, mostly in pencil, on 20 × 20.5 cm ruled paper, with a few passages, as noted, in ink or in typescript. As there are differences from the published text, the references indicated below are not always an exact match.

The manuscript collates as follows:

A chronology for 1918–24, on stationery of The Panhellenic, New York, 1 p.

Outline for parts 5 and 6, paginated 1–8.

Notes for parts 6 to 14, 11 p.

Preface, paginated 1–3. Dated "Cairo - October 23rd 1932."

Part One [1]–(2), marked "rough draft," three drafts, paginated 1–6, 1–16, and 4; (3)–(4), paginated 1–31; (8)–(16), paginated 1–26; (16)–(22), paginated 1–43.

Part Five (3), a single, unpaginated page; (8), two drafts, the first, paginated 1–2, with the heading "Part 6," and 2–4; also another draft for p. 4; (9), five drafts, paginated 1, 1–2, and 1–4, 1, and 2; (10), paginated 1–4; (10)–(11), paginated 3–7.

Part Six [1], paginated 1–10; (3), three drafts, paginated I–IV, I–III, I–II; (4)–(9), two drafts, paginated 1–5 and I–V; [1], two drafts, paginated I–VIII and I–VI; (4)–(9), two drafts, paginated 6–31, 31[bis]–38, and I–III; (11)–(17), paginated 1–43; (20)–(22), paginated 1–16.

Part Seven, complete, paginated 1–18.

Part Eight (1)–(4), two continuous drafts, paginated 1–11 and 1–8; possibly an early draft, paginated 1–100 [page 1 starts in mid-sentence].

Part Nine (complete), paginated 1–5 and 5A–D, 6–78. Pages 6–10, 14, and 16–29 are in typescript, with pencil cancellations, corrections, and annotations. Partial draft of the beginning, in ink, entitled "Chapter I," paginated 1–13; also a stray p. 9; also another draft, in pencil, paginated 2–7. Draft headed "Chapter 2," paginated 1–18; on the verso of the unpaginated title page, unidentified draft (apparently also for *Present indicative*); two pages of unrelated notes at the end. (4), paginated 1–2; (16), a one-page draft headed "ch. 16 / extra page."

An apparently discarded draft, beginning "Descriptive writing is generally disappointing," possibly for Part Nine, paginated 1–4.

Miscellaneous drafts concerning Japan, possibly discards from Part Nine: "The Temple of Heaven," 2 p.; "Chapter 3," paginated 1–3; "Japan / Tokyo," paginated 1–7; unidentitied, paginated 1–5; and unidentified, 3 p.

Draft, possibly discarded, concerning Gertrude Lawrence and "Poor little rich girl," paginated I–III.

Unidentified, unpaginated drafts, including two pages of drafts for songs, 5 p.

Diary, dated Rio de Janeiro, Nov. 17, n.y., paginated 1–4.

Diary, dated Petropolis, Nov. 30, n.y., paginated 1–6.

Present indicative was first published by William Heinemann Ltd in 1936.

FRKF 410d

PALMER COX (1840–1924)

Brownie Calendar, 1893

12 original pencil and watercolor drawings on paper, signed. All are 23 × 28 cm, with the calendar for the month in pencil alternatively in the bottom right or bottom left corner; each drawing is mounted on cardboard.

The Brownie year book. New York: McLoughlin Bro's., publishers, n.d. [1896].

Folio, 14 unpaginated leaves, 24 × 31 cm.

FRKF 60

FRANCIS DE CROISSET (1877–1937)

Papers of Louis Robin relating to Francis de Croisset

I. LETTERS

From Francis de Croisset to Robin

With the exceptions of the following, the large majority of the more than 200 letters and cards are undated with no place indicated. The correspondence deals in great detail with relations between Croisset and his publishers and, especially, the press. There are mentions of several of his works, notably the play *Chérubin*, which he co-adapted in 1905 as an opéra-comique set to music by Massenet.

[1901 July, Paris*] ALS, 1 p.

[1901 Aug., Paris*] ALS, 1 p.

[1902 Jan. 19, Paris*] ALS, 1 p.

[1902 Sept. 18, Paris*] ALS, 1 p.

1903 Jan. 5, London, telegram

1903 Feb. 21, Cannes, telegram

1903 March 7, Nice, telegram

1903 Aug. 1, Bagnères-de-Luchon, telegram

1903 Aug. 2, Bagnères-de-Luchon, telegram

1903 Aug. 7, Biarritz, telegram

1903 Aug. 11, Bagnères-de-Luchon, telegram

1903 Aug. 12, Bagnères-de-Luchon, telegram

1903 Sept. 5, Brussels, telegram

1903 Oct. 26, The English Grand Hotel, Teneriffe[S], ALS, 3 p.

1903 Oct. 31, The English Grand Hotel, Teneriffe[S], ALS, 5 p.

1903 Oct. 31, The English Grand Hotel, Teneriffe[S], ALS, 2 p.

1903 Nov. 15, Algiers, telegram

[1905 Sept. 11, Paris*] ALS, 1 p.

[1905 Sept. 15, Bagnères-de-Luchon*] ALS, 1 p.

[1905 Oct. 24, Paris*] ALS, 1 p.

1906 March 5, Hôtel Westminster, Nice[S], ALS, 2 p.

1906 March 19, Nice, telegram

1906 March 23, Nice, telegram

1906 March 26, Nice, telegram

1906 Oct. 14, La Tour, ALS, 4 p.

1909 Feb. 10, Nice, telegram

1909 Dec. 29, Hôtel de la Plage, Cannes[S], ALS, 2 p.

1910 April 4, Grasse, telegram

1910 May 20, ALS, on one side of a card printed 11, place des États-Unis [Paris], mourning border.

1911 March 22, Nice, telegram

1911 March 22, Grasse, telegram

[1914 Sept. 19?, Brussels*] ALS, 1 p.

1916 Jan. 24, Hôtel Terlinck, La Panne-Bains[S], ALS, 2 p.

1919 Jan. 28, ALS on one side of a card printed 11, place des États-Unis, Paris.

1921 Dec. 25, n.p., ALS, 1 p.

1922 March 5, Continental-Hotel, Berlin[S], ALS, 2 p. (env)

1924 March 31, ALS on one side of a card printed Villa Croisset, Grasse.

[1920s] Dec. 6, La gazette de Paris[S], ALS, 1 p.

1926 June 16, 12, Boulevard Flandrin. XVIe. [Paris][S], TLS, 1 p.

1928 Jan. 16, Saint-Bernard, Hyères[S], TLS, 1 p.

1928 Oct. 17, 199, Boulevard St Germain. VIIe.[S], TLS, 1 p.

1929 March 27, 199, Boulevard St Germain. VIIe.[S], TLS, 1 p.

1929 Oct. 13, 199, Boulevard St Germain. VIIe.[S], TLS, 1 p.

1929 Dec. 23, 199, Boulevard St Germain. VIIe.[S], TLS, 1 p.

1930 June 27, 199, Boulevard St Germain. VIIe.[S], ALS, 1 p.

1931 Jan. 8, La Mamounia, Hotel transatlantique, Marrakech[S], ALS, 1 p.

1931 May 5, 199, Boulevard St Germain, TLS, 1 p.

1931 July 7, 199, Boulevard St Germain. VIIe.[S], TLS, 1 p.

1931 Dec. 7, 199, Boulevard St Germain, TLS, 1 p.

1931 Dec. 10, TLS on one side of a card printed 199, Boulevard St Germain. VIIe.

1932 March 16, 199, Boulevard St Germain, TLS, 1 p.

1932 June 17, TLS on a card printed 199, Boulevard St Germain. VIIe. (env)

1932 Dec. 8, 199, Boulevard St Germain. VIIe.[S], TLS, 1 p.

1934 Jan. 2, [Hotel] George V[S], TLS, 1 p.

1936 July 8, 44, avenue Gabriel. XIIIe, TLS, 1 p.

1936 Dec. 16, 44, avenue Gabriel. XIIIe[S], TLS, 1 p.

Also, ALS from Germaine de Croisset to Robin, on stationery of 199, boulevard Saint-Germain, n.d., 1 p.

From Georges Ricou to Robin

Many letters are on the stationery of the Théâtre national de l'Opéra-Comique, Paris[S] (=Opéra-Comique[S]). The correspondence includes details about singers and performances. The names mentioned include Marguerite Carré, Geneviève Vix, Lucien Muratore, Jeanne Hatto. The wartime letters document Ricou's service as a lieutenant at the front.

1912 April 4, Opéra-Comique[S], TLS, 2 p.

1912 April 8, Opéra-Comique[S], TLS, 2 p.

1912 April 10, Opéra-Comique[S], TLS, 2 p.

1912 April 11, Opéra-Comique[S], TLS, 1 p.

1912 April 12, Opéra-Comique[S], TLS, 1 p.

1916 Jan. 16, n.p., APCS

1916 Sept. 13, n.p., ALS, 1 p.

1917 June 30, n.p., ALS, 4 p.

1918 May 6, n.p., ALS, 4 p.

1921 May 12, Comédie Française [Paris][S], TLS, 1 p.

1926 Jan. 9, Opéra-Comique[S], ALS, 2 p.

1926 March 2, Opéra-Comique[S], TLS, 1 p.

1926 May 23, Opéra-Comique[S], TLS, 1 p.

1932 Jan. 6, n.p., ALS, 1 p.

Undated

ANS, Opéra-Comique[S], on one side of a printed card.

ANS, Opéra-Comique[S], on one side of a printed card.

ANS, "Jeudi," Opéra-Comique[S], on both sides of a printed card.

ANS, "Samedi," Opéra-Comique[S], on one side of a printed card.

ANS, "Samedi," Opéra-Comique[S], on one side of a printed card.

ANS, [191?] Opéra-Comique[S], on one side of a printed card.

ALS, Comédie Française [Paris][S], 1 p.

ALS, "Mercredi," Comédie Française [Paris][S], 1 p.

ALS, "Dimanche," Comédie Française[S], on both sides of a printed card.

ALS, "Lundi," n.p., 1 p.

Georges Ricou was secrétaire général of the Opéra-Comique.

To and from Robin

Pierre Bertrand, ALS to Robin, 1958 Oct. 23, Paris, 1 p. Bertrand succeeded Robin as Croisset's secretary.

Robin, TL to Philippe de Croisset, 1958 Nov. 10, n.p., 1 p., carbon copy. Philippe de Croisset, TLS to Robin, 1958 Nov. 13, Marie-Claire, Paris[S], 1 p.

Robin, TL to Éditions Bernard Grasset, 1958 March 19, n.p., 1 p., carbon copy. Éditions Bernard Grasset, TLS to Robin, 1958 March 21, Paris, 1 p.

Maurice Noël, TLS to M. de Chateaubriant, 1959 Dec. 4, Le Figaro littéraire, Paris[S], 1 p.

Jean Senard, TLS to Robin, 1960 May 31, Le Figaro littéraire[S], 1 p.

Robin, TL to the Nouvelles littéraires [1962 April 25] n.p., 1 p., carbon copy. Nouvelles littéraires, TLS to Robin, 1962 May 9, Paris, 1 p.

The correspondence deals with Robin's frustrated efforts to publish the Croisset correspondence.

II. OTHER PAPERS

Le tour de main

Autograph fragment, 3 p., from Croisset's three-act comedy, premiered in Nice in 1906.

LETTER TRANSCRIPTS

"Francis de Croisset / a) au début de / sa vie littéraire / des Nuits de quinze ans au Paon / Lettres à Louis Robin, son secrétaire"

Partly handwritten, partly typewritten manuscript, 100 p. Signed by Robin at the end.

Accompanied by a partial handwritten and typewritten transcription of the letters. With another copy of the same manuscript, typewritten throughout, with manuscript title page, each 96 p. Also, AN in pencil in Robin's hand with an alternative title for his projected volume: "Pages / de la vie littéraire / à la belle époque / 220 letters / de Francis de Croisset / à son secrétaire," and other notes by Robin.

CLIPPINGS

Caricature of Croisset by Sem from *Le Journal*, n.d.

Caricature of Croisset as a peacock by C. Léandre, from an unidentified journal, in color, 1902. The caption reads: "- Qui, mieux que moi, pouvait faire le Paon?"

Article on Croisset by Fernand Rooman, from *Le Gardénia* (Antwerp) for March 1908.

J. Desbouchères's article on Croisset in the *Revue illustrée* 25:15 (10 Aug. 1910), together with the cover, illustrated with a photograph of Croisset.

Various clippings relating to Croisset, especially from the time of his death in 1937.

EPHEMERA

Printed announcement of a banquet hosted by the Association générale des étudiants de Paris in Croisset's honor, 1905.

Printed, illustrated menu of a luncheon hosted in honor of Croisset, n.d.

Publisher's announcement for Croisset's posthumous travel volume *La côte de Jade* (Paris: Bernard Grasset, 1938); with a quotation from the book written in Robin's hand on another sheet of paper.

Printed announcement of the wedding of Germaine de Croisset and Count Roger de Montebello, 1933.

III. PHOTOGRAPHS OF CROISSET

As a young man. By Nadar, oblong black-and-white portrait (22 × 16.5 cm).

Small round portrait printed on a card (11 × 17 cm), signed and inscribed to Robin. Printed credit on the verso to DuGuy, Art & Photographie, 368, rue St Honoré, Paris.

Sepia photographic portrait (10.5 × 17 cm), signed and inscribed to Robin. Printed credit on the verso to DuGuy, Art & Photographie, 368, rue St Honoré, Paris.

Black-and-white photographic portrait by Rehbinder (16 × 22 cm), signed by the photographer and signed and inscribed to Robin by Croisset (Oct. 1926). Printed credit on the verso to Vogue-Studio, Wladimir Rehbinder, directeur, 9, rue Saint-Florentin, Paris.

Sepia photograph showing Frédéric Mistral and Jean Richepin in the same carriage as Francis de Croisset and his bride, Marie-Thérèse Bischoffsheim, née de Chevigné, on their wedding day in 1910 (18 × 13 cm).

Postcard photograph by Bryer & Bert, Paris.

CROISSET / ROBIN PAPERS
London, Sotheby's, 5 Dec. 1991, lot 485.
FRKF 1412

GABRIELE D'ANNUNZIO (1863–1938)

Letter to Reynaldo Hahn

n.d. [Paris?] ALS, 1 p., confirming a luncheon appointment.

Paris, Laurin-Guilloux-Buffetaud-Tailleur (Drouot), 8 Feb. 1985, lot 115.
FRKF 658.2

ALPHONSE DAUDET (1840–97)

L'Arlésienne

Three notebooks containing manuscripts and drafts for the play, 177, 138, and 114 p., [ca. 1871–72]

A 14.5 × 18.5 cm ruled notebook (stationer's ticket of Susse Frères), paginated (not in Daudet's hand) [1]–177 (odd numbers only), bound in black paper boards decorated with blind-tooled floral patterns. Inscribed by Daudet in the upper right corner on the verso of the free front endpaper: "Pour Julia: / le plus long le premier." This notebook is written mostly in black ink, with passages in pencil toward the end and some corrections and additions in pencil throughout. It includes an early version of the entire play ([1]–[104]); drafts for various scenes in act 2 ([106]–[116]); several drafts for act 1, First Tableau, scene 1 (117–37); a draft for act 2, Third Tableau, scenes 1–5 ([138]–[152]); a draft for act 2, Second Tableau, scene 5 (153–57); a draft for act 2, Third Tableau, scenes 4–5 (157–[70]); and a draft of a scene between Frédéri and the Gardian in the Fourth Tableau (171–75). On p. [2] (verso of the free front endpaper), [4], and 177 (recto of the free rear endpaper), sketches of the set in Daudet's hand, in pen-and-ink and pencil.

An 11 × 16.5 cm ruled notebook, paginated (not in Daudet's hand) 1–[138] (odd numbers only), bound in grey-brown marbled paper with purple cloth spine, and with a small octagonal label on the front board marked, in Daudet's hand: "L'Arlésienne." On p. 3, in Daudet's hand: "L'Arlésienne / Drame rustique en cinq tableaux" and list of characters. The notebook is written in black ink, with some passages, corrections, and additions in pencil. It is an incomplete draft of the play, stopping at the beginning of act 3, Fifth Tableau, scene 3.

A 15.5 × 18.5 cm ruled notebook, paginated (not in Daudet's hand) 1–[114] (odd numbers only), bound in modern purple boards and spine, original beige paper wrappers bound in; on the front wrapper, in Daudet's hand: "L'Arlésienne." On p. 1, in Daudet's hand: "L'Arlésienne / Drame rustique en cinq tableaux" and list of characters. The manuscript is written in black ink throughout, with occasional doodles (heads and faces) at the bottom of the page. It includes an incomplete draft of the play, stopping in the middle of act 3, Fifth Tableau, scene 1 (1–109); a list of proverbial expressions, possibly for use in the play (111); a draft of act 2, First Tableau, scenes 1 and 2, the beginning only ([112]–[114]).

Heinrich Schütz to Henry Miller, p. 58–59.
Paris, Hervé Chayette (Drouot), 1 July 1985, lot 29.
FRKF 1297

Note to Reynaldo Hahn

n.d., Paris, ANS on his printed visiting card.

Paris, Laurin-Guilloux-Buffetaud-Tailleur (Drouot), 8 Feb. 1985, lot 115.
FRKF 658.3

CLAUDE DEBUSSY (1862–1918)

I. MUSIC MANUSCRIPTS

Le balcon

Holograph manuscript of this song for voice and piano on a poem by Charles Baudelaire, 1888, 8 p. Notated in black ink, with a few pencil markings, on two separate bifolia housed in a third bifolium (the third page of which is the last page of music) of tall 24-staff paper (blind stamp of Lard-Esnault). There is no title page. At the top of the first page of music, in Debussy's hand: "Le Balcon." Dated Jan. 1888 at the end. The manuscript was presented by Debussy to his friend Paul Poujaud.

Published in 1890 in *Cinq poèmes de Charles Baudelaire*.
Lesure 70/I.
Paris, Laurin-Guilloux-Buffetaud-Tailleur (Drouot), 16 Dec. 1988, lot 55.
FRKF 1354

Chevaux de bois

Holograph manuscript of this song for voice and piano on a text by Paul Verlaine, 1885, 5 p. Notated in black ink on both sides of two sheets and the recto of one sheet of tall, self-ruled 15-staff paper. Dated at the end: "Paris (10 = 1 - 85 x.)" [i.e. 10 Jan. 1885]. The date is followed by Debussy's monogram (AD). Mutilated: the tops of the leaves are torn and singed, with loss of musical text in the first system at the top of each page. At the bottom of p. [1], note in Debussy's hand: "(Exagérez l'accent des notes marquées du signe)."

Published in 1888 and republished in 1903 as no. IV ("Paysages belges. Chevaux de bois") in *Ariettes oubliées*.

Lesure 63/IV.
London, Sotheby's, 28 May 1986, lot 377.
FRKF 1138

Colloque sentimental

Holograph manuscript of this song for voice and piano on a text by Verlaine, n.d., 4 p. Notated in black ink on p. [1], [3], [5], and [7] of a gathering of two nested bifolia of tall 22-staff paper (almost illegible oval blind stamp: Lard?). On p. [1], above the first system, in red pencil: "III. Colloque sentimental." An early, different version of the song published in 1904 as no. 3 of the second series of *Fêtes galantes*.

Formerly in the Legouix and Jean-Marie Martin collections.
Lesure 114/III.
London, Sotheby's, 28 May 1986, lot 378.
FRKF 1139

La fille aux cheveux de lin

Holograph manuscript of this song for voice and piano on a poem by Leconte de Lisle, n.d., 9 p.

> The song is written in black ink, with pencil additions and corrections, on p. [2] to [7] of a gathering of three nested bifolia of tall, self-ruled 12-staff paper; the second leaf, presumably blank, of the first bifolium is missing.
>
> On p. [1] in Debussy's hand: "la fille aux cheveux de / Lins. / Chanson Ecossaise / poesie de Leconte de Lisle"; also on p. [1], dedication: "a Mme Vanier / qui a réalisé ce probleme / que, ce n'est pas la musique / qui fait la / beauté du chant … / mais le chant, qui fait la / beauté de la musique. / (surtout pour [this last word added in pencil] la mienne.) / L'auteur humble et reconnaissant. / Ach. Debussy."
>
> On p. [7], note in Debussy's hand: "Tout ce que je / pense avoir de bon, / avec le cerveau est / la dedans - / Voyez et jugez / Ach. Debussy." Also signed "Ach. Debussy" at the bottom of p. [8], which is another draft of the end of the song. On p. [9], unrelated sketches (counterpoint exercises?). Additional musical jottings in pencil on p. [7], [8], and [9].

Dated 1881 by Lesure and Grove.
Lesure 15.
London, Sotheby's, 29 Nov. 1985, lot 48.
FRKF 1029

Intermezzo pour orchestre

Holograph manuscript of the transcription for piano four-hands. The manuscript is written in black ink on eleven single leaves of 16-staff paper (with traces of stubs suggesting it was previously bound), beginning on the verso of the first leaf and continuing on the recto of the ten following leaves, numbered 1 to 10 in the upper right corner.

On the cover: "Intermezzo. / pour orchestre. / (Partition piano a 4 mains). / Cl. Ach. Debussy / 21 Juin 1882." Also on the cover is the following epigraph: "La mysterieuse îles des esprits se dessinait vaguement aux lueurs du clair de lune; la résonaient des jours délicieux, la flottaient des danses nébuleuses. Les sons devenaient de plus en plus suaves: la ronde tourbillonait plus entrainante… (Henri Heine, Intermezzo)." Additional corrections and markings in black and blue pencil throughout. Folio 1v is entirely cancelled in red pencil.

Lesure 40.
Marburg, Stargardt, 5–6 March 1985, lot 782.
FRKF 809

Jeux

Manuscript, in short score, chiefly in the hand of a copyist, partly in Debussy's hand, with annotations by the composer and by Diaghilev and Nijinsky, n.d. [1912], 43 p.

> The manuscript is written in black ink, with annotations and additions in black and blue pencil, on two gatherings of four nested bifolia and one gathering of three nested bifolia of tall 19-staff paper (blind stamp of L. Andrieu), paginated 1–42, and a single leaf (verso only written in Debussy's hand) of tall 22-staff paper.
>
> On the title page, in black ink, in an unidentified hand (not the copyist's), title "Jeux"; and, in blue ink, in the hand of Serge Lifar: "Partition / de Vaslav Nijinsky / [signed:] Serge Lifar / avec les Notations / de Debussy, [added in pencil:] de Diaghilev / et de Nijinsky." Stamp of Lifar on the title page; stamp of Durand on the title page and throughout.
>
> Annotated throughout, beginning on p. 5, in pencil, in two Russian hands. Numerous markings in Debussy's hand throughout, in pencil or black ink. These consist in corrections or alterations to the music, tempo or dynamic indications, and staging indications. The additional page, corresponding to an alternative ending, is entirely in Debussy's hand.

See Debussy's letters to Durand, 1912 Nov. 1 [actually Sept. 1] and 1912 Sept. 12, in *Correspondance*, p. 1542–3.
Lesure 133.
London, Sotheby's, 9 May 1984, lot 149.
FRKF 301

Madrid

Holograph manuscript, incomplete, of this song for voice and piano, n.d., 1 p.

> Notated in black ink on p. [2] of a bifolium of tall, self-ruled laid 18-staff paper. On p. [1], in Debussy's hand: "Madrid / paroles / Musset / musique / de Bussy." Comprises only 18 measures. The vocal line is present, but the words are missing.
>
> Signed and inscribed at the bottom of the page: "A mes bons Amis / P. Vidal et Passerieu / leur vieil ami / Ach de Bussy." At the top of p. [1] unidentified sketches, in pencil, notated in

pencil on a system of two staves. Dated, in an unidentified hand, 1880; dated 1879 by Grove (with the title "Madrid, princesse des Espagnes").

Lesure 1.
Marburg, Stargardt, 8–9 June 1982, lot 622.
FRKF 14

Marche écossaise sur un thème populaire

Holograph manuscript sketches, n.d., 1 p. Notated in black ink on the recto of a single sheet of tall 16-staff paper (16.5 × 24.5 cm). Notated on two 4-staff systems and corresponding to the first 7 measures. According to Lesure, this piano version dates from 1890 and was in the collection of D.-E. Inghelbrecht.

Lesure 83.
FRKF 287

Ode bacchique

Holograph manuscript of this duet for soprano and tenor with piano accompaniment, n.d., 10 p. Notated in black ink on both sides of sheets of tall 16-staff paper, paginated [1]–11, not in Debussy's hand. On the title page, in Debussy's hand: "a Madame Vasnier. / Ode Bachique. / (tirée d'Hymnis comedie Lyrique de Th. de Banville) / Musique Ach. Cl. Debussy." On an additional sheet, two short related drafts, evidently a discard of the original p. 7 (the sixth page of music).

From the collection of Arturo Toscanini.
Dated 1882 by Lesure and Grove.
Lesure 41.
London, Sotheby's, 26 May 1983, lot 17.
FRKF 120

L'ombre des arbres

Holograph manuscript of this song for voice and piano, on a poem by Verlaine, 1885, 2 p. Notated in black ink on the first two pages of a bifolium of 15-staff paper (blind stamp of Lard-Esnault). No title. At the top of p. [1] in Debussy's hand: "Andante (dans un sentiment de tristesse rêveuse)."

Bound in pale green, red, and yellow marbled paper and cream-colored vellum corners and spine, with author and title gold-tooled on thin black leather on spine. Dated Paris, 6 Jan. 1885, at the bottom of the second page.

Published in 1888 in *Ariettes, paysages belges et aquarelles* and republished in 1903 as no. 3 in *Ariettes oubliées*.
Lesure 63/III.
FRKF 713

Pelléas et Mélisande

Holograph manuscript of the opera, in short score, 1893–1901, 131 leaves. Written chiefly in black ink, with additions and corrections in blue or red ink, black pencil, blue or red pencil, and two different shades of green pencil, on the rectos (with occasional additions on the versos) of sheets of tall 26, 30-staff paper (blind stamps of Lard-Esnault or Lard-Esnault Bellamy).

Collation:

Act 1: On title page, in Debussy's hand: "Pélléas et Mélisande. / 1er Acte" and stamp of the New England Conservatory of Music; foliated (beginning on the next folio) 1–23 in blue pencil, in Debussy's hand; dated at the end "Dec - 93. / Janv. Fev. 94." A revision of a passage from 12r is written on 11v.

Act 2: On title page, in Debussy's hand: "Pélléas et Mélisande. / (2ème Acte)"; foliated (beginning on the next folio) 1–19 in red pencil, in Debussy's hand; marked at the end "(finis / 17. Aout. 95)." Folio 17 was removed by Debussy at an unknown date (but after 1901) and folded in four (evidently by him), and bears an autograph inscription in the lower right corner, perpendicular to the staves: "Pour le Docteur René Vaucaire / Claude Debussy, / (Pèllàs et Melisande) / 2e Acte : 3e Scène." A revision of two measures from 15r is on 14v, and a revision of two measures from 18r is on 17v (the verso of the Vaucaire folio).

Act 3: On title page, in Debussy's hand: "Pélléas et Mélisande. 3ème Acte"; foliated (beginning on the next folio) 1–33 in black pencil, possibly in Debussy's hand; there is no date at the end. The music at the bottom of 6r (on the words "Je n'ouvrirais [sic] plus les mains cette" [nuit]) continues for 3 measures on 6v, where an additional 2 measures (corresponding to a different passage) are notated in blue pencil. Four small drafts are notated in pencil and black ink on 14v (notes for the orchestration). On 17v, new draft, in black ink, with the text in pencil, for the passage "Elle est très délicate …" On 19v, continuation of 19r. The entire passage (13 measures on 19r, 26 measures on 19v), immediately following Golaud's words "sans affectation …," cancelled in red pencil; the revised version of the ending of the scene is drafted, in red ink, on 20r.

Act 4: On title page, in Debussy's hand: "Pélléas et Mélisande. / 4eme acte"; foliated in Debussy's hand (beginning on the next folio) 1–4 in blue pencil and 5–33 in red pencil; dated at the end: "Sept. Oct. 93. / Mai. 95. / Janvier 1900. / Sept. 1901." At the bottom of 9v, revision of the 4-measure passage (on 9r) "Vous espérez voir quelque chose dans mes yeux …" At the bottom of 19v, partial rewriting in fair copy of the 10 orchestral measures at the beginning of scene 5. On 31v, 4 measures drafted in pencil.

Act 5: On title page, in Debussy's hand: "Pèlléas et Mélisande. / 5eme acte"; foliated (beginning on the next folio) 1–17 in blue pencil, in Debussy's hand. On 11v, two sketches in pencil, representing a total of 3 measures.

Bound in cream-colored cloth, with purple fillet on the edges of both boards; on the front board, in purple lettering: "Pelléas / et / Mélisande / (esquisse)"; on the spine, also in purple lettering: "Pelléas / et / Mélisande." On the verso of the front board, bookplate of the New England Conservatory of Music Library, gift of [in manuscript:] "Mr. Eben D. Jordan, " and "Cabinet 45." At the bottom, in pencil, in the same hand: "Transferred to this Library from the Office safe. / [Sept. 1911?]" On the front free endpaper, library slip stamped "Library use only" and filled out, in most cases in the hand of a librarian, with names of patrons and the dates of their visits, including Arthur Honegger (8 Jan. 1929), Gustav Holst (26 April 1929), Artur Schnabel (2 April 1930), [André?] Morize and Léon Vallas (5 Nov. 1932), Edward Lockspeiser (27 Oct. 1960), and Rudolf Kolisch (Oct. 1967). The last date recorded is 6 Feb. 1969.

See David A. Grayson, *The genesis of Debussy's Pelléas et Mélisande* (Ann Arbor: UMI Research Press, 1986), especially p. 159–63. See also Vincent Giroud, "*Pelléas et Mélisande*: Le manuscrit Koch de l'université Yale," *Revue musicale de Suisse Romande* 55:2 (June 2002): 42–51.
Lesure 93.
New York, Christie's, 21 May 1982, lot 16.
Marburg, Stargardt, 8 June 1982, lot 626 (Vaucaire folio).
FRKF 15,15.1

II. LETTERS

To Émile Baron

1887 Jan. 5 [Rome*] ALS, 3 p. (env), a humorous letter of reproach for not writing; also mentions his monogrammed stationery and Jean Ajalbert's *Paysages de femmes*. Signed A Debussy. Red AD monogram on stationery. *Correspondance*, p. 58.

FRKF 558a

To Pierre de Bréville

[1894 Feb. 16?] "Vendredi," n.p., ALS, 2 p., concerning a concert of Grieg songs by Esther Sidner; also mentions Glazunov. *Correspondance*, p. 194–95.

Paris, Laurin-Guilloux-Buffetaud-Tailleur (Drouot), 28 June 1983, lot 80.
FRKF 286

To Lilly Debussy

Letters are autograph, signed, and sent from Paris unless otherwise noted.

1899

April: 21 (1 p.); 24 (2 p., with envelope marked "1ere de toutes" in Lilly's hand); 27 (1 p.)

May: 1 (3 p.); 5 (3 p.); 8 (3 p., with *pneumatique* envelope); 12 (2 p.); 15 (3 p.); 19 (4 p. on 2 sheets, with unaddressed env); 22 (3 p., env); 23–24 (6 p., env); 26 (3 p., env); 27 (6 p., with envelope, annotated by Lilly); 29 (7 p., env); 31 (3 p., env)

June: 1 (1 p., env); 2 (3 p., env); [7] (1 p.); 12 (2 p., *pneumatique* envelope); [15?] ("Jeudi soir," 3 p.); 16 (1 p., printed *carte pneumatique fermée* on the address side); 17 (6 p. on 3 sheets, env); 18 (i.e. 19, 3 p.); 20 (i.e. 21, "Mercredi," 1 p., printed *carte pneumatique fermée* on the address side); 20 (i.e. 21, "Mercredi," 3 p., env); [22] (1 p., env)

July: 3 (3 p., *pneumatique* envelope); 4 (3 p., env)

July–Aug.: marked June 1899 on envelope but dated July–Aug. 1899 in *Correspondance*, 7 p.

1900

April: 25 (2 p.)

1902

July (all Hotel Cecil, Strand. W.C. London[S]): [15] (4 p., env); 16 (1 p., env); [17] ("Jeudi," 3 p., env); 18 (6 p., env)

1903

April: 27 (London, telegram); 27 (Hotel Cecil, Strand. W.C., London[S], 2 p., env); 27 (Hotel Cecil, Strand. W.C., London[S], 3 p., env); 30 (London, telegram)

May: 1 (Hotel Cecil, Strand. W.C., London[S], 3 p., env); 29 (58, rue Cardinet [Paris][S] 2 p., env); [30] (58, rue Cardinet[S], 4 p.); 31 (58, rue Cardinet[S], 3 p., env)

June (all 58, rue Cardinet[S]): 1 (4 p., env); 2 (3 p., env); 3 (2 p., env); 4 (3 p., env, annotated "lettre Saxophone" by Lilly); 5 (2 p., env)

December: 19 (2 p., env)

1904

July: 16 (4 p., env); 19 (4 p.); 24 (3 p., env, annotated by Lilly); 28 (2 p., env); 30 (3 p., env, together with a receipt for 100-franc money order in Debussy's name, also postmarked 30 July 1904)

August: 11 (Dieppe*, 4 p., env. This is the letter in which Debussy tells Lilly that he is leaving her); [22] (1 p., env)

September: 14 (Dieppe*, 3 p., env)

1905

February: [13] ("Lundi soir," 1 p., with *pneumatique* envelope); [18] ("Samedi," 1 p., env, dated in Lilly's hand); [22] ("Mercredi," 1 p., env, dated in Lilly's hand); [26, 1905?] ("Dimanche 5h," 1 p.); [Feb. 1905?] (2 p.)

March: 22 [i.e. 21] ("Mardi," 1 p., env, blank, sealed with green wax); 22 (4 p., env)

A *pneumatique* envelope, postmarked 8 June 1899, belongs with a letter not in the collection; see *Correspondance*, p. 493.

Rosalie Texier (1875–1932), known as Lilly (Debussy usually spelled the name with 2 *l*'s), became Debussy's wife on 18 Oct. 1899. Originally from northern Burgundy, she had worked as a model for a Parisian couture house and was a close friend of Debussy's mistress, Gabrielle (Gaby)

Dupont. Lilly tried to kill herself after Debussy left her in July 1904 for the singer Emma Bardac, who became his second wife four years later.

The correspondence was formerly in the collection of the French music critic Émile Vuillermoz (1878–1960). *Correspondance*, p. 468–70, 472, 474–78, 480–92, 493–94, 498–501, 503–06, 510–14, 556, 675–78, 726–29, 733–40, 807, 852–58, 861–64, 884–87, 890–91.
FRKF 197

To Serge Diaghilev

1917 May 20, 80, avenue du Bois de Boulogne [Paris]^S ALS, 2 p., concerning Ballets russes performances at the Châtelet. *Correspondance*, p. 2113.

1917 May 26 [on back of envelope: Paris] ALS, 1 p. Mentions Fauré's *Pavane*, Stravinsky's *Petrushka*, and Leonid Massine. Sent via *pneumatique*. On the back of the letter, possibly in Diaghilev's hand: "Las Meninas / 1916." *Correspondance*, p. 2116.

Both formerly in the collection of Serge Lifar, with his stamp printed in red.
London, Sotheby's, 9 May 1984, lots 150–51.
FRKF 302–03

To Paul Dukas

[1896 June 24, Paris*] ALS, 2 p. (env), concerning *Pelléas et Mélisande*. *Correspondance*, p. 318.

1901 March 13 [Paris*] ALS, 1 p. (env), inquiring about a reply to a previous letter. *Correspondance*, p. 589.

FRKF 535a, 558b

To Louis Émie

1916 Dec. 25, n.p., ALS, 1 p., concerning *M. Croche*. *Correspondance*, p. 2063.

Paris, Laurin-Guilloux-Buffetaud-Tailleur (Drouot), 12 June 1984, lot 206.
FRKF 470

To Edwin Evans

1908 Aug. 28 [Paris] 80, avenue du Bois de Boulogne^S, ALS, 2 p. Declines an invitation by the London Philharmonic Society to conduct *Images*. *Correspondance*, p. 1111–12.

London, Sotheby's, 29 Nov. 1985, lot 46.
FRKF 1076

1909 April 18 [Paris*] ALS, 2 p. (env), concerning *Pelléas et Mélisande*. *Correspondance*, p. 1170.

London, Christie's, 16 Oct. 1985, lot 180.
FRKF 1019

To Mr. and Mrs. Eugène Fromont

1901 Aug. 28 [Bichain] ALS to Eugène Fromont, 2 p., concerning *Pour le piano*; also mentions the *Trois nocturnes* and *Pelléas et Mélisande*. *Correspondance*, p. 615.

1905 March 30, n.p., ALS to Eugène Fromont, 2 p., concerning *Pelléas et Mélisande*; also mentions the *Suite bergamasque*. *Correspondance*, p. 893.

1905 April 21, n.p., ALS to Madame Fromont, 2 p., concerning the *Suite bergamasque*, the *Rêverie*, and *Pour le piano*. *Correspondance*, p. 903–04.

Paris, Laurin-Guilloux-Buffetaud-Tailleur (Drouot), 3 July 1985, lots 40, 42, 43.
FRKF 847–49

To Georges Hartmann

1899 Jan. 15, 58, rue Cardinet [Paris]^S ALS, 2 p., concerning the *Trois nocturnes*. *Correspondance*, p. 448.

London, Christie's, 5 May 1982, lot 145.
FRKF 16

To Maurice Kufferath

1906 Aug. 19, "Gd Hotel-Château de Pueys, près Dieppe," ALS, 1 p., concerning modifications to the role of Pelléas for Edmond Clément. *Correspondance*, p. 964.

Paris, Librairie de l'Abbaye catalogue 273 (1983), no. 120.
FRKF 285

To Louis Laloy

1907 March 8, 64, avenue du Bois de Boulogne [Paris]^S ALS, 3 p., concerning Ravel's *Histoires naturelles*. *Correspondance*, p. 998–99.

See *Claude Debussy*, exhibition catalogue, Bibliothèque nationale, 1962, p. 55, no. 202.
Paris, Ader-Picart-Tajan (Drouot), 11 June 1982, lot 60.
FRKF 161

To Pierre Louÿs

[1894 July 27] "Vendredi soir (Minuit)" [Paris*] ALS, 2 p. (env). Mentions *Pelléas et Mélisande*; also a dinner with André Gide and Paul Valéry. *Correspondance*, p. 215–16.

Paris, Laurin-Guilloux-Buffetaud-Tailleur (Drouot), 16 March 1984, lot 35.
FRKF 423

1898 Sept. 24, n.p. ALS, 1 p., a letter of apology and explanation. *Correspondance*, p. 420.

Paris, Jean Morelle (Drouot), 14 Dec. 1983, lot 203.
FRKF 245

[1898?] n.p., ALS, 1 p., a letter of thanks and confirming a rendez-vous. *Correspondance*, p. 436.

Paris, Les Argonautes, Nov. 1983 catalogue, no. 42.
FRKF 839

[1901 Oct. 26] "Samedi" [Paris*] ALS, 1 p., concerning the *Trois nocturnes*. Carte pneumatique. *Correspondance*, p. 622.

See Drouot auction catalogue of 23 Feb. 1973, lot 50.
FRKF 839

To Gabriel Mourey

1913 Nov. 17, 80, avenue du Bois de Boulogne [Paris]^S ALS, 2 p., concerning *La flûte de Pan*, now known as *Syrinx*. *Correspondance*, p. 1696.

New York, Christie's, 16–17 Dec. 1983, lot 409.
FRKF 152

To André Poniatowski

"Jeudi. Février 1893," ALS, 10 p. Mentions Massenet's *Werther*, Gounod's *Faust*, Ambroise Thomas's *Hamlet*; also mentions Gustave Charpentier, Berlioz, and works by Palestrina and Victoria. Discusses his *String Quartet* and *Proses lyriques*. *Correspondance*, p. 113–17. Formerly in the collection of Sacha Guitry.

Paris, Ader-Picart-Tajan (Drouot), 11 June 1982, lot 59.
FRKF 160

To Émile Vuillermoz

1913 June 24 [Paris*] ALS, 1 p., *pneumatique*, concerning the Debussy gala of 19 June 1913. *Correspondance*, p. 1633.

Paris, Librairie de l'Abbaye catalogue 268 (1983), no. 133.
FRKF 500

To "Cher Monsieur"

1903 Dec. 30, 58, rue Cardinet [Paris]^S ALS, 2 p., concerning the *Trois nocturnes*. *Correspondance*, p. 812–13.

Sotheby's, New York, 15 Oct. 1982, lot 138.
FRKF 5

III. PRINTED MUSIC

Cinq poèmes de Ch. Baudelaire. [Paris: L. Parent] 1890.

Folio, [4 l.], 1–35 [+1] p. No music publisher's number. The name of the author appears on the title page as Claude A. Debussy. Printed on verso of title page: "Tirage unique à 150 exemplaires. / Nos. 1 à 50 sur papier de Hollande. / - / Exemplaire N° 38."

Original parchment-like wrappers bound in brown, green, blue, and gold marbled paper boards with cream-colored vellum corners and spine (stamp of F. Hauttecoeur). Thin black leather label on spine, with author and title gold-tooled. Signed by Debussy in red ink on verso of title page. Several small musical corrections, also in red ink, throughout.

Lesure 70.
Paris, Laurin-Guilloux-Buffetaud-Tailleur (Drouot), 3 July 1985, lot 39.
FRKF 865

Images. 2e Série pour Piano seul. I. Cloches à travers les feuilles. Paris: A. Durand & Fils, 1908.

Folio, 1–7 p. Music publisher's number: D. & F. 6994 (1). Lesure 105.

Bound with the following seven printed items and manuscript copy:

Images. 2e Série pour Piano seul. II. Et la lune descend sur le temple qui fut. Paris: A. Durand & Fils, 1908.

Folio, 1–5 p. Music publisher's number: D. & F. 6994 (2). Lesure 105.

Images. 2e Série pour Piano seul. III. Poissons d'or. Paris: A. Durand & Fils, 1908.

Folio, 1–13 p. Music publisher's number: D. & F. 6994 (3). Lesure 105.

Estampes pour le piano. I. Pagodes. II. La Soirée dans Grenade. III. Jardins sous la pluie. Paris: A. Durand & Fils, 1903.

Folio, 1–24. Music publisher's number: D. & F. 6326 (1–3). Lesure 108.

Pelléas et Mélisande. Extraits transcrits pour piano à 2 mains et piano à 4 mains par Léon Roques. Duo à la Fontaine: (Acte II). Piano à 2 mains. Paris: A. Durand, 1906.

Folio, 1–11. Music publisher's number: D. & F. 6691. Lesure 93.

Pelléas et Mélisande. Extraits transcrits pour piano à 2 mains et piano à 4 mains par Léon Roques. Les cheveux: (Acte III). Piano à 2 mains. Paris: A. Durand, 1906.

Folio, 1–12. Music publisher's number: D. & F. 6731. Lesure 93.

Pelléas et Mélisande. Extraits transcrits pour piano à 2 mains et piano à 4 mains par Léon Roques. La mort de Pelléas: (Acte IV). [Piano à 2 mains]. Paris: A. Durand, 1906.

Folio, 1–12. Music publisher's number: D. & F. 6744. Lesure 93.

Noël des enfants qui n'ont plus de maison. Chant et piano. (Textes français et anglais). Paris: A. Durand & Fils, 1916.

Folio, 1–7. Music publisher's number: D. & F. 9418. Also, manuscript copy in purple ink, in an unidentified hand, on seven tall sheets of 12-staff paper (words lacking). Lesure 147.

Bound in vellum, the front board stamped in gold with two fishes and stylized algae, with three algae also decorating the back board.

FRKF 20232

Le martyre de Saint-Sébastien / mystère en cinq actes / de / Gabriele d'Annunzio / Musique de / Claude Debussy / Partition pour Chant et Piano / Transcription par André Caplet. Paris, A. Durand & Fils, Éditeurs, 1911.

Folio, [8], 1–104 p. Music publisher's number: D. & F. 8171.

Bound in quarter beige morocco and purple and green marbled paper boards. On the spine: "Debussy / Le martyre / de / St Sébastien / D.E. Inghelbrecht." Original paper covers bound in. Inscribed by Debussy in the upper right corner of the title page: "pour D.E. Inghelbrecht. / Affectueux remerciements. / Claude Debussy. / Juin 1911." Annotated throughout by Inghelbrecht in black, blue, and green pencil. The notes are both textual and musical.

Lesure 130.
New York, Christie's, 5 May 1982, lot 146.
FRKF 17

Pelléas et Mélisande: Drame lyrique en 5 actes et 12 tableaux de Maurice Maeterlinck, musique de Claude Debussy. Partition pour chant et piano. Paris: E. Fromont, Éditeur, copyright 1902.

[8], [1]–283 [+ 1] p. Music publisher's number: E. 1416. F.

Original limp green cloth binding, with the title and Debussy's monogram in gold lettering on the front board. On the spine: "M. Maeterlinck / et / C. Debussy / Pelléas Et Mélisande / 1902." Ownership inscription of baritone Jean Périer (1869–1954), the first Pelléas, in the upper right corner of the title page.

Lesure 93.
FRKF 535h

Printemps: suite symphonique. Paris: Durand, n.d.

Folio, [4], 1–98. Orchestral score.

"Nouvelle édition" printed at the top of the title page. Copyright statement dated 1913. Signed by Charles Munch on the recto of the flyleaf; also with his stamp at the bottom of the flyleaf and at the top of the title page. Marked up by Munch in black, blue, and red pencil.

Printemps was orchestrated by Henri Busser in 1912.

Lesure 68.
Paris, Hervé Poulain (Drouot), 5 April 1984, lot 9.
FRKF 438

IV. EPHEMERA

Pelléas et Mélisande

Program for a performance at the Théâtre National de l'Opéra-Comique, Paris, on 27 Nov. 1906. [1–24] p. The cast includes Jean Périer (Pelléas), Hector Dufranne (Golaud), Félix Vieuille (Arkel), Mary Garden (Mélisande), and Suzanne Brohly (Geneviève). On p. [18]: "Notes sur Pelléas et Mélisande" (by Eugène d'Harcourt, extracted from *Le Figaro* for 1 May 1902).

FRKF 535g

LÉO DELIBES (1836–91)

Lakmé: opéra en 3 actes. Poëme de MM. Edmond Gondinet & Philippe Gille. Paris: Au Ménestrel [Heugel & Fils], 1883.

Folio, [8], I–VI, 1–275 [+1] p. Piano-vocal score, first edition. Music publisher's number: H. 5683. Inscribed by Delibes on the recto of the flyleaf: "à Madame A. Proust / Hommage très respectueux / de l'auteur / Léo Delibes / février 84." Bound in purple cloth, author and title gold-tooled on black leather on spine; also, gold-tooled initials J.P. [Jeanne Proust] at the bottom of the spine. Original pictorial cover bound in.

Paris, Ader-Picard-Tajan (Drouot), 22 Nov. 1985, lot 143.
FRKF 1359

Letter to "Mon cher ami"

[1883] "Lundi soir," 220, rue de Rivoli [Paris]^S ALS, 3 p., concerning *Lakmé*; probably to Georges Hartmann.

Marburg, Stargardt, 5–6 March 1985, lot 783.
FRKF 810

JEAN DESBORDES (1906–44)

Letters to Alice Turpin

The letters, listed here by first lines, are all autograph, signed, and without date and place unless otherwise noted.

"Mademoiselle, Je pars demain en Seine-et-Marne" [ca. 1928] 1 p.

"Mademoiselle, J'aurais besoin de revoir encore les épreuves" [ca. 1928] 1 p.

"Mademoiselle, Je suis triste pour hier" [ca. 1928] 1 p.

"Mademoiselle, Je rentre à l'instant," Paris, 1 p.

"Mademoiselle, comme je suis navré," 1 p.

"Mademoiselle, je voudrais tellement vous remercier," *carte pneumatique* [Paris*] 1928, 1 p.

"Chère Mademoiselle, Merci de tout votre dévouement," Montereau, 2 p.

"Chère Amie, Nous avons été bien surpris hier soir" [ca. 1928] 1 p.

"J'ai attendu votre coup de telephone," *carte pneumatique*, [Paris*] 1928, 1 p.

"Chère Alice, Madame Bousquet m'a telephone," *carte pneumatique* [Paris*] 1928, 1 p.

"Chère Alice, Je me suis trop avancé," 1 p., in pencil.

"Chère Alice, Surtout n'oubliez pas" [Paris, 1928 July 27*] 1 p.

"Ma petite Alice, Je rentre et je me couche," 2 p.

"Petite chérie, J'ai eu le coeur inondé de joie" [Paris, 1928 Aug. 6*] 1 p.

"Chérie, Je me suis expliqué votre absence," marked "Pneu" [Paris, 1928 Aug. 8*] 1 p.

"Si je vous abandonne, chère petite Alice," 55, rue Nollet [Paris] 1 p.

"Ma chère petite Alice, Voilà, nous sommes installés," dated "16" without month [1929?]. Roquebrune, 1 p.

"Chère Alice, J'ai été assez étonné de ne pas recevoir de réponse" [1929 or later, Paris?] 5, rue Changarnier, XIIe^S, 2 p.

The correspondence refers to the publication of Desbordes's *J'adore*, issued by Bernard Grasset in 1928, as well as to Desbordes's affair with Alice Turpin.

See under Cocteau.
Paris, Laurin-Guilloux-Buffetaud-Tailleur (Drouot), 12 June 1984, lot 32.
FRKF 458

MAURICE DONNAY (1859–1945)

Letter to Reynaldo Hahn

1926 Feb. 27, Paris, ANS on both sides of a card, looking forward to their collaboration.

See under Hahn.
Paris, Laurin-Guilloux-Buffetaud-Tailleur (Drouot), 8 Feb. 1985, lot 115.
FRKF 658.4

LORD ALFRED DOUGLAS (1870–1945)

"Stones for bread"

Autograph manuscript, 1 p., n.d. Incipit: "Ah, woe to us who look for asphodel…" At the head of manuscript [not in Douglas's hand?]: "Sonnet / By Lord Alfred Bruce Douglas." At the bottom of the manuscript: "page 2."

Published in *The Complete Poems of Lord Alfred Douglas, including Light Verse* (London: Martin Secker, 1928), p. 119, with the date 1913. The printed incipit is: "A woe to us…"

London, Sotheby's, 21 July 1983, lot 420.
FRKF 349

Letter to Lucie Delarue-Mardrus

1930 Feb. 13, 35, Fourth Avenue, Hove, Sussex^S, ALS, 4 p., concerning her book *Les amours d'Oscar Wilde* (Paris, 1929). Mentions Robert Ross and *De Profundis*. Accompanied by a French translation, typescript with manuscript corrections, 3 p.

See Christie's, London, 28 Nov. 1990, lot 167; Sotheby's, New York, 14 June 1993, lot 143; and Sotheby's, London, 19 July 1994, lot 153.
Paris, Ader-Picard-Tajan (Drouot), 11 June 1982, lot 67.
FRKF 163

Letters to Mrs. Shore

1942 Aug. 22, 1, St. Ann's Court, Nizzels Avenue, Hove 2, Sussex^S, ALS, 2 p.

1942 Oct. 14, 1, St. Ann's Court, Nizzels Avenue, Hove 2, Sussex^S, ALS, 2 p.

Mrs. Shore, formerly Robinson, a fortune-teller consulted by Oscar Wilde.

See Christie's, London, 28 Nov. 1990, lot 168, and Sotheby's, London, 19 July 1994, lot 151.
London, Sotheby's, 8 Dec. 1983, lot 169.
FRKF 272

PAUL DUKAS (1865–1935)

I. MUSIC MANUSCRIPTS

Ariane et Barbe-Bleue

Holograph fragment, in short score, from the prelude to act 2, n.d., 1 p. Notated in purple ink on a single sheet of tall 20-staff paper. The fragment comprises 6 measures, notated on two 3-staff systems. At the top of the page, in Dukas's hand: "Voilà de l'inédit / qui sera un jour / toujours encorbeau [sic]."

Paris, Laurin-Guilloux-Buffetaud-Tailleur (Drouot), 29 April 1982, lot 49.
FRKF 8

"Ariane et Barbe-Bleue (Moralité à la façon des contes de Perrault)," autograph manuscript of Dukas's essay on his opera [1910], 13 p., in ink, with corrections in the composer's hand and pencil corrections and annotations in a different hand. With an envelope marked in pencil (not in Dukas's hand) "Ariane / P.D." and dated "Lundi de Pâques 1910 / Versailles," and various jottings on the back.

First published as "Un inédit de Paul Dukas / 'Ariane et Barbe-Bleue' (Moralité à la façon des contes de Perrault)" in the special Dukas issue of the *Revue musicale*, vol. XVII, no. 166 (May–June 1936): 324–27. Note p. 324: "Ce commentaire sur la signification poétique et musicale du personnage d'Ariane a été écrit par Paul Dukas en 1910. Il l'a donné la même année à M. Robert Brussel qui nous l'a communiqué." Reprinted in: Paul Dukas, *Les écrits de Paul Dukas sur la musique. Avant-propos de G. Samazeuilh* (Paris: Société d'éditions françaises et internationales, 1948), p. 623–26.

FRKF 9

Dukas's opera *Ariane et Barbe-Bleue*, on a libretto by Maurice Maeterlinck, was premiered at the Opéra-Comique in Paris on 10 May 1907.

La fleur

Holograph manuscript of this chorus for voice and orchestra, 1887, 20 p. Written in black ink on five nested bifolia of 22-staff paper (blind stamp of Lard-Esnault), paginated 1–20 by the composer. The manuscript begins on the verso of the outer bifolium. Scored for 2 flutes, 2 oboes, english horn, 2 clarinets, 2 bassoons, 2 horns in F, strings, and SATB.

On the cover, in Dukas's hand: "La Fleur / Choeur à 4 voix et orchestre." At the top of p. 1: "La Fleur (Poésie de Millevoye)." Signed and dated 13 April 1887 at the end.

Listed by Grove as unpublished.
Paris, Ader-Picart-Tajan (Drouot), 11 June 1982, lot 71.
FRKF 165

Polyeucte

Holograph manuscript draft, in short score, of this concert overture, 1891, 6 p. Notated in black ink, with corrections in red ink and a few more in pencil, on three nested bifolia of tall 32-staff paper (blind stamp of Lard-Esnault); paginated 1–6 in Dukas's hand.

At the top of p. 1, in Dukas's hand: "Je consens, ou plutôt j'aspire à ma ruine / Monde, pour moi tu n'es plus rien / Polyeucte (ouverture pour la tragédie de Corneille)." Signed and dated 16 Sept. 1891 at the end. On the verso of p. [1] is a fragment, in full score, of an apparently unrelated, unidentified stage work. Inscribed in pencil, in Dukas's hand: "Ouverture de Polyeucte / 2e Esquisse."

Paris, Laurin-Guilloux-Buffetaud-Tailleur (Drouot), 16 Oct. 1991, lot 124.
FRKF 1392

Velléda

Holograph manuscript, in short score, of this cantata, 1880–81, 57 p. Notated in black ink, with additional markings in black pencil, on the recto sides of individual sheets of tall 22-staff paper (blind stamp of Lard-Esnault), stitched with pink thread, and foliated by the composer I–VII (Prelude) and 1–50. On title page, in blue pencil, possibly in Dukas's hand: "Velléda." The prelude is scored for two pianos. At the top of p. I, in Dukas's hand: "Prélude" and, in parentheses, the following epigraph: "elle chantait dans la tempête et semblait se jouer / dans les vents (Chateaubriand - Les martyrs)." Signed and dated "80–81" at the end.

Paris, Laurin-Guilloux-Buffetaud-Tailleur (Drouot), 15 Dec. 1989, lot 63.
FRKF 1348

II. LETTERS

To G. Jean-Aubry

[1919 July 27, Kilburn*] "Mardi soir," ALS, 2 p. (env), concerning Falla and *The three-cornered hat*.

1919 July 30 [Paris] ALS, 1 p. Mentions Albéniz, Falla, and Debussy.

London, Sotheby's, 9 May 1985, lots 91–92.
FRKF 766.1–2

To Gustave Samazeuilh

1932 Aug. 27, n.p., ALS, 4 p. Mentions Charles Bordes, Henry Prunières, P.-J. Toulet, Ravel, Franck, d'Indy, Wagner, and Fauré.

Paris, Ader-Picart-Tajan (Drouot), 11 June 1982, lot 70.
FRKF 164

ALEXANDRE DUMAS (1824–95)

An album containing manuscripts and photographs relating to Alexandre Dumas fils's novel and play *La dame aux camélias*, 1843–84 and n.d.

The album contains the following documents:

> Passport in the name of Alphonsine Plessis, rentière, for a trip to London, stamped and dated 25 Jan. 1846. The passport gives Alphonsine Plessis's physical characteristics and is signed by her. Countersigned on the verso by the head of Chancery, 26 Jan. 1846.
>
> A printed bill, completed in manuscript, from Ragonot, Fleuriste, rue de la Paix, N° 14, dated 9 Nov. 1843, for flowers purchased from Dec. 1842 through Feb. 1843. On the verso: "Mme Dupleci" The bill predates the time of Duplessis's liaison with Dumas fils. It includes seven orders for camellias.
>
> Manuscript bill for medical visits by Dr Davaine and Messrs Chomel and Louis: "Note des visites faites par le Dr Davaine à Madame Duplessis dans sa dernière maladie." Dated Paris, 8 Feb. 1847. The total number of medical visits between May 1846 and Feb. 1847 is given as 177 visits and 7 consultations. Duplessis died on 3 Sept. 1847.
>
> Marie Duplessis to Agénor, duc de Guiche, "Jeudi" [21 July 1842*, received in London] Paris, ALS, 2 p. (env), a love letter, signed Marie Duplessis.
>
> Photograph of a portrait of Antoine Alfred Agénor de Gramont, duc de Guiche, then duc de Gramont (1819–80), Minister of Foreign Affairs in May–Sept. 1870.
>
> Photograph of an unidentified portrait.
>
> Alexandre Dumas fils to Sarah Bernhardt, 1884 Jan. 28, n.p., ALS, 3 p., presenting to her a copy of *La dame aux camélias* with his break-up letter to Marie Duplessis bound in.
>
> Alexandre Dumas fils to Marie Duplessis [1845] Aug. 30, "minuit," n.p., unsigned letter, 1 p., breaking off the relationship. Crowned monogram embossed in upper left corner. Reproduced in facsimile in Micheline Boudet. *La fleur du mal: la véritable histoire de la Dame aux camélias* (Paris: Albin Michel, 1993).
>
> Gustave Le Vavasseur to an unidentified correspondent, 1869 Oct. 28, n.p., ALS, 4 p., concerning Marie Duplessis.
>
> Alexandre Dumas fils. Carte-de-visite photograph.
>
> [Empress Eugénie ?] Carte-de-visite photograph.
>
> Alexandre Dumas fils as a young man [?] Carte-de-visite photograph.
>
> Sarah Bernhardt. Sepia photographic portrait by Waléry, Paris (17 × 22 cm).
>
> Original photograph of an unidentified young man.

The album is bound in vellum, with a gold-tooled decorative border along the edges on the recto of both boards and a single gold fillet on the verso.

Alphonsine Plessis, a.k.a. Marie Duplessis (1824–47), Alexandre Dumas's mistress (and subsequently Franz Liszt's) and the original model for the Marguerite Gautier of his novel *La dame aux camélias* (1848). Verdi's *La traviata* (1853) was inspired by Dumas's 1852 stage adaptation of his novel.

FRKF 675

HENRI DUPARC (1848–1933)

Extase

Holograph manuscript of this song for voice and piano, on a poem by Henri Cazalis [i.e. Jean Lahor], n.d., 2 p.

> Notated in black ink on p. [2]–[3] of a bifolium of tall 15-staff paper (blind stamp of Lard-Esnault).
>
> On title page, in Duparc's hand: "A Monsieur Camille Benoit / Extase. / Poésie de H. Cazalis. / H. Duparc." Dedication, title, author of the poem repeated at the top of p. [2]. Signed "H. Duparc" at the end. Stamped "Gravé" at the top of p. [2]. Music publisher's number (EB et Cie 63) marked in blue pencil on title page.

Dated 1874, rev. 1884 by Grove.

L'invitation au voyage

Holograph manuscript of this song for voice and piano on a poem by Charles Baudelaire, n.d., 6 p.

> Notated in black ink on p. [2] to [7] of two nested bifolia of tall 15-staff paper (blind stamp of Lard-Esnault). On title page, in Duparc's hand: "L'Invitation au Voyage / poésie de Ch. Baudelaire / H. Duparc." Author of text, dedication, title repeated at the top of p. [2]. Signed "H. Duparc" at the end. Stamped "Gravé" on title page. Music publisher's number (EB et Cie 60) marked in blue pencil on title page.

Dated 1870 by Grove.
Heinrich Schütz to Henry Miller, p. 60–61.

Lamento

Holograph manuscript of this song for voice and piano, on a poem by Théophile Gautier, n.d., 3 p.

> Notated in black ink on p. [1]–[3] of a bifolium of tall 15-staff paper (blind stamp of Lard-Esnault), nested within another such bifolium serving as wrappers. On the front of the outer bifolium, in Duparc's hand: "Lamento / Poésie de Théophile Gautier / H. Duparc." At the top of p. [1], also in Duparc's hand: "A Monsieur Gabriel Fauré / Poésie de Théophile Gautier / Lamento." Signed "H. Duparc" at the end. Stamped "Gravé" at the top of p. [1]. Music publisher's number (EB et Cie 66) marked in blue pencil on title page.

Dated 1883? by Grove.

Le manoir de Rosemonde

Holograph manuscript of this song for voice and piano, on a poem by Robert de Bonnières, n.d., 3 p.

> Notated in black ink on p. [1]–[3] of a bifolium of tall 15-staff paper (blind stamp of Lard-Esnault), nested within a similar bifolium serving as wrappers. On the front of the outer bifolium, in Duparc's hand: "Le manoir de Rosemonde / Poésie de Robert de Bonnières / H. Duparc." Title and author of the poem repeated at the top of p. [2]. Signed "H. Duparc" at the end. Stamped "Gravé" at the top of the title page. Music publisher's number (EB et Cie 65) marked in blue pencil on title page.

Dated 1879 (?82) by Grove.

Phidylé

Holograph manuscript of this song for voice and piano, on a poem by Leconte de Lisle, n.d., 6 p.

> Notated in black ink on p. [2]–[7] of two nested bifolia of tall 15-staff paper (blind stamp of Lard-Esnault). On the front of the outer bifolium, in Duparc's hand: "Phidylé / Poésie de Leconte de Lisle / H. Duparc." At the top of p. [1], also in Duparc's hand: "A Monsieur Ernest Chausson / Poésie de Leconte de Lisle / Phidylé." Signed "H. Duparc" at the end. Stamped "Gravé" at the top of the title page. Music publisher's number (EB et Cie 64) marked in blue pencil on title page.

Dated 1882 by Grove.

Sérénade florentine

Holograph manuscript of this song for voice and piano, on a poem by Henri Cazalis [Jean Lahor], 2 p.

> Notated in black ink on p. [2] and [3] of a bifolium of tall 15-staff paper (blind stamp of Lard-Esnault). On p. [1] in Duparc's hand: "Sérénade florentine / Poésie de Henri Cazalis / H. Duparc." At the top of p. [2], also in Duparc's hand: "Poésie de H. Cazalis / A Monsieur Henry Cochin / Sérénade Florentine." Signed "H. Duparc" at the end. Stamped "Gravé" at the top of p. [2]. Music publisher's number (EB et Cie 61) marked in blue pencil on title page.

Dated 1880–81(?83) by Grove.

Testament

Holograph manuscript of this song for voice and piano, on a poem by Armand Silvestre, n.d., 5 p.

> Notated in black ink, with a correction in blue pencil, on p. [2]–[6] of two individual bifolia, stitched together, of tall 15-staff paper (blind stamp of Lard-Esnault). On p. [1] in Duparc's hand: "A Madame Henri de Passus. / Testament / mélodie pour voix de mezzo-soprano ou baryton. / poésie de A. Silvestre / H. Duparc." Signed "H. Duparc" at the end. Pasted-in cancel on p. [4], affecting one measure (all three staves). Stamped "Gravé" at the top of p. [2]. Music publisher's number (EB et Cie 67) marked in blue pencil on title page.

Dated 1883(?85) by Grove.

La vague et la cloche

Holograph manuscript of this song for voice and piano, on a poem by François Coppée, n.d., 8 p.

> Notated in black ink on two separate bifolia of tall 15-staff paper (blind stamp of Lard-Esnault), housed within another similar bifolium serving as wrappers. On the front of the outer bifolium, in Duparc's hand: "A Monsieur Vincent d'Indy / La Vague et la Cloche / (mélodie pour voix et basse) / Réduction d'orchestre par Vincent d'Indy / H. Duparc." At the top of p. [1], also in Duparc's hand: "A Monsieur Vincent d'Indy / Poésie de François Coppée / La Vague et la Cloche / (mélodie pour voix de basse) / Réduction pour piano par Vincent d'Indy." At the bottom of p. [1], in pencil, not in Duparc's hand: "cette mélodie est publiée avec orchestre." Signed "H. Duparc" at the end. Stamped "Gravé" at the top of the title page. Music publisher's number (EB et Cie 62) marked in blue pencil on title page.

Dated 1871 by Grove. The original orchestral version was reduced by d'Indy; a second edition is Duparc's own reduction.

DUPARC SONGS
Paris, Laurin-Guilloux-Buffetaud-Tailleur (Drouot), 16 Oct. 1991, lots 134–41.
FRKF 1393–1400

ANTONIN DVOŘÁK (1841–1904)

O sanctissima

Holograph manuscript of the revised version of this motet for soprano and alto with organ accompaniment, 1890, 2 p. Notated in black and red ink on both sides of a single sheet of tall 24-staff paper. The text and part of the dynamic markings are in red.

At the top of p. [1] in Dvořák's hand: "'O Sanctissima' upraveno pro Sopr a Alt Vysoká / 18 28/5 90 / Ant. Dvořák." The organ part is not notated. Originally composed in 1879.

Burghauser 95b.
London, Sotheby's, 29 Nov. 1985, lot 54.
FRKF 1030

Symphony no. 8 in G major

Holograph manuscript of Dvořák's own arrangement for piano four-hands, of the second movement of his eighth symphony, 1890, 11 p. Notated in black ink, with corrections in red ink and an additional note in pencil, on three individual bifolia of oblong 12-staff paper, paginated 1 to 12 [sic, for 11].

At the top of p. 1, in Dvořák's hand: "II. Adagio / [in red ink] Druhá veta pro piano na 4 ruce (z G=Sinfonie) / aranzoval / Ant. Dvořák." Dated at the end Prague, 27 Oct. 1890.

Burghauser 518.
Lion Heart Autographs catalogue, 1985.
FRKF 574

Letter to Alfred Littleton

[1884 Oct.] n.p., ALS, 4 p. in English. Mentions a work identified as *The wedding gown*; also refers to Gounod. On p. [4], a 12-measure musical quotation from *The wedding gown*, notated on two systems of two staves. Marked "rec.d Oct 31/84" in the upper left corner of p. [1].

FRKF 557

EDWARD VII, KING OF ENGLAND (1841–1910)

Letter to Frederick Leighton

n.y. Nov. 22, Marlborough House[S], ALS, 3 p., accompanied by a letter from Francis Knollys (as private secretary) to Leighton, 1895 Jan. 1, Sandringham, Norfolk[S], 4 p., conveying the Prince of Wales's congratulations on Leighton's peerage.

See Christie's, London, 28 Nov. 1990, lot 169; and Sotheby's, New York, 17 Dec. 1992, lot 83.
London, Phillips, 24 Oct. 1985, lot 586.
FRKF 1012

PIERCE EGAN (1772–1849)

Letter to Daniel Egerton

1834 Feb. 18, Dublin, ALS, 1 p., concerning a forthcoming production.

FRKF 648

SIR EDWARD ELGAR (1857–1934)

I. MUSIC MANUSCRIPTS

Concerto for violin and orchestra in B minor, op. 61

Autograph manuscript with instructions and proof corrections for the first edition (violin and piano score) of the *Violin concerto*, with three autograph musical quotations on hand-drawn staves, with heading on both pages: "Corrections for Violin Solo," signed at the end and dated 16 Oct. 1910, 2 p. The corrections were evidently sent to Elgar's publisher, Novello and Co.

London, Sotheby's, 9 May 1985, lot 71.
FRKF 760

Four choral songs, op. 53

Holograph manuscript of "There is sweet music," 1908, 21 p., in black ink on five individual bifolia of tall 16-staff paper and an additional sheet at the end, mounted on a stub, paginated 1–21. At the top of p. 1, in Elgar's hand: "There is sweet music / part song for S.A.T.B. / The words by Tennyson / the music by Edward Elgar / op. 53 N° 1." At the bottom of the page, footnote, relating to the first tenor part: "Some contraltos should sing with the 1st Tenors"; also, note in the lower right corner: "I think the arrangement for piano is the best that can be done under the circumstances!!! It is better to keep the two keys separate." Signed at the bottom of the last page and dated "Roma / Gennaio 1908."

A setting of the Choric Song (first verse only) from Tennyson's poem "The lotos eaters." See Craggs, p. 79, with the date 1907. The songs were first published by Novello in 1908.

Heinrich Schütz to Henry Miller, p. 100–01.
New York, Lion Heart Autographs, catalogue (1985).
FRKF 570

Symphony no. 3

Pencil draft, in short score, for Elgar's projected Third Symphony, on a half-sheet of music paper (26 × 19 cm), representing a total of 10 measures, 1933, 1 p. Marked "Symphony" in dark blue ink, in capital letters, at the top, with the following inscription in the left margin: "E. Somerville Tattersall / To A / Perfect Host / from an / imperfect guest / Edward Elgar / Rutland Arms / Newmarket / 10th May 1933."

London, Sotheby's, 9 May 1985, lot 81.
FRKF 763

II. LETTERS

To Charles Long

1931 April 13, Marl Bank, Rainbow Hill, Worcester[S], ALS, 1 p.
1932 June 7, Brooks's, London[S], ALS, 2 p.
1932 Oct. 26, Marl Bank, Worcester[S] (embossed), TLS, 1 p.
1934 June 21, Worcester, ALS, 1 p.

London, Phillips, 24 Oct., 1985, lot 552.
FRKF 1009

To Harvey Marsh

1902 March 13, Craeg Lea, Wells Road, Malvern[S], ALS, 7 p. (env), concerning a concert organized by the Worcestershire Philharmonic Society. Mentions performances of *Cockaigne* under Weingartner.

FRKF 383

To Gertrude Walker

1887 Dec. 21, 4 Field Terrace, Bath Road, Worcester^S, ALS, 3 p. (env), enclosing the title page, in proof, of a new song and asking for her permission to dedicate it to her.

Accompanied by the title page of *Through the long days* (London: Stanley Lucas, Weber & Co., n.d.), inscribed: "Miss Gertrude Walker / From Edward Elgar / Apr:3: 1887"; and the title page of *As I laye a-thynkynge* (London: Beare & Son, n.d.), inscribed: "With the composer's compliments / May 1888."

Gertrude Walker, later Jenner, singer and friend of Elgar. See Robert Anderson, "Gertrude Walker: an Elgarian Friendship," *Musical Times* CXXV (1884): 698–700.

London, Sotheby's, 9–10 May 1985, lots 67–68.
FRKF 759.1–2

III. PRINTED WORKS

The Kingdom: an oratorio. London: Novello and Company, Limited; New York: The H.W. Gray Co., 1906.

[i]–[xii], [1]–189 [+ 1] p. Vocal score, "Novello's original octavo edition." Music publisher's number: 12286. Signed and dated "Worcester 1908" by Elgar on the title page, with a musical quotation ("To hear their sighing"). Bound in black machine-grained leather, worn.

Presented by Elgar to William Henry Reed (1877–1942), founding member of the London Symphony Orchestra and author of *Elgar as I knew him* (London: Victor Gollancz, 1936) and *Elgar* (London: J.M. Dent & Sons, 1939).

London, Sotheby's, 9–10 May 1985, lot 72.
FRKF 761

The music makers: Ode by Arthur O'Shaughnessy set to music for contralto solo, chorus, and orchestra. London: Novello and Company, Limited; New York: The H.W. Gray Co., 1912.

[i]–[vi], [1]–86 p. Vocal score, "Novello's original octavo edition." Music publisher's number: 13704. Bound in dark green machine-grained leather, with monogram "W.H.R." on the front board, in the lower right corner.

Inscribed "To W.H.R. from E.R. / Christmas 1912" on the recto of the flyleaf, and, further down on the same page, in Elgar's hand: "To W.H. Reed: / "Musicians thinke our / Soules are harmonies." / (Sr. Tho. Davies) / Edward Elgar: / June 9:1913."

London, Sotheby's, 9–10 May 1985, lot 75.
FRKF 762

EUGÉNIE DE MONTIJO, EMPRESS OF THE FRENCH (1826–1920)

Letters to Stendhal

[1839 Dec.] to "Monsieur," n.p., ALS, 3 p., giving news of the political situation in Spain.

[1840] to "Mon cher Monsieur," n.p., ALS, 3 p., reporting on a trip to Toledo.

Both letters are signed: "E. Guzman et Palafox." The letters are dated by Stendhal. The first letter is annotated in his hand at the top of the first page: "Lue en Janvier 40 / Répondu le 7 août 1841." Stendhal, *Correspondance générale*, VI:281–82 and 435–36.

Accompanied by a letter from Paca [Francisca] Portocarrero y P[alafox], later Duchess of Berwick and Alba, to Stendhal [Madrid, Dec. 1840], 2 p., also dated by Stendhal. Stendhal, *Correspondance générale*, VI:436–37.

With an autograph note in an unidentified hand, transcribing an article from *Le Pays* for 22 Jan. 1853, and an additional note in the same hand concerning the three letters to Stendhal.

Paris, Ader-Picard-Tajan (Drouot), 22 Nov. 1985, lot 41.
FRKF 1368

TREYER EVANS

"Wot's he sayin' Bob?"

Pen-and-ink cartoon on paper (21.5 × 30.5 cm) mounted on cardboard, signed at the lower right corner. Underneath the drawing, manuscript caption in pencil: "1st Loafer (as Frenchman asks him a question): 'Wots' he sayin' Bob?' / 2d [Loafer] 'dunne, - 'it 'im in the ea[letters missing] ole.'"

London, Christie's, 21 July 1981, lot 246.
FRKF 107

MANUEL DE FALLA (1876–1946)

I. MUSIC MANUSCRIPT

Soneto a Córdoba

Manuscript, partly holograph, of this song for voice and harp on a poem by Góngora, 1927, 3 p.

> Notated in black ink on p. [2] to [4] of a single bifolium of 26-staff paper (stamped Sociedad de autores espanoles, Madrid), numbered 26 at the bottom of each page.
>
> The music is in the hand of a copyist, while the words, and various corrections and additions, are in Falla's hand with a few additional corrections in pencil, apparently in Falla's hand. On p. [1] title "Soneto" in Falla's hand. At the top of p. [2]: "A Córdoba / Soneto de Gongora / Manuel de Falla." At the end, in Falla's hand: "Granada 1585 / Granada 1927."

Gallego LXXII; Crichton, p. 46.
FRKF 841

II. LETTERS

Unless otherwise noted the letters are in French.

To [Mme de Chaumont-Quitry]

> 1920 Feb. 3, Paris, ALS, 2 p. on mourning stationery. Mentions *Le tricorne*.

London, Sotheby's, 29 Nov. 1985, lot 64.
FRKF 1077

To Claude Debussy

> 1916 May 14, Madrid, ALS, 4 p. (env), concerning the death of Enrique Granados; also mentions *El amor brujo*, *Mélodies espagnoles*, and *Noches en los jardines de España*. Debussy, *Correspondance*, p. 1991–92 (published from a draft).

London, Sotheby's, 23 Nov. 1984, lot 440.
FRKF 541

To [Emma Debussy?]

> 1924 April 15, Granada, ALS, 4 p. Mentions *L'après-midi d'un faune* and *Nuages*, as well as *El retablo de maese Pedro*.

FRKF 724.5

To Serge Diaghilev

All are ALS dated from Madrid, with envelopes, on mourning stationery with red monograms. From the collection of Serge Lifar, with his stamp printed in red.

> 1919 April 30, 3 p. concerning *Le tricorne*; mentions Picasso; also refers to *El retablo de maese Pedro*.
>
> 1919 May 24, 4 p., concerning *Le tricorne*, *Noches en los jardines de España*, Arbós's orchestration of Albéniz's *Iberia*; mentions Massine, Picasso, and Martínez Sierra. *Heinrich Schütz to Henry Miller*, p. 118–19.
>
> 1919 July 28, 3 p. Mentions the death of his mother as he was about to leave for London to attend the premiere of *Le tricorne*.

London, Sotheby's, 9 May 1984, lots 167–69.
FRKF 305, 304, 306

To Edwin Evans

> 1921 Aug. 3, Granada, ALS, 4 p. on mourning stationery, announcing he is sending him two Cancioneros.
>
> 1929 Jan. 2, Granada, ALS, 3 p. Mentions Gustav Holst.

London, Christie's, 16 Oct. 1985, lots 183, 186.
FRKF 1018, 1013

To G. Jean-Aubry

Unless otherwise noted, all autograph letters, signed.

> 1910 May 29, Paris, 1 p. Mentions *La vida breve* and Marguerite Long.
>
> 1910 June 7, Paris, 3 p., concerning his giving a performance of his works.
>
> [1911 Feb. 8, Paris*] 1 p. Mentions Ravel.

FRKF 724

> 1911 June 18, Paris, 2 p. Mentions S. Berchut.
>
> 1912 April 2, Paris, 2 p., concerning a concert.
>
> 1912 April 11, Paris, 1 p. Mentions Ricardo Viñes.
>
> 1913 Jan. 3, Paris, 2 p. Mentions André Messager.

FRKF 1147

> 1913 June 19, Paris, 3 p. Mentions *Le sacre du printemps*, Turina, *La vida breve*, *Noches en los jardines de España*.

London, Sotheby's, 29 Nov. 1985, lot 62.
FRKF 1054

> 1913 Oct. 17, Paris, 3 p. Mentions Albéniz, Turina, and *Noches en los jardines de España*.

London, Sotheby's, 9–10 May 1985, lot 82.
FRKF 764.1

1914 Jan. 14, n.p., 1 p. on mourning stationery, concerning *La vida breve*.

FRKF 724

1914 May 8, n.p., 1 p. on mourning stationery.

FRKF 1147

1917 June 29, Madrid, 4 p. (env). Mentions *El corregidor y la molinera*, as well as Mme Albéniz, Turina.

FRKF 725

1919 Aug. 19, Madrid, 5 p. on mourning stationery, concerning Diaghilev and *Le tricorne*.

London, Sotheby's, 23 Nov. 1984, lot 441.
FRKF 542

1920 Sept. 16, Madrid, 3 p. on mourning stationery.

FRKF 1147

1920 Oct. 18, Granada, 3 p. on mourning stationery. Mentions *Noches en los jardines de España* and *El amor brujo*, as well as Albert Carré.

London, Sotheby's, 28 May 1986, lot 396.
FRKF 1127

[1920 Dec. 23, Granada*] APCS

London, Sotheby's, 9–10 May 1985, lot 83.
FRKF 764.2

1921 March 15, Granada, APCS, concerning the title of his *Tombeau de Claude Debussy*.

London, Sotheby's, 29 Nov. 1985, lot 66.
FRKF 1055

1923 Oct. 23, Granada, 4 p. (env), concerning *El retablo de maese Pedro*.

FRKF 725

1924 March 14, Granada, 4 p. (env). Mentions *Psyché*, *La vida breve*, and *El retablo de maese Pedro*.

1924 Sept. 11, Granada, TLS, 4 p. (env), concerning *El retablo de maese Pedro*.

London, Sotheby's, 9–10 May 1985, lots 84, 85.
FRKF 764.3-4

1924 Sept. 29, Granada, 4 p. (env), concerning *Psyché*; also mentions Lorca.

London, Sotheby's, 23 Nov. 1984, lot 442.
FRKF 543

1925 Sept. 2, Granada, TLS, 1 p., concerning *Psyché* and including a 3-measure musical quotation.

London, Sotheby's, 9–10 May 1985, lot 87.
FRKF 764.6

1926 April 16, Granada, TPCS, concerning *Psyché*.

FRKF 842

1928 June 22, Granada, TLS, 1 p. (env). Mentions the premiere of *El retablo de maese Pedro*.

1929 Jan. 2, Granada, 7 p., declining the suggestion of an honorary doctorate at Oxford.

London, Sotheby's, 9–10 May 1985, lots 86, 88.
FRKF 764.5, 764.7

1929 Feb. 5, Granada, 3 p. Mentions *El retablo de maese Pedro*.

FRKF 724

1929 March 5, Granada, TLS, 1 p. (env). Mentions *Atlántida* and the *Harpsichord concerto*.

London, Sotheby's, 29 Nov. 1985, lot 65.
FRKF 1078

1929 April 15, n.p. [Granada?] APCS

1935 June 24, Lanjarón, APCS, partly in Spanish.

FRKF 1147

To Roland-Manuel

1938 April 17, Granada, TLS, 2 p., in Spanish. Mentions the death of Maurice Ravel.

Paris, Paul Renaud (Drouot), 14 May 1986, lot 90.
FRKF 1194

To an unidentified female friend

1930 July 7, Granada, ALS, 3 p., possibly to Misia Sert; mentions *L'Atlántida*, addressed to "Bien chère amie."

London, Sotheby's, 28 May 1986, lot 401.
FRKF 1128

GABRIEL FAURÉ (1845–1924)

I. MUSIC MANUSCRIPTS

Dolly, op. 86

Manuscript copy of an early version of the *Berceuse*, [ca. 1862], 4 p., in black ink on p. [2]–[5] of two nested bifolia of tall 18-staff paper. On p. 1, in Fauré's hand: "Canson din lé jardi / Gabriel Fauré." The two piano parts are on facing pages. Possibly in the hand of one of Fauré's students, according to Jean-Michel Nectoux.

FRKF 679.1

Mai

Holograph manuscript of this song for soprano voice and piano, on a poem by Victor Hugo, n.d., 2 p., in black ink on both sides of a single sheet of tall 22-staff paper (blind stamp of Lard). At the top of p. [1] in Fauré's hand: "N° 4 / Mai! / à Madame H. Garnier." Dated 1862 by Grove.

FRKF 679.2

Mazurke in B-flat

Written in black ink, with additions in pencil, on p. [2]–[3] of a bifolium of tall 20-staff paper (blind stamp of Lard). On p. 1, in Fauré's hand: "Mazurke / Gabriel Fauré"; at the top of p. [2], also in Fauré's hand: "Morceau de piano en / forme de Mazurka." Dated ca. 1865 by Grove.

FRKF 679.5

Nocturne for piano, no. 5, in B-flat major, op. 37

Holograph manuscript, 1884, 11 p., notated in black ink, with additional markings in pencil, on both sides of sheets of tall 18-staff paper, paginated 1–10 by the composer, with an unnumbered cancelled page between 6 and 7.

On the title page, in Fauré's hand: "à Madame Marie P. Christofle / 5ème Nocturne / op. 38 [crossed out] 37 / Gabriel Fauré." At the top of p. 1, also in Fauré's hand: "à Madame Marie P. Christofle. / 5me Nocturne. / (en Si♭ majeur) / Gabriel Fauré, op. 37." At the bottom of p. 1, in a different hand, music publisher's number: "J. 2281.5.H." Signed and dated Louveciennes, Aug. 1884 at the end. Pasted-on revision on p. 3.

Heinrich Schütz to Henry Miller, p. 74–75.

Bound with the following two items:

Berceuse for violin and piano, op. 16

Holograph draft, incomplete, n.d., 3 p., notated in black ink on tall 18-staff paper. At the top of p. [1] in Fauré's hand: "Berceuse / Gabriel Fauré."

Followed by a complete manuscript of the violin part, also written in black ink on tall 18-staff paper on the recto of the first page of the following manuscript:

Andante for violin and piano, op. 75

Holograph manuscript of the violin part, n.d., 2 p., notated in black ink on 18-staff paper (numerous revisions pasted on both pages). At the top of p. [1] in Fauré's hand: "Andante pour violon et piano / Gabriel Fauré." Unidentified sketches, in pencil, on the verso of p. [2].

FRKF 901a–c

Piano sonata

Holograph manuscript, 1863, 10 p., notated in black ink, with additional pencil markings, on p. [3] to [12] of three nested, stitched bifolia of tall 20-staff paper (blind stamp of Lard). On p. [1] in Fauré's hand: "Sonate / pour le piano / Allegro - Menuet - Final / Gabriel Fauré." At the top of p. [3], dedication: "dédié à ma nièce Marguerite." Signed and dated 6 April 1863 at the end.

FRKF 1107

Puisque j'ai mis ma lèvre

Holograph manuscript of this song for voice and piano, on a poem by Victor Hugo, 1863, 3 p., in black ink on pages [2]–[4] of a bifolium of tall 20-staff paper (blind stamp of Lard). On p. [1] in Fauré's hand: "Poésie de Victor Hugo / mise en musique par Gabriel Fauré." Signed "Gabriel Bébé Py-Fauré" [?] and dated 2 Oct. 1863 at the end. Unidentified 9-measure sketch at the top of p. [1], notated on one staff. Date of composition given by Grove as 8 Dec. 1862.

FRKF 679.4

Rêve d'amour

Holograph manuscript of this song for voice and piano, on a poem by Victor Hugo, 1864, 2 p., in black ink on pages [2] and [3] of a bifolium of tall 20-staff paper (blind stamp of Lard). On p. [1] in Fauré's hand: "Poësie de Victor Hugo / mise en musique par Gabriel Fauré." At the top of p. [2]: "dédiée à Madame Claire de Gomiecourt." Signed and dated 5 May 1864 at the end.

FRKF 679.3

Valse de Faust

Holograph manuscript of Fauré's transcription of the Waltz from act 2 of Charles Gounod's *Faust*, arranged for flute, violin, and piano, n.d., 16 p., in black ink, with a few additional markings in black and blue pencil, on pages [3]–[18] of an unsewn gathering of five nested bifolia of tall 18-staff paper (blind stamp of Lard). On p. [1] in Fauré's hand: "Valse de Faust / dérangée / avec un rare bonheur / à l'usage / d'un piano, d'un violon / et / d'une flûte / par il maëstro / Joseph Barbanchu."

Not in Grove.
FRKF 678

II. LETTERS

None published in Fauré, *Correspondance*, ed. Jean-Michel Nectoux (Paris: Flammarion, 1980).

To André Beaunier and Jeanne Raunay

[1917] Sept. 2, Le Gui, avenue des Chèvrefeuilles, Saint-Raphaël[S], ALS, 2 p., addressed to "Bien chers amis." Mentions the first *Cello sonata* and the second *Violin sonata*.

[1918, Winter] Nice, ALS, 2 p. Mentions Alfred Jarry's *Ubu Roi* and confusions between him and Gabriel Faure.

Paris, Laurin-Guilloux-Buffetaud-Tailleur (Drouot), 19 March 1986, lots 52–53.
FRKF 1116–17

To Mme de Chaumont-Quitry

[1897 July 2?] n.p., ALS, 1 p., declining an invitation. Date pencilled on the letter in an unknown hand.

Paris, Laurin-Guilloux-Buffetaud-Tailleur (Drouot), 12 June 1984, lot 211.
FRKF 471

To Henriette Fuchs

[date illegible, Paris*] ALS, 1 p., enquiring about her participation in a concert with pieces by Gounod and himself. "Telégramme" printed on the address side.

Paris, Laurin-Guilloux-Buffetaud-Tailleur (Drouot), 12 June 1984, lot 217.
FRKF 475.1

To Madame Girard

[1899 Dec. 12, Paris*] ALS, 1 p.

[before 1900] "Jeudi," Grand Café d'Apollon, Aix-en-Provence[S], ALS, 2 p.

[1902 Jan. 17, Nice*] ALS, 1 p.

[1902 Jan. 23, Nice*] ALS, 1 p.

[1912 Feb. 1*] Roubaix, APCS

1918 Dec. 16, Conservatoire national de musique et de déclamation, Paris[S], ALS, 2 p., concerning *Pénélope*.

1919 March 29, Monte Carlo, ALS, 2 p.

Undated: 5 ALS, n.p., each 1 p.

Paris, Daniel Offret (Drouot), 18 Nov. 1985, lot 23.
FRKF 980

To Willy Rehberg

n.d., n.p., ALS, 4 p. Comments on his correspondent's move to Geneva.

Paris, Laurin-Guilloux-Buffetaud-Tailleur (Drouot), 12 June 1984, lot 216.
FRKF 475.2

To unidentified recipients

1910 April 26, Das Römerbad, Ems[S], ALS to "bien cher ami," 4 p. Mentions Paul Dukas.

1911 Jan. 19, Conservatoire national de musique et de déclamation [Paris][S] ALS, 2 p. Mentions Robert de Montesquiou.

1919 Feb. 26, Conservatoire national de musique et de déclamation[S], ALS to "cher ami," 3 p. Mentions Camille Bellaigue's article on *Pénélope*.

1923 June 27, Annecy-le-Vieux, ALS to "cher ami," 2 p. Mentions Paul Léon, Paul Dukas, Henri Rabaud, and Roger-Ducasse; also mentions the Isola brothers, Albert Carré, Queen Elizabeth of Belgium, *Pénélope*, and the *Trio*.

Paris, Laurin-Guilloux-Buffetaud-Tailleur (Drouot), 12 June 1984, lots 212–15.
FRKF 472–75

GEORGES FEYDEAU (1862–1921)

Monologues

Holograph manuscript, 1878–80, 57 p., in black ink on the recto pages of a bound notebook, paginated 1–37 only.

The manuscript contains the following. Each monologue is preceded by a title page and is signed and dated at the end.

"Le Potache / Scène de la vie de collège / monologue en vers / A Mlle Octavie d'Andor," July 1878, 8 p.

"La Petite Révoltée / Scène en vers / A Melle Julia Depoix," March 1880, 14 p.

"Ma Cuisinière / monologue [in prose] / A Félix Galipeaux," 16 March 1880, 10 p.

"Le Mouchoir / Monologue en vers / 1ere Epreuve [sic]," Nov. 1880, 12 p.

"Le Mouchoir! / Monologue en vers. / 2e Epreuve / Revue et corrigée," Dec. 1880, 7 p., also signed on the title page.

On p. [1] autograph presentation inscription: "A mon bon ami Arsias de Béarn / En vers c'est tout ce que j'ai fait! / Aujourd'hui je te l'offre en livre! / Peut-être un jour viendra, qui sait? / Où tu le vendras à la livre! / G Feydeau / Samedi 21 mai 1881." Bound in brown marbled paper boards with brown morocco spine. Top edge gilt; author and title ("Monologues") gold-tooled on spine. Bookplates of [Arsias de Béarn?] and Marcel Silvain.

All recorded in Talvart except for "Ma Cuisinière," published 1880–83. See Talvart, 5:406–7.
Paris, Laurin-Guilloux-Buffetaud-Tailleur (Drouot), 12 Dec. 1985, lot 87.
FRKF 959

GUSTAVE FLAUBERT (1821–80)

Letters to Louise Colet

1853 May 26, "Nuit de jeudi 1 h," [Rouen*] ALS, 7 p. (env). *Correspondance*, II:332–36.

1853 Dec. 28, "Mercredi, 11 h du soir," n.p., ALS, 6 p. *Correspondance*, II:493–95.

Paris, Laurin-Guilloux-Buffetaud-Tailleur (Drouot), 12 June 1984, lots 42–43.
FRKF 459–60

Letters to Ernest Feydeau

[1858 Dec. 26, Croisset] ALS, 2 p. *Correspondance*, II:848–49.

[late 1858 or early 1859] n.p., ALS, 1 p. "La IVe partie est superbe - superbe." Concerning *Daniel*. Not located in *Correspondance*.

Paris, Charavay, 18 Dec. 1985, lots 145–46.
FRKF 935–36

FOUGASSE (CYRIL KENNETH BIRD, 1887–1965)

"A sense of direction"

Original pen-and-ink cartoon on Whatman's water colour sketching board (27 × 38 cm), comprising a sequence of twelve vignettes, each with a manuscript caption underneath. On the verso, stamp indicating that the cartoon has been published in *Punch*.

London, Christie's, 21 July 1981, lot 247.
FRKF 98

"Official Extravagance"

Original pen-and-ink cartoon on Whatman's water colour sketching board (27 × 38 cm), signed in the lower right corner. Underneath the drawing, manuscript caption in ink: "Official Extravagance. / '… and then take the case of the Post Office: I notice that the walls of every single one of their telephone-boxes are actually decorated by hand, when it stands to reason that it would be very much cheaper to have the design printed!'" On the verso, stamp indicating that the cartoon has been published in *Punch*.

London, Christie's, 21 July 1981, lot 246.
FRKF 108

ANTOINE QUENTIN FOUQUIER-TINVILLE (1746–95)

Letter to Citizen "Rabau Pommier"

[1793 Oct. 9] Paris, ALS, 1 p., to Jacques-Antoine Rabaut-Pomier requesting documents to assist his case against Marie Antoinette, dated "Le 18 du premier mois deux.ème décade de l'an 2 eme de la république une et indivisible." The recipient is identified as "député à la Convention nationale."

Mounted in an album also containing the following prints:

Fouquier-Tinville, plate by Audibran after Raffet (10 × 12.5 cm).

"Fouquier-Tinville, né à Hérouan [etc.]," biography of Fouquier-Tinville, illustrated by plate after Raffet (12 × 15.5 cm) and another plate showing the Tribunal révolutionnaire in action (14.5 × 4.5 cm).

Fouquier-Tinville, plate by Florensa after Lacauchie (11 × 17 cm).

"Les Français sous la Révolution: L'accusateur public," plate by Massard after Baron (11 × 15 cm).

"XVIIIe siècle / Convention / A.ne Q.in Fouquier Tinville / Accusateur public" (8.5 × 15 cm). Hand-colored.

"Fouquier-Tinville," plate by Portman (9 × 14.5 cm).

New York, Sotheby's, 14 Feb. 1986, lot 461.
FRKF 988

CÉSAR FRANCK (1822–90)

Aimer

Holograph manuscript of this song for voice and piano on a poem by Joseph Méry, 1849, 6 p., notated in black ink on p. 1 to [6] (only the first 4 are paginated) of a gathering of two nested bifolia of tall 16-staff paper (blind stamp of C.A.F.), placed within an additional bifolium serving as wrappers. On the front of the outer bifolium, in Franck's hand: "Mélodies / (S'il est un charmant gazon / 3 exemplaires) / Aimer, Robin Gray, / Combien j'ai douce souvenance, Ninon, L'émir de Bengador." On top of p. 1, also in Franck's hand: "Aimer." Dated 28 Feb. 1849 at the end.

Fauquet, p. 242–43; 885.
London, Sotheby's, 29 Nov. 1985, lot 70.
FRKF 1031

Les Béatitudes

Holograph manuscript of this oratorio for voice soloists, chorus, and orchestra, in full score, 1879, 537 p., notated in black ink, with additional notations (not by Franck) in black, blue, and red pencil, on both sides of sheets of tall 26-staff paper (blind stamp of Lard-Esnault), paginated 1–535. There is no title page, but a manuscript dedication page ("A Madame / César Franck. / 10 Juillet 1879.") and a manuscript table of contents. At the top of p. 1, in Franck's hand: "Les Béatitudes / Prologue." Fair copy, with the piano accompaniment notated on the bottom two staves.

Bound in dark blue boards with black morocco corners and spine. Gilt fillet along the edges and on spine; on the spine: "Les / Béatitudes / Orchestre & réduction / César Franck."

Fauquet, p. 902–05.
Heinrich Schütz to Henry Miller, p. 72–73.
Paris, Boisgirard (Drouot), 22 May 1985, lot 139.
FRKF 646

Rébecca

Holograph manuscript, in short score, of the aria and scene "O Seigneur Dieu, qui protèges mon maître" and the duet "Seigneur, vous paraissez avoir fait longue route" from this oratorio, 1881, 13 p. Notated in black ink on 13 pages, paginated from 3 onward, of tall 18-staff paper (blind stamp of Lard-Esnault), with rehearsal letters highlighted in red pencil. On the title page, in blue pencil, possibly not in Franck's hand: "Eliézer / Rebecca." At the top of p. [1] in Franck's hand: "Air et Scène"; on p. 5: "Duo." Inscribed at the bottom of p. 13: "à mon ami et excellent interprète / Monsieur Hermann Léon / 17 Mars 1881 / 1ere Audition / César Franck."

Rébecca, "scène biblique" on a text by Paul Collin, was first performed, with piano accompaniment, by the Société chorale d'amateurs Guillot de Sainbris in March 1881; the date given by Grove (15 March) does not match the one in this manuscript.

From the collection of Sacha Guitry.
Fauquet, p. 906.
London, Sotheby's, 29 Nov. 1985, lot 71.
FRKF 1032

FREDERICK II, KING OF PRUSSIA (1712–86)

I. LETTERS

To the king of the Two Sicilies

The letters, all signed, and one page in length, are written in French in secretarial hands and convey news of births, marriages, and deaths in the Prussian royal family. Dated from Berlin and with envelopes, unless otherwise noted.

To Charles VII, king of Naples

 1740 Sept. 27
 1742 Jan. 9
 1743 May 28
 1748 Dec. 10
 1750 April 4
 1757 June 30, on mourning stationery
 1757 Aug. 11
 1758 June 13
 1758 Nov. 4

To Ferdinand IV, king of Naples

 1762 June 23, Breslau
 1765 July 15, Charlottenburg

1767 May 7
1767 July 26, Charlottenburg
1767 Oct. 5
1770 May 26
1771 March 8
1771 Nov. 12
1772 Nov. 19
1773 Jan. 11
1773 Nov. 5
1773 Dec. 10
1777 Sept. 17
1779 Feb. 25, Breslau
1780 Jan. 15, on mourning stationery
1780 May 2
1782 Jan. 2
1782 May 28
1783 Jan. 5 (no env)
1786 March 9

Also, LS to the Marquis de Montallegre, 1739 June 17, Ruppin, 1 p.

See Christie's, London, 28 Nov. 1990, lot 172.
FRKF 1288

To Herzog Karl von Braunschweig

1732 April 23, Nauen, ALS, 1 p., in French, addressed to "Monsieur Mon très cher Frère."

Accompanied by: *Ein unveröffentlichter Jugendbrief Friedrichs des Grossen. Den Teilnehmern an der Generalversammlung der Gesellschaft der Bibliophilen, Berlin 16. Oktober 1921, überreicht von Iwan Bloch* [Berlin, 1921], a single, loose bifolium of wove paper nested within wrappers. The title is taken from the front wrapper. Unnumbered copy from an edition of 300. Introduction on p. [1]–[2], colophon on p. [2], facsimile of the letter on p. [3].

Marburg, Stargardt, 26 Nov. 1985, lot 1251.
FRKF 1282

To Prince Ferdinand of Prussia

1772 March 25, Potsdam, LS, 1 p., in French, addressed to "mon très cher Frère."

Marburg, Stargardt, 5 March 1985, lot 1284.
FRKF 835

To Michael Gabriel Fredersdorf

[1757 March] 4, n.p., ALS, 1 p.

Marburg, Stargardt, 26 Nov. 1985, lot 1254.
FRKF 1285

To King Friedrich Wilhelm of Prussia

1736 Nov. 2 [Rheinsberg] ALS, 2 p. Thanks his father for a gift of pheasants, mentioning his sister Philippine, duchess of Brunswick and Wolfenbüttel, and the Prince of Miran (Duke Karl of Mecklenburg-Strelitz).

Heinrich Schütz to Henry Miller, p. 20–21.
Marburg, Stargardt, 26–27 Nov. 1985, lot 1252.
FRKF 1283

To Captain von Lipsky

1757 Feb. 20, Dresden, 1 p. Copy in a secretarial hand, marked "copia" in the upper left corner.

See Christie's, London, 16 Dec. 1991, lot 289.
Marburg, Stargardt, 5–6 March 1985, lot 1282.
FRKF 833

To Obristleutnant von Quaden

1757 March 19, Dresden, 1 p. Copy in a secretarial hand, including the letter from Quaden to Frederick II, dated Berlin, 1757 March 16.

See Christie's, London, 16 Dec. 1991, lot 289.
Marburg, Stargardt, 5–6 March 1985, lot 1282.
FRKF 833

To Kommissär Stoeckhardt

1782 Oct. 9, Potsdam, LS, 1 p., concerning a new alloy in cannon manufacturing.

Marburg, Stargardt, 5–6 March 1985, lot 1286.
FRKF 837

To General von Tauentzien

1784 Sept. 2, Potsdam, LS, 1 p., transmitting an enclosed order to be transmitted to all infantry generals and officers in Silesia. Accompanied by the order, signed by Frederick the Great, 3 p., criticizing the behavior and tactics recently adopted by some officers.

London, Christie's, 29 May 1986, lot 46.
FRKF 1287

To Major General von Winterfeld

1783 July 7, Potsdam, LS, 1 p., concerning a soldier named Wigand.

Marburg, Stargardt, 5–6 March 1985, lot 1287.
FRKF 838

To Commander von Wobersnow

1757 March 9, Dresden, ALS, 1 p., concerning payment of gun-money to retiring captains.

See Christie's, London, 16 Dec. 1991, lot 289.
Marburg, Stargardt, 5–6 March 1985, lot 1282.
FRKF 833

Other letters

1740 July 5, Berlin, LS, 1 p., to the council of an unidentified Prussian town, thanking them for their condolences on the death of his father, King Friedrich Wilhelm I.

Marburg, Stargardt, 26–27 Nov. 1985, lot 1253.
FRKF 1284

1779 Dec. 28, Berlin, LS, 1 p., "An die Porcellain Manufactur," concerning a craftsman from the Meissen factory named Hanefeld; also mentions Andreas Sigismund Margraff.

See Christie's, London, 16 Dec. 1991, lot 290.
Marburg, Stargardt, 5–6 March 1985, lot 1285.
FRKF 836

II. MISCELLANEOUS

Les matinées royales, ou l'art de régner

Manuscript, in the hand of a copyist, of this work attributed to Frederick II, n.d., 146 p. The manuscript comprises seven paginated gatherings, with traces of stitching, collating as follows: 1–18 [+ 2, blank]; 1–24, 25–48, 49–72, 73–96, 97–121 [101 omitted in numbering], 122–125 [+ 4]. Occasional underlinings in red pencil ("votre oncle henry," p. 31; "mon frere henry," p. 53).

Title on p. 1 of the first section: "Idée de la personne, de la manière de vivre / et de la cour du Roi de Prusse / par / feu Milord Tirconel / ambassadeur de France à la cour prussienne."

The second section has no general title and is organized in seven "matinées," some with sub-sections. References to "mon cher neveu" indicate that it is conceived as a series of lessons.

Premier[e] matinée: origine de notre maison (p. 1–3); de la position de mon Royaume (p. 3–4); du sol de mes etats (p. 4); des moeurs des habitans (p. 4–6).

Seconde matinée: de la religion (p. 6–15).

Troisieme matinée: de la justice (p. 15–20).

Quatrieme matinée: de la politique (p. 20–34); de la politique particuliere (p. 22); dans mes voyages (p. 22–24); a la revue de mes troupes (p. 24–27); dans les belles lettres (p. 27–29); dans le petit detail (p. 29–30); dans l'habillement (p. 30–31); dans le plaisirs (p. 31–34).

Cinquieme matinée: de la politique d'Etat (p. 34) premier principe (p. 35–39), second principe (p. 39–41), troisieme principe (p. 41–44).

Sixieme matinée: du militair (p. 44–75).

Septieme matinée: de la finance (p. 75) This last part contains a number of tables concerning taxes, a "Memoire envoyé a la province de Minden" (p. 97), and detailed analyses of taxation of various commodities (salt, wood, tobacco, etc.) and services (post).

On p. [128] a plan, in the form of a graph, for the reimbursement of the national debt. There is an incomplete table of contents on p. [129].

First published in 1766 as *Les matinées royales, ou Entretiens sur l'art de régner*. Also attributed to Voltaire.

Paris, Laurin-Guilloux-Buffetaud-Tailleur (Drouot), 3 July 1985, lot 67.
FRKF 851

ANNIE FRENCH (1872–1965)

"While Listening to the 'Wireless' 1940"

Bound album containing pen-and-ink and watercolor drawings, 1940, 160 p. The album is a sort of ledger with every other leaf perforated into detachable coupons; it measures 8.5 × 21 cm and is bound in blue-green boards and blue sheepskin spine. It is foliated 1–139, with several irregularities in the numbering and an index to the illustrations on three leaves at the end.

Provenance signature on the verso of the front board: "Ex libris/ Annie French." On the flyleaf, autograph title in Annie French's hand: "Idle / sketches / while / listening to / the news etc / on the / 'wireless' / Begun August / 1940 / 2nd year / of / the war." On the page following the index, autograph note: "I bought this / book in the bargain / basement in / Kennards / Croydon / for fourpence hapenny / (meant for shop accounts?)." A number of drawings are pasted on; several have captions in the hand of the author.

London, Christie's, 14 May 1985, lot 206.
FRKF 1421

LUDWIG GABILLON (1825–96)

Letter to a friend

n.d., Unterstützung-Verein "Schröder" [Berlin?]^S ALS, 3 p. On the last page, blank, unidentified pencil drawing of a face in an unknown hand.

Ludwig Gabillon: actor, stage director, and superintendent of the Burgtheater.

Marburg, Stargardt, 5–6 March 1985, lot 907.
FRKF 824b

JOHN GALSWORTHY (1867–1933)

Letter to W. Hecht

1928 Nov. 2, Bury House, Bury, nr. Pulborough, Sussex^S, ALS, 2 p., giving permission to print a letter by him on an unspecified issue.

London, Christie's, 23 March 1984, lot 70.
FRKF 435

MARY GARDEN (1877–1967)

Letter to Jules Brasseur

[1908 April 23, Paris*] ALS, 1 p., in French, declining an invitation. Printed "carte pneumatique" on the address side.

FRKF 535b

JEAN GENET (1910–86)

Les bonnes

Carbon typescript, corrected, 75 p., with manuscript additions, n.d.

Collation: [t.p.], [1], 2–7, [9], 10–11, [11 bis], 12–21, 21 bis, 22, 22 ter, 23–30, 30 bis, 30 ter, 30 quater, 31, [17 unnumbered p.], 41–47, [47 bis], [47 ter], 48–61.

The corrections are in black or blue ink or pencil and occur on the verso sides of typed pages, or are written on pasted-in sheets or slips of ruled paper. On title page, in Genet's hand: "Les bonnes," cancelled and replaced by "Mesdemoiselles Lemercier." Note in pencil in upper left corner, possibly not in Genet's hand: "3 ex." Title "Mesdemoiselles Lemercier" repeated, in manuscript, at the top of p. [1].

Bound in beige cloth, with brown and dark green leather labels on spine and fore edges; author and title gold-tooled on spine. Mock reference letters for Solange Lemercier pasted on both fixed endpapers.

Les bonnes was first performed in Paris in April 1947 and first published in *L'Arbalète* 12 (May 1947). This manuscript, which corresponds neither to the text in *L'Arbalète* nor to the two versions published in a single volume in 1954 by Jean-Jacques Pauvert, may be an intermediate version.

See Jean Genet, *Théâtre complet*, ed. Michel Corvin and Albert Dichy (Paris: Gallimard, Bibliothèque de la Pléiade, 2002), p. 1048–50 and 1080–81.
Heinrich Schütz to Henry Miller, p. 138–39.
FRKF 1248d

L'enfant criminel

Autograph manuscript, n.d., 10 p., in blue ink, mostly on the recto sides of nine folio-size sheets of ruled paper and an additional 4to-size sheet of ruled paper; paginated in pencil in an unidentified hand. At the top of p. 1, title: "L'enfance criminelle." Page 10 is evidently a supplement, marked 1 and corresponding to the same figure at the bottom of p. 9.

Commissioned as a radio talk in 1949; rejected by the radio, it was first published by Paul Morihien in 1949 in the volume *L'enfant criminel & 'Adame Miroir*. See also Genet, *Oeuvres complètes*, Vol. 5 (Paris: Gallimard, 1979), p. 377–93. Neither published version includes the text of p. 10.

Paris, Ader-Picard-Tajan (Drouot), 22 Nov. 1985, lot 156.
FRKF 1369

Notes on homosexuality

Autograph manuscript in the form of an ALS to Jean-Paul Sartre, n.d., n.p., 4 p., in dark blue ink on the recto sides of four tall sheets of ruled paper. Incipit: "On n'a pas eu le temps de parler. Relativement à la pédérastie voici ma théorie que je vous propose." Signed "Genet" at the end.

FRKF 1248a

Letter to the Préfet de Police

n.d. [1957] n.p., autograph draft, 2 p., concerning *Le balcon*. Together with three pages of autograph notes and comments to Genet by Jean-Paul Sartre, written in black ballpoint pen on the recto sides of three tall sheets of ruled paper.

FRKF 1248b

ROSEMONDE GÉRARD (1866–1953)

"Causerie" on the theater

Untitled holograph manuscript [1945], 8 p., with pasted-on clippings with extracts of the texts read as part of the causerie. Accompanied by an ALS to André Saudemont [1945 Nov. 27, Paris*] 1 p., enclosing the manuscript.

Rosemonde Gérard married Edmond Rostand in 1889.

Paris, Le Roux-Mathias (Drouot), 19 April 1985, lot 240.
FRKF 716c

EDWARD GERMAN (1862–1936)

"Rolling down to Rio"

Holograph manuscript of this song for voice and piano, on a poem by Rudyard Kipling, n.d. [1903], 4 p. Notated in black ink, with additional markings in black pencil, on a bifolium of tall 19-staff paper.

> Housed in a bifolium of tall 20-staff paper (A.L. No. 14.), on the front of which is the following inscription in German's hand: "The original MS. of / 'Rolling down to Rio' / from the / 'Just So' Song Book / Words by / Rudyard Kipling / Music by / Edward German / (Signed by the Author & Composer)." At the top of p. [1] of the manuscript, also in German's hand: "N° [7 cancelled] 12 'Rolling down to Rio' / [signed:] Rudyard Kipling / Edward German." Initialed by German at the end. Pasted-on revisions on p. [2] and [4].

New York, Christie's, 16 Nov. 1984, lot 256.
FRKF 366

LÉON POTIER, DUC DE GESVRES (ca. 1620–1704)

Legal document

Document printed in Paris by P. Gisset, sur le Pont S. Michel, à l'Ecrevisse Royale, and dated 9 July 1703, concerning the transfer by gift of the Duc de Gesvres's properties to his son Bernard-François Potier, marquis de Gesvres.

> Folio, [4] p. Inscription at the end indicating that the copy is made for the Duc de Gesvres, "a la descharge de Mr C[?] et de M. le Comte de Lignières."

In a beige folder with the printed title: "Catalogue des autographes précieux provenant du cabinet de M. N. Yéméniz et de documents historiques et nobiliaires provenant des cabinets de D'Hozier, Chérin, Chevillard, Clairambault, Lainé, Courcelles, Saint-Allais, etc. etc." (Paris: Étienne Charavay, n.d.), No. 547.

Léon Potier de Gesvres, duc de Gesvres from 1669 until 1704, governor of Paris. His son Bernard-François Potier de Gesvres (1655–1739), duc de Gesvres from 1704 until 1722, became governor of Paris on his father's death. See *Dictionnaire de biographie française*.

Paris, Laurin-Guilloux-Buffetaud-Tailleur (Drouot), 3 July 1985, lot 67.
Apparently part of FRKF 851

ANDRÉ GIDE (1869–1951)

"Oscar Wilde"

Holograph manuscript, n.d. [1901], 24 p., in black ink on the recto sides of 24 folio-size leaves (22 × 33.5 cm), numbered in pencil in the upper right corner. Corrected in black ink or pencil throughout in Gide's hand, with additional markings in pencil, presumably in the hands of the typesetters, whose names (Jules, M. Hoyau, M. Marcoux [?], M. Roulleau, M. Marcel) appear on ff. 1, 4, 7, 10, 13, 15, 17, 19, 21, and 23. Signed "André Gide" at the end.

Bound in blue-grey morocco with dark green silk doublures; double fillets of gold in the borders of the verso sides of both boards. Binding signed "Asper, Genève" in gold tooling at the bottom of the verso of the front board. On the verso of the free front endpaper, bookplate of Count Alain de Suzannet.

Published in *L'Ermitage, revue mensuelle de littérature et d'art* 13:6 (June 1902): 401–29; reprinted in *Prétextes* (Paris: Mercure de France, 1903) and in *Oscar Wilde: in memoriam* (Paris: Mercure de France, 1910).

See Talvart, 7:44 (no. 24).
Heinrich Schütz to Henry Miller, p. 92–93.
New York, Breslauer [ca. 1982], lot 103.
FRKF 90

Letter to Jean Cocteau

> 1945 March 11, Alger, ALS, 2 p. Looks forward to resuming relations after the war; mentions Denoël.

Paris, Laurin-Guilloux-Buffetaud-Tailleur (Drouot), 16 March 1984, lot 51.
FRKF 424

Letters to Marcel Proust

[1921 May 3] "Mardi," n.p., ALS, 3 p. Kolb XX:239–41.

[1921 May 13] n.p., ALS, 5 p. Kolb XX:261–62.

1922 April 13, n.p., ALS, 1 p. Kolb XXI:129.

Paris, Ader-Picard-Tajan (Drouot), 22 Nov. 1985, lots 139–41.
FRKF 1381–83

W. S. GILBERT (1836–1911)

Letter to Lionel Brough

1888 [June corrected to] July 17, 12 Breakspears, Uxbridge, ALS, 3 p.

The English actor Lionel Brough (1836–1909) was in the original casts of Gilbert's *La vivandière* (1868) and *The Mountebanks* (1892).

London, Christie's, 5 May 1982, lot 151.
FRKF 19

Letter to W. Hecht

1904 May 11, Hotel Kaiserhof, Wiesbaden^S, ALS, 1 p., concerning an unidentified play.

London, Christie's, 23 March 1984, lot 70.
FRKF 435

Letter to Arthur T. Poyser

1908 April 6, Grim's Dyke, Harrow Weald^S, ALS, 1 p., giving permission to quote a song from *The Yeomen of the Guard*.

London, Sotheby's, 9–10 May 1985, lot 212.
FRKF 779a

JEAN GIONO (1895–1970)

Letter to Georges Auric

n.d, n.p., ALS, 1 p., on a carbon typescript, signed and headed "Poeme extrait de … accompagnés de la flûte / de Jean Giono."

No collaboration between Giono and Auric is listed in Grove.

London, Sotheby's, 29 Nov. 1985, lot 278.
FRKF 1047e

UMBERTO GIORDANO (1867–1948)

Marina

Holograph manuscript, in full score, of this one-act opera, n.d. [ca. 1889] 261 p., in black ink on tall 24-staff paper, unpaginated. On title page, in Giordano's hand: "Poca favilla gran fiamma seconda. / Dante. / Marina. / Melodramma in un atto. / Personaggi / Lambro / Daniele / Montenegrini / [Lambro:] Baritono. / [Daniele:] Baritono. / Marina, sorella di Daniele … Soprano. / Giorgio Lascari, uffiziale serbo … Tenore. / Coro di soldati montenegrini e donne montenegrine. / La scena è nel Montenegro. Epoca della guerra serbo-montenegrina." Marked "Fine" at the end.

Bound in light brown crocodile skin, with a decorative pattern roll-tooled in black along the outer edges, and white silk doublures.

Marina, melodrama in one act on a libretto by Enrico Golisciani, was Giordano's submission to the 1889 Sonzogno contest, where it placed sixth.

Heinrich Schütz to Henry Miller, p. 78–79.
London, Christie's, 29 May 1986, lot 414.
FRKF 1182

ALBERT GLATIGNY (1839–73)

Le fer rouge. France et Belgique: chez tous les libraires [i.e. Brussels: J.H. Briard], 1870.

[6] + 73 [+ 3] p. Illustrated allegorical frontispiece celebrating the defeat of Napoleon III at Sedan, printed in red. One of the copies printed on China paper. Paper wrappers bound in. Also bound in, ALS from Glatigny to an unidentified friend, n.d., n.p., 4 p., concerning mostly Corsica, with mentions of Villemessant and Louis Blanc.

Bound in blue morocco, all edges gilt; author's name and title gold-tooled vertically on the spine. The binding is signed M. Lortic in gold at the bottom of the verso of the front board. On the verso of both boards, gold-tooled frise. Double endpapers in pink marbled paper.

Brussels, Simonson, 19 May 1984, lot 182.
FRKF 368

ALEKSANDER KONSTANTINOVICH GLAZUNOV (1865–1936)

"Einlage zur ¾ Variation im Todtentanz von Franz Liszt"

Holograph manuscript fragment of this piece for piano, 1931, 1 p. Notated in black ink on the recto of a single sheet of tall 10-staff paper. At the top of the page, in Glazunov's hand: "Einlage zur Variation ¾ im Todtentanz von Fr. Lizst [sic]." Dated at the bottom 24 April 1931.

With inscription to Herr Petri: "Hochgeehrter und lieber Herr Petri, mir gefällt gar nicht die von Siloti revidierte Einlage vor der ¾ Variation. Ersternet [?] sind zufällig anstadt 7–8 Takte, wobei die letzten 2 sind ganz *styllos*. Hiermit erlaube ich mir Ihnen die 7 Takte, wie ich sie meine, zu empfehlen. / Ihr ganz ergebenen / Alexander Glazunow."

No work of this title listed in Grove or in *Alexander Glazunow* (Frankfurt: Belaieff, n.d. [1998]). Marburg, Stargardt, 26 Nov. 1985, lot 772.

FRKF 1149

Finnish Fantasy, op. 88

Holograph manuscript of this orchestral work, 1909, 50 p. Notated in black ink, with additional markings in black, red, and blue pencil, on separate bifolia of large, square-shaped 24-staff paper (N° 52a (1) Iurgenson v Moskve), paginated 1–50 by the composer. At the top of p. 1, in Glazunov's hand: "Fantaisie Finnoise / Alexandre Glazounow / op. 88 –" Also on p. 1, in a different hand, autograph mention of Belaieff, Leipzig, and music publisher's number 2898. Initialed and dated St. Petersburg, 20 Feb. 1910 at the end.

Heinrich Schütz to Henry Miller, p. 102–03.

FRKF 225

CHARLES GOUNOD (1818–93)

I. MUSIC MANUSCRIPTS

Choeur de chasseurs "Où sommes nous?"

Holograph manuscript of this part-song (the first bass line only), 1855, 2 p. Notated in black ink on both sides of a tall sheet of blue 12-staff paper. At the top of the first page, in Gounod's hand: "Choeur de Chasseurs. (n° 2.) 1ère Basse." Dated 1855 by Grove.

FRKF 993

George Dandin

Holograph manuscript, in full score, of this unfinished opéra-comique after Molière's comedy [1873–74], 207 p. Notated in black and purple ink on a combination of bifolia and single leaves of tall 24-staff paper. In each number, the music begins on the verso of a title page.

The manuscript comprises the following sections, with titles in Gounod's hand:

Overture, 56 p. "George Dandin / Comédie en trois actes, en prose / de Molière. / Musique de Charles Gounod. / Ouverture. / Ch. Gounod."

Act 1, scene 2, Melodrama, 2 p. "Duo / Lubin-George Dandin. / (Acte I. Scène 2me.)" The spoken dialogue is written out in Gounod's hand.

Act 1, scene 8, Trio, 16 p. "Réparation d'honneur. / (Clitandre, George Dandin, Mr de Sotenville.) / Act I. Scène 8." The large signature of Georgina Weldon is written across several pages in black or blue pencil, partly erased in some instances.

Act 2, scene 4, Duet, 15 p. "Duo. / (Angélique, George Dandin.) / Acte II. Scène 4." Large signature of Georgina Weldon in blue pencil across the title page and every other page.

Act 2, scene 7, Duet/ Two versions.

Version A, 12 p. Notated partly in purple ink. "Duo. / (Lubin, George Dandin.) / Acte II, Scène 7." Large signature of Georgina Weldon in blue pencil across the title page and every other page.

Version B, 23 p. Notated in black ink on a different paper (24-staff, Lard-Esnault). "Duo. / (Lubin, George Dandin.) / Acte 2. Sc. 7.)"

Act 2, scene 9, Trio, 28 p. "Trio. / (George Dandin, Mr et Mme de Sotenville.) / Acte II, Scène 9.)" Large signature of Georgina Weldon in black pencil across the title page and every other page. Incomplete: the orchestration and vocal lines are lacking from p. [5] on, to resume on p. [18] (two measures of orchestration only; the words are lacking on p. [21] and [23–26].

Act 3, scene 8, Recitative and scene, 7 p. "Récitatif et Scène. / (Angélique.) / Acte III, Scène 8." Large signature of Georgina Weldon in red pencil across the title page and every other page. Only the recitative is present.

Act 3, scene 14, Quintet, 34 p. "Quintette. / (Angélique, Claudine, George Dandin, Mr et Mme de Sotenville). / Acte III, Sc. 14." Large signature of Georgina Weldon in red and black pencil across the title page and every other page.

Act 3, scene 15, Aria, 14 p. "Complainte. / (George Dandin.) / Acte III, Scène 15 et dernière." At the end, calligraphed in Gounod's hand: "fin de George Dandin."

See Laurin-Guilloux-Buffetaud-Tailleur (Drouot), Paris, 20 June 1977, lot 37.

London, Sotheby's, 17 May 1990, lot 124.
FRKF 130

Lutter, aimer

Holograph manuscript of this a cappella quartet for two tenors and two basses, n.d. [ca. 1880?], 4 p., in black ink, with additional notations in red pencil, on a single bifolium of tall 26-staff paper (blind stamp of Lard-Esnault). At the top of p. [1] in Gounod's hand: "Lutter, aimer. / (Quatuor vocal, dédié à Joseph Heyberger.)" Dating suggested by a manuscript note in pencil in an unidentified hand.

Not in Grove.
Lion Heart Autographs, catalogue (1985).
FRKF 575a

Le médecin malgré lui

Holograph manuscript, in full score, of this opéra-comique after Molière's comedy, 1857, 576 p. Notated in black ink, with additional markings in red pencil (notably tempo and dynamics indications), on tall bifolia of 30-staff paper (Lard-Esnault). The bifolia are numbered in the overture and in some of the numbers but not all. There is no title page. At the top of p. [1] in Gounod's hand: "Le Médecin malgré lui. / Ouverture." Signed and dated 1857 at the end.

Bound in boards lined with dark green Annonay paper; dark green morocco spine; on the spine, inlays on patent leather between double gilt fillets. Gold-tooled on spine: "Ch. Gounod / Le médecin / malgré lui / Manuscrit."

Heinrich Schütz to Henry Miller, p. 52–53.
FRKF 1401

O Sanctissima

Holograph manuscript, n.d., 2 p., in black ink on p. [2] and [3] of a single bifolium of 12-staff paper. It comprises 16 measures (with indication of a pp da capo), noted on four, 4-staff systems. On title page: "O Sanctissima. / Motet à la Ste Vierge. / pour Mezzo Sop. et Tenor." Written in A-flat for mezzo-soprano, tenor, and organ accompaniment; the tempo indication is Moderato quasi andantino.

Not in Grove.
Marburg, Stargardt, 5–6 March 1985, lot 804.
FRKF 811

La Toussaint. Hymne sacré

Holograph manuscript, n.d., 3 p., in black ink on three pages of 12-staff paper. The title is written on a separate bifolium, in which the manuscript proper is inserted. Inscribed by the composer "à mon élève et amie R. Jousset. Ch. Gounod." For soprano or tenor voice and piano. Undated, author of text unidentified. Incipit: "Ouvrez-vous, cieux des cieux!"

Not in Grove.
FRKF 384

Unidentified work for piano four-hands

Written on two separate bifolia of tall 24-staff paper (blind stamp, possibly of Lard-Esnault), the beginning in purple ink, the last three pages in black ink, with additional notations in blue pencil. Signed at the end "Ch. Gounod." In C major, marked moderato.

Lion Heart Autographs, catalogue (1985).
FRKF 575b

II. MANUSCRIPTS

Eulogy given at Bizet's funeral

Pencil draft of Gounod's eulogy at Bizet's funeral [June 1875], 2 p., together with an ANS from Anna Gounod on a visiting card ("Madame Ch. Gounod") to Ludovic Halévy, n.d., presenting the document to him in the hope he might give it someday to Bizet's son.

Paris, Oger-Dumont (Drouot), 14 Feb. 1985, lot 47.
FRKF 692c

La reine de Saba

Holograph list of the numbers in the opera, on stationery of Ville de Paris, Écoles communales, Direction de l'Orphéon [late 1850s], 3 p., with a pencilled note in Ludovic Halévy's hand at the top of the first page: "Note autographe de Ch. Gounod / Ludovic Halévy."

Gounod's *La reine de Saba* was premiered at the Paris Opéra on 28 Feb. 1862.

Paris, Oger-Dumont (Drouot), 14 Feb. 1985, lot 47.
FRKF 692a

III. LETTERS

To Alphonse Daudet

1880 June 21, n.p., ALS, 1 p., offering a song to be inserted in the play *Jack* (premiered in Jan. 1881).

Paris, Laurin-Guilloux-Buffetaud-Tailleur (Drouot), 1 July 1986, lot 107.
FRKF 1161

To Georges Hainl

1860 Sept. 14, Montretout, ALS, 2 p., concerning *Le médecin malgré lui*.

FRKF 1408

To Léonie Halévy

1872 June 7, Tavistock House, Tavistock Square [London]^S (pink paper), ALS, 4 p. Mentions *Le médecin malgré lui*, his Requiem mass, and Bizet's *Djamileh*.

Paris, Oger-Dumont (Drouot), 14 Feb. 1985, lot 49.
FRKF 693

To Ludovic Halévy

1882 Oct. 27, Saint-Cloud, ALS, 1 p.

[1882] "Vendredi," n.p., ALS, 2 p., concerning *L'abbé Constantin*.

1883 Sept. 9, n.p., ALS, 2 p.

n.d., n.p., ALS, 1 p., a letter of recommendation for the bearer.

n.d., n.p., ALS, 1 p., in the third person, transmitting a message on behalf of Édouard Dubufe.

Paris, Oger-Dumont (Drouot), 14 Feb. 1985, lot 50.
FRKF 694

Other letters

To an unidentified male correspondent

1874 Jan. 26, London, Tavistock House, Tavistock Square, ALS, 4 p., concerning his recent work (the *Messe de Sainte Cécile*, *Jeanne d'Arc*, the *Missa S.S. Angeli Custodes*, the oratorio *L'Annonciation*, and other religious compositions); mentions his dream to visit Palestine and Jerusalem. Addressed to "Mon cher enfant! mon fils!" Possibly to Georges Bizet.

Marburg, Stargardt, 5–6 March 1985, lot 805.
FRKF 812

To an unidentified female student

n.d., "à table" [Paris?] ALS, 2 p., concerning *Roméo et Juliette*. On p. [1] in the upper left corner, in the hand of Ludovic Halévy: "Lettre à [blank]."

Paris, Oger-Dumont (Drouot), 14 Feb. 1985, lot 50.
FRKF 694.5

IV. PRINTED MUSIC

La Rédemption

Complete bound engraved version of the full score, possibly a proof copy, without title page. [London: Novello, Ewer, 1882?].

352 p., 27 × 34 cm. Music publisher's number: [Novello, Ewer] 6345. The text is printed in both English and French throughout, the English text being on top. At the top of page 1, manuscript inscription in black ink, underlined twice, in an unidentified hand: "Not published."

Presentation inscription to Camille Saint-Saëns on the recto of the first page, blank: "A mon cher Camille Saint-Saëns / Mon Camille, Je t'offre avec bonheur cette oeuvre que tu aimes et à laquelle ton nom demeure attaché dans mon souvenir. Seulement:

> Ce volume ne prêteras
> Sans nul prétexte absolument:
> A l'éditeur obéiras
> En ceci scrupuleusement.
> Ch. Gounod"

The inscription is followed by a manuscript musical quotation of 3 measures on one staff ("Le Verbe s'est fait chair"), identified as belonging with p. 308.

Bound in quarter brown morocco and buckram. On front board, in gilt lettering: REDEMPTION. On the spine, which is partly missing, one can still read (in English): "Full score / Ch. Gounod." On the verso of the front board, large manuscript inscription in black ink: "No 19."

The work was first performed at the Birmingham Festival in 1882. The English text was by the Rev J. Troutbeck.

See: *The Redemption: a sacred trilogy / written and composed by Charles Gounod* (London; New York: Novello, Ewer and Co. [1882?]). (Novello, Ewer and Co. 6345)
London, Sotheby's, 26–27 May 1983, lot 29.
FRKF 121

V. MISCELLANEOUS

Pencil drawing of the profile of a woman in antique headgear, signed and dated "Ch. Gd / 30 avril 1880." On a single sheet of paper (15 × 19.5 cm), with a note in the hand of Ludovic Halévy: "Dessin de Gounod, signé / fait le 30 avril 1880 à la Commission des auteurs dramatiques / Ludovic Halévy."

Paris, Oger-Dumont (Drouot), 14 Feb. 1985, lot 47.
FRKF 692b

ENRIQUE GRANADOS (1867–1916)

Cartas de amor

Holograph fragment from this piano piece, n.d. The 8-measure fragment is written on a half sheet of 12-staff paper, marked 148 in red pencil in an unidentified hand. At the top of the page, in Granados's hand: "Valses / cartas de amor / E Granados." Above the first measure of music: "Continuacion."

Accompanied by a TLS from Antoni Carreras of the Royal Academy of Medicine, Barcelona, to Jack Bornoff, 1982 April 8, 1 p., enclosing the manuscript.

Paris, Hervé Poulain (Drouot), 5 April 1984, lot 16.
FRKF 442

KATE GREENAWAY (1846–1901)

Flower girls

Pencil with watercolor drawing on paper (16.5 × 11.5 cm), signed with initials and dated "Christmas 1896."

New York, Christie's, 30 Oct. 1985, lot 455.
FRKF 962

EDVARD GRIEG (1843–1907)

Letters to Gerhard Schjelderup

1906 July 4, Troldhaugen, ALS, 8 p., concerning *Peer Gynt*; also mentions Wagner and Richard Strauss. Benestad, I:630–32.

1906 Dec. 4, Kristiana, ALS, 8 p., concerning *Peer Gynt* and the *Ballade for piano*, op. 24; mentions Bjornson, Sinding, and Svendsen. Benestad, I:632–33.

Gerhard Schjelderup (1859–1933), Norwegian composer.

London, Sotheby's, 10 May 1984, lots 59, 62.
FRKF 327–28

YVETTE GUILBERT (1865–1944)

Letters to Eugène Bertrand

[1897 Oct. 25] n.p., ALS, 3 p. Date in the hand of Ludovic Halévy.

n.d., "5 heures," n.p., ALS, 2 p., concerning a recommendation for a protégée (probably Marie Lauzac).

Eugène Bertrand (1834–99) was director of the Paris Opéra from 1892 to 1899.

Accompanied by two clippings concerning the lawsuit brought against Guilbert by the Concert-Parisien, identified in Halévy's hand as being from *Le Temps* for 11 April 1892 and from *Le Matin* for 15 April 1892.

Paris, Oger-Dumont (Drouot), 14 Feb. 1985, lot 51.
FRKF 695

Letter to Ludovic Halévy

[1897 Oct. 20] Paris*, ALS, 1 p., concerning her protégée Marie Lauzac; mentions Victorien Sardou. Printed "Carte pneumatique fermée" on the address side. Dated by Ludovic Halévy.

Paris, Oger-Dumont (Drouot), 14 Feb. 1985, lot 51.
FRKF 695.5

SACHA GUITRY (1885–1957)

Je t'aime!

Autograph manuscript of this play, 1919, 89 p., in black ink on both sides of individual sheets of heavy folio-size paper, mounted on stubs and bound in half red morocco and reddish marbled paper boards, with raised bands on spine. Paginated by Guitry: [4], 1–97 [+ 1] p., some pages blank.

Manuscript half-title: "'Je t'aime' / comedie en cinq actes." With a verse dedication "à Yvonne / et à Printemps," 4 stanzas of 4 lines each, initialed S.G. at the bottom. On title page: "Je t'aime!" [replacing cancelled title "Pour / vivre / heureux ..."] / comedie en 5 actes / par / Sacha Guitry / [addition in blue ballpoint pen:] Manuscrit de Je t'aime! / offert à Marcel Achard parce / que j'aime à la fois ses pièces / et lui-même / Sacha Guitry."

Original full-page pen-and-ink and wash drawing on p. [38] showing three black musicians. On p. 89, 91, 93, and 95, stage maps, lists of props, and descriptions of costumes for each of the acts. Laid in: ALS to [Marcel Achard?] on stationery of 18, avenue Elisée-Reclus [Paris], n.d., 1 p., offering to incorporate into the manuscript [of *Je t'aime?*] modifications made to the text for performances.

Talvart, 7:377
Heinrich Schütz to Henry Miller, p. 120–21.
Paris, Ader-Picard-Tajan (Drouot), 19 Feb. 1986, lot 72.
FRKF 1367

Un monde fou

Autograph drafts for this comedy in four acts, n.d., 87 p., in black ink and pencil, with corrections in red and black pencil, on the recto sides (with occasional drafts on the versos) of 87 leaves, with irregular pagination. Verse preface on p. 1–2. At the top of p. 1, in Guitry's hand: "Un monde fou / comédie nouvelle en 4 actes / par / Sacha Guitry." Evidently incomplete, with multiple drafts for a single passage.

First performed in Nov. 1938; according to Harding, p. 156–57, it was the last play Guitry wrote for his third wife, Jacqueline Delubac.

Not in Talvart.
Paris, Laurin-Guilloux-Buffetaud-Tailleur (Drouot), 12 Dec. 1985, lot 102.
FRKF 948

Letter to Reynaldo Hahn

n.d., Savoy Hotel, London[S], ALS, 7 p., concerning their operetta *Mozart*. On the verso of the last page, ALS from Hahn to "Mon cher Ed," n.d., n.p., 2 p.

Paris, Laurin-Guilloux-Buffetaud-Tailleur (Drouot), 8 Feb. 1985, lot 115.
FRKF 658.5

REYNALDO HAHN (1874–1947)

I. MUSIC MANUSCRIPTS

SONGS AND PIANO PIECES

A collection of manuscript songs and piano pieces by Hahn from the collection of Cléo de Mérode. The manuscripts are bound together, as follows, after a series of printed songs (see below under Printed music).

Adoration

Holograph manuscript of this song for voice and piano, 1891, 4 p., in black ink on p. [1]–[4] of a bifolium of tall 20-staff paper (blind stamp of Lard-Esnault) nested within another bifolium serving as wrappers. On the front of the outer bifolium, in Hahn's hand: "Adoration / R.H." On p. [1], title: "Hymne à Cléo - " Initialed and dated at the end: "Paris, Avril–Mai 91."

Comme un cri

Holograph manuscript of this song for voice and piano, 1891, 3 p., in black ink on both sides of a single leaf and page 3 of a bifolium of tall 16-staff paper (blind stamp of Lard-Esnault), the first page of which serves as cover. On cover, in Hahn's hand: "Comme un cri—! / Poésie de Banville / R.H. / 8 avril 1891." At the top of p. [1]: "Comme un cri — / (Poésie de Th. de / Banville)." Initialed and dated at the end: "8 Juin 1891 / de 11 h à midi m-[one word cropped by the binder] / tout d'un trait."

Contour mélodique improvisé

Holograph manuscript of this piece for piano, 1891, 1 p., in pencil on p. [1] of a bifolium of tall 20-staff paper (blind stamp of Lard-Esnault). On the preceding title page, in pencil, in Hahn's hand: "Contour mélodique improvisé / en voiture ouverte. / 3 Juin 91." At the top of p. [1]: "Contour mélodique improvisé"; initialed at the bottom of the page and dated at the end: "3 Juin 91. 10 h du matin, / Boulevard Malesherbes, / en voiture ouverte."

Notturno alla Italiana

Holograph manuscript of this piano piece, 1891, 5 p., in black ink on p. [3]–[7] of two nested bifolia of tall 8vo-size 12-staff paper (blind stamp of Lard-Esnault). On p. [1] in Hahn's hand: "Notturno alla Italiana. / R.H. / Parigi 1891." Initialed at the end.

Good-bye

Holograph manuscript of this piano piece, 1891, 1 p., in black ink on the recto of one sheet of tall 18-staff paper (oval blind stamp cropped by the binder), nested within an additional bifolium. On the front of the outer bifolium, in Hahn's hand: "Good-bye. / R.H. / Paris, Juin 1891." Initialed and dated at the end: "Paris Juin 1891."

Offrande

Holograph manuscript of this song for voice and piano, n.d., 4 p., in black ink on p. [3]–[4] of the same bifolium as "Good-bye" and p. [3]–[4] of its outer bifolium. At the top of p. [3] of the first bifolium, in Hahn's hand: "à Vous. / Offrande. (P. Verlaine)." Dated 1891 by Grove.

Improvisazione

Holograph manuscript of this piano piece, 1891, 4 p., in black ink on p. [3]–[6] of two nested bifolia of tall 8vo-size 12-staff paper (blind stamp of Lard-Esnault). On p. [1] in Hahn's hand: "tirée du recueil: 'fleur de mon âme' / N° 17. / Improvisazione! / R.H." The same title and note are also at the top of p. [3]. Initialed and dated at the end: "1er Juin 1891. / 2 h du matin."

Portrait

Holograph manuscript of this piano piece, n.d., 7 p., in black ink on p. [3]–[9] of three nested bifolia of tall 8vo-size 12-staff paper (blind stamp of Lard-Esnault); the second leaf of the second bifolium has been excised. On p. [1] in Hahn's hand: "Portrait / R.H." At the top of p. [3], dedication: "à Cléo - " Initialed at the end.

Tristesse …

Holograph manuscript of this piano piece, 1891, 4 p., in black ink on the recto sides of four leaves, possibly conjoined, of tall 14-staff paper (blind stamp of Lard-Esnault), foliated in Hahn's hand and preceded by a title page on the same paper. On title page, in Hahn's hand: "Les Impressions / Tristesse … / Paris. 15 Avril 1891 / R.H." At the top of p. [1]: "Les Impressions. / Tristesse." Initialed and dated at the end: "14 avril 1891 / 7 h du matin / J'ai eu la fievre toute la nuit."

Regrets

Holograph manuscript of this piano piece, 1891, 4 p., in black ink on p. [3]–[6] of a gathering of two nested bifolia of tall 18-staff paper (blind stamp of Lard-Esnault). On p. [1] in

Hahn's hand: "(Les Impressions: / recueil.) / Regrets — / 29 avril 1891." At the top of p. [3]: "(Les Impressions, recueil / n° 27) / Regrets ... / 'Vous n'avez rien compris à ma simplici[té] / Rien, ô ma pauvre enfant ...' (poésie de Paul Ver[laine])." Dated at the end: "Mercredi 29 Avril 1891. / de minuit à / une heure du / matin. / (le Mage.)"

Le mage, opera in five acts by Massenet on a libretto by Jean Richepin, was premiered at the Paris Opéra on 16 March 1891.

Fleur de mon âme

Holograph manuscript of this song for voice and piano, 1891, 4 p., in black ink on p. [3–4] and [7–8] of three nested bifolia of tall 20-staff paper (blind stamp of Lard-Esnault). On the front of the outer bifolium, in Hahn's hand: "Fleur de mon âme ... / R.H." At the top of p. [1]: "Fleur de mon âme ... / Poésie de Th. Gautier." Signed and dated at the end: "Reynaldo Hahn / 1891."

Pièces d'amour

Holograph manuscript of these piano pieces, 1891, 12 p., on both sides of seven sheets, possibly conjoined, of tall 18-staff paper (blind stamp of Lard-Esnault).

> On the recto of the first leaf, in Hahn's hand: "Quelques pièces tirées du recueil: / 'Pièces d'amour' / Reynaldo Hahn / Eté de 1891 - loin de / Pari[s]." At the top of p. [2]: "5 [written over 3] pièces tirées du recueil: / 'Pièces d'amour' - / N° 5. - Grands yeux. - " This piece initialed and dated at the end, on p. [3]: "Münster am Stein. / 8 Juillet 1891 / Beau soleil / !!!!! / 8 h, matin."
>
> At the top of p. [4]: "(Pièces d'amour) / N° 2 / à un mouchoir (!) - ..." This piece initialed and dated at the end, on p. [6]: "Münster am Stein. / au loin - / 3 Juillet 91. / 11 h du soir."
>
> At the top of p. [7]: "(Pièces d'amour) / N° 9. - Chatain doré sur fond clair." This piece dated at the end, on p. [9]: "Münster am Stein. / au loin - / 9 Juillet 91. / 6 h soir / (un peu fati[gué] / Tout d'un trait / 10 minutes / chouff!!"
>
> At the top of p. [10]: "(Pièces d'amour) / Mens divinior - (Souffle plus divin!)." This piece dated at the end, on p. [11]: "Hambourg dans l'Elbe / 18 Septembre."
>
> At the top of p. [12]: "(Pièces d'amour) / *** / 'Ange plein de bonté connaissez-vous / l'angoisse?' / Ch. Baudelaire)." This piece signed and dated at the end, on p. [13]: "20 Septembre 1891 / Minuit. J'ai / passé toute la jour[née] / à travailler: je s[uis] / brisé. - "

Laid in, in the same volume:

L'incrédule

Holograph manuscript of this song for voice and piano, n.d., 3 p., in black ink on the recto sides of three single leaves of oblong 14-staff paper (blind stamp of Lard-Esnault). Lacking the piano accompaniment, except for the first two measures. At the top of p. [1] in Hahn's hand: "L'incrédule. - (Poésie de Paul Verlaine.)" Signed at the end.

FRKF 1111a–m

Les feuilles blessées

Holograph manuscript of the first eight songs of this cycle for voice and piano, on poems by Jean Moréas, 1901–06, 37 p. Notated in blue ink, with additional pencil markings, on the recto sides of sheets of tall 20-staff paper. On title page, in blue ink, in Hahn's hand: "Les feuilles mortes / Stances. / 1 Dans le ciel est dressé le chêne / séculaire - / 2 Encor sur le pavé ... / 3. Quand reviendra l'automne ... / 4. Belle lune d'argent ... / 5. Quand je viendrai m'asseoir ... / [in pencil:] 6. Eau printannière."

The manuscript comprises the following:

1. "'Encor sur le pavé sonne mon pas nocturne' / (Stances) / Jean Moréas," 4 p., numbered II at the top of p. 1, signed and dated July 1901 at the end; on a blank sheet bound after p. 4, autograph note by Henri Heugel [?]: "M. Douin / Manuscrit à graver avec grand soin / Hahn / 19.9.03."

2. "Dans le ciel est dressé le chêne séculaire - / (Jean Moréas)," numbered I at the top of p. [1], 4 p., signed and dated Hamburg, Aug. 1901 at the end.

3. "Quand reviendra l'automne avec / ses feuilles mortes ... / Jean Moréas," two manuscripts, the first numbered III at the top of p. [1], 3 p. each, both signed and dated at the end, the first 1903, the second Versailles, 1903.

4. "4 / Belle lune d'argent / (Les Stances) / Jean Moréas," with a dedication to Georges Vaudoyer on the title page, which is also signed and dated 1904, 5 p., signed and dated Paris, Munich, Versailles, 1904 at the end.

5. "Quand je viendrai m'asseoir ... / (Jean Moréas)," signed and dated 1904 on the title page, numbered V at the top of p. [1], 5 p., signed and dated Versailles, Oct. 1904 at the end.

6. "Eau printannière. / (J.M.)," initialed and dated 1905 on title page, 4 p., signed and dated Versailles, Nov. 1905 at the end.

7. "(Les Stances) / Donc vous allez fleurir encor ... / J.M.," numbered VII at the top of p. [1], 4 p., signed and dated 1906 at the end, with an autograph note by Heugel to Charles Douin, 2 March 1906, on the verso of p. 4 and with publisher number H. et Cie 22879 in an unidentified hand.

8. "Les feuilles mortes / Compagne de l'éther," initialed on the title page, 5 p., signed and dated 1906 at the end, with a note from Heugel to Douin, 18 April 1906, on the title page.

Bound in after "Compagne de l'éther":

> *Les feuilles blessées: stances de Jean Moréas. [...] IX. Pendant que je médite. Musique de Reynaldo Hahn*. Paris: Au Ménestrel, n.d. Folio, 4 p. Music publisher's number: H. & Cie 23,209.

Les feuilles blessées: stances de Jean Moréas. [...] X. Roses en bracelet. Musique de Reynaldo Hahn. Paris: Au Ménestrel, n.d. Folio, 2 p. Music publisher's number: H. & Cie 23,210. Dated at the end: "Constantinople / Printemps 1906."

Les feuilles blessées: stances de Jean Moréas. [...] XI. Aux rayons du couchant. Musique de Reynaldo Hahn. Paris: Au Ménestrel, n.d. Folio, 5 p. Music publisher's number: H. & Cie 23,211. Dated at the end: "Salzbourg / Août 1906."

Bound in the same volume:

L'obscurité / Choeur sans accompagnement

Holograph manuscript of this a cappella chorus on a text by Victor Hugo, 1897, 5 p., in blue ink on the recto sides of sheets of tall 18-staff paper (Joh. Aug. Böhme, Hamburg, No. 11), foliated by Hahn. Initialed and dated 1897 on the title page; signed and dated Hamburg, Oct. 1897 at the end. At the top of p. 1, dedication in pencil: "à Madame Duglé"; and, in blue ink, also in Hahn's hand: "L'Obscurité / Poésie de V. H. / (O. et B.)" The entirety of p. 1 is a pasted-on cancel.

Bound with:

L'obscurité: choeur à 4 voix mixtes sans accompagnement. Paroles de Victor Hugo. Musique de Reynaldo Hahn. Paris: Au Ménestrel, n.d. Folio, 4 p. Music publisher's number: H. & Cie 21,984. Dated 1897 at end. Presentation inscription on front wrapper: "à Madame Duglé, ce / choeur dont, grâce à elle, L'obscurité? / a cessé! / Respectueux et affectueux / hommage. / Reynaldo Hahn / 1904." The score also bears a printed dedication to Angèle Duglé, née Aubé, niece of Gounod, voice teacher and friend and patron of Hahn.

Bound in pink and grey marbled paper boards with corners and spine in red morocco; top edge gilt. Spine decorated with gold-tooled floral motifs. Also gold-tooled on spine: "Reynaldo / Hahn / Les / feuilles / blessées / Stances / de J. Moréas."

London, Sotheby's, 1 Dec. 1993, lot 395.
FRKF 1422a–d

Ivresse

Holograph music manuscript of this piano piece, 1906–09, 2 p. Notated in black ink on p. [2] and [3] of a bifolium of tall 18-staff paper (blind stamp of Lard-Esnault). On p. [1] in Hahn's hand: "Le rossignol éperdu. / Ivresse." Also on p. [1] copyright mention and music publisher's number (H. & Cie 29,177) marked in pencil. Manuscript epigraph at the top of p. [2]: "Noie mon souffle de ton haleine! que / mes lèvres s'écrasent à baiser tes mains! ... (Flaubert)." Initialed and dated at the end: "Paris 1906–Versailles 1909."

FRKF 1126

II. DIARIES

1897–99

Autograph diary for 1897–99, 144 p., in an exercise book, bound in beige buckram, written in black or blue ink and, occasionally, pencil.

The manuscript is abundantly corrected and marked up in ink or blue pencil. Two counts: 1 through [61], then, from the entry dated 12 Dec. 1897, 1 through 83. The initial entry is dated 15 April 1897, the last 7 Aug. [1899]. A blank, grey page is glued on the verso of p. 14 and another leaf of the same paper is inserted, on which the death of Hahn's father on 14 June 1897 is recorded. On the recto of the free front endpaper, in blue ink: "Vu."

Topics covered in the diary include: the death of Brahms (15 April 1897); Lamoureux and Colonne (17 April 1897); Gabriel Fauré (10 June 1897); Sarah Bernhardt (28 June 1897 and passim); Octave Mirbeau (26 July 1897); trips to Germany (Aug.–Oct. 1897, Feb.–March 1899); *Parsifal* (3 Sept. 1897); Marie van Zandt (3 Nov. 1897); Stéphane Mallarmé (3 Nov. 1897 and 10 Sept. 1898); Gustave Moreau (12 Dec. 1897 and 23 April 1898); the Dreyfus Affair (17 Jan. 1898, 7 Aug. 1899); Gounod's *Philémon et Baucis* (24 Feb. 1898); a trip to London (June–July 1898). There are references to Hahn's *Trio* (5 Aug. 1897), his *Nuit d'amour bergamasque* (25 Oct. 1897), *L'île du rêve* (22 March 1898), and *La carmélite* (2 June 1899).

A number of passages were published in the Juvenilia section of *Notes (journal d'un musicien)* (Paris: Librairie Plon, 1933).

Heinrich Schütz to Henry Miller, p. 88–89.
Paris, Laurin-Guilloux-Buffetaud-Tailleur (Drouot), 3 July 1985, lot 78.
FRKF 853

1901–02

Autograph diary concerning Sarah Bernhardt [1901]–02, 82 p., in an exercise book (17 × 21.5 cm) bound in limp light blue leather.

Only the first ten pages are paginated (with 2 leaves paginated 6 and 7) and written on both sides, after which the writing is almost entirely on the recto of each leaf until the entry dated 8 Sept., where both sides are used through the end.

The diary begins with a long entry dated "Mardi 31 Juillet." The first six pages of the notebook are in pencil, the rest is in blue or black ink, with abundant corrections (evidently made at a later stage). There are four blank leaves between the entries dated Aug. 4 and 6. On the recto of one of those leaves, two pencil drawings showing details of furniture; similarly, two blank leaves between the Aug. 12 and 14 entries, and a single blank leaf between Aug. 15 and 21. The last entry, left incomplete and cancelled in blue pencil, is dated "Dimanche 4 mai 1902." On the cover, in pencil, S.B. in capital letters. The diary includes an account of Sarah Bernhardt in Edmond Rostand's *L'Aiglon*.

Paris, Laurin-Guilloux-Buffetaud-Tailleur (Drouot), 3 July 1985, lot 77.
FRKF 852

III. LETTERS

To Céleste Albaret

[1922 Nov.] Regina Hotel, Paris, autograph telegram, 2 p., concerning Proust's last illness.

Paris, Ader-Picard-Tajan (Drouot), 22 Nov. 1985, lot 142.
FRKF 1384

To Gabriel Astruc

[1913 July 13*] 9, rue du Commandant Marchand [Paris]^S, ALS, 1 p.

Marburg, Stargardt, 26 Nov. 1985, lot 780.
FRKF 1150

To Emmanuel Bondeville

[1923? Toulon?] ALS on two postcards, concerning *Ciboulette*.

London, Sotheby's, 28 May 1986, lot 421.
FRKF 1130

To Albert Carré

[1900 Oct. 12, Paris*] ALS, 1 p., concerning *La carmélite*. Printed "Carte pneumatique fermée" on the address side.

[1906] Aug. 23, Munich, ALS, 4 p., concerning *Don Giovanni* and *Le nozze di Figaro*.

[ca. 1912 April 20] n.p., ALS, 11 p., on mourning stationery, concerning performances of *Don Giovanni*; mentions Jean Périer and *Pelléas*.

Paris, Laurin-Guilloux-Buffetaud-Tailleur (Drouot), 1 July 1986, lots 118–19, 121.
FRKF 1163–64, 1166

To General Cuny

[1927 May 17, Paris*] ALS, 1 p., conveying his regrets.

n.d., n.p., ALS, 3 p., addressed to "Mon colonel." Mentions Marguerite Herleroy.

Either Olivier Adolphe Amédée Cuny (1844–1929), named general in 1900, or Charles Cuny (1867–1931), named general in 1922.

FRKF 669

To Demetz

[1906 Feb. 18] n.p., ALS, 2 p., concerning "l'affaire du festival Mozart." Dated in an unidentified hand, possibly the recipient's.

Marburg, Stargardt, 26 Nov. 1985, lot 780.
FRKF 1150.5

To Édouard Detaille

n.d. [Paris] 9, rue Alfred de Vigny^S, ALS, 1 p., congratulations on a portrait.

n.d., n.p., ANS, 1 p., on mourning stationery, a message of congratulations. Written on the recto of a card.

Paris, Laurin-Guilloux-Buffetaud-Tailleur (Drouot), 12 June 1984, lot 222.
FRKF 476

To Maurice Donnay

The letters deal mostly with the operetta *Malvina*, premiered at the Gaîté-lyrique in March 1935, of which Donnay was one of the co-librettists. Though undated, they are from the years 1934–35.

ALS, Hotel Astoria & Arc Romain, Aix-les-Bains^S, 2 p.

Paris, Laurin-Guilloux-Buffetaud-Tailleur (Drouot), 3 July 1985, lot 79.
FRKF 854

ALS, n.p., 2 p.

Marburg, Stargardt, 5 March 1985, lot 88.
FRKF 813

ALS, Hotel Astoria & Arc Romain, Aix-les-Bains^S, 3 p.
ALS, n.p., 4 p.

Paris, Laurin-Guilloux-Buffetaud-Tailleur (Drouot), 19 March 1986, lot 60.
FRKF 1118

ALS, Les Fleurs, Bénerville^S, 3 p.

Marburg, Stargardt, 12 June 1986, lot 678.
FRKF 1329

To Louis Hennevé

[ca. 1914–18] n.p., ALS, 1 p., concerning a polemical exchange.

Paris, Laurin-Guilloux-Buffetaud-Tailleur (Drouot), 1 July 1986, lot 122.
FRKF 1167

To Marguerite Herleroy

[1920 Dec. 16, Paris*] ALS, 1 p.

[1922 Oct. 7, Paris*] ALS, 1 p., concerning the casting of Massenet's *Manon*. Recommends the baritone Robert Couzinou.

1924 Oct. 24, Paris, TLS, 1 p.

[1944?] Dec. 6., n.p., APCS, dated by the recipient.

[1944 Dec. 18, Monte Carlo*] APCS

1945 Jan. 11 [postmark undecipherable] APCS

The following letters have no year or no date

April 26, Versailles, ALS, 1 p.

Oct. 17, n.p., ALS, 4 p.

Oct. 28, n.p., ALS, 2 p., comments on her records.

Gd Hôtel Montré, Bordeaux^S, ALS, 3 p.

7, rue Greffuhle [Paris]^S ALS, 2 p.

no month, 15, 7, rue Greffuhle, APCS

n.p., ALS, 1 p.

ANS on both sides of a visiting card, accompanied by an undated autograph recommendation for Marguerite Herleroy, in draft and fair copy, 3 p. and 1 p., on stationery of Hôtel Regina, Paris.

Marguerite Herleroy (1883–[after 1944]), Antwerp-born soprano, a pupil of Pauline Viardot, and a longtime friend of Hahn. See also under Saint-Saëns.

FRKF 669

To Paul Hervieu

[1911 Feb. 15, Paris*] ALS, 1 p., concerning a legal case involving Hahn and Catulle Mendès.

n.d., 9, rue du Commandant Marchand [Paris]^S ALS, 1 p., a letter of congratulation.

Paris, Laurin-Guilloux-Buffetaud-Tailleur (Drouot), 19 March 1986, lot 61.

FRKF 1119

To Tristan [Klingsor]

n.d., 7, rue Greffuhle, VIIIe [Paris]^S ALS, 2 p., congratulating him on a publication.

London, Sotheby's, 28 May 1986, lot 421.

FRKF 1130.1

To Mme Henry Lapauze

[1911 Nov. 23, Paris*] ALS, 1 p., marked "pneumatique" in Hahn's hand on the address side.

[1911 Nov. 25, Paris*] ALS, 1 p.

[1911 Dec. 2, Paris*] ALS, 1 p.

[1913 July 8, Paris*] ALS, 1 p., on mourning stationery.

[1914 Nov.? 23, Paris*] ALS, 1 p.

n.d., Hôtel de Paris, Monte-Carlo^S, ALS, 2 p.

n.d., n.p., APCS, possibly sent from England; the card shows a reproduced painting of Dickens.

FRKF 731

To Madeleine Lemaire

n.d., 9, rue Alfred de Vigny [Paris] ALS, 2 p., concerning a recommendation made on her behalf to André Messager.

Marburg, Stargardt, 5–6 March 1985, lot 809.

FRKF 814

To Pierre Loti

[1899 Feb.?] Hamburg, ALS, 3 p., congratulating him on his military promotion.

Paris, Laurin-Guilloux-Buffetaud-Tailleur (Drouot), 1 July 1986, lot 117.

FRKF 1162

To Ernest Moret

1892

[Nov. 10, Paris*] ANS on both sides of a calling card (env)

1894

[Jan. 15] "Dimanche" [Paris*] ALS, 1 p. (env)

[Jan. 22, Paris*] ANS on one side of a calling card (env), with a short musical quotation and referring to César Cui's *Le flibustier*, premiered on that day at the Opéra-Comique.

[Jan. 31, Paris*] "Lundi," ALS, 2 p. (env)

[July 24] "Mardi," Paris*, ALS on embossed stationery, 3 p. (env)

[July 27] "Jeudi," Paris*, ALS, 1 p. (env)

[Nov. 12, Paris*] ALS, 1 p., "Télégramme," printed on the address side.

[Dec. 27] Paris*, ALS, 2 p. (env)

[Dec. 30] Paris*, ALS, 3 p. (env)

1895

[Jan. 2] Paris*, ALS, 3 p. (env)

July 16, Saint-Germain-en-Laye*, ALS, 8 p. (env), mentions Massenet.

[July 26] Saint-Germain-en-Laye*, ALS, 1 p. (env)

[Aug. 3] "Mon Logis" Rue de Poissy 69 bis St Germain-en-Laye^S but postmarked Paris, ALS, 3 p. (env), mentions Proust and Massenet.

Aug 10*, "Samedi," Dieppe, ALS, 4 p. (env), mentions Proust.

[summer?] "Vendredi," Beg Meil, ALS, 2 p., mentions Proust and Massenet.

Aug 11, Dieppe, ALS, 8 p. (env)

[Dec. 14] Paris*, ALS, 3 p. (env), mentions Proust and Saint-Saëns.

1896

[Feb. 21] Paris*, ALS, 2 p. (env)

[April 8] "Lundi soir," Paris*, ALS, 4 p. (env), concerning Massenet's *Cendrillon*.

[April 27?] Paris*, ALS, 2 p. (env)

[Aug. 3] Saint-Cloud*, ALS, 6 p. (env), mentions Édouard Risler and Charles Levadé.

[Paris?, postmark illegible] ALS, 3 p. (env), mentions Jacques-Émile Blanche and Proust's *Les plaisirs et les jours*.

Before 1898

n.p., ALS, 3 p. (env), refers to *L'île du rêve*.

1898

[Feb. 2] Paris*, ALS, 3 p. (env)

[Feb. 4] Paris*, ALS, 3 p. (env), concerning Saint-Saëns's *Ascanio*; with a musical quotation.

[June 18] "Lundi," Paris*, ALS, 2 p. (env), mentions Massenet and Robert de Montesquiou.

Undated

n.p., ALS, 2 p., concerning Messager's *Madame Chrysanthème*.

Ernest Moret (1871–1949) was a fellow student in composition in Massenet's class at the Conservatoire and a close friend of Hahn's at the time. In addition to the names mentioned, the correspondence discusses their work.

Paris, Couturier-Nicolaÿ (Drouot), 7 March 1985, lot 52.
FRKF 643

To Marcel Proust

n.d. [ca. 1921 May] n.p., ALS, 4 p. Kolb XIX: 281.

Paris, Ader-Picard-Tajan (Drouot), 24 Nov. 1986, lot 174.
FRKF 1181

To Ann Weil

1910 [23 March, Paris*] ANS, 1 p. (env). The note simply says: "Aimez Mozart!"

Paris, Laurin-Guilloux-Buffetaud-Tailleur (Drouot), 1 July 1986, lot 123.
FRKF 1168.1

Other letters

To a critic

[1908?] "Samedi," Hotel Cecil [London]^S, ALS, 11 p., concerning *Prométhée triomphant*.

Paris, Laurin-Guilloux-Buffetaud-Tailleur (Drouot), 1 July 1986, lot 120.
FRKF 1165

To a composer

n.y., Nov. 25, Paris, ALS, 4 p., on mourning stationery. On his music and the tendencies of modern music.

Paris, Laurin-Guilloux-Buffetaud-Tailleur (Drouot), 12 Dec. 1985, lot 104.
FRKF 947.2

To a friend

n.y., April 17, n.p., ALS, 2 p., concerning a female musician, probably a singer.

London, Sotheby's, 28 May 1986, lot 421.
FRKF 1130.2

To a musician

n.d., Paris, ALS, 2 p., concerning a rehearsal schedule.

Paris, Laurin-Guilloux-Buffetaud-Tailleur (Drouot), 1 July 1986, lot 123.
FRKF 1168

To a poet

n.d., n.p., ALS, 3 p., congratulating him on his poetry and feeling for music.

Paris, Laurin-Guilloux-Buffetaud-Tailleur (Drouot), 1 July 1986, lot 123.
FRKF 1168.2

To "Cher ami"

n.d., n.p., ALS, 2 p., concerning changes to be made to the text of *Malvina*. Possibly to Maurice Donnay.

Marburg, Stargardt, 5–6 March 1985, lot 808.
FRKF 813

To "Cher maître et ami"

[1911, Paris?] ALS, 3 p., enclosing an ALS to M. le Président, n.d., n.p., 3 p., concerning Catulle Mendès and *La fête chez Thérèse*.

Paris, Laurin-Guilloux-Buffetaud-Tailleur (Drouot), 12 Dec. 1985, lot 103.
FRKF 947.1a–b

To "Madame"

[1940?] 7, rue Greffulhe [Paris] VIIIe^S, ALS, 2 p. Mentions his departure for Arles to attend the Daudet festivities.

Paris, Laurin-Guilloux-Buffetaud-Tailleur (Drouot), 3 July 1985, lot 79.
FRKF 854.5

To a female recipient

[ca. 1909?] Hôtel Métropole, Brussels⁵, ALS, 2 p., concerning *Le bal de Béatrice d'Este*.

FRKF 732

IV. PRINTED MUSIC

La Fête chez Thérèse: Ballet-pantomime en deux actes de Catulle Mendès. Chorégraphie et Mise en Scène de Mme Stichel. Musique de Reynaldo Hahn. Partition piano seul. Paris: Au Ménestrel, Heugel & Cie, copyright 1910.

Folio, [8], 1–169 [+ 3] p. Music publisher's numbers: H. & Cie 25, 625–628; 24, 630–631. Stamp of Heugel on p. [5]. In original decorated wrappers. Inscribed by Reynaldo Hahn, on the front wrapper: "A Madame André Messager / son respectueux confrère et ami / Reynaldo Hahn / 1910."

FRKF 516

Portraits de peintres: pièces pour piano d'après les poésies de Marcel Proust. Dédiées à José Maria de Hérédia. 1. Albert Cuyp. 2. Paul Potter. 3. Anton Van Dyck. 4. Antoine Watteau. Paris: Au Ménestrel, Heugel et Cie., 1896.

In four fascicles, each in a blue wrapper with red and black lettering. Printed at the head of each fascicle: "A Madame Madeleine Lemaire." All folio: 5 p.; 3 p.; 3 p.; 5 p. Music publisher's numbers: H. & Cie 18,387–390.

The special edition, each piece preceded by a page (included or not in the pagination) with the relevant poem by Proust and a lithographed portrait of the painter, the four fascicles housed in a grey portfolio stamped with a blue and green floral pattern, with the title "Portraits de peintres" on the front board and tied with a pink ribbon. At the head of the first fascicle, presentation inscription by Proust [to Hahn?]: "Quis nobis Deus haec olia fecit? / Je le remercie bien respectueusement, avec la seule chose que je sache faire, avec des chansons / Son reconnaissant et dévoué ami / Marcel Proust."

FRKF 1366

A collection of printed songs

All are inscribed to Cléo de Mérode and bound in purple Annonay Paper boards and blue goatskin spine. On the recto of the front flyleaf, doodles, sketches of profiles, and note, apparently in Reynaldo Hahn's hand: "Recueil des stupidités / sorties de la plume inepte / de cet imbécile de / Rinalda [P crossed out] Kalm." Also bound with manuscripts of various songs, see above under Music manuscripts.

The collection comprises the following:

Si mes vers avaient des ailes! ... Poésie de Victor Hugo. Paris: G. Hartmann & Cie [1888?].

Folio, 3 p. Music publisher's number: G.H. & Cie 2007. Printed mention "[N°] 3. En MI (Ton original)" underlined in blue pencil on cover. Pencil annotations (fingering), possibly in Hahn's hand. Inscribed on cover: "à Cléo / avec toute mon / admiration. / R.H. / Juin 1891."

FRKF 1111q

Rêverie. Poésie de Victor Hugo. Paris: G. Hartmann & Cie [1888?].

Folio, 5 p. Printed on cover: "N° 2" [i.e. version in E-flat, the original key]. Music publisher's number: G.H. & Cie 2006. Inscribed on the title page: "à Cléo -. / admiration prosternée. / R.H. / Juin 1891."

FRKF 1111p

Mai. Poésie de François Coppée. Paris: G. Hartmann & C.ie [1889?].

Folio, 3 p. Music publisher's number: G.H. & Cie 2146 (2). Printed mention "2. En SOL BÉMOL (Ton original)" underlined in blue pencil on cover. Inscribed on cover: "à Mademoiselle Cléo de Merode. / homage sincère. / R.H. / Juin 1891."

FRKF 1111o

Aubade espagnole. Chantée dans L'Obstacle de M. Alphonse Daudet. Paris: G. Hartmann & C.ie [1890?].

Folio, 7 p. Music publisher's number: G.H. & Cie 2255. Printed mention "Édition originale pour choeur de voix d'hommes et ténor solo ou duo de ténor et baryton" underlined in blue pencil on cover. Inscribed on cover: "à Cléo / R.H. / Juin 1891."

FRKF 1111n

DANIEL HALÉVY (1872–1962)

Un épisode. Paris: Cahiers de la Quinzaine [1907].

[1]–72 [+ 14] p. No title page. The title is taken from the cover and the half-title on p. [11]. On the back cover: "sixième cahier de la neuvième série." In the original paper wrappers.

Paris, Laurin-Guilloux-Buffetaud-Tailleur (Drouot), 3 July 1985, lot 140.

FRKF 900.2

FROMENTAL HALÉVY (1799–1862)

I. MUSIC MANUSCRIPT

La tentation

Holograph manuscript, in full score, of this "opéra-ballet," ca. 1832, 383 p. Notated in black ink, with additional markings in red and blue pencil, on tall 20 or 22-staff paper. On the recto of the second folio, in pencil, possibly in a dealer's hand: "Halévy / La Tentation. / Opéra en 5 actes. / Partition d'orchestre. / compl. 380 ff. / (1832)." Initialed J.H. at the end.

Bound in bright green cloth, with dark green morocco corners and spine; on the spine, raised bands, author and title gold-tooled. Tipped in on the recto of the first folio, blank, TLS from Edward N. Waters, acting chief, Music Division, The Library of Congress, Washington, D.C., to Raymond Arthur Davies in Montreal, 1957 May 13, 1 p., concerning this manuscript.

La tentation, opéra-ballet by Halévy and Casimir Gide, libretto by Cavé and Coralli, was premiered at the Paris Opéra on 20 June 1832.

Heinrich Schütz to Henry Miller, p. 32–33.
FRKF 579

II. LITERARY MANUSCRIPT

"Notice sur la vie et les travaux de Mr. Paul Delaroche"

Holograph manuscript, n.d., 38 p., in black ink, with additions and corrections in pencil, mostly on individual bifolia, paginated [1], 2–25, 25 bis, 26–27, 29–31. There is no p. 28. Placed in an additional bifolium, serving as wrappers, with this note on the front, in the hand of Ludovic Halévy: "F. Halévy / notice sur Paul Delaroche / Manuscrit / Manuscrit de / mon oncle / Ludovic Halévy."

Not listed in Grove.
Paris, Oger-Dumont (Drouot), 14 Feb. 1985, lot 52.
FRKF 681.1

III. LETTERS

Unless otherwise noted, all of the letters in this section were purchased as one lot: Paris, Oger-Dumont (Drouot), 14 Feb. 1985, lot 52, and were accessioned as FRKF 681.

To Alexandrine Halévy

[1844] Aug. 4, Paris*, ALS, 4 p. (env), with messages from Flore and Mélanie Halévy.

Originally housed in a bifolium, serving as wrappers, annotated in the hand of Ludovic Halévy: "Halévy (Fromental) Août 1841." Not located in Galland.

1850 Jan. 2, n.p., ALS. Contains a verse epistle entitled "A Mr. de St. Georges." Galland, p. 103–05.

n.d., "Vendredi," n.p., ALS, 1 p. Galland, p. 245.

Also, seven short poems addressed to Alexandrine Halévy, the first one signed by Léonie Halévy, others in the hand of Fromental Halévy. Dated ca. 1842 in a note in the hand of Ludovic Halévy.

Alexandrine Halévy, née Lebas, known as Nanine, wife of Léon Halévy.

To Léon Halévy

[1847 Nov. 5] n.p., ALS, 2 p., dated in an unidentified hand. The letter begins on the last page of an undated ALS from Léonie Halévy. Galland, p. 57.

[1852 June 15] "Mardi," n.p., ALS, 1 p. (env). Dated by the recipient. Galland, p. 103.

n.y., "Samedi 30 8," n.p., ALS, 2 p. Suggested dating: 1847, 1852, or 1858. Galland, p. 242.

[1858 Oct. 28] "Jeudi 28," n.p., ALS, 1 p. Galland, p. 162.

The following letters are undated with no place mentioned:

ALS, 1 p. Galland, p. 243.

ALS, "Dimanche 28," 1 p. Not located in Galland.

ALS, "Mardi," 1 p. Galland, p. 243.

ALS, "Vendredi soir," 1 p. Galland, p. 243.

ALS, "Mercredi 13 J.," 1 p. Suggested dating: 1848. Galland, p. 243.

ALS, 2 p. Suggested dating: after 1855. Galland, p. 244.

ALS, "Samedi," Galland, p. 245.

ALS, "Mercredi," 1 p. Galland, p. 244.

Originally housed in two bifolia serving as wrappers, annotated in the hand of Ludovic Halévy, the first: "F. Halévy / quatre lettres à mon père / Et des petits vers de mon oncle et de / mes tantes Léonie, Flore et Mélanie / 1842"; the other: "F. Halévy / Lettres à mon père / IIIIIII = 7."

To Léonie Halévy

[1860 Aug.] "Lundi 13," n p., ALS, 3 p. Galland, p. 185.

To Ludovic Halévy

1853

March, n.p., ALS, 1 p. Galland, p. 107–08.

May 18, Paris, ALS, 3 p. Galland, p. 108–09.

June 17, Auteuil, ALS, 3 p., enclosing a letter of the same date to Madame Charles Rodrigues. Galland, p. 111–12.

July 2, Auteuil, ALS, 1 p. Galland, p. 113.

1854

[March] "Dimanche," n.p., ALS, 1 p. Galland, p. 118.

[Dec. 21] n.p., ALS, 1 p. Galland, p. 131.

1855

Jan. 14, n.p., ALS, 1 p. Galland, p. 131–32.

1856

Oct., n. p., ALS, 1 p. Galland, p. 142.

[Dec. 15] "Mercredi," n,p, ALS, 1 p. Galland, p. 143.

Dec., Conservatoire impérial de Musique, Paris[S], ALS, 1 p. Galland, p. 143.

1857

July, n.p., ALS, 1 p. Galland, p. 147.

Aug. 11, n.p., ALS, 1 p. Galland, p. 148.

Oct. 12, n.p., ALS, 1 p. Galland, p. 151.

1858

[March 20] "Samedi," n.p., ALS, 1 p. Galland, p. 157.

June 5, Paris, ALS, 1 p. Galland, p. 159.

July 2, n.p., ALS, 1 p. Galland, p. 159.

July 15, n.p., ALS, 1 p. Galland, p. 160.

July 17, n.p., ALS, 1 p. Galland, p. 161.

July 17, n.p., ALS, 1 p. Galland, p. 161.

Dec., n.p., ALS, 2 p. Galland, p. 163.

1860

July 11, n.p., ALS, 4 p. Galland, p. 176.

July 18, n.p., ALS, 2 p. Galland, p. 177.

Aug., n.p., ALS, 1 p. Not located in Galland.

Aug. 21, Tréport, ALS, 4 p. Galland, p. 185–86.

Sept. 2, Saint-Germain-en-Laye, ALS, 2 p. Not located in Galland.

Sept. 17, n.p., ALS, 1 p. Galland, p. 188–89.

Nov. 15, n.p., ALS, 2 p. Galland, p. 189–90.

1861

July 25, Bas-Prunay, par Marly-le-Roi, ALS, 3 p. Galland, p. 199–200.

No year

March 25, n.p., ALS, 2 p. Not located in Galland.

May 7, n.p., ALS, 1 p. Not located in Galland.

Many letters are evidently dated by Ludovic Halévy. Originally housed in three bifolia serving as wrappers, annotated in the hand of Ludovic Halévy, 1860.

To François-Joseph Heim

1844 Oct. 6, n.p., ALS, 1 p.

n.y., Dec. 17, n.p., ALS, 1 p.

1850 Feb. 1, n.p., ALS, 1 p., to Mrs. Heim.

The above letters in a folder annotated by Ludovic Halévy and in other, unidentified hands. None of the three letters located in Galland.

Undated

ALS, "Mardi soir," n.p., 1 p. Galland, p. 245.

ALS, "Mercredi," n.p., 1 p. Galland, p. 221. Attributed by Galland to "a colleague."

François-Joseph Heim (1787–1865), painter, member of the Académie des Beaux-Arts (elected 1829).

To Hippolyte Lebas

n.d., "Vendredi," n.p., ALS, 1 p. Galland, p. 246.

n.d., n.p., ALS, 1 p. Galland, p. 247.

Originally housed in a folder marked, in the hand of Ludovic Halévy: "F. Halévy / Lettre à M. Le Bas."

To Auguste Maquet

[1851 or 1856] April 1, ALS, 1 p. Galland, p. 248.

To Monsieur Potier

n.y. July 30, ALS, 1 p., recommendation for tenor Charles-Marie Wicard. Galland, p. 136.

Potier was chef du chant à l'opéra, Saint-Germain-en-Laye.

Marburg, Stargardt, 5–6 March 1985, lot 783.

FRKF 810.5

To Anatole Prévost-Paradol

1849 Aug. 16, n.p., ALS, 1 p., annotated by Ludovic Halévy. Galland, p. 69.

Anatole Prévost-Paradol (1829–70), son of Léon Halévy and Lucinde Paradol. Appointed minister of France in Washington, he committed suicide when France declared war on Prussia.

To Henri Vernoy de Saint-Georges

[late 1840] n.p., ALS, 1 p., probably to Saint-Georges according to Galland. Galland, p. 27–28.

[1849] Dec. 8, n.p., ALS, 5 p. Galland, p. 74–75.

1852 Dec. 5, n.p., ALS, 3 p. Galland, p. 104–05.

1854 Sept. 12, Paris, ALS, 1 p. Not located in Galland.

[1855 June 29] "Vendredi 29 J," Fromont, ALS, 8 p. Galland, p. 134–35.

n.d., "Jeudi 1er," n.p., ALS, 1 p. Galland, p. 273.

n.d., n.p., ALS, 1 p., concerning his nomination to the Legion of Honor. Not located in Galland.

n.d., n.p., ALS, 1 p., mentioning Scribe. Not located in Galland.

Originally housed in a bifolium, serving as wrappers, annotated in unidentified hands.

Henri Vernoy de Saint-Georges (1801–75), novelist and librettist, collaborator of Halévy for *L'artisan* (1827), *Le roi et le batelier* (1827), *Ludovic* (1833), *L'Éclair* (1835), *La reine de Chypre* (1841), *Le Lazzarone* (1844), *Le Val d'Andorre* (1848), *La fée aux roses* (1849), *Le Juif errant* (1852), *Le nabab* (1853), *Jaguarita l'Indienne* (1855), and *La magicienne* (1858).

To Monsieur [Seurre?]

1859 [Jan.] 5, n.p., ALS, 1 p. Apologizes for missing a meeting and conveys his wishes for the new year. Galland, p. 164.

Other letters

To "Mon cher confrère"

[1861] "Samedi 3 août," n.p., ALS, 1 p., concerning the Rome voyage of a certain Schwartz. Galland, p. 200.

FRKF 681

To "Mon cher confrère"

1861 Aug. 12, Institut impérial de France, Académie des Beaux-Arts, Paris^S, ALS, 2 p., concerning an article by Berlioz. Galland, p. 200–01.

Paris, Oger-Dumont (Drouot), 14 Feb. 1985, lot 41.
FRKF 689.5

To "Cher & excellent confrère"

n.d., "Lundi soir," n.p., ALS, 2 p., postponing a meeting. Galland, p. 221–22.

IV. MISCELLANEOUS

Clipping of an article from the *Revue politique et littéraire*, 1885 Aug. 10, with the text of a letter from Halévy to Adolphe Crémieux, 1861 April 14. With an annotation by Ludovic Halévy.

Paris, Oger-Dumont (Drouot), 14 Feb. 1985, lot 52.
FRKF 681

LÉON HALÉVY (1802–83)

Holograph poems

"Les larmes du cerf," n.d., n.p., 1 p.

"L'Ecrin," n.d., n.p., 1 p.

Paris, Oger-Dumont (Drouot), 14 Feb. 1985, lot 52.
FRKF 681.16

GEORGE FRIDERIC HANDEL (1685–1759)

Haec est Regina, HWV 235

Manuscripts, in the hands of copyists, one of them Giuseppe Antonio Angelini, of the following parts:

Concertino. Notated in black ink, in the hand of Angelini, on a gathering of two nested, stitched bifolia of oblong 9-staff paper. On the front of the outer bifolium, in Angelini's hand: "Antofona P.ª / Concertino / Hec est Regina / Del Sig. G.F. Hendel."

First violin. Notated in black ink on p. [2] and [3] of a single bifolium of tall 10-staff paper. On p. [1] in a copyist's hand: "Violino P.º / Concerto Grosso / Antif.ª P.ma / Hec est Regina Virginum / Canto solo / Con v-v. / Del Sg. G.F. Hendel."

First violin (second copy). Notated in black ink, in Angelini's hand, on p. [2] and [3] of a single bifolium of tall 9-staff paper. On p. [1] in Angelini's hand: "Violino P.º / Concerto Grosso / Antif.ª P.ª / Hec est Regina / Canto Solo Con v-v. / Del Sig. G.F. Hendel."

Second violin. Notated in black ink, in Angelini's hand, on p. [2] and [3] of a single bifolium of tall 9-staff paper. On p. [1] in Angelini's hand: "Violino S.º / Concerto Grosso / Antif.ª P.ª / Hec est Regina / Canto Solo Con v-v. / Del Sig. G.F. Hendel."

Second violin (second copy). Notated in black ink on p. [2] and [3] of a single bifolium of tall 10-staff paper. On p. [1] in a copyist's hand: "Violino 2.º / Concerto Grosso / Antif.ª P.ma / Hec est Regina Virginum / C. solo / Con v.v. / Del Sg. G.F. Hendel."

Viola. Notated in black ink, in Angelini's hand, on p. [2] and [3] of a single bifolium of tall 9-staff paper. On p. [1] in Angelini's hand: "Viola / Della Antif.ª P.ª / Hec est Reggina / Canto Solo Con VV. / Del Sig. G.F. Hendel." At the top of p. [2]: "Violetta."

Bass. Notated in black ink on p. [2] and [3] of a single bifolium of tall 10-staff paper. On p. [1] in a copyist's hand: "Contrabasso / Antif.ª P.ma / Hec est Regina Virginum / C. solo / Con v.v. / Del Sg. G.F. Hendel."

Soprano solo. Notated in black ink, in Angelini's hand, on p. [1] to [3] of a single bifolium of tall 9-staff paper. At the top of p. [1] in Angelini's hand: "Antif.ª P.ª Canto Solo Con Stro. Del S. Hendel." One correction in Handel's hand on p. [2].

Organ. Notated in black ink on p. [2] and [3] of a single bifolium of tall 10-staff paper. On p. [1] in a copyist's hand: "Organo / Antifona Prima / Canto solo con strumen.ti / Per La B.V. del Carmine / Del Sig. G.F. Hendel."

Laudate pueri, HWV 237

Manuscripts, in the hands of copyists, one of them Angelini, of the following parts:

Concertino. Notated in black ink on three gatherings of four nested, stitched bifolia of oblong 9-staff paper. On the front of the first gathering, in a copyist's hand: "Concertino / Laudate Pueri Dominum / A cinque con violini / violette e oubue / Del sig: G.F. Hendel"; at the top of the page, signature of E. Goddard and annotation in his hand: "From the Colonna Library / For the Festival of the Madonna del Carmine."

First oboe. Notated in black ink on a gathering of two nested, stitched bifolia and an additional bifolium of tall 9-staff paper. At the top of the first page, in a copyist's hand: "Ouboé Primo."

Second oboe. Notated in black ink on a single gathering of two nested, stitched bifolia of tall 10-staff paper. At the top of the first page, in a copyist's hand: "Ouboé S.º"

First violin. Notated in black ink on two gatherings of two and three nested, stitched bifolia of tall 9-staff paper. On the front of the first bifolium, in a copyist's hand: "Violino Primo / Laudate Pueri."

Second violin. Notated in black ink on two gatherings of two and three nested, stitched bifolia of tall 9-staff paper. On the front of the first bifolium, in a copyist's hand: "Violino S:º / Laudate Pueri."

Viola. Notated in black ink on a gathering of three nested, stitched bifolia of tall 9-staff paper. On the front of the first bifolium, in a copyist's hand: "Alto / Violetta."

Violoncello or viola da gamba. Notated in black ink on a gathering of three nested, stitched bifolia of tall 9-staff paper. On the front of the first bifolium, in a copyist's hand: "Tenore / Violetta Gª"

First soprano. Notated in black ink, in Angelini's hand, on two gatherings of two nested, stitched bifolia of tall 9-staff paper. At the top of the first page, in Angelini's hand: "Canto Pº"

Second soprano. Notated in black ink on a gathering of two nested, stitched bifolia of tall 10-staff paper. At the top of the first page, in a copyist's hand: "Sop:no Secondo Concertato."

Alto (first chorus). Notated in black ink, in Angelini's hand, on a gathering of two nested, stitched bifolia of tall 9-staff paper. At the top of the first page, in Angelini's hand: "Alto / P.º / Ch.º"

Tenor (first chorus). Notated in black ink, in Angelini's hand, on a gathering of two nested, stitched bifolia of tall 9-staff paper. At the top of the first page, in Angelini's hand: "Tenore / P.º / Ch.º"

Bass (first chorus). Notated in black ink on a gathering of two nested, stitched bifolia of tall 10-staff paper. At the top of the first page, in a copyist's hand: "Basso / P.º / Ch.º"

Soprano (second chorus). Notated in black ink on a gathering of two nested, stitched bifolia of tall 10-staff paper. At the top of the first page, in a copyist's hand: "Sop:no C:º Ripienº"

Alto (second chorus). Notated in black ink on a gathering of two nested, stitched bifolia of tall 9-staff paper. At the top of the first page, in a copyist's hand: "Alto S:º Choro."

Tenor (second chorus). Notated in black ink on a gathering of two nested, stitched bifolia of tall 9-staff paper. At the top of the first page, in a copyist's hand: "Tenore di Ripieno. / Sº Choro."

Bass (second chorus). Notated in black ink on a gathering of two nested, stitched bifolia of tall 9-staff paper. At the top of the first page, in a copyist's hand: "Basso S:º Rip."

Organ (continuo). Notated in black ink on two gatherings, stitched together, of two nested bifolia and a single bifolium of tall 10-staff paper. On the front page of the first gathering, in a copyist's hand: "Continuo / Organo. / Primo Choro / Laudate Pueri à cinque / con Ripieni Stromenti / Del Sig: G.F. Hendel / [in a different hand, possibly Handel's]: senza part."

Bass (continuo). Notated in black ink on two gatherings of three and two nested, stitched bifolia of tall 9-staff paper. On the front page of the first gathering, in a copyist's hand: "Violone / Continuo / Laudate Pueri / Organo Sº Chº"

Saeviat tellus inter rigores, HWV 240

Manuscripts, in the hands of copyists, one of them Angelini, of the "Concertino" and "Canto Solo" parts.

Soprano solo. Notated in black ink on two gatherings of two nested, stitched bifolia of tall 9-staff paper. The first gathering is in Angelini's hand. At the top of the first page, in Angelini's hand: "Motetto à Canto solo Con VV. Del S. Hendel." With a few corrections in Handel's hand.

Concertino. Notated in black ink on three gatherings of four, four, and two nested, stitched bifolia of oblong 9-staff paper. On the front page of the first gathering, in a copyist's hand: "Concertino / Motett"; also, signature of E. Goddard.

Heinrich Schütz to Henry Miller, p. 16–17.

Te decus virgineum, HWV 243

Manuscripts, in the hand of Angelini, of the following parts:

Concertino. Notated in black ink on p. [2]–[4] of a single bifolium of oblong 9-staff paper. On the front of the outer bifolium, in Angelini's hand: "Antif.ª 2.ª / Concertino."

First violin. Notated in black ink on p. [2] and [3] of a single bifolium of tall 9-staff paper. On the front of the outer bifolium, in Angelini's hand: "Violino P:mo / Concerto

Grosso / Antif.ª 2.ª / Te Decus Virgineum / Alto solo / Con V.V. / Del S.e G.F. Hendel."

First violin (second copy). Notated in black ink on p. [2] and [3] of a single bifolium of tall 9-staff paper. On p. [1] in Angelini's hand: "Violino P.º / Concerto Grosso / Antif.ª 2.ª / Te Decus Virgineum / Alto Solo Con VV. / Del Sig. G.F. Hendel."

Second violin. Notated in black ink on p. [2] and [3] of a single bifolium of tall 9-staff paper. On p. [1] in Angelini's hand: "Violino S.º / Concerto Grosso / Antif.ª 2.ª / Te Decus Virgineum / Alto Solo / con V.V. / Del S.e G.F. Hendel."

Second violin (second copy). Notated in black ink on p. [2] and [3] of a single bifolium of tall 9-staff paper. On p. [1] in Angelini's hand: "Violino Sº / Concerto Grosso / Antif.ª 2.ª / Te Decus Virgineum / Alto Solo Con V.V. / Del. S.e G.F. Hendel."

Violone [cello?]. Notated in black ink on p. [2] and [3] of a single bifolium of tall 9-staff paper. On p. [1] in Angelini's hand: "Violone / Antif.ª 2.ª / Alto Solo Con VV. / Te Decus / Del Sig. G.F. Hendel"

Bass. Notated in black ink on p. [2] and [3] of a single bifolium of tall 9-staff paper. On p. [1] in Angelini's hand: "Contrabassi / Antif.ª 2.ª / Alto Solo Con VV / Te Decus / Del Sig. G.F. Hendel."

Alto solo. Notated in black ink on p. [1]–[3] of a single bifolium of tall 9-staff paper. On p. [1] in Angelini's hand: "Alto Solo con VV. Antif.ª 2.ª Sig. Hendel."

Organ. Notated in black ink on p. [2]–[4] of a single bifolium of tall 9-staff paper. On p. [1] in Angelini's hand: "Organo / Antif.ª 2.ª / Te decus virgineum / Alto solo / con v.v. / Del S.e G.F. Hendel." Also, signature of E. Goddard and annotations in his hand: "From the Colonna Library / For the Festival of the Madonna del Carmine."

Also present is an original wrapper inscribed in an 18th-century hand: "Hendel / Antifona Pma = Hac est Regina - / Sda = Te decus virgineum / = Per la Madonna del Carmine." Also with the signature of E. Goddard and the note in his hand: "From the Colonna Library." Another annotation in a different, more recent hand: "Composed at Rome July, 1707. / For the Festival of the Madonna del Carmine."

HANDEL SCORES

Provenance: purchased at auction by the English collector Edward Goddard (1792–1878); sold at Sotheby's, London, on 4 Feb. 1878 (lot 325); purchased by the musicologist W.H. Cummings (1831–1915) and given by him to the singer Eva Nellie Brown; sold by her son Peter Plummer at auction in 1985.
London, Sotheby's, 29 Nov. 1985, lot 97.
FRKF 1085a–d

DUDLEY HARDY (1867–1922)

Pen-and-ink cartoon on thick paper (25 × 34 cm), signed in the lower left corner and dated [19]11, showing visitors at an art show. The caption, written in ink on a piece of paper pasted at the bottom, reads: "What do you say to this glorious landscape Mr. B?" "It isn't hung quite straight." Above the pasted-on paper, in pencil: "Very thin line down," and, in red pencil, "This drawing to be returned to D.H."

London, Christie's, 21 July 1981, lot 249.
FRKF 99

JOSEPH HAYDN (1732–1809)

"Specificazione di tutte Le Opere"

Autograph document, n.d. [but 1783 or after] 2 p., in black ink on both sides of a tall sheet of paper. The document lists 73 operas performed at Esterhaza. It includes works by Anfossi, Cimarosa, Gluck (*Orfeo*), Jommelli, Paisiello, Piccini, Salieri, Sarti, and, at the end of the list, numbered 63–73, eleven by Haydn himself: *Il mondo della luna*, *Acide*, *La canterina*, *Lo speziale*, *L'incontro improviso*, *Le pescatrice*, *L'infedeltà delusa*, *L'isola disabitata*, *La fedeltà premiata*, *Orlando paladino*, and *Armida*.

Hamburg, Hauswedell und Nolte, 24 Nov. 1983, lot 2317.
FRKF 240

HUGO VON HOFMANNSTHAL (1874–1929)

Elektra

Autograph manuscript, n.d., 68 p., in black ink on the recto sides of single sheets of laid paper.

On the title page, in Hofmannsthal's hand: "H. v. Hofmannsthal / Elektra / Tragödie in einem Aufzug / frei nach Sophokles. / Dramatis personae / Klytämnestra / Elektra / Chrysothemis / die Töchter / A'gisth / Orest / der Pfleger des Orest / [the next 2 added to the right:] die Vertraute / die Schleppträgerin / ein junger Diener / ein alter Diener / der Koch / die Aufseherin / Die Dienerinnen."

Foliated 1–7, a–i, k–p, α–τ, a.–i., k.–p., α–λ. The last foliation, cancelling an ε, may also be read as 2. There are two blank sheets at the end.

See Hugo von Hofmannsthal, *Sämtliche Werke* VII, *Dramen* 5, ed. Klaus E. Bohnenkamp and Mathias Mayer (Frankfurt: S. Fischer Verlag, 1997), in particular p. 317–18. *Heinrich Schütz to Henry Miller*, p. 94–95.
FRKF 341

Das Märchen der 672. Nacht

Autograph manuscript, 1895, 30 p., in black ink and black pencil on the recto sides (except for four folios) of individual leaves of laid paper.

> The manuscript is in two sections. The first part, foliated 1–3, is an outline of the plot. At the top of p. 1, in Hofmannsthal's hand: "19. April 1895 (Reconvalescenz nach der Influenza) / Das Märchen der 672ten Nacht." The second section is the draft of the story, foliated a.–e., [one unpaginated leaf], f., [α.]–[χ], [unpaginated leaf]. On title page, in Hofmannsthal's hand: "Das Märchen der 672ten Nacht / Von dem jungen Kaufmannssohn und seinen vier / Dienern"; dated April 1895 in the lower left corner.

See Hugo von Hofmannsthal, *Sämtliche Werke* XXVIII, *Erzählungen* 1, ed. Ellen Ritter (Frankfurt: S. Fischer Verlag, 1975), p. 201–06.
FRKF 226

Letter to "Herr Director"

> 1925 Sept. 10, Bad Aussee, ALS, 1 p., to the head of a cinematographic company, concerning the film version of *Der Rosenkavalier*.

Marburg, Stargardt, 5–6 March 1985, lot 201.
FRKF 800

ALFRED EDWARD HOUSMAN (1859–1936)

Letters to Charles Wilson

> 1927 March 12, Trinity College, Cambridge, ALS, 1 p. (env), concerning Housman's edition of Lucan.
>
> 1927 Aug. 7, Trinity College, Cambridge, ALS, 3 p. (env), declining to contribute his autograph.

See Christie's, New York, 17 May 1991, lot 121; see also Sotheby's, New York, 7 Dec. 1992, lot 127.
New York, Christie's, 22 Nov. 1985, lot 56.
FRKF 1268

Other letters

To Mrs. Burkitt
> 1933 May 19 [Cambridge] ALS, 2 p., declining an invitation at St. Homer.

To S.M. Ellis
> 1917 Nov. 7, Cambridge, ALS, 1 p. (env), declining a request to send a photograph.

To Mr. Wilson
> 1930 March 21, Cambridge, ALS, 1 p., declining an invitation.

To "Dear Madam"
> 1933 June 7, Cambridge, ALS, 1 p., in pencil, concerning his place of birth.

To "My dear Sir"
> 1920 Jan. 22, Cambridge, ALS, 1 p., a thank you note for a book.

From Philip Lee Warner to Grant Richards
> 1914 June 30, London, TLS, 1 p., concerning proofs of *A Shropshire Lad*. Annotated by A.E. Housman.

All the above from the collection of Perry Molstad. Accompanied by a typed note from G.F. Sims to Molstad 1961 June 13, quoting to him letters from Housman to Mrs. Grant Richards.

See Christie's, New York, 7 June 1990, lot 59; Sotheby's, New York, 7 Dec. 1992, lot 126.
New York, Sotheby's, 16 May 1984, lot 644.
FRKF 314

GEORGES HÜE (1858–1948)

Note

> ANS to an unidentified female recipient on one side of a card, n. d. 7, rue Volney [Paris]^S, concerning a rehearsal at the Opéra.

Paris, Laurin-Guilloux-Buffetaud-Tailleur (Drouot), 1 July 1986, lot 118.
FRKF 1163.5

JEAN HUGO (1894–1984)

Letter from Jacques Lemarchand

1924 June 23, Bernard Grasset, Éditeur, Paris[S], TLS, 1 p., concerning Radiguet's novel *Le bal du comte d'Orgel*.

FRKF 1245.A09

VALENTINE HUGO (1887–1968)

Album amicorum

A small oblong album, bound in red boards, comprising 40 unpaginated sheets of 6-staff music paper (15 × 9 cm), 15 of which are inscribed, preceded by 4 blank sheets and followed by 3 blank sheets. In a red slipcase.

At the bottom of the verso of fourth blank sheet, facing the first page [1] of music paper, date (possibly in Jean Cocteau's hand?): "1er mai 1919."

Contents by page:

[1] Signatures of Jean Cocteau, Erik Satie, Albert Thomas, and André Mater, and date (in Satie's hand): "7 Août 1919."

[3] Pen-and-ink drawing of Georges Auric's profile by Cocteau, dated 29 May 1919.

[7] Music manuscript, signed G[eorges] A[uric], comprising 12 measures notated on single staves, to words [by Cocteau] beginning "Coupe à ta muse les cheveux Picasso."

[9] "Initiales," holograph 4-line poem by Raymond Radiguet, signed R.R. and dated May 1920.

[11] 5 measures of music by Auric, notated in pencil on a single staff, unsigned, n.d.

[13] "théâtre," holograph 4-line poem by Cocteau, unsigned. See *Oeuvres poétiques complètes*, p. 204–05.

[15] Profile of Auric by Cocteau, n.d., unsigned.

[17] Drawing by Cocteau showing a hand and a bilboquet, with a holograph 4-line poem, titled underneath "Mr Mater jouant au / bil / bo / quet le Dimanche," unsigned, n.d. Not located in *Oeuvres poétiques complètes*.

[19] "Marie Laurencin," 8-measure musical quotation by Auric on single staves, set to words [by Cocteau] beginning "Entre les fauves et les cubists," unsigned, 25 May, n.y. The song was published in *Huit poèmes de Jean Cocteau* (1918).

[21] and [23] "La carpe," 8-measure musical quotation by Francis Poulenc, in blue ink on 2 staves (first 3 measures) for piano, followed by a vocal line on a single staff, signed and dated 30 July, n.y. From *Le Bestiaire, ou Le Cortége d'Orphée*; Schmidt 15a.

[25] "je suis un menteur" written ca. 50 times in an unidentified hand in microscopic characters, unsigned, dated 20 Aug. 1919.

[29] Drawing signed Jean Hugo [but possibly by Cocteau] with the inscription (possibly in Cocteau's hand) "Je vous aime de toute mon âme belle espagnole," n.d.

[33] "Adieu, New-York!" music manuscript by Auric, comprising 23 measures notated on single staves, marked etc. at the end, unsigned, n.d.

[36] Unattributed drawing of a woman with the caption in pencil (not in Cocteau's hand): "Cocteau et la belle Rousse."

Accompanied by the following documents:

ALS from Auric to René Berthelot, 1970 Feb. 22, Berghotel Prätschli, Arosa[S], 2 p. (env)

ALS from Darius Milhaud to René Berthelot, 1970 Feb. 28, 10 Boulevard de Clichy Paris XVIII[S] (embossed), 1 p. (env), with a typed questionnaire with Milhaud's responses.

ALS from Jean Hugo to [René Berthelot?] 1981 Oct. 4, Lunel, 2 p.

ALS from Jean Marais to [René Berthelot?] 1983 Oct. 31, n.p., 1 p.

Printed invitation to the funeral of Auric on 22 Nov. 1983.

Paris, Ader-Picard-Tajan (Drouot), 19 June 1984, lot 314.
FRKF 534

VICTOR HUGO (1802–85)

Album

Album containing manuscripts by Hugo, letters to and from him, and other documents relating to him. Bound in red and green marbled paper boards with red morocco corners and spine; gold-tooled on the spine: "Dossier / sur / Victor / Hugo."

The contents of the album are as follows:

Hugo, ALS to "Monsieur le rédacteur de l'Indépendance Belge," 1862 Jan. 21, Hauteville House [Guernsey], 2 p., on the death penalty and refuting the authorship of verse published in the Belgian journal and attributed to him.

—, ALS to an unidentified correspondent, 1868 May 17, Hauteville House, 1 p., concerning his dog named Sénat.

La voix de Guernesey, proof of this poem in 8 parts, with autograph corrections [1867?], 1 p., inscribed on the verso: "A mon excellent ami / M. Eug. Van Bemmel / Victor Hugo" and dated Hauteville House, Nov. 1867.

"Hugo, Le Comte Victor - de l'Académie française." Unidentified manuscript in black ink (Hugo's name in red ink) on the first page of a bifolium. The text is a general, somewhat critical appreciation of Hugo and quotes a 4-line parody of his poetic style at the end.

Béranger, Pierre Jean de, ALS to Hugo, 1830 March 15, n.p., 4 p., concerning *Hernani*.

Joanny, Jean-Baptiste, known as Bernard Brisebarre, ALS to Hugo, 1830 June 6, n.p., 1 p., concerning *Hernani*. The Comédie-Française actor Joanny created the part of Don Ruy Gomez de Silva in Hugo's play.

Hugo, ALS to the Proviseur of the Collège de Bourbon, [1830 14 April*] n.p., 1 p., concerning a performance of *Hernani*.

—, ALS to Louis Boulanger [1828 Oct. 11, Paris*], 3 p. Mentions "Le pacha," from *Les Orientales*.

—, ALS to an unidentified poet, n.y. April 21, Hauteville House, 2 p., congratulating the recipient on his book.

—, ALS to Astolphe de Custine, n.y. May 11, Paris, 7 p., concerning Naples; also mentions Custine's companion Sainte-Barbe.

La fin de Satan. Autograph fragment, n.d., 1 p., 85 lines in black ink on a long, narrow piece of paper, beginning with the line "Cependant il était question dans la ville …" from "Celui qui est venu."

Unidentified prose fragment, possibly for *Post-scriptum de ma vie*, n.d., 1 p., in brown ink on a long, narrow sheet of paper, beginning with the sentence "On abat un rocher, on abat un chêne, on abat un chien." Together with a note in an unidentified hand, concerning the two manuscripts above, 1 p.

Hugo, ALS to Adolphine Bonnet, [1864*] May 15, H[auteville] H[ouse], 1 p. (env), together with an ANS from Hugo to the same, n.d., and a small dried bough sewn to a piece of paper; and three envelopes addressed to her, posted from Guernsey but not in Hugo's hand.

Two envelopes, mailed from Guernsey, one of them in Hugo's hand, addressed to Emmanuel Baratel in Villefranche de Lauraguais, postmarked 1862 and 1865.

Hugo, ALS to M. Plon, 1868 Dec. 6, H[auteville] H[ouse], 1 p., concerning songs composed by Alphonse Dami to the words of "Autre guitare" ("Comment, disaient-ils") from *Les rayons et les ombres* and "Autre chanson" ("L'aube naît") from *Les chants du crépuscule*.

—, ALS to his son Charles Hugo, [1846*] Sept. 26, Villequier, 4 p.

Maréchale Oudinot, duchess of Reggio, LS to Jacques-Alexandre Bernard Law, marquis de Lauriston, 1821 April 30, Paris, 1 p., requesting a pension for Hugo on behalf of the Duchesse de Berry. Docketed by Lauriston and with indications, in a secretarial hand, that the request has been granted.

Les contemplations. Autograph manuscript fragment from the poem "Pleurs dans la nuit," in black ink on a short piece of paper; 3 lines beginning "Voyez des longs fusils …"

Quatre-vingt-treize. Manuscript fragments in black ink on a yellow and a white sheet of paper. The fragment on the yellow sheet begins with the words "Ne sachant d'où lui vient ce secours …" ("Radoub," Part 3, Book 4, 10); the other begins "Voici le trajet que suivait la mèche …" ("Ce que fait l'Imânus," Part 3, Book 2, 14). With an autograph transcription in an unidentified hand.

Dieu. Manuscript fragment in black ink on a small piece of paper, comprising 6 lines beginning "Oui, je te le redis, calcule, additionne …" from "Les voix." With 2 additional lines, beginning "Est-ce [Dieu]"? on the verso. With an autograph transcription in an unidentified hand.

La fin de Satan. Autograph fragment from "Ceux qui parlaient dans le bois," on the recto of a small piece of thin blue paper, comprising 10 lines beginning "Chaque jour rayonnant/éclatant qui passe dans/sous les cieux …"

[*Théâtre en liberté*]. Fragment, possibly for *La forêt mouillée*, in black ink on a small piece of paper, comprising 7 lines beginning "Il dit aux fleurs …"

Unidentified fragment, written in black ink on a small piece of paper, beginning "Je me tâte, je me pince …" On the accompanying transcription: "Gavroche"

Hugo, ALS to an unidentified correspondent, n.y., Dec. 26, n.p., 2 p., a recommendation for Alphonse Petit.

—, ALS to an unidentified composer, 1860 July 2, H[auteville] H[ouse], 1 p., giving his permission to set the poem "Les enfants pauvres" from *L'art d'être grand-père*.

"Au peuple." Printed proclamation, dated Jersey, 31 Oct. 1852 and signed Victor Hugo, Fombertaux, Philippe Faure at the bottom, 1 p. Annotation in Hugo's hand on the verso.

"Victor Hugo," lithograph by Delpech, n.d. 18 × 25 cm

"Victor Hugo," lithograph, signed Alophe, n.d., Paris: Aubert (Galerie de la Presse, de la Littérature et des Beaux-Arts). 21 × 28.5 cm

"Victor Hugo en 1830," unidentified lithograph. 22 × 27.5 cm

"V. Hugo," lithograph by Pollet after Deveria. Paris: Blaisot, n.d. 21 × 19.5 cm

[Victor Hugo], lithograph by Masson. Paris: Chardon aîné et Aze, n.d. Accompanied by 2 lithographically reproduced manuscript lines: "Haine vigoureuse de l'anarchie / tendre et profond amour du peuple / Victor Hugo." 16 × 24 cm

"V. Hugo," copperplate engraving by Leguay. Paris: Sartorius, n.d. 8.5 × 13.5 cm

[Victor Hugo], lithograph by Chenay, accompanied by the lithographically reproduced caption in Hugo's hand: "Victor Hugo / Hauteville House / janvier 1860." 7 × 11 cm

[Mme Paul Meurice], sepia carte-de-visite photograph.

[Victor Hugo in the late 1870s?], carte-de-visite photograph by J. Maes.

[Victor Hugo in the late 1860s?], carte-de-visite photograph (oval portrait) by Pierre Petit.

[Victor Hugo in the late 1860s?], carte-de-visite photograph (rectangular portrait) by Pierre Petit.

[Victor Hugo and his grandaughter], carte-de-visite photograph by Garnier Arsène, Guernsey.

[Victor Hugo and his two grandchildren], carte-de-visite photograph.

Large sepia photograph of Hugo and his family at Hauteville House, showing Paul Meurice, Lockroy, and Juliette Drouet, in addition to Alice, Georges, and Jeanne Hugo. 24 × 17 cm

[Victor Hugo in the late 1870s], sepia postcard photograph by Nadar.

Envelope of a letter addressed by Hugo to Amédée Méreaux, 1870 July 4, Guernesey*.

Les hommes d'aujourd'hui. Dessins de Gill. Victor Hugo. No 1. Paris, n.d. [1878?] 4 p. Text by Félicien Champsaur, color portrait of Hugo by Gill on cover.

Centenaire de Victor Hugo 1802–1902. Printed subscription bulletin for the commemorative plaquette by René Rozet published by Christofle.

Paris, Laurin-Guilloux-Buffetaud-Tailleur (Drouot), 29 March 1985, lot 52.

FRKF 961

Letter to an unidentified recipient

1869 May 7, n.p., ALS, 2 p., concerning *L'homme qui rit*.

Paris, Charavay, 18 Dec. 1985, lot 1.

FRKF 937

Profils et grimaces

Vacquerie, Auguste (1819–95). *Profils et grimaces*. Paris: Michel Lévy frères, éditeurs, 1856.

8vo. [4], [1]–328 [+2] p. Bound in green morocco, with a rectangular pattern of blind-tooled double-fillets on both boards. All edges gilt. Raised bands, and author and title on spine. Multicolored marbled paper endpapers; bookplate of Paul Meurice. On first page, blank, presentation inscription: "Offert respectueusement / à Madame / Paul Meurice. / Auguste Vacquerie." Autograph typographical corrections 4, 11, 12, 63, 67, 282, 293, and 322.

One of the extra-illustrated copies, with the following material, by page number. The photographs are pasted in.

Title page, verso: photograph of Mme Paul Meurice. 7 × 9.3 cm

Folio inserted after the title page: autograph manuscript, signed, of "A Madame Paul Meurice." a 6-stanza poem, signed and dated at the end: "Auguste Vacquerie / Guernesey, Hauteville-house, 9 juillet 1856."

1: photograph with the manuscript caption: "V.H. / par A.V." 7.2 × 8 cm

9: photograph with the manuscript caption: "Marine-terrace. / par Ch. Hugo" 8.8 × 6.7 cm

10: photograph with the manuscript caption: "La main de Victor Hugo. / par A. V." 7.1 × 6.4 cm

19: photograph with the manuscript caption: "Le bas de Hauteville-house / A.V." 7.4 × 4.1 cm

20: photograph with manuscript caption: "le général / Mezzaros / proscrit / hongrois. / pelisse donnée / par le / sultan. / C[harles] H[ugo]." 6.8 × 7.7 cm

24: bound opposite: original pen-and-ink drawing by Victor Hugo: "Bossue chinoise." 7.7 × 10.7 cm

28: photograph with manuscript caption "Rochers de la grève de Jersey / C.H." 6.2 × 8 cm

29: photograph with manuscript caption "A[uguste] V[acquerie] / par A[uguste] V[acquerie]." 6.4 × 7.7 cm

34: bound opposite: original pen-and-ink drawing by Victor Hugo: "Vous voilà donc! idole de mon âme!" 5.5 × 8.5 cm

36: photograph of Vacquerie, signed "A.V." 4.5 × 6.4 cm. Underneath, manuscript note, underlined: "(nous ressemblons à un homme qui a la colique.)"

37: photograph with manuscript caption: "Le petit Le Flo / par A.V." 7.4 × 7.6 cm. Underneath, manuscript note: "(Alfred de Musset devant les critiques.)"

53: photograph [La petite Le Flo?]. 6 × 6 cm. Underneath, manuscript note: "(Alfred de Musset devant le public.)"

54: photograph with the manuscript caption: "A. V. / par A. V." 6.9 × 7.8 cm

61: photograph with manuscript caption, "La serre de Marine-terrace. — par A.V." 7 × 9.7 cm

62: photograph with manuscript caption: "V.H. / par A.V." 3.4 × 3.4 cm

62: bound opposite, untitled original pen-and-ink drawing by Victor Hugo, showing two figures, one of them seated, holding a whip [?], the other a hunchback, bowing his head. 8.8 × 8 cm

67: photograph with manuscript caption, "ANSON, barbier de V.H. à Jersey. — par A.V." 6 × 5.8 cm

68: bound opposite: original pen-and-ink drawing by Victor Hugo: "individu qui fait des visites." 7.6 × 9.5 cm

73: photograph with manuscript caption: "Une ferme de Jersey / par Ch. H." 7.4 × 9 cm

74: photograph with manuscript caption: "V.H. / A.V." 5.5 × 6 cm. Manuscript note underneath: "(Effet de [printed title: PHEDRE] sur le génie.)"

74: bound opposite: original pen-and-ink drawing by Victor Hugo: "Hippolyte." 11.5 × 9.8 cm

76: bound opposite: original pen-and-ink drawing by Victor Hugo: "le cerf d' Hippolyte." 11 × 7.2 cm

78: photograph of a cat asleep in front of a window, with manuscript caption: "Effet de Phèdre sur les bêtes. — A.V." 9.5 × 6.3 cm

79: photograph with manuscript caption: "Madame Victor Hugo. / A.V." 5.2 × 5 cm

84: photograph with manuscript caption: "Les petits Le Flo / C.H. Jersey." 7.4 × 7.4 cm. Underneath, manuscript note: "(Emmeric se rappelle une petite fille avec laquelle il a été élevé.)"

85: photograph showing Victor Hugo leaning against a gate, with manuscript caption: "V.H. / C.H." 7.2 × 7.2 cm

89: photograph [of Hugo?]. 6 × 6 cm.

90: photograph of Charles Hugo with manuscript caption: "C.H. / A.V." 3 × 5 cm

92: photograph with manuscript caption: "Mad. V.H. / A.V." 2 × 2.8 cm

93: photograph with manuscript caption: "Léopoldine — dessin d'Édouard Dubufe — phot. par A.V." 5 × 5.6 cm

95: octagonal photograph of Charles Hugo with manuscript caption: "Charles / par A.V." 3 × 3.5 cm, partly cropped by the binder.

96: photograph of Adèle Hugo with manuscript caption: "Mlle Adèle Victor Hugo. — par Aug. V." 2 × 3 cm

97: bound opposite: original pen-and-ink drawing by Victor Hugo: "jeune soldat." 5.2 × 8 cm

98: photograph with the manuscript caption: "La terasse de Hauteville-house. (Ch. – V.H. – Victor.) par A.V." 7.3 × 6.1 cm

99: photograph with the manuscript caption: "Ce que Victor Hugo, Charles et Victor regardent. – A.V." 9.4 × 6.5 cm

100: photograph with the manuscript caption: "A. V. à sa fenêtre de Marine-terrace. / – A. V." 7.6 × 8.2 cm

101: photograph with the manuscript caption: "Ce qu' Auguste Vacquerie regarde. / – A.V." 8.7 × 7.1 cm

102: photograph with manuscript caption: "Victor Hugo et Charles faisant des armes. — A.V." 10 × 7.2 cm

107: photograph with the manuscript caption: "Restes d'un château. Jersey. / – par Ch. H." 9.3 × 9.9 cm

108: photograph with the manuscript caption: "Eugène Delacroix. / A.V." 4.2 × 4.8 cm

110: photograph with manuscript caption: "Le Rocher des Proscrits Jersey — par C.H." 8 × 10.5 cm, caption slightly cropped by the binder.

111: photograph with manuscript caption: "V.H. dans / le Rocher / des Proscrits. / C.H." 6.7 × 8.1 cm

114: photograph with manuscript caption: "La chambre de V. H. à Marine-terrace." 7.9 × 5.5 cm

115: photograph with manuscript caption: "A. V. / La main de Mad. V. H." 7.8 × 5.7 cm

119: photograph with manuscript caption: "V. H. sur la grève. Jersey. / – C. H." 7.2 × 8.8 cm

120: photograph with manuscript caption: "Costume / de paysan / hongrois. / Sandor / Téléki. / par C.H." 7 × 8 cm

123: photograph of Vacquerie in profile, signed "A.V." 7.5 × 5 cm

124: photograph of Victor Hugo seated, with manuscript caption "V.H. / C.H." 7.2 × 8 cm

129: photograph of a landscape. 3 × 2.9 cm

130: photograph with the manuscript caption: "Le jardin voisin. Jersey. / A. V." 8.8 × 7.7 cm

132: bound opposite: autograph manuscript by Vacquerie, beginning with the words "L'amour du fils contrariant la haine du père …" [see p. 130 of *Profils et grimaces*] concluding "c'est tout ce qu'Hémon avait dans le coeur" [p. 135], 8 pages (recto sides only), the text cropped by the binder at the bottom of the page.

135: photograph of Paul Meurice, with manuscript caption: "P.M. / A.V." 4.5 × 5.5 cm

136: photograph with the manuscript caption: "Dessin d'Eugène Delacroix. / Photographié par Auguste Vacquerie" 5.6 × 5.9 cm

137: photograph with the manuscript caption: "Dessin de Victor Hugo / Photographié par Auguste Vacquerie" 6.2 × 6.8 cm

138: photograph with the manuscript caption: "Paul Meurice. / par Aug. Vacquerie" 6.7 × 7 cm

140: photograph of Vacquerie, with manuscript caption: "A.V. par C.H." 2.3 × 5 cm

141: photograph of Mrs. Hugo seated in the garden, with manuscript caption: "Mad. V.H. par A.V." 2.8 × 6.1 cm

154: photograph of Adèle Hugo with an umbrella, with manuscript caption: "Mlle Adèle Victor Hugo par C.H." 6.1 × 7.6 cm

155: photograph with manuscript caption: "Madame / Paul / Meurice. / Jersey / 1853 / A.V." 6.5 × 8.1 cm

161: photograph of rocks. 4 × 4.5 cm

162: photograph with manuscript caption: "Jersey. / C. H." 7 × 8 cm

165: photograph of a rock. 5 × 5.3 cm

166: photograph of Victor Hugo (right profile), with manuscript caption: "V.H. / A.V." 7 × 7.6 cm

177: photograph of the house from the garden side, with manuscript caption: "Hauteville-house / par A.V." 6.3 × 9.6 cm

178: photograph with manuscript caption: "Le jardin de Marine-terrace, un jour qu'il tombait de la tragédie. A.V." 8.6 × 7 cm

181: bound opposite, original pen-and-ink drawing by Victor Hugo: "BONSOIR." 8 × 11.6 cm

182: photograph with the manuscript caption: "Eug. Delacroix. / Aug. Vacquerie." 4.4 × 4.5 cm

194: photograph of Vacquerie (left profile), with manuscript caption "A.V. par A.V." 7 × 9 cm

195: photograph of Victor Hugo (right profile, in front of a curtain), with manuscript caption "V.H. par A.V." 7.5 × 8 cm

206: photograph of rocks. 2.5 × 2.6 cm

207: photograph of Vacquerie wearing a cap. 7.8 × 6.6 cm. Underneath, manuscript note: "(Costume d'un lettré prospère.)"

208: bound opposite, original pen-and-ink drawing by Victor Hugo: "CONSERVATOIRE / A tous les coeurs bien nés que la patrie est chère!" Drawn on the back of an envelope. 8.5 (at its widest) × 12.2 cm

215: photograph of Victor Hugo with his hand behind his head, signed "par C.H." 7 × 9.5 cm

216: photograph of Mrs. Hugo seated, with manuscript caption: "Mad. V.H. / par C.H." 38 × 40 cm

216: bound opposite, untitled original pen-and-ink drawing by Victor Hugo, representing a seated character holding out enormous hands toward another, angry-looking character. 14 × 7.5 cm

226: photograph of Mrs. Hugo reading, with manuscript caption: "Madame Victor Hugo — A.V." 7.4 × 9.1 cm

227: photograph of Charles Hugo, with manuscript caption: "C.H. / par A.V." 6.5 × 8 cm

243: photograph of Vacquerie with manuscript caption: "A.V. / A.V." 7.2 × 6.5 cm. Cropped by the binder.

244: photograph of Victor Hugo seated, with his hand under his chin, with manuscript caption: "V.H. / A.V." 1.6 × 4.6 cm

248: photograph with manuscript caption: "V.H. / dans le / Rocher / des / Proscrits. / C.H." 6.8 × 8 cm

250: photograph of leaves. 6.8 × 3.3 cm

251: photograph of Mrs. Hugo (left profile), with manuscript caption: "Mad. V.H. / A.V." 4.4 × 4.8 cm

253: group photograph, with manuscript caption: "Hauteville-house. (Mad. V.H. - Victor - Charles - V.H.) par A.V." 7 × 9.3 cm

254: photograph with the manuscript caption: "Léopoldine H. (d'après une peinture de L. Boulanger.) A. V." 4.7 × 6.3 cm

255: photograph of Adèle Hugo, with manuscript caption: "Adèle H. (d'après une peinture de Boulanger) A.V." Another line of text was cropped by the binder. 2.5 × 4 cm

256: photograph of Victor Hugo with his hand in his hair, with manuscript caption: "V.H. / (Rocher / des / Proscrits) / C.H." 7 × 8 cm

264: photograph with manuscript caption: "Porte de la serre de Marine-terrace — A.V." 7 × 2.5 cm

265: oval photograph of Mrs. Hugo in the greenhouse, with manuscript caption: "Madame V.H. / par / Auguste V." 6 × 7.5 cm

273: photograph with the manuscript caption: "Charles et Victor. A. V." 6.4 × 7.7 cm

274: photograph with the manuscript caption: "Madame de Girardin. / Jersey. 1853. C. H." 6.7 × 7.5 cm

280: bound opposite: original pen-and-ink drawing by Victor Hugo: "la tragédie." 5 × 10 cm

281: photograph of Victor Hugo seated, with manuscript caption: "Victor / A.V." 6 × 6.2 cm

282: photograph of Paul Meurice, with manuscript caption: "Paul M. / Auguste V." 5 × 6.7 cm

284: photograph with manuscript caption "A.V. / A.V." 4.5 × 4.5 cm

285: photograph of Mrs. Vacquerie, with manuscript caption: "La mère de / l'auteur / A.V." 6.6 × 7.9 cm

317: bound opposite: original pen-and-ink drawing by Victor Hugo: "mathématicien." 5.8 × 11 cm

325: photograph with the manuscript caption: "Ernest Lefevre. / par Aug. Vacquerie." 6.9 × 8 cm

[326]: photograph with the manuscript caption: "A. V. / par / A.V." 7 × 9.5 cm

See Antoine Coron, ed., *Des livres rares depuis l'invention de l'imprimerie* (Paris: Bibliothèque nationale de France, 1998), p. 240–41, and Françoise Heilbrun and Danielle Molinari, eds. *Victor Hugo: photographies de l'exil* (Paris: Musée d'Orsay and Maison de Victor Hugo, 1998), especially p. 90–94.
Heinrich Schütz to Henry Miller, p. 50–51.
Paris, Ader-Picard-Tajan (Drouot), 20 March 1985, lot 69.
FRKF 568

LUIGI ILLICA (1857–1919)

Letter to Lina Mascagni

[ca. 1911] n.p., ALS, 6 p., on Mascagni's philandering; mentions Giuseppe Verdi and Teresa Stolz.

London, Sotheby's, 26–27 Nov. 1987, lot 316.
FRKF 1341.2

VINCENT D'INDY (1851–1931)

Note to an unidentified friend

[ca. 1905?] AN on a visiting card. Mentions a trip to Poland.

Paris, Laurin-Guilloux-Buffetaud-Tailleur (Drouot), 3 July 1985, lot 27.
FRKF 845c

Letter [to Reynaldo Hahn]

1924 Nov. 6, Paris, ALS, 1 p., concerning a concert of his music to be conducted by Hahn.

Paris, Laurin-Guilloux-Buffetaud-Tailleur (Drouot), 8 Feb. 1985, lot 115.
FRKF 658.6

JOHN IRELAND (1879–1962)

The forgotten rite

Holograph full-score manuscript of this work for orchestra, 1913, 18 p., written in black ink on tall 20-staff paper, with additional notes and corrections in black and blue pencil. The first three pages are unnumbered, the remainder paginated 4 to 18. At the head of the manuscript: "Prelude. John Ireland:" On the title page, in Ireland's hand: "The Forgotten Rite / Prelude for orchestra: / by / John Ireland. / written in 1913. / time of performance 7 minutes. / 14A Gunter Grove / [crossed out: 54 Elm Park Mansions] / Chelsea S.W. / tel: 883 Kensington."

Holograph transcription for piano four hands, n.d., 7 p., in black ink on 16-staff paper, paginated 1–7 in blue pencil, with additional notes and corrections in black pencil. At the end of the manuscript, in black pencil: "6½ minutes." On the title page, in Ireland's hand: "Prelude / for orchestra: / by John Ireland: / (arrangement for pianoforte duet) / 54 Elm Park Mansions / Chelsea S.W."

Bound in cream-colored cloth. On front board, in gold lettering: "John Ireland. (framed by a single gold fillet) / Prelude." Tipped on the recto of the free front endpaper is a note on stationery marked The Studio / 14a. Gunter Grove, / Chelsea, S.W.: "This volume contains the original score of 'the Forgotten Rite,' and a piano arrangement of it, both in the author's handwriting. In several details this score differs from the final published version. It was presented to Kenneth A. Wright, Esq., on Sept: 8, 1928, by his friend John Ireland."

Accompanied by two autograph letters from Ireland to Kenneth Wright, 1928 Sept. 8 and 10 [London] 1 p. and 2 p., both concerning *The forgotten rite* and the gift of the manuscript.

"This prelude was Ireland's first important orchestral work. It was inspired by his love for the Channel Islands, especially Jersey, and his admiration for the writings of Arthur Machen" (Craggs, *John Ireland*, p. 35–36). The orchestral score and piano scores were both first published by Augener in London in 1918.

London, Sotheby's, 29 Nov. 1985, lot 109.
FRKF 1084a–b

Sea Idyll

Holograph manuscript of this piano suite in three movements, 1899–1900, 20 p. Notated in black ink, with additional pencil markings, on five separate bifolia and a single sheet of tall 12-staff paper, housed in an additional bifolium, serving as wrappers, of which only the front leaf survives.

On the front outer leaf, in Ireland's hand: "Sea Idyll / by / John N. Ireland / If lost, please return to / 62 Limerston St / Chelsea S.W." Dated 17 Dec. 1899 on p. [4] of the fourth bifolium, at the end of the second movement, with the following epigraph: "'If he is unequal, he will presently pass away; but those … no longer a mate for frogs & worms, dost soar & burn with the gods of the empyrean.' Emerson." Also dated 5 Jan. 1900 at the end. Pasted-down cancels on p. [4] of the third bifolium and on p. [1] of the fourth. Two pasted-on cancels on the last page.

Apparently an early version of this piece, a later version of which exists in manuscript in the British Library. See Craggs, *John Ireland*, p. 9.

London, Sotheby's, 29 Nov. 1985, lot 108.
FRKF 1039

WASHINGTON IRVING (1783–1859)

A history of New York from The Beginning of the World to the end of the Dutch dynasty; containing, among Many Surprising and Curious Matters, the Unutterable Ponderings of Walter the Doubter, the Disastrous Projects of William the Testy, and the Chivalric Achievements of Peter the Headstrong - the Three Dutch Governors of New Amsterdam; Being the Only Authentic History of the Times that Ever Hath Been or Ever Will Be Published. By Diedrich Knickerbocker ... The whole Embellish'd by Eight Pictures from the Hand of Maxfield Parrish, Esqre. New York: Published by R.H. Russell, Anno Domini, MCMIII [1903].

One leaf blank, [i]–[xxxiv], 1–[299] [+ 8 leaves of plates], 1 leaf blank. 23 × 31 cm. Bound in brown cardboard boards, backed with buckram, top edge gilt. Illustrated cover by Maxfield Parrish on front board, with title: "Knickerbocker's / History / of New York / By Washington Irving / R.H. Russell [publisher's monogram] New York"; spine blank. Bookplate of Roderick Terry.

On copyright page: "Composition and Electrotyping by D.B. Updike, The Merrymount Press, Boston / Presswork by The University Press, John Wilson and Son, Cambridge, U.S.A." Second edition. The first appeared in 1900. See Langfeld, p. 82 (without mention of this second edition).

The illustrations by Parrish are bound in as follows:

Frontispiece ("And Oloffe bethought him ..."), dated 1898.

[after p. 24:] "They introduced among them rum ...," dated 1899.

[after p. 44:] Saint Nicholas, n.d.

[after p. 80:] "Wouter Van Twiller: 'The first morning ...,'" n.d.

[after p. 140:] "Blacksmiths," n.d.

[after p. 188:] Concerning Witchcraft, n.d.

[after p. 238:] "A phalanx of oyster-fed Pavonians ...," n.d.

[after p. 278:] "The first movement of the governor ...," n.d.

This copy is illustrated throughout with pen-and-ink and watercolor drawings by William Henry Drake. All but the first are signed "W.H.D" in red ink. The illustrations, which are either full-page (as specified) or in the margin or at the bottom of printed pages, are as follows. Untitled illustrations are described in square brackets.

On verso of free front endpaper: "The Seal of New Netherland."

On first leaf, blank, recto: "Peter Stuyvesant Governor of New Amsterdam (1647–1664)" (portrait and seal).

On first leaf, blank, verso: "Washington Irving" (bust).

p. [xii], full-page: "Diedrich Knickerbocker (writing the History of New York)"; p. xvi: "Diedrich Knickerbocker 'poking about town'"; p. [xxiv]: "Diedrich prying"; p. [xxx]: [Diedrich saluting]; p. [xxxii], full-page: "Theories and Speculations"; p. [xxxiii], [three owls and a vignette with Diedrich and his book with two Dutchmen smoking pipes and drinking beer]; p. [xxxiv], full-page: "Diedrich resting."

p. 1: "The Orange and Black (the shadow) [arrow] The Dutch National Colors"; p. 2: [griffin]; p. 5: "The Earth," "The Earth's Orbit," "The Sun"; p. 6: "The great Egg of night and the Celestial Bull"; p. 7: "René Descartes," "Plato"; p. 8: [tortoise, snake, the earth]; p. 9: [the sun, the earth, the moon]; p. 11: [balloons inscribed with names of scientists: Buffon, Darwin, Herschel, etc.]; p. 12–13: "Noah's Ark"; p. 14: "Phoenician vessel," "Chinese Junk," "Viking Explorers"; p. 15: "Christoval Colon (clumsily nicknamed) Columbus," "The Log-Book of the good NOAH"; p. 16: "Indian Pottery," "Indian Wigwams"; p. 17: "Indian bow and arrows," "Indian Implements of shell," "Indian Moccasins, or shoes"; p. 18: "Marco Polo," "Charles Darwin"; p. 19: "American Indian Chief Sixteenth Century"; p. 20: "American Indian Warrior 1585"; p. 24: [Indian]; p. 31: [Dutch peasant at sunset]; p. [32]–[33]: "New Amsterdam 1624"; p. [34]: "Master Hendrick Hudson's Goode ship 'The Half-Moon'"; p. 35: "Hendrick Hudson"; p. 40: "Master Richard Blome"; p. 42: "Master Adrian Block"; p. 43: "The Retreat"; p. 45: "Admiral Martin Van Tromp"; p. 46: "The Sage Oloffe's dream"; p. 48: "A remarkable fog"; p. 49: "Abraham Hardenbroeck," "Winant Ten Broeck," "Jacobus Van Zandt"; p. 62: "Vander Donck (The Great Historian)"; p. 63: "Master Juet," "Jolly Topers"; p. 64: "A Sachem"; p. 65: "Dominic Heckwelder"; p. 69: [drinking scene]; p. [74], full-page: "Wouter Van Twiller"; p. [76], full-page: "Map of the Battery 1664 / The Duke's Plan of the Towne of Mannados"; p. 81: [knife and tobacco-box]; p. 82: "Wandel Schoonhover," "Barent Bleecker," scales; p. 89: "The Burgomaster's Little Joke"; p. 91: [rooftops with weathercocks]; p. 94: "Dutch Courtship"; p. 98: [cherub with beer tankard];

p. 100: "Killian Van Rensellaer"; p. 104: "The Battery"; p. 108: [putti and heart]; p. 112: "A Squatter"; p. 117: "The Courier"; p. [118], full-page: "The first church and Governor's house"; p. [119]: "Dutch Wind Mill"; p. [120], full-page: "William the Testy"; p. 124: "Knowledge is Power"; p. 127: "Popping the question in New Amsterdam"; p. 130: "Exit Jacobus Van Curlet"; p. 136: [debtor in prison]; p. 141: "Dutch Tavern New Amsterdam 1679"; p. 143: "Robert Chevit"; p. 144: "The Long and Short Pipes"; p. 147: [monument to Jan Jansen Alpendam]; p. 150: [cats and dogs]; p. 153: "The Hieroglyphic Sign"; p. 157: "The Goblins of the Kattskill Mountains"; p. [158], full-page: "The first brick house in the City"; p. [159]: "The Water Gate. Wall Street"; p. [160], full-page: "Anthony Van Corlear The Trumpeter"; p. 165: [attroupement in front of a proclamation]; p. 169: "Will Cottington," "Alicrsander Partridg"; p. 170: "Hans Reimer Oothout"; p. 171: "A Yankee Lawyer"; p. 172: [Puritan and Dutchman shaking hands]; p. 177: "The Sancho Panza Historian"; p. 179: "Everet Ducking," "Jacobus Van Carlet"; p. 180: portrait; p. 182: "Two Lean Hungry Looking Yankees"; p. 187: "John Josselyn, Gent."; p. 189: [cat in the moon and witch on broom]; p. 195: [old Keldermeester appearing to the general in a dream]; p. [196], full-page: "Terrific

Battle at Fort Christina"; p. [197]: "Trinity Fort / Originally called / Fort Casimir (New Sweden)"; p. [198], full-page: "Gen'l Van Poffenburgh attacks the sunflowers and pumpkins"; p. 200: "Jan Printz Governor of New Sweden"; p. 202: "Ruins of the fortress 'Helsenborg' (Musquito Castle.)"; p. 203: "Jan Claudius Risingh"; p. 204: [beer tankard]; p. 205: "Captain Bobadil"; p. 206: "Sven Schüte otherwise called Skytte"; p. 207: "Fort Christina"; p. 208: "Dirk Schuiler (or Skulker)"; p. 212: "Saint Nicholas"; p. 217: "Anthony's Nose / Hudson River"; p. 218: "Van Dams. Suy Dams," "Van Pelts," "Hoppers," "Cloppers"; p. 219: "Jacobus Varra Vanger," "Brooklyn Ferry House and Ferry Boats"; p. 220: "Van Groll," "Gardeniers," "Van Hoesens," "Couenhovens (of Sleepy Hollow)," "Van Kortland"; p. 221: "Jacobus Van Poffenburgh," "Van Higginbottoms," "Knickerbockers," "Van Vlotens," "Van Nests"; p. 222: "The Art of Retreat"; p. 224: "Michael Paw"; p. 225: "Peter Stuyvesant and Beëlzebub"; p. 228: [Skytte and his garrison marching out]; p. 233: "The Damien farmhouse (now the site of the Equitable Building)"; p. 234: "Van Tassels," "Van Giesons," "Van Wart," "Vander Spiegles," "Van Winkles"; p. 235: "Van Wyck," "Van Dyke," "Vander Hoofs," "Van Gelder," "Vander Belts" p. 236: "Van Bunschotens," "Stoffel Brinkerhoff," "Bensons," "Browers"; "Stoutenburghs"; p. 237: "Spitter Splutter / Dunder Blitzen"; p. 238: "Van Arsdales," "Dyckmans," "Van Blarcoms," "Van Rippers," "Waldrons," "Onderdonks"; p. 239: "Van Brunts," "Van Hornes," "Schermerhorns," "Quackenbosses," "Vander Lyns," "Carrebrantzes"; p. 240: [three-cornered hat and mosquito]; p. 242: "Homer"; p. 245: "Mynheer William Beekman," "Wolfert Van Horne," "Brom Van Bummel"; p. 246: "The Great Seal of England. Province of New York 1688 to 1689"; p. [247]: "The 'Bouwerie' Gov Stuyvesant's Home," "The first street on East River"; p. [248], full-page: "t'Fort nieuw Amsterdam op de Manhattans"; p. 252: "Ten Broecks," "Rutgers," "Ten Eycks," "Harden Broecks"; p. 253: "Platter-breeches"; p. 255: "A young belle from Holland"; p. 257: "Chief of the Tribe"; p. 258: "Lord Baltimore"; p. 259: "A Council of War"; p. 262: "Dominie Aegidius Luyck"; p. 264: "Little Trumpeters"; p. 265: "Charles II"; p. 266: "An Hostile Fleet"; p. 270: "The State House New Amsterdam 1650"; p. 273: [Brick house, windmill, goose on perch]; p. 276: "'The White Hall' / Governor Stuyvesant's City House"; p. 279: "Col Nicholas"; p. 283: "An Old Dutch Burgher"; p. 285: [the burgomasters kicked down the stairs by Stuyvesant's wooden leg]; p. 288: "Preserved Fish," "Determined Cock"; p. 289: "Burgomaster Roerback"; p. 290: "The British Officers"; p. 293: "De Ruyter"; p. 295: "Hardkoppig Peter's Wooden Leg"; p. 298: "The Egg"; p. [299]: "The End" [hourglass].

Drake has also embellished titles and initials with decorations in red ink.

Born in New York on 4 June 1856, Drake studied at the Académie Jullian in Paris and is best known as one of the illustrators of the first edition of Rudyard Kipling's *Jungle Book* (1894). See the entries on him in Benezit and Thieme-Becker.

See Christie's, New York, 7 June 1990, lot 40.
FRKF 80

MAX JACOB (1876–1944)

Signed but undated autograph notes, 1 p., in black ink on the verso of a single sheet of ruled paper, comprising a 12-line poem, under the heading "chapitre trois," and, under the heading "chapitre quatre," four paragraphs of poetic prose.

London, Sotheby's, 29 Nov. 1985, lot 278.
FRKF 1047d

HENRY JAMES (1843–1916)

I. LETTERS

Unless otherwise noted, the letters described below are not recorded in Edel. Except where noted, they have the accession number FRKF 138a–ar. Many of the letters are written on printed stationery of James's residences and clubs, abbreviated as follows:

Reform Club, Pall Mall, S.W. [London] = Reform Club^S

Lamb House, Rye, Sussex = Lamb House^S

21 Carlyle Mansions, Cheyne Walk, S.W. [London] = Carlyle Mansions^S

34 De Vere Gardens. W. [London] = De Vere Gardens^S

The Athenaeum, Pall Mall, S.W. [London] = Athenaeum^S

To Mrs. Rodolph Adlercron (formerly Hester Bancroft)

1906 March 27, Reform Club^S, ALS, 3 p. (env)

1907 July 8, Lamb House^S, ALS, 2 p. (env)

1913 May 11, Carlyle Mansions^S, ALS, 2 p. (env)

1913 July 8, Carlyle Mansions^S, ALS, 1 p. (env)

1914 July 15, Lamb House^S, ALS, 2 p. (env)

1914 Aug. 1, Lamb House^S, ALS, 2 p. (env)

1914 Sept. 3, Lamb House^S, TLS, 2 p. (env)

1915 April 8, Carlyle Mansions^S, ALS, 1 p. (env)

[1915 June 8*] "Monday a.m.," Carlyle Mansions^S, ALS, 2 p. (env)

n.d., "Tuesday p.m.," Lamb House^S, ALS, 2 p.

London, Sotheby's, 8 Dec. 1983, lot 218.
FRKF 274

To Mrs. Bancroft

[1892* March 21], Reform Club^S (embossed), ALS, with mourning envelope

[1892*] June 9, Siena, ALS, 4 p., on mourning stationery (env)

[1892*] Sept. 27, De Vere Gardens^S, ALS, 4 p., with mourning envelope

1895 Feb. 13, De Vere Gardens^S, ALS, 4 p. (env)

1898 Dec. 21, Lamb House^S, TLS, 2 p. (env)

1901 Feb. 18, 105 Pall Mall S.W. [London] ALS, 8 p. (env)

1901 June 2, Lamb House^S, ALS, 4 p. (env)

1901 June 18, Lamb House^S, ALS, 2 p.

[1901 June 20] "Wednesday," Lamb House^S, ALS, 2 p. (env)

1901 Aug. 13, Lamb House^S, ALS, 4 p. (env)

[1901] Sept. 15, Lamb House^S, ALS, 2 p. (env)

1902 Jan. 15, Lamb House^S, ALS, 2 p. (env)

1902 March 8, Lamb House^S, ALS, 4 p. (env)

1902 Nov. 17, Lamb House^S, ALS, 2 p. (env)

1903 Feb. 6, Reform Club^S, ALS, 6 p.

1903 Feb. 14, Reform Club^S, ALS, 1 p.

1903 April 3, Reform Club^S, ALS, 4 p.

1903 April 21, Reform Club^S, ALS, 3 p.

1903 July 14, Lamb House^S, ALS, 2 p. (env)

1905 Dec. 31, 109 Pall Mall, S.W., ALS, 2 p.

n.d., "Friday noon," De Vere Gardens^S, ALS, 2 p., (env)

n.y., Dec. 13, Dresden, ALS, 4 p.

n.y., March 21, De Vere Gardens^S, ALS, 4 p., on mourning stationery

n.d., "Thursday," Reform Club^S, ALS, 3 p.

Accompanied by an original photograph of Mrs. Adlercron with her two children, taken by Frank Urwin, n.d., Grantham, (15 × 10 cm).

London, Sotheby's, 8 Dec. 1983, lot 216.
FRKF 275

Also, 1898 March 21, De Vere Gardens^S, TLS, 3 p. (env), concerning *What Maisie knew*.

See Christie's, London, 28 Nov. 1990, lot 192; see also Sotheby's, New York, 17 Dec. 1992, lot 134.
London, Sotheby's, 8 Dec. 1983, lot 217.
FRKF 273

To Grace Edith Barnes

[1904 or 1905] "Tuesday p.m.," 36 West 10th St. [New York] ALS in pencil, 4 p., enclosing tickets (not present).

1907 March 4, Lamb House^S, ALS, 2 p. Mentions Roger Fry.

G.E. Barnes was John La Farge's assistant.

To Hugh[?] Bell

n.d., "Monday a.m.," King's Cot, Windsor[S], ALS, 3 p. Apologizes for canceling an appointment.

To Mrs. Hugh Bell

[1890] Oct. 12, De Vere Gardens[S], ALS, 8 p., concerning *The American*.

[1893*] Feb. 10, De Vere Gardens[S], ALS, 4 p. (env), concerning Mrs. Bell's plays.

1900 Oct. 6, Lamb House[S], ALS, 4 p. (env). Mentions Elizabeth Robins.

Also, a loose envelope, postmarked 1893 Oct. 5

To G. Bloede

[1875?] March 21 [London*] 3 Bolton Street, W., ALS, 4 p. (env), concerning a poem submitted by his correspondent.

To John E. Brown

n.y. Oct. 15, 3 Bolton St. Piccadilly W. [London] ALS, 1 p., declining to write for *The Independent*.

To Thomas Bushby

1914 April 20, Carlyle Mansions[S], ALS, 2 p. (env), addressed to "Dear Mr. Postmaster."

To Madame Cantagalli

[1887] Jan. 26 [Florence*] Hotel du Sud, ALS, 2 p. (env). Mentions Violet Paget (Vernon Lee).

To Lady Cecil

1908 Oct. 28, ALS on both sides of a card printed: Lamb House
1910 May 27, Hill Hall, Theydon Bois, Epping[S], ALS, 3 p.
1911 Dec. 7, Reform Club[S] (mourning), ALS, 4 p. (env)
1912 Sept. 10, Lamb House[S], ALS, 2 p. (env)
1912 Sept. 15, Lamb House[S], ALS, 2 p.
1913 Sept. 27, Lamb House[S], ALS, 2 p.

London, Sotheby's, 22 July 1985, lot 414.

FRKF 881

To R.W. Chapman

1913 Jan. 21, 21 Carlyle Mansions / Cheyne Walk / S.W., ALS, 3 p., a response to the announcement of Chapman's engagement.

FRKF 222

To Sybil Colefax

1914 Jan. 19, Carlyle Mansions[S], ALS, 1 p. Accepts an invitation.

1914 Jan. 29, Carlyle Mansions[S], ALS, 1 p. Extends an invitation.

To Lady Colvin

1903 July 14, Lamb House[S], ALS, 2 p. "I am immensely touched by your remembrance …"

To Julia Daudet

[1896] June 12, De Vere Gardens[S], ALS, 14 p., concerning George Meredith; mentions the publication of *The other house*.

Heinrich Schütz to Henry Miller, p. 86–87.

1897 April 12, De Vere Gardens[S], ALS, 4 p. Thanks her for sending him her *Notes sur Londres* (Paris: E. Fasquelle, 1897).

1901 Jan. 16, Athenaeum[S], ALS, 7 p. Mentions *A little tour of France*.

1906 Dec. 19, Lamb House[S], ALS, 2 p. Thanks her for sending him her *Au bord des terrasses, poésies* (Paris: A. Lemerre, 1906).

1907 April 19, 58, rue de Varenne, ALS, 2 p. Mentions a dinner the next day with Léon Daudet and his wife.

The letters are all in French.

To A.E. Drinkwater

1909 Jan. 19, ALS on one side of a card printed: Lamb House. Thanks for the return of a book.

The recipient was secretary of the Independent Stage Society.

To Anstey Guthrie

[1892] "Monday," 34 de Vere Gdns. W., ALS, 1 p., on mourning stationery
n.d., "Tuesday," De Vere Gardens[S], ALS, 1 p.

Guthrie was a contributor to *Punch* under the name Anstey.

To [Anna?] Hallowell

1874 Feb. 11, Florence, ALS, 6 p.

To Aline Harland

1907 May 19, Hotel de Russie, Rome, ALS, 6 p. "The immense pleasure I have in this news of you from dear old Kensington Corner …"

To William Heinemann

[1895 Jan. 5] "Saturday," De Vere Gardens[S], ALS, 2 p., written on the day of the failure of *Guy Domville*.

1895 Feb. 13, De Vere Gardens[S], ALS, 2 p.

To Mrs. F.H. Hill

n.y. April 17, 3 Bolton Street W. [London] ALS, 2 p., concerning Christina Rogerson, involved in the Dilke case.

To Miss Holman Hunt

n.d., 58, rue de Varenne [Paris][S], ALS, 4 p., explaining why he will not be able to meet with her in Rye.

Miss Holman Hunt was one of the two daughters of the painter William Holman Hunt (1827–1910).

FRKF 221

To William James, Jr.

1910 Oct. 20, 36 West 10th Street [New York][S], ALS, 8 p. (env). Mentions Edith Wharton, her sister-in-law Mrs. Jones, and John La Farge.

FRKF 223

To R.U. Johnson

1913 Aug. 8, Lamb House[S], ALS, 6 p.

To Jean-Jules Jusserand

[1892] Aug. 9, De Vere Gardens[S], ALS, 6 p., addressed to "Mon cher ami" but otherwise in English.

Also, a letter from Elise Jusserand to Grace Nichols, on mourning stationery of 5, avenue Montaigne [Paris] 4 p., concerning Katherine Loring and James.

To Kenneth Kinloch-Cooke

[1891] Dec. 19, De Vere Gardens[S], ALS, 4 p., concerning James's essay on Mrs. Humphry Ward.

To John La Farge

1904 July 21, Lamb House[S], TLS, 1 p., concerning James's forthcoming voyage to the United States; mentions William James.

To Miss Larpent

1904 July 21, Lamb House[S], ALS, 2 p.

1910 Jan. 6, Lamb House[S], ALS, 1 p. (env)

To Miss Leupp

1905 Nov. 30, Lamb House[S], ALS, 1 p., enclosing a check. Note in pencil in an unidentified hand: "Raising funds for Bryn Mawr College."

To Katharine Peabody Loring

[1887] Feb. 28, Palazzino Alvisi [Venice] ALS, 4 p., concerning Alice James and Louisa Loring.

To Lady Macmillan

1897 July 19, Bournemouth, Bath Hotel, TLS, 1 p., addressed to Mrs. Frederick.

1914 Dec. 4, Carlyle Mansions[S], TLS, 2 p.

The recipient was the wife of Sir Frederick Orridge Macmillan (1851–1936), the publisher.

To Lady Mallet

[1899 Aug 23*] Lamb House[S], ALS, 2 p. (env), a letter of apology.

To Mrs. Otto H. Matz

1905 March 11, University Club, Chicago[S], ALS, 2 p. (env), a letter of apology.

To S.S. McClure

1897 July 20, Bournemouth, Bath Hotel, ALS, 2 p. Mentions receiving proofs.

To Mr. and Mrs. Payne

n.y., Jan. 8, Reform Club[S] (embossed), ALS, 1 p. Declines an invitation to a Dickens masquerade. Written in the third person.

To Jocelyn Persse

n.d., "Tuesday midnight," Reform Club[S], ALS, 4 p., concerning a dinner engagement. Not in Gunter & Jobe.

Jocelyn Dudley Persse (1873–1943), nephew of Lady Gregory and a close friend of James in the last decade of his life.

To Countess Edith Peruzzi

[1887] Jan. 27, Hotel du Sud [Florence] ALS, 1 p., accepting a dinner invitation.

FRKF 138

1890 Aug. 30, De Vere Gardens^S, ALS, 4 p.

New York, Christie's, 22 Nov. 1985, lot 65.

FRKF 1270

1899 Aug. 1, Lamb House^S, ALS, 4 p.

1901 Oct. 10, Lamb House^S, ALS, 10 p.

Edith Marion Story, daughter of the American sculptor William Wetmore Story.

FRKF 973.1, 973.3

To James B. Pinker

1908 March 24 and 25, Edinburgh, 2 telegrams, concerning the premiere of James's *The high bid*.

1909 Oct. 20, Lamb House^S, ALS, 1 p., acknowledging the receipt of a royalty check.

To Elizabeth Robins

1896 Feb. 22, Gloucester, telegram

1897 March 6, De Vere Gardens^S, ALS, 4 p. Mentions Eleanor Calhoun and Virginia Bateman.

1901 Feb. 2, Athenaeum^S, ALS, 10 p. (env)

1905 June 30, The Mount, Lenox, Mass.^S, ALS, 8 p. (env), about sailing back to Europe together.

[1906 March 30] Reform Club^S, ALS, 4 p. (env), concerning her brother Raymond Robins. Marked "not of course published" in Elizabeth Robins's hand in upper left corner of p. 1.

[1906 April 12*] "Wednesday night," Reform Club^S, ALS, 3 p. (env)

[1906] May, Reform Club^S, ALS, 4 p. Mentions the San Francisco earthquake.

[1907] "Monday a.m.," Reform Club^S, ALS, 6 p. (env)

1907 Oct. 9, Lamb House^S, ALS, 2 p., concerning *Summersoft* (also called "Mrs. Gracedew").

n.d., on stationery of The Athenaeum, Pall Mall. S.W. [crossed out in James's hand, and replaced by:] 79 Grosvenor St. W. [London] ALS, 4 p. Mentions letting De Vere Gardens.

To George Smalley

1915 Sept. 11, Carlyle Mansions^S, TLS, 4 p., concerning James's renunciation of his American citizenship. Accompanied by a small clipping with the headline "Henry James, Englishman."

FRKF 220

To Marie Souvestre

1897 March 27, De Vere Gardens^S, TLS, 2 p.

1897 March 28, De Vere Gardens^S, TLS, 2 p.

1897 March 31, De Vere Gardens^S, TLS, 3 p.

1897 April 2, De Vere Gardens^S, TLS, 1 p.

The letters all have to do with an appointment; the first one mentions Mme Allard [Julia Daudet's mother?] and the Daudets. All letters are marked "dictated" on p. 1 in upper left corner.

Marie Souvestre ran a school for English girls and was acquainted with Lytton Strachey, to whom she taught French. See Edel IV:116.

To Lady Stephen

n.y., June 18, 3 Bolton St. Mayfair [London] ALS, 2 p., declining an invitation.

Lady Stephen, wife of James Fitzjames Stephen.

To [Thoby?] Stephen

n.y, May 3, De Vere Gardens^S, ALS, 3 p., concerning a visit.

To Mrs. Stimson

1900 June 28, Lamb House^S, ALS, 4 p.

FRKF 973.2

To Mrs. Julian Sturgis

1904 April 13, Reform Club^S, ALS, 4 p., addressed to "Dearest Mrs. Julian."

FRKF 973.5

To Millicent, Duchess of Sutherland

1903 Dec. 23, Lamb House^S, ALS, 6 p. Edel IV:302–03.

Lady Millicent Fanny St Clair Erskine, eldest daughter of the 4th Earl of Rosslyn, married successively the 4th Duke of Sutherland, Major P.D. Fitzgerald, and Lt. Col. G.E. Hawes.

FRKF 973.4

To Mrs. Trower

[1894?] Nov. 11, De Vere Gardens^S, ALS, 1 p., accepting an invitation.

To Miss Tuckerman

n.d., Lamb House^S, ALS, 2 p. (fragment, only p. 7 and 8 are present), concerning *The Princess Casamassima*.

To Allan Wade

1912 July 17, Lamb House^S, ALS, 1 p., enclosing a check as a contribution to the Independent Stage Society's efforts against censorship; the recipient was the Society's secretary.

To Mrs. Walford

[1891] Nov. 27, De Vere Gardens^S, ALS, 4 p. Mentions Wolcott Balestier.

To Sydney Waterlow

1910 Sept. 10, Chocorua, N.H., ALS, 6 p., on mourning stationery

1911 Jan. 19, 21 East Eleventh Street [New York]^S, ALS, 4 p., on mourning stationery

1911 Aug. 19, Hill, Theydon Mount, Epping^S, ALS, 10 p.

1911 Sept. 2, Hill, Theydon Mount, Epping^S, ALS, 4 p.

1912 Oct. 21, Lamb House^S, TLS, 3 p., marked "Dictated" on p. 1 in upper right corner

1913 April 22, Carlyle Mansions^S, ALS, 1 p.

1913 April 24, Carlyle Mansions^S, ALS, 2 p.

1913 May 3, Carlyle Mansions^S, ALS, 2 p.

[1913] July 10, Carlyle Mansions^S, ALS, 2 p.

1913 July 25, Carlyle Mansions^S, ALS, 4 p.

1913 Aug. 27, Carlyle Mansions^S, ALS, 2 p.

1913 Sept. 5, Carlyle Mansions^S, ALS, 4 p.

Sydney Waterlow (1878–1944), diplomat, subsequently ambassador to Greece.

To S.W. [Sarah Butler Wister?]

n.d., Lamb House^S, ALS, 1 p., suggesting a meeting.

Other letters

To "My dear Sir"

1905 March 26, Hotel Van Nuys, Los Angeles^S, ALS, 2 p. Refuses permission to reprint his article on Trollope.

To an unidentified correspondent

n.d, n.p., ALS, 2 p. (fragment, only p. 8 and 9 are present), concerning *The two magics*.

II. MISCELLANEOUS

John Pollock to J.B. Pinker, 1911 Jan. 16 [London] 21 Hyde Park Place, ALS, 3 p., concerning a cut made in James's play *The saloon*. Quotes a cablegram received from James in New York.

FRKF 138

A National Bank of Boston check for $150 made out to Henry James as payment of a story sold to the *Atlantic Monthly*, 25 June 1868. Endorsed by James on the reverse.

FRKF 138

WILLIAM TRAVERS JEROME (1859–1934)

The famous hypothetical question in the trial of Harry K. Thaw for the murder of Stanford White. Prepared by William Travers Jerome [and] Francis P. Garvan. Made into this book by Boehm & Rathbone [New York, 1907].

[1–10], [1]–39 [+ 5] p.; 22 × 29 cm. De Luxe edition, "specially printed and bound for Subscribers," no. 171 of an edition of 250 copies. Bound in full green shagreen, with the short title gold-tooled on the front board.

Accompanied by a printer's dummy used for engraving the book, with pencil annotations and, in the margins, original drawings and caricatures in pen, pencil, and pen-and-watercolor, signed by the American artists who contributed to the book: C. Allan Gilbert, H. Richard Boehm, Ike Morgan, Julius Hess, Sewell Collins, C.D. Williams, N.H. Loomis, "Scar," M. Stein, Irving S. Cobb, Homer Davenport, Archie Gunn, L.W. Burgess, J.J. Casey, W. Morgan, G. Hyman, T. Powers, and others. Housed in a red cloth folder, with the half-title gold-tooled on the front board as on the cover of the printed book.

A set of unbound proofs for the book.

A group of clippings and autograph notes, most of them unrelated to the Thaw trial, evidently originating from H. Richard Boehm, and including a postcard photograph of W.T. Jerome and unidentified original photographs, mostly family pictures, some showing bullfighting scenes.

New York, Sotheby's, 13 Dec. 1983, lot 420.

FRKF 187

ROBERT KASTOR

Drawings

Seventy-five pen-and-ink drawings, signed, of 19th- and 20th-century musicians and composers, along with their autographs, most with musical quotations, ca. 1891–1935. The drawings, usually after photographs, are on various kinds of paper, measuring ca. 24 × 30 cm. Some are identified or dated on the verso. Each drawing is signed by Kastor unless otherwise noted. The collection comprises portraits of the following:

Bruch, Max, with a 2-measure unidentified musical quotation in the composer's hand, signed by him, and dated 14 Feb. 1902 on the verso.

Bruneau, Alfred, with a 4-measure musical quotation in the composer's hand from act 2 of his opera *Le rêve*, signed, n.d.

Busoni, Ferruccio, with a 6-measure musical quotation from his *All'Italia* in pencil, in the composer's hand, signed and dated by him Paris, Feb. 1909.

Casals, Pablo, with an unidentified 2-measure musical quotation in his hand, signed and dated by him 1933 (and on the verso Paris, May 1933).

Chaminade, Cécile, with a 4-measure musical quotation from a song ("Si tu pouvais venir …") in the composer's hand, signed, and dated 14 April 1899 on the verso.

Charpentier, Gustave, with an 8-measure musical quotation from *Julien, ou La vie du poète*, act 4, scene 1, in the composer's hand, signed, and dated 17 April 1914 on the verso.

Colonne, Édouard, signed by the conductor and dated 10 Jan. 1900 on the verso.

Cortot, Alfred, with an inscription in the pianist's hand, signed, and dated 6 Dec. 1933 on the verso.

Cui, César, with a 6-measure musical quotation in the composer's hand from act 1, scene 1 of his opera *Le flibustier*, signed and dated by him St. Petersburg, 22 Feb. 1897.

Debussy, Claude, not signed by Kastor, with a 2-measure musical quotation in the composer's hand from *Pelléas et Mélisande*, signed, and dated March 1911 on the verso.

Diémer, Louis, with a 3-measure musical quotation in the composer's hand from his *Orientale* for piano, no. 3, op. 36, signed and dated by him Paris, 30 Dec. 1899.

Dubois, Théodore, with a 4-measure musical quotation in the composer's hand, from his *La chanson de ma mie*, signed by him, n.d.

Dukas, Paul, with a 4-measure musical quotation in the composer's hand from *Ariane et Barbe-bleue*, signed, and dated 17 March 1911 on the verso.

Duparc, Henri, with an inscription by Duparc, signed, and dated 12 April 1921 on the verso.

Dvořák, Antonin, with a 5-measure musical quotation from act 3 of *Rusalka*, noted in short score in the composer's hand, signed and dated by him Prague, 7 Oct. 1901.

Elgar, Edward, with a 3-measure musical quotation from *The Apostles* in the composer's hand, signed, and dated 3 March 1907 on the verso.

Enesco, Georges, with a 3-measure musical quotation from *Oedipe* in the composer's hand, signed and dated by him 1935, and dated on the verso Paris, Jan. 1935.

Erlanger, Camille, with a 3-measure musical quotation in the composer's hand from act 1 of his opera *Le fils de l'étoile*, signed and dated by him 1904, dated 3 May 1904 on the verso.

Falla, Manuel de, with a 4-measure musical quotation from *El amor brujo* in the composer's hand, signed and dated by him 12 Nov. 1923.

Fauré, Gabriel, with a 3-measure musical quotation in the composer's hand from his song "Les matelots," signed, n.d.

Gevaert, François-Auguste, with a 23-measure fragment from a religious choral composition in the composer's hand, signed and dated by him Brussels, 1 April 1896.

Glazunov, Aleksandr Konstantinovich, with a 3-measure musical quotation in the composer's hand from his *Violin concerto*, op. 82, signed, and dated 25 July 1909 on the verso.

Godard, Benjamin, with a 3-measure musical quotation in the composer's hand from his *Chanson arabe*, signed and dated by him 1891.

Goldmark, Carl, with a 3-measure musical quotation in the composer's hand from *Merlin*, signed by him from Vienna and dated 28 March 1902 on the verso.

Grechaninov, Aleksandr Tikhonovich, with a 5-measure musical quotation in the composer's hand from his *String quartet* in G major, op. 2, signed and dated by him Paris, 31 March 1927.

Grieg, Edvard, signed by the composer, and dated Dec. 1897 on the verso.

Honegger, Arthur, with a 2-measure musical quotation in the composer's hand from his ballet *Sémiramis*, signed and dated by him Jan. 1934.

Hubay, Jenö, with a 6-measure musical quotation in the composer's hand from his opera *A cremonai hegedüs*, signed, and dated 22 June 1910 on the verso.

Hüe, Georges Adolphe, with a 3-measure musical quotation in his hand from act 2 of his opera *Dans l'ombre de la cathédrale*, signed by him, and dated 15 May 1922 on the verso.

Humperdinck, Engelbert, with a 4-measure musical quotation from the first movement of the *Maurische Rhapsodie* in the composer's hand, signed and dated 1901 by him, and dated 24 Jan. 1901 on the verso.

Indy, Vincent d', with a 6-measure musical quotation from *Fervaal*, act 1, scene 1, in the composer's hand, notated for strings and flute, signed by him, and dated 1894.

Joachim, Joseph, with a 4-measure musical quotation in the violinist's hand from his *Konzert in ungarischer Weise*, op. 11 (measures 2–4, and the first half of measure 5 of the beginning of the solo violin part), signed and dated by him Berlin, 24 March 1900.

Joncières, Victorin, with an 8-measure musical quotation in

the composer's hand from his drame lyrique *Le chevalier Jean*, signed and dated by him 29 June 1891.

Koubetzky, A., with a 9-measure musical quotation from Wagner's *Siegfried*, act 2, scene 3, in the conductor's hand, inscribed, signed, and dated by him Paris, 24 Aug. 1909.

Kreisler, Fritz, with a 2-measure musical quotation from *Schön Rosmarin* in the violinist-composer's hand, signed by him, and dated May 1933.

Kubelík, Jan, with an unidentified 3-measure musical quotation in the hand of the composer, signed by him and dated 25 May 1905.

Landowska, Wanda, with a 3-measure musical quotation from *Podolanka* in Landowska's hand, signed by her, and dated 1917, with an inscription to Kantor.

Lecocq, Charles, with a 4-measure musical quotation from *La fille de Madame Angot* in the composer's hand, signed by him, n.d.

Lehar, Franz, with an 8-measure musical quotation from *Die lustige Witwe* in the composer's hand, signed, and dated 14 Dec. 1910 on the verso.

Leoncavallo, Ruggiero, with a 2-measure musical quotation from *La bohème*, act 1, in the composer's hand, signed and dated by him Paris, 15 Oct. 1899.

Leroux, Xavier, with a 6-measure musical quotation from *Astrarté* in the composer's hand, signed, and dated by him 27 Sept. 1900.

Mascagni, Pietro, with a 3-measure musical quotation from *Cavalleria rusticana* in the composer's hand, signed, and dated July 1899 on the verso.

Massenet, Jules, with a 3-measure musical quotation from *Le mage* in the composer's hand, signed by him, n.d.

Menuhin, Yehudi, with a 4-measure musical quotation from Beethoven's *Violin concerto* in the violinist's hand, signed, and dated Dec. 1931 on the verso.

Messager, André, with a 4-measure musical quotation from *La Basoche*, act 2, in the composer's hand, signed by him, n.d.

Mottl, Felix, with a 4-measure musical quotation from Berlioz's overture *Le carnaval romain* in the conductor's hand, in pencil, signed, and dated 21 Jan. 1897 on the verso.

Nikisch, Arthur, signed by the conductor, and dated 18 April 1911 on the verso.

Paderewski, Ignace Jan, with an unidentified 3-measure musical quotation in the pianist's hand, signed by him, n.d.

Perosi, Lorenzo, with a 2-measure musical quotation in the composer's hand from his *La risurrezione di Cristo*, signed, and dated Paris, 27 Feb. 1899 on the verso.

Pierné, Gabriel, with a 3-measure musical quotation in the composer's hand from the "Fête des fous" from his symphonic poem *L'an mil*, signed and dated by him Nov. 1903.

Prokofiev, Sergei, not signed by Kastor, with an unidentified 2-measure musical quotation in the composer's hand, signed and dated by him 1933, and dated 16 Dec. 1933 on the verso.

Puccini, Giacomo, with a 2-measure musical quotation from *La bohème* ("Mi chiamano Mimi") and a presentation inscription in the composer's hand, also signed and dated by him Torre del Lago, 14 Dec. 1899.

Pugno, Raoul, with a 4-measure musical quotation in the composer's hand from his ballet *La danseuse de corde*, signed by him, n.d.

Rachmaninoff, Sergei, with a 3-measure musical quotation (the first theme of the last movement from *Kolokola* [The bells]) in the composer's hand, signed and dated by him Paris, April 1930.

Ravel, Maurice, with a 3-measure musical quotation in the composer's hand from the "Forlane" of his *Le tombeau de Couperin*, signed and dated by him Nov. 1922.

Roussel, Albert, with a 3-measure musical quotation from *Padmâvatî*, act 2, in the composer's hand, signed, and dated 29 Oct. 1923 on the verso.

Saint-Saëns, Camille, with a 4-measure musical quotation from *Ascanio*, act 1, in the composer's hand, signed, n.d.

Sarasate, Pablo de, with a 6-measure musical quotation in the composer's hand from his *Zigeunerweisen* for violin, op. 20, signed and dated by him Paris, 20 Feb. 1899.

Sauer, Emil, with a presentation inscription by the pianist, signed ("Emil v. Sauer") and dated by him Madrid, 6 Dec. 1932.

Schillings, Max von, with a 3-measure musical quotation in the composer's hand from his *Mona Lisa*, signed and dated by him Berlin, March 1925.

Schmitt, Florent, with an unidentified 1-measure musical quotation in the composer's hand, signed, and dated Nov. 1922 on the verso.

Sibelius, Jean, with a 7-measure musical quotation from *Valse triste* in the composer's hand, signed, and dated 25 April 1921 on the verso.

Sousa, John Philip, with a 4-measure musical quotation in the composer's hand from *The stars and stripes forever*, signed and dated by him 1921, and dated March 1921 on the verso.

Strauss, Richard, with a 4-measure musical quotation (the main theme from *Ein Heldenleben*) in the composer's hand, signed, and dated 26 Sept. 1901 on the verso.

Stravinsky, Igor, with a 1-measure musical quotation from *L'oiseau de feu* in the composer's hand, inscribed, signed, and dated by him Berne, 2 April 1917.

Thibaud, Jacques, with an unidentified 1-measure musical quotation in the violinist's hand, inscribed, signed and dated by him Paris, 7 April 1933.

Thomas, Ambroise, with an unidentified 4-measure musical quotation from *Mignon* in the composer's hand, signed, n.d.

Toscanini, Arturo, with an unidentified 4-measure musical quotation in the conductor's hand, signed and dated by him 25 March 1925.

Verdi, Giuseppe, signed by the composer, n.d.

Vidal, Paul, with a 4-measure musical quotation in the composer's hand from his ballet *La maladetta*, notated for violins and flutes, signed and dated by him 15 Aug. 1896.

Wagner, Siegfried, with a 5-measure musical quotation in the composer's hand from his opera *Bruder Lustig*, signed, and dated 23 Nov. 1910 on the verso.

Walter, Bruno, with a 6-measure musical quotation from the overture to Mozart's *Die Entführung aus dem Serail* in the conductor's hand, signed and dated by him Paris, March 1930.

Weingartner, Felix, with a 6-measure musical quotation in the hand of the conductor from his Symphony no. 2 in E-flat, op. 29, signed and dated by him Paris, 10 May 1905.

Widor, Charles-Marie, with an unidentified 4-measure musical quotation (for voice) in the composer's hand, signed by him, n.d.

Ysaÿe, Eugène, with an unidentified 2-measure musical quotation and presentation inscription in the violinist's hand, signed and dated by him Brussels, Oct. 1901.

According to Bénézit, Kastor was a member of the Société des artistes français as of 1894. A further series of his drawings of writers and artists is in the general collections of the Beinecke Library.

Lion Heart Autographs, New York, Nov. 1984.
FRKF 361 a–z, aa–zz, ba–bw

KEPPEL FAMILY

An album relating chiefly to members of the Keppel family and containing the following letters and documents:

Caroline, princess of Wales (1768–1821)

- To "Dr. Baillie"

  1807 Feb. 20, LS, 4 p., on mourning stationery, signed "CP"

  Dr. Matthew Baillie was royal physician.

Charlotte Augusta, princess of Great Britain (1796–1817)

- To Lady Albemarle

  1805 Nov. 12, ALS, 3 p., signed "Charlotte"

- To Lady de Clifford

  [ca. 1814] ALS, 3 p., signed "Charlotte." Across the page is a pasted-on clipping on a visit of the Princess of Wales to Windsor, mentioning Lady de Clifford.

Princess Charlotte Augusta of Wales, daughter of George IV, first wife of Leopold of Saxe-Coburg, later king of the Belgians; Lady de Clifford, her governess, whose daughter Elizabeth Southwell Keppel married the fourth Earl of Albemarle.

Leopold I, king of the Belgians (1790–1865)

- To Lady Anne Amelia Keppel Coke, Countess of Leicester

  1831 Feb. 17 [?] Buckingham Palace, ALS, 4 p.

  1834 Nov. 2, Brussels, ALS, 3 p.

  1842 July 4, Buckingham Palace, ALS, 3 p.

  Anne Amelia Keppel Coke, wife of Thomas William Coke, 1st Earl of Leicester.

Augustus Frederick, Duke of Sussex (1773–1843)

- To "Dear Coke" [Thomas William, Earl of Leicester]

  n.d., n.p, ALS, 2 p.

- To Lady Anne Amelia Keppel Coke, Countess of Leicester

  1823 Dec. 23, Tunbridge Wells, ALS, 3 p.

  1824 Nov. 4, Nottingham, ALS, 3 p.

  1829 Jan. 16, Cambridge, ALS, 4 p.

  1833 Oct. 10, Darlington, ALS, 4 p.

  1835 Jan. 13, St. Araph, ALS, 4 p., on mourning stationery

  1837 Aug. 8, Hampton [?] Palace, ALS, 4 p., on mourning stationery

  1839 Feb. 17, St. Araph, ALS, 2 p.

- To an unidentified lady

  All are autograph letters, signed, addressed to "Dear Jane" or "My dear Jane" and unless otherwise noted were written from Kensington Palace, London. The letters dated 8 Oct. through 13 Nov. 1840 are on mourning stationery.

  1821

  February: 7 (Royal Pavillion, Brighton, 3 p.)

  1840

  October: 8 (4 p.); 12 (4 p.); 13 (2 p.); 14 (1 p.); 15 (4 p.); 16 (2 p.); 17 (4 p.); 19 (2 p.); 22 (4 p.); 23 (1 p.); 24 (2 p.); 26 (4 p.); 28 (2 p.); 29 (2 p.); 30 (1 p.); 31 (2 p.)

  November: 2 (3 p.); 3 (2 p.); 4 (1 p.); 5 (2 p.); 9 (2 p.); 13 (4 p.)

  December: 7 (Wimbledon Palace [London] 4 p.); 11 (Wimbledon Palace, 4 p.)

  1842

  August: 31 (4 p.)

  September: 27 (Sandbeck [?] Palace [London] 4 p.)

  October: 9 (Streatham, 2 p.)

- To Sir Henry Keppel

  1834 [place not deciphered] ALS, 4 p., on mourning stationery

Mary, Duchess of Gloucester (1776–1857)

- To Thomas Keppel

1840 Oct. 10, ALS, 4 p., on mourning stationery, with a reference to Holckham Hall, seat of the Keppel family.

Mary Louisa Victoria, Duchess of Kent (1786–1861)

- To Anne Amelia Keppel Coke, Countess of Leicester

  1835 Aug. 9, Tunbridge Wells, LS, 3 p., on mourning stationery, signed "Victoria"

George Thomas Keppel, 6th Earl of Albemarle (1799–1891)

- To Edward Ellice

  1883 March 14, ALS, 3 p.

  Edward Ellice, second husband of Lady Anne Amelia Keppel Coke.

Also, LS from Miss Coke to Major Keppel, n.y. Oct. 21, Pierremont, 1 p., on mourning stationery and written in the third person.

Other material:

Charles William Wentworth Fitzwilliam, Earl Fitzwilliam, to Lord Albemarle, 1857 Nov. 20, "Wentworth Woodhouse," ALS, 4 p., with a postscript in another hand.

Three letters from members of the Albemarle family to "Willie" [William George Keppel?]

  1900 Jan. 9, Guards Club [London] ALS, 2 p., signed "Your affectionate cousin."

  n.d., "Saturday," Quidenham Park, Attleborough[S], ALS, 2 p., signed "Your affectionate uncle."

  n.y. Dec. 7, from "Bury" to "Dear Willy," Quidenham Hall, Thetford[S], ALS, 2 p.

Joseph Chamberlain to "Dear Mr Boyle," 1900 Oct. 4, Highbury, Moor Green, Birmingham[S], ALS, 3 p., congratulating him on his "fight for the Empire."

Five newspaper clippings, with mentions of Admiral Sir Henry Keppel and the visit of the Duke of Edinburgh to China.

Thirty-four envelope cuttings, showing the address side. Most are addressed to Thomas Keppel; some are addressed to Lady Anne Keppel [mid to late 1830s].

Thomas Keppel. *To my parishioners*. Fakenham: Printed by G.N. Stewardson, [1863]. Printed on a single 8vo-size bifolium, paginated [1], 2–3. Dated at the end: "N. Creake, Jan. 6, 1863."

The album is bound in red morocco (binder's ticket: Fletcher, Norwich), with a triple gold fillet and a gold-tooled decorative motif on both boards; on spine, raised bands, gold-tooled decorations, and crown and swan motif at the bottom, as well as the title: "M.S. Letters." Inscribed on the verso of the free front endpaper: "William George Keppel / From / Fanny Keppel / 1872."

London, Sotheby's, 22 July 1985, lot 366.
FRKF 889

JEROME KERN (1885–1945)

Five songs from *Cover Girl*

Long Ago (And Far Away) / Words by Ira Gershwin. [New York] T.B. Harns, 1944.

Make Way For To-morrow / Words by Ira Gershwin and E.Y. Harburg. [New York] T.B. Harns, 1944.

Sure Thing / Words by Ira Gershwin. [New York] T.B. Harns, 1944.

Put Me To The Test / Words by Ira Gershwin. [New York] T.B. Harns, 1944.

Cover Girl / Words by Ira Gershwin. [New York] T.B. Harns, 1944.

[20] p. In a brown morocco binding. Title on front board: 5 SONGS / BY / JEROME KERN / FROM / COVER GIRL / WORDS BY / IRA GERSHWIN. / 1944 / RITA HAYWORTH. Presentation inscription to Rita Hayworth on free front endpaper: "For Rita Hayworth / This souvenir with the / devotion of hers / faithfully / Jerome Kern / June, 1944." All are scores for voice and piano, with guitar chords.

Cover Girl, the Columbia Pictures Corporation motion picture directed by Charles Vidor and starring Rita Hayworth and Gene Kelly, had its premiere at Radio City Music Hall on 30 March 1945.

Boston, Daniel F. Kelleher Co., 22 July 1982, lot 127.
FRKF 10

JESSIE M. KING

Three original drawings

[The mermaid's farewell] Pen-and-ink and pencil on vellum (20 × 29 cm), signed in the lower right corner, 1948.

"Youth's Challenge." Pen-and-ink and pencil on vellum (12.5 × 21 cm), signed in the lower right corner, n.d. Also titled, at the top of the drawing: "Dalbeattie Youth Centre."

"And I will give you a coach and six." Unfinished pen-and-ink and pencil drawing on vellum (36 × 28 cm), heightened with black and orange watercolor. The full caption, calligraphed in capital letters in the upper left corner, reads: "And I will give you a coach / and six / Six black horses as black / as pitch Lady will you / walk Lady will you / talk Lady will you / walk and talk with me?" Inscribed [?] to Sir John Fry in the right margin.

See Christie's, New York, 7 June 1990, lots 73–75.
See also Sotheby's, New York, 17 Dec. 1992, lot 143.
FRKF 81a–c

CHARLES KINGSLEY (1819–75)

Sermons

Autograph manuscripts of 15 sermons, 1852–74, 265 p., in black ink, with occasional corrections in black or blue pencil, on nested, stitched bifolia of various types of paper. The manuscripts are considerably corrected and reworked. Some of them are initialed CK on the first page.

The sermons are as follows:

2 Corinthians 3:4–5 (1852 Aug. 29; also 1855, 1857), 26 p.

2 Corinthians 8:1–2 (1859 March 13; also 1864, 1867), 12 p.

Romans 8:15–17 (Eversley, last Sunday in 1860; also 1862, 1865, 1868, and 1874), 11 p.

Ephesians 3:20 (1860; also 1864, 1868), 18 p.

John 2:11 (1862 Jan.; also 1864, 1868), 16 p.

Matthew 13:29 (5th Sunday after Epiphany, 1862; also 1867), 16 p.

Revelation 13:17 (Whitsunday 1862), 7 p.

Isaiah 44:24–29 (1st Sunday after Epiphany, 1863; also 1865), 20 p.

Ezekiel 11:4 (1863 Sept. 20; also 1869), 27 p.

Ecclesiastes 11:18–19 (1863), 16 p.

Psalms 121:1–8 (Eversley, 1868 Sept. 27), 12 p.

Micah 6:5–8 (Eversley, 20th Sunday after Trinity, 1869), 24 p.

2 Kings 23:3–4, 25–26 (Eversley, 1869), 22 p.

Proverbs 1: 20–24 (1869 Nov. 10 and 1870 Nov. 6, both dates cancelled), 14 p.

Luke 9:16–17 (n.d.), 24 p.

New York, Charles Hamilton, 8 Feb. 1985, lot 84.
FRKF 561

RUDYARD KIPLING (1865–1936), PURPORTED AUTHOR

"The handiest man"

Manuscript poem in black ink on both sides of a sheet of ruled paper, n.d. Incipit: "While you're shouting for Tommy & cheering Jack …"

Purportedly "given by Kipling to the chief engineer on the boat on which he traveled to South Africa," according to the 1984 Christie's catalogue, but actually a forgery.

See Christie's, New York, 7 June 1990, lot 78.
London, Christie's, 28 March 1984, lot 180.
FRKF 295

J.C.B. KNIGHT

Pen-and-ink cartoon on heavy cardboard (23.5 × 31 cm), n.d., signed in the lower left corner, showing a couple at the theater, while a violent confrontation is taking place on stage between a man, holding a gun, and a woman. The caption, written in pencil at the bottom, reads: She - "I can't bear it" He - "My dear it's only acting" She - "No - I mean that picture. Why don't they put it straight?"

London, Christie's, 21 July 1981, lot 249.
FRKF 97

CHARLES KOECHLIN (1867–1950)

Letters to Hermann Scherchen

1931 Dec. 25, Paris, ALS, 3 p. Mentions Romain Rolland and discusses several of his own works.

1937 May 11, Paris, ALS, 1 p., concerning the manuscript of his *Symphony*.

1950 Aug. 23, Villers-sur-Mer, ALS, 6 p. The last 4 pages list orchestral works by Koechlin, with his comments.

Paris, Laurin-Guilloux-Buffetaud-Tailleur (Drouot), 1 July 1986, lots 163–64.
FRKF 1169–70

See also under Myers, Rollo.

ÉDOUARD LALO (1823–92)

Letter to Pablo de Sarasate

1879 Nov. 18, n.p., ALS, 4 p., concerning the *Symphonie espagnole*, the projected ballet *Le Roi des Aulnes*, and the first *String Trio*; mentions Vaucorbeil, Jean-Baptiste Faure, and Saint-Saëns's *Étienne Marcel*. Below the date, in an unidentified hand (Sarasate?): "Lalo, Paris."

Marburg, Stargardt, 5–6 March 1985, lot 826.
FRKF 815

JEAN LANNES, DUC DE MONTEBELLO (1769–1809)

Letter to the Administration centrale de la Haute-Garonne

[1799 Nov.] 24 Frimaire an VIII, Lectoure, ALS, 1 p., concerning a libelous attack on his chief of staff, Adjutant General Étienne Bartier. On printed stationery, corrected in Lannes's hand. Addressed to "Citoyens administrateurs."

Nassau, Bahamas, Fiduciary Company Ltd, 25 June 1984, lot 133.
FRKF 320

EDWARD LEAR (1812–88)

I. MANUSCRIPTS AND DRAWINGS RELATING TO *A BOOK OF NONSENSE*

A folio-size album (32 × 46 cm) containing, in three sequences, 49 pasted-in pen-and-ink drawings on oblong pieces of paper (ca. 20 × 10.5 cm except where noted), each illustrating an autograph limerick, as well as additional material, n.d. [1835–40?], 38 p.

The *Book of nonsense* limericks are as follows, numbered as indicated in parentheses:

"There was an old Sailor of Compton …" (27)
"There was an old person of Rheims …" (35)
"There was an old person of Cheadle …" (28)
"There was an old person of Cadiz …" (26)
"There was an old man of Coblenz …" (19.5 × 13 cm, "N° 1")
"There was an old man of Leghorn …" (19.5 × 13 cm, "N° 2")
"There was an old man of Nepaul …" (19.5 × 13 cm, "N° 3")
"There was an old man of Calcutta …" (19.5 × 13 cm, "N° 4")
"There was an old man of the Hague …" (19.5 × 13 cm, "N° 5")
"There was an old man of Bombay …" (19.5 × 13.5 cm, "N° 6")
"There was a soldier of Bicester …" and "When a bull with one poke …," illustrated limerick in 2 parts (19.5 × 13 cm, "N° 7" and "N° 8")
"There was a sick man of Tobago …"; "Till one day, to his bliss …"; and "To a roast leg of mutton you may go …" illustrated limerick in 3 parts (19.5 × 13 cm, "N° 9," "N° 10," and "N° 11")
"There was an old person of Sparta …" (lithograph, proof, 22.5 × 15 cm, initialed E.L. in reverse)
"There was an old Lady of Prague …" (6)
"There was an old man of Orleans …" (29)
"There was an old man of the Isles …" (32)
"There was an old Man of Bohemia …" (25)
"There was an old man of the Dee …" (33)
"There was an old person of Ischia …" (1)
"There was an old man of the South …" (8)
"There was an old man of New York …" (31)
"There was an old man of the Nile …" (lithograph, proof, 22.5 × 15 cm, initialed E.L. in reverse)
"There was an old person of Prague …" (19)
"There was an old person of Rhodes …" (21)
"There was an old Man of Jamaica …" (20)
"There was an old Lady whose folly …" (lithograph, proof, 22.5 × 15 cm, initialed E.L. in reverse)
"There was an old man of Apulia …" (23)
"There was an old man of Madras …" (24)
"There was an old man of Moldavia …" (10)
"There was an old person of Troy …" (lithograph, proof, 22.5 × 15 cm, initialed E.L. in reverse)
"There was an old person of Buda …" (lithograph, proof, 22.5 × 15 cm, initialed E.L. in reverse)
"There was an old man of the Coast …" (lithograph, proof, 22.5 × 15 cm, initialed E.L. in reverse)
"There was an old man of Corfu …" (11)
"There was an old man of Vienna …" (16)
"There was an old man of the East …" (9)
"There was an old person of Burton …" (37)
"There was an old person of Leith …" (2)
"There was an old Man who forgot …" (3)
"There was an old person of Hurst …" (4)
"There was an old man of Dundee …" (5)
"There was an old man of the North …" (7)
"There was an old lady of Poole …" (unnumbered, 16 × 10 cm)

"There was an old man of Vesuvius …" (12)

"There was an old man of the Cape …" (13)

"There was an old Man of Cape Horn …" (14)

"There was an old person of Ems …" (15)

"There was an old man of the West …" (17)

"There was an old man of Quebec …" (18)

"There was an old man of Peru, who watched his wife making a stew" (22)

"There was an old man of th'Abruzzi …" (30)

"There was an old person of Gretna …" (36)

Pasted in the album is the following additional material:

[Monkeys], 4 pencil drawings on a single sheet (29.5 × 18.5 cm)

Visit to Captain Hornby, illustrated story in 8 brown pen-and-ink drawings on oblong pieces of paper (ca. 18.5 × 11 cm), numbered 1–8, with captions in Lear's hand.

"Rich & rare were the gems she wore …," 4 pen-and-ink drawings illustrating the poem by Thomas Moore, on oblong pieces of paper (18 × 11.5 cm), numbered 1–4.

"Ye banks & braes's bonny Doon" [sic], 4 pen-and-ink drawings illustrating the poem by Robert Burns, on oblong pieces of paper (18 × 11 cm), numbered 1–4.

[An encounter with a gander], story in 3 episodes, 3 brown pen-and-ink drawings with captions on a single sheet of paper (11.5 × 18.5 cm)

"Oh! Pan! / You dear old man! -," poem, illustrated with a black pen-and-ink caricature on paper (19 × 20 cm)

Untitled black pen-and-ink drawing on paper showing a male and a female bird dressed as humans (19 × 17.5 cm)

"A moving spectacle seen in Prescot. Nov. 10. 1836," brown pen-and-ink drawing on paper (23 × 18.5 cm)

"Scene at Lambeth Palace," brown pen-and-ink drawing on paper (18.5 × 11 cm)

"He threw both his eyes up to heaven," brown pen-and-ink drawing on paper (18.5 × 11.5 cm)

"The clough and crow to roost are gone," brown pen-and-ink drawing on paper (16 × 11.5 cm)

"2. The owl sits on the tree," brown pen-and-ink drawing on paper (14 × 11.5 cm)

"Both child & nurse are fast asleep," brown pen-and-ink drawing on paper (16.5 × 11 cm)

"Il Riposo in Italia," brown pen-and-ink drawing on paper (20 × 16 cm)

"7. If a bee alights upon your nose …," brown pen-and-ink drawing on paper (23 × 19 cm)

"The Mistletoe hung in the castle hall …" and "And the Baron beheld with a father's pride," 2 brown pen-and-ink drawings on paper (23 × 14 cm) illustrating the poem by Thomas Haynes Bayly.

"Go where glory waits thee …" and "But when friends are nearest …," 2 brown pen-and-ink drawings on paper (18.5 × 11 cm) illustrating the poem by Thomas Moore.

"Ah! name not the hour …," brown pen-and-ink drawing on paper (19 × 11.5 cm)

"Goosy goosy gander," brown pen-and-ink drawing on paper (16 × 10 cm)

[Nick and the bottle], illustrated story, in 6 brown pen-and-ink drawings on oblong pieces of paper (16 × 10.5 cm), each accompanied by an autograph caption.

"My mother did not speak …" and "Old Robin fed them both," 2 brown pen-and-ink drawings, accompanied by autograph captions, on oblong pieces of paper (23 × 14.5), the second numbered 8.

[Daniel O'Rourke], illustrated story in 13 black pen-and-ink drawings on tall or oblong pieces of paper (ca. 18 × 11 cm), each accompanied by an autograph caption.

[Two goats], one wearing glasses and drinking a glass of wine, with a smaller goat in the background, pencil on paper (19 × 16 cm)

"She's all my Fanny …," 3 drawings, numbered 1–3, illustrating a poem, brown pen-and-ink on oblong pieces of paper (18 × 11 cm)

The remainder of the material in the album, apparently unrelated to Lear, includes maritime pencil drawings, prints of Plymouth, Brussels, Devonport, and Oporto, a pencil and wash drawing and five pen-and-ink drawings, four signed "G. Hornby" and two dated 1837.

Contemporary binding: greenish paper board, with brown calf corners and spine. On the verso of the original front board, pictorial border showing roses and large pasted-on bookplate, inscribed by hand "R. Reynolds / 10 King St / Manchester" (a note in the same hand is found on an otherwise blank page toward the end of the album).

From the collections of Admiral Sir Phipps Hornby and Hans P. Kraus.
See Christie's, London, 11 Dec. 1969, lot 163.
Schiller, p. viii–ix.
See *Lear in the original: drawings and limericks by Edward Lear for his Book of nonsense, now first printed in facsimile, together with other unpublished nonsense drawings; with an introduction and notes by Herman W. Liebert* (New York: H.P. Kraus, 1975).
Exhibited: "Edward Lear, 1812–1888," London, Royal Academy of Arts, April–July 1985 (no. 72b in the catalogue).
Heinrich Schütz to Henry Miller, p. 40–41.
FRKF 64

Seventy-nine pen-and-ink drawings, each illustrating an autograph limerick, 80 [i.e. 79] p., n.d. [early 1840s?]. The drawings are on oblong sheets of three kinds of blue paper (20.5 × 12.5 cm), foliated 1–80 in Lear's hand, and pasted on the recto sides in a notebook of blue paper; originally bound in two notebooks, now rebound in a modern Sangorski & Sutcliffe binding. Drawing and limerick no.

11 are missing (the page is blank). There are 3 blank pages between 45 and 46.

The incipits are as follows:

1. "There was an old Lady whose folly …"
2. "There was a young Lady of Norway …"
3. "There was an old person of Rhodes …"
4. "There was an old man of the Nile …"
5. "There was an old man of the North …"
6. "There was a young [Lady cancelled] person …"
7. "There was an old man of Jamaica …"
8. "There was an old man who cried 'Hush!' …"
9. "There was an old man on some rocks …"
10. "There was an old man of the West - Who wore a pale plum coloured vest"
12. "There was an old man of Wrkein …"
13. "There was an old man of Peru … So he sat on a chair - "
14. "There was an old parson of Burton …"
15. "There was a young Lady of Sweden …"
16. "There was a young Lady of Hull …"
17. "There was an old man who said - 'How - shall I flee from this horrible cow?'"
18. "There was an old man of Dundee …"
19. "There was an old person whose legs …"
20. "There was a young Lady of Dorking …"
21. "There was an old man of the West, Who never could get any rest"
22. "There was an old man on the coast …"
23. "There was an old man whose delight …"
24. "There was an old person of Troy …"
25. "There was an old person of Tartary …"
26. "There was an old person of Rheims …"
27. "There was an old man who said- 'See! I have found a most beautiful bee!'"
28. "There was a young Lady whose Eyes …"
29. "There was a young Lady of Parma …"
30. "There was a young Lady of Smyrna …"
31. "There was an old man of Apulia …"
32. "There was an old Lady of Prague …"
33. "There was an old man of the Cape …"
34. "There was an old person of Dover …"
35. "There was an old person of Cadiz …"
36. "There was a young Lady of Poole …"
37. "There was an old man of Coblenz …"
38. "There was a young Lady of Russia …"
39. "There was an old man of Sodore …"
40. "There was an old man of Leghorn …"
41. "There was an old man of the South …"
42. "There was an old man of the east …"
43. "There was an old man of Columbia …"
44. "There was an old man of Killkenny …"
45. "There was an old person so silly …"
46. "There was an old sailor of Compton …"
47. "There was a young Lady of Bute …"
48. "There was a young Lady of Portugal …"
49. "There was an old person of Sparta …"
50. "There was an old man of Marseilles …"
51. "There was an old man of Kamsckatka [sic] …"
52. "There was a young Lady of Turkey …"
53. "There was an old man whose repose …"
54. "There was an old man whose despair …"
55. "There was an old person of Sidon …"
56. "There was an old man of Madras …"
57. "There was an old person whose mirth …"
58. "There was a young girl of Majorca …"
59. "There was an old Lady of Leeds …"
60. "There was an old man in a boat …"
61. "There was an old man of Vesuvius …"
62. "There was a young Lady of Welling …"
63. "There was a young person of Wales …"
64. "There was an old man of Peru … / So he ran up & down"
65. "There was an old man of New York …"
66. "There was an old man of th'Abruzzi …"
67. "There was an old person of Ischia …"
68. "There was an old man of the Isles …"
69. "There was an old man of Moldavia …"
70. "There was an old man of Bohemia …"
71. "There was an old person of Buda …"
72. "There was an old man whose desire …"
73. "There was an old man who said - 'Well!, this is a remarkable bell!'"
74. "There was an old person of Calais …"
75. "There was an old man at a casement …"
76. "There was an old person of Dutton …"
77. "There was an old man with a light …"
78. "There was an old person of Gretna …"
79. "There was an old man who said 'O!-' …"
80. "There was an old man who made bold …"

From the collection of Ada Duncan of Naughton House, Fife.
Exhibited: "Edward Lear, 1812–1888," London, Royal Academy of Arts, April–July 1985 (no. 74 in the catalogue).
Schiller, p. ix.
London, Sotheby's, 20 June 1986, lot 647.
FRKF 1361

Thirty-six drawings, each illustrating an autograph limerick, n.d. [1835–40?], 36 p. Black pen-and-ink drawings, with limericks calligraphed underneath in black ink on the recto sides of 36 oblong leaves of an unpaginated album bound in dark red sheepskin with red morocco corners and spine; spine gilt, reddish marbled paper endpapers.

The limericks are the following:
  "There was an Old Derry down Derry …"
  "There was an Old Man with a beard …"
  "There was an Old Man with a nose …"
  "There was an Old Man on a hill …"
  "There was an Old Man with a gong …"
  "There was an Old Man in a tree …"
  "There was an Old Man of Kilkenny …"
  "There was an Old Man in a boat …"
  "There was an Old Man of Madras …"
  "There was an Old Man of the Isles …"
  "There was an Old Man who supposed …"
  "There was a Young Lady of Norway …"
  "There was an Old Man of Vienna …"
  "There was an Old Person whose habits …"
  "There was an Old Person of Cadiz …"
  "There was a Young Lady whose nose …"
  "There was an Old Man of Apulia …"
  "There was an Old Man of Peru …"
  "There was a Young Lady of Lucca …"
  "There was an Old Man of Cape Horn …"
  "There was an Old Man of Bohemia …"
  "There was an Old Person of Rheims …"
  "There was an Old Man on some rocks …"
  "There was an Old Man of the Coast …"
  "There was an Old Man in a pew …"
  "There was an Old Man who said …"
  "There was a Young Lady of Hull …"
  "There was an Old Man of the East …"
  "There was an Old Person of Tartary …"
  "There was a Young Girl of Majorca …"
  "There was a Young Lady of Prague …"
  "There was a Young Lady of Parma …"
  "There was an Old Man of Aôsta …"
  "There was a Young Person of Burton …"
  "There was an Old Person of Spain …"
  "There was a Young Lady of Clare …"

From the collection of Philip J. Mead.
Schiller, p. xi.
London, Christie's, 29 May 1986, lot 203.
FRKF 1255

Eighty-six pen-and-ink drawings, each illustrating an autograph limerick, n.d. [late 1870s], 86 p. The drawings are on the recto sides of the first 86 leaves of an oblong notebook (24 × 13.5), bound in brown cloth.

The limericks are as follows:
  "There was an old Man with a Beard …"
  "There was a young lady of Ryde …"
  "There was an old Man with a nose …"
  "There was an old man on a hill …"
  "There was an old Person of Chili …"
  "There was a young Person of Smyrna …"
  "There was an old Man with a gong …"
  "There was a young Lady whose bonnet …"
  "There was an old Man with a flute …"
  "There was a young Lady, whose chin …"
  "There was an old man in a boat …"
  "There was a young Lady of Portugal …"
  "There was an old Man of Moldavia …"
  "There was an old Man of Madras …"
  "There was an old Person of Leeds …"
  "There was an old man of Peru … So he tore off his hair"
  "There was an old Person of Hurst …"
  "There was a young Person of Crete …"
  "There was an old Man of the Isles …"
  "There was an old Person of Buda …"
  "There was an old Man of Columbia …"
  "There was a young lady of Dorking …"
  "There was an old Man of Vienna …"
  "There was an old Person whose habits …"
  "There was an old Man of Marseilles …"
  "There was an old Person of Cadiz …"
  "There was an old Person of Basing …"
  "There was a young lady of Bute …"
  "There was a young lady whose eyes …"
  "There was a young lady of Norway …"
  "There was a young lady whose nose …"
  "There was a young lady of Turkey …"
  "There was an old man of Apulia …"
  "There was an Old Man with a poker …"
  "There was an Old Man of the North …"
  "There was a young lady of Poole …"
  "There was an old Man on whose nose …"
  "There was an old Man of Nepaul …"
  "There was an old Man of Abruzzi …"
  "There was an old person of Rhodes …"
  "There was an old Man of Peru, who watched his wife making a stew"

"There was an old Man of Melrose …"
"There was a young lady of Lucca …"
"There was an old man of Bohemia …"
"There was an old Man of Vesuvius …"
"There was an old Man of Cape Horn …"
"There was an old Lady whose folly …"
"There was an old Man of Corfu …"
"There was an old Man of the South …"
"There was an Old Man of the Nile …"
"There was an old person of Cromer …"
"There was an old Person of Troy …"
"There was an old Man of the Dee …"
"There was an old Man of Dundee …"
"There was an old person of Tring …"
"There was an old Man on some rocks …"
"There was an old Man of Coblentz …"
"There was an old Man of Calcutta …"
"There was an old Man in a pew …"
"There was an Old Man who said. 'How, - shall I flee from this horrible Cow?'"
"There was a young Lady of Hull …"
"There was an Old Man of Whitehaven …"
"There was an old Man of Leghorn …"
"There was an old Man of the Hague …"
"There was an old Man of Jamaica …"
"There was an old person of Dutton …"
"There was a young lady of Tyre …"
"There was an Old Man who said, 'Hush! I perceive a young bird in a Bush'"
"There was an old man of the Coast …"
"There was an old Person of Bangor …"
"There was an old Man with a beard …"
"There was an Old Man of the West …"
"There was an old Person of Anerly …"
"There was an old Person of Spain …"
"There was an old Man who said 'Well! will nobody answer this bell?'"
"There was a young Lady of Wales …"
"There was a young lady of Welling …"
"There was an old Person of Tartary …"
"There was an old Person of Chester …"
"There was an old Man with an owl …"
"There was a young lady of Sweden …"
"There was a young Girl of Majorca …"
"There was an old Person of Burton …"
"There was an old Person of Ewell …"
"There was a young lady of Palma …"

"There was a young Lady of Clare …"

From the collection of Dudley Massey of Pickering and Chatto, subsequently sold by Bernard Quaritch Ltd to Justin Schiller.
Exhibited: "Edward Lear, 1812–1888," London, Royal Academy of Arts, April–July 1985 (no. 75b in the catalogue).
Schiller, p. xi–xii.
FRKF 82

Illustrated limerick on a single oblong sheet (20 × 12.5 cm).

"There was an old person of Ramleh …"

London, Sotheby's, 9 Dec. 1985, lot 649.
FRKF 1021

II. DRAWINGS

"And the dish ran away with the spoon"

Pen and brown ink drawing on blue paper (20.5 × 16.5 cm), unsigned, with the caption in Lear's hand.

London, Sotheby's, 21 Nov. 1985, lot 55.
FRKF 1095

[Owl and parrots]

Pen-and-ink drawing on paper (17.5 × 12.5 cm), showing an owl, a parrot, two smaller parrots, and a fantastic bird perched on a branch, with a Greek landscape in the background. Signed "E. Lear" in the lower right corner.

London, Sotheby's, 10 July 1986, lot 38.
FRKF 1254

[Romulus and Remus]

Four pen-and-ink drawings on paper (18 × 11.5 cm), numbered 1 to 4 in the upper left corner. Each drawing is signed and has a caption in Lear's hand.

London, Sotheby's, 9 Dec. 1985, lot 648.
FRKF 1087

Self-caricature, in profile, standing

Pen-and-ink on paper (13 × 21 cm), signed and dated Oct. 1870.

London, Sotheby's, 9 Dec. 1985, lot 650.
FRKF 1025

"A walk on a windy day"

Nine pen-and-ink drawings on paper (12.5 × 10 cm), preceded by an extra one (10.5 × 11 cm), 1860, 10 p. The first drawing shows a man seated, with a bird on his lap. It is signed "L." and dated "December 26. 1860." The other nine drawings are numbered by Lear and all carry a caption. Mounted in an album bound in dark blue morocco, with gold fillet along the edge of both boards, and author and title gold-tooled on front board; raised bands and double gilt fillets on the spine; all edges gilt, pale purple marbled paper endpapers.

London, Christie's, 9 July 1985, lot 47.
FRKF 1307

Illustrated story in eight scenes

Eight pen-and-ink drawings on individual sheets of cream-colored laid paper, 13.5 × 9.5 cm, dated 28 Feb. 1842.

The captions are as follows:

1. "Mr. L[ear] sets out for a walk - but is amazed at the high wind."
2. "Mr. L. loses his hat - & contemplates the flight thereof from a serene staircase."
3. "Mr. L. avails himself of his umbrella to fly after his lively hat."
4. "Mr. L. is joined in the chase of his lively hat by some familiar and affectionate jackdaws."
5. "Mr. L. rests on the branch of a tree, & converses with one of the familiar & affectionate jackdaws."
6. "Mr. L. descends to the earth & recovers his lively hat by means of 2 ingenious infants."
7. "Mr. L. is shocked to find a hole in his lively hat."
8. "Mr. L. returns home in a superfluous & unsatisfactory manner."

London, Christie's, 5 May 1982, lot 110.
FRKF 72

III. LETTERS

To "Allan"

1874 Feb. 18, Agra, ALS, 2 p. Refers to traveling in India.

FRKF 342a

To "Dear Arthur"

n.d., "27 Duke St. St. James" [London] ALS, 4 p. Mentions his correspondent's family in Rome.

London, Phillips, 28 March 1985, lot 419A.
FRKF 867

To Laura Campbell

1893 Oct. 21, Genoa, ALS, 2 p. (env), illustrated with a drawing of Lear carrying a parasol and riding astride an elephant. Signed "Bombyx Major."

n.d., n.p., ALS, 4 p., with an illustration showing three people around a dinner table about to eat three live birds.

FRKF 517a–b

To Mrs. George Coombe

1868 May 5, Ajaccio, Hotel Ottavi, ALS, 4 p., illustrated on p. 1 with a drawing showing Lear and three others riding on an elephant, and on p. 4 with the head of a Corsican woman.

London, Sotheby's, 15 Dec. 1982, lot 141.
FRKF 114

Also, an envelope inscribed (not in Lear's hand): "A letter written by Edward Lear to Mrs George Coombe (little Laura Willett's great great grandmother)."

FRKF 342b

To Miss Duncan

1865 Jan. 3, "61, Promenade des Anglais" [Nice] ALS, 3 p., illustrated with a drawing of Lear escorted by two frogs.

London, Sotheby's, 22 July 1985, lot 135.
FRKF 885

To "My dear Francis"

1867 Sept. 12, Winchester, ALS, 4 p., illustrated on p. [1] with a drawing of a pig, marked "E LEAR."

London, Sotheby's, 18 Dec. 1985, lot 96.
FRKF 1002

To Frederick W. Gibbs

1871 March 27, Villa Emily, San Remo, ALS, 4 p.
1872 Aug. 27, Allestree Hall, Derby[S], ALS, 3 p.
1873 Oct. 13, Grand Albergo di Genova, Genoa, ALS, 4 p.
1883 Nov. 18, Villa Tennyson, San Remo, ALS, 4 p.
1884 Jan. 23–24, Villa Tennyson, San Remo, ALS, 4 p.

London, Sotheby's, 10 July 1986, lot 91.
FRKF 1251

To "my dear Gussie"

1882 May 6, Villa Tennyson, San Remo, ALS, 3 p., illustrated on p. [2] with a small self-caricature.

London, Sotheby's, 10 July 1986, lot 89.
FRKF 1253

1883 Oct. 18, Villa Tennyson, San Remo, ALS, 4 p., illustrated on p. [4] with a drawing of three animals playing musical instruments.

London, Sotheby's, 18 Dec. 1986, lot 74.

FRKF 1349

To Miss Mandeville

1868 March 14, Villa Montaret, ALS, 3 p., commenting on the two pen-and-ink "monograms" on page 4 of the letter, one of them showing a pagoda, the other a ham.

London, Christie's, 5 May 1982, lot 113.

FRKF 75

To Lady Susan Percy

1840 Dec. 22, Via Felice [Rome] ALS, 1 p., enclosing "little scratches on 'stocking paper'" as a Christmas present. The letter is written in the third person.

1844 March 29 [Rome] ALS, 2 p. (env), enclosing three drawings for her amusement. On p. 2 is a self-caricature of a tiny Lear attacking an enormous ham with giant fork and knife. The caption reads: "Who first introduced salt meat into the Navy? Give it up? - Noah -: because he took Ham into the Ark." Inside envelope: "Mr. Lear presents his respect to Lady Susan Percy, and sends her some representations of frightful facts which occurred 3 or 4 hours ago.- "

London, Christie's, 5 May 1982, lots 112, 111.

FRKF 74, 73

To Miss Renshaw

1883 July 15, Mendrisio, Canton Ticino, Switzerland, ALS, 4 p., concerning his drawing of Bab el Kalabahe, his "50 Corsican children" [i.e. drawings of Corsica], illustrations to Tennyson, and an exhibition of his work in Wardour Street.

London, Sotheby's, 15 Dec. 1982, lot 146.

FRKF 109

To Mrs. Scrivens

1875 July 27 [8 Duchess Street] ALS, 3 p. On p. 3, self-caricature of Lear holding a leg of mutton (referred to in the body of the letter).

FRKF 342b

To William Wetmore Story

n.d., No. 19 Hotel d'Angleterre [Paris] ALS, 3 p. Mentions Thackeray; also refers to his painting of Bassae.

To Mrs. William Story

n.d., V. Condotti, ALS, 2 p. Mentions Robert and Elizabeth Barrett Browning. Accompanied by a paper print of a photograph of Lear, with a facsimile of his signature (13 × 20 cm).

London, Sotheby's, 10 July 1986, lot 90.

FRKF 1250

To Mrs. Gurney Sutton

[1870] May 7, Maison Guichard [Cannes] ALS, 2 p. Contains a humorous alphabet.

FRKF 62

To Emily Tennyson

1855 Nov. 11, Stoke Newington, ALS, 12 p. Discusses Franklin Lushington's stay in Capri. On p. 1, pen-and-ink illustration showing the first of his "Tennyson Landscapes."

London, Sotheby's, 16 July 1984, lot 99.

FRKF 508

To F.T. Underhill

1878 July 28, Monte Generoso, Canton Ticino, ALS, 2 p.

1879 June 14, Villa Emily, San Remo, ALS, 2 p.

1880 Sept. 26, Gd Hotel, Varese, Lombardia, ALS, 2 p., with an enclosed slip of paper with the address, in Lear's hand, of Sibylla, Lady Lyttleton.

1880 Dec. 25, Villa Emily, San Remo, ALS, 4 p.

1881 Feb. 11, Villa Emily, San Remo, ALS, 4 p.

1884 Oct. 1, Villa Tennyson, San Remo[S], ALS, 3 p.

1886 Feb. 14, Villa Tennyson, San Remo, ALS, 2 p.

1886 April 24, Villa Tennyson, San Remo[S], ALS, 3 p.

1886 May 11, Hôtel de Londres, Genoa, ALS, 4 p.

1886 Oct. 26, Villa Tennyson, San Remo, 3 p.

1887 June 2, Edward Lear Villa Tennyson San Remo[S], ALS, 1 p.

1887 July 11, Edward Lear Villa Tennyson San Remo[S], ALS, 1 p.

The correspondence conveys personal news and discusses artistic matters as well as financial transactions. There are references to Lear's oil views of Damascus and Taormina and his Tennyson illustrations. There are mentions of Lady Lyttleton, Lord Northbrook, Underhill's pupil Arnold Congreve, the death of Lionel Tennyson, as well as comments on children.

FRKF 63

To Mrs. Richard Ward

1873 July 5, Villa Emily, San Remo, ALS, 3 p. (env). Illustrated, on p. 3, with ten miniature pen-and-ink renderings of paintings by Lear.

London, Bloomsbury Book Auctions, 30 Nov. 1983, lot 185.
FRKF 243

1873 Aug. 25, Villa Emily, San Remo, ALS, 3 p., with front side of envelope. Illustrated, on p. 2, with a pen-and-ink drawing of Lear astride an elephant, and, on p. 3, two caricatures after Lear's own "Evening - on the Via Appia" and "Morning, near the Pinetree of Redicicoli."

London, Sotheby's, 29 June 1982, lot 248.
FRKF 69

To Digby Wyatt and his wife

1863 Sept. 29, n.p., ANS to Mrs. Wyatt on a small piece of paper, 1 p., illustrated with a tiny drawing of two cats and a parrot.

London, Sotheby's, 10 July 1986, lot 92.
FRKF 1252

1863 Dec. 24, 15 Stratford Place, Oxford St [London] ALS to Mrs. Wyatt, 3 p., concerning *Parrots*, with mentions of Sotheby's and Quaritch; also mentions a view of the Citadel of Corfu.
1866 Sept. 20, 15 Stratford Place, Oxford St, ALS to Digby Wyatt, 2 p., a humorous letter in fanciful spelling.

London, Sotheby's, 15 Dec.1982, lot 143.
FRKF 112

1866 Oct. 24, "Thratford Plaithe, Okthford Thtreet" [London], ALS to Mrs. Wyatt, 3 p., a humorous letter spelled in imitation of a lisp caused by toothache, and containing a 19-line poem in two stanzas, beginning "O Thuthan Thmith! Thweet Thuthan Thmith!"
1868 May 7, Ajaccio, Corsica, ALS to Mrs. Wyatt, 4 p., a description of Corsica, illustrated on p. 1 with a Corsican moufflon and the head of a Corsican woman.

London, Sotheby's, 15 Dec. 1982, lots 140, 142.
FRKF 115, 113

1868 Sept. 4, 15 Stratford Place, Oxford St., ALS to Mrs. Wyatt, 3 p. Contains a humorous poem with names of fanciful German cities.

London, Sotheby's, 15 Dec. 1982, lot 143.
FRKF 112

1869 June 29, Gd Hotel du Louvre, Paris, ALS to Lady Wyatt, 4 p., illustrated at the bottom of p. [4] with four small drawings showing insect-like women.

New York, Swann Galleries, 3 May 1990, lot 323.
FRKF 1360

1872 July 31, 6 Chandos Street, Cavendish Square [London] ALS to Lady Wyatt, 4 p. Contains a humorous report on a visit to the zoo.

London, Sotheby's, 15 Dec. 1982, lot 143.
FRKF 112

1872 Nov. 26, San Remo, ALS to Lady Wyatt, 4 p. Lear gives his place of residence as "Willerhemmerley" and reports on his trip to India.

London, Sotheby's, 29 June 1982, lot 503.
FRKF 71

1875 April 16, n.p., ALS to Lady Wyatt, 2 p., a jeu d'esprit consisting in using the word "mint," underlined each time, in 39 instances in the same number of lines.
1881 July 30, Mendrisio, Canton Ticino, Switzerland, ALS to Lady Wyatt, 4 p., giving personal news; illustrated on p. 4 with a self-caricature and a small drawing showing silhouettes of four Ticinians carrying large triangular baskets.

London, Sotheby's, 15 Dec. 1982, lots 144–45.
FRKF 110–11

To unidentified recipients

1879 March 14, Villa Emily, San Remo, ALS to "My dear Madam," 1 p. Apologizes for using stationery he had already written on. On p. [3], three riddles, signed and dated San Remo, 14 March 1879. On p. [4], beginning, crossed out, of a letter to "My dear William Evans," Villa Emily, San Remo, 7 February 1879.

London, Christie's, 27 March 1985, lot 176.
FRKF 871

n.d., fragment of an ALS, with a pen-and-ink drawing by Lear on one side showing a view of his studio, 11.5 × 9 cm, paginated 3 and 4.

FRKF 342

IV. MISCELLANEOUS

Original photograph of Lear in middle age (6 × 9.5 cm).

London, Sotheby's, 10 July 1986, lot 89.
FRKF 1253

Draft of a 4-line poem in Cockney, beginning "Some people their attention fixes …," written on the verso of the front side of an envelope postmarked Bath, 27 August 1868 and addressed in an unknown hand to "E. Lear Esq, 15 Stratford Place, Oxford Street, London."

London, Sotheby's, 15 Dec. 1982, lot 143.
FRKF 112

CHARLES LECOCQ (1832–1918)

I. MUSIC MANUSCRIPTS

La fille de Madame Angot

Holograph full-score manuscript for the ballet, n.d., 25 p., notated in purple ink on oblong 22-staff paper. At the bottom of the first page, in black and red pencil: "La fille de madame Angot / Ballet pour l'Eden." Additional notes and corrections in black ink and pencil. At the top of p. 1: "Danse générale"; at the top of p. 16: "Pas de Clairette"; p. 20, "Pas du comique"; p. 22: "Le comique et Clairette." On p. 20, a 15-measure revision on a folded paste-up. Bound in quarter black morocco and grey marbled paper boards.

"Pour la fameuse reprise de 1888, à l'Eden Théâtre, Lecocq écrivit le ballet des Fariniers qui se danse au troisième acte." Schneider, *Les maîtres de l'opérette française*, p. 174.

FRKF 281

Miscellaneous sketches

An oblong sketchbook of 131 sheets of 14-staff paper, containing drafts, n.d., mostly in pencil, occasionally in black ink, and usually notated on systems of two staves. Some of the texts are in English. Includes sketches for *La Camargo* (1878), *Le grand Casimir* (1879), *La jolie Persane* (1879), *Janot* (1881), *Plutus* (1886), *Les grenadiers de Mont-Cornette* (1887), and *Ali-Baba* (1887). Bound in dark brown limp sheepskin.

FRKF 537

II. LETTERS

To Louis Gallet

1894 Sept. 18, ALS on both sides of a card printed: 14, Rue de Nanterre. Asnières, 2 p.

1895 Feb. 19, n.p., ALS, 2 p., concerning a possible collaboration.

FRKF 503

FRANZ LEHAR (1870–1948)

Letters to Hans Hinkel

1938 Sept. 7, Vienna, ALS, 1 p. Mentions *Die lustige Witwe*.

1938 Sept. 25, Vienna, ALS, 1 p. Mentions *Die lustige Witwe*.

London, Sotheby's, 29 Nov. 1985, lot 115.
FRKF 1079

1938 Nov. 8, Berlin, ALS, 1 p., concerning *Die lustige Witwe*.

London, Sotheby's, 9–10 May 1985, lot 112.
FRKF 767.1

1939 Jan. 22, Berlin, ALS, 4 p. (env). Mentions Hitler and *Giuditta*.

London, Sotheby's, 29 Nov. 1985, lot 116.
FRKF 1080

1939 June 18, Vienna, ALS, 3 p. Mentions *Die lustige Witwe*.

1939 Nov. 5, Vienna, ALS on one side of a card. Mentions *Frasquita*.

London, Sotheby's, 9–10 May 1985, lot 113–14.
FRKF 767.2–3

1942 July 9, Vienna, ALS, 2 p. Mentions *Paganini*, *Giuditta*, and *Friederike*.

London, Sotheby's, 29 Nov. 1985, lot 114.
FRKF 1053

Hans Hinkel (1901–60), Reichskulturverwalter. All letters except 1939 June 18 and Nov. 5 have the salutation "Heil Hitler!"

RUGGIERO LEONCAVALLO (1857–1919)

I. OPERAS AND OPERETTAS

A chi la giarrettiera?

Holograph manuscript, in short and full score, of this operetta, 1918, ca. 290 p.

> The short score is written in pencil, with additional markings in red ink and red pencil, on a combination of nested and separate bifolia of tall 14-staff paper, paginated 1 through 126, with traces of stitching. In lieu of a title page is a facsimile of the cover of the first edition. The stamp of G. Venturini, Florence, is found on p. 1 and throughout. Signed and dated Viareggio, July 1918 at the end.
>
> The full score is written in pencil, with additional markings in red pencil, on 19 gatherings of nested or separate bifolia of tall staff paper preprinted for instrumentation, usually cut at the bottom, and irregularly paginated. On title page, in an unidentified hand: "R. Leoncavallo / A chi la giarrettiera? / (Operetta in 3 Atti) / Ouverture." Signed and dated Viareggio, July 1918 at the end. The vocal lines are present but the text is lacking. The last two gatherings are apparently discarded drafts, with the names of the characters crossed out in red.
>
> Both the short- and the full-score manuscripts lack act 3, no. 1; the short score lacks act 3, no. 3.

"*A chi la giarrettiera?*," operetta in three acts on a libretto by Edmondo Corradi, was premiered at the Adriano Theater in Rome on 16 Oct. 1919 (Leoncavallo had died on 9 August).

London, Sotheby's, 17 Nov. 1983, lot 130.
FRKF 228.130.1–2

Avemaria

Holograph drafts for a projected opera, n.d. The manuscript comprises the following:

> 1. Sketches in short score, in pencil, on pages [1] to [4] of two nested bifolia of 14-staff paper. The passage is scored for tenor and offstage chorus and begins with Leone's words "Ecco: il tuo nome ha detto la campana."
>
> 2. Short-score draft, incomplete, of a setting of the Ave Maria, in pencil, on both sides of a single leaf of 12-staff paper.
>
> 3. Two pages of short-score drafts, in pencil, on p. [2] and [3] of a single bifolium, beginning with the words "Non dire no."
>
> 4. Four pages of rough sketches, in pencil, on a single bifolium of 12-staff paper.
>
> 5. Two orchestral fragments in full score, in pencil, on both sides of a single, large sheet of 12-staff paper. The two pieces are scored for violin, oboe, tambourine, and keyboard. The first, lasting 18 measures, has the heading "Solenne"; the second, present in the first 6 measures only, is entitled "Danza."
>
> 6. Three systems of 2 staffs, noted in pencil on p. [1] of a single bifolium. Marked at the top of the page: "scherzetto orchestra / Daniello e Avemaria."
>
> 7. The beginning of act 1, scene 1, for soloists and chorus, drafted in short score, in pencil, on 12 pages (the first 11 of which are paginated), of four nested bifolia of 12-staff paper, with 2 staffs added in manuscript on p. 9 and [12]. At the top of p. 1: "Atto I / Scena prima / Avemaria / Leoncavallo" and the indications Andantino, with two alternative metronomic markings ($\quarternote = 60$ or $\eighthnote = 152$). The characters are given as Venditrice di carciofi (soprano), Venditrice di mele (soprano), Ragazzo venditore di limoni dolci (mezzo soprano), Salvatore (tenore), Maruzzaro (tenore), Riccotaro (baritono), Venditore di carne di majale (baritone), Venditore di franfellicchi (basso), Venditore di cottone (basso), Maestro di scuola (bass), and Il scrivatore pubblico (spoken role).
>
> 8. A single leaf of 12-staff paper with 12 measures of rough sketches in pencil.

The fragments are housed in a single bifolium serving as folder. On its front, in pencil, possibly not in Leoncavallo's hand: "Avemaria / Manoscritto."

Described by Sotheby's as a projected opera on a libretto by Luigi Illica and Enrico Cavacchioli, the work is not listed by Grove.

London, Sotheby's, 17 Nov. 1983, lot 129.
FRKF 228.129

La coupe et les lèvres

Holograph full-score manuscript for act 1, scenes 2 and 3, and short-score manuscript copy for act 5, scene 3, n.d.

> The manuscript for act 1, scenes 2 and 3 (part 1) is written on a gathering of nested and individual bifolia and loose sheets of 20-staff paper, paginated 1 to 18, with traces of stubs and stitching. The manuscript of act 5, scene 3 (part 2) is written on six nested bifolia, stitched together, of 16-staff paper.
>
> There are title pages for both parts. On the front cover of the first part, in Leoncavallo's hand: "A. de Musset / La coupe et les lèvres / Scènes deux et trois / mises en musique / avec accomp.t de Piano Violon et Violoncelle / par / R. Léoncavallo." On the front cover of the second part, in a copyist's hand: "A de Musset / La coupe et les lèvres / Dernière scène entre Deidamia et Frank / Musique de / R. Léoncavallo."
>
> Part 1 is entirely in Leoncavallo's hand: it is noted on two systems of 10 staffs. The text and stage directions are in French throughout. At the end is the word "Fin," in Leoncavallo's hand. On the verso of p. 18, additional drafts in pencil, noted on four 3- and 4-staff systems.
>
> Part 2 is written in ink in the hand of a copyist, with additional pencil markings in Leoncavallo's hand, some of textual nature (including Italian translations for certain passages), others concerning the violin and cello parts, not otherwise present, and a few markings in blue pencil.
>
> The setting of act 1, scenes 2 and 3, stops at the words for the

Voice: "Alors, lève-toi donc, car ton jour est venu," and does not include the encounter with Stranio and Belcolore that ends the scene in Musset's play. The setting of act 5, scene 3, begins halfway through the scene, with Frank's words "C'est bien toi! - je te tiens, - toujours fraîche et jolie" and ends before the dénouement, with Déidamia's words "j'ai gardé ton trésor."

Not among Leoncavallo's works listed in Grove.
London, Sotheby's, 17 Nov. 1983, lot 121.
FRKF 228.121.3

Goffredo Mameli

Holograph manuscript, in full score, and fragments of the short-score manuscript of this opera, with preparatory notes, 1916, ca. 520 p.

The full-score manuscript is written in pencil, with additional markings in red pencil, on gatherings of nested bifolia of tall 37-staff paper preprinted for instrumentation, signed at the end, n.d. At the top of p. [1] of act 1, in Leoncavallo's hand: "Mameli / Episodio I / R. Leoncavallo." *Collation:* "Preludietto," I–IV; act 1, [1]–217; Intermezzo, a–o; act 2, 1–189.

The short-score drafts are written in pencil on two gatherings of nested 16-staff paper and two loose bifolia. The first bifolium and gathering comprise the Preludietto and the end of the first episode and the intermezzo; the second gathering and bifolium is entitled "L'alba / Episodio II° / Leoncavallo" and is signed and dated Viareggio, 17 Feb. 1916 at the end.

The preliminary notes are written in black and blue ink in a folio-size ruled notebook in brown papers with a printed paper label entitled "Alba Italica / R. Leoncavallo." At the top of p. 1, in Leoncavallo's hand: "Goffredo Mameli / riassumito di varie biografie e studi."

Goffredo Mameli, "azione storica" on a libretto by Leoncavallo and Gualtiero Belvederi, was premiered at the Teatro Carlo Felice in Genoa on 27 April 1916.

London, Sotheby's, 17 Nov. 1985, lot 125.
FRKF 228.125, 1–2

Maiá

Holograph manuscript, in short score, and partly holograph full-score manuscript, 1907–09, 234 and ca. 800 p.

Short score

The short-score manuscript is written in pencil, with additions in black and red ink and blue and red pencil, on stitched gatherings of nested bifolia of tall 14-staff paper, paginated throughout in Leoncavallo's hand. The music is set to the original French text throughout.

Collation: Act 1, 78 p.; act 2, 94 p.; act 3, 62 p. Each act is bound separately in green paper covers, calligraphed in black ink and red watercolor ("P. Berel / R. Leoncavallo / Maia / I° [II° / III°] Atto"). Acts 1 and 3 have separate title pages, calligraphed in blue and red pencil: "P. Berel / Maïa / Ir [IIIme] acte / R. Leoncavallo/ Brissago / 1907 -"

On the last page, not numbered, of the act 1 manuscript, note in pencil in Leoncavallo's hand: "comin.to Mese di Marzo 1907 / (1° atto) / finito mese di ?" At the end of the act 2 manuscript, on p. [96], note in pencil: "finito il 26 Marzo 1908 dopo il 3° atto"; on the last page of the act 3 manuscript, note in pencil: "finito la composizione il 17 Gennaio 1908 (dopo il 1° atto)."

Also, additional sketches, in short score, three of them identified as "Nouveau choeur 1er acte," "Nuova scena finale," "Intermezzo II° atto," 64 p.

Full score

The full score is written in black ink, with additional markings in black, blue, or red pencil, on separate bifolia of tall 33-staff paper preprinted for instrumentation. There are two title pages, both in the hand of a copyist, one written in blue pencil, one in black ink.

Collation: Act 1, 1–166; "Intermezzo / qui précède l'acte II," 1–25; act 2, 1–242; act 3, 1–138. Revised passages: "Nouvelle chanson à boire de Torias" (act 2), 1–14; "Nouvel Andante de Maïa" (act 3), [1–14]; "Nouveau final, II acte," 1–58 (signed and dated Brissago, Aug. 1910 at the end); "Nouveau final 3me acte," 1–[43]. On the last page of act 3, in Leoncavallo's hand: "Fini d'orchestrer à Rapallo / le 11 mars 1909 / R. Leoncavallo." The orchestral parts are in Leoncavallo's hand, the vocal lines and words (in French) in that of a copyist.

Maiá, drama lirico in three acts, on a libretto by Paul de Choudens under the pseudonym Paul Berel, was premiered, in an Italian translation by Angelo Nessi, at the Costanzi Theater in Rome on 15 Jan. 1910.

London, Sotheby's, 17 Nov. 1983, lot 124.
FRKF 228.124.1–2

Malbruk

Holograph manuscript, in short score, incomplete, of this opera, ca. 1909, 263 p.

The manuscript is written in pencil, with a few passages and annotations in black ink and blue pencil, on separate bifolia, stitched together, of tall 14-staff paper. There are two paginations in act 1, one continuous, one for each number. The manuscript is placed in an additional bifolium serving as wrappers, marked, possibly not in Leoncavallo's hand: "Originale / Malbruk / R. Leoncavallo."

The manuscript comprises the following: Overture, [19] p.; act 1, 101 [i.e. 104] p.; act 2, [68] p.; act 3 (incomplete), [19] p. Also, 53 pages of additional drafts, some of them set to the French version of the text. There are special title pages for the "Canzone delle corne" (act 1) and for the "Coretto della ronda" and "Mattinata / Coro-Waltzer" (act 2). Some sections are signed at the end.

London, Sotheby's, 17 Nov. 1983, lot 123.
FRKF 228.123

Another manuscript, in full score, written in black ink, with additional markings in blue pencil, on tall 24-staff paper, and comprising the following sections:

1. "Petit-Duo" (for Basilide and Apollonius, the words in French), 10 p., paginated 543–52.

2. [title not in Leoncavallo's hand:] "Présentation du corps du ballet," 8 p., paginated 1–8.

3. [title not in Leoncavallo's hand:] "Defilé des Soldats de Malbrouck," 9 p., paginated 9–17.

The three sections are housed in a loose bifolium of 28-staff paper marked in blue pencil, possibly in Leoncavallo's hand: "Granadinas / L'Alguasiles," and, in black pencil, also possibly in Leoncavallo's hand: "Aschemberg."

Malbruck, *fantasia comica medioevale* in three acts, on a libretto by Angelo Nessi, was premiered at the Teatro Nazionale in Rome, on 19 Jan. 1910. The French edition of the piano-vocal score (*Malbrouk s'en va-t-en guerre*. Paris: Eschig, 1910) credits Maurice Vaucaire as co-author of the libretto.

FRKF 1414

The Manicuring Girl

Holograph manuscript, in full score, of act 2 of this operetta, signed in various places, n.d. [but ca. 1918–19], 180 p.

Notated in pencil, with additional markings in blue pencil, on seven gatherings of nested bifolia of tall 33-staff paper preprinted for instrumentation, cut at the bottom. Only the Duet and Finale are paginated by the composer. On title page, in Leoncavallo's hand: "'The Manicuring Girl' / Atto II / Musica di Leoncavallo / N° 1 / Ecran cinématographique -." The words "Parole di R. de Simone" were scratched out at the top of the page.

At the head of the first page of music in the first gathering, also in Leoncavallo's hand: "'Ecran cinématographique' / R. Leoncavallo"; on p. [1] of the second gathering: "Intermezzo N° 1 [1 B cancelled] 2"; on p. [1] of the third gathering: "Tempo di Valse / Scorza (tenore) e Coro / N° 4 [3 cancelled]"; on p. [1] of the fourth gathering: "N° 5 / Quintetto" (labelled "Quintette" at the top of the first page of music); on p. [1] of the fifth gathering: "N° 6 [5 cancelled] / Duetto"; on p. [1] of the sixth gathering: "n° 7 [6 cancelled] / Chanson comique" (labelled "Depart pour le Vesuve" at the top of the first page of music); on p. [1] of the seventh gathering: "Gran finale II° / N° 8 & 9 [7 cancelled]." The vocal lines are present but the words are lacking, except in a few instances (e.g. the Quintet and Duet), where they appear in French.

Accompanied by a manuscript of the act 2 Intermezzo, in short score, possibly in the hand of a copyist, 7 p. Also, a separate sheet of tall 14-staff paper, marked by Leoncavallo "The Manicuring Girl / Gran Finale II," with annotations in another hand.

Not in Grove.

FRKF 1415

Pierrot au cinéma

Libretto and manuscript drafts, partly holograph, in short and full score, of this unpublished operetta, ca. 1919, ca. 340 p.

Libretto

The libretto is present in three typescript versions: the first entitled "Capriccio d'amore [annotation in pencil, possibly in Leoncavallo's hand: 'Pierrot'] / Sketch - Balletto / in due parti (Da uno spunto di Trület) / di Luigi Bonelli / Versi di Arturo Franci / Musica di Ruggiero Leoncavallo," with manuscript corrections by Leoncavallo, 21 p., stamped "G. Venturini / Editore / Firenze"; the second entitled "Pierrot al cinematografo / Operetta in un atto / Parole di C. Trulet / Traduzione di Cip / Musica di R. Leoncavallo," 14 p., stamp of Venturini, with inscription in Leoncavallo's hand, in blue pencil, on the verso of the last leaf; the third entitled "Pierrot al cinema / Parole di C. Trulet / Musica di R. Leoncavallo / Testo italiano di / Arturo Franci," stamp of Venturini, 11 p., incomplete.

Together with the libretto are two manuscript versions, one of them in Leoncavallo's hand, and a typescript version with a carbon copy, of a song beginning "O mio Pierrot, perdono …," subtitled on the typescripts "Parole e Musica di R. Leoncavallo."

Short score

The short-score manuscript is written chiefly in pencil, with some additions in red ink and blue pencil, chiefly on nested bifolia of tall 14-staff paper. On the title page, in Leoncavallo's hand: "A Mad.me Emilia Laus / âme vibrante d'art / et de charité, l'ami / Leoncavallo / Pierrot au cinema / Comedie en un acte / Paroles de Trulet / Musique de Leoncavallo / [stamp of G. Venturini]."

The manuscript, previously bound (traces of stitching), comprises the following sections, as labelled in Leoncavallo's hand. Many sections are signed by the composer and stamped by G. Venturini.

1. "Petite ouverture," holograph, 7 p.

2. "N° 1 / Ecran cinématographique / Un splendide yacht traverse les flots en pleine mer," holograph, 3 p.; with a copy, not holograph, annotated and signed by Leoncavallo, 4 p.

3. "N° 2. Duettino Tenore Soprano," holograph, 5 p.; with 3 copies, not holograph, one without the words.

4. "N° 3 [and 3 bis] / Couplets de Pierrot," holograph, 6 p.

5. "N° 4 / Mélodie de Pierrette," holograph, 3 p. [and] "Musique de scène," holograph, 2 p. followed by a title page (possibly not in Leoncavallo's hand) for "N° 6 / Valse de Pierrot."

6. "N° 5 / Mélodie de Pierrette," holograph, 3 p.

7. "Pianoforte / Pantomima / Musica di Ruggiero Leoncavallo," in an unidentified hand, 18 p.

8. "No. 6. Valse de Pierrot," 2 p., in black ink, probably in the hand of a copyist.

9. "Fox-trot," holograph, 3 p.

10. "No. 9 / Ensemble final," holograph, 2 p.

Also in Leoncavallo's hand is the draft for a "Minuetto," 3 p. (the vocal line is on the third page).

Several of the manuscripts above have an annotation, initialed or signed [signature not deciphered] and dated 19 September 1955.

Also in Leoncavallo's hand are 16 pages of drafts, with the heading "Danza delle ancelle."

Other sections, not holograph, are:

"Pierrot au cinéma / Tango," 5 p., inscribed, signed, and dated Viareggio, 13 Aug. 1918, by Leoncavallo.

"Pierrot au cinéma / Gavotte," 2 p.

"Pierrot au cinéma / Valse," 4 p.

"Pierrot au cinéma / Rigaudon," 3 p.

"Pierrot au cinéma / Menuet," 3 p.

All the above manuscripts are docketed, dated Florence, 8 July 1925, with the signatures of Luigi Perrocchi, Achille Pierattini, and Silla [?] Pierattini Testa.

Further manuscript sections, generally present in two copies each, none of them holograph, are entitled: "Gavotte di Leoncavallo / dal Pierot [sic]"; "Fox-trott per pianoforte"; "Minuetto / Quartetto / Soprano-Tenore-Caratteristica donna-Caracteristico uomo"; "Danza e coro orientale"; "Alzata di Sipario / Entrata cori / Sestetto"; "Duettino comico / Fox-trott"; "Gran Walzer"; "All[egro] Moderato"; "Serenata (tenore)"; "Danza buffonesca"; "Coro e danza"; "(Tango) - Duetto comico"; "Duettino comico-fox-trott"; "Duettino comico (Soubrette e Buffo)"; "Melodia per soprano"; "Duetto soprano-tenore"; "Tango - arrang: di S. Allegra"; "Notturno."

Some of those manuscripts contain pencilled notes dated Florence, 1955. All the above are in short score. There is also a full-score manuscript, in a copyist's hand, of "Valzer di Pierrot," 13 p.

The short-score manuscript is accompanied by a printed cover maquette [?] for "Pierrot au cinéma / Un atto e Pantomima di C. Trulet / Musica di Ruggiero Leoncavallo" (Florence: G. Venturini, n.d.).

Full score

The full-score manuscript is complete and evidently all in Leoncavallo's hand; it is written in pencil, with additional markings in blue and red pencil, on nine gatherings of nested bifolia of large, tall staff paper preprinted for orchestration, cut at the bottom. At the bottom of the first page of each section is the stamp of G. Venturini, Florence, with the date 1919 filled in in blue pencil.

It comprises the following sections: "Petite ouverture," 33 p.; "N° 2 / Duettino Soprano-Tenore," [14 p.]; "N° 3 / Couplets de Pierrot," [8] p.; "N° 4 [changed into 5 in a different hand] / Musique de scène," 8 p.; "N° 5 [5 partly erased] / Mélodie soprano," 10 p.; "N° 6 / Valse de Pierrot," 13 p.; "N° VII / Mélodie de Pierrette," 8 p.; "[7 bis added, not in Leoncavallo's hand] Morceau de bravoure / ajouté," [8] p.; "N° 8 / Pantomima," [81] p.

Also in full score are the following dance arrangements, written in ink on tall 24-staff paper, numbered 1 to 7 and 10–12 in an unidentified hand, most of them signed "R. Leoncavallo" at the end (but probably not by Leoncavallo): 1. Tango, 5 p.; 2. Duettino comico, 6 p.; 3. Duetto, 14 p.; 4. Duettino comico, 10 p.; 5. Danze e coro delle campane, 11 p.; 6. Danza buffonesca, 5 p.; 7. Serenata per tenore e intermezzo atto 2°, 4 p.; 10. Sestetto, 18 p.; 11. Danza e coro orientale, 10 p.; 12. Quartetto-Minuetto, 4 p. All marked "Sì" in pencil at the top of the first page in an unidentified hand.

Accompanied by miscellaneous, unrelated papers.

These include three Bollettin[i] di Dichiarazione e Mandat[i] alla Società Italiana degli Autori ed Editori, Roma, filled out and signed by Jeanne Puel Leoncavallo, for the songs "Ma Suzon" and "Vieni, amor mio" and an unidentified "Teste del pezzo di Ruggiero Leoncavallo" [?]; a leaflet of samples entitled *Klaviermusik aus dem Verlage von Max Brockhaus*, Leipzig, including five pieces by Leoncavallo, marked by pencil; carbons of handwritten letters from Jeanne Leoncavallo, 1936; lists of works, an invoice, and miscellaneous notes, possibly in Leoncavallo's hand.

Not listed in Grove.
London, Sotheby's, 17 Nov. 1983, lot 131.
FRKF 228.131.1

La reginetta delle rose

Holograph manuscript, in short score, n.d., 232 p., mostly in pencil, with passages in black ink and additions in blue pencil and black and red ink, on various types of tall paper.

Each act is placed in a bifolium serving as wrappers, labelled in blue pencil, the whole originally housed in an additional bifolium labelled, in Leoncavallo's hand: "La Reginetta delle Rose / 1° Originale / Leoncavallo."

Collation (including separate title pages for numbers within each act): act 1, [59] p.; act 2, [102] p.; act 3, [70] p. Accompanied by a fragment titled "Intermezzo al 2° atto," 1 p., in a separate blank bifolium.

La reginetta delle rose, operetta in three acts, on a libretto by Giovacchino Forzano, was premiered at the Teatro Costanzi, Rome, and at the Politeama Giacosa, Naples, on 24 June 1912.

London, Sotheby's, 17 Nov. 1983, lot 127.
FRKF 228.127

Der Roland von Berlin

Holograph manuscripts of the libretto and short score of this opera, 1903, 577 p.

The libretto is written in black, red, and purple ink and black and blue pencil on both sides of tall sheets of unruled paper, paginated 1 to 71. Pages 67–70 are a "Nuovo finale," in black and purple ink; additional pencil notes on the verso of p. 71. On the title page, in Leoncavallo's hand: "Il Rolando / Dramma storico in 4 atti / di / R. Leoncavallo / Tratto dal romanzo: Il Rolando di Berlino / di / W. Alexis." A number of revisions are written on paste-on pieces of paper.

The short score is written in pencil on gatherings of nested bifolia, stitched together, of tall 12- or 16-staff paper (with occasional supplementary staves in manuscript). The first 11 pages of act 1 are missing. The score begins with the words (for L'Elettore): "Per cielo! Il caso è nuovo!" The remainder of the manuscript collates as follows: act 1, 11–[196] p.; act 2, [91] p.; act 3, [112] p.; act 4, scene 1, 1–66 [i.e. 1–68, as numbers for pages 2 and 4 were accidentally omitted from the numbering; act 4, scene 2, [49] p.

On title page of act 2, in Leoncavallo's hand: "Atto II° / Il Rolando / Dramma lirico in 4 Atti / Parole e musica di / R. Leoncavallo / Prima idea al lapis." The subtitle for act 3 simply reads "Opera in 4 atti" and is dated Brissago, June 1903. At the end of act 3, signature of Leoncavallo and date, in French: "Samedi 4 Juillet / 1 heure ½ du matin." There are two separate title pages for the two tableaux of act 4, reading simply: "Quadro I° [–II°] / Il Rolando / Atto IV / R. Leoncavallo / Prima idea al lapis." Marked "Fine dell' opera" and signed at the end.

Der Roland von Berlin, *historisches Drama* in four acts, on a libretto by the composer after Willibald Alexis's *Der Roland von Berlin* (translated into English as *The Burgomaster of Berlin*) was premiered at the Städtische Oper, Berlin, on 13 Dec. 1904.

Heinrich Schütz to Henry Miller, p. 96–97.
London, Sotheby's, 17 Nov. 1983, lot 122.
FRKF 228.122

Zazà

Holograph manuscript, in short score, of a large part of act 1 of the opera, n.d., 161 p.

> The manuscript begins with the words for the chorus "Ma brava! Ma brava!" (p. 12 of the piano-vocal score) and continues until the end of the act. Notated in pencil, with a few additional markings in black ink, on sixteen gatherings of varying numbers of nested bifolia and single leaves of 12-staff paper (27 × 33 cm), with traces of stitching, placed in an additional bifolium, the third page of which is the last page of the act.
>
> Across an additional leaf of different 12-staff paper, possibly the remainder of an additional protective wrapper, in blue pencil, in Leoncavallo's hand: "Zaza / Appunti"; unidentified sketches on the verso, notated in black ink.

Zaza, *commedia lirica* in four acts, on a libretto by the composer after the play by Pierre Berton and Charles Simon, was premiered at the Teatro lirico in Milan, on 10 Nov. 1900.

London, Sotheby's, 17 Nov. 1983, lot 126.
FRKF 228.126

Zingari

Holograph manuscript, in short score, n.d., 171 p., mostly in pencil, with passages in black ink, with additions in red and blue pencil, chiefly on nested bifolia of tall 14-staff paper, housed in an additional bifolium serving as wrappers, marked "Zingari / Leoncavallo" in the composer's hand.

> *Collation:* Episode 1, [86] + [2] p.; Intermezzo, [4] p.; Episode 2, 1–[57] p. Also, miscellaneous sketches in pencil, [24] p. There is a title page for each episode, the first labelled, in Leoncavallo's hand: "I Episodio / Zingari / Dramma Lirico in Due Episodi / E. Cavacchioli e G. Emmanuele / Musica di / R. Leoncavallo / Firenze e Montecatini / da Aprile al 15 Agosto / consegnato l'orchestrazione."

Zingari, *dramma lirico* in two acts on a libretto by Enrico Cavicchioli and G. Emanuel, after Pushkin's *Tsygany*, was premiered at the London Hippodrome on 16 Sept. 1912.

London, Sotheby's, 17 Nov. 1983 lot 128.
FRKF 228.128

II. OTHER WORKS

Écho

Holograph full-score manuscript of this work for chamber orchestra, 1884. Notated in ink (with a few additional markings in pencil) on 12 unnumbered pages of 24-staff paper. On the title page, possibly in a copyist's hand: "Echo / Scène idyllique" and, in Leoncavallo's hand: "Mandolines 1ere et 2e Mandole et Orchestre / R. Leoncavallo." Dated in Leoncavallo's hand in the lower right corner: "Bruxelles Juillet 1884." The name of a dedicatee has been erased at the top; only the words "A" and "L'autore" are left. The title and composer's signature also appear at the top of the first page of music. The work, in A major, is scored for two mandolins (one offstage), mandola, flutes, oboes, clarinets, bassoons, horns, and strings. The tempo indication is Cantabile sost°. In a grey folder marked (not in Leoncavallo's hand): "Eco / Manoscritto originale / Inedito."

Not in Grove.
London, Sotheby's, 17 Nov. 1983, lot 121.
FRKF 228.121.2

"Invocazione all'Italia / (dall' Op. Mameli) / Corni in Fa / 3° e 4°"

Title page only (not holograph).

FRKF 1414

"Mattinata"

Autograph parts, notated in black ink, possibly in Leoncavallo's hand, on tall 12-staff paper (G.B.T. Casa Musicale Pietro Napoli, Livorno), for the following instruments: cello, 2 p., marked "N° 3 / R. Leoncavallo / Mattinata / Cello"; flute, 1 p., marked "N° 3 / Mattinata / R. Leoncavallo / Flauto 1mo in Do."

FRKF 1414

Pantins vivants

Holograph manuscript of this minuet for full orchestra, n.d., 12 p. Notated in black ink on four nested bifolia of tall staff paper preprinted for instrumentation, cut at the bottom, paginated 1–12 by the composer. On title page, in Leoncavallo's hand: "[These two words printed in red:] Pantins Vivants - / - Menuet - / de / - R. Leoncavallo - / - Partitura grande orchestra -"

At the top of p. 1, also in Leoncavallo's hand: "Pantins Vivants / Minuetto / [signed:] R. Leoncavallo." Signed at the end. On the last page of the outer bifolium, in pencil: "M. Leoncavallo / # 121 / Via S. Andrea / Firenze."

London, Sotheby's, 17 Nov. 1983, lot 121.
FRKF 228.121.1

"Serenata"

Autograph parts, fragments, comprising the beginning of the flute part and a sheet, unfilled, for the harp, marked "N° 7" at the top.

FRKF 1414

"Serenata Medioevale"

Holograph manuscript, in short score, on a text by Angelo Nessi, n.d., 5 p. Notated in black ink, the words in red ink, on a bifolium and the recto of a single sheet of tall 12-staff paper (G.B.T. Casa Musicale Pietro Napoli, Livorno). The title and text of the poem are written, in Leoncavallo's hand, on the verso of the single leaf. Possibly relating to *Malbruk*.

Not in Grove.
FRKF 1414

"Tarantella"

Autograph parts, notated in black ink, possibly in Leoncavallo's hand, on tall 12-staff paper (G.B.T. Casa Musicale Pietro Napoli, Livorno) for the following instruments: "Ottavino," 3 p.; "Trombe 1ma e 2nda in Fa," 3 p.; "Tromba 3za in Fa," 2 p.; "G. Cassa - Tamburi - Triangolo," 2 p.

FRKF 1414

"Tempo di Valse"

Holograph manuscript, incomplete, notated in black ink, with indications of orchestration in red ink, on bifolia or individual sheets of tall 12-staff paper (G.B.T. Casa Musicale Pietro Napoli, Livorno), paginated I–X; also, the timpani part, 1 p.

FRKF 1414

"Valse mélancolique"

Holograph fragment, in short score, notated in black ink on p. [2] and [3] of a bifolium of tall 12-staff paper (G.B.T. Casa Musicale Pietro Napoli, Livorno), 2 p.

FRKF 1414

Unidentified songs

In F major. Notated in black ink, without the words, on individual sheets of tall 12-staff paper (G.B.T. Casa Musicale Pietro Napoli, Livorno), the beginning in two different versions, 6 p.

In E-flat major. Notated in black ink, without the words, on a bifolium of tall 12-staff paper (G.B.T. Casa Musicale Pietro Napoli, Livorno), 4 p.

FRKF 1414

Unidentified sketches

Two fragments, each notated in ink on small oblong leaves (16.5 × 13 cm) of 10-staff paper, foliated 1 and 2. The first, marked "And.te en sourdine," in D-flat major, comprises 21 measures, notated on a single staff. The second, also notated on a single staff, is in D major and comprises 17 measures. Additional drafts in pencil are on the verso, notated on four systems of 2 staffs and two single staffs. Another fragment, on both sides of the top part of a torn sheet, is notated in ink on two systems of 2 staffs and totals 21 measures.

These sketches were found among the manuscripts of *La coupe et les lèvres* but appear to be unrelated.

London, Sotheby's, 17 Nov. 1983, lot 121.

FRKF 228.121.3

Sketches, notated in black ink, usually in short score, on bifolia or individual sheets of tall 12-staff paper (G.B.T. Casa Musicale Pietro Napoli, Livorno), 35 p. Accompanied by a folder marked "Epido Re," with notes in an unidentified hand, n.d.

FRKF 1414

III. LETTERS

All letters are in French.

To Georg Droescher

1908 June 7, Brissago (Switzerland), ALS, 4 p. concerning *Maiá* and Choudens.

FRKF 794

To Adolph Fürstner and his wife

1893
April 23, Milan, from Berthe Leoncavallo to Mrs. Fürstner, ALS, 4 p.
May 19, London, ALS, 4 p.
Oct. 30, 16, via Vivajo [Milan] ALS, 4 p.

1894
Feb. 10, Berlin, ALS, 2 p.
[Feb.?] n.p., to Mrs. Fürstner, ALS, 3 p. (env)
Feb. 28, n.p. ("Hotel Central"), ALS, 3 p.
June 14, Milan, ALS, 10 p.
July 18, Marienbad, ALS, 8 p.
Nov. 17, Milan, ALS, 6 p.
Nov. 26, n.p., ALS, 3 p.
Dec. 27, n.p., ALS, 8 p.

1895
March 9, Milan, ALS, 8 p.
March 11, Milan, telegram
April 4, Bologna, ALS, 3 p.
April 9, Rome, ALS, 6 p. (env)
April 22, Milan, ALS, 4 p.
May 6, Milan, ALS, 3 p.
May 12, Milan, ALS, 8 p.
May 29, Augsburg [?] ALS, 8 p.
June 9, Milan, ALS, 6 p.
June 11, Milan, ALS, 2 p.
June 26, Milan, telegram
Aug. 14, Cannero (Lago Maggiore), ALS, 8 p., enclosing a letter from the publisher Tedeschi, not present, with a request that it be returned.
Aug. 21, Cannero (Lago Maggiore), ALS, 4 p.
Sept. 18 [?] Cannero (Lago Maggiore), ALS, 4 p.
Oct. 14, Milan, ALS, 8 p.
Oct. 19, Milan, ALS, 14 p.
Oct. 25, n.p., ALS, 12 p.
Nov. 2, 16, via Vivajo, ALS, 4 p.
Nov. 9, Milan, ALS, 6 p.
Dec. 16, Milan, ALS, 3 p.
Dec. 25, Milan, ALS, 4 p.

1896
Jan. 2, 16, via Vivajo, ALS, 4 p.
Feb. 28, Rome, ALS, 4 p.
July 10, Brissago, Lago Maggiore, ALS, 12 p.
Dec. 28, Pallanza (Lac Majeur), ALS, 7 p.

1897
June 20, Berlin, ALS, 2 p., annotations in pencil in an unidentified hand on an adjoining page.

With drafts of letters from Adolph Fürstner to Leoncavallo:
1895 Aug. 21, Arenstein [?] AL, 3 p. (with postal receipt)
1896 July 18, Engelberg, AL, 3 p.
n.d., n.p., AL, 1 p.

Also, "Es war ein Traum …," autograph poem, dated 1 January 1893. Marked at the top: "Poesie: Dorémi / Musik R. Leoncavallo."

The Berlin music publisher issued *Der Bajazzo*, the German version of *I Pagliacci*, in 1892. The correspondence discusses the possibility of future contracts and refers to the revision, publication, and premiere of *Chatterton*, the success of *I Medici* in Germany, the composition of *La vie de bohème*, and the commission of *Der Roland von Berlin*. Disparaging comments are made about fellow composers Mascagni (especially concerning *I Rantzau* and *Silvano*), Franchetti, Cilea, Coronaro, Giordano, and Samaras (especially *La martire*). The letter of 28 Feb. 1896 reports on "the terrible fiasco of Puccini's Bohème." There are requests for financial assistance and help on behalf of the composer's brother and discussions of the financial situation of Sonzogno, his rivalry with Ricordi, and transactions with the Bolognese publisher A. Tedeschi. The dating of several letters is in pencil, apparently not in Leoncavallo's hand. Some are accompanied by typed English translations.

FRKF 205

To Ernst von Hesse-Wartegg

1905 Oct. 26, Brissago, ALS, 4 p. Mentions Minnie Hauk and his *Ave Maria* and *I Pagliacci*.

Marburg, Stargardt, 12 June 1986, lot 706.
FRKF 1331

To Sir James Rennell Rodd

1916 May 28, Florence, ALS, 2 p., concerning *Goffredo Mameli*.

London, Bloomsbury Auctions, 7 March 1984, lot 95.
FRKF 492

To Cosima Wagner

1894 July 28, Bayreuth, ALS, 2 p. (env). Regrets not being able to accept her invitation.

London, Sotheby's, 19 Nov. 1985, lot 882.
FRKF 996

Other letters

To "Altesse"

1901 May 2, Milan, ALS, 4 p., concerning *La bohème* and complaining about Gustav Mahler and Puccini. Possibly addressed to Archduke Eugen.

Marburg, Stargardt, 12 June 1986, lot 705.
FRKF 1330

To an unidentified friend

1896 Dec. 28, Pallanza, ALS, 3 p. Mentions *La vie de bohème*, *I Pagliacci*, and *Der Roland von Berlin*.

Marburg, Stargardt, 26–27 Nov. 1985, lot 809.
FRKF 1151

To an unidentified publisher

1901 June 21, Milan, ALS, 4 p., concerning two possible works, both in collaboration with Victor Capoul, to be entitled *Le clown* and *Pazzariello*.

Paris, Le Roux-Mathias (Drouot), 19 April 1985, lot 283.
FRKF 720

IV. PRINTED WORK

Ave Maria. Preghiera per voce di tenore con accompagnamento di arpa ed harmonium ad lib. Brissago, Switzerland: privately printed, 1905. Three unbound bifolia, paginated 3–9, in illustrated wrappers (signed E.B.).

Printed dedication in upper right corner of front cover: "A Sua Santità / PIO X / Sommo Pontefice." On back cover: "Ateliers artistiques A. Trüb & Cie., Aarau (Suisse)." Accompanied by an undated form letter from Leoncavallo, Brissago, advertising the sale of his *Ave Maria* to benefit victims of the Sept. 1905 earthquake in Montalto Uffugo, Calabria, with an autograph postscript in the composer's hand.

See: Leoncavallo. *Ave Maria; a cura di Alessandra Bertacchi* (Bologna: Ut Orpheus Edizioni, 1997).
FRKF 280

LEOPOLD I, KING OF THE BELGIANS (1790–1865)

Documents and memorabilia relating to the marriage of Leopold I, king of the Belgians, and Princess Charlotte of England.

Marriage treaty, in black ink, in a secretarial hand, on a gathering of five nested bifolia, sewn with a navy blue ribbon connected to nine seals on the ninth and last page. The signatures next to the seals are those of the archbishop of Canterbury and Lords Eldon, Harrowby, Bathurst, Sidmouth, Liverpool, and Castlereagh, as well as Nicholas Vansittart and the Baron de Just. The treaty is dated London, 13 March 1816. Laid in are an "Additional Article," in the same secretarial hand, 2 p., also dated London, 13 March 1816, with the same seals and signatures, and a ratification of the marriage, 1 p., dated London, 21 May 1816, sealed and signed by Castlereagh and Baron de Just. In an envelope dated 29 Aug. 1840 and inscribed by Leopold I: "My English Marriage / treaty signed - / 1816."

Also, calligraphed document, dated 25 May 1816, signed by George IV as Prince Regent at the top and countersigned by John Fisher, bishop of Salisbury, conferring on Leopold I the right to sit in the Royal Chapel at Windsor in his capacity as knight and companion of the Order of the Garter; written on vellum backed with navy blue silk, with blue and gold tassel, in a gilt silver case with tassel.

Illuminated appointment of negotiators for marriage treaty with a seal, in a gilt silver case with arms and tassels; and ratification of the marriage treaty, also with a seal in gilt silver case and tassels.

Accompanied by twelve letters from Robert Banks Jenkinson, 2nd earl of Liverpool, prime minister of England, to Prince Leopold of Saxe-Coburg, all concerning the living arrangements and expenses of Prince Leopold and his wife:

1816

March 21, Fife House, LS, 3 p.
March 22, Fife House, LS, 4 p.
March 27, Fife House, LS, 2 p.
March 29, Fife House, LS, 4 p.

May 1, Fife House, ALS, 3 p.

Oct. 24, Walmer Castle [Kent] ALS, 6 p.

Nov. 5, Walmer Castle, ALS, 3 p.

1817

Feb. 19, Fife House, ALS, 1 p.

Sept. 16, Walmer Castle, ALS, 1 p.

1819

Aug. 1, Coombe Wood, ALS, 1 p.

1820

Jan. 27, Coombe Wood, ALS, 2 p., on mourning stationery.

June 30, Fife House, LS, 3 p.

London, Christie's, 16 Oct. 1985, lot 31.
FRKF 1096.1–5

MICHEL MAURICE LÉVY (1883–1965)

La rivière de la forêt

Printed version of this song for voice and piano on a poem by Pierre Louÿs. An offprint from *Madame & Monsieur* [?], two sides of a single sheet, numbered 2 and 3. Numbered at the bottom 1471–72. At the top of the page: "Madame & Monsieur / à Geneviève Vix / La Rivière de la Forêt / Chansons de Bilitis. / Musique de / Michel Maurice Lévy / Paroles de / Pierre Loüys [sic]."

Cinq chansons de Bilitis (La rivière de la forêt. - Bilitis. - Tendresses. La rencontre. - Les danses au clair de lune), by Michel Maurice Lévy, was published by Senart in Paris in 1921.

Neither the work nor the composer is in Grove.
FRKF 499.5

FRANZ LISZT (1811–86)

I. MUSIC MANUSCRIPTS

Ballade for piano, no. 1, A. 117

Holograph manuscript draft of an early version of this piece for piano, n.d., 1 p., in black ink on the first page of a bifolium of 8vo-size 16-staff paper. Signed "F. Liszt" at the end. The work is dated 1845–49 by Grove. It was first published by Kistner in Leipzig in 1849.

London, Sotheby's, 17 May 1990, lot 147.
FRKF 1305

Freischütz Fantasie, A. 68

Holograph draft for part of this fantasia on themes from Weber's opera, n.d. [ca. 1840], 4 [+ 1] p., in black ink, with one correction in red pencil, on a bifolium of tall 12-staff paper (an extra staff hand-drawn on p. [1]), the additional page being a cancel originally sealed on the entire p. [2]. On p. [4], across the left margin, in an unidentified hand: "Manuscript von Liszt. Freischütz Fantasia"; and, in another hand: "Aus dem Nachlass von Berthold Kellermann."

The *Fantasie* is based on the motifs "Und ob die Wolke sie verhülle" (act 3) and the act 1 Waltz.

London, Sotheby's, 29 Nov. 1985, lot 117.
FRKF 1033

Für Männergesang, nos. 4 and 5

Holograph manuscript of these two choruses for a cappella male chorus [1860], written on two oblong sheets attached with adhesive, numbered 3–4 and 1–2, of 18-staff paper (evidently cut from a taller sheet). The first chorus is on p. 3 and 4, the second on p. 1 and 2. They are both notated on 3-staff systems. A number of corrections and deletions on p. 4.

No. 4, beginning with the indication "Gehalten und sehr fest betont," is the second version, in E-flat, of *Trost I* (M. 22, "Es rufet Gott uns mahnend"), on a text by T. Meyer-Merian. No. 5, marked "Mässig bewegt, mit inniger Erfüllung, mit halber Stimme," is the second version, in G major, of *Nicht gezagt* (M. 23), also on a text by Meyer-Merian. Both were first published by Kahnt in Leipzig in 1861.

Inscription at the end: "Vorliegendes Manuscript ist eigenhändig von Dr. Franz Liszt geschrieben. Die betreffende Composition für Männerchor ist bei C. F. Kahnt in Leipzig erschienen. Dies Herrn Hetz zur Beglaubigung." Signed A.W. Gottschalk.

Paris, Laurin-Guilloux-Buffetaud-Tailleur (Drouot), 3 July 1985, lot 102.
FRKF 855

Grosses Konzertsolo (Grand solo de concert), A. 167

Holograph manuscript fragment, n.d., in black ink, with additional markings (notably fingerings) in pencil and red ink, on a single bifolium, paginated 7 through 10 in red pencil in the upper right corners. The staves are manuscript and number ten per page, except on p. 9 where Liszt added an additional one at the bottom. At the top of p. 7, in red ink, in an unidentified hand: "Manuscript von Dr Liszt. Aus 'Grosses Concertsolo von Fr. Liszt.' [illegible] 7ber / 11. 52."

The piece is the original version of the *Concerto pathétique* for two pianos. "Liszt composed a *Grand solo de concert* [S175a] as a solo competition piece—a concert Allegro in sonata form—for the Paris Conservatoire by 1850. He prepared a version of it with orchestral accompaniment, probably in collaboration with Raff—who was working under Liszt's instructions—before 1851 [S365]. He extended the solo work by adding the Andante sostenuto theme and all the material connected with it in 1851, publishing the work as *Grosses Konzertsolo* [S176]. The two-piano version was made probably by late 1855, and was performed on many occasions from 1856." Leslie Howard, *Critical notes to Ferenc Liszt, Grosses Konzertstück & Concerto pathétique for two pianofortes* ([Edinburgh]: The Hardie Press, 1998. Liszt Society Publications, Vol. 9).

Marburg, Stargardt, 5–6 March 1995, lot 833.
FRKF 816

Ich möchte hingehn, N. 31

Holograph manuscript (incomplete) of this song for tenor and piano, n.d., in black ink on oblong 14-staff paper, on three pages, the first two of which are numbered in Liszt's hand. The middle section (measures 71 through 133) is lacking.

On the verso of page 3, the composer has written: "Strophen aus der Fremde - / ('Ich möchte hingehn wie das Abendrot;') / Gedichtet von Herwegh, / für eine Tenor Stimme / mit Clavier Begleitung / von / Franz Liszt - / auf einer 2ten Platte, den geistreichen Verfasser der / 'Melodie der Sprache' / Louis Köhler / freundschaftlich gewidmet."

Bound in green paper boards. On front board, gold-tooled on darker green leather label: "En hommage … / S.E.M. Aloïs Vollgruber / Ambassadeur d'Autriche en France"; and on a smaller label: "Pont-à-Mousson / 27 mai 1955." On spine, gold-tooled on green leather label: "Franz Liszt - Strophen aus der Fremde."

Tipped in before the manuscript is an engraved portrait of Liszt after Deveria, captioned "Litz" [sic] and credited: "Paris, Rosselin, Quai Voltaire 23 / Imp. Lemercier Paris."

Published in Berlin by Schlesinger in 1859, and in a revised version by Kahnt in 1860. See *Musikalische Werke*, VII:2, p. xii–xiii. The dedicatee was the piano teacher and music critic from Königsberg, Christian Louis Heinrich Köhler (1820–86).

FRKF 385

Réminiscences de La Juive, A. 20

Holograph manuscript draft fragment of this "paraphrase" for piano, n.d., 4 p., in black ink, with corrections in black and red pencil, on a bifolium of tall 16-staff paper, paginated 27–30. The manuscript is incomplete, beginning at the second variation, preceded by the last seven measures (all cancelled) of the first. Signed and inscribed on p. [4]: "F Liszt / al mio amico / Monsignore Lottin de Laval."

Réminiscences de La Juive, fantaisie brillante sur des motifs de l'opéra de Halévy was composed in 1835 (the same year as the first performance of the opera) and published in Paris by Schlesinger the following year.

Heinrich Schütz to Henry Miller, p. 36–37.
London, Sotheby's, 9–10 May 1985, lot 118.
FRKF 769

Resignazione (Ergebung), E. 28

Holograph draft of this piece for keyboard (piano or organ), 1877, 4 p., in black ink, with corrections in red ink and red and blue pencil, on a bifolium of oblong 8-staff paper, with an additional two staves pasted-in at the top of p. [1]. Signed, titled, and dated at the end: "Resignazione / ('Ergebung') / 25 Octobre 77 - Roma."

For unspecified keyboard instrument. First published in facsimile in August Göllerich, *Franz Liszt* (Berlin: Marquardt & Co., 1908); published as a work for piano in Liszt, *Neue Ausgabe sämtlicher Werke/New Edition of the Complete Works* (Kassel and Budapest, 1970–), I/12. Dated 1877–81 by Grove.

FRKF 1146

Seconde marche hongroise (Ungarischer Strummarsch), A. 112

Holograph manuscript of the revised version of this piece for solo piano, 1875, 6 p., in black ink, with corrections in red pencil, on a bifolium and a single leaf of tall 20-staff paper. Dated at the end "14 Octobre 75. / Villa d'Este / FL." At the bottom of p. [6] is a 17-measure "ossia" section.

First published in Berlin by Schlesinger in 1876.

Paris, Pierre Cornette de Saint-Cyr (Drouot),
25 May 1984, lot 64.
FRKF 709

II. LETTERS

To Berthold Kellermann

1879 Aug. 29, Bayreuth, ALS, 3 p. (env), concerning Wagner, with references to *Parsifal* and the *Ring*. Not in *Briefe* II.

Marburg, Stargardt, 5–6 March 1995, lot 836.
FRKF 818

To Eduard Liszt

1857 March 26, ALS, Weimar, 16 p. Mentions Meyerbeer and discusses at length the First Piano Concerto, including ten musical quotations. *Briefe* I: 270–76.

1860 July 9, Weimar, ALS, 9 p. Mentions Peter Cornelius and Hans von Bülow. *Briefe* I:359–62.

1864 Sept. 7, Weimar, ALS, 4 p. Mentions Wagner. Not in *Briefe* II.

London, Sotheby's, 29 Nov. 1985, lots 121, 124, 126.
FRKF 1056–58

1872 Nov. 6, Horpács[S], ALS, 3 p. Mentions Bayreuth and *Der Ring der Nibelungen*. *Briefe* II:177–78.

London, Sotheby's, 28 May 1986, lot 444.
FRKF 1129

To Marie Lynen

1882 July 16, Bayreuth, ALS, 2 p. Mentions Saint-Saëns, Wagner, and *Parsifal*.

1886 May 8, Weimar, ALS, 3 p. (env). Announces his departure for Bayreuth and the marriage of his granddaughter.

Both letters are in French. Not in *Briefe* II.

Paris, Laurin-Guilloux-Buffetaud-Tailleur (Drouot), 12 June 1984, lots 229, 235.
FRKF 477

To Carl Reinecke

1849 May 30, Weimar, ALS, 4 p., in French, concerning Wagner, with mentions of *Tannhäuser* and references to Gluck, Handel, and Weber; also about Schumann, with references to *Faust* and *Genoveva*. *Briefe* I: 76–78.

Marburg, Stargardt, 5–6 March 1995, lot 834.
FRKF 817

To Marchese Francesco Sampieri

1839 Jan. 14, [Florence*] ALS, 2 p. and address leaf, addressed to "mon cher Marquis," concerning a concert. In French. Not in *Briefe* I.

London, Sotheby's, 9–10 May 1985, lot 117.
FRKF 768

To an unidentified recipient

1828 April 1, n.p., ALS to "Le redacteur de la Reunion," 3 p. and address leaf.

FRKF 564

III. PRINTED MUSIC

L'Etoile du soir: romance sans paroles, de l'Opéra: Tannhäuser, de R. Wagner, transcrite pour piano par F. Liszt. Paris: J. Meissonnier Fils, n.d. [ca. 1849].

Folio, [1]–7 p. Music publisher's number: J.M. 2734.

Bound in contemporary sheepskin; possibly a proof copy. Inscribed by Wagner at the bottom of the title page: "An Madame / Jessie Laussot / am Abend seiner Abreise / von Bordeaux, Sonnabend 18ten [May 1850?] / abends 7 uhr. / R.W." Jessie Laussot and Wagner had an affair in the spring of 1850; see Ernest Newman, *The life of Richard Wagner*, vol. 2, p. 146.

London, Sotheby's, 29 Nov. 1985, lot 248.
FRKF 1037

IV. MISCELLANEOUS

Pencil caricature of Liszt on paper (13 × 16.5 cm), unsigned, n.d. [late 19th century?], showing Liszt in clerical costume, in profile, with a large nose.

London, Sotheby's, 9–10 May 1985, lot 121.
FRKF 770

ANITA LOOS (1894–1981)

I. MANUSCRIPTS

"Daisy"

(Title is sometimes spelled "Daisey")

Typescript of an early version of this comedy in three acts, 1956, ca. 155 p. Typed on title page and folder: Untitled play / July 27, 1956.

Another version, typescript, carbon, with autograph corrections, n.d., ca. 93 p. Title printed on folder: "Every girl needs a parlor"

Another version of act 1, typescript, 4 copies (the last incomplete), 1960, 28 and 21 p. Stamped "Jun 14 1960."

Another version, n.d., ca. 100 p.

Another version, typescript, ca. 1962, ca. 100 p., with an autograph note in Loos's hand: "Read this on April 8 - 1962"

Another version of act 1, largely made up of cut-and-paste typescript fragments, with autograph corrections, n.d., ca. 28 p.

Another version of act 1, act 2 (stamped "April 1 1959"), and notes (stamped "March 21 1959"), typescript, n.d., 75 p. Marked "Daisey" on folder.

Another version, complete, typescript with pencil corrections, 117 p. Title "Daisey" corrected to "Daisy" on folder.

Another version of act 1, typescript, [ca. 1962], 73 p. Autograph annotation by Loos on p. 1: "Re-read / May 28th – 1962."

Another version of act 2, typescript, n.d., 32 p.

Another version of act 1, typescript, incomplete, n.d., 24 p.

Fragments of act 2, typescript, some with pencil annotations, n.d., ca. 70 p.

Two unidentified fragments, typescript, n.d.

No play with this title is recorded among Loos's published works.

Unidentified works

Included are fragments of collaborations with Ludwig Bemelmans and "Charlie" (Charles MacArthur). Some possibly relating to "Daisy." Accompanied by an envelope marked "Bemmy's material." Unidentified drafts are also present in Loos correspondence with Bemelmans.

Fragment, titled "Chandelier," typescript, n.d., 1 p. Illustrated with a pencil drawing showing four men carrying a chandelier.

Fragments, 12 p., typescript, manuscript, and pencil illustrations for sets and costumes.

Fragment, typescript, illustrated, n.d., 3 p., accompanied by an additional sheet marked "Charlie".

"The one I love the best," typescript, n.d., 2 p. Marked "Charlie" in manuscript, and in typescript, "For the blurb."

"The one I love the best / Details of Conversations," typescript, 1953, 11 p. Marked "Charlie" in manuscript on the title-page. Dated 20–21 November 1953.

"To The One I Love the Best," typescript, 1953, 4 p. Marked "For Charlie" in manuscript on the title-page.

Five preparatory drawings for sets, in pencil on tracing paper.

"21,000 Monuments and 60,000 Objects Are Under the Protection of the State," typescript, n.d., 2 p.

"Walk in Hollywood," autograph manuscript, illustrated, n.d., 5 p. Written in pencil on the recto of five large sheets.

Fragments of drafts or notes, typescript, n.d., 3 p.

II. CORRESPONDENCE

From Pierre Barillet

rue Vineuse[S] = on the stationery of 3, rue Vineuse, XVIe [Paris]

1952

Aug. 22, Kerbastic, Gestel, Morbihan[S], ALS, 2 p.

Sept. 14, 3, rue Vineuse, 16ème, ALS, 2 p.

Sept. 24, n.p., ALS, 2 p.

Nov. 1, rue Vineuse[S], ALS, 4 p.

Nov. 13, Metz, ALS, 2 p.

Nov. 29, rue Vineuse[S], ALS, 2 p., with a typed note.

Dec., "Vendredi 5," rue Vineuse[S], ALS, 2 p.

1953

Feb. 8, "Sunday," rue Vineuse[S], ALS, 2 p.

Feb. 14, rue Vineuse[S], ALS, 4 p.

Feb. 20, rue Vineuse[S], ALS, 4 p.

March 10, rue Vineuse[S], ALS, 2 p.

March 14, rue Vineuse[S], TLS, 1 p., with autograph postscript.

April 2, n.p., TLS, 2 p., with autograph postscript.

April 15, Rome, TLS, 2 p.

April 20, n.p., TLS, 2 p.

April 26, n.p., TLS, 1 p.

May 1, rue Vineuse[S], ALS, 2 p.

May 4, rue Vineuse[S], TLS, 1 p.

May 16, "Saturday night," rue Vineuse[S], TLS, 2 p.

May 25, rue Vineuse[S], ALS, 2 p.

July 17, Monaco, ALS, 2 p.

Aug. 24, n.p., TLS, 2 p.

Sept. 22, "Tuesday," Bastide du Roy, Antibes, ALS, 2 p.

Dec. 14, 3, rue Vineuse, 16ème, TLS, 2 p.

1954

Jan. 13, n.p., TLS, 2 p.

March 1, 3, rue Vineuse, 16ème, TLS, 2 p.

April 3, Paris, TLS, 2 p.

May 19, n.p., TLS, 1 p.

June 14, Paris, TLS, 2 p., with autograph postscript.

Oct. 11, n.p., TLS, 2 p.

Oct. 24, 3, rue Vineuse, 16ème, ALS, 2 p.

Oct. 26, 3, rue Vineuse, 16ème, ALS, 2 p.

Nov. 21, n.p., ALS, 2 p.

Dec. 28, n.p., ALS, 2 p.

1955

July 19, La Fiorentina, Saint-Jean-Cap-Ferrat[S], ALS, 4 p.

Aug. 31, n.p., ALS, 2 p.

Nov. 13, 3, rue Vineuse, 16ème, ALS, 2 p.

Dec. 19, n.p., TLS, 1 p.

1956

Jan. 22, "Sunday," n.p., ALS, 2 p.

Jan. 25, "Wednesday," n.p., ALS, 2 p.

March 21, n.p., ALS, 2 p.

April 28, n.p., TLS, 1 p.

1957

March 14, n.p., ALS, 2 p.

June 28, Sitges (Spain), ALS, 4 p.

[Sept. 30, Amsterdam*] APCS

Dec. 26, Paris, TLS, 2 p.

1958

Feb. 17, 3, rue Vineuse, 16ème, TLS, 2 p.

April 1, Paris, TLS, 2 p.

May 19 [Fontvieille*] APCS, also signed by Jean-Pierre Grédy.

July 22, Paris, TLS, 2 p.

1959

Feb. 13, 3, rue Vineuse, 16ème, TLS, 2 p.

Feb. 23, 3, rue Vineuse, 16ème, TLS, 1 p.

May 17, Paris, TLS, 2 p.

1960–77

1960 Aug. 1 [Fontvieille*] APCS

[1960 Dec. 27, Villars-sur-Ollon*] APCS

1961 Feb. 16, n.p., TLS, 1 p.

1961 June 11, Paris, TLS, 2 p.

1961 Sept. 19, n.p., ALS, 2 p.

1962 Jan. 5, n.p., TLS, 2 p.

1962 Dec. 25 [Villars-sur-Ollon*] APCS

1963 Aug. 30, Azeitao (Portugal), TLS, 2 p.

1963 Dec. 9, rue Vineuse, ALS, 2 p.

1963 Dec. 30, Villa Noailles, Hyères[S], ALS, 4 p.

1965 April 21, Florence, APCS

1977 Sept. 2, Valmont, Glion-sur-Montreux[S], ALS, 2 p.

Undated

ALS, 13 Sept., n.p., 1 p.

TLS, "Thursday," n.p., 1 p.

ALS, "Thursday," rue Vineuse[S], 2 p.

ALS, "Tuesday 23," rue Vineuse[S], 2 p.

ALS, "Monday 29," rue Vineuse[S], 2 p.

ALS, "Sunday night," rue Vineuse[S], 2 p.

ALS, "Monday 11," rue Vineuse[S], 2 p.

ALS, "Saturday 13," n.p., 4 p.

ALS, 13 Aug., Château Légier, Fontvieille[S], 2 p.

ALS, "Tuesday," n.p., 2 p.

The letters are all in English. Accompanied by carbon copies of 3 typed letters from Loos to Barillet, 1953 March 24 and April 6 and 1954 March 18, 2 p. each. Also accompanied by a black-and-white photograph showing Anita Loos at a table with Pierre Barillet, Mrs. John Wilson (née Natalie Paley), and Clifton Webb at the Empire Room in the Waldorf Astoria Hotel, n.d., New York (20 × 25 cm).

Pierre Barillet, French playwright, collaborator of Jean-Pierre Grédy on many successful comedies, including adaptations of plays by Anita Loos.

From Cecil Beaton

1948 July 14, 8 Pelham Place, S.W.7 [London][S], TLS, 2 p.

[1968 Jan. 23, Bora-Bora*] APCS

1968 Aug. 28, St-Regis-Sheraton, New York[S], TLS, 1 p.

1968 Nov. 20, Raffles, New York[S], TLS, 1 p.

No year

April 12, 8 Pelham Place, S.W.7[S], ALS, 2 p.

April 15, 8 Pelham Place, S.W.7[S], ALS, 1 p.

Aug. 8, 8 Pelham Place, S.W.7[S], ALS, 3 p.

Nov. 3, 8 Pelham Place, S.W.7[S], ALS, 3 p.

Undated

4 ALS, 8 Pelham Place, S.W.7[S], each 2 p.

ALS, 8 Pelham Place, S.W.7[S], 1 p.

ALS, Mereworth Castle, Maidstone, Kent[S], 1 p.

ALS, The Beverly Hills Hotel[S], n.d., 3 p.

ALS, Capri, "date unknown," 1 p.

ANS on a Christmas card.

Also, TL from Loos to Beaton, n.y. July 19, n.p., 2 p.

From Ludwig Bemelmans

1954 Oct. 27, Town & Country, New York[S], TLS, 1 p., to "Charlie" (Charles MacArthur)

1955 Dec. 4, Ludwig Bemelmans[S], TLS, 1 p.

1955 Dec. 4, n.p., TLS, 1 p., addressed to "My dear collaborators," 3 copies.

1956 Jan. 17, Claridge's, London[S], TLS, 1 p.

1956 Dec. 8, Town & Country, New York[S] (verso), TLS, 2 p., illustrated with 3 pencil drawings.

1956 Dec. 25, Hôtel Ritz, Paris[S], TLS, 2 p.

1957 Sept. 4, Hôtel Ritz, Paris[S], TLS, 1 p.

Undated

TLS, n.p., 4 p., illustrated with a set design in pencil.

TLS, "Full moon, Saturday," n.p., 2 p.

ALS, Hôtel Ritz, Paris[S], 4 p.

TL, n.p., 6 p.

Accompanied by a TL from Loos to Bemelmans, 1955 Nov. 18, n.p., 2 p.; a TLS to Nunnally Johnson, 1956 Oct. 20, New York, 4 p.; and an unidentified manuscript, 4 p.

From Jean-Pierre Grédy

1951 Oct. 1, Paris, ALS, 2 p.

1952 Oct. 22, Paris, ALS, 4 p.

1954 Feb. 24, Paris, ALS, 2 p.

1961 Jan. 28, Paris, telegram

1961 Jan. 30, Paris, ALS, 6 p.

1961 June 11, Paris, ALS, 6 p.

1961 July 20, Saint-Tropez, ALS, 2 p.

1962 Sept. 29, Paris, ALS, 2 p.

1962 Nov. 16, Paris, ALS, 4 p.

1962 Dec. 31, Paris, ALS, 2 p.

1964 April 13, Paris, ALS, 2 p.

1964 April 14, Paris, ALS, 2 p.

1964 May 9, Paris, ALS, 6 p.

1964 May 27, Paris, ALS, 4 p.

1964 June 20, Paris, ALS, 2 p.

1971 Oct. 8, Kurhotel Montafon, Schruns[S], ALS, 5 p.

1973 May 26, Vineuil, ALS, 2 p.

[1973 Sept. 10, Paris*] APCS

1974 June 4, Château des Buspins, Daubeuf-près-Vatteville[S], ALS, 3 p.

1974 Dec. 8, Château des Buspins, Daubeuf-près-Vatteville[S], ALS, 2 p.

1976 Dec. 27, Les Buspins, ALS, 2 p.

Undated

ALS, "Thursday the 25th of Sept," Paris, 2 p.

ALS, "Sunday," n.p., 2 p.

APCS, 24 Feb.

The letters are all in English. Accompanied by carbon copies of 2 typed letters from Loos to Grédy, 1962 Oct. 5, 2 p., and 1974 Dec. 23, 1 p.

Jean-Pierre Grédy, French playwright, collaborator of Pierre Barillet.

From Miriam Howell

1966 March 10, Ashley Famous Agency, Inc., New York[S], TLS, 1 p., from her secretary.

From Aldous Huxley

1926 May 14, Congress Hotel and Annex, Chicago[S], ALS, 1 p.

1926 July 5, The Athenaeum, Pall Mall, S.W.1. [London][S], ALS, 2 p.

1926 July 21, London, ALS, 2 p.

1941 April 26, ANS, 1 p.

1947 March 26, Wrightwood, California, TLS, 1 p.

1947 April 22, Los Angeles, TLS, 2 p.

1947 July 4, Wrightwood, California, TLS, 2 p.

1947 July 27, Wrightwood, California, TLS, 2 p.

[1947 Sept. 22, Taos*] APCS, also signed by Frieda [Lawrence] and "Angelina."

1947 Dec. 22, Los Angeles, ALS, 2 p.

1949 Jan. 16, Sage and Sun Apts., Palm Desert, California, ALS, 2 p.

1949 Feb. 14, Sage and Sun, Palm Desert, California, TLS, 1 p.

1949 Aug. 5, Wrightwood, California, TLS, 1 p.

1949 Nov. 15, 740 North Kings Road, Los Angeles[S], ALS, 2 p.

1949 Dec. 25, Los Angeles, telegram

1949 Dec. 27, Los Angeles, TLS, 2 p.

[1950 Oct. 17, Missouri*] APCS

1950 Nov. 15, Los Angeles, TLS, 2 p.

1953 Jan. 2, Los Angeles, ALS, 4 p.

1953 April 24, Los Angeles, ALS, 2 p.

[1953 June 9, Coeur d'Alene*] APCS

1953 Aug. 14, n.p., ALS, 2 p.

1955 Feb. 12, Los Angeles, ALS, 2 p.

1955 Aug. 24, Guilford, Connecticut, TLS, 1 p.

1955 Dec. 27, Los Angeles, TLS, 2 p.

1956 March 25, 740 N. Kings Road, Los Angeles[S], ALS, 4 p.

1956 April 4, Los Angeles, ALS, 2 p.

1956 Dec. 19, on stationery of 740 N. Kings Road, cancelled by hand to "3276 Deronda Dr., Los Angeles," ALS, 3 p.

1957 Jan. 18, Los Angeles, TLS, 1 p.

1957 Feb. 22, Los Angeles, TLS, 1 p.

Undated

n.p. TLS, 2 p.

Feb. 14, n.p., ANS on one side of a card.

From Addison Mizner

1928 March 7, Addison Mizner, Architect, Palm Beach, Florida[S], TLS, 2 p.

From Wilson Mizner

1927 Dec. 22, Famous Players-Lasky Corporation, Paramount Studios, Hollywood[S], TLS, 2 p.

1928 July 27, The Ambassador, Los Angeles[S], TLS, 3 p.

1928 Aug. 11, The Ambassador, Los Angeles[S], TLS, 1 p.

1929 Jan. 31, Los Angeles, telegram

1930 Dec. 30, Los Angeles, telegram

1931 May 9, Hollywood, telegram

1932 June 22, San Francisco, telegram

Also, undated ALS, State Narcotic Hospital[S], n.d., 3 p., written in pencil, signed "The Faculty," and purportedly reporting on the internment of "her son Willie."

III. OTHER PAPERS

"Adieu to the Ritz" by Ludwig Bemelmans, proofsheets, 4 p.

"Mizner"
  Material relating to Loos's projected biography of Wilson Mizner, possibly to be entitled "A child's life of Wilson Mizner" [?].

  Book proposal, typescript, carbon, n.d., 3 p.

  Typescript fragments, n.d, ca. 35 p.

  Verse account of Mizner, typescript with autograph corrections, n.d., 2 p. Incipit: "Wilson Mizner, Frisco's boy …"

  TL from Loos to Edwin Baird, *Real America Magazine*, 1933 July 28, 2 p., carbon, concerning Mizner.

  Mizner, Wilson. "Why has California gone back?," typescript, n.d., 3 p., 2 copies.

  Typed copy of a letter from Mizner to Simon and Schuster, 1932 May 31, Burbank, California, 1 p.

  TLS from [Mizner?] to his parents, 1928 March 20, Los Angeles, 2 p.

  Also, various newspaper and magazine clippings relating to Mizner.

ANITA LOOS PAPERS
Huxley letters acquired from George MacManus, Philadelphia. Remaining papers: New York, Swann Galleries, 14 June 1984, lots 154–57, 164, 173.
FRKF 192, 1431

PIERRE LOTI (1850–1923)

Letter to Reynaldo Hahn

n.d., n.p., ALS on both sides of a card, inviting Hahn to stay with him.

Paris, Laurin-Guilloux-Buffetaud-Tailleur (Drouot), 8 Feb. 1985, lot 115.
FRKF 658.7

Letter to the Marquise de Montebello

[ca. 1891] n.p., ALS, 3 p., on mourning stationery. Mentions a passage he wishes to submit to her from his account of his trip to the Orient and the impending marriage of Léon Daudet and Jeanne Hugo.

Paris, Laurin-Guilloux-Buffetaud-Tailleur (Drouot), 29 April 1982, lot 83.
FRKF 65

LOUIS-PHILIPPE, KING OF THE FRENCH (1773–1850)

Letters to Napoléon, duc de Montebello

1847 Feb. 3, Neuilly, ALS, 2 p. (env). Thanks for an attention shown to Queen Marie-Amélie.

Paris, Laurin-Guilloux-Buffetaud-Tailleur (Drouot), 29 April 1982, lot 94.
FRKF 66

1847 July 30, Neuilly, ALS, 1 p., mentioning an illness of his son the Prince de Joinville.

Nassau, Bahamas, Fiduciary Company Ltd, 25 June 1984, lot 155.
FRKF 321

Napoléon Lannes, second duc de Montebello (1801–74), French ambassador to the court of Naples in 1838–47 (and later in St. Petersburg), minister of foreign affairs in 1839 and Ministre de la Marine in 1847.

LOUISE D'ORLÉANS, WIFE OF LEOPOLD I, KING OF THE BELGIANS (1812–50)

Manuscript diary

1850 May 14 to Sept. 7, 67 p., written in French in a ruled notebook, paginated throughout by the queen, and bound in dark blue boards with corners and spine in dark blue calf. At the top of the first page, in Queen Louise's hand: "Notes et Journal / 1850."

The first entry is dated "Buckingham Palace, 14 Mai 1850," the last "Samedi 7" [Sept.]. The queen died in Ostend on 11 Oct. The entry dated "Mercredi 28 [Aug.]" records the death at Claremont, Surrey, on 26 August, of King Louis-Philippe of the French, the father of Queen Louise.

Laid in, blank mourning envelope containing dried ferns and an ecclesiastical calendar for 1850.

London, Christie's, 16 Oct. 1985, lot 32.
FRKF 1293

PIERRE LOUŸS (1870–1925)

I. LITERARY MANUSCRIPTS

"Le livre des eaux et de la nuit"

A collection of manuscript and printed materials gathered by Louÿs with a view to a verse collection, which was not published. Items 1–9 are printed; items are 1 p. and undated, unless otherwise noted. The collection comprises the following:

1. "L'aube de la lune," from *Le Mercure de France* for Oct. 1894.

2. "Le retour d'Adonis," from *Le Mercure de France* for April 1894.

3. "Jour d'hiver," from *La revue blanche*.

4. "Envoi," from *La revue blanche*, on verso of the preceding item.

5. "Les pêcheurs," from *La revue blanche*.

6. "Sirène mourante," from *La revue blanche*, on verso of the preceding item.

7. "Scènes dans la Forêt des Nymphes: Le matin; Le soir; La nuit," from *La revue blanche*, 3 p. Also, autograph manuscript version of "Le matin."

8. "Aquarelles passionnées: La danse; L'amazone," from *Le Mercure de France*, April 1894.

9. "L'ombre," proof [?] on a large folio sheet.

10. "Trouée," typescript.

11. "Pégase," typescript, on verso of the preceding item.

12. "La prairie," typescript, 2 versions, 1 p. each.

13. "Au premier matin bleu …," typescript, with autograph corrections by Louÿs, dated "1889 / 5–8 novembre 1890 / 3 mars 1891 / 10 janvier 1901 / (dates à jamais mémorables)."

14. "Chèvre-pieds," typescript.

15. "Quand tu marches à la brune …," autograph manuscript.

16. "Elle est au ciel; son corps est penché sur le Monde …," autograph manuscript.

17. "A la nymphe de Sumène," autograph manuscript, 3 p., dated Lapras, 17 Aug., n.y. Also, "To the nymph of Sumene," uncredited English translation, typescript, 2 p.

18. "Mantones y capas," autograph manuscript, dated "Séville. 15 février 95." Previous title, partly cancelled: "Mantones de Manila."

19. "Elles marchent sur le bout …," autograph manuscript, dated 1–19 Nov. 1894.

20. "Chevelures! pleurs de saules!" autograph manuscript, dated 2–19 Nov. [1894?].

21. "Enfants qui revenez de la terre nocturne …," autograph manuscript.

22. "Ariane, Seigneur, fut le seul labyrinthe …," autograph manuscript.

Also, a gathering, paginated 39–48, with traces of stitching, comprising the poems "XX / Le matin"; "XXI / Le soir"; "XXII / La nuit"; "XXIII / Les pêcheurs"; "XXIV / Sirène mourante."

Housed in a clothbound folder, with a paper label marked, in Louÿs's hand: "Le Livre des Eaux et de la Nuit." Accompanied by a description, in French, of the manuscript, with an English postscript certifying its authenticity, signed by J.J. Champenois, 1929 March 19, on stationery of The United French Publishers, New York, 1 p.

New York, Sotheby's, 22 May 1985, lot 332.
FRKF 1365

II. MUSIC MANUSCRIPTS

Holograph manuscripts

"La célèbre romance de Khadidja / transcrite spécialement pour Mlle L. de H. / Paroles de M.M. J. Barbier et M. Carré / Musique de Georges Bizet," 1 p., n.d., notated in black ink on a small sheet of 12-staff paper (blind stamp of Lard-Esnault). Vocal line only. A parody of *Carmen*, marked "Mouvement de valse lente."

"La romance de sentiment champêtre idiot," on a small blank sheet, in pencil, marked at the top: "pour 'Sic,'" 11 measures, notated on three individual staves.

Autograph card, in pencil; on one side, the sketch of a female head, on the other side a short musical quotation, marked "Automob. Ragtime," and various addresses (including that of Robert de Flers).

A short musical quotation in pencil on the verso of an envelope stamped "Mustel, père & fils harmoniums d'art & celestas" and addressed to "Monsieur Pierre Louÿs / 29 Rue de Boulanvilliers / Paris 16e"; readdressed to "Maison Carrée / Biarritz / Basses Pyrénées," postmarked Paris, 27 March 1903.

A 5-measure musical quotation in purple ink, with additions in blue and red pencil, on a fragment of music paper, marked "Feierlich ♩. = 60."

A 7-measure musical quotation in purple ink on a blank sheet, marked "La romance XVIIIe. (pour 'Sic')."

"Le bel aviateur / valse," in purple ink on p. [1] and [3] of a single bifolium of tall 12-staff paper (blind stamp of Lard-Esnault / Ed. Bellamy Sr.). The manuscript is in four parts: I. "La rencontre"; II. "L'aviateur parle"; III. "La jeune fille répond en baissant les yeux"; IV. "Persée et Andromède." It is notated on a single staff, except for the end of the first part. Additional humorous comments. At the end: "Ordre: 1.2.3.4.2.3.4.1 ce qui fait huit parties."

"L'Anniversaire / Romance chantée par trois zoizos," in pencil on two single sheets of tall 8-staff paper, the music notated on single staves, with abundant humorous comments.

A 5-measure musical quotation, notated in pencil on a small sheet of blank paper, with the heading "Lent et triste."

"Marche Triomphale pour le retour de Pierre Bracquemond," in purple ink on one side of a half-sheet of 12-staff paper, marked "P.L. Op. 115 / Feierlich (♩. = 60)."

Seven small loose sheets of paper with unidentified musical quotations, in ink or pencil.

A 12-measure musical quotation on a small sheet of paper, in purple ink and marked "Vif / pour une chanson populaire."

A 2-measure musical quotation in purple ink, with additions in red and blue pencil, on a fragment of music paper.

A 23-measure musical quotation in blue ink, on 2 single staves, on a small sheet of laid paper, marked "Ah! s'il est dans votre village," with additional notes in pencil.

An 8-measure musical quotations in purple ink on 4 systems of 2 staves, marked "♩ = 142" and signed "Richard Strauss"; at the bottom, in pencil, in an unidentified hand: "(Pierre Louÿs.)"

No compositions by Louÿs are listed in Grove.
FRKF 499.5

Manuscript in the hand of Claude Debussy

"Chanson des rois mages," song for voice and piano, n.d. The manuscript is on p. [2]–[4] of a single bifolium of tall 24-staff paper (blind stamp of LE/Ed. Bellamy Sr.). The music is notated in black ink, the words in blue ink. On title page, in blue ink, in Debussy's hand: "à Madame Henri de Régnier. / Chanson des Rois Mages. / Paroles de / Henri Heine / Musique de / Pierre Louÿs."

Presented by Louÿs to his mistress Marie de Régnier (in literature Gérard d'Houville), wife of the poet Henri de Régnier, to celebrate the birth of Pierre de Régnier, her son by Louÿs.

FRKF 499

III. LETTERS

To Claude Debussy

ALS in the form of a musical manuscript, n.d., n.p., 3 p., written in blue ink on three sides of a single bifolium of 12-staff paper (blind stamp of Flammarion & Vaillant) in the form of a duet for two voices and piano. The voices are Pierre Louÿs and "L'ombre de Debussy." The jocular text makes references to Jacques-Émile Blanche, Vincent d'Indy, and André Gide. The first 5 bars contain various indications of tone but are silent. There are scattered indications of orchestration throughout. Not in Borgeaud.

Paris, Jean Morelle (Drouot), 14–15 Dec. 1983, lot 202.
FRKF 244

[1894 July 31, Constantine*] ALS, 7 p. (env), "Innombrables lettres, non moins innombrables télégrammes …" On page 6 is a music manuscript of a "Romance en la mineur" ("Khadidja m'attend …"), supposedly by Bizet.

[1894 Dec. 23?] n.p. ALS, 3 p., "J'ai rarement été tourmenté d'indécision comme ce matin." Mentions Alfred Vallette and Debussy's *String quartet* and *Prélude à l'Après-midi d'un faune*.

[1895 Oct. 1*] "8 Vendémiaire 104" [Paris*] ALS, 3 p. (env), "Impossibilité absolue d'être chez moi ce soir—" On p. 4, blank, a few notes by Debussy, recording a rendez-vous with Ernest Chausson at Le Chernoy near Versailles, as well as the name of Lerolle-Bonheur [Henry Lerolle?].

1896 July 24, Cercle du Casino de Houlgate[S], ALS, 4 p., "Ton erreur, (si tu en fais une) c'est de croire …"

1897 Feb. 22, "Fontaine-Bleue" [but Algiers*] ALS, 3 p. (env), "J'ai eu une pleuropneumonie …" Mentions José-Maria de Heredia as well as works by Alfred Bruneau and Emmanuel Chabrier.

[1897*] April 15, "Fontaine-Bleue" [but Algiers*] ALS, 3 p. (env), "… quatre mois sont passés." Mentions Jean de Tinan.

1898 Feb. 5, Cairo, ALS, 4 p. (env), "Pas de nouvelles de toi." Mentions René Peter, the Dreyfus Affair, and *Cyrano de Bergerac*.

[1898*] April 20, "en mer," ALS, 7 p. (env), "Je ne me suis pas encore remis …" Mentions Puccini, René Peter, and *Pelléas et Mélisande*.

[1899 Feb. 6*] "47 février (environ)," Grand Hôtel du Petit Louvre, Marseille[S], ALS, 2 p. (env), "Je viens de voir une chose tout à fait digne d'être photographiée …" Describes Marseilles; mentions René Peter.

None of the letters is in Borgeaud.
Paris, Laurin-Guilloux-Buffetaud-Tailleur (Drouot), 14 Dec. 1983, lots 193–202.
FRKF 244.5

n.d., n.p., ALS, 1 p., signed with the initials P.L. Contains a purported musical quotation from *Esclarmonde*, signed "Massenet," and inscriptions, signed, from Victor Hugo, Paul Valéry, and Edgar Degas. Not in Borgeaud.

Paris, Laurin-Guilloux-Buffetaud-Tailleur (Drouot), 16 Nov. 1983, lot 161.
FRKF 251

To an unidentified correspondent

[1901 Feb. 7] n.p., ALS, 3 p., concerning the performance that evening of a recitation of twelve poems from his *Chansons de Bilitis* with musical accompaniment by Debussy.

FRKF 727

See also under Lévy, Michel Maurice.

LUDWIG I, KING OF BAVARIA (1786–1868)

Letter to Clemens von Zimmermann

1859 Dec. 29, Munich, ALS, 1 p.

The recipient was then director of the Neue Pinakothek.

Marburg, Stargardt, 5–6 March 1985, lot 966.
FRKF 830

LUDWIG II, KING OF BAVARIA (1845–86)

Letter to Hans von Bülow

1869 Feb. 26, n.p., ALS, 4 p. (env), concerning *Tannhäuser* and *Das Rheingold*, with mention of bass-baritone August Kindermann.

London, Sotheby's, 14–15 April 1982, lot 376.
FRKF 77

Letter to Count von Holstein

n.d., n.p., ALS, 1 p., informing Holstein (equerry in charge of the royal stud) of his arrival. Dated by Sotheby's ca. 1870.

London, Sotheby's, 14–15 April 1982, lot 377.
FRKF 78

Letter to Cardinal Quaglia

1866 Jan. 31, Monaco, LS, 1 p. (env). Thank you note, in Italian, signed "Ludovico."

London, Sotheby's, 14–15 April 1982, lot 375.
FRKF 76

MAURICE MAETERLINCK (1862–1949)

Letter to [Maximilian Harden?]

n.d. [1891?] Oostacker par Gand [Ghent] ALS, 3 p., concerning his article about Harden in the *Frankfurter Zeitung*.

Paris, Ader-Picard-Tajan (Drouot), 22 Nov. 1985, lot 210.
FRKF 1371

Other letters

To "cher Monsieur"

n.y. May 23, Paris, ALS, 3 p., concerning *Pelléas et Mélisande*.

Paris, Ader-Picard-Tajan (Drouot), 22 Nov. 1985, lot 210.
FRKF 1371

To "Monsieur et cher Maître"

1902 Jan. 16, Paris, ALS, 4 p., concerning *Monna Vanna*. Probably to Jules Claretie, administrateur of the Comédie-Française; mentions Lugné-Poë and an unidentified actor.

Maeterlinck's play *Monna Vanna* was premiered at Lugné-Poë's Nouveau Théâtre in Paris on 17 May 1902.

See Christie's, London, 28 Nov. 1990, lot 199; see also Sotheby's, New York, 17 Dec. 1992, lot 161.
Marburg, Stargardt, 5–6 March 1985, lot 279.
FRKF 801

To an unidentified recipient

1904 Oct. 16, Luneray, ALS, 3 p. Mentions *Pelléas et Mélisande* and *Intérieur*.

FRKF 535C

GUSTAV MAHLER (1860–1911)

"Selbstgefühl!"

Manuscript, in the hand of F. Weidig, of this song for voice and piano, with holograph annotations by Mahler, n.d. Notated in black ink on p. [1] to [4] of a single bifolium of 12-staff paper. A few indications in pencil are by Mahler; others, in black and red pencil, are evidently in a different hand. The title of the song is written across the top of p. [1].

In brown wrappers, marked at the top, in Mahler's hand: "Heft III Nro 5," and with a large blue paper label with the song title and an inscription in Mahler's hand: "Hohe Lage: G-dur / Tiefe Lage: F-dur." The text is from Brentano and Arnim's *Des Knaben Wunderhorn*. First published in *Lieder und Gesänge* (Mainz, 1892).

London, Sotheby's, 10 May 1984, lot 103.
FRKF 330

"Starke Einbildungskraft"

Manuscript, in the hand of F. Weidig, of this song for voice and piano, with holograph annotations by Mahler, n.d. Notated in black ink on p. [2] and [3] of a single bifolium of 12-staff paper. A few indications in pencil were added by Mahler. The title of the song is written across p. [1].

In brown wrappers, marked at the top "Heft II Nro 4" in Mahler's hand, and with a large blue paper label with the song title and an inscription in Mahler's hand: "N.B. Muss für beiden Ausgaben transponirt werden (Anmerkung für den Setzer). / Hohe Lage: C-dur / Tiefe Lage: A-dur." The text is from Brentano and Arnim's *Des Knaben Wunderhorn*. First published in *Lieder und Gesänge* (Mainz, 1892).

London, Sotheby's, 10 May 1984, lot 98.
FRKF 329

MARIA MALIBRAN (1808–36)

Le matelot

Manuscript, possibly holograph, of this song for voice and piano, n.d., 2 p. Notated in black ink on p. [2] and [3] of a bifolium of tall 16-staff laid paper. On p. [1] in Malibran's hand: "Le Matelot / Anglais." On p. [2] in upper right corner, signature of Malibran. The text of the song is in English.

London, Sotheby's, 29 Nov. 1985, lot 156.
FRKF 1034

Letter to Baroness [James?] de Rothschild

1830 March 26, ALS, 2 p., in the third person, accepting an invitation for 3 April.

Paris, Oger-Dumont (Drouot), 14 Feb. 1985, lot 17.
FRKF 682

Letter to the Marchese Francesco Sampieri

[1834] April 24 [Bologna] ALS, 1 p. Mentions the first performance of Bellini's *Norma*.

London, Sotheby's, 9–10 May 1985, lot 10.
FRKF 757

PIETRO MASCAGNI (1863–1945)

I. MUSIC MANUSCRIPTS

A. OPERAS

Nerone

Holograph manuscript, in full score, of this opera, 1933–34, 293 p. Notated in black ink, with rehearsal numbers in red pencil and additions in black pencil or blue ink, on both sides of individual sheets of tall elephant-size 36-staff paper preprinted for instrumentation. Bound, in three volumes, in red cloth and purple morocco spine with author and title gold-tooled on spine.

Paginated 1–71 (act 1) and 1–87 (act 2) by the composer and 1–135 (act 3) in a different hand. There is no title page. At the top of p. 1, title "Nerone" in Mascagni's hand.

Signed and dated, in all cases from Rome, at the bottom of the following pages:

> Act 1: 21 April 1934, p. 13; 24 April 1934, p. 23; 28 April 1934, p. 28; 7 March 1934, p. 32; 8 March 1934, p. 36; 9 March 1934, p. 40; 11 March 1934, p. 45; 16 March 1934, p. 53; 19 March 1934, p. 60; and 16 April 1934, at the end of act 1 (p. 71).
>
> Act 2: 22 Nov. 1933, p. 6; 24 Nov. 1933, p. 10; 25 Nov. [year cropped], p. 17; 26 Nov. 1933, p. 20; 27 Nov. 1933, p. 26; 28 Nov. 1933, p. 31; 29 Nov. 1933, p. 33; 30 Nov. 1933, p. 36; 4 Dec. 1933, p. 42; 7 Dec. 1933, p. 46; 7 Dec. 1933, p. 48; 9 Dec. 1933, p. 52 and 54; 12 Dec. 1933, p. 64; 9 Jan. 1934, p. 72; 10 Jan. 1934, p. 75; 14 Jan. 1934, p. 82; and 16 Jan. 1934, at the end (p. 87).
>
> Act 3: 23 Jan. 1934, p. 21; 24 Jan. 1934, p. 27; 27 Jan. 1934, p. 38; [date and place cropped] p. 43; 2 Feb. 1934, p. 46; 3 Feb. 1934, p. 49; 4 Feb. 1934, p. 54 and 58; 5 Feb. 1934, p. 61; 9 Feb. 1934, p. 69; 11 Feb. 1934, p. 76; 12 Feb. 1934, p. 81; 17 Feb. 1934, p. 86; 25 Feb. 1934, p. 100; 26 Feb. 1934, p. 104; 27 Feb. 1934, p. 111; 28 Feb. [year cropped], p. 116; 1 March 1934, p. 119; 4 March 1934, p. 128; and 6 March 1934 at the end (p. 135).

Nerone, opera in three acts on a libretto by Giovanni Targioni-Tozzetti, was premiered at the Teatro alla Scala, Milan, on 16 January 1935.

Flury W16 (p. 153–55).
Heinrich Schütz to Henry Miller, pp. 132–33.
London, Sotheby's, 11 Nov. 1982, lot 35.
FRKF 2

Pinotta

Holograph manuscript, in full score, of the Coro di Filatrici, signed at end, 1884, 11 p. Notated in black ink on three nested bifolia and a single sheet of tall 24-staff paper.

On front cover, in Mascagni's hand: " - Coro di Filatrici - / con accomp.to di piena orchestra - / - composto da - / - Pietro Mascagni - / - Milano Giugno 1884 -" Inscribed on front cover: "Al mio caro Mario, / che tanto ha fatto per me / in questa occasione, col / suo affetto e con la sua / competenza, offro in / ricordo queste faville / sfuggite dal maglio, / nel giorno della prima / presentazione al pubblico / di 'Pinotta'. / San Remo, / 23 Marzo 1932. / = P. Mascagni ="

Pinotta, Mascagni's first opera, written in the early 1880s, was first performed in San Remo on 23 March 1932.

Flury W15 (p. 151–53).
London, Sotheby's, 27 Nov. 1987, lot 314.
FRKF 1339

Sì

Partial holograph manuscript, in full score, of this operetta, comprising nos. 7 (Finale to act 1) and 9–10, 1919, 151 p. Notated in black ink, with additional markings in black, red, and blue pencil, on gatherings of nested, stitched bifolia of monogrammed tall 24-staff paper preprinted for instrumentation, paginated (odd pages only, not in Mascagni's hand) 141 to 355.

> At the top of p. 141, in the hand of a copyist: "= Finale I° = Atto I°"; at the top of p. 217, in the hand of a different copyist: "Coretto e duettino del Corteo nuziale (Sì e Luciano) / N° 9"; at the top of p. 233, also in the hand of a copyist: "Duetto della Seduzione (Vera e Luciano) / N° 10."

The orchestration is in Mascagni's hand, the words and vocal lines in that of a copyist. Signed and dated Ardenga, 24 Sept. 1919, on p. [216]; Ardenga, 10 Sept. 1919, at the bottom of p. 231; and Ardenga, 29 Sept. 1919, at the bottom of p. 355.

Sì, operetta in three acts on a libretto by Carlo Lombardo and Arturo Franci, was premiered at the Quirino Theater in Rome on 13 Dec. 1919.

Flury W13 (p. 139–41).
FRKF 362a

B. OTHER WORKS

Alla gioia

Holograph manuscript, in short score, of this unfinished cantata for solo voices (soprano, tenor, baritone, and bass), chorus, and orchestra, on Schiller's "Ode to joy," in the Italian translation by Andrea Maffei, 1881–82, 75 p., in black ink with occasional corrections in pencil, on oblong 12- and 10-staff paper, paginated (usually odd numbers only) 1–82.

The manuscript comprises the following numbers:

1. No. 1. Introduzione (Tenore e coro), signed and dated at the end "Di Casa = Livorno 12 Luglio 1881."

2. No. 3 [sic] Quartetto con coro (sop. ten. bar. b.), signed and dated at the end "Livorno 31 ottobre 1881 = Di Casa."

3. Coretto, signed and dated at the end "Di Casa = Livorno 14 Novembre 1881."

4. Aria di Soprano, signed and dated at the end "Di Casa = Livorno 23 Gennaio 1882." On the last page [27] of this number, autograph note, signed: "Bravo Pietro, quest' aria / è un piccolo capolavorino / A. Soffredini."

5. Corale. This section ("Il libro delle offese") stops after the sixth measure.

6. Duetto (sop. ten.). A 6-measure sketch, notated on a 2-staff system, without words.

7. Unidentified 15-measure sketch for a chorus, without the words.

8. Corale, signed and dated at the end "Livorno 14 Dicembre 1881 = Di Casa."

9. Unidentified section, beginning with an orchestral passage leading to a solo for the tenor and a choral section, signed and dated at the end "[Di] Casa = Livorno 9 Febbrajo 1882." The last 8 pages are on a different, 10-staff paper.

10. Unidentified section, beginning with an orchestral passage, leading to a solo for the bass and a quartet, signed and dated at the end "Livorno 23 Gennaio 1882 = Di casa."

11. Unidentified choral section, with the accompaniment only partly sketched in, signed and dated at the end "Livorno 28 Gennaio 1882 = Di cas.a."

A partial manuscript of the same work is at Harvard. See Barbara Mahrenholz Wolff, *Music Manuscripts at Harvard* (Cambridge, Mass.: Harvard University Library, 1992), p. 107.

Listed in Grove as unpublished.
Flury W47 (p. 164–65).
FRKF 538

Canzone popolare

Holograph manuscript of this piece for flute, violin, cello, and piano, 1882, 4 p. Notated in black ink on a bifolium and a single sheet of oblong 10-staff paper. On the title page, in Mascagni's hand: "Canzone Popolare / - per Flauto, Violino, Pianoforte e Violoncello - / - di / - Pietro Mascagni - / - Allievo dell'Istituto Cherubini in Livorno - / - Milano 1 Giugno 1882 - / = P. Mascagni =" Also signed and dated 1 June 1882 at the end.

Listed in Grove as unpublished.
Flury W110 (p. 173).
Marburg, Stargardt, 12 June 1986, lot 729.
FRKF 1332

In filanda

Holograph manuscript, in short score, of this cantata, 1880–81, 98 p. Notated in black ink, with occasional annotations, corrections, and cancellations in black and red pencil, in a notebook bound in red Annonay paper boards with light brown sheepskin spine.

The manuscript comprises the following sections:

"Preludio," 5 p., signed at the end and dated "Livorno 22 Dicembre 1880 = / = Di Casa ="

"1. Coro d'Introduzione," 8 p., signed at the end and dated "Livorno 10 Dicembre 1880 = / = Di Casa ="

"Recitativo [added in pencil, possibly in another hand: e Preghiera]" 14 p., signed at the end and dated "Livorno 14 Dicembre 1880 = / = Di Casa ="

[Aria di Ninetta] 6 p., signed at the end and dated "Livorno 2 Dicembre 1880 = / = Di Casa ="

"Recitativo," 4 p., signed at the end and dated "Livorno 5 Gennajo 1880 [sic, evidently for 1881] = / = Di Casa ="

"Terzetto," 8 p., signed at the end and dated "Livorno 17 Dicembre 1880 = / = Di Casa ="

"Recitativo," 2 p., signed at the end and dated "Livorno 4 Gennajo 1881 = / = Di Casa =" Title across the page, in red pencil: "Filatrici / Coro"

"Strofe delle filatrici," 8 p., signed at the end and dated "Livorno 18 Dicembre 1880 = / = Di Casa ="

[Orchestral interlude] 4 p., signed at the end and dated "Livorno 7 Gennajo 1881 = / = Di Casa ="

"Recitativo," 3 p., signed at the end and dated "Livorno 5 Gennajo 1880 [for 1881?] = / = Di Casa ="

[Aria di Beppo] 3 p., signed at the end and dated "Livorno 3 Dicembre 1880 = / = Di Casa ="

"Recitativo," 3 p., signed at the end and dated "Livorno 5 Gennajo 1880 [for 1881?] / = Di Casa ="

"Finale," 30 p., signed at the end and dated "Livorno 3 Gennajo 1881 = / = Di Casa ="

Tipped in on the recto of the last leaf: printed program for the first performances, at the Istituto Musicale Cherubini in Leghorn, on 9 and 11 Feb. 1881, conducted by Alfredo Soffredini, with the composer at the piano, 1 leaf.

On the recto of the front flyleaf, in an unidentified hand: "Pietro Mascagni / In Filanda / Bozzetto lombardo / Cantata für Solostimmen / und Orchester / (ungedruckt) / Klavierauszug (1880)." On the back flyleaf, note in the same hand indicating that the full-score manuscript is in the Pierpont Morgan Library, purchased in Dec. 1980 in Hamburg.

Pencil sketches of male profiles, possibly in Mascagni's hand, on both front and back flyleaves.

Listed in Grove as unpublished.

Flury W44 (p. 164).
London, Sotheby's, 29 Nov. 1985, lot 158.
FRKF 1036

Inno ad Adelaide Cairoli

Holograph manuscript of this song for voice and piano, 1898, 5 p. Notated in black ink on both sides of a single leaf and the first three pages of a separate bifolium of tall 12-staff paper (blind stamp of G. Venturini). Incipit: "O nome immortal." On p. [1] in Mascagni's hand: "= Ad Adelaide Cairoli =" Signed at the end and dated Rome, 3 Dec. 1898. Also on the last page, above the date: "All' amico carissimo Ott. Pilade Mazza."

Listed in Grove as unpublished.
Flury W83 (p. 169).
London, Sotheby's, 28 May 1986, lot 475.
FRKF 1143

Invocazione alla madonna

Holograph manuscript, in a version with organ accompaniment, of this choral piece with orchestral accompaniment, 1932, 4 p. Notated in black ink on a bifolium of tall 12-staff paper (Edizione musicale "Adriatica," Bari, "Universal" 12**).

The manuscript occupies the first three pages; on p. [4] is a revised, expanded version of the first few measures, with manuscript title above: "Invocazione alla Madonna." Signed and dated Leghorn, 6 Aug. 1932 on p. [3].

Flury W39a (p. 163).
London, Sotheby's, 26–27 Nov. 1987, lot 319.
FRKF 1344

C. LIBRETTO

Isabeau

Comments and corrections, in Mascagni's hand, to Luigi Illica's libretto for *Isabeau*, n.d., 16 p., in black ink on the recto sides of 16 oblong leaves. Bound in modern red and green marbled paper boards, with a crimson leather label on the front board that reads: "Pietro Mascagni / Modifiche al libretto / di / Isabeau / Autografo."

Isabeau, leggenda drammatica in three acts, on a libretto by Illica, was premiered in Buenos Aires on 2 June 1911.

Accompanied by:

Isabeau: leggenda drammatica in tre parti di Luigi Illica; musica di Pietro Mascagni. Milan: Edoardo Sonzogno, 1910.

[1–15], 16–63 [+ 1] p. In original blue paper wrappers, with title, authors, and publisher gold-tooled at the bottom center and Sonzogno's monogram blind-tooled in the lower left corner of the front cover. A few pencil annotations in the margins.

Flury W10 (p. 120–22).
FRKF 793.1–2

II. LETTERS

To Lina Mascagni, his wife

1893 Feb. 28, Venezia, ALS, 4 p., concerning *I Rantzau*; also mentions *Cavalleria rusticana*. Signed "Piero."

1895 Oct. 29, de la Reine d'Angleterre, Budapest[S], ALS, 6 p., concerning *Guglielmo Ratcliff*; also mentions *Cavalleria rusticana*.

Paris, Hervé Poulain (Drouot), 5 April 1984, lots 21–22.
FRKF 439–40

To Maria Mascagni, his aunt

1889 Oct. 29, Cerignola, ALS, 4 p.

1890 Oct. 21, Leghorn, ALS, 3 p.

1890 Oct. 30, Cerignola, ALS, 4 p., with two postscripts from Lina Mascagni.

1890 Dec. 27, Cerignola, ALS, 3 p. (env), with a postscript from Lina Mascagni.

Also, two empty envelopes addressed to Maria Mascagni in Mascagni's hand, postmarked 1889 March 28 and 1890 July 9.

London, Sotheby's, 26–27 Nov. 1987, lot 315.
FRKF 1340

To Mario Mascagni, his cousin

1919 Aug. 15, Ardenza-Leghorn, ALS, 2 p.

1923 Oct. 2, Ardenza-Leghorn, ALS, 2 p.

1930 June 3, Palace, Turin[S], ALS, 2 p.

1930 June 14, Reale Accademia d'Italia, Rome[S], ALS, 3 p. Mentions *Isabeau*.

1930 June 27, Reale Accademia d'Italia, Rome[S], ALS, 4 p. Mentions *Il piccolo Marat*.

1930 Aug. 12, Grand Corallo, Leghorn[S], ALS, 4 p. Mentions Puccini's *La bohème* and various other operas he is conducting, including *Cavalleria rusticana*.

1930 Sept. 16, Grand Corallo, Leghorn[S], ALS, 7 p. Mentions Puccini's *La bohème* and his own *Cavalleria rusticana*, *Zanetto*, and *Isabeau*. With a postscript from Lina Mascagni.

1932 March 25, San Remo, ALS, 2 p., concerning *Pinotta*.

1932 May 25, Reale Accademia d'Italia, Leghorn[S], ALS, 4 p., concerning *Pinotta*.

1932 Aug. 8, Grand Corallo, Leghorn[S], ALS, 4 p. Mentions *L'amico Fritz*, *Iris*, *Cavalleria rusticana*, as well as Rossini's *Il barbiere di Siviglia* and Leoncavallo's *I Pagliacci*.

1932 Aug. 11, Grand Corallo, Leghorn[S], ALS, 2 p. Mentions *Iris*, *L'amico Fritz*, *Il piccolo Marat*, *Le maschere*, as well as Rossini's *Il barbiere di Siviglia*.

1932 Sept. 17, Grand Corallo, Leghorn[S], ALS, 2 p. Mentions *Nerone*, *Pinotta*, and *L'invocazione alla Madonna*.

1932 Dec. 12, Grand Corallo, Leghorn[S], ALS, 1 p.

1933 April 7, San Remo, Miramare Continental Palace[S], ALS, 4 p. Mentions *Pinotta* and *Cavalleria rusticana*.

1933 July 2, Hotel Plaza, Rome[S], ALS, 4 p. (env), concerning *Nerone*.

1933 Oct. 6, Palace, Turin[S], ALS, 6 p. (env), concerning *Nerone*; also mentions *Pinotta* and *Cavalleria rusticana*.

1934 May 3, Reale Accademia d'Italia, Leghorn[S], ALS, 4 p., concerning *Nerone*.

1934 June 18, ALS on both sides of a card printed: Reale Accademia d'Italia, Leghorn, concerning *Nerone*.

1934 July 2, Reale Accademia d'Italia, Rome[S], ALS, 4 p., concerning *Nerone*; also mentions Catalani's *Loreley*, Puccini's *Turandot*, and Giordano's *Andrea Chénier*.

1934 July 27, Palace, Turin[S], ALS, 2 p., concerning *Nerone*.

1935 Aug. 7, Hotel Hungaria Szálló, Szeged[S], ALS, 4 p. Mentions *Cavalleria rusticana*.

1935 Dec. 12, Grand Corallo, Leghorn[S], ALS, 2 p., concerning *Nerone*.

1935 Dec. 17, Grand Corallo, Leghorn[S], ALS, 5 p., concerning *Nerone*.

1935 Dec. 19, "19 December 1935-XIV," Grand Corallo, Leghorn[S], ALS, 4 p. (env), concerning *Nerone*.

1937 Sept. 17, "17 Set[tembre] 1937.XV.," Reale Accademia d'Italia, Rome[S], ALS, 2 p.

1938 Sept. 22, "22 Settembre 1938.XVI.," Reale Accademia d'Italia, Leghorn[S], ALS, 2 p. Mentions *Le maschere* and symphonies by Haydn, Tchaikovsky, and Dvořák.

Undated

[ca. 1932?] Grand Corallo, Leghorn[S], ALS, 5 p. Mentions *L'amico Fritz* and *Il barbiere di Siviglia*. Possibly incomplete, or fragments of two different letters. There is no opening salutation.

[ca. 1932] Hotel Corso-Splendid, Milan[S], ALS, 3 p., enclosing proofs of *Nerone*, which are not present, and giving three corrections, with a musical quotation in each case; also mentions the *Rapsodia satanica*. Also enclosing the manuscript text for the title page and the list of musical numbers in *Nerone*.

Also, autograph copy of a letter from Mascagni to "Caro Maestro Arturo Rossato," n.d., Bolzano. Accompanied by empty envelopes addressed by Mascagni to his uncle, and postmarked Leghorn, 1910 Aug. 16 and 1921 Oct. 23, and Pesaro, 1927 June 28.

London, Sotheby's, 26–27 Nov. 1987, lots 318, 320.
FRKF 1343, 1345

To Renzo Rossi

1932 March 19, Miramare Continental Palace, San Remo[S], ALS, 4 p. (env), concerning *Pinotta*.

London, Sotheby's, 26–27 Nov. 1987, lot 316.
FRKF 1341.1

III. PHOTOGRAPHS

Mascagni and his wife in a group of soldiers, one on each side of them, five standing on steps (16.6 × 11.6 cm). Inscribed by Mascagni at the top: "Al carissimo Mario Mascagni / Ricordo di Tolmezzo, Luglio 1916 / P. Mascagni."

Another photograph of the same group, with an additional soldier, standing on the same level in front of a house (16.4 × 11.6 cm). Inscribed by Mascagni at the top: "A Mario Mascagni / per ricordo grato / Tolmezzo, Luglio, 1916 - / = P. Mascagni ="

Mascagni at the age of 27. Sepia photographic portrait (16.5 × 21.5 cm) printed on the verso of the cardboard mount: Bettini / Livorno. Inscribed by Mascagni at the top: "Alla mia Carissima Zia Maria, per ricordo / dei bei giorni passati a S. Miniato, oggi che me ne / vade a malincuore; / lascio questo ritratto / con grato animo. - / 13 ottobre '90 = / P. Mascagni ="

Black-and-white photograph of an oil portrait of Mascagni by J.N. Pellis (15 × 11.5 cm). In small block letters, in lower left corner: "Al maestro insigne / Pietro Mascagni / con ammirazione ed affetto / J.N. Pellis / [1916?]." Signed (or inscribed) J.N. Pellis in lower right corner. Inscribed by Mascagni on matting: "al mio caro Mario / Tolmezzo - Luglio 1916 - / P. Mascagni." Painter not traced in any of the bibliographical sources.

London, Sotheby's, 26–27 Nov. 1987, lot 317.
FRKF 1342.1

JULES MASSENET (1842–1912)

I. MUSIC MANUSCRIPTS

Massenet's music manuscripts are described in six groups:

A. OPERAS
B. STAGE MUSIC
C. ORATORIOS
D. ORCHESTRAL MUSIC
E. SONGS
F. INSTRUMENTAL MUSIC

A. OPERAS

Amadis

Manuscript of Jules Claretie's libretto for the opera [n.d. but probably 1910], 68 p. The manuscript is in Massenet's hand throughout, written in black ink, with corrections in blue and red pencil, on the recto sides of single oblong sheets (20.5 × 15.5 cm), foliated A–B and 1–66.

> On fol. 1: "Amadis / [erased: de Gaule] / Opéra légendaire en quatre actes / [erased: quatre tableaux] / dont un prologue. / [erased: poème de Jules Claretie / musique de J. Massenet]." Pasted-on cancels on the upper half of fol. 41 and in the middle of fol. 57. Folios 10–27 (from the beginning of act 2, originally called 2nd tableau) were previously numbered 1–18. Exceptionally for Massenet at the end of his life, there is a folio 13.
>
> Accompanied by an ALS (printed "Carte pneumatique" on the address side) from Massenet to Jules Claretie [1911 June 15, Paris*] 1 p., concerning *Amadis*. Also accompanied by a typed description, at the back of which is the typed note: "Collection Jean Farger. Fontainebleau."
>
> In original black sheepskin clasp folder, with inlaid calf labels on the front board and spine. The one on the front board reads: "Amadis / Paroles de Jules Claretie / Musique de Massenet / Opéra composé à / l'aide de ces feuillets / écrits et corrigés / par / Jules Massenet" and the one on the spine: "Manuscrit / d'Amadis." On the reverse of the front board, octagonal paper label pasted in, inscribed, in Massenet's hand: "Poème / d'Amadis."

Amadis was premiered posthumously at Monte Carlo on 1 April 1922.

FRKF 539a

Bacchus

Holograph "brouillon d'orchestre," i.e. manuscript draft of the full score, without any vocal parts, incomplete, n.d. [1908], 377 leaves. Notated in black ink, with additional annotations in black and blue pencil (a few in red) on the recto sides of individual sheets, torn at the top (ca. 30 × 32.5 cm) and foliated by Massenet. Rehearsal numbers are marked in blue pencil, while corrections are generally made in ink and highlighted in blue pencil.

Collation:

> Act 1: 1–12 (foliated 12/12 bis), 14–43; pasted-on corrections on fol. 7, 28. Marked at the end, in black ink: "Fin du 1er acte - Prologue." There is no rehearsal number 13; it is replaced by 12 bis.
>
> Act 2, originally housed in a bifolium of tall music paper, torn at the top, marked, in blue pencil: "Bacchus / orchestre / 2° acte": 1–12, 12 bis, 14–74 [75–106 missing], 107–185; pasted-on (originally pinned-in) corrections on fol. 70, 72, 111, 120, 140, 143, 154, 155, 179, 183, 185. Marked at the end, in blue pencil: "Fin du 2° acte."
>
> Act 3, 2nd tableau, originally housed in a bifolium of tall music paper, torn at the bottom, marked, in blue pencil: "3e acte / 2° tableau / orch.": 1, 1 bis, 2–12, 12 bis, 14–110; pasted-on corrections on fol. 12 bis, 14, 39, 40, 41, 52, 59, 61, 67, 78, 84. Short, unidentified draft on fol. 110v. Marked at the end, in ink: "Fin du 3e acte."
>
> Act 4, originally housed in a bifolium of tall music paper, torn at the bottom, marked, in blue pencil: "Bacchus / orchestre / (4e acte)" (also with a list of the instruments involved): 1–12, 12 bis, 14–38, 38 bis (marked "ancien 35"), "ancien 36," "ancien 37," "ancien 38," 39–52, 53A, 53B, 53C, 53E, 53F, 53G, 53–61; pasted-on (originally pinned-in) corrections on fol. 36, 38 bis, 53C, 53D, 53E. Marked at the end, in ink: "Fin."

FRKF 904

Cléopâtre

Holograph "brouillon d'orchestre," n.d. [ca. 1912], 290 leaves. Notated in black ink, with additional annotations in black, red, and blue pencil, on the recto sides of individual sheets, torn at the top (ca. 30 × 34 cm) and foliated by Massenet. Rehearsal numbers are marked in blue pencil up to 133, in red pencil afterwards, while corrections are generally made in ink and highlighted in blue pencil.

Originally housed in four hard folders with green Annonay paper boards and dark grey cloth spines, with paper labels on front boards marked, in Massenet's hand: "Cléopâtre / acte 1er [2d / 1er & 2e / tableaux [3ème / 4ème]"; act 2, 2nd tableau was housed in a paper folder marked in blue pencil: "Cléopâtre / 2° acte / 2° tableau."

Collation:

> Act 1, 1–12, 12 bis, 14–82; pinned-in cancels on fol. 32, 39, 58. Rehearsal number 13 is marked 12 bis. Marked in ink at the end: "fin du 1er acte."
>
> Act 2, 1st tableau: 1–12, 12 bis, 14–52; pinned-in cancels on fol. 22, 43, 45, 52. Fol. 49–52 are on a different, lighter paper. Marked at the end: "fin du 1er tableau du 2e acte."

Act 2, 2nd tableau: 1–12, 12 bis, 14–38; pinned-in cancels on fol. 1, 36. Marked at the end: "fin du 2d tableau du 2d acte."

Act 3, 1–12, 12 bis, 14–76; pinned-in cancels on fol. 6, 26. Large excision on fol. 65. Four measures are on fol. 19v (beginning one measure before rehearsal number 305). Tears at the tops of fol. 35 and 36 cropped or removed the foliation. Marked at the end: "fin du 3ème acte."

Act 4, 1–12, 12 bis, 14–52; pinned-in cancels on fol. 22, 27.

FRKF 912

Hérodiade

Holograph manuscript, in short score, of the original version of the opera, 1879–80, 340 p. Notated in black and purple ink, with additional corrections in black, blue, and red pencil, on the verso sides (unless otherwise noted) of individual sheets of tall 28-staff paper (blind stamp of Lard-Esnault). Passages cancelled in ink or blue pencil.

Bound in heavy light grey boards. On the front board, title lettered in red-brown with dark brown shading. Also on the front board, in purple ink, in Massenet's hand: "premier manuscrit / mars 1879 / J. Massenet" (the signature faded and barely legible). On the spine, in Massenet's hand: "Hérodiade / partition / (p[ian]o et chant / manuscrite. / J. Massenet / 1879. / 1re rep.: Bruxelles - Paris / 19 Xbre 1881. 1er fév. 84." Purple marbled endpapers.

On the verso of the front free endpaper, in purple ink unless otherwise noted, in Massenet's hand: "Hérodiade / opera en cinq actes et 7 tableaux / représenté pour la 1ere fois / [in pencil:] le lundi 19 Xbre /81 - 7½ du soir / à Bruxelles / Théâtre de la Monnaie / Jean [in pencil:] Vergnet / Hérode [in pencil:] Manoury / Phanuel [in pencil:] Gresse / Vitellius [in pencil:] Fontaine / Hérodiade [in pencil:] Deschamps / Salomé [in pencil:] Marthe Duvivier / une jeune babylonienne [in pencil:] Lonati - / [in the middle of the page:] à mes bons amis de Passy / Camille Claude et sa femme, / j'offre ce manuscrit / en souvenir reconnaissant de leur intérêt / pour cet ouvrage et de leur amitié / pour l'auteur / J. Massenet / Passy. 28 oct. 1880 / 8 heures du soir. / [in lower left corner:] représenté à Paris (en quatre actes / et sept tableaux) / Théâtre Italien / le 1er février 1884 / Salomé, Fidès Devriès / Hérodiade, Tremelli / Jean, Jean de Reszké / Herode, Maurel / Phanuel, Edouard de Reszké / - "

Collation:

Act 1 [in black ink, with occasional corrections in purple ink]: 1–4, 4 bis, 4 ter, 5–30, 30v [in purple ink, foliated 31 bis], 31, 32 [almost entirely cancelled], 33–50; [in purple ink:] 51–55; [in black ink:] 57 [foliated "56 et 57"], 58–62, [62v, in purple ink], 64 [foliated 63/64], 65–70; pasted-on cancels found on fol. 1, 25. Autograph notes on fol. 12, 31 bis, 34, 39, 42, 51, 55, 58, 62v, 63/64, 67, 70, dated between 21 March 1879 and 3 March 1880.

At the end, in black ink: "fin du 1er acte. / Paris - Mercredi 14 mai 1879. / 5 heures du soir."

Act 2, 1st tableau [in black ink, with occasional corrections in purple ink]: 1 (marked at the top: "2d acte / Hérodiade"), 2–8, 8v [in purple ink], 9–12, 12v [foliated 13], 14–35, 35v [foliated 36], 37–38; pasted-on cancel on fol. 15. Autograph notes on fol. 1, 5, 8v, 17, 18, 22, 23, 34, 38, dated between 5 June 1879 and 13 March [1880]. Marked in ink at the end: "fin du 1er tableau - (2nd acte)."

Act 2, 2nd tableau [in black ink, with occasional corrections in purple ink]: 1–48; [in purple ink:] 49; [in black ink:] 51 [foliated 50/51], 52–55. Autograph notes on fol. 10, 24, 31, 41, 42, dated between 11 and 14 July 1879. Marked in ink at the end: "fin du 2d acte." Pasted-on cancels on fol. 1, 12, 19, 50, 51.

Act 3 [in black ink, with occasional corrections in purple ink]: 1 (marked at the top: "Hérodiade / opéra en 5 actes et 7 tableaux / [3ème acte]"), 2–5, 5v [paginated 6], 7–15; [in purple ink:] 16, 17, 18 [foliated 18/21], 22 (headed, at the top: "Divertissement [nouveau]"), 23–39, 40 [foliated 40/45], 40v [foliated 46 bis], 46–47, 47v [foliated 48 bis], 48, 48v [paginated 40 bis], 49, 49v [paginated 50 bis], 50–56, 56v [paginated 56 bis], 57, 57v [paginated 57 bis], 62 [paginated "58–62"], 63–71; pasted-on cancels on fol. 1, 13, 15, 48. Autograph notes on fol. 7, 11, 15, 17, 22, 25, 30, 31, 32, 48, 49, 50, 52, 55, 56 bis, 62, 66, 68, 71, dated between 18 July 1879 and 5 July 1880. Marked at the end: "(fin du 3ème acte)."

Act 4 [in purple ink]: 1 (marked at the top: "Hérodiade / opéra en 5 actes, et 7 tableaux / acte IV. / Le Saint-Temple / à Jérusalem"), 2–6, 6v [foliated 6 bis], 11 [foliated 7/11], 12–21, 22 [foliated "nouveau 22"], 23–25, 28, [in black ink:] 29 (headed "Marche Sainte"), 30–38, 38v [not foliated], 39–41; [in purple ink:] 42–47, 49 [foliated 48/49], 50–69, 71 [foliated 70/71], 72–89; pasted-on cancels on fol. 2, 5, 28, 30, 31, 50, 51, 53, 81. Autograph notes on fol. 1, 4, 6, 11, 15, 21, 25, 28, 29, 33, 36, 38v, 42, 51, 53, 56, 58, 59, 61, 68, 69, 89, dated from 30 September 1879 to 15 Aug. 1880. Marked at the end "fin du 4ème acte."

Act 5 [in black ink]: 1 (marked at the top: "Hérodiade / opéra en 5 actes et 7 tableaux / Acte V. 1er tableau."), 2–12, 18–26, 27 (marked at the bottom: "fin du 1er tableau du 5e acte"), 28 (marked at the top: "Hérodiade / acte V / 2d tableau"), 29–31, 31v [paginated 31 bis], 32–36, 36v [paginated 36 bis], 37–40, 40v [not paginated]; pasted-on cancels on fol. 1, 5. Autograph notes on fol. 1, 3, 7, 9, 10, 11, 21, 24, 26, 27, 28, 30, 33, 34, 37, dated between 13 Sept. 1879 and 4 Jan. 1880. Marked at the end "fin de l'opéra," signed "J. Massenet," and dated "Passy, dimanche 4 janvier 80. / 11 h du matin."

Heinrich Schütz to Henry Miller, p. 70–71.
London, Sotheby's, 23 Nov. 1984, lot 482.
FRKF 544

Panurge

Holograph "brouillon d'orchestre," n.d. [ca. 1912], 422 leaves. Notated in black ink, with additional annotations in black, red, and blue pencil, on the recto sides of individual sheets, torn at the top (ca. 29.5 × 33 cm) and foliated by

Massenet. Rehearsal numbers are marked in red pencil, while corrections are generally made in ink and highlighted in blue pencil.

Originally housed in three light brown folders, marked in Massenet's hand, in red pencil: "brouillon," and in blue pencil: "Panurge / 1er [2d / 3e] acte / orchestre."

Collation:

Act 1: 1–12, 14–114; pasted-on (originally pinned-in) cancels on fol. 5, 20, 78, 81. There is no rehearsal number 13 or 12 bis: as for the foliation, the numbering skips from 12 to 14.

Act 2: 1–12, 14–184; pasted-on (originally pinned-in) cancels on fol. 6, 15, 60, 61, 63, 65, 127, 129, 140. Excision on fol. 6.

Act 3: 1–12, 14–126; pasted-on (originally pinned-in) cancels on fol. 1, 52, 68, 69, 98, 119. On verso of folio 1, cancelled draft of the first five measures. Marked "Fin" at the end. Laid in with act 3: manuscript draft, apparently of an early version of the solo violin in the act 3 Intermède, notated on the recto of a fragment of a large sheet, 23 measures.

FRKF 903

Roma

Holograph "brouillon d'orchestre," n.d. [ca. 1909–10], 337 leaves. Notated in black ink, with additional annotations in black, red, and blue pencil, on the recto sides of individual sheets, torn at the top (ca. 30 × 33.5 cm) and foliated by Massenet. Rehearsal numbers are marked in blue pencil, while corrections are generally made in ink and highlighted in blue or red pencil. The overture is on sheets of lighter paper, also torn at the top and of smaller size (28.5 × 31.5 cm), and has a separate count of rehearsal numbers from the rest of the opera.

The various acts were originally separated by imitation-wood brown cardboard dividers, marked by Massenet, in red pencil: "brouillon / Roma" and, in blue pencil: "orchestre / 1er [2° / 3ème / 4ème / 5ème] acte."

Collation:

Overture: 1–12, 12 bis, 14–44. At the top of p. 1, in Massenet's hand: "Ouverture [cancelled: tragique]."

Act 1: 1–12, 12 bis, 14–48 (foliated 48/49), 50–61; pasted-on (originally pinned-in) correction found on fol. 56. Marked at the end, in blue pencil: "Fin du 1er acte."

Act 2: 1–12, 12 bis, 14–23 (foliated 23/24), 25–41, 41 bis, 42; pasted-on (originally pinned-in) correction found on fol. 12. Marked at the end, in ink: "Fin du 2e acte." Folios 17–42 are on the same lighter paper as the overture.

Act 3: 1–12, 12 bis, 14–48 (foliated 48/36), 37 [bis]–48 [bis], 49–83; pasted-on (originally pinned-in) or tipped-in corrections on fol. 30, 35, 37 [bis], 48 [bis], 65, 67, 74, 75, 76, 79, 80, 82. Marked at the end, in ink: "fin du 3e acte." Folios 36–47 are on the same lighter paper as the overture. Miscellaneous drafts on fol. 1v–21v and 24v–25v: several drafts for *Don Quichotte*, one including a vocal line (to the words "Placez votre main pure ô noble chevalier," the last words of act 3), fol. 1v; draft, in short score, of the overture to *Roma*, foliated, in reverse order, 1 [i.e. 12v] to 9 [i.e. 2v] (also on verso of 12 bis); rough sketches for the overture, paginated 1–2, 7 bis, and marked "à intercaler page 8" (14v–17v); unidentified sketches (18v–19v); draft of an unidentified song, marked "ténor" (20v); draft of a "Panis angelicus" with organ accompaniment, notated on 3-staff systems (21v); unidentified drafts, some with text (24v–25v).

Act 4: 1–12, 12 bis, 14–78; pasted-on (originally pinned-in) or tipped-in corrections on fol. 5, 6, 28, 38, 56, 67. Marked at the end, in ink: "fin du 4e acte."

Act 5: 1–12, 12 bis, 14–41; pasted-on (originally pinned-in) corrections on fol. 17, 19, 21, 22, 23, 38. Marked at the end, in ink: "fin du 5e acte."

FRKF 895

Thérèse

Holograph "brouillon d'orchestre," n.d. [ca. 1907], 216 leaves. Notated in black ink, with additional annotations in black, blue, and red pencil, on the recto sides of individual sheets (blind stamp of Lard-Esnault), torn, generally at the bottom (ca. 30 × 30.5 cm), and foliated by Massenet. Rehearsal numbers are marked in blue pencil, while corrections are generally made in ink and highlighted in blue pencil. Annotations and corrections in red pencil only on three folios in act 1, numerous in act 2. One correction in green pencil, act 2, fol. 58.

Originally housed in two light brown folders, marked in Massenet's hand, in red pencil: "Thérèse," and in blue pencil: "Thérèse / Orch[estre] / 1er [2d] acte"; other annotations indicate that both were originally for the manuscripts of acts 2 and 5 of the piano-vocal manuscript score of *Ariane*.

Collation:

Act 1: 1–12, 12 bis, 14–112; pasted-on addition, folded, on fol. 87. On fol. 30v, 31v, and 32v, draft, incomplete, of the "Menuet d'amour" that opens act 2, foliated 1–3; on fol. 56v, unidentified draft, in full score, cancelled, foliated 48. Marked "Thérèse" at the bottom of fol. 45.

Act 2: 1–12, 12 bis, 14–104. On fol. 99, in red pencil, "le parlé." Marked "Fin" in red pencil at the end.

FRKF 905

B. STAGE MUSIC

Les Érinnyes

Holograph full-score manuscript of the incidental music to the tragedy by Leconte de Lisle (1872–76). Notated in black ink, with additional markings in red ink, and black, blue, and red pencil, on the recto sides of tall 30-staff paper (blind stamp of Lard-Esnault), foliated by the composer (including 13). On the first folio, in Massenet's hand: "Les Erinnyes / Tragédie antique en 2 parties / - Leconte de Lisle - / Partition-Orchestre."

Collation:

Nos. 1 and 2: 1–2, 2 bis, 3–23, with pasted-on revisions on fol. 1, 2, and 4; no. 3: 1–11, with pasted-on revisions on fol. 3 and 11; no. 4: 1–24, with autograph notes on 2v and pasted-on revision on fol. 5, 11, 12, 13, 14, 16, 18, 19; "Divertissement / n° 1" (labelled "Suite du n° 4"): [1]–24; "Divertissement / n° 2" (also labelled "Suite du n° 4"): [1]–6; "Divertissement / n° 3" (also labelled "Suite du n° 4"): [1]–32, with pasted-on revisions on fol. 6, 21, 25, and 27; no. 5: 1–8; no. 6: 1–6; no. 7: 1–13; no. 8: 1–5, with added no. 8 bis notated, in black ink, on 5v; no. 9: 1–24, [24v], 25–27, with fol. 10 cancelled and marked "Coupure - (enchaînez de suite)" and pasted-on revisions on fol. 11 and on 16 and 17 (the entire page in both cases), 18, and 24; no. 10: 1–14, with pasted-on revision on fol. 3.

Pasted on the verso of the flyleaf, autograph note on a half-sheet of laid paper, giving the list of numbers to be copied.

Pasted on fol. 11v in no. 3, autograph note on a half-sheet of laid paper: "Sont utiles à copier exactement / 1° = les répliques - / 2° et les paroles dans les mélodrames / exactement au dessus des mesures - / il faudra réserver toujours / un espace pour graver une / traduction."

At the end of the Divertissement, no. 3, on fol. 32, in Massenet's hand: "Fin du divertissement / Paris. / Mercredi 4 Janvier 1876. / minuit ½."

No. 6 was previously sealed with a sheet of laid paper, folded and glued on fol. 1 and 6v. Also pasted on 6v, autograph note on a half-sheet of laid paper: "n° 7 = ce morceau est gravé / jusqu'à la lettre E. / comme orchestration c'est exact et pareil / - Seulement l'indication et réplique des / voix n'est pas indiqué, le morceau / étant gravé comme orchestre seul."

In no. 9, fol. 24v, is a "Version, pour terminer au concert," with "on termine par la / Marche argienne / 12 fev: 83 / J.M" at the bottom of the page in blue pencil.

At the end of the manuscript (no. 10, fol. 24r), autograph note: "Fin des Erinnyes / Novembre 1872 Paris / Janvier '73 Fontainebleau / Paris - nov: Décembre '75 - Paris / Hiver 1876 / J. Massenet."

Bound in brown green Annonay paper boards, vellum spine with black leather label marked "Massenet / Les / Érinnyes / Partition d'orchestre."

Les Érinnyes was premiered at the Théâtre de l'Odéon on 6 Jan. 1873 and, in the revised version, at the Théâtre-Lyrique de la Gaîté, in May 1876.

FRKF 910

Jérusalem!

Holograph short-score manuscript and full-score draft ("brouillon d'orchestre") of the incidental music to the play by Georges Rivollet, n.d. [1912], 35 + 47 leaves.

The manuscript short score was originally housed in five beige folders, marked in ink, in Massenet's hand: "'Jérusalem!' / acte I. [II. / III. / IV. / V.] / (musique de scène)." The music is written in black ink, the text and stage directions in red ink, on the recto sides of 35 individual sheets of tall 20-staff paper (blind stamp of Lard-Esnault), foliated separately for each act: act 1, 1–2; act 2, 1–9; act 3, 1–8; act 4, 1–4, 4 bis, 5–11 (pasted-on corrections on fol. 9); act 5, 1–3. Marked at the end, in ink: "Fin de 'Jérusalem!'" There are additional markings in blue pencil and in black pencil (the latter not in Massenet's hand).

The brouillon d'orchestre was housed in a bifolium of music paper, cut at the top, marked "Orchestre" in blue pencil, in Massenet's hand, with the additional indication, in black pencil: "j'ai commencé le mardi 3 mars." It is written in black ink, with additional markings in blue pencil and a few more in red pencil, on the recto sides of single sheets, torn at the top (ca. 30 × 34 cm), of tall music paper, foliated by Massenet. Most corrections are made in ink and highlighted in blue pencil.

Collation:

1–4; 1 (marked in upper left corner: "fin de l'acte I"); 1 (marked at the top: "La Casa nuova"), 2–4; 1 (marked in upper left corner: "scène 2ème"), 2; 1 (marked at the top: "acte 2 - scène 4m"), 2; [unpaginated folio, marked in upper left corner: "acte 2 / scène 5m"]; 1 (marked in upper left corner: "même scène 5"); 1 (marked in upper left corner "fin de l'acte"); 1 (marked at the top: "Siloé"), 2–5; 1 (marked at the top: "La Procession"), 2–4; 1 (marked at the top: "reprise de la Procession sortie"), 2–[4] (marked at the end "fin du 3e acte"); [1] (marked in upper left corner: "acte 4m Entr'acte"), 2–3; 1 (marked at the top: "Entr'acte St Sépulchre"), 2–6; 1 (marked in upper left corner: "Les lépreux"), [unpaginated, with folded pasted-on addition], 2 (with folded pinned-in addition, marked "La vision" in red pencil), 3; 1 (marked in upper left corner: "fin du 4e acte"), 2; 1 (marked at the top: "Entr'acte 5e acte"), 2; 1 (marked in upper left corner: "acte 5 scène 2n"). Rehearsal numbers, marked in blue pencil, are continuous throughout. Rehearsal number 13 is marked "12 bis."

Jérusalem! a play in five acts, in prose, by Georges Rivollet, stage music by Massenet, was premiered at Monte Carlo on 17 Jan. 1914.

FRKF 894, 894.5

C. ORATORIOS

Ève

Holograph manuscript, in full score, 1874, 183 p. Notated in black ink, with additional notations in black, blue, and red pencil, on the recto sides of tall sheets of 26-staff paper (blind stamp of Lard-Esnault), foliated by Massenet.

On fol. 1, in the upper right corner, in Massenet's hand: "Ève / mystère pour soli, orchestre / & choeurs."

Collation:

1–13, 13 bis, 13 ter, 14, 14 bis, 14 ter, 15–124, 124 [bis], 125–178. From fol. 144 to the end, the pages were refoliated from four numbers down. Pasted-on revisions found on fol. 6, 7, 12, 21, 27, 30, 37, 48, 83, 100, 101, 108, 124, 131, and 147. At the bottom of fol. 178: "fin d'Ève / Dimanche 1er novembre / 1874. / J. Massenet."

Bound in white Annonay paper boards, with vellum spine. Black leather label on spine, marked "Massenet / Ève / Partition / d'orchestre."

FRKF 907

La terre promise

Holograph full-score manuscript of this oratorio, 1897–99, 225 p. Notated in black ink, with additional markings in black, blue, and red pencil on the recto sides of tall sheets of 28-, 32-, and 35-staff paper (blind stamp of Lard-Esnault), foliated throughout by Massenet. Fol. 13 is foliated 12 bis.

At the top of fol. 1, in Massenet's hand: "La Terre Promise. / Oratorio en trois parties. / 1ère partie / Moab (L'alliance) / 'Gardez les préceptes du Seigneur / 'afin que vous possédiez cet excellent / 'pays où vous entrerez ainsi que Dieu / 'l'a juré à vos pères (Deutéronome)." At the top of fol. 87: "La Terre Promise / 2de partie / Jéricho (La Victoire) / 'Le peuple ayant jeté de grands cris, / 'Les murailles de Jéricho tombèrent / 'jusqu'aux fondements et chacun entra dans la ville / [cancelled: 'par l'endroit qui se trouva vis-à-vis de lui -] / Josué." At the top of fol. 177: "La Terre Promise / 3ème partie / Chanaan (la terre promise) / 'Il renvoya ensuite le peuple / chacun dans ses terres' / (Josué)."

Autograph note at the end (fol. 225): "cet ouvrage a été / commencé à Aix-les-Bains 1897. / continué à Pourville Juin 1898. / et terminé à / Egreville le 17 août 1899. / J.M."

Bound in beige and turquoise marbled paper boards, with vellum spine. Octagonal dark brown leather label on front board, with double gilt fillet on the edges, marked, in gold tooling: "La terre promise / Manuscrit / Partition d'orchestre"; on the spine, light brown leather label, marked, in gold-tooling: "La / terre promise / Manuscrit / Partition d'orchestre."

La terre promise, oratorio on a text by Massenet drawn from the translation of the Old Testament by Silvestre de Sacy, was premiered in Paris, at Saint-Eustache, on 15 March 1900.

FRKF 896

La Vierge

Holograph full-score manuscript of this oratorio on a text by Charles Grandmougin, 1878–80, 327 p. Notated in black ink, with additional notations in red and purple ink and black, blue, and red pencil, on the recto sides of sheets of tall 26-, 30-, or 36-staff paper (blind stamp of Lard-Esnault), foliated continuously by Massenet 1–327.

On fol. 1, in Massenet's hand: "La Vierge / légende sacrée en quatre scènes / poème de Ch: Grandmougin / musique de J. Massenet." On fol. 7v, added indications in red ink concerning the offstage orchestra. On fol 71, autograph note dated 2 Aug. 1878; pasted-on revisions on fol. 161, 212, 238, 276.

At the bottom of fol. 223 (4eme scène / L'Assomption / Prélude / Le dernier sommeil de la Vierge), autograph note: "Je désire que ce morceau / soit exécuté à l'occasion de mon enterrement. / J.M. / (été 1878 - Font[ainebl]eau)." On fol. 225v, variant for the first three bars of fol. 226, with autograph note: "je préfère cette / variante / pour les 1eres mesures / de la page suivante / août 1878 / J.M."

Fol. 228–88 have various additional foliations 1–25 in the upper left corner. On fol. 289 (L'Assomption / n° 14), cut, indicated in blue pencil, with autograph note at the bottom of the page: "J'ai l'intention de couper / ces 8 premières mesures - / on commencerait à la 9ème mesure ff. / Paris / 16 X 1878 / J. Massenet." Also, autograph note in purple ink in the middle of the page: "Orchestre / supplémentaire / en se servant des huit instrumentistes qui / ont joué les fanfares / de la 3me scène / Ajouté le 30 avril 1880 / à propos des / concerts de l'Opéra." These additions are found on fol. 295v to the end.

On fol. 324–26, additions in red "à défaut de gd orgue," with explanatory autograph note at the bottom of fol. 324. At the bottom of fol. 327: "Fin de 'la Vierge' / 22 août 1878 / 10 h du matin / Fontainebleau J. Massenet."

Bound in two volumes in dark green Annonay paper boards with vellum spine; on the spine, black leather label marked, in gold tooling: "Massenet / La Vierge / Orchestre / Ier [sc]ene [2eme / scene] [3e scen[e]] [4eme scène]." Volumes 1 and 2 disbound by the library; the original bindings are preserved with the manuscript.

La Vierge was premiered at the Paris Opéra on 22 May 1880.

FRKF 897

D. ORCHESTRAL MUSIC

Marche solennelle

Holograph full-score manuscript of this march for full orchestra, 1881, 45 p. Notated in purple and black ink on the recto sides of tall sheets of 36- (fol. 1–3 and 36–45) and 28-staff paper (fol. 4–35) (blind stamp of Lard-Esnault), foliated by Massenet (including 13).

> At the top of fol. 1, in Massenet's hand: "Marche Solennelle / J. Massenet." In the middle of the page, note in black ink: "tous les passages écrits / à l'encre noire seront exécutés / à défaut de fanfare - / La copie doit les reproduire / dans les parties en cas d'urgence / en ayant soin d'écrire les / passages <u>exactement en mesure</u> / et en petites notes / à la place des pauses et des silences / de façon à ce que la mesure / soit exacte - / peut-être sur une ligne au dessus / des parties, en indiquant: / 'à défaut de fanfare'"; at the bottom of the page, autograph notes: "Lundi 28 février 81 / 11½ matin / déjeuner Cl[aude] à la maison" and "Mardi gras / 1er mars / 81 / 2 h."

> The bottom of fol. 45 has been torn out, leaving only the first lines of two autograph notes: "cette Marche solennelle a été …" and "fin de la preparation …"

> For the choral parts at the end, only vocal lines, without text, are present.

> On fol. 41, note in black ink at the bottom of the page: "paroles à adapter sur tout le passage choral. / - sentiment d'un hymne, d'un hosanna, / ou d'un chant de fête dans un style pompeux -" Autograph notes on fol. 4, 6, 12, 18, 22, 31, and 33 (recording the fire of the Printemps department store and concerning the projected "Phoebé").

Bound in dark green Annonay paper boards, vellum spine with black leather label marked "Massenet / Marche / solennelle / Orchestre." On the front board, paper label marked, in Massenet's hand: "Marche solennelle / pour orchestre, fanfare, gd orgue / & choeur - / partition d'orchestre / manuscrit / J. Massenet."

Written for the inauguration of the Beethoven Hall in Barcelona, where Massenet himself conducted the premiere in April 1881. Published, in full score, by Heugel in 1897, and in a piano four-hand arrangement.

FRKF 909

Scènes alsaciennes

Holograph full-score manuscript of this symphonic suite, 1881, 112 p. Notated in black ink on the recto sides of individual leaves of tall 28-staff paper (blind stamp of Lard-Esnault), foliated by Massenet. Additional markings in blue pencil and black pencil (many of the latter evidently not in Massenet's hand).

Collation:

> [title page], 1–25, 26 (marked at the top: "Scènes alsaciennes / (Souvenirs) / n° 2 - <u>Au cabaret</u>"), 27–62, 63 (marked at the top: "Scènes alsaciennes / (Souvenirs) / n° 3 <u>Sous les tilleuls</u>"), 64–70, 71 (marked at the top: "Scènes alsaciennes / (Souvenirs) / n° 4. <u>Dimanche soir</u>"), 72–90, 91 (marked at the top: "[cancelled in pencil: (Retraite française)" with note in purple ink: "il faut obtenir un effet très lointain, / d'abord—puis, le crescendo et / le decrescendo bien ménagé"), 92–112.

> On title page, in Massenet's hand: "Scènes alsaciennes / (Souvenirs) / (7eme Suite d'orchestre) / J. Massenet / (Partition d'orchestre / été 1881.)" Also on the title page, in Massenet's hand: "AVIS / copier 4 cartons militaires / pour 4 trompettes Si♭ / et 4 cartons militaires / pour 4 tambours / 31 Jan / 82 / JM"; and a second note, in pencil, cancelled, n.d.: "AVIS / pour la copie des clairons / et tambours sur des petits / cartons / militaires / JM." Music publisher's number (G.H. 1312) added at the bottom in pencil and inked over, not in Massenet's hand.

> At the top of fol. 1, dedication, written in purple ink: "à mon ami Edouard Colonne / chef d'orchestre des concerts [cancelled: de l'association artistique] du Châtelet." Also on fol. 1, in Massenet's hand: "Scènes alsaciennes / (7ème suite d'orchestre) / (Souvenirs) / J. Massenet / <u>n° 1. Dimanche matin</u>." Pasted-on cancels found on fol. 3 and 56.

> Autograph notes on fol. 1, 7, 17, 26, 46, 53, 55, 62, 63, 70, 71, 85, 90, 95, 98, 104, 112, dated between 26 July and 30 Aug. 1881.

Originally bound in dark green Annonay paper boards, vellum spine with black leather label marked "J. Massenet / Scènes / alsaciennes / Partition / d'orchestre." Disbound by the library; the original binding is preserved with the manuscript.

The *Scènes alsaciennes* were premiered under Colonne on 19 March 1882.

FRKF 902

Scènes hongroises

Holograph full-score manuscript of this symphonic suite, 1871–75, 65 p. Notated in black ink, with additional markings in black, blue, and red pencil, on the recto sides of tall sheets of 26-staff paper (blind stamp of Lard-Esnault), foliated by the composer (including 13). At the top of fol. 1, in Massenet's hand: "à M. et Mme Georges Bizet / Scènes Hongroises / 2d suite d'orchestre. / J. Massenet."

Collation:

> No. 1: 1–20, with pasted-on revisions on fol. 1, 13, and 14; no. 2: 1–11; no. 3: 1–5; "Cortège, bénédiction nuptiale et sortie de l'église": 1–34, with pasted-on revisions on fol. 17.

> At the bottom of no. 1, fol. 20: "Paris - octobre 71 / Fontainebl. 30 mai 1875." At the bottom of no. 2, fol. 11: "Paris 8re 71 / Fontainebleau 75 / 31 mai." At the bottom of no. 3, fol. 5: "(8re 71) / Font: 1er Juin 1875." At the bottom of the last page ("Cortège," fol. 34r): "fin de la 2d Suite / (Scènes Hongroises) / Paris - octobre 71 / Fontainebleau / Janvier 1875."

Bound in white, red, and green Annonay paper with vellum spine; on the spine, black leather label marked: "Massenet / Scènes / hongroises / Orchestre."

Premiered by Pasdeloup in Nov. 1871; first published by Hartmann in 1880.

FRKF 893

Scènes napolitaines

Holograph full-score manuscript of this symphonic suite, 1878, 85 p. Notated in black ink, with corrections and additions in pencil, and additional markings in red and blue pencil, on the recto sides of tall sheets of 28-staff paper (blind stamp of Lard-Esnault), foliated by the composer (including 13).

> On title page, in Massenet's hand: "Voici l'ordre et la légende de ce morceau: / 1° La Danse - / 2° La Procession - / et / l'Improvisateur - / 3° La Fête - [this numbering replacing a previous one, scratched out] / à mon ami Arban / Scènes Napolitaines / 5e suite d'orchestre," The dedication at the top of the page is in a different ink.
>
> At the bottom of the last page: "fin des Scènes Napolitaines. / refait et terminé 22 juin 1878, Font[ainebleau] J. Massenet." Also on the last page, in the lower left corner: "1ere exécution: 1866."

Bound in dark green Annonay paper boards, vellum spine with black leather label marked "Massenet / Scènes / napolitaines / Orchestre."

FRKF 911

Suite parnassienne

Holograph full-score manuscript draft ("brouillon d'orchestre"), without the vocal parts, of this symphonic suite with soloists and chorus on words by Maurice Léna, n.d. [1912?], 64 leaves. Notated in black ink, with additional markings in blue and red pencil, on the recto sides of tall individual sheets, torn at the top (ca. 30 × 34 cm) and foliated in Massenet's hand. Rehearsal numbers, marked in blue pencil, are continuous throughout. Corrections are usually made in ink and highlighted in blue pencil.

Originally housed in beige folders, the first marked by Massenet "Suite Parnassienne" in blue pencil, the other, in ink: "Orchestre / Suite Parnassienne," and in red pencil: "brouillon."

Collation:

> [part I]: 1 (marked in black ink, at the top: "Uranie"), 2–12, 12 bis, 13–14. Rehearsal number 13 is marked 12 bis.
>
> [part II]: 1 (marked at the top: "Clio"), 2–12, 12 bis, 14–15, [unpaginated folio, on different, thicker paper, corresponding to rehearsal numbers 41–43, marked "Euterpe" in blue pencil]; pinned-in cancel found on fol. 5.
>
> Rehearsal numbers 44–49 are not present.
>
> [part IV]: 1 (marked at the top: "Suite Parnassienne. / N° 4 / Calioppe / (L'épopée) / titre à mettre avant & avec les tromp[ettes] / et la déclamation"), 2–12, 12 bis, 14–34.

Autograph note pinned-in on fol. 1 of part I: "Les six solistes (pris dans les premiers violons de l'orchestre) seront placés, ainsi que la 2e harpe, en dehors de l'estrade des musiciens; ils seront invisibles pour le public et leur sonorité devra paraître venir de loin."

Published posthumously by Heugel in 1913.

FRKF 906

Suite théâtrale

Holograph manuscripts, in short and full score, and "brouillon d'orchestre" of this symphonic suite for solo voice and orchestra, n.d., 150 leaves and 26 p.

> The short score, incomplete, is written in black ink, with some annotations in pencil (not in Massenet's hand) on the recto sides of individual sheets of tall 20-staff paper, foliated 11–34 in Massenet's hand (fol. 13 paginated 12 bis). It includes the last 12 measures of part I (beginning two measures before rehearsal number 47) and continues until the end. Copyright statement ("Copyright 1913 / H & Cie 25.853") written in pencil at the bottom of fol. 11 in an unidentified hand. Pasted-in correction on fol. 32–33.
>
> The full score, also incomplete, is written on both sides of 13 sheets of heavy tall 26-staff paper, paginated 1–26 by Massenet (p. 13 paginated 12 bis). The rehearsal numbers are written in blue pencil. The score ends five measures after rehearsal number 14. At the top of p. 1, in Massenet's hand: "Partition / d'orchestre. / le poème, de M. Léna. / la musique, de J. Massenet. / Suite Théâtrale / (pour orchestre, voix et / déclamation.) / la tragédie. / la comédie. / la danse." Stamped "Gravé"; copyright statement added in ink at the bottom of the page, in an unidentified hand: "Heugel & Cie, 1913 / H et C / 26085."
>
> The orchestral draft ("brouillon d'orchestre") is written in black ink, with corrections and annotations in blue and red pencil, on the recto sides of 107 individual sheets, foliated by Massenet, torn at the top, of tall music paper. Corrections are generally made in ink and highlighted in blue pencil. The rehearsal numbers are in blue pencil.
>
> *Collation:* 1–12, 12 bis, 14–107; pasted-on (originally pinned-in) correction on fol. 14. Folio 70 is cut up and held together by fragments from the border of a sheet of postage stamps. At the top of fol. 1, in red pencil, in Massenet's hand: "Suite théâtrale"; at the top of fol. 32: "II. La comédie."

FRKF 908, 908.5

Unidentified fragment

Possibly from an orchestral work, in full score, n.d., 1 p. Notated in black ink on the recto of a single sheet of tall 24-staff paper (blind stamp of Lard-Esnault), foliated 7 in blue pencil, with rehearsal number 5 in red pencil. On the evidence of the handwriting, the fragment dates from the last period of Massenet's life, possibly as late as 1910. The first measure is marked "lento," the second "piu agitato."

London, Christie's, 5 May 1982, lot 156.
FRKF 20

E. SONGS

Chanson pour elle

Partly holograph manuscript of the orchestral version of this song for soprano voice, on a poem by Henri Maigrot, n.d. [1897 or later], 22 p. Notated in black ink, with additional markings in blue pencil, on the recto sides of tall sheets of 18-staff paper, foliated in Massenet's hand. Only the orchestration is in the composer's hand, the vocal line and words are in that of a copyist.

The version for voice and piano of *Chanson pour elle* was published by Heugel in 1897 with a dedication to Georgette Bréjean-Gravière (later Bréjean-Silver).

FRKF 844

Mienne!

Holograph manuscript of this song for soprano or tenor and piano, on a poem by Ernest Laroche, 1893, 7 p. Notated in black ink, with a few additional pencil markings, on the recto sides of seven single sheets of tall 20-staff paper (blind stamp of Lard-Esnault), foliated in Massenet's hand. At the top of p. 1, in Massenet's hand: "Mienne! / poésie d'Ernest Laroche." At the end of the manuscript: "Pont de L'arche / samedi 25 août / 93 5 h du soir - temps splendide. J. Massenet."

Paris, Dominique Vincent (Drouot), 21 Dec. 1984, lot 202.
FRKF 703

Soir de printemps

Holograph manuscript of this melodrama for voice and piano, on a poem by Gabriel Martin, 1893, 5 p. Notated in black ink on the recto sides of five single sheets of tall 20-staff paper (blind stamp of Lard-Esnault), foliated in Massenet's hand, placed in a bifolium serving as wrappers. On p. [1] of the outer bifolium, in Massenet's hand: "Soir de printemps / poésie de Gabriel Martin / accompagnement de Massenet." Signed and dated at the end: "Massenet / St Raphaël - 21 déc /93. / après-midi -"

Published with the subtitle "Declamatorium" (Paris: Heugel, 1894).

Paris, Dominique Vincent (Drouot), 21 Dec. 1984, lot 203.
FRKF 704

F. INSTRUMENTAL MUSIC

"Le Bac, petite improvisation pour piano"

Holograph manuscript, 1879. Notated in black ink on p. [2] to [4] of a single bifolium of 14-staff paper (blind stamp: Porel?). At the top of p. [2]: "Le Bac / Improvisation pour le piano—" At end: "Trouville / Maison Barbantane, 13 août 79. / Mercredi onze heures ¼ du matin / J. Massenet." In B-flat. The tempo indication is: Andantino, calme. 49 measures. Evidently unpublished: not in the seven (untitled) *Improvisations* (Paris: Hartmann, 1875).

Not in Grove or Irvine.
New York, Sotheby's, 25 May 1983, lot 38.
FRKF 91

Fantaisie for cello and orchestra

Holograph manuscript of the transcription for cello and piano of this work for cello and orchestra, 1896–97, 37 p. Notated in black ink, with corrections highlighted in blue pencil, on the recto sides of 37 single sheets of tall 16-staff paper, foliated by Massenet (folio 13 numbered 12bis), housed in a bifolium serving as wrappers.

On p. [1] of the outer bifolium, in Massenet's hand: "à mon ami J. Hollman / Fantaisie / pour Violoncelle et orchestre / J. Massenet / transcription pour / p° et vlle / (automne) 1896 = (printemps) 1897." Solo passage written on two folded, pasted-on pieces of paper on folio 11. Pasted-on cancels on fol. 14, 16, and 22.

The orchestral version was published by Heugel in 1897.

Paris, Dominique Vincent (Drouot), 21 Dec. 1984, lot 204.
FRKF 705

II. LITERARY MANUSCRIPT

"La fille de Jephté"

Holograph manuscript synopsis, in Massenet's hand throughout, of the libretto of a projected opera in four acts and eight tableaux, n.d., in black ink, with corrections in black and blue pencil, on two different types of paper placed inside a folded sheet of laid paper serving as wrappers. On the front wrapper: "La fille de Jephté / opéra en 4 actes / et 5 tableaux / 1er acte - l'exil / 2e acte - la coupe des Ammonites / 3e acte - la maison de Jephté / 4e acte (1er tableau) / la crypte ? - / (2e tableau) / la salle des sacrifices." Pages [1]–[3] are a plot summary, written on the same kind of laid paper; p. [5]–[19], written on wove paper, a detailed synopsis.

The manuscript was once bound; traces of stubs and stitching.

> Tipped in at the end: TLS, with autograph additions, from [Jean?] Gaudefroy Demombynes to Jean Farger, 1946 May 12, Rowayton, Connecticut, 1 p. (env), concerning "La fille de Jephté." Also accompanied by an ALS from Eugène Borrel to [Jean Farger?] on stationery of the Société française de musicologie, Paris, 1946 June 26, 2 p.; and by a TLS from Paul-Marie Masson to Jean Farger, on the same stationery, 1946 Aug. 8, 1 p., both about "La fille de Jephté." Masson was president of the Société française de musicologie. Farger is described as "Ingénieur du son" and his address is given as 17, rue Béranger, Fontainebleau.

"La fille de Jephté" is unknown to Grove and to Irvine.
FRKF 501

III. LETTERS

To [Eugène?] Manuel

1877 May 2, Paris, ALS, 1 p., conveying thanks.

London, Christie's, 5 May 1982, lot 156.
FRKF 20.5

To [Mathilde Marchesi]

1888 Feb. 9, The Hague, ALS, 4 p., reporting on the success of her pupil Sybil Sanderson in *Manon*.

Paris, Hervé Chayette (Drouot), 21 May 1984, lot 94.
FRKF 710

To Octave Mirbeau

1891 July 22, Paris, ALS, 3 p., recommending an architect from Rouen for Mirbeau's neighbors.

Paris, Dominique Vincent (Drouot), 6 Dec. 1984, lot 272.
FRKF 662a

To Pauline Viardot

n.d., "Samedi soir," n.p., ALS, 1 p., offering a duettino for piano [four-hands?] to Viardot's daughters. Blind stamp of "B.D."

Paris, Le Roux-Mathias (Drouot), 19 April 1985, lot 297.
FRKF 721.1

Other letters

To unidentified recipients

[1896 Oct. 27] n.p., ALS, 2 p., recommending a female candidate for a [voice?] competition. Dated in an unidentified hand. Blind stamp of "B.D."

n.d., "Samedi," n.p., ALS, 1 p., concerning a female student. Blind stamp of "B.D."

n.d., ANS on both sides of a visiting card (printed: "Monsieur Massenet"). Blind stamp of "B.D."

Paris, Le Roux-Mathias (Drouot), 19 April 1985, lot 297.
FRKF 721.2–4

To an unidentified recipient

1873 March 7, Paris, ALS, 1 p., cancelling an engagement on the grounds of ill health.

Paris, Laurin-Guilloux-Buffetaud-Tailleur (Drouot),
12 Dec. 1985, lot 133
FRKF 928

To an unidentified female correspondent

1901 July 17, Égreville, ALS, 2 p.

1905 Feb. 23, Paris, ALS, 3 p., giving the address of the poet D. Mytis (whose poetry he set to music).

1912 Feb. 17, Palais de Monaco [Monaco]^S, ALS, 2 p., reporting on the premiere of *Roma*.

Paris, Ader-Picard-Tajan (Drouot), 28 June 1985, lot 225.
FRKF 1335

IV. PRINTED MATERIAL

Amadis: opéra légendaire en quatre actes dont un prologue. Poème de Jules Claretie. Musique de J. Massenet. Paris: Au Ménestrel, Heugel, copyright 1922.

[1]–35 [+ 1] p. Libretto.

FRKF 539b

ROBIN MAUGHAM (1916–81)

Papers relating to his uncle W. Somerset Maugham and the Maugham family, arranged in seven sections:

- I. MANUSCRIPTS BY ROBIN MAUGHAM
- II. ROBIN MAUGHAM DIARIES
- III. ROBIN MAUGHAM RESEARCH FILES
- IV. MAUGHAM FAMILY PAPERS
  - A. WILLIAM MAUGHAM PAPERS
    1. *Sermons*
    2. *Incoming correspondence*
    3. *Personal papers*
  - B. LETTERS TO GEORGE MAUGHAM
  - C. ROBERT MAUGHAM PAPERS
  - D. MISCELLANEOUS PAPERS
- V. SUBJECT FILES
- VI. BOOKS RELATING TO W. SOMERSET MAUGHAM AND THE MAUGHAM FAMILY
- VII. PHOTOGRAPHS
  - A. ORIGINAL PHOTOGRAPHS
  - B. PHOTOGRAPHIC FILES
    1. *People*
    2. *Places*

I. MANUSCRIPTS BY ROBIN MAUGHAM

Somerset and all the Maughams

"Family book / Robin's copy," typescript, ca. 131 p.

Autograph manuscript, on recto and verso pages of a tall notebook, 156 p., with a few typescript passages pasted on and related material laid in.

"Sermons (notes on & copies of)," typed transcripts of sermons by William Maugham, ca. 50 p.

"Childhood in Paris" by Violet Williams-Freeman Hammersley, in three parts; typescript, three copies.

Correspondence and notes, including letters from Derek Hammersley, Cynthia Maugham, Diana [Maugham?], and corrected proofs of an essay on Lord Maugham, paginated 539–74.

Robin Maugham's *Somerset and all the Maughams* was published in London by Longmans and Heinemann in 1966.

II. ROBIN MAUGHAM DIARIES

1956

Autograph diary, 12 Dec., 2 p., with a typed copy, 1 p.

1959

"W.S.M. and Maughams generally," autograph manuscript, 10–13 Aug., 11 p. Foliated 1–9, with a typed copy, 8 p.

1961

Manuscript diary, 5 May and 1 Nov., 18 p., with a typed copy, 12 p. Contains entries unrelated to W. Somerset Maugham.

1962

"Hotel Le Beau Rivage / Lausanne Ouchy," autograph manuscript, 27 April–4 Aug., 41 p. Foliated 11–38.

"Westmoreland," manuscript, 12 Oct., 5 p., foliated 1–4, with 4 typed copies, 3 p. each.

"Lunch WSM Dorchester," autograph diary, 24 Oct., 5 p. Foliated 1–4, with a typed copy, 3 p.

"Villa Mauresque," autograph diary, 24 Dec., 17 p. Foliated 19–33, with a typed copy, 13 p.

1963

["Mrs. Violet Hammersley talking about W.S.M"] autograph diary [June] 8 p. Foliated 1–6, with two typed copies, 6 p. each.

1963–64

"Villa Mauresque / 15 Nov 1963," autograph diary, 15 Nov. 1963–26 Jan. 1964, 33 p., foliated 1–20, plus six pages of pasted-on newspaper clippings. In bound notebook with paper label reading: "90th Birthday / Maugham Diaries / 15 November 1963 / to 25 January 1964." With a typed copy, 30 p.

1964

"(Alan's night out episode) / 5 June 1964 / [cross] / Please God come back and help us," manuscript diary, 5–11 June, 25 p. Foliated 1–16, with a typed copy, 20 p.

1965

"Villa Mauresque / Saturday May 15, 1965," autograph diary, 15–18 May, 21 p. Foliated 1–16. In bound notebook with paper label reading: "Maugham Diaries / May 1965." With a typed copy, 19 p.

"Villa Mauresque / 1 July 1965," autograph diary, 1–8 July 1965, 16 p. Foliated 1–15. In bound notebook with paper label reading: "Maugham Diaries / 1 July 1965." With a typed copy, 12 p.

1966

"20 Jan 66 / The end of WSM as told to me by Alan Searle," autograph diary, 4 p., with a typed copy and a page of newspaper clippings, 4 p.

III. ROBIN MAUGHAM RESEARCH FILES

"Maughams in America"
> Correspondence with American historical societies and others, miscellaneous notes, and a photograph [early 1960s]. The letters are addressed to Hector Bolitho or Derek Peel.

"Maughams of Brough, Appleby &c."
> Correspondence to Derek Peel, a manuscript Maugham family tree, labelled "provisional pedigree," maps, postcards, and miscellaneous printed ephemera.

"Maughams of London"
> Correspondence to Derek Peel, mostly concerning Robert Maugham, miscellaneous notes, typed copies and photostats of official documents, and printed ephemera.

"W.S.M. and his brothers"
> Copy of the certificate of baptism of Frederic Herbert Maugham, documents relating to Henry Neville Maugham, printed ephemera and typed notes relating to the church in Whitstable, two issues of *The Cantuarian* (vol. XXVII, no. 6, and vol. XXIX, no. 1), biographical notes, and typed records of interviews.

"Maughams (& Snells) in France"
> Correspondence of Robin Maugham and Derek Peel, a marriage certificate for Robert Ormond Maugham and Edith Mary Snell (1863), legal papers concerning the estate of R.O. Maugham, and a file containing biographical and bibliographical information on Anne Snell.

"Maughams of Lincolnshire"
> Correspondence with Derek Peel and information concerning Moulton and the Rev. William Maugham and his descendants, as well as printed ephemera and a photostat of the will of John Maugham (1703).

"Family"
> Letters to and from Beldy Maugham, correspondence with the British Embassy in Paris, and miscellaneous correspondence files relating to W. Somerset Maugham and the Maugham family.

Maugham family tree
> Autograph, 2 p.

Miscellaneous
> Clippings, either originals or photostats, by or concerning W. Somerset Maugham, arranged in four ring folders. Also, typed transcripts of articles and excerpts by or concerning W. Somerset Maugham, two ring folders, miscellaneous newspaper clippings concerning W. Somerset Maugham, and miscellaneous photostats and photocopies of articles relating to him.

IV. MAUGHAM FAMILY PAPERS

A. WILLIAM MAUGHAM PAPERS

1. *Sermons*
> All are autograph; many are recorded as having been delivered several times; only the earliest date is shown.

Acts 10:38, 15 Dec. 1765

Acts 5:38–39, 3 Nov. 1790

Ephesians 5:11, 24 March 1793

Ephesians 5:15, 14 Sept. 1794
1 Corinthians 14:20, 28 Sept. 1794
1 Corinthians 14:20, 5 Oct. 1794
Galatians 4:18, 26 Oct. 1794

Hebrews 11:7, 3 May 1795
Hebrews 11:7, 31 May 1795
Ephesians 5:11, 1 Nov. 1795
Romans 13:12–13, 29 Nov. 1795

Psalms 33:17–18, 31 July 1796
John 8:32, 4 Sept. 1796

Romans 8:13, 1 Jan. 1797
1 Thessalonians 4:11, 22 Jan. 1797
Romans 10:2, 7 May 1797
James 1:27, 29 July 1797
Psalms 90:12, 6 Aug. 1797
Psalms 37:3, 29 Oct. 1797
Exodus 14:13–14, 19 Dec. 1797
Proverbs 22:1, 21 Dec. 1797
Proverbs 29:25, 24 Dec. 1797

Romans 6:21, 17 Feb. 1798
John 13:35, 1 April 1798
Psalms 76:10, 29 Nov. 1798

Mark 16:20, 20 Jan. 1799
Hebrews 11:1, 24 Feb. 1799
Job 4:7, 17 Nov. 1799
Luke 15:13, 1 Dec. 1799
Luke 15:17, 15 Dec.1799

Romans 8:5, 23 March 1800
Luke 14:16–18, 6 April 1800
Luke 14:16–18, 13 April 1800
Titus 2:14, 11 May 1800
Psalms 37:38, 1 June 1800
Isaiah 11:9, 6 July 1800

John 8:29, 31 Aug. 1800
Matthew 24:12, 26 Oct. 1800
Galatians, 6:9, 21 Dec. 1800

John 13:17, 8 March 1801
Proverbs 3:35, 21 June 1801
1 Timothy 1:5, 23 Aug. 1801
Proverbs 4:23, 11 Oct. 1801
1 Timothy 2:1–2, 25 Oct. 1801
2 Peter 3:9, 29 Nov. 1801
Acts 5:38–39, 20 Dec. 1801
1 Peter 4:9–10, 21 Dec. 1801
John 4:9, 25 Dec. 1801

John 3:19, 21 Feb. 1802
John 18:37, 7 March 1802
Ecclesiastes 2:26, 4 April 1802
John 3:12, 20 June 1802
Acts 17:30, 4 July 1802
Philippians 1:22–23, 11 July 1802
John 12:35, 1 Aug. 1802
Proverbs 21:30, 5 Sept. 1802
Psalms 127:1–2, 3 Oct. 1802

Proverbs 1:7, 23 Jan. 1803
Proverbs 1:7, 30 Jan. 1803
Acts 16:30, 6 Feb. 1803
Acts 16:30, 13 Feb. 1803
Matthew 13:41–42, 17 April 1803
Luke 9:56, 24 April 1803
Acts 2:4, 29 May 1803
Acts 2:4, 5 June 1803
Luke 9:56, 12 June 1803
Acts 4:32, 24 July 1803
1 Kings 8, 11 Sept. 1803
Titus 2:11–12, 13 Nov. 1803

Luke 20:38, 1 Jan. 1804
Luke 20:38, 29 Jan. 1804
1 Timothy 6:6, 24 June 1804
Jeremiah 9:4, 29 July 1804

Psalms 100:1, 17 March 1805
Romans 11:26, 2 June 1805
Hebrews 9:27, 23 June 1805
Hebrews 9:27, 30 June 1805
Psalms 98:1, 5 Dec. 1805

Proverbs 16:7, 2 Nov. 1806
John 18:38, 23 Nov. 1806

John 4:9, 1 Feb. 1807
1 Peter 2:21, 27 March 1807, 2 versions
Titus 2:13, 12 April 1807
2 Thessalonians 3:10, 2 Nov. 1807
Romans 10:3, 22 Nov. 1807

Luke 2:10–11, 25 Dec. 1808

Acts 24–25, 4 Oct. 1812

Romans 6:23, n.d. [end missing]
"On the King's recovery," n.d.
"I should now have done …," unidentified fragment, n.d.
Titus 3:1–2, n.d.

2. *Incoming correspondence*

From Edmund Chalmer
    1782 Nov. 16, London, ALS, 1 p.

From Mary Crips
    1800 Jan. 12, Torpoint, ALS, 2 p., concerning the death and debts of Theophilus Maugham. Addressed to Mrs. Maugham.

From Mr. Elliott
    1753 Feb. 17 [Cambridge] Magd[alene] College, ALS, 2 p.

From Abraham Emanuel
    1800 Oct. 27 [Plymouth] ALS, 1 p.
    1801 March 6 [Plymouth] ALS, 1 p.
    Both concerning the late Theophilus Maugham.

From Theophilus Maugham [Thomas Reid]
    1794 April 2, Sheerness, ALS, 2 p., to his brother William Farringdon Maugham.
    1796 March 3, Spithead, ALS, 2 p.
    1798 May 10, Plymouth, ALS, 2 p.
    1798 Oct. [i.e. Nov.] 9, Plymouth, ALS, 3 p.
    1798 Nov. 24, Plymouth, ALS, 3 p., addressed to "Dear Brother."
    1798 Dec. 19, Plymouth, ALS, 3 p.
    1799 Jan. 18, Plymouth, ALS, 3 p.
    1799 Feb. 13, H.M.S *Ethalion* at sea, ALS, 2 p.
    [1799] April 10, Plymouth, ALS, 2 p.
    [1799] n.d., "Meddeterain Streats" [i.e. on board H.M.S. *Ethalion*] ALS, 3 p.
    1799 Dec. 13, off Brest, ALS, 2 p.
    n.d., n.p. ALS, 2 p.

From William Farringdon Maugham
    1790 Dec. 2, London, ALS, 3 p., to his brother John Maugham.
    1799 April 29, London, ALS, 3 p., to his mother.
    1805 July 12, London, ALS, 2 p.

From John Webbe
    1802 June 19, Navy Pay Office [Plymouth] ALS, 2 p., concerning Theophilus Maugham.

3. *Personal papers*

Certificate, printed on parchment and filled in by hand, in the name of Thomas, bishop of Ely, concerning the consecration as deacon of William Maugham of Magdalene College, Cambridge, 18 March 1753.

Certificate, printed on parchment and filled in by hand, in the name of Matthew, bishop of Ely, concerning the ordination of William Maugham of Magdalene College, Cambridge, on 21 September 1755.

Printed declaration, signed by Maugham and countersigned by Matthew, bishop of Ely, promising to abide by the liturgy of the Church of England, 21 September 1755, 1 p.

Printed document confirming the appointment of William Maugham as curate of the chapel of Moulton, Moulton, Lincolnshire, 11 June 1782.

Foster & Bonner, manuscript account statement, 1814 Jan. 16–July

Memorandum concerning Maugham, 1762 Sept. 12.

The moral penman: a new copy-book, Latin and English, *after a manner never before extant. For the use of schools.* By George Bickham … bound manuscript copy, n.d. 20 p.

Last will and testament of Thomas Reid [i.e. Theophilus Maugham] 1 July 1800, 1 p., marked "copy."

Last will and testament, written in a secretarial hand on a large sheet of parchment, dated 10 Oct. 1814. Accompanied by an autograph note by Maugham concerning his will, n.d.

A catalogue of the household furniture, books, brewing vessels, farming utensils, &c. Of the Revd. Wm. Maugham, deceased, of Moulton, which will be sold at auction, on the premises, by John Bamford, on Friday and Saturday, the 8th and 9th days of July, 1814. Spalding: D. Dann, printer [1814]. Broadside, 43 × 57 cm.

Miscellaneous and unidentified correspondence, 9 items.

See *Somerset and all the Maughams*, p. 7–35.

B. LETTERS TO GEORGE MAUGHAM

From Emanuel and Lucy Eleanor [Maugham] Andrew

n.d., Boston, Ohio, ALS, 4 p., from both Emanuel and Lucy Eleanor Andrew, addressed to "Dear uncle."

1839 April 11, New York, ALS, 4 p., from Emanuel.

1840 May, Boston, Ohio, ALS, 4 p., signed Emanuel and Eleanor Andrew.

1841 Dec. 16, Boston, Ohio, ALS, 4 p., signed Emanuel and Eleanor Andrew.

1843 Jan. 3–31, Boston, Ohio, AL, 2 p., no signature; the end of the letter is apparently missing.

1843 Sept. 21, Boston, Ohio, ALS, 2 p.

1845 March 23, Boston, Ohio, ALS, 3 p., from Eleanor Andrew, reporting on the death of Emanuel on 10 March 1845.

See *Somerset and all the Maughams*, p. 47–53.

C. ROBERT MAUGHAM PAPERS

Pocket diary kept during a tour of France and Germany, 1820. Places visited include Calais, Douai, Cambrai, Antwerp, Mézières, Sedan, Trier, Bingen, Coblenz, Bonn, Cologne. 61 p., with miscellaneous loose notes laid in. With a typed copy, 27 p.

Scrapbook, [1840–50], ca. 50 p., containing chiefly poetic clippings and the following manuscript material, all pasted on blue paper: "Select sentences," calligraphic manuscript, unsigned, 1 p.; "Select sentences," calligraphic manuscript, 2 p., signed at the end "Robert Maugham, September 1805"; [More "select sentences"], calligraphic manuscript, 1 p., also signed at the end "Robert Maugham, September 1805"; "Epitaph on a young lady," manuscript inscription on a drawing of a tomb, n.d.; "Reflections on a tomb," calligraphic manuscript, illustrated, 1 p.; "Industry," signed "Robert Maugham," 1 p.; "The Country Alehouse. From the Deserted Village," calligraphic copy, 3 p.; "Anthem," calligraphic manuscript, signed at the end "Montague / Christ's Hospital," 1 p.; "The Village School-Master / From The Deserted Village," calligraphic manuscript, 1 p.; colored crayon drawing of a flower, signed E.G. Frances; "At early dawn the farmer rose," unidentified manuscript, 1 p.

An accompanying note on an envelope, in the hand of Robin Maugham, expresses doubt on the scrapbook's provenance.

Robert Maugham, W. Somerset Maugham's grandfather. See *Somerset and all the Maughams*, p. 72–90.

D. MISCELLANEOUS PAPERS

Manuscript sermon on Psalms 51:17, 5 April 1713, 8 p., with a pencil note in the hand of George R. Maugham, indicating that it was written by the Rev. Farringdon Reid of Marsham, Nots., rector of Somerley, Leicestershire.

Passport in the name of Thomas Crewe, 12 April 1802, possibly with no connection to the Maugham family.

Manuscript commonplace book, with ownership inscription of Ann Jane Edmondson, 29 Aug. 1825, 38 p., in at least two different hands. Contains: "Maternal affection, extract from a funeral sermon"; miscellaneous poems, many unidentified, including several by Felicia Hemans; a few children's drawings, laid in; a loose cyanotype photograph. Bound in calf, with gilt decorative borders on both boards, spine missing.

Newspaper clipping, ca. 1862–63, concerning the discovery of a coffin containing the remains of William Maugham's favorite parrot.

Letters from A.A. Snell and C.O. Maugham, most to Dorothy Yarde and "Dear Mabel," 1874–1905 and n.d., typed copies.

Certified copy of the entry of the marriage of Elizabeth Mary Somerset Maugham and Vincent Rudolph Paravicini, London, 20 July 1936.

V. SUBJECT FILES

Gardner-Serpollet steam car

W. Somerset Maugham. Portrait by H.A. Freeth, 1946, etching on paper (15 × 26.5 cm). Signed and numbered 13/75 by Freeth.

Morgan, Louise. "Somerset Maugham," from *Writers at work* (London: Chatto & Windus, 1927), carbon typescript.

Books given by W. Somerset Maugham. [Canterbury:] The King's School, Canterbury, n.d., 32 p. Mimeographed typescript.

Typed notes for a film on W. Somerset Maugham, n.d., 21 p., with a typed chronology of W. Somerset Maugham's life, 4 p.

VI. BOOKS RELATING TO W. SOMERSET MAUGHAM AND THE MAUGHAM FAMILY

Brander, Laurence. *Somerset Maugham: a guide*. Edinburgh and London: Oliver & Boyd, 1963.

8vo, [i]–vi, [1]–222. Bright blue cloth publisher's binding with author, title, and publisher's device gold-tooled on spine. In green and orange dust jacket with lettering in white and green.

Brophy, John. *Somerset Maugham*. London, New York, Toronto: Longmans, Green & Co., n.d. (Published for The British Council and the National Book League).

[1]–48 p.; 21.5 cm. On half-title: "Bibliographical Series of Supplements to 'British Book News' on Writers and Their Work, General Editor Bonamy Dobrée." On cover: "Writers and their Work no. 22." In green paper wrappers.

(Canterbury) *The pilgrim's guide to the royal and ancient city of Canterbury. The official guide …* Canterbury: printed by Gibbs & Sons Ltd, 1962/63.

[1]–76 p. [+ folding map bound in before p. 1]; 18.5 cm. In pictorial purplish red paper wrappers. On cover: "The official guide and historical record."

Cordell, Richard. *Somerset Maugham: a biographical and critical study*. London, Melbourne, Toronto: Heinemann, 1961.

8vo, [i]–xi, [1], 1–250 [+ ill. front.]. In dust jacket. The first chapter is profusely annotated by Robin Maugham.

Deed, B.L. *A history of Stamford School*. N.p.: printed for the School, 1954.

8vo, [i]–ix, [3], 1–138 [+ 2 p.] [+ ill. front.]. Reddish brown cloth publisher's binding, with title and author gold-tooled on spine. On verso of title page: "Printed in Great Britain at the University Press, Cambridge (Brooke Crutchley, University Printer)." Inscribed by the author on verso of front board: "Robin Maugham / with best wishes, / Basil Deed / 5 May 1962."

Dover College Register. Fourth edition 1871–1924. Edited by C.L. Evans. Dover: printed by G.W. Grigg and son, "St George's Press," Worthington Street and York Street, 1924.

8vo, [1]–250 p. [+ ill. front.]. Cream-colored cloth binding, with title, school seal, and date gold-tooled on front board; both boards and spine also decorated with three black horizontal stripes. Three entries under Maugham on p. 139–40.

Edwards, D.L. *A history of the King's School, Canterbury*. London: Faber and Faber, 1957.

8vo, [1]–224 p. [+ ill. front.]. Bright blue cloth publisher's binding, with title, author, and publisher gold-tooled on spine. In light grey dust jacket with black lettering and red devices.

Goldsmith, Oliver. *An abridgment of the history of England, from the invasion of Julius Caesar, to the death of George II. By Dr. Goldsmith. The continuation to April, 1813, by an eminent historian. Ornamented with a frontispiece, and with heads by Bewick*. Gainsborough: printed by and for Henry Mozley, 1813. At the head of the title page: "Greatly enlarged, being brought down to April, 1813."

[frontispiece], 12mo, 416 p. Bound in plain calf. Ownership inscription on the flyleaf: "Thomas Maugham / Moulton / Feb. 23rd / 1814." Two other ownership inscriptions on the verso of the front board, one "G.M. Stubbins," with "his great niece" noted in another hand, the other not deciphered, dated 1914.

(King's School, Canterbury) *A brief survey of the King's School, Canterbury*. [Canterbury: printed by Gibbs and Sons Ltd, 1962?].

[1]–27 [+ 1] p. ; 18.5 cm. Foreword by J.P. Newell on p. [1], dated Oct. 1962: "… written by Canon Shirley." In pink paper wrappers. Title taken from cover.

Liddell, Robert. *An object for a walk*. London: Longmans, 1966.

8vo, [8], [1]–212 [+ 2] p. In pictorial dust jacket.

Lincolnshire: a country of infinite charm. With 534 places and 118 pictures. London: Hodder and Stoughton Limited, 1952. At the top of the title page: "The King's England." On verso of the title page: "First published July 1949, second impression 1952."

8vo, [i]–x, 1–451 [+ 1] p. [+ 30 leaves of plates]. Red cloth publisher's binding, with title and series title black-tooled on front board and on the spine (where the publisher's name also appears). In dark blue dust jacket; the title on the dust jacket is given as: "Arthur Mee's Lincolnshire." Note on p. [v] indicating that the volume was edited by Claude and Lois Scanlon and Sydney Warner.

MacCarthy, Desmond. *William Somerset Maugham 'The English Maupassant': an appreciation.... With a bibliography.* [London]: William Heinemann, 1934.

1–22 [+ ill. front.]; 18.5 cm. In yellow paper wrappers with green lettering. Title taken from cover.

Maugham, Frederic Herbert Maugham, first Viscount. *The case of Jean Calas.* London: William Heinemann Ltd., 1928.

8vo, [6 + 1 ill. front.], i–ix, [1], 1–204. Plain brown cloth publisher's binding, with title, author, and publisher gold-tooled on spine. Printed note tipped in between frontispiece and title page: "The author, since this book was in type, has been appointed to be a Judge of the Supreme Court."

—. *Lies as allies, or Hitler at war.* London, New York, Toronto: Oxford University Press, 1941.

[1]–64 p.; 18 cm. In grey and red paper wrappers. Signed by [Lord Maugham?] on cover.

—. *Lies as allies, or Hitler at war.* London, New York, Toronto: Oxford University Press, 1941.

[1]–64 p.; 18.5 cm. In brick red paper wrappers; on verso of front wrapper: "Printed in Canada and published by the Oxford University Press, Amen House, Toronto." Together with a printed slip: "With the compliments of the Oxford University Press, University Avenue, Toronto 2"; also with a TLS from Sir Humphrey Milford to Viscount Maugham, on stationery of Oxford University Press, Oxford, 24 March 1941, 1 p.

Maugham, Henry Neville. *The book of Italian travel (1580–1900). With four illustrations in photogravure by Hedley Fitton.* London: Grant Richards; New York: E.P. Dutton & Co., 1903.

8vo, [2], [i]–ix, [3], [1]–458 [+ 2] p. [+ 4 leaves of plates]. Dark blue cloth publisher's binding, with title and Y-shaped decorative device gold-tooled on front board; title, publisher, and a different decorative pattern on spine; top edge gilt. Inscribed by the author on flyleaf: "My friend Aunt Julia / from the / nephew & author / H N M / 1903."

—. *Richard Hawkwood: a romance.* Edinburgh and London: William Blackwood and Sons, 1906.

8vo, [8], [1]–368 [+ 16 leaves of advertisements]. Bound at the end: Catalogue of Messrs Blackwood & Sons' Publications, dated 7/06. Red cloth publisher's binding, with title and subtitled black-tooled on the front board, separated by a decorative device; title, subtitle, author, and publisher gold-tooled on the spine.

Maugham, Robert. *The act 6 & 7 Victoriae, Cap. 73; for consolidating and amending several of the laws relating to attorneys and solicitors practising in England and Wales; with an introduction and analysis of the act, and copious notes, shewing the effect of the alterations.* London: E. Spettigue, Law Bookseller and Publisher, 1843.

8vo, [i]–xiv, [1]–65 [+ 1] p. Bound in brown cloth boards with blind-tooled decorations on both boards and with title and author printed on paper label on front board. Ownership signature on title page: "John Abbott / 10 Charlotte Street / Bedford Square."

—. *Outlines of character: consisting of The great character, The English character, — Characteristic classes in relation to happiness, — The gentleman, — External indications of character, — Craniology, — The poet, — The orator, — Literary characters, — The periodical critic, — The man of genius.* Second edition. London: printed by J. and C. Adlard, 23, Bartholomew Close; for Longman, Hurst, Rees, Orme, Brown, and Green, Paternoster Row, 1823.

8vo, [1–2], [i]–xiv, 3–306 p. [+ ill. front.] Bound in quarter red sheepskin and green marbled paper; marbled edges; spine gilt, with raised bands; gold-tooled on spine: "Character / outlines / By / Robt. Maugham / Secretary / The Incorpd. / Law Society / 1823"; green and purple marbled endpapers. Presentation copy, inscribed by the author on the half-title: "S.W. Sweet Esq.re / With the author's resp[ect]." Bookplate of the Duke of Sussex, identified in a note in pencil on the verso of the front free endpaper. On both sides of the flyleaf, long note in black ink, dated in pencil "AD 1886" in an unidentified hand, concerning the book and its author.

—. *Outlines of the law of real property; or readings from Blackstone and other text writers; including the alterations to the present time.* London: E. Spettigue, Law Bookseller and Publisher, 1842.

8vo, 17 p.l., [1]–410 p. One folding table bound between p. 220 and 221. Grey cloth binding, with double blind-tooled fillet along the edges; on spine, gold-tooled: "Outlines / of / law / Real / property." Bookseller's ticket: Wildy & Sons Ltd., London. Ownership signature of Wightman Wood on the recto of front free endpaper. Unidentified pencilled notes throughout.

—. *A treatise on the law of attornies, solicitors, and agents; with notes and disquisitions.* London: J. & W.T. Clarke, law-booksellers and publishers, 1825.

8vo, [i]–xxxv, [1], [1]–502. Rebound in green boards with dark purple cloth spine. Ownership signature on flyleaf: "E.J. Holland / Linc. Inn / Dec.r /62"; also on flyleaf, ownership stamp of William Barnard, L.L.B., Trinity College, Camb[ridge].

(Maugham, W. Somerset) *A comprehensive exhibition of the writings of W. Somerset Maugham, drawn from various private collections and libraries. With a preface by the author. May 25 through August 1, 1958. Albert M. Bender Room, Stanford University Library.* Stanford, California: Stanford University Press, 1958.

24 unpaginated leaves; 22.5 cm. Printed note on verso of title page: "The exhibition was arranged and the catalogue compiled by J. Terry Bender, chief of the division of special collections and keeper of rare books to the Stanford University Libraries." In grey paper wrappers, with title of exhibition printed on a red rectangular background.

[Mordaunt, Elinor]. *Gin and bitters. By A. Riposte.* New York: Farrar & Rinehart, Incorporated, 1931.

8vo, [6], [1]–306. Black cloth publisher's binding, with title, author's pseudonym, and publisher gold-tooled on front board and spine.

Rawnsley, Willingham Franklin. *Highways and byways in Lincolnshire. With illustrations by Frederick L. Griggs.* London: Macmillan and Co., Limited, 1914.

8vo, [i]–xviii, [2], [1]–519 [+ 1 p.]; folding map bound after p. [520]; 4 p. of advertisements for The Highways & Byways Series. Blue cloth publisher's binding, with title and illustrator gold-tooled on front board and title, author, and publisher gold-tooled on spine; top edge gilt.

Snell, Anne Alicia. *Aline ou la chaumière suisse. Avec gravures dans le texte.* Rouen: Mégard et Cie, libraires-éditeurs, 1890. On half-title: Bibliothèque morale de la jeunesse, 3e série in-8°.

8vo, [1]–159 [+ 1] p. In grey paper wrappers.

—. *Les deux chaumières. Avec gravures dans le texte.* Rouen: Mégard et Cie, libraires-éditeurs, 1891. On half-title: Bibliothèque morale de la jeunesse, 3e série in-8°.

8vo, [1]–157 [+ 3] p. In grey paper wrappers.

—. *Les filles du capitaine. Avec gravures dans le texte.* Rouen: Mégard et Cie, libraires-éditeurs, 1890. On half-title: Bibliothèque morale de la jeunesse, 1re série in-8°.

8vo, [1]–224 p. In grey paper wrappers.

—. *Isabelle Verneuil ou la pension Montbrison. Avec gravures dans le texte.* Rouen: Mégard et Cie, libraires-éditeurs, 1890. On half-title: Bibliothèque morale de la jeunesse, 3e série in-8°.

8vo, [1]–160 p. In grey paper wrappers; front wrapper and half-title largely missing.

VII. PHOTOGRAPHS

A. ORIGINAL PHOTOGRAPHS

Maugham, Frederic Herbert, first Viscount Maugham

As a child, sepia photograph by Le Jeune, Paris, n.d., mounted on a 6 × 9.5 cm card.

As a young boy, sepia photograph by Le Jeune, Paris, n.d., mounted on a 10.5 × 15.5 cm card.

As a young man, photograph by Stearn, Cambridge, "Lent 1899," mounted on a 10.5 × 16.5 cm card.

In a group photograph entitled "Headquarters Central Detachment Special Constabulary, Section IX (Lincoln's Inn)," issued as a postcard, n.d., 13 × 8.5 cm.

Playing cricket, n.d., 12 × 16.5 cm.

Playing sports at St. Moritz, photograph Foto-Flury, St. Moritz, n.d., 10 × 15 cm.

Passport photograph, stamped on verso 24 July 1931.

Portrait photograph by J. Russell & Sons, London, mounted on cardboard, 17 × 22.5 cm.

With Robin Maugham as a young child, Littlestone, Kent, n.d., 9 × 9 cm.

As Lord Chancellor, oil portrait by Sir Gerald Kelly, photograph by Paul Laib, London, mounted on cardboard, 19 × 28 cm.

With his daughter Kate Mary Bruce, n.d., 11 × 15 cm.

Maugham, Helen Mary, Lady

As a young woman, uncredited sepia photograph, 10 × 15 cm, mounted on two different kinds of heavy paper.

With Robin Maugham as a baby, colored photograph by Lyddell Sawyer, London [ca. 1916] mounted on cardboard, 12.5 × 19 cm.

With Robin Maugham as a young child, Littlestone, Kent, n.d., 9 × 9 cm.

Maugham, Robert (d. 1862)

Sepia portrait photograph, face retouched, 16.5 × 21 cm, mounted on heavy carboard.

Maugham, Robert Ormond

Oval sepia photographic portrait by M. Alophe, Paris, n.d., mounted on 6 × 10 cm card.

Standing, sepia photograph by August Adler, Dresden, mounted on 6 × 10 cm card.

Terracotta statuette by J. Boehm, four amateur photographs, 8.5 × 12 cm.

Maugham, Robin

In front of the entrance door to Villa Mauresque, May 1965, 8 × 11 cm.

Maugham, W. Somerset

At age 17, sepia photograph by London Stereoscopic Company, mounted on a 10.5 × 16.5 cm card.

As a young adult, sepia photograph by Elliott & Fry, London, mounted on a 13.5 × 19 cm card.

With Robin Maugham, n.d. [1960s?], 7 × 7 cm.

W. Somerset Maugham [photograph by Robin Maugham? early 1960s?], 6 × 4.5 cm.

Contact sheet for 14 pictures taken by Robin Maugham at the Villa Mauresque, 1959.

Sepia photograph by Paul Laib of an unidentified portrait of W. Somerset Maugham, 22.5 × 28 cm.

Photograph by Paul Laib of an unidentified portrait of W. Somerset Maugham, 22.5 × 20 cm.

Snell, Anne Alicia

Sepia photograph, printed on paper, n.d., 6 × 9 cm.

Snell, Edith Mary

Photograph by H.S. Mendelssohn, London, n.d., mounted on cardboard, 15 × 22 cm.

Cragg House, Brough, Westmorland

3 photographs by John T. Hill, Murton, Appleby, 21 × 16.5 cm.

Moulton, Lincolnshire

[photograph by Robin Maugham?], 11 black-and-white prints, 13.5 × 8.5 cm.

B. PHOTOGRAPHIC FILES

1. *People*

Back, Barbara

Haxton, Gerald

Maugham, Charles

Maugham, Elizabeth

Maugham, Frederic Herbert Maugham, first Viscount, including a picture with Noel Coward and others

Maugham, Helen Mary, Lady

Maugham, Henry Macdonald

Maugham, Henry Neville

Maugham, Robert

Maugham, Robin

Maugham, Sophie (Barbara Sophia von Scheidlin)

Maugham, Syrie

Maugham, William (photograph of a drawing)

Maugham, W. Somerset

    At the King's School, Canterbury, ca. 1888

    As a young man

    Miscellaneous portraits

    With Frederic Herbert Maugham at Bad Gastein, n.d.

    With Robin Maugham, at Parker's Ferry, 1945

    With Robin Maugham at a Longmans cocktail party, 1955

    At the opening of the science laboratory, 1958, and at the Maugham Library, 1961, at the King's School, Canterbury

    With Robin Maugham on the terrace of the garden at Villa Mauresque, 1959

    At Hotel Beau-Rivage, Ouchy, April 1962, photograph by Robin Maugham

    At Villa Mauresque, 1964, photograph by Robin Maugham

    At his 90th birthday, 25 Jan. 1964

    At Villa Mauresque in May 1965, photograph by Robin Maugham

    At Villa Mauresque in July 1965

    W. Somerset Maugham's funeral service, 1965

    With Barbara Back

    With Barbara Back and Gerald Haxton

    With Alan Searle, photograph by Robin Maugham

Searle, Alan, and Robin Maugham at Villa Mauresque, May 1965

Searle, Alan

Snell, Anne Alicia

Snell, Edith Mary

Snell, Rose Ellen

Somerset, Henry, Sir

2. *Places*

Nelson Doubleday's cottage in Yemassee, N.C.

Old Grammar School, Appleby

Old School Buildings, Moulton, Lincolnshire

Old Vicarage, Whitstable

Parker's Ferry

Suresnes, France

Syrie Maugham's villa, Le Touquet

Tye House, Hartfield

Villa Mauresque, Saint-Jean-Cap-Ferrat, exterior, interior, garden, W. Somerset Maugham's Rolls Royce

Whitstable

ROBIN MAUGHAM PAPERS
FRKF 191

WILLIAM SOMERSET MAUGHAM (1874–1965)

Letter to Charles Hanson Towne

1924 Dec. 18, Myrtle Bank Hotel and Hotel Titchfield, Jamaica[S], TLS, 1 p., concerning the terms of a contract.

New York, Sotheby's, 16 May 1984, lot 644.
FRKF 312

GUY DE MAUPASSANT (1850–93)

"La vocation"

Holograph manuscript, n.d. [ca. 1887?], 11 p., in black ink on both sides of three nested bifolia, paginated 1–10, the last page unpaginated. Signed "Guy de Maupassant" at the end.

Bound with four unsigned illustrations by Maupassant in the style of Steinlen, each depicting a woman; one is pen-and-ink and wash, the others a combination of pen-and-ink, wash, and crayon. Bound in purple marbled paper boards with dark brown cloth spine. Bookplate of Casimir de Woznicki. Laid in: ALS from Casimir de Woznicki to [Édouard?] Champion, 1921 May 15, Paris, 1 p., presenting the manuscript as a gift to the recipient.

No short story with this title located in Talvart or in Maupassant, *Contes et nouvelles*, ed. Louis Forestier (Paris: Gallimard, Bibliothèque de la Pléiade, 1974–79). Dating suggested in the auction catalogue description.

Paris, Boisgirard (Drouot), 22 May 1985, lot 64.
FRKF 644

MAXIMILIAN, EMPEROR OF MEXICO (1832–67)

I. LETTERS AND DOCUMENTS

Printed document signed by Maximilian, conferring the imperial order of Guadalupe on Don Ventura Rivera. Dated Chapultepec, 6 July 1866. Numbered 1102 in the upper left corner. Countersigned by José Maria Gonzales, Prio encargado de la Gran Cancelleria. With an official note from the chancery confirming registration on the verso.

London, Sotheby's, 10 May 1984, lot 336.
FRKF 337

Letter to "Ministerio de Fomento"

1865 Aug. 12, Chapultepec, LS, 2 p., concerning the construction of a railroad between Vera Cruz and Puebla. Countersigned by an undersecretary on behalf of the minister of public works.

London, Sotheby's, 10 May 1984, lot 337.
FRKF 338

Letter to Dr. Rosenthal

1866 April 26, Chapultepec, LS, 2 p.

Geneva, L'autographe, catalogue 6, 1984.
FRKF 488

II. AUGUST JILEK PAPERS RELATING TO MAXIMILIAN AND CHARLOTTE

A. CORRESPONDENCE RECEIVED

Alexandrine, duchess of Coburg
  1867 July 11, Hallenberg bei Koburg, ALS on mourning stationery, 4 p. (env)

Carl Ludwig of Habsburg, archduke
  1866 Nov. 3, n.p., ALS, 5 p.
  1868 Jan. 5, Vienna, document, signed, 1 p.

Clémentine d'Orléans, duchess of Coburg-Kohary
  1867 July 8, Ebenthal near Vienna, ALS on mourning stationery, 2 p. (env), in French, with notes on verso of last page.

Corio, Marchese (Mexican ambassador to the Belgian court). All letters are in Italian.
  1866
    Nov. 2, Paris, ALS on mourning stationery, 4 p.
    Dec. 26, Brussels, ALS, 3 p.
  1867
    Jan. 18, Brussels, ALS, 12 p.
    Feb. 7, Brussels, ALS, 2 p., cut away at the top of pages 1–2.
    Feb. 24, Brussels, ALS, 4 p.
    March 2, Brussels, ALS, 4 p.
    March 5, Brussels, ALS, 4 p.
    March 11, Brussels, ALS, 4 p.
    March 13, Brussels, ALS, 4 p.
    May 8, Brussels, ALS, 4 p.
    May 14, Brussels, ALS, 4 p.
    May 17, Brussels, ALS, 4 p.
    n.d., n.p., ALS, 4 p.

Couvay, vicomte de (financial adviser to King Leopold II)
  1866 Nov. 5, Brussels, ALS on mourning stationery, 3 p.
  1866 Nov. 28, Brussels, ALS on mourning stationery, 3 p.
  1867 Feb. 23, Brussels, ALS on mourning stationery, 3 p.
  1867 March 26, ALS on mourning stationery, 3 p.
  1867 June 10, Brussels, ALS, 3 p.
  1867 June 14, Brussels, ALS, 2 p.

Fischer, Augustin, S.J.
  1866 Nov. 27, Orizaba, ALS, 2 p.
  1866, Dec. 11, Orizaba, ALS, 2 p.
  1866, Dec. 29, Puebla, LS in a secretarial hand, 1 p.

Flandres, Philippe de Belgique, comte de
  1866
    Dec. 27, Brussels, ALS on mourning stationery, 1 p.
  1867
    Jan. 10, n.p., ALS on mourning stationery, 1 p.

Jan. 28, Brussels, ALS, 1 p.
Feb. 5, Düsseldorf, ALS, 1 p.
Feb. 20, Düsseldorf, ALS, 1 p.
Feb. 22, Düsseldorf, ALS, 1 p.
March 10, Brussels, ALS, 1 p.
March 27, Brussels, ALS, 1 p.
April 19, Brussels, ALS, 1 p.
April 22, Brussels, ALS, 1 p.
May 12, n.p., ALS, 1 p.
June 23, Paris, ALS, 1 p. (abundantly corrected by Jilek).
July 20, n.p., ALS on mourning stationery, 1 p.

Dr. Fritsch (assistant to Riedel and physician to HRH Sophie)
1866
Oct. 15, Ischl, ALS, 3 p.
Oct. 21, Ischl, ALS, 2 p.
Oct. 27, Ischl, telegram
Nov. 22, Salzburg, ALS, 2 p.
Dec. 19, Vienna, ALS, 3 p.
Dec. 27, Vienna, ALS, 3 p.
1867
Jan. 8, Vienna, ALS, 2 p.
Jan. 13, n.p., ALS, 2 p.
March 3, Vienna, ALS, 2 p.
Accompanied by a telegram from HRH Sophie to Graf Bombelles, date not deciphered.

Grunne, Eugénie, comtesse de
[1867] Jan. 28, Brussels, ALS, 2 p.
[1867] March 4, Brussels, ALS, 2 p.
[1867] June 23, ALS, 4 p.

Guggenthal, Victor von
1867 Aug. 28, Caskieben in Aberdeenshire, ALS, 3 p.

Kuhacsevich, Jacob von (treasurer to Maximilian)
1868, Oct. 10, Vienna, ALS, 1 p. (env). Accompanied by a copies of letters from Kuhacsevich to Radonetz, 1865 Nov. 2, Chapultepec, and from Jellinek (royal gardener at Miramar) to Maximilian, 1865 Sept. 25, 6 p.

Mrs. Kuhacsevich (lady-in-waiting of Empress Charlotte)
1865 Nov. 10, Mexico City, ALS, 4 p.
1866 Jan. 27, Mexico City, ALS, 4 p.
1866 April 10, Mexico City, ALS on mourning stationery, 4 p.

Loosey [?], Carl F. (Austrian consular official)
1867 Feb. 15, New York, ALS, 2 p.

Machold, J., professor
1865 July, n.p., ALS, 3 p. (env)

Maximilian of Austria, emperor of Mexico
1865 Feb. 10, Chapultepec, ALS, 4 p.
1865 Dec. 22, Chapultepec, ALS, 9 p.
1866 Jan. 7, Cuernavaca, ALS, 8 p.
1866 Feb. 4, Cuernavaca, ALS, 3 p.
1866 April 26, Chapultepec, ALS, 8 p.

Pont, baron du (secretary to Maximilian)
1867 Feb. 13, Vienna, ALS, 2 p.

Dr. Riedel (director of lunatic asylum in Vienna)
1866
Oct. 18, Vienna, ALS, 4 p.
Oct. 25, n.p., ALS, 4 p.
Nov. 10, n.p., ALS, 5 p.
Dec. 5, n.p., ALS, 4 p.
Dec. 16, Vienna, ALS, 3 p.
Dec. 27, Vienna, ALS, 4 p.
1867
Jan. 4, Vienna, ALS, 4 p.
Jan. 16, Vienna, ALS, 4 p.
Feb. 4, n.p., ALS, 4 p.
Feb. 28, Vienna, ALS, 4 p.
March 15, n.p., ALS, 3 p.
March 16, n.p., ALS, 3 p.
April 13, n.p., ALS, 4 p.
June 3, n.p., ALS, 3 p.
June 7, n.p., ALS, 4 p.
[July 9] n.p., ALS, 4 p.
July 9, n.p., ALS, 4 p.
July 21, n.p., ALS, 4 p.

B. OUTGOING CORRESPONDENCE

(n.p. unless indicated)

Alexandrine, duchess of Coburg
n.d., draft, 2 p.

Carl Ludwig of Habsburg, archduke
[1866] April 28 to Nov. 25, drafts, 4 p.

Corio, Marchese
[1867] Feb. 18 to March 6, drafts, 5 p.

Couvay, vicomte de
1866 Nov. 18, draft, 4 p.
1866 Dec. 3, draft, 4 p.
[1867 late June], draft, 4 p.

Crenneville, Gräfin
[1866–67] Dec. 14 and Feb. 3, drafts, 3 p.
[1866–67] Nov. [18?] to June 3, drafts, 4 p.
[1866–67?] July 5, draft, 3 p.

Fischer, Augustin, S.J.
1867 Jan. 14 and 25, drafts, 1 p.

Flandres, Philippe de Belgique, comte de
[1867] Jan. 1 to March 15, drafts, 4 p.
[1867] April 8, draft, 1 p.
[1867] July 7, draft, 2 p.
[1867] April 27 to July 25, drafts, 3 p.

Dr. Fritsch
[1866] Oct. 18 and 25, drafts, 2 p.
[1866] Nov. 27, draft, 2 p.
[1866–67] Dec. 29 to Jan. 15, drafts, 4 p.
[1867] Jan. 26 to May 22, drafts, 2 p.

Maximilian of Austria, emperor of Mexico
- 1864 Oct. 7, Trieste, ALS, 8 p. (env), with an ANS on the recto of the envelope.
- 1864 Dec. 14, Trieste, ALS, 4 p. (env), with a list of books, 4 p.
- 1865 May 30, Vienna, ALS, 10 p. (env), with notes in shorthand on an additional page.
- 1865 July 15, Vienna, ALS, 8 p. (env), with a list of mottoes to be included in the inside decoration at Miramar, 3 p.
- 1865 Nov. 10, Vienna, ALS, 6 p. (env)
- 1866 March 8, Vienna, ALS, 4 p. (env), with a tipped-in ANS by J. Machold on p. 2.
- 1866 July 30, Vienna, ALS, 8 p. (env)
- 1866 Aug. 24, Vienna, ALS, 4 p. (env)
- 1867 Jan. 25, ALS, 3 p., draft

Together with "Concepte von Briefen an S. Majestät den Kaiser Maximilian von Mexico," autograph manuscript, [1866] Oct. 15 to 1867 Jan. 14, 7 p. Accompanied by a small turquoise letter case, with "Meine Briefe an den Kaiser Maximilian nach Mexico" gold-tooled on the front board, with vine decorations in the four corners.

Poliakovich (Austrian embassy councilor in Mexico)
- 1865 Oct. 30, Vienna, ALS, 2 p. (env)

C. PERSONAL PAPERS

"Journal über den Verlauf der Geisteskrankheit Ihrer Majestät der Kaiserin Charlotte von Mexico in Miramar vom 10 October 1866 bis [29] Juli 1867." Autograph diary, 50 p. Signed and dated Vienna, 1 August 1867 at the end.

Accompanied by an affidavit, in French, signed by Jilek, Riedel, Dr. Bulkens, director of the lunatic asylum in Gheel, Belgium, and Dr. Machek, physician to Empress Charlotte at Miramar, dated Miramar, 17 July 1867. Also accompanied by copies of telegrams, annotated by Jilek; a draft of a letter to Dr. Bulkens, Jul 20, n.y., 2 p.; and a floor plan of the "Gartenhaus" at Miramar, n.d., 1 p.

D. ADDITIONAL PAPERS

LS from Leopold I, king of the Belgians, to the President of the Republic of Chile, 29 July 1857, 1 p. Announcing the marriage of his daughter Charlotte to Archduke Maximilian of Austria.

Manuscript, signed, in the hand of Empress Charlotte, 1866, 36 p. A long extract copied from *Murray's handbook for travellers, concerning Rome and St Peter's*, written in black ink on nine nested bifolia of folio-size paper. Signed by the empress and dated 20 October 1866 at the end. Note by Jilek at the top of p. [1].

Manuscript document entitled "Geheime Instruktionen," signed by Radonetz, Castle prefect in Miramar, and Graf Bombelles, chief chamberlain to Maximilian, Xonaca, 20 December 1866, 4 p.

Copies of birth certificates for two children of Jilek, Vienna, 1870.

Death and burial certificate for Jilek, Trieste, 12 November 1898.

Various newspaper clippings relating to Mexico, the Austrian imperial family, and Jilek himself, including an announcement of his death.

August Jilek (1819–98), personal physician to Maximilian and Charlotte. The papers relate mostly to the crisis of 1866 and the subsequent internment of Empress Charlotte. Earlier papers relate to the construction and embellishment of Miramar, the imperial couple's residence on the Adriatic coast near Trieste.

FRKF 1417

FELIX MENDELSSOHN-BARTHOLDY (1809–47)

I. MUSIC MANUSCRIPTS

Concerto for piano, no. 2 in D minor, op. 40

Holograph manuscript of the complete solo part, n.d., 18 p. Notated in black ink on nine leaves of tall 16-staff paper, the last page conjoined with the title page, which is blank on the verso. On the title page, in Mendelssohn's hand: "Concerto." Written mostly on 2-staff systems, except for some orchestral tutti notated on two additional staves below. The lower eight staves on p. [15] are a pasted-on cancel.

Placed in a blue folder (recycled wrappers of *Trois duos concertans pour piano et violon sur des thèmes favoris … par Henri Herz et C.P. Lafont* (Paris: Troupenas, n.d.), marked on the front: "Porzia Gigliucci from/ uncle Alf./ Genoa 1864" and on the inside cover: "Autograph copy of / the second concerto in D [sic] / by Felix Mendelsohn [sic] Bartholdy / presented to me by the author / J. Alfred Novello." Porzia Gigliucci (1845–1938) was the daughter of the singer Clara Novello.

London, Phillips, 15 Nov. 1990, lot 57.
FRKF 1308

Laudate pueri, op. 39

Holograph manuscript of this motet for two soprano and alto soli, women's chorus, and organ, [1830], 8 p. Notated in black ink on the four pages of the two separate bifolia of 15-staff paper. Above the first bar of music on the first page of the first bifolium, in Mendelssohn's hand: "No. 3 [sic] Laudate pueri"; and above the first bar on p. [5]: "No.

2 Terzett" ["Beati omnes qui timent Dominum"]. There are a number of corrections in both parts.

Written in 1830 and revised in 1837–38. First published in *Drei Motetten für weibliche Stimmen mit Orgel Begleitung* (Bonn: N. Simrock, 1830).

London, Sotheby's, 10 May 1984, lot 109.
FRKF 332

Lieder ohne Worte, op. 85, no. 5, "Lied"

Holograph manuscript, 1847, 2 p., notated in black ink on two facing pages, unnumbered, of a music album otherwise blank (ticket of R. Ackermann, Jnr.) comprising 64 leaves, its pages measuring 20.5 × 25.5 cm, bound in maroon sheepskin with embossed frames and hand-tooled gold fleurons on both boards. The pages are of 12-staff paper, the staves surrounded by a blind decorative border.

Signed and inscribed by Mendelssohn at the end: "zum Andenken / an Miss Cavendish / Felix Mendelssohn Bartholdy / London den 6ten Mai / 1847." On the verso of the free front endpaper, ownership inscription: "Caroline F. Cavendish."

London, Sotheby's, 9–10 May 1984, lot 108.
FRKF 331

Oedipus at Colonos, op. 93

Manuscript, in short score, in the hand of a copyist, of the chorus "Zur rossprangenden Flur," from the incidental music to Sophocles' play *Oedipus at Colonos*, n.d., 15 p. Notated in ink, with the English translation in pencil, on four separate bifolia of tall 12-staff paper, paginated [1] to 15.

At the top of p. [1] in Mendelssohn's hand: "Chor aus dem Oedipus zu Kolonos" and the inscription: "Herrn Grote / Zu freundlichem Andenken / Felix Mendelssohn Bartholdy." On p. [16], unidentified manuscript entitled "Styrian air," notated in pencil.

Contemporary marbled wrappers, with the following inscription on the flyleaf: "Chorus in the Oedipus in Colonna / by Felix Mendelssohn Bartholdy (given by him to G.G. in April [1848 cancelled] 1847) / at Eccleston St. 1847."

Laid in: visiting card ("Mr Grote. 12, Savile Row") with the following note on the back: "Mendelssohn's original score of chorus in 'Oedipus' music, with autograph presentation to George Grote, Historian of Greece."

London, Sotheby's, 9–10 May 1985, lot 152.
FRKF 771

Verleih' uns Frieden

Partly holograph manuscript of this chorus with piano accompaniment, n.d., 4 p. Notated in black ink on a single bifolium of 16-staff laid paper. Only the piano part is in Mendelssohn's hand, the words and choral parts are in another, unidentified hand. The title, "Verleih uns Frieden," is written in Mendelssohn's hand at the top of the manuscript. The name of the composer, spelled Mendelssohn-Bartholdi, is written in pencil in a different hand. At the bottom of the first page, in pencil: "Otto v. Blankenburg."

Accompanied by a Maggs Bros. invoice recording the sale of the manuscript on 29 July 1922 to Sigismund Goetze, Esq., for the sum of £13.10; also by an autograph English translation of the words, in an unidentified hand.

According to Grove, which only records a version for chorus and orchestra, the work is dated 10 Feb. 1831 and was dedicated to E.H.W. Verkenius; it was first heard in Leipzig on 30 Oct. 1839. Published in vol. 14/A/2 of *Felix Mendelssohn Bartholdy's Werke: Kritisch durchgesehene Ausgabe*, ed. Julius Rietz (Leipzig: Breitkopf und Härtel, 1874), p. 77.

London, Bloomsbury Book Auctions, 30 Nov. 1983, lot 131.
FRKF 242

"Volkslied" [i.e. Winterlied], op. 19a, no. 3
"Gruss," op. 19a, no. 5
"Abschied"

Holograph manuscript of these three songs for voice and piano, n.d., 3 p. Notated in black ink on p. [1]–[3] of a single bifolium of oblong 14-staff paper. At the top of p. [1] in Mendelssohn's hand: "Volkslied," and, in the top right corner, in a different hand, a note indicating that the songs are in his hand. "Volkslied" occupies four systems on p. [1] and three systems on p. [2]. Above the fourth system, in Mendelssohn's hand: "Gruss," which also occupies the system at the top of p. [3]. The text of the second stanza is written out in Mendelssohn's hand. Underneath, in Mendelssohn's hand: "Abschied"; this song occupies the next three systems, with the text of the second stanza written out in Mendelssohn's hand.

"Gruss" is a setting of a poem by Heine; "Volkslied" is based on a Swedish song. "Abschied" ("Es weh'n die Wolken über Meer") is listed by Grove with no source identified.

London, Sotheby's, 17 May 1990, lot 40.
FRKF 1303

II. OTHER MANUSCRIPTS

Album

Autograph manuscript album illustrating his 1829 tour of Scotland [late 1846 or early 1847], 25 leaves. Oblong album (pages, 23 × 16 cm) containing pencil drawings on the recto sides of the first 25 leaves, with a poem by Karl Klingemann copied in black ink, in Mendelssohn's hand, generally on the same page, or, in three instances ("Ben More," "Oban," and "Loch Lomond 12r August"), on the opposite page. On the recto of the front free endpaper, in Mendelssohn's hand: "Reise-gedichte von Carl Klingemann Esqre / für die Zeichenbücher / von / Felix Mendelssohn Bartholdy Esqre."

The album contains the following drawings, dated as indicated:

1. "Frühstück," 27 June
2. "York," 23 July
3. "Durham," 24 July
4. "Edinburgh zum Erstenmale, Sonntag 26 July. / Salisbury Crags"
5. "Dreigespräch auf dem Dache der Abbei Melrose," 31 July 1829
6. "Edinburgh von Weiham," 1 Aug.
7. "Im Wirthause zu Blair Athal," 2 Aug.
8. "Der Birnamswald, der Birnamswald," n.d.
9. "Dunkeld d. 2r Aug. Herzoglicher Wasserfall"
10. "Ball und Souper / Dunkeld," 2 Aug. (drawing entitled "Ein Regenbogen schien über dem Wasserfall")
11. "Pass von Killiecrankie," 3 Aug. 1829
12. "Bruar Falls, Blair Athol," 3 Aug. 1829
13. "Tummel Bridge," 4 Aug.
14. "Stille im Lärmen. Moness Fall," 4 Aug.
15. "Am Loch Tay auf dem Weg nach Killin," 5 Aug.
16. "Ben More," 5 Aug.
17. "Inveruran," 6 Aug.
18. "Oban" (Robert Bruce's Rock), 7 Aug.
19. "Loch Awe," 9 Aug.
20. "Taynuilt zwischen Oban und Inverary," 9–10 Aug.
21. "Loch Lomond," 12 Aug.
22. "Dumbarton Castle," 12 Aug.
23. "Am Loch Lomond," 13 Aug.
24. "Auf der Euphrosyne, Loch Lomond den 13r August— Ein Lied in Volkston, auf einer Wasserfahrt zu singen"
25. "Trossachs," 13 Aug.

Bound in brown cloth, covered in the modern period with a protective red and blue cloth.

On 31 Jan. 1847, Mendelssohn wrote to his longtime friend Karl Klingemann (1798–1862) that he was sending him this album, in which he had copied both Klingemann's poems and his own drawings from their 1829 tour. See *Felix Mendelssohn-Bartholdys Briefwechsel mit Legationsrat Karl Klingemann in London*, hrsg. und eingeleitet von Karl Klingemann (Essen: G.D. Baedeker, 1909), p. 319.

Heinrich Schütz to Henry Miller, p. 42–43.
London, Christie's, 28 March 1984, lot 136.
FRKF 294

Autograph album-leaf

Album-leaf, signed, with a black pen-and-ink drawing of an Alpine village in Mendelssohn's hand and a musical quotation, in two parts, of a setting of a folk song beginning with the words, also notated in Mendelssohn's hand, "Mein Vater ist ein Appenzeller." On the left of the drawing are two other short musical quotations, the first inscribed "Aufruf des Herrn," the second "Echo des Herrn Preusser."

The caption under the drawing reads: "Auf der Wengern Alp, am Sonntag den 21 August 1842." The one under the song reads: "Plötzliche Antwort des jungen Führers aus Amstag."

Signed "Felix Mendelssohn Bartholdy." Anonymous presentation inscription by Mendelssohn ("zu freundlicher Erinnerung an alle vier") in the lower right corner, dated Leipzig, 29 September 1842.

London, Sotheby's, 17 May 1990, lot 39.
FRKF 1302

III. LETTERS

To E. Buxton

1843 April 30, to E. Buxton of Ewer & Co, Leipzig, ALS, 2 p., in English, concerning his *Festgesang* written for the 1840 Gutenberg festival (and subsequently adapted as the Christmas carol "Hark! the herald angels sing"). Also enclosing a note for Moscheles, which is not present. Note by a former owner pasted on p. [3]. Stamp of Rawlins Collection - Historical Docs. and A.L.S.

Kenneth Rendell Catalogue 169.
FRKF 397

1844 March 28, to E. Buxton at Ewer & Co., Berlin, ALS, 1 p., in English, concerning Mendelssohn's incidental music to *A Midsummer Night's Dream*; includes a 33-measure musical quotation from the Finale.

London, Sotheby's, 28 May 1986, lot 487.
FRKF 1141

To Fanny Mendelssohn Hensel

1840 Nov. 14, Leipzig, ALS, 3 p. Contains two musical quotations. Felix Mendelssohn-Bartholdy, *Briefe 2: Aus den Jahren 1830 bis 1841* (Leipzig: Hermann Mendelssohn, 1863), p. 240–43.

London, Sotheby's, 29 Nov. 1985, lot 162.
FRKF 1081

To Friedrich Kistner

1844 Nov. 15, Berlin, ALS, 1 p. Mentions Chopin.

Carl Friedrich Kistner (1797–1844), music publisher.

Marburg, Stargardt, 26 Nov. 1985, lot 839.
FRKF 1152

To J. Alfred Novello

1846 Feb. 13, Leipzig, ALS, 1 p., in English, concerning *Elijah*, the first performance of which took place in Birmingham Town Hall on 26 Aug. of that year.

London, Sotheby's, 17 Nov. 1983, lot 138.
FRKF 229

To Simrock

1838 Jan. 2, Leipzig, ALS, 2 p.

London, Sotheby's, 29 Nov. 1985, lot 163.
FRKF 1082

To an unidentified friend in London

1832 Sept. 5, Berlin, ALS, 2 p. Contains one musical quotation.
FRKF 386

IV. MISCELLANEOUS

Auf Wiedersehn

An album leaf with a manuscript song entitled "Auf Wiedersehn." The song, with piano accompaniment, is 13 measures long and written in black ink, in Mendelssohn's hand, on two 3-staff systems on the recto of a single, oblong leaf (16 × 13 cm), with embossed decorative border, further embellished with flowers and decorative botanical motifs in watercolor. The manuscript is dated Leipzig, 22 Jan. 1840 at the bottom, with the dedication: "An Fräulein Elise Meerti zum Andenken von Cécile und Felix M.B."

Bound in half dark blue morocco and blue and red marbled paper. On the spine: "Mendelssohn - Auf Wiederschhr [sic]." Bookplate of Dr. Lucien-Graux. Accompanied by two locks of hair of Cécile and Felix Mendelssohn, wrapped individually in leaves of laid paper and placed in a small mourning envelope, pasted on a sheet of brown paper, on which is also pasted a small sheet of paper, folded, containing a leaf identified as coming from Mendelssohn's grave.

Marburg, Stargardt, 5–6 March 1985, lot 845.
FRKF 819

GIAN CARLO MENOTTI (1911–)

"Dorme Pegaso"

Holograph manuscript of this song for voice and piano [ca. 1967], 1 p. Notated in black ink on the recto of a single sheet of tall 16-staff paper. At the top of the page, in Menotti's hand: "Per Marc Pincherle con simpatia e amicizia / Gian Carlo Menotti / Dorme Pegaso (dai Canti della lontananza) / Parigi 1968." Dated 13 Feb., n.y., at the bottom of the page.

Menotti's *Canti della lontananza*, a cycle of seven songs on texts by the composer, was published by Schirmer in New York in 1967.

Boston, Daniel Kelleher, 22 July 1982, lot 153.
FRKF 11

WILLIAM MEREDITH (1919–)

Papers relating to James Merrill

I. LETTERS FROM JAMES MERRILL TO WILLIAM MEREDITH

[1947 Sept. 9, New York*] APCS
[1947 Sept. 24] "Wednesday night," New York, ALS, 3 p.
[1947 Oct. 7] "Tuesday," n.p., ALS, 2 p.
[1947 Oct. 16] "Tuesday," n.p., ALS, 2 p.
[1947 Oct. 19] "Sunday night," New Canaan, ALS, 2 p.
1947 Nov. 1, n.p., James Ingram Merrill$, ALS, 2 p.
1948 Jan. 6, n.p., ALS, 1 p., with a typescript poem: "Variations: the air is sweetest that a thistle guards," 4 p. (*Collected Poems*, p. 19–22)
[1948 Feb. 11, Palm Beach*] APCS
1948 June 26, Georgetown, ALS, 1 p.

1948 July 8, n.p., ALS, 2 p.

[1948] July 15, n.p., ALS, 2 p.

[1948] July 30, n.p., ALS, 2 p.

1948 Aug. 7, n.p., ALS, 2 p.

[1948?] Sept. 11, Bard College, Annandale-on-Hudson[S], ALS, 1 p.

[1948] Sept. 27, "Monday," Bard College[S], ALS, 2 p.

1948 Nov. 2, Bard College[S], ALS, 1 p.

1948 Dec. 13, Bard College[S], ALS, 1 p.

1948 Dec. 14, Bard College[S], ALS, 1 p.

1949 Jan. 27, n.p., ALS, 2 p.

1949 April 14, Merrill's Landing, Palm Beach[S], ALS, 2 p.

1949 April 14, Merrill's Landing, Palm Beach[S], ALS, 2 p., a second letter sent the same day.

1949 July 7, n.p., JIM[S], ALS, 2 p.

[1949 July 14, New York*] APCS

1949 July 25, n.p., JIM[S], ALS, 2 p.

1949 July 29 [New York*] APCS

1949 Oct. 27, n.p., JIM[S], ALS, 2 p.

1950 March 19, n.p., ALS, 1 p.

1950 April 4, French Line[S], ALS, 2 p., on board the *De Grasse* (filled in in Merrill's hand).

[1950 May 21, Naples*] APCS

1950 June 4, Rome, JIM[S], TLS, 1 p.

1950 June 26, Cassis, JIM[S], ALS, 2 p.

1950 Aug. 3, Salzburg, TLS, 1 p., on verso: "The charioteer of Delphi," typescript (*Collected Poems*, p. 74–75)

1950 Sept. 11, Florence, TLS, 2 p. At the end of the letter, typescript poem: "How unforgettably the fire that night …" ("Fire Poems," *Collected Poems*, p. 59)

1950 Sept. 28, Paris, TLS, 2 p.

[1950?] Nov. 1, Palma de Mallorca, TLS, 1 p., on the verso, typescript poem: "Olive Grove." (*Collected Poems*, p. 60)

1951, "The twelfth day of Christmas," Palma de Mallorca, TLS, 2 p.

1951 Feb. 16, n.p., ALS, 3 p.; on p. 2, autograph sonnet: "Orfeo." (*Collected Poems*, p. 97)

[1951?] March 14, n.p., TLS, 1 p., on the verso, typescript poems: "The octopus"; "Thistledown." (*Collected Poems*, p. 61)

1951 July 7, n.p., TLS, 1 p. At the top of the letter, typescript poem: "Who guessed amiss the riddle of the Sphinx." (*Collected Poems*, p. 76)

1951 Aug. 30, Rome, TLS, 2 p.

1951 Nov. 18, n.p., ALS, 2 p.

1951 Dec. 16, Ritz, Paris[S], ALS, 2 p.

1952 Feb. 1, n.p., TLS, 2 p.

1952 Feb. 8 [Rome*] ALS, 1 p.

[1952] "Good Friday," Graz, ALS, 3 p.

[1952?] May 8 [Athens*] APCS

1952 July 16, Rome, TLS, 1 p.

1952 Nov. 12, Rome, ALS, 1 p.

[1952, Turkey*] APCS

1953 March 4, New York, TLS, 1 p.

1953 July 7, The Orchard, Southampton, Long Island[S], ALS, 2 p.

1954 April 12, David Noyes Jackson[S], TLS, 1 p.

1954 Aug. 25, n.p., TLS, 1 p.

1954 Nov. 4 [Rome] TLS, 1 p.

[1955 Nov. 16*] Amherst, APCS

[1956 Jan. 26, Amherst*] APCS

1956 March 5, Amherst, Amherst College[S], TLS, 1 p.

[1956] Nov. 26 [Hong Kong*] APCS

[1956? Ceylon*] APCS

n.p., n.d., TLS, 1 p. Postmarked Bevoglu, Turkey, 22 Jan. 1957 according to a note by Meredith

[1957 April, London] TLS, 1 p.

[1957] May 4, de France & Choiseul[S], ALS, 2 p.

1957 May 12, de France & Choiseul[S], ALS, 2 p.

[1957] June 5, Stonington, ALS, 2 p.

[1957] June 30, Ponte Vedra Beach, Florida, ALS, 2 p.

[1957] n.p., ALS, 1 p.

1958 Feb. 3, Santa Fe, ALS, 1 p.

[1958] March 6, n.p., ALS, 1 p.

[1958 May 26] 107 Water Street, Stonington[S], ALS, 2 p.

[1958 July 22, Stonington*] APCS

[1958*] Oct. 28 [Japan*] APCS

1958, "Xmas," n.p., ANS on a card

1959 Jan. 31, Pension Biederstein, Munich[S], ALS, 2 p. (env)

1959 Aug. 1, n.p., TLS, 1 p.

[1959 Oct. 11] "8:40 a.m.," n.p., ALS, 1 p.

[1960 Aug. 10, Stonington*] APCS

[1960 Aug. 20*] Munich, APCS

1961 July 15, n.p., ALS, 1 p.

[1964 April 14] "Tuesday," n.p., APCS

1965 March 9, n.p., TLS, 1 p., with autograph postscript

[1967*] April 23 [Madison*] APCS

1967 Nov. 14, n.p., ANS, 2 p.

[1968 May 9, Jamaica*] APCS

1969 Jan. 27, n.p., ALS, 1 p.

1969 March 15, ANS on one side of a card of Villa Serbelloni, Bellagio

1969 May 13, Stonington, ALS, 2 p.

1969 Oct. 27, n.p., James Merrill[S], ALS, 1 p. (env)

1973 Jan. 18, n.p., ALS, 2 p.

1973 June 5, n.p., ANS, 1 p., attached to "The great American poem," typescript, photocopy, 1 p.

1974 Jan. 25, 107 Water Street, Stonington[S], ALS, 2 p. (env)

[1974?] Dec. 1 [New York*] APCS

1975 Jan. 22, Athens, TLS, 1 p.

1975 April 4 [Athens*] TLS, 1 p.

1975 Dec. 13, ANS on one side of a card printed 107 Water Street, Stonington (env), enclosing an invitation to a reception for Merrill at the Lyman Allyn Museum, Connecticut College.

1979 Jan. 6, ANS on one side of a card printed 107 Water Street, Stonington (env)

1979 Sept. 23 [Greece*] APCS

1981 April 21, ALS on both sides of a card printed 107 Water Street, Stonington (env)

Undated and without year

ALS, May 2, n.p., 2 p.

ALS, "Sat. 16 April," n.p., 1 p.

APCS [Arizona? postmark illegible]

ALS, July 22, n.p., 1 p.

TLS, May 15, n.p., 1 p.

ALS, Oct. 21, Voices, Vinalhaven, Maine[S], 2 p.

ANS, "Sunday," n.p.

APCS [Oct. 23*, year not legible, Greece*] with a postscript from David Jackson

ANS, "Monday, a.m.," n.p., on the reverse of an envelope

APCS [year not deciphered, Iran*]

ALS, April 23, Poros, JIM[S], 1 p.

TLS, May 8, n.p. [Italy] 1 p.

TLS, June 9 [Rome] JIM[S], 1 p.

TLS, July 15, n.p. JIM[S], 1 p.

TLS, "Friday," n.p., 2 p.

ALS, "Wed. 8th," The Orchard, Southampton, Long Island[S], 2 p.

TLS, Sept. 13, Rome, 1 p.

TLS, Oct. 11, n.p., 1 p.

TLS, Jan. 17, Canefield House, St. Thomas, Barbados[S], 2 p.

TLS, June 23, n.p., 1 p.

ALS, Nov. 2, Gritti Palace-Hotel, Venice[S], 2 p.

ALS, Aug. 12, n.p., on both sides of a card printed JIM

TLS, Sept. 16, American President Lines[S], 1 p.

ALS, Jan. 15, New York, 1 p.

ALS, "Monday evening," n.p., James Ingram Merrill[S], 2 p.

ALS, "Sunday 1:30 A.M.," Merrill's Landing, Palm Beach[S], 1 p.

TL (incomplete?), n.d., n.p.

2 envelopes, [1968 June 24, Stonington*] and [Greece*], date undeciphered

Also, ALS to Dear Robert, n.y., Feb. 1, n.p., 1 p.

Also, TLS from Meredith to Merrill, 1975 Feb. 12, n.p., 1 p., photocopy

II. LETTERS FROM OTHERS

Julian P. Boyd

1948 Oct. 29, The Library, Princeton University[S], TLS, 1 p.

1948 Nov. 4, The Library, Princeton University[S], TLS, 1 p., with an autograph postscript.

n.y. Dec. 8, One Twenty Broadmead, Princeton[S], ALS, 1 p.

Francis Brown

1958 Dec. 4, *The New York Times Book Review*[S], TLS, 1 p.

Charles E. Merrill

1950 Sept. 7, The Orchard, Southampton, Long Island[S], TLS, 2 p.

1950 Nov. 6, from his secretary, Seventy Pine Street, New York[S], TLS, 1 p.

Hellen Merrill Plummer

n.y. March 29, n.p., ALS, 2 p.

n.y. Feb. 2, n.p., ALS, 2 p.

Also, printed announcement of the marriage of Hellen Ingram Merrill to William Leroy Plummer, 1950.

"Pete"

1948 Nov. 29, Schools of English, University of Virginia, Charlottesville[S], TLS, 1 p.

"Tony"

1948

June 6, London, TLS, 2 p.

[June 28, London] TLS, 2 p.

July 20, Paris, TLS, 2 p.

Aug. 17, Paris, TLS, 2 p.

Sept. 7, Paris, TLS, 4 p.

Sept. 24, Excelsior, Naples[S], TLS, 5 p.

Oct. 1, Florence, TLS, 8 p.

Oct. 23, Florence, TLS, 4 p.

Nov. 6, Florence, TLS, 6 p.

Nov. 29, Florence, TLS, 3 p.

III. MANUSCRIPTS OF POEMS BY JAMES MERRILL

"Poem in spring" ("Being born of earth, we've come to sit …"). Typescript, 1 p., on the verso, autograph note to Meredith [Nov. 1948]. *Collected poems*, p. 15.

"Figures in a legendary glade." Typescript, 1 p. *Collected poems*, p. 31–32.

"First poems / James Merrill." Carbon typescript, 30 p. See *Collected poems*, p. 3–50.

"For Proust." Typescript, 1 p., inscribed at the bottom: "Bill from Jim / and again thank you / for yesterday / 17 Nov 58." *Collected poems*, p. 139–40.

"The grape cure." Typescript, 1 p. *Collected poems*, p. 29–30.

"The greenhouse." Typescript, 1 p., inscribed at the bottom: "J.M. / to / W.M.," with the note: "This is the only poem of the past 14 months. You may have seen it already, too, in the Oct. Poetry. Alas." *Collected poems*, p. 63.

"H.P." Typescript, photocopy, 1 p. Published as "Hubbell Pierce (1925–1980)." See *Collected poems*, p. 828.

"Hour-Glass." Holograph, 1 p., dated 12 June 1949 at the bottom. *Collected poems*, p. 16.

"The house." Holograph, 1 p., inscribed at the end: "W.M. from J.M. / 14 March 1949." *Collected poems*, p. 50.

"Lines composed at sunset." Typescript, 1 p. No poem with that title in *Collected poems*.

"Of the lives lost." Typescript, 1 p. No poem with that title in *Collected poems*.

"Periwinkles." Typescript, 1 p. *Collected poems*, p. 48.

"Q: Always no longer where a moment ago it buzzed …" Holograph, 1 p., inscribed at the bottom: "Dec 1948 / J.I.M." No poem with that title or incipit in *Collected poems*.

"The reconnaissance." Typescript, 1 p., inscribed at the bottom: "WMM / from JIM." *Collected poems*, p. 156.

"Roger Clay's proposal." Typescript, 1 p., signed J.I.M. at the bottom and dated 6 Feb. 1962. *Collected poems*, p. 155.

"Tintype before sailing." Typescript, carbon, 1 p. Note by Meredith at the top: "with letter of 7 July 49." No poem with that title in *Collected poems*.

"Willow." Holograph, 1 p., inscribed at the end: "W.M. from J.M. / 25 March 1949." *Collected poems*, p. 49.

"Wreaths for the Warm-Eyed." Holograph, 2 p. *Collected poems*, p. 18.

Also:

"Hark, all you ladies that do sleep!" Manuscript copy in Merrill's hand, 2 p. Note at the end: "Words & music by Thomas Campion."

Miscellaneous notes on poems, possibly in Merrill's hand, 2 p., and three stanzas from Apollinaire's "La chanson du mal aimé," possibly copied in Merrill's hand, 1 p.

IV. PHOTOGRAPHS

Rollie McKenna. Black-and-white photographs of Merrill
 Wearing glasses, [early 1950s] (17.5 × 12 cm)
 In profile, ca. 1970 (11.5 × 15.5 cm)
 Holding a cat, ca. 1970 (20.5 × 25 cm)
 Sitting on a sofa, ca. 1970 (25 × 20.5 cm)
 Reading, ca. 1970 (20.5 × 25 cm)
 Holding a cigarette, ca. 1970 (20.5 × 25 cm)
 Sitting, with his elbow on a chair, ca. 1970 (25 × 20.5 cm)
 With his hands on his cheeks, a Japanese print in the background, ca. 1970 (20.5 × 25 cm)

Three amateur black-and-white photographs (6 × 9 cm)
 Romanesque statue-column
 Glass on a windowsill in Florence
 Rooftops in France or Italy

V. MISCELLANEOUS

Drawing
 "An Arriere-Pensée (Right) confronted by An Esprit de l'Escalier / drawn by j. merrill at Annandale-on-Hudson May 1949." Pen-and-ink drawing on p. [4] of a Nov. 1948 Bard College poetry conference program.

Leaves from a Kabuki program, with a few annotations by Merrill.

Typed list of addresses for James I. Merrill and David Jackson, Sept. 1956 to March 1957, 1 p.

MEREDITH / MERRILL PAPERS
FRKF 676

PROSPER MÉRIMÉE (1803–70)

Drawings

Three pen-and-ink drawings on a folio-size sheet of paper, numbered 1 to 3 from bottom to top, and captioned respectively, in fanciful spelling:

> 1. "Reie monstrueuse péchet à Dieppe / le 1er Avril 1849, voillié le / moniteur du deuze du maisne moit."
> 2. "Le grend serrepant de Mere."
> 3. "poison volen della Calyphornie."

Autograph note at the top: "au Ministère des Cultes, par Mr Mérimée de l'Académie / française, le mercredi 2 Mai 1849. / Gal de Guillermy [?]"

Paris, Boisgirard (Drouot), 22 May 1985, lot 67.
FRKF 645

Letter to "Monsieur le Duc"

> 1853 June 26, Paris, ALS, 1 p., asking for an interview with Napoleon III to thank him for favor.

Marburg, Stargardt, 5–6 March 1985, lot 279.
FRKF 802

ANDRÉ MESSAGER (1853–1929)

Letter to Victor Wilder

> [1891 Sept. (15?), Paris*] ALS, 1 p. Printed: "Télégramme" on the address side. Concerning the receipt of tickets for a concert or opera performance.

FRKF 535d

GIACOMO MEYERBEER (1791–1864)

Letter to Léonie Halévy

> 1849 April 9, Paris, LS, 2 p., inviting her to the premiere of *Le prophète*. In a secretarial hand. Not in *Briefwechsel und Tagebücher*, vol. 4.

Paris, Oger-Dumont (Drouot), 14 Feb. 1985, lot 55.
FRKF 696.5

Letters to Ernest Reyer

> 1863 May 17, Berlin, ALS, 1 p., concerning the Grand Prix de composition musicale given by the Institut de France.
>
> n.d., n.p., ALS, an invitation to dine with Berlioz and others.

Paris, Oger-Dumont (Drouot), 14 Feb. 1985, lot 55.
FRKF 696

Other letters

Letter to an unnamed director of the Paris Opéra
> n.d., ALS, 1 p., agreeing to participate in a benefit raffle.

Paris, Oger-Dumont (Drouot), 14 Feb. 1985, lot 55.
FRKF 696.7

Letter to an unidentified correspondent
> 1832 April 10, n.p., ALS, 2 p., in French. Mentions *Robert le diable* in Liège and a projected new work on a text by Scribe and Alexandre Dumas. The recipient evidently lived in Brussels. Not in *Briefwechsel und Tagebücher*, vol. 2.

Paris, Oger-Dumont (Drouot), 14 Feb. 1985, lot 19.
FRKF 683

DARIUS MILHAUD (1892–1974)

Letters to Eric Bentley

> 1960 Jan. 5, 10 Boulevard de Clichy, Paris XVIII^S, ALS, 2 p.
>
> 1962 Jan. 28, n.p., ALS, 1 p.

Undated or without year
> TLS, Sept. 11, n.p., 2 p.
>
> ALS, Sept. 18, Florence, 1 p.
>
> ALS, "Tuesday," n.p., 2 p.
>
> ALS, "Tuesday," Florence, 1 p.
>
> TLS, Nov. 23, 10 Boulevard de Clichy, Paris XVIII^S, 1 p.
>
> TLS, Oct. 27, 10 Boulevard de Clichy, Paris XVIII^S, 1 p.

In English, mostly concerning Milhaud's "Songs of Courage." Accompanied by a music manuscript fragment in Milhaud's hand, with the heading "Song of Mother Courage," initialed by Milhaud at the end, and comprising 14 measures notated in black ink on a single staff.

FRKF 576a

Mother courage, op. 379

Ozalid and photocopies (unless otherwise noted), annotated by Milhaud and Eric Bentley, of Milhaud's manuscript, in short score, of his music for the play by Bertold Brecht, two sets with differing annotations, each paginated 1–34, 1959.

The two sets include the following sections:

1. "Song of Mother Courage (Sc.1)"
2. "Song of Mother Courage (Scene 7)"
3. "Song of Mother Courage (after scene 8)"
4. "Song of Mother Courage (male chorus) (end scene 12)"
5. Song of the Soldier
6. "Yvette's song from Mother Courage = Fraternization"
7. Song of the Great Capitulation
8. "Army Chaplain's Song"
9. Soldier's Song
10. "Song of the Great Souls of this Earth"
11. "Lullaby"
12. "Corrections in the Song of the Army Chaplain," holograph manuscript, 1 p., with an ANS from Milhaud to Bentley on the lower half of the sheet
13. "Interlude I (before scene 2)," dated "Florence, 5 Sep 1959"
14. "Interlude II (before scene 3)"
15. "Interlude III (before scene 4)"
16. "Interlude IV (before scene 5)"
17. "Interlude V (beginning with scene 6)"
18. "Interlude VI"
19. "Interlude VII"
20. "Interlude VIII (before scene 9)"
21. "Interlude IX (before scene 11)."

At the top of the first page of the first set, note in Milhaud's hand: "All the songs of Mother Courage will be sung an octave lower by Miss Prassinou / Milhaud," with an additional note in Bentley's hand: "corrected by EB / Sept 25 / 59."

FRKF 576b

HENRY MILLER (1891–1980)

Tropic of cancer

Typescript, with autograph additions and corrections. The manuscript is bound in four volumes, in grey linen, with brown leather labels on the spine with author and title gold-tooled. It collates as follows:

Volume 1

Two manuscript title pages. The first, on stationery of Henry Miller 18 Villa Seurat Paris XIVe, reads: "Tropic of Cancer / Vol. I / First draft / Original Version"; the second is on a plain sheet of paper, stamped "W.A. Bradley / 5, rue St-Louis-en-l'île / Paris-IVe" and reads: "Property of / Henry V. Miller / 4, Ave. Anatole France / Clichy (Seine) - France / 'Tropic of [cancelled: Capricorn] Cancer' / by / Anonymous / I."

Paginated 1–15, 15–35, [36 cancelled as:] 40, 41–47, 46–51, 13–14, 17–22; 25; 27, 29–34, 41–42, 42a–h, 43; 43–44; 1–13, 29–37, 14–15, 20–25; [1], 2–4 (these last four pages on verso of stationery of Vanves-Cinéma, Paris), 14–28, 4–5 (5 a cancel pasted on the verso of a sheet of Vanves-Cinéma stationery), 7, [unpaginated, headed "Nanavati"], 5, 15–22, 20–25; 26–45, 26–45, 36–68, 70–80 (with another draft on the verso of p. 48–79), 80–88; 50, 51–53, 58–61, 63, 65–71, 74–86.

Volume 2

52–65, 67–68, 66, 66 [another draft on the verso], 67, 67 [another draft on the verso], 68, 68 [another draft on the verso], 70–71, 73–79 [another draft on the verso of p. 70 through 79], 76–87, 83–88, 91–97, 91, 91, 92–93, 93, 94, 94, 94, 95–97; 98–111, 112–120, 107–112; 112–114, [six unpaginated folios], 113–118, 118a, 121, 123, 125–126, 126–129, [1 (headed: Part 2. The Last Book)], 2–13, [13 unpaginated folios, consisting of pasted-on typescript fragments]; 1–7 (also pasted-on typescript fragments), [25 more unpaginated folios consisting of pasted-on typescript fragments); [manuscript title page on stationery of Henry Miller 18 Villa Seurat Paris XIVe: "Tropic of Cancer / First Draft / Original Version / Vol. II."]; [second title page on a plain sheet of paper, stamped "W.A. Bradley / 5, rue St-Louis-en-l'île / Paris-IVe": "Property of / Henry V. Miller / 4, Ave. Anatole France / Clichy (Seine) - France / 'Tropic of Cancer' / by / Anonymous / II"]; 46–51; 80–82, 2–7, 16–19, 6–8, [1], 2, 254–260, [1], 2–9 (manuscript draft on verso of 7 and 8); [1]–2: [1]–2–3, 5, 9 (the last five pages on verso of stationery of American University Union in Europe, Paris); 1–8; [1], 2–8, [unpaginated, manuscript heading: "Crazy Cock"], 9–11; [1], 2–7, 69–75; 84–87, 87–90; 70–74. Before the section headed "Crazy Cock" are several versions of the "Bezegue, Inc." section.

Volume 3

214–225, 225–235, 223–244; 1–6, [unpaginated], 2–5, [unpaginated folio marked in red pencil: "Tropic / original / pages"]; [manuscript title page on stationery of Henry Miller 18 Villa Seurat Paris XIVe: "Tropic of Cancer / First Draft / Original Version / Vol. III."]; [second title page on a plain sheet of paper: "Tropic of Cancer / Excised pages"]; 1–22, 2–22, 215–224; [1, headed: Volume 2. (The Last Book)], 2–7; [1, headed: Entr'acte], 2–7, 262–272, 215–219, 226–234, 236–240, 242–243, 245–254, 257–262, 253–274; 107–111; 112–114, 280–283, 283a, 284–290, 294, 301–302, 305–327; [unpaginated folio marked, in red pencil: "Tropic / Original pages"].

Volume 4

88–106, 136–144, 149–150, 48–50 (another draft, typed with blue and black ribbon, on verso of these last three pages),

87–89, 196, 206, 104a, 233, [1, headed: Henri Matisse], 2–4 [unpaginated], 7–8; [1], 2–4 (these last five pages on verso of Vanves-Cinéma stationery), 124–125, 127–133, 141, 125–139, 59–70; [1, cancelled heading: The Thchekowa Woman], 2–5 (these last five pages on verso of Vanves-Cinéma stationery), 76–83, 88–106; [1, headed: Wednesday; Paris], 2–3, [4]; [1, headed: Wednesday Morning, Paris], 2–9 (these last nine pages on stationery of American University Union in Europe, Paris); [1, headed: Letter to Rona], 2–5; [1, headed: Letter from Marcienne], 2–3, 52–57; 58–65; 273–279, 279a; 68–73; 157–167, 167a, 142–145, 145–147, 147–157, 159, 164–170, 163, 165, 168–173, 173a, 175, 178–179, 181–182, 174; 175–179; 180–189, 193–195, 197a, 197–214.

The typescript comprises both ribbon and carbon copies, on various types and various sizes of paper, including bright yellow and pink paper. Many pages are entirely or partly cancelled.

Heinrich Schütz to Henry Miller, p. 130–31.
New York, Sotheby's, 14 Feb. 1986, lot 429.
FRKF 986

Letters to Karl G. Karsten

[1934 Nov. 26*] Paris, TLS with autograph postscript, 4 p. (env)

[1935 Sept. 12*] Paris, TLS with autograph postscript, 1 p. (env)

Concerning *Tropic of cancer*.

FRKF 1281

A.A. (ALAN ALEXANDER) MILNE (1882–1956)

I. MANUSCRIPTS

When we were very young

Autograph manuscript, n.d., 58 p., in pencil or black ink of various types on the recto sides of sheets of different kinds of paper, foliated in pencil in an unidentified hand.

Accompanied by a "Note for the Owner of the MS - in case it is of any interest." Autograph note, 1925, 2 p., in black ink on the recto sides of two quarto-size sheets of laid paper. Signed and dated 2 April 1925 at the end.

Also with an ALS from Milne to "My dear E.V.," on stationery of 13, Mallord Street, Chelsea, S.W.3. [London], 3 April 1925, 1 p., concerning the manuscript of *When we were very young*.

Also accompanied by *When we were very young*, typescript, with autograph corrections in the hand of Milne, n.d., 59 p. Typed on the recto sides of quarto-size pages of laid paper, foliated 1 to 54 by the author, with four additional pages foliated 3, 4, 11, and 14. Preceded by a page inscribed in Milne's hand: "Messrs Methuen & Co Lt / 36 Essex St. / W.C.2 / from A:A:Milne."

"Just before We Begin"

Holograph manuscript of the preface to *When we were very young*, n.d. [ca. 1924], 2 p., in black ink, with additional pencil markings. Preceded by a manuscript title page for the book, 1 p. and followed by a manuscript table of contents, 2 p.

Accompanied by an ALS from Milne to Owen D. Winters of New York City, on stationery of 13, Mallord Street, Chelsea, S.W.3., 21 Dec. 1925, 1 p. (with envelope); and an ALS from Milne to Carl H. Pforzheimer, on stationery of Cotchford Farm, Hartfield, Sussex, 30 Aug. 1945, 1 p., (with envelope), together with a carbon copy of a TLS from Pforzheimer to Milne, New York, 16 July 1945, 2 p., all concerning the above manuscript.

Heinrich Schütz to Henry Miller, p. 126–27.

Another copy, in black ink on the recto sides of two pages of quarto-size wove paper. Preceded by an autograph title page, marked "Methuen" in pencil, in a different hand, and followed by an autograph table of contents, 2 p.

II. PRINTED MATERIAL

Milne, A.A., *When we were very young*. Serialized in *Punch Magazine*, volume CLXVI, Jan.–June 1924:

No. 4305, (9 Jan.): I. Brownie; II. In the Fashion; III. Before Tea.

No. 4306, (16 Jan.): IV. Puppy and I.

No. 4307, (23 Jan.): V. Disobedience.

No. 4308, (30 Jan.): VI. The King's Breakfast.

No. 4309, (6 Feb.): VII. Rice Pudding; VIII. The Alchemist.

No. 4310, (13 Feb.): IX. Teddy Bear.

No. 4311, (20 Feb.): X. Buckingham Palace; XI. At the Zoo.

No. 4312, (27 Feb.): XII. Nursery Chairs.

No. 4313, (5 March): XIII. If I were a King; XIV. Half-way Down.

No. 4314, (12 March): XV. Lines and Squares.

No. 4315, (19 March): XVI. Spring Morning; XVII. Growing Up.

No. 4316, (26 March): XVIII. Market Square.

No. 4317, (2 April): XIX. Sand-between-the-Toes; XX. Independence.

No. 4318, (9 April): Auto-suggestion. Not identified as part of series.

No. 4319, (16 April): XXXI [sic, for XXI]. Little Bo-Beep and Little Boy Blue.

No. 4320, (23 April). No poem in this issue.

No. 4321, (30 April): XXII. The Three Foxes.

No. 4322, (7 May). No poem in this issue.

No. 4323, (14 May). No poem in this issue.

No. 4324, (21 May): XXIII. Jonathan Jo.

No. 4325, (28 May). No poem in this issue.

No. 4326, (4 June): XXIV. Missing.

No. 4327, (11 June). No poem in this issue.

No. 4328, (18 June): XXV. Happiness.

—. *When we were very young… With decorations by Ernest H. Shepard.* London: Methuen & Co. Ltd., 1924.

8vo., [i]–x, [1 l.], 1–99 [+ 1] p. Bound in blue cloth, gold fillet along the edges of front board. On front board, three gold-tooled figures; on back board, one figure gold-tooled (Christopher Robbin peeping through curtains). Author, title, and publisher gold-tooled on spine. In lettered and illustrated dust jacket.

—. *When we were very young.* New York: E.P. Dutton & Co. 1924.

8vo., [i]–xii, [1 l.], 1–100 [+ 2] p. "This Special Edition of *When We Were Very Young* is limited to five hundred copies." Pictorial cover with dark green cloth spine; dark green top edge; pictorial dust jacket.

Six drawings … illustrating poems from When we were very young by A.A. Milne. London: Methuen & Co. Ltd, n.d.

Six prints in a large portfolio, each identified as no. 49 from an edition of 250. Title and captions on printed labels pasted on the inside of the portfolio.

Proofs of six pages with Milne's poems and the illustrations by E.H. Shepard, printed on India paper, each marked "proof" at the bottom and signed by Milne and Shepard. The poems are the following: "Lines and Squares"; "Happiness"; "Vespers"; "Hoppity"; "Teddy Bear"; and "The King's Breakfast."
FRKF 408

Fraser-Simson, Harold. *Fourteen songs from "When we were very young." Words by A.A. Milne. Music by H. Fraser-Simson. Decorations by E.H. Shepard.* London: Methuen & Co., Ltd., 1924.

Folio, [1 l.], [1]–34. Music publisher's number: M. & C°. 101. In original dark grey boards with printed label and brown cloth spine.

—. *Fourteen songs from "When we were very young." Words by A.A. Milne. Music by H. Fraser-Simson. Decorations by E.H. Shepard.* New York: E.P. Dutton & Company, 1925.

Folio, [1 l.], [1]–34. In original pale blue boards with printed label and dark red cloth spine, with green printed dust jacket.

—. *The King's Breakfast. Words by A.A. Milne. Music by H. Fraser-Simson. Decorations by E.H. Shepard.* London: Methuen & Co., Ltd. [and] Ascherberg, Hopwood & Crew, Ltd., 1925.

25 × 17.5 cm, [I]–VI, [1]–17 [+ 1] p. Music publisher's number: M. & C°. 103. Pink and white pictorial boards with dark blue cloth spine, pictorial pink and white dust jacket.

—. *More "Very Young" songs. From "When we were very young" and "Now we are six." Words by A.A. Milne. Music by H. Fraser-Simson. Decorations by E.H. Shepard.* London: Methuen & Co. Ltd., 1928.

Folio, [3 l.], 1–40 [+ 2] p. Music publisher's number: M. & Co. 108. No. 39 from an edition of 100 signed and numbered copies, signed by Milne, Fraser-Simson, and Shepard. In original grey boards with printed label and dark blue cloth spine.

The Very Young Calendar 1930. Verses by A.A. Milne. Decorations by E.H. Shepard. New York: E.P. Dutton & Co., Inc. [1930].

Twelve sheets of thick paper and a cover (20 × 25.5 cm) tied together at the top with a blue cord. At the bottom of the title page: "Lettered by A.E. Taylor."

The King's breakfast and other selections from A.A. Milne. Illustrations by Ernest H. Shepard. New York: E.P. Dutton & Co., Inc., 1947.

13 unpaginated leaves, 23.5 × 19 cm. In pictorial boards and pictorial dusk jacket.

When We Were Very Young note paper. A.A. Milne / E.H. Shepard. New York: E.P. Dutton & Company, n.d.

Stationery and envelopes, together with a reply card, in a pictorial box.

Miscellaneous clippings, photostats, and transcripts.

See also under Shepard, Ernest H.

A.A. MILNE MATERIALS unless otherwise noted London, Sotheby's, 10 July 1986, lot 199.
FRKF 1298

ROBERT DE MONTESQUIOU-FÉZENSAC (1855–1921)

"Valse lente"

Autograph manuscript of this poem, n.d., 1 p., in purple ink on pink paper with bubble-like spots.

Paris, Couturier-Nicolaÿ (Drouot), 7 March 1985, lot 44.
FRKF 642

Les chauves-souris: clairs-obscurs. Paris: Georges Richard, 1892.

[10], [1–8], 9–262, [627–32] [+6] p. No. 10 of 100 copies. On title page: "Deuxième ouvrage carminal." Presentation inscription to Henriette, marquise d'Eyragues, 1892 April 29, on a preliminary page. Bookplate, with "Mademoiselle Henriette de Montesquiou" written in Montesquiou's hand.

Full green morocco binding, signed Marius Michel. Top edge gilt with incised bat decoration. Raised bands, with author and title gold-tooled on spine. Gold fillets on inside front and back boards. Double gold fillets on board edges and endcaps. Green silk endpapers. Bat decorations on front board, inside front and back boards, and endpapers. Gold tooled on front board: "Qu'est-ce chauve-souris? – Mystère de mystère …"

FRKF 647

Sabliers et lacrymatoires: élégies guerrières et humaines. Paris: Bibliothèque internationale d'édition, Edward Sansot, Editeur, 1917.

[I]–VI, [1]–317 [+ 3] p. + frontispiece page. No. 1 of 15 copies on Japon impérial, untrimmed. The dedication copy, with a presentation inscription on the first page, blank: "A / Monsieur Anatole France. / Cher et Illustre Maître, / quelqu'un me dit que vous avez exprimé / le désir de voir paraître une continuation des 'Offrandes', / Vos désirs sont des ordres / Elle paraît sous un vocable qui lui crée des devoirs, / dont j'espère qu'elle ne se montrera pas tout à fait / indigne. / Votre respectueusement affectionné. / Robert de Montesquiou. / 917"

The printed dedication to Anatole France is on p. [V]–VI. In the original paper wrappers.

Paris, Couturier-Nicolaÿ (Drouot), 7 March 1985, lot 254.
FRKF 652

Letter to Reynaldo Hahn

1907 Nov. 18, Neuilly, ALS, 2 p., inviting him to a reception in honor of Grand Duchess Marie.

Paris, Couturier-Nicolaÿ (Drouot), 2 Dec. 1987, lot 152.
FRKF 1295

MARIA MANUELA KIRKPATRICK, CONDESA DE MONTIJO (d. 1879)

Letter to Stendhal

[1840] June 27, n.p., ALS, 7 p. The year is added in Stendhal's hand. Stendhal, *Correspondance générale*, VI:364.

Accompanied by a biographical note on the Countess de Montijo, also referring to the letter.

Paris, Ader-Picard-Tajan (Drouot), 22 Nov. 1985, lot 40.
FRKF 1370

FRANCESCO MORLACCHI (1784–1841)

La rosa appassita

Holograph manuscript of this song for voice and piano on a text by Felice Romani, 1834, 4 p. Notated in black ink on p. [1]–[4] of a small oblong bifolium of 10-staff paper. At the top of p. [1] in Morlacchi's hand: "La rosa appassita / Romanza in forma d'Elegia / Morlacchi in Dresda / il 25 marzo 1834." The words are probably in the hand of a copyist.

London, Sotheby's, 29 Nov. 1985, lot 156.
FRKF 1034A

GEORGE MORROW

Undated pen-and-ink cartoon on board (oblong, 34.5 × 26 cm), signed at the lower left corner, and showing an angler in conversation with a passer-by. The caption is written in ink at the bottom and reads: *Helpful passer-by* "Excuse me, sir, but I think you have caught a fish" *The novice* "Yes, yes, I know. But I'm looking to see whether I take the hook out of the fish or the fish off the hook."

Pasted on the back is a printed ticket for the "St. Dunstan's Day" sale to benefit the Blinded Soldiers' and Sailors' After-Care Fund, with the words: "Original sketch / Geo Morrow" added in ink. The title given in the auction catalogue is "How to fish."

London, Christie's, 21 July 1981, lot 249.
FRKF 102

IGNAZ MOSCHELES (1794–1870)

Letter to Emilie [Roche?]

1842 July 8, London, ALS, 1 p., with a short musical quotation.

Paris, Oger-Dumont (Drouot), 14 Feb. 1985, lot 20.
FRKF 684

WOLFGANG AMADEUS MOZART (1756–91)

Gavotte, K. 300

Holograph manuscript, 1778, 2 p. Notated in black ink on both sides of a single sheet of 16-staff paper (23 × 30 cm). At the top of page 1, in Mozart's hand: "// Gavotte //," and the date: Paris, 1778.

Also on p. 1, in the upper right corner, in the hand of Georg von Nyssen: "von Mozart und seine Handschrift." In the upper left corner: "No 50." At the bottom of the page are a red seal and another inscription, in the hand of Carl August André: "Aus den Nachlass des grossen Tonmeisters überreicht dies Blatt zu geneigter Erinnerung an Herrn Minister von Eisendecker unter Verbürgung der Echtheit der Handschrift Mozarts / Frankfurt a/M 24 Dezember 1855 C.A. André."

In B-flat major; scored for two oboes, two horns in E-flat, two bassoons, and strings. Possibly a discarded movement from the ballet *Les petits riens*, K. 299b. Published for the first time in 1963, from a photostat in the Salzburg Mozarteum, in *Neue Ausgabe sämtlicher Werke* II:6/2, 46.

Accompanied by an ALS from Carl August André to Herr Minister Wilhelm von Eisendecker, Frankfurt, 24 Dec. 1855, 1 p., presenting the Mozart manuscript as a token of gratitude for arranging for the purchase of a piano by Graf Otto von Bismarck-Schönhausen, then Prussian delegate to the federal diet in Frankfurt.

See Banks, C.A., and J. Rigbie Turner. *Mozart: prodigy of nature* [exhibition catalogue] (New York: Pierpont Morgan Library; London: British Library), 1991, p. 40 and 45.

Heinrich Schütz to Henry Miller, p. 22–23.
New York, Sotheby's, 14 Dec. 1983, lot 112.
FRKF 139, 139.5

ROLLO MYERS (1892–1985)

The Rollo Myers papers are described in seven groups:

I. MANUSCRIPTS OF WORKS BY ROLLO MYERS
II. OTHER MANUSCRIPTS AND RESEARCH FILES
III. INCOMING CORRESPONDENCE
IV. MANUSCRIPTS BY CHARLES KOECHLIN
V. PHOTOGRAPHS
VI. PRINTED MATERIAL
VII. MISCELLANEOUS PAPERS

I. MANUSCRIPTS OF WORKS BY ROLLO MYERS

Debussy

Holograph manuscript, n.d., 79 p., written in a 4to-size notebook of ruled paper in moleskin boards. Inscribed on the verso of the front board: "Ernest Myers / Balliol Nov. 3. 1865" and, in Myers's hand: "Rollo Myers / Balliol 1910–1913." On title page, in Myers's hand: "M.S. of / my book on / Debussy."

Erik Satie

Manuscript of Part Three, 1947, 101 p., in black ink in a 4to-size notebook, dated 24 July 1947 at the end.

II. OTHER MANUSCRIPTS AND RESEARCH FILES

Chabrier

"Chabrier," typescript with autograph corrections, n.d., 6 p. Possibly incomplete; paginated 3–9.

Debussy

"Debussy," typescript with autograph corrections, 1979, 9 p.

"Frontispiece," typescript, carbon, 1 p.

"Some first performances," typescript with autograph corrections, 4 p.

"Acknowledgements," typescript with autograph corrections, 1 p.; typescript with autograph corrections, 2 p.; carbon typescript, 2 p.

"Sources," typescript with autograph corrections, 7 p.

"Bibliographie debussyste," printed extract from an unidentified source, paginated [129]–143, with annotations in Myers's hand.

Autograph notes on Debussy, written in blue ballpoint pen in a spiral-bound 4to-size ruled notebook, n.d. [1960s].

Unsigned woodcut representing Debussy in profile.

Debussy. Sinfoniia si minor / Symphonie en si mineur. For piano four-hands [Moscow, 1933?], photocopy, 23 p.

Miscellaneous photocopies, photographs, newspaper clippings relating to Debussy.

Fauré

"The chamber music of Gabriel Fauré," typescript, carbon, n.d., 5 p.

Koechlin

"Ch. Koechlin," typescript, carbon, of Myers's article on Koechlin for the *Grove Dictionary of Music*, 15 p. At the top of p. [1] in Myers's hand: "My article in Grove." Date of Koechlin's death added in pencil.

Ravel

"Ravel," typescript with autograph corrections, 5 p. Autograph notes on Ravel, written in blue and red ballpoint pen in a spiral-bound 4to-size notebook, n.d.

Satie

Autograph notes on Satie, written in black and blue ballpoint pen in a 4to-size ruled notebook in moleskin cover, n.d.

Miscellaneous

Autograph notes on Chabrier, Milhaud, Satie, Debussy, and Ravel, written in pencil and black, blue, and red ballpoint pen in a tall notebook. Together with a typed version of a speech by Paul Valéry published in *Pièces sur l'art* (Paris: Gallimard, 1934) and two pages of miscellaneous notes on contemporary French music.

Fragment of a talk or concert presentation. Typescript with autograph corrections, 2 p. concerning Fauré, Déodat de Séverac, and Granados.

III. INCOMING CORRESPONDENCE

From Suzy Charles-Koechlin

1959 April 8, Paris, ALS, 2 p., concerning Myers's book on Satie.

From Cyril Clemens

1974 Nov. 27, Kirkwood, Missouri, *Mark Twain Journal*[S], TLS, 1 p., offering Myers honorary membership in the Mark Twain Society.

From Jean Cocteau

1947 April, Milly-la-Forêt, ALS, 1 p., with a note by Myers indicating that the letter concerns the preface to the French edition of his book on Satie.

1949 Dec., n.p., ALS, 1 p.

1952 Oct. 11, n.p., ALS, 1 p. (env)

1956 Feb. 11, Suvretta House, St Moritz[S], ALS, 1 p.

1957 Dec. 11, Milly-la-Forêt, ALS, 1 p.

With three envelopes, unassigned, postmarked 1951, 1955, and 1956. Also with a photocopy of "Satie est mort, vive Satie," typescript, corrected, signed Jean Cocteau at the end.

From Andrzej Jankowski

1977 April 27 [Kingston-upon-Thames] ALS, 2 p.

From Jonathan Cape, Ltd.

1976 Feb. 6, London, TLS, 1 p., concerning Debussy.

From Charles Koechlin

1947 Dec. 26, Paris, ALS, 2 p., enclosing an article on atonal music.

1948 Nov. 17, Paris, ALS, 2 p. (env). Mentions Satie and Debussy.

1948 Dec. 10, Paris, ALS, 2 p. (env)

1948 Dec. 27, Paris, ALS, 5 p. (env), concerning Myers's book on Satie.

1949 Jan. 7, Paris, ALS, 1 p. (env)

1949 Jan. 25, Paris, ALS, 2 p. (env). Mentions his compositions *La loi de la jungle* and *Les bandar-log*.

1949 Feb. 25, Paris, ALS, 2 p.

1949 March 8, Paris, ALS, 3 p. (env), concerning Debussy and Koechlin's orchestration of *Khamma*.

1949 March 26, Paris, ALS, 2 p. (env)

1949 April 14, Paris, ALS, 2 p. (env)

1949 April 20, Villers-sur-Mer [Paris*] ALS, 2 p. (env)

1949 April 24, Paris, ALS, 1 p. (env)

1949 May 3, n.p. [Paris?] ALS, 1 p. (env)

From Francis Poulenc

[1946 July] London, APCS. Dated by Myers.

n.d. [Noizay?] APCS

From Yvonne Tiénot

1972 March 8, Paris, ALS (env), about Myers's *Modern French Music*.

From "Valentine"

1984 April 1, n.p., ALS, 2 p., in French. With a postscript from "André."

From an unidentified writer

1983 June 6, APCS in French.

1984 July 4, APCS

With a signature cut from a letter, n.d.

IV. MANUSCRIPTS BY CHARLES KOECHLIN

"Notes sur la vie et l'oeuvre de Ch. Koechlin." Autograph manuscript in Koechlin's hand, written on both sides of six oblong sheets, paginated 1 to 12. The postscript is dated 26 Feb. 1949.

"Notes sur l'orchestration d'oeuvres d'autres compositeurs." Autograph manuscript in Koechlin's hand, written on the recto of a single sheet. One annotation in Myers's hand.

"Quelques réflexions, au sujet de la musique atonale." Autograph manuscript in Koechlin's hand, written on the recto sides of 17 oblong sheets, paginated 1 to 17. Signed and dated at the end Dec. 1947. Note in Myers's hand at the top of p. 1: "Published in Music Today. Editor: R.M."

V. PHOTOGRAPHS

Jean Cocteau

Photograph of a drawing by Cocteau showing him, according to a note in Myers's hand, in his Oxford robes after his honorary doctorate. (14 × 9 cm) The drawing bears the annotation "Milly" and an inscription to Mary Hoeck, also according to a note by Myers.

Claude Debussy

Copy of a photograph of Debussy (17 × 21.5 cm) standing in front of a house, with his hat on the grass before him.

Francis Poulenc

Photograph (20 × 15 cm) showing Poulenc at the piano with Pierre Bernac. Inscribed in Poulenc's hand at the top: "pour notre cher ami Myers - très amicalement / Francis Poulenc. Noël 1936"; also signed by Bernac.

Photograph (11.5 × 11 cm) showing Poulenc playing the harpsichord four-hands with Wanda Landowska. Inscribed at the top in Poulenc's hand: "Chez Wanda à Lakeville, pour mon cher Rollo très affectueusement / Poulenc." Manuscript note on the verso: "photo H. Landskoff."

Group photograph

Unidentified group photograph, dated by Myers Feb. 1979 on the verso. Stamped Atelier photographique Yobal Laboye, Castres, on the verso.

VI. PRINTED MATERIAL

Calvocoressi, Michel-Dimitri. *Charles Koechlin*. Paris: Éditions Maurice Senart [1924]. (Collection "Nos Musiciens")

[1–7], 8–30 [+ 2] p. Presentation inscription on title page: "à Mr Rollo H. Myers / avec mes meilleurs sentiments / Ch. Koechlin / mai 1949." Disbound.

Cocteau, Jean. *Cock and Harlequin: Notes concerning Music. Translated from the French by Rollo H. Myers. With a portrait of the Author and two Monograms by Pablo Picasso.* London: The Egoist Press, 1921.

[1–7], 8–57 [+ 3] p., 1 pl. Laid in is an unidentified newspaper clipping with review of the translation.

Erik Satie [comic book]. Scenario: Daniele Strozecki; dessin: Gilles Frechet. Arcueil: Centre culturel communal d'Arcueil, n.d. [1975–80?].

Myers, Rollo. *Erik Satie. Traduit de l'anglais par Robert Le Masle.* Paris: Gallimard, 1959. (collection "Leurs figures")

8vo, [1–7], 8–200 [+ 2] p.

—. *Music since 1939*. London: Longmans, Green & Co. for the British Council, 1947.

8vo, [i]–vii, [viii], 9–48, photographic frontispiece and 7 leaves of photographic plates.

Renaudin, Pierre. [*Charles Koechlin*]. Paris: Cathelineau, 1952.

10 fol., unpaginated. On cover, facsimile of the signature of Ch. Koechlin and three measures of music notated on a two-staff system, initialed and dated 8–9 June 1949. Laid in: photograph of Charles Koechlin in 1947 by Paul / Saint-Étienne. Inscribed to Rollo Myers by Suzy Charles-Koechlin.

Volta, Ornella. *Erik Satie.* Paris: Seghers, 1979. (coll. Seghers/Humour)

[1–8], 9–157 [+ 3] p. Inscribed by the author on the half-title: "Pour Monsieur / Rollo Myers / Satiste Emérite / l'hommage d' / Ornella Volta/"

Miscellaneous printed items

Animation action culturelle. Bulletin, Acte centre d'animation culturelle Bures Orsay, no. 12 (May–June [1975]). Cover and p. [4] devoted to Satie.

"The art of Claude Debussy." *Rhythm* (Nov. 1911), offprint, photocopy.

Clippings about Jean Cocteau, 1955–71, and n.d.

Clippings about music and other subjects.

A Flower Given to my Daughter, song by Albert Roussel, words by James Joyce. Paris: Durand, c1948. 2 copies.

"Hommage à Erik Satie." Mimeographed document, n.p. [1975], 26 p. Preface by Philippe Gaucher. Autograph correction by Myers on p. 3.

The Musical Quarterly, LXIII: 4 (Oct. 1977). Contains Myers's "A Music Critic in Paris in the Nineteen-Twenties," p. 524–44.

The Musical Quarterly, LXIV: 4 (Oct. 1978). Contains Myers's "The Opera That Never Was: Debussy's Collaboration with Victor Segalen in the Preparation of *Orphée*," p. 485–506. Together with an ALS from Annie Joly-Segalen to Myers, on stationery of 11, avenue du Lycée Lakanal, Bourg-la-Reine, 25 Nov. [1978?] 2 p.; an ALS from Éliette Segalen to Myers, Paris, n.d., 2 p.; and a printed program from the French Ministry of Culture and Communication entitled "Centenaire de Victor Segalen" (Paris, 1978).

"Ravel, Maurice." From the fifteenth edition of *Encyclopedia Britannica*, offprint, 1974, 4 copies.

Scrapbook of clippings, including reviews of writings by Myers, and articles and letters to editors by him, ca. 90 p., some detached. Clippings dated ca. 1939–ca. 1972.

Music by Myers:

Une danseuse, song, words by Jean Cocteau (Paris: Senart, ca. 1922)

Deux histoires naturelles, song, words by Jules Renard (Paris, Éditions de la Sirène, copyright 1922)

Feuilles mortes, for piano (Paris: Deiss, copyright 1926)

Je peux regarder le soleil en face, song, words by Jean Cocteau (London: Chester, copyright 1947)

Noël, song, words by Théophile Gautier (Paris: Senart, ca. 1920)

Transformation. Mimeographed journal, n.p., n.d. Contains Myers's "The Solitude of Satie," 2 p.

VII. MISCELLANEOUS PAPERS

Pedigree 2. Essington, Hughes, and Clarke

Printed document, n.p., n.d., 6 copies. 4to, unbound quire. Accompanied by engraved portraits of Lieut. Charles Griffin Clark R.N., (1790–1850); Gordon Wyatt Clark about 1875; Henry Welch (1796–1876); Mrs. Henry Welch née Thornton (1798–1870); Admiral Sir William Essington, K.C.B.; Mrs. Matthew Clark, née Squibb (1793–1873); and George Squibb (1764–1831).

Unidentified

Manuscript in English, concerning Egyptology, in black ink on three tall, nested bifolia, bound in dark blue cloth, with "A Manuscript," gold-tooled on the front board, n.d., 12 p.

Two documents, one with the printed heading "Secunda clace, vale dos reales: para el Bienio de mil ochocientos veinte y siete; y viente y ocho"; the other with a stamp of "Republica de Chile" and the printed heading "Tersera clase dos reales." Both signed by several individuals, one representing the Chilean Mining Association, 1827. With a related bookdealer's bill.

Calligraphic manuscript, in Arabic, 1 p.

ROLLO MYERS PAPERS

London, Phillips, 27 June 1985, lots 619, 622.

FRKF 876, 880

NAPOLÉON III, EMPEROR OF THE FRENCH (1808–73)

Letter to Macaire et Cie

[1831] Sept. 30 [Arenenberg] ALS, 1 p., concerning a letter to Mr. Carteret and a letter to Mr. Botte, a jeweller in Geneva.

Hamburg, Hauswedell und Nolte, 22 May 1984, lot 1662.
FRKF 318

Letters to Jean-Martial Bineau

1852 Jan. 28 [Paris?] ALS, 1 p., concerning a report to be published in *Le Moniteur*; mentions Achille Fould.

[1852 Sept. 27] Marseilles, ALS, 1 p. Mentions financial transactions and his successful trip to Marseilles. Date from docket mark.

Jean-Martial Bineau (1805–55), an engineer and railroad expert, was Louis-Napoléon's minister of public works in 1849–51 and became finance minister following the coup d'état of 2 Dec. 1852.

Paris, Dominique Vincent (Drouot), 12 March 1984, lot 316.
FRKF 425

Letter to the editor of the *Journal du peuple*

1841 Dec. 9, Ham, ALS, responding to an attack in the *Journal*.

Paris, Hervé Chayette (Drouot), 21 May 1984, lot 177.
FRKF 712

NAPOLÉON III, EMPEROR OF THE FRENCH (1808–73)
EUGÉNIE DE MONTIJO, EMPRESS OF THE FRENCH (1826–1920)
EUGÈNE-LOUIS-NAPOLÉON, PRINCE IMPÉRIAL (1856–79)

An album of autograph letters, manuscripts, and memorabilia, compiled by Pierre de Bourgoing, ca. 1849–95, with unrelated manuscript documents. The collection comprises the following, listed in the order in which they appear in the album:

Three carte-de-visite photographs of Napoléon III, Empress Eugénie, and the Prince Impérial.

Laid in: a blank sheet of paper and matching envelope, both with mourning border, from the stationery of Empress Eugénie at Farnborough.

Manuscript marriage contract, in a secretarial hand, between Baron Philippe de Bourgoing and Anna Léonie Dollfus, 1856 June 22, Saint-Cloud, 1 p., signed by Napoléon III.

Napoléon III
  Autograph letters, signed, to Philippe de Bourgoing
    1871 Aug. 27, Chislehurst, 2 p.
    1872 Sept. 12, West Cowes, 1 p.

Empress Eugénie
  Letters to Mme de Bourgoing and Philippe de Bourgoing. All but the first four items are on mourning stationery.
    1870 Sept. 15, n.p., AL to Mme de Bourgoing, 3 p.
    1870 Sept. 17, n.p., AL to Philippe de Bourgoing, 4 p.
    1871 July 20, n.p., LS to Mme de Bourgoing, 4 p.
    1872 Sept. 30, Camden Place [Chislehurst] ALS to Mme de Bourgoing, 3 p.
    [1873?] Aug. 29, Camden Place^S, ALS to Philippe de Bourgoing, 3 p.
    n.y. April 21, Villa de la Haute, Posilippo, ALS to Mme de Bourgoing, 2 p.
    n.y. June 8, Farnborough, ALS to Mme de Bourgoing, 1 p.
    n.y. Aug. 28, Arenenberg, par Ermalingen, C.^ton de Thurgovie^S, ALS to Mme de Bourgoing, 4 p.
    n.y. Dec. 9, Prince's Gate, S.W. [London] ALS to Philippe de Bourgoing, 2 p.
    1882 April 29, Nice, ALS to Mme de Bourgoing, 3 p.
    1892 Jan. 2, Farnborough Hill, Farnboro', Hants.^S, ALS to Pierre de Bourgoing, 2 p.
    1893 Jan. 2, Farnborough Hill, Farnboro', Hants.^S, ALS to Pierre de Bourgoing, 3 p.
    1896 Jan. 1, n.p., ANS to Pierre de Bourgoing, on both sides of a card.
    n.y. April 28, Villa de la Haute, Posilippo, ALS to Pierre de Bourgoing, 2 p.

Napoléon III
  ALS to Monsieur le Ministre, 1849 July 11, "Elysée Nationale" [Paris] 1 p., demanding the release of M. de Fauchécourt from Sainte-Pélagie. Signed "Louis-Napoléon Bonaparte."

Eugène-Louis-Napoléon, Prince Impérial
  Pen-and-ink drawing of a soldier, with a two-line caption in the hand of Pierre de Bourgoing, with pencilled explanations initialed by Bourgoing.
  Letters to Pierre de Bourgoing
    1872 Aug. 31, Cowes, ALS, 2 p., signed "Louis-Napoléon"

n.d. [after 1873] Arenenberg, par Mannenbach, C.^ton de Thurgovie^S, ALS, 1 p., signed "Napoléon"

n.d. [after 1873] n.p., ALS, 1 p., on monogrammed stationery; signed "Napoléon"

1877 Oct. 15, Camden Place, Chislehurst^S, ALS, 2 p., signed "Napoléon"

Pen-and-ink drawing of a soldier [by the Prince Impérial?] n.d. Camden Place, Chislehurst^S, ALS, 3 p., signed "Napoléon"

Telegrams

Empress Eugénie. Four telegrams to Pierre de Bourgoing, ca. 1902–06, London and Farnborough, signed Comtesse Pierrefonds.

Napoléon III or Eugène-Louis-Napoléon, telegram to Philippe de Bourgoing, n.d., Paris.

Eugène-Louis-Napoléon, Prince Impérial. Two telegrams to Philippe or Pierre de Bourgoing, 1875, 1877, Chislehurst, Florence.

Eugène-Louis-Napoléon, Prince Impérial, to Pierre de Bourgoing, 1877 Oct. 13, Chislehurst.

Empress Eugénie to Philippe or Pierre de Bourgoing, 1878 Nov. 18, Chislehurst, signed Comtesse Pierrefonds.

Philippe de Bourgoing to Pierre de Bourgoing, [1879] June 20, Paris, announcing the death of the Prince Impérial.

Empress Eugénie to Philippe de Bourgoing, [year not deciphered] Jan. 14, Paris; to Philippe or Pierre de Bourgoing, 1881 Jan. 3, Chislehurst; to Pierre de Bourgoing, 1882 April 22, Nice, this last telegram conveying condolences of the death of Philippe de Bourgoing. All three telegrams are signed Comtesse Pierrefonds.

Eugène-Louis-Napoléon, Prince Impérial

Pencil drawing of a soldier made for Pierre de Bourgoing, 1862, with a pencil annotation in the hand of Philippe de Bourgoing.

Pencil drawing, signed "louis napoléon," 1862, with a caption in the hand of Philippe de Bourgoing: "Mr. de Griand [?] / pêchant un requin / 14 8bre 1862 / St Cloud."

Two pen-and-ink drawings, on a single sheet of paper, representing Tropmann, as identified by the caption in blue pencil, signed "Bon de Bourgoing / Ecuyer de SM 1867." The teenage serial killer Jean-Baptiste Tropmann (ca. 1850–70) was guillotined in Jan. 1870.

Empress Eugénie

Pencil drawing of a tree, 1839, with a caption in red pencil signed Bon de Bourgoing."

Eugène-Louis-Napoléon, Prince Impérial

Doodles, writing exercises, etc., 1 p., on ruled paper, presumably in the hand of the Prince Impérial, n.d. [early 1860s].

Two pen-and-ink drawings [by the Prince Impérial?, mid-1870s?] Arenenberg, par Ermalingen, C.^ton de Thurgovie^S.

Pen-and-ink drawing of two musketeers, with a pencil caption in the hand of Pierre de Bourgoing indicating that they were made by the Prince Impérial at Arenenberg.

Two pen-and-ink drawings [by the Prince Impérial?] on envelope stamped: "Service de l'Empereur (Maison de l'Impératrice)."

Pencil drawing, with pencil caption in the hand of Pierre de Bourgoing: "portrait (?) du général / ministre de la Guerre / fait par le Prince Impérial / Chislehurst 1879."

Pen-and-ink doodles [by the Prince Impérial?].

Printed prayer, with printed signature Napoléon, the text in red and blue gothic script, with a decorated initial and decorated capitals on green, red, or gold background, and with a border decorated with bees, [1870s?].

Printed invitation on blue paper for a gathering at Chislehurst on 16 March 1874, with a "carton d'introduction," embossed with the Napoleonic monogram and signed by Philippe de Bourgoing.

Printed address by the Prince Impérial, [1874] 1 p.

Printed "carton d'introduction" in the name of Pierre de Bourgoing and badge, on purple paper, for the funeral of the Prince Impérial at Chislehurst [1879].

Printed pass for Pierre de Bourgoing, signed by Brigadier General Campbell and countersigned by the Duke of Bassano, for the funeral of the Prince Impérial [1879].

Invitation, in the name of Pierre de Bourgoing, to the funeral of the Prince Impérial [1879].

Two printed prayers, one in French, one in English, in memory of the Prince Impérial, on cards with mourning borders [1879].

Printed notification, in the name of Philippe de Bourgoing, of mourning etiquette following the death of Napoléon III, dated Chislehurst, 1873 Jan. 10, and printed memorial card, in English, and printed pass for the funeral of Napoléon III, 1873 Jan. 15.

Printed insurance policy, completed in manuscript, in the name of J. Cariben aîné, from the Compagnie Royale d'Assurances contre l'Incendie, 1843 June 15.

Manuscript marriage contract between Jean Barron, carpenter in Macau (Gironde) and Jeanne Ladie, Castelneau, 1741 Jan. 7, 3 p.

Eugène-Louis-Napoléon, Prince Impérial

Pen-and-ink drawing showing horses and riders, initialed L.N., 1868, with a caption in the hand of Philippe de Bourgoing [?] indicating that it was made at the Camp in Châlons on 6 Sept. 1868.

Manuscript legal document, signed, concerning a complaint by Jean Dussat, carpenter in Macau, 26 Brumaire V [16 Nov. 1796] 4 p.

Empress Eugénie
> ANS to Pierre de Bourgoing on both sides of a card, n.d., n.p., on mourning stationery

Eugène-Louis-Napoléon, Prince Impérial
> Draft of an ALS to his godmother, the queen of Sweden, n.d., n.p., 1 p., with a note in purple ink in the hand of Philippe de Bourgoing [?] indicating that the last part of the letter is in the hand of a secretary.
>
> Four pen-and-ink and wash drawings of riders on horses, a pen-and-ink and wash drawing of a soldier, and a pen-and-ink and wash drawing of a military position, with an explanatory note in the hand of Pierre [?] de Bourgoing, Metz, 4 Aug. [1870?].

Bound in uniform green morocco (stamp of Gruel at the bottom of the spine), both boards stamped in gold with the arms of Napoléon III and the imperial bee at each corner. The bee is also stamped in gold five times between the raised bands on the spine, as is the word "Souvenirs." All edges gilt.

Baron Philippe de Bourgoing (1827–82) was equerry to Napoléon III and, after 1870, a Bonapartiste member of the Chambre des Députés. His son Pierre (1855–1916) was a childhood friend of the Prince Impérial. See *Dictionnaire de biographie française*.

See Christie's, London, 16 Dec. 1991, lot 313.
Heinrich Schütz to Henry Miller, p. 62–63.
FRKF 743

JACQUES OFFENBACH (1819–80)

I. MUSIC MANUSCRIPTS

Offenbach's music manuscripts are described in seven groups:

A. OPERETTAS, OPÉRAS-BOUFFES, AND OPÉRAS-COMIQUES
B. INCIDENTAL MUSIC
C. CHORAL MUSIC
D. SONGS
E. DANCE MUSIC
F. MUSIC FOR CELLO
G. MISCELLANEOUS SKETCHES

A. OPERETTAS, OPÉRAS-BOUFFES, AND OPÉRAS-COMIQUES

L'amour chanteur

Holograph manuscript, in full score, n.d., 80 p. Notated in black ink, with additional pencil markings (not in Offenbach's hand) on separate bifolia, stitched together, of oblong 24-staff paper (blind stamp of Lard-Esnault). Calligraphed on the title page, not in Offenbach's hand: "L'amour chanteur. / Musique de J. Offenbach. / Grande partition." The numbering and captions at the top of the sections are in the same hand.

The manuscript comprises the following sections, marked, as indicated, in Offenbach's hand:

 1. "Introduction" (labelled and signed by Offenbach).
 2. "No. 1" (not in Offenbach's hand).
 3. Marked "N° 2" on the outer bifolium, Quartet ("Prenez garde!").
 4. Marked "no. 3," Couplets for Guillaume ("On comblait partout d'éloges …").
 5. Marked "no. 4 bis / Récitatifs" (four recitatives, noted on three pages of a single bifolium).
 6. Marked "Air de Popelinet / n° 5" ("Plus prompt qu'une bombe").
 7. Marked "no. 6 / air" ("A toi que j'adore …"), with a note on p. 1: "Je prie le copiste de baisser d'un ton tout ce morceau."

L'amour chanteur, operetta in one act on a libretto by Charles Nuitter and L'Épine, was premiered at the Théâtre des Bouffes-Parisiens on 5 Jan. 1864.

FRKF 59

Apothicaire et perruquier

Holograph full-score manuscript, notated in black ink on oblong 24-staff paper (blind stamp of Lard-Esnault). On title page, the original title, "Le mariage par les cheveux," is written and crossed out in Offenbach's hand, replaced by the word "Apothicaire" in red pencil in an unknown hand, after which Offenbach has added "et Perruquier." The word "Ouverture" is also in Offenbach's hand. Also on the cover, in blue pencil: "Mr Caspers / 1 Rue St Claude au Marais," and, in black pencil, at the bottom: "Alexandrine" [?]

The score comprises the following numbers (all under the heading "Le mariage par les cheveux"), all labelled in Offenbach's hand:

"Ouverture," 11 p.

"n° 1 Romance de Boudinet," 3 p., annotations in ink and pencil in a different hand.

"n° 2 Romance de Chilpéric," 3 p., with an annotation in pencil in a different hand.

"n° 3 Duo entre Sempronia et Chilpéric," 9 p., annotations in pencil in a different hand.

"n° 4 Quatuor," 6 p., annotations in red pencil, possibly in Offenbach's hand, and in black pencil, in a different hand.

"n° 5 Duo," 7 p., annotations in pencil in a different hand.

"n° 6 Couplets," 4 p., annotations in pencil in a different hand.

"n° 7" [Finale], 5 p., annotations in red pencil, possibly in Offenbach's hand, and in black pencil, in a different hand.

Bound with *La bonne d'enfant*. Dark red marbled paper boards, red morocco spine. On the spine: "Partition / manuscrite / J. Offenbach / Un mariage / par / les cheveux / La / bonne / d'enfant / J.O."

Apothicaire et perruquier, opérette-bouffe in one act, on a libretto by Élie Frébault, was premiered at the Théâtre des Bouffes-Parisiens on 17 Oct. 1861.

FRKF 234a

La baguette

Holograph draft fragment, in full score, for this opéra-comique. The six pages of drafts are written in black ink, with additional drafts in pencil, on a loose bifolium and a single sheet of oblong 24-staff paper (blind stamp of Lard-Esnault), numbered 3 and 4 in Offenbach's hand (replacing a previous foliation), while the pages are renumbered 9 to 14, in blue pencil in a different hand. At the top of p. 9, in pencil, not in Offenbach's hand: "Kalinsky – La Baguette." At the top of p. 11, in Offenbach's hand: "2d acte." The draft is for an ensemble (quartet?) for unidentified characters, beginning with the words (cancelled): "elle a vingt ans elle est née à …"

La baguette, opéra-comique in two acts, libretto by Henri Meilhac and Ludovic Halévy, is listed by Grove among unperformed works, with the alternative title *Fédia*, and dated 1862.

FRKF 236.08

Barbe-Bleue

Holograph full-score manuscript fragment of an early or intermediate version, 13 p. Notated in black ink on four oblong bifolia, numbered 6 to 9, of 24-staff paper (blind stamp of Lard-Esnault). The fragment ostensibly belongs to the last scene of act 3, but neither text nor music corresponds to the published score. It begins with Popolani's words "Est-ce vous Monseigneur," leading to a reprise of Barbe-Bleue's act 1 song "Je suis Barbe Bleue ô gué / Jamais veuf ne fut plus gai" and a confrontation between Barbe Bleue and his former wives as he is trying to take back Boulotte's bridal ring. There are some erasures and passages crossed out.

Barbe-Bleue, opéra-bouffe in three acts, libretto by Henri Meilhac and Ludovic Halévy, was premiered at the Théâtre des Variétés in Paris on 5 Feb. 1866.

FRKF 288

La boîte au lait

Holograph manuscript, in short score, of act 4, no. 2, 1876, 4 p. Notated in black ink and pencil on p. [1]–[4] of a bifolium of oblong 24-staff paper (blind stamp of Lard-Esnault), nested within another bifolium serving as wrappers. On the front of the outer bifolium, in Offenbach's hand: "La Boîte au lait / J.O. / 4eme acte n° 2." Signed by the composer at the top of p. [1] and dated Paris, 14 Oct. 1876. The words ("C'est mon amour qui remplacait [sic] mon ame") are written in pencil.

La boîte au lait, opéra-bouffe in four acts, libretto by Jules Noriac and Eugène Grangé, was premiered at the Théâtre des Bouffes-Parisiens on 3 Nov. 1876.

Marburg, Stargardt, 26 Nov. 1985, lot 869.
FRKF 1153

La bonne d'enfant

Holograph full-score manuscript, in black ink on oblong 20-staff paper (blind stamp of Lard-Esnault). The headings, the list of instruments at the beginning of each number, and some tempo indications are in the hands of copyists. The orchestration is in Offenbach's hand throughout, while the piano reduction at the bottom appears to be in a different hand. There is no title page. At the top of p. 1, title: "La Bonne d'Enfant." Throughout, in pencil, at the bottom of the pages: "H et Cie 1934." Bound with *Apothicaire et perruquier* (see above).

The score comprises the following numbers, identified in the hand of a copyist:

"Ouverture," 12 p.

"N° 1 Duo," 22 p. The words on the first nine pages are in a different hand; also with pencil annotations in a different hand.

"N° 2 Duo," 15 p., pencil annotations in a different hand.

"N° 3," 11 p.

"N° 4," 5 p.

"N° 5 [in a different hand:] Trio," 21 p., also with pencil annotations in a different hand.

La bonne d'enfant, opérette-bouffe in one act, on a libretto by Eugène Bercioux, was premiered at the Théâtre des Bouffes-Parisiens on 14 Oct. 1856.

FRKF 234b

Les contes d'Hoffmann

Partial, largely holograph manuscript, with parts in the hand of Ernest Guiraud, 1880 and n.d., ca. 390 p. The manuscript comprises the following sections:

Act 1, no. 1 - Introduction

Title page, on a single sheet of oblong 24-staff paper (blind stamp of Lard-Esnault) in the hand of a copyist: "1er Acte / N° 1 / Les contes d'Hoffmann." The word "Introduction" was subsequently added in blue pencil, in a different hand. A portion of the opening chorus, in full score, comprising 20 pages, numbered 19 to 38 in pencil in an unidentified hand. The fragment is written in black ink on two single sheets and four individual bifolia of oblong 24-staff paper (blind stamp of Lard-Esnault). It appears to be mostly in a copyist's hand, with a few markings in another hand.

An alternative version of the Muse's aria, notated, chiefly in the hand of Ernest Guiraud, on two individual bifolia and the recto of a single sheet, all of tall 24-staff paper (blind stamp of Lard-Esnault), beginning with the words "soin de trouver son excuse …" and ending "Elle est sur la …" with a pencilled reference to p. 32 of the "partition à l'italienne." It is paginated 23–31 in pencil, in an unidentified hand. The first page is headed "Suite de la page 23."

Act 1, no. 2

Manuscript, notated in full score, the vocal line and piano accompaniment in the hand of a copyist, the orchestration in Guiraud's hand, from the beginning to Lindorf's words "Va-t-en au [diable]." Written on both sides of a single sheet and two individual bifolia, numbered respectively 1 and 2–3, of oblong 24-staff paper (blind stamp of Lard-Esnault). At the top of fol. 1r: "N° 2 Les Contes d'Hoffmann (André [sic, for Andrès] et Lindorf) Gde Partition."

Act 1, no. 4

A fragment in Offenbach's hand, on two individual bifolia of oblong 24-staff paper (blind stamp of Lard-Esnault) numbered 9 and 10 in Offenbach's hand. The fragment, which contains only the vocal lines and the bass lines, begins with Hermann's words "Oh! oh! d'où vient cet air faché" and ends at "Va pour Kleinzach." Note in pencil (not in Offenbach's hand) in the upper right corner of both bifolia: "Fin du n° 4 (1e acte) Remplacé."

Act 1, no. 5 - Couplets et Andante

A fragment, notated in short score in Offenbach's hand on both sides of a single sheet and three sides of an unnumbered bifolium of oblong 18-staff paper (blind stamp of Lard-Esnault), beginning with the words, for the chorus, "[Klein]zach, clicclac [sic] / trictrac" (end of the second verse of the Kleinzach song) until the end of the number. The role of Hoffmann is notated in bass clef.

Act 1, no. 6 - Finale

A fragment in Offenbach's hand, written on two individual bifolia (numbered 3 and 4 in his hand) and a single sheet (numbered 5) of oblong 24-staff paper (blind stamp of Lard-Esnault). The fragment, which contains only the vocal lines and the piano accompaniment at the bottom, begins with the words for the chorus "Nous serons un jour dans le même cas" and ends at Lindorf's words "Pour en guérir cher oison" (second verse, not retained, of the duettino). At the top of the first bifolium, in blue pencil, in an unidentified hand: "(feuilles supprimées) (N° 6. 1e acte.)"

A fragment from the same duet, notated in the hand of a copyist (text and piano accompaniment only) on a single, oblong sheet of 24-staff paper (blind stamp of Lard-Esnault), beginning "-tiendrait cher poison" and ending with the words, sung in unison, "cher supôt de Luci[fer] / cher échappé de l'en[fer]."

Act 2, no. 7 - Récitatif et scène

A fragment in Offenbach's hand, on three individual bifolia, numbered 1–3 in his hand, of oblong 24-staff paper (blind stamp of Lard-Esnault). The fragment, which contains only the vocal lines and the piano accompaniment at the bottom, begins with Hoffmann's words "Allons courage et confiance" and ends with the words (not retained in the final version) "Je tremble." At the top of the first bifolium, in pencil, in an unidentified hand: "2e acte (n° 1) remplacé."

Nicklausse's song "Une poupée aux yeux d'émail," in short score, partly in Offenbach's hand, on the recto sides of two individual sheets. At the top of the first sheet, in Offenbach's hand, "2d acte fin du n° 1." The manuscript ends with the words "Tout pour la physi[que]," followed by the pencilled indication, not in Offenbach's hand: "laisser en blanc."

Act 2, no. 8 - Récitatif et trio

A fragment corresponding to an earlier state of the words and music. This section of the manuscript is entitled, on a small sheet of paper pasted on the first page: "Contes d'Hoffmann / Morceaux coupés / Partition manuscrite." On p. [1] of the outer bifolium, detached, in Offenbach's hand: "Hoffmann / 2nd acte / n° 2 / 1 Recit - Hoffmann Niclausse / 2 Recit - Hoffmann Niclause et Coppelius / 3. Trio - Hoffmann Nicklaus et Coppelius." The fragment is notated (vocal lines and piano accompaniment only) on eight unnumbered, individual bifolia and the recto of a single sheet of oblong 24-staff paper (blind stamp of Lard-Esnault). It begins with Nicklausse's words "Elle ne rêve plus j'espère" and continues until the end of the trio.

Manuscript notated in full score, the vocal lines in the hand of a copyist, the orchestration in Guiraud's hand, on seven individual bifolia of oblong 24-staff paper (blind stamp of Lard-Esnault), housed in an eighth forming wrappers, with a single sheet inserted in the third bifolium. The manuscript ends on p. [4] of the outer bifolium. The fragment begins with Coppélius's words "C'est moi, Coppélius" and continues until the end of the trio. Marked, in the hand of a copyist on p. [1] of the outer bifolium: "Les contes d'Hoffmann / (2e acte) N° 2 Trio"; in blue pencil, in another hand: "n° 8"; and in pencil, in a different hand: "supprimé."

Act 2, no. 9 - Choeur et scène

A fragment, in Offenbach's hand, notated (words and piano accompaniment only) on three individual bifolia and both sides of a single sheet of oblong 24-staff paper (blind stamp of Lard-Esnault), numbered respectively 6–8 and 8 bis. The fragment begins with Spalanzani's words "Fort bien Cochenille" and continues through half of the second verse of Olympia's song. At the top of p. [1] in pencil, not in Offenbach's hand: "(feuilles supprimées) 2e acte n° 3," and, in blue pencil, "9."

Another fragment, notated in short score in Offenbach's hand on p. [1] through [3] of a single bifolium of oblong 24-staff paper (blind stamp of Lard-Esnault), comprising the two verses of Olympia's song and ending with Spalanzani's words "Allons mes[sieurs]."

Act 2, no. 10 - Scène et romance

A fragment in the hand of a copyist, on a single bifolium of oblong 22-staff paper (blind stamp of Lard-Esnault), with the heading "N° 4 (Les Contes d'Hoffmann) 2e Acte"; also marked, in blue pencil: "Supprimé / Remplacé." The fragment begins with the words "Ils se sont éloignés …" and comprises the vocal lines only.

A fragment notated in the hand of a copyist (vocal line only) on an individual bifolium and both sides of a single sheet of oblong 22-staff paper (blind stamp of Lard), numbered respectively 2 and 3, beginning with Hoffmann's words "Ah! vivre deux" and ending with the word "[a]mour."

Act 2, no. 11

A fragment of recitative, in full score, in Guiraud's hand, on a single sheet of tall 24-staff paper (blind stamp of Lard-Esnault), beginning with Nicklausse's words "Par ma foi si tu savais" and ending with Hoffmann's words "Dieu puissant." Marked in pencil at the top: "Suite n° 10."

A fragment of the same number, in full score, the vocal lines in the hand of a copyist, the orchestration in Guiraud's hand, on both sides of a single sheet of oblong 24-staff paper (blind stamp of Lard-Esnault), beginning with the words "foi si tu savais" and ending with "pas en vie."

A fragment of the récitatif dialogué between Nicklausse and Hoffmann, in full score on a single bifolium of oblong 24-staff paper (blind stamp of Lard-Esnault), numbered 4 (not in Offenbach's hand) and paginated 19–[22], the vocal lines in the hand of a copyist, the orchestration in Guiraud's hand, beginning "Ecoute écoute, écoute ce joyeux signal …" and ending with the words "malheureux fou suivez la belle / ah! pauvre fou, qui riez d'elle …"

A fragment, in Offenbach's hand, in short score, on a bifolium and recto of a single sheet of oblong 20-staff paper (blind stamp of Lard-Esnault). The fragment begins with the words "Tu me fuis," comprises the duettino "Oui, pauvre(s) fou(s)," and ends at Coppélius's entrance. At the top of p. [1] in pencil, not in Offenbach's hand: "2e acte n° 5."

A fragment of the concluding section (in G major) of the same duettino, the vocal lines in the hand of a copyist, the orchestration in Guiraud's hand, on a single bifolium of oblong 24-staff paper (blind stamp of Lard-Esnault), numbered 5 [?] (not in Offenbach's hand), in the hand of a copyist, beginning with the words "qui vs appelle à ses genoux / L'amour m'appelle à ses genoux" and ending "dont aucune âme ne doit jaillir / bientôt une âme en doit jaillir."

Another fragment, in a copyist's hand, in short score, on an oblong sheet of 12-staff paper, beginning with the end of the duettino and continuing through the end of Coppélius's recitative.

Act 3, no. 13 - Romance

A fragment (the vocal line only) on two individual bifolia and both sides of a single sheet of oblong 22-staff paper (blind stamp of Lard), numbered respectively 1–2 and 3 and comprising the entire aria. Marked at the top of p. [1], not in Offenbach's hand: "Andante / (Les Contes d'Hoffmann) / Romance d'Antonia."

Act 3, no. 16 - Récitatif et duo

A fragment of the recitative, in full score, on both sides of two single sheets and a bifolium of oblong 24-staff paper (blind stamp of Lard-Esnault), paginated in pencil, in an unknown hand, 3–4, 5–6, and 7–10, and notated in full score, beginning with Hoffmann's words "[sépa]rés? Je l'ignore" and ending "me console Antonia!" There are additional markings in blue pencil. All eight pages are cancelled in pencil.

Act 3, no. 17A - Trio-finale

Manuscript, in the hand of a copyist, of the entire number, notated (vocal lines only) on eight numbered individual bifolia of oblong 22-staff paper (blind stamp of Lard). Marked at the top of p. [1], not in Offenbach's hand: "N° 6 / (Les Contes d'Hoffmann) / Trio."

Act 3, no. 17B

Manuscript of the melodrama (marked "On parle") for the end of the scene, in Guiraud's hand, in full score on the recto of a single sheet of tall 24-staff paper (blind stamp of Lard-Esnault). The melodrama is the repeat of the "C'est une chanson d'amour …"

A fragment from the last scene, in short score, in the hand of a copyist, on four sides of a single bifolium of 14-staff paper (blind stamp of Lard), beginning with Antonia's words "C'est une chanson d'amour" and ending with Nicklausse's "Malheureux!"

Act 4, Entr'acte and no. 18

On p. [1] of the outer bifolium, in Offenbach's hand: "Les contes d'Hoffmann / 4eme Acte / n° 1 / J.O."; in another hand, in blue pencil: "ancien 4e acte," and in pencil, in yet another hand: "Entracte et n° 18."

Also, a 3-measure musical sketch, in pencil, in Offenbach's hand.

Manuscript, in full score, with piano reduction at the bottom of the page, partly in Offenbach's, partly in Guiraud's hand, beginning with Hoffmann's words "Messieurs silence un refrain amoureux …" until the end of the barcarolle. The manuscript is written on two individual bifolia and a single sheet, numbered respectively 1, 2, and 3 in Offenbach's hand, of oblong 24-staff paper (blind stamp of Lard-Esnault), and placed in a fourth bifolium serving as wrappers. The words and the piano accompaniment, which is present only in the first bifolium, are in Offenbach's hand. The manuscript was completed in full score by Guiraud, beginning with p. [2] of the outer bifolium (first 5 measures of the entr'acte) and the first three pages of bifolium 1. At the top of bifolium 1, in Offenbach's hand: "St Germain 20 Juin 80."

Act 4, no. 18 bis - sortie

Manuscript, in Guiraud's hand, notated in full score on p. [1]–[3] of a single bifolium of tall 24-staff paper (blind stamp of Lard-Esnault). At the top of p. [1] in an unidentified hand, "Nous allons perdre notre argent."

Act 4, no. 18 ter

An orchestral passage, in full score, in Guiraud's hand, notated in black ink, with pencil additions, on both sides of a single sheet of tall 24-staff paper (blind stamp of Lard-Esnault). Marked in blue pencil at the top: "18 ter."

Another orchestral passage, notated in full score in ink, the last 4 measures in pencil, in Guiraud's hand, on four systems, on the recto of a single sheet of tall 24-staff paper (blind stamp of Lard-Esnault). Marked at the top, in black and blue pencil: "n° 18 ter Melodrame (A) / repl: (nous avons beaucoup souffert)."

Act 4, no. 18 quater

An orchestral passage, notated in ink in full score, in Guiraud's hand, on two systems, on the recto of a single sheet of tall 24-staff paper (blind stamp of Lard-Esnault). Marked at the top, in ink: "n° 18 quater / Mélodrame."

Act 4, no. 20

Full-score manuscript, partly in Offenbach's, partly in Guiraud's hand, beginning with the words for the chorus "Giulietta palsambleu" and ending with the reprise of the barcarolle. The manuscript collates as follows: three individual bifolia, followed by two single sheets, followed by seven individual bifolia, with a single sheet laid in the third, followed by a single sheet, stitched with the previous two bifolia; all of oblong 24-staff paper (blind stamp of Lard-Esnault), paginated 1 to 47, and placed in an outer bifolium serving as wrappers. The words and piano accompaniment are in Offenbach's hand, the orchestration in Guiraud's hand. Numerous cancellations, including the whole of p. 31. Beginning on p. 24 and through p. 30, the text and piano accompaniment are in a third, unidentified hand. The orchestration stops on p. 38 and is afterward limited to a few indications or sketches in pencil. On p. [1] of the outer wrapper, in Offenbach's hand: "Contes d'Hoffmann / 4eme acte / n° 4 / J.O." The "n° 4" was subsequently corrected to n° 3, then n° 2. "N° 20," replacing "n° 19" also appears in blue pencil at the top of the page.

A fragment notated in short score, in Offenbach's hand, on the four sides of a single bifolium, numbered 7, of oblong 18-staff paper (blind stamp of Lard-Esnault), beginning with Hoffmann's words "Tiens mes cartes …" and ending with "Voyez le jour aimez." The last page (corresponding to the song "L'amour lui dit la belle," notated in G major) is cancelled in its entirety.

Act 4, no. 22 - Duo

Manuscript fragment in short and full score on the four sides of a single bifolium of oblong 24-staff paper (blind stamp of Lard-Esnault), beginning with Giulietta's words "Ton ami dit vrai" and ending with Hoffmann's words "te quitter non." The vocal lines and piano accompaniment are in the hand of a copyist, the orchestration is in Guiraud's hand.

Act 4, no. 22 bis

An orchestral passage, notated in full score, in Guiraud's hand, on two systems, on the recto of a single sheet of tall 24-staff paper (blind stamp of Lard-Esnault). Marked at the top, in pencil: "22 bis."

Act 5, intermède

Corrected proof sheets from the Choudens orchestral score (music publisher's number A.C. 5303), marked up and corrected in blue pencil (possibly in Guiraud's hand), with an additional manuscript sheet, the whole paginated 1 to 17 and entitled "n° 24 Intermède." The proof sheets comprise the Prélude, act 2 Entr'acte, and act 4 Entr'acte. The intermède was published by Choudens as part of a *Suite d'orchestre des Contes d'Hoffmann*, edited by Ernest Guiraud.

Act 5, no. 23

Manuscript of the chorus "Folie," in Guiraud's hand, on three systems on the recto of a single sheet of tall 24-staff paper (blind stamp of Lard-Esnault). Only the first two bars of orchestration are present. Marked at the top of the page, in black ink: "Contes d'Hoffmann 5eme acte n° 1"; and, in blue pencil: "Supprimé."

Act 5, no. 24

A fragment beginning with the spoken words: "Au diable l'amour et vive l'ivresse," leading to a repeat of the "Glou glou" chorus, and ending with a repeat of the chorus "Jusqu'au matin remplis mon verre." The fragment is largely in Guiraud's hand, with the vocal lines in a different penmanship, written on a combination of nested bifolia and individual sheets (with traces of stubs) of tall 24-staff paper (blind stamp of Lard-Esnault).

The fragment is paginated 1 to 12 in blue pencil. At the top of the first page, also in blue pencil: "N° 24."

An orchestral passage, in full score, in Guiraud's hand, notated on both sides of a single sheet of tall 24-staff paper (blind stamp of Lard-Esnault). Marked in ink, at the top of p. [1]: "A / Contes d'Hoffmann 5me acte"; and, in blue pencil: "24."

Act 5, no. 25

End of the reprise of the Kleinzach song (3 bars only), notated in full score, in Guiraud's hand, on the recto of a single sheet of tall 24-staff paper (blind stamp of Lard-Esnault). Marked in ink at the top: "B"; and in blue pencil: "25."

Melodrama (words and music) notated in full score in Guiraud's hand on the recto of a single sheet of tall 24-staff paper (blind stamp of Lard-Esnault), beginning with the words "Qui êtes vous? Olympia? Brisée" and ending with "A vous le dernier couplet." Marked in pencil, at the top: "25."

Fragment of Stella's arioso "Ah! C'est en vain que mes amours," in short score, in Guiraud's hand, on the recto of a single sheet of tall 24-staff paper (blind stamp of Lard-Esnault), beginning with the words "coeur pour toujours."

Two fragments of an orchestral passage, in full score in Guiraud's hand on the recto of a sheet and both sides of a second sheet of tall 24-staff paper (blind stamp of Lard-Esnault), paginated 1 and 2 and 3 respectively.

Unidentified fragment

A sheet of tall 24-staff paper with 1 measure of music in full score, with notes for the engraver in Guiraud's hand, referring in particular to cuts in no. 10.

Originally from the collection of Raoul Gunsbourg.
Heinrich Schütz to Henry Miller, p. 68–69.
London, Sotheby's, 22–23 Nov. 1984, lot 505.
FRKF 545

Le Décaméron

Partial holograph full-score manuscript, comprising the following numbers:

no. 2: in black ink on three unpaginated bifolia of oblong 20-staff paper. At the top of the first page, in Offenbach's hand: "à Saint Charles / n° 2 / Air de danse"; a different hand has added: "(Décameron)." There are a few corrections in pencil throughout.

FRKF 284

no. 3: in black ink on the first eight pages, unnumbered, of a gathering of three nested bifolia of oblong 20-staff paper (blind stamp of Lard-Esnault). At the top of p. [1] in Offenbach's hand: "n° 3"; in another hand, in pencil: "Vous allez chanter comme prelude un de nos jolis airs / chantez quelques instants." Above the first measure of each of the four vocal parts, in Offenbach's hand: "transposé/e en si."

no. 4: in black ink on the first ten pages, unnumbered, of a gathering of three nested bifolia of oblong 20-staff paper (blind stamp of Lard-Esnault). At the top of p. [1] in Offenbach's hand: "nº 4 / La vie"; in another hand, in pencil: "Comme un conseil antique arrive à leurs oreilles / c'est très bien à parler on n'est pas toujours prompt / celles qui n'auront rien à dire, chanteront -" The vocal line is missing, save for a few words and notes on p. [7], [8], and [9].

no. 6: in black ink on the first six pages, unnumbered, of a gathering of two nested, sewn bifolia of oblong 20-staff paper (blind stamp of Lard-Esnault). At the top of p. [1] in Offenbach's hand, in ink: "nº 6" and, in pencil: "comme du naufrageur ecouterent [?]"; in another hand, in pencil: "prêtèrent en silence un[e] attentive oreille / comme."

no. 8: in black ink on the first six pages, unnumbered, of a gathering of two nested, sewn bifolia of oblong 20-staff paper (blind stamp of Lard-Esnault). At the top of p. [1] in Offenbach's hand, in ink: "nº 8."

Nos. 3, 4, 6, and 8 are placed in an additional bifolium serving as wrappers, marked in pencil, in an unidentified hand: "Air de danse / Lydia / Le Décaméron ou la Grotte d'Azur."

Paris, Dominique Vincent (Drouot), 12 March 1984, lot 322.
FRKF 429

Le Décaméron, ou La grotte d'azur, légende napolitaine in one act by Joseph Méry, was premiered at the Salle Herz in May 1855 ("semi-staged play with songs" according to Grove).

La duchesse d'Albe

Holograph drafts, in full score, for part of the work, n.d., 25 p. Notated in black ink, with some markings in pencil, on six bifolia and a single sheet of oblong 24-staff paper (blind stamp of Lard-Esnault). Beginning with an ensemble at the Père de Rita's words "Voici l'instant de la justification …" The words are then missing, though some of the vocal lines are present, while the orchestral accompaniment is barely sketched in. The text is present again with the words (marked "Recit") "et voici celle à qui la Reine veut l'unir" and the fragment ends on the words "votre souveraine qui vous transmet ses volon-[tés]."

London, Sotheby's, 28 May 1986, lot 504.
FRKF 1142

Holograph manuscript fragment from the German version, 4 p., n.d. The manuscript, in Offenbach's hand, is written on a single bifolium, paginated 47–48 and 57–58, of tall 24-staff paper. It evidently is of two different passages, the first beginning "O Juil'ya," the second with the words "Kind mein Kind." Only the vocal lines and 2 measures from the accompaniment are present.

Marburg, Stargardt, 19 June 1984, lot 884.
FRKF 486

La duchesse d'Albe, opéra-comique in three acts on a libretto by Jules Henri Vernoy, marquis de Saint-Georges, was commissioned by Adolphe Adam for the Théâtre-Lyrique and composed in 1847–48. After the theater closed owing to the 1848 Revolution, Offenbach tried in vain to have it performed in Cologne in a German version.

Élodie, ou le forfait nocturne

Manuscript, in a copyist's hand, of a piano version of the Romance du charcutier from *Élodie*, n.d. Notated in black ink, with additional pencil annotations, on p. [3] of a single bifolium of 16-staff paper (blind stamp of Dantier). On p. [1] in the copyist's hand: "Romance du Charcutier / extraite / de l'Opérette: / Élodie ou le forfait nocturne / musique de J: Offenbach et L. Amat."

Grove lists *Élodie* under Offenbach's contributions to works by other composers. The one-act operetta, libretto by Léon Battu and Hector Crémieux, was premiered at the Théâtre des Bouffes-Parisiens on 19 Jan. 1856.

FRKF 236.10

Entrez, messieurs, mesdames

Holograph manuscript, in full score, of the orchestral introduction, n.d. Notated in black ink, with additional markings in pencil, on the first three pages of a single, unnumbered bifolium of oblong 24-staff paper (blind stamp of Lard-Esnault). At the top of p. [1] in red pencil, possibly in Offenbach's hand: "Messieurs Mesdames (3 coups)"; and, in black pencil: "en la / transposer cet entr'acte 1 ton plus haut / en la." (The score is in G major.) At the top and the bottom of p. [2] in black and red pencil: "rideau."

As the word "entr'acte" suggests, this is possibly recycled from another work from Offenbach's Comédie Française repertory.

Entrez, messieurs, mesdames, prologue on a libretto by Joseph Méry and J. Servières (pseudonym of Ludovic Halévy), was premiered at the Bouffes-Parisiens (Salle Marigny) on 5 July 1855.

FRKF 236.11

Fantasio

Partial and partly holograph full-score manuscript of act 1. Notated in black ink on oblong 24-staff paper (blind stamp of Lard-Esnault). On the title page: "Fantasio / Introduction" (in Offenbach's hand); and "Fantasio / Partitur" in red pencil in an unidentified hand. The manuscript comprises the following numbers:

OFFENBACH [189]

"No. 3 nouveau," in blue pencil in Offenbach's hand, 10 p., on three bifolia, numbered 1 to 3 in his hand.

"Elsbeth / Fantasio / N° 4 / 1er acte," not in Offenbach's hand, 12 p., with annotations in pencil, in German, not in his hand, the text accompanied by a German translation.

"n° 5," in Offenbach's hand; also marked "n° 5 (ancien)" in another hand, 20 p.

"N° 5 bis / Musique de scène de Fantasio (1er acte) / 1° Danse de Fantasio / 2° Marche de Fantasio," in Offenbach's hand, and at the top of the following page, in his hand: "Marche du passant," 3 p.

"1er acte / Fantasio / n° 6," in Offenbach's hand, 7 p., with the heading "Marche" in his hand and, in a different hand: "Choeur des Pénitents."

"1er acte / Fantasio / n° 7," in Offenbach's hand, 8 p.

Unidentified fragment of no. 2, "Ballade," 2 p., beginning with the words "[i]-ci m'asseoir" and ending "comme un point sur un i."

Unidentified, but no. [1], beginning with orchestral introduction[?] without the words except for "-ble qui n'aimât changer avec eux," 10 p., in the hand of a copyist throughout.

Unidentified, 4 p., beginning with Faccio's words "mais puisque tu le sais" and ending with "Oui je"; another fragment of the same number [?] in Offenbach's hand, 4 p., beginning with the words "entreprise baroque" and ending "voilà pourquoi je vais"; another fragment of the same number, in a copyist's hand, 17 p., beginning with the words "vais à la cour" and ending "dans le calme de la nuit," the text only partially filled in, also in German.

According to Christie's, the annotations in German are in the hands of E. Mautner and Richard Genée (co-librettist of *Die Fledermaus*).

In a modern binding, boards decorated with gold floral and geometric patterns on a dark brown background, spine in vellum. Printed label on the front board: "J. Offenbach / Fantasio / Acte I Nr 3–7."

Fantasio, opéra-comique in three acts after Musset's comedy, on a libretto by Paul de Musset and Charles Nuitter, was premiered at the Opéra-Comique on 18 Jan. 1872, and in Vienna on 21 Feb. of the same year. The rest of the manuscript is in the British Library.

London, Christie's, 28 March 1984, lot 139.
FRKF 279

Le fifre enchanté

Holograph full-score manuscript of no. 2, in black ink, with some additional notations in pencil in another hand, on 14 pages spread over four independent bifolia, numbered 1 to 4 in Offenbach's hand, of oblong 24-staff paper (blind stamp of Lard-Esnault), placed in a fifth, unnumbered bifolium serving as wrappers. On the front of the outer bifolium, at the top, in Offenbach's hand: "n° 2 / Duo." In another hand, in pencil: "Le Fifre enchanté / Coraline et Popelinet." At the top of the first page of music, not in Offenbach's hand: "N° 2 enfin parler à ta belle maîtresse. Chut! Silence!" The duo is between Coraline and Popelinet and begins with the words: "Pas de bruit …"

Marburg, Stargardt, 22–23 March 1983, lot 913.
FRKF 216

Holograph full-score manuscript of the finale, in black ink, with some additional notations in pencil in another hand, on 13 pages spread over four independent bifolia, numbered 1 to 4 in Offenbach's hand, of oblong 24-staff paper (blind stamp of Lard-Esnault), placed in a fifth, unnumbered bifolium serving as wrappers. On the front of the outer bifolium, at the top, in Offenbach's hand: "n° 8 / Final." In another hand, in pencil: "Le Fifre enchanté." At the top of the first page of music, not in Offenbach's hand: "N° 8 Finale. Il faut le souffle du Diable. Vous allez voir." The characters involved are Coraline, Rigobert, Mme Robin, Mr Robin, and Popelinet. The sung text begins: "C'est un procureur qu'on demande …"

FRKF 59.5

Le fifre enchanté, operetta in one act, libretto by Charles Nuitter and Étienne Tréfeu, was premiered at Bad Ems on 12 July 1864 and revived in Paris at the Théâtre des Bouffes-Parisiens on 30 Sept. 1868.

La Foire Saint-Laurent

Holograph manuscripts for five numbers for this opéra-comique, 1876 and n.d.

No. 21, in black ink on the four pages of a single bifolium of oblong 24-staff paper (blind stamp of Lard-Esnault), nested within another bifolium serving as wrappers. On the front of the outer bifolium, in Offenbach's hand: "La Foire St Laurent / J.O. / 2d Acte, n° 5." At the top of the first page of music, in Offenbach's hand: "Paris," and signature. In short score, with the piano accompaniment on the bottom two staves.

No. 22, in black ink on the first five pages of two loose bifolia of oblong 24-staff paper (blind stamp of Lard-Esnault), nested within another bifolium serving as wrappers. On the front of the outer bifolium, in Offenbach's hand: "N° 4," cancelled in pencil in another hand and replaced by "n° 3." Signed by Offenbach and dated Paris, 13 Oct. 1876 at the top of the first page of music. In short score, with the piano accompaniment on the bottom two staves.

No. 23, in black ink on 12 pages of three bifolia, numbered 1 to 3 in Offenbach's hand, of oblong 24-staff paper (blind stamp of Lard-Esnault), nested within another bifolium serving as wrappers. On the front of the outer bifolium, in Offenbach's hand: "La Foire / J.O. / 2d Acte, n° 2." In short score, with the piano accompaniment on the bottom two staves.

No. 24, full-score manuscript in black ink on both sides of two single leaves, paginated 1 to 4, of 24-staff paper (blind stamp of Lard-Esnault), nested within a bifolium serving as wrappers. On the front of the outer bifolium, in pencil, in an unidentified hand: "La Foire Saint Laurent." The fragment begins "-semble Etes vous folle" and ends with the words "oui je t'aime."

No. 25, full-score manuscript, 8 p., in black ink on both sides of a single, unnumbered leaf, a bifolium numbered 4, and both sides of a single leaf, numbered 5, of 24-staff paper (blind stamp of Lard-Esnault), nested within the same bifolium as the fragment from no. 24. The fragment begins with the words "dans la terre sur la boutique" and ends "Entrons tous / Deux sous deux."

La Foire Saint-Laurent, opéra-bouffe in three acts, libretto by Hector Crémieux and A. de Saint-Aubin, was premiered at the Folies-Dramatiques on 10 Feb. 1877.

FRKF 236.12

Geneviève de Brabant

Holograph full-score manuscript of a quintet written for the revised version.

Notated in black ink on three unnested bifolia, numbered 1 to 3, and the recto of a single leaf, numbered 4, of oblong 24-staff paper (with two additional lines for the percussion at the bottom), with numerous corrections and deletions in blue and red pencil. The manuscript is placed in a fourth, unnumbered bifolium serving as wrappers. On the front wrapper, in ink, not in Offenbach's hand: "(Chatte Blanche)." Signed by Offenbach and dated 2 Feb. 1875 at the top of p. 1. Also at the top of p. 1, in another hand, in pencil: "pas autant de besogne que j'en voudrais"; at the end of the manuscript, in the same hand: "à 18 bis." The ensemble is written for Armide, Narcisse, Siffroi, Martel, and Golo, replacing five different names, crossed out. The text of the ensemble begins with the words "Au sein des fleurs où vit Armide ..." This particular number was reused for a revival of *La chatte blanche*.

Geneviève de Brabant, opéra-bouffe on a libretto by Adolphe Jaime and Étienne Tréfeu, was premiered at the Théâtre des Bouffes-Parisiens in Paris on 19 Nov. 1859; the revised version in three acts, libretto by Hector Crémieux, was premiered at the Théâtre des Menus-Plaisirs on 26 Dec. 1867, and an expanded version, in five acts, at the Théâtre de la Gaîté on 25 Feb. 1875.

Also, see below under G. Miscellaneous sketches.

New York, Sotheby's, 25 May 1983, lot 44.
FRKF 92

Les Géorgiennes

Holograph manuscript, in full score, 262 p. Notated in black ink, with some annotations in pencil, on bifolia and individual leaves, generally numbered by Offenbach, of oblong 24-staff paper (blind stamp of Lard-Esnault). A few pages, and some headings and indications, are in the hands of copyists. On title page, in the hand of a copyist: "Les Géorgiennes. / Opéra Bouffe / En Trois Actes. / Musique de J. Offenbach. / Grande Partition."

The score comprises the following sections, labelled (unless specified otherwise) in Offenbach's hand:

"Introduction / Feroza"

[in the hand of a copyist:] "N° 1. Choeur d'introduction / Romance de Mirza"

"Chanson Turc [sic] / Feroza / J.O."

"1er acte n° 3"

"n° 4 / [in another hand:] 1er Acte / Feroza"

"1er Acte 4 Bis"

"n° 5 / Final du 1er Acte / Choeur, chanson de la vigne, conjuration / Feroza / J.O."

"Entr'acte et—Introduction du 2d acte"

"N° 3 / Entrée des Tambours / Eintritt der Tambour [sic]"

"n° 4"

"n° 4 bis"

"2nd acte / Duo / Ferosa - Cefalon [?]"

"N° 6 2d acte"

"2° acte n° 7 Final"

"Introduction du 3eme acte"

[not in Offenbach's hand:] "Feroza 3e acte N° 1 / [in a different hand] Partitur des III Akt" "N° 2"

[not in Offenbach's hand:] "3e Acte Feroza / N° 3"

"n° 4 Ferosa 3eme acte"

Bound in heavy blue boards. Octagonal paper label on front board, marked, in the hand of a copyist: "Die schönen Weiber / aus Georgien / Partitur."

Les Géorgiennes, opéra-bouffe in three acts on a libretto by Jules Moineaux and Camille du Locle, was premiered at the Théâtre des Bouffes-Parisiens on 16 March 1864.

FRKF 506

La jolie parfumeuse

Discarded sketches, comprising the following:

1. Holograph short-score manuscript of an aria for Poirot in act 3, in black ink, on 10 pages over three single bifolia, numbered 1–3 in Offenbach's hand, of oblong 24-staff paper (blind stamp of Lard-Esnault), placed in a fourth bifolium serving as wrappers. At the top of the outside bifolium, in the composer's hand: "n° 2 3eme acte," and, in pencil, in another hand: "Parfumeuse / coupe."

2. Holograph manuscript fragment of another aria [?] for Poirot, 5 p., beginning with the words "[ma] foi non" and end-

ing "un lingot ah cher"; written on a single bifolium of oblong 24-staff paper (blind stamp of Lard-Esnault), numbered 2 in Offenbach's hand, followed by a single leaf, numbered 3, placed in a third, unnumbered bifolium, the first page of which appears to be the beginning of the piece, though the vocal line is lacking and only the first 3 bars are sketched in in full score. Marked "Parfumeuse" in pencil across the front of the outer bifolium and "Parfumeuse / coupé" on the first page of bifolium 2.

3. Additional sketches, 11 p., partly in full score, partly in short score, on an unnumbered single leaf, a single leaf numbered 2 in Offenbach's hand, a bifolium numbered 3, and two unnumbered leaves (the second of which does not follow directly), all of oblong 24-staff paper (blind stamp of Lard-Esnault). The fragment begins "Commencez par ôter ces voiles" and ends with Rose's words "ah! tant d'au[dace?]." The leaves are placed in an additional bifolium serving as wrappers, on the front of which are 10 measures of sketches. Marked in pencil, not in Offenbach's hand: "Parfumeuse / coupe."

La jolie parfumeuse, opéra-comique in three acts, libretto by Hector Crémieux and Ernest Blum, was premiered at the Théâtre de la Renaissance on 29 Nov. 1873.

Paris, Dominique Vincent (Drouot), 12 March 1984, lot 327.
FRKF 434

Lischen et Fritzchen

Autograph sketch for the beginning of Friztchen's Couplets (no. 1). Notated in black ink on both sides of a single sheet of oblong 22-staff paper. At the top is written: "n° 1." The manuscript consists of the first 7 measures of the piano accompaniment and the first 14 measures of the vocal line. The name of the character is given as "Fritzerl."

Lischen et Fritzchen, "conversation alsacienne" in one act, libretto by P. Dubois [Paul Boisselot], was premiered at Bad Ems on 21 July 1863 and revived at the Théâtre des Bouffes-Parisiens in Paris on 5 Jan. 1864.

FRKF 236.15

Madame Favart

Manuscript drafts, 11 p., n.d. (ca. 1878), in black ink on 24-staff paper (with two additional lines for the percussion at the bottom).

The drafts comprise a single sheet numbered "a" and written in full score, marked "all.gro vivo," beginning with the words (for the chorus) "Ah cela … Pénétrer près du Roi …" (the text is written over a previous, different text noted in pencil); a single, unnumbered bifolium, with Offenbach's signature at the top, with just the vocal line and piano accompaniment, beginning with the words "… Dieu regarde-le, regarde-moi …"; a single sheet, in full score, numbered 3 bis, beginning "vante votre grace …"; and a bifolium, numbered 4, also in full score, beginning "quittent la place Et quoi que je fasse …" to the end of the number. An additional unnumbered bifolium serves as wrappers.

Folio 3 bis and bifolium 4 appear to be an early draft of the end of no. 20 (Air: "J'entrai dans la royale tente …"). Neither the music nor the text match the published Choudens score. The rest of the manuscript seems to be discarded material for the same scene. Marked in pencil across the front wrapper (apparently not in Offenbach's hand): "Coupures à voir."

New York, Sotheby's, 25 May 1983, lot 46.
FRKF 94

Madame l'archiduc

Holograph manuscript, in short score, of act 2, no. 2, 1874, 20 p. Notated in black ink on five separate bifolia, numbered 1–5 in Offenbach's hand, of oblong 24-staff paper (blind stamp of Lard-Esnault), placed within an additional bifolium serving as wrappers. On the front of the outer bifolium, in Offenbach's hand: "Madame l'archiduc / 2° acte n° 2 / J.O." Signed by Offenbach at the top of p. [1] and dated Aix, 28 June 1874. The manuscript begins with Marietta's words "Le capitaine" and goes until the end of the trio.

Madame l'archiduc, opéra-bouffe in three acts, libretto by Albert Millaud [and Ludovic Halévy], was premiered at the Théâtre des Bouffes-Parisiens on 31 Oct. 1874.

Paris, Laurin-Guilloux-Buffetaud-Tailleur (Drouot), 28 May 1986, lot 227.
FRKF 1160

Mesdames de la Halle

Manuscript, in the hand of a copyist, of part of no. 7 (Septuor bouffe). Notated in ink on both sides of a single sheet of oblong 20-staff paper, which appears to be a cancel, on the evidence of the traces of glue in the four corners. The discarded side comprises 11 measures, beginning with the words "[Mon] âme se déchire," and consists of the vocal parts only. The other side consists of 33 measures, also beginning "mon âme se déchire," with the bass accompaniment for the first 12 measures only.

Mesdames de la Halle, opéra-bouffe in one act, libretto by Armand Lapointe, was premiered at the Théâtre des Bouffes-Parisiens on 3 March 1858.

FRKF 237

Nuit d'Espagne

Holograph manuscript draft, in full score, of a scene from this unfinished work for soloists and chorus, n.d., 49 p. Notated in black ink on tall 22-staff paper, paginated 59–107 (not in Offenbach's hand). At the bottom of p. 59, in pencil, in an unidentified hand: "[cancelled: D d'Albe] Nuit d'Espagne." Only the string parts are present (but not complete). The vocal lines and text are intermittently notated.

Bound in greenish gray marbled paper boards and green morocco; on the spine: "Offenbach / La duchesse d'Albe."

Nuit d'Espagne (or *Nuit en Espagne*, but neither title may be Offenbach's) is an uncompleted project, dating probably from the years 1845–50, of which only one act survives; not in Grove or Yon.

London, Sotheby's, 9–10 May 1985, lot 170.
FRKF 772

Die Rheinnixen / Les fées du Rhin

Holograph manuscript, in short score, n.d., ca. 195 p. Notated in black ink, with pencil additions and corrections, on individual bifolia of oblong 24-staff paper (blind stamp of Lard-Esnault). The French text is in Offenbach's hand, the German text, in pencil, in the hand of Alfred von Wolzogen. Stage directions are present throughout, in Offenbach's hand.

The manuscript comprises the following sections, as labelled by Offenbach:

> No. 1, "Introduction" (signed "Jacques Offenbach" at the top of p. 1) is written on bifolium 1 and first two pages of bifolium 2; no. 2, "air," on bifolium 2, p. [3] through bifolium 1 [bis], p. [2]; no. 3 (previously marked 4 in Offenbach's hand), "Marche des paysans," from bifolium 1 [bis], p. [2] through bifolium 3, p. [2]; no. 5, "Trio," from bifolium 3, p. [3] through a single folio numbered 5; no. 6 (previously marked "n° 1" in Offenbach's hand), "Choeur de soldats," bifolium 6, p. [1] through bifolium 7, p. [1]; no. 7 (previously 8 in Offenbach's hand), "Chanson à boire," from bifolium 7, p. [2] through bifolium 9, p. [1].

> The next section is preceded by a title page with the heading, in Offenbach's hand: "Recit de Ulrich avec choeur / et / Final / du 1er acte" and comprises the following: one bifolium, marked "no. 9" (not in Offenbach's hand); no. 10, marked in Offenbach's hand "Final," eight bifolia and p. [1–2] of a ninth, numbered 1–9 in Offenbach's hand.

> The section corresponding to act 2 is housed in a bifolium serving as wrappers and marked in pencil (not in Offenbach's hand) "Fées du Rhin / (alle[mand] et Français)" and comprises seven bifolia and two single folios, numbered 1–7 and 2 bis and 4 bis in Offenbach's hand. The numbers are identified in German, not in Offenbach's hand. The only one identified by Offenbach is "Trio bouffe" (folio 2 bis, recto). At the end of bifolium 7, p. [2], in Offenbach's hand: "fin de 2nd Acte."

> Act 3 comprises ten bifolia, numbered 1 to 10 in Offenbach's hand, and two single folios, numbered 1 bis and 1 ter, also in his hand. Bifolium 1 is marked "3eme acte" in Offenbach's hand and signed "J. Offenbach." On bifolium 1, p. [3], the indication "n° 2 / Ballet" (music not present) is changed to "N. 17" in an unidentified hand. An unidentified hand has also filled in sections left blank by Offenbach with reference numbers. At the top of bifolium 8, p. [2] in Offenbach's hand: "Final."

> The manuscript of act 4 is housed in a bifolium serving as wrappers and marked, in Offenbach's hand, "4eme acte / Les Fées du Rhin / Hedwig et Conrad / [two words not deciphered]." It comprises six bifolia, numbered 1–6 in Offenbach's hand, and an additional three bifolia, numbered 1–3, also in his hand. At the top of bifolium 6, p. [4], which is otherwise blank, in Offenbach's hand: "Duo d'Edwige et d'Ulrich"; at the top of bifolium 1, 2nd series, in his hand: "Duo dramatique."

> The last section, housed in a bifolium serving as wrappers, is marked "Finale" in Offenbach's hand. It comprises three bifolia and a single folio, numbered 1–3 and 3 bis in his hand.

Holograph manuscript of act 2, nos. 13–15, in full score, 61 p. Notated in black ink, with additions and corrections in black, red, and blue pencil, on a gathering of six nested, stitched bifolia, followed by a single bifolium; a gathering of four nested, stitched bifolia, also followed by a single bifolium; and a gathering of three nested, stitched bifolia, all of oblong 24-staff paper (blind stamp of Lard-Esnault). The orchestration and musical annotations (in French) are in Offenbach's hand, the words (in German only) and vocal lines usually in the hand of a copyist and occasionally in Offenbach's hand.

> The first gathering begins at the end of no. 12 at Hedwig's words "[Und dass ihr] Sang" and ends (on p. [4] of the single bifolium) with the passage in unison following Conrad's first statement of "Gold ist [gar eine schöne Sache]"; the second gathering begins at the end of the second repeat of the ensemble "Gold ist gar eine schöne Sache" and ends (on p. [4] of the single bifolium) in the middle of the ensemble "Er dienet unserer Sache"; the third gathering begins just before the third and final repeat of "Gold ist gar eine schöne Sache" and ends at Armgard's words "Du sollst gerettet sein!" There is also an additional page, cut in half, entirely in Offenbach's hand, evidently a cancel for an unidentified passage from no. 14. Numerous passages cancelled throughout.

Paris, Laurin-Guilloux-Buffetaud-Tailleur (Drouot), 30 June 1987, lot 148.
FRKF 1112

Partly holograph full-score manuscript of act 3 of the opera, 164 unpaginated leaves of oblong 24-staff paper, including six blank pages.

> The last page, comprising only 3 measures of music, is present only as a fragment, pasted on the free back endpaper. The vocal lines and words are generally in the hand of a copyist, while several passages (e.g. the end of no. 25) are in Offenbach's. The list of instruments is also in the hand of a copyist, with additions and corrections by Offenbach. Some tempo indications are in Offenbach's hand.

Numerous passages throughout are cancelled in black, blue, or red pencil. Page [1] is a cancel, formerly sealed with red wax. It is preceded by a page with 7 bars, entirely in Offenbach's hand, with the heading, also in his hand: "Introduction du 3eme acte"; on the right side are the stamp of the Hof-Operntheater and the title, not in Offenbach's hand: "Die Rhein Nixen / 3ter Partitur / 4.2.64." On the recto of the cancelled page, in a copyist's hand: "Musique de J. Offenbach. / Acte Quatrième. / Grande Partition." The music begins on the verso. There is another cancel (4 measures substituted for 7) three pages before the end of no. 28 ("duo").

Dark green cloth binding. On front board, on an octagonal paper label, stamped "Kaiser:König:Hof-Operntheater," in the hand of a copyist: "Archiv Nº 323. / 4 / 2 / 64 / Die Rhein Nixen. / Oper in drei Akten. Ins. v. Ruitter [sic]. Musik von J. Offenbach. / Partitur." On front free endpaper, stamp of "Kaiser:König:Hof-Operntheater" and title (not in Offenbach's hand): "Archiv Nº 323. / 4 / 2 / 64 / Die Rhein Nixen. / Grosse romantische Oper in drei Akten von Ruitter [sic] deutsch bearbeitet von Freiherrn von Wolzogen. / Musik von Jaques [sic] Offenbach. / Partitur / 3ter Akt."

Paris, Laurin-Guilloux-Buffetaud-Tailleur (Drouot), 23 June 1989, lot 108.

FRKF 1347

Holograph manuscript of act 4, nos. 26–27, in full score, n.d., 24 p.

Notated in black ink on a gathering of six nested, stitched bifolia of oblong 24-staff paper (blind stamp of Lard-Esnault). Portions of the text, in German, are in Offenbach's hand, the rest in another hand. Begins with Armgard's words "Frantz! Frantz!" (followed by his "Ja, es ist Wahrheit") and ends with Conrad's words "Was wollet ihr?" Numerous cancellations in black or blue pencil.

Paris, Laurin-Guilloux-Buffetaud-Tailleur (Drouot), 30 June 1987, lot 148.

FRKF 1112

Holograph manuscript of the text of the last scene (including stage directions), with musical example set on the text "Que votre coeur de père …"

At head of manuscript: "après le duo d'Edwige et d'Ulrich." Notated in black ink on two 8vo bifolia of laid paper with the monogram "JO" embossed on the first page of each bifolium. The musical example, on p. [4], comprises only the first 14 measures. Accompanied by a carbon copy of a typewritten transcription.

Marburg, Stargardt, 19–30 Nov. 1983, lot 927.

FRKF 146

A single leaf of sketches for 12 measures, notated in ink (the text in pencil) on two staves on a sheet of 24-staff paper (blind stamp of Lard-Esnault). The text is in German.

FRKF 236.23

Die Rheinnixen, Grosse romantische Oper in four acts, libretto by Offenbach and Charles Nuitter, was premiered at the Hofoper in Vienna, in a translation by Alfred von Wolzogen, on 4 Feb. 1864.

Robinson Crusoé

Holograph rough sketches for the duet between Robinson and Vendredi, n.d., written in black ink and pencil on the four pages of a single bifolium, numbered 1 in Offenbach's hand, of 24-staff paper (blind stamp of Lard-Esnault). The manuscript is in short score, with the piano accompaniment notated on the bottom two staffs. The first and fourth pages are cancelled in ink. The text is present only on p. [4], beginning with the words "il vient un jour où l'on voit un sourire …"

Robinson Crusoé, opéra-comique in three acts, libretto by Eugène Cormon and Hector Crémieux, was premiered at the Opéra-Comique on 23 Nov. 1867.

FRKF 236.24

Le Roi Carotte

Autograph manuscript, incomplete, 1870, in black ink on oblong 24-staff music paper (blind stamp of Lard Esnault), with corrections in ink and pencil. The manuscript comprises:

1. Two bifolia, not nested, within a third bifolium serving as wrappers: The title page reads: "Roi Carotte / 1er acte. / 1er tableau. Number for Fridolin and chorus Fridolin: 'Le cas est assez délicat …'" In short score.

2. Two bifolia, not nested, within a third bifolium serving as wrappers (wrappers torn, missing one sheet); 2 single sheets and one bifolium. "Le Roi Carotte / [crossed out:] 1er acte Nº 1 1er tableau." Below, in blue pencil: "Nº 1." Inscribed (not in Offenbach's hand): "Mr P.A. Dumas / 24 rue Notre-Dame des Victoires Number for Fanfarinet 'En fait d'amour je me proclame instruit à fond …'" The bifolium is marked 4 in the upper right corner. May be incomplete. In short score. At top of first page of bifolium 4, sketches for the chorus.

3. Five numbered bifolia, not nested, within a sixth bifolium serving as wrappers. On front wrapper: "Roi Carotte / 1er acte / 1er tableau / Duo." In blue pencil: "Nº 5," corrected in ink as 3. Part of the text is written out in pencil under the vocal line. Duet for Cunégonde and Fridolin: "Ah vous sortez du couvent."

4. A single sheet, numbered 1 in upper right corner, "en route / gaiement" (on Rataplan chorus), continuing on the first two pages of a bifolium numbered 2 in upper right corner.

5. A single, unnumbered bifolium, with the end or part of a duet: "Viens [donc?] fuyons / Fuir et pourquoi."

6. Four bifolia numbered 6, 9, 11, 12: For soloists (Fridolin, Robin, Piperlo, Schnaps) and chorus, from "pipe et pas de courroux mais fume …" Bifolium 9 is a fragment from same; on p. [4]: "choeur des armures." Bifolia 11, 12: end of the same number.

7. Five consecutive bifolia, numbered 1 to 5, in a sixth bifolium serving as wrappers, torn, first page of bifolium present: "Le Roi Carotte / N° 9 (corrected in pencil as 7) / 1er acte / 4 eme Tableau." In blue pencil: "N° 9" (corrected in black pencil as 7). At top of bifolium 1: "& melodrame - n° 9 / seulement choeurs," and date: "16 juin 70." Ensemble for Fridolin, Truc, Koffre, Traccz, and Schnaps, and a chorus of Courtisans and Tailleurs ("Plus éclatant que l'éclatante aurore …").

8. A single, unnumbered bifolium, one voice: "-fin vraiment c'est assommant …" continuing on to two bifolia numbered 5 and 6. Followed by two bifolia numbered 5 and 6, beginning "le pied de grue sur mon escalier. Ah quel ennui, ah quel tourment …"

9. A single, unnumbered sheet, beginning with stage direction "ayant envie d'éternuer" and text "ma Princesse …" (ensemble on verso), continuing on five bifolia numbered 10, 11, 12, 13, and 14 (split). Incomplete.

10. One bifolium, numbered 2: ensemble with chorus beginning "Celui-ci fut Ottokar …" continuing on to a single leaf numbered 3 (with additional sketches, in reverse, on five staves, at the top).

11. A single sheet, marked in pencil: "Acte III / 10e tableau / n° 21 Duo de l'anneau / Fridolin et Cunégonde"; with 8 additional bars of drafts on a 6-staff system. Beginning: "Quoi puissance souveraine et couronne de roi …"

12. A single unnumbered sheet, at the top of which is: "Acte 3e / 2° Tableau / Scene 1ere Replique - Robin: Il n'y a que ça à faire." Eleven bars of music, scored for strings, on a 5-staff system. Above the third bar: "(Replique) Et voici ma replique."

Le roi Carotte, opéra-comique in four acts, libretto by Victorien Sardou after E.T.A. Hoffmann, was premiered at the Théâtre de la Gaîté in Paris on 15 Jan. 1872.

Paris, Laurin-Guilloux-Buffetaud-Tailleur (Drouot), 30 June 1987, lot 150.
FRKF 1113

Tromb-Al-Ca-Zar

Holograph manuscript of the "Ali Baba" waltz, in short score, notated in black ink on a single leaf of 12-staff paper. A text, which gives the waltz its name ("Ali Baba la chou" etc.), is written under the last 17 bars of the right-hand part. An unknown hand (seemingly not Offenbach's) has corrected Ali into Ala throughout. The work, in F major, has 58 measures. At the top of the manuscript, in pencil, in an unidentified hand: "Valse d'Offenbach" and an unidentified signature.

Tromb-Al-Ca-Zar, ou Les criminels dramatiques, "bouffonnerie musicale" in one act on a libretto by Charles Dupeuty and É. Bourget, was premiered at the Théâtre des Bouffes-Parisiens on 3 April 1856.

Also listed by Grove as "Alababa," ca. 1855.
FRKF 236.04

La vie parisienne

Holograph manuscript fragment from no. 6 (act 1, finale), on both sides of a single leaf of 24-staff paper. Only the vocal line and part of the bass accompaniment are notated. The text begins with the indication "Presto" and the words "[en-]cor Hurrah Hurrah Hurrah Je viens de débarquer" from the Bresilian's aria.

La vie parisienne, opéra-bouffe in five (then four) acts, libretto by Henri Meilhac and Ludovic Halévy, was premiered at the Théâtre du Palais Royal on 31 Oct. 1866; the revised version was premiered at the Théâtre des Variétés on 25 Sept. 1873.

FRKF 237

Whittington

Holograph full-score manuscript of no. 23 [?] [Air …], 4 p., n.d. [ca. 1874]. Notated in black ink, on 12 staves, on two half sheets, glued together, of Lard-Esnault paper (27 × 17.5 cm). At the top of the manuscript, in Offenbach's hand: "Voyage / act II / n° 10a / Offenbach." The vocal line is without text and is marked simply as "song."

This number was recycled by Offenbach into the revised version of *Le voyage dans la lune*, given at the Variétés in 1878 with the famous Thérésa.

New York, Sotheby's, 25 May 1983, lot 47.
FRKF 95

Holograph full-score manuscript of no. 33. Notated in black ink on two independent bifolia of 24-staff paper (blind stamp of Lard-Esnault), numbered 1 and 2 in Offenbach's hand, and nested in two additional bifolia serving as wrappers. On p. [1] of the first outer bifolium, in ink: "Dick Whittington / Introduction instrumentale," and in pencil: "A Voir," neither in Offenbach's hand. On p. [1] of the second outer bifolium, in ink, in Offenbach's hand: "n° 5 / 2d Tableau / n° 1" and, in pencil, not in his hand: "?? Whittington." The number is for "Le sonneur" [?], "Le capitaine," and a "Choeur des moines" [?], and begins with the words "Courons sur sa trace …" The scoring is incomplete.

FRKF 236.34

Whittington, grand opéra bouffe-férrie in three acts on a libretto by Charles Nuitter and Étienne Tréfeu, translated by Henry Brougham Farnie, was premiered at the Alhambra Theatre in London on 26 Dec. 1874.

B. INCIDENTAL MUSIC

Le barbier de Séville

Full-score manuscript, in the hand of A. Roques, of Offenbach's stage music for Beaumarchais's play, 42 p., 1852. The manuscript is notated in black and blue ink on oblong 16-staff paper, numbered 165 to 208 in an unidentified hand. On p. 165, title: "Le Barbier de Séville / arrangé pour le Théâtre Français / Partition / A.R. Paris 25 7bre 1852."

The score comprises the following numbers:

> p. 166: "Air de Lindor" (without the words).
>
> p. 167–78: "1er Entr'acte = sur l'air = veux-tu ma rosinette = arrange Pour Orchestre = A.R. ="
>
> p. 179–83: "2° Entracte."
>
> p. 184–85: "Air de Rosine" ("quand dans la plaine …").
>
> p. 187–89: "Air Traditionel [sic] de Bartholo (3eme acte) / dans le Barbier de Séville / Partition / A.R. Paris 7bre 1852" ("veux-tu ma Rosinette …").
>
> p. 191–202: "Orage."
>
> p. 203–08: "Boléro."

FRKF 236.09

Le mariage de Figaro

Full-score manuscript, in the hand of A. Roques, of Offenbach's stage music for Beaumarchais's play, 15 p., 1852. The manuscript is notated in black ink on oblong 16-staff paper, numbered 145 to 159 in an unidentified hand. On p. 145, title: "Mariage de Figaro / (orchestré pour le Théatre Français) / Partition / A.R. Paris ce 15 7bre 1852."

The score comprises the following numbers:

> p. 146: "2° acte / n° 1 / romance" (without the words) also p. 146: "4eme acte / = réplique = du n° 2."
>
> p. 147–52: "Réplique = il faut bien souffrir ce qu'on ne peut empêcher."
>
> p. 152–53: n° 5 "(Réplique) (Diantre soit des femmes qui fourent des épingles partout)."
>
> p. 154–55: "(replique) (elle etoit cachetée d'une Epingle qui là outrageusement pique)."
>
> p. 155–56: "(replique) (c'est une drole de tête)."
>
> p. 157: "(replique) = attendez je vais le faire déchanter."
>
> p. 158–59: "5ème acte (replique) Tous me feront honneur et plaisir."

On the last page, bound with the manuscript and numbered 164, 6 measures of unidentified drafts in Offenbach's hand, notated on two staves.

FRKF 236.16

C. CHORAL MUSIC

Agnus Dei

Partly holograph manuscript of this setting of the liturgical text, 7 p., in two parts, both on oblong 14-staff paper (some with the blind stamp of Lard-Esnault). The first, on the recto of a leaf numbered 99 in pencil (not in Offenbach's hand), is entirely holograph and comprises the soprano line and the organ (or piano?) accompaniment for the third verse ("Agnus Dei … Dona nobis pacem"); the second, in the hand of a copyist, is an incomplete set of parts, bound as follows:

> p. 109–10: "Soprano solo."
>
> p. 107: "2e soprano solo."
>
> p. 105: "1°" [tenor?] headed "Marchand" (possibly in Offenbach's hand).
>
> p. 101: "2°" [tenor?] headed "Tajan" (possibly in Offenbach's hand).
>
> p. 103: "1° Basse."

At the head of p. 99, not in Offenbach's hand: "N° 28."

Grove lists an *Agnus Dei* for solo, chorus, and organ, dated 1858.

FRKF 236.02

Après le jour

Largely holograph manuscript parts for this ballad for soprano, baritone, chorus, and orchestra. On title page, in Offenbach's hand: "Choeur et Ballade / après le jour / Parties de choeur Quatuor et / Parti[ti]on"; and in pencil, not in Offenbach's hand: "No. 1." Also a memorandum in three points in Offenbach's hand, headed "attention à faire," cancelled.

The manuscript comprises:

> 1. The piano part, in Offenbach's hand, with vocal lines and words in black ink on p. [2]–[4] of a single bifolium of tall 18-staff paper (blind stamp not deciphered, possibly Lard-Esnault), with the heading "n° 1" in Offenbach's hand.
>
> 2. The first soprano solo part, notated in Offenbach's hand on single staves on a bifolium and the recto of a single leaf of tall 12-staff paper (blind stamp not deciphered), marked "n° 1 / 1er Soprano Solo" in Offenbach's hand.
>
> 3. The second soprano solo part, notated in Offenbach's hand on single staves on the first three pages of a bifolium of tall

12-staff paper (blind stamp not deciphered), marked "n° 2 / 2em Soprano (Solo)" in Offenbach's hand.

4. The baritone part, with parts of the choral interventions and accompaniment, notated in Offenbach's hand on single staves on the first three pages of a bifolium of tall 12-staff paper (blind stamp of Lard-Esnault); cancel (for the bottom 3-staff system) pinned in at the bottom of p. 1.

5. The first soprano choral part, in three copies, only the first in Offenbach's hand throughout, all three notated on the first three pages of a bifolium of tall 12-staff paper (blind stamp of Lard-Esnault). At the top of p. [1] in Offenbach's hand in two of the copies: "N° 1 / 1er Soprano / Introduction - Choeur et Ballade."

6. The second soprano choral part, in three copies, only the first in Offenbach's hand throughout, all three notated on the first three pages of a bifolium of tall 12-staff paper (blind stamp of Lard-Esnault for copy 2, not deciphered in the others). At the top of p. [1] in Offenbach's hand, in copy 1: "2eme Soprano / Introduction et Ballade"; in copy 2: "n° 1 / Introduction Choeur et Ballade"; cancel pinned in p. [2] of copy 2, for the middle 3-staff system. Unidentified sketches on p. [4] of the first copy.

7. The first tenor choral part, in six copies, only the first in Offenbach's hand throughout, the first two notated on the four pages of a bifolium of tall 12-staff paper, the other four on 12- or 14-staff paper (blind stamps of Lard-Esnault and not deciphered). At the top of p. [1] of copy 1, in Offenbach's hand: "1er Tenor / Introduction et Ballade"; corrections in Offenbach's hand in several other copies.

8. The second tenor choral part, in six copies, only the first in Offenbach's hand throughout, notated on the first three pages of bifolia of tall 12- and 14-staff paper (blind stamps of Lard-Esnault and not deciphered). At the top of p. [1] of copy 1, in Offenbach's hand: "2eme Tenor / Introduction Choeur et Ballade."

9. The first bass choral part, in six copies, only the first in Offenbach's hand throughout, notated on the first three pages of bifolia of tall 12- and 14-staff paper (blind stamps of Lard-Esnault and Dardart). At the top of p. [1] of copy 1, in Offenbach's hand: "Pre Basse / Introduction Choeur et Ballade" (the last four words also in his hand in one other copy).

10. The second bass choral part, in six copies, only the first in Offenbach's hand throughout, notated on the first three pages of bifolia of tall 12- and 14-staff paper (blind stamps of Lard-Esnault, Dardart, and Dantier Fils). At the top of p. [1] of copy 1, in Offenbach's hand: "2ème Basse / Introduction Choeur et Ballade" (the last four words also in his hand in one other copy).

11. The first violin part, on the verso of a single sheet and the first seven pages of two nested bifolia of tall 12-staff paper (no blind stamp located), marked at the top of the first page in Offenbach's hand: "Introduction Choeur et Ballade," and on the recto of the first sheet, in pencil, possibly in Offenbach's hand: "n° 1 / Choeur d'Introduction / Violon 1°"

12. The second violin part, on pages [2]–[8] of two nested bifolia of tall 12-staff paper (no blind stamp located), marked on the recto of the first sheet, in pencil, possibly in Offenbach's hand: "n° 1 / 2° Violon / Choeur d'Introduction." Pasted-in cancel on p. [8].

13. The viola part, on pages [2]–[8] of two nested bifolia of tall 12-staff paper (no blind stamp located), marked on the recto of the first sheet, in pencil, possibly in Offenbach's hand: "n° 1 / Alto / Choeur d'Introduction." Pasted-in cancel at the top of p. [8].

14. The cello and double bass part, in two copies, on pages [2]–[8] of two nested bifolia of tall 12-staff paper (no blind stamp located), marked on p. [2] in Offenbach's hand in copy 1 only: "Choeur Introduction et Ballade" and, on the recto of the first sheet of copy 1, in pencil: "n° 1. Introduction Ballade." Pasted-in cancel at the top of p. [8] in copy 1.

Some of the text and vocal lines are present in all the instrumental parts.

The work is dated 1846 by Grove.

FRKF 540

Ave Maria

Holograph rough draft of this choral work for soprani, tenors, and basses, in black ink on pages [1] and [2] of a single bifolium of oblong 16-staff paper. Noted on seven 4-staff systems, without accompaniment. On p. [3] are brief, unidentified sketches, only the first of which, notated on four staffs, appears to be related.

Dated ca. 1865 by Grove.

FRKF 236.07

Sérénade, for male choir

Manuscript of the tenor part in the hand of a copyist, on the recto of a single sheet of 12-staff paper. At the top of the page: "Nr 41 / 1er Ténor / Sérénade." Only the vocal line is present. At the bottom, in pencil, in an unidentified hand: "autographe de sa femme Herminie."

FRKF 237

D. SONGS

"Absence"

Holograph manuscript of this song for tenor or soprano voice and piano, n.d., notated in black ink on two pages, possibly belonging to a single oblong bifolium of 16-staff paper. The pagination is not in Offenbach's hand. Only part of the piano accompaniment is present. At the top of the manuscript, in Offenbach's hand: "Absence" and in another hand "N° 29" on p. 2 and "N° 46" on p. 3. On p. 4, unidentified sketches in pencil, notated on one staff and representing 9 measures. The poem by Théophile Gautier is the same as the one set by Berlioz (first two verses) in *Les nuits d'été*.

Not listed in Grove.
FRKF 236.01

"Aimons sur l'onde harmonieuse"

Holograph manuscript of this song for soprano or tenor voice and unspecified accompaniment, in black ink on a single folio of 12-staff paper, torn at the bottom (blind stamp of Lard-Esnault). The manuscript comprises the vocal line and only the first 3 bars of the accompaniment (noted on one staff only). The text begins: "Aimons sur l'onde harmonieuse / Où Venise victorieuse / Un jour montra comme Vénus / Ses charmes nus." At the top of the manuscript, in pencil, in an unidentified hand: "Nº 59."

Not listed in Grove.
FRKF 236.03

"Hier la nuit d'été"
"Roses et papillons"

Holograph manuscripts for these songs for soprano or tenor voice and piano, written in ink and pencil on six pages of 16-staff paper. They appear to be a succession of three bifolia, bound together in а contemporary binding.

> On p. [3] of the first bifolium, a draft of "Roses et papillons," the vocal line only (in the upper left corner, in pencil, not in Offenbach's hand: "nº 32") and on p. [1] of the second bifolium, a brief sketch for the beginning of "Hier la nuit d'été" (limited to the first eight words, written in Offenbach's hand: "moi j'étais devant toi, plein de joie"). The same pages contain various drafts in pencil, possibly for "Roses et papillons," notated on two 3-staff and two 2-staff systems, without words.
>
> On p. [2] and [3] of the second bifolium, another, complete manuscript of "Roses et papillons," the piano part also not sketched in; on p. [4] of the second bifolium, a first draft of "Hier la nuit d'été," the vocal line mainly, with only 3 bars of the piano accompaniment (with additional sketches in ink and pencil at the bottom, possibly for the piano accompaniment, both notated on one staff).
>
> On p. [1] of the third bifolium, another complete draft (vocal line only) of "Hier la nuit d'été," with the text written out in its entirety at the bottom, in Offenbach's hand (in the upper left corner, in pencil, not in Offenbach's hand: "nº 7").
>
> Traces of foliation, not in Offenbach's hand: 88 (on p. [2] of the first bifolium), 81 ter (on p. [3] of the second bifolium), 81 bis (on p. 1 of the third bifolium).

Neither song is listed in Grove.
FRKF 236.13; 236.25

"Jeune fillette reste coquette"

Holograph manuscript of this song, n.d., in black ink on a single sheet of 10-staff laid paper, cropped at the bottom. In the upper right corner, in pencil, not in Offenbach's hand: "Jeune Fillette." Above the first bars of music, in Offenbach's hand: "en répétant ce doux refrain." Only the vocal line is present.

Not listed in Grove.
FRKF 236.14

"Minuit amène le mystère"

Holograph manuscript of this song for soprano or tenor voice and piano, in black ink on the second and third pages of a single bifolium of 12-staff paper (blind stamp of Lard-Esnault). On p. [1], title in pencil, not in Offenbach's hand: "Le mystère de minuit / Nº 53." The author of the words is not identified in Grove.

FRKF 236.17

"Nocturne"

Holograph manuscript of this song for soprano or tenor voice and piano, on a poem by Henri Vernoy de Saint-Georges, 3 p., notated in black ink on the second, third, and fourth pages of a single bifolium of 12-staff paper. On p. [1], title in pencil, not in Offenbach's hand: "Nocturne / Nº 60." At the top of p. [2] in Offenbach's hand: "Nocturne. Paroles de Mr de St Georges musique / de Jacques Offenbach." Incipit: "Aux bois ma bergère jolie …" Listed by Grove as "Aux bois ma bergère, nocturne." Also on p. [1], 5 bars of rough sketches notated on one staff in Offenbach's hand.

FRKF 236.18

"Pablo, boléro"

Holograph manuscript of this song for two voices and piano, n.d., 8 p. Only the first measure of the piano accompaniment is present. Notated in black ink on one side of a single leaf, the four pages of a bifolium, and the first three pages of another bifolium of 12-staff paper. Incipit : "Pablo reprends ta mandoline …" Listed by Grove as being for soprano and tenor.

FRKF 236.19

"Le ramier blessé"

Holograph manuscript of this song for soprano or tenor. Notated in black ink on the second and third pages of a bifolium and the first page of another bifolium of 12-staff paper (blind stamp of Lard-Esnault). At the top of p. [2]

in Offenbach's hand: "Le Ramier blessé." On p. [1] in pencil, not in Offenbach's hand: "Le ramier blessé / N° 56." Only the vocal line is present. Incipit: "Autour de moi quand tout dort …"

Not listed in Grove.

FRKF 236.22

"Le sylphe"

Manuscript, in the hand of a copyist, of this song for soprano or tenor voice, cello, and piano, n.d., 18 p., in three 4-staff systems per page, on five nested bifolia, stitched together, of 12-staff paper (blind stamp of Lard-Esnault). On cover, in red ink: "(Piano) / Le Sylphe / musique de / J. Offenbach." Numerous corrections in pencil, in an unidentified hand, on p. [4]–[9], suggest that part of the music was adapted, with alternative words, as a duet for Robinson and Vendredi in *Robinson Crusoé* (on the words: "A toi notre existence!"). Words by Leube according to Grove. Incipit: "Toi qu'en ces murs pareille aux rêveuses Sylphides …"

FRKF 236.30

"La tramontane"

Holograph manuscript of this song for soprano or tenor voice and piano, in black ink on the second and third pages of a single bifolium of 12-staff paper (traces of Lard-Esnault blind stamp). On p. [1] in pencil, not in Offenbach's hand: "La Tramontane." Also on p. [1], unidentified sketches, in ink, scattered over five staffs. More such sketches on p. [4]. The last 6 bars at the top of p. [3], representing an original, more developed ending, are cancelled. Incipit: "Au loin mugit la tramontane …" The author of the text is not identified in Grove.

FRKF 236.31

E. DANCE MUSIC

Polka

Holograph manuscript short score and ten orchestral parts.

The piano score is written in black ink on the second and third pages of a single bifolium of oblong 14-staff paper (blind stamp of Lard-Esnault); the second trio is written on the recto of a single sheet of similar paper. The first four systems are written on a cancel, pasted in. The title, "Polka," in Offenbach's hand appears above the first measure. On p. [1] in pencil, not in Offenbach's hand: "Polka." In C major.

The parts are for the following instruments (the headings in quotation marks are in Offenbach's hand): [first violin], "2d Violin," [viola], "Basse" [cello], "Basse" [double bass], "Flute," "Clarinette," "Piston en la," [oboe/piccolo?], [oboe/piccolo?].

They are written on single sheets of 12-staff paper (some with the blind stamp of Lard), with the exception of the last, which is on the verso of a smaller sheet of paper (blind stamp of Lard-Esnault), torn at the bottom.

FRKF 236.21

Suite de danses en ut majeur

Holograph manuscript of the second flageolet part, notated in black ink on the recto of a single sheet of oblong 10-staff paper. At the top of the page, in Offenbach's hand: "2°" On the verso, unidentified sketches in black ink.

FRKF 236.27

Suite de valses

Fragmentary holograph full-score manuscript, notated in ink on 17 unnumbered pages of 17-staff laid paper. At the top of p. [1], in pencil, not in Offenbach's hand: "Fragment de valses, vers 1840." Pages [1]–[6] are untitled; p. [7]–[9] are headed no. 1; p. [10]–[13] no. 2; and p. [14]–[17] no. 3. Only the first violin part is present most of the time, though lacking on p. [2] and [3] where only the bass line is present. Other parts are occasionally present.

FRKF 236.28

Suite de valses

Fragmentary holograph full-score manuscript, in black ink on 32 pages of 18-staff paper (traces of Lard-Esnault blind stamp), foliated 1 to 16. Only the first 27 measures are fully orchestrated. The string section is complete through folio 4v, with some wind parts. Afterward, the first violin is the only section present, save for the trombones on folio 8v and 9r. At the top of folio 1r, in pencil, not in Offenbach's hand: "vers 1840–45 Suite de danses incomplete." The opening section is not titled; at the beginning of folio 3r: "Tempo 1°"; at the beginning of folio 5r: "1 Valse."

Scored for piccolo and flute, oboe, clarinet in A, horns in D and G, bassoons, cornet à piston, ophicleides, trumpet in D, trombone, timpani, drum, triangle, bass drum, cymbals, and strings.

FRKF 236.29

Valse pour orchestre en la majeur

Fragmentary holograph full-score manuscript, notated in black ink on the first page of a single 16-staff bifolium. Only 16 measures and the first violin part are present.

FRKF 236.32

Valse pour orchestre en mi majeur

Fragmentary holograph full-score manuscript, notated in black ink on the first page of a single 16-staff bifolium. Only 24 measures and the first violin part are present.

FRKF 236.33

Unidentified

Partial holograph full-score manuscript of a dance. Notated in black ink on three leaves, paginated in pencil, not in Offenbach's hand, 25 to 30, of 16-staff paper. A section marked "Trio" begins at the third measure of p. 25. The word "Coda" appears at the top of p. 28. Only the Trio section is fully scored. The rest comprises mostly the first violin part and occasional sections for the woodwinds.

FRKF 236.36

F. MUSIC FOR THE CELLO

Concerto militaire

Holograph manuscript, incomplete, of the opening allegro, with only the first 14 bars of accompaniment notated. Written in black ink on a single leaf of oblong 6-staff paper. At the top of the page, two unidentified pencil drawings, possibly by a child. On the verso, unidentified sketches: 6 measures in black ink on one staff; 5 measures in pencil, also on one staff; "Andante," in black ink, 11 measures, in G major. At the top of the page, five more caricature-like drawings in pencil and, in a child's hand, the words: "Meine liebe Herminie" (Offenbach's wife Herminie d'Alcain).

Three rough sketches for the andante, notated in black ink on a single sheet of 12-staff paper, representing respectively 3, 8, and 6 bars. The middle sketch is the principal theme, according to a note by Antonio de Almeida, whose collection included the manuscript of the entire work.

FRKF 236.05–06

Les plaintes de la châtelaine

Autograph manuscript of this "Rêverie" for cello and piano, 1850, 4 p. Signed and dated at the top: "La Rozelle, 27 août 1850 / Les Plaintes de la chatelaine . / Rêverie composée par / Jacques Offenbach." Notated in black ink, with a few corrections and additions in pencil, on a single bifolium of 12-staff paper. The piano part is present in its entirety, but much of the cello line is missing, save for measures 3, 28–29, 34, 46–47, 50–51, 54–60, 62–64, 67–77, and 91 to the end.

New York, Sotheby's, 25 May 1983, lot 45.

FRKF 93

Polka composée expressément pour Mme la comtesse de Chabrillan

Holograph manuscript, in black ink on p. [2] and [3] of a single bifolium. The cello part appears only in the trio section (measures 30–53). At the top of p. [2] in Offenbach's hand: "Polka composée expressément pour Madame la Comtesse de Chabrillan." On p. [1] in pencil, not in his hand: "Polka / N° 16." In A major. Dated 1851 by Grove.

FRKF 236.20

Sérénade for cello and piano

Holograph manuscript, n.d., in black ink on the recto of a single leaf of oblong 14-staff paper (a 15th staff added in Offenbach's hand). The title, "Sérénade," is written at the top, also in his hand. The cello part appears to be incomplete. On the verso are various unidentified sketches in both ink and pencil, written in both directions. The longest has 30-odd measures. Two others are marked "Rondo" (one of them, at the top of the page, is also marked "in G dur"). In the upper right corner of the recto, inscription in dark blue ink, signed "Korman" [?] and identifying the piece as an autograph of Offenbach "tiré des papiers de ce compositeur."

FRKF 236.26

G. MISCELLANEOUS SKETCHES

A disbound album of sketches for various works [ca. 1860], comprising single leaves and single or nested bifolia of oblong 16-staff paper (blind stamp of Lard-Esnault), written on both sides and paginated in pencil (not in Offenbach's hand) 1 to 142 (through most of the album, odd numbers only except 108, 110, and 142). The sketches are generally in black ink, with a few in pencil, and written on 2- and 3-staff systems.

Phénice. Sketches, in short score, with occasional indications of orchestration, for this unfinished opéra-comique, on a libretto by Clairville and Siraudin, 1860 (p. 1–[62]).

p. 1. Above the first sketch, in Offenbach's hand: "Ritournelle Empereur."

[2]. The vocal line of the sketch at the bottom is to the text: "Bonjour cousine … C'est vrai que je suis timide mais malgré moi malgré moi j'ai peur."

3. Above the first staff, in the center: "duo." The third sketch is described as "Quintette," beginning with the words "C'est elle." Above the third system: "Andantino." At the bottom of the page, before the last system: "Après l'andante."

[4]. At the bottom of the page, before the final system: "Duo / anfang."

5. Several sketches for characters identified as Sylvain, Albert, and Flora, and on the text: "Il te manque deux notes."

[8]. Sketches on the text "Sacrilege / Allons il est fou Allons laissons-le / Albert."

[10]. At the top of the page: "Choeur d'introduction"; in the outer margin next to the first system: "en fa"; farther down: "C'est demain fête au vil[lage]."

11. Above the third system: "choeur infernal."

[12]. At the top of the page: "Chanson"; below the vocal line: "C'est le vin … qui nous met en train." Farther down: "Choufleuri / 28 mai 60." Underneath, sketches for a duet between Turnulu and Verneria.

13. At the top of the page: "Lento / Rheinweinlied"; the following sketch is to the words "Le Pauvre Docteur il est fou il est fou à lier."

[14]. Names of characters at the top: Phenice, Sylvain; above the second system: "duo"; text under the vocal line: "Invisible dis-tu ma pupille invisible"; at the bottom: "Fuyons le pauvre Docteur il est fou" and "Le pauvre docteur je le plains."

[16]. Above the first sketch: "Duo Flora Quevedo / oui jeune et jolie"; in the outer margin, next to the third system: "Trio bouffe."

17. In the inner margin, above the third system: "Reinlied"; above the fourth system, "choeur" and the words: "Bravo ah que c'est bien [?] cela"; below the first staff of the last system: "Bravo oui c'est bien cela."

[18]. Above the first sketch: "1er Duo 2d act[e]"; under the vocal line: "Oui jeune et jolie / mon cousin rêvait."

19. Above the first system: "valse 3eme acte"; in the inner margin, next to the second system: "choeur / demain j'entendrai tout …"; under the next system: "je voudrais — -mais mais je ne peux pas"; above the fourth system: "Romance Flora dehors avec acct solo de deux cors differemment places."

[20]. Above the second system: "Scene 5 3ème acte"; above the fourth system: "Diable"; in the outer margin, next to the fifth system: "Chant du diable."

21. Above the first system: "Final"; under the second system: "voyez le pauvre Docteur."

[22]. Above the first system: "Flora Sylvain."

23. Above the first system: "Final 2eme"; below the first staff: "Les vendangeurs"; under the first staff of the third system: "marche pour l'arrivée du vin."

[24]. Under the first staff of the third system: "La maladie"; in the outer margin next to the fourth system: "Choeur des vignerons."

25. Above the first system: "Galop"; above the second system: "Trio"; above the third system: "Duo."

[26]. Above the first system: "Duetto"; text above and under the first staff of the second system: "tristement je suis très gai"; above the third system: "duo choeur" and the words "je suis heu-reux"; above the fourth system: "Choeur villa[geois?]."

27. Above the first system: "duo"; above the second system: "Phe[nice] Syl[vain]"; under the first staves of the second and third systems: "lalalalalala … c'est pourtant bien facile"; above the fourth system: "Phe (à part) Syl (à part)."

[28]. Notes for orchestration in the outer margin.

29. Below the first staff of the second system: "Bonjour maître."

31. Below the first staff of the third system: "mon Dieu"; below the first staff of the third system: "finir très brusquement"; above the staff: "Le Docteur"; below the staff: "Voyons parlez Flora"; above the sixth system: "apres l'ensemble a 4 temps"; below the first staff: "meme mon [not deciphered] mais" and "je veux parler"; above the staff: "Albert"; below the staff, and continuing into the following system: "silence silence silence."

[32]. Above the first system: "Duo 4eme."

33. Above the second system: "Valse."

35. Above the second system: "Andante Duetto."

[36]. Above the first system: "Chanson Diable"; below the first staff of the third system: "Venez tous bien vite au bal infernal."

[38]. Above the first system: "Duetto"; above the fourth system: "Valse 2ter Theil"; below the first staff of the sixth system: "ah c'est charmant."

[40]. Above the fourth system: "Bravo c'est vrai."

41. Note at the top of the page: "pour discours pour le concours" [rest not deciphered]; underneath, still above the first system: "Ritournelle / Espagne"; under the first staff of the fifth system: "quel est le tour ici"; under the first staff of the seventh system: "Silence et."

[42]. Above the first system: "Andante Septuor ou Quatuor"; in the outer margin, next to the second system: "17 mars 60"; the same date is repeated next to the third system, above the words "marche Introduction"; above the fourth system: "Fanfare à 3 notes"; in the outer margin, next to the fifth system: "5 avril."

43. Above the first system: "Duo bouffe Flora le Docteur (la bouche fermée et reflechissant"; below the first staff: "Voyons expliquez-vous / hum … hum"; above the third system: "Choeur d'introduction"; in the outer margin: "30 mars"; below the first staff: "achetez nos fleurs et nos fruits."

[44]. In the outer margin, next to the second system: "4eme / Fin."

45. Below the first staff of the first system: "Clochettes" and undeciphered words.

[46]. Above the first staff of the fifth system: "Choeur"; below the staff: "Elle n'est pas mal de figure"; below the first staff of the sixth system: "pour finir tout le monde."

[48]. Below the first staff of the second system: "les choeurs entrent peu à peu [?]" [the rest undeciphered; also an undeciphered note at the bottom of the page].

51. Above the first system: "Entendez la cloche qui."

[52]. In the outer margin, next to the fourth system: "Trio / marche"; above the first staff: "Sultan"; in the outer margin, next to the fifth system: "Marche / Sultan"; in the outer margin, next to the sixth system: "Andante / Romain."

53. Above the third system: "1er Echo."

[54]. Above the second system: "Fin"; below the first staff: "le vin le vin bois-le."

55. Above the first system: "Tyrolienne"; below the first staff of the second system: "et sûrement c'est ça."

[56]. Above the second staff of the seventh system: "tres fort"; below the staff: "Quatuor à l'unisson même la contrebasse."

57. In the inner margin, next to the fourth system: "Valse / pas trop / vite."

[58]. Above the first system: "Il faut agir avec mystê[re]."

59. Above the first system: "Choeur des vignerons"; below the first staff: "Ohne Begleitung."

61. Above the third system: "Arriver en fa pour le chant à cause du piston."

[62]. Above the first system: "Polonaise."

Listed by Grove as possibly in three acts; not mentioned by Yon.

Unidentified stage music or ballet. Miscellaneous sketches, in short score, 1859 (p. 63–[70]).

63. Above the first system: "Menuet."

65. At the top of the page: "14 8bre [18]59"; above the second system: "Valse lente."

[66]. Above the first system: "Valse"; above the sixth system: "Valse lente."

[68]. Above the first system: "Marche villageoise"; above the third system: "Marche Paysanne."

69. Undeciphered word above the first system; in the inner margin, next to the third system: "Introdu[ction]"; in the inner margin, next to the fourth system: "ouverture."

[70]. In the outer margin, next to the third system: "Marche / Fée"; above the sixth system: "Chas[se]."

Le papillon. Sketches, in short score [1860?] (p. 71–[82]).

71. Above the first system: "Modera[to]"; above the fourth system: "All.to presque valse."

72. In the outer margin, next to the second system: "2de Scene."

[74]. In the outer margin, next to the fourth system: "Orage"; below the first staff of the sixth system: "le Bain"; at the end of the system, above the staff: "la chasse."

75. In the inner margin, next to the first system: "Scene / de la foret / Livry-Merante"; above the second system: "Sommeil."

[76]. Above the third system: "Polka"; above the seventh system, in the middle of the page: "Trio."

77. Above the third system: "Andantino"; above the fourth system: "Trio"; above the fifth system: "chasse au papillon."

79. Above the first system: "Valse des ombres"; in the inner margin, next to the first system: "Introd[uction]"; above the seventh system: "entrée du Bucheron."

[80]. In the inner margin, next to the second system: "Ouverture"; in the inner margin, next to the third system: "Ballet / Marche."

81. Above the first system: "Marche."

Le papillon, ballet in four tableaux on a libretto by Saint-Georges and Marie Taglioni, was premiered at the Paris Opéra on 26 Nov. 1860.

Daphnis et Chloé. Sketches, in short score, for this operetta (p. [82]–[102]).

[82]. In red pencil, in the outer margin, next to the third and fourth systems, not in Offenbach's hand: "Daphnis et Chloé"; above the fourth system: "fin Duo"; in the outer margin, next to the sixth system: "Ritournelle."

83. Above the first system: "Golo"; in the outer margin, in the middle of the page: "milieu du Duo"; underneath, above the staff: "Duetto"; two systems down, below the staff: "la petite est charmante"; above the system at the bottom: "[one word undeciphered] menuet / Chloé."

[86]. Above the third system: "Introduction"; above the sixth system: "Oui c'est bien là le ri [?]"; toward the middle of the page, below the first staff: "Essayons."

[88]. Below the first staff of the second system: "Je viens du grand opéra"; in the outer margin, next to the fifth system: "choeur d'ouverture."

[92]. Below the eighth staff: "silence si vla qu'il [one word undeciphered]"; in the outer margin, next to the following staff: "La folle"; above the first staff: "aussitot que la lumière"; below the staff: "le comte Ori [sic]"; in the outer margin, two staves down: "Enfant Prodigue."

[94]. At the top of the page, tiny caricature representing a round face; above the first system: "Juif errant"; in the outer margin, beginning one-third down the page: "Cadet Roussel / Dagobert / Bergère / Giroflé -Girofla / Manon / Marechal de Saxe / Mme Denis"; above the second line of the second system: "Malgré la [Bataille?]"; above the next staff: "La Palisse"; below the next staff: "il etait un' bergere" and "que [tu es?] belle fille."

97. In the middle of the page, above the third system: "Choeur."

[98]. Below the first line of the third and fourth systems: "non rien ne vaut à mes yeux qu'un joli petit Bezigue à deux / qu'un petit petit Bezigue à deux"; in the middle of the page, above the middle staff of the seventh system: "[glo?] la folie."

[100]. Above the first system, in pencil: "Duo"; under the first staff of the second system: "oui c'en est fait frappe frappe."

101. Above the third system: "Quand minuit sonne à notre Dame."

[102]. In the outer margin, next to the fourth system: "Roi Dagobert."

Daphnis et Chloé, operetta in one act on a libretto by Clairville and Jules Cordier, was premiered at the Bouffes-Parisiens on 27 March 1860.

Geneviève de Brabant. Sketches, in short score, for the first version of this opéra-bouffe [1859?] (p. 103–42).

[104]. Below the second staff of the first system: "de la part de Charles Martel"; above the second system: "à Boire."

105. Below the second staff: "non c'est pas moi c'est pas."

[106]. In the upper left corner, caricature of a head. At the top of the page: "fin"; in the outer margin, next to the second system: "Ritournelle de la Poule"; above the tenth staff: "Benissons."

108. Below the seventh staff: "Juste ciel qu'ai-je fait quelle [sic] est donc mon forfait" then "2de reprise en la au lieu de re"; below the first line of the penultimate system: "Rends nous le à notre amour"; at the bottom of the page: "Lancelot - Cico / Locrin - [Stern?]."

109. Above the first system: "Duetto / in g mol"; below the fifth staff: "Qua qua qua qua qu'a"; below the seventh staff: "et moi vous me plantez vous me plantez la"; below the next staff: "moi si froid votre epoux" [etc.]; below the next staff: "que fait Eglantine"; below the penultimate staff: "si cependant quelques cavaliers \ étaient assez galants pour se mesurer Golo est la" [etc.].

110. Above the first system: "a Paris dans mon quartier / m.t de polka"; below the fifth staff: "souper a la maison d'or"; above the fourth system: "Complainte"; below the sixth system: "Bounm zim boum boum."

111. Above the fifth system: "Choeur"; below the staff: "Voilà bien le vin que j'aime oui le vin que j'aime."

[112]. Above the first system: "Ronde"; in the outer margin, next to the third system: "Duo"; above the staff: "quoi Reinold en ces lieux"; in the outer margin, next to the sixth system: "Rondo"; to the right, under the staff: "vous allez voir nous allons voir."

113. In the inner margin, next to the third system: "n° 9"; above the staff: "le voila"; under the staff: "celui qui reflètent sur nos cours [?]"; above the seventh system: "parlez le voulez vous"; above the eighth system: "fin."

[114]. Below the ninth staff: "à Paris"; above the last system: "choeur"; below the staff: "en chasse"; above the staff, to the right: "Bouche fermée [en étant?]."

115. Above the first system: "gai compagnon"; below the first staff of the second system: "Voilà bien le vin que j'aime"; above the penultimate system: "Chanson toujours piano jusqu'a la fin"; in the inner margin, next to the last system: "Refrain."

117. Above the first system: "Introdu[ction] clarinette"; in the inner margin, next to the second system: "Refrain"; above the lower staff: "c'est le vin que toujours j'aime."

[120]. Above the fourth system: "Trio de la marche."

121. In the inner margin, next to the third system: "n° 2"; above the staff: "Altamor interoge [sic] la."

[122]. Above the first system: "arrivée du Prince suite de la marche."

123. In the inner margin, next to the fourth system: "Ballet / c moll"; above the sixth system: "Polonaise"; above the same system, in the middle of the page: "Trio"; also some financial calculations in the lower right corner.

[124]. Above the first system: "Prince"; in the outer margin, next to the first system: "après la fête."

[126]. Above the second system, in pencil: "Comte de Morny. 4 avril."

137. Below the first system: "Pif paf pif"; below the first staff of the ninth system: "Dieu protège notre empire."

139. Below the first staff: "c'est trés bien c'est trés bien"; at the end of the staff: "Dieu des combats veille sur."

[140]. Below the first staff of the fourth system "je suis soldat."

See above under *Geneviève de Brabant* in group A.

Paris, Dominique Vincent (Drouot), 12 March 1984, lots 326, 323, 325, 324.
FRKF 430–33

Unidentified sketches, 2 p., in black ink on both sides of a single leaf of oblong 24-staff paper with a (barely legible) blind stamp of Lard-Esnault (?). Numbered 200 in pencil in an unidentified hand in upper right corner. The sketches occupy most of the recto, save for one staff, and are usually written on two staves. There are only three sketches on the verso, one of them on three staves.

Marburg, Stargardt, 19–30 Nov. 1983, lot 926.
FRKF 145

A leaf of sketches, notated in black ink on 21-staff paper. At the top of the recto, in Offenbach's hand: "Romance."

FRKF 387

Holograph full score of a partial number from an unidentified work, 12 p., in ink on three consecutive, independent bifolia, numbered 4, 5, and 6 in Offenbach's hand, of oblong 24-staff paper. A moderato section, with the indication "on parle," begins on the first page of bifolium no. 4, followed by the ensemble launched by Guiotti on the words "Sur ce front fait pour la couronne …" The manuscript ends with the four gypsies' word "Achetons."

FRKF 236.35

Holograph manuscript of an unidentified overture. Notated in black ink on 19 pages, the first 18 of which are numbered in Offenbach's hand, in a gathering of six nested bifolia, sewn together, of oblong 18-staff paper (blind stamp of Lard-Esnault). On p. 1, in Offenbach's hand: "Introduction"; in pencil, in another hand: "ouverture primitive / (mariage aux lanternes)." Page 14 is a cancel, sewn to the verso of p. 13. On p. [19], after the end of the overture, holograph manuscript of a 10-measure "Andante non troppo" for strings, possibly unrelated; on p. [20], a similar 9-measure draft in pencil.

FRKF 451

Fragments and sketches accessioned as Frederick R. Koch Foundation 237

A single sheet of oblong 24-staff paper, with 6 measures of music in ink on a single staff and 18 measures on a 2-staff system.

A fragment torn from a larger sheet, comprising three different sketches notated in ink. The first, of 38 measures, marked "a dur"; the second, 19 measures; the third, 8 measures. More unidentified sketches are present on the verso.

Unidentitied sketches notated on both sides of the first sheet, torn at the bottom, of a bifolium of oblong 12-staff paper, with some indications of orchestration.

A sheet, torn laterally, with sketches on both sides. The words "Senza" and "Il Canto de amor" appear on one side.

Fragment of an unidentified stage work, notated in full score on both sides of a single sheet of torn 24-staff paper. The passage begins with the words "en toi j'espère, ô Dieu sauveur … du militaire au noble Coeur …"

Fragment of an unidentified stage work, notated in full score on both sides of a single sheet of oblong 20-staff paper, beginning with the words "doit attention," followed by the indication "Marche."

A single leaf of oblong 12-staff paper (traces of Lard-Esnault blind stamp), with three unidentified sketches of a few bars each on the recto.

A single leaf of oblong 12-staff paper, with two short musical sketches on the recto, one with text underneath (not deciphered).

A single leaf of oblong 24-staff paper (blind stamp of Lard-Esnault) with five unidentified short sketches, the first with the heading (in Offenbach's hand): "304 Les Amazones" (?), the second: "Serenade 137 - Grenier."

A single leaf of 12-staff paper; on the recto, two short unidentified sketches, one with the names of two characters (M …, Duc?).

A single leaf of tall 12-staff paper, torn at the top and the bottom; pencil sketches for an unidentified work for cello and piano on both sides.

Fragment of a leaf with a vocal line, on four staffs, for soprano voice, to the text: "… soeur morte d'amour - je pleure encor ma soeur morte d'amour."

A single leaf of tall 24-staff paper with a vocal line for an unidentified character in a possibly abandoned work. The text is: "[Je suis le père Cy-] rille Dévot compagnon et je parcours la Castille prêchant maint sermon."

A single bifolium of tall 20-staff paper, with two short sketches, one on p. [1], the other on p. [4].

A single leaf of oblong 24-staff paper with a draft, notated on three systems of five and six staffs, possibly for a chorus or an ensemble. The only words present appear to read "Hm - hm."

A single leaf, torn, of oblong 12-staff paper, with drafts of a canon in pencil and ink, notated on the recto on two 3- and 4-staff systems.

A single bifolium of oblong 24-staff paper (blind stamp of Lard-Esnault), numbered 8 in Offenbach's hand, and comprising empty measures numbered 11 to 63. A few sketches, in full score, follow on p. [3] and [4].

A single bifolium of tall 12-staff paper, with two brief sketches notated in ink on p. [1].

A single leaf of tall 14-staff paper (blind stamp of Lard-Esnault) with sketches on both sides. On the recto, in ink, 19 measures, with the indications "G dur" and, under the second measure: "unis"; there are also shorter sketches of 4 measures each farther down. On the verso, 4 measures sketched in ink, with the indication "D dur," and more sketches, totalling ca. 45 measures, notated in pencil: one with the indication "fin," another marked "Adagio, E dur," another "e moll," another "G dur."

Fragment of a single leaf, with a tenuto piano chord and the following text, to be spoken by a character named Nanette: "Eh ben v'la comme j'y cours … Ah j'ai trop peur, sauvons-nous -"

A single leaf of tall 12-staff paper with five short sketches, notated in ink on the recto, the first two on 2-staff systems, the fourth with the indication "H dur" and undeciphered words under the staff.

A single sheet of oblong 6-staff paper with sketches in pencil, totalling about 20 measures, with the indications "C moll" (?) and "Bass."

A single sheet of tall 20-staff paper; at the top, 6 measures notated on a 2-staff system, and below, two short sketches, one in ink, the other in pencil.

Text of a chorus notated, possibly by a copyist, on a single bifolium, with the heading "2de Basse / All° Moderato," beginning with the words (evidently from a chorus) "Camarades entendez-vous au loin la Diane résonne." The music is absent.

Manuscript, notated in ink in the hand of a copyist, of an unidentified work, for voice and piano, without the words. Only the last 11 bars (bass line only) and the words "pour finir" at the end appear to be in Offenbach's hand. The manuscript is on p. [2] and [3] of a single bifolium of 12-staff paper in four systems with a line for the words (blind stamp of Lard-Esnault).

A single sheet of 14-staff paper with various unidentified sketches notated in ink and in pencil on both sides.

A fragment of a sheet with various unidentified fragments notated in ink and in pencil on both sides.

A single sheet of 12-staff paper with various drafts notated in ink and in pencil on the recto.

A single sheet of 12-staff paper with two short drafts, both notated in ink on two-staff systems.

A half-sheet, torn, with a fragment of a work, possibly for horns and piano, notated in ink on two 3-staff systems, on one side, and on the other side a different fragment, notated on a 2-staff system.

A single sheet of oblong 12-staff paper with two short drafts notated in ink on a 4-staff system.

A single bifolium, numbered 29, of 20-staff paper (blind stamp of Lard-Esnault); on the first two pages, an incomplete full-score draft, limited to a single line, possibly for the oboe.

A single sheet of 12-staff paper; on one side, the words "N° 4" (cancelling a 2) in Offenbach's hand, and on the other, in the opposite direction, a fragment of an unidentified work, notated on a 3-staff system, with only the piano accompaniment present (13 measures).

A single sheet of badly soiled 16-staff paper with various sketches in pencil on one side, two of them with the indications "minuetto" and "h moll."

A single sheet of 15-staff paper with various sketches in ink and in pencil, the last two with the indications "All.to" and "d dur."

A fragment of a large sheet with two short sketches notated in ink.

A single leaf, torn, of 20-staff paper, with ca. 15 sketches, notated in ink and in pencil, on both sides, one of them with the indication "marche."

A small piece of paper cut from a larger sheet, with a 16-measure draft notated in ink.

A short fragment notated in ink on two staffs on a small piece of paper cut from a larger sheet.

A single sheet of 12-staff paper with two drafts notated in ink.

A single sheet of 12-staff paper with five short drafts notated in ink, one marked "a mol." On the other side, an unidentified manuscript of 17 measures (an additional measure is cancelled), in G major, possibly for the cello, notated in ink on one staff, in a copyist's hand.

A single sheet, numbered 5, of torn 24-staff paper, with a fragment of an unidentified work, in full score, on both sides. The vocal line begins "Sois protecteur pendant la guerre …"

A single sheet of oblong 20-staff paper with two short sketches notated on one side, one in pencil, the other in ink.

A single sheet of oblong 24-staff paper with five short sketches notated in pencil on the recto.

A single sheet of oblong 24-staff paper (blind stamp of Lard-Esnault), with a fragment of a full-score manuscript notated in ink on both sides, with only one line complete and one more additional bar of accompaniment.

A single bifolium of green 18-staff paper with the beginning of an unidentified full-score manuscript on the first page, only a few measures for the flute and horns. At the top of p. [4], in reverse, is a 15-measure draft with the heading "final."

A single sheet of oblong 20-staff paper with six short fragments on the recto, four notated in ink, two in pencil.

A single bifolium of 16-staff paper with an incomplete full-score draft notated in ink on the first two pages.

A single bifolium of 16-staff paper with an incomplete full-score draft, possibly related to the previous one, also notated in ink on the first two pages.

A small piece of paper, torn from a larger sheet, with three drafts notated in ink, the first with the heading "Rondo mi / E dur," the second "harmonies"(?).

A single leaf of 14-staff laid paper with various fragments notated on both sides in ink and pencil.

A small piece of paper, torn from a larger sheet, with a fragment notated in ink on a 2-staff system on one side, and on the verso three small fragments notated in ink and in pencil.

Fragment of a sheet with short drafts notated in ink on both sides.

Fragment of a sheet with five staffs of drafts notated in pencil.

A single leaf of oblong 18-staff paper with a 10-measure fragment notated on a 3-staff system (only piano accompaniment is present) on one side, and on the verso, four short fragments notated in ink and in pencil.

A small piece torn from a larger sheet with four short drafts notated in ink on one side.

A single bifolium of 12-staff paper with a 5-measure draft on a 2-staff system at the top of p. [1]. Two additional measures are cancelled.

A single sheet of 16-staff paper with seven short drafts on both sides, notated in ink and in pencil, one of them with the heading "Rondo / a dur."

Part of a sheet (numbered 9 in Offenbach's hand) of oblong 24-staff paper, torn in the middle, with a fragment of an unidentified work for the stage, in full score. The words on the recto are "au bruit des marches triomphales sonnez encor, roulez toujours …"; and on the verso "Qu'Allah me damne je suis sultane," while the chorus sings "Crions vivat."

A single sheet of 20-staff paper with ca. eight short sketches notated in ink on the recto, some with text (not deciphered).

A single sheet of oblong 24-staff paper (blind stamp of Lard-Esnault), marked at the top, in pencil, in Offenbach's hand: "n° 4 et 5," with two sketches notated in ink on 2 and 3-staff systems on the recto.

A single bifolium of oblong 24-staff paper (blind stamp of Lard-Esnault); on p. [1] the opening of a full-score draft, marked "All.ro vivo," with only the first violin part present.

A single bifolium of 24-staff paper (traces of blind stamp of Lard or Lard-Esnault) with a fragment notated in ink on two 5-staff systems on p. [1], totalling 16 measures.

A single sheet of oblong 24-staff paper (traces of blind stamp of Lard or Lard-Esnault) with a fragment, in full score, of an unidentified work for the stage. On the recto, 6 blank measures numbered 2 to 7, followed by 12 measures of a violin line, continuing on the verso, and the start of a vocal line beginning with the words "Dieu sois mon guide …"

A single sheet of oblong 24-staff paper (blind stamp of Lard-Esnault) with 8 measures lightly sketched in ink and in pencil, and cancelled.

A single sheet of oblong 24-staff paper (blind stamp of Lard-Esnault), numbered "4 bis" in Offenbach's hand, with an unidentified fragment notated in ink in full score on both sides, totalling 33 measures, begining with 15 measures numbered 1–8, 1–4, a1a, b2b, c3c. The scoring starts at measure 16, numbered aaa, and continues on the verso (to ggg), followed by an unnumbered measure, a repeat of the aaa–ggg numbering, and 3 unnumbered measures.

A single sheet of oblong 20-staff paper (blind stamp of Lard-Esnault) with two drafts on the recto, both notated in ink, the second on a 2-staff system and with the heading "Entrée de la cour."

FRKF 237

A sketch leaf of tall 24-staff paper (blind stamp not deciphered) with short drafts, in ink or in pencil, on both sides. At the top of the recto, in Offenbach's hand: "Carraud"; on the verso, in the margin, toward the middle of the page, also in his hand: "Grenadiers."

Paris, Ader-Picard-Tajan (Drouot), 18 Dec. 1985, lot 280.
FRKF 933

II. LETTERS

To Ernest L'Épine

1865 March 13, Vienna, ALS, 4 p., on the death of the Duc de Morny.

FRKF 733

To "Mr Mayer"

n.d., "mercredi" [note in pencil in another hand: "été 1879"] n.p., ALS, 2 p. Concerns sending a manuscript (of *La fille du tambour major*, according to a note in the same unidentified hand) and mentions the London publishing firm of Cramer, Wood & Co.

n.d., n.p., ALS, 2 p. Concerns a letter to Cramer, Wood & Co. and a request for 1,000 francs owed according to a contract.

FRKF 291

To his daughter Pepita

[1875 July 8, Aix-les-Bains*] Théâtre de la Gaité, Paris[S], ALS, 4 p. (env). Reports on a concert at the Casino of Aix-les-Bains; mentions Zulma Bouffar and *La vie parisienne*.

Marburg, Stargardt, 19 June 1984, lot 885.
FRKF 480

To Auguste Pittaud-Deforges

[ca. 1855?] "Samedi soir," n.p., ALS, 3 p., concerning the prologue, *Entrez Messieurs, Mesdames*. On the back of the letter, in Offenbach's hand: "Monsieur Deforges."

FRKF 292

To Alfred von Wolzogen

All are autograph letters, signed, in French.

[1860]

March 3, Théâtre des Bouffes-Parisiens, Passage Choiseul, Rue Monsigny, Direction [Paris][S] (blue), 4 p.

1863

[1863 spring?] "Donnerstag," n.p., 3 p.

March 26, 11 Rue Laffitte [Paris] 4 p., asking if Wolzogen would translate *Die Rheinnixen*

April 17, Berlin, 3 p.

May 4, Vienna, 1 p.

May 31, n.p., 3 p.

June 1, n.p., 2 p.

June 4, Étretat, 1 p.

[summer? 1863?] "Mercredi," n.p., 1 p.

[summer 1863] n.p., 3 p.

June 10, n.p., 3 p.

June 19, n.p., 3 p.

June 19, Étretat, 3 p.

June 29, n.p., 1 p.

July 7, n.p., 4 p.

July 12, n.p., 2 p.

July 19, Ems, 3 p.

Aug. 4, Étretat, 4 p., with three musical examples.

[summer 1863] "Dimanche," Étretat, 1 p.

Aug. 30, Berlin, 4 p., with pasted-on correction on p. 4.

[summer 1863] "Lundi," n.p., 3 p.

Sept. 10, Vienna, 4 p.

Oct. 20, Paris, Théâtre des Bouffes-Parisiens[S], 4 p., with a musical example.

Nov. 4(?), "Mercredi," n.p., 4 p.

1864

Jan. 20, n.p. [Vienna?] 3 p.

[Jan.] n.p. [Vienna?] 3 p.

Undated

"Mercredi, 6 hrs ½," Breslau, 1 p.

"ce mercredi," Vienna, in the hand of Herminie Offenbach, 3 p.

The letters have to do with the collaboration between Wolzogen and Offenbach on the translation and staging of *Die Rheinnixen*.

With an ALS from Alfred von Wolzogen to Offenbach, 1860 Jan. 30, Breslau, 3 p. Mentions *Orphée aux enfers* and requests information on the Bouffes-Parisiens and the Théâtre Déjazet. In French. Probably a retained draft; several passages crossed out.

Accompanied by a clipping: "Feuilleton. Die Rhein-Nixen. Grosse romantische Oper in 3 Acten, von J. Offenbach," from *Die Presse*, Vienna, 6 Feb. 1864, 2 leaves.

Marburg, Stargardt, 19–30 Nov. 1983, lots 928–29.
FRKF 147, 147.5, 148

To unidentified correspondents

n.y., Feb. 11, Théâtre des Bouffes-Parisiens [Paris][S] (blue), ALS to an unidentified friend, 2 p., concerning the singer Adolphe Jaime fils.

Paris, Le Roux-Mathias (Drouot), 19 April 1985, lot 302.
FRKF 722

1874 Sept. 2, Biarritz, ALS, 4 p. Mentions *Orphée aux enfers* and *Whittington*; also Victorien Sardou and Étienne Tréfeu.

New York, Sotheby's, 22 May 1985, lot 415.
FRKF 747

Third-party correspondence

n.d., n.p., ALS from Sophie Schloss to Herminie Offenbach, 1 p., written in the third person on a fragment of music paper, regretting to have missed the recipient. Unidentified sketch by Offenbach on the verso.

FRKF 237

EUGENE O'NEILL (1888–1953)

Letter to Eugene O'Neill, Jr.

[1924 Jan. 22*] Brook Farm, Ridgefield, Connecticut[S], ALS, 1 p. (env), concerning a production of Strindberg's *The ghost sonata* at the Provincetown Playhouse.

New York, Christie's, 18 Oct. 1988, lot 1523.
FRKF 1423

GIOVANNI PACINI (1796–1867)

"Bocca di Paradiso"

Holograph manuscript of a song for voice and piano, 1850, 2 p., written in black ink on both sides of a single leaf of oblong 9-staff paper. Signed "Jean Pacini" on p. [1] in the upper right corner and inscribed "à B[?] l'année 1850." Above the signature, in another hand: "originale, inedito, dal celebre [Pacini]."

FRKF 536

Letters to Francesco Maria Piave

1863 Feb.? 2, Pescia, ALS, 1 p.

1867 April 14, Pescia, LS, 3 p., in a secretarial hand, first part in verse. There are mentions of Pacini's operas *Don Diego di Mendoza* and *Berta di Varnol*, both on libretti by Piave.

1867 May 18, Pescia, LS, 2 p., in a secretarial hand and in verse throughout.

London, Sotheby's, 29 Nov. 1985, lot 176.
FRKF 1083

FERDINANDO PAËR (1771–1839)

I. LETTERS

To Gilbert-Louis Duprez

1838 Jan. 30, Liste Civile, Musique du Roi, Paris^S, ALS, 1 p., conveying an invitation from the queen to appear in a scene from Roulz's *Lara* at a concert on 7 Feb.

Paris, Oger-Dumont (Drouot), 14 Feb. 1985, lot 22.
FRKF 685

To Monsieur Louis

1827 May 12, P[aris] ALS, 4 p. Mentions his operas *Numa Pompilio* and *Le maître de chapelle*, as well as difficulties with Domenico Barbaja, a letter from whom he encloses. (The enclosure is not present.)

Kenneth Rendell Catalogue 169.
FRKF 399

II. MANUSCRIPT DOCUMENTS

A collection of manuscript memoranda

All the documents are signed by Paër as "Directeur des Théâtres de la Cour"; all but the first two are on the stationery of the Maison de S.M. l'Empereur et Roi. Service du Grand Chambellan.

"Maison de S.M. l'Empereur et Roi. Service du Grand Chambellan. Etat pour Monsieur Crivelli, P^{er}. Tenor, pour ses Services au théâtre de la Cour." 1811 Nov. 25, 1 p., concerning the cantata *Éloïse* and the opera *Didon*.

"Maison de S.M. l'Empereur et Roi. Service du Grand Chambellan. Etat du Service extraordinaire de la musique au théâtre de la Cour, en Xbre." 1811 Dec. 31, 1 p., concerning two horn players, an oboist, and a bassoonist who appeared in performances of the operas *Mérope* and *Nina*.

"Théâtre des Tuileries. Mémoire des Ouvrages faits pour le Théâtre de Sa Majesté L'Empereur et Roi au palais Des Tuilleries par Bédel Tapissier Rue des trois frères Nº 19." 1813 Feb., 3 p., concerning the "Opéra des Baccantes" and Molière's *Tartuffe*. On p. [3] is an "État de la somme due au Sr Isabey dessinateur …" Signed by Jean-Baptiste Isabey and countersigned twice by Paër.

"Théâtre de St. Cloud. Mémoire de Peintures de Décorations faites pour le Théâtre de la Cour, d'après les dessins de M. Isabey Déssinateur du Cabinet de Sa Majesté, et des Théâtres de la Cour. Par Cicéri Peintre des Théâtres de la Cour et du Grand Opéra." 1813 June, 4 p., concerning the sets for *Aline, reine de Golconde* (presumably the opera by Berton), performed at Saint-Cloud on 24 June 1813. Signed by Jean-Baptiste Isabey and countersigned by Paër. On p. [4] is the "État de la somme due à Mr Isabey … et à M. Ciceri."

"Théâtre de St. Cloud. Mémoire des peintures des Décorations faites pour le Théâtre de la Cour, d'après les dessins de M. Isabey Déssinateur du Cabinet de Sa Majesté, et des Théâtres de la Cour. Par Cicéri Peintre des Théâtres de la Cour et du Grand Opéra." 1813 July, 3 p., concerning the set for the operas *Montano* [Berton's *Montano et Stéphanie*] and *Ser-Marc Antonio*. Signed by Jean-Baptiste Isabey and countersigned by Paër. On p. [3] is the "État de la somme due à Mr Isabey … et à M. Ciceri."

"Memoire des Ouvrages faits pour Sa Majesté L'Empereur et Roi par Bedel Tapissier Rue des trois frères Nº 19. Savoir Theatre de St Cloud." 1813 July, 4 p., concerning the decoration of a Palais Gothique. Signed by Jean-Baptiste Isabey and countersigned by Paër. On p. [4] is the "État de la somme due à M. Isabey […] et à M. Bedel."

"Théâtre de St. Cloud. Mémoire des Ouvrages de serrurerie faite et fournie dans le Courant du mois de Juillet 1813, pour les Théatres de la Cour." 1813 Aug. 2, 4 p., concerning, among others, the decoration for the opera *Montano*. Signed by Jean-Baptiste Isabey and countersigned by Paër. On p. [4] is the "État de la somme due à Mr. Isabey … et à Mr. Mignon …"

"Petit Théâtre Portatif. Mémoire des Peintures des Décorations faites pour le Théâtre de la Cour, d'après les déssins de M. Isabey, Déssinateur du Cabinet de Sa Majesté, et des Théâtres de la Cour. Par Ciceri, Peintre des Théâtres de la Cour et du Grand Opéra." 1813 Sept. 14, 2 p., concerning the operas *Ser-Marc Antonio* and *Didon*. Signed by Jean-Baptiste Isabey and countersigned by Paër. On p. [2] is the "État de la somme due à M. Isabey … et à M. Ciceri."

"Théâtre de St. Cloud. Mémoire de peintures de Décorations faites pour le Théâtre de la Cour, d'après les dessins de M. Isabey, Dessinateur du Cabinet de Sa Majesté, et des Théâtres de la Cour. Par Ciceri Peintre des Théâtres de la Cour et du Grand Opéra." 1813 Oct. 17, 2 p., concerning *Le mariage de Figaro*, "Opéra Seria," *Zoraim*, and *Raoul, Sir de Créqui*. Signed by Jean-Baptiste Isabey and countersigned by Paër.

"Théâtre de la Cour. Mémoire de peintures de Décorations faites pour le Théâtre de la Cour, d'après les dessins de M. Isabey, Déssinateur du Cabinet de Sa Majesté, et des Théâtres de la Cour. Par Ciceri Peintre des Théâtres de la Cour et du Grand Opéra." 1813 Nov. 15, 2 p., concerning a Palais Gothique for the Petit Théâtre Portatif and the opera *Paul et Virginie* at the Théâtre de Saint-Cloud. Signed by Jean-Baptiste Isabey and countersigned by Paër.

"Théâtre des Thuileries. Mémoire de Peintures et Décorations faites Palais Egiptien, pour Minur "II," Tragédie, par Le Maire, Peintre en Décors, rue St Marceau, N° 29." 1814 Jan. 12, 1, 3 p. Signed by Jean-Baptiste Isabey and countersigned by Paër.

Paris, Laurin-Guilloux-Buffetaud-Tailleur (Drouot), 12 March 1984, lot 331.
FRKF 428

RENÉE PARNY

Autograph manuscript concerning the premiere of Edmond Rostand's *L'Aiglon*, n.d., 2 p.

Renée Parny, wife of the novelist Jérôme Tharaud, was part of the original cast of *L'Aiglon* in 1900.

Paris, Le Roux-Mathias (Drouot), 19 April 1985, lot 240.
FRKF 716b

WALTER PATER (1839–94)

Letter to Oscar Wilde

[1890 Feb., Oxford] ALS, 1 p., confirming a dinner invitation.

See Christie's, New York, 7 June 1990, lot 99; Sotheby's, New York, 17 Dec. 1992, lot 199.
New York, Christie's, 22 Nov. 1985, lot 102.
FRKF 1274

GIOVANNI BATTISTA PERGOLESI (1710–36)

La fenice sul rogo, ovvero La morte di San Giussepe

Holograph full-score manuscript of this oratorio, n.d., 172 p., written in black ink on a combination of separate bifolia and (most of the time) gatherings of two nested bifolia of oblong 12-staff paper, numbered (gatherings and single bifolia) 1 to 21 in a contemporary hand; the three gatherings that form the overture are unnumbered.

There is no title page. On the front of the outer bifolium of the first gathering, the words "Parte prima" in a contemporary hand, possibly Pergolesi's. In a different hand, the figure "VI"; yet in a different hand, a shelfmark: "86c / Arm° A." On the last page (the first page of the bifolium numbered 21) in Pergolesi's hand: "Finis / Laus Deo, Beate Virgini / Beatoq: Josepho."

See Barry S. Brook, "Recent developments in Pergolesi research, performance, and publication (May, 1986)," in Francesco Degrada, ed. *Studi Pergolesiani / Pergolesi Studies* 2, Scandicci (Florence): La Nuova Italia Editrice, 1988, p. 3–6.
Paymer 64 (listed as "doubtful work").
Heinrich Schütz to Henry Miller, p. 18–19.
FRKF 706

JEAN PÉRIER (1869–1954)

Undated note [1907, Monte Carlo] on a visiting card ("Jean Perier / à l'Opéra-Comique"). Dated Monte Carlo, 19 April 1907 in a different hand.

Périer premiered the part of Pelléas.

FRKF 535e

WILLIAM J. PERLMAN (1889?–1954)

Theater letters

A collection of letters concerning the theater. Some are addressed to Elizabeth F. Hague, secretary of The Playwrights Club. Many are in response to a questionnaire sent to playwrights for a projected book on the theater.

Abbott, George. TLS, 395 Riverside Drive, New York[S] [1929] Jan. 31, 2 p., to Miss Hague.

Anderson, Maxwell. ANS on the original TLS from Perlman dated 25 Jan. [1929] 1 p.

Barry, Philip. ALS, The University Club [New York][S] 1929 Feb. 25, 4 p.

Behrman, S.N. ALS, Five Thirty-Five Fifth Avenue, New York[S], 1929 May 3, 1 p.

Bennett, Arnold. Photograph of a TLS, 75 Cadogan Square, S.W.1. [London][S] 1929 Feb. 2, 2 p.

Bourdet, Édouard. TLS, La Villa Blanche, Tamaris-sur-Mer[S], 1929 Feb. 11, 2 p., in French, with a manuscript translation.

Brown, Martin. TLS, Villa Gardénia, Monte Carlo[S], 1929 Feb. 11, 2 p.

Carpenter, Edward Childs. TLS, The Murray, 66 Park Avenue, New York[S], 1929 Jan. 25, 1 p.

Cohan, George M. TLS, Geo. M. Cohan Productions[S], New York, 1924 Feb. 11, 1 p.

Coward, Noel. ALS from Coward's secretary, Nöel [sic] Coward[S], n.p., 1929 April 24, 1 p.

—. ALS, Office of the Manager, 111 Ebury Street, S.W.1 [London][S] 1929 May 17, 1 p. (env)

—. TLS, Nöel [sic] Coward[S], n.p., 1937 Jan. 18, 2 p.

—. TLS from Coward's secretary, Nöel Coward[S], n.p., 1937 Oct. 12, 1 p., with carbon copies of three letters from Perlman to Coward, Los Angeles, 1937 Jan. 23, Aug. 27, and Sept. 1, 1 p. each.

Craven, Frank. TLS, Longacre Theatre, New York[S], n.d., 1 p.

Crothers, Rachel. TLS, 575 Park Avenue, New York[S], 1937 Feb. 5, 2 p. (env), with a carbon copy of a letter from Perlman, Los Angeles, 1937 Feb. 18, 1 p.

Galsworthy, John. Typed transcription of a letter, Biarritz, 1929 Feb. 8, 1 p. (carbon copy)

Gold, Michael. TLS, New Masses[S], New York, n.d., 2 p.

Goodman, Jules Eckert. TLS, Kenapeek, Peekskill, N.Y.[S], 1929 May 3, 1 p.

Granville-Barker, Harley. ALS, El Conquistador Hotel, Tucson, Arizona[S], 1929 Jan. 29, 1 p. (env)

Green, Paul. TLS, Raleigh Road, Chapel Hill, N.C.[S], 1937 Jan. 19, 2 p. Also, carbon copy of a letter from Perlman, Los Angeles, 1927 Jan. 23, 1 p.

Gribble, Harry Wagstaff. ALS, Hotel Bristol, New York[S], 1929 Jan. 30, 6 p.

Hamilton, Clayton. ALS, The Players, New York[S], 1924 Feb. 8, 1 p., to Miss Hague, with a typed transcription (carbon copy)

Hart, Moss. TLS, 29 West 46th Street [New York] 1933 Nov. 6, 1 p.

—. TLS, Dear Ruth, 1501 Broadway, New York[S], 1945 Aug. 9, 1 p. Also, carbon copy of a letter from Perlman, Los Angeles, 1946 Dec. 14, 1 p.

Hellman, Lillian. TLS, Pleasantville, N.Y., 1947 Jan. 6, 1 p.

Hodge, William. ALS, Hotel Astor, New York[S], n.d., 1 p., to Miss Hague, with a typed transcript.

Hopwood, Avery. ALS, The Blackstone, Chicago[S], n.d., 2 p.

Howells, William Dean. Typed note, signed, n.p., n.d., 1 p. Under the typed heading: Association for the Publication of Individual War History.

Kaufman, George S. TLS, 200 West 58th Street, New York[S], 1924 Dec. 8, 2 p.

Kelly, George. TLS, Rosalie Stewart & Bert French Productions Inc., New York[S], 1924 Feb. 12, 1 p., to Miss Hague.

Kennedy, Charles Rann. TLS, The Bennett School, Millbrook, N.Y.[S], 1929 June 5, 2 p.

Langner, Lawrence. TLS, Fourteen West Eleventh Street [New York][S] 1929 Feb. 1, 2 p.

Levy, Benn. TLS from his secretary, 66, Church Street, S.W.3. [London][S] 1937 March 23, 1 p.

Lindsay, Howard. TLS, New York, 1946 Dec. 30, 1 p.

Lothar, Rudolph. TLS, Berlin, 1929 Feb. 25, 3 p., in German.

Mantle, Burns. TLS, Seasongood Road, Forest Hills Gardens, Long Island[S], 1937 Jan. 9, 1 p. Also, carbon copy of a letter from Perlman, Los Angeles, 1937 Sept. 8, 1 p.

Marquis, Don. TLS, Hollywood, 1929 April 29, 3 p.

Munro C.K. (Charles Kirkpatrick). ALS, 3 Queen's Road Studios, London[S], 1929 Feb. 4, 2 p.

Nicholson, Kenyon. TLS, 154 East 39th Street, 1924 Feb. 9, 1 p., to Miss Hague.

Odets, Clifford. TLS, n.p., 1937 Aug. 3, 1 p.

O'Marr, Elizabeth. Signature on a carbon copy of a TL from Perlman, Los Angeles, 1937 April 28.

O'Neill, Eugene. Typed transcript of a letter, n.p., n.d., 1 p., carbon copy. Also, carbon copy of a letter from Perlman to O'Neill, Los Angeles, 1937 May 13, 1 p.

Pollock, Channing. TLS, 240 West 98th Street, New York[S], 1929 Feb. 5, 2 p.

Raphaelson, Samson, TLS, 58 Central Park West [New York] 1929 Feb. 5, 2 p.

—. TLS, Riviera Country Club, Los Angeles[S], 1937 Feb. 18, 1 p., with a typed response, signed, to the questionnaire.

Reinhardt, Max. TLS to Agnes A. Porter, 2201 Maravilla Drive, Hollywood[S], 1937 June 22, 1 p. (env)

Rice, Elmer. TLS, Hotel Walton, New York[S], 1929 Feb. 1, 1 p.

Richman, Arthur. ALS, n.p., 1929 Jan. 31, 2 p.

Schnitzler, Arthur. TLS, Sternwartestrasse 71, Vienna[S], 1929 March 2, 1 p., in German.

Selwyn, Edgar. TLS, Selwyn and Company, Inc., New York[S], 1924 Dec. 3, 1 p.

Shaw, Irwin. TLS, New York, 1946 Dec. 26, 1 p.

Sherwood, R.E. TLS, 597 Fifth Avenue, New York[S], 1929 Jan. 29, 1 p.

Snow, Norman. 3 TLS, Dodd, Mead & Company, New York[S], 1937 April 5, Aug. 26, and Oct. 22, each 1 p., with copies of three letters from Perlman, Los Angeles, 1937 Aug. 21, Aug. 31, and Oct. 28, each 1 p.

Stewart, Donald Ogden. TLS, Upper Jay, N.Y., 1937 June 4, 1 p., with a typed response to the questionnaire, carbon with pencil corrections, signed, 2 p.

Strong, Austin. ALS, Hotel Weylin, New York[S], n.d., 4 p., to Miss Hague.

Thomas, Augustus. TL, n.p., 1929 Feb. 9, 1 p.

Wassermann, Jakob. TLS, Altaussee, 1929 Sept. 21, 1 p. (env), in German.

Weiman, Rita. TLS, 103 East 86th Street, New York[S], 1929 Feb. 21, 2 p.

Wilde, Percival. TLS, Sharon, Connecticut[S], 1924 Feb. 13, 1 p., to Miss Hague.

Williams, Jesse Lynch. 2 TLS, Princeton, New Jersey[S], 1929 Jan. 30 and Feb. 7, 1 and 2 p. respectively, the first from his secretary.

Also, typed table of contents for projected book on the theater.

See Christie's, New York, 17 May 1991, lot 129.
FRKF 79

ROGER PEYREFITTE (1907–2000)

Letters to Léonce Peillard

1957 March 12, 15, avenue Hoche, VIIIe [Paris][S], ALS, 1 p., correcting a mistake in a text of his.

1957 March 17, 15, avenue Hoche, VIIIe[S], ALS, 1 p.

1961 Jan. 17 [Fiesole?] APCS

London, Sotheby's, 28 May 1986, lot 183.
FRKF 1238b

ILDEBRANDO PIZZETTI (1880–1968)

Black-and-white photographic portrait of Pizzetti (14 × 8.5 cm), inscribed by the composer at the bottom: "alla gentile Signora Maria Mascagni / con rispettuosa mia cordialità / da Roma / 18-6-951 / Ildebrando Pizzetti."

London, Sotheby's, 26–27 Nov. 1987, lot 317.
FRKF 1342.2

AMILCARE PONCHIELLI (1834–86)

I. MUSIC MANUSCRIPT

Omaggio a Donizetti

Holograph full-score manuscript of the second movement of this cantata ("Qui del delubro …"), n.d., 25 p., written in black ink on tall 20-staff paper, numbered in pencil. At the top of p. 1 in Ponchielli's hand: "Cantata a / Donizetti / N° 2. Dopo il Coro d'Introduzione / Rec.o e Romanza / pr Sop.o con / Cori."

Omaggio a Donizetti, for soprano solo, women's chorus, harmonium, piano, and strings, on a text by Antonio Ghislanzoni, was premiered in Bergamo in 1875.

Marburg, Stargardt, 19 June 1984, lot 894.
FRKF 487

II. LITERARY MANUSCRIPT

Autograph synopsis for two libretti based on Shakespeare, n.d., 7 p., in black ink on two bifolia of tall paper, joined with adhesive, ruled in black and red, paginated in pencil (not in Ponchielli's hand).

The manuscript is incomplete, beginning at act 3, scene 11a, for a libretto synopsis based on *Measure for Measure*, which ends on p. 3 with a brief summary of act 5 and the comment: "Ma questo dramma non va per melodramma"; on p. 4–7, synopsis for "Racconti d'inverno di Shakespeare" (*A winter's tale*). Neither work is listed by Grove among Ponchielli's works or projects.

FRKF 1106

III. LETTERS

To Antonio Ghislanzoni

All are autograph letters, signed, unless otherwise noted.

1873
    March 14, Cremona, 3 p.
    April 14, Milan, 4 p.
    April 28, Cremona, 2 p.
    [mid to late May] "Domenica," Cremona, 2 p.
    May 21, Cremona, 1 p.
    [mid to late June] Cadenabbia, 2 p.
    Aug. 27, Cremona, 4 p.

1874
- Feb. 5, Milan, 4 p.
- [Feb. 6–7] n.p. 4 p.
- [mid to late Feb.] n.p., 1 p.
- April 9, Milan, 1 p.
- [April 12] "Domenica," n.p., 3 p.
- April 14, Milan, 4 p.
- [June] n.p., 3 p.
- June 14, Milan, 3 p.
- June 23, Milan, 3 p. Miscellaneous notes [in Ghislanzoni's hand?] on p. [4]
- [July 20–25] "Domenica," n.p., 3 p.
- Aug. 17, Milan, 3 p.
- Aug. 19, Milan, 2 p.
- Sept. 3, Milan, 4 p.
- Oct. 12, Milan, 2 p.
- Nov. 26, Milan, 4 p.
- Dec. 8, Leghorn, 3 p.

1875
- Jan. 15, Palermo, AL, 4 p., apparently incomplete
- Feb. 1, Palermo, AL, 4 p., apparently incomplete
- [mid to late March] n.p. 1 p.
- April 1, Milan, 3 p. Miscellaneous notes [in Ghislanzoni's hand?] on p. [4]
- April 5, Milan, 4 p.
- April 9, Milan, 2 p.
- April 13, Milan, 4 p.

1876
- March 23, Milan, 3 p.
- May 15, n.p., 4 p.
- Sept. 13, Cremona, 4 p.
- Oct. 23, Barco, 2 p.

1877
- Jan. 23, Rome, 1 p.
- May, Rome, 2 p.
- July 5, Rome, 2 p.
- July 7, Rome, 3 p.
- July 9, Rome, 4 p.
- July 24, Rome, AL, 4 p., apparently incomplete

1878
- Feb. 11, Rome, 4 p.
- May 8, Milan, 2 p.
- Nov. 11, Milan, 3 p.
- Nov. 22, Milan, AL, 2 p., apparently incomplete
- Nov. 27, Milan, 3 p.
- Dec. 14, Milan, 3 p.

1879
- March 15, Milan, 1 p.

1883
- July 21 [place undeciphered] 1 p.

1884
- June 14, Milan, 3 p.
- July 8, n.p., 3 p.

1885
- April 14, Milan, AL, 4 p., apparently incomplete
- May 9, Milan, 4 p.
- May 15, n.p., 3 p.
- [May] "Sabbato 23," n.p., 4 p.
- May 26, Milan, 3 p.
- May 29, Milan, 4 p.
- June 10, Milan, 3 p.
- June 14, Milan, 3 p.
- June 20, Milan, 4 p.
- June 24, Milan, 3 p.
- Aug. 10, Brescia, 4 p., concerning *Marion Delorme* and mentioning singers Pantaleoni and Lhérie, as well as Giulio Ricordi and Durand, also with a reference to *I lituani*.
- [Aug.–Sept.] n.p., 3 p.
- [Fall] "Sabbato," Turin, 3 p.
- Nov. 21, "Via S. Damiano 26" [Milan] 2 p.
- Dec. 10, Milan, 2 p.
- Dec. 22, Milan, 4 p.
- Dec. 28 [Piacenza] 4 p.

The undated letters are dated in pencil in an unidentified hand.

Antonio Ghislanzoni (1824–93) wrote the librettos for Ponchielli's *I lituani* (1874) and the unfinished *I mori di Valenza* (also 1874), but the correspondence discusses several others of Ponchielli's works, notably *Marion Delorme* (1885), as well as other composers, especially Verdi.

Letters of 13 Sept. 1875 and 10 Aug. 1885: Marburg, Stargardt, 5–6 March 1985, lot 868–69.
FRKF 820.1–2

The rest of the correspondence:
FRKF 898

To Francesco Maria Piave

1867 Nov. 4, Cremona, ALS, 4 p., concerning the libretto for an unidentified project.

London, Sotheby's, 9–10 May 1985, lot 176.
FRKF 773

BEATRIX POTTER (1866–1943)

The Owl and the Pussy Cat

Five preparatory drawings to illustrate Edward Lear's poem, pen-and-ink and watercolor. Another series of ten small illustrations, pen-and-ink, on both sides of a sheet of paper (18 × 23 cm).

The first verse of the poem is quoted in full under the first two vignettes; shorter quotations accompany three others.

London, Sotheby's, 19 June 1986, lot 713.
FRKF 1424

FRANCIS POULENC (1899–1963)

I. MUSIC MANUSCRIPTS

Les animaux modèles

Autograph manuscript notebook with preparatory notes and a musical quotation, 1942, 33 p. The manuscript occupies the first 17 leaves, unpaginated, of a 30-leaf oblong notebook (leaves 17.5 × 12.5 cm), bound in boards with a brown decorative pattern and two leather straps. Written in black ink, it is a detailed synopsis, including a sketch of a set on fol. [3r] ("Plantation possible du décor") and a single 3-measure musical quotation on fol. [3v]. On title page, in Poulenc's hand: "Notes / pour "Les animaux et leurs / hommes." On fol. [29v], in reverse, title, in his hand: "Notes pour la musique / de scène de / Périclès." No such project is recorded in Grove.

Les animaux modèles, ballet in one act after La Fontaine *Fables*, was premiered at the Paris Opéra on 8 Aug. 1942.

Schmidt 111, p. 312–21.
FRKF 742

Banalités

Holograph manuscript of this song cycle for voice and piano on poems by Guillaume Apollinaire, 1940, 18 p. Notated in black ink, with a few annotations in red pencil, on both sides of nine leaves torn from a spiral-binder notebook of tall 20-staff paper, with an additional leaf serving as title page.

> On the title page, in Poulenc's hand: "Banalités / 5 mélodies sur des poëmes / de Guillaume Apollinaire / I. Chanson d'Orkenise / II. Hôtel / III. Fagnes de Wallonie / IV. Voyage à Paris / V. Sanglots / musique de Francis Poulenc / 1940." At the top of the same page, also in his hand: "ce cahier appartient à / Francis Poulenc / 5 rue de Médicis / Paris"; at the bottom of the page, in a different hand, music publisher's number: "M.E. 6232 1 à 5."

> At the end of "Chanson d'Orkenise," dated: "Paris / Novembre / 1940"; at the end of "Hotel," dated: "Noizay / octobre 1940"; at the end of "Fagnes de Wallonie," dated: "Paris / Novembre / 1940"; at the end of "Voyage à Paris," dated: "Noizay - Octobre / 1940"; at the end of "Sanglots, dated: "Paris / Novembre / 1940." Incomplete: missing the first page of "Sanglots"; also out of order: the first page of "Hôtel" is on the verso of the last page of "Voyage à Paris," while the second page of "Hôtel" is on the recto of the first page of "Fagnes de Wallonie."

From the collection of Pierre Bernac.
Schmidt 107, p. 307–09.
Paris, Oger-Dumont (Drouot), 14 Feb. 1985, lot 70.
FRKF 919

Les biches

Two short-score manuscripts of this ballet, in the hand of a copyist, with annotations by the composer and by Bronislava Nijinska.

> Manuscript 1, 103 p. (unpaginated), is calligraphed in black and red ink on tall 15-staff paper. It comprises the following numbers (titles in red): Ouverture; Rondeau; Chanson dansée; Adagietto; Jeu; Rag-Mazurka; Coda; Andantino; Petite chanson dansée; Final.

> All the staging indications are in Poulenc's hand, in red. There are also markings in pencil in a different hand (evidently Nijinska's), some of them in Russian. Also, a number of additions in red ink in the copyist's hand, and deletions, additions, and corrections in pencil, possibly in Poulenc's hand. On title page, in the copyist's hand: "Les Biches. / Ballet avec Chant. / en 1 Acte. / Francis Poulenc." In Poulenc's hand, date "(1923)" and dedication: "à madame José-Maria Sert." Stamps of Ballets russes and of Serge Lifar (printed in purple). On p. [3] and various other pages, stamps of the music copyist R. & J. Jakob, Paris, and of the Ballets russes.

> Bound in limp pale green cloth. On front board, white paper label in the upper left corner, marked "Les Biches" in ink. On recto of front free endpaper, purple stamp of Lifar, and annotation in his hand: "Avec Notations de Poulenc et de Br. Nijinska [signed:] Serge Lifar."

FRKF 299

> Manuscript 2, 43 p., entirely in the hand of a copyist, comprises two gatherings, stitched together, of seven and five bifolia of tall 14-staff paper. There are no outer wrappers. The manuscript lacks the Chanson dansée pour l'ensemble des danseuses et danseurs and the Rag-Mazurka, both simply listed on p. 38, as well as the Petite chanson dansée and the Final, both mentioned at the end. On the title page: "A Madame J.M. Sert. /

Les Biches. / Ballet avec Chant. / Francis Poulenc." Purple stamp of Lifar. n.d.

Schmidt 36, p. 100–13.
London, Sotheby's, 9–10 May 1984, lot 188.
FRKF 299.5

Ce doux petit visage

Holograph manuscript of this song with piano on a poem by Paul Éluard, 1939, 2 p. Notated in black ink on p. [2] and [3] of a bifolium of oblong 14-staff paper (G.B.T. 1112). On p. [1] in Poulenc's hand: "Pour Alice - tendrement / Francis / Rien que ce doux petit visage … / Poesie de / Paul Eluard / Musique de / Francis Poulenc / avril / 1939." At the top of p. [2], dedication: "à la mémoire de Raymonde Linossier." Marked at the end, in pencil, "1'42" and dated: "Noizay / avril 1939." Stamped "gravé" on both p. [1] and [2]; music publisher's number (12064 R.L. et Cie) in manuscript at the bottom of p. [2] and [3].

Schmidt 99, p. 295–96.
Paris, Laurin-Guilloux-Buffetaud-Tailleur (Drouot), 19 March 1986, lot 151.
FRKF 1120

La guirlande de Campra

Holograph manuscript, in full score, of "Matelote provençale," Poulenc's contribution to this collective work for small orchestra, 1952, 9 p. Notated in dark blue ink, with additional corrections in red ballpoint pen, on pages [3] to [11], paginated 1 to 9 in Poulenc's hand, of a gathering of three nested bifolia of oblong 16-staff paper. On the front of the outer bifolium, in Poulenc's hand: "à Roger Bigonnet / très amicalement / Francis Poulenc / Matelotte [sic] provençale / (sur un thème de Campra) / pour orchestre / Francis Poulenc / juin 52." At the top of p. 1, also in Poulenc's hand: "Matelotte [sic] provençal / (sur un thème de Campra) / Francis Poulenc / juin 52." Signed and dated Noizay, June 1952, at the end.

La guirlande de Campra, variations sur un thème de Campra, a collective work with contributions from Auric, Honegger, Daniel-Lesur, Roland-Manuel, Sauguet, and Tailleferre, was published in 1954 by Salabert in Paris.

From the collection of Pierre Bernac.
Schmidt 153, p. 421–23.
London, Sotheby's, 29 May 1986, lot 290.
FRKF 1144

Un joueur de flûte berce les ruines

Holograph manuscript of this work for solo flute, 1942, 1 p. Notated in black ink on one page of a bifolium, with four printed staves. In the upper left corner is a woodcut showing a sculpted grotesque figure playing a flute. On the right is the following title, printed in black ink capital letters: "Un joueur de flute / berce les ruines." Underneath the printed title is the following inscription in Poulenc's hand: "Pour Madame / Paul Vincent-Vallette / en très respectueux hommage / Fr. Poulenc." Signed and dated 1942 at the bottom of the page. On p. [4] of the bifolium, printed indication: "Joueur de flute / Sculpture de la maison de l'abbé Grécourt." Dated 1941 by Schmidt, based on another manuscript.

First published in 2000 by Chester Music, with a foreword by Ransom Wilson.

Not in Grove.
Schmidt 114, p. 323, as "Untitled Piece for Solo Flute."
London, Sotheby's, 9–10 May 1985, lot 182.
FRKF 775

Main dominée par le coeur

Holograph manuscript of this song on a poem by Paul Éluard, 1946, 5 p. Notated in blue ink on 14-staff paper on five unnumbered pages of two nested bifolia. The music begins on the first page of the inner bifolium and ends on page 3 of the outer bifolium. There are a few corrections in black and red pencil. On cover, in Poulenc's hand: "Main dominée par le coeur / (titre provisoire) / - / Paul Eluard Francis Poulenc / - " Dated at the end: "Noizay, Aug. 1946." At the top of the first page, dedication: "à Marie-Blanche" [de Polignac].

Schmidt 135, p. 374–76.
FRKF 283

… Mais mourir

Holograph manuscript of this song for voice and piano on a poem by Paul Éluard, 1947, 2 p. Notated in black ink on p. [2] to [4] of a single bifolium of oblong 12-staff paper (G.B.T. 1112). On p. [1] in Poulenc's hand: "Brouillon définitif / à la mémoire de Nus[c]h / … mais mourir / Paul Eluard / Francis Poulenc / 1947." Dated at the end: "Noizay / [cancelled: Septembre] Octobre 47."

Schmidt 137, p. 377–79.
Paris, Oger-Dumont (Drouot), 14 Feb. 1985, lot 68.
FRKF 918a

Mélancolie

Holograph manuscript of this work for solo piano, 1940, 10 p. Notated in dark blue ink on p. [3] to [12], paginated 1 to 10, of a gathering of four nested bifolia of tall 24-staff paper. On p. [1] in Poulenc's hand: "Mélancolie / Francis

Poulenc." Also stamped "Gravé," with music publisher's number "M.E. 6231" handwritten at the bottom. At the top of p. 1, dedication "à Raymond Destouches" and autograph inscription: "Pour mon cher petit / Raymond bien / affectueusement / son grand ami / Francis / 1941." Dated at the end: "Talence / Brive / juin / août 1940."

Schmidt 105, p. 304–05.
Paris, Ader-Picard-Tajan, 18 Dec. 1985, no. 340B.
FRKF 934

Miroirs brûlants. 1. "Tu vois le feu du soir"

Holograph manuscript of this song for voice and piano on a text by Paul Éluard, 1938, 5 p. Notated in black ink, with a few corrections in red pencil, on p. [3] to [7] of a gathering of two nested bifolia of oblong 12-staff paper (G.B.T. 1112). On p. [1] in Poulenc's hand: "Deux Poèmes de / Paul Eluard / I. / II. / Francis Poulenc / 1938." At the top of p. [3], dedication "à Pierre Bernac" and inscription: "pour mon vieux Pierre / en souvenir de notre cher travail / d'Anost, avec / ma vieille amitié. / Francis." Dated at the end "Autun 1938."

From the collection of Pierre Bernac.
Schmidt 98, p. 293–95.
Paris, Oger-Dumont (Drouot), 14 Feb. 1985, lot 68.
FRKF 918b

Montparnasse

Holograph manuscript of this song for voice and piano on a poem by Guillaume Apollinaire, 1941–45, 5 p. Notated in black ink on p. [3] to [7] of a gathering of two nested bifolia of tall 18-staff paper (Durand & Cie). Dated at the end: "Noizay - Paris / Septembre 41 – Janvier 45." On p. [1] in Poulenc's hand: "Montparnasse / Poëme de / Guillaume Apollinaire / musique de / Francis Poulenc."

From the collection of Pierre Bernac.
Schmidt 127, p. 356–57.
Paris, Oger-Dumont (Drouot), 14 Feb. 1985, lot 71.
FRKF 920

Paul et Virginie

Holograph manuscript of this song for voice and piano on a poem by Raymond Radiguet, 1946, 3 p. Notated in dark blue ink on p. [2]–[4] of a single bifolium of tall 16-staff paper. On p. [1] in Poulenc's hand: "à Lucien Daudet / Paul et Virginie / R. Radiguet Fr. Poulenc." Stamped "Gravé" and marked, in a different hand: "M.E. 6482 / 1 epreuve en noir / in/40 Jésus / édition séparée." Dated at the end: "Noizay / août 46."

Schmidt 132, p. 370–71.

Paris, Oger-Dumont (Drouot), 14 Feb. 1985, lot 73.
FRKF 922

Un poème

Holograph manuscript of this song for voice and piano, on a poem by Guillaume Apollinaire, 1946, 2 p. Notated in dark blue ink on p. [2] and [3] of a single bifolium of tall 16-staff paper. On p. [1] in Poulenc's hand: "à Luigi Dallapiccola / Un Poëme / G. Apollinaire Fr. Poulenc." Stamped "Gravé" and marked, in a different hand: "M.E. 6484." Dated at the end: "Le Tremblay / 27 juillet / 1946."

From the collection of Pierre Bernac.
Schmidt 131, p. 369–70.
Paris, Oger-Dumont (Drouot), 14 Feb. 1985, lot 72.
FRKF 921

Le portrait

Holograph manuscript of this song for voice and piano on a text by Colette, 1938, 5 p. Notated in black ink on p. [3]–[7] of two nested bifolia of oblong 12-staff paper (G.B.T. 1111). On the front cover, in Poulenc's hand: "Le Portrait. / Poëme de Colette / Francis Poulenc / 1938." At the top of p. 1: "à Hélène Jourdan Morhange."

From the collection of Pierre Bernac.
Schmidt 92, p. 278–79.
Paris, Oger-Dumont (Drouot), 14 Feb. 1985, lot 67.
FRKF 917

Rosemonde

Holograph manuscript of this song for voice and piano, on a poem by Guillaume Apollinaire, 1954, 3 p. Notated in black ink on p. [1]–[3] of a single bifolium of tall 16-staff paper. On p. [1] in Poulenc's hand: "à la Comtesse Pastré / Rosemonde / Poëme / de Guillaume / Apollinaire / Musique de / Francis Poulenc." Dated at the end: "Noizay / mai / 1954."

From the collection of Pierre Bernac.
Schmidt 158, p. 430–31.
Paris, Oger-Dumont (Drouot), 14 Feb. 1985, lot 76.
FRKF 923

Sonata for flute and piano

Holograph manuscript draft, 1956–57, 30 p. Notated in black ink, with corrections in red and blue ballpoint pen, on two gatherings of six and four tall bifolia of 12-staff paper (embossed Flammarion), the first paginated 1–17 (first and second movements), the second 1 to 13 (third movement). Pages 18–19 (first gathering) and 14–16 (second gathering) are paginated but blank. At the top of p. 1 (first gathering): "à mémoire de Madame Elizabeth Sprague Coolidge / Sonate / pour flute et piano / monstre / [addition in red pencil:] Brouillon / Pour mon ange / gardien, le cher / Docteur Chevalier / tendrement / Poulenc." At the top of p. 1 (second gathering), in red ballpoint pen: "brouillon." Dated on p. 11 (first gathering) at the end of the first movement: "Majestic / Cannes / Decembre / 56"; and at the bottom of p. 13 (second gathering), at the end of the third movement: "Majestic / Cannes / Décembre / mars / 57."

Schmidt 164, p. 455–66.
Heinrich Schütz to Henry Miller, p. 144–45.
Paris, Offret-Daniel (Drouot), 16 April 1985, lot 16.
FRKF 639

II. LETTERS

Unless noted, the letters described below are not in Poulenc's *Correspondance 1910–1963*.

To Stéphane Audel

[1955] "Jeudi," n.p., ALS, 1 p., concerning *Dialogues des carmélites*.

Paris, Laurin-Guilloux-Buffetaud-Tailleur (Drouot), 1 July 1986, lot 233.
FRKF 1171

To Georges and Nora Auric

[1932*] Jan. 12, Noizay, ALS to Nora Auric, 6 p. (env), concerning the concerto for two pianos and orchestra; also mentions Serge Lifar, Darius Milhaud's *Maximilien*, Erik Satie's *Le piège de Méduse*, Henri Sauguet, Ravel's *Concerto in G*, Cocteau, and Paul Hindemith. *Correspondance*, p. 360–61.

[1933 Jan. 23*] Paris, ALS to Nora Auric, 8 p. (env), concerning *Le Bal Masqué*; also mentions Ravel's *Concerto pour la main gauche*. *Correspondance*, p. 381–82.

London, Sotheby's, 21 May 1987, lots 482–83.
FRKF 1320–21

[1936 Aug. 25] "mardi," Hotel du Commerce, Uzerche[S], ALS to Georges Auric, 4 p. Mentions the death of Pierre-Octave Ferroud, Pierre Bernac, and the *Litanies à la vierge noire*. *Correspondance*, p. 424–26.

London, Sotheby's, 28 May 1986, lot 514.
FRKF 1132

[1937 Aug. 17*] Anost, Saône-et-Loire, ALS to Nora Auric, 2 p. (env). Mentions his *Mass in G* and his working sessions with Pierre Bernac. *Correspondance*, p. 447–48.

[1938 Sept. 11*] Noizay, ALS to Nora Auric, 4 p. (env), concerning the *Litanies à la vierge noire*; mentions Nadia Boulanger.

London, Sotheby's, 21 May 1987, lots 484–85.
FRKF 1322–23

[1940 Aug. 20, Brive-la-Gaillarde*] ALS to Georges Auric, 4 p. (env). Mentions Darius Milhaud, Jacques Ibert, Marc Chadourne and his wife, Yvonne Printemps and Pierre Fresnay, and *Les animaux et leurs hommes*. *Correspondance*, p. 500–01.

[1940] Noizay, ALS to Georges Auric, 2 p. Mentions Stravinsky and a composition entitled "Dimanche de mai." *Correspondance*, p. 495.

London, Sotheby's, 28 May 1986, lots 512, 515.
FRKF 1318–19

[ca. 1949 or 1950] "Dimanche," Le Grand Coteau, Noizay[S], ALS to Nora Auric, 4 p., concerning his piano concerto; also mentions Toscanini.

London, Sotheby's, 21 May 1987, lot 486.
FRKF 1324

[1953?] "mardi," Sept. 22, n.p., ALS to Georges Auric, 4 p., concerning *Dialogues des carmélites*, the *Stabat Mater*, and Monteverdi's *Orfeo*. *Correspondance*, p. 768–69.

London, Sotheby's, 28 May 1986, lot 518.
FRKF 1131

To Pierre Bernac

[1940] July 10, Cahors, ALS, 4 p. *Correspondance*, p. 497–98.

[1944 July 29] "samedi," n.p., ALS, 2 p. Mentions *Les mamelles de Tirésias*. *Correspondance*, p. 566–67.

[1944?] "Dimanche," n.p., ALS, 4 p. Mentions *Les mamelles de Tirésias*. *Correspondance*, p. 570–71.

[ca. 1944] "16," Larche, ALS, 2 p. Mentions *Les mamelles de Tirésias*.

[1945] ANS, n.p., 1 p., on the verso of a TLS from Philippe Erlanger, Association Française d'Action Artistique [Paris][S] 1945 Sept. 25, 1 p.

[ca. 1945] "samedi," n.p., ALS, 6 p. Mentions his stage music for Armand Salacrou's *Le soldat et la sorcière*.

[1945 Sept.] "lundi 10," n.p., ALS, 6 p. Mentions *Le soldat et la sorcière*. *Correspondance*, p. 604–05.

[1946 Aug.] "Dimanche," n.p., ALS, 2 p., concerning Radiguet and the song *Paul et Virginie*. *Correspondance*, p. 627.

[ca. 1947] "samedi," Noizay, ALS, 2 p. Mentions his stage music for Molière's *Amphitryon*.

[ca. 1947] Sept. 23, Noizay, ALS, 4 p. Mentions *Les mamelles de Tirésias* and *Amphitryon*.

[1948] July 18, Le Tremblay, ALS, 8 p., concerning *Calligrammes*. *Correspondance*, p. 646–47.

[ca. 1950] "mercredi," Cannes, ALS, 4 p. Mentions the *Stabat Mater*.

[1950 Aug.] ALS, Le Tremblay, 2 p., concerning *La fraîcheur et le feu*. Also, manuscript table of contents for "La Fraicheur et le Feu / 7 Mélodies sur 1 poëme / de Paul Eluard," 1 p. *Correspondance*, p. 691–92.

1950 Aug. 29, n.p., ALS on both sides of a card, 2 p. *Correspondance*, p. 694.

[1953 Jan. 6] "mardi," Hôtel Beau-Rivage, Ouchy-Lausanne[S], ALS, 4 p. Mentions Charlie Chaplin and the *Entretiens avec Claude Rostand*. *Correspondance*, p. 745–46.

[1953 March 26] APCS, incomplete. *Correspondance*, p. 751.

[1953 Aug.] "samedi 22," n.p., ALS on three cards, 6 p., concerning *Dialogues des carmélites*; also mentions Pierre Fournier. *Correspondance*, p. 757–58.

1953 Sept. 1, n.p., ALS, 8 p., concerning *Dialogues des carmélites*; with two short musical examples. *Correspondance*, p. 760–61.

[1953 Sept. 11] "Vendredi," n.p., ALS on two cards, 4 p., concerning *Dialogues des carmélites*. *Correspondance*, p. 764.

[1953 Dec. 7] "lundi," n.p., ALS, 4 p., concerning *Dialogues des carmélites*; also mentions *Concert champêtre* and Hugues Cuénod. See *Correspondance*, p. 773–74, no. 1.

[1953] Dec. 8, n.p., ALS on both sides of a card, concerning *Dialogues des carmélites*. With two short music quotations, one of 4 measures, the other of 3 measures. *Correspondance*, p. 773.

[1953 Dec. 13] "Dimanche," n.p., ALS on two cards, 4 p., concerning *Dialogues des carmélites*. See *Correspondance*, p. 774, n. 1.

[1953 Dec. 18] "vendredi," Lausanne, ALS, 4 p. Mentions the *Concert champêtre* and *Dialogues des carmélites*; also the Cluytens recording of *Les mamelles de Tirésias*. See *Correspondance*, p. 774, n. 1.

[1953] Dec. 19, Hotel Beau-Rivage, Ouchy-Lausanne[S], ALS, 4 p., concerning *Dialogues des carmélites*. *Correspondance*, p. 777.

[1954] n.p., ALS, 1 p., concerning *Dialogues des carmélites*. On the verso of a TLS from Claude Delvincourt to Poulenc, 1954 Jan. 27, Conservatoire national de musique[S], 1 p.

[1954 July 28] "mercredi" n.p., ALS, 10 p., concerning *Dialogues des carmélites*. *Correspondance*, p. 796–98.

[1954 Aug.] "mardi" [Noizay] ALS, 5 p., concerning *Dialogues des carmélites*; also mentions Robert Fizdale. *Correspondance*, p. 802–03.

[1955 Sept. 9] "Vendredi," Noizay, ALS, 5 p., concerning a recording of his songs. *Correspondance*, p. 828.

[1956] Aug. 17, n.p., ALS, 6 p., concerning *Dialogues des carmélites*; also mentions *Le travail du peintre*. *Correspondance*, p. 846–48.

[1956] "Dimanche," Hôtel Beau-Rivage, Ouchy-Lausanne[S], ALS, 6 p. Mentions *Le travail du peintre*, an unidentified sonata, and the *Entretiens avec Claude Rostand*.

[1957 Jan.] "Jeudi," Gr. Hotel Continental, Milan[S], ALS, 2 p., concerning *Dialogues des carmélites*. *Correspondance*, p. 858–59.

[1957] March 8, Hotel Majestic, Cannes[S], ALS, 4 p. Mentions Pierre Boulez. *Correspondance*, p. 864–65.

[1957] July 12, Touring-Hotel Bristol, Cologne[S], ALS, 4 p., concerning *Dialogues des carmélites*. *Correspondance*, p. 873–74.

[1958 March] "Jeudi," Blue Bar, Cannes[S], ALS, 4 p., concerning *La voix humaine*. *Correspondance*, p. 887–88.

1958 Easter, Saint-Raphaël, ALS, 8 p., concerning *La voix humaine*. *Correspondance*, p. 891–93.

[1958] Aug. 11, Tourrettes-sur-Loup, ALS, 4 p., concerning *La voix humaine*. *Correspondance*, p. 897–98.

[1958 Oct. 4] "samedi," Villa d'Este, Cernobbio, Lago di Como[S], ALS, 4 p., concerning *Dialogues des carmélites*; also mentions Ildebrando Pizzetti and Denise Duval, as well as other singers. *Correspondance*, p. 900–01.

[1959] Aug. 20, n.p., 4 p. ALS, concerning the *Gloria*. *Correspondance*, p. 931–32.

[1959 Dec.] "samedi soir," n.p., ALS, 2 p., concerning the Fréjus disaster.

1960

Feb. 26, Hotel Wyndham, New York[S], ALS, 2 p., concerning *Les mamelles de Tirésias* in New York. *Correspondance*, p. 941–42.

[March 2] "mercredi," Hotel Ambassador, Chicago[S], ALS, 2 p. Mentions Duval. *Correspondance*, p. 942–43.

[July] "Lundi" [Rocamadour?] APCS. Mentions the *Gloria*. *Correspondance*, p. 947.

Sept. 5, n.p., ALS, 4 p. Mentions *La voix humaine* and *Dialogues des carmélites*. *Correspondance*, p. 958.

[Sept.] "mercredi," n.p., ALS, 4 p. Mentions *La voix humaine* with Duval in England. *Correspondance*, 959–60.

1961

[Jan.] "jeudi matin" [Boston] ALS, 2 p., concerning the *Gloria*. *Correspondance*, p. 970–71.

[Jan. 23] "Lundi" [New York] ALS, 2 p., concerning the *Gloria*. *Correspondance*, p. 973.

1962

Feb. 6, n.p., ALS, 2 p. Mentions the *Gloria* at Aspen.

March 26, n.p., ALS, 4 p. Mentions the *Sept répons des ténèbres*. *Correspondance*, p. 990.

July 3, Rocamadour, ALS, 6 p. Mentions Gérard Souzay, among much other musical news.

July 14, Bagnols-en-Forêt, ALS, 3 p. *Correspondance*, p. 996.

July 28, n.p., ALS, 2 p., a report on the Aix-en-Provence festival, mentioning Darius Milhaud's *Les malheurs d'Orphée*.

Aug. 20, n.p., ALS on two cards, 4 p.

Nov. 8, n.p., ALS, 4 p., concerning Nadia Boulanger, the *Sonata for clarinet and piano*, and *Les mamelles de Tirésias*.

Nov. 10, n.p., ALS, 2 p. Mentions the *Sonata for oboe and piano*.

Undated or without year

ALS, "jeudi," n.p., 2 p., concerning *Dialogues des carmélites*.

ALS, Feb. 14, n.p., 2 p., reporting on a concert in Algiers.

ALS, "vendredi," Turin, 2 p., reporting on a concert.

ALS, "31," Rome, 4 p. Mentions the *Piano Concerto*; also mentions Jane Bathori.

ALS, March 14, Naples, 3 p. Mentions Gino Penno, Renata Tebaldi, and Ebe Stignani in *Aida*; also mentions Ingrid Bergman and Roberto Rossellini.

ALS, "vendredi," Grand Hotel Continental, Milan^S, 2 p. Reports on Tebaldi and Giuseppe di Stefano in *Tosca* and Mario del Monaco and Leonie Rysanek in *Otello*.

ALS, "samedi" [Noizay] 2 p. Mentions *La voix humaine* and Bartók's *Bluebeard's Castle*.

ALS, "vendredi," n.p., 2 p., concerning *Dialogues des carmélites*; mentions Tebaldi in *Aida*. Addressed to "Chère Pierre."

ALS on both sides of two cards, "vendredi," n.p., 4 p., concerning *Dialogues des carmélites*.

APCS [Rocamadour?]

ALS, "mardi soir," n.p., 4 p., concerning the Parisian premiere of *Dialogues des carmélites*.

ALS, "lundi," n.p., 4 p., concerning a concerto [for two pianos?].

ALS, "lundi," n.p., 2 p., concerning *Dialogues des carmélites*.

ALS, "lundi" [after 1958] n.p., 4 p. Mentions *Dialogues des carmélites* [London premiere] and *La voix humaine*.

ALS, "lundi," n.p., 3 p. Mentions *Les mamelles de Tirésias*.

ALS, July 30, n.p., 2 p. Mentions *Les mamelles de Tirésias*.

ALS, "vendredi, n.p., 1 p.

Paris, Oger-Dumont (Drouot), 14 Feb. 1985, lots 79–81.
FRKF 924–26

To Louis Chevalier

[1956 July] Evian, ALS, 1 p., dated in pencil, possibly by the recipient.

1960 Aug. 12, n.p., 2 p.

1961 July 30, n.p., ALS, 1 p.

1962 Nov. 13, Bagnols-en-Forêt, ALS, 1 p.

n.d., "Dimanche," n.p., ALS, 4 p.

n.y. April 28, n.p., ALS, 4 p.

n.y. June 6, n.p., ALS, 1 p.

n.d., "Mercredi," n.p., ALS, 2 p.

n.d. [Rome?] APCS

n.d., n.p., ALS, 1 p.

n.d., Noizay, ALS on one side of a card

Louis Chevalier was Poulenc's doctor, and the correspondence deals largely with his health.

Paris, Offret-Daniel (Drouot), 16 April 1985, lots 18–23.
FRKF 640.1–6

To Serge Diaghilev

1919 April 28, Paris, ALS, 2 p. Mentions G. Jean-Aubry, Misia Sert (Edwards), and the *Rapsodie nègre*. From the collection of Serge Lifar, with his red stamp. *Correspondance*, p. 89.

London, Sotheby's, 9 May 1984, lot 186.
FRKF 307

To Pierre Fournier

1962 Nov. 1, Cannes, 2 p., addressed to "cher enfant." Mentions the *Sonata for oboe and piano*. *Correspondance*, p. 1004–05.

Paris, Laurin-Guilloux-Buffetaud-Tailleur (Drouot), 19 March 1986, lot 152.
FRKF 1121

To G. Jean-Aubry

[1919 June 10*] "Jeudi 8" [Pont-sur-Seine, Aube*] ALS, 2 p. (env), concerning *Le bestiaire*.

London, Sotheby's, 29 Nov. 1985, lot 180.
FRKF 1075

1919 June 10, Pont-sur-Seine, TLS, 3 p. (env). Mentions *Le bestiaire* as well as Stravinsky and Ravel. *Correspondance*, p. 92–93.

London, Sotheby's, 28 May 1986, lot 513.
FRKF 1133

[1919 Nov. 8*] "Vendredi, 23 rue de Monceau" [Paris] ALS, 2 p. (env). Mentions Honegger and *Cocardes*.

London, Sotheby's, 9–10 May 1985, lot 178.
FRKF 774.2

[1920*] June 22, n.p., ALS, 2 p. (env), concerning a proposed concert in London.

Paris, Laurin-Guilloux-Buffetaud-Tailleur (Drouot), 12 Dec. 1985, lot 159.
FRKF 930

[1921 Oct. 17*] ALS on two post cards, 3 p. (env). Mentions Malipiero's *Quartet*, Stravinsky's *Concertino*, and Bartók's *Second Quartet*, as well as Rubinstein and Milhaud.

London, Sotheby's, 29 Nov. 1985, lot 181.
FRKF 1074

[1921 Oct. 25, Paris*] "Dimanche soir," ALS, 2 p. (env). Mentions Malipiero and a planned string quartet.

Paris, Laurin-Guilloux-Buffetaud-Tailleur (Drouot), 12 Dec. 1985, lot 160.
FRKF 931

[1922 April] "samedi 15" [Paris*] ALS, 1 p. (env), concerning the program of a concert of his piano music in Le Havre.

London, Sotheby's, 9–10 May 1985, lot 177.
FRKF 774.1

[1922] Sept. 18 [Tours*] ALS, 3 p. (env), concerning the proof of a text on him in Chester's "Miniatures" series.

London, Sotheby's, 9–10 May 1985, lot 179.
FRKF 774.3

[1923 Sept. 26, Paris*] APCS, concerning *Les biches*.

London, Sotheby's, 9–10 May 1985, lot 180.
FRKF 774.4

To Roland-Manuel

[1943 Nov. 8*] Noizay, ALS on both sides of three cards (env). Congratulates him on his work on Debussy and Ravel; mentions Stravinsky. *Correspondance*, p. 547.

[1950] March 1, Carmel, California, ALS, 4 p. Mentions Denise Duval and *L'heure espagnole*. *Correspondance*, p. 683–84.

[1954 Feb. 6] "Samedi," Hotel Majestic, Cannes^S, ALS, 4 p. concerning Bernac and the Conservatoire; also mentions Honegger, Boulez, Delvincourt, Chabrier, and *Dialogues des carmélites*. *Correspondance*, p. 784–85.

Paris, Paul Renaud (Drouot), 14 May 1986, lots 113, 119, 120.
FRKF 1195–97

To M. Monod

[1954 March 26] "vendredi," Semiramis Hotel, Cairo^S, ALS, 4 p. Mentions *Dialogues des carmélites*.

M. Monod was the French Consul in Alexandria (see *Correspondance*, p. 786–87, n. 3).

London, Sotheby's, 9–10 May 1985, lot 183.
FRKF 776

To Ricardo Vinès

[1917 Aug. 25, Paramé*] ALS, 4 p. (env), mentioning Debussy and Ravel. *Correspondance*, p. 54–55.

Paris, Laurin-Guilloux-Buffetaud-Tailleur (Drouot), 12 Dec. 1985, lot 158.
FRKF 929

To an unidentified friend

[1942] Noizay, ALS, 2 p., concerning *Les animaux modèles*.

Paris, Laurin-Guilloux-Buffetaud-Tailleur (Drouot), 12 Dec. 1985, lot 161.
FRKF 932

III. MISCELLANEOUS

Pencil sketch of Poulenc by Christian Bérard (17 × 22 cm). Titled "Francis Poulenc" and signed by Bérard. n.d.

Paris, Ader-Picard-Tajan, 18 Dec. 1985, lot 340.
FRKF 927

MARCEL PROUST (1871–1922)

I. MANUSCRIPTS
   A. *A la recherche du temps perdu*
   B. OTHER MANUSCRIPTS
II. LETTERS BY PROUST
III. LETTERS TO PROUST
IV. PRINTED BOOKS
V. MISCELLANEOUS MATERIAL

I. MANUSCRIPTS

A. *A la recherche du temps perdu*

Pléiade references are to the Tadié edition.

A l'ombre des jeunes filles en fleurs

Manuscript fragments and corrected proof, pasted on large sheets of thick paper, marked in blue pencil as indicated in the upper left corners.

"3èmes épreuves / N° 4," 6 proof clippings and one manuscript fragment (32 × 50 cm). Corresponds to Pléiade, 1:462–69.

Paris, Boisgirard (Drouot), 22 May 1985, lot 78.
FRKF 741

"N° 9," 18 proof clippings and 11 manuscript fragments (65 × 50 cm). Corresponds to Pléiade, 1:506–15.

FRKF 190.1

"N° 15," 9 proof clippings and 6 manuscript fragments (64.5 × 49.5 cm). Corresponds to Pléiade, 1:543–53.

Paris, Laurin-Guilloux-Buffetaud-Tailleur (Drouot), 16 Nov. 1983, lot 202.
FRKF 444

"N° 13," 21 proof clippings and 12 manuscript fragments (64.5 × 50 cm). Corresponds to Pléiade, 1:548–59.

"4èmes épreuves N° 3," 17 proof clippings and 10 manuscript fragments (65 × 49.5 cm). Corresponds to Pléiade, 1:611–23.

FRKF 1225

"N° 18," 11 proof clippings and 10 manuscript fragments (64 × 50 cm). Corresponds to Pléiade, 2:4–13.

Paris, Laurin-Guilloux-Buffetaud-Tailleur (Drouot), 17 June 1987, lot 120.
FRKF 1208

"[Premi]ères [?] épreuves / N° 26," 18 proof clippings and 8 manuscript fragments (63 × 47.5 cm). Corresponds to Pléiade, 2:79–88.

Paris, Ader-Picard-Tajan (Drouot), 17 Oct. 1984, lot 156.
FRKF 498

"2èmes épreuves" and "N° 28," 13 proof clippings and 7 manuscript fragments (63 × 47.5 cm). Corresponds to Pléiade, 2:96–105.

Paris, Laurin-Guilloux-Buffetaud-Tailleur (Drouot), 17 June 1987, lot 121.
FRKF 1209

"Cahier violet / N° 6," 6 proof clippings and 8 manuscript fragments (64.5 × 50 cm). A large portion of the sheet was cut out and subsequently pasted over. Corresponds to Pléiade, 2:164–71.

New York, Christie's, 17 Dec. 1983, lot 513.
FRKF 157

"Page 23," 12 manuscript fragments (64 × 48 cm). The whole upper right corner cut out. Corresponds approximately to Pléiade, 2:249–54.

FRKF 1225

"Cahier violet / N° 24," 9 manuscript fragments (33 × 48 cm). Corresponds approximately to Pléiade, 2:250–56.

FRKF 190.2

"Cahier violet / N° 29," 17 manuscript fragments (64.5 × 47.5 cm). Corresponds to Pléiade, 2:259–69.

London, Sotheby's, 17 Nov. 1983, lot 202.
FRKF 235

"Cahier violet / N° 34," 3 proof clippings and 7 manuscript fragments (28 × 50 cm.). Corresponds to Pléiade, 2:302–04.

FRKF 190.3

Le côté de Guermantes

Corrected galleys (*placards*), with manuscript additions, 1919, 59 folios.

The first series of *placards*, numbered 1 to 12, corresponds to Pléiade, 2:310–452, beginning with "A l'âge où les noms …" The second series, comprising *placards* numbered 32 to 48, corresponds to Pléiade 2:695–884, from "leur naissance. Car le soir du brouillard …" to the end of the novel. In the upper left corner of *placard* 1, pasted-on printed label: "Prière de retourner ces épreuves corrigées et signées à M. Gallimard," with manuscript note, possibly in Proust's hand: "Corrigées le 27 mai 1919." Similar labels are found on *placard* 7, with the manuscript date 11 June 1919, and on *placard* 9 (16 June 1919). Together with *placard* 10, manuscript draft, beginning "Enfin il reçut cette lettre de réconciliation qu'il avait bien je pense imaginée plusieurs milliers de fois …" and ending "de le pouvoir, donc de le faire." (Not located in Pléiade 2, ca. 422ff or 451ff.)

At the bottom of the first side of *placard* 32, long manuscript addition consisting of two pages glued one above the other, beginning "le cri de leur rage et de leur stupéfaction" and ending "et dans l'intervalle se jetant sur les militaires." (Pléiade, 2:698–99.)

At the bottom of the second half of *placard* 44, long manuscript addition consisting of two sheets glued side by side, beginning at "Je regardais M. de Charlus" and ending "qui m'a perfidement calomnié, dis-je à M. de Charlus." (Pléiade, 2:843–48.)

Shorter manuscript additions at the bottom of the second half of *placard* 38 and at the bottom of the first half of *placard* 43.

The corrections are made in black ink, the longer ones circled in blue pencil. The second sides of *placards* 34, 45, and 47 are entirely uncorrected.

FRKF 188

La prisonnière

Autograph draft fragment on two pieces of paper glued together (11 × 27.5 cm), numbered "39" in Proust's hand at the bottom. Marked in pencil on the verso, in an unidentified hand: "dos[sier] rouge / intitulé / 2e partie de / l'Episode / soirée Verdurin / quai Conti." Concerning Vinteuil; corresponds to Pléiade, 3:756–57.

Paris, Ader-Picard-Tajan (Drouot), 22 Nov. 1985, lot 130.
FRKF 1378

B. OTHER MANUSCRIPTS

"A Daniel Halévy, en le regardant pendant le premier quart d'heure de colle"

Autograph poem, [13 May 1888], 2 p., in black ink on both sides of a sheet torn from a notebook (red rule on the left). Incipit: "Tamisé, le soleil égoutte des pleurs d'or …"

Autograph note by Halévy on p. [2], beginning: "Proust (Marcel) retenue du Dimanche 13 mai 1887."

Écrits de jeunesse, p. 140–41.
Paris, Laurin-Guilloux-Buffetaud-Tailleur (Drouot), 12 Dec. 1985, lot 162.
FRKF 946

"A Wafflard, Brack ou Collardeau …"

Autograph poem on Reynaldo Hahn, n.d. [1909], 2 p., on both sides of a single sheet of paper (19.5 × 17.5 cm), originally folded in four.

Lettres à Reynaldo Hahn, p. 170–71.
London, Sotheby's, 28 May 1986, lot 217.
FRKF 1210

"Chanson sur Robert"

Autograph poem, n.d., [1893?], 2 p., comprising 24 lines, beginning "Droit comme un piquet, sec comme une pierre / Ou qu'est son charme?" A satire on Robert de Montesquiou.

See Christie's, New York, 7 June 1990, lot 102.
London, Sotheby's, 9–10 May 1985, lot 368.
FRKF 788

"Hélas seul de tant d'illustres …"

Autograph poem, n.d. [Nov.–Dec. 1906], 2 p., addressed to Reynaldo Hahn. At top of poem is the following note: "Je vous enverrai suite. Mais ne laissez pas traîner à cause de plaisanteries idiotes de Chevigné et sur la Pourtalès."

Kolb VI:298–99.
London, Sotheby's, 29 Nov. 1985, lot 375.
FRKF 1070

"Lettre de recommandation à Madame Urgèle, fée, pour Mr. Daniel Halévy. artiste dramatique"

Autograph manuscript, signed, n.d., [ca. 14 May 1888], n.p., 1 p., in purple ink on the first page of a folio-size bifolium.

Kolb XXI:549–50.
Paris, Laurin-Guilloux-Buffetaud-Tailleur (Drouot), 12 Dec. 1985, lot 173.
FRKF 941

"La mort d'une grand-mère"

Autograph manuscript [1907], 4 p. Draft of an article published in *Le Figaro* for 23 July 1907, on the death of Mme de Rozières, grandmother of Robert de Flers.

Paris, Ader-Picard-Tajan (Drouot), 22 Nov. 1985, lot 118.
FRKF 1374

"Notes sur des notes"

Clippings of a newspaper review by Reynaldo Hahn, with autograph annotations by Proust, n.d. [1908?], 1 p. The article is a review of a concert by the Concerts Lamoureux and of a revival of Wagner's *Götterdämmerung* at the Paris Opéra, conducted by André Messager. The date of the article is given as 15 Nov. 1908. Mounted on heavy board.

FRKF 677

Les plaisirs et les jours

Autograph draft of a fragment from "Violante ou la mondanité," beginning "Les personnes du monde sont si médiocres que Violante n'eut qu'à desirer …" The manuscript is written in purple ink on p. 4, of an undated letter to his mother. See *Les plaisirs et les jours*, p. 42.

Paris, Boisgirard (Drouot), 22 May 1985, lot 77.
FRKF 736

"Fragments de comédie italienne," early autograph drafts [ca. 1895–96], 6 p., written in black ink on a loose bifolium and three single leaves of ruled paper (red rule on the left), paginated 2–5, the unpaginated leaf with the heading: "Supplément à la page 4 pour intercaler après les 2 premières lignes de la page 4, avant III." At the top of p. 2 is the following table of contents, cancelled: "I. Portrait de Madame. II. Etude pour le portrait de Madame Z. III. Etudes pour le portrait de Madame Z. IV. Portrait de M. Y."

The manuscript contains the following sections:

"II. / Je vous vis tout à l'heure pour la première fois, Cydalise …," p. 2–4 and unpaginated, corresponding more or less to section VI:I ("Cires perdues") of "Fragments de comédie italienne" (*Les plaisirs et les jours*, p. 56–57).

"III. Myrto, spirituelle bonne et jolie mais qui donne dans le chic," p. 4–5, corresponding more or less to section II ("Les amies de la comtesse Myrto") of "Fragments de comédie italienne" (*Les plaisirs et les jours*, p. 52–54).

"IV. Témoin d'une scène un peu légère …," p. 5, corresponding to section III ("Heldémone, Adelgise, Ercole") of "Fragments de comédie italienne" (*Les plaisirs et les jours*, p. 54). Signed at the bottom of p. 5.

Paris, Laurin-Guilloux-Buffetaud-Tailleur (Drouot), 12 Dec. 1985, lot 172.
FRKF 942

"Le roman de l'inconscient"

Autograph manuscript, [1913], 4 p. Heavily corrected draft on the four sides of a folded 8vo-size sheet, paginated 2–5, of this introduction to *Du côté de chez Swann*, prepared for Proust's interview with E.J. Bois on 12 Nov. 1913.

Paris, Ader-Picard-Tajan (Drouot), 22 Nov. 1985, lot 121.
FRKF 1375

"Le roman épistolaire"

Holograph manuscript of fragments of a projected "Roman épistolaire à quatre" by Proust with his friends Daniel Halévy, Fernand Gregh, and Louis de La Salle.

The manuscript comprises the following:

> 1. Letter dated "Paris 4 août 93" in Proust's hand, 9 p. (the first eight numbered). "Non je ne vous oublie pas mon abbé …" Signed "Gouvres-Dives."
>
> 2. Letter dated "Rambouillet 5 août" in Halévy's hand, 6 p. "Cher Monsieur l'abbé, Je vais prendre un congé de quinze jours …" Signed "Milleroy."
>
> 3. Undated letter, "St Moritz," in Proust's hand, 2 p. "Ah! mon cher petit abbé vous ne m'aimez pas soumise …" Signed "Gouvres-Dives."
>
> 4. Undated letter, "Saint Moritz," in Proust's hand, 8 p. "Je suis ici depuis hier mon cher abbé …" Signed "G.D."

Écrits de jeunesse, p. 225–71.
See Jean-Yves Tadié, *Marcel Proust* (Paris: Gallimard, 1996), p. 210–13.
See also below, Letters to Daniel Halévy.
Marcel Proust: l'écriture et les arts, no. 46.
Paris, Laurin-Guilloux-Buffetaud-Tailleur (Drouot), 3 July 1985, lot 138.
FRKF 857Z

"Sentiments filiaux d'un parricide"

Fragment of a scrapbook containing original clippings of Proust's article, published in *Le Figaro* for 1 Feb. 1907. The scrapbook fragment consists of two unbound gatherings of three bifolia each, paginated respectively 265 to 276 and 277 to 288.

The following clippings are also present, as described in ink in an unidentified hand:

> "Richard Wagner à sa couturière … Monde Artiste 27 janvier 1907," p. 265–66.
>
> "Tschaïkowsky sur Wagner … Propos Artistiques 25 janvier 1907," p. 266–68.
>
> "Van Blanenberghe / Une mère tué [sic] par son fils … Temps 26 Janvier 1907," p. 269–72.

> "Van Blanenberghe" [a different article, no citation], p. 273.
>
> "Marcel Proust / Van Blarenberghe … Figaro, 1er Février 1907," p. 274–85.
>
> "Tristan Bernard … Figaro 6 fevrier 1907," p. 286–87.
>
> "Nietzche [sic] sur Wagner … Ménestrel, 9 Février 1907," p. 287.
>
> "Stéphen Heller sur Berlioz" [beginning only, no citation], p. 288.

Paris, Laurin-Guilloux-Buffetaud-Tailleur (Drouot), 3 July 1985, lot 139.
FRKF 858

Sésame et les lys

Autograph fragments of Proust's translation of John Ruskin's *Sesame and lilies*, n.d., 7 p. Written in black ink on the verso sides (and in one instance on both sides) of sheets of ruled paper of different sizes, consisting in two cases of two sheets glued one at the bottom of the other. Paginated 164–65, 167, 169–70 in black ink, with a second pagination (197–98, 200, 202–03) in blue pencil; one smaller leaf unpaginated. On p. 164, in the upper left corner, in pencil, "M. Saumoneau" (presumably the typesetter).

Proust's translation of *Sesame and lilies* was published by the Mercure de France in 1906.

Paris, Ader-Picard-Tajan (Drouot), 22 Nov. 1985, lot 113.
FRKF 1418

"Sonnet: En pensant à Daniel pendant qu'on marque les absents"

Autograph manuscript of a poem, [10 May 1889], 1 p. Written in black ink on the recto of an upside-down sheet torn from a notebook (red rule on the right). Signed: "Marcel Proust" at the bottom. Incipit: "Ses yeux sont comme les noires nuits brillantes …" Upper right corner torn, with loss of one word in the title.

Écrits de jeunesse, p. 155.
Paris, Laurin-Guilloux-Buffetaud-Tailleur (Drouot), 12 Dec. 1985, lot 164.
FRKF 945.2

"Sonnet: Pédérastie"

Autograph manuscript of a poem, [1887], 1 p., in purple ink on the recto of a ruled sheet torn from a notebook (blue rule on the left). Incipit: "Si j'avais un gros sac d'argent d'or ou de cuivre …" Inscribed at the top: "A Daniel Halévy"; initialed at the bottom: "M.P."

Écrits de jeunesse, p. 149.
Marcel Proust: l'écriture et les arts, no. 43.

Paris, Laurin-Guilloux-Buffetaud-Tailleur (Drouot), 12 Dec. 1985, lot 163.
FRKF 945.1

II. LETTERS BY PROUST

To his mother

Several of the letters dated in September 1899 are on the stationery of Splendide Hôtel & Gd Hôtel des Bains, Évian-les-Bains, abbreviated Splendide Hôtel[S].

[1887] Sept. 24, n.p. [Auteuil?] ALS, 4 p, with a postscript in the hand of Proust's grandmother. Kolb I:99–100. *Marcel Proust: l'écriture et les arts*, no. 10.

See Christie's, New York, 7 June 1990, lot 103.
FRKF 670a

[1888 Sept. 5] n.p. [Auteuil] on engraved stationery reading "Dimanche," ALS, 4 p. Kolb I:108–09.

Paris, Ader-Picart-Tajan (Drouot), 11 June 1982, lot 174.
FRKF 167

[1896 Sept. 16] "Mercredi," n.p., ALS, 4 p. Kolb II:123–24.
FRKF 1222

[1896 Sept. 19, Paris*] ALS, 1 p. Kolb II:127.
FRKF 670c

1899

[Sept. 10] "Dimanche 1h½," n.p., ALS, 12 p. Kolb II:304–05.
[Sept. 11] "Lundi 1h½," Splendide Hôtel[S], ALS, 8 p. Kolb II:306–09.
[Sept. 12] "Mardi 2 heures," Splendide Hôtel[S], ALS, 13 p. Kolb II:310–13.
[Sept. 13] "Mercredi 1 heure," Splendide Hôtel[S], ALS, 4 p. Kolb II:314–16.
[Sept. 14] "Jeudi 1 heure ½," n.p., ALS, 18 p. Kolb II:318–21.
[Sept. 15] "Vendredi 3 heures," n.p [Evian] ALS, 11 p. Kolb II:322–23.
[Sept. 16] "Samedi 3 heures," n.p. [Evian] ALS, 12 p. Kolb II:325–27.
[Sept. 17] Splendide Hôtel[S], ALS, 6 p. Kolb II:329–31.
[Sept. 18 or 19] n.p., ALS, 4 p. Incomplete, beginning with the words: "j'avais pu mieux faire …," and without the end of the letter. Kolb II:332–33.
[Sept. 20] "Mercredi 2 heures," n.p., ALS, 8 p. Kolb II:335–37.
[Sept. 22] "Vendredi 1 heure," Splendide Hôtel[S], ALS, 8 p. Kolb II:338–41.
[Sept. 24] "Dimanche 1 heure ½" n.p., ALS, 8 p. Kolb II:343–45.
[Sept. 25 or 26] Splendide Hôtel[S], ALS, 6 p. Kolb II:346–48.
[Sept. 28 or 29] "Couché à une heure," Splendide Hôtel[S], ALS, 7 p. Kolb II:350–52.
[Sept. 29 or 30] Splendide Hôtel[S], ALS, 4 p. Kolb II:353–55.

FRKF 340

[1902 Oct. 17] "Vendredi," Hôtel de l'Europe, Amsterdam[S], ALS, 2 p. Kolb III:163–65. *Marcel Proust: l'écriture et les arts*, no. 63.

[1902 Dec. 6] n.p., ALS, 4 p. Kolb III:190–91. *Marcel Proust: l'écriture et les arts*, no. 14.

[1903 March 9] n.p., ALS, 8 p. Kolb III:265–68.

[1903 March 18–19] n.p., ALS, 3 p. Kolb III:275–76.

[1903? April] n.p., ALS, 1 p. Kolb III:292.

[1903 May?] n.p., ALS, 2 p. Kolb III:327–28.

[ca. 1903 May?] n.p., ALS, 1 p. Kolb III:328.

[1903 July?] n.p., ALS, 1 p. Kolb IV:424.

[1903 July 16] n.p., ALS, 6 p. Kolb III:373–74.

[ca. 1903 Dec.] n.p., ALS, 1 p., on mourning stationery. Kolb III:445.

[1903?] n.p., ALS, 1 p. Kolb III:357.

[1904 May or June?] n.p., ALS, 2 p. Kolb IV:143–44.

[1904 June 22?] n.p., ALS, 1 p. Kolb IV:167–68.

[1904 Aug. 11] Yacht Hélène[S], ALS, 11 p. Kolb IV:209–13.

[1904 Aug. 15] "Lundi soir" [Paris] ALS, 8 p. (mourning env). Kolb IV:216–18.

[1905, end of Aug.] n.p., ALS, 1 p. on mourning stationery. On verso: "Madame." Kolb V:162. This may be Proust's last letter to his mother, who died on 26 Sept. 1905.

n.d, n.p., ALS, 1 p. Kolb III:467.

London, Sotheby's, 26–27 May 1983, lot 190.
FRKF 137

To André Beaunier

[ca. 1912 Nov. 10] n.p., ALS, 4 p. Kolb XI:371–73.

Paris, Ader-Picard-Tajan (Drouot), 19 June 1984, lot 265.
FRKF 529.2

[1912 Dec. 20] n.p., ALS, 3 p. Kolb XI:375.

Paris, Ader-Picard-Tajan (Drouot), 19 June 1984, lot 264.
FRKF 529.1

[1913 Dec. 8] n.p., ALS, 4 p. Kolb XII:366–68

Paris, Ader-Picard-Tajan (Drouot), 11 June 1982, lot 180.
FRKF 173

To Robert de Billy

[ca. 1892 Aug. 19] n.p., ALS, 2 p., on both sides of an oblong pink card. Kolb I:181.

[after 1905 Sept. 13] n.p., ALS, 3 p., on mourning stationery. Kolb V:340.

Paris, Laurin-Guilloux-Buffetaud-Tailleur (Drouot), 12 June 1984, lot 108.

FRKF 461.1–2

[1911 April (8?)] n.p., ALS, 7 p. Kolb X:278–79.

Paris, Laurin-Guilloux-Buffetaud-Tailleur (Drouot), 3 July 1985, lot 146.

FRKF 862

[1919 late Oct.] n.p., ALS, 19 p. Kolb XVIII:446–49.

See Christie's, New York, 7 June 1990, lot 111.
New York, Sotheby's, 15 Oct. 1982, lot 294.

FRKF 61

To Gustave Binet-Valmer

[ca. 1921 June 4] 44 rue Hamelin [Paris] ALS, 7 p. Kolb XX:314–15.

Paris, Ader-Picart-Tajan (Drouot), 11 June 1982, lot 182.

FRKF 175

To Jacques Boulenger

[1921 March 5] n.p., ALS, 5 p. Date written in pencil, and partly erased, at the top of p. 1, possibly in Boulenger's hand. Kolb XX:116–17.

FRKF 211

[1921 March 21] n.p., ALS, 5 p. Kolb XX:144–45.

FRKF 209

[1921 July 12] [Paris*] ALS, 8 p. Kolb XX:394–96.

Paris, Boisgirard (Drouot), 22 May 1985, lot 84.

FRKF 740

[1921 Aug. 26] n.p., ALS, 14 p. (env). Envelope addressed to: Monsieur Jacques Boulenger / Directeur de l'Opinion / 4 rue Chauveau-Lagarde; marked "Personnelle." Date (1921 Aug. 30) written in pencil (in Boulenger's hand?) at top of p. 1. Kolb XX:421–23.

FRKF 210

[1921 Nov. 26] n.p., ALS, 9 p. (env). Date written in pencil at the top of p. 1. Kolb XX:530–32.

FRKF 730.1

1922 March 22, Paris, TLS, 2 p. (env). Kolb XXI:93.

FRKF 208

A single envelope addressed to Boulenger in Proust's hand, postmarked Aug. 1921.

FRKF 210

To Princesse Alexandre de Caraman-Chimay

[ca. 1903 Nov. 26] n.p., ALS, 4 p., on mourning stationery. Kolb XVI:395–96.

n.d., "Dimanche soir," n.p., ALS, 4 p., on mourning stationery. Kolb XVI:397–98.

[ca. 1917 Aug. 23] 102 bd Haussmann [Paris] ALS, 8 p., concerning Emmanuel Bibesco's suicide. Kolb XVI:216–17.

Paris, Ader-Picard-Tajan (Drouot), 13 Dec. 1984, lot 427.

FRKF 673.1–3

To the Marquis Illan de Casa Fuerte

[1903 Feb. 12] "Jeudi," n.p., ALS, 3 p. Kolb X:395.

Paris, Laurin-Guilloux-Buffetaud-Tailleur (Drouot), 16 Nov. 1983, lot 198.

FRKF 252

[early 1907?] n.p., ALS, 3 p. "Je ne pense pas que la plus tendre collaboration des couleurs de l'aurore …" Addressed to "Illan!" Not located in Kolb.

London, Sotheby's, 28 May 1986, lot 218.

FRKF 1211

n.d., n.p., ALS, 3 p. "Ce petit mot est pour vous dire que j'étais mourant …" The unstamped envelope is addressed in Proust's hand to "Monsieur le Marquis de Casa-Fuerte / 5 Boulevard Jules Sandeau." Not located in Kolb.

Paris, Ader-Picard-Tajan (Drouot), 22 Nov. 1985, lot 128.

FRKF 1377

To Mme Anatole Catusse

[1904 Nov.] n.p., ALS, 4 p., on mourning stationery. Kolb IV:344–45.

[ca. 1906 Sept. 16] n.p., ALS, 4 p., on mourning stationery. Kolb VI:213.

[ca. 1907 Jan. 21] n.p., ALS, 5 p., on mourning stationery. Kolb VII:38–39.

[1907 Feb.] n.p., ALS, 4 p., on mourning stationery. Kolb VII:92.

From the James Gilvarry Collection.
See Christie's, New York, 7 June 1990, lot 107.
New York, Christie's, 7 Feb. 1986, lot 221.
FRKF 969

[ca. 1907 Oct. 5] n.p., ALS, 4 p., on mourning stationery, with a postscript in pencil. Kolb VII:285–86.

FRKF 194

[ca. 1907 Oct. 15] n.p., ALS, 4 p., on mourning stationery. Kolb VII:294–295.

[1908 Feb. 28] "Vendredi," n.p., ALS, 1 p., on mourning stationery. Kolb VIII:54.

[1914 Sept. 8] [Cabourg*] ALS, 1 p. Kolb XIII:302.

From the James Gilvarry Collection.
See Christie's, New York, 7 June 1990, lot 107.
New York, Christie's, 7 Feb. 1986, lot 221.
FRKF 969

[1915 early Feb.] n.p., ALS, 7 p. Kolb XIV:48–50.

See Christie's, New York, 7 June 1990, lot 107.
New York, Sotheby's, 14 Feb. 1986, lot 507.
FRKF 982

[1917 late Nov.] n.p., ALS, 8 p. Kolb XVI:323–25.
[1917 Dec.] n.p., ALS, 4 p. Kolb XVI:353–54.

From the James Gilvarry Collection.
See Christie's, New York, 7 June 1990, lot 107.
New York, Christie's, 7 Feb. 1986, lot 221.
FRKF 969

To Henri Cazalis

[ca. 1906 Feb., Paris] 45 rue de Courcelles, ALS, 4 p., on mourning stationery. Kolb VI:33–34.

Paris, Ader-Picart-Tajan (Drouot), 11 June 1982, lot 176.
FRKF 169

To Julia Daudet

[ca. 1909 Nov. 19] n.p., ALS, 5 p. Kolb XII:409–10.

London, Sotheby's, 29 June 1982, lot 187.
FRKF 68

To Lucien Daudet

[1909, early Oct.] n.p., ALS, 4 p. "J'arrive de Cabourg, bien incapable d'écrire mais non pas de pleurer de toutes mes forces …" Partially published in Kolb XXI:643–44.

Paris, Ader-Picard-Tajan (Drouot), 22 Nov. 1985, lot 255.
FRKF 1385

To Maurice Duplay

[ca. 1910 Sept. 8] Cabourg, ALS, 8 p. Kolb X:166–68.

Paris, Laurin-Guilloux-Buffetaud-Tailleur (Drouot), 29 March 1985, lot 60.
FRKF 958

To Jacques Faure-Biguet

[1922 June 9 or 10] n.p., ALS, 1 p. Kolb XXI:251.

FRKF 353

To Gaston Gallimard

[1922, early Jan.] n.p., ALS, 9 p. Kolb XXI:24–25.

Paris, Ader-Picard-Tajan (Drouot), 22 Nov. 1985, lot 135.
FRKF 1379

To Henri Ghéon

[1914 Jan. 3, Paris*] ALS, 16 p. (env). Kolb XIII:22–27.
[1914 Jan. 7, Paris*] ALS, 8 p. (env). Kolb XIII:37–39.
[ca. 1922 Aug. 17] [Paris*] ALS, 4 p. (env). Kolb XXI:421–22.

Paris, Laurin-Guilloux-Buffetaud-Tailleur (Drouot), 12 Dec. 1985, lots 176–78.
FRKF 938.1–3

To Reynaldo Hahn

[ca. 1906 June 24] n.p., ALS, 2 p. Kolb XVI:400–01.

FRKF 502

[1906 Sept. 18 or 19] n.p., ALS, 5 p., on mourning stationery. Kolb VI:215–17.

FRKF 702

[1907 Jan.] n.p., ALS, 2 p. Kolb VII:42.
[1907 Feb. 8] n.p., ALS, 2 p., with a drawing of a rebus on the second page. Kolb VII:74.
[1907?] n.p., ALS, 3 p., with an ink drawing of two heads on the last page. Kolb VII:284–85.

[1908 Jan.] n.p., ALS, 4 p., on mourning stationery. Kolb VIII:33–34.

Paris, Laurin-Guilloux-Buffetaud-Tailleur (Drouot), 10 April 1987, lots 134–37.
FRKF 1214–17

[1908 April 10] Paris, telegram. Kolb VIII:87.

Paris, Ader-Picart-Tajan (Drouot), 11 June 1982, lot 179.
FRKF 172

[1912 Jan.] n.p., ALS, 3 p. Ink drawing ("L'agneau mystique") below the signature. Kolb XI:29.

Paris, Laurin-Guilloux-Buffetaud-Tailleur (Drouot), 10 April 1987, lot 138.
FRKF 1218

[1912 Aug.–Sept.] n.p., ALS, 4 p. Kolb XI:193–94.

FRKF 730.3

n.d., n.p., ALS, 3 p. "Morchat, rentre avec crise de sortie …" Not located in Kolb.

Paris, Laurin-Guilloux-Buffetaud-Tailleur (Drouot), 16 Nov. 1983, lot 200.
FRKF 253

To Daniel Halévy

[1888? May 22?, Paris] ALS, 7 p. Kolb XXI:552–53.

Paris, Laurin-Guilloux-Buffetaud-Tailleur (Drouot), 12 Dec. 1985, lot 170.
FRKF 943

[1891 July] n.p., ALS, 4 p. on mourning stationery, transmitting a recommendation to Ludovic Halévy for a young actress named Mlle Cam. Dated in ink by Daniel Halévy in the upper right corner. Kolb XXI:559–60.

[1893 July 20] [Paris*] "ce même jeudi 5 h" [i.e. 20 July] ALS, 2 p. (env), concerning the "Roman épistolaire." Kolb IV:413.

[1893 July 20 but postmarked July 21] "9, bd Malesherbes" [Paris] ALS, 2 p. (env), concerning the "Roman épistolaire." Signed "Pauline." Kolb IV:414–15.

[1893 Aug. 4?, Paris?] ALS, 4 p., concerning the "Roman épistolaire." Numbered "I" in Halévy's hand. Kolb IV:416.

[1893 Aug. 19] "Samedi," n.p., ALS, 4 p. Numbered "II" in Halévy's hand. Kolb IV:418.

[ca. 1893 Aug. 21, St Moritz] ALS, 2 p., concerning the "Roman épistolaire." Kolb IV:420.

Paris, Laurin-Guilloux-Buffetaud-Tailleur (Drouot), 3 July 1985, lots 137–38.
FRKF 856–57

[ca. 1907 Dec. 10] "102 bd Haussmann" [Paris] ALS, 10 p. Kolb XXI:618–20.

[ca. 1907 Dec. 10] n.p., ALS, 2 p. Kolb XXI:621.

[ca. 1907 Dec. 18] n.p., ALS, 7 p. Kolb XXI:622–23.

[1907 mid–Dec.] n.p., ALS, 7 p. on mourning stationery. Kolb XXI:623–25.

Paris, Laurin-Guilloux-Buffetaud-Tailleur (Drouot), 3 July 1985, lot 140.
FRKF 900.1

[ca. 1907 Dec. 18] n.p., ALS, 6 p., on mourning stationery. Kolb XXI:626–27.

[1908 Jan.] n.p., ALS, 5 p., on mourning stationery. Kolb XXI:628–29.

[1908 Jan.] n.p., ALS, 2 p., on mourning stationery. Kolb XXI:630–31.

Paris, Laurin-Guilloux-Buffetaud-Tailleur (Drouot), 3 July 1985, lot 139.
FRKF 858

[1908 Jan.] n.p., ALS, 8 p. Kolb XXI:631–32.

Paris, Laurin-Guilloux-Buffetaud-Tailleur (Drouot), 3 July 1985, lot 141.
FRKF 859

[1908 May or June] n.p., ALS, 4 p. This letter of condolence on the death of Ludovic Halévy also contains the celebrated anecdote concerning Proust signing the guest book of the duc de Gramont. Kolb XVIII:584–86.

Paris, Laurin-Guilloux-Buffetaud-Tailleur (Drouot), 3 July 1985, lot 139.
FRKF 858

[ca. 1913 Dec.] n.p., ALS, 4 p. Kolb XIV:348–49.

Paris, Laurin-Guilloux-Buffetaud-Tailleur (Drouot), 3 July 1985, lot 143.
FRKF 860

[1914 Nov. 16] n.p., ALS, 3 p. Kolb XIII:331.

Paris, Laurin-Guilloux-Buffetaud-Tailleur (Drouot), 12 Dec. 1985, lot 174.
FRKF 940

To Laure Hayman

[1906 Sept. 13, Versailles*] ALS, 8 p., on mourning stationery (env). Kolb VI:205–07.

Paris, Ader-Picart-Tajan (Drouot), 11 June 1982, lot 177.
FRKF 170

[1922 May 18] n.p., ALS, 8 p. Kolb XXI:208–09.

Paris, Boisgirard (Drouot), 28 May 1986, lot 108.
FRKF 1223

To Robert d'Humières

[1899 Feb. 2] n.p., ALS, 6 p. Kolb XIV:333–34.

Paris, Ader-Picard-Tajan (Drouot), 22 Nov. 1985, lot 110.
FRKF 1373

To Georges de Lauris

[1909 March] n.p., ALS, 6 p. Kolb IX:61–62.

[1910 July 13] "Mercredi," n.p., ALS, 8 p. Kolb XVI:403–04.

Paris, Laurin-Guilloux-Buffetaud-Tailleur (Drouot), 19 March 1986, lots 166–67.
FRKF 1219–20

To Berthe Lemarié

[ca. 1918 July 23] n.p., ALS, 4 p. Kolb XVII:320–21.

Paris, Ader-Picart-Tajan (Drouot), 11 June 1982, lot 181.
FRKF 174

To Charles Levadé

1894 Dec. 25, n.p., ALS, 4 p. (env). Kolb XII:396–97.

New York, Sotheby's, 25 May 1983, lot 50.
FRKF 96

To Robert de Montesquiou-Fezensac

[1894 May 21] n.p., ALS, 3 p., small red monogram in the upper left corner. Kolb I:293–94.

Paris, Boisgirard (Drouot), 28 May 1986, lot 107.
FRKF 1224

[1895] Jan. 3, n.p., ALS, 4 p, on stationery with small red "MP" monogram and a second small monogram. Kolb I:358–59.

FRKF 730.2

[1899 June 21–25] n.p., ALS to "Mon cher Comte," 3 p., on stationery with small red monogram. Kolb II:289. Montesquiou's *Les Perles rouges: 93 sonnets historiques, avec quatre eaux-fortes inédites de Albert Besnard*, was published by Fasquelle in 1899.

FRKF 360

[1905 April 27] "Jeudi," n.p., ALS, 4 p., on mourning stationery with small red monogram. Kolb V:114–15.
FRKF 206

[1905 May 16] "Mardi soir," n.p., ALS, 8 p., on mourning stationery. Kolb V:149–51.

Paris, Laurin-Guilloux-Buffetaud-Tailleur (Drouot), 17 June 1987, lot 127.
FRKF 1213

[1905 June 29] n.p., ALS, 4 p., on stationery with red monogram. Kolb V:270–71.

FRKF 195

[1905 Aug.] n.p., ALS, 2 p. Kolb V:337.

FRKF 701

[1906 May 29] n.p., ALS 6 p., on mourning stationery with small red monogram. Kolb VI:88–89.

FRKF 195

[1917 Nov. 3] n.p., ALS, 4 p., on stationery with small red monogram. Kolb XVI:277.

FRKF 207

[1921 April 18 or 19] n.p., ALS, 12 p., on stationery with small red monogram. Kolb XX:194–95.

Paris, Ader-Tajan (Drouot), 20 Dec. 1991, lot 233.
FRKF 1404

To Louisa de Mornand

[1905 May 21] n.p., ALS, 7 p., on mourning stationery. Kolb V:165–66.

FRKF 1212

To Gabriel Mourey

[ca. 1905 July 12] n.p. ALS, 4 p., on mourning stationery. Kolb XIII:365–66.

FRKF 359

To Albert Nahmias

[1912 April] n.p., ALS, 4 p. (env with two postscripts). Kolb XI:95–96.

1913 Dec. 6, Paris, telegram. Kolb XII:363.

1913 Dec. 7, Paris, telegram. Kolb XII:365–66.

Also, three empty envelopes addressed to Nahmias, postmarked Paris, 1912 Dec. 23 [see Kolb XI:329], 1919 Aug. 28 [Paris?], and n.d., n.p.

Paris, Ader-Picart-Tajan (Drouot), 11 June 1982, lots 176, 179.
FRKF 171–72

To Pauline Neuburger

[1880*] Sept. 5, Auteuil, ALS, 2 p. (env). Kolb I:93.

Paris, Ader-Picart-Tajan (Drouot), 11 June 1982, lot 173.
FRKF 166

To [Pierre d'Orléans]

[ca. 1899] Nov. 30, "Jeudi," 9, boulevard Malesherbes [Paris] ALS, 16 p., concerning the Dreyfus Affair. The identification of the recipient is proposed by Kolb XIV:335–38.

Paris, Ader-Picard-Tajan (Drouot), 22 Nov. 1985, lot 109.
FRKF 1372

To René Peter

[ca. 1911 Dec. 30?] n.p., ALS, 6 p. Kolb XVI:405–06.

Paris, Ader-Picard-Tajan (Drouot), 13 Dec. 1984, lot 296.
FRKF 671

To Jacques Porel

[1919 May 27] n.p., ALS, 8 p. Kolb XVIII:240–42.
[ca. 1919 Oct. 22] n.p., ALS, 1 p. Kolb XVIII:436.

Paris, Boisgirard (Drouot), 22 May 1985, lots 81, 83.
FRKF 738.1-2

To Réjane

[1919 July?] n.p., ALS, 4 p. Kolb XVIII:317–18.

Paris, Boisgirard (Drouot), 22 May 1985, lot 80.
FRKF 737

To J.-H. Rosny

[1921 Nov. or Dec.] 44, rue Hamelin [Paris] ALS, 4 p. Kolb XX:585.

Paris, Ader-Picard-Tajan (Drouot), 22 Nov. 1985, lot 132.
FRKF 1387

To Marie Scheikévitch

[1921 June 25*] 44, rue Hamelin [Paris] ALS, 8 p. (env). Kolb XX:361–62.

London, Sotheby's, 9–10 May 1985, lot 369.
FRKF 789

To Misia (Edwards) Sert

[1919 May 5, Paris*] ALS, 8 p. (env). Kolb XVIII:201–03.

Paris, Boisgirard (Drouot), 22 May 1985, lot 82.
FRKF 739

To Geneviève Straus

[ca. 1906 May 9] n.p., ALS, 2 p., on mourning stationery. Kolb XIV:343–44.

Paris, Laurin-Guilloux-Buffetaud-Tailleur (Drouot), 3 July 1985, lot 145.
FRKF 861

To Gustave Tronche

[1920 Aug. 27] n.p., ALS, 6 p. Kolb XIX:415–16.
FRKF 195

To Fernand Vandérem

[1920 Jan. 15] 44, rue Hamelin [Paris] ALS, 10 p. Kolb XIX:68–70.

Paris, Laurin-Guilloux-Buffetaud-Tailleur (Drouot), 16 Nov. 1983, lot 201.
FRKF 254

To Jean-Louis Vaudoyer

[1910 July 18] Grand Hotel, Cabourg[S], ALS, 8 p. (env, in a secretarial hand). Kolb X:141–43.

Paris, Laurin-Guilloux-Buffetaud-Tailleur (Drouot), 19 March 1986, lot 168.
FRKF 1221

To Mme Vittoré

[ca. 1918 Nov. 11] n.p., ALS, 4 p. Kolb XVII:457.

Paris, Ader-Picard-Tajan (Drouot), 22 Nov. 1985, lot 127.
FRKF 1376

To his grandmother, Mme Nathé Weil

[1885 or 1886, summer] JJ. Biraben, Hôtel de la Paix, [Salies-de-Béarn][S], ALS, 3 p. Kolb I:94–96.

Paris, Ader-Picart-Tajan (Drouot), 11 June 1982, lot 175.
FRKF 168

To Gabriel de Yturri

[1905 June 29] n.p., ALS, 3 p., on stationery with small red monogram. Kolb V:271–72.

FRKF 195

Other letters

To "Monsieur"

[1922] n.p., ALS, 4 p. Kolb XIX:362–63.

Paris, Ader-Picard-Tajan (Drouot), 22 Nov. 1985, lot 137.
FRKF 1380

To "Cher ami"

n.d., n.p., ALS, 1 p. "Vous êtes très gentil de m'avoir annoncé vos fiançailles …" [Possibly Kolb XIX:105, early Feb. 1920, to Comte Pierre de Polignac]

FRKF 196

III. LETTERS TO PROUST

From Jean Cocteau

1919 Aug. 7, n.p., ALS, 1 p., thanking him for an inscribed copy of *A l'ombre des jeunes filles en fleurs*. Kolb XVIII:368.

Paris, Ader-Picard-Tajan (Drouot), 22 Nov. 1985, lot 138.
FRKF 1336

From his mother, Mme Adrien Proust

[1888 Sept. 6] Salies, ALS, 4 p. Incomplete. Kolb I:111.

Paris, Ader-Picart-Tajan (Drouot), 11 June 1982, lot 174.
FRKF 167

1890
All of the letters dated in 1890 are on mourning stationery.

[June 26?] "Jeudi 3 h[eure]s," Auteuil, ALS, 4 p. Kolb I:142–43.
[July 14] "Lundi 14, 6 hrs ¾ soir," Auteuil, ALS, 4 p. Kolb I:143–44.
[Aug. 1?] "Vendredi, 3 h[eure]s," Auteuil, ALS, 2 p. Kolb I:145. *Marcel Proust: l'écriture et les arts*, no. 11.
[Aug. 5] "Mardi," n.p., ALS, 2 p. Kolb I:146.
[Aug. 10] "Dimanche matin," n.p., ALS, 4 p. Kolb I:147.
[Aug. 11] "Lundi midi," Auteuil, ALS, 4 p. Kolb I:148–49.
[Aug. 14] "Jeudi mat[in]" Auteuil, ALS, 6 p. Kolb I:150–51.
[Aug. 18] "Lundi 3 h[eure]s" [Paris] ALS, 6 p. Kolb I:151–52.
[Aug. 18] n.p., ALS, 4 p. Kolb I:152–53.
[Aug. 19] "Mardi 3 h[eure]s," Auteuil, ALS, 3 p. Kolb I:153–54.
[Aug. 21?] "Jeudi matin," Auteuil, ALS, 4 p. Kolb I:154–55.
[Aug. 22] "Vendredi midi," Auteuil, ALS, 4 p. Kolb I:156–57.
[Aug. 28] "Jeudi midi," Auteuil, ALS, 6 p. Kolb I:157–58.

FRKF 193

[1896 Oct. 20] "Mardi soir 7 heures," ALS, 4 p. Kolb II:135–36.

FRKF 670b

1903
[ca. July 17] "6h½," n.p., ALS, 1 p. Kolb III:377.
[Aug. 12] "Mercredi soir 8½," Grand Hôtel Victoria, Interlaken[S], ALS, 4 p. Kolb III:393–94.
Aug. 18, Splendide Hôtel[S], ALS, 4 p. Kolb III:399.
Aug. 19, Splendide Hôtel[S], ALS, 4 p. Kolb III:402–03.
[Aug. 20] "Jeudi matin," Splendide Hôtel[S], ALS, 2 p. Kolb III:405–06.
[Aug. 23] n.p., "Samedi 3 hr," ALS, 4 p. Kolb III:411–12.
[Aug. 24*] "Lundi," Evian, ALS, 1 p. Kolb III:413.
[Aug. 27] "Jeudi 27," [Evian] ALS, 2 p. Kolb III:414–15.

London, Sotheby's, 26–27 May 1983, lot 190.
FRKF 137

n.d., "Mardi," n.p., ALS, 3 p. "Nous n'avons vraiment pas de chance pour le Cap Fréhel …" See under *Les plaisirs et les jours*. Not located in Kolb.

Paris, Boisgirard (Drouot), 22 May 1985, lot 77.
FRKF 736

From Geneviève Straus

[1920] March 15, n.p., ALS, 2 p., concerning Robert de Montesquiou. Kolb XIX:158–59.
[1920] 104, rue de Miromesnil [Paris][S], ALS, 3 p., concerning *Le côté de Guermantes*.
1920 Sept. 28, Versailles, APCS
1920 Oct. 23, Versailles, ALS, 2 p. Kolb XIX:548–49.
[ca. 1920] "Lundi," 15, rue Berthier, Versailles[S], ALS, 4 p. Mentions *Le côté de Guermantes* and F. Halévy's *Charles VI*.
[1921] May 27 [i.e. 21] "Samedi," 104, rue de Miromesnil[S], ALS, 4 p., concerning *Sodome et Gomorrhe*. Kolb XX:285–86.
1921 June 10, Versailles, ALS, 2 p., concerning an article by Léon Daudet and *Le côté de Guermantes*. Kolb XX:330–31.
[1921 June 22] "Mercredi," Versailles, ALS, 4 p., concerning Léon Daudet and *Sodome et Gomorrhe*. Kolb XX:360.
[1922] "Dimanche," n.p., ALS, 2 p. (printed "Pneumatique" on the recto), concerning *Sodome et Gomorrhe*.
[1922] May 13, 104, rue de Miromesnil[S], ALS, 4 p., concerning *Sodome et Gomorrhe*. Kolb XXI:183–84.
n.d., "mardi," 104, rue de Miromesnil[S], ALS, 2 p.
n.d., n.p., APCS written on both sides.

n.d., n.p., APCS written on both sides, thanking him for a gift of flowers.

Paris, Laurin-Guilloux-Buffetaud-Tailleur (Drouot), 12 Dec. 1985, lot 175.

FRKF 939

IV. PRINTED BOOKS

Du côté de chez Swann. Paris: Bernard Grasset, 1914 [i.e. 1913]. (*A la recherche du temps perdu*)

[2] 1–523, [+ 8] p.

Bound in half dark brown morocco and grey marbled papers. Top edge gilt. On the spine: "Marcel / Proust / Du côté / de chez Swann / 1923 [sic]." Original wrappers bound in. The date on the wrappers is 1913. The *achevé d'imprimer* is dated 8 Nov. 1913. Bound at the end are 8 pages of advertisements.

Tipped in after the front wrapper: ALS to Louis de Robert, n.d., n.p., 9 p. (not located in Kolb). Pasted on blank page facing the *achevé d'imprimer*: clipping from bookdealer's catalogue advertising *placards* from the projected volumes 2 and 3 of the abortive Bernard Grasset edition of *A la recherche du temps perdu*.

Accompanied by: A clipping from a bookdealer's catalogue (Maurice Dussarp, 64, rue du Rocher, Paris) advertising the sale of Louis de Robert's set of the five first titles of *A la recherche du temps perdu*. A typed note and a clipping concerning Proust and Louis de Robert. A photograph (with the Mondial Photo-Press stamp on the back) showing Jacques-Émile Blanche, Édouard Champion, M. Charpentier, and Pol Neveux in front of Blanche's portrait of Proust exhibited at the Galerie Charpentier [1934?].

FRKF 654g

A l'ombre des jeunes filles en fleurs. Paris: Éditions de la Nouvelle Revue Française, 1918. (*A la recherche du temps perdu*, tome II)

[1–6], 7–443 [+ 5] p. First edition. *Achevé d'imprimer* dated 30 Nov. 1918.

Inscribed on the recto of the flyleaf: "A Monsieur le Comte Robert de Montesquiou en hommage d'une affection admirative et respectueuse qui ne s'est pas démentie depuis vingt cinq ans Son fidèle et reconnaissant / Marcel Proust."

Full dark brown calf (stamp of Muser), raised bands on spine, with author, title, and date gold tooled; all edges gilt. Full dark brown calf doublures. Original paper wrappers bound in.

Paris, Ader-Picard-Tajan (Drouot), 4 June 1986, lot 107.

FRKF 1226

A l'ombre des jeunes filles en fleurs. Paris: Éditions de la Nouvelle Revue Française [1918]. (*A la Recherche du temps perdu*, tome II)

[1–6], 7–443, [+ 5] p. *Achevé d'imprimer* dated 30 Nov. 1918.

Inscribed by Proust to Louis de Robert: "A Louis de Robert, Au meilleur ami de mon premier livre Avec toute la reconnaissante tendresse de son / Marcel Proust." Tipped in after the front wrapper: ALS to Louis de Robert, "8 bis rue Laurent Pichat" [Paris, ca. mid-July 1919] 4 p. Kolb XVII:328–29.

Bound in half dark brown morocco and grey marbled papers. Top edge gilt. On the spine: "Marcel / Proust / A l'ombre / des jeunes filles / en fleurs / 1918." Original wrappers bound in. On wrappers: "Troisième édition."

FRKF 654a

A l'ombre des jeunes filles en fleurs. Paris: Éditions de la Nouvelle Revue Française, 1920. (*A la recherche du temps perdu*, tome II)

Two 4to volumes, in unbound quires (each consisting of two nested bifolia), uncut, as issued; [1–6], 7–250 [+ 1 blank leaf]; [1–6], 7–228 [+ 8 p., including a 4-page "Catalogue général" of Éditions de la Nouvelle Revue française]. Accompanied by a lithograph of the portrait of Proust by Jacques-Émile Blanche, without signature or number. *Achevé d'imprimer* at the end of the second volume, dated 28 Feb. 1920. Hors-commerce copy, numbered 0 on verso of title page, of 50 copies printed on "Papier Bible."

In a beige paper folder housed within a hard folder with pochoir-decorated boards tied with a black and a white ribbon. Autograph inscription on verso of the front board: "Nina from Walter [Berry] / July 14th 1926."

FRKF 1225

Another copy, numbered XXVII on verso of title page.

FRKF 190.4

Le côté de Guermantes I. Paris: Éditions de la Nouvelle Revue Française, 1920. (*A la Recherche du temps perdu*, tome III, "Édition originale")

[1–8], 9–279 p. *Achevé d'imprimer* dated 17 Aug. 1920. Two leaves of errata bound at the end. No. 394 of the 1040 copies on Papier vélin pur fil Lafuma.

Bound in half dark brown morocco and grey marbled papers. Top edge gilt. On the spine: "Marcel / Proust /

Le côté / de / Guermantes / I / 1920." Tipped in after the front wrapper: ALS to Louis de Robert [shortly before 26 May 1921] n.p., 4 p. Kolb XX:293–94.

FRKF 654b

Le côté de Guermantes II - Sodome et Gomorrhe I. Deuxième édition. Paris: Éditions de la Nouvelle Revue Française, 1921. (*A la Recherche du temps perdu*, tome IV)

[1–6], 7–282, [+ 2] p. *Achevé d'imprimer* dated 30 April 1921.

Bound in half dark brown morocco and grey marbled papers. Top edge gilt. On the spine: "Marcel / Proust / Le côté / de / Guermantes / II / Sodome / et Gomorrhe / I / 1921." Inscribed by Proust to Louis de Robert: "à Louis de Robert, son ami consolé, admiratif et reconnaissant / Marcel Proust."

FRKF 654c

Sodome et Gomorrhe II. Paris: Éditions de la Nouvelle Revue Française, 1922. (*A la Recherche du temps perdu*, tome V)

3 volumes. Volume 1: [1–6], 7–230, [+ 2 p.]. *Achevé d'imprimer* dated 10 April 1922. Volume 2: [1–6], 7–236, [+ 2 p.]. Achevé d'imprimer dated 3 April 1922. Volume 3: [1–6], 7–237, one leaf blank. Achevé d'imprimer dated 3 April 1922.

Bound in half dark brown morocco and grey marbled papers. Top edge gilt. On the spine: "Marcel / Proust / Sodome / et / Gomorrhe / II / * [**] [***] / 1922." Inscribed by Proust to Louis de Robert: "Cher ami / Je viens d'être si malade que je n'ai presque pas pu faire d'envois de mes livres. Mais vous savez que la dernière pensée du malade sera pour le premier ami de Swann. La scène (Mlle Vinteuil) qui vous y choquait, vous apparaîtra expliquée, nécessaire, à la fin du 3e tome de ce S. et G. II (si toutefois vous avez la patience d'aller jusque là). Souvent peut-être vous serez tenté de fermer un si long volume et continuerez-vous par amitié pour votre dévoué et reconnaissant / Marcel Proust." Tipped into volume 1, after front wrapper, ALS to Louis de Robert [July or August 1913] n.p., 11 p. Partially published in Kolb XII:237–39; see also XXI: 180–81.

FRKF 654d-e-f

V. MISCELLANEOUS MATERIAL

"Une peine abimait …"

Autograph manuscript of a poem by Daniel Halévy, corrected throughout by Proust, [ca. 1887], 3 p. The poem is written in black ink on p. [1] and [2] of a loose bifolium.

Proust's underlinings and corrections are on p. [1] to [3] and are in purple and in black ink.

Paris, Laurin-Guilloux-Buffetaud-Tailleur (Drouot), 12 Dec. 1985, lot 165.

FRKF 944

David Levine. Caricature of Marcel Proust, proof on cream-colored laid paper, signed and dated D. Levine 63.

FRKF 61

GIACOMO PUCCINI (1858–1924)

I. MUSIC MANUSCRIPTS

A. OPERAS

La fanciulla del West

Miscellaneous holograph sketches, n.d., 45 p. Notated in black pencil or black ink, on one or both sides of single sheets and individual bifolia of tall 12-staff paper. Includes sketches for the Bible reading scene in act 1 (after rehearsal number 50, beginning with Joe's words "E qui da noi non fa?"); also act 1, following rehearsal number 90 (on Castro's words "alla Madonna Canyada"); act 2, between rehearsal numbers 24 and 26 (at Minnie's words "Ah, le mie rose!") and between rehearsal numbers 54 and 55 (on Dick Johnson's words "Ho sognato d'andarmene con voi"); one sketch, presumably for act 2, is headed "Gioco."

Schickling 78.A.2.
FRKF 989

Another fragment, also in pencil, with an addition in red pencil, on both sides of a tall sheet of 12-staff paper. Corresponds to act 1, after rehearsal number 73, beginning with Minnie's words "[Sarete] stanco" and ending with Johnson's words "Fermai il cavallo."

Schickling 78.A.I.73
FRKF 282

Madama Butterfly

Holograph manuscript draft fragment, in short score, for act 2, part 1, n.d., 4 p. Notated in black ink on a single bifolium of tall 12-staff paper. Begins at rehearsal number 50, six measures before Butterfly's reentrance with the words "E questo? … e questo? …" and ends at the third measure following rehearsal number 54. Inscription to Alfredo Caselli at the top of p. [1], dated June 1908.

Schickling 74.A.II.50.
FRKF 573

Holograph manuscript drafts, in short score, for Pinkerton's act 3 aria, "Addio, fiorito asil," [1904], 4 p. Notated in pencil, mostly in 4-staff systems, on a single bifolium of oblong 14-staff paper. Two drafts for the whole aria are present, the first one on p. [1] and [2], the second on p. [3] and [4]. The first draft leads to a repeat of Sharpless's words "Andate, il triste vero apprenderà," the second to the exchange between Butterfly and Suzuki ("E qui, E qui …").

Signed and marked "Rimaneggiamenti!" in the bottom right corner of the first page. Presented by Puccini to Giovanni Zenatello, who first sang the aria in the revised version of *Madama Butterfly*, premiered at Brescia in May 1904. Subsequently in the possession of Maria Cebotari and Sir Clifford Curzon.

Schickling 74.A.III.27.a.
London, Sotheby's, 29 Nov. 1985, lot 187.
FRKF 1040

Tosca

Holograph manuscript, in short score, of the opening of act 3, n.d., 4 p. Notated on 4-staff systems in black ink, with additional corrections in pencil, on p. [1]–[4] of a single bifolium of tall 12-staff paper. The passage begins at rehearsal number 4 and ends 6 bars after rehearsal number 7 (p. 279–82 of the revised Ricordi edition).

Schickling 69.A.III.4.a.
London, Sotheby's, 29 Nov. 1985, lot 186.
FRKF 1026

Turandot

Holograph sketches, n.d., 1 p. Notated in pencil on the recto side of a single sheet of tall 12-staff paper, foliated "a" in the upper left corner. There are three brief sketches, the first to the words "un chi affronta il ci-"; the second with the words "Lento / Liu / cantato da pochi soprani," and, in the left margin "Marcia [?] Morte Liù"; the third with the words "Cercono" [?] and "al c[not deciphered] della luna."

Schickling 91.A.I.2.a.
FRKF 989.5

B. OTHER WORKS

"Inno a Diana"

Holograph manuscript of this song for voice and piano on a text by Carlo Abeniacar, 1897, 3 p. Notated in black ink, with additional markings in blue pencil, on the first three pages of a bifolium of tall 12-staff paper. At the top of p. [1] in Puccini's hand: "Inno a Diana." Signed and dated 12 Dec. 1897 at the end.

(Another manuscript of the same song, in the hand of a copyist, with autograph annotations by Puccini, and accompanied by a letter from Puccini to Abeniacar, was acquired by the Beinecke in 1998. London, Sotheby's, 21 May 1998, lot 308.)

From the collection of Carl Hein.
London, Sotheby's, 15 Oct. 1982, lot 164A.
FRKF 6

II. OTHER MANUSCRIPTS

"I motivi di terra e di acqua"

Autograph manuscript, n.d. [ca. 1919–20], 5 p., in black ink on loose leaves, one of them on Torre del Lago stationery, with brief notes on verso of p. 1. Mentions *Tosca* and *La rondine*.

FRKF 734

III. LETTERS

Many of the letters are on printed stationery of Puccini's residences, abbreviated as follows:

Via Verdi[S] = on stationery of Via Verdi, 4, Milan
Torre del Lago[S] = on stationery of Torre del Lago, Toscana
Viareggio[S] = on stationery of Viareggio, Via Buonarroti

To Giovacchino Forzano

1916 June 5, Torre del Lago, ALS, 1 p., concerning *La rondine*.

London, Sotheby's, 29 Nov. 1985, lot 188.
FRKF 1073

To Angelo Magrini (with related material)

1918 Feb. 28, Viareggio, ALS, 1 p.
1918 Oct. 13, Viareggio, ALS, 1 p.
1918 Nov. 11, Torre del Lago[S], ALS, 1 p.
1919 Aug. 10 [Viareggio*] APCS
1919 Oct. 22, ALS with blue sticker of Torre del Lago, 1 p.

1920

Jan. 13, ALS on both sides of an oblong card printed Torre della Tagliata, Orbetello

Jan. 15, ALS on both sides of an oblong card printed Torre della Tagliata, Orbetello

Feb. 6, Torre della Tagliata, Orbetello[S], ALS, 3 p.

March 3, Via Verdi[S], ALS, 1 p.

March 6, Via Verdi[S], ALS, 2 p.

[June 20] Savoy Hotel, London[S], ALS, 2 p.

July 18, Torre del Lago[S], ALS, 2 p.

July 21, Torre del Lago[S], ALS, 2 p.

July 23, Torre del Lago[S], ALS, 1 p.

[Aug. 10, Bagni di Lucca*] APCS

Aug. 24, Torre del Lago[S], ALS, 2 p.

Sept. 6, Torre del Lago[S], ALS, 1 p.

[Dec. 19] Torre della Tagliata, Orbelleto[S], ALS, 2 p.

[Dec. 28?] "Martedì," Torre della Tagliata, Orbelleto[S], ALS, 2 p.

Dec. 28, Torre della Tagliata, Orbelleto[S], ALS, 3 p.

Dec. 29, Torre della Tagliata, ALS, 1 p.

1921

Jan. 15, Via Verdi[S], ALS to Erminia Magrini, 1 p. (env)

Jan. 17, Via Verdi[S], ALS, 2 p.

Jan. 23, Via Verdi[S], ALS, 2 p.

Jan. 26, Via Verdi[S], ALS, 2 p.

Feb. 6, Via Verdi[S], ALS to Erminia Magrini, 2 p.

Feb. 12, Via Verdi[S], ALS, 2 p.

Feb. 12, Via Verdi[S], ALS to Erminia Magrini, 2 p.

[Feb. 24, Milan*] APCS. On the correspondence side, Puccini has pasted and annotated a clipping from the *Corriere della sera*. Signed and dated 24 Feb. 1921 on the verso.

March 6, Via Verdi[S], ALS, 2 p.

[March 17] "Giovedi," Hôtel de Paris, Monte Carlo[S], ALS, 4 p.

[March 19?] "Sabato," Hôtel de Paris, Monte Carlo[S], ALS, 3 p.

April 9, Via Verdi[S], ALS, 2 p.

April 10, Via Verdi[S], ALS, 2 p.

April 10, Milan, APCS to Erminia Magrini, Egyptian postcard, written on the picture side, representing the Pyramids.

April 12, Via Verdi[S], ALS, 1 p.

April 22, Via Verdi[S], ALS, 1 p.

April 26, Via Verdi[S], ALS, 2 p.

July 12, Torre del Lago[S], ALS, 2 p.

[Aug. 18, Munich*] APCS to Erminia Magrini

Sept. 24, Torre del Lago[S], ALS, 2 p.

1922

[Feb. 2, Milan*] APCS, written on the picture side, reporting on the success of *Il trittico*.

Feb. 3 [Viareggio*] APCS

Feb. 18, Via Verdi[S], ALS, 1 p.

May 27, La Lettura, Rivista Mensile del Corriere della Sera, Milan[S], 2 p.

[July 20] Viareggio[S], ALS, 2 p.

[July 29] Viareggio[S], ALS, 2 p.

Aug. 13, Viareggio[S], ALS, 2 p.

Aug. 17, Viareggio[S], ALS, 2 p.

[Nov. 5] "Domenica," Hotel Lotti, Paris[S], ALS, 2 p.

Nov. 27 [Cisterna di Roma*] APCS

[Nov. 28] "Martedi" [Cisterna di Roma*] APCS

Dec. 28 [Milan*] APCS

Dec. 30, Via Verdi[S], ALS, 1 p.

1923

[Jan. 2] Via Verdi[S], ALS, 1 p.

[Jan. 11] "Giovedi sera," Via Verdi[S], ALS, 1 p.

Jan. 30, Via Verdi[S], ALS, 2 p.

Feb. 6, Via Verdi[S], ALS, 2 p.

Feb. 16 [Milan*] APCS

Feb. 21 [Milan*] APCS

Feb. 21, Via Verdi[S], ALS, 1 p.

Feb. 22, Via Verdi[S], ALS, 1 p.

Feb. 27, Via Verdi[S], ALS, 1 p.

March 10, n.p., ALS, 2 p.

[May 20, Vienna*] APCS to Erminia Magrini, written by Angelo Magrini, with an inscription and the signature of Puccini.

July 3, Viareggio[S], ALS Giacomo Puccini, 2 p.

July 6, Viareggio[S], ALS, 4 p.

[Aug. 11, Viareggio*] APCS

Aug. 22 [St. Moritz*] APCS, also signed by Tonio Franca.

Sept. 21, Giacomo Puccini, Viareggio[S], ALS 1 p.

Oct. 9 [Vienna*] APCS

Oct. 14 [Vienna*] APCS, printed postcard of Hotel Bristol Vienna.

Oct. 16, Vienna, telegraph. Mentions *Manon Lescaut*.

Oct. 17 [Vienna*] APCS

Oct. 17, Hotel Bristol, Vienna[S], ALS from Elvira Puccini to Magrini, 3 p.

[Oct. 22, Vienna*] APCS

Oct. 22, Vienna, ALS, 2 p.

Oct. 29, Hotel Bristol, Vienna[S], ALS, 4 p.

[Nov. 26] "Lunedi" [Roma*] APCS

[Nov. 29] "Giovedi," Sottosegretario di Stato per le Belle Arti[S], ALS, 2 p.

1924

Feb. 2, Giacomo Puccini, Viareggio[S], ALS, 2 p.

Feb. 24, Giacomo Puccini, Viareggio[S], ALS, 2 p.

[April 6, Viareggio*] APCS, illustrated with a photograph of Giacomo Puccini.

May 2, Via Verdi[S], ALS, 1 p.

May 6, Via Verdi[S], ALS, 1 p.

May 18, Giacomo Puccini, Viareggio[S], ALS, 2 p.

[June 13, Salsomaggiore*] APCS

Aug. 7, Viareggio[S], ALS, 2 p.

Nov. 7 [Brussels*] APCS

Nov. 17 [Brussels] ALS, 2 p., in pencil.

Undated

ALS, Torre del Lago[S], 1 p.

Accompanied by the following material

Correspondence after Puccini's death and concerning his final illness

- To Magrini, 1924

  Nov. 17, n.p., ALS from Elvira Puccini, 4 p.

  [Nov. 19, Brussels*] APCS from Antonio Puccini

  Nov. 19, ALS from Fosca Puccini, Milan, 8 p.

  Nov. 22, telegram from Antonio Puccini, Brussels

  Dec. 4, ALS on both sides of a card from Piero Massoni, n.p.

  Dec. 6, ALS from Fosca Puccini, Milan, 4 p., on mourning stationery

  Dec. 6, ALS from Antonio Puccini, Viareggio, 3 p., on mourning stationery

  Dec. 11, ALS from Pietro Panichelli, Pisa, 4 p.

  Dec. 20, ALS from Elvira Puccini, Milan, 4 p., on mourning stationery

- From Magrini to his wife, 1924, all from Brussels

  [Nov. 25] "Martedì sera," Hotel Metropole[S], ALS, 6 p., with a postscript from Fosca Puccini.

  Nov. 28, APCS

  Nov. 28, telegram

  Nov. 29, 2 telegrams, reporting that Puccini is in desperate condition.

  Nov. 29, telegram, reporting the death of Puccini at 11:30.

  Nov. 29, Angelo Magrini, Armatore, Viareggio[S], ALS, 8 p.

  Nov. 30, telegram

- To Magrini from Antonio Puccini

  1925 Feb. 2, Milan, ALS, 4 p., on mourning stationery

  undated, Viale Carducci 80[S], 1 p. Also signed by Giuseppe Adami.

- To Erminia Magrini from Elvira Puccini

  1928 July 31, n.p., ALS, 2 p., a letter of condolence on the death of the Magrinis' son.

Additional correspondence

ALS to Puccini from Rodolfo Morandi [1922 Dec. 14*] Albergo d'Italia, Novara[S], 4 p. (env)

ALS to Magrini from Rodolfo Morandi [1922 Dec.?] n.p., 2 p.

TL from Magrini to Morandi, 1922 Dec. 27, carbon copy

APCS, blank, inscribed on the picture side (representing Turandot) by Hariclea Darclée, 1923 July, to an unidentified recipient.

ALS to Puccini from Hubert Marischka, 1923 May 19, n.p., in German.

Photographs

Sepia photograph of Puccini (11 × 15 cm; E. Sommariva, Milan), with autograph inscriptions: "All carissimo Angiolino Magrini / ricordo di vivace amicizia / Giacomo Puccini" and "Torre del Lago / 1919 / Nov."

Sepia photograph of Puccini on his death bed (Castineau [?]), dated 29 Nov. 1924 (18 × 24 cm).

Two photographs of the drawing of Puccini on his deathbed by Henri Logelain.

Four photographs of Puccini's funeral in Brussels: three are black-and-white (19.5 × 25 cm) and stamped Favresse P., Brussels, on the verso; the fourth is sepia (18 × 24 cm), stamped Photo Reportage Belge, and shows Magrini, together with Puccini's son Antonio and Puccini's old violin teacher Alfonso Frosoli, identified on the verso.

Additional material relating to Puccini

"Il club non ancora batterato," manuscript document, signed by Puccini, Rodolfo Morandi, Guido Marotti [?], Guido Torrese, Francesco Farrelli, Guido Mosattini, G. Ricciotti Baccelli, Giovacchino Forzano, Antonio Puccini, P. Pistolesi, and two others, dated Viareggio, 21 Nov. 1918, 4 p.

Printed announcement for a Requiem mass for Puccini on the 30th anniversary of his death [1954], with a printed reproduction of a black-and-white photograph of Puccini by A.B[?] (10 × 16 cm) affixed.

Two blank postcards representing "Giacomo Puccini a Celle di Val di Roggio" (two different group scenes).

A postcard showing Puccini and four others, addressed to Magrini, stamped 10 Aug. 1918.

Unrelated additional material

APCS from Giuseppe Adami to unidentified, 1920 Aug.

APCS from Ceccardo Roccatagliata Ceccardi [to Magrini?] 1916 July 1, Viareggio

ALS from Giovacchino Forzano to Erminia Magrini, 1918 Nov. 24, Viareggio, 3 p.

ALS from Giovacchino Forzano to Magrini, 1920 Nov. 27, Milan, 1 p.

APCS from Moses Levy to Magrini, 1923 April 29, Tunis

AL from Magrini to Pietro Pancrazi, 1921 Feb. 16, Angelo Magrini, Armatore, Viareggio^S, 2 p., draft

APCS from Renato Simoni to Magrini [1921 Dec. 31, Naples*]

ANS on a card with mourning border from Ernesto Battista to Magrini, 1918 Feb. 22, Villa Gerassi

ALS from Ernesto Battista to Magrini, 1919 April 5, Trent, 1 p.

ALS from Ernesto Battista to Magrini, on both sides of a card, 1919 Dec. 25, Trent

Printed invitation addressed to Magrini for dinner with the Italian Minister in Berlin, May 16, n.y.

Printed program of a children's event in honor of Magrini, signed by [the children?], Collina, 1917 Aug. 19

"Iuda, tragedia di Enrico Pea in versi prosati od in prosa versata a ... piacere," typescript, with one manuscript addition in an unidentified hand), 4 p.

Various unidentified postcards, evidently from family members, and documents.

FRKF 994

To Leopoldo Mugnone

1897 Feb. 17, Milan, ALS on Ufizio Telegrafico di Milano forms, 3 p. (env), concerning the cancellation of performances, probably of *La bohème*.

London, Sotheby's, 10 May 1984, lot 141.
FRKF 333

To Plinio Nomellini

1903 Feb. 5, Milan, ALS, 4 p.

1903 April 24 [Torre del Lago*] APCS

[1903 April 27] n.p., ALS, 4 p.

1903 Aug. 27, n.p., ALS, 2 p.

1903 Oct. 1 [Torre del Lago*] APCS

[1903 Dec. 7, Torre del Lago*] APCS

1904 Aug. 5, Boscolungo Abetone (Serra Bassa)^S, ALS, 1 p.

1905 Jan. 22, Via Verdi^S, ALS, 1 p.

1905 Feb. 8, Via Verdi^S, ALS, 1 p.

[1905 Oct.*] "Giovedì," Via Verdi^S, ALS, 1 p. Mentions *Madama Butterfly*.

1906 April 3, n.p., ALS, 2 p.

1907 Jan. 14, Kaiserin Auguste Victoria, Hamburg-Amerika Linie^S, ALS, 3 p.

[1907 May 5] "Domenica," Via Verdi^S, ALS, 1 p.

1907 May 19, Via Verdi^S, 19 May 1907, ALS, 1 p.

1907 June 4, London, APCS

[1908 March 23*] APCS

1908 June 3, Via Verdi^S, ALS, 1 p.

1913 Jan. [2]1, n.p., APCS, concerning the bust of Puccini by Pavel Trubetskoi.

[1917 May 15, Torre del Lago*] APCS

n.d., n.p., ALS, 2 p., marked "inpettissima"

The Leghorn-born painter Plinio Nomellini (1866–1943), a Torre del Lago resident as of 1902, was a close friend of Puccini.

FRKF 843

To Sybil Seligman

1908 April 8, Via Verdi^S, ALS, 1 p.

Kenneth Rendell Catalogue 169.
FRKF 398

1909 March 6, Torre del Lago^S, ALS, 1 p. Partly torn, with loss of text on the left side.

FRKF 792

To Francesco Tamagno

1888 Dec. 31, Milan, ALS, 2 p.

1889 Feb. 21, Milan, ALS, 2 p.

1892 Jan. 11, Milan, ALS, 4 p.

1892 Jan. 13, Milan, ALS, 3 p., concerning Puccini's *Edgar*, the title role of which Tamagno sang in Madrid in 1892.

1892 Jan. 15, Milan, ALS, 2 p.

1892 Jan. 16, Milan, ALS, 4 p., with three musical quotations of 10, 1, and 2 measures respectively.

FRKF 1109

To Alfredo Vandini

1893
[Nov. 29, Milan*] APCS

1894
Jan. 2 [Milan*] ALS, 2 p. (env)
June 4 [Torre del Lago*] APCS
[Nov. 21, Torre del Lago*] APCS

1896
[March 1, Naples*] APCS
[April 2, Torre del Lago*] APCS

1897
Jan. 25, Milan, APCS
[Feb. 28, Milan*] APCS to Alfredo Caselli.
[late Nov.] n.p., ALS, 2 p.
Dec. 23, Milan, APCS

1898
Jan. 31, Milan, APCS

[Feb. 25, Paris*] APCS

March 9, Milan*] ALS, 3 p. (env)

[March, postmark undecipherable] APCS, illustrated with a scene from *La bohème*.

[May 14, Paris*] APCS

June 14, Paris, telegram

[June 29, Torre del Lago*] APCS

[late Sept.] n.p., ALS, 2 p.

[Nov. 6, Torre del Lago*] APCS

Nov. 12 [Torre del Lago*] ALS, 3 p. (env)

[Nov. 20, Torre del Lago*] APCS

Nov. 21, Torre del Lago, telegram

Nov. 27, Torre del Lago, ALS, 3 p. (env)

1899

[March 5*, place on postmark not legible] APCS

[Aug. 18] [Boscolungo*] APCS

Sept. 23, Torre del Lago, APCS

[Oct.] n.p., ALS, 4 p.

[Oct. 4, Torre de Lago*] APCS

Oct. 10, Torre del Lago, ALS, 2 p.

[Oct., Milan*] ALS, 2 p. (env). Dated third week of Oct. by Dieter Schickling.

Oct. 27, Milan, APCS

Oct. 31 [Torre del Lago*] APCS

[Nov. 22, Torre del Lago*] APCS

[Nov. 29, Torre del Lago*] APCS

[Dec. 8, Torre del Lago*] APCS

1900

[Jan. 16] Paris, ANS, 1 p. To Victorien Sardou.

[Jan. 31, Viareggio*] APCS. The postcard illustration is act 3 of *Tosca*.

[July 18, London*] APCS

1901

Jan. 23, telegram, signed Giulio [Ricordi]

Jan. 24, Rome, telegram, signed Giulio [Ricordi]

Jan. 25, Rome, telegram, signed Tito [Ricordi]

Feb. 16, n.p., ALS, 2 p.

[April 16, Milan*] APCS

[May 27*] "Lunedi," Grand Hotel & de Milan^S, ALS, 1 p. (env)

[June 25] [Torre del Lago*] APCS. The illustration shows Puccini at Torre del Lago.

[July 25] [Cutigliano*] APCS

[Dec. 30, Milan*] APCS

1902

[Feb. 8, Milan*] APCS

[March 8, Milan*] 2 APCS

[March 9, Milan*] 2 APCS

[March 9] "Domenica" [Milan*] APCS

[March 15, Viareggio*] APCS

[April 1, Torre del Lago*] APCS

[May 1, Viareggio*] APCS

[mid-May] n.p., ALS, 3 p.

May 13, Torre del Lago, ALS, 3 p.

[May 31, Viareggio*] APCS

[July 15] [Viareggio*] APCS

[Dec. 1, Turin*] Torre del Lago^S (blue), ALS, 2 p. (env)

[Dec. 10, Torino-Roma*] APCS

[Dec. 12, Torre del Lago*] APCS

1903

[Jan. 21] [Milan*] APCS

[March 11, Torre del Lago*] APCS

[March 14, Viareggio*] APCS

[April 2, Viareggio*] APCS

[May 26, Torre del Lago*] APCS

[June 20, Torre del Lago*] APCS

[June 22, Torre del Lago*] APCS. The illustration side represents Marcello in act 3 of *La bohème*.

Sept. 18 [Torre del Lago*] APCS

Oct. 1, Théâtre national de l'Opéra-Comique, Paris^S, ALS, 2 p.

Nov. 20, Torre del Lago, telegram

Nov. 24 [Torre del Lago*] APCS

[Dec. 25, Torre del Lago*] APCS

1904

[Jan. 27, Milan*] ALS, 1 p.

Feb. 2, Milan, ALS, 1 p.

[Feb. 8, Milan*] ALS, 1 p.

Feb. 27, Milan, ALS, 1 p.

March 8 [Milan*] ALS, 1 p.

April 1 [Torre del Lago*] ALS, 1 p.

April 19 [Torre del Lago] ALS, 1 p.

[May 20, Brescia*] APCS

May 29, Brescia, telegram

[Nov. 30, Torre del Lago*] APCS

[Dec. 25, Torre del Lago*] APCS

1905

Jan. 25, Via Verdi^S, ALS, 1 p.

March 25, ANS on both sides of a telegram receipt dated from Torre del Lago

March 30, Torre del Lago, ALS, 1 p.

[March] n.p., ALS, 1 p.

[May 19*] Via Verdi^S, ALS, 1 p.

[June, Buenos Aires] APCS

June 7, Las Palmas, APCS

Sept. 11 [Torre del Lago?] APCS

[Sept. 23*] Torre del Lago^S, ALS, 1 p.

[Nov. 21, Bolgheri*] APCS

1906

Jan. 21 [Naples*] ALS, 1 p.

[Jan. 31*] "mercoledì," Cav. Angiolo Valiani & Figli, Caffé Ristorante, Rome^S, ALS, 2 p. (env)

Feb. 13, The Grand Hôtel Baglioni, Florence^S, ALS, 2 p.

May 3, Via Verdi^S, ALS, 1 p.

Aug. 22, Boscolungo Abetone^S (Serra Bassa.), ALS, 1 p.

Oct. 24 [Paris*] ALS, 1 p.

1907

Jan. [2]6 [New York*] APCS

April 10, Torre del Lago^S, ALS, 1 p.

[April 28*] Torre del Lago^S, ALS, 1 p.

June 6, London, APCS

July 31, Torre del Lago^S, ALS, 1 p.

1908

[Jan. 8, Milan*] APCS

[Jan. 11, Milan*] APCS

[Jan. 28] [Milan*] APCS. The reverse shows the Villino Puccini in Boscolungo-Abetone, with a note in the composer's hand: "Mia casa, 28.1.08."

Feb. 24, Naples, telegram

[Feb., Milan] ALS, 2 p.

March 15, n.p., ALS, 1 p.

April 21, Torre del Lago^S, ALS, 1 p.

June [23] Chiatri, ALS, 1 p.

Dec. 29, Torre del Lago^S, ALS, 1 p.

1909

Jan. 14, Torre del Lago^S, ALS, 1 p.

[Feb. 16] "Martedì," Capalbio (Maremma Toscana)^S, ALS, 2 p.

[Feb. 20] Hôtel de Milan, Rome^S, ALS, 1 p.

[March 25*] "Giovedi" Torre del Lago^S, ALS, 1 p.

April 18, Torre del Lago^S, ALS, 1 p.

June 3 [Paris*] APCS

July 8, Torre del Lago^S, ALS, 1 p.

Oct. 3, Torre del Lago^S, ALS, 1 p.

Dec. 5, Torre del Lago^S, ALS, 1 p.

Dec. 17, Via Verdi^S, ALS, 1 p.

Dec. 22, Via Verdi^S, ALS, 1 p.

1910

Jan. 29, Via Verdi^S, ALS, 1 p.

April 3 [Torre del Lago*] ALS, 1 p. (env)

[June 11, Paris*] APCS

[June 17, Paris*] APCS

[Oct. 20, Torre del Lago*] APCS

[30 Dec.*] Torre del Lago^S, ALS, 1 p.

1911

[Feb. 8*] Torre del Lago^S, ALS, 2 p.

[Feb. 15*] Torre del Lago^S, 1 p.

March 3, Via Verdi^S, ALS, 1 p.

April 2, Torre del Lago^S, ALS, 1 p.

[April 5*] Torre del Lago^S, ALS, 1 p.

[April 15, Milan*] APCS

June 1, Via Verdi^S, ALS, 1 p.

[June 6] Hôtel Regina, Rome^S, ALS, 3 p. (env)

July 1, Torre del Lago^S, ALS, 1 p.

[July 4, Torre del Lago*] APCS

July 6, Torre del Lago^S, ALS, 1 p.

[Oct. 22, Torre del Lago*] APCS. On the picture side, photograph of Puccini.

Oct. 24, Torre del Lago^S, ALS, 1 p.

[Dec. 4, Naples*] APCS

1912

Jan. 2 [Milan*] APCS

[April 3] "mercoledì," Hôtel de Paris, Monte-Carlo^S, ALS, 2 p. (env)

April 12, Via Verdi^S, ALS, 1 p.

Dec. 14, Via Verdi^S, ALS, 1 p.

[Dec. 23*] Via Verdi^S, ALS, 1 p.

1913

March 29 [Berlin*] APCS

[April 1, Berlin*] APCS

April 3, Via Verdi^S, ALS on both sides of a card (env)

April 5, Milan, telegram

April 9, Torre del Lago^S, ALS, 1 p.

[April 12, Torre del Lago*] APCS

[April 16, London*] APCS

[May 12*] Torre del Lago^S, ALS on both sides of a card (env)

July 2, Milan, APCS. Illustration is a photograph of Puccini.

[July 5, Viareggio*] APCS

[Sept. 25*] Torre del Lago^S, ALS on both sides of a card (env)

[Dec. 18, Milan*] APCS

Dec., Milan*] ANS on the front of a calling card (env)

1914

[Dec. 30, Milan*] APCS

1915

Feb. 11, Via Verdi^S, ALS, 1 p.

Feb. 13, Via Verdi^S, ALS, 1 p.

[Feb. 20, Milan*] APCS

March 8, Torre del Lago[S], ALS, 1 p.

May 12, Rome, telegram

July 10 [Torre del Lago*] APCS

Dec. 18 [Torre del Lago*] APCS

1916

[Feb. 17*] Torre del Lago[S], ALS, 1 p.

[Feb. 18] Torre del Lago[S], ALS, 1 p.

March 29 [Torre del Lago*] APCS

[Oct. 31] Torre del Lago[S], ALS, 1 p.

Dec. 24, Via Verdi[S], ALS, 1 p.

1917

[Jan. 11*] Via Verdi[S], ALS, 1 p.

Jan. 15, ANS on the front of a visiting card

Jan. 16, Via Verdi[S], ALS, 1 p.

Jan. 18, Via Verdi[S], ALS, 1 p.

Jan. 29, Via Verdi[S], ALS, 1 p.

March 14 [Monte Carlo*] APCS

May 4, Via Verdi[S], ALS, 2 p. (env)

June 8, Torre del Lago[S], ALS, 1 p.

[Aug. 2, Viareggio*] APCS

1918

[Jan. 3, Viareggio*] APCS

1919

[July] ALS, 3 p.

July 14, Torre del Lago[S], ALS, 1 p.

1920

May 21, Torre del Lago, ANS on both sides of a telegram receipt

Oct. 2, [Pistoia*] APCS, also signed by Elvira, Giorgio, and Gino.

Oct. 18 [Vienna*] APCS

Dec. 27, ANS on both sides of a calling card

Dec. 28 [Ortebello*] APCS

1921

April 1, Torre del Lago[S], ALS, 1 p.

April 8, Milan, APCS

June 22, Torre del Lago[S], ALS, 1 p.

July 4, Hotel Quirinal, Rome[S], ALS, 2 p. (env)

Sept. 16, Torre del Lago[S], ALS, 2 p. (env)

Nov. 10, Hotel Quirinal, Rome[S], ALS, 1 p.

1922

June 2, Viareggio, APCS

1923

March 19, Viareggio[S], ALS, 1 p.

Nov. 27, Hotel Quirinal, Rome[S], ALS, 1 p. (env)

1924

Sept. 27 [Viareggio*] APCS

Undated

ALS [after 1900] Hôtel de Milan, Rome[S], 1 p. (env)

ALS, Hôtel de Milan, Rome[S], 1 p. (env)

ALS, "venerdì," n.p., 1 p.

ALS, n.p., 1 p. (env)

ALS, n.p., 3 p.

ALS, Grand Continental Hôtel, Rome[S], 1 p.

ALS, n.p., 1 p.

APCS [Milan*, date undecipherable]. Reproduction of a Rembrandt painting on the correspondence side.

APCS [Viareggio, 31 July*, year not deciphered]

APCS [postmark undecipherable]

ALS, Rome, written on a telegram form

The collection came with the following additional material:

ALS from Puccini to Morichini, Hôtel de Milan, Rome[S], n.d. [mid-March 1902] 2 p. (env)

ANS to Carlo Biagini on both sides of a calling card, n.d. (env)

Autograph draft of a telegram from Puccini to the Sindaco Monti, n.p. [second week of Jan. 1900] 1 p.

Autograph telegrams from Puccini to the following, n.d., but second week of Jan. 1900.

Cappelletti belle arti, Lucca
Circolo Bohème, Bologna, n.p.
Direzione Teatro Comunale Trieste, n.p.
The Filarmonica Livornese, n.p.
The Fratelli Giannini, Bari, n.p.
Maestro Giorgi, n.p
The Onorevole Luporini, Lucca, n.p.
Prefetto Anarratone, Bari, n.d.
Preside Ginnasio, Lucca, n.p.
Ximenes, Nicola Tolentino, n.p.
An unidentified recipient, n.p.

Autograph telegrams from Puccini to the following:

Giulio Ricordi, [27 Jan. 1901] Rome, and n.d., [but dated 16 Jan. 1900 by Schickling] n.p.
Pagni, Torre del Lago, n.d., signed Oronte.
Mazzini, Rome, n.d.

"I Lucchesi di Roma a Giacomo Puccini / 8 novembre 1893." Illustrated menu. Inscribed by Puccini to Vandini on the verso, with a musical quotation from *Manon Lescaut*, Rome, 9 Nov. 1893.

Original photograph (8 × 7.5 cm) of Puccini after a car accident in 1903, with a clipping on the subject pasted on the verso.

Telegram [to Puccini?] signed Gigi, Rome, n.d.

AN in Puccini's hand, 1 p.

The correspondence covers the entirety of Puccini's career, with references to all of his works and to his interpreters, librettists, colleagues, and rivals: Caruso, Destinn, Leoncavallo, Mascagni, Mugnone, Ruffo, Scotti, Storchio, Toscanini, Verdi, and Zandonai, among others.

FRKF 707

To Maurice Vaucaire

1906 Aug. 8, Boscolungo Abetone[S] (Serra Bassa.), ALS, 2 p., concerning his draft libretto of *La femme et le pantin*, after Pierre Louÿs (eventually set to music by Zandonai in 1911 under the title *Conchita*). In French.

FRKF 290

IV. PRINTED MUSIC

La fanciulla del West: opera in tre atti (dal drama di David Belasco) di Guelfo Civinini e Carlo Zangarini. Musica di Giacomo Puccini. Opera completa. Riduzione di Carlo Carignani. Milan [et al.]: G. Ricordi & C.; New York: Boosey & Co., copyright 1910.

Quarto, 1–333 [+ 1] p. Music publisher's number 113300. Vocal score, first edition, with a printed dedication to Queen Alexandra of England. In the original illustrated wrappers.

The page with the cast list is inscribed by the composer, cast, and other personalities associated with the world premiere of the work at the Metropolitan Opera, New York, on 10 Dec. 1910. In addition to Puccini, the signers include Arturo Toscanini (the conductor), Giulio Gatti-Casazza (the Met's director general), J. Speck (the stage manager here described as "Régisseur général"), and Emmy Destinn (Minnie), Enrico Caruso (Dick Johnson), Pasquale Amato (Jack Rance), Adamo Didur (Ashby), Antonio Pini-Corsi (Happy), Albert Reiss (Nick), Dinh Gilly (Sonora), Angelo Badà (Trin), Giulio Rossi (Sid), Vincenzo Reschiglian (Bello), Pietro Audisio (Harry), Glenn Hall (Joe), Bernard Bégu (Larkens), Andrès de Segurola (Jake Wallace), Edoardo Missiano (José Castro), Georges Bourgeois (Billy Jackrabbit), and Marie Mattfeld (Wowkle). Accompanied by a printed invitation from the Board of Directors of the Metropolitan Opera Company to Mr. M.H. Halperson (the name is filled in by hand) for the reception held in Puccini's honor in the foyer of the Met following the opening night performance.

Heinrich Schütz to Henry Miller, p. 104–05.
London, Sotheby's, 21 Nov. 1990, lot 208.
FRKF 1406

ARTHUR RACKHAM (1867–1939)

The Peter Pan Portfolio, by Arthur Rackham, from Peter Pan in Kensington Gardens, by J.M. Barrie. London: Hodder & Stoughton [1910].

3 preliminary leaves and 12 colored mounted plates (55 × 50 cm), each preceded by a printed caption on the recto of an additional leaf. Printed on the recto of the sheet preceding the title page: "This Copy of The Peter Pan Portfolio is dedicated to Mr. J.M. Barrie by the Artist, the Publishers and the Engravers." Signed by Rackham and the two publishers. At the bottom of this page, in pencil, in Barrie's hand: "To Michael [Llewellyn Davies] / from his / J.M.B. / Christmas 1910."

Bound in cream-colored vellum, with restored white silk ties and in a restored light green cloth box constructed from the front board of the original vellum cover. On cover: "This edition is limited to 100 copies for Great Britain and Ireland, numbered and signed by the publishers, and with each plate signed by Arthur Rackham." According to Latimore and Haskell, p. 39, only 20 copies were actually printed. Inscribed in black ink in the upper right corner of the cover: "To Michael [Llewellyn Davies] / from J.M.B. / Jan. 1911."

With two storage tickets that were affixed to the original box, one with the name of Mrs. John Llewellyn-Davies.

FRKF 119

RAYMOND RADIGUET (1903–23)

I. MANUSCRIPTS

Le bal du comte d'Orgel

Partial, uncorrected carbon typescript copy of the novel [ca. 1922], presumed to have been typed by Georges Auric at Le Piquey in 1922.

Collation:

[1], 2–17, 20–37, 38–77 [in two copies, interleaved]. This section corresponds roughly to p. 1–90 of the first edition of the novel (Paris: Bernard Grasset, 1924).

1–54, 55–58 [two copies, interleaved], 59–65, [66]. This section corresponds to p. 160–239 of the novel.

An intermediate version of the text, without Cocteau's revisions.

See Arnaud, p. 300 and 322. See also Radiguet, *Le bal du comte d'Orgel, édition critique établie par Andrew Oliver et Nadia Odouard* (Paris: Lettres modernes, 1993), vol. I, p. lxxiii–lxxiv.

Paris, Couturier-Nicolay (Drouot), 2 Dec. 1987, lot 211.
FRKF 1296

Les joues en feu

Proofs, corrected by Jean Cocteau, of the first edition of this verse collection, published posthumously by Bernard Grasset in 1925. The proofs comprise manuscript maquettes for the cover and for the title page and preliminaries, and ten galleys bearing the stamp of "Imp[rimerie] F. Paillart / Abbeville (Somme)" and the date 7 March 1925.

Hamburg, Hauswedell und Nolte, 20–21 May 1985, lot 2040.
FRKF 796.1

Holograph manuscript and partial typescript of the preface and manuscripts of four poems, n.d., 11 p., written in black ink on the recto sides of loose folio-size sheets of onionskin paper, only the preface paginated, 1–2 and 1–3. At the top of p. 1, in Radiguet's hand: "Sans titre"; in pencil, in a different hand: "Préface joues en feu." The carbon typescript comprises only the first two pages. The manuscript poems are: "Vénus démasquée," 1 p.; "L'étoile de Vénus," 1 p.; "Septentrion, dieu de l'amour," 2 p.; "Élégie," 1 p. The last page is a "Note de l'Editeur" in Cocteau's hand.

FRKF 1245.A03

"Tohu"

Autograph manuscript of this tale, n.d., 1 p., in black ink on two pages glued one on top of the other. The top part is on the verso of a fragment from an unidentified commercial ledger concerning French colonies and showing the dates 1916–17. Marked "page 8" in red ink, in an unidentified hand, in the upper right corner. Original title erased: "[Illegible] de Tohu."

First published in *Sic*, No. 35 (Dec. 1918). See *Oeuvres complètes*, p. 489.

FRKF 189

II. MISCELLANEOUS

[Deux cahiers manuscrits, reproduits en fac-similé]. Facsimiles of two notebooks by Radiguet [Paris: D. Jaconet pour É. Champion, 1925].

Untitled notebooks in grey and brick red covers (both 16.5 × 22 cm), 11 and 20 unnumbered leaves, mostly filled in on the recto sides. The rear wrapper of the first notebook is written out on both sides. Note by Jean Cocteau, facsimile, on fol. [19r] of the second notebook. At colophon, on fol. [20r] of the second notebook: "La phototypie de ce manuscrit a été faite par Daniel Jaconet pour Édouard Champion. / Achevé de tirer le 4 mars 1925 à cent trente exemplaires dont dix sur Japon de A à J tous chiffrés à la main par Jean Cocteau et signés." The reproduction of Cocteau's pen-and-ink portrait of Radiguet, as noted in the Harvard University Library record, is not present in part 1.

The first notebook is a portrait of Montparnasse in the post-1918 era, the second seems to relate to Radiguet's novel *Le diable au corps*.

Hamburg, Hauswedell und Nolte, 20–21 May 1985, lot 2040.
FRKF 796.2

Time Magazine, LXIV:26 (27 Dec., 1954), containing "The Devil in the Book," an article on Radiguet's *Le diable au corps*.

Clipping from an unidentified English or American newspaper, n.d., reporting the arrest by mistake of a millionaire named Guy Radiguet.

FRKF 1245.supp A

MAURICE RAVEL (1875–1937)

I. MUSIC MANUSCRIPTS

A. WORKS BY RAVEL

A la manière de Borodine

Holograph manuscript of this piece for piano solo, n.d., 2 p. Notated in black ink on p. [2] and [3] of a bifolium of tall 24-staff paper (blind stamp of Lard-Esnault). At the top of p. [2] in Ravel's hand: "à la manière de ... / Borodine / Valse"; in another hand: "Maurice Ravel." Signed at the end. Pencil markings by the engraver throughout. At the bottom of p. [2], not in Ravel's hand: "U.S.A. Copyright 1914 / by A. Zunz Mathot Editeur Paris / 11 Rue Bergère"; music publisher's number (Z. 729 M), also found at the bottom of p. [3].

Composed in 1913 according to Grove.

London, Sotheby's, 25 Nov. 1985, lot 192.
FRKF 1041

A la manière de Emmanuel Chabrier

Holograph manuscript of this piece for piano solo, 2 p., in black ink, with corrections and addition in red ink and black pencil, on p. [2] and [3] of a bifolium of tall 24-staff paper (blind stamp of Lard-Esnault / Ed. Bellamy Sr.). At the top of p. [2] in Ravel's hand: "à la manière de. - / Emmanuel Chabrier / paraphrase sur un air de Gounod (Faust IIe acte)." Underneath, in pencil, in another hand: "Maurice Ravel." Signed at the end by the composer. In the bottom left corner of p. [2], not in Ravel's hand: "U.S.A. Copyright 1914 / by A. Zunz Mathot Editeur Paris / 11 Rue Bergère"; music publisher's number (Z. 731 M) added at the bottom of p. [2] and [3]. On p. [1] in pencil, in an unidentified hand: "no 3." Pencil markings by the engraver.

Composed in 1913 according to Grove.

FRKF 515

Berceuse sur le nom de Gabriel Fauré

Holograph manuscript of this piece for violin and piano, 1922, 3 p. Notated in black ink, with a few corrections in red ink and engraver's markings in pencil, on p. [2]–[4] of a single bifolium of oblong 12-staff paper. On p. [1] in Ravel's hand: "pour Claude Roland-Manuel / Berceuse / sur le nom de Gabriel Fauré / [a short musical explanation, also to be read upside-down from the system of notes used, introduced by a treble clef in one direction and a bass clef in the other]." At the bottom of p. [2], not in Ravel's hand, copyright statement, Durand et Cie., 1922, and music publisher's number (D.F. 10270). Signed at the end and dated: "Lyons la Forêt / Septembre 1922." Stamp of Durand on p. [1], twice.

Paris, Paul Renaud (Drouot), 14 May 1986, lot 139.
FRKF 1114

Fugue on a theme by Reber

Holograph manuscript, 1900, 4 p. Notated in black ink on the four sides of a single bifolium of 24-staff paper, on 4-staff systems, with the exception of the opening. On p. [1] in Ravel's hand: "Sujet de Reber." Additional pencil sketches on p. [4]. Dated 31 May 1900 at the end.

A student exercise.

Paris, Laurin-Guilloux-Buffetaud-Tailleur (Drouot), 3 July 1985, lot 149.
FRKF 864

Un grand sommeil noir

Holograph manuscript of this song for voice and piano on a poem by Paul Verlaine, 1895, 2 p. Notated in black ink, with corrections in pencil on p. [2] and [3] of a bifolium of tall 12-staff paper. Signed and dated 6 Aug. 1895 at the end. On p. [1], title in Ravel's hand: "Un grand sommeil noir / P. Verlaine." Unidentified sketches on p. [1] and [4].

London, Christie's, 27 March 1985, lot 214.
FRKF 869

Sites auriculaires

Holograph manuscript of this work for two pianos, n.d. [1895–97], 13 p., in black ink, with a few erasures and corrections and a few markings in blue pencil, on 12-staff paper (blind stamp of Lard-Esnault). The manuscript comprises: a single sheet paginated 1–2, two nested bifolia paginated 3–10, two single sheets paginated 11–13, followed by another single sheet, blank. Title on p. 1, in Ravel's hand: "Sites Auriculaires."

The work is in two parts: The first, "Habanera," is on p. 1–7; the second, "Entre cloches," on p. 8–13. The "Habanera" is preceded by the epigraph: "Au pays parfumé que le soleil caresse / Ch. Baudelaire."

Sites auriculaires was premiered on 5 March 1898 at the Société nationale de musique, by Marthe Dron and Ricardo Viñes. The work was withdrawn by the composer and published only in 1975 by Salabert in Paris. The "Habanera," orchestrated by Ravel, became the third movement of his *Rapsodie espagnole* (1907–08).

Heinrich Schütz to Henry Miller, p. 84–85.
Paris, Laurin-Guilloux-Buffetaud-Tailleur (Drouot), 3 July 1985, lot 148.
FRKF 863

Sonata for violin and piano

Autograph draft of the opening of the *Sonata for violin and piano*, signed and dated May 1927, 1 p., on the recto of a single sheet of oblong 16-staff paper. The draft, written in pencil, corresponds to the first 20 bars of the first movement.

New York, Christie's, 16–17 Dec. 1983, lot 436.
FRKF 153

B. WORKS ARRANGED BY RAVEL

Debussy. Nocturnes

Holograph manuscript of Ravel's transcription of "Nuages" and "Fêtes" for piano four-hands, n.d., 18 p.

"Nuages" is written in black ink on a bifolium and a single sheet, taped together, of tall 32-staff paper (blind stamp of Lard-Esnault / Ed. Bellamy Sr.), paginated 1–6 (not in Ravel's hand; p. 6 is blank).

"Fêtes" is written on three nested bifolia and a single sheet, taped together, of tall 30-staff paper (blind stamp of Lard-Esnault / Ed. Bellamy Sr.), paginated 7–19. Pages 7 through most of 12 are in purple ink; the remainder is in black ink, with tempo indications in black ink throughout. There are some additional markings in pencil in the engraver's hand. On p. 1 in Ravel's hand: "Nocturnes / Claude Debussy / Transcription pour 2 pianos 4 mains / I Nuages / [in pencil, not in Ravel's hand:] par Maurice Ravel." On p. 7, in Ravel's hand: "II. Fêtes" and engraver's stamp (A. Gulon).

Published in 1909 according to Grove.

Paris, Laurin-Guilloux-Buffetaud-Tailleur (Drouot), 16 Nov. 1983, lot 208.
FRKF 256

Debussy. Prélude à l'après-midi d'un faune

Holograph manuscript of Ravel's transcription for piano four-hands, n.d. 10 p.

Notated in black ink, with additional autograph annotations in blue pencil and other markings (some not in Ravel's hand) in black pencil, on three nested bifolia of tall 28-staff paper (blind stamp of Lard-Esnault / Ed. Bellamy Sr.), paginated [1]–10 in Ravel's hand. At the top of p. [1] in Ravel's hand: "Prélude à l'après-midi d'un faune / Claude Debussy / Transcription à 4 mains / par Maurice Ravel." At the bottom of p. [1], in a different hand, name and address of the publisher E. Fromont and initials E.F. Pasted-on correction on p. [1]. Pencil markings by the engraver.

Published in 1930 according to Grove.

Paris, Laurin-Guilloux-Buffetaud-Tailleur (Drouot), 16 Nov. 1983, lot 207.
FRKF 255

Debussy. Sarabande

Holograph manuscript of Ravel's orchestration of this movement from *Pour le piano*, 1922, 9 p.

Notated in black ink, with additional markings (most not by Ravel) in red ink and in pencil, on a combination of separate bifolia and single sheets of tall 30-staff paper, paginated [1]–9. The first page is a single sheet glued on the inside of a bifolium serving as wrappers, with the last two pages of the manuscript on its second leaf.

On the front of the outer bifolium, in pencil, not in Ravel's hand: "Sarabande & Danse (Ravel)" and engraver's markings. At the top of p. [1] in Ravel's hand: "Sarabande / Claude Debussy." At the bottom of the page, in another hand: "Copyright by Jean Jobert 1923 / Paris, Jean Jobert, Editeur, 44, Rue du Colisée / J.J. 192 / Tous droits d … [completed in pencil, possibly in Ravel's hand:] exécution, de repro- / duction & d'arrangements réservés." Signed and dated Nov. 1922 at the end. Pencil markings by the engraver.

Published in 1923 according to Grove.

Paris, Laurin-Guilloux-Buffetaud-Tailleur (Drouot), 16 Nov. 1983, lot 210.
FRKF 258

Debussy. *Tarantelle styrienne*

Holograph manuscript of Ravel's orchestration, 1922, 32 p.

Notated in black ink, with additional holograph markings in red ink and a large number of pencil markings, most evidently not in Ravel's hand, on both sides of sheets of tall 24-, 28-, and 30-staff paper, paginated [1]–32. At the top of p. [1] in Ravel's hand: "Danse / Claude Debussy / [not in Ravel's hand:] Orchestrée par Maurice Ravel." At the bottom of the page, in the same second hand: "Copyright by J. Jobert 1923 / Paris. Jean Jobert, Editeur, 44 Rue du Colisée / J.J. 193 / Tous droits." Signed and dated Dec. 1922 at the end. Pencil markings by the engraver.

Published as *Danse* in 1923, according to Grove.

Paris, Laurin-Guilloux-Buffetaud-Tailleur (Drouot), 16 Nov. 1983, lot 209.
FRKF 257

Mussorgsky. *Khovanshchina*

Partial holograph manuscript of Ravel's orchestration of Mussorgsky's unfinished opera, n.d. [1913], 40 p.

The manuscript is in two sections, both written in black ink, with additional markings in pencil, on bifolia of tall 40-staff paper. The first section is in two gatherings, stitched together, of four and two nested bifolia; the second comprises a single gathering of three nested bifolia. The first section is paginated 1–24; the second, 1–16, both in Ravel's hand. At the top of p. 1 of the first section, in pencil, in an unidentified hand: "Khovantchina / Orch. Ravel / 1er acte [the rest undeciphered]." At the bottom of p. 24, in an unidentified hand: "Kohvantchina [sic] par Ravel / Col. / Serge Lifar"; also, note in pencil, in a different hand: "page 40 / de la grande / Partition."

The first section begins at rehearsal number 1 bis and ends four measures after rehearsal number 29. At the top of p. 1 of the second section, in the upper right corner, not in Ravel's hand: "Khovantchina / par Ravel / Col. Serge Lifar." Also at the top of p. 1 of the second section, in pencil, not in Ravel's hand: "Khovantchina 2e acte Chanson de Kouska avec choeurs," and, in a different hand: "page 246 de la grande partition." The second section begins at rehearsal number 126 and ends five measures after rehearsal number 141. Purple stamp of Serge Lifar on the first and last pages of each section.

Reported as lost by Grove.

London, Sotheby's, 11 Nov. 1982, lot 45.
FRKF 3

II. LITERARY MANUSCRIPT

Letter to *Le Figaro*

Manuscript draft concerning *L'heure espagnole*, n.p. [1911], 5 p., the first page on the verso of mourning stationery. Accompanied by a clipping from *Le Figaro* with the text of the letter as it appeared, in much reduced form, on 17 May 1911. Partly published in Stuckenschmidt, p. 103–04, identified as being "among the notes Jean Godebski left to the writer René Chalupt for the preparation of his book on Ravel." See also Orenstein, p. 118.

L'heure espagnole, on a libretto by Franc-Nohain, was premiered at the Opéra-Comique on 19 May 1911.

London, Sotheby's, 14–15 April 1982, lot 63.
FRKF 26

III. LETTERS

Many of Ravel's letters are on the printed stationery of his residence, abbreviated as follows:

Le Belvédère[S] = on the stationery of Le Belvédère / Montfort l'Amaury (S.& O.)

Unless otherwise noted, the letters are not in Orenstein.

To [Edmond Bonniot?]

1916 June 21, n.p., ALS, 3 p., concerning mostly Ravel's wartime service, his health, and the state of his camionette Adelaide.

Bonniot was the son-in-law and literary executor of Stéphane Mallarmé as well as Ravel's personal doctor. Their house near Fontainebleau, in Valvins (where the poet died), was next to the one of Ravel's friends Cipa and Ida Godebski.

New York, Sotheby's, 15 Oct. 1982, lot 165.
FRKF 7

To Félix Brunetière

1931 Dec. 26, Ateliers mécaniques Bonnet[S], Levallois, ALS, 1 p., reserving the right to conduct his *Concerto in G* with Marguerite Long as soloist.

London, Sotheby's, 29 Nov. 1985, lot 196.
FRKF 1071

To Hélène Kahn Casella

1913 April 2, Clarens-Montreux, hôtel des Crêtes, ALS, 7 p.; p. 3–7 are headed "destiné au Comité de la S.M.I. ou, à défaut, à M. Gustave Samazeuilh." Orenstein, p. 126–28.

[ca. 1913] n.p., ALS, 3 p.

1913 April 8, Clarens, APCS

1914 Feb. 14, Saint-Jean-de-Luz, APCS

1914 March 21, Saint-Jean-de-Luz, APCS. Orenstein, p. 135.

1914 March 28, Saint-Jean-de-Luz, ALS, 4 p. (env)

1914 April 8, Saint-Jean-de-Luz, ALS, 4 p. (env)

1914 April 10, Fuenterabbia, APCS

1914 July 4, Ongi Ethori, St-Jean-de-Luz^S, ALS to Alfredo Casella, 4 p.

1914 July 18, Saint-Jean-de-Luz, APCS. Orenstein, p. 139.

1914 Aug. 29, Saint-Jean-de-Luz, APCS to Alfredo Casella

1914 Sept. 21, Ethori, St-Jean-de-Luz^S, ALS, 4 p.

1916 Jan. 5, Paris T.M.C.R., rue de Vaugirard no. 156, APCS

1916 June 2, APCS [stamped "Convois automobiles, section de (rest illegible)"]

1916 Oct. 8, ALS [on the envelope: "hôpital temporaire no. 20, salle 7, Châlons s/M"] 3 p.

[1916 Oct. 17*] Châlons-sur-Marne, APCS to Alfredo Casella from a doctor [signature illegible]

1916 Oct. 18, Châlons-sur-Marne, APCS

1919 Jan. 19, Megève, ALS, 4 p. (env). Orenstein, p. 169.

1919 Sept. 10, Saint-Cloud, ALS on a card, 2 p. (env)

1919 Dec. 2, Lapras, ALS, 1 p.

1920 Jan. 15, Lapras, ALS, 1 p.

1920 March 24, Lapras, ALS on a card, 2 p. (env), on mourning stationery

1920 July 18 [Saint-Sauveur, Eure*] APCS

1920 Aug. 24, La Bijeannette [i.e. Château de Bigeannette, Saint-Sauveur, Eure] ALS on a card, 2 p. (env), on mourning stationery

1921 June 16, Paris, ALS, 3 p. (env)

1921 July 25, Le Belvédère^S, ALS, 4 p. (env)

1921 Dec. 8, ALS, 1 p. [stamped on address side: Le Belvédère, Montfort-l'Amaury (S & O)]

1922 Jan. 17, Paris, Durand & Fils, Editeurs^S, ALS, 1 p. (env)

[1922 May 18*] "Jeudi," Montfort l'Amaury, ALS, 1 p. ["carte pneumatique"]

1922 July 29, Le Belvédère^S, ALS, 4 p. (env)

1922 Sept. 20, Le Frêne [Lyons-la-Forêt, Eure] APCS

1923 Jan. 8, Le Belvédère^S, ALS, 1 p.

1923 Feb. 7, Le Belvédère^S, ALS, 1 p.

1923 March 30, Le Belvédère^S, ALS, 1 p.

1923 July 27, Le Belvédère^S, ALS, 1 p.

1923 Aug. 2, Le Belvédère^S, TLS, 1 p.

[1923 Sept. 9*] Le Belvédère^S, ALS, 1 p.

1923 Oct. 9, Le Belvédère^S, TLS, 1 p.

1923 Dec. 27, Le Belvédère^S, TLS, 1 p.

1924 Feb. 13, Le Belvédère^S, TLS, 1 p. (window env)

1924 June 18, Le Belvédère^S, TLS, 1 p. (window env)

1924 Aug. 26, APCS stamped: Le Belvédère, Montfort-l'Amaury

1924 Nov. 24, Le Belvédère^S, TLS, 1 p.

1925 April 23, Le Belvédère^S, ALS, 1 p.

[1925 Sept. 5*] APCS stamped: Le Belvédère, Montfort-l'Amaury

1925 Nov. 5, APCS stamped: Le Belvédère, Montfort-l'Amaury

1926 June 3, Paris, ALS, 1 p. ["carte pneumatique"]

1926 Aug. 14, APCS stamped: Le Belvédère, Montfort-l'Amaury

1926 Sept. 24 [Montfort-l'Amaury*] APCS

1927 Jan. 6, APCS stamped: Le Belvédère, Montfort-l'Amaury

1927 Feb. 27, Edinburgh, APCS. Also signed by Gérard Hekking.

1927 July 22, Le Belvédère^S, ALS on a card, 2 p. (env)

1928 April 14, "de Grand Canyon à Buffalo," APCS

1929 Feb. 13, Le Belvédère^S, ALS, 1 p.

1929 Dec. 27, n.p., ALS [decorated card] 2 p.

1930 May 6, Le Belvédère^S, ALS, 1 p.

1930 May 15, Le Belvédère^S, ALS, 1 p.

1930 Sept. 9, Le Belvédère^S, ALS on a card, 2 p., transmitting a letter to Toscanini, which is not present.

1930 Sept. 19, Le Belvédère^S, ALS on a card, 1 p. (env)

1931 Feb. 4, Le Belvédère^S, ALS, 1 p.

1931 March 17, Le Belvédère^S, ALS, 1 p.

[1937*] April 16, Paris, ALS, 1 p. (year also in pencil)

Hélène Kahn was married to Alfredo Casella from 1907 until their divorce in 1919. Topics covered in the letters include projected concerts at the S.M.I. including music by Debussy, Milhaud, Satie, Schoenberg, and Stravinsky. Among Ravel's works mentioned are the *Trio*, *La valse* (long entitled "Wien"), *Daphnis et Chloé*, the *Chansons hébraïques*, the *Trois poèmes de Stéphane Mallarmé*, *Tzigane*, and the *Sonata for violin and cello*. There are references to Claire Croiza, Ninon Vallin, and Arturo Toscanini, notably in connection with the famous performance of *Boléro* in 1930. Among composers mentioned are Lili Boulanger, Maurice Delage, Florent Schmitt, Stravinsky, and Casella himself, while the final letter conveys condolences on the death of Karol Szymanowski. A few letters, as indicated, are to Alfredo Casella.

FRKF 1110

To Mme Jean Cruppi

1905 Aug. 27, Hôtel des bains de mer, Roscoff[S], ALS, 4 p. Mentions the *Sonatine* and a symphonic project. Orenstein, p. 79–80.

Paris, Ader-Picart-Tajan (Drouot), 11 June 1982, lot 188.
FRKF 176

To Serge Diaghilev

1917 Jan. 12, 1, rue de Chazelles. XVIIe [Paris][S], ALS, 3 p., agreeing to compose a ballet on a libretto by Francesco Cangiullo. Orenstein, p. 164.

From the collection of Serge Lifar, with his stamp printed in red and purple.
London, Sotheby's, 9 May 1984, lot 203.
FRKF 308

To Mme Fernand Dreyfus

1918 Sept. 10, Saint-Cloud, ALS to "ma chère marraine," 4 p. Orenstein, p. 166–67.

Paris, Paul Renaud (Drouot), 14 May 1986, lot 52.
FRKF 1187

To Edwin Evans

1910 Jan. 4, 4, avenue Carnot [Paris] XVIIe.[S], ALS, 3 p., on mourning stationery. Mentions *Daphnis*.

London, Sotheby's, 29 Nov. 1985, lot 191.
FRKF 1059

1914 May 31, Paris (back of envelope), ALS, 4 p (env). Sends cuts for *Daphnis*, comments on Diaghilev, Lalo, *Le rossignol*.

1914 June 7, n.p., ALS, 3 p. Quotes (in English) his letter to several London newspapers protesting against performances of *Daphnis* without chorus.

1914 July 20, Ongi Ethori, Saint-Jean-de-Luz[S], ALS, 4 p. (env)

1914 July 31, Ongi Ethori, Saint-Jean-de-Luz[S], ALS, 4 p.

London, Christie's, 16 Oct. 1985, lots 196–99.
FRKF 1014–17

To Mme Henry Ghys

1912 Nov. 27, 4, avenue Carnot, XVIIe [Paris][S], ALS on both sides of a card

1914 Sept. 26, Ongi Ethori[S], 23, rue Sopite, St-Jean-de-Luz, ALS, 3 p. (env)

FRKF 726a

To Xavier Cyprian (Cipa) Godebski

[1908 Feb.*? Levallois (back of envelope)] ALS, 2 p. (env). Orenstein, p. 95–96.

1908 March 26, Levallois (back of envelope), ALS, 4 p. (env)

[1908 Sept. 3 Paris*] ALS, 4 p. (env)

[ca. 1908] n.p. ALS, 2 p.

1909 March 14, 4, avenue Carnot [Paris] ALS, 7 p., on mourning stationery (env). Orenstein, p. 102–03.

1910 April 10 [Avon*] ALS, 4 p. (env)

1910 April 16, Valvins, ALS, 1 p.

1910 April 25, Valvins (back of envelope), ALS, 4 p. (env). Orenstein, p. 110–11.

1911 Feb. 25 [Paris*] ALS, 1 p.

1911 March 22, La Grangette [Vulaines-sur-Seine] ALS, 4 p. (env). Orenstein, p. 116–17.

1911 June 2 [Paris*] ALS, 4 p. (env)

1911 June 16, n.p., ALS, 3 p.

[1911 Dec. 29, Paris*] ALS, 2 p. (env)

1913 April 4, Hôtel-Pension des Crêtes, Clarens-Montreux, APCS

1913 Oct. 12, Saint-Jean-de-Luz, ALS, 1 p.

[1914 Jan. 16, Paris*] ALS, 2 p. ("pneumatique")

[1914 Feb. 14*] Saint-Jean-de-Luz (back of envelope), ALS, 4 p. (env)

1914 June 28, Saint-Jean-de-Luz, ALS, 4 p. (env), with notes in an unidentified hand on verso.

1914 Aug. 3, Saint-Jean-de-Luz, ALS, 4 p.

1914 Aug. 20, Saint-Jean-de-Luz, ALS, 4 p. Orenstein, p. 141–42.

1916 April 5, Convois automobiles, Section T.M. 171, par B.C.M., APCS

1916 July 4, 15e section du parc automobile par B.C.M., Paris (on envelope), ALS, 3 p. (env)

1916 July 27, 38e section du parc automobile par B.C.M., Paris (on envelope), ALS, 4 p. (env)

1919 Jan. 21, Hôtel du Mont-Blanc, Megève, APCS

1920 July 9, Saint-Sauveur, APCS

1922 April 11, Le Belvédère, Montfort L'Amaury, ALS, 4 p. (env). Orenstein, p. 198–99.

1922 May 10 [Montfort L'Amaury*] ALS, 1 p. (env)

1924 Feb. 14, Montfort L'Amaury, TLS, 1 p. Orenstein, p. 223.

1927 Dec. 14, Le Belvédère, Montfort L'Amaury, ALS, 1 p. Orenstein, p. 254.

Also, APCS to Jean Godebski, Clarens, 1913 April 12; two visiting cards, one dated 1923 Nov. 15; and one undated photograph showing Ravel [at Montfort l'Amaury?].

London, Sotheby's, 14–15 April 1982, lot 61.
FRKF 24

To Ida Godebski

1905

Aug. 9 [Paris*] ALS, 8 p. (env). Orenstein p. 77–78.

Aug. 23, Morgat, ALS, 2 p., also signed by Maurice Delage.

Sept. 4, Portrieux-Saint-Quay, ALS, 4 p. (env)

1906

Aug. 18, Levallois (back of envelope), ALS, 4 p. (env). Orenstein, p. 87–88.

Aug. 26, Hermance, ALS, 4 p. (env)

Sept. 13, Hermance (back of envelope), ALS, 4 p. (env)

Oct. 22 [Paris*] APCS, also signed by Léon-Paul Fargue (env)

1907

July 11, n.p., ALS, 4 p.

July 27, Morlaix, APCS (env)

Aug. 13, Grand-Hôtel de la Plage, Morgat, ALS, 2 p., also signed by Delage.

Oct. 8, Legallois (back of envelope), ALS, 4 p. (env)

Nov. 15, Levallois (back of envelope), ALS, 4 p. (env)

[Dec. 23, Paris*] ALS, 4 p. (env)

1908

Jan. 20, Levallois (back of envelope), ALS, 7 p. (env). Orenstein, p. 93–94.

June 19, n.p., ALS, 8 p. Orenstein, p. 98.

July 17, Levallois (envelope), ALS, 7 p. (env)

[Aug. 5*] Levallois (back of envelope), ALS, 4 p. (env)

Sept. 3, Levallois (back of envelope), ALS, 2 p. (env)

Sept. 16, Valvins, ALS, 4 p. (env)

Sept. 18, Valvins (back of envelope), ALS, 8 p. (env)

Sept. 24, Valvins, ALS, 4 p. (env)

[Sept.] Valvins, ALS, 4 p. Orenstein, p. 99–100.

1910

May 10, Valvins (back of envelope), ALS, 6 p. (env)

July 29, Paris, ALS, 4 p., on mourning stationery

Aug. 4, Paris (back of envelope), ALS, 4 p. (env)

Sept. 27, Paris (back of envelope), ALS, 4 p. (env). Orenstein, p. 114–15.

[ca. 1910–14] "Samedi," n.p., ALS, 2 p.

1911

July 19, Ciboure, ALS, 4 p. (env). Orenstein, p. 119.

1912

Aug. 2, Saint-Jean-de-Luz, ALS, 5 p. (env)

Sept. 8, Saint-Jean-Pied-de-Port, APCS (env), also signed by Gustave Samazeuilh.

Sept. 24, Saint-Jean-de-Luz, ALS, 5 p.

Oct. 7, Saint-Jean-de-Luz, ALS, 5 p. (env)

1913

Aug. 27, Saint-Jean-de-Luz, ALS, 2 p. on a card (env)

[before 1914] n.p., ALS, 2 p., also signed by Michel-Dimitri Calvocoressi.

1914

[early 1914?] Paris (verso), ALS, 1 p. (env)

March 19, Saint-Jean-de-Luz, ALS, 4 p. (env)

March 25, Saint-Jean-de-Luz, ALS, 4 p. (env)

April 4, Geneva, APCS (env)

April 8, Saint-Jean-de-Luz, ALS, 4 p. Orenstein, p. 135–36.

Sept. 8, Saint-Jean-de-Luz, ALS, 8 p.

Sept. 18, Saint-Jean-de-Luz, ALS, 4 p. (env)

1916

March 9, Section annexe du triage du personnel, Viroflay, APCS (env)

March 28, Convois automobiles, Section T.M. 171, par B.C.M., APCS (env)

April 2, n.p., ALS, 4 p.

April 14, Ambulance automobile chirurgicale, Secteur 36, par B.C.M, Paris, APCS

May 9, Convois automobiles, Section T.M. 171, par B.C.M., Paris, ALS, 3 p. (env)

June 11, 15e section de parc automobile, par B.C.M., Paris (on envelope), ALS, 2 p. (env)

June 16, 15e section de parc automobile, par B.C.M., Paris (on envelope), ALS, 2 p. (env)

June 21, n.p. ALS, 2 p.

June 26, 15e section de parc automobile, par B.C.M., Paris (on envelope), ALS, 2 p. (env)

Aug. 16, section de parc automobile, par B.C. M., Paris (on envelope, torn), ALS, 2 p. (env)

Aug. 22, 38e section de parc automobile, par B.C.M., Paris (on envelope), ALS, 3 p. (env)

Sept. 4, 38e section de parc automobile, par B.C.M., Paris (on envelope), ALS, 4 p. (env)

Sept. 21, Section automobile de place n°9, Châlons-sur-Marne (on envelope), ALS, 1 p. (env)

Sept. 26 [Hôpital temporaire n°20, Châlons-sur-Marne*] ALS, 3 p. (env)

Oct. 5, Hôpital temporaire n°20, Châlons-sur-Marne (on envelope), ALS, 4 p. (env)

Oct. 11, Hôpital temporaire n°20, Châlons-sur-Marne (on envelope), ALS, 2 p. (env)

Oct. 17, n.p., ALS, 2 p.

[1916?] 15e section de parc automobile, par B.C.M., Paris (on envelope), envelope only.

1917

Feb. 14, Section automobile de place, Châlons-sur-Marne n°9, (on envelope), ALS, 4 p. (env)

March 19, Section automobile de place n°9, Châlons-sur-Marne, APCS

1918
Nov. 6, Saint-Cloud, ALS, 1 p.
Nov. 11, Saint-Cloud, ALS, 1 p. Orenstein, p. 167–68.

1919
Jan. 14, Megève, ALS, 4 p. (env). Orenstein, p. 168–69.
Feb. 12, Megève, ALS, 4 p. (env)
Feb. 25, Megève, 2 APCS
March 6, Megève, ALS, 4 p. (env)
March 17, Megève, ALS, 4 p. (env)
March 30, Annecy, ALS, 4 p. (env)
May 24, Saint-Cloud, ALS, 4 p. (env). Orenstein, p. 173–74.
Sept. 2, Saint-Cloud, ALS, 2 p. on a card (env). Orenstein, p. 174–75.
Sept. 19, Saint-Cloud, ALS, 4 p. (env)
Dec. 27, Lapras [Lamastre*] ALS, 1 p. Orenstein, p. 177–78.

1920–30
1920 Jan. 15, Lapras, ALS, 4 p. Orenstein, p.178–79.
1920 May 21, Saint-Sauveur (front of envelope), 2 p. (env)
1920 July 17 [Saint-Sauveur] ALS, 2 p., on mourning stationery on a card (env)
1920 Sept. 24, Lyons-la-Forêt, ALS, 4 p. (env)
1920 Sept. 26, Lyons-la-Forêt, ALS, 1 p.
1921 March 17 [Montfort l'Amaury] APCS
1921 June 29, Montfort l'Amaury, ALS, 1 p.
1923 March 23, Montfort l'Amaury, ALS, 1 p.
1923 June 17, "Yacht 'le Formidable,' en rade de Montfort l'Amaury," APCS
1923 Aug. 14, Montfort l'Amaury, TLS, 1 p.
1924 July 26, Montfort l'Amaury, APCS
[1924? Aug. 26, Montfort l'Amaury *] envelope only
1924 Oct. 13, Montfort l'Amaury, TLS, 1 p.
1928 Feb. 16, "De Portland à Denver," Portland Limited[S], ALS, 4 p. (env)
1930 May 8, Montfort l'Amaury, ALS, 2 p. on card. Orenstein, p. 271.
n.d., n.p. ALS, 1 p.

The sculptor Xavier Cyprian ("Cipa") Godebski (1864–1937) and his wife Ida (1872–1935) were Ravel's closest friends and supporters, and soon became, in Marcel Marnat's words, "his adoptive family." The correspondence mentions many of his works, including *L'heure espagnole*, *Gaspard de la nuit*, *Le tombeau de Couperin*, *Ma Mère l'Oye* (whose original, piano four-hand version is dedicated to the Godebski children, Jean and Marie ["Mimie"], both mentioned regularly in the letters), *Daphnis et Chloé*, the *Trio*, the *Sonatine*, *La Valse* (from the early project referred to as "Vienne" or "Wien"), *Boléro*, *Tzigane*, *L'enfant et les sortilèges*, and the *Sonata for violin and cello* (which Godebski did not like). The letter of 1908 March 26 enclosed a clipping of Pierre Lalo's negative review of the *Rapsodie espagnole* and contains Ravel's angry comments. Other topics covered include fellow composers (Debussy, Delage, Dukas, Durey, Fauré, Satie, Schmitt, Séverac, Stravinsky), difficulties with the Opéra-Comique about *L'heure espagnole*, Gatti-Casazza's interest in the same work and its success at Covent Garden, Ravel's despair at the declaration of war, the reasons for his enlisting in the automobile division, life in the army, his dislike of Paris, his apolitical views, his atheism, the health of his parents, especially his affection for and concern about his mother, his triumphant 1928 visit to the United States. On a lighter note, the postcard to Jean Godebski (1913 April 12), a publicity display for a preserve factory, is annotated by Ravel: "attribué à Chardin / Musée de Clarens."

London, Sotheby's, 14–15 April 1982, lot 62.
FRKF 25

To Jeanne Hatto

1922 Jan. 31 [stamped on verso: Le Belvédère, Montfort-l'Amaury (S-&-O)] ALS, 1 p. Mentions the completion of the *Sonata* ("Duo") *for violin and cello*. Orenstein, p. 193.

New York, Christie's, 16–17 Dec. 1983, lot 437.
FRKF 154

To Franz Josef Hirt

1927 Jan. 23, Le Belvédère[S], ALS, 1 p., expressing concern about not hearing from Mme de Wateville.

Marburg, Stargardt, 19 June 1984, lot 902.
FRKF 481

To G. Jean-Aubry

1907 March 23, Levallois (back of envelope), ALS, 4 p., concerning Ravel's songs. Orenstein, p. 90.

London, Sotheby's, 28 May 1986, lot 528.
FRKF 1136

1907 Oct. 26, Levallois (back of envelope), ALS, 2 p. (env), sending family addresses and a musical variant for a song to a text by Verlaine (on the words "ce vieux vin de Chypre est ex-"). Orenstein, p. 93.

London, Sotheby's, 23 Nov. 1984, lot 514.
FRKF 546

1908 Sept. 17, Valvins par Avon (S & M)^S, ALS, 1 p.

FRKF 840

1911 Aug. 5, Ciboure, ALS, 4 p. (env), concerning *Daphnis et Chloé*.

London, Sotheby's, 28 May 1986, lot 530.
FRKF 1135

1912 Jan. 2 [Paris*] ALS, 4 p. (env), concerning *Ma Mère l'Oye*; also mentions *Daphnis et Chloé*, Raoul Gunsbourg, and Jacques Rouché.

FRKF 726b

1912 Feb. 3, Paris (back of envelope), ALS, 3 p. (env), concerning planned stage performances of *Ma Mère l'Oye*.

London, Sotheby's, 23 Nov. 1984, lot 516.
FRKF 547

1912 Feb. 15, n.p., ALS, 1 p., concerning an invitation from "Madame de S.P."

FRKF 289b

1912 May 4, Monte Carlo, APCS. Mentions *Daphnis et Chloé*.

FRKF 558c

1912 July 19, Saint-Jean-de-Luz, ALS, 3 p., concerning "L'heure fantasque" [i.e. *L'heure espagnole*].
1913 Feb. 18, 4, avenue Carnot. [Paris] XVIIe.^{S}, ALS, 2 p. (env). Mentions Mauclair and Carraud.

FRKF 840

1914 Nov. 15 [Paris*] APCS. Mentions *La cloche de Termonde* [?] and "Vienne" [i.e. *La valse*].

London, Sotheby's, 9–10 May 1985, lot 191.
FRKF 777.2

1918 July 11, Saint-Cloud, ALS, 3 p. (env). Mentions a projected concert with Ravel playing *Le tombeau de Couperin*.

London, Sotheby's, 29 Nov. 1985, lot 193.
FRKF 1060

1918 [Oct.] 15, Saint-Cloud, ALS, 4 p. (env). Mentions the *Introduction et allegro pour harpe* and *Le tombeau de Couperin*.

FRKF 840

1919 July 18, Saint Cloud [but Paris*] ALS, 4 p. (env). Mentions *Le tombeau de Couperin*, Falla, and Lord Berners.

London, Sotheby's, 9–10 May 1985, lot 190.
FRKF 777.1

1920 Sept. 24, APCS [reproduction of a photograph, annotated by Ravel, of "Le Frêne," Lyons-la-Forêt (Eure)]. Mentions a projected article on Schoenberg.

FRKF 558c

1922 May 10, Le Belvédère, ALS, 1 p., concerning a planned trip to England.

FRKF 840

1922 June 9, Le Belvédère^S, ALS, 1 p., concerning a planned trip to London; mentions Robert Casadesus.

FRKF 289a

1922 June 18, Le Belvédère, ALS, 1 p. Mentions the *Sonata for violin and cello*.

London, Sotheby's, 9–10 May 1985, lot 192.
FRKF 777.3

1922 Aug. 10, Le Frêne / Lyons-la-Forêt / Eure^S, ALS, 4 p. (env). Mentions the Aeolian [Hall?], Defaure, and Henry Février.

FRKF 558c

1923 Feb. 21, Le Belvédère, ALS, 1 p. Mentions a recital by pianist Jean Duhem.
1924 June 19, Le Belvédère, TLS, 1 p. (window env). Mentions *L'enfant et les sortilèges* and transmitting a letter.

FRKF 840

1924 Nov. 20, Le Belvédère^S, TLS, 1 p. (window envelope). Mentions the third of the *Mélodies hébraïques*, *Tzigane*, and *L'enfant et les sortilèges*; also discusses Mussorgsky.

FRKF 558c

1925 Oct. 29, Le Belevédère^S, TLS, 2 p., concerning mostly a concert he is to conduct. Typed in red.

London, Sotheby's, 29 Nov. 1985, lot 195.
FRKF 1072

1927 July 25, Hôtel d'Athènes, Paris^S, ALS in pencil, 1 p. (env), concerning Jean-Aubry's visit to Montfort-l'Amaury.

FRKF 558c

1928 July 4, Saint-Jean-de-Luz, ALS, 1 p. (env), concerning [a trip to?] Oxford.

1928 Aug. 24, Le Belvédère, ALS, 1 p., concerning the death of Jacques Durand.

FRKF 840

To Jean Jobert

1922 June 8, ALS, 1 p. Orenstein, p. 202.

1922 June 26, ALS, 1 p.

1922 Oct. 15, ALS, 1 p.

1923 Feb. 8, ALS, 4 p. Orenstein, p. 209.

1923 Feb. 21, ALS, 1 p.

1923 March 23, ALS, 1 p.

1924 April 14, TLS, 1 p. Orenstein, p. 225–26.

1926 April 22, ALS, 1 p.

1926 Sept. 5, APCS

1927 Feb. 21, ALS on both sides of a card. Orenstein, p. 247.

1928 Aug. 27, ALS, 1 p.

All on stationery of Le Belvédère / Montfort l'Amaury (S.&O.). Jean Jobert, the Parisian music publisher, published Ravel's orchestrations of Debussy's *Sarabande* and *Danse*. The correspondence also mentions Paul Paray, Ida Rubinstein, and the composition of *Boléro*.

FRKF 238

To Abbé Joseph Joubert

1913 May 5 [Paris*] ALS, 1 p. Orenstein, p. 124.

The recipient, organist at the Luçon Cathedral, was preparing his 8-volume anthology *Les maîtres de l'orgue contemporain*.

London, Christie's, 5 May 1982, lot 167.
FRKF 21

To Hélène Jourdan-Morhange

1922 May 13, Le Belvédère, 13 May 1922, ALS, 1 p.

1923 Aug. 4, Le Belvédère, TLS, 1 p., reporting on an accident to his finger.

Paris, Laurin-Guilloux-Buffetaud-Tailleur (Drouot) 19 March 1986, lots 178–79.
FRKF 1122–23

To Mme Alfred Madoux-Frank

1926 April 23, Le Belvédère^S, ALS, 1 p. Mentions the *Chansons madécasses*. Orenstein, p. 243.

1931 Feb. 5, Le Belvédère^S, ALS, 1 p. Mentions the *Piano concerto in G*. Orenstein, p. 274.

London, Sotheby's, 23 Nov. 1984, lots 520–21.
FRKF 548.1–2

To Alma Mahler

1920 Aug. 30, La Bijeannette, ALS on both sides of a card, mourning stationery. Thanks her for an invitation and mentions Mme Paul Clemenceau.

Marburg, Stargardt, 26 Nov. 1985, lot 882.
FRKF 1154

To Roland-Manuel

1913 Oct. 7, Saint-Jean-de-Luz (on envelope), ALS, 4 p. Discusses *Placet futile* and mentions Émile Vuillermoz. Orenstein, p. 133.

1918 May 1, Saint-Cloud, ALS, 4 p. News from the war, also mentions *Le tombeau de Couperin*.

1919 Dec. 22, Lapras, ALS, 4 p. Mentions Samazeuilh and Chalupt, *Ma Mère l'Oye*, *Daphnis*, Debussy's *Fantaisie*, and the composition of "Wien" (i.e. *La valse*).

1920 Aug. 1, 7, avenue Léonie, St. Cloud (S et O)^S, ALS, 1 p. Mentions *L'enfant et les sortilèges* and the *Sonata for violin and cello*.

1921 Oct. 29 [stamped on address side: Le Belvédère, Montfort-l'Amaury (S & O)] ALS, 1 p. Mentions Darius Milhaud and the composition of the *Sonata for violin and cello*.

1921 Dec. 8 [stamped on address side: Le Belvédère, Montfort-l'Amaury (S & O)] ALS, 1 p. Mentions Reynaldo Hahn.

1923 June 26, Le Belvédère^S, ALS, 4 p. Mentions Stravinsky's *Noces*.

1924 Apr. 10, Le Belvédère^S, TLS, 1 p. Mentions Germaine Tailleferre and *Tzigane*.

Paris, Paul Renaud (Drouot), 14 May 1986, lots 41, 51, 53–54, 56–57, 59, 61.
FRKF 1185–86; 1188–93

To Édouard Mignan

1923 June 20, Le Belvédère^S, ALS, 3 p. (env). Comments on Mignan's *Rapsodie* and its use of whole-tone scales. Orenstein, p. 216–17.

Paris, Ader-Picard-Tajan (Drouot), 19 June 1984, lot 352.
FRKF 531

To Henri Rabaud

1922 April 19, Le Belvédère^S, ALS, 1 p. Apologizes for not being able to serve on the composition contest at the Conservatoire.

London, Sotheby's, 29 Nov. 1985, lot 194.
FRKF 1061

To Misia Sert

1906 July 19 [Paris?] ALS, 4 p. Mentions Willy (Henry Gauthier-Villars) and "Vienne" (i.e. *La Valse*). Orenstein, p. 85–86.

London, Sotheby's, 14–15 April 1982, lot 62.
FRKF 25.5

1920 Jan. 10, Lapras, ALS, 4 p., concerning *Daphnis et Chloé* and *La Valse*; mentions Diaghilev.

FRKF 992

1921 March 10, Montfort l'Amaury, ALS, 1 p., concerning Ravel's efforts on behalf of Nicolas Obouhov.

FRKF 388

Other letters

To an unidentified English correspondent

1920 May 21, La Bijeannette. St Sauveur (Eure & Loir), ALS on both sides of a card with mourning border, concerning James Elroy Flecker. Orenstein, p. 183.

FRKF 212

To "Mon capitaine"

1916 July 31, n.p., ALS, 2 p. Request for a leave from the army to visit his mother.

FRKF 213

To "cher ami"

[1922? Paris?] ALS, 1 p., in pencil, on the verso of a blank bill of Hôtel d'Athènes, 21, rue d'Athènes, Paris (IXe). Apologies for not being able to wait and hoping to see his correspondent at Mussorgsky's *Tableaux d'une exposition*, first heard on 19 Oct. 1922.

FRKF 296

IV. MISCELLANEOUS

Photographic portrait of Ravel at the piano (oblong, 16 × 19 cm), inscribed: "à Madame Alma Mahler / hommage de respectueuse affection / Maurice Ravel / Wien I/II/20."

The credit line reads: "Copyright by Durand & Cie. Éditeurs, Paris. 1914."

FRKF 394

LEONARD RAVEN–HILL (1867–1942)

Undated pen-and-ink cartoon on heavy cardboard (oblong, 27 × 34.5 cm), signed in the lower left corner, showing two hunters in a mountain landscape. The caption, written twice, identically, one version crossed out in pencil, reads: "Exhausted stalker 'Oh, shoot the darn stag yourself!'"

London, Christie's, 21 July 1981, lot 249.
FRKF 99

OTTORINO RESPIGHI (1879–1936)

I. MUSIC MANUSCRIPTS

A. WORKS BY RESPIGHI

"Abbandono"

Holograph manuscript of the vocal line of this song on a text by Annie Vivanti, n.d., 2 p. Notated in black ink on both sides of a single sheet of tall 12-staff paper. The accompaniment is notated just for the first measure, on a single staff. At the top of p. [1] in Respighi's hand: "Abbandono"; at the very top, ownership signature of Chiarina Fino Savio. At the end, note in her hand: "Questa pagina è stata scritta dal Maestro Respighi a Rovereto nel 1912 la sera stessa del concerto. Si era smarrita la musica, lui l'accompagnò a memoria … io … leggendola per la seconda volta!!!"

Published in 1910 in *Sei melodie*, P 089 (2).

London, Sotheby's, 26–27 Nov. 1987, lot 380.
FRKF 1338.1

Antiche cantate d'amore. "Al tramontar del giorno"

Holograph manuscript, in short score, of this song after Pasquini, n.d., 8 p. Notated in black ink with a few corrections in pencil, the words in red ink, on a gathering of two nested, stitched bifolia of tall 12-staff paper (Luigi Dàmaso, Turin). At the top of p. [1] in Respighi's hand: " - Antiche

Cantate d'amore - / 1637 – 1710 - B. Pasquini." Round stamp of C. Fino Savio at the top of p. [1] and on p. [8].

In green paper wrappers. Calligraphed on an octagonal paper label: "B. Pasquini / Antiche cantate d'amore / 1637–1710"; in pencil, above the title: "Armonizzate da Respighi"; at the bottom, in red ink: "Chiarina Fino Savio 11.vi.1924." Also, pink ownership label printed "Chiarina Fino Savio" and reproduction of a photograph, possibly of her, on inside front cover.

P 098 no. 1
London, Sotheby's, 26–27 Nov. 1987, lot 380.
FRKF 1338.3

"La fine"

Holograph manuscript of this song for voice and piano on a text by Rabindranath Tagore, n.d., 10 p. Notated in black ink, with a few pencil annotations, on a gathering of three bifolia of tall 12-staff paper (B. & H. Nr. 5. C. / 11. 12.). On the front of the outer bifolium, in Respighi's hand: " - alla Signora Chiarina Fino Savio - / (V) / - La Fine - / (Rabindranath Tagore) / Poemetto lirico / per mezzosoprano e pianoforte / - Ottorino Respighi - " Rectangular stamp of Chiarina Fino Savio, Torino, on both sides of the front cover.

Published in 1918 in *Cinque liriche*, P 108 (5). Premiered by Chiarina Fino Savio in March 1917.

London, Sotheby's, 26–27 Nov. 1987, lot 380.
FRKF 1338

Prelude in B flat on a chorale by Bach

Manuscript in black ink over six pages of two nested, stitched bifolia of tall 12-staff paper. On front of first bifolium: "Preludio in Si♭ magg. - sopra un corale di Bach - per organo" and the dedication: "Roma 15 Novembre 1914 / Al rag. Vittorio Scotti in ricordi della visita al mio studio. / OR." Signed and dated on front of first bifolium June 1912; also dated June 1912 at the end.

Possibly the unpublished *Preludio per organo*, P 056.

New York, Christie's, 16–17 Dec. 1983, lot 438.
FRKF 155

Quanta invidia mi fai

Full- and short-score manuscripts and a set of parts, partly holograph, for this cantata for soprano and string orchestra, 1917.

> The full-score manuscript is written in Respighi's hand in black ink, with additional annotations in black, red, and blue pencil, on a gathering of four nested, stitched bifolia of tall 16-staff paper, placed within an additional bifolium serving as wrappers, 12 p. On the front of the outer bifolium, calligraphed in a copyist's hand: "Benedetto Marcello / 1686–1739 / 'Quanta invidia mi fai, bel gelsomino' / Cantata per Soprano e Orchestra d'archi / Realizzazione di 'Ottorino Respighi' / Partitura / e parti d'orchestra staccate." On the front of the first bifolium, in pencil, in a copyist's hand: "Partitura d'orchestra"; in Respighi's hand: "Benedetto Marcello (1686–1739) / 'Quanta invidia mi fai, bel gelsomino' / Cantata per Soprano e Orchestra d'archi / Realizzazione di Ottorino Respighi / (Ottobre 1917)." Also dated Oct. 1917 at the end. Round stamps of C. Fino Savio throughout.

> The short score is written in black ink, with corrections in pencil, the words in red ink, on a gathering of three nested, stitched bifolia of tall 12-staff paper (Luigi Dàmaso, Turin), 12 p.

> In green paper wrappers. Calligraphed on an octagonal paper label: "B. Marcello / Quanta invidia mi fai …"; at the bottom, in red ink: "Chiarina Fino Savio 11.vi.1924." Also, pink ownership label printed "Chiarina Fino Savio," her round stamps, and reproduction of a photograph, possibly of her, on inside front cover.

> The parts, written mostly in the hand of a copyist, are the following: Violino 1°, 2 p., 5 copies; Violino 2d°, 2 p., 4 copies (one of them with an unrelated part notated in pencil on the fourth page); Viola, one copy in Respighi's hand, 3 p., the other two, 2 p.; Violoncello, one copy in Respighi's hand, 3 p., the other two 2 p.; Contrabasso, 2 p., two copies. Round stamps of Chiarina Fino Savio.

> With another copy of the short-score, in the hand of a copyist, 11 p. Round stamps of Chiarina Fino Savio.

P 098 no. 2
London, Sotheby's, 26–27 Nov. 1987, lot 380.
FRKF 1338.4

Re Enzo

Manuscript, in short score, in the hand of a copyist, of the part of Lauretta in this opera comica, n.d. [ca. 1905], 27 + 14 p. The manuscript, written in black ink throughout on tall 12-staff paper, is in two parts: the first, on two gatherings of four and three nested, stitched bifolia paginated 1–26, comprises four numbers (act 1: Stornello-duetto, Lauretta e Isabella; "O viso d'incanto"; act 2: "Io non so cosa"; act 3: Recit.vo e Romanza di Lauretta); the second part, on two unpaginated gatherings, sewn together, one of two nested bifolia, one of a single bifolium and a single leaf, is headed "Duetto."

> The first part, on both sides of the first page and on the last page, bears the round stamp of C. Fino Savio. At the end of the second part, note in Respighi's hand: "N.B. La calma ed il benessere ritornorno su queste Respighiane pagine, mercè le cure assidue del chirurgo ostetrico Ernello … Una parola d'encomio al sullodato elastico(*) libero docente - / (*) per informazioni rivolgersi alla signora Lauretta / Felsina 31 - Gennaio 12 [19]05."

On the cover of part 1, note in pencil, possibly in the hand of Chiarina Fino Savio: "Re Enzo / manoscritto Respighi / tenore Lavarello (Ernello)." Pencil corrections and annotations throughout.

Ernello Lavarello was in the cast of *Re Enzo* at the opera's premiere at the Teatro del Corso, Bologna, on 12 March 1905.

P 055
London, Sotheby's, 26–27 Nov. 1987, lot 380.
FRKF 1338.2

B. WORKS ARRANGED AND ORCHESTRATED BY RESPIGHI

Alexander Porfir'evich Borodin. *Arabian melody*

Holograph manuscript of Respighi's orchestration, 1920, 7 p. Notated in black ink, with additional markings in red pencil, on both sides of tall 24-staff paper. On title page, in Respighi's hand: "Borodine - Mélodie arabe / Istrumentazione di Ottorino Respighi. / (1920)."

FRKF 122.01

Frédéric Chopin. *Polonaise*, op. 40, no. 1

Holograph manuscript of Respighi's orchestration, n.d., 15 p. Notated in black ink, with additional markings in black and red pencil, on both sides of tall 24-staff paper. On title page, in Respighi's hand: "Chopin - Polonaise - (Op. 40 n° 1.) / Istrumentazione / Ottorino Respighi." Unidentified draft, fragment, on verso of p. 15.

FRKF 122.02

Moritz Moszkowski. *Waltz for piano*, op. 57, no. 5

Holograph manuscript of Respighi's orchestration, 1920, 30 p. Notated in black ink, with additional markings in red and blue ink and in black, red, blue, and purple pencil, on both sides of tall 20-staff paper. On title page, in Respighi's hand: "Moszkowski / Valzer d'amore / Op. 57 n° 5 / Istrumentazione di Ottorino Respighi / (Settembre 1920)." Dated 2 Sept. 1920 at the end.

FRKF 122.03

Giovanni Paisiello. *La serva padrona*

Holograph manuscript, in short and full score, of Respighi's arrangement of Paisiello's opera buffa, 1920, 196 p.

The short-score manuscript is written in black ink, with pencil corrections (mostly in the hand of Serge Diaghilev), on both sides of sheets of tall 16-staff paper, paginated 1–85 (followed by a blank sheet paginated 99). Some portions (text and music) may be in the hand of a copyist. There is no title page. At the top of p. 1, in Respighi's hand: " - Paisiello - / La serva padrona / Recitativi e istrumentazione di Ottorino Respighi." Numerous cuts and corrections by Diaghilev throughout. On p. 85, title page, in Respighi's hand, for the "Balletto per la 'Serva padrona' / di Giovanni Paisiello." The ballet (a single number) is notated, in short score, on the verso. Purple stamp of Serge Lifar on p. 1.

The full-score manuscript, entirely holograph, is written in black ink, with additional markings in blue pencil, on nested or separate bifolia of tall 20-staff paper, paginated 1–112. At the top of p. 1, in Respighi's hand: "Paisiello / La Serva padrona / Recitativi e istrumentazione di Ottorino Respighi." The words are missing on p. 101–10. The "Balletto per la Serva padrona di Paisiello" is on p. 111. On the verso, paginated 112, fragment, marked [rehearsal number?] 77, evidently a recitative for Uberto introducting the Ballet. Purple stamp of Serge Lifar on p. 1.

Formerly in reddish brown paper wrappers, the front of which has been preserved. It is inscribed in blue pencil, in Respighi's hand: "Paisiello / La Serva padrona / Recitativi e istrumentazione / di / Ottorino Respighi / Marzo 1920."

There is no record of a performance of Respighi's arrangement of Paisiello's *La serva padrona*.

Heinrich Schütz to Henry Miller, p. 124–25.
London, Sotheby's, 9 May 1984, lot 205.
FRKF 298, 298.5

Nikolay Andreyevich Rimsky-Korsakoff. *Orientale*

Holograph manuscript of Respighi's orchestration of Rimsky-Korsakoff's *Orientale* for voice and orchestra, n.d., 5 p. Notated in black ink, with additional markings in black and red pencil, on both sides of tall 24-staff paper. On title page, in Respighi's hand: " - Orientale - Rimsky-Korsakow."

FRKF 122.04

Mikhail Ivanovich Glinka. *Ruslan i Lyudmila*
Nikolay Andreyevich Rimsky-Korsakoff. *Sadko*

Holograph manuscript of Respighi's orchestration of three extracts from Glinka's *Ruslan i Lyudmila* and one from Rimsky-Korsakoff's *Sadko*, 1920, 31 p. Notated in black ink, with additional markings in black, red, and blue pencil, on both sides of tall 20-staff paper.

On cover, in Respighi's hand: "Glinka. Dal Russlan e Ludmila: / Marcia / Danza orientale / Vivace. / Rimsky-

Korsakow - dal Sadko: Canzone indiana / Istrumentazione di Ottorino Respighi / Marzo 1920." On cover, in large letters, in pink pencil, not in Respighi's hand: "Indiana."

FRKF 122.03, 122.06

Aleksandr Afanasy Spendiaryan.
Canzone tartara

Holograph manuscript of Respighi's orchestration, 1920, 14 p. Notated in black ink, with additional markings in black, red, and blue pencil, on both sides of tall 16-staff paper. On cover, in Respighi's hand: "Canzone Tartara / (di A. Spendiarow.) / Istrumentazione di Ottorino Respighi / (Maggio 1920)." Undeciphered note in pencil, not in Respighi's hand, on cover. Notes in an unidentified hand on p. 15.

FRKF 122.07

Peter Illich Tchaikowsky. *Les saisons*

Holograph manuscript of Respighi's orchestration of two pieces from Tchaikovsky's suite, 1920, 17 p. Notated in black ink, with additional markings in black, red, and blue pencil, on both sides of tall 20-staff paper. On title page, in Respighi's hand: "Ciaikowsky / (Agosto - Autumno) / Trascrizione per Orchestra / di Ottorino Respighi / (Marzo 1920)." On p. [12], in Respighi's hand: "(No. 2) (Ottobre)."

FRKF 122.08

II. LETTERS

To Serge Diaghilev

1917 Aug. 29, Bologna, ALS, 2 p., concerning Alessandro Scarlatti; also mentions Leonid Massine.

From the collection of Serge Lifar, with his stamp printed in red.
London, Sotheby's, 9 May 1984, lot 204.
FRKF 309

To Chiarina Fino Savio

1911 (?)
Feb. 4, Bergamo, telegram
[Mar 29, Bologna*] envelope only
[Apr. 12, Bologna*] envelope only
[Jun 16, Bologna*] envelope only

1912
Jan. 1, Bologna, ALS on both sides of a card

Jan. 28, Bologna, ALS on both sides of a card (env). Mentions *Aretusa*.

Feb. 12, Bologna, ALS, 3 p. (env)

Feb. 18, Bologna, ALS on both sides of a card

March 1, Rome, telegram

March 7, Rome, telegram

March 14, Bologna, ALS on both sides of a card. Mentions *Aretusa*.

March 16, Rome, telegram

March 18, Rome, telegram

March 19, Bologna, ALS on both sides of a card

March 19 [?] Bologna, telegram

March 19, Milan, telegram

March 21, Rome, telegram

March 23, Rome, telegram

March 24, Turin, telegram from Giuseppe Fino to Respighi (copy)

March 29, Rome, telegram

May 5, Bologna, ALS, 3 p. (env). Mentions *Noël ancien*.

May 13, Bologna, ALS, 2 p. (env)

May 19, Bologna, ALS, 3 p.

May 25, Bologna, ALS, 3 p. (env). Mentions *Noël ancien* and *Notte*.

May 29, Bologna, ALS on both sides of a card (env)

[June 8*] envelope only

June 15, Bologna, ALS, 3 p. (env). Mentions *Semirama* and *Marie Victoire*.

July 13, Bologna, ALS, 3 p. (env)

July 23, Bologna, APCS from Respighi and two other, unidentified correspondents

[July 30, Bologna*] envelope only

Sept. 24, Bologna, ALS, 3 p. (env). Mentions *Marie Victoire*.

Oct. 7, Bologna, ALS, 3 p., concerning *Marie Victoire*.

Oct. 16, Bologna, ALS, 3 p. Mentions *Semirama*, *Marie Victoire*, and the "threat" of a *Tristan* at the Teatro Communale.

Oct. 21, Bologna, ALS, 3 p. (env). Mentions *Marie Victoire*, *Noël ancien*, *Notte*.

Nov. 2, Bologna, ALS, 3 p. Mentions *Marie Victoire*.

Nov. 24, Bologna, ALS, 5 p. Mentions *Marie Victoire* and the *Notturno per orchestra*.

n.d., Grand Hotel Fiorina, Turin[S], ALS, 1 p. (env)

1913
Jan. 4, Bologna, ALS, 2 p.

Jan. 13, Bologna, ALS, 2 p. (env), concerning a tour in Germany.

March 14–15, Rome, ALS, 4 p. (env). Mentions *Aretusa*.

March 30, Rome, ALS, 2 p. (env)

April 13, Rome, ALS on both sides of a card (env). Mentions *Aretusa*.

May 20, Rome, ALS, 3 p. (env). Mentions *Notte*, *Noël ancien*, and *Marie Victoire*.

July 28, Bologna, ALS, 2 p. (env). Mentions *Nebbie* and another song, as well as *Marie Victoire*.

Nov. 10, Rome, ALS, 2 p. Mentions *Aretusa*.

Nov. 10, Rome, ALS to Giuseppe Fino, 1 p.

Nov. 30, Rome, ALS on both sides of a card

Dec. 10, Rome, ALS on both sides of a card

Dec. 30, Bologna, ALS, 3 p. (env)

1914

Jan. 9, Rome, ALS on both sides of a card (env)

Jan. 9, Rome, telegram

Jan. 25, Bologna, telegram

Jan. 28, Rome, ALS, 4 p. Mentions *Aretusa*.

Jan. 31, Rome, ALS, 2 p. (env). Mentions *Aretusa*.

Feb. 5, Rome, APCS written on both sides

Feb. 13, Rome, telegram

Feb. 15, Rome, ALS, 1 p.

Feb. 18, Rome, telegram

March 12, Rome, APCS written on both sides, to Giuseppe Fino.

March 19, Rome, ALS, 3 p. (env)

April 2, Harmonia, Rivista italiana di musica, Rome[S], ALS, 3 p. (env)

April 12, Bologna, ALS, 2 p. (env). Mentions *La sensitiva*.

[Apr 30, Roma*] envelope only

May 1, Rome, ALS, 1 p. (env)

May 13, Rome, ALS, 3 p. (env). Mentions *La sensitiva* and *Marie Victoire*.

May 20, Rome, ALS on both sides of a card (env). Mentions *La sensitiva*.

May 23, Bologna, ALS, 3 p. (env)

June 1, Bologna, ALS, 2 p. (env). Mentions *La sensitiva*.

June 11, Rome, ALS, 3 p. (env). Mentions *La sensitiva*.

July 1, Rome, ALS on both sides of two cards (env). Mentions *La sensitiva*.

July 8, Rome, ALS on both sides of a card

July 12, Bologna, APCS, on both sides. Mentions *La sensitiva*.

July 22, Bologna, ALS, 3 p. (env). Mentions *La sensitiva*.

July 31, Bologna, ALS on both sides of a card (env). Mentions *Il tramonto*.

Aug. 31, F. Bongiovanni, Bologna[S], ALS to Giuseppe Fino, 2 p.

Sept. 7, Bologna, ALS on both sides of a card (env)

Sept. 23, Bologna, ALS, 2 p. (env). Mentions *La sensitiva*.

Sept. 28, Bologna, ALS, 2 p. (env). Mentions *Il tramonto*.

Oct. 5, Bologna, ALS, 2 p. (env)

Oct. 8, Bologna, ALS on both sides of a card (env)

Oct. 27, Liceo Musicale di S. Cecilia, Rome[S], ALS, 3 p. (env)

Nov. 10, Rome, ALS on both sides of a card (env)

Dec. 17, Bologna, ALS, 2 p. (env). Mentions Riccardo Zandonai.

Dec. 24, Bologna, ALS, 4 p. (env)

Dec. 31, Bologna, ALS, 2 p. (env). Mentions *Il tramonto*.

1915

Jan. 25, Rome, ALS on both sides of a card (env). Mentions his *Sinfonia drammatica*.

Jan. 29, Rome, ALS, 4 p. (env). Mentions *Marie Victoire*.

March 7, Rome, ALS, 2 p. (env). Mentions *La sensitiva*.

March 9, Rome, ALS, 3 p. Mentions *La sensitiva*.

March 13, Rome, ALS, 3 p. (env). Mentions *Marie Victoire*.

May 2, Rome, ALS, 2 p. (env)

May 11, Rome, ALS on both sides of two cards (env). Mentions *Il tramonto*.

May 22, Bologna, APCS written on both sides. Mentions *Il tramonto*.

June 21, Bologna, ALS on both sides of two cards (env)

June 24, Bologna, ALS, 2 p. (env). Mentions *La sensitiva*.

[Aug. 10, Levanto*] envelope only

[Sept. 18, Roma*] envelope only

Sept. 23, Bologna, ALS, 2 p.

Oct. 10, Levanto, ALS on both sides of a card and one side of a second card

Oct. 18, Bologna, ALS, 3 p. (env). Mentions *La sensitiva* and Stravinsky's *Petrushka*.

Oct. 30, Rome, ALS, 2 p. (env). Mentions *La sensitiva* and *Il tramonto*.

Nov. 10, Rome, ALS on both sides of a card. Mentions *Marie Victoire*.

Dec. 18, Rome, ALS on both sides of a card and one side of a second card

1916

Jan. 5, Bologna, ALS on both sides of a card. Mentions *Prince Igor*.

Jan. 15, Rome, ALS on both sides of a card. Mentions *La sensitiva*.

Jan. 23, Rome, ALS, 2 p. (env). Mentions *La sensitiva* and *Il re Enzo*.

Feb. 10, Rome, ALS on both sides of a card (env). Mentions *Il tramonto*.

Feb. 14, Rome, ALS on both sides of a card (env)

March 3, Rome, ALS on both sides of a card (env). Mentions *La sensitiva*.

April 2, Bologna, ALS, 6 p. (env)

April 11, Rome, ALS, 2 p. (env)

June 5, Tizziano Eremo, ALS on both sides of a card (env)

June 28, Eremo, ALS on both sides of two cards (env). Mentions *La bella addormentata nel bosco*.

July 9, Levanto, ALS, 2 p. (env)

Aug. 5, Levanto, ALS, 2 p. (env)

Aug. 16, Levanto, ALS, 2 p. (env)

Sept. 19, Levanto, ALS, 2 p. (env)

Oct. 9, Bologna, ALS, 2 p. Mentions *La bella addormentata nel bosco*.

Oct. 23, Bologna, APCS written on both sides. Mentions *La sensitiva*.

Oct. 26, Rome, ALS, 2 p. Mentions *La sensitiva*.

1917

Feb. 18, Rome, ALS, 4 p. (env). Mentions *Il Tramonto* and the *Violin Sonata*.

[April 5, Florence*] envelope only

April 15, Rome, ALS, 4 p. (env)

May 14, Rome, ALS, 2 p. (env). Mentions *Aretusa*.

June 17, Rome, ALS, 3 p. Mentions *Aretusa*.

June 23, Rome, ALS, 2 p. (env)

July 2, Rome, ALS, 2 p. (env)

July 9, Bologna, ALS, 3 p. (env). Mentions working on "Voci della chiesa."

Sept. 3, Bologna, ALS, 3 p. (env)

Nov. 28, Rome, ALS, 2 p. (env). Mentions *La sensitiva*.

Dec. 8, Rome, ALS, 2 p. Mentions *La sensitiva*.

Dec. 21, Rome, ALS, 2 p. (env)

1918

Jan. 27, Rome, ALS, 4 p. (env). Mentions *La sensitiva*.

Feb. 5, Rome, ALS, 2 p. Mentions *Il tramonto* and *La sensitiva*.

March 27, Rome, ALS, 2 p. Mentions Ildebrando Pizzetti.

April 1, Rome, APCS written on both sides. Mentions Pizzetti.

[April 21, Rome*] envelope only

May 6, Rome, ALS, 3 p. (env)

[Nov. 18, Bologna*] envelope, Società per il risveglio della vita cittadina in Bologna[S], and clipping announcing a concert by Respighi and Chiarina Fino Savio.

Nov. 5, Rome, ALS, 4 p. (env). Mentions *Il flauto di Pane* and *Le fontane di Roma*.

Dec. 11, Rome, APCS written on both sides. Mentions *Il flauto di Pane*.

Dec. 29, Rome, APCS written on both sides. Mentions *Il flauto di Pane*, *La sensitiva*, and Arturo Toscanini.

1919

Jan. 29, Rome, ALS, 3 p. Mentions the *Violin Sonata* and *Il flauto di Pane*.

10 Feb., Rome APCS written on both sides

Feb. 27, Rome, ALS, 6 p. (env). Mentions *Il flauto di Pane*.

March 7, Rome, ALS, 2 p.

[May cancelled by the recipient] April [?] 9, Rome, ALS, 3 p. (env)

May 8, Rome, ALS, 3 p. Mentions *Le fontane di Roma*.

July 29, Anacapri, ALS, 6 p. (env). Mentions *La boutique fantasque*.

[1919] "Lunedì." Rome, ALS, 1 p. Mentions *La sensitiva*.

1920–32

1920 July 16, Cavalese (Trentino), ALS, 4 p.

1921 Sept. 7, Laverio, Lago Maggiore, ALS from Elsa Respighi, 4 p. (env)

1925 [Nov. 16, Rome*] envelope only

1932 April, Rome, ANS on one side of a card

Also, fragment of a letter, dated on the verso 1914 May 20, 1 p.; and the last page of a letter [ca. 1918] mentioning *Il flauto di Pane*.

Many letters have pencil annotations by Chiarina Fino Savio. There are some envelopes for which letters are not present.

Accompanied by:

APCS to Respighi from his father, written on both sides, 1914 Aug. 18, Bologna. Mentions Chiarina Fino Savio.

TLS from Respighi to "Caro Maestro," 1929 Nov. 1, Rome, 1 p.

[G.M. Marini?] ALS to Respighi, 1918 Sept. 25, Società del Quartetto, Bologna[S], 2 p. (env), concerning Respighi's *String Quartet*.

ALS to Respighi, 1918 Sept. 18, Bologna, Società per il risveglio della vita cittadina in Bologna[S], 1 p., signed on behalf of the council.

Telegram from Maria Adelaide, princess of Savoy, to Chiarina Fino, n.y. April [?] 21.

Mezzo-soprano Chiarina Fino Savio premiered Respighi's cantata *Aretusa* in 1911 and he wrote several other vocal compositions for her; as this correspondence shows, she became a close friend and confidante. A few letters, where noted, are addressed to Giuseppe Fino, Chiarina's husband.

London, Sotheby's, 26–27 Nov. 1987, lot 379.
FRKF 1337

III. PRINTED MUSIC

Cinque liriche. Milan: G. Ricordi e C., copyright 1918.

Folio, 1–31 [+ 1] p. Music publisher's number: 117191-96. P 108. The songs are as follows: 1. "I tempi assai lontani" (Percy Bysshe Shelley), dedicated to Chiarina Fino Savio, p. 1–5; 2. "Canto funebre" (Shelley), dedicated to Adriana Clementi, p. 6–10; 3. "Par les soirs …" (Jacques d'Adelsward-Fersen), dedicated to Adriana Clementi, p. 11–16; 4. "Par l'étreinte …" (Jacques d'Adelsward-Fersen), dedicated to Anna Amfiteatroff, p. 17–20; 5. "La fine" (Rabindranath Tagore), dedicated to Chiarina Fino Savio, p. 21–31.

In dark green wrappers with calligraphic manuscript title in black and red: "Signora Chiarina Fino Savio / Cinque Liriche /

Musica di / Ottorino Respighi." Pencil annotations, possibly by Chiarina Fino Savio, for songs 4 and 5. On p. 23 ("La fine," measures 22–25), pasted-on manuscript variant, possibly in Respighi's hand. Round stamp of Chiarina Fino Savio.

Deità silvane: cinque liriche di Antonio Rubino musicate da Ottorino Respighi. Milan: G. Ricordi & C., copyright 1917.

Folio, [2], 1–25 [+ 1] p. Music publisher's number: 117081-86. P 107. Round stamp of C. Fino Savio on the title page. Inscribed on the verso of the title page: "per la Signora / Chiarina Fino Savio / Ottorino Respighi / Roma 22 Dicembre 1917."

E se un giorno tornasse … Recitativo per mezzo soprano con accompagnamento di pianoforte. Poesia di Vittoria Aganoor-Pompilj imitata da Maeterlinck. Milan [et al.]: G. Ricordi e C., copyright 1909.

Folio, [2], 1–3 [+ 1] p. P 096. Music publisher's number: 117459. Provenance: Chiarina Fino Savio.

Pini di Roma: poema sinfonico per orchestra. Trascrizione per pianoforte a quattro mani. Milan: G. Ricordi e C., copyright 1925.

Folio, [6], 1–31 [+ 1] p. P 142. Provenance: Chiarina Fino Savio.

Quattro liriche per canto e pianoforte su parole di poeti armeni. Milan: G. Ricordi & C., copyright 1922.

Folio, 1–16 [+ 2] p. Music publisher's number: 118784-88. P 132. Printed at the top of p. 1: Ad Elsa / Quattro Liriche / Antica poesia popolare armena / Musica di / Ottorino Respighi / (1921). Provenance: Chiarina Fino Savio.

"Razzolan sopra a l'aja, le galline." *4 Rispetti toscani. 4. Razzolan sopra a l'aja, le galline.* Bologna: F. Bongiovanni, copyright 1915.

Folio, 1–8 p. P 103 (4). Music publisher's number: F. 589 B. Printed at the top of p. 1: Alla Signora Argia Pini / Razzolan, sopra a l'aja, le galline … / IV. / (Tono originale) / Dai "Rispetti Toscani" / di Arturo Birga / Musica di / Ottorino Respighi. Front wrapper illustrated by C.F. Zanetti (printed in blue). Provenance: Chiarina Fino Savio.

"Scherzo." *Scherzo. Parole di Carlo Zangarini.* Bologna: Francesco Bongiovanni, n.d. [1906?].

[1], 2–3 [+ 1] p. [printed on a single bifolium]. Music publisher's number: F. 238 B. P 068. Printed at the top of p. 2: Alla Signorina Maria Pedrazzi / Scherzo / Parole di C. Zangarini / Ottorino Respighi. Printed on cover: N° 238 - per soprano e mez. sopr. Provenance: Chiarina Fino Savio.

Sei liriche. Prima serie. Bologna: F. Bongiovanni, copyright 1912. P 090 (1-6)

1. *O falce di luna*
Folio, 1–5 p. The title is taken from the cover. Printed at the top of p. 1: Alla signora Chiarina Fino Savio. / O falce di luna / G. D'Annunzio / Ottorino Respighi. Music publisher's number: F. 481 B. Wrappers illustrated by V. Venturini. Round stamp of Chiarina Fino Savio on cover and p. 1; also, her manuscript ownership signature in upper right corner of cover ("Chiarina Fino") and pencilled annotation in her hand: "Questo e mio!"

2. *Van li effluvi de le rose*
Folio, 1–3 [+ 1] p. The title is taken from the cover. Printed at the top of p. 1: Alla signora Chiarina Fino Savio. / Van li effluvi de le rose / G. D'Annunzio II. / Ottorino Respighi. Music publisher's number: F. 482 B. Wrappers illustrated by V. Venturini. Manuscript ownership signature of Chiarina Fino Savio in upper right corner of cover.

3. *Au milieu du jardin*
Folio, 1–3 [+ 1] p. The title is taken from the cover. Printed at the top of p. 1: Alla signora Chiarina Fino Savio. / Au milieu du jardin / Jean Moréas / III. / Ottorino Respighi. Music publisher's number: F. 483 B. Wrappers illustrated by C.F. Zanetti (printed in green). Provenance: Chiarina Fino Savio.

4. *Noël ancien*
Folio, [cover], 2–5 [+ 1] p. The title is taken from the cover. Printed at the top of p. 2: Alla signora Chiarina Fino Savio. / Noel ancien / IV. / Ottorino Respighi. Music publisher's number: F. 484 B. Wrappers illustrated by V. Venturini. Manuscript ownership signature of Chiarina Fino Savio in upper right corner of cover.

5. *Serenata Indiana*
Folio, [1]–6 [+ 2] p. The title is taken from the cover. Printed at the top of p. 2: Alla signora Chiarina Fino Savio. / Serenata indiana / P.B. Shelley / V. / Ottorino Respighi. Music publisher's number: F. 485 B. Wrappers illustrated by V. Venturini. Manuscript ownership signature of Chiarina Fino Savio in upper right corner of cover; also on cover, "respighi" written in red pencil (not in his hand). Variant for measure 8 pencilled at the top of p. 3, possibly in Respighi's hand.

6. *Pioggia*
Folio, [cover], 2–7 [+ 1] p. The title is taken from the cover. Printed at the top of p. 2: Alla signora Chiarina Fino Savio / (Soprano) Pioggia / (Vittoria Aganoor Pompili) / VI / Ottorino Respighi. Music publisher's number: F. 486a B. Soprano version. Wrappers illustrated by C.F. Zanetti (printed in blue). Ownership [?] inscription at the top of cover: "Mary Modi Phocea [?]." Provenance: Chiarina Fino Savio.

Sei liriche. Seconda serie. Bologna: F. Bongiovanni [copyright 1912]. P 097 (1, 6)

1. *Notte*
Folio, 1–4. At the top of p. 1: I. / Alla signora Chiarina Fino Savio. / Notte. / (mezzo soprano) / Parole di Ada Negri. / Musica di / Ottorino Respighi. Music publisher's number:

F. 521 B. Lacking wrappers. Round stamp of Chiarina Fino Savio at the top of p. 1; also, in blue pencil, possibly in her hand: "3 minuti"; annotations in pencil throughout.

6. Nel giardin
Folio, 1–7 [+ 1] p. At the top of p. 1: Alla signora Chiarina Fino Savio. / Il giardino. / (Tono originale) / Parole di / F. Rocchi. / VI. / Musica di / Ottorino Respighi. Music publisher's number: F. 526 B. Front wrapper illustrated by C.F. Zanetti (printed in blue).

"Sopra un aria antica." *Quatro liriche (dal poema paradisiaco di Gabriele D'Annunzio). Canto e pianoforte. IV. Sopra un aria antica.* Bologna: Pizzi & C., copyright 1921.

Folio, 1–9 [+ 1] p. P 125. Music publisher's number: P. 275 & C. Printed at the top of p. 1: IV. / Sopra un' aria antica / (tono originale) / G. D'Annunzio / Ottorino Respighi / (1920). Round stamp of Chiarina Fino Savio on cover and throughout.

"Soupir." *Sei melodie. 6. Soupir.* Bologna: F. Bongiovanni, copyright 1910.

Folio, 1–6. P 089 (6). Printed at the top of p. 1: A Mademoiselle Hortense Nunziante di Mignano / Soupir / Sully Prudhomme / VI / O. Respighi. Front wrapper illustrated by Venturini. Round stamp of Chiarina Fino Savio on both wrappers and p. 1.

Stornellatrice. Parole di C. Zangarini e A. Donini. Bologna: F. Bongiovanni, copyright 1906.

[1–2], 3 [+ 1] p. [printed on a single bifolium]. Music publisher's number: P. 268 B. P 069. Printed at the top of p. [2]: Alla Signorina Maria Pedrazzi / Stornellatrice / Poesia di C. Zangarini / e di A. Donini / Ottorino Respighi. Version for mezzo soprano or baritone. Annotated in pencil on cover and throughout. Provenance: Chiarina Fino Savio.

"Viene di là, lontan lontano." *4 Rispetti toscani. 3. Viene di là, lontan lontano.* Bologna: F. Bongiovanni, copyright 1915.

Folio, [1], 2–11 [+ 1] p. Music publisher's number: F. 588 B. P 103 (3). Printed at the top of p. 2: Alla Signora Argia Pini / Viene di là, lontan lontano ... / III. / (Soprano) / (Tono originale) / Dai "Rispetti Toscani" / di Arturo Birga / Musica di / Ottorino Respighi. The title is given as "Vieni di là, lontan lontano" on cover. Front wrapper illustrated by C.F. Zanetti (printed in blue). Provenance: Chiarina Fino Savio

RESPIGHI PRINTED MUSIC
FRKF 1338.6a–o

IV. MISCELLANEOUS

Typescript note, with an autograph correction, unsigned, n.d. [1938?], 1 p., concerning a ballet composition by Respighi entitled "Scherzo veneziano."
FRKF 122

RIDGEWEY

"Iccups"

Pen-and-ink cartoon on paper (26 × 20.5 cm), n.d., mounted on board, with pencilled caption underneath: "Leader of waits: 'Ere Bill go a bit steady! That sounded more like 'Iccups!' / Indignant [cancelled: musician] artist: 'What do you mean - sounds like 'iccups? That was 'iccups!'" Signed on the lower right side.

London, Christie's, 21 July 1981, lot 249.
FRKF 100

ARTHUR RIMBAUD (1854–91)

I. LETTERS

To his family Both addressed to "Mes chers amis"

1884 May 29, Aden, ALS, 3 p. Pléiade, p. 386–87.

Paris, Boisgirard (Drouot), 28 May 1986, lot 109.
FRKF 1277

1885 Oct. 22, Aden, LS, 2 p., about leaving his job in Aden and dealings in arms sale. Pléiade, p. 405–06.

Paris, Jean Morel (Drouot), 14–15 Dec. 1983, lot 263.
FRKF 246

From Paul Bourde

1888 Feb. 29, Argelès, ALS, 4 p., concerning the situation in Abyssinia, while informing Rimbaud of his growing literary reputation in Paris. Not in Pléiade; partially published in Alain Borer, *Un sieur Rimbaud, se disant négociant* (Paris: Lachenal et Ritter, 1984), p. 79.

Paul Bourde (1851–1914), once a schoolmate of Rimbaud in Charleville, later a journalist and colonial administrator.

Paris, Jean Morel (Drouot), 14 Dec. 1983, lot 264.
FRKF 247

II. PRINTED WORKS

Les illuminations / Notice par Paul Verlaine. Paris: Publications de La Vogue, 1886.

> 103 [+ 1] p. Red brick wrappers bound in. On front wrapper, pasted-in label of "Léon Vanier / Libraire-Éditeur / 19, Quai Saint-Michel, Paris." First edition. No. 161 on Hollande from an edition of 200 copies (30 on Japan, 170 on Hollande), numbered on the half-title, verso.
> Bound in brown morocco, all edges gilt, author's name and title gold-tooled on the spine. Quadruple gold fillet on verso of both boards, pale blue and red marbled paper endpapers.

Reliquaire: poésies. Préface de Rodolphe Darzens. Paris: L. Genonceaux, 1891.

> [I]–XXVIII, 1–152 p. Inscribed to "Mon cher Jean" by Darzens. Bound in red morocco; two quadrupled fillets along the edges, separated by a black fillet. A similar decor on the spine, with raised bands, and author, title, and year gold-tooled. All edges gilt. Green morocco and green silk doublures, with a quintuple fillet along the edges on the versos of boards. Stamped A. & R. Maylander at the bottom of the verso of front board. White paper wrappers bound in. In slipcase decorated in red marbled paper. Bookplate of Bibliothèque Jacques Odry.

Une saison en enfer. Bruxelles: Alliance typographique (M.-J. Poot et compagnie), 1873.

> [1]–53 [+ 1] p. First edition. Original paper wrappers bound in. Bound in uniform red morocco, stamped Alix; all edges gilt; on spine, raised bands and author, title, and date gold-tooled. Gilt border on the verso of both boards, pink marbled paper doublures. In slipcase decorated with red and grey marbled paper. Bookplate of Bibliothèque Jacques Odry.

Heinrich Schütz to Henry Miller, p. 64–65.

Les stupra / sonnets. Paris: Imprimerie particulière, 1871 [i.e. 1923].

> 10 unpaginated leaves. No. 122 from an edition of 175 copies (25 on Japan) numbered on the half-title, verso. Original paper wrappers. Bookplate of Bibliothèque Jacques Odry.

RIMBAUD PRINTED WORKS
Brussels, Simonson, 19 May 1984, lots 261–64.
FRKF 369–71

LOUIS DE ROBERT (1871–1937)

Papa

Autograph manuscript of this novel, 1895, 216 p., in black ink, with additional markings in pencil, on the verso side of 8vo-size sheets of paper (14 × 21.5 cm). At the top of p. 1, in Robert's hand: "Louis de Robert / 1895 / Papa / [Original title, cancelled:] La remplaçante." Names of typesetters throughout the manuscript.

Bound in grey and brown marbled paper, brown morocco corners and spine; spine with raised bands and author, title, and word "MS." gold-tooled.

Accompanied by the printed book: Louis de Robert. *Papa.* Paris: Bibliothèque-Charpentier, 1896.

> 8vo, 4 l., 1–310 p. Presentation inscription on the half-title: "A ma jeune maman / Tout ce qui m'aime et tout / ce que j'aime au monde. / Louis de Robert / - 14 Juin 1896 -" Bound in grey and brown marbled paper, brown morocco corners and spine; spine with raised bands and author and title gold-tooled. Bound in: original yellow paper wrappers and two letters:
>
> Proust, Marcel. ALS to Louis de Robert, [1897 Oct. 25], "Lundi," n.p., 7 p. Kolb XVI:391–93.
>
> Loti, Pierre. ALS to Louis de Robert, n.d., n.p., 2 p., concerning *Papa.*

FRKF 653a–b

FREDERICK ROLFE, BARON CORVO (1860–1913)

Letter to "Dear Sirs"

> 1909 Nov. 7, Venice, ALS, 4 p., concerning his search for a new literary agent and financial support. Written in red ink; possibly a retained draft, with a number of corrections and deletions.

FRKF 270

Ballade of boys bathing. Holborn [London]: Apud Guidonem Londinensem [Officina Mauritiana], 1972.

Printed on p. [2] and [3] of a single, folded sheet. Colophon on p. [4]. No. 102 from an edition of 200 copies. First separate publication; first published in *The Art Review* for April 1890. With an envelope printed: Ballade of boys bathing /

by Frederick W Rolfe / Baron Corvo / apud Guidonem Londinensem impressa / 2.

See Woolf, p. 143.
New York, Swann Galleries, 11 Dec. 1986, lot 378.
FRKF 1260

SIGMUND ROMBERG (1887–1951)

Viennese Nights: A Vitaphone Operetta. Produced by Warner Brothers. Books and lyrics by Oscar Hammerstein 2nd; Music by Sigmund Romberg; Director Alan Crosland; Musical Conductor Louis Silvers; Edited by Harold McLernon; Photography by James Van Trees and Frank Good; Mixer George Groves; Art Director Max Parker. Vocal score. New York: Harms Inc., 1930.

Piano-vocal score. Music publisher's number: 8511-170. Bound in brown pebble-grain cloth; top edge gilt; title and composer gold-tooled on front cover and spine; dark purple marbled endpapers. Inscribed on the verso of the front free endpaper: "To / Max Parker / Sincerely / Oscar Hammerstein 2 / Sigmund Romberg / Hollywood / July 18/30"; also signed by James C. Van Trees, next to his name, on the title page.

FRKF 755

FÉLICIEN ROPS (1833–98)

Letter to "mon cher Liesse"

n.d., n.p., ALS, 2 p.

FRKF 663

GIOACHINO ROSSINI (1792–1868)

I. MUSIC MANUSCRIPTS

Cantata per Francesco I imperatore d'Austria

Holograph manuscript, in full score, of this cantata for soprano, two tenors, chorus, and orchestra, n.d. [1819], 47 p. Notated in black or dark brown ink on twelve bifolia, numbered in Rossini's hand, of oblong 16-staff paper.

At the top of the first page, in Rossini's hand: "Cantata." On the verso of the last leaf, in an unidentified hand: "Cantata del Sig[nore] Rossini fatta in occasione della festa dell' Imperatore, l'anno 1818." On p. [2] of bifolium 12, after the recitative, notes in Rossini's hand: "però colle nuove parole che sono composte nello stesso metro"; and "Qui si cambia Scena. Si suona e canta il coro dell' altra Cantata colle Bande a questo succede il Baletto Tirolese, indi il Balabile dell' altra Cantata; riserbando per la veduta ultima dei ritratti la musica Germanica qui scritta e che il Sig. Calegare agiusterà per Le Bandè." The "Musica Germanica" (i.e. the Austrian national anthem, "Gott! erhalte Franz den Kaiser," set to Haydn's music) is notated on the facing page, on three staves.

Note on the verso of the rear flyleaf, in German, in the hand of a previous owner, indicating that the manuscript was once in the collections of Bellini and Giovanni Battista Perucchini.

Bifolium 11, missing when the manuscript was sold at Sotheby's, resurfaced in 1991 and was acquired by the collector to be reunited with the rest of the manuscript.

First performed at the Teatro San Carlo, Naples, on 9 May 1819, in honor of the visit of Francis I. First published in Rossini, *Tre cantate napoletane*, a cura di Ilaria Narici, Marco Beghelli, Stefano Castelvecchi (Pesaro: Fondazione Rossini, 1999, Edizione critica II/4).

Heinrich Schütz to Henry Miller, p. 26–27.
London, Sotheby's, 29 Nov. 1985, lot 202.
FRKF 1042, 1042A

Scherzo for piano

Holograph manuscript of this piano piece, 1850, 3 p. Notated in black ink on two separate sheets of oblong 10-staff paper. There is no title. Autograph inscription on p. [3]: "All' amico mio Carissimo / Angelo Martinez / Gioachino Rossini / Firenze 30 Giugno 1850."

FRKF 990

II. LETTERS

To Ignaz Moscheles

1842 Sept. 10, Bologna, ALS, 1 p., in French. Rossini thanks the Bohemian composer for his involvement in the London premiere of his revised *Stabat Mater*.

London, Christie's, 5 May 1982, lot 168.
FRKF 22

To Francesco Sampieri

All are autograph letters, signed.

1821–43

[1821 or 1822] 1 p., on p. 3 of a letter from Isabella Colbran to Rossini, n.y., Aug. 15, n.p., 2 p.

[ca. 1821–22] n.p., 1 p.

[1823] June 9, Venice, 1 p.

[1823] n.p., 1 p.

[1823?] n.p., 1 p.

[1828 Feb. 9*, Paris] 3 p. Mentions *Moïse*.

1830 Aug. 12, Castenaso, 1 p.

[1833*] April 3, Bologna, 1 p.

[1833*] April 14, [Bologna*] 1 p.

1833 May 28, Paris, 1 p.

1834 Aug. 25, Théâtre Royal Italien, Paris[S], 2 p.

[1835?] "Lunedi," n.p., 1 p.

[1837?] March 15, "Dal Licevo," 1 p.

1838 April 17, Bologna, 2 p.

1840 Oct. 31, n.p., 1 p.

1842 July 28, n.p., 1 p.

1843 Nov. 3, n.p., 1 p.

1844

March 15, n.p., 1 p.

March 21, Bologna, 1 p.

April 2, Bologna, 1 p.

April 6, Bologna, 1 p.

April 12, Bologna, 1 p.

April 22, Bologna, 1 p.

May 6, Bologna, 1 p.

May 10, Bologna, 1 p.

May 16 [Bologna*] 2 p.

May 21, Bologna, 1 p.

May 27, Fossa Alta, 1 p.

June 1, Bologna, 1 p.

June 11, Bologna, 1 p.

July 9, Bologna, 1 p.

Aug. 2, Bologna, 2 p.

Sept. 8, Bologna, 1 p.

Sept. 20, Bologna, 1 p.

Sept. 24, Bologna, 2 p.

Sept. 27, Bologna, 1 p.

Oct. 1, Bologna, 1 p.

Oct. 3, Bologna, 1 p.

Oct. 4, Bologna, 1 p.

Oct. 5, n.p., 2 p.

Oct. 8, Bologna, 1 p.

Oct. 16, Bologna, 3 p.

Oct. 18, Bologna, 1 p.

1845

May 5, Bologna, 1 p.

May 24, Bologna, 1 p.

Dec. 17, "Da casa," 1 p.

1846

April 8, Bologna, 1 p.

Undated or without year

30 March, n.p. 1 p.

n.p., 2 p., mentioning bass Nicolas Levasseur. In French.

"Martedi," n.p., 1 p.

"Mercoledi," n.p., 1 p.

"Mercoledi," n.p., 2 p.

"Mercoledi," n.p., 1 p.

"Giovedi," n.p., 1 p.

"Giovedi," n.p., 1 p.

8 ALS, n.p., 1 p. each

Also, ALS from Isabella Rossini to Francesco Sampieri [ca. 1840] "Domenica," 1 p.

Marchese Francesco Sampieri (1790–1863), fellow composer and friend of Rossini. The correspondence contains references to *Semiramide*, *Maometto II*, *Moïse*, and *Otello*. See *Giachino Rossini, lettere e documenti*, ed. Bruno Cagli and Sergio Ragni (Pesaro: Fondazione Rossini, 1992–), 3 vols. issued so far.

London, Sotheby's, 9–10 May 1985, lot 193.
FRKF 729

III. MISCELLANEOUS

Sepia photograph of Rossini (5.5 × 9 cm), mounted on a piece of cardboard (19 × 24.5 cm), inscribed: "Offert à Madame Ingres / L'heureuse Femme du peintre Italien /

Disciple de la Grande Ecole quoique / né en France / G. Rossini / Paris, ce 30 Avril 1863."

Paris, Oger-Dumont (Drouot), 14 Feb. 1985, lot 95 bis.
FRKF 699

EDMOND ROSTAND (1868–1918)

L'Aiglon. Drame en six actes, en vers. Représenté pour la première fois au Théâtre Sarah Bernhardt le 15 mars 1900. Paris: Librairie Charpentier et Fasquelle, 1900.

6 leaves, [1–3] 4–262, [2] p. Large paper copy (21.5 cm) printed on Japan paper. On verso of half-title: "Exemplaire imprimé spécialement pour Madame Sarah-Bernhardt." Inscribed by Rostand to Sarah Bernhardt on recto of first page, blank: "L'Aiglon n'est plus qu'un livre, et le voici, Madame, N'ouvrant que des feuillets et regrettant ses ailes … Les ailes qu'il avait quand vous lui prêtiez celles Qui vous pendent, Sarah, des deux côtés de l'âme! Edmond Rostand Saint-Brice[?], 1901."

Original wrappers, signed by René Lalique, bound in. Bound in cream-colored morocco. On the front board is an inlay of green and gold morocco showing an eaglet in the sun. All edges gilt. Raised bands. Author and title gold-tooled on spine. In the center of the spine is a gold-tooled cardinal's monogram. Red and green cloth doublures. The binding is signed and dated "Ch. Meunier 1906" at the bottom of the verso of the front board. On the verso of the front free endpaper is the bookplate of Count Alain de Suzannet.

Laid in is a ticket reading: "Ce livre a figuré à l'exposition "Dix Siècles de Livres français" (Lucerne, 9 juillet – 2 octobre 1949) sous le n° 267 du catalogue." Accompanied by an ALS from Rostand to "chère amie" [i.e. Sarah Bernhardt], n.d., n.p., 2 p., thanking her for sending flowers.

London, Sotheby's, 27 Nov. 1984, lot 369.
FRKF 674a–b

"La première de L'Aiglon"

Unidentified autograph manuscript, unsigned, n.d., 4 p. The author of the manuscript, who indicates that he later performed the part of Flambeau at the Théâtre de la Porte-Saint-Martin, does not indicate which role he played at the premiere.

Paris, Le Roux-Mathias (Drouot), 19 April 1985, lot 240.
FRKF 716b

Letter to Sarah Bernhardt

n.d., n.p., ALS, 3 p., responding to a letter of recrimination.

Paris, Le Roux-Mathias (Drouot), 19 April 1985, lot 240.
FRKF 716a

Letter to Constant Coquelin

[1899] n.p., ALS, 2 p., concerning his participation in *L'Aiglon*. Addressed to "Mon cher Coq."

Paris, Hervé Chayette (Drouot), 21 May 1984, lot 129.
FRKF 711

MAURICE ROSTAND (1891–1968)

Letter to M. Mercereau

n.d., "3, rue de Tilsitt" [Paris] ALS, 2 p., cancelling a reading engagement.

Paris, Le Roux-Mathias (Drouot), 19 April 1985, lot 240.
FRKF 716b

ALBERT ROUSSEL (1869–1937)

Pâdmavatî

Holograph sketches, in short score, for act 2 of this opéra-ballet, n.d., 44 p. The manuscript is written in black ink, with corrections in black and red pencil, on individual leaves of tall 18-staff paper (blind stamp of Lard-Esnault / Ed. Bellamy Sr.).

Collation:

"2d Acte / Prélude," 8 pages numbered 1 to 8 in Roussel's hand, ending with the words (for the chorus) "et que jaillisse la fin!"

Draft of the duet between Ratan-Sen and Pâdmavatî, paginated 17 to 22, beginning with Ratan-Sen's words "Ce n'est pas la mort que je redoute" and ending "La mort va nou[s]." At the top of p. 17, in pencil: "(p. 151 mes. 5)."

Drafts for the final scene, paginated 1–16, beginning 13 measures before the words (for the chorus) "Sur la pierre" and ending in the middle of a choral passage (words not present). At the top of p. 1, in pencil: "(p. 173 mes. 6)"; on p. 16, next to the last system at the bottom, in pencil: "(p. 200 mes. 3) / Manquent ici 13 mes." Pages 8–12 originally paginated 1–5; pages 13–15 originally paginated 1–3. On the verso of p. 1 and 2, cancelled drafts for the duet, both beginning with the words

"[Ce n'est pas la] mort que je redoute …" On the verso of p. 8, cancelled draft of the passage beginning "Pâdmavatî, songez aux mères qui verront leurs enfants égorgés."

Additional drafts, paginated 1–4 and 6–6b in blue pencil, with other, unidentified drafts, mostly in pencil, on the verso of each sheet.

Pâdmavatî, opéra-ballet on a libretto by Louis Laloy, was composed chiefly in 1912–14, completed in 1919, and premiered at the Paris Opéra on 1 June 1923.

Heinrich Schütz to Henry Miller, p. 106–07.
FRKF 556

Le testament de la tante Caroline

Holograph manuscript, in short score, of this opera buffa, n.d., 156 p. Notated in black ink, with a few pencil corrections, on both sides (generally) of individual sheets or bifolia, separate or nested, of tall 20-staff paper (Lard-Esnault Supérieur 251.20). Act 1 paginated 1–36 and 27–48 in Roussel's hand; act 2, 1–53; act 3, 1–43. The one-page prelude to act 2 and two-page prelude to act 3 are not paginated.

Le testament de la tante Caroline, opéra-bouffe in three acts on a libretto by Nino [N. Weber] was first performed in Olomouc (Czechoslovakia) on 14 Nov. 1936 (as *Testament Tety Karoliny*) and at the Opéra-Comique in Paris on 11 March 1937. According to Grove, it was written ca. 1932–33.

FRKF 708

ANTON RUBINSTEIN (1829–94)

String quartet in A-flat major, op. 106, no. 1

Holograph manuscript, n.d., 19 p., in black ink, with additional markings in black pencil and red ink, on five nested bifolia and a single sheet (laid in the middle) of tall 20-staff paper, paginated 1 to 19 by the composer. On the title page, in Rubinstein's hand: "Deux / Quatuors / pour 2 Violons, Alto et Violoncelle / composés / par / Ant. Rubinstein / op. 106 / N° I"; at the bottom of the page, in red ink, in a different hand, music publisher's number 1619. At the top of p. 1, also in Rubinstein's hand: "a Monsieur Jean Becker / Quatuor N° 1."

Boston, Daniel Kelleher, 22 July 1982, lot 217.
FRKF 12

RUDOLF, CROWN PRINCE OF AUSTRIA (1858–89)

Letter to Joseph von Pausinger

1888 Sept. 13, Belovar, ALS, 3 p. (env), concerning a bear hunt organized for Edward, Prince of Wales, the future Edward VII.

London, Sotheby's, 18 May 1989, lot 315.
FRKF 1309

MAURICE SACHS (1906–45?)

Letter to "Robert chéri"

n.d., n.p., ALS, 1 p.

Paris, Laurin-Guilloux-Buffetaud-Tailleur (Drouot), 12 June 1984, lot 112.
FRKF 462

HENRI VERNOY DE SAINT-GEORGES (1801–75)

Letters to Fromental Halévy

n.y., June 30, n.p., ALS, 6 p., a letter of recrimination concerning plans for a work called *Le laurier*; mentions Émile Perrin, Léon Carvalho, and the tenor Joseph Barbot.

n.d., n.p., ALS, 4 p., concerning *Jaguarita l'Indienne* and *Le laurier*; also mentions Perrin.

Paris, Oger-Dumont (Drouot), 14 Feb. 1985, lot 52.
FRKF 681.18

CAMILLE SAINT-SAËNS (1835–1921)

I. MUSIC MANUSCRIPTS

Élégie in D major for violin and piano, op. 143

Holograph manuscript, 1915, 9 p. Notated in black ink on two separate bifolia of oblong 14-staff paper, paginated [1]–8 by the composer and housed in an additional bifolium serving as wrappers. On the front of the outer bifolium, in Saint-Saëns's hand: "à Sir Henry Heyman / Elégie / pour Violon et Piano / C. Saint-Saëns." Signed and dated July 1915 at the end.

Ratner 139.
Boston, Daniel Kelleher, 22 July 1982, lot 222.
FRKF 13

The Promised Land, op. 40

Holograph manuscript of the full-score and piano-vocal score of this oratorio, n.d., 325 p.

The full-score manuscript is written in black ink, with additional markings in black, blue, and red pencil, on both sides of tall sheets of 36-staff paper (blind stamp of Lard-Esnault), paginated 1–85, 1–36, and 1–44 in the composer's hand. On title page, also in his hand: "The promised Land. - 1rst Part. / Prelude." At the top of p. 1, in pencil, not in Saint-Saëns's hand: "The Promised Land / Camille Saint-Saëns / op. 140." The manuscript lacks the two unaccompanied chorales. Pages 25–44 of part 3 have been repaginated.

Bound in reddish brown marbled paper boards, with corners and spine in red morocco; on spine, gold-tooled title with gilt fillets and fleur-de-lys.

The short-score manuscript is written in black ink on separate bifolia of oblong 14-staff paper (blind stamp of Lard-Esnault), paginated by Saint-Saëns and arranged in four sections labelled a–d, each housed in an additional bifolium serving as wrappers, with the corresponding alphabetical letter written in the upper left corner of the wrapper and each bifolium.

Collation: Section a, 1–12; section b, 1–66; section c, 1–44; section d, 1–38. Section a is labelled, in Saint-Saëns's hand: "Introduction"; section b: "The Promised Land. / 1rst Part."; section c: "The promised Land / 2d Part"; and section d: "The promised land / 3d Part."

The Promised Land, oratorio on a text by Hermann Klein, was premiered at the Three Choirs Festival, held at Gloucester Cathedral, in 1913.

Heinrich Schütz to Henry Miller, p. 108–09.
London, Phillips, 14 June 1989, lot 21.
FRKF 1388, 1352

Trio for piano, violin, and cello in F major, op. 18

Holograph manuscript, 1864, 57 p. Notated in black ink, with additional markings (some in the engraver's hand) in black and blue pencil, on both sides of sheets of tall 24-staff paper, paginated by the composer. The pagination is irregular: 1–38, 35–36 [repaginated 39–40 in an unidentified hand], [41–47 paginated in the same unidentified hand], 48–57. At the top of p. 1, not in composer's hand: "Trio / Camille Saint-Saëns." Music publisher's number ("J.M. 730") written in the same hand at the bottom of the page. Signed and dated Oct. 1864 at the end. Drawing of a fleur-de-lys by Saint-Saëns on p. 30 (end of the andante).

Ratner 113.
London, Sotheby's, 29 Nov. 1985, lot 209.
FRKF 1043

II. LETTERS

Many of Saint-Saëns's letters are on printed stationery indicated as follows:
rue de Courcelles^S = rue de Courcelles 83 bis, Paris
rue de Longchamp^S = rue de Longchamp 17, Paris

To Gabriel Astruc

[1908 July 3, Paris*] ALS, 1 p. Printed "carte pneumatique" on the address side.

FRKF 795.01

To Edmond Audran

1896 May 8, Milan, ALS, 3 p. Mentions the *Second Violin Sonata*. Embellished with a decorated initial and the drawing of a flower.

Paris, Laurin-Guilloux-Buffetaud-Tailleur (Drouot), 19 March 1986, lot 190.
FRKF 1125

To Lucien Augé de Lassus

1887 March 11, Paris, ALS, 1 p.

1893

Jan. 20, Algiers, ALS, 3 p.

Feb. 3, Algiers, ALS, 2 p.

Feb. 14, Algiers, ALS, 1 p.

[Feb.?] on stationery showing an unidentified private residence, ALS, 4 p.

Feb. 22, Algiers, ALS, 2 p.

Feb. 26, Algiers, ALS, 4 p.

Feb. 27, Algiers, ALS, 2 p.

Feb. 28, Algiers, ALS on both sides of a card.

March 1, Algiers, 1 March 1893, ALS, 4 p.

March 2, Algiers, ALS, 1 p.

March 8, Algiers, ALS, 2 p.

March 10, Algiers, ALS, 4 p.

March 18, Algiers, ALS, 1 p.

March 24 [n.y., 1893?] Algiers, ALS, 1 p.

April 15, Grand Hôtel Beauvau, Marseilles^S, ALS, 1 p.

Sept. 4, Asnières, ALS, 2 p. Decorated initial.

Sept. 6, Asnières, ALS, 2 p.

Oct. 10, Paris, ALS, 3 p.

1905

Jan. 21, Institut de France [Paris]^S ALS, 1 p.

April 7, Hotel Freienhof, Thun^S, ALS, 2 p.

June 29, Pallanza, ALS, 4 p. Decorated initial.

July 8 [1905?] rue de Longchamp^S, ALS, 3 p.

July 10, rue de Longchamp^S, ALS, 2 p.

n.d. [1905 July?] rue de Longchamp^S, ALS, 3 p.

n.d. [1905 July?] rue de Longchamp^S, ALS, 1 p.

July 14, Hotel Freienhof, Thun^S, ALS, 2 p.

July 20, Thun, ALS, 3 p.

July 21, Thun, ALS, 3 p.

Aug. 1, n.p., ALS, 2 p.

[Aug., Thun?] ALS, 2 p.

Aug. 6, Thun, ALS, 2 p.

Oct. 9, rue de Longchamp^S, ALS, 2 p.

Oct. 11, n.p., ALS, 3 p., on mourning stationery.

Oct. 26, rue de Longchamp^S, ALS, 2 p.

Dec. 11, Genoa, ALS, 3 p.

n.d., AN on both sides of a card, to Mme Augé de Lassus.

1906

Feb. 5, Hotel de Paris, Monte-Carlo^S, ALS, 2 p.

March 18, Monte Carlo, ALS to Mme Augé de Lassus, 5 p.

[1906, Monte Carlo?] ALS, 3 p.

July 18, rue de Longchamp^S, ALS, 3 p.

Oct. 19, Le Havre, ALS, 1 p.

Nov. 13, Hotel Gotham, New York^S, ALS, 2 p.

1908

May 3, n.p., ALS, 3 p.

June 12, Grosvenor Hotel, London^S, ALS to Mme Augé de Lassus, 2 p.

Nov. 24, Nuevo Gran Hotel de Inglaterra, Barcelona^S, ALS, 3 p.

Dec. 10, Nuevo Gran Hotel de Inglaterra, Barcelona^S, ALS, 3 p.

1909

March 28 [1909?] Nouvel Hôtel de Paris, Monte-Carlo^S, ALS, 2 p.

April 4, Palais de Monaco^S, ALS to Mme Augé de Lassus, 2 p. Drawing of flower.

April 15, Paris, ALS, 2 p.

June 2, rue de Longchamp^S, ALS to Mme Augé de Lassus, 3 p.

Aug. 17, Dieppe, ALS to Mme Augé de Lassus, 2 p.

Aug. 29, Dieppe, ALS, 2 p.

Sept. 19, rue de Longchamp^S, ALS, 3 p.

Sept. 25, rue de Longchamp^S, ALS to Mme Augé de Lassus, 2 p.

Sept. 27, rue de Longchamp^S, ALS, 3 p.

Oct. 4, rue de Longchamp^S, ALS to Mme Augé de Lassus, 3 p.

1910

Jan. 18, Luxor Hotel, Luxor^S, ALS to Mme Augé de Lassus, 2 p. (env)

Jan. 31, Cairo, ALS to Mme Augé de Lassus, 2 p.

April 25 [April 24*] rue de Longchamp[S], ALS to Mme Augé de Lassus, 2 p. (env)

June 27, Paris, ALS, 4 p.

Aug. 3, ALS to Mme Augé de Lassus, 3 p. Drawing of flower.

1911–1921

1911 Feb. 25, Excelsior Hotel, Algiers[S], ALS to Mme Augé de Lassus, 2 p.

1913 June 23, rue de Courcelles[S], ALS, 2 p.

1913 July 1, Ruhl Hotel, Vichy[S], ALS, 2 p.

1915 March 9, rue de Courcelles[S], ALS to Mme Augé de Lassus, 2 p.

1916 Nov. 1, rue de Courcelles[S], ALS to Mme Augé de Lassus, 1 p.

1918 March 29, Cannes, ALS to Mme Augé de Lassus, 2 p.

1918 April 5, Cannes, ALS to Mme Augé de Lassus, 2 p. (env)

1921 May 30 [Paris*] ALS to Mme Augé de Lassus, 1 p. (env)

Undated and with no place

ALS, 1 p.

ALS, "Lundi," 1 p.

APCS [Egypt?]

ALS, "Samedi," 2 p.

ALS, "Vendredi," 1 p.

With two drafts for the libretto of *L'ancêtre*, one in the hand of Augé de Lassus, one in the hand of Saint-Saëns, [1905], 2 p.

Lucien Augé de Lassus (d. 1914), librettist of Saint-Saëns's *Phryné* (1893) and *L'ancêtre* (1905).

FRKF 795.07

To [Ernest?] Bloch

1914 Feb. 19, rue de Courcelles[S], ALS, 1 p., concerning Marguerite Herleroy in *Phryné*.

FRKF 505

To Aristide Cavaillé-Coll

1890 Oct. 6, n.p., ALS, 2 p., a recommendation for [Paul?] Fauchey.

FRKF 795.02

To Georges Clemenceau

1920 April 13, Paris, ALS, 2 p. Mentions Lloyd George and Alexandre Millerand.

Paris, Laurin-Guilloux-Buffetaud-Tailleur (Drouot), 8 Feb. 1985, lot 166.
FRKF 656

To Arthur Dandelot

1911 Oct. 19, rue de Courcelles[S], ALS on both sides of a card (env), acknowledging receipt of J.-G. Prodhomme's *Gounod*. Accompanied by an autograph note by Dandelot.

1915 Dec. 1, rue de Courcelles[S], ALS, 2 p. (env), concerning Dandelot's "Matinées du Palais de Glace." Accompanied by autograph notes by Dandelot.

1919 Nov. 15 [Paris*] ALS, 1 p. (env)

[1921] April 16 [Paris*] ALS, 2 p., on mourning stationery (env), concerning the farewell of Mr. de Brozick.

FRKF 795.03

To Paul Fauchey

[1907 June 10, Paris*] ALS, 1 p.

1918 May 1, Cannes, ALS, 1 p., a peace offering.

FRKF 795.04

To Gabriel Geslin

[1894, Paris*] ALS, 1 p. Printed: "Télégramme" on the address side.

[1894 May 3, Paris*] ALS, 1 p. Printed: "Télégramme" on the address side.

1897 May 5, Paris, telegram

1898 April 26, Lyons, ALS, 2 p.

[1909?] May 17, Las Palmas, ALS, 2 p.

n.d., "Vendredi," Théâtre des Arts, Rouen[S], ALS, 2 p.

n.d., "Jeudi," London, ALS, 2 p.

Gabriel Geslin, Saint-Saëns's secretary and travelling companion.

FRKF 795.05

To Raoul Gunsbourg

1915 Oct. 22, rue de Courcelles[S], ALS, 3 p., concerning *Phryné*; also mentions *L'ancêtre*.

FRKF 795.06

To Reynaldo Hahn

1906 May 16 [Paris?] ALS, 2 p.

1921 Nov. 10, n.p., ALS, 1 p. Congratulates him on conducting an unidentified Saint-Saëns work.

1921 Dec. 3, Marseilles, ALS 2 p. Mentions *Ascanio*.

Paris, Laurin-Guilloux-Buffetaud-Tailleur (Drouot), 8 Feb. 1985, lot 166.
FRKF 657b

To Marguerite Herleroy

1910 March 3, Hôtel de Paris, Monte-Carlo[S], ALS, 3 p.

1910 April 10, R. de Longchamp 17 [Paris] ALS, 1 p.

[1910?] May 28, n.p., ALS, 2 p.

1910 June 4, Grosvenor Hotel, Belgravia, London, S.W.[S], ALS on both sides of a card.

1911 Feb. 8, Excelsior Hotel, Algiers[S], ALS, 1 p.

1912 May 2, rue de Courcelles[S], ALS, 2 p.

1912 May 31, ALS, 2 p.

1912 June 28, rue de Courcelles[S], ALS, 2 p.

[1912?] rue de Courcelles[S], ALS, 2 p.

1913 May 20, Hotel des Trois Couronnes, Vevey[S], ALS, 2 p.

1913 Sept. 11, Hotel Cecil, Strand, London, W.C.[S], ALS, 2 p.

1914 Jan. 14, rue de Courcelles[S], ALS, 2 p.

[1914?] Jan. 18, rue de Courcelles[S], ALS, 2 p.

1915 July 12, n.p., ALS, 1 p.

1915 Sept. 1, rue de Courcelles[S], ALS, 1 p.

[1915?] rue de Courcelles[S], ALS, 2 p.

1915 Sept. 23 [Paris*] ALS, 1 p.

1915 Nov. 2, n.p., ALS, 2 p.

1915 Nov. 9, rue de Courcelles[S], ALS, 2 p.

1915 Nov. 11, n.p., ALS, 2 p.

1915 Nov. 17, rue de Courcelles[S], ALS, 2 p.

1915 Nov. 17, rue de Courcelles[S], ALS, 2 p. Contains attacks on Astruc and Richard Strauss.

1915 Nov. 20, rue de Courcelles[S], ALS, 2 p.

1915 Nov. 23, rue de Courcelles[S], ALS, 3 p.

1915 Dec. 2, n.p., ALS, 2 p.

[1915 Dec.?] "Mercredi," n.p, ALS, 2 p.

1916 Jan. 14, rue de Courcelles[S], ALS, 2 p.

1916 Feb. 15, rue de Courcelles[S], ALS, 2 p., accompanied by a clipping headed "A l'Opéra-Comique," concerning *Phryné*.

1916 Sept. 10, Bourbon-l'Archambault, ALS, 2 p.

1916 Sept. 20, Bourbon-l'Archambault, ALS, 2 p.

[late 1916] rue de Courcelles[S], ALS on both sides of a card.

1917 Dec. 3, n.p., ALS, 1 p.

1918 May 6, Cannes, ALS, 2 p.

1918 June 1, Compagnie des Chemins de Fer P.L.M. Lyon, Gare de Perrache[S], ALS, 3 p.

1918 June 16, Hôtel du Parc, Bourbon-l'Archambault[S], ALS, 3 p.

[1918?] June 17, n.p., ALS, 2 p.

[1918?] "Dimanche," Le Grand Hotel, Marseille[S], ALS, 1 p.

n.d. [1919?] n.p., APCS [view of the Grand Hôtel, Hammam R'hira, Algeria]. Musical quotation, signed, inscribed "à Madame Herleroy."

1919 Feb. 4, Hammam R'hira, ALS, 1 p.

1919 Feb. 19, Hammam R'hira, ALS, 2 p. Contains a disparaging reference to *Cavalleria rusticana*.

1919 Feb. 19, Hammam R'hira, telegram

1919 Feb. 23, Hammam R'hira, ALS, 2 p.

[1919?] May 11, n.p., ALS, 1 p.

1921 May 26, n.p., ALS, 2 p.

1921 July 4, n.p., ALS, 1 p.

1921 Aug. 29, Hotel du Palais, Poitiers[S], ALS, 1 p.

Undated or no year given

ALS on both sides of a card, 29 May, n.p.

ALS, n.p., 1 p.

ALS, "Dimanche," n.p., 2 p.

ALS, n.p., 1 p.

ALS, Bourbon-l'Archambault, 2 p.

ALS, 20 Nov., n.p., 1 p. Drawing of flower.

ALS, rue de Courcelles[S], on both sides of a card.

ALS, "Vendredi," rue de Courcelles[S], on both sides of a card. Mentions Pierre-Barthélémy Gheusi.

ALS, rue de Courcelles[S], on one side of a card.

ALS, "Mardi," rue de Courcelles[S], on one side of a card.

ANS, n.p. (env)., on one side of a card ("Vous êtes divine").

Also, ALS from Valentine Nussy-Saint-Saëns to Marguerite Herleroy, 1938 Nov. 20, Paris, 2 p., congratulating her on her Legion of Honor.

Soprano Marguerite Herleroy (1883–after 1944) sang the title role in Saint-Saëns's *Phryné*, notably at the Gaîté-Lyrique in Paris. In addition to *Phryné*, the letters discuss *La princesse jaune*, *L'ancêtre*, *Hélène*, *Le timbre d'argent*, *The Promised Land*, *Proserpine*, *Ascanio*, *La nuit*, and various songs; they also mention Sybil Sanderson, Albert Carré, Raoul Gunsbourg, and Jacques Rouché. See under Reynaldo Hahn.

FRKF 505

To Sir Henry Heyman

1915 Dec. 14, rue de Courcelles[S], ALS, 3 p. Mentions *The Promised Land* and the *Élégie*.

1916 Nov. 24, Paris, ALS, 2 p., concerning the Paris premiere of the *Élégie* the previous evening; also mentions *Hail, California!* Drawing of a flower.

1919 Nov. 8, Paris, ALS, 2 p. Mentions the *Élégie*. Accompanied by a printed concert program for a "Festival Saint-Saëns=Fauré," Paris, Salle Gaveau, 23 Nov. 1916, including the *Élégie*.

Boston, Daniel Kelleher, 22 July 1982, lot 222.
FRKF 13.5

To Fernand Le Borne

1902 Nov. 17, n.p., ALS, 2 p.

n.p., n.d., ALS, 3 p. (env), concerning *Le Déluge*.

[1909*] Aug. 4, rue de Longchamp[S], ALS, 2 p. (env), concerning a contract with Pathé.

1910 May 26, n.p., ALS, 2 p.

1910 May 26, n.p., ALS, 1 p., also concerning the program of a concert.

1910 May 27, n.p., ALS, 3 p.

1910 Sept. 7, Gd Hotel Astoria et de l'Arc Romain, Aix-les-Bains[S], ALS, 1 p.

1910 Sept. 28, n.p., ALS, 2 p.

[1910] Oct. 1, Paris, ALS, 2 p.

1911 Jan. 31, Excelsior Hotel, Algiers[S], ALS, 1 p. (env), clearing a misunderstanding.

Fernand Le Borne (1862–1929), French composer. The 1910 letters concern the program of a concert and mention Eugène Ysaÿe and Joseph Hollmann.

Paris, Laurin-Guilloux-Buffetaud-Tailleur (Drouot), 1 July 1986, lots 264–67.
FRKF 1173–76

To Lucien L'Hoest

[1908*] Oct. 26, Monaco, ALS, 2 p., on mourning stationery (env, postmarked 1908 Feb 27), concerning a symphony by L'Hoest.

FRKF 795.08a

To L. Marbeau

1919 Oct. 15, rue de Courcelles, 83 bis, ALS, 2 p., thanking his correspondent for sending him his book *Lettres d'une opérée*.

Paris, Laurin-Guilloux-Buffetaud-Tailleur (Drouot), 1 July 1986, lot 268.
FRKF 1177.2

To Pierre Monteux

1919 Aug. 19, Paris, ALS, 3 p. (env), concerning *The Promised Land*, *Hail, California!*, the *Psaume CL*, and, especially, *Hymne à Victor Hugo*, with a short musical quotation from this last work; also mentions *Phryné*, *Henry VIII*, and *Ascanio*, and singers Emma Eames and Jean Lassalle.

New York, Sotheby's, 22 May 1985, lot 365.
FRKF 745

To Émile Renaud

1898–1911

1898 Sept. 14, Paris, ALS, 2 p.

1905 Nov. 11, Paris, ANS on both sides of a card.

1906 Sept. 15, Paris, ANS on both sides of a card.

1907 March 5, Palais de Monaco[S], ALS, 2 p.

1907 Aug. 5, Zürich, ALS, 2 p.

1907 Aug. 12, Paris, ALS, 2 p.

1907 Aug. 12, n.p., ALS, 1 p.

1908 April 21, n.p., ALS, 2 p.

1908 April 23, n.p., ALS, 2 p., concerning the divorce of Gabriel Geslin.

1909 Nov. 3, rue de Longchamp[S], ALS, 2 p.

1909 Dec. 28, Cairo, ALS, 2 p.

1910 April 21, n.p., ANS on both sides of a card. Drawings of flowers.

1910 July 2, n.p., ALS, 1 p. Decorated initial.

1910 Nov. 2, n.p., ANS, 1 p.

1911 July 5, n.p., ANS on both sides of a card.

1911 Dec. 16, Grand Hôtel des Bains de la Station Thermo-Minérale d'Hammam-r'Irha[S], ALS, 2 p.

1911 Dec. 26, Grand Hôtel des Bains de la Station Thermo-Minérale d'Hammam-r'Irha[S], ALS, 2 p. Decorated initial.

1912

April 27, rue de Courcelles[S], ALS, 3 p., with a double postscript, one cancelled, on p. [4]. Drawing of flower.

May 6, rue de Courcelles[S], ALS, 1 p.

[June 24, Paris*] ALS, 1 p.

Oct. 10, rue de Courcelles[S], ALS, 2 p. Presented as "un Acrostiche en prose!"

Dec. 1, n.p., ALS, 1 p.

1913

April 1, rue de Courcelles[S], ALS, 3 p., with a drawing of a fish; mentions *Proserpine*.

April 3, Palace Hôtel, Brussels[S], ALS, 1 p.

April 19, rue de Courcelles[S], ALS, 2 p.

May 14, rue de Courcelles[S], ALS, 2 p. Illustrated with the drawing of a flower and ornamented initials.

July 12, n.p., ALS, 2 p.

Nov. 14, Grand Hotel Beauvau, Marseilles[S], ALS, 2 p., in the form of a short story.

1914

March 7, rue de Courcelles[S], ALS, 2 p. Mentions *Le timbre d'argent*.

March 28, Palais de Monaco[S], ANS on both sides of a card.

April 3, rue de Courcelles[S], ALS, 2 p.

April 7, n.p., ALS, 2 p.

April 12, Palais de Monaco[S], ALS, 2 p.

June 14, n.p., ALS, 2 p. Mentions *La princesse jaune*, *Phryné* and *Proserpine*.

June 19, rue de Courcelles[S], ANS on both sides of a card.

July 20, rue de Courcelles[S], ALS, 2 p.

July 23, n.p., ALS, 2 p., with a humorous drawing in the shape of a mock musical quotation.

Aug. 13, rue de Courcelles[S], ANS on both sides of a card.

Aug. 26, rue de Courcelles[S], ALS, 2 p.

Aug. 29, rue de Courcelles[S], ALS, 2 p.

Sept. 1, rue de Courcelles[S], ALS, 2 p

Oct. 8, rue de Courcelles[S], ALS, 1 p.

Oct. 27, rue de Courcelles[S], ALS, 3 p. Illustrated with a drawing of a flower.

Oct. 30, rue de Courcelles[S], ALS, 2 p.

Nov. 4, rue de Courcelles[S], ALS, 2 p., with an embellished initial.

Dec. 3, rue de Courcelles[S], ALS, 3 p. Mentions Jules Barbier and *Psyché*, as well as his arrangement for two pianos of the Liszt sonata.

Dec. 19, rue de Courcelles[S], ANS on both sides of a card.

1915

Jan. 5, rue de Courcelles[S], ANS on both sides of a card.

Jan. 28, rue de Courcelles[S], ALS, 3 p.

April 3, rue de Courcelles[S], ALS, 3 p. Mentions *The Promised Land*.

Aug. 2, rue de Courcelles[S], ALS, 3 p. Mentions California and San Francisco.

Aug. 13, rue de Courcelles[S], ANS on one side of a card.

Sept. 17, Hotel du Parc, Bourbon-l'Archambault[S], ALS, 3 p.

Sept. 28, Bourbon-l'Archambault, ALS, 2 p. Illustrated with a drawing of a flower.

Dec. 20, rue de Courcelles[S], ALS, 2 p., with an embellished initial. Mentions *Henry VIII*.

1916

Jan. 26, rue de Courcelles[S], ALS, 2 p. Mentions *Samson et Dalila*.

Feb. 19, rue de Courcelles[S], ALS, 3 p. Mentions *Phryné* and *The Promised Land*.

Undated, but before 1912

ANS on both sides of a card, n.p.

ANS on both sides of a card, "lundi," n.p.

ALS, "Vendredi," n.p., 2 p.

ANS on both sides of a card, "Samedi," n.p.

ALS, "Dimanche," n.p., 3 p.

ALS, "Dimanche," n.p., 2 p., on mourning stationery.

ALS, "Mardi," n.p., 2 p.

ALS, "Dimanche," n.p., 2 p., with decorated initial.

ALS, "Mardi," n.p., 1 p.

ALS, 18 March, Hôtel de Paris, Monte Carlo[S], 3 p. Mentions *Phryné*.

ALS, "Lundi;" n.p., 2 p.

ALS, Sept. 1, Gd Hotel Astoria et de l'arc romain, Aix-les-Bains[S], 2 p.

ALS, n.p., 1 p.

ANS, "Mercredi," rue de Courcelles[S], on both sides of a card. Drawing of flower.

AN, rue de Courcelles[S], on one side of a card, a "calligramme" in the shape of glasses.

Undated, but after 1912

ANS, March 10, rue de Courcelles[S], on both sides of a card.

ANS, Dec. 1, rue de Courcelles[S], on both sides of a card.

ALS, rue de Courcelles[S], 2 p. Mentions *La fille de Madame Angot*.

ALS, n.p., 2 p.

ANS, n.p., with a drawing of a flower and a decorated initialed signature, 1 p.

ALS [probably after 1912] rue de Courcelles[S], 3 p. Illustrated with drawings of a train, a one-note musical quotation, and a butterfly.

Undated

AN, Grand Hotel Beauvau, Marseilles[S], 1 p., a 4-line humorous poem, illustrated with a drawing of a devil.

ANS May 16, n.p., on one side of a card.

AN, rue de Courcelles[S], on one side of a card.

ALS, n.p., 1 p.

Also, ALS to Émile Renaud from the Association des artistes musiciens [Paris] 1899 June 1, a letter of appreciation, signed by eleven committee members.

Émile Renaud, once organist of the Royal Chapel at Versailles, became one of Saint-Saëns's closest friends (they used the form "tu" as of 1912) and the correspondence reveals an unusually unbuttoned and humorous aspect of the composer's personality. It also contains many references to Gabriel Geslin.

Letter of 1914 Dec. 3
Marburg, Stargardt, 19 June 1984, lot 912.
FRKF 482.5

Renaud correspondence [except letter of 1914 Dec. 3]
FRKF 1105

To [Henry Roujon]

1908 Nov. 8 [Paris?] ALS, 4 p., concerning Erckmann-Chatrian; also mentions Manuel Garcia and Verdi and *Les vêpres siciliennes*.

Paris, Dominique Vincent (Drouot), 6 Dec. 1984, lot 272.
FRKF 662b

To M. de Saint-Chaffray

[before 1854] "Vendredi," n.p., ALS, 1 p.

[1854 Oct. 15?] "Dimanche matin," n.p., ALS, 2 p., announcing his visit while declining a dinner invitation.

1855 Oct. 2, n.p., ALS, 3 p., concerning a composition, possibly a song, on a text by Saint-Chaffray.

n.d., "Vendredi," n.p., ALS, 2 p.

Paris, Laurin-Guilloux-Buffetaud-Tailleur (Drouot), 1 July 1986, lot 263.
FRKF 1172

To Caroline de Serres

1900 Dec. 30, Bône (Algeria), ALS, 3 p., on mourning stationery, concerning his stay in Algeria. Mentions Liszt and the *Faust-Symphonie*.

London, Christie's, 27 March 1985, lot 248.
FRKF 868

To Edouard Silas

[ca. 1871?] "Mardi," n.p., ALS, 3 p., concerning a concert of Silas's music and the dedication to him of a "petite gavotte."

[1871?] "Mardi / Ella matinée's day" [London?] ALS, 3 p.

[1893?] "Saturday" [London?] ALS, 3 p., concerning his honorary doctorate at Cambridge.

n.y., June 2, "9 Park Mall, Regent Park" [London] ALS, 1 p.

Edouard Silas (1827–1909), Dutch organist and composer.

FRKF 795.09b

To Marie Trélat

[1901*] Sept. 28 [Paris*] ALS on both sides of a card (env)

FRKF 795.08b

To Auguste Vacquerie

1894 Dec. 1, Narbonne, ALS, 2 p., concerning *Proserpine*; also mentions *Samson et Dalila*.

Paris, Laurin-Guilloux-Buffetaud-Tailleur (Drouot), 19 March 1986, lot 189.
FRKF 1124

To various unidentified recipients

1872 Feb. 2, Paris, ALS, 2 p., on mourning stationery.

FRKF 795.09a

1879 Oct. 16, Paris, ALS, 1 p., to a composer, concerning a symphony to be performed by Colonne.

FRKF 795.10

1880 May 26, Paris, ALS, 3 p., to a musician, concerning a concert at which two pieces by the recipient will be performed.

FRKF 795.11

1881 May 19, Barcelona, ALS, 2 p., to "cher et illustre confrère," concerning the composition of a hymn to Victor Hugo.

Paris, Ader-Picard-Tajan (Drouot), 19 June 1984, lot 356.
FRKF 532

1887 March 30, Paris, ALS, 2 p., possibly to a fellow composer.

FRKF 795.12

1889 April 30, Saint-Germain, ALS, 3 p., cancelling a social engagement.

FRKF 795.13

[1890?] Oct. 17, Saint-Germain, ALS, 4 p., on mourning stationery, to a friend. Mentions *Samson et Dalila*.

FRKF 977

1893 Jan. 22, Algiers, ALS, 3 p., concerning Gounod and *Don Juan*.

Paris, Laurin-Guilloux-Buffetaud-Tailleur (Drouot), 1 July 1986, lot 268.
FRKF 1177

1894 July 29, Paris, 2 p. Mentions Pablo de Sarasate.

FRKF 795.14

[ca. 1894?] "Samedi," n.p., ALS, 2 p., concerning a dinner invitation.

FRKF 795.15

1895 Dec. 24, Grand Hotel de Milan[S], ALS, 1 p. Mentions obtaining Opéra tickets from Mr. Maillard.

FRKF 795.16

SAINT-SAËNS [269]

1896 Jan. 6, Naples, ALS, 2 p.

FRKF 795.17

1896 July 19, n.p., ALS, 3 p., to a friend. Mentions *Proserpine*, *La princesse jaune*, *Le timbre d'argent*, *Phryné*, and Léon Carvalho.

Marburg, Stargardt, 19 June 1984, lot 910.
FRKF 482

1896 Oct. 22, Hôtel de la Poste, Brussels[S], ALS, 1 p. Mentions Léon Carvalho.

FRKF 795.18

1896 Nov. 17, ALS on both sides of a card, "Grand Hôtel Collet," n.p.

FRKF 795.19

1899 Feb. 20, Las Palmas, ALS, 2 p., to a friend.

FRKF 795.20

1900 Aug. 18, Béziers, ALS, 3 p., on mourning stationery.

FRKF 795.21

1902 May 7, n.p., ALS, 3 p. Discusses the form of opéra-comique and mentions *Déjanire* and Fauré's *Prométhée*.

Marburg, Stargardt, 26 Nov. 1985, lot 892.
FRKF 1155

1905 Nov. 10, Paris, ALS on both sides of a card.

FRKF 795.23

1908 Sept. 25 [Paris?] ALS, 2 p.

FRKF 795.24

1909 Aug. 9 [Paris] ALS, 2 p. Mentions the Futurist Manifesto and his response to Marinetti.

Saint-Saëns's letter to Marinetti is in the Marinetti Papers in the Beinecke Library.

Paris, Ader-Picard-Tajan (Drouot), 19 June 1984, lot 280.
FRKF 530

1909 Dec. 9, Luxor, ALS, 2 p., concerning Geslin's divorce.

FRKF 795.26

[ca. 1909?] "Vendredi," rue de Longchamp[S], ALS, 2 p., concerning "l'affaire Geslin."

FRKF 795.25

1910 April 3, Palais de Monaco, Monaco[S], ALS, 2 p., to a female recipient. Mentions Mlle Ravaud [Alice Raveau?] and his song "Les violons dans le soir."

London, Sotheby's, 19 Nov. 1985, lot 928.
FRKF 997

1910 June 30, n.p., ALS, 3 p., concerning *L'ancêtre* and *L'heure espagnole*; mentions Albert Carré and Alice Raveau.

FRKF 795.27

[1911?] Feb. 15 [Algiers?] ALS, 1 p.

FRKF 795.28

1911 Aug. 8, Paris, ALS, 3 p, to a newspaper editor, on questionnaires and declining to contribute to a journal.

FRKF 795.29

1913 April 9, rue de Courcelles[S], ALS, 2 p., to unidentified friends, concerning *Proserpine* and *Le timbre d'argent*; also mentions Pierre Barbier.

Paris, Ader-Picard-Tajan (Drouot), 19 June 1984, lot 280.
FRKF 530.5

1913 April 15, rue de Courcelles[S], ALS, 2 p., to a friend.

FRKF 795.30

1913 May 5, rue de Courcelles[S], 1 p., to a composer and friend.

FRKF 795.31

1913 May 14, Hotel Suisse, Geneva[S], 3 p., to a friend.

FRKF 795.32

1915 Feb. 25, n.p., 2 p., to a friend, regretting not being able to attend a committee meeting.

FRKF 795.33

1915 Sept. 24, Hotel du Parc, Bourbon l'Archambault[S], ALS, 3 p., to a musician. Mentions *Proserpine*.

FRKF 795.34

1916 Feb. 22, Hôtel-Restaurant du Chapon fin, Bordeaux[S], ALS, 2 p., concerning the performance of one of his works (probably *The Promised Land*).

FRKF 795.35

1916 Feb. 28, Paris, 2 p., to a musician. Mentions *Phryné* and his bad relations with the Opéra-Comique.

FRKF 795.34a

1916 March 16, n.p., ALS, 1 p., to a friend. Mentions *Hélène*; members of the cast listed at the bottom, possibly in another hand.

FRKF 795.36

1918 May 10, Cannes, APCS

FRKF 795.37

1918 Nov. 21, n.p., ALS, 1 p., to "mon cher Pierre." Mentions Vincent d'Indy.

Paris, Laurin-Guilloux-Buffetaud-Tailleur (Drouot), 1 July 1986, lot 268.
FRKF 1177.1

1919 April 5, Marseilles, ALS, 2 p., to a writer. Addressed to "Mon cher poête."

FRKF 795.38

1919 June 6, Paris, ALS, 1 p., declining an invitation to write a preface. Mentions *Hélène*.

FRKF 795.39

1920 June 18, n.p., ALS, 1 p.

FRKF 795.40

[1921?] Feb. 21, n.p., ALS, 3 p.

FRKF 795.41

Undated

ANS, n.p., 1 p.

FRKF 795.42

ALS, Berck-sur-Mer, 1 p., to "cher Maître."

FRKF 795.44

ANS on both sides of a card, "Rue de Longchamp 17"

FRKF 795.45

ALS to a friend, "23 Upper Baker St." [London] 2 p.

FRKF 795.46

ALS to a woman, 14, rue Monsieur-le-Prince [Paris][S] 2 p., postponing a talk on the first part of Haydn's *The seasons* for Concordia members.

Paris, Laurin-Guilloux-Buffetaud-Tailleur (Drouot), 8 Feb. 1985, lot 166.
FRKF 657a

ALS, "Samedi," n.p., 2 p. Mentions the "Danse macabre" and the "Carnaval? de Guiraud."

Paris, Ader-Picard-Tajan (Drouot), 13 Dec. 1984, lot 343.
FRKF 672

Other letters

Mlle de Charny [?] to Saint-Saëns

[1917?] Nov. 1, Nemours, Algeria, ALS, 2 p., thanking for assistance; the writer was evidently a singer.

E.W. Wallington to Hermann Klein

1913 March 6, Buckingham Palace[S], TLS, 1 p., concerning *The Promised Land*.

E.W. Wallington, private secretary to the Queen; Hermann Klein, librettist of *The Promised Land*.

FRKF 795.48–49

III. PRINTED MUSIC

Henry VIII: Opéra en 4 Actes. Poème de Léonce Détroyat & Armand Silvestre. Traduction allemande de Hermann Wolff. Traduction italienne de A. de Lauzières. Partition Chant et Piano par Léon Delahaye. Paris: Durand & Schoenewerk, [1883].

Quarto, [8], 1–384 p. Piano-vocal score, first edition. Music publisher's number: 3083.

Bound in dark blue cloth, author (as "C. de S. Saëns") and title gold-tooled on brown leather label on spine. Initials M.P. [Marcel Proust] blind-tooled on front board. On the recto of the front free endpaper, note in red ballpoint pen: "partition de Marcel Proust / offerte par Madame / Robert Proust / 1935 / Jacques Guérin -"

Paris, Ader-Picard-Tajan (Drouot), 22 Nov. 1985, lot 143.
FRKF 1358

IV. MISCELLANEOUS

Autograph memorandum, n.d., n.p., 1 p., a critique of an unidentified printed score, with page references.

FRKF 795.47

Autograph note, n.d., n.p., 1 p., concerning military music; with a one-measure musical quotation giving the range of a flute.

FRKF 795.43

Autograph statement signed, n.d., n.p., 1 p., concerning Verdi; also mentioning Chabrier.

London, Sotheby's, 23 Nov. 1984, lot 529.
FRKF 549

Newspaper clipping entitled "Les Grands Concerts," from *Le Figaro*. The article is signed Henri Quittard.

FRKF 795.50

GEORGE SAND (1804–76)

Letter to Josef Dessauer

n.d., "Vendredi," n.p., ALS, 1 p., with a note by Delacroix, signed with a cross, and initialed by Chopin. Incipit: "Delacroix qui vous adore veut que vous veniez ce soir chez moi." Not in Lubin IV, not in *Lettres retrouvées*.

FRKF 521

Letter to Camille Pleyel

[1839*] April 2, Marseilles, ALS, 3 p., ordering a piano as a surprise gift for Chopin. Lubin, XXV:332–33.

FRKF 519

Letters to Pauline Viardot

[1841 Jan. 30] n.p., ALS, 1 p. Mentions Chopin and Érard. Lubin, V:219–20.

FRKF 520

[1843 June 16, Nohant] ALS, 1 p. Mentions Chopin. Lubin, VI:180–82.

Paris, Ader-Picard-Tajan (Drouot), 19 June 1984, lot 358.
FRKF 533

VICTORIEN SARDOU (1831–1908)

Letters to Mme Senterre

1894 March 19 [postmark illegible] ALS, 1 p. (env)
n.d. [postmark illegible] ALS, 1 p. (env)

Both mention Sarah Bernhardt.

Paris, Laurin-Guilloux-Buffetaud-Tailleur (Drouot), 12 June 1984, lot 114.
FRKF 463

SIEGFRIED SASSOON (1886–1967)

"Aids to reflection. Stephen"

Autograph manuscript, 1933, 3 p., in red, blue, and green ink, with a title page embellished with watercolor, on the recto sides of two nested, stitched 8vo-size bifolia, in decorated paper wrappers. A small commonplace book, evidently made for presentation to Stephen Tennant, containing quotations from Edgar Allan Poe, Francis Bacon, Thomas Hardy, Percy Bysshe Shelley, John Keats, Walter de la Mare, Edmund Blunden, Paul Verlaine (in French), Omar Khayyam, James Elroy Flecker, and Christina Rossetti. Dated 21 April 1933 at the bottom of the last page.

London, Sotheby's, 14 Oct. 1987, lot 864.
FRKF 1425

Letters to Stephen Tennant

1930 Nov. 6, n.p., ALS, 1 p., addressed to "Illustrious Don Stefano" and signed "your loving kangar." Mounted on an illustrated frontispiece to an early edition of *Los suenos de don Francis de Quevedo*.

1951 Aug. 16, [Heytosbury?] ALS, 1 p. (env), enclosing a printed announcement of the publication of *Common chords*, with a manuscript addition. Accompanied by a photographic postcard showing an exhibition case devoted to Sassoon. Inscribed by Sassoon on the verso: "Combridges' [sic] Book Shop at Hove."

London, Sotheby's, 14 Oct. 1987, lot 867.
FRKF 1430

ERIK SATIE (1866–1925)

I. MUSIC MANUSCRIPTS

Parade

Manuscript, in a copyist's hand, of a reduction for piano four-hands of Satie's ballet, with extensive annotations by Jean Cocteau and a few by Leonid Massine [1917].

> The manuscript comprises 29 leaves of 12-staff paper, paginated as follows: [title page], 1–14, 13 bis, 14 bis, 15–16, 15 bis, 16 bis, 17–30, 29 bis, 30 bis, 31–32, 31 bis, 32 bis, 33–44, 43 bis, 44 bis, [45]–48.
>
> On the title page: "Piano à quatre mains. / Parade. / Ballet. / Thème de: Jean Cocteau. / Musique de: Erik Satie. / Rideau, Décor et Costumes de [later insertion: Pablo] Picasso. / Chorégraphie de: Massine." Purple stamp of Serge Lifar and numerous annotations by Cocteau in all directions, in black ink and in pencil. On recto of free front endpaper, purple stamp of Lifar and annotation in his hand: "Parade / Partition de Satie / de Cocteau / de Massine / Ballets Russes de Diaghilev / 1917 / Col. Serge Lifar."
>
> The two piano parts are written on facing pages. The annotations by Cocteau are in black pencil and green or red ink. Massine's annotations, in Russian, are in black pencil. Lifar's purple stamp appears passim. The pages marked "bis" are primarily textual and are mostly in Cocteau's hand, with interventions from Massine and possibly others. The incipits are as follows:
>
> p. 13 bis and 14 bis: [Le Manager] "UN - HOMME - BIEN - AVERTI - EN - VAUT - DEUX!"
>
> p. 15 bis and 16 bis: [Le Manager de la petite Américaine] "C'EST UN CRIME DE - TUER - EN - SOI - LA - CURIOSITÉ"
>
> p. 29 bis and 30 bis: "L'appareil Mors [sic] tout seul"
>
> p. 31 bis and 32 bis: [Manager de l'acrobate] "PRENEZ / VOS / JAMBES / A / VOTRE / COU …"
>
> p. 43 bis and 44 bis: "Cris des trois managers ensemble"
>
> The additional musical notations in pencil that appear on p. 13, 14, 16, 20, 22, 32 bis, are possibly in Satie's hand.

Bound in black sheepskin, with the title "PARADE," slanted, gilt-tooled, in the middle of the front board.

This manuscript is not mentioned in Cocteau, *Théâtre complet*, p. 1577–78.
Heinrich Schütz to Henry Miller, p. 114–15.
London, Sotheby's, 9 May 1984, lot 214.
FRKF 297

Sonnerie pour réveiller le bon gros rois des singes

Holograph manuscript, signed, of this fanfare for two trumpets in C, 1921, 1 p. Notated in black ink on 10-staff paper. Full title given in Satie's hand as: "Sonnerie pour réveiller le bon gros Roi des Singes (lequel ne dort toujours que d'un oeil)." Signed at the end and dated 30 Aug. 1921.

FRKF 379

II. NON-MUSIC MANUSCRIPT

Paul et Virginie

Autograph manuscript notebook and autograph note in Satie's hand toward this unrealized project in collaboration with Jean Cocteau and Raymond Radiguet, n.d., 7 p. Written in black ink on the recto sides of the first six leaves of a ruled notebook ("Le Fénelon," Papeterie de l'Éperon, Paris, 17 × 22 cm) and a separate fragment from a sheet of music paper. The notebook contains a synopsis, scene by scene, for act 1, and ends at the heading for act 2. The single sheet is entitled: "Les diverses Tessitures de 'Paul et Virginie' / considérées au point de vue 'timbre.'"

This manuscript is not mentioned in Cocteau, *Théâtre complet*, p. 1624–25.
Paris, Ader-Picard-Tajan (Drouot), 4 June 1986, lot 122.
FRKF 1180

III. LETTERS

To Jean Cocteau

> [1916 July 31] "Lundi matin" [Paris*] ALS, 1 p. Printed "carte pneumatique" on the address side. *Correspondance*, p. 250.
>
> [1916 Nov. 20] "Lundi matin" [Paris*] ALS, 1 p. Mentions Roland-Manuel, Cyprian Godebski, and Mme Claude Debussy. Printed "carte pneumatique" on the address side. *Correspondance*, p. 266–67.
>
> [1918 April 7] "Dimanche gras" [Paris*] ALS, 2 p. Mentions Auric and Winnaretta (Singer), princesse de Polignac. *Correspondance*, p. 326.
>
> [1918 Oct. 22] "Mardi midi" [Paris*] ALS, 2 p. Mentions Auric and Louis Durey. *Correspondance*, p. 343.
>
> [1920 Aug. 26] n.p., ANS in pencil, 1 p. Mentions Caryathis. *Correspondance*, p. 421–22.
>
> [1921 July 25*] "1923 Dec. 25," Arcueil-Cachan, ALS, 2 p. Mentions Hébertot, Kisling, and Georges Braque. *Correspondance*, p. 451–52.
>
> 1921 July 28, Arcueil-Cachan, ALS, 2 p, concerning *Paul et Virginie*; mentions Derain and Radiguet. *Correspondance*, p. 452.
>
> [1921 Aug. 3] Arcueil-Cachan, APCS. Mentions Derain, Hébertot, Radiguet, and Pierre Bertin. *Correspondance*, p. 453.
>
> 1921 Aug. 26, Arcueil-Cachan, ALS, 2 p., concerning *Paul et Virginie*; mentions Poulenc. *Correspondance*, p. 455–56.

SATIE [273]

1921 Aug. 31 [Paris?] APCS, concerning *Paul et Virginie*. *Correspondance*, p. 456.

1921 Sept. 5, Arcueil-Cachan, ALS, 2 p., concerning *Paul et Virginie*. *Correspondance*, p. 457–58.

1921 Oct. 28, Arcueil-Cachan, ALS, 2 p., concerning Derain. *Correspondance*, p. 464.

All of the above are tipped in a slim album bound in blue cloth.

From the collection of Jacques Guérin.
Paris, Ader-Picard-Tajan (Drouot), 4 June 1986, lot 121.
FRKF 1179

To Roland-Manuel

1919 March 15, Arcueil-Cachan, ALS, 2 p., concerning *Socrate*. *Correspondance*, p. 356.

n.d., n.p., ALS, 4 p., a humorous letter, with no form of salutation. Incipit: "J'ai peut-être été un peu vif." Not located in *Correspondance*.

Paris, Paul Renaud (Drouot), 14 May 1986, lots 22, 26.
FRKF 1183–84

To Misia Edwards (Sert)

1919 April 27 [i.e. 26] [Paris*] ALS, 2 p., concerning Diaghilev and *Parade*. "Carte pneumatique" printed on the address side. *Correspondance*, p. 362–63.

Paris, Laurin-Guilloux-Buffetaud-Tailleur (Drouot), 1 July 1986, lot 281.
FRKF 1178

IV. PRINTED MUSIC

Sports & divertissements. Musique d'Erik Satie. Dessins de Ch. Martin. Paris: Publications Lucien Vogel, 1914.

Oblong folio, 23 leaves, including one colored plate, 44.5 × 39.5 cm. No. 343 of the 675 ordinary copies, from a total edition of 900, numbered at the colophon. The preface by Satie is dated 15 May 1914. Ownership inscription on colophon page: "Property of / Rollo Myers."

London, Phillips, 27 June 1985, lot 623.
FRKF 1419

V. MISCELLANEOUS

Cartulaire de l'église métropolitaine d'art de Jésus conducteur, no. 1 (May 1895). Three contributions by Satie on p. [1] under the headings "Suprématiales" and "Confrériales."

FRKF 1419

HENRI SAUGUET (1901–89)

Letters to Pierre Bernac

1963 Aug. 6, Coutras (Gironde), ALS, 3 p., concerning the creation of Friends of Francis Poulenc.

1963 Aug. 22, Coutras (Gironde), ALS, 2 p., concerning concerts by boys' choirs; also mentions Henri Barraud and Darius Milhaud.

Paris, Oger-Dumont (Drouot), 14 Feb. 1985, lot 83.
FRKF 698

FRANZ SCHUBERT (1797–1828)

I. MUSIC MANUSCRIPTS

Als ich sie erröten sah, D. 153

Holograph manuscript, incomplete, of this song for voice and piano, on a poem by B.A. Ehrlich, 1815, 4 p. Notated in black ink on a bifolium of tall 12-staff paper. At the top of p. [1] in Schubert's hand: "Als ich Sie erröten sah. / Gedicht von Ehrlich. / Frz Schubert m[ano]p[ropr]ia / den 19. Februar [1]815." The final 14 bars are lacking.

London, Sotheby's, 17 May 1990, lot 233.
FRKF 1356

Morgenlied, D. 381
Abendlied, D. 382

Holograph manuscripts of these songs for voice and piano on texts by an unidentified author, 3 p. Notated in black ink on p. [1] and on p. [2–3], respectively, of a single bifolium of oblong 16-staff paper. At the top of p. [1] in Schubert's hand: "Morgenlied. Sch[ubert]m[anu]p[ropria] Den 24. Februar 1816. / Franz Schubert mpia." The text of stanzas 2–4 is written at the bottom of the page in Schubert's hand. At the top of p. [2] in Schubert's hand: "Abendlied. Schmp Den 24. Februar 1816. / Franz Schubert mpia." The text of stanzas 2 and 3 is written in Schubert's hand at the top of p. [3].

Marburg, Stargardt, 26–27 Nov. 1985, lot 900.
FRKF 1156

Fantasy in F minor, for piano four-hands, D. 940

Holograph draft and sketches, 1828, 24 p. notated in black ink on a separate bifolium, a gathering of three nested bifolia, and another separate bifolium, all of oblong 12-staff paper. At the top of the first page, in Schubert's hand: "Fantasia. / Jänuar 1828 / frz Schubert m[anu]pr[opr]ia."

See Franz Schubert, *Fantasie in f-Moll D 940 für Klavier zu vier Händen: Entwurf* in the Pierpont Morgan Library, New York; *eigenhändige Reinschrift in der Musiksammlung der Österreichischen Nationalbibliothek*. Facsimile edition, edited by Hans-Joachim Hinrischen, introduction by Günter Brosche (Tutzing: H. Schneider, 1991).

Heinrich Schütz to Henry Miller, p. 28–29.
FRKF 214A

Romanze, D. 114

Fragment, partly holograph, from the first version of this song for voice and piano, on a text by Friedrich von Matthisson. The manuscript is written in black ink on both sides of an oblong sheet of 16-staff paper. It begins "Fräulein hörchte" and ends with the words "Der Vater gruft." The words are in the hand of a copyist, the music, tempo, and expressive markings in Schubert's hand. Dated by Grove Sept. 1814.

Marburg, Stargardt, 19–20 June 1984, lot 917.
FRKF 489

II. LETTER

To Joseph Gross

[1821] [Vienna?] ALS, 1 p., concerning his *Deutsche Tänze*, op. 9. With a pencilled note indicating that the "Überbringer" referred to in the letter is Joseph Hüttenbrenner, younger brother of the composer Anselm Hüttenbrenner.

Marburg, Stargardt, 26–27 Nov. 1985, lot 901.
FRKF 1157

III. PRINTED MUSIC

Erlkönig. Ballade von Göthe, in Musik gesetzt und Seiner Excellenz dem hochgebohrnen Herrn Herrn Moritz Grafen von Dietrichstein in tiefer Ehrfurcht gewidmet von Franz Schubert. 1tes Werk. Vienna: in Comission bey Cappi und Diabelli, [1821]. D. 328 (A)

[1–3], 4–15 [+1] p. First edition, with the ownership inscription of Augusta Sachs [?] on the front wrapper. Initialed and numbered by Schubert at the bottom of p. [16]: "FSmp [Franz Schubert manu propria] 91."

Marburg, Stargardt, 19–20 June 1984, lot 918.
FRKF 490

CLARA SCHUMANN (1819–96)

Piano variations on a theme by Robert Schumann, op. 20

Holograph manuscript of Variation VI, n.d., 1 p. Notated in black ink on the verso side of a single album leaf (22.5 × 14 cm) with a blue decorative border and the 6 staves also printed in blue. At the top of the page: "Var: VI. / Clara Schumann. / Op:20." Pasted on a sheet of paper, inscribed: "Der lieben verehrten / Frau Natalie Macfarren / von / Clara Schumann. / Landau April 1869."

Letter to her son Ferdinand Schumann

1884 July 11, Obersalzberg bei Berchtesgaden, ALS, 4 p.

Paris, Oger-Dumont (Drouot), 14 Feb. 1985, lots 30–31.
FRKF 680, 686

ELISABETH SCHUMANN (1888–1952)

Letters to Hugo Burghauser

1937 Nov. 29, Hyde Park Hotel, Knightsbridge, London[S], ALS, 2 p.

1938 Jan. 19, Hotel Meurice, New York[S], ALS, 2 p.

1938 April 14, Nice, APCS

1940 Feb. 8, n.p., TLS, 1 p. Drawings in an unidentified hand on the verso.

1941 July 16, Bird Cage Studio, Rockport, Maine[S], ALS, 2 p.

1942 June 27, Rockport, Maine, ALS, 3 p.

1942 Aug. 11, Bird Cage Studio, Rockport, Maine[S], ALS, 2 p.

1943 Feb. 27, n.p., ANS on the recto of a visiting card (env)

1943 June 28, Bird Cage Studio, Rockport, Maine[S], ALS, 2 p.

1943 July 26, Bird Cage Studio, Rockport, Maine[S], ALS, 2 p.

1944 Oct. 26, Reno, ALS, 2 p.

1945 Oct. 9, n.p., ALS, 3 p.

1950 June 16, R.M.S. "Caronia," Cunard Line[S], ALS, 4 p.

1951 July 16, New York, ALS, 4 p.

1951 Sept. 23, West Wycombe Park, Bucks[S] (embossed), ALS, 2 p.

Accompanied by miscellaneous printed ephemera concerning Strauss and Elisabeth Schumann.

London, Sotheby's, 27–28 Nov. 1986, lot 637.
FRKF 1363

MARIE SCHUMANN (1841–1929)

Letter to Johannes Brahms

1896 Aug. 17 [Frankfurt] ALS, 8 p. Mentions Hanslick.

Paris, Oger-Dumont (Drouot), 14 Feb. 1985, lot 32.
FRKF 687

ROBERT SCHUMANN (1810–56)

I. MUSIC MANUSCRIPTS

Die Blume der Ergebung, op. 83, no. 2

Holograph manuscript of this song for voice and piano on a text by Friedrich Rückert, n.d., 5 p. Notated in black ink on p. [3]–[7] of a gathering of two bifolia of oblong 10-staff paper with an embossed decorative border. On p. [1] in Schumann's hand: "Die Blume der Ergebung / von / F. Rückert." The title and Rückert's name are repeated at the top of p. [3]. Signed "R. Schumann" at the end. Dated 1850 by Grove.

Accompanied by an ALS from G.F. Bainbridge, private secretary to the Duke of Edinburgh, to Thomas Pettit, Esq., on stationery of Clarence House, St. James's, 1893 Jan. 3, 2 p., concerning this manuscript, then evidently in the possession of the Duke of Edinburgh.

London, Sotheby's, 17 May 1990, lot 49.
FRKF 1300

Fest-Ouvertüre, op. 123

Holograph manuscript of Schumann's own arrangement for piano four-hands of this cantata, n.d., 7 p. The manuscript is written in black ink, with a few additions in red pencil, on two single bifolia of tall 24-staff paper. On p. [1] in the upper right corner, in pencil, in an unidentified hand: "Op. 123."

The *Fest-Ouvertüre*, for tenor, chorus, and orchestra, on Matthias Claudius's *Rheinweinlied*, was composed in 1853 and premiered in Düsseldorf on 17 May 1853.

Marburg, Stargardt, 19–20 June 1984, lot 925.
FRKF 491

Herbstlied, op. 89, no. 3
In's freie, op. 89, no. 5

Holograph manuscript drafts for these two songs for voice and piano on texts by Wilfred von der Neun (Friedrich Wilhelm Schöpff), 1850, 2 p. Notated in black/dark brown ink on both sides of a single sheet of tall grey 24-staff paper; abundantly corrected. On the recto are the last 24 bars of *Herbstlied*, dated at the end "D[resden] 11ten Mai 1850"; on the verso, the first 31 measures of *In's freie*.

Heinrich Schütz to Henry Miller, p. 46–47.
London, Sotheby's, 29 Nov. 1985, lot 218.
FRKF 1044

II. LETTERS

To Friedrich Kistner

1840 July 26 [Leipzig] ALS, 1 p., concerning the publication of *Myrten*.

London, Sotheby's, 9–10 May 1985, lot 198.
FRKF 728

To [Carl Reinecke?]

1849 April 9 [Dresden] ALS, 4 p., concerning *Variations on Bach's first French Suite*. Includes one musical quotation. Jansen 340 (p. 301).

Marburg, Stargardt, 5–6 March 1985, lot 890.
FRKF 821

To Heinrich Schmidt

[1843 Dec.?] n.p. ALS, 1 p.

Marburg, Stargardt, 19 June 1984, lot 926.
FRKF 483

To Karl Friedrich Wecker

1854 Jan. 22, Hannover, ALS, 2 p. Mentions Clara Schumann and Joseph Joachim. With a note on the address side in the hand of Otto Schmöll, Wecker's grand nephew, dated Vienna, 1944 Sept. 1.

Marburg, Stargardt, 5–6 March 1985, lot 891.
FRKF 822

EUGÈNE SCRIBE (1791–1861)

I. MANUSCRIPT

Une femme qui se croit veuve

Autograph manuscript of this comedy in three acts, n.d., 56 p., written in black ink, with occasional pencil corrections, on the first 54 pages of a sewn gathering of 40 bifolia. Signed "Eugène Scribe" at the end.

No play with this title is in Scribe's *Oeuvres complètes* (Paris: Dentu, 1874–85); not in BnF printed or online catalog.

Paris, Le Roux-Mathias (Drouot) 19 April 1985, lot 244.
FRKF 718a

II. LETTERS

To Josef Dessauer

n.y. Sept. 9, Séricourt, ALS, 2 p., declining a commission.

Marburg, Stargardt, 26–27 Nov. 1985, lot 285.
FRKF 1276

To "Monsieur Henriot libraire"

[1840 Oct.] n.p., ALS, 3 p. Mentions *Le verre d'eau*, *Le lion amoureux*, and *La favorite*.

Paris, Le Roux-Mathias (Drouot), 19 April 1985, lot 244.
FRKF 718b

To Nestor Roqueplan

1849 Feb. 13, n.p., ALS, 2 p., concerning rehearsals for *Le prophète*.

Paris, Le Roux-Mathias (Drouot), 19 April 1985, lot 243.
FRKF 717b

To the president and members of the Commission de l'opéra

1831 June 7, Paris, ALS, 3 p., concerning his pension; lists the works he has contributed and mentions the yet unperformed *Robert le diable*.

Paris, Le Roux-Mathias (Drouot), 19 April 1985, lot 243.
FRKF 717a

GEORGE BERNARD SHAW (1856–1950)

Letter to George Alexander

1914 May 24, 10 Adelphi Terrace, W.C. [London][S] ALS, 2 p., concerning the staging of *Pygmalion*.

London, Sotheby's, 22 July 1985, lot 327.
FRKF 888

Letters to Frederick H. Evans

Typescript copy, carbon, with manuscript corrections, 95 p., stitched together. In a slipcase with bookplate of Frederick H. Evans. Accompanied by: *Forty-three original drawings by Aubrey Beardsley: The collection of Frederick H. Evans of London. To be sold Thursday evening, March Twentieth at 8:15 o'clock* (New York: The Anderson Galleries, 1919), 10 p., an auction catalogue.

New York, Swann Galleries, 9 May 1985, lot 62.
FRKF 651

ERNEST H. SHEPARD (1879–1976)

Drawings for A.A. Milne's *When we were very young*

Unless otherwise noted, these 62 preparatory drawings on 59 sheets are in pencil on paper. They include:

- "Bad Sir Brian Botany," 5 drawings pasted on a large sheet of paper, with an additional drawing on the sheet, signed in the lower right corner.
- "At home," initialed in the lower left corner.
- "Before tea," initialed in the lower left corner.
- "Three Foxes," signed in the lower right corner.
- "Three foxes" and "Politeness," 2 drawings mounted together, both signed in the lower right corner.
- "At the zoo," unsigned.
- "Rice pudding." 3 small drawings pasted on a large sheet of paper, the first signed in the lower left corner, the other two initialed in the lower right corner.
- "The King's Breakfast," signed in the lower right corner.
- "Daffodownlilly," initialed in the lower right corner.
- "Disobedience," signed in the lower left corner.
- "The island" [previous title, "Desert Island," cancelled], initialed in the lower right corner.
- "Jonathan Jo," signed in the lower left corner.
- "Nursery chairs," signed in the lower right corner.

"Twinkletoes," signed in the lower left corner.

"Four friends," initialed in the lower right corner.

"Waterlilies," 2 drawings, matted together, both signed in the lower right corner.

"Happiness," signed in the lower right corner.

"Spring morning," 2 drawings, matted together, both initialed in the lower left corner.

"Lines & Squares," signed in the lower right corner.

"Brownie" and "Independence," 2 drawings matted together, the first initialed in the lower left corner, the second signed in the lower left corner.

"Corner of the Street," initialed in the lower right corner.

"Summer afternoon," signed in the lower left corner.

"Wrong House," signed in the lower left corner.

"In the fashion," initialed in the lower left corner.

"Market Square," 2 drawings matted together, one signed in the lower left corner, the other signed center right.

[Title not deciphered], signed in the lower right corner.

"Happiness" and "The Christening," 2 drawings matted together, one signed in the lower right corner, the other initialed in the lower right corner.

"The Alchemist" and "If I were king," 2 drawings matted together, the first signed in the lower right corner, the other initialed in the lower right corner.

"Growing up," "Twinkletoes," and "Shoes with laces," 3 drawings on a single sheet of paper, signed in the lower left corner.

"Vespers," not signed.

"Hoppity," signed in the lower right corner.

"Buckingham Palace," 2 drawings, numbered 1 and 2, matted together, both initialed in the lower right corner.

"Missing," signed in the lower right corner.

"Teddy Bear," unsigned.

"Mirror" and "Halfway Down," 2 drawings matted together, both signed in the lower right corner.

"Hoppity," signed in the lower right corner.

"Verses 1 to 4," signed in the lower left corner.

"Shoes and Stockings," initialed in the lower left corner.

"C.R. wiggling his toes," pencil and graphite, initialed in the lower right corner.

"Knights and Ladies," initialed in the lower right corner.

"Shoes and stockings" and "Mirror," 2 drawings on a single sheet, signed in center right.

"Little Bo-Peep and Little Boy-Blue," signed in the lower right corner.

"Invaders," signed in the lower left corner.

Accompanied by the following letters from Ernest H. Shepard to Carl H. Pforzheimer, all on the stationery of Long Meadow, Longdown, Guildford, concerning Pforzheimer's purchase of the original drawings for *When we were very young*.

1928 June 30, ALS, 1 p.

1928 Dec. 26, ALS, 1 p., to "Dr. Rosenbach"

1929 Jan. 26, ALS, 4 p. and autograph receipt, 1 p. (env)

Also, TLS from F.B. Adams, Jr. to Carl H. Pforzheimer, 1954 June 24, The Pierpont Morgan Library, New York[S], 1 p., requesting permission to borrow the manuscript of *When we were very young* for exhibition, and a receipt, signed by Herbert Cahoon, 1954 Oct. 26, The Pierpont Morgan Library, New York[S], concerning the loan of three of the drawings to the Morgan Library for a children's literature exhibition from Nov. 1, 1954, to Feb. 28, 1955, 1 p.

London, Sotheby's, 10 July 1986, lot 199.
FRKF 1298

CLAUDE ALLIN SHEPPERSON (1867–1921)

"Elizabeth and her English Garden"

Two pen-and-ink cartoons on paper (each 24.5 × 17 cm) mounted on Whatman's water colour sketching board, both signed, the first at bottom center, the second at bottom left. The one at the top is captioned "The Rose Border," the one at the bottom "Bedding-out Plants."

The title is an allusion to Elizabeth von Arnim's *Elizabeth and her German Garden*, first published in 1898.

London, Christie's, 21 July 1981, lot 251.
FRKF 104

[Guy Mannering]

Pen-and-ink drawing on board (13 × 21 cm), mounted on heavy board, for an illustration to Sir Walter Scott's *Guy Mannering*, showing the hero, a stranger, and a female gypsy; signed in the lower right corner. Pasted on the back is this inscription, written in pencil on board: "Guy Mannering / Ere Mannering, somewhat struck by the man's gesture & insolent tone of voice, had made any answer, the gypsy had emerged from her vault & joined the stranger. He questioned her in an undertone, looking at Mannering. – 'A shark alongside – eh?'" No edition of *Guy Mannering* illustrated by Shepperson is listed in the *British Museum Catalogue*.

London, Christie's, 21 July 1981, lot 251.
FRKF 106

[Is that butter?]

Pen-and-ink cartoon on paper (36 × 26 cm) mounted on heavy board, signed in ink at lower left and in pencil, underneath the drawing, in the lower right corner. Manuscript caption on the verso: "Guest - Who has just been introduced by the hostess to her niece - gazing fixedly beyond her, at the tea-table / ' How d'you [cancelled: do] — Is that BUTTER?'"

Published in *Punch*, 19 June 1917.

London, Christie's, 21 July 1981, lot 251.
FRKF 103

JEAN SIBELIUS (1865–1957)

I. MUSIC MANUSCRIPTS

Harpolekaren och hans son, op. 38, no. 4

Holograph manuscript of this song for voice and piano, n.d., 6 p. The manuscript is written in black ink on two nested bifolia of 20-staff paper (B & H. Nr 12. C.). It is notated in systems of 4 staves (the second blank) and occupies six pages, of which only 1 and 3–5 are paginated, beginning with the front of the outer bifolium. On p. 1 is the signature of Ida Ekman in the upper right corner. In Sibelius's hand: "Harpolekaren och hans son. / (Ur 'Vapensmeden') / V. Rydberg / Jean Sibelius."

Harpolekaren och hans son (The harper and his son), a setting of a text by Viktor Rydberg (1828–95), was published in 1904.

London, Sotheby's, 17 Nov. 1983, lot 177.
FRKF 230.3

Jag ville, jag vore i Indialand, op. 38, no. 5

Holograph manuscript of this song for voice and piano, n.d., 5 p., written in black ink, with additional corrections in blue pencil, on two nested bifolia (the outer one detached) of 12-staff manuscript ruled for solo and keyboard (B. & H. Nr 5.C.). It begins on the first page of the inner bifolium and occupies five pages, numbered 1 to 5 by the composer. Inscribed by the composer in pencil, on the side of the first page of the outer bifolium: "Fru Ida Ekman." Signed by Ida Ekman in the upper right corner of the same page.

The title is in her hand: "Sibelius. / Jag ville jag vore. / (Manuscript)."

On p. 1, in Sibelius's hand: "Jag ville, jag vore. / (Gustav Fröding) / Jean Sibelius."

"Jag ville, jag vore i Indialand" (I wished I dwelled in India land"), on a text by Gustaf Fröding (1860–1911), was composed in 1904.

London, Sotheby's, 17 Nov. 1983, lot 178.
FRKF 230.4

Soluppgång, op. 37, no. 3

Version for voice and piano

Holograph manuscript , n.d. [1898], 3 p., written in dark blue ink, with a few additional pencil annotations, on p. [2] to [4] of a single bifolium of 20-staff paper At the head of the manuscript, on p. [2] in Sibelius's hand: "Soluppgång. / (Tor Hedberg) / Jean Sibelius." On p. [1] in the hand of Ida Ekman: "Sibelius. / Soluppgång / (Manuscript)." Page [1] is also signed by Ida Ekman in the upper right corner. A first draft of measures 43–45 at the top of p. [4] is cancelled.

Set to a poem by the Swedish poet Tor Hedberg (1862–1931), *Soluppgång* was composed in 1898 and premiered in Helsinki in 1902 by Ida Ekman. It was first published in 1902.

Heinrich Schütz to Henry Miller, p. 90–91.

Version for voice and orchestra

Holograph manuscript, n.d., 9 p., written in black ink with a few additional annotations in black and red pencil. The manuscript occupies 9 pages, paginated 1 through 9, spread over a gathering of one single and two nested bifolia, stitched together, of 24-staff paper (B & H. Nr 14. A.).

On the first page of the first bifolium, signature of Ida Ekman in the upper right corner and the following dedication: "Till Ida Ekman / den oförlikneliga / 'Sibelius-sangersken' / med [?]nemhet fran / Jean Sibelius." The title *Soluppgång* is also written below in red pencil. At the top of p. 1 is the signature of Ida Ekman in the upper right corner and, in Sibelius's hand: "Soluppgang / Tor Hedberg / Sang med piano eller / Orchester arrangemang / Jean Sibelius / Op 37 N= 3."

This orchestral version is not recorded by Grove.

London, Sotheby's, 17 Nov. 1983, lot 175–76.
FRKF 230.1–2

DAME EDITH SITWELL (1887–1964)

Letter to Christian Bérard

n.d. "Saturday," Sesame Imperial Club, London[S], ALS, 2 p., confirming an invitation.

Monaco, Sotheby's, 11 Oct. 1991, lot 411.
FRKF 1391c

GEORGIA SITWELL (1905–80)

Letter to "cher ami"

n.y. Aug. 6, Weston Hall, Towcester, Northants.[S], ALS, 3 p., concerning some information to be forwarded to the Duchess of Winchester, whose address is given on p. [2], in French.

Monaco, Sotheby's, 11 Oct. 1991, lot 411.
FRKF 1391d

OSBERT SITWELL (1892–1969)

Letter to Boris Kochno

1935 May 28, 2, Carlyle Square, S.W.3. [London][S] TLS, 1 p., concerning Walton; mentions the *First Symphony*.

Monaco, Sotheby's, 11 Oct. 1991, lot 411.
FRKF 1391b

THÉOPHILE ALEXANDRE STEINLEN (1859–1923)

Correspondence with Germaine Perrin

Unless otherwise noted, the letters are ALS. The dates of letters from Germaine Perrin are marked with superscript GP.

1922

July: [12[GP]] ("mercredi 4 hs," Lausanne*, 1 p., with cryptic annotations by Steinlen); [17] ("lundi 5 h," 73 rue Caulaincourt, [Paris][S], 1 p.)

1923

July: 13 (n.y. [afternoon], 21 R[ue] Caulaincourt, [Paris], 1 p.); 13 ([evening], Paris, 1 p.); [13[GP]] (n.y. "Vendredi," n.p., 2 p.); 15 (n.y., n.p., 4 p.); 16 (n.y., "Atelier," [Paris?], 2 p.); [17*] (Persan-Beaumont*, APCS); [17[GP]] ("Jeudi," Lausanne*, 1 p., env); 18 (73 [Rue] Caul[aincour]t, [Paris], 2 p.); 19 (73 [Rue Caulaincourt], [Paris], 2 p.); 20 (Paris, 2 p.); [21*] ("2 h ½," 21 Rue Caul[aincourt], [Paris], 1 p.); 21[GP] (n.y., n.p., 2 p.); 23 ([morning], Jouy[-la-Fontaine], 1 p.); 23 (n.y. [afternoon], Jouy-la-Fontaine, 2 p.); 26 (Jouy[-la-Fontaine], 2 p.); 27 (Maurecourt*, 1 p.); 29 ([evening], Jouy[-la-Fontaine], 2 p.); 29 (Paris*, 1 p.); 30 (n.y. [afternoon], Paris, 2 p.); 30 ([evening], Paris, 2 p.); 31 (n.y. [morning], Paris, 4 p.); 31 (n.y. [afternoon], Jouy[-la-Fontaine], 2 p.)

August: 1 ([morning], Maurecourt*, 1 p); 1 ([afternoon], Jouy[-la-Fontaine], 1 p.); 1 (n.p., APCS); 2 (n.y., Jouy[-la-Fontaine], 2 p.); [3[GP]] ("Samedi," Corvay, La Tuilière, 2 p., env); 4 (n.y., Jouy[-la-Fontaine], 6 p.); [5[GP]] ("Dimanche soir," Publier*, 2 p., env); 6 (Jouy[-la-Fontaine], 1 p.); 6[GP] ("2 hs," n.p., 2 p.); [6[GP]] ("Lundi soir," Publier*, 2 p., env); 7 (Maurecourt*, 1 p.); 8[GP] ([morning], Publier*, 2 p., env); [8[GP]] ("Mercredi soir," Evian-les-Bains*, 2 p., env); 9 (n.y., Jouy[-la-Fontaine], 4 p.); [9[GP]] ("Jeudi soir," Publier*, 4 p., env); 10 ([evening], Paris, 1 p.); 10 (Jouy[-la-Fontaine], 1 p.); 11 (Jouy[-la-Fontaine], 1 p.); 11[GP] (Publier*, 4 p., env); 12 (Jouy[-la-Fontaine], 1 p.); [13] ("Lundi," Maurecourt*, 1 p.); 13[GP] (Lenk, 2 p., env); 14 (Jouy[-la-Fontaine], 1 p.); [14[GP]] ("mardi," Lenk, 6 p., env); 15 (Jouy[-la-Fontaine], 1 p.); 16 ([afternoon], Jouy[-la-Fontaine], 1 p.); 16 (n.y. [evening], Jouy[-la-Fontaine], 4 p.); 16[GP] (Lenk*, 2 p., env); [17[GP]] ("vendredi soir," Lenk*, 3 p., env); 18 (n.y. [afternoon], Jouy[-la-Fontaine], 4 p.); 18 ([evening], n.p., 1 p.); 18 (n.y., Jouy[-la-Fontaine], 4 p.); [18[GP]] ("samedi soir," Lenk*, 4 p., env); 20 (Jouy-[la-Fontaine], 1 p.); 20[GP] (Lenk, 2 p., env); [21[GP]] ("mardi matin," Lenk, 2 p., env); [22[GP]] ("mercredi matin," Switzerland*, APCS, env); [22[GP]] ("mercredi soir," St. Moritz*, 2 p., env); [24[GP]] ("vendredi soir," Lugano, 4 p., env); 26 (Jouy[-la-Fontaine], 1 p.); [26[GP]] ("Dimanche 4 hs," Lausanne, 2 p., env); [27] ("Lundi," "Gare de Maurecourt," 1 p.); 27 (n.y., n.p., 4 p.); 27[GP] (n.y., Lausanne, 3 p.); 28 ([morning], Jouy[-la-Fontaine], 1 p); 28 (21 Rue Caulaincourt XVIIIe, [Paris][S], 1 p.); [28[GP]] ("Mardi midi," Lausanne*, 2 p., env); 29 (n.y., Jouy[-la-Fontaine], 4 p.); 30 (n.p., 4 p.); 31 (Jouy[-la-Fontaine], 1 p.)

September: 1 (n.y., Paris, 2 p.); 1 (n.y., 21 Rue Caulaincourt XVIIIe, [Paris][S], 2 p.); [1[GP]] ("Samedi 3 hs," Lausanne*, 2 p., env); 2 (n.y., Jouy[-la-Fontaine], 2 p.); [2[GP]] ("Dimanche," Lausanne*, 2 p., env); 3 (Jouy[-la-Fontaine], 1 p.); 4 (n.y., Jouy[-la-Fontaine], 1 p.); [4[GP]] ("Mardi 3 hs," Lausanne*, 2 p., env); 5 (Jouy[-la-Fontaine], 1 p.); 7 (Jouy[-la-Fontaine], 1 p.); 9 (n.y., Jouy[-la-Fontaine], 2 p.); 10 (Jouy[-la-Fontaine], 1 p.); 11 (Paris, 1 p.); 14 (Jouy[-la-Fontaine], 1 p.); 15 (Paris, 1 p.); [16[GP]] ("Dimanche," Lausanne*, 2 p., env); 20 (Maurecourt*, 1 p.); 21 (Jouy-la-Fontaine, 1 p.); 23[GP] (n.y., n.p., 2 p.); 24 (n.y., Paris, 1 p.); 26 ([evening], Paris*, 1 p.); 26 (n.y., n.p., 1 p.); 27 (Paris, 1 p.); [28] ("Vendredi soir," Paris, 1 p.); 29 (Paris*, 1 p.)

October: 1 (Paris, 1 p.); [3] ("mercredi matin," Paris*, 1 p.); 4 (Paris*, 1 p.); 5 (Paris*, 1 p.); [6] ("Samedi soir," Paris*, 1 p.); [8] ("lundi," Paris*, 1 p.); 9 (Paris, 1 p.); [16] ("Mardi," Paris*, 1 p.); 17 (Paris, 1 p.); 23 (Paris, 4 p.); 30 (Paris, 1 p.)

November: [16] ("Vendredi," Paris, 1 p.)

Undated

ALS, "vendredi matin," 21 R[ue] C[aulaincour]t, 4 p.
ALS, "samedi," [Paris] 1 p.
ALS, "mardi 5 h matin," n.p., 2 p.
ALS, "mardi soir," n.p., 10 p.
ALS, "mercredi," n.p., 2 p.
ALS, "vendredi 11 h.," n.p., 2 p.

Also, three empty envelopes addressed to Steinlen by Germaine Perrin, postmarked 2, 5, and 14 August 1923.

The following letters from Germaine Perrin were in an envelope marked, in her hand: "Etaient dans le portefeuille le 13 décembre 1923" [the day Steinlen died]:

1923 July 26, Corvay, ALS, 2 p.
[1923] Aug. 1, Champanges, ALS, 4 p.
1923 Nov. 13, n.p., ALS, 1 p.
1923 Dec. 10, n.p., ALS, 1 p.
n.d., "mardi," n.p., ALS, 1 p.
n.d., "Lundi soir," n.p., ALS, 2 p.

Undated letters from Germaine Perrin:

ANS, "mercredi," n.p., 1 p.
ALS, "Lundi," n.p., 2 p.
ALS, "Dimanche," n.p., 2 p.
ALS, "Mercredi 7 hs soir," Corvay, 2 p.
ALS, "vendredi soir 10 hr," Champanges, 2 p.
ALS, "vendredi soir," n.p., 2 p.
ALS, "lundi," n.p., 2 p.
ALS, "jeudi soir," n.p., 2 p.
ALS, "samedi," Lausanne, 1 p.
ALS, "vendredi soir," n.p., 3 p.
ALS, "Samedi soir 9 hs ½," Champanges, 4 p.
ALS, "Mardi soir," n.p., 2 p.
ALS, "Samedi soir 7 hs," n.p., 2 p.
ALS, "Jeudi 7 hs. soir," Champanges, 2 p.
ALS, "Mardi soir," n.p., 2 p.
ALS, "Dimanche," n.p., 2 p.
ALS, "lundi soir," n.p., 2 p.
ALS, "Mercredi," Corvay, 1 p.

Accompanied by the following material:

Two ALS to Germaine Perrin from her mother, one on both sides of a card, 1923 Dec. 14, n.p.; the second n.d., "Dimanche," [but after 1923 Dec. 14] n.p, 6 p. On the death of Steinlen.

Nine autograph postcards and letters from pupils from a school in Yverdon, Switzerland [Aug.–Sept. 1923] thanking Steinlen for visiting their class in [early July?] 1923.

The correspondence documents the tender friendship that developed between Steinlen and Germaine Perrin in the last months of his life. The possibility of a marriage is discussed.

Paris, Laurin-Guilloux-Buffetaud-Tailleur (Drouot), 18 Dec. 1984, lot 282.
FRKF 655

STENDHAL (PSEUDONYM OF HENRI BEYLE, 1783–1842)

"Testament de H.M. Beyle né à Grenoble en 1783"

Autograph manuscript, signed, 1835, 1 p., leaving his possessions to his sister Pauline; also mentions Romain Collomb, Domenico di Fiori, and Prosper Mérimée. Dated 8 Feb. 1835. *Correspondance générale*, V:391.

Paris, Ader-Picard-Tajan (Drouot), 22 Nov. 1985, lot 43.
FRKF 1386

Letter to Henri de Latouche

[1825] "ce Jeudi à 2 h.," n.p., ALS, 2 p., concerning Rossini's *Semiramide*. Signed H. Beyle. *Correspondance générale*, III:545–46.

Marburg, Stargardt, 5–6 March 1985, lot 355.
FRKF 804

Vies de Haydn, de Mozart et de Métastase. Paris: de l'imprimerie de P. Didot, l'aîné, imprimeur du roi, 1817.

[i]–viii, [7]–468 [+ 4]. Annotated in pencil throughout by a contemporary reader. Bound in uniform beige morocco by Huser; all edges gilt; on spine, raised bands and author and title in gold lettering; beige morocco and vellum doublures.

Second edition, a reissue of the 1814 edition with a new title page and 3 pages of errata.

Paris, Ader-Picard-Tajan (Drouot), 20 March 1985, lot 102.
FRKF 569

GEORGE STERLING (1869–1926)

"The black hound bays"

Autograph manuscript of this poem, signed, n.d., 4 p., in pencil on the recto of four legal-size mimeographed sheets of a "Report on dredging or placer ground," paginated 1–4 in Sterling's hand. At the top of p. 1, in his hand: "The Black Hound Bays / (Dedicated to all readers of the Sat. Eve. Post)." First published in *Hesperian* (San Francisco, 1930). See Johnson, p. 63.

Lilith

Autograph manuscript of act 1, scenes 2–4 of this dramatic poem, signed, n.d., 14 p. Written in pencil on the recto sides of ruled legal-size paper, paginated 1–14 in Sterling's hand. At the top of p. 1, in his hand: "Lilith. / An allegory of temptation." First published by A.M. Robertson in San Francisco in 1919.

See Johnson, p. 25–26.
From the collection of Estelle Doheny.
Camarillo, California, Christie's, 1–2 Feb. 1988, lot 966.
FRKF 1346.1–2

ROBERT STOLZ (1880–1975)

Ich glaub' mein Glaserl hat ein Loch!

Holograph manuscript of this song for voice and piano, 1965, 3 p. The manuscript is written in pencil on p. [1]–[3] of a bifolium of 12-staff paper (stamped ATV Nr.2). At the top of p. [1] in Stolz's hand: "'Ich glaub' mein Glaserl hat ein Loch!' / Text: Aldo von Pinelli / Musik: Robert Stolz." Signed and dated 30 Aug. 1965 with a presentation inscription to Walter Slezak at the end. Miscellaneous notes on p. [4].

Accompanied by an ALS from Stolz to Slezak, 1945 Dec. 30, New York, 1 p.

New York, Sotheby's, 22 May 1985, lot 424.
FRKF 748, 748.5

OSCAR STRAUS (1870–1954)

Eine Frau, die weiss, was sie will

Autograph 8-measure quotation from this operetta, in blue ink on a half-sheet of staff paper with the following dedication: "To my dear friend Walter Slezak / who created this song / with all good wishes / Oscar Straus / New York, 1946."

Ein Walzertraum

Holograph manuscript, in short score, of Franzi's entrance aria, 1906–07, 6 p. The manuscript is written in pencil on both sides of three leaves of 12-staff paper (J.E. N° 20). At the top of p. [1] in Straus's hand: "N° 10 Entréelied (Franzi) mit Chor." With a torn cover of a J.E. music book with the following inscription, in ink, in Straus's hand: "Original manuscript score 'Walzdream' / Oscar Straus / 1906/07."

Letters to Hugo Klein

1895 June 21, Mödling, ALS, 4 p. Mentions various compositions, including walzes.

1897 Nov. 5, Mainz, ALS, 3 p. (env)

New York, Sotheby's, 22 May 1985, lots 425–26.
FRKF 750, 749, 750.5

ALICE STRAUSS
FRANZ STRAUSS

Letters to Hugo Burghauser

1947 April 10, Garmisch, TLS, 1 p., from Alice Strauss.

1948 Jan. 27, Montreux Palace Hotel, Montreux[S], TLS, 1 p., from Alice Strauss.

1948 April 10, Garmisch, TLS, 1 p., from Alice Strauss.

1948 May 9, Garmisch, TLS, 1 p., from Alice Strauss; mentions Karl Böhm and Igor Stravinsky.

1948 Nov. 3, Montreux-Palace, Montreux[S], ALS, 3 p.

1954 Sept. 25, Dr. Franz Strauss, Garmisch[S], TLS, 1 p., from Franz Strauss.

[1956 Dec. 19, Garmisch*] APCS, from Franz Strauss.

1966 Feb. 5, Dr. Franz Strauss, Garmisch[S], TLS, 1 p., from Franz Strauss, with an autograph postscript in his hand.

1966 Feb. 24, Dr. Franz Strauss, Garmisch[S], TLS, 1 p., from Franz Strauss.

1976 Dec. 26, Dr. Franz Strauss, Garmisch[S], TLS, 1 p., from Alice Strauss.

1978 July 21, n.p., ALS on both sides of a card, from Alice Strauss.

1979 Oct. 11, Garmisch, ALS, 1 p., from Alice Strauss.

[1980?] Jan. 8, Dr. Franz Strauss, Garmisch[S], TLS, 1 p., from Alice Strauss.

Accompanied by:

Printed card with mourning border, dated Garmisch, Sept. 1949 (env), signed by Franz Strauss, acknowledging condolences received on his father's death.

Printed card with mourning border, dated Garmisch, May 1950, with an autograph note by Franz Strauss, acknowledging condolences received on his mother's death.

Photocopy of a TLS from Richard Strauss to "Sehr geehrter Herr Doktor," 1948 Nov. 5, Montreux, 1 p., concerning Maria Jeritza.

Carbon copies of two typed letters from Hugo Burghauser to Franz Strauss, n.d., New York, each 1 p.

Carbon copies of two typed letters from Burghauser to Maria Jeritza, 1976 Dec. 31, New York, 2 p., and 1977 Feb., New York, 1 p.

Autograph note in Burghauser's hand, concerning Maria Jeritza.

Miscellaneous clippings and printed ephemera concerning Strauss and Elisabeth Schumann.

The correspondence deals largely with the unsuccessful attempts of the Strauss family to persuade Maria Jeritza to let them have access to the manuscript of Richard Strauss's song *Malven*, which the composer had presented to her in 1948.

London, Sotheby's, 27–28 Nov. 1986, lot 647.
FRKF 1364.1a–c, 1364.2b

JOHANN STRAUSS (1825–99)

Letter to Gustl

[ca. 1892?] n.p., ALS, 8 p., a denunciation of the musical establishment.

FRKF 356

RICHARD STRAUSS (1864–1949)

I. MUSIC MANUSCRIPTS

Der Arbeitsmann, op. 39, no. 3

Holograph manuscript, in full score, of the orchestral version of this song on a poem by Richard Dehmel, 1918, 14 p. Notated in black ink on four nested bifolia of tall 30-staff paper (B. & H. Nr. 54. A.), paginated 1–14 by the composer. On title page, in Strauss's hand: "Herrn Dr Fritz Sieger / freundschaftlichst gewidmet. / Der Arbeitsmann / (Richard Dehmel) / für eine Singstimme und grosses Orchester / von / Richard Strauss / op. 39 / Aufführungsrecht und / alle Rechte der mechanischen / Vervielfältigung vom Componisten vorbehalten." At the top of p. 1, also in Strauss's hand: "Der Arbeitsmann (Richard Dehmel) / Richard Strauss op. 39/III." Dated Garmisch, 19 Dec. 1918 at the end.

London, Sotheby's, 27 Nov. 1986, lot 645.
FRKF 1353

Malven

Holograph manuscript of this song on a poem by Betty Knobel, 1948, 2 p., in blue ink on p. [1–2] of a bifolium of oblong 14-staff Hug & Co. paper. At top of manuscript, in Strauss's hand: "Malven (Betty Knobel)." Signed in upper right corner and dated Montreux, 23 Nov. 1948, at the end. Inscribed: "Der geliebten Maria diese letzte Rose!"

First published by Boosey & Hawkes, London, in 1985.

Heinrich Schütz to Henry Miller, p. 140–41.
New York, Sotheby's, 11 Dec. 1984, lot 809.
FRKF 389

September

Holograph manuscript on this song on a poem by Hermann Hesse, 1948, 4 p. Written in black ink with corrections in blue ballpoint pen on a bifolium of oblong 14-staff Hug & Co. paper. At top of manuscript, in Strauss's hand: "September (Hermann Hesse) / Richard Strauss." Dated at the end: "Pontresina, 14. Aug. 1948." Autograph inscription: "'Der schönsten Frau der Welt,' der erhabenen 'Kaiserin,' grossmächtigsten 'Prinzessin,' Mari-adne, Marie-andl - Maria Jeritza, der Gütigen und ihrem lieben Gatten in D(i)emut zu Weihnachten 1948. Richard Strauss Montreux, 26 Oktober 1948."

FRKF 392

II. LETTERS

To Emmy Destinn

1902 Sept. 22, Charlottenburg [Berlin]^S ALS, 1 p. Mentions *Feuersnot*.

Marburg, Stargardt, 5–6 March 1985, lot 907.
FRKF 824a

To Maria Jeritza and Irving Seery

1927 Dec. 26, Vienna, ALS, 2 p. Mentions *Der Rosenkavalier*, *Salomé*, *Josefslegende*, and *Die aegyptische Helena*.

1928 Jan. 21, Vienna, ALS, 3 p. (env). Mentions Hofmannsthal and *Die aegyptische Helena*.

FRKF 390–91

STRAUSS [283]

1948

 July 25, Hotel Saratz, Pontresina[S], ALS, 3 p. (env). Mentions the *Rosenkavalier* manuscript.

 Aug. 5, Pontresina, APCS

 Aug. 20, Hotel Saratz, Pontresina[S], ALS, 2 p. (env)

 Aug. 28, Montreux-Palace, Montreux[S], ALS, 1 p.

 Oct. 26, Montreux-Palace, Montreux[S], ALS, 2 p. (env)

 Oct. 31, Montreux-Palace, Montreux[S], ALS, 3 p.

 Nov. 6, Montreux, RCA Radiogram, asking for $1,000 in banknotes or travellers' checks.

 Nov. 8, Montreux-Palace, Montreux[S], ALS, 2 p., concerning the copy of the *Rosenkavalier* manuscript.

 Nov. 8, Montreux-Palace, Montreux[S], ALS, 1 p.

 Nov. 16, Montreux-Palace, Montreux[S], ALS, 2 p. (env), with traces of tears and adhesive tape repairs. Mentions the manuscripts of *Till Eulenspiegel*, *Don Juan*, and *Tod und Verklärung*.

 Nov. 24, Montreux-Palace, Montreux[S], ALS, 20 p. (env)

1949

 Feb. 2, Montreux, TLS, 1 p.

 Feb. 5, Montreux-Palace Hôtel, Montreux[S], TLS, 2 p.

 Feb. 13, Montreux-Palace, Montreux[S], ALS, 2 p. (env). Mentions *September*.

 March 7, Montreux-Palace, Montreux[S], ALS, 3 p.

 April 20, Montreux, TLS, 1 p.

 [May 1, Montreux*] n.p., ALS on two sides of a card (env), transmitting addresses for Dr. Franz Reichenbach and Ralph Hawkes.

 June 18, Garmisch, TL on a card (env), on reverse is an uncredited photograph of Strauss in old age, signed.

 July 1, Garmisch, TLS, 2 p. (env)

With six additional envelopes with postmarks dated 1948–49 and undeciphered.

Also, three letters from Franz Strauss to Jeritza.

 1944 Jan. 20, Montreux-Palace, Montreux[S], ALS, 4 p.

 1948 Sept. 30, Garmisch, TLS, 2 p. (env). Mentions Klaus Mann and Alma Mahler.

 1949 Jan. 20 [postscript, Jan. 27] n.p., ALS, 2 p., in English.

With two envelopes printed by the Landespostdirektion, Berlin, with Strauss commemorative stamp, postmarked 1954 Sept. 18; on the reverse are stamps of the Internationale Richard Strauss Gesellschaft and a stamped date of receipt (1954 Oct. 14). One envelope is addressed to Maria Jeritza-Seery, the other to Irving Seery.

The 1948–49 correspondence deals mostly with the sale of manuscripts of works by Strauss, using Jeritza as an intermediary.

FRKF 393

To Gustav F. Kogel

 1896 Oct. 25, Florence, APCS. Mentions *Don Juan*, *Macbeth*, and *Also sprach Zarathustra*.

Marburg, Stargardt, 5–6 March 1985, lot 906.
FRKF 823

To Gustav Mahler

 1901 Jan. 28, Charlottenburg, ALS, 1 p.

FRKF 395

To Ernst Schlesinger

 1928 June 19, Garmisch[S], ALS, 2 p.

 1929 July 22, Garmisch, ALS, 4 p. (env)

 1929 July 29, Garmisch, ALS, 3 p.

 1929 Aug. 14 [Taormina] APCS, with a photograph of Strauss on the reverse.

 1929 Sept. 3, Hotel Saratz, Pontresina[S], ALS, 2 p.

 1929 Sept. 27, Garmisch[S], ALS, 3 p.

 1931 June 25, Hotel Verenahof, Baden[S], ALS, 1 p.

 1931 July 30, Garmisch[S], ALS, 3 p. (env)

 1932 July 21, Garmisch[S], ALS, 4 p. (env)

 1933 Feb. [21?] Garmisch[S], ALS, 2 p.

 1937 Dec. 27, Taormina, APCS, with a photographic portrait of Strauss on the reverse.

 1938 Sept. [14?] Hotel Verenahof-Ochsen, Baden bei Zürich[S], ALS, 1 p. (env)

Two unidentified additional envelopes, postmarked Garmisch and Taormina.

Accompanied by a typescript carbon of a letter from the Bundesminister für Finanzen to Strauss, 1931 July 27, Vienna.

Ernst Schlesinger, Strauss's lawyer.

London, Sotheby's, 22 May 1985, lot 429.
FRKF 753

To Wolfgang Schneditz

 1942 June 2, Garmisch, ALS, 1 p. (env)

Marburg, Stargardt, 5–6 March 1985, lot 909.
FRKF 825

To Leo Slezak

 1923 July 12, ALS on both sides of a card printed "On board S.S. 'Vestris'" (env). Discusses Maria Olczewska and Wagner's *Rienzi*.

1935 Dec. 17, Garmisch[S], ALS, 2 p. (env), concerning a projected film adaptation of *Der Rosenkavalier*.

New York, Sotheby's, 22 May 1985, lots 427–28.
FRKF 751–52

III. PRINTED MUSIC

Morgen! [Facsimile edition of the manuscript in the Robert Owen Lehman Foundation]. Vienna: Bundesministerium für Unterricht, 1964. On title page: "Zum hundertsten Geburtstag von Richard Strauss." No. 628 from an edition of 1000 copies.

London, Sotheby's, 27–28 Nov. 1986, lot 647.
FRKF 1364.2b

Der Rosenkavalier: Schluss-Szene. Faksimile nach dem Autograph in der Österreichischen Nationalbibliotek. Vienna: Österreichische Nationalbibliotek, 1964.

> 20 unpaginated leaves, including 15 fascimile leaves. One of 1,000 copies. English translation of the afterword by Leopold Nowak bound in at the end. Bound in dark blue cloth, with black morocco corners and spine, with double gold fillets along the corners and along the spine; author and title gold-tooled on spine.

From the library of Maria Jeritza.
London, Sotheby's, 26 May 1988, lot 1592.
FRKF 1355

IV. PHOTOGRAPHS

Strauss and Maria Jeritza. Sepia photograph (12.5 × 22 cm), ca. 1928. Mounted on cardboard with the following inscription in Strauss's hand: "der dankbare Komponist der Helena / Richard Strauss." On the verso, unsigned autograph inscription, partly cropped, also in Strauss's hand: "… getreuen Geburtshelfer Dr Ernst Schles[inger]."

Postcard photograph of Strauss with a young boy on his knees, n.d. Stamped on the verso "Setzer, Photo-Bildnisse, Wien, VII. Museumstrasse 3."

Autograph of Strauss on a card. With an envelope, postmarked Munich [year not deciphered], addressed to Otto Lessmann in Charlottenburg.

New York, Sotheby's, 22 May 1985, lot 431.
FRKF 744b–d

Strauss in 1948. Black-and-white photographic portrait (7 × 10 cm). Note in pencil on the verso, in the hand of Hugo Burghauser: "Montreux Palace Hotel Terrasse 1948." Stamped on the verso: Bildstelle Wachtl, Wien.

Strauss in conversation with an unidentified man. Oblong black-and-white photograph of (27 × 20 cm). Stamped on the verso: Photographia Edith. Heinz Köhler & Cia., Rua do Ouvidor, 94.

London, Sotheby's, 27–28 Nov. 1986, lot 647.
FRKF 1364.2b

IGOR STRAVINSKY (1882–1971)

I. MUSIC MANUSCRIPTS

Cinq pièces faciles

The manuscript is calligraphed in black ink on thirteen, non-nested bifolia of 10-staff oblong paper (21 × 14.5 cm), paginated 1 to 53 in Stravinsky's hand, housed in two nested bifolia serving as wrappers, p. 53 being the third page of the inner bifolium.

> On the front cover, in pencil (not in Stravinsky's hand): "IGOR STRAWINSKY / CINQUE PIECES / FACILES / pour piano à 4 m. / [Main droite facile] / 1) ANDANTE / 2) ESPANOLLA / 3) BALALAIKA / 4) NAPOLITANA / 5) GALOP." On page [1] of the inner bifolium, dedication in Stravinsky's hand: "Très respectueusement / dédié à / Madame Eugenie Errazuriz / Igor Strawinsky / Morges Avril 1917." The manuscript is signed at the end and dated: Morges, 3 April 1917.

Together with a manila envelope, postmarked [9?] April 1917 and addressed in Stravinsky's hand to: "Madame E. Errasuriz / 60. Av. Montaigne / Paris."

New York, Sotheby's, 14 Dec. 1983, lot 118.
FRKF 143

Étude pour pianola

The manuscript, calligraphed in black ink, occupies ten pages, numbered 1 to 10 in Stravinsky's hand, of two nested bifolia, with two additional bifolia nested in these, of oblong 15-staff paper ("S" embossed on p. 1). The music is noted on two 6-staff systems. The title is calligraphed on p. [1] of the first bifolium: "IGOR STRAWINSKY / [double waving line] / ETUDE POUR PIANOLA." Signed at the end and dated Morges, 10 Sept. 1917.

In bright orange and purple paper wrappers with the manuscript title in black ink: "IGOR STRAWINSKY / ETUDE / POUR / PIANOLA." On p. [1] of the second bifolium, dedication: "Respectueusement dédié / à /

Madame Eugenia Errazuriz / Igor Strawinsky / Morges / 10 Septembre 1917."

Not listed in Grove.
New York, Sotheby's, 14 Dec. 1983, lot 119.
FRKF 144

Renard

Holograph manuscript of the piano-vocal score, 1916, 153 p. Notated in black and red ink, with additional markings in black pencil throughout, in an oblong notebook of bound bifolia of 10-staff paper; paginated I–IV (introduction) and 1–149 by the composer.

> At the top of p. 1, in Stravinsky's hand, in black ink: "Baika / pro / lisu, petukha, / kota da barana. / Veseloe predstavlenie / c peniem i musykoi / Igora Stravinskago"; and, in red ink: "Renard / histoire burlesque / chantée et jouée, / faite pour la scène. / composée par / Igor Stravinsky / mise en français par C.-F. Ramuz." The text and stage indications are in the two languages throughout, the Russian in black ink, the French in red ink.

> On the verso of the two leaves preceding p. I, pasted-on "Obshchee zamechanie" / "Remarque générale," both texts in Stravinsky's hand. Signed and dated Morges, 1916, in Russian and in French, on p. 147; both signatures cancelled in pencil, with note [to the engraver?] in pencil, in French, indicating that they have to be moved to p. 149, where a similar indication is found.

> On the verso of p. 147, stub indicating that the following page has been excised. At the top of p. 148, in black ink, in Stravinsky's hand: "Marche / aux sons de laquelle les acteurs quittent / la scène"; and, in pencil: "Shestvie. / Laisser la place pour la traduction russe."

Hardbound, with boards and spine decorated with pink paper with black motifs; bicolor orange and green endpapers; in a beige cardboard slipcase lined with green paper.

From the collection of Eugenia Errazuriz.
Heinrich Schütz to Henry Miller, p. 112–13.
London, Sotheby's, 16 Dec. 1983, lot 117.
FRKF 142

II. LETTERS

To Lord Berners

> 1917 Sept. 8, Morges, ALS, 2 p., in French, a plea for financial help from Diaghilev; also mentions Jose Maria Sert and Misia (Edwards). From the collection of Serge Lifar, with his stamp printed in purple.

London, Sotheby's, 9 May 1984, lot 217.
FRKF 310

To Michel-Dimitri Calvocoressi

> 1911 April 20, Beaulieu-sur-Mer, ALS, on both sides of a card, in French, concerning Calvocoressi's translations of his songs *Vesna* and *Rosyanka*. Also mentions his *Scherzo fantastique* and a funeral song on the death of Rimsky-Korsakoff.

Kenneth Rendell Catalogue 169.
FRKF 400

To Jean Cocteau

> [1914 Feb. 26, Leysin*] APCS, written on both sides, in French, in blue ink, crosswritten in red ink. Mentions *Le rossignol*, *Petrushka*, and Pierre Monteux.

London, Sotheby's, 9–10 May 1985, lot 208.
FRKF 778

To "cher ami"

> n.d., n.p., autograph card, signed, a New Year's greeting in French.

New York, Christie's, 16–17 Dec. 1983, lot 437.
FRKF 154.5

SIR ARTHUR SULLIVAN (1842–1900)

I. MANUSCRIPTS

The absent-minded beggar

Autograph music quotation, signed, n.d., notated in black ink on a 2-staff system, and titled, in Sullivan's hand: "last 8 bars (coda) of 'Ab:Min:Beg:' March." The quotation is actually 12-measures long.

Accompanied by:

> *The absent-minded beggar: song. The words by Rudyard Kipling; the music by Arthur Sullivan*. London: published for "The Daily Mail" Publishing Company by Enoch & Sons, copyright 1899.
> Folio, [1]–9; the four bifolia (including the cover) are tied with a navy blue ribbon. Printed on special paper, with an additional title and a cover lettered in gold. Inscribed in Nov. 1899 "For Charles Enoch" and signed by Kipling and Sullivan on p. [1].

> *The absent-minded beggar: song. The words by Rudyard Kipling; the music by Arthur Sullivan*. Published for "The Daily Mail" Publishing Company by Enoch & Sons, copyright 1899.
> Folio, [1]–9 p. Regular edition.

London, Christie's, 16 Nov. 1984, lot 234.
FRKF 365, 365.5

Ivanhoe

Autograph manuscript listing the characters in *Ivanhoe* and recording the scenes in which they appear, n.d., 1 p.

Ivanhoe, opera in three acts, on a libretto by J. Sturgis, was premiered at the Royal English Opera House on 31 Jan. 1891.

London, Sotheby's, 9–10 May 1985, lot 212.
FRKF 779b

II. PRINTED MUSIC

The Martyr of Antioch: Sacred musical drama. The words selected and arranged from Milman's poem, The music composed by Arthur Sullivan. The accompaniment arranged for the pianoforte from the full score by Eugène d'Albert. London: Chappel & Co., 50, New Bond Street [1880].

[8*], [i]–iv, 1–215 [+1] p. At bottom of the title page: "This work was composed expressly for, and performed for the first time at the Leeds triennial musical festival, Octr. 15th 1880." Music publisher's number 16997.

Bound in brown morocco by Zaehnsdorf, with author and title gold-tooled on the front board and on both boards a triple gold fillet along the edges with four small floral motifs at each corner. The same motifs also on the spine, with raised bands and the title and author gold-tooled. All edges gilt. Manuscript dedication on the verso of the first page, otherwise blank: "Presented to His Royal Highness Prince Leopold R.G. / by His Royal Highness' faithful servant / Arthur Sullivan / Dec: 1880." Bookplate of H.R.H. The Duke of Albany, K.G.

Accompanied by an engraved portrait of H.H. Milman, print of the ship *Strathurd*, and notes of a former owner.

London, Sotheby's, 22 May 1987, lot 536.
FRKF 1389

ARTHUR SYMONS (1865–1945)

"A song of bought flowers"

Autograph manuscript of this poem, signed at the end and dated 11 May 1889, 2 p.

"Books and a man"

Autograph manuscript, signed, of this essay, written on the recto sides of six leaves of ruled paper. Also, typescript, with autograph corrections, 4 p.

"On some first nights"

Autograph manuscript of this essay, signed, n.d., 28 p., written in ink on 28 leaves of ruled paper, irregularly paginated (occasionally with double pagination) and with abundant corrections and deletions in ink and pencil.

Accompanied by APCS to Maggs Brothers [1925 Feb. 8, Sidmouth*] concerning "Some first nights." With a TLS from Maggs Brothers to J.M.C. Kennedy, Esq., 1925 Feb. 9, transmitting the above APCS from Symons.

See Sotheby's, New York, 17 Dec. 1992, lot 237.
New York, Christie's, 16–17 Dec. 1983, lot 447–49.
FRKF 179–81

"William Blake as a Painter"

Autograph manuscript of this essay, n.d., 21 p., in black and purple ink, with annotations in pencil, on two different kinds of ruled paper. The title is in pencil on an additional sheet. Signed at the end.

New York, Christie's, 16 Dec. 1984, lot 450.
FRKF 182

DEEMS TAYLOR (1885–1966)

London Town

Holograph manuscript of this song from the incidental music to Clemence Dane's *Will Shakespeare*, n.d., 2 p. The manuscript is written in black ink on p. [2] and [3] of a bifolium of tall 12-staff paper (Schirmer No. 9). On p. [1] in Taylor's hand: "London Town / 'Will Shakespeare,' Act I - Henslowe"; and, at the top of p. [2]: "To Walter Slezak, with admiration for a superb artist / Deems Taylor / London Town / Clemence Dane / Henslowe & Players / Deems Taylor / From the incidental music to Winthrop Ames's production of / 'Will Shakespeare.'"

New York, Sotheby's, 22 May 1985, lot 424.
FRKF 748A

PETER ILICH TCHAIKOVSKY (1840–93)

I. LETTERS

To Hermann Laroche [G.A. Larosh]

[1885] July 3, Maidanovo, ALS, 4 p. (env). Mentions Berlioz.

London, Sotheby's, 29 Nov. 1985, lot 227.
FRKF 1062

To Marie Lynen

1893 Jan. 17, Paris, ALS in French, 1 p. (env). Announces his departure for Cambridge and regrets not being able to visit her in Antwerp. Envelope addressed to "Madame Marie de Lynen."

Paris, Laurin-Guilloux-Buffetaud-Tailleur (Drouot), 12 June 1984, lot 253.
FRKF 478

To Carl Reinecke

1892 Jan. 12 [1891 Dec. 21 old style] Kiev, ALS in French, 4 p. (env), concerning *Roméo et Juliette*.

Marburg, Stargardt, 5–6 March 1985, lot 917.
FRKF 826

To Vasilii Sapelnikov

1889 Oct. 19, Moscow, ALS, 4 p. Mentions *The sleeping beauty*, the *Violin Concerto*, and Rimsky-Korsakoff.

London, Sotheby's, 29 March 1985, lot 231.
FRKF 1064

II. MISCELLANEOUS

Cabinet photograph of Tchaikovsky by Müller & Pilgram, Leipzig (10.5 × 16.5 cm). Inscribed by the composer to Miss Smyth, 11 Feb. 1888.

London, Sotheby's, 29 Nov. 1985, lot 229.
FRKF 1063

SIR JAMES EMERSON TENNENT (1804–69)

Album

Illustrated album with manuscripts and autographs laid in (when specified) or mounted. The album measures 27 × 34.5 cm, with contents as follows:

Illustrated frontispiece, signed, by David Roberts, dated 1860.

David Roberts, ALS to Lady Tennant, 21 July 1860, 7 Fitzroy St. [London], 2 p., concerning his contribution to the album. (laid in)

Stanfield, Clarkson. "Webley Castle, South Wales." Watercolor on paper (17 × 24.5 cm), signed in the lower left corner and dated 1850 in the lower right.

Doyle, Henry. Untitled drawing [two children reading on a lake shore]. Watercolor on paper (17.5 × 22 cm), signed in the lower left corner, n.d.

Southey, Robert. Autograph inscription (two lines), signed and dated Keswick, 24 July 1824.

Hogg, James. "Journey of the soul." Autograph poem, 2 p., signed and dated Altrine Lake, 9 July 1824, at the end.

Hervieu, M.D. [?] "The stream of life." Autograph poem, 1 p., signed at the bottom, Dublin, n.d.

Wordsworth, William. "She dwelt among the untrodden ways …," from *Lyrical Ballads*. Autograph poem, 1 p., signed at the bottom and dated Crystal Mount, 26 July 1824.

Coleridge, Hartley. "Fair is the page, and smooth …" Autograph poem, signed, 1 p., n.d.

Wilson, John. Unidentified poem on both sides of a sheet foliated 3, signed and dated Windermere, 27 July 1824, 2 p.

Doyle, Richard. "A flight of fancy." Watercolor on paper (17 × 20.5 cm), signed in the lower left corner.

—. ALS to "My dear Tennent," 1 April 1845, C.G. [Covent Garden?], 4 p., concerning his contribution to the album. (laid in)

Cunningham, Allan. "The Mariners Song." Autograph poem, 1 p. Signed at the bottom, n.d.

Galt, John. "To Sir Walter Scott (written when Marmion was first published)." Autograph poem, 1 p., signed at the bottom and dated London, 8 Aug. 1824.

Wilson, John. "Sonnet / The evening cloud." Autograph poem, 1 p., signed at the bottom, Windermere, n.d.

Campbell, Thomas. ANS, n.d., 1 p. On the verso of the same sheet: Bowring, Sir John. Autograph poem, signed and dated London, 13 Sept. 1824, at the bottom.

Pepe, Gabriele. Short prose inscription in Italian, beginning "Tra gli uomini le cose tutte sono così passagiere …," signed and dated London, 1 Oct. 1824.

Van de Welde, W. "Temple of the Sacred Tooth at Kandy." Pen-and-wash drawing on paper (21 × 13.5 cm), signed in the lower right corner, n.d.

Malcolm, John. "Lines on the death of Lord Byron." Autograph poem, 3 p., signed at the end and dated Edinburgh, 16 July 1824. On verso of p. [3]: Roche, H., "Commissaire du comité grec de Paris," ANS, dated Nauplion, 16 April 1825. In French, beginning "Le plus beau jour de ma vie est celui de m'être trouvé au milieu du Sénat de la Grèce …"

Jones, J.E. "The Right Hon. J. Whiteside M.P. / Sketched during the Trial of D. Monneth." Pencil drawing on paper (11.5 × 17 cm), n.d.

Koraes, Adamantios. A 3-line manuscript quotation from Pindar, in Greek, signed, n.d.

Irving, Washington. Manuscript inscription, beginning "'The mind,' Seneca observes …," signed and dated Paris, 25 Oct. 1824.

Warden, David Bailie. Manuscript quotation from Marcus Aurelius, 1 p., signed and dated Paris, 26 Oct. 1824.

Grégoire, Henri. Short inscription in French, signed "Grégoire E[….]," n.d.

O'Connor, Arthur. Autograph inscription, 2 p., beginning "May your generous efforts be crown'd with success …," signed "A. Condorcet O'Connor," n.d.

Knox, William. "The field of Gilboa." Autograph poem, 2 p., signed and dated Belfast, 15 Jan. 1824.

Carlyle, Thomas. "The night moth." Autograph poem, 2 p., signed and dated Paris, 1824.

Atkins, J. "Miss Bathurst / drowned in the Tiber at Rome 1823." Pencil drawing on paper (15 × 20 cm), heightened with crayon.

Sgricci, Tommaso. "Imprecazione d'Ecuba a Paride sulla Morte." Autograph poem, 1 p., initialed at the bottom. On the verso: Tennent, R.J. "Napoleon's grave." Autograph poem, 1 p., signed and dated Florence, 8 Dec. 1824.

Targioni-Tozzetti, Antonio. Short inscription in Latin, signed and dated Florence 11 Dec. 1824.

Malcolm, John. "The warrior's dirge." Autograph poem, 1 p., signed and dated Paris, 29 Oct. 1824.

Bollante, Abbate. Short inscription in Arabic, signed and dated Malta, 8 March 1825 [?]. Bollante is identified in a pencilled note as working at the Library of the Grand Master, Malta.

Laing, Alexander Gordon. ANS, Malta, 8 March 1825, 1 p.

Nicholl, A. "Hermitage of St. Finbar, Co. Cork." Watercolor on paper (22 × 18 cm), signed in the lower right corner.

Wright, Waller Rodwell. "Ο ΔΗΜΟΣ ΙΩΝΙΟΣ ΤΟΙΣ ΒΡΕΤΑΝΝΟΙΣ ΕΥΧΑΡΙΣΤΙΑΣ ΕΝΕΚΑ." Autograph inscription in Greek, dated La Valetta, 10 March 1825. On the verso: Fletcher, Henry. "Lines written in a copy of Mrs Tighe's Poems." Autograph poem, 1 p., dated Malta, 10 March 1825.

Guilford, Lord. Short autograph inscription in Greek, signed Guilford, Chancellor of the Ionian Academy, n.d.

Psalidas, Athanasios. Inscription in Greek, dated Nauplion, 1825.

Piccolo, Professor. Short quotation in Greek from Sophocles' *Ajax*, dated Corfu [15 March] n.y. [1825?]

Lusignan, James. Two inscriptions, one from Matthew, one from "Runic ode" by Finnur Magnússon, with Icelandic and Danish versions and Latin translation, 1 p., signed and dated Corfu, 18 March 1825.

Santa Rosa, Santorre. Short Latin quotation, dated Nauplion, 1 April 1825.

Atkins, J. Portrait of an unidentified man, pen-and-ink and wash on paper (7.5 × 9.5 cm), signed in the lower left corner.

Porro, Count. ANS in Italian, Nauplion, 1 April 1825.

Palma, Alerino, conte. ANS in Italian, n.p., n.d.

Kalerdji, Nikolai. ANS in Russian, Nauplion, 5/17 April 1825. Described in a pencilled note as a "Russian Greek."

Ducas, Adam. ANS in Greek, Nauplion, 7 April 1825.

Pecchio, Count. Short quotation in Italian, signed and dated Nauplion, 26 April 1825.

Stanfield, Clarkson. "At Rochester." Watercolor on paper (17.5 × 25 cm), signed at the bottom.

Trikoupes, Spyridon. ANS in Greek, Nauplion, 29 April 1825.

Rheineck, Freiherr von. ANS in German, Nauplion, 22 April 1825.

Gamba, Pietro, conte. Manuscript copy of Byron's poem "On this day I complete my thirty-sixth year," preceded by an ANS in Italian, n.d., 3 p.

Suzzo, Michel. ANS and inscription, Nauplion, 25 April 1825. In Arabic and French. Signed: "Michel Suzzo, préfet d'Athènes."

Kriese, Antonio. ANS in Greek, Nauplion, 15/27 May 1827. Described in a pencilled note as Vice Admiral of the Greek fleet.

Miaoulis, Antonio. ANS in Greek, n.p., 16/28 May 1825.

Doyle, Richard. Untitled watercolor on paper (17.5 × 22 cm), signed and dated 1845 in the lower left corner.

Hikesios. Greek translation of and excerpt from Sir Walter Scott's poem "Lay of the last minstrel," 1 p., signed and dated Crete, 1/13 June 1825.

Canaris, Constantino. ANS in Greek, 18 July [1825].

Mavrocordato, Prince. ANS in Greek, n.p., n.d.

Petraki, Anargyre. ANS, Athens, 24 July 1825. In Greek and French.

Stanhope, Leicester Fitzgerald Charles, fifth Earl of Harrington. ANS, n.p., n.d. On the verso: Tennent, Robert James. "Ancient of days! August Athena!" Autograph poem, signed and dated Athens, 24 July 1825.

Jellicoe, J.L. "The house in which Lord Byron died in Missolonghi." Pen-and-ink and watercolor on paper (11.5 × 11 cm). Mounted underneath is a four-line quotation from Byron, possibly in Tennent's hand.

Sombasi [?], Giacomachi. ANS in Greek, n.p., 1825. Described in a pencilled note as "Late Greek Admiral."

Hunt, Leigh. "Wishes for Greece / 1822." Manuscript poem, 3 p., signed at the end.

Morgan, John. "Bygone days." Autograph poem, 2 p., signed at the end.

Proctor, Bryan Waller. "All things which live and are …" Autograph poem, 1 p. Initialed at the end and dated 25 Jan. 1826.

Bentham, Jeremy. Autograph inscription [his address], dated 30 Jan. 1826.

Watts, Alaric Alexander. "Lines suggested by a portrait by Sir Peter Lely supposed to be that of Nell Gwynn." Autograph poem, 5 p., signed at the end. On the verso of the last page: "Dedicatory stanzas / To William Wordsworth Esq." Autograph poem, 2 p., initialed M.J.J. at the end.

Doyle, James. "The legend of Sir Gareth of Orkney." Four pen-and-ink and watercolor drawings on paper (16 × 19 cm), with manuscript captions. Initialed at the end.

McEwen, W.D.H. "The Dial of Ahaz." Autograph poem, 2 p., Belfast, n.d.

Knowles, James Sheridan. Autograph inscription, Belfast, 19 May 1826.

Roscoe, William. "Graecia victrix." Autograph poem, 2 p., signed at the end.

M'Crie, Thomas. Autograph inscription, n.p., n.d. On the verso: Borras, J. "Epigrama." Autograph poem, 1 p., signed at the end.

P., R. "Song." Autograph poem, 1 p., Belfast, n.d., initialed at the end.

Nicholl, A. "Fruit women of Ceylon." Pencil drawing on grey paper (18.5 × 13.5 cm), heightened with white.

Landon, Letitia Elizabeth. "Song"; "There is a flower haunting …" Two autograph poems, 1 p., the first signed, the second initialed.

Roberts, Emma. "Alas I have no splendid gift …" Autograph poem, 1 p., signed at the end.

Cranmore, R.T. "When thro' life unblest we rove …" Manuscript score for voice and piano, 1 p. Dated Sept. 1826.

Wiffen, Jeremiah Holmes. "To a lady." Autograph poem, 1 p., signed and dated London, 11 Dec. 1827.

Hervey, TK. "The Temple of Jupiter Olympias at Athens." Autograph poem, 2 p., signed at the end.

Thackeray, William Makepeace. ANS to "My dear Ea," n.y., Monday, 24 Jermyn Street [London], 1 p. On the facing page: pen-and-ink drawing showing two dwarfs and a maiden, initialed by Thackeray in the lower left corner.

Hofland, B. "To a Border of Roses in the Garden of White Knights." Autograph poem, 1 p., signed at the end. On verso: Carne, John. "To fairest Greece for ever left behind …" Autograph poem, 1 p., signed at the end.

Croly, George. Autograph inscription in Greek and note, 1 p., initialed at the end.

Pringle, Thomas. "Not in vain the Patriot dies …" Autograph poem, 1 p., signed at the end.

Stanfield, Clarkson. ALS to Sir J. Emerson Tennent, 19 March 1860, The Green Hill, Hampstead, 2 p., concerning a contribution to the album.

Stanfield, Clarkson. "At Ancona." Pencil and watercolor on beige paper (13.5 × 22.5 cm), initialed in the lower right corner.

Roscoe, Thomas. "Sonnet / Dante banished from Florence"; "Graecia liberata." Two autograph poems, 3 p., both signed at the end.

Unidentified. "Elie House / Colanbo." Watercolor on paper (24.5 × 18.5 cm).

Kennedy, Will. "To my absent love." Autograph poem, 1 p., signed at the end.

Trueba y Cosío, Joaquín Telesforo de. ALS to J. Emerson Tennent, 5 Jan. 1829, London, 1 p. In English, including "Epigrama," autograph poem in Spanish.

Howard, F. Illustration for *As you like it*. Pencil on paper (24.5 × 19 cm).

Richardson, D.S. "Mornings." Autograph poem, signed and dated 7 Jan. 1829 at the end.

Wade, Joseph Augustine. "Louise! A Sketch." Autograph poem, signed and dated 10 Jan. 1829 at the end.

Doyle, Annette. [Tulips]. Watercolor on paper (17 × 21.5 cm), signed Annette in the lower left corner.

Wade, Joseph Augustine. "Song of the Harebell, from The Songs of the Flowers." Manuscript score of this song for voice and piano, 1 p., signed at the end and initialed in the lower right corner.

Buckingham, J.S. "Lines adapted to the Air of 'Montalambert,' heard during a Calm at Sea." Autograph poem, 2 p., signed and dated London, 26 Jan. 1829.

Poole, John. ALS to [Sir James Emerson Tennent], 26 Jan. 1829, London, 1 p.

Porter, Jane. Autograph inscription, 1 p., signed and dated Esher, 17 Feb. 1829 at the end.

Porter, Anna Maria. "Lines suggested by an unknown female [?] portrait." Autograph poem, 1 p., signed and dated Esher, 18 Feb. 1829 at the end.

Nicholl, A. "The Giants' Causeway." Watercolor on paper (22.5 × 18 cm), signed in the lower right corner.

Wyle [?], Thomas. "The Arab Sheik to his Tribe." Autograph poem, 3 p., signed and dated London, 11 April, n.y., at the end.

Doyle, Charles. "A pilgrimage." Pen-and-ink drawing on paper (21 × 17 cm), signed "Charles" in the lower left corner.

Read, William. "Farewell to the World!" Autograph poem, 4 p., signed and dated Belfast, 6 Sept. 1830, at the end. Identified in a note as "Author of Rouge et Noir."

Franklin, John. "Oh woe be to the ship …" Poem, calligraphed in red and blue, with illuminated initials, and illustrated with two pen-and-ink drawings, one at the beginning and one at the end, 4 p. The poem is initialed at the end. Signed "John Franklin, 1845" in the lower right corner of the second drawing.

Croly, George. "Sappho - from an antique gem." Autograph poem, 1 p., initialed at the end.

Porter, Jane. "Youth's Prayer." Autograph poem, 1 p., signed and dated Lower Belgrave Street, Eaton Square, 15 May 1845, with an inscription: "Copied for my very dear young friend Eleanor Emerson Tennent."

Cruikshank, George. 2 ALS to Sir James Emerson Tennent, Anwell St. [London], 20 and 25 June 1845, 2 p. and 1 p. respectively, the earlier letter with envelope, both concerning his contribution to the album. Earlier letter laid in.

—. "A dreadful state of suspense." Pen-and-ink and watercolor drawing on paper (18.5 × 23 cm), signed in the lower right corner.

Dickens, Charles. Autograph inscription, signed and dated 17 May 1860. Also, ALS to Sir James Emerson Tennent, 17 May 1860, Tavistock House, Tavistock Square, London W.C.[S], 1 p. *Letters*, Pilgrim Edition, IX:254.

Print [Pied Piper?] signed at the bottom "S.G.[…] del. 1864" (7 × 10 cm).

Nicholl, A. "The chatty bazaar." Pencil drawing on gray paper (19 × 12 cm), heightened with white.

Stanfield, Clarkson. [A Franciscan monk.] Watercolor on paper (17.5 × 24.5 cm), signed in the lower left corner.

Doyle, John. Autograph inscription, signed and dated 2 Aug. 1860.

—. ALS to Sir James Emerson Tennent, n.d., n.p., 1 p., concerning his contribution to the album.

Collins, Wilkie. "Count Fosco at the Opera." Autograph manuscript, 2 p., signed and dated 1 Dec. 1860 at the end, with the note: "From 'The Woman in White.'"

—. ALS to Sir James Emerson Tennent, 3 Dec. 1860, 12 Harley Street [London][S], 3 p., concerning his contribution to the album.

Millen, W.S. "Sir J. Emerson Tennent KCS." Print (11 × 13.5 cm).

Stanfield, Clarkson. "Domus Hospitium Canterbury." Watercolor on paper (17.5 × 16.5 cm), signed in the lower right corner.

Nicholl, A. "Moorish Marriage Procession, Ceylon." Pencil drawing on beige paper (25.5 × 17.5 cm), heightened with white, signed in the lower left corner, 1848.

—. "1800 stone steps, Sacred Mountain of Mehintibai [?]." Pen-and-ink drawing on beige paper (15 × 24 cm).

[Bird]. Unidentified pen-and-ink drawing on paper (11 × 16 cm).

Nicholl, A. "Alligators, Pool … Ceylon." Watercolor on paper (24.5 × 19 cm). Signed in the lower right corner.

Bound in turquoise morocco, signed M.M. Holloway, London, with quadruple gilt fillet and decorative pattern on the edges of both boards; raised bands, ornamented with a thin gilt fillet, on the spine, decorated throughout with a pattern similar to the one on the boards. Gold-tooled on spine: "Autographs / and / sketches." All edges gilt, pink silk doublures, with a triple gold-tooled fillet on all edges of the verso of both boards, and a double fillet on the facing page, with fleur-de-lys like patterns in the corners.

Sir James Emerson Tennent (1804–69), author of *A picture of Greece in 1825, as exhibited in the personal narratives of James Emerson, Count Pecchio, and W.K. Humphreys* (London, 1826), M.P. for Belfast (1832–42), secretary of the India Board (1841–43), civil secretary to the government of Ceylon (1845–50), governor of St. Helena (1850–52), M.P. for Lisburn (1852), secretary to the Board of Trade (1852–67). Knighted 1845, baronet 1867.

FRKF 1426

JEAN DE TINAN (1874–98)

Un document sur l'impuissance d'aimer. Frontispiece de Félicien Rops. Paris: [Librairie de L'Art indépendant] 11, rue de la Chaussée d'Antin, 1894.

[14] + 145 + 3 p. No. 9, on China, from an edition of 310 (5 on Japan, 5 on China, 300 on Dutch paper), numbered on the half-title verso. With the Rops frontispiece present in three printings (black, red, and green). Original brown paper wrappers bound in. On verso of back wrapper, in pencil, in Tinan's hand: "Mon exempl. / T."

Bound in half brown morocco and beige marbled paper. Tipped in: ALS from Stéphane Mallarmé to Jean de Tinan, Paris, n.y., April, on both sides of a card, concerning *Un document sur l'impuissance d'aimer*. Bookplates of Raoul Simonson and Bibliothèque Jacques Odry.

Brussels, Simonson, 19 May 1984, lot 277.
FRKF 373

SIR HERBERT BEERBOHM TREE (1853–1917)

Letter to W. Hecht

n.y. Feb. 18, Her Majesty's Theatre [London][S] ALS, 3 p., concerning *L'étrangère* by Alexandre Dumas fils.

London, Christie's, 23 March 1984, lot 70.
FRKF 435

JOAQUÍN TURINA (1882–1949)

Letters to G. Jean-Aubry

1912 Feb. 18, Paris, ALS in French, 2 p. Mentions Manuel de Falla and a concert of Spanish music by the Quatuor Lejeune.

[1920 March 12*] ALS on both sides of his visiting card, in French (env), about Falla and *The three-cornered hat*.

London, Sotheby's, 9–10 May 1985, lots 89, 92.
FRKF 765.1–2

UNIDENTIFIED

ALS from an unidentified actor to "Cher Monsieur," 1900 Aug. 16, Chateau de Condé par Guignicourt, Aisne^S, 3 p., concerning a possible engagement in Egypt; mentions Lucien Guitry and William Busnach's play *L'assommoir*, written with Octave Gastineau after Émile Zola's novel.

Paris, Le Roux-Mathias (Drouot), 19 April 1985, lot 240.
FRKF 716d

Document from the War Council of Vienna, 1761 May 22, concerning the Seven Years War. Signed by Graf von Harrach and Graf von Neipperg.

Marburg, Stargardt, 26–27 Nov. 1985, lot 1253.
FRKF 1284

RALPH VAUGHAN WILLIAMS (1872–1958)

Letter to Gwen Raverat

[1931] July 12, Dorking, ALS, 4 p., concerning his *Job*, a masque for dancing, on a scenario by Raverat and Geoffrey Keynes, premiered in Cambridge on 5 July 1931.

Sotheby's, London, 14–15 April 1982, lot 85.
FRKF 27

GIUSEPPE VERDI (1813–1901)

I. MANUSCRIPTS

Ernani

Autograph working copy in Verdi's hand of the libretto by Francesco Maria Piave, n.d. [1843–44]. The manuscript is written in black ink on an unsewn gathering of nine unnumbered and unpaginated quarto-size bifolia placed in another bifolium serving as wrappers, the whole forming an unbound fascicle.

> On front wrapper in Verdi's hand: "Ernani" and the following note in Piave's hand: "Questo MS. è tutta copia di mano / del M.ro Verdi il quale sopra / questo ha composto la sua musica / F.M. Piave / Venezia 23 marzo 1854." Abundant corrections and revisions in Verdi's hand, mostly in black ink, some in pencil.
>
> The sections are laid out as follows: fols. [2r]–[7r]: Parte 1a. / Il Bandito; fols. [7v]–[12r]: Parte Seconda / L'Ospite; fols. [12v]–[16r]: Parte Terza / La Clemenza; fols. [16v]–[19v]: [part 4, no heading].
>
> The text of part 4 is not in consecutive order: on fols. [16v] and [17r], in a different penmanship, Verdi has written out the text of the final scene (no. 14 in the published score); then follows an earlier version of scenes 3 through 6; the last scene is missing. Laid in between fols. [16] and [17] is a single octavo-size bifolium (blind-stamped: Bath, with a crown), in Piave's hand, comprising an alternative version of act 4, scene 1 (opening chorus) and the beginning of scene 2 (Ernani's recitative).

See Philip Gossett's afterword in: *Giuseppe Verdi. Ernani*, edited by Claudio Gallico (Chicago and London: The University of Chicago Press; Milan: Ricordi, 1985), p. [lxv]–[lxvii].
Heinrich Schütz to Henry Miller, p. 38–39.
London, Sotheby's, 9–10 May 1985, lot 219.
FRKF 781

"Pro memoria per Piave"

Memorandum to Francesco Maria Piave concerning *Rigoletto*, in black ink in the form of six numbered paragraphs on the first page of a quarto-size bifolium. n.d.

London, Sotheby's, 9–10 May 1985, lot 226.
FRKF 783.6

II. LETTERS

Many of Verdi's letters are dated from his home, St Agata, near Busseto.

To Count Opprandino Arrivabene

> 1862 June 4, Paris, ALS, 1 p., concerning his travels and thanking him for sending croissants. *Verdi intimo*, p. 20.
>
> 1863 March 22, Paris, ALS, 3 p., concerning his trip to Andalusia and *Les vêpres siciliennes*. *Verdi intimo*, p. 24–25.

London, Sotheby's, 14–15 April 1982, lots 86–87.
FRKF 28–29

> 1863 March 31, Paris, ALS, 3 p. *Verdi intimo*, p. 25.

London, Sotheby's, 26 May 1983, lot 92.
FRKF 123

> 1863 May 25, Paris, ALS, 3 p., concerning *Les vêpres siciliennes*. *Verdi intimo*, p. 26–27.
>
> 1863 July 15, Paris, ALS, 3 p. Mentions the impending premiere of *Les vêpres siciliennes* and the Érard piano he is bringing back from Paris. *Verdi intimo*, p. 27–28.
>
> 1863 July 20, Paris, ALS, 1 p. Announces travel plans for his return to Italy. *Verdi intimo*, p. 28.
>
> 1863 Dec. 14, Busseto, ALS, 1 p., concerning business dealings via Rothschild. *Verdi intimo*, p. 32.

London, Sotheby's, 14–15 April 1982, lots 88, 90, 89, 91.
FRKF 30, 32, 31, 33

> 1864 Feb. 16, Genoa, ALS, 1 p. Mentions the Italian Parliament and a letter published in the *Gazetta del Popolo*. *Verdi intimo*, p. 36.
>
> 1864 Feb. 22, Genoa, ALS, 1 p. Announces his departure for Turin. *Verdi intimo*, p. 37.

London, Sotheby's, 26 May 1983, lots 93–94.
FRKF 124–25

1864 March 29, Busseto, St. Agata, ALS, 2 p. Mentions Gounod's *Mireille* and Rossini's *Petite messe solennelle*. *Verdi intimo*, p. 38–40.

London, Sotheby's, 14–15 April 1982, lot 92.
FRKF 34

1865 Feb. 1, Cremona, ALS, 1 p. Reports that he has been composing. *Verdi intimo*, p. 45.

London, Sotheby's, 26 May 1983, lot 95.
FRKF 126

1865 April 25, Busseto, S Agata, ALS, 3 p. Quotes letters received from Léon Carvalho and Léon Escudier reporting on the success of *Macbeth* in Paris. *Verdi intimo*, p. 51–52.

1865 April 28, Busseto, ALS, 3 p. Mentions Manzoni, *Macbeth* in Paris, and the Duke of Rivas. *Verdi intimo*, p. 52–54.

London, Sotheby's, 11 Nov. 1982, lots 67–68.
FRKF 1097–98

1865 June 14, Busseto, ALS, 3 p. Discusses a business deal and mentions Franco Faccio's *Amleto*. *Verdi intimo*, p. 57.

London, Sotheby's, 17 Nov. 1983, lot 196.
FRKF 231.07

1865 Dec. 31, Paris, ALS, 3 p. Mentions the beauties of Haussmann's Paris, Meyerbeer's *L'Africaine*, Wagner's *Tannhäuser*, and *La forza del destino* and *Don Carlos*. *Verdi intimo*, p. 61.

London, Sotheby's, 11 Nov. 1982, lot 70.
FRKF 1100

1866 March 24, Piacenza, ALS, 2 p. Mentions *Don Carlos*. *Verdi intimo*, p. 69–70.

1866 April 6, St Agata, ALS, 3 p., concerning *Don Carlos*. *Verdi intimo*, p. 70.

London, Sotheby's, 17 Nov. 1983, lots 197–98.
FRKF 231.08–09

1866 Sept. 28, Paris, ALS, 2 p. Mentions rehearsals of *Don Carlos*. *Verdi intimo*, p. 72.

London, Sotheby's, 14–15 April 1982, lot 93.
FRKF 35

1867 Feb. 8, Paris, ALS, 2 p., on mourning stationery. On the death of his father; mentions rehearsals of *Don Carlos*. *Verdi intimo*, p. 76.

London, Sotheby's, 26 May 1983, lot 96.
FRKF 127

1867 June 16, St Agata, ALS, 4 p., on mourning stationery. Mentions *Don Carlos* and discusses the political state of Italy. *Verdi intimo*, p. 78–79.

London, Sotheby's, 14–15 April 1982, lot 94.
FRKF 36

[1867 July 25, Busseto] ALS, 1 p., on mourning stationery, concerning the death of Antonio Barezzi. *Verdi intimo*, p. 79.

London, Sotheby's, 17 Nov. 1983, lot 199.
FRKF 231.10

[1867] Aug. 4 [Genoa] ALS, 1 p., on mourning stationery. Reports that he lacks the will to go to Paris. *Verdi intimo*, p. 80.

1868 March 13, Genoa, ALS, 2 p., in praise of Cremonese delicacies. *Verdi intimo*, p. 84.

London, Sotheby's, 26 May 1983, lot 97–98.
FRKF 128–29

1868 April 9, Genoa, ALS, 2 p., concerning Cremonese biscotti and Italian politics. *Verdi intimo*, p. 85.

London, Sotheby's, 14–15 April 1982, lot 95.
FRKF 37

1868 Aug. 27, St Agata, ALS, 3 p., on his refusal of the Cross of the Crown of Italy; mentions Emilio Broglio, then minister of education. *Verdi intimo*, p. 96–97.

London, Sotheby's, 17 Nov. 1983, lot 201.
FRKF 231.11

1869 March 23, Genoa, ALS, 3 p. Mentions *Rigoletto* in Paris, the *Requiem* (originally planned as a Mass for Rossini), *Don Carlos*, *La forza del destino*, and Camille du Locle and Émile Perrin. *Verdi intimo*, p. 101–03.

London, Sotheby's, 14–15 April 1982, lot 96.
FRKF 38

1869 Dec. 30, Genoa, ALS, 4 p. Mentions the *Requiem*. *Verdi intimo*, p. 114–15.

1870 May 19, S Agata, ALS, 4 p. Discusses Federico Ricci's *Una follia a Roma*. *Verdi intimo*, p. 119–20.

London, Sotheby's, 11 Nov. 1982, lots 69, 72.
FRKF 1099, 1101

1871 Jan. 1, Genoa, ALS, 2 p. Mentions corresponding with Cairo. *Verdi intimo*, p. 122.

London, Sotheby's, 14–15 April 1982, lot 97.
FRKF 39

[1871 Feb. 24] Genoa, ALS, 3 p., concerning composer Romualdo Marenco; mentions Mariani. *Verdi intimo*, p. 128.

London, Sotheby's, 17 Nov. 1983, lot 203.
FRKF 231.20

1871 Sept. 2, St Agata, ALS, 3 p. Announces the completion of *Aida* and discusses the question of melody. *Verdi intimo*, p. 134–36.

1872 Jan. 13, Milan, ALS, 3 p. Mentions rehearsals of *Aida* in Milan and *La forza del destino*. *Verdi intimo*, p. 137.

[1872 Feb. 9] Milan, ALS, 2 p. Reports on the Milan premiere of *Aida* the night before. *Verdi intimo*, p. 138–42.

London, Sotheby's, 14–15 April 1982, lots 98–100.
FRKF 40–42

1872 Dec. 29, Naples, ALS, 2 p. Complains about the situation of Neapolitan theaters. *Verdi intimo*, p. 152–53.

London, Sotheby's, 26 May 1983, lot 99.
FRKF 130

1873 April 16, St Agata, ALS, 4 p. Mentions the *String Quartet*, the San Carlo premiere of *Aida*, the success of *La forza del destino* in Piacenza and Bari, and Amilcare Ponchielli. *Verdi intimo*, p. 156–58.

London, Sotheby's, 11 Nov. 1982, lot 75.
FRKF 1102

1873 Oct. 25, St Agata, ALS, 3 p. Discusses the state of cultural affairs in France. *Verdi intimo*, p. 162–63.

London, Sotheby's, 26 May 1983, lot 100.
FRKF 131

1874 July 21, St Agata, ALS, 4 p. Discusses reviews of the *Requiem* in Paris, with mentions of Johannès Weber and Alexis Azevedo. *Verdi intimo*, p. 176–77.

London, Sotheby's, 14–15 April 1982, lot 103.
FRKF 43

1874 Aug. 15, St Agata, ALS, 2 p. Mentions *Aida* and the *Requiem*. *Verdi intimo*, p. 177–78.

London, Sotheby's, 17 Nov. 1983, lot 205.
FRKF 231.13

1875 March 29, Genoa, ALS, 1 p. Regrets not being able to go to Rome. *Verdi intimo*, p. 181.

1876 Oct. 9, St Agata, ALS, 3 p. Discusses recent trips and refers to the international political situation. *Verdi intimo*, p. 189.

1877 [Jan.] 2, Genoa, ALS, 3 p. On Italian politics and reporting. *Verdi intimo*, p. 193.

London, Sotheby's, 14–15 April 1982, lots 104–06.
FRKF 44–46

1879 Sept. 3, St Agata, ALS, 3 p. Mentions his benefit concert in Milan for flood victims. *Verdi intimo*, p. 237–39.

London, Sotheby's, 26 May 1983, lot 101.
FRKF 132

1880 April 19, Milan, ALS, 3 p. Reports on a performance of two of the *Quattro pezzi sacri* in Milan. *Verdi intimo*, p. 244–46.

London, Sotheby's, 14–15 April 1982, lot 107.
FRKF 47

1880 June 24, St Agata, ALS, 4 p. Reports on a painting and sculpture exhibition in Turin. *Verdi intimo*, p. 258–59.

London, Sotheby's, 26 May 1983, lot 102.
FRKF 133

1880 Sept. 14, St Agata, ALS, 4 p. Mentions Boito and announces the completion of the *Otello* libretto. *Verdi intimo*, p. 259–60.

London, Sotheby's, 14–15 April 1982, lot 108.
FRKF 48

1881 Dec. 23, Genoa, ALS, 4 p. Reports on a visit to Milan and mentions Boito, Faccio, and Ricordi. *Verdi intimo*, p. 294.

London, Sotheby's, 26 May 1983, lot 103.
FRKF 134

1883 March 15, Genoa, ALS, 3 p., concerning the four-act *Don Carlos*. From the collection of Arturo Toscanini. *Verdi intimo*, p. 300.

1884 March 18, Genoa, ALS, 3 p. Mentions Pius IX, Quintino Sella, and Piroli. *Verdi intimo*, p. 310–11.

London, Sotheby's, 17 Nov. 1983, lots 208–09.
FRKF 231.15–16

1884 June 10, S Agata, ALS, 4 p. Mentions Puccini. *Verdi intimo*, p. 311–15.

London, Sotheby's, 11 Nov. 1982, lot 79.
FRKF 1103

1884 Dec. 24, Genoa, ALS, 4 p. Discusses musical trends in Italy. *Verdi intimo*, p. 317.

London, Sotheby's, 17 Nov. 1983, lot 210.
FRKF 231.17

1884 Dec. 29, Genoa, ALS, 3 p. Reports on *Don Carlos* in Milan. *Verdi intimo*, p. 305–06.

1885 March 16, Genoa, ALS, 4 p., about composer Giovanni Sgambati. *Verdi intimo*, p. 318–19.

London, Sotheby's, 26 May 1983, lots 104–05.
FRKF 135–36

1886 Jan. 19, Genoa, ALS, 2 p. On the death of Ponchielli. *Verdi intimo*, p. 331.

London, Sotheby's, 11 Nov. 1982, lot 80.
FRKF 1104

1886 March 17, Genoa, ALS, 3 p. Mentions *Otello* and Victor Maurel. *Verdi intimo*, p. 330–31.

London, Sotheby's, 17 Nov. 1983, lot 211.
FRKF 231.18

To M. Bagier

1863 May 16, Paris, ALS in French, 3 p., concerning the *Inno delle nazioni*; mentions Escudier. From the collection of Arturo Toscanini.

London, Sotheby's, 17 Nov. 1983, lot 195.
FRKF 231.06

To Leone Emanuele Bardare

1853 Jan. 1, Rome, ALS, 1 p., concerning *Il trovatore*. From the collection of Arturo Toscanini.

London, Sotheby's, 17 Nov. 1983, lot 192.
FRKF 231.03

To Salvatore Cammarano

1848 Dec. 20, Paris, ALS, 1 p., concerning *La battaglia di Legnano*.

FRKF 352

To Camille du Locle

1894 Dec. 20, Genoa, ALS, 2 p. (env), concerning *Otello* and *Falstaff*. Addressed to Du Locle in Capri. Inscribed by Du Locle on the last page: "Lettre de Verdi offerte à Mademoiselle Giuseppina Orsolini par son tout dévoué Camille du Locle."

London, Sotheby's, 21 May 1987, lot 551.
FRKF 1326

To Léon and Marie Escudier

1845 Sept. 20, Busseto, ALS to Marie Escudier, 2 p. Mentions *Attila* and meeting with Léon Pillet.

Marburg, Stargardt, 29–30 Nov. 1983, lot 987.
FRKF 149

1847 April 8, Milan, ALS to Marie Escudier, 2 p., concerning *Macbeth* and *I masnadieri*; mentions Jenny Lind and Benjamin Lumley. From the collection of Arturo Toscanini.

London, Sotheby's, 17 Nov. 1983, lot 191.
FRKF 231.02

1852 April 30, n.p., ALS to Léon Escudier, 3 p., concerning *Jérusalem* and *Il trovatore*.

FRKF 158

To Antonio Ghislanzoni

1870 July 18, St Agata, ALS, 3 p., concerning *Aida*.

Marburg, Stargardt, 21 June 1984, lot 948.
FRKF 484

To Ferdinand Hiller

1877 April 18, Busseto, ALS in French, 4 p., concerning the *Requiem* and the *String Quartet*. From the collection of Arturo Toscanini.

London, Sotheby's, 17 Nov. 1983, lot 207.
FRKF 231.14

To Vincenzo Luccardi

[1845] [June 7, Milan*] ALS, 1 p. "Tu sei il piu bel matto …"

1845 Oct. 17, Milan, ALS, 1 p. Mentions *Giovanna d'Arco*. Abbiati 1:596.

1846 Feb. 11, Venezia, ALS, 1 p. On the address side, draft of a letter (in Luccardi's hand?). Concerns *Attila*. Abbiati 1:600.

1848 July 14, Paris, ALS, 1 p. Abbiati 2:23.

1848 Nov. 21, Paris, ALS, 3 p., concerning *La battaglia di Legnano*. Abbiati 1:775–76.

[1852] Nov. 5 [Piacenza*] ALS, 1 p. Mentions Piave and *La traviata*. Abbiati 2:176.

1853 Sept. 28, Busseto, ALS, 1 p. "Volontieri ti renderei il piccolo servigio che mi chiedi …"

1853 Nov. 12, Paris, ALS, 1 p. "T'ho scritto prima di partire da Busseto …"

[1854?] n.p., ALS, 1 p., concerning *La traviata*. Abbiati 1:502–03.

1856 April 6, Busseto, ALS, 3 p. Mentions *Giovanna d'Arco*, *Stiffelio*, and *La battaglia di Legnano*. Abbiati 2:355–56.

1857 [March 27*] Busseto, ALS, 1 p., concerning *Simon Boccanegra*. Abbiati 2:398.

1857 July 29, Rimini, ALS, 1 p. Abbiati 2:435.

1857 Aug. 25, Busseto, AL, 2 p. "Se tu avessi potuto rispondarmi prima …"

1858 Feb. 7, Naples, ALS, 1 p., concerning *Gustavo III (Un ballo in maschera)*; also mentions *Simon Boccanegra*. Abbiati 2:469.

1858 Feb. 18, Naples, ALS, 1 p., concerning *Gustavo III*; also mentions *Simon Boccanegra* and *Aroldo*. Abbiati 2:474.

1858 Feb. 27, Naples, ALS, 2 p., concerning *Gustavo III* (or *Una vendetta in domino*); also mentions *Simon Boccanegra*. Abbiati 2:474–75.

1858 March 8 [Naples*] ALS, 1 p. "Resterò ancora in Napoli 7 od 8 giorni circa."

1858 March 22, Naples, ALS, 1 p., concerning *Gustavo III* (or *Una vendetta in domino* or *Adalia degli Adimari*). Abbiati 2:475–76.

1858 Nov. 21, Naples, ALS, 1 p., concerning an impending trip to Rome.

1859 March 15, Civitavecchia, ALS, 2 p. Abbiati 2:532.

1859 April 26, Busseto, ALS, 2 p., concerning the loss of the diploma Verdi was awarded by the Accademia filarmonica di Roma.

1859 May 18, Busseto, ALS, 1 p. "Questa volta colla tua del 10 …"

1860 Jan. 12, Genoa, ALS, 1 p. "E' fiato gettato di scrivere …," with a postscript by Giuseppina Verdi.

1860 April 5, Busseto, ALS, 3 p. "Ieri m'arrivo la cassa del ritratto che tu hai spedito …"

1860 May 12, Busseto, ALS, 2 p. "Ho fatto quanto m'hai detto per la statuetta …"

1860 June 10, Busseto, ALS, 2 p. Mentions Faccio's *Amleto*.

1860 Dec. 7, Genoa, ALS, 2 p. Mentions *Un ballo in maschera*.

1862 Feb. 27, Paris, ALS, 3 p. Mentions Caroline Douvry-Barbot and *Un ballo in maschera*. Abbiati 2:687.

1862 March 10, Paris, ALS, 3 p. Mentions Caroline Douvry-Barbot. Abbiati 2:687–88.

1862 July 26, Busseto, ALS, 2 p. (env.). "Fra il 20 e il 23 d'agosto partirò …"

1863 Jan. 13, Madrid, ALS, 2 p. (env). Mentions *La forza del destino*. Abbiati 2:726.

1863 Feb. 17, Madrid, ALS, 3 p. Mentions *La forza del destino*. Abbiati 2:730.

1863 Sept. 7, St Agata, ALS, 3 p. "Sono sorpreso nel sentire come tu non abbia ricevuto mie lettere …"

1863 Dec. 16, Busseto, ALS, 1 p. (with recto of envelope). "Io mi trovo qui in mezzo alla nebbia …"

1864 June 28, Genoa, ALS, 2 p. (env). "Ho tardato tanto a risponderti …" [postmarked 1862].

1864 Nov. 29, Busseto, ALS, 2 p. Mentions a recent visit from Piave.

1864 Dec. 31, Busseto, ALS, 1 p. (env). "Fra le tante lettere che ho ricevute …"

1865 June 19, Busseto, ALS, 3 p. (env), concerning Verdi's private oratory at St. Agata.

1866 April 14, St Agata, ALS, 1 p. (env). Mentions *Don Carlos*.

1866 May 2, Busseto, ALS, 3 p. "Ho ricevuto la tua lettera con entro il permesso …"

[1867 May 15, Busseto*] ALS, 3 p., with mourning envelope addressed to Luccardi in Paris. Mentions Escudier and an impending visit to Paris.

[1867 July 23, Busseto*] ALS, 1 p., on mourning stationery (env). Announces the death of Antonio Barezzi.

1868 May 8, St Agata, ALS, 2 p. (env). Abbiati 3:192–93.

1869 Nov. 30, Genoa, ALS, 3 p. (env). "Ho ricevuto la carta tua dal 27 …"

1870 Jan. 1, Genoa, ALS, 2 p. "Auguro a te pure ed alla tua famiglia …"

1870 Feb. 3, Genoa, ALS, 1 p. (env). "Povero Vaselli!!"

[1870 April, Parma] ALS, 1 p. "Sono a Parma per le prove d'Aida …"

1870 Oct. 26, St Agata, ALS, 1 p. (env), concerning *Aida*.

1870 Dec. 30, Genoa, ALS, 3 p. (env), concerning *Aida*.

"Sabato," n.p., ALS, 2 p. "Ricevo oggi la tua e prima di partire per St Agata rispondo subito."

FRKF 118

1871 June 9, St Agata, ALS, 3 p. (env), concerning *Aida* and the situation in France; mentions Draneht Bey. From the collection of Arturo Toscanini.

London, Sotheby's, 17 Nov. 1983, lot 204.
FRKF 231.12

To Andrea Maffei

1845 Sept. 12, Busseto, ALS, 2 p., concerning *Attila*.

London, Sotheby's, 21 May 1987, lot 542.
FRKF 1325

To Ignazio Marini

1841 Nov. 15, Milan, ALS, 2 p., concerning *Oberto*, and giving the text of a new cavatina; mentions Temistocle Solera. With one musical quotation.

See Philip Gossett's Afterword in: *Giuseppe Verdi. Ernani*, edited by Claudio Gallico (Chicago and London: The University of Chicago Press; Milan: Ricordi, 1985), p. [lxv].
London, Sotheby's, 9–10 May 1985, lot 218.
FRKF 780

To Count Nani Mocenigo

1844 [Jan.?] 28, Venice, ALS, 1 p., concerning *Ernani*. Addressed to "Alla Nobile Presidenza del Gran Teatro La Fenice." In the hand of Piave and signed by both him and Verdi.

London, Sotheby's, 9–10 May 1985, lot 220.
FRKF 782

To Carlo Panattoni

1891 Feb. 7, Genoa, ALS, 3 p. (env). Mentions Nuitter, Pacini, Royer, and *Le trouvère*. Envelope addressed to: "Avv[ocato] Carlo Panattoni, Deputato al Parlamento."

FRKF 504

To Francesco Maria Piave

1843 June 16, Milan, ALS, 1 p., concerning a projected *Cromwell*.

1843 Aug. 8, Milan, ALS, 2 p., concerning the projected *Allan Cameron*.

1843 Aug. 19, Milan, ALS, 2 p., concerning *Allan Cameron*.

1843 Aug. 27, Milan, ALS, 1 p., concerning *Allan Cameron*.

1843 Oct. 2, Milan, ALS, 3 p., concerning the libretto of *Ernani*.

1843 Oct. 10, Cassano, ALS, 2 p., concerning the libretto of *Ernani*.

1843 Oct. 19, [Cassano*] ALS, 1 p., concerning *Ernani*.

1844 April 2, Milan, ALS, 1 p., concerning *Ernani*.

[1844] [April 18, Milan*] ALS, 1 p., concerning a projected *Lorenzino* and *I due Foscari*.

1844 May 9, Milan, ALS, 1 p., concerning *I due Foscari*.

1844 May 14, Milan, ALS, 2 p., concerning the libretto of *I due Foscari*.

[1844] [May 22, Milan*] ALS, 2 p., concerning *I due Foscari*; also mentions Pacini.

1844 Sept. 9, Busseto, ALS, 1 p., concerning *I due Foscari*; also mentions Donizetti.

FRKF 85

[1844?] [Nov. 30, Milan*] ALS, 2 p., concerning *I due Foscari*; also mentions Pacini and Samuele Levi's *Giuditta*. Includes a musical notation.

[1845] [Nov. 17, Milan*] ALS, 3 p., concerning *Attila*; mentions Temistocle Solera.

London, Sotheby's, 9–10 May 1985, lots 221–22.
FRKF 783.1–2

[1845] [April 12, Milan*] ALS, 3 p. Discusses the *Attila* project and mentions Mme de Staël's *De l'Allemagne*.

[1845] [Nov. 24, Milan*] ALS, 3 p., concerning *Attila*, with references to *Nabucco*, *Giovanni d'Arco*, *Guillaume Tell*, and *Robert le diable*.

[1845] [Nov. 28, Milan*] ALS, 2 p., concerning *Attila*, with a reference to *I due Foscari*.

FRKF 85

[1846] [Aug. 22, Milan*] ALS, 3 p., concerning *Macbeth* and *Il corsaro*, with references to the projected *Cromwell*; mentions Ricci and Maffei.

London, Sotheby's, 9–10 May 1985, lot 223.
FRKF 783.3

1846 Sept. 2, Milan, ALS, 1 p., concerning *Macbeth*.

[1846 Sept. 4, Milan] ALS, 2 p. "Eccoti lo schizzo del Macbet …"

FRKF 85

1846 Sept. 14, Milan, ALS, 2 p., concerning *Il corsaro* and *Macbeth*. From the collection of Arturo Toscanini.

London, Sotheby's, 17 Nov. 1983, lot 190.
FRKF 231.01

[1846] [Sept. 22, Milan*] ALS, 3 p., concerning *Macbeth*. Mentions Count Mocenigo.

1846 Oct. 23, Milan, ALS, 1 p., concerning *Macbeth*.

1846 Oct. 29, Milan, ALS, 2 p., concerning *Macbeth*. Mentions Count Mocenigo.

FRKF 85

1846 Nov. 9, Milan, ALS, 2 p., concerning *Macbeth*.

London, Sotheby's, 29 Nov. 1985, lot 223.
FRKF 1065

[1846] [Dec. 3, Milan*] ALS, 3 p., concerning *Macbeth*; includes a draft of the libretto for act 2, scene 1.

[1846] [Dec. 10, Milan*] ALS, 6 p., concerning *Macbeth*; includes a draft of the libretto for act 4.

[1846] [Dec. 22, Milan*] ALS, 3 p., concerning *Macbeth*; includes an outline of the last scene of act 4.

FRKF 85

[1846] [Dec. 26, Milan*] ALS, 1 p.

London, Sotheby's, 29 Nov. 1985, lot 235.
FRKF 1066

[1847] [Jan. 21, Milan*] ALS, 1 p., concerning *Macbeth*.

[1847] [Feb. 14, Milan*] ALS, 1 p., concerning *Macbeth*.

1847 March 26, Milan, ALS, 2 p., reporting on the premiere of *Macbeth*.

1850 April 28, Busseto, ALS, 3 p. Mentions the plays *Kean* and *Le comte Herman* (both by Alexandre Dumas), *Stradella*, *Stiffelius*, and *Le roi s'amuse* [i.e. *Rigoletto*].

1850 May 6, Busseto, ALS, 3 p., concerning *Rigoletto*; mentions *Ernani*.

FRKF 85

[1850 May 29, Piacenza*] ALS, 2 p.

London, Sotheby's, 29 Nov. 1985, lot 237.
FRKF 1068

[1850] [June 3, Cremona*] ALS, 2 p., concerning *Rigoletto*.

1850 Oct. 22, Busseto, ALS, 1 p., concerning *Rigoletto*; also discusses *Stiffelio*.

FRKF 85

1850 Nov. 28, Busseto, ALS, 2 p., concerning *Rigoletto* and *Stiffelio*.

London, Sotheby's, 9–10 May 1985, lot 224.
FRKF 783.4

1850 Nov. 29, Busseto, ALS, 2 p., concerning *Rigoletto*.

1851 Jan. 14, Busseto, ALS, 2 p., concerning *Rigoletto*.

[1851 Jan. 20, Borgo S. Donnino*] ALS, 3 p., concerning *Rigoletto*.

1851 Jan. 24, Busseto, ALS, 1 p., concerning *Rigoletto*.

FRKF 85

[1851 Jan. 31, Borgo S. Donnino*] ALS, 2 p., concerning *Rigoletto*.

London, Sotheby's, 29 Nov. 1985, lot 236.
FRKF 1067

1851 Feb. 5, Busseto, ALS, 3 p., concerning *Rigoletto*. With a one-page postscript by Giuseppina Strepponi.

1851 Feb. 7, Busseto, ALS, 1 p., concerning *Rigoletto*.

1851 March 25, Busseto, ALS, 1 p., concerning *Rigoletto*.

1851 Nov. 15, Busseto, ALS, 1 p., concerning *Stiffelio*.

FRKF 85

1854 Feb. 10, Paris, ALS, 3 p., concerning *Les vêpres siciliennes*; mentions Boracchi and Sophie Cruvelli.

London, Sotheby's, 9–10 May 1985, lot 225.
FRKF 783.5

1854 March 16, Paris, ALS, 2 p., concerning *La traviata*; mentions Antonio Gallo, Ricordi, and singers Maria Spezia and Coletti. From the collection of Arturo Toscanini.

London, Sotheby's, 17 Nov. 1983, lot 193.
FRKF 231.04

1856 July 31, Busseto, ALS, 1 p., concerning the revision of *Stiffelio* [i.e. *Aroldo*]

[1856 Aug. 23, Enghein-les-Bains*] ALS, 2 p., concerning *Aroldo*; also mentions *Ernani* and Meyerbeer's *Les Huguenots*.

FRKF 85

[1856 Oct. 21, Paris*] ALS, 2 p., concerning *Il trovatore* and *Simon Boccanegra*; mentions Maria Spezia. From the collection of Arturo Toscanini.

London, Sotheby's, 17 Nov. 1983, lot 194.
FRKF 231.05

1857 Feb. 5, St Agata, ALS, 2 p., concerning *Aroldo*. Mostly in the hand of Giuseppina Strepponi, signed by Verdi with a postscript and the address in his hand.

London, Sotheby's, 9–10 May 1985, lot 227.
FRKF 783.7

1861 Aug. 5, Busseto, ALS, 3 p., concerning *La forza del destino*; also mentions *Ernani*, *Il trovatore*, *La traviata*, *Un ballo in maschera*, and *Simon Boccanegra*, as well as Ricordi and Maffei.

1861 Aug. 6, Busseto, ALS, 3 p., concerning *La forza del destino*.

1861 Aug. 13, Busseto, ALS, 2 p., concerning *La forza del destino*; also mentions Enrico Tamberlick.

[1861 Aug.] ALS, 3 p., concerning *La forza del destino*. "Eccoti il quart' atto." Dated late Aug. by Baker.

[1861 Sept.] ALS, 1 p., concerning *La forza del destino*. "Va bene la scena …"

[1861 Sept. 25, Busseto*] ALS, 1 p., concerning *La forza del destino*. Includes one musical notation.

[1861 Nov. 5, Busseto*] ALS, 4 p., concerning *La forza del destino*. The fourth page is an additional draft for the libretto pasted on p. 3.

[1861 Nov. 10, Busseto*] ALS, 3 p., concerning *La forza del destino*.

[1861 Nov. 20, Busseto*] ALS, 3 p., concerning *La forza del destino*; also mentions Ricordi. With a postscript by Giuseppina.

[1861 Nov.?] ALS, 1 p., concerning *La forza del destino*.

[1861 Nov. 22, Milan*] ALS, 1 p., concerning *La forza del destino*.

1861 Dec. 14, St. Petersburg, ALS, 2 p., concerning *La forza del destino*.

[1862 Jan.] [St. Petersburg*] ALS, 1 p., concerning *La forza del destino*; mentions Emma La Grua.

[1864 Dec.] ALS, 1 p., concerning the revision of *Macbeth*. "Per non perder tempo ho fatto la musica dell' aria …"

1864 Dec. 15, St Agata, ALS, 2 p., concerning the revision of *Macbeth*.

1864 Dec. 20, n.p., ALS, 1 p., concerning the revision of *Macbeth*.

[1865 Jan.] ALS, 1 p., concerning the revision of *Macbeth*. "Nelle strofe del duetto finale ..." Dated by Baker.

1865 Jan. 28, St Agata, ALS, 4 p., concerning the revision of *Macbeth*; includes a draft libretto for act 4, scenes 9–11.

[1865] Feb. 1, n.p., ALS, 2 p., concerning the revision of *Macbeth*.

FRKF 85

1869 June 19, Busseto, ALS, 1 p. Mentions rehearsals of *Bianca* and Medini, the first Ramfis in *Aida*.

London, Sotheby's, 9–10 May 1985, lot 231.
FRKF 783.9

To Giulio and Tito Ricordi

1853 Nov. 7, Paris, ALS to Tito Ricordi, 2 p., concerning *Rigoletto*, *Il trovatore*, and *Luisa Miller*; mentions singers Mario, Marietta Alboni, Emilia Frezzolini, and Italo Gardoni.

London, Sotheby's, 21 May 1987, lot 647.
FRKF 1327

1884 Dec. 9, Genoa, ALS to Giulio Ricordi, 2 p. (env), asking Ricordi to arrange for him to receive subscriptions to the Milanese press.

Marburg, Stargardt, 26 Nov. 1985, lot 939B.
FRKF 1158

1886 April 2, Paris, ALS to Giulio Ricordi, 4 p., concerning *Otello* and *La traviata*; also mentions Massenet's *Le Cid* and its interpreters, Rose Caron and Jean de Reszke, and Reyer's *Sigurd*. Includes one musical notation to describe the range of the tenor J.-V. Duc.

London, Sotheby's, 17 May 1990, lot 279.
FRKF 1301

To Alphonse Royer

1856 July 20, Venice, ALS, 2 p., congratulating Royer on his appointment as director of the Opéra; mentions *Il trovatore*.

Paris, Oger-Dumont (Drouot), 14 Feb. 1985, lot 65.
FRKF 700

To "Car[issi]o Sezzi"

1856 July 19, Venice, ALS, 1 p. Discusses travel plans to Paris.

Marburg, Stargardt, 29–30 Nov. 1983, lot 988.
FRKF 150

To Alfredo Soffredini

1896 [but possibly earlier] Dec. 11, Genoa, ALS, 2 p., concerning *Falstaff*. From the collection of Arturo Toscanini.

London, Sotheby's, 17 Nov. 1983, lot 212.
FRKF 231.19

To Francesco and Margherita Tamagno

1880 Feb. 28, Paris, ALS, 1 p., concerning *Otello*; mentions Arrigo Boito.

1886 Jan. 30, Genoa, ALS, 3 p., concerning *Otello*.

1887 Jan. 11, Milan, ALS to Margherita Tamagno, 1 p. (env)

FRKF 1108

To Ermanno Wolf-Ferrari

1896 June 15, Busseto, ALS, 1 p. (env), turning down a request.

London, Sotheby's, 28 May 1986, lot 605.
FRKF 1134

Other letters

To an unidentified correspondent

[ca. 1871] n.p., ALS, draft, concerning *Aida*.

London, Sotheby's, 9–10 May 1985, lot 239.
FRKF 783.10

Antonio Barezzi to Francesco Maria Piave

1844 March 20, ALS, 3 p. Quotes a letter from Verdi, dated 16 March 1844, reporting on the premiere of *Ernani* in Venice. Barezzi was Verdi's father-in-law.

FRKF 85

Giuseppina Verdi to Francesco Maria Piave

[1859 Nov. 3, Parma*] ALS, 1 p. The address is in Verdi's hand.

London, Sotheby's, 9–10 May 1985, lot 228.
FRKF 783.8

III. MISCELLANEOUS

Carte-de-visite photograph of Verdi, n.d. [ca. 1850] 10 × 6.5 cm. Reproduced from the portrait of Verdi by Disdéri.

London, Sotheby's, 17 May 1990, lot 279.
FRKF 1301

PAUL VERLAINE (1844–96)

I. MANUSCRIPTS

"A celle qu'on dit froide"

Holograph manuscript of this poem, 1889, 2 p., written in black ink on two sheets of laid paper, numbered 2 and 3, both glued on a sheet of cream-colored paper. On the left of the second sheet, facing the poem, two pen-and-ink drawings by Verlaine representing Gothic windows. Signed and dated Sept. 1889 at the end.

First published in *Femmes* (n.p. [Brussels: Kistemaekers], 1891). See *Oeuvres poétiques complètes*, p. 532–33 and 1220–22.

Paris, Jean Morelle (Drouot), 14–15 Dec. 1983, lot 333.
FRKF 248a

"A Raoul Ponchon"

Holograph manuscript of this poem, n.d. [1891], 1 p., in black ink on the recto of a half-sheet of Assistance publique paper. The title, "Raoul Ponchon, condamné," was cancelled, then rewritten at the top of the half-sheet, followed by the epigraph (from Ponchon's *Les vieux messieurs*): "… cet autre commençait à manger de la merde." Signed at the end.

Published as "A Raoul Ponchon (Conseils dans sa manière)" in *Invectives* (Paris: Léon Vanier, 1896). See *Oeuvres poétiques complètes*, p. 946 and 1317.

Paris, Jean Morelle (Drouot), 14–15 Dec. 1983, lot 336.
FRKF 248c

"Balanide"

Holograph manuscript of the poem, 1890, 1 p., in black ink on a half-sheet of Assistance publique paper (12.5 × 21 cm). At the top of the page, numbering XVII bis. Dated in pencil at the bottom: "Hôpital Broussais. Janvier 90." Small cross after the title and footnote in Verlaine's hand: "seul fragment intégral d'un livre détruit: D'aucuns."

First published in *"Hombres" (Hommes)* [Paris: Albert Messein, 1904]. See *Oeuvres poétiques complètes*, p. 1406–07.

Heinrich Schütz to Henry Miller, p. 80–81.
Paris, Laurin-Guilloux-Buffetaud-Tailleur (Drouot), 12 June 1984, lot 130.
FRKF 467

"Nouvelles notes sur Rimbaud"

Holograph manuscript of this essay, 1895, 8 p., in black ink on eight octavo sheets of cream and light green laid paper (watermarks of Universal and Original Island Mill respectively). Verlaine has cancelled and modified a previous title ("Diverses notes …" [?]). On the verso of p. 5, cancelled title: "Les Tablettes d'un lézard / par / Paul Paillette." Signed by Verlaine and dated Oct. 1895 at the end.

See *Oeuvres en prose complètes*, p. 973–76.
Paris, Jean Morelle (Drouot), 14–15 Dec. 1983, lot 337.
FRKF 248b

"Vaucochard (au peuple)"

Holograph fragment of *Vaucochard et fils* Ier, n.d., 2 p. The manuscript is written in black ink on both sides of a sheet of gray paper (13 × 21 cm). It begins "Mes amis, mes enfants, vous demandez ici …" and ends with the words "Sire, parlez plus bas. (Sera continué très prochainement)."

See *Oeuvres complètes*, I: 1359–61.
Paris, Laurin-Guilloux-Buffetaud-Tailleur (Drouot), 12 June 1984, lot 127.
FRKF 464

II. LETTERS

To Ernest Delahaye

[1873 May 15] "Jeudi," Jehonville, ALS, 4 p., illustrated on p. [2], [3], and [4] with self-caricatures in purple ink, with captions. The one on p. [4] is in two parts and has the captions "Nous," showing Verlaine and Rimbaud parting at the French-Belgian border, and "Lui," showing Rimbaud drinking and smoking at a café table. *Correspondance générale*, p. 310.

Paris, Laurin-Guilloux-Buffetaud-Tailleur (Drouot), 19 March 1986, lot 200.
FRKF 1278

To Leo d'Orfer

1884 Sept. 2, Coulommes par Attigny, ALS, 1 p., concerning mostly manuscripts of poems by Rimbaud. Published partially in *Correspondance générale*, p. 873.

Paris, Jean Morelle (Drouot), 14 Dec. 1983, lot 330.
FRKF 248d

1887 Oct. 23 [Paris*] ALS, 3 p., concerning *Sagesse* and *Parallèlement*; also gives autobiographical details and mentions Leconte de Lisle and Rimbaud. *Oeuvres complètes*, I: 1271–73.

Paris, Laurin-Guilloux-Buffetaud-Tailleur (Drouot), 12 June 1984, lot 128.
FRKF 465

To Louis Jullien

1887 Nov. 21 [Paris] ALS, 5 p. Discusses future financial arrangements; mentions *Amour, Parallèlement, Bonheur*, and the *Mémoires d'un veuf*; also mentions Charles Morice.

Louis Jullien was the head doctor of the St. Lazare Hospital.

Paris, Laurin-Guilloux-Buffetaud-Tailleur (Drouot), 12 June 1984, lot 129.
FRKF 466

To Léon Vanier

[1886 Jan. 14] n.p., ALS, 2 p. Addressed to "O bien aimé libraire et éditeur trez-prétieux"; mentions *Les mémoires d'un veuf*, which Vanier published in 1886. Dated in a different hand.

1888 Aug. 13, n.p., ALS, 2 p., concerning *Romances sans paroles* and *Les poètes maudits*. Also mentions Cazals and Rimbaud.

Paris, Laurin-Guilloux-Buffetaud-Tailleur (Drouot), 16–17 Nov. 1983, lots 235, 238.
FRKF 263, 266

To an unidentified recipient

1884 Aug. 31, n.p., ALS, 2 p., concerning *Jadis et naguère*, also mentions *Amour, Les poètes maudits*; mentions Forain, René Ghil, and others. Possibly to Léon Vanier. Not in *Correspondance générale*.

Paris, Laurin-Guilloux-Buffetaud-Tailleur (Drouot), 16–17 Nov. 1983, lot 237.
FRKF 265

III. PRINTED WORKS

Bonheur. Paris: Léon Vanier, Éditeur / 19, quai Saint-Michel, 1891.

[4] + [1]–120 [+ 2] p. No. 14 of 55 copies on Hollande. Large paper copy, untrimmed.

Bound in before the half-title: original pencil drawing of Verlaine, signed Aman-Jean. Tipped in: ALS from Verlaine to Jean Moréas, n.y., "Mercredi 11 h." n.p., 1 p., concerning a rendez-vous; also mentions Germain Nouveau.

Bound in dark red morocco, with a single fillet along the edges. Spine with raised bands and author, title, and year gold-tooled. Dark red silk doublures. On verso of boards, triple gold fillet along the edges. Original brown paper wrappers bound in. On last page, otherwise blank, unsigned autograph note recording the purchase of this book at Vanier's store on 9 June 1893 and the sale of a similar copy auctioned in 1922 at the Meilhac sale. Bookplates of Pierre Duché and "EAP."

Confessions: notes autobiographiques. Portrait par Anquetin. Paris: Publications du "Fin de siècle" / 59, rue de Provence / 1895.

[2], [1]–246 [+ 6] p. [+ 2 leaves of plates]. No. 2 of 30 on Hollande. Large paper copy, untrimmed. Bound in after the half-title page: portrait of Verlaine by Louis Anquetin, signed by Verlaine. Bound in after the title page: portrait of Verlaine by an unidentified artist, dated 17 March 1869, printed on Japan paper with the pencil inscription "Verlaine à 25 ans." Tipped in: ALS from Verlaine to "Mon cher ami," 1894 Oct. 12 [Paris] rue de Vaugirard, 4, hôtel de Lisbonne, 2 p., concerning *Confessions*.

Bound in half red morocco and red marbled paper. Top edge gilt. Spine with raised bands and author, title, and year gold-tooled. Reddish brown marbled end papers. Original wrappers bound in. Bookplates of Pierre Bellanger, Bibliothèque Jacques Odry, and Raoul Simonson.

Liturgies intimes / Mars 1892. Paris: Bibliothèque du Saint-Graal [1892].

[8], [1]–31 [+ 1] p. Frontispiece portrait of Verlaine by Hayet. In original white paper wrappers. On front wrapper: "Bibliothèque du Saint-Graal / Nº 1." One of the 50 copies on Vélin, from a total edition of 375. Laid in: publisher's announcement for *Liturgies intimes*, mentioning a de-luxe edition with illustrated cover by Cazals. Laid in: original watercolor drawing on a sheet of laid paper, folded in the middle (37 × 25 cm), initialed FAC [F.A. Cazals] and dated 1890 in the lower right corner; also with the annotation: "frontispiece pour Liturgies intimes." The drawing, which is in fact the projected illustrated cover, represents Verlaine, from the back, facing a seashore, with a large apparition of an angel holding a chalice, standing in a conch-like nacelle with a cross in front. Also laid in: photo-lithograph of the drawing by Hayet showing Verlaine's mother on her death bed. Pasted in on p. [1]: ALS on two sides of a card from Cazals to André Hugon, [1938 May 5*], Villemomble, concerning his projected illustrated cover for *Liturgies intimes* and mentioning the Hayet plate. Laid in: ALS from Cazals to André Hugon, 1939 Jan. 24, 1 p., requesting the return of the watercolor and Hayet plate.

In a quarter purple morocco chemise, with author and title gold-tooled on spine, and pink marbled paper slipcase. Bookplate of Bibliothèque Jacques Odry.

Les mémoires d'un veuf. Paris: Léon Vanier, Libraire-éditeur / 19, quai Saint-Michel, 1886.

[4] + [1]–224 p. Copy no. 22 of 22 on Hollande. Large paper copy, untrimmed, original brown wrappers bound in. Tipped in: ANS from Verlaine to Léon Vanier, 1887 Feb. 10, asking him to give a copy of the book to Cazals. Laid in: ALS from Verlaine to Vanier, 1889 Jan. 11, 2 p., concerning *Mémoires d'un veuf, Parallèlement, Jadis et naguère*, and *Les poètes maudits*; also mentions Cazals. Bookplate of Bibliothèque Jacques Odry.

Bound in quarter brown morocco (stamp of Semet et Plumelle) and brown marbled paper, separated by a gold fillet. Top edge gilt. Spine with raised bands and gilt fleurons, with author, title, and year gilt-stamped. Pink marbled paper endpapers.

Brussels, Simonson, 19 May 1984, lots 284, 290, 299, 301.
FRKF 374–77

Les poètes maudits: Tristan Corbière, Arthur Rimbaud, Stéphane Mallarmé. Paris: Léon Vanier, 1884.

[1–4], [I]–IV, [5]–56 + three additional leaves of plates. Printed note on title page: "(Cet ouvrage n'est tiré qu'à 253 exemplaires)." Stamped R in red on p. [2]. In the original paper wrappers.

FRKF 577

PAULINE VIARDOT (1821–1910)

Letters to Bernhard Cossmann

n.y. July 3, n.p., ALS, 2 p. on monogrammed stationery. Mentions the Rubinstein *Cello Sonata*.

n.d., "Vendredi," n.p., ALS, 1 p., concerning music lessons.

n.y. Dec. 11, "Dimanche," n.p., ALS, 1 p.

London, Sotheby's, 19 Nov. 1985, lot 954.
FRKF 1005

Letter to Henri Reber

n.d., n.p., ALS, 3 p., on monogrammed stationery, cancelling an engagement.

Paris, Le Roux-Mathias (Drouot), 19 April 1985, lot 317.
FRKF 723

Letter to Mme Zimmermann

n.d., "Lundi 16," n.p., ALS, 2 p., an invitation to an event at which Chopin, George Sand, and Ary Scheffer, among others, will be present.

Paris, Oger-Dumont (Drouot), 14 Feb. 1985, lot 36.
FRKF 688

Letter to an unidentified recipient

1863 Dec. 21, Baden-Baden, ALS, 4 p., on monogrammed stationery, about a concert program, including Schubert's *Erlkönig*, Bellini's *La sonnambula*, and Gluck's *Orphée*.

London, Sotheby's, 19 Nov. 1985, lot 953.
FRKF 998

Printed "Notice biographique" filled out in Viardot's hand, n.d. [but after 1849], 1 p., in black ink on the recto of a 13.5 × 16 cm sheet of paper. Listed among her roles are Fidès and Gluck's Orphée.

Paris, Le Roux-Mathias (Drouot), 19 April 1985, lot 317.
FRKF 723.5

FÉLIX VIEUILLE (1872–1953)

AN on a visiting card ("Félix Vieuille / de l'Opéra-Comique"), n.d., n.p., a note of thanks.

Vieuille premiered the part of Arkel in *Pelléas et Mélisande* in 1902.

FRKF 535f

HEITOR VILLA-LOBOS (1887–1959)

Fantasia de movimentos mistos

Holograph manuscript, in short score, of the arrangement for violin and piano, 1921, 28 p., written in black ink, with corrections in black and red pencil, on seven nested bifolia and a single sheet, sewn, and paginated [1] to 28. At the top of p. [1] in the composer's hand: "Fantaisie de / mouvements mixtes / pour violon et orchestre / A Paulina d'Ambrosio / H. Villa-Lobos / Rio 1921 / I. Alma convulsa (Tourment) / Réduction pour Violon et Piano."

According to the auction catalog, despite the mention that the manuscript is the reduction for violin and piano, the presence of many indications for orchestration suggests that it is a fair copy of the short score.

Paris, Hervé Poulain (Drouot), 5 April 1984, lot 33.
FRKF 443

VOLTAIRE (1694–1778)

Autograph manuscript on religion, n.p., n.d., in black ink on a small octavo bifolium of laid paper (10 × 16 cm). The text begins "cherche la vraye relligion elle doit etre universelle …"

At the bottom of p. 1 is the signature: "Yontchin." The text on p. 2 begins "tout persecuteur est ennemi de dieu et des hommes." A few fragmentary lines in transferred ink are barely decipherable on p. 3, which was trimmed. They include the words "Yontchin" and "jesuite."

Marburg, Stargardt, 5–6 March 1985, lot 376.
FRKF 805

Letter to Charles Palissot de Fontenoy

[1757] Aug. 15 [Ferney] Les Délices, ALS, 3 p., concerning Guymond de la Touche's play *Iphigénie en Tauride*; mentions Claude-Pierre Patu and Anne-Marie de Luxembourg, princesse de Robecq. *Correspondance* IV:1070–71 (Besterman 4837).

Marburg, Stargardt, 5–6 March 1985, lot 377.
FRKF 806

RICHARD WAGNER (1813–83)

I. MUSIC MANUSCRIPTS

"Attente," WWV 55
"Les deux grenadiers," WWV 60
"Mignonne," WWV 57

Holograph drafts for these three songs for voice and piano, n.d., 4 p.

> Notated in black ink and pencil on p. [1] to [4] of a tall bifolium with 14 hand-drawn staves, foliated 305 and 306 in an unidentified hand. On p. [1], draft of "Mignonne, allons voir si la rose," on the poem by Pierre de Ronsard, notated on a 2-staff system, the first 15 measures in black ink, the rest in pencil. Incomplete: stops at the word "ter[nir]." At the bottom of the page, doodles in black ink using bits of texts from both "Mignonne" and "Les deux grenadiers." On p. [2] and [3], drafts for "Attente" notated in black ink on 3-staff systems. At the top of p. [2] in Wagner's hand: "Attente / Victor Hugo." Incomplete: the music stops after measure 22; only the text is notated thereafter. On p. [4], pencil drafts, incomplete, for "Les deux grenadiers," on a French translation of Heine's "Die beiden Grenadiere"; the words are written only through measure 17.

Dated 1839 ("Attente," "Mignonne") and 1839–40 ("Les deux grenadiers") by Grove.

London, Sotheby's, 9–10 May 1985, lot 245.
FRKF 784a–c

"Attente," WWV 55
"Extase," WWV 54

Holograph manuscript, incomplete, of these two songs for voice and piano, both to texts by Victor Hugo, n.d., 2 p.

> Notated in black ink on both sides of a single sheet of tall hand-drawn 24-staff paper, "Attente" on the recto, "Extase" on the verso. "Attente" lacks the first 12 measures; "Extase" comprises only the first 12 measures of the piano accompaniment, without words or vocal line. Accompanied by the first printing of "Attente" in the journal *Europa* (Stuttgart, 1842), 2 p.

Both songs dated 1839 by Grove.

London, Sotheby's, 29 Nov. 1985, lot 245.
FRKF 1045a–c

Die Meistersinger von Nürnberg, WWV 96. *Preislied*

Holograph manuscript, the vocal line only, 1866, 1 p.

> Notated in black (brown) ink on the recto of a large sheet of paper (31 × 40 cm). At the top, in Wagner's hand: "Die Selige Morgentraum - / Deut-weise." At the bottom, also in Wagner's hand: "Gedichtet zu Eva's von Stolzing Preise." Initialed at the end of the last staff and dated 24 Dec. 1866 at the bottom.

> The text of the three verses is written, in Wagner's hand throughout, below the vocal line. On a separate sheet of paper, autograph presentation inscription to Arturo Toscanini from Eva Chamberlain-Wagner: "Arturo Toscanini / dem meisterlichen Priester heiliger Deutscher Kunst, dem von Gott gesandten, theuren Mann, sei dieses Blatt gewidmet welches die Tochter Richard Wagners, von ihrer Mutter einst empfing und das sie nun in Bayreuths feierlich ernstester Stunde mit dankerfüller Begeisterung in seine wunderhätigen treuen Hände giebt." Signed and dated: "Bayreuth, Festspieljahr 1930."

London, Sotheby's, 17 Nov. 1983, lot 214.
FRKF 233

II. LITERARY MANUSCRIPTS

Lohengrin

Autograph manuscript of the libretto for the opera, 1845, 29 p., in black ink, with additions and corrections in red ink and in black pencil, on a gathering of eight nested bifolia of tall laid paper (21.5 × 35 cm), written on both sides, foliated 1–16 in an unidentified hand. Outer bifolium is wove paper.

> On the front of the outer bifolium is the following inscription: "Von des deutschen [grosses] Meisters / eigner Hand / geschrieben / schenke ich (Fritz Weiss K.S. Hopofernsänger) dieses / werthvolle Manuscript / meinem lieben werthen Wilhelm (Trinius) / Richard Wagner schenkte es an / Carl Ritter (Schwager der Johanna Wagner) / dessen Bruder Alexander od. Sascha Ritter / Franzisca Wagner zur Frau hat / Darauf empfing es der Klaviervirtuoso / Rudolf Wehner / und als dieser d. 8. Octbr. 1857 starb, kam / es in meine Hände / Fritz Weiss." Written below in pencil, in an unidentified hand: "Dresden, July 1868."

> The text begins on the first page of the second bifolium, preceded by the title in Wagner's hand: "Lohengrin / Romantische Oper / in 3 Acten," followed by the list of characters. Signed and dated at the end Dresden, 27 Nov. 1845. Together with an 8-line fragment written on a small piece of gray paper, beginning with Lohengrin's words "O Elsa! Was hast du mir angethan!" in the last scene, originally laid in. The corresponding passage is on fol. 15r of this manuscript.

Described in J. Kapp, "Die Urschrift von Richard Wagners 'Lohengrin'-Dichtung," *Die Musik* XI (1911–12), 88–93;

and O. Strobel, "Die Urgestalt des 'Lohengrin': Wagners erster dichterischer Entwurf," *Bayreuther Festspielführer* (1936), 141–71.

London, Sotheby's, 29 Nov. 1985, lot 246.
FRKF 1035

Siegfrieds Tod

Autograph manuscript of the libretto for the earliest version of *Götterdämmerung*, 1848, 38 p., in black ink on a gathering of ten nested, sewn bifolia of two different kinds of tall wove paper (21 × 33.5 cm), written on both sides, unpaginated. On the front of the outer bifolium, in Wagner's hand: "Siegfrieds Tod." The text begins on the first page of the second bifolium. At the top of the page, in parentheses: "12 Nov. [18]48." On the same page, below: "Siegfrieds Tod / Eine grosse Heldenoper in drei Akten," followed by a list of the characters. Signed and dated at the end Dresden, 28 Nov. 1848. On p. [34], an 8-measure musical quotation, notated on two staves, perpendicular to the text. Many corrections, revisions, and cancellations throughout.

See John Deathridge, Martin Geck, and Egon Voss, *Wagner Werk-Verzeichniss*, Mainz and New York: Schott, 1986, p. 393.

Heinrich Schütz to Henry Miller, p. 44–45.
London, Sotheby's, 10 May 1984, lot 176.
FRKF 334

III. LETTERS

Unless otherwise noted, not located (or published to date) in *Sämtliche Briefe*.

To Franz Brendel

1852 Feb. 4 [Zürich] ALS, 4 p. Mentions productions of *Tannhäuser* in Schwerin and *Lohengrin* in Weimar, the role of music criticism, and a projected article on Beethoven's Coriolan overture.

1853 Feb. 4, Zürich, ALS, 2 p. *Sämtliche Briefe*, V:177–79.

1853 Feb. 7, Zürich, ALS, 2 p. *Sämtliche Briefe*, V:182–83. On an article concerning composers of "pure music" writing for the stage, with references to Weber and Schumann.

Franz Brendel, editor of *Neue Zeitschrift für Musik*.

London, Sotheby's, 14–15 April 1982, lots 157, 164.
FRKF 50, 52

To Hans von Bülow

1868 March 13, Tribschen, ALS, 3 p. Discusses the interpretation of Mozart and includes a musical quotation of the main theme of the second movement of the Symphony no. 39 in E-flat major, K. 543.

London, Sotheby's, 14–15 April 1982, lot 257.
FRKF 55

To Julius Cornet

1844 July 19, Dresden, ALS, 1 p., concerning *Rienzi* and *Das Liebesmahl der Apostel*. Partially published in *Sämtliche Briefe*, II:386–87.

London, Sotheby's, 9–10 May 1985, lot 246.
FRKF 785

To Ferdinand Heine

1850 Sept. 14, Zürich, ALS, 3 p. Mentions *Lohengrin* in Weimar conducted by Liszt, plans to set *Siegfrieds Tod* to music, his article "Das Judenthum in der Musik," published in *Neue Zeitschrift für Musik* under the pseudonym K. Freigedank, frustrated hopes to have the *Tannhäuser* overture performed in Paris, and Meyerbeer's *Le prophète*. *Sämtliche Briefe*, III:406–09.

London, Sotheby's, 14–15 April 1982, lot 150.
FRKF 49

To Baron August von Loën

1871 Nov. 3, Lucerne, ALS, 3 p. Discusses plans for the Bayreuth theater and announces a visit to the site.

The recipient was intendant of the Weimar Opera House and chairman of the Bayreuth Patronage Committee.

London, Sotheby's, 14–15 April 1982, lot 272.
FRKF 56

To Francesco Lucca

1861 Nov. 14, Vienna, ALS in French, 4 p., concerning the sale of rights to *Tannhäuser* and *Rienzi* for Italy; also a reference to *Tristan und Isolde*.

London, Sotheby's, 10 May 1984, lot 177.
FRKF 335

To Anton Mitterwurzer

1853 Feb. 28, Zürich, ALS, 4 p. Mentions Tichatschek, the original Tannhäuser, *Der fliegende Holländer*, and urges Mitterwurzer to get a copy of his newly completed poem for *Der Ring des Nibelungen*. *Sämtliche Briefe*, V:206–08.

Anton Mitterwurzer (1818–76), baritone, premiered the part of Wolfram in *Tannhäuser*.

London, Sotheby's, 14–15 April 1982, lot 166.
FRKF 53

To Count Julius von Platen-Hallermund

1860 Jan. 27, Paris, ALS, 4 p., concerning *Tristan und Isolde*. *Sämtliche Briefe*, XII:44–45.

FRKF 991

To Robert Prölz

1877 Nov. 25, Bayreuth, ALS, 3 p., concerning Prölz's *Geschichte des Hoftheaters zu Dresden*.

Marburg, Stargardt, 5–6 March 1985, lot 921.
FRKF 828

To Hans Richter

1876 June 13, Bayreuth, ALS, 1 p. Discusses the rehearsal for the *Ring* scheduled that evening. With fragment of an envelope.

Hans Richter conducted the first performance of the tetralogy at Bayreuth on 13–17 Aug. 1876.

London, Sotheby's, 14–15 April 1982, lot 279.
FRKF 57

To Carl Riedel

1877 Aug. 5, Bayreuth, ALS, 1 p. Discusses interpretation; contains a musical quotation from J.S. Bach's motet *Singet dem Herrn ein neues Lied*, BWV 225.

Carl Riedel (1827–88), German choirmaster and composer.

London, Sotheby's, 14–15 April 1982, lot 285.
FRKF 58

To Princess Carolyne Sayn-Wittgenstein

[1854 Nov., Zürich] ALS, 6 p. Discusses the composition of *Die Walküre*, where Wagner has reached the act 2 Todesverkündigung, and discusses Liszt's failure to have *Tannhäuser* produced in Berlin and his hopes to obtain an amnesty from King Friedrich Wilhelm IV. *Sämtliche Briefe*, VI:285–87.

London, Southeby's, 14–15 April 1982, lot 181.
FRKF 54

To Georg Unger

1875 Oct. 20, Bayreuth, ALS, 4 p. (env). Mentions Karl Scherbarth, Julius Hey, and Hermann Levi.

Tenor Georg Unger (1837–87) sang the role of Siegfried at the first Bayreuth *Ring* the following year.

Marburg, Stargardt, 5–6 March 1985, lot 920.
FRKF 827

Other letters

To the director of the opera house at Schwerin

1852 Oct. 28, Zürich, ALS, 4 p., concerning the forthcoming production of *Lohengrin*.

London, Southeby's, 15 April 1982, lot 162.
FRKF 51

To an unidentified friend [Hans von Bülow?]

[ca. 1867?] n.p., ALS, 1 p. Mentions Ludwig II of Bavaria.

London, Sotheby's, 9–10 May 1985, lot 249.
FRKF 787

IV. PRINTED MUSIC

Tannhäuser / und / der Sängerkrieg auf Wartburg; / grosse romantische Oper in 3 Acten / von / Richard Wagner. / Partitur. / Als Manuscript von der Handschrift des Componisten auf Stein gedruckt. Dresden, 1845.

450 pages, 36 cm. In original boards. Dated 8 July 1849 and signed "Tichatscheck" on the title page. Pencilled notes from a previous owner on verso of back free endpaper. One of the 100 copies of the full-score manuscript, written on a "paper especially prepared for the subsequent copying process" and reproduced lithographically in the spring of 1845 by the Dresden publisher C.F. Meser at Wagner's expense. A number of copies were presented to friends, notably Spohr and Schumann. "Shortly after the edition had been produced, [Wagner] had a copyist make small corrections in all the copies, and these were written in ink." (Strohm, p. VII)

A comparison between the corrections in this copy and the one in the collections of the Irving S. Gilmore Music Library, Yale University (M1500 W134 T16 M5++), shows a number of variants. Similar corrections in ink have been found on pages 1, 9, 17, 25, 26, 35, 40, 43, 68, 101, 121, 125, 149, 150, 153, 184, 185, 187, 190, 217, 224, 225, 237, 254, 255, 260, 311, 315, 328, 331, 353, 356, 386, 398, 399, 410, 414, 427, 429, 432, 434, and 436. Some of the corrections, written in ink in the Yale Music Library copy, are written in pencil in this copy, apparently in Wagner's own hand: see p. 285, 335, 338, 339, 339, 342, 343, 344, 345, 346, 347, 348, 381, 442, and 443; the ones on p. 319 are in red ink and red pencil. The presence of occasional pencilled crosses or jottings in the margin suggests that this was used by Wagner as a marked-up copy: see p. 36, 150, 151, 172, 173, 186, 237, 260, 315, 318, 321, 353, 356, 429. A number of pencilled corrections or indications of tempo or expressive markings are not present in the Yale Music Library copy: p. 50, 93, 155, 167, 175, 176, 186, 190, 318, 411, 416, 417, 418, 419, 421, 422, 423, 424, 425, 426, 429, 433, and 435. At the end of Elisabeth's act 2 intervention "Zurück von ihm," the placement of the pause on the words "Erlöser litt" has been modified in red pencil; in the Rome Narration, on the word "ewig" (Tannhäuser: "Wo nun dein Reiz mir ewig lacht"), one note is modified in the vocal line (E-sharp changed to C-sharp).

The Bohemian tenor Joseph Tichatschek [Josef Tichacek] (1807–86) sang the title role in the first performance of *Tannhäuser* in Dresden on 19 Oct. 1845 (having sung the first Rienzi three years before). The signature partly covers an earlier inscription that had been erased.

Cecil Hopkinson. *Tannhäuser: an examination of 36 editions* (Tutzing: Hans Schneider, 1973, Musikbibliographischen Arbeiten, 1), p. 6–9 and 45–48. See Richard Wagner. *Tannhäuser und der Sängerkrieg auf Wartburg*, edited by Reinhard Strohm (Mainz: Schott, 1980, Richard Wagner. Sämtliche Werke, V,1), p. VI-VII.
FRKF 1

V. MISCELLANEOUS

Announcement of the marriage of Wagner to Cosima von Bülow. Document, in Cosima Wagner's hand, Lucerne, 25 Aug. 1870, 1 p. Signed "Richard Wagner" and "Cosima Wagner [geb Liszt]."

London, Sotheby's, 9–10 May 1985, lot 247.
FRKF 786

SIR HUGH WALPOLE (1884–1941)

Letter to Miss M. Dunkels

[1917 Oct. 1, London*] ALS, 1 p. (env), enclosing a check.

London, Christie's, 23 March 1984, lot 70.
FRKF 435

SIR WILLIAM WALTON (1902–83)

I. MUSIC MANUSCRIPTS

Walton's music manuscripts are described in ten groups.

A. OPERAS
B. BALLET MUSIC
C. STAGE MUSIC
D. FILM MUSIC
E. SYMPHONIC MUSIC
F. MUSIC FOR WIND AND BRASS ENSEMBLES
G. CHORAL WORKS
H. VOCAL MUSIC
I. CHAMBER MUSIC
J. PIANO MUSIC

A. OPERAS

The bear, C. 79

Partial holograph manuscript of the vocal score of this opera in one act on a libretto by Paul Dehn and the composer, after Anton Chekhov, n.d. [1965–67], 40 p. Notated in pencil on various types of paper (H. Colom - B. Aires, Zurich Schutzmarke Hug & Co. Nr. 12, Stamp. music. f.lii de Marino Napoli), paginated 1–16, 16a, 17–23, 23 revised, 24–37. Laid in after p. 22, a photostat marked 22 revised. This final section of Walton's reduction for voice and piano of *The Bear*, the only portion that is extant, starts at rehearsal figure 66 and goes to the end of the opera.

Craggs, p. 144–45.
FRKF 604

Troilus and Cressida, C. 62

Holograph manuscript, in full score, of the opera, [1947]–54, 517 p. Notated in pencil on both sides of tall sheets of 32-staff paper, paginated by the composer. Three volumes bound in dark blue rexine.

Collation:

Vol. 1: paginated 1–44, [47], 48–182; cancelled passages noted on p. 9, 14, 30, 35, 36, 37, 44, 66, 97, 98, 127, 138, 139, 177, and 178. On p. [47], otherwise blank, note in Walton's hand: "Cut to page 48." The upper half of p. 82 is covered by a blank cancel. Laid in, typed label of Oxford University Press (previously taped on front cover): "Full score / Act I / Troilus and Cressida / by / William Walton / Original manuscript / [in manuscript:] (Revised 1955)."

Vol. 2: paginated 1–171; cancelled passages noted on p. 57 and 146. Laid in, typed label of Oxford University Press (previously taped on front cover): "Full score / Act II / Troilus and Cressida / by / William Walton / Libretto by Christopher Hassall / Original MS."

Vol. 3: paginated 1–166. Cancelled passages noted on p. 54, 57, 81–85, 90, 91, 101, 111, 117–118, 130, and 156. Traces of repagination from 110 onwards. Laid in, two typed labels of Oxford University Press (previously taped on top of each other on front cover): "Full score / Act IIII / Troilus and Cressida / by / William Walton / Original manuscript"; " "Full score / Act III / Troilus and Cressida / by / William Walton / Original manuscript version / [in manuscript:] (Revised 1955)."

Autograph note at the end: "End of Opera / To my wife / 13.9.54." Stamp of Oxford University Press throughout.

Accompanied by the following material:

"At the haunted end of the day," revised manuscript version (transposed from B-flat minor to G minor), in full score, notated in pencil on tall 32-staff paper, paginated 33–41; also, a revised p. 69, in full score; and revisions to act 3, p. 19, notated in blue and black pencil of the full-score manuscript; as well as seven pages of additional revisions or sketches, in full score.

"At the haunted end of the day," variant ending, notated in pencil on a tall strip of paper initially taped on a photocopy of the relevant page from the full-score manuscript, paginated 40; marked, in Walton's hand "special ending for aria."

"Act I, (special ending for aria – overlay)," notated in pencil on a tall strip of paper initially taped on a photocopy of the relevant page from the full-score manuscript, paginated 151.

Two pages of revisions, written in blue ballpoint pen, marked in pencil, in Walton's hand: "Revisions Nov. 74."

A revision of the passage "The gods compel me," notated in pencil on a sheet, foliated 80.

One alteration to act 1, p. 55, notated in pencil on a strip of paper pasted on a photocopy of the relevant passage in the vocal score.

Three pages of alterations to act 3, notated in short score on two sheets of tall 14-staff paper, paginated A and C, affecting 11 passages; one alteration to act 3, notated in short score on a strip of music paper, dated April 1976 in Walton's hand; four pages of alterations, also dated April 1976, affecting 8 passages in acts 1, 2, and 3; six pages (paginated only 1 through 5) of alterations to acts 3, 2, and 1 (in that order), affecting ca. 20 passages; one alteration to act 1 ("Their vengeance would destroy us"), noted on a strip of paper, marked "out of date (see 19.1.76)"; alterations on a strip of music paper, dated Feb. 1976; and alterations on three strips of music paper, joined with adhesive.

See William Walton, *Troilus and Cressida*, edited by Stuart Hutchinson (Oxford and New York: Oxford University Press, 2003. Walton Edition, vol. 1), p. vii–xvii and xx–xxv.
Craggs, p. 116–22.
Heinrich Schütz to Henry Miller, p. 142–43.
FRKF 580

B. BALLET MUSIC

Devoirs de vacances, C. 39b

Holograph manuscript, in short score, of the "Galop final" of this ballet by Boris Kochno, choreographed by John Taras, to *Music for children*, n.d. [but 1949], 7 p. Notated in pencil on two nested bifolia of tall 12-staff paper (watermarked P.M. Fabriano). On title page, in Walton's hand: "Galop Final." In another hand: "(written as an extra finale / for Boris Kochno's ballet / Music for Children, 1949–50 (?) / W.W. thinks Kochno has a score."

See William Walton, *Instrumental Music*, edited by Michael Aston (Oxford and New York: Oxford University Press, 2003. Walton Edition, vol. 20), p. vi–vii and xv.
Craggs, p. 77.
FRKF 624D

The first shoot, C. 29

Holograph manuscript of the arrangement for brass band [1981], 48 p. Notated in pencil on both sides of individual leaves of tall 16-staff paper (Scomegna A 16.70), paginated 1–50 (pages 10 and 15 are blank). On title page, in Walton's hand: "In Mem. / C.B. Cochran and his Young Ladies / 'The First Shoot' / ballet / devised by Frederick Ashton & Cecil Beaton / Music revised and arranged for Brass Band by / William Walton / 'Follow the Sun' Adelphi Theatre 1936." Originally stapled with p. 39, a 4-measure revision notated on a strip of 23.5 × 10.5 cm paper.

Craggs, p. 59–61.
FRKF 594

The quest, C. 49

Manuscript, partly holograph, partly in the hand of an unidentified orchestrator, of this ballet, in full score, n.d. [1943], 201 p. Notated in pencil, with additional markings in blue or red pencil, on gatherings of nested bifolia of tall 32-staff paper, mostly unpaginated, housed in a dark blue folder with printed label of Oxford University Press. On title page, in Walton's hand: "Dedicated to the / Sadler's Wells Ballet Company / and in particular to / Ninette, Margot, Constant, Bobbie & Freddie / The Quest / A ballet in five scenes from Spenser's 'Fairie Queene'. / Choreography by Frederick Ashton. / Scenery by John Piper. / Music by William Walton." The section not in Walton's hand is the last (Variation 7) of the Seven Deadly Sins.

Also, full-score manuscript of the ballet, in the hand of a copyist, n.d. [1943], 230 p. Notated in black ink, with additional markings in blue pencil, on gatherings of nested bifolia of tall 24-staff paper (G & T).

Collation: 1–57 [Scene I], 1–42 (Scene II), brief notation on an unnumbered page, 1–40 (Scene III), [1–6] (Variation.7.Pride), 1–26 (Scene 3. Continued), 1–25 (Scene IV), 1–22 [23, 24] (Scene V). On title page, not in Walton's hand: "The Quest / William Walton." With a bifolium of tall 21-staff paper, containing 9 measures of music, in full score, in the hand of Vilem Tausky, corresponding to transitional passages for the suite arranged from the ballet (C. 49a).

Also, a title page on a loose leaf, marked (not in Walton's hand): "William Walton / Ballet Suite / The Quest / arranged from the original score / Vilem Tausky."

Craggs, p. 93–96.
FRKF 605A–B

C. STAGE MUSIC

Christopher Columbus, C. 46

Holograph manuscript, in full score, of the incidental music to Louis MacNeice's play, n.d. [1942], 133 p. Notated in pencil, with additional markings in blue and red pencil, on different sizes of tall paper, bound together in grey boards; pasted-on typescript fragments of the text are found throughout. Stamp of The British Broadcasting Corporation throughout. The manuscript comprises the following sections, as titled by Walton unless otherwise indicated:

Act I:
"Introduction & chorus," 16 p.
[Title not in Walton's hand:] "Background: Columbus & Prior," 3 p.
[Title not in Walton's hand:] "Recitation & Chorus," 6 p.
"Fanfares / & / Court Music," 2 p.
"Male chorus / No-no-never again!" 5 p. (paginated 6–10)
"Beatriz's Song," 3 p.
"Melody of Beatriz's Song c/f into Kyrie," 1 p.
"Chorus 'Granada has fallen' / Background music," 19 p.
"Fanfares / Fanfare and background," 2 p.

Act II:
"Introduction. Port music," 8 p.
"Woman's song 'There be three ships' / Background music on Beatriz's Song / Drumming," 3 p. (paginated 15–17)
"'Per Dominum' / Litany of the Saints / Capstan Shanty," 2 p. (paginated 18–19)
"Shanty 'We're gone away' / & / Sea music," 5 p. (paginated 20–24)
"Night music," 3 p. (paginated 25–27)
"Gold-gold-gold," 6 p. (paginated 28–33)
"Speaking Chorus / Look-Look-Look / & Te deum," 7 p. (paginated 34–40)
"Indian chorus / Fanfare / Reprise Indian chorus / [Reprise Indian chorus, indicated by ditto marks]," 7 p. (paginated 41–47)

"Background & speaking chorus," 21 p.
[partly erased:] "Final chorus," 15 p.

Craggs, p. 89–90.
FRKF 623

Macbeth, C. 43

Holograph manuscript, in full score, of the incidental music to Shakespeare's tragedy, n.d. [1941–42], 76 p. Notated in pencil, with additional markings (not all in Walton's hand) in red ink, red pencil, and black crayon, on a combination of separate and nested bifolia of 18- and 24-staff paper, arranged in sections usually tied together with pink string. The score comprises the following sections, labelled by Walton:

"Macbeth / Act I Sc. I" [numbered 1 and 2 in a different hand], 11 p.
"Macbeth Act I" [numbered "3 (& 4)"], 2 p.
"Macbeth Act I between Scs. V & VI / Festal entrance music" [numbered 5], 4 p.
"Macbeth Act I between Scs. VI & VII / Festal & Banquet music 1–5" [numbered 6], 6 p.
"Macbeth Act I Sc 7 / Banquet music cont." [numbered 7], 5 p.
[not in Walton's hand:] "Act 1. Banquet music 3" [numbered 8], 5 p.
"Macbeth Act I Sc 7 / Banquet music cont." [numbered 9], 7 p.
"Macbeth Act II before Sc I" [numbered 10], 2 p.
"Macbeth Act II sc 2" [numbered 11–13], 3 p.
"Act II Sc 4" [numbered 14/14a/14b], 1 p., with 1 p. of notes
"Macbeth Act III before scene I" [numbered 15], 1 p., notated in ink
"Macbeth Act III sc II / Witches Music" [numbered 16], 14 p.
"Macbeth Act III Sc II" [labelled "Apparitions" in a different hand, and numbered 17a–c], 6 p.
"Macbeth Act III Sc II March of the eight kings" [numbered 18], 4 p.
"Macbeth Act III before Sc I" [numbered 15], and "Act III between Scs 3–4" [numbered 19], with note at the bottom: "over for 20, 21, 22," 1 p.
"Act III between Scs. 5 & 6," "6–7," and "7–8" [numbered 20–22], 1 p.
"Macbeth Act III between Scs 8 & 9," "9–10," and "10–11" [numbered 23–25], 1 p.
"During Sc 11 Act III" [numbered 26–27], 1 p.
"Macbeth / Act III / Final Lines" [numbered 28], 3 p.

Housed in a brown folder stamped: "The Gielgud / 'Macbeth' / Music by Walton"; tipped in inside the folder, "Music plot, Macbeth," typescript with markings in blue pencil.

Craggs, p. 84–85.
FRKF 581

D. FILM MUSIC

As you like it, C. 31

Holograph manuscript, in full score, of the music for the film by Paul Czinner after Shakespeare's play, n.d. [1936], 113 p. Notated in pencil, chiefly on gatherings of nested bifolia of tall 22- or 27-staff paper, some with printed instrumentation. The manuscript comprises the following sections:

"Title Music," 21 p.

"Under the Greenwood Tree," in short score, 2 p.

"Reel II / [Fountain Scene]," 30 p.

"Reel III N° 5 (after Dukes Exit)," 6 p.

"Reel 4 No. 3 / Sunrise," 6 p.

"Reel V Dinner Scene," 3 p.

"Snake Scene / (on a theme by Dr Paul Czinner)," 4 p.

"Reel X / Procession," 16 p.

[no title: Prelude leading and Choral Ballet], 17 p.

"Reel X / Hymn," 8 p.

"Final Pass-out," 2 p.

The music appears to be in Walton's hand throughout, but many annotations seem to be in a different hand. The choral parts are notated in the Hymn but not in the Choral Ballet section. Accompanied by 19 pages of miscellaneous drafts.

Craggs, p. 62–63.

FRKF 608, 636

The Battle of Britain, C. 81

Largely holograph manuscript, in full score, of the film music [1969], 151 p. Written (except where noted) in pencil on sheets of tall 20-staff paper (Curci, Naples). The manuscript comprises the following sections (titled by Walton unless otherwise specified):

"4 M I / The young Siegfrieds," 12 p.; "Music Cue and Times," typescript, 2 p., tipped in on title page and on verso of p. 12.

"2M2 & 3MI," 2 p., "Music Cue and Times," typescript, 2 p., tipped in on title page and on verso of p. 2.

"6MI," 8 p.; "Music Cue and Times," typescript, 2 p., tipped in on title page and on verso of p. 8.

"6M2," 2 p.; "Music Cue and Times," typescript, 1 p., tipped in on title page.

"6M3," 3 p.; "Music Cue and Times," typescript, 1 p., tipped in on title page.

"7.M.1," 4 p.; "Music Cue and Times," typescript, 1 p., tipped in on title page.

"9M2 / 'Gay Berlin,'" 8 p.; "Music Cue and Times," typescript, 1 p., tipped in on title page.

"10.M.1," 6 p.; "Music Cue and Times," typescript, 2 p., tipped in on title page and on verso of p. 6.

"14.M.3," 8 p., photocopy.

"Introduction to March for record," 4 p.; written on 28-staff paper (G.B.T.[?])

The following sections are written on bifolia and single sheets of oblong 14-staff paper (A.L. No. 41):

"A nightingale sang in Berkeley Square" (with the heading "small group version"), 9 p.

"A nightingale sang in Berkeley Square" (with the heading "Band Version"), 12 p.

The following are photocopies or photostats, some with autograph annotations in several hands, including Walton's:

"3M2" (marked "Transposed score"), 9 p.

"5.M.I," 14 p.

"12.M.I," 17 p.

"14.M.I and II," 7 p.

"14.M.3," 8 p.

"14.M.3A," 3 p.

"End Titles / (14.M.3)," 2 p.

"'The Battle of Britain' - March," 2 p. (2 copies)

"Horst Vessel Song," 4 p.

Craggs, p. 147–48.

FRKF 585

Escape me never, C. 28

Holograph manuscript, in full score, of the music for the film by Paul Czinner after the play by Margaret Kennedy, n.d. [1934], 93 p. Notated in pencil on gatherings of nested bifolia or individual sheets of tall 24-staff paper. The manuscript comprises the following sections:

"Title Music," 10 p.

"N° 2 / Venetian scene," 20 p.

"Car & Baker's Shop," 6 p.

"Well Head N° 1," 40 p.

"Dolomites," 16 p., paginated 41–56.

"Reel 3 N° 3 Heavenly R." and "No. 4 after father's child," 1 p.

The music appears to be in Walton's hand throughout; some of the annotations are in a different hand.

Craggs, p. 56–57.

FRKF 609

The First of the Few

See under Symphonic Music, *The Spitfire*

Hamlet, C. 54

Holograph manuscript, in full score, of the music for the film version of Shakespeare's tragedy, directed by Laurence Olivier [1947], 129 p. Notated in pencil, with additional markings (usually not in Walton's hand), in red, blue, or green pencil and red ballpoint pen, on separate or nested bifolia of tall 24- or 32-staff paper. The manuscript comprises the following sections, labelled by Walton unless otherwise indicated:

[Title not in Walton's hand:] "Funeral March," 8 p.

"Ham. / 2 M. I. Sc. 17–19" [in a different hand: "Something rotten in the state of Denmark"], 2 p.

"Ham. / 5 M.I. / & / 5 M.3" [in a different hand: "The Ghost"], 4 p.

"Hamlet / 3.M.4. Sc. 32" [in a different hand: "Oh that this too too solid flesh"], 3 p.

"Hamlet / 4.M.I Sc. 41–45" [in a different hand: "The house of Polonius"], 2 p.

"Ham. / 4.M.2. Sc 54–56," 3 p.

"Ham. / 5.M.2," 4 p.

"Hamlet / 6.M.I. Sc 106" [in a different hand: "O cursed spite that ever I was born to set it right"], 4 p.

"Hamlet / 7.M.I. Sc. 128" [in a different hand: "Ophelia and Hamlet"], 3 p.

"Ham / 8.M.I" [in a different hand: "Prelude: 'To be or not to be'"], 9 p.

"Ham / 8.M.2," 1 p.

"8.M.3 Sc 163 / New measurement" [in a different hand: "The players' entrance"], 2 p.

"Hamlet / 8.M.4. Sc. 166-8 / New measurement," 3 p.

"Ham / 9 M.I. Sc 159–60," 1 p.

[in a different hand:] "The entry of the Court," 4 p.

"Hamlet 9.M.3 Sc. 181–198" [in a different hand: "The players scene"], 10 p.

"Hamlet / 9.M.3 Sc 181–198 (continued)" [in a different hand: "Players' Scene (cont)"], 3 p.

"Retake 9.M.4 (formerly 8.M.4) / Sc 165–168" [in a different hand: "The play's the thing"], 3 p.

"Hamlet / 11.M.1 Sc 204–210" [in a different hand: "Hamlet and the Queen: the Ghost"], 11 p.

"Hamlet / 11.M.2. / 13 [corrected as 18?].M.I. / 3.M.I / 3.M.2," 1 p.

"Hamlet / 13.M.I Sc 242" [in a different hand: "Ophelia by the stream"], 10 p.

"Ham / 14.M.2 Sc 274" [in a different hand: "Hamlet's letter to Horatio"], 4 p.

"Hamlet / 14.M.3 Sc 283–285" [in a different hand: "The death of Ophelia"], 3 p.

[title not in Walton's hand:] "Hamlet / 15.M.I. Sc. 300 / & / 16.M.I. Sc 306–10," 1 p.

"Hamlet / 17.M.2 Sc. 321," 3 p.

"Ham. / Duel Sc. / [Title not in Walton's hand:] 18MI," 15 p.

[cancelled:] "Original / Ham / I.M.I.," 10 p.

Also, "In youth, when I did love," unaccompanied song, holograph, notated in black ink on 16-staff paper, 1 p. First Gravedigger's song.

Craggs, p. 105–07.

FRKF 583

Henry V, C. 50

Partial holograph manuscript, in full score, of the music for the film after Shakespeare's tragedy, directed by Laurence Olivier, ca. 1943–44, 35 p. Written mostly in pencil, with additional markings (not all by Walton) in blue pencil, black, or red crayon, or red ballpoint pen, on separate or nested bifolia of tall 24-staff paper. The manuscript comprises the following sections, titled by Walton unless otherwise indicated:

"Reel 11 / Bourbon: 'The sun doth gild,'" 9 p.

"Reel 11 (shot 143 p. 96) / Henry: 'God be with you all,'" 3 p.

"Reel 12 (shot 147 p. 98) / Henry: '- gentle herald,'" [also marked, in a different hand: "Suite - Henry V / No. 3 Charge & Battle"], 6 p.

[title page cancelled] "Reel 14 (shot 273 page 135) / Burgundy: 'Alas she hath from France,'" 4 p. At the bottom of p. 1, note in pencil, in the hand of Alan Frank of Oxford University Press: "This solo passage is based on a French folk-song (Baïlèro) from Chants d'Auvergne, collected by J. Canteloube. It is used by permission of Heugel et Cie., Paris."

[not in Walton's hand:] "Titles II B / No chorus," 3 p.

[not in Walton's hand:] "Titles II C / Henry V / Sop & Alt," 5 p. (incomplete).

Fragment of the end titles, marked "48 h" in the upper left corner, notated on a single sheet of tall 24-staff paper (Zurich Schutzmarke Nr. 2), 2 p.

The "Charge and Battle" manuscript, previously in the collection of Halsted B. Vander Poel, was acquired in 2004 by the Beinecke Library (London, Christie's, 3 March 2004, lot 356).

See William Walton, *Henry V: A musical scenario after Shakespeare, for speaker, mixed chorus, children's choir (optional), and orchestra. The text of Walton's music adapted by Christopher Palmer*. Edited by David Lloyd-Jones (Oxford: Oxford University Press, 1999. Walton Edition, vol. 23), particularly p. xi.

See also Craggs, p. 96–99.
FRKF 582

Richard III, C. 63

Holograph manuscript, in full score (with portions in short score), of the music for the film, directed by Laurence Olivier after Shakespeare's tragedy, 1955, 229 p. Notated in pencil, with additional markings (usually not by Walton) in blue pencil or black or red crayon, on separate bifolia of tall 24- or 30-staff paper. The manuscript comprises the following sections, labelled by Walton unless otherwise indicated:

"Opening titles," 11 p. (pages numbered 1–3 and 2–9). On p. 4, pencil annotation in Walton's hand: "Meno mosso / con prosciuto [sic], agnello e confitura di fragole"; marked "Recorded 29/3/55"

"I.M.1," 1 p.; marked "Recorded 24/2/55"

"I.M.2" [Fanfares], 1 p.; [on same page] "I.M.3," 3 p.; [on p. 4 of the same bifolium] "I.M.4.," 1 p., all notated on a single bifolium of tall 12-staff paper; marked "recorded," n.d.

"I.M.5.B" [also labelled "No 4 in Suite"], 5 p.; marked "Recorded 22/2/55"

"2.M.I.A," 6 p. "Recorded 22/2/55"

"2 M.I.B" 5 p. "Recorded 25/2/55"

"2.M.2," 4 p. "Recorded 22/2/55"

[cancelled:] "3.M.I.," 1 p. "Recorded 24/2/55"

[cancelled:] "3.M.2," 3 p. "Recorded 24/2/55"

"4.M.1," 6 p. "Recorded 22/2/55"

"4.M.2," 5 p. "Recorded 22/2/55"

"4.M.3," 2 p. "Recorded 24/2/55"

"5.M.1," 3 p. "Recorded 22/2/55"

[cancelled:] "5.M.2" [also labelled: "Suite No 3"], written on a bifolium of tall 20-staff paper, 2 p. "Recorded 22/2/55"

[cancelled:] "6.M.I," written on a bifolium of tall 20-staff paper, 3 p.; marked "22/2/55"

"6.M.2," 2 p. "Recorded 22/2/54" [i.e. 1955]

"7 M.I," 2 p. "Recorded 22/2/55"

"7.M.2," 2 p., in short score, notated in ink with, pencil corrections, on a bifolium of tall 12-staff paper, entitled "Elegy" at the top of p. [1]

"7.M.3," 1 p. "Recorded 25/2/55"

"8.M.I," 7 p. "Recorded 25/2/55"

"8.M.2," 5 p. "Recorded 22/2/55"

"9.M.I.," 4 p. "Recorded 25/2/55"

"9.M.2," 3 p. "Recorded 25/2/55"

[cancelled:] "9.M.3," 1 p. "Recorded 22/2/55"

"9 M 4 / 9 M. 5 / 10.M.1," 3 p. "Recorded 25/2/55"

"10.M 2," 1 p.; [on next page] "12.M 4," 2 p.; [on p. 4 of the same bifolium:] "13. M 1," 1 p.; marked on p. [4] "Recorded 22/2/55"

"10.M.3," 3 p. "Recorded 25/2/55"

"12.M.I," 2 p. "Recorded 30/3/55"

"12.M.2," 3 p. "Recorded 25/2/55"

"12.M.3," 2 p. "Recorded 25/2/55"

[cancelled:] "13.M.2," 5 p. "Recorded 25/2/55"

"13.M.3," 3 p. "Recorded 24/2/55"

"14.M.1," 5 p. "Recorded 25/2/55"

"14.M 2," 10 p. "Recorded 30/3/55"

"15.M.1," 6 p. "Recorded 30/3/55"

"15.M.2A," 7 p. "Recorded 30/3/55"

"15.M.2B," 1 p. "Recorded 30/3/55"

"15.M.3. / 15.M.4" [labelled in another hand "A variant of the opening titles"], 8 p. "Recorded 29/3/55"

"16.M.I," 3 p. "Recorded 29/3/55"

"16.M.2" [labelled "Ghosts" in a different hand], 18 p. "Recorded 31/3/55"

"17.M.I," 6 p. "Recorded 29/3/55"

"17.M.2," 19 p. "Recorded 29/3/55"

"18.M.I," 18 p. "Recorded 30/3/55"

"18.M 2," 3 p. "Recorded 30/3/55"

"18.M.3," 5 p. "Recorded 30/3/55"

"18.M.4A. / & / 18.M.4B," 5 p.

"18.M.4.C & End Titles," 13 p. "Recorded 30/3/55"

"Fanfares Reel 16 & 17," 1 p.

Craggs, p. 124–25.
FRKF 584

E. SYMPHONIC MUSIC

Capriccio burlesco, C. 80

Holograph manuscript, in full score, of this piece for orchestra, 1968, 48 p., bound in grey boards. Notated in pencil on both sides of tall sheets of 28-staff paper (G.B.T. 28), paginated 1–42 by Walton. On title page, in Walton's hand: "[Cancelled: Philharmonic Overture N.Y. 68] Capriccio burlesco / William Walton." On the verso of the title page, autograph note: "Commissioned by the New York Philharmonic." On the facing page, above the orchestration and timing, autograph dedication: "To André Kostelanetz." Initialed and dated Forio, 5 Sept. 1968, at the end. Laid in are second copies (discards?) of p. 1, 2–3, 18–19, and 42.

Craggs, p. 146–47.
FRKF 598

Concerto for viola and orchestra, C. 22

Holograph manuscript, in full score, of the second (revised) score of the original version of the *Viola Concerto* [1929], 100 p. On the front of the outer bifolium of the first gathering, in Walton's hand: "Viola Concerto / William Walton." Notated in black ink, with occasional pencil corrections and markings, on three gatherings of nested bifolia of tall 28-staff paper (watermarked J. Daguerre No. 1).

Collation:

I, [1]–[27]; pasted-on cancels noted on [4–5], [8–9], [10–12], [14–16], [18–21], and [26–27].

II, 1–29; pasted-on cancels noted on p. 2, 16, 17, and 18.

III, [1–44]; pasted-on cancels noted on [5–7], [9–12], [14–16], [29–30], and [34–37], [40].

Also, holograph manuscript, in full score, of the revised version, [1961], 118 p. Notated in pencil on both sides of tall 28-staff paper, paginated 1–118 in Walton's hand. Stamp of Oxford University Press throughout. On front cover, in Walton's hand: "Concerto for viola and orchestra / [in another hand: reduced] / William Walton." At the top of p. 1, also in Walton's hand: "To Christabel / Concerto for viola and orchestra / William Walton."

See William Walton, *Concerto for viola and orchestra*, edited by Christopher Willington (Oxford and New York: Oxford University Press, 2002. Walton Edition, vol. 12), p. v–xx.
Craggs, p. 47–49.
FRKF 586A–B

Concerto for violin, C. 37

Holograph manuscript, in full score, of the revised version, 1943, 142 p.

Notated in pencil, with additional markings in blue pencil, on both sides of tall sheets of 24-staff paper (watermarked L.J.C.), paginated 1–142, and bound in dark blue cloth. Gold-tooled on front board: "William Walton / Violin Concerto." At the top of p. 1, in Walton's hand: "for Jascha Heifetz." Autograph note at the end of the manuscript: "New York. 2/6/39. Revised 30/11/43." Laid in is an analysis of the concerto in Walton's hand, with musical examples, written in pencil on two single sheets of tall 18-staff paper, 3 p.

On the flyleaf, stamp of Oxford University Press and notes indicating that the score was used by Sir Malcolm Sargent to conduct the work, twice in 1950 and once again in 1952, by Norman Del Mar in 1950, and by Walton himself for the 1950 recording and for a performance with the Royal Philharmonic Orchestra in 1955.

Craggs, p. 70–72.
FRKF 597

Concerto for violoncello and orchestra, C. 65

Holograph manuscript sketches, in short and full score, for the *Cello Concerto*, n.d. [1955–56], 47 p.

The short-score drafts are written in pencil on two gatherings of nested bifolia of tall 12- and 16-staff paper (Stamp. music. f.lli de Marino Napoli), with taped-on cancels. They comprise drafts for the second and third movements. On the front of the outer bifolia, in pencil, not in Walton's hand: "William Walton / Cello Concerto / II [III] / Piano score."

The full-score drafts are written on the recto sides of two sheets of tall 24-staff paper (one sheet foliated 23c).

Craggs, p. 129–30.
FRKF 627

Crown imperial, C. 32

Holograph manuscripts, in full and short score, of Walton's first *Coronation March*, 1937, 45 and 11 p.

The full-score manuscript is written in pencil on both sides of tall sheets of 24-staff paper (watermarked L.J.C.), paginated 1–45. Page 1 is glued to the front brown paper wrapper, marked (not in Walton's hand): "Coronation March. / (1937.) / 'Crown Imperial.' / William Walton." Pages 2–17 are supplied in reduced facsimile.

The short-score manuscript is written in pencil, in 4-staff systems, on a gathering of four nested bifolia of tall 16-staff paper (A.L. No. 10).

Craggs, p. 64–65.
FRKF 595A–B

Façade, second suite for orchestra, C. 12e

Manuscript, in full score, partly holograph, partly in the hand of a copyist, with annotations by Constant Lambert, 63 p. Notated in black ink or pencil, with additional markings in black, blue, and red pencil, on various types of tall paper, originally bound in white cardboard boards with typed label pasted on the front board. Numbers 1, 2, 3, and 5 are in the hand of a copyist, numbers 4 and 6 are Walton's holograph. Pencilled annotations in various hands throughout. The manuscript comprises the following sections:

"I. Fanfare," 4 p.

"II. Scotch Rhapsody," 10 p.

"6. Country dance," 8 p.

"8. Noche espagnola," written in pencil in Walton's hand on a gathering of four nested, stapled bifolia of tall 18-staff paper (Durand & Cie), 14 p.

"Popular Song," 15 p.

"Foxtrot. 'Old Sir Faulk,'" in Walton's hand, written in pencil on two nested and two separate bifolia of tall 24-staff paper, 13 p.

Craggs, p. 33–34.
FRKF 638B

Granada Prelude, C. 75

Holograph manuscript, in full score, of the music commissioned by Granada Television, 1962, 34 p. Notated in pencil on both sides of separate bifolia of tall 32-staff paper (G. Ricordi & C.), paginated 1–34 by the composer (Prelude), followed by six unnumbered pages (Call Signs and End Music), placed within two additional bifolia, the second page of the inner one being the first page of music. On the front of the second bifolium, in Walton's hand: "'Granada' Prelude - End Music - Call Signs / William Walton." Housed in a light brown paper folder, marked (in a different hand): "Granada / Prelude / MS. / Renamed Prelude for Orchestra / (July 1982) / 1962."

Craggs, p. 139–40.
FRKF 601

Improvisations on an impromptu of Benjamin Britten, C. 82

Holograph manuscript, in full score, of these variations for full orchestra, n.d. [1970], 58 p. Notated in pencil on both sides of sheets of tall 28-staff paper (G.B.T.), paginated 1–58 by the composer, and bound in grey cardboard. On title page, in Walton's hand: "To the San Francisco Symphony Orchestra, / Josef Krips Conductor and Music Director, / in memory of Adeline Smith Dorfman / Improvisations on an Impromptu of Benjamin Britten / William Walton." Initialed at the end. Stamp of Oxford University Press on the title page.

Craggs, p. 149–51.
FRKF 622

Johannesburg Festival Overture, C. 66

Holograph manuscript, in full score, of this concert overture, 1956, 67 p. Notated in pencil on both sides of tall sheets of 30-staff paper (F.lii de Marino, Napoli), paginated 1–42 and 47–71 by the composer; bound in dark blue rexine, with typed Oxford University Press label pasted on the front board. On title page, in Walton's hand: "Johannesburg Festival Overture (1956) / William Walton." Dated at the end Forio d'Ischia, 31 May 1956. Pages 42 and 47 are glued together.

Accompanied by two sheets removed from the original manuscript, written on both sides, and paginated 42–45 (originally accessioned with the *Cello Concerto* as FRKF 627a); and four sheets, in photocopy, paginated 40–47, with p. 41–46 cancelled in pencil in Walton's hand.

See William Walton, *Overtures*, edited by David Lloyd-Jones (Oxford and New York: Oxford University Press, 2002. Walton Edition, vol. 14), p. x and xiv–xv.

Craggs, p. 130–31.
FRKF 630

March for A history of the English speaking peoples, C. 70

Holograph manuscript, in full score, 1959, 22 p. Notated in pencil on both sides of individual sheets of tall 30-staff paper (f.lii de Marino, Napoli), paginated 1–22 by the composer; in grey paper wrappers. On title page, in Walton's hand: "March for 'A History of the English Speaking Peoples' / William Walton." Dated 1959, in a different hand, on the front wrapper.

Craggs, p. 135.
FRKF 632

Music for children, C. 39a

Holograph manuscript, in full score, of the arrangement *Music for Children* for full orchestra, n.d. [1940–41], 37 p. Notated in pencil on two gatherings of nested bifolia of tall 24-staff paper, paginated 1–37 by the composer; bound in brown printed Oxford University Press wrappers, filled in by hand (not Walton's). There are two title pages; the second, in Walton's hand, reads: "Music for children / William Walton."

FRKF 624C

The National Anthem, C. 60

Holograph manuscript, in full score, of Walton's arrangement of "God Save the Queen" for full orchestra, n.d. [1953], 3 p. Notated in pencil on p. [2]–[4] of a bifolium of tall 32-staff paper. On the front page of the bifolium, not in Walton's hand: "God Save the Queen / arranged by / Sir William Walton."

Craggs, p. 115.
FRKF 626

Orb and sceptre, C. 59

Holograph manuscript, in full score, of Walton's second *Coronation March*, 1953, 33 p. Notated in pencil on separate bifolia of tall 32-staff paper, paginated 2–[23] and 33–42 by the composer, housed in an additional bifolium serving as wrappers. On the front of the second bifolium (recto of p. 1), in Walton's hand: "Orb and Sceptre / Coronation March (1953) / by / William Walton."

Craggs, p. 113–14.
FRKF 628

Partita for orchestra, C. 67

Holograph manuscript, in full score, of this orchestral suite in three movements, n.d. [1957], 113 p. Notated in pencil on both sides of tall sheets of 30-staff paper (f.lii de Marino, Napoli), paginated 1–113 by the composer; bound in dark blue rexine, with typed printed label of Oxford University Press taped on the front board. On the title page, in Walton's hand: "To / George Szell and the Cleveland Orchestra / Partita / for / Orchestra / William Walton." On the verso of the title page, also in Walton's hand: "Commissioned by the Cleveland Orchestra for its 40th Anniversary season." Green stamp of Oxford University Press in several places.

Craggs, p. 131–32.
FRKF 631

Portsmouth Point, C. 17

Holograph manuscript, in full score, of this overture for orchestra, n.d. [1924–25], 41 p. Notated in pencil, with additional markings in blue pencil, on fourteen nested bifolia of tall 20-staff paper, placed within two additional bifolia serving as wrappers. On the front of the outer bifolium, in black ink, in Constant Lambert's hand: "Portsmouth Point. / an Overture / (after a print by Rowlandson) / for / Orchestra / by / W.T. Walton." On the front of the second bifolium, in pencil, in Walton's hand: "Portsmouth Point. / An / Overture (after a print by Thomas Rowlandson) / for / Orchestra / by / W.T. Walton." Also marked at the top of the same page: "British Section" and, at the bottom: "Time of performance is 5½ to 6 mins."

A manuscript copy, in Constant Lambert's hand, n.d. [1926?], 45 p., written in black ink, with additional markings in red ink and black and blue pencil, on a gathering of eleven nested bifolia of tall 30-staff paper, paginated 1–[45], placed within two outer bifolia, each with the same title, in black ink, as the manuscript above.

See William Walton, *Overtures*, edited by David Lloyd-Jones (Oxford and New York: Oxford University Press, 2002. Walton Edition, vol. 14), p. v–vii and xii.
Craggs, p. 40–41.
FRKF 588A–B

Prologo & fantasia, C. 100

Partial holograph manuscript, in full score, of this piece for orchestra, n.d. [1981–82], 51 p. Notated in pencil on both sides of sheets of tall 24- and 32-staff paper (G.B.T.), paginated 1–14, 19–28, 1–11, 5–6, 5–12, 14–15, and 21–24; six more pages are photocopies, four in a copyist's hand. The whole is housed in an additional bifolium serving as wrappers.

At the top of the first page, in Walton's hand: "Prologo & Fantasia."

Craggs, p. 164.
FRKF 610

Scapino, C. 40

Holograph manuscript, in full score, incomplete, of this concert overture, n.d. [1940], 29 p. Notated in black ink, with additional markings in black and blue pencil, on both sides of sheets of tall 32-staff paper, paginated 1–39 by the composer; bound in blue-green rexine. On front board, in gold lettering: "Full score / William Walton / Scapino / Comedy Overture." On title page, in Walton's hand: "For / Dr. F.A. Stock and the Chicago Symphony Orchestra / in commemoration of the 50th anniversary of its foundation / Scapino / a / Comedy Overture / for / full orchestra / (after an etching from J. Callots 'Balli di Sfessania' 1622) / by / William Walton." Stamp of Oxford University Press on title page. Lacks p. 20–25, 34–37, and 40–79. Dated 1941, not in Walton's hand, on front cover.

See William Walton, *Overtures*, edited by David Lloyd-Jones (Oxford and New York: Oxford University Press, 2002. Walton Edition, vol. 14), p. vii–viii and xiii–xiv.
Craggs, p. 78–81.
FRKF 625

Siesta, C. 19

First and second proofs of violin I and II, viola, violoncello, contrabass, flute (piccolo), oboe, clarinet I and II, bassoon and horn I and II parts for the second, revised edition [1962]. The proofs all bear the stamp of Henderson & Spalding as well as the imprint and copyright of Oxford University Press. The first proofs are corrected by Walton in red ink. The dedication "To Stephen Tennant" is crossed out in each case, with the indication "out." The clarinets part is abundantly corrected in black, red, and blue pencil. A note by Walton, in red ink, reads: "This part will have to be re-engraved throughout on 2 staves. It is impossible for 2 players to play from 1 stave." There are no corrections on the second proofs. Accompanied by a loose quire from an unidentified songbook, containing "Four Songs" and "Metamorphosis."

Siesta, for small orchestra, was originally composed in 1926 and published in 1929 by Oxford University Press. The revised edition, also published by Oxford University Press, came out in 1963; see Craggs, p. 43.

London, Sotheby's, 9 May 1985, lot 254.
FRKF 1428

Sinfonia concertante for piano and orchestra, C. 21

Holograph manuscript, in full score, of the original version, [1927], 84 p.

> Notated in black ink, with additional markings in pencil, on two gatherings of nested bifolia of tall 30-staff paper. On the front of the outer wrapper of the first gathering, in Walton's hand: "Sinfonia concertante / for / orchestra / with / pianoforte (continuo) / by / William Walton"; at the top, in another hand: "Original version." The manuscript of a different, intermediate version was acquired by the Beinecke at auction in 2000 (London, Sotheby's, 9 Dec. 1999, lot 265).

Craggs, p. 45.

Holograph manuscript, in full score, of the revised version, [1943], 69 p.

> Notated in pencil, with additional markings (not all in Walton's hand) in red or blue pencil, on both sides of sheets of tall 24-staff paper (watermarked L.J.C.), paginated 1–69 in Walton's hand, and bound in dark greenish blue rexine. Typed Oxford University Press label on front board: "Full score (original M.S. copy) / 'Sinfonia concertante' (revised) / by / William Walton / [in manuscript:] revised / version." On title page, in Walton's hand: "Sinfonia Concertante / for / orchestra (with pianoforte obbligato) / William Walton / (1926–7 revised 1943)."

Craggs, p. 46.

Manuscript, mostly in a copyist's hand, of the piano part, [ca. 1943], 31 p.

> Notated in black ink, with additions and corrections (some in Walton's hand) in pencil and green ink, on three gatherings of nested bifolia of tall 12-staff paper, numbered 1–3. Page 5 of the second gathering is cancelled and rewritten entirely, in Walton's hand, on the recto side of a tall sheet of 14-staff paper.

See William Walton, *Sinfonia concertante*, edited by Lionel Friend (Oxford and New York: Oxford University Press, 2004, Walton Edition, vol. 11).
FRKF 587A, C, B

The Spitfire

Holograph manuscript, in full score, of this prelude and fugue for orchestra arranged from the film music for *The First of the Few*, n.d. [1942–43], 32 p. Notated in pencil, with additional markings in blue and red pencil, on both sides of sheets of tall 24-staff paper, housed in a dark blue rexine binder, with typed Oxford University Press label. On title page, in Walton's hand: "Prelude and Fugue ('The Spitfire') / from / Leslie Howard's film / 'The First of the few.'"

Craggs, p. 87–88.
FRKF 607

Symphony no. 1, C. 27

Holograph manuscript, in full score, 1933 [but 1932–35], 178 p.

> Notated in black ink, with additional markings in blue ink or black, red, or blue pencil, on gatherings of nested bifolia of two kinds of tall 28-staff paper, written on both sides, the first three movements paginated (not by Walton) 1–125, the last (by Walton) 1–53; bound in light brown boards.

> The first movement is on 31 × 44 cm paper (watermark of Daguerre No. 1), the other three on 29 × 39 cm paper (also watermarked Daguerre No. 1). Pasted on the front board, on a printed Oxford University Press label, not in Walton's hand: "Walton / Symphony. / This score should only be used when / absolutely necessary. It may / not be identical with the printed / score." Unsigned title page calligraphed in black ink (with additional pencil traces) by Rex Whistler: "To Imma / Freifrau Von Doernberg / Symphony / William Walton / .MCMXXXIII." At the bottom of p. 1, pencilled note in Walton's hand: "Engraver Note: / All repeat bars to be engraved in full. / Disregard all pencil marks red blue or ordinary." A similar note is on p. 20. Pasted-on cancels noted on p. 9 (first movement) and 3, 51, and 52 (fourth movement). Several pages of the last movement, including the first three pages, are notated in blue ink.

See William Walton, *Symphony No. 1*, edited by David Lloyd-Jones (Oxford and New York: Oxford University Press, 1998. Walton Edition, vol. 9), especially p. xi.
Craggs, p. 55–56.
FRKF 593

Symphony no. 2, C. 68

Holograph manuscript, in full score, 1959–60, 117 p.

> Notated in pencil on both sides of tall sheets of 32-staff paper (G. Ricordi & C.), paginated 1–117 by the composer; bound in bright blue cloth with typed Oxford University Press label pasted on the front board. On title page, in Walton's hand: "Symphony No. 2 / William Walton / Dedicated to the Royal Liverpool Philharmonic Society / which commissioned this work." At the bottom of p. 52 (end of the first movement), autograph note: "Jan '59, revised Feb. March '60 / Forio d'Ischia"; at the bottom of p. 71 (end of the second movement), autograph note: "Jan–Feb '60 / Forio d'Ischia." Dated Forio d'Ischia, 22 July 1960 at the end. Dated 1960, not in Walton's hand, on the front label.

> Accompanied by the manuscript of the original version of the first movement, written in pencil on both sides of loose sheets of tall 30-staff paper (f.lii de Marino, Napoli), paginated 1–48 by the composer.

See William Walton, *Symphony No. 2*, edited by David Russell Hulme (Oxford and New York: Oxford University Press, 2006. Walton Edition, vol. 10), especially p. xii. Craggs, p. 132–34.

FRKF 634, 634a

Variations on a theme by Hindemith, C. 76

Holograph manuscript, in full score, 1963, 104 p.

> Notated in pencil on both sides of tall 32-staff paper (G. Ricordi & C.), paginated 1, 1–103 by the composer, and bound in bright blue cloth. On title page, in Walton's hand: "To Paul & Gertrud Hindemith / Variations on a Theme by Hindemith / Written in honour of the 150th Anniversary of the Royal Philharmonic Society / by / William Walton." At the bottom of p. 1, autograph note: "From the 2nd mov. of Hindemith's Concerto for Vlc. & Orch. (1940). By permission of Edition Schott. Mainz." Dated at the end Forio, 6 Feb. 1963.
>
> Accompanied by 55 pages of drafts and discards, also in full score, written on a combination of 28- and 32-staff paper.

Craggs, p. 141–42.

FRKF 600

Varii capricii, C. 86a

Holograph manuscript, in full score, of this free transcription of the "Five Bagatelles for Guitar," n.d. [1975–76], 44 p.

> Notated in pencil on both sides of tall 28-staff paper (G.B.T.), paginated 2–45. On title page, in Walton's hand: "Varii Capricci (free transcriptions of Five Bagatelles for Guitar)." Accompanied by an alternative version of no. 5, also written in pencil, and on the same type of paper, paginated 1–17. On the title page, in Walton's hand: "Varii Capricci No. 5 2nd version / W.W."
>
> Laid in at the end is an alternative coda, written in short score on a strip of paper (22 × 12.5 cm), for the ballet version of *Varii Capricci* (Craggs C86b). This was written by William Walton four days before his death and, according to a handwritten note on the verso of the page, was received by Robin Langley at Oxford University Press the day Walton died [8 March 1983].

Craggs, p. 154–55.

FRKF 613a–c

F. MUSIC FOR WIND AND BRASS ENSEMBLES

Anniversary fanfare, C. 89

Holograph manuscript of this fanfare for brass and percussion written for the EMI 75th anniversary concert, n.d. [1973], 6 p. Notated in pencil on both sides of individual sheets of tall 12-staff paper (Stamp. music. f.lii de Marino Napoli), paginated 1–6 by the composer. On title page, in Walton's hand: "Fanfare for the 75th anniversary of E.M.I / for / 9 Trumpets in B-flat (3.2.2.2) / 4 Tenor Trombones / 3 Bass Trombones / Timpani & Percussion / to be immediately followed by Coronation March 'Orb & Sceptre' (1953)."

Craggs, p. 157.

FRKF 615

Fanfare for the National, C. 92

Holograph manuscript of this fanfare for brass and percussion to mark the official opening of the National Theatre, 1976 [but written in 1974?], 8 p. Notated in pencil on three nested bifolia of 14-staff paper (monogram M on a treble clef), paginated 1–8 by the composer. On title page, in Walton's hand: "Fanfare for the National / W.W" and date, 1976, not in Walton's hand.

Craggs, p. 159–60.

FRKF 617

Medley for brass band, C. 29b

Holograph manuscript of this abortive competition piece, which includes an arrangement from the ballet *The first shoot*, n.d. [1981], 45 p. Notated in pencil on individual sheets of tall 18-staff paper (Scomegna A 18.70), paginated 1–34 and 31–42 by the composer. On title page, in Walton's hand: "Medley for Brass Band / W.W."

Craggs, p. 59–61.

FRKF 612

Salute to Sir Robert Mayer on his 100th Birthday, C. 97

Holograph manuscript of the introduction to the National Anthem, scored for trumpets and trombones, n.d. [1979], 1 p. Notated in pencil, on three 6-staff systems, on the recto of a single sheet of tall 18-staff paper (G.B.T.). At the top of the page, in Walton's hand: "Introduction to the National Anthem."

Craggs, p. 162–63.

FRKF 620

Title music for the BBC TV Shakespeare Series, C. 96

Holograph manuscript, in full score, of the opening fanfare for winds and percussion, for the BBC Television's Shakespeare series, [1977], 1 p. Notated in pencil, on two 11- and 12-staff systems, on the verso of a single sheet of

24-staff paper. On the recto, in Walton's hand: "Opening Fanfare Shakespeare TV series 25 seconds."

Craggs, p. 161–62.
FRKF 619

G. CHORAL WORKS

Antiphon, C. 94

Holograph manuscript of this anthem for chorus and organ on words by George Herbert, 1977, 8 p. Notated in pencil on both sides of individual sheets of tall 14-staff paper (monogram M on treble clef), paginated 1–8 by the composer, and placed in a bifolium of the same paper, on the second page of which is the first page of music. On title page, in Walton's hand: "Antiphon / George Herbert" and dated 1977 (not in Walton's hand).

See William Walton, *Shorter choral works without orchestra*, edited by Timothy Brown (Oxford and New York: Oxford University Press, 1999. Walton Edition, vol. 6), p. xi and xix–xx.
Craggs, p. 160–61.
FRKF 618

Cantico del sole, C. 90

Holograph manuscript of this motet for unaccompanied mixed chorus, n.d. [1973–74], 10 p. Notated in pencil on both sides of individual sheets of tall 14-staff paper (G.B.T. Ricordi & C.), paginated 1–10 by the composer. On title page, in Walton's hand: "To / Sir Robert & Lady Mayer / Cantico del Sole / S. Francesco d'Assisi / Motet for mixed voices a capella / William Walton."

See William Walton, *Shorter choral works without orchestra*, edited by Timothy Brown (Oxford and New York: Oxford University Press, 1999. Walton Edition, vol. 6), p. x and xviii.
Craggs, p. 157–58.
FRKF 616

Coronation Te Deum, C. 58

Holograph manuscript, in short score, n.d. [1953], 34 p. Notated in pencil on both sides of individual sheets of tall 16-staff paper, paginated 1–34 by the composer. On the recto of the first sheet, in Walton's hand: "Coronation Te Deum / William Walton."

Craggs, p. 111–12.
FRKF 629

Gloria, C. 72

Holograph manuscripts, in short and full score, of this anthem for soloists, chorus, and orchestra, 1961, 80 and 111 p.

The short-score manuscript is written in pencil on single sheets and separate bifolia of tall 16-staff paper (Stamp. music. f.lli de Marino Napoli), housed within an additional bifolium serving as wrappers, paginated 1–80 by the composer (p. 1 is the second page of the outer bifolium). On the front of the outer bifolium, not in Walton's hand: "Gloria in excelsis Deo / William Walton / 1961." Accompanied by 24 additional pages of drafts and discards.

The full-score manuscript is written in pencil on the recto sides of single sheets of tall 36-staff paper (ruled on one side only), paginated 1–111 by the composer, and housed in a light blue cloth folder, on which is pasted a typed label of Oxford University Press. There is no title page or heading.

Craggs, p. 136–37.
FRKF 603A–B

Jubilate Deo, C. 87

Holograph manuscript of this anthem for double mixed chorus and organ, 1972, 10 p. Notated in pencil on both sides of individual sheets of tall 14-staff paper (G.B.T.), paginated 1–10 by the composer, and housed in a bifolium of the same paper. On the front of the bifolium, not in Walton's hand: "William Walton / Jubilate Deo / 1972." At the top of p. 1, in Walton's hand: "Jubilate Deo."

See William Walton, *Shorter choral works without orchestra*, edited by Timothy Brown (Oxford and New York: Oxford University Press, 1999. Walton Edition, vol. 6), p. ix–x and xviii.
Craggs, p. 156.
FRKF 614

King Herod and the cock, C. 95

Holograph manuscript of this Christmas carol for unaccompanied mixed voices, n.d. [1977], 2 p. Notated in pencil on two half-sheets, taped together, of paper monogrammed M on a treble clef, and a single sheet of tall 12-staff paper (Stamp. music. f.lii de Marino Napoli). The words are present only on the single sheet.

See William Walton, *Shorter choral works without orchestra*, edited by Timothy Brown (Oxford and New York: Oxford University Press, 1999. Walton Edition, vol. 6), p. xi and xx.
Craggs, p. 161.
FRKF 621

A litany, C. 1

Holograph manuscript of this anthem for unaccompanied four-part chorus on a text by Phineas Fletcher, 1916, 4 p. Notated in black ink on a bifolium of tall 12-staff paper. At the top of p. [1] in Walton's hand: "A Litany / W.T. Walton." Dated at the end (in a later hand): "Easter 1916." The word "Chris[tmas]" was first written then erased.

Also, seven individual parts for an earlier version, for first, second, third, and fourth trebles, notated in pencil on four sheets of 12-staff paper torn in two, and a second copy of the second, third, and fourth treble parts written in pencil on both sides of three smaller strips of paper.

See William Walton, *Shorter choral works without orchestra*, edited by Timothy Brown (Oxford and New York: Oxford University Press, 1999. Walton Edition, vol. 6), p. vi and xv.
Craggs, p. 13.
FRKF 591a–b

Missa brevis, C. 78.

Holograph manuscript of this mass for double mixed chorus and organ, 1966, 15 p. Notated in pencil on both sides of individual sheets of tall 16-staff paper, paginated 1–15 by the composer. On title page, in pencil, not in Walton's hand: "Missa brevis / William Walton / 1966."

See William Walton, *Shorter choral works without orchestra*, edited by Timothy Brown (Oxford and New York: Oxford University Press, 1999. Walton Edition, vol. 6). p. ix and xvii–xviii.
Craggs, p. 143–44.
FRKF 635

H. VOCAL MUSIC

Anon in love, C. 71a

Holograph manuscript, in full score, of the orchestral version of this song cycle for tenor and small orchestra, on texts from anonymous 16th- and 17th-century lyrics, [1971], 23 p. Notated in pencil on both sides of individual sheets of 24-staff paper (G.B.T.), paginated 1–23 by the composer. There is no title page. The date 1960 [year of the premiere of the original version] figures, not in Walton's hand, on the protective folder, stamped by Oxford University Press.

Craggs, p. 135–36.
FRKF 633

Child's song

Holograph manuscript of this song for voice and piano on a poem by Swinburne, 1918, 3 p. Notated in black ink on p. [2]–[4] of a single bifolium of tall 12-staff paper (R.C.1). At the top of p. [2] in Walton's hand: "Childs' Song / Swinburne / W.T. Walton" Dated July 1918 at the end.

See Craggs, p. 165.
London, Sotheby's, 22 Nov. 1989, lot 266.
FRKF 1334

Façade, C. 12

Partly holograph manuscripts of various movements, some in the hand of Constant Lambert, of the entertainment on texts by Edith Sitwell, n.d. [but ca. 1922–79], 145 p. Notated in pencil or black ink on various types of paper. The manuscript comprises the following sections, to which alphabetical letters (A–W) were assigned arbitrarily (not in Walton's hand) at an unknown stage:

"Fanfare" (E), in pencil on both sides of a single sheet of tall 16-staff paper, 2 p.; also, proof, photocopy (V5), with autograph pencil corrections by Walton, 1 p.

"1 Hornpipe / 2 En famille / 3 Mariner Man" (G), in pencil on two nested bifolia of tall 16-staff paper, 7 p.; on the title page, manuscript table of contents for *Façade* (Fanfare and 12 numbers).

"En famille" (F), in pencil on a bifolium and a single sheet of tall 16-staff paper, 5 p.; another version (K), in pencil on sheets of tall 16-staff paper (stamp of J & W Chester Ltd.), 7 p.; another version (W), in ink, in the hand of a copyist, with corrections in black or red pencil and blue ink, on individual sheets of tall 24-staff paper, 6 p., numbered [1]–2 and 4–7. Additional sketches, in blue ink and pencil, on the verso of p. 7.

"Mariner man (group 1)" (L), in pencil on p. [2] and [3] of a bifolium of tall 12-staff paper, 2 p.; another version (Q), in black ink in the hand of a copyist, the vocal line and words in pencil in that of Constant Lambert, on a bifolium of tall 16-staff paper, 3 p.

"The Octogenerian" [sic] (C), in black ink, with pencil corrections, on both sides of single sheets of tall 12-staff paper, 5 p., followed by "Through Gilden Treillises," 6 p., the first page cancelled, with additional pencil sketches on the verso of p. [11].

[Came the Great Popinjay] "Herodiade's Flea" (V1), in pencil on both sides of a single sheet of tall 30-staff paper, 2 p.; also, proof, photocopy (V10–12), with autograph pencil corrections by Walton, 3 p.; also, photocopy of an unidentified manuscript (V2–4), with autograph pencil corrections and annotations by Walton, 3 p.

"Tarantella" (I), in pencil on both sides of individual sheets of tall 14-staff paper (blind stamp of J & W Chester Ltd.), 6 p.

"Mazurka" (H), in pencil on both sides of single sheets of tall 14-staff paper (blind stamp of J & W Chester Ltd.), 8 p.

"Nos. [cancelled: 7.8.9.] 4.5.6. / Small Talk / By the lake / Said King Pompey" (B), in black ink, with pencil corrections, on both sides of separate sheets of tall 12-staff paper, 12 p.

"Something lies beyond the scene" (N), in black ink on p. [1]–[3] of a bifolium of oblong 14-staff paper, 3 p.; another version

(M), in pencil on both sides of two sheets of tall 16-staff paper (stamp of J & W Chester Ltd.), 3 p.; a third version (O), in black ink, the words in pencil, on a gathering of two nested bifolia of tall 16-staff paper, the music in the hand of a copyist, the vocal line and words in that of Constant Lambert, 6 p. (title given as "Something lies beyond").

"[cancelled: No 22] Aubade 14. / [cancelled: No 23 The owl] Fox trot 15." (D), in black ink, with corrections and additions in pencil, on both sides of sheets of tall 12-staff paper, 10 p. The title of No. 23 is given as "The white owl" at the top of the first page of music.

"Daphne" (R), in black ink in the hand of a copyist, the words and vocal line in pencil, in that of Constant Lambert, on two nested bifolia of 16-staff paper, 7 p.; on title page, in pencil, in the hand of Lambert: "Query revise / Not in this perf"; also, proof, photocopy (V6–9), with autograph corrections by Walton in pencil and blue ballpoint pen, 4 p.

"The Last Galop," photocopy of an early version (T), written [in black ink] on oblong 15-staff paper, 5 p. The title is spelled "The last gallop."

"March" (J), incomplete manuscript, in pencil, on the first three pages of a single bifolium of tall 16-staff paper (blind stamp of J & W Chester Ltd.), labelled (not in Walton's hand) "Sketch for 'March'" on p. [4], 3 p.; also, another version (P), in black ink, in the hand of a copyist, without the words, on a bifolium and a single sheet of tall 16-staff paper, 4 p.; on the title page, in pencil, in the hand of Constant Lambert: "Don't use"; also, photocopy of an early version (S), written on oblong 14-staff paper, 2 p.

Also, manuscript table of contents (A) for the 1951 edition, in Walton's hand, with additional notes in other hands, in blue ink, with additions in black ink and pencil, on the first three pages of a bifolium of tall 12-staff paper. On p. [1]: "To Constant Lambert / Façade / An entertainment / with poems by / Edith Sitwell / & music by / William Walton."

Also, a manuscript (U) entitled "Façade 2 / Poems by Edith Sitwell / Music by William Walton" (the title page in two versions, one cancelled), written in pencil on tall sheets cut at the bottom (30 × 27 cm), paginated 1–23 by the composer, and comprising the following numbers:

"1 Came the Great Popinjay"
"2 Aubade"
"3 March"
"4 Madam Mouse Trots"
"5 The Octogenarian"
"6 Gardener Janus Catches a Naiad"
"7 Water Party"
"8 Said King Pompey"

On the verso of the first (cancelled) title page, table of contents and dedication "To Cathy Berberian." On the verso of the list of instruments, discarded page from "Came the Great Popinjay," marked "Old" at the top.

See William Walton, *Façade Entertainments*, edited by David Lloyd-Jones, with a preface by Stewart Craggs (Oxford and New York: Oxford University Press, 2000. Walton Edition, vol. 7), p. v–xi, xiii–xvii, and xix–xxxvi.
Craggs, p. 19–30.
FRKF 638A

The forsaken merman, C. 4

Holograph manuscript, in short score, of this cantata for soprano and tenor soli, double female chorus, and orchestra on a text by Matthew Arnold, 1916, 20 p. Notated in pencil (the first 13 pages) and black ink in a tall notebook of 12-staff paper in dark purple wrappers. At the top of p. [1] in Walton's hand: "No I / 'The Forsaken Merman' / for / tenor and soprano solo, chorus & orchestra / Matthew Arnold / W.T. Walton" Dated Summer 1916 at the end.

Craggs, p. 14.
London, Sotheby's, 9 May 1985, lot 253.
FRKF 1429

In honour of the city of London, C. 33

Holograph manuscript, in short score, incomplete, of this cantata for chorus and orchestra [1937], 25 p. Notated in pencil, with additions in red pencil, on both sides of single sheets of tall 14-staff paper, placed within a bifolium of the same paper, paginated 1 to 25; p. 1 is the second page of the outer bifolium. On the front of the outer bifolium, in Walton's hand: "In Honour of the City of London / a poem by / William Dunbar / set to music for chorus and orchestra by / William Walton." The manuscript ends at the penultimate line of the third verse.

Craggs, p. 67–68.
FRKF 596

Love laid his sleepless head

Holograph manuscript of this song for voice and piano on a text by Swinburne, 1918, 3 p. Notated in black ink, with one correction in pencil, on p. [2]–[4] of a single bifolium of tall 12-staff paper (R.C.1). At the top of p. [2] in Walton's hand: "Song." Dated at the end July 1918.

See Craggs, p. 165.
London, Sotheby's, 22 Nov. 1989, lot 265.
FRKF 1333

A Lyke-wake song

Holograph manuscript of this song for voice and piano on a poem by Swinburne, 1918, 4 p. Notated in black ink, with additions in pencil, on two separate bifolia, one of tall 14-

staff paper (B.C. No. 3), one of tall 12-staff paper. On the first page of the first bifolium, in black ink, in Walton's hand: "A Lyke Wake Song." At the top of p. [2]: "A Lyke-wake song / Swinburne / W.T. Walton." Dated July 1918 at the end. On the second bifolium is a copy, in a different script, but probably in Walton's hand, of the first 28 measures of the song.

See Craggs, p. 165.
London, Sotheby's, 22 Nov. 1989, lot 268.
FRKF 1351

A Song for the Lord Mayor's Table, C. 74

Holograph manuscript, in short score, of this song cycle for soprano and orchestra, n.d. [1962], 32 p. Notated in pencil on a combination of nested bifolia and single sheets of tall 12-staff paper (Stamp. music. f.lii de Marino Napoli), each section paginated by Walton. The manuscript comprises the following sections, titled by Walton:

> "In Honour of the City of London / A Song for the Lord Mayor's Table / A song-cycle devised by Christopher Hassall / music by / William Walton / No I The Lord Mayor's Table Thomas Jordan," 8 p.
> "II / Glide gently (William Wordsworth)," 3 p.
> "III / Wapping Old Stairs (Anon.) / 1790," 5 p.
> "No IV Holy Thursday (William Blake) / 1789," 4 p.
> "The Contrast (Charles Morris 1798)," 7 p.
> "No VI Rhyme (Anon. 18th century)," 5 p.

Also, holograph manuscript of the arrangement for small orchestra, 1962 [but 1970], 85 p. Notated in pencil on both sides of tall sheets of 24-staff paper (G.B.T.), paginated 1–85 by the composer. On title page, in Walton's hand: "A Song for the Lord Mayor's Table / A song cycle devised by / Christopher Hassall."

Craggs, p. 138–39.
FRKF 602A–B

Tritons, C. 8

Holograph manuscript of this song for voice and piano on a text by William Drummond, 1920, 4 p. Notated in black ink, with additional markings (not all by Walton) in red ink and blue pencil, on a bifolium (now split) of tall 12-staff paper. At the top of p. [1] in Walton's hand: "Tritons. / W. Drummond / [Not in Walton's hand:] C.E. 2239 / W.T. Walton / (1920)." At the bottom of p. [1], not in Walton's hand: "Copyright 1921 by J. Curwen & Sons Ltd." Page 3 is cancelled in its entirety and rewritten on p. 4, in Walton's hand but in a different script.

Craggs, p. 17.
FRKF 589

The Twelve, C. 77a

Holograph manuscript, in full score, of this anthem for mixed voices and orchestra, on words by W.H. Auden, 1965, 45 p. Notated in pencil on both sides of individual sheets of tall 24-staff paper (G.B.T. 24), paginated 1–45 by the composer. On title page, in Walton's hand: "The Twelve / An anthem for the Feast of any Apostle / words by W.H. Auden / music by William Walton."

Craggs, p. 143.
FRKF 599

I. CHAMBER MUSIC

Passacaglia, C. 98

Holograph manuscript of this piece for solo cello, 1982 [but 1979–80?], 6 p. Notated in black felt-tip pen on individual sheets of tall 18-staff paper (Scomegna A 18.70), paginated 1–4. On title page, in Walton's hand: "Passacaglia / for / 'Cello Solo." The date, 1982, is not in Walton's hand. Cancelled draft on the verso of p. 3; there is also a "new page 4."

Craggs, p. 163.
FRKF 611

Quartet for strings (1922), C. 11

Holograph manuscript, 1922, 132 p. Notated in black ink on three gatherings of nested bifolia of oblong paper cut to the dimensions 31 × 10.5 cm, and paginated respectively 1–22, 1–62, and 1–52. Pages 48–51 of the last movement are lacking. On the front of the first gathering, in Walton's hand: "Quartet / (chosen for the International Festival of Contemporary Chamber Music at Salzburg. 1923) / I / (Moderato)" and the autograph presentation inscription: "for / Bumps / from / William. / Sept 28th 1936." Initialed and dated 1920–2 at the end of the first and second movements; signed and dated Amalfi, 23 Nov. 1922 at the end of the third movement.

Craggs, p. 18–19.
FRKF 590

Quartet for strings (1947), C. 53

Holograph manuscript of the *String Quartet in A minor*, n.d. (1947), 48 p. Notated in black ink on the recto sides of sheets of tall 24-staff paper, folded and glued at the bottom, while the right margin is highlighted by a pasted-on strip of paper. Paginated [1]–48. At the top of p. [1] in Walton's hand: "To / Ernest Irving / String Quartet in A minor / William Walton."

Craggs, p. 103–04.
FRKF 606A

Sonata for string orchestra, C. 53a

Manuscript, partly holograph, partly in the hand of Malcolm Arnold, of this arrangement of the *String Quartet in A minor*, n.d., 66 p. Notated in pencil in Walton's hand (the first three movements) and in black ballpoint pen in Arnold's hand (fourth movement) on separate bifolia (first three movements) and a gathering of nested bifolia (fourth movement) of tall 18-staff paper (G.B.T.), paginated 1–66 by the composer and by Arnold, and housed in two additional bifolia. On p. [4] the outer bifolium, in Walton's hand: "Sonata for String Orchestra / (adapted from String Quartet 1947)."

Craggs, p. 104–05.
FRKF 606B

Toccata for violin and piano, C. 13

Holograph manuscript, n.d. [1922–23], 28 p. Notated in black ink on an unpaginated gathering of nine nested bifolia of tall 12-staff paper (R.C.1), written on both sides. On the front of the outer bifolium in Walton's hand: "Toccata / for / violin and pianoforte. / W.T. Walton." Also, autograph note at the top: "Please return to / The British Music Society / 3, Berners Street. London. WI."

Craggs, p. 38–39.
FRKF 592

J. PIANO MUSIC

Duets for children, C. 39

Holograph manuscript of the first version, for piano solo, of these nine pieces, n.d. [1940], 9 p.

> Notated in pencil on three nested bifolia of tall 16-staff paper (G. Schirmer). On the title page, in Walton's hand: "Tunes for my niece." At the top of p. [1]: "for Elizabeth."

Holograph manuscript of the definitive version for piano four-hands, 1940, 18 p.

> Notated in pencil, with additional markings in red ink and red pencil, on five nested bifolia of tall 14-staff paper (G. Schirmer), paginated 1–18 by the composer. On the title page, in Walton's hand: "Duets for children / by William Walton." Also on the title page, in blue ballpoint pen: "for Alfred Chenhalls (Cheney) / in the celebration (surtax!) / from / William / May 15th 1940." At the top of p. 1 in Walton's hand: "To Elizabeth and Michael."

See William Walton, *Instrumental Music*, edited by Michael Aston (Oxford and New York: Oxford University Press, 2003. Walton Edition, vol. 20), p. v–vi and xiv–xv.
Craggs, p. 75–76.
FRKF 624A–B

II. LETTERS

To Edwin Evans

[1942 May 13, London*] ALS, 2 p. (env), concerning *Façade*.

London, Sotheby's, 29 Nov. 1985, lot 251.
FRKF 1069

To Boris Kochno

1949 Nov. 4, Forio d'Ischia, ALS, 1 p.

1949 Nov. 7, Forio d'Ischia, ALS, 1 p.

1950 Feb. 5, Forio d'Ischia, ALS, 2 p., concerning *Devoir de Vacances*.

Monaco, Sotheby's, 11 Oct. 1991, lot 411.
FRKF 1391a

To Elizabeth Lutyens

1945 May 7, Ashby St. Ledgers, Rugby[S], ALS, 1 p., sending a financial contribution.

1951 Jan. 28, Forio d'Ischia, ALS, 1 p., regarding a Unesco project. Incomplete.

1953 July 17, Lowndes Cottage, Lowndes Place, London, S.W.I.[S], TLS, 1 p. Notes (in Luytens's hand?) on the verso, concerning Wittgenstein.

1959 Jan. 25, San Felice, Forio d'Ischia, Prov. di Napoli, Italy[S], ALS, 1 p. Mentions Stravinsky and *Belshazzar's Feast*, as well as a composition for clarinet by Lutyens.

1962 May 22, San Felice, Forio d'Ischia[S], ALS, 2 p. (env). A letter of condolence on the death of Edward Clark.

1976 Aug. 3, La Mortella, Forio d'Ischia, Italy[S], ALS, 2 p. Mentions *Troilus and Cressida*.

Elizabeth Lutyens (1906–83), the British composer, daughter of Sir Edwin Lutyens and wife of BBC producer Edward Clark.

London, Sotheby's, 29 Nov. 1985, lot 252.
FRKF 1051

III. PRINTED MUSIC

Belshazzar's Feast, for Mixed Choir, Baritone Solo and Orchestra. Text selected and arranged from the Holy Bible by Osbert Sitwell. German Translation by Beryl de Zoete and

Baronin Imma Doernberg. London: Oxford University Press, 1931.

> Vocal score, first edition. [i]–[xii], [1]–120 p. The cover design, initialed in the lower right corner, is by Gino Severini. Inscribed on p. [xii]: "for / Edward Clark / from / William Walton / Nov. 12th 1931."

Belshazzar's Feast, commissioned by Edward Clark on behalf of the BBC, was first performed in Leeds on 8 Oct. 1931.

London, Sotheby's, 29 Nov. 1985, lot 250.
FRKF 1052

EVELYN WAUGH (1903–66)

Letter to Joseph Brewer

[ca. 1925 May] "Friday," Newlands Corner, Merrow Downs, Guildford[S], ALS, 7 p. Not in *The Letters of Evelyn Waugh*.

Brewer was an American classmate of Waugh's at Oxford; the letter evokes their days at the university and mentions Ibsen's *The wild duck*.

London, Sotheby's, 7 Dec. 1999, lot 296.
FRKF 1433

CARL MARIA VON WEBER (1786–1826)

Letters to Gottfried Weber

All are autograph letters, signed.

1810
> April 15 [Darmstadt] 3 p.
> [June 18 Darmstadt] 3 p. The second page is in a different hand.
> Aug. 21, Darmstadt, 1 p.
> Aug. 30, Darmstadt, 2 p.
> Sept. 9, Frankfurt, 1 p.
> Sept. 23, Darmstadt, 1 p.
> Sept. 28, Darmstadt, 1 p.
> Oct. 8, Darmstadt, 1 p.
> Oct. 12, Darmstadt, 2 p.
> Oct. 23, Frankfurt, 1 p.

1811
> Jan. 8, Darmstadt, 2 p.

> Jan. 15, Darmstadt, 2 p., with a postscript by Meyerbeer.
> [Feb., Darmstadt] 2 p., with a postscript by Meyerbeer.
> Feb. 20, Giessen, 2 p.
> Feb. 27, Würzburg, 2 p.
> March 10, Augsburg, 1 p. Accompanied by a "Circulare" in five different hands, dated 10 March 1811, and signed by "Melos" [C.M. von Weber], "G[iu]sto" [Gottfried Weber], "the unknown" [Alexander von Dusch], "Philodikaios" [Meyerbeer] and "Triole" [Johann Gänsbacher].
> March 22, Munich, 3 p.
> April 30, Munich, 3 p.
> May 16, Munich, 1 p.
> July 3, Munich, 2 p.
> July 8, Munich, 1 p.
> July 19, Munich, 3 p.
> Aug. 2, Munich, 1 p.
> Aug. 16, Wolfberg bei Konstanz, 3 p.
> Aug. 23, Schaffhausen, 1 p.
> Aug. 30, Zürich, 1 p.
> Sept. 14–16, Bern, 5 p.
> Oct. 9, Basel, 2 p., with a musical quotation.
> Nov. 15, Munich, 2 p.
> Nov. 29, Munich, 2 p.
> Dec. 31 [Munich] 3 p.

1813
> Jan. 26–27 [Prague] 3 p.
> March 9, Prague, 6 p. with music quotations.
> June 21, Prague, 1 p. The beginning is missing.
> July 14, Prague, 2 p.

1814
> Jan. 29, Prague, 3 p.
> May 5, Prague, 6 p.
> Nov. 3, Prague, 4 p.

1815
> Jan. 30, Prague, 3 p.
> Aug. 20, Munich, 3 p., with a pasted-on clipping from the *Münchener Politische Zeitung* for 5 Aug. 1815 reporting on a concert given by Weber.
> Sept. 16, Prague, 2 p.

1816
> Feb. 2, Prague, 4 p.
> April 24, Prague, 2 p.
> Sept. 17, Prague, 2 p.

1817
> March 6, Dresden, 2 p.
> July 21, Dresden, 1 p., enclosing a list of books, 4 p.

Sept. 8, Dresden, 1 p.

1822

April 22, Dresden, 3 p., with clipping from *Briefe von C.M. Weber*, p. 22–24.

May 13, Dresden, 2 p., with pasted-on clipping from *Briefe*.

Nov. 8, Dresden, 1 p., with pasted-on clipping from *Briefe*, p. 24–25.

Dec. 2, Dresden, 2 p., with pasted-on clipping from *Briefe*, p. 25–26.

1824

March 19, Dresden, 1 p., with pasted-on clipping from *Briefe*, p. 30.

March 22, Dresden, 1 p., with pasted-on clipping from *Briefe*, p. 30–31.

June 13, Dresden, 1 p.

Oct. 11, Dresden, 2 p.

1825

April 8, Dresden, 1 p.

Aug. 15, Ems, 1 p.

Sept. 4, Dresden, 1 p., with pasted-on clipping from *Briefe*.

Oct. 17, Dresden, 1 p., with musical quotation.

Nov. [29?] Dresden, 3 p., with three musical quotations, and a pasted-on clipping from *Weitere Nachtrichten*, p. 304.

1826

Feb. 3, Dresden, 1 p., accompanied by a clipping from *Briefe*, p. 39–40.

Several letters are signed "Melos."

The jurist, amateur composer, and music critic Gottfried Weber (1779–1839) was C.M. von Weber's best friend. The letters discuss the latter's career (such as his triumphant concert in Munich on 11 Nov. 1811) and works (the *Beherrscher der Geister* overture, the *Bassoon Concerto* in F major, the *Piano Concerto* no. 2 in E-flat major, *Silvana*, *Abu Hassan*, and *Euryanthe*, among others). Apart from Meyerbeer, the letters mention fellow composers E.T.A Hoffmann and Franz Danzi; music publishers Johann Anton André and Nicolaus Simrock; singers Ludwig Berger and Caroline Brandt; Friedrich Kind, librettist of *Der Freischütz*; and Castil-Blaze, who adapted the work in French.

Published: Werner Bollert and Arno Lemke, eds., "Carl Maria von Webers Briefe an Gottfried Weber," *Jahrbuch des Staatlichen Instituts für Musikforschung Preussischer Kulturbesitz*, 1972, p. 7–103. See also Lemke, "Einige Anmerkungen zur Freundschaft zwischen Carl Maria von Weber und Gottfried Weber" and Bollert, "Anmerkungen zu Carl Maria von Webers Briefe an Gottfried Weber," *Jahrbuch der Staatlichen Instituts für Musikforschung Preussischer Kulturbesitz*, 1973, p. 72–75 and p. 76–135, respectively.

Marburg, Stargardt, 29–30 Nov. 1983, lot 1005.
FRKF 151

JAMES McNEILL WHISTLER (1834–1903)

Letters to William Michael Rossetti

[1867] June 26 [London] ALS, 4 p.

[1867] Dec. 11 [London] ALS, 3 p.

[1867 Dec. 16] "Monday" [London] ALS, 3 p.

[1872 Sept. 3, London] ALS, 3 p.

[1881 April 3] Arts Club, Hanover Square [London] W.S (embossed), ALS, 1 p.

The 1867 letters concern his proposed expulsion from the Burlington Fine Arts Club.

See Christie's, New York, 17 May 1991, lot 139; see also Sotheby's, New York, 17 Dec. 1992, lot 248. New York, Christie's, 14 May 1985, lot 110.
FRKF 637

REX WHISTLER (1905–44)

Letters to Stephen Tennant

All are autograph letters, signed and, unless otherwise noted, illustrated.

1924 April 8, Pinner, 1 p.

1924 Aug. 5, "Slade" [London] 4 p.

1924 Aug. 27, Farnham Common, 4 p. (env)

1924 Sept. 12, Farnham Common, 4 p.

[1924 Sept. 27] "Saturday," Farnham Common, 2 p.

[1924 Sept. 29] "Monday (8 o'clock!)," Farnham Common 2 p.

["Latest Sept 1924"] n.p., fragment of an ALS, 4 p.; only p. 5–[8] are present.

[1924? Oct. 6] "Tuesday," "Slade" [London] 4 p. (env), in pencil.

[1924 Oct. 10] "Friday," Farnham Common, 4 p. (illustrated env)

[1924 Oct. 13] "Monday, Slade," 4 p.

1925 [May 15] "Friday," Farnham Common, 6 p.

1925 July 13, Farnham Common, 4 p. (env)

[mid-1920s] "Slade," 2 p. Not illustrated. Clipping from the *Daily Mirror* pinned on, showing the film actress Mae Murray at Longchamp.

[1929] July 16, Rome, 4 p. (illustrated env)
"1930 Autumn," XX Fitzroy Street [London] 2 p.
[1929? 1930?] 20 Fitzroy Street, 2 p.
["1933 Summer?"] "Thursday," 20 Fitzroy Street, 4 p.
[1935] April 12, 20 Fitzroy Street, 2 p.; incomplete.
[1936 Sept. 15] "Tuesday night, late," 20 Fitzroy Street, W.1., 2 p. (env)
[1920s] 2 incomplete ALS, n.p., each 2 p., the first marked P.S.

Together with the following material:

Autograph, hand-painted Christmas card, in an envelope postmarked London, 24 Dec. 1937.
Illustrated envelope postmarked London [1?] July 1925, enclosing a review of a Cézanne exhibition clipped from the *Evening Standard* for 30 June 1925.
Three calligraphed and illustrated envelopes, postmarked London, 15 Aug. 1924 and undeciphered.
Illustrated and calligraphed envelope postmarked London, 15 Oct. 1924.
Two envelopes postmarked London, 7 Oct. 1924 and 2 July 1925 (illustrated).

London, Sotheby's, 15 Dec. 1987, lot 326.
FRKF 1310

CHARLES-MARIE WIDOR (1844–1937)

ANS on one side of a card to an unidentified correspondent, n.d., n.p. Concerning a concert at the Institut by the English pianist Evelyn Howard Jones.

Paris, Dominique Vincent (Drouot), 6 Dec. 1984, lot 272.
FRKF 662c

OSCAR WILDE (1854–1900)

I. MANUSCRIPTS

De Profundis

Typescript, with manuscript corrections, n.d., 142 p. Typed in blue ribbon on the recto sides of 142 leaves (20 × 25.5 cm), preceded by a title page, foliated [1]–142. On the title page, in typescript: "Manuscript. / of / 'De Profundis.'" Working typescript of *De Profundis*, typed on one side only.

Stitched with a thin purple cord and bound in thick beige paper wrappers in a slipcase of similar paper, with typed labels: "De Profundis MS." pasted on the front and the spine; also inscribed on the front by Robert Ross: "Property of Robert Ross / Mayfair Chambers / 13 Little Grosvenor Street / Mayfair / W.," and by Carlos Blacker: "Property of C.P. Blacker / Stanley Green / Surrey. 1934."

Also a copy (purple ribbon) with a different title page: "Manuscript of / 'De Profundis,'" foliated [1]–139; "CB / Torquay 30th June 1913" on a preliminary page. A second copy (also purple ribbon), with yet a different title page: "Manuscript / - of - / 'De Profundis,'" foliated [1]–135, signed by Blacker on a preliminary page.

Accompanied by an ALS from Robert Ross to Carlos Blacker, on stationery of 13, Little Grosvenor Street, London, W., 1913 May 14, 1 p., concerning the *De Profundis* typescript. With a clipping from *The Sunday Express* for 16 Dec. 1928, concerning Wilde.

London, Sotheby's, 10 July 1986, lot 152.
FRKF 1403a–b

"To L.L."

Autograph manuscript, n.d. [ca. 1885], 1 p. Written in black ink on the recto side of a large sheet of laid paper (watermark of De La Rue & Co, London). Incipit: "You have only wasted your life …" A poem addressed to Lilly Langtry.

See Christie's, London, 28 Nov. 1990, lot 231.
London, Sotheby's, 18 Dec. 1985, lot 120.
FRKF 1008

II. LETTERS

To Carlos Blacker

1897 July 12, Berneval-sur-Mer, près Dieppe, ALS, 12 p. (env). *Complete Letters*, p. 911–12.
[1897 Aug. 4] Café Suisse, Dieppe^S, ALS, 2 p. (env). *Complete Letters*, p. 921.

London, Sotheby's, 10 July 1986, lots 128, 130.
FRKF 1205, 1207

To Rose Coghlan and Elizabeth Marbury

[1893 Autumn] drafts of telegrams to each of them, n.p. 1 p., notes by a previous collector on the verso. Mounted on a sheet of paper with a magazine photograph of Wilde pasted on the right. *Complete Letters*, p. 573.

London, Phillips, 16 Feb. 1884, lot 403.
FRKF 277

III. MISCELLANEOUS

Forgery of an ALS from Wilde to Leonard C. Smithers, n.d., "Monday," Paris, 3 p.

FRKF 1203

WILHELM I, EMPEROR OF GERMANY (1797–1888)

Document with the signature of Wilhelm I, dated Berlin, 17 March 1863, 1 p.

Marburg, Stargardt, 5–6 March 1985, lot 1286.
FRKF 837

WILHELM II, EMPEROR OF GERMANY (1859–1941)

Letters to Miss Mary Montagu

1905 Oct. 17, ALS on both sides of a card, Neues Palais [Potsdam].

[1906]–1907 Christmas and New Year, n.p., ANS on the verso of a postcard showing the S.M.S. "Deutschland."

1908 Feb. 27, Berlin, ALS on both sides of a card.

1908 March 5, n.p., ALS on both sides of a card.

1908 May 1, Achilleion, Corfu[S], ALS, 4 p.

1908 Aug. 27, Metz, ALS, 4 p.

1908 Nov. 21, Neues Palais, ALS on both sides of a card.

1909 April 27, Achilleion, Corfu[S], ALS, 4 p.

1909 Oct. 13, Jagdschloss Hubertusstock, ALS, 4 p.

[1909]–1910 Christmas and New Year, n.p., 2 ANS on the versos of postcards, one showing William II on the deck of a ship, the other showing the deck of a ship.

1910 Jan. 8, Neues Palais, ALS, 4 p.

1910 May 1, Schloss Wiesbaden[S], ALS, 4 p.

1910 June 7, Neues Palais, telegram, 2 p.

1910 Oct. 10, Cadinen, Westpreussen[S], ALS, 4 p.

1911 Aug. 24, Schloss Wilhelmshöhe[S], ALS, 4 p.

1911 Dec. 17, Neues Palais, ALS, 3 p.

[1911]–1912 Christmas and New Year, n.p., ANS on the verso of a postcard showing William II.

1912 May 7, Achilleion, APCS

1912 Nov. 25, Neues Palais, ALS, 3 p.

1913 July 22, Balholm, ALS, 2 p.

1913 Oct. 1, n.p., APCS

[1913]–1914 Christmas and New Year, n.p., 2 ANS on the versos of postcards, one showing William II hunting, the other showing William II reviewing troops in Berlin.

1914 May 3, Achilleion, ALS, 2 p.

n.d., n.p., ALS, 3 p.

Also, ALS on both sides of a card from William II to Lord Charles Thomas Montagu-Douglas-Scott, 1905 Oct. 7, Pillau, addressed to "My dear Admiral Montagu."

The letters are all in English. Accompanied by 43 additional postcards showing William II or places associated with him, four of them with annotations in his hand (1911 and n.d.)

See Christie's, London, 28 Nov. 1990, lot 237.
Marburg, Stargardt, 26–27 Nov. 1985, lot 1062.
FRKF 1290

HUGO WOLF (1860–1903)

I. MUSIC MANUSCRIPTS

Beherzigung

Holograph manuscript of this song for voice and piano, on a poem by Goethe, n.d. [1887], 2 p. Notated in black ink on both sides of a single sheet of tall 12-staff paper (J.E. & Co. no. 12). At the top of p. [1] in Wolf's hand: "Beherzigung / (Goethe)"; in red pencil, in another hand: "N° 4." Published in 1888 as no. 4 of *Sechs Gedichte von Scheffel, Mörike, Goethe und Kerner*. Date of composition given as 1 March 1887 by Grove.

Heinrich Schütz to Henry Miller, p. 76–77.
London, Sotheby's, 29 Nov. 1985, lot 256.
FRKF 1038

Ich stand in dunkeln Träumen

Holograph manuscript of this song for voice and piano on a text by Heinrich Heine, 1878, 2 p. Notated in black ink on both sides of a sheet of tall 18-staff paper. At the top of p. [1] in Wolf's hand: "Wien am 26. Mai [1]878. / Aus dem Lieder-Cyklus von / H. Heine / II. / Hugo Wolf." Dated again "29. Mai [1]878" at the end. Published in 1903 in *Lieder aus der Jugendzeit*.

London, Sotheby's, 28 May 1986, lot 624.
FRKF 1140

Mir träumte von einem Königskind

Holograph manuscript of this song for voice and piano on a text by Heinrich Heine, 1878, 3 p. Notated in black ink on both sides of a single sheet of tall 18-staff paper. Measures 11–24 are cancelled in blue pencil and rewritten on a separate half-sheet, with a pencilled note in Wolf's hand. At the top of p. [1] in Wolf's hand: "Wien am 16. Juni [1]878. / Aus dem Lieder-Cyklus von / H. Heine / Hugo Wolf." Dated again "16. Juni" at the end. First published posthumously in 1927.

Marburg, Stargardt, 26–27 Nov. 1985, lot 957.
FRKF 1159

Wie des Mondes Abbild zittert

Holograph manuscript of this song for voice and piano, 1880, 1 p., written in black ink on both sides of a single sheet of 18-staff paper. Signed at the top of the first page and dated Vienna, 13 Feb. 1880. Also at the top of p. [1] in Wolf's hand: "Aus dem Liederstrauss v. H. Heine." Numbered XII in roman numerals above the first staff. Not published during Wolf's lifetime.

London, Sotheby's, 23 Nov. 1984, lot 554.
FRKF 550

II. LETTERS

To Oskar Grohe

1895 June 24, Matzen, ALS, 2 p. (env), concerning *Der Corregidor*.

London, Sotheby's, 28 May 1986, lot 628.
FRKF 1137

To Heinrich Potpeschnigg

1897 May 17, Vienna, APCS, concerning Gustav Mahler and *Der Corregidor*. Signed "Wolfing."

London, Christie's, 5 May 1982, lot 185.
FRKF 23

ERMANNO WOLF-FERRARI (1876–1948)

I. MUSIC MANUSCRIPTS

Wolf-Ferrari's music manuscripts are described in eight groups:

A. OPERAS
B. VOCAL MUSIC
C. CHORAL MUSIC
D. ORCHESTRAL MUSIC
E. CHAMBER MUSIC
F. PIANO MUSIC
G. ORGAN MUSIC
H. MISCELLANEOUS

Unless otherwise noted, the Wolf-Ferrari scores constituted lot 630 in the Sotheby's (London) auction of 28 May 1986. Most items in sections B–H are not in Grove, except where noted.

A. OPERAS

Gli amanti sposi

Holograph manuscript draft, in short score, and miscellaneous sketches, 1921 and n.d., 234 p. Notated in black ink and pencil on a combination of single sheets and separate or nested bifolia of tall 12-staff paper, each act housed in an additional bifolium serving as wrappers. On title page inserted before act 1: "Honny soit qui mal y pense / Atto I°."

Manuscripts for act 1 comprise a continuity draft, written in ink on the verso sides of bifolia nested two by two, and paginated 1–37, with occasional pencil drafts on the facing pages; and miscellaneous sketches.

The manuscript for act 2 is also preceded by a title page with the original title. It comprises a continuity draft in pencil, paginated 1–80, and three additional pages of sketches.

The manuscript for act 3 contains the same title page, with the old title corrected as *Gli amanti sposi*. It comprises a continuity draft, paginated 1–30, with an additional folio 19–20, cancelled, and a double set of p. 22–27.

The act 2 intermezzo is notated separately, on a bifolium and three individual sheets of tall 14-staff paper (Schutzmarke No. 6), and dated Feb. 1921 in the upper corner of p. [1]. Followed by miscellaneous sketches.

Gli amanti sposi, opera giocosa in three acts, on a libretto by Luigi Sugana, Giuseppe Pizzolato, Enrico Golisciani, and Giavacchino Forzano after Goldoni, was premiered at the Teatro La Fenice, Venice, on 19 Feb. 1925.

FRKF 1200.01

L'amore medico

Holograph manuscript draft, in short score, with a fragment of the overture, in full score, and miscellaneous additional drafts, 1910–12, 202 p.

The short-score draft, abundantly corrected throughout, is written in ink and in pencil on a combination of individual bifolia and single sheets of tall 16-staff paper, generally on both sides, each act housed in an additional bifolium serving as wrappers. The first is marked "[in pencil] L'amore medico primo schizzo / [in ink] Atto Primo," the second "[in pencil] Der Liebhaber als Artz / [in ink] Atto II°." A large part of act 2 is written on 12-staff paper. In four instances, towards the middle of act 1, the text is written in pencil on an otherwise blank page, opposite the music. Act 1 is dated 10 May 1910 on p. [1], in upper right corner, and 14 June 1912 at the end. Act 2 is undated.

The partial manuscript of the overture is written in black ink on eight pages of two separate bifolia of tall 24-staff paper, paginated 1–8 by Wolf-Ferrari. At the top of p. 1, in his hand: "Der Liebhaber als Artz / (L'amore medico) / Ouverture / W. Wolf-Ferrari."

L'amore medico, commedia musicale in two acts on a libretto by Enrico Golisciani after Molière, was premiered in Dresden, as *Der Liebhaber als Artz*, on 4 Dec. 1913.

FRKF 1200.02

La bona mare

Holograph sketches, in short score, for an unrealized opera, 1940, 14 p. Notated in pencil on the recto sides of twelve single sheets, foliated 1–12, and both sides of a single sheet, unfoliated, of tall 12-staff paper (Sünova Nr. 4), housed within a bifolium of the same paper serving as wrappers. On the outside wrapper, in pencil, in Wolf-Ferrari's hand: "La bona mare / Atto I / 30 Agosto [19]40."

FRKF 1200.09

Cenerentola

Largely holograph manuscript, incomplete, 1898, ca. 250 p. The manuscript comprises the following:

1. An incomplete draft of act 1, in full score, notated in black ink on separate bifolia of tall 24-staff paper, paginated [1]–60, 65–76 and 115, 115 [bis]–19, with another set of bifolia paginated 111–19, signed and dated 21 April 1898 at the top of p. 1; with another manuscript of the first 46 measures, notated in black ink on the first three pages of a bifolium of tall 30-staff paper; and a manuscript of the last 13 pages of the act, also in full score, in the hand of a copyist, paginated 239–51; together with miscellaneous additional drafts, one of which is dated 23 March 1898.

2. A draft of act 2, in short score, notated in black ink on two gatherings combining bifolia and single sheets of oblong 14-staff paper, paginated [1]–33.

3. Incomplete draft of act 3, in short score, partly in the hand of a copyist, the Italian text in black ink, the German text and stage directions in red ink, on paper of different sizes, paginated at the bottom 1–46; a second section paginated 218–29, and a single leaf (the final measures) paginated 230.

4. Eight sheets of miscellaneous drafts, one page in full score.

Cenerentola, fiaba musicale in three acts, on a libretto by Maria Pezzè-Pascolato after Charles Perrault, was premiered at the Teatro La Fenice, Venice, on 22 Feb. 1900 and in a revised version in Bremen on 31 Jan. 1902.

FRKF 1200.14

La dama boba

Holograph manuscript draft, in short score, and draft of the full score, 1937, ca. 380 p.

The short-score draft is written in pencil on the recto sides (with additional sketches on the versos) of individual sheets of tall 12-staff paper (Sünova Nr. 4). Each act is housed in a bifolium serving as wrappers. On the front of the one for act 1, in Wolf-Ferrari's hand: "finito lo schizzo in 96 giorni." Act 1 is paginated 1–56; at the bottom of p. 56: "finito l'atto primo il giorno 21 Maggio." Act 2 is paginated 1–58, and act 3, 1–55. Dated 2 Aug. 1937 at the end.

The full score is written in pencil, with occasional corrections and additions in red pencil, on separate bifolia or individual sheets, paginated 2–138 (acts 1 and 2) and 1–75 (act 3), of various types of tall 12- and 24-staff paper (some of it Sünova 24 zeilig). Rehearsal numbers are marked in red pencil. At the bottom of p. 72: "Fine atto Primo"; on p. 138, "Fine dell'Atto II°."

Laid in: autograph draft of a portion of the libretto (ending with the words: "Maria!" "Gabriele!"), in Wolf-Ferrari's hand, 1 p.; also a half-page with unidentified sketches.

Also, a pencilled draft, in short score, incomplete, for the overture, written on the recto sides of two single sheets of tall 12-staff paper, foliated 1 and 2, and marked at the top, in Wolf-Ferrari's hand: "Ouverture / Boba."

La dama boba, commedia lirica in three acts on a libretto by Mario Ghisalberti after Lope de Vega, was premiered at the Teatro alla Scala, Milan, on 1 Feb. 1939.

FRKF 1200.17

Le donne curiose

Holograph draft, in short score, and miscellaneous sketches, n.d., 123 p.

The draft is written in black pencil, with additions in red pencil, on a combination of nested bifolia, separate bifolia, and individual sheets of tall 12-staff paper. There is a continuous section, marked "Atto I" at the beginning, on all sides of five nested bifolia, unpaginated, the accompaniment notated on one or two staves; and an unidentified section, paginated 0 to 21 bis. A few additional sketches, in ink, are laid in.

The sketches comprise a section paginated 76–81 and various drafts, grouped together under the heading "Donne Curiose / Schizzi." They include two oblong sheets of 22-staff paper, both notated in ink.

Also present is a single sheet from the holograph full score, in ink, marked at the end "Fine del II° atto."

Le donne curiose, commedia musicale in three acts on a libretto by Luigi Sugana after Goldoni, was premiered as *Die neugierigen Frauen* at the Hofoper, Munich, on 27 Nov. 1903.

FRKF 1200.18

I gioielli della Madonna

Miscellaneous holograph drafts and sketches, in short score, 1908 and n.d., 304 p. The manuscript comprises:

1. An autograph synopsis of act 1, written in black and red ink and black pencil, 17 p. At the top of p. [1] in Wolf-Ferrari's hand: "Prospetto del Primo atto." With a short autograph listing of the numbers in act 1 and a 4-page musical outline of the act, with the thematic material laid out, numbered 1–16.

2. Skeleton draft headed "Parte prima," only the beginning paginated 1–4; one section, containing the vocal lines only, is housed in a bifolium labelled "Per Zangarini."

3. Holograph manuscript, in short score, of the act 2 Intermezzo, in black ink, with pencil annotations, on p. 1 through 5 of a gathering of two nested bifolia of tall 12-staff paper.

4. Two skeleton drafts of act 2, one paginated 1 to 52 (one section is also paginated 101–10 and, farther down, 119–22), the other incomplete and irregularly paginated 7–23, with sections taped together.

5. Holograph manuscript, in short score, of the act 3 Intermezzo, in black ink, with pencil annotations, on p. 1 through [6] of a gathering of two nested bifolia of tall 12-staff paper.

6. Incomplete skeleton draft of act 3, signed and dated 20 Jan. 1908 at the top of p. 1, paginated 1–13 (many pages with a double pagination); other sections paginated 1–10, 6–7, and 131–34. Laid in, a quire, paginated 33–48, from an unidentified edition of Wilhelm Hauff's *Märchen-Almanach auf das Jahr 1826*, comprising the end of *Die Geschichte von dem Gespensterschiff* and the beginning of *Die Geschichte von der abgehauenen Hand*.

7. A section headed "Duetto e finale III," consisting of a single sheet, foliated 1, and two bifolia, numbered 2 and 3, no. 3 with two single sheets laid in, paginated b–e.

8. Unidentified sketches.

I gioielli della Madonna, opera in three acts (drawn from Neapolitan life), on a libretto by Carlo Zangarini and Enrico Golisciani based on a synopsis by the composer, was premiered as *Der Schmuck der Madonna* at the Kurfürstenoper, Berlin, on 23 Dec. 1911.

FRKF 1200.26

Das Himmelskleid

Miscellaneous holograph drafts and sketches, 1922 and n.d., 634 p., written mostly in pencil on bifolia or individual sheets, usually of tall 12-staff paper. The manuscript comprises:

1. Two holograph manuscripts of the prelude, in short score, both in ink on two separate bifolia, paginated 1–8; also, a draft in pencil, 4 p.

2. Partial draft of act 1, in black ink, with corrections and annotations in pencil and red ink, clearly belonging to the same draft as one for the prelude, and paginated 9–24, 177–96, 245–56, 273–84, 349–83; there is another set of p. 365–83.

3. A draft of act 1, in pencil, possibly incomplete, paginated 1–10, 10 bis, 11–18, 18 [bis]–19, 20–31, 31b, 32–33, 33 bis/34, 35–39, 39 bis, 40–58; with additional sketches throughout; also, miscellaneous sketches in pencil and black ink, on a gathering of five nested bifolia. Dated 1 Aug. 1922 on the title page.

4. Another draft of act 1, in pencil, with occasional additions or corrections in black or red ink, on gatherings of nested bifolia and single bifolia, numbered 1 to 9, followed by bifolia numbered 1–7, with the words in both German and Italian; the manuscript ends five bars after rehearsal number 383.

5. A skeleton draft of act 3, in pencil, paginated 1–9, 9 bis, 10, 10 bis, 11, 11 bis, 12–20, 20 [bis], 21–29. Marked "Fine" at the end.

6. A skeleton draft of act 3, in pencil, paginated 1–78, 89 [sic, for 79]; marked "Fine" at the end.

7. Miscellaneous sketches in a bifolium labelled "Himmelskleid / Veste di Cielo / Schizz[o]"; some, possibly for act 1.

8. A bundle of sketches, in black pencil and red ink, housed in a bifolium serving as wrappers and labelled "Chaos (?) Himmelskeid." Followed by a few pages of additional sketches.

Das Himmelskleid [La veste del cielo], "Legende" in three acts, on a libretto by Wolf-Ferrari after Charles Perrault, was premiered at the National Theater, Munich, on 21 April 1927.

FRKF 1200.28

Irene

Partly holograph manuscripts of this opera on a libretto by the composer, 1895 and n.d., 213 p. The manuscripts comprise:

1. A full-score manuscript of acts 1 and 2, in black ink on tall 32-staff paper, bound in two volumes: vol. 1 paginated 1–124, vol. 2 paginated 1–[91].

2. An early autograph draft of the libretto, in black ink on eight nested bifolia of ruled paper, with corrections in red ink, entitled "Opera in quattro atti," and lacking most of act 3.

3. A partial draft of the libretto of the Prologue and the beginning of act 1, in pale black ink on both sides of three separate sheets.

4. A complete autograph libretto, in three acts, in black ink on six nested bifolia of plain paper. On the title page: "Irene / [cancelled: Re Oro.] / Dramma in musica / in tre atti / di / Ermanno Wolf-Ferrari / 1895."

5. A partial manuscript, in short score, in the hand of a copyist, written on gatherings of varying numbers of bifolia of tall 12-staff paper, act 1 paginated [1]–94, act 2 [1]–40, act 3 (incomplete) 1–30.

6. A manuscript of act 2, in full score, in the hand of a copyist, unpaginated.

7. Loose sketches, 20 p., written in black ink and in pencil on two kinds of oblong 14-staff paper.

Unperformed and unpublished according to Grove.

FRKF 1200.30

I quattro rusteghi

Holograph drafts and sketches, in short score, n.d., 170 p. Notated in ink and black pencil on a variety of papers. The manuscript comprises the following:

1. Autograph libretto for act 2, written in black ink on a gathering of four bifolia of ruled paper, paginated [1] to 10 (6 and 7 blank), with unrelated pencilled notes on the last page.

2. Incomplete draft of act 1, written in black ink on six numbered gatherings of bifolia of tall 16-staff paper, prepared for the full score, but with vocal lines and text only, with the piano accompaniment at the bottom occasionally sketched in, in ink or pencil. Incomplete: ends at Margarita's words "Ma che bestion!"

3. Draft of the act 2 Intermezzo and miscellaneous drafts, heavily reworked, in pencil and black and red ink.

4. Heavily corrected draft for act 3, written in black ink, paginated 1–25. Note in pencil taped on p. 5.

5. Pencil draft for a portion of act 2, beginning with Lucieta's words "Varda, varda," paginated 1–11; with a few additional pages of unidentified drafts.

I quattro rusteghi, commedia musicale in three acts, on a libretto by Luigi Sugana and Giuseppe Pizzolato after Goldoni, was premiered at the Hofoper, Munich, as *Die vier Grobiane*, on 19 March 1906.

Heinrich Schütz to Henry Miller, p. 98–99.

FRKF 1200.45

Il segreto di Susanna

A portion of the holograph short-score manuscript and miscellaneous drafts, 9 p. The short-score manuscript is written in ink on the recto sides of a bifolium and a single sheet of tall 12-staff paper (B. & H. Nr. 1. C.), paginated in pencil 40–42. The drafts are in black ink and pencil on a bifolium and a single sheet of smaller tall 12-staff paper, starting from both directions.

Il segreto di Susanna, interlude in one act on a libretto by Enrico Golisciani, was premiered at the Hofoper, Munich, as *Susannes Geheimnis*, on 4 Dec. 1909.

FRKF 1200.51

Sly

Holograph draft, in short score, for act 2, drafts for act 3, and miscellaneous sketches, 1926 and n.d., 330 p. Written mostly in pencil on a variety of papers.

The draft for act 2 is written in pencil, with occasional corrections or annotations in red pencil or red ink, on the recto sides of single sheets of three kinds of tall 12- or 16-staff paper (one is Sünova Nr. 4), foliated 1–3, 3 bis, 4a–c, 5, 5 bis, 6a–b, 7a–b, 8, 9a, 9 bis, 10, 10 bis, 11, 11 bis, 12, 12 bis, 13, 14, 15a, 15 bis, 16 bis, 16, 16a, 16 bis [i.e. ter], 17a, 17 bis, 18, 18 bis, 19–26, 27a–c, 28a–c, 29, 30 [paginated 30/31], 32 [paginated 32/33], 34–35, 36 [paginated 36/37], 38–41, 42a [paginated 42a–b], 42c–d, 43a–d, 44a–c, 45 [housed in a bifolium also numbered 45, with a revised draft of the same passage], 46, 47a–b, 48–54, 55a–c, 56a–b, 57–58, 165 [bifolium, the second and third pages of which are a revision of 58], 59–63, 64a–c, 65a–b, 66a–b, 67–73. Additional sketches on the verso of some pages. Laid in after fol. 25, an unnumbered bifolium with an extended 4-page revision corresponding to a passage marked by crosses on fol. 25; the same occurs after 27 b and 46 (a single sheet in both cases; the latter instance is a passage for the chorus). Housed in a bifolium serving as wrappers, labelled in pencil "Sly / Atto 2º" and dated at the top 10 Aug. 1926.

Drafts for act 3, in short score, are paginated 1a–1b, 2–7, 7 bis, 8–11, 11b, 12–13, 14–16 (i.e. one page marked "14–16"), and 17–30.

The sketches are in pencil, housed in two bifolia serving as wrappers, one labelled "Chaos" [?]. The sheets are foliated but not continuously and are in no clear order. They include an early version of the beginning of act 2. Additional sketches include a draft for the final scene, comprising a single sheet, foliated 19 (beginning with Sly's words "In questo instante"), and 13 additional sheets, foliated 24–25, 26 bis, 27–29, 29 bis, 30–31, 31 [bis], 32 [an early version of the last measures], 32 [bis]–34 [another version of the ending]. Miscellaneous other drafts include a fragment from act 1, in fair copy, written in ink on a single bifolium paginated 89–92, and corresponding to p. 53–55 of the piano-vocal score, and a skeleton draft of the end of act 1. Other drafts are discards from act 2.

Sly, ovvero La leggenda del dormiente risvegliato, dramma lirico in three acts and four scenes on a libretto by Giovacchino Forzano (inspired by an episode from Shakespeare's *The taming of the shrew*), was premiered at the Teatro alla Scala, Milan, on 29 Dec. 1927.

FRKF 1200.55

La vedova scaltra

Holograph draft, in short score, and miscellaneous sketches, 1929, 378 p.

> The complete draft is written, mostly in pencil, generally on the recto sides of single sheets of tall 12-staff paper (Sünova Nr. 4), with occasional sketches on the verso. Each act is housed in an additional bifolium serving as wrappers. A pencilled note at the top of the one containing the first act indicates that it was begun on 10 April 1929 and completed on 28 April. The wrapper for act 2 bears the date 29 April; the one for act 3 is dated 12 Oct. Act 1 is foliated 1–98; act 2 [parts I and II] 99–151, 152 [foliated 152/153], 154–61; act 2, part III is paginated 1–42; act 3 is foliated 1–15, [unpaginated folio, 16 crossed out], 16–67, 67 bis, 68–74, 74 bis, 75–76, 76 bis, 77–92.
>
> Additional sketches in pencil and black ink, on five gatherings of five nested bifolia of tall 12-staff paper, with single sheets, some laid in. One of them is dated 3 Aug. 1929; another one bears a reference, in ink, to A. Henseler's biography of Offenbach (Berlin, 1930). An additional gathering, paginated 1–14 with additional material laid in, is for the beginning of act 2; it is dated 29 April 1929.

La vedova scaltra, *commedia lirica* in three acts, libretto by Mario Ghisalberti after Goldoni, was premiered at the Rome Opera on 5 March 1931.

FRKF 1200.77

Unidentified opera

Holograph draft of act 1, in short score, incomplete, of an unidentified work for the stage, 1932, 81 p. Notated in pencil on the recto sides of individual sheets of tall 12-staff paper (Sünova Nr. 4), paginated 1–60, with occasional sketches on the verso sides. Two duplicate pages 56 and 57 are filed at the end. On the front of the bifolium serving as wrappers, in Wolf-Ferrari's hand: "Atto Primo / Luglio 1932." The work has evidently a Middle-Eastern setting, with characters named Il Guardiano, Habab, Leila, Mirza, Mohammed etc.

FRKF 1200.74

B. VOCAL MUSIC

Canzone di Dante

Holograph manuscript and two drafts of this song for voice and piano, 1897, 8 p.

> The manuscript is written in black ink and pencil on a single bifolium of oblong 8-staff paper. It is headed at the top of p. [1]: "Canzone di Dante. Wolf Ferrari 4 Giugno 1897." The words and vocal line are present throughout but only the left hand of the piano part is notated, with the exception of the first four measures of the right hand, written in pencil.

> One of the drafts is also written in ink, on both sides of a single sheet of oblong 12-staff paper. The piano right hand is also missing. The other draft is in black ink and pencil, on p. [1] and [4] of a bifolium of tall 12-staff paper, and is notated on 2-staff systems. Incipit: "Quantunque volte, lasso!"

FRKF 1200.11

Die drei Röselein

Holograph manuscript of this song for voice and piano on words by Friedrich Silcher, n.d. [early 1900s?], 3 p. Notated in black ink, with pencil corrections, on the first three pages of a bifolium of tall 12-staff paper. At the top of p. [1] in Wolf-Ferrari's hand: "Die drei Röselein / Volkslied / E. Wolf Ferrari."

FRKF 1200.19

Mailied

Holograph manuscript of this song for voice, on a poem by Goethe, with violin, cello, and piano accompaniment, n.d., 7 p. Notated in black ink on a bifolium and a single sheet of tall 12-staff paper; in addition, copies of the violin and cello parts on two single sheets of the same paper. At the top of p. [1] in Wolf-Ferrari's hand: "Mailied / von Goethe." Incipit: "Wie herrlich leuchtet mir die Natur!"

FRKF 1200.33

Neig schöne Knospe

Holograph manuscript of this song for voice and piano, possibly on a text by Friedrich von Bodenstedt, n.d., 1 p. Notated in blue ink on a single sheet of oblong 9-staff paper (B & H. Nr. 9. C.). Considerable water damage at the top makes the first staff almost illegible. At the top of the page, in Wolf-Ferrari's hand: "Wolf Ermanno / Mirza-Schaffy."

FRKF 1200.34

Ogni pena più spettata

Holograph manuscript of this song (vocal line only), on an unidentified text, n.d., 1 p. Notated in black ink on the verso side of a single sheet of oblong 6-staff paper (B. & H. Nr. 30. C.), marked #3 at the top. Could be related to the vocal manuscript of "Canto notturno."

FRKF 1200.73

Rispetti, op. 11

Holograph manuscript and sketches of these four untitled songs for voice and piano on an unidentified text. The manuscript is written in black ink on a gathering (the first three pages of which are blank) of three nested bifolia of tall 12-staff paper. The drafts are written in black ink and pencil on two individual sheets and a bifolium of the same paper. There is no title or signature. Dated 1902 by Grove.

FRKF 1200.47

Rispetti, op. 12

Holograph draft of these four songs for voice and piano, 1902, 8 p. Notated in black ink and pencil on the first eight pages of a gathering of three nested bifolia of tall 12-staff paper. At the top of p. [1] in Wolf-Ferrari's hand: "Rispetti 3" and date in pencil: "(24 Ottobre 1902)."

FRKF 1200.48

Scena di Orfeo

Holograph manuscript of a scene for tenor solo and chorus, with piano accompaniment, n.d., 7 p. Notated in black ink, with corrections in pencil, on the first seven pages of a gathering of two bifolia of oblong 14-staff paper (Litolff, Braunschweig). At the top of p. [1] in Wolf-Ferrari's hand: "Scena di Orfeo / Ermanno Wolf." A resetting of the text by Calzabigi set to music by Gluck, beginning with the chorus "D'orror l'ingombrino," till the end of the scene.

FRKF 1200.50

[Six songs]

An Emma, Oh! Menschenherz, was ist dein Glück?, Strimpellata, La serenata, Stornello, Salmo 100

Holograph manuscript of six songs for voice and piano on texts by Friedrich Schiller, Nicolaus Lenau, Arrigo Boito, Ludwig Uhland, unidentified, and from the Bible, 1892, 19 p. Notated in black ink on a gathering of five nested bifolia of tall 12-staff paper, with traces of stitching. On p. [1] in Wolf-Ferrari's hand: "An Emma / (Fragment) / Von Schiller"; p. [6]: "*** / Lenau"; p. [8]: "Strimpellata / Arrigo Boito"; p. [10]: "La Serenata / (Da Lodovico Uhland) / trad Benedetto Prina"; p. [14]: "Stornello"; p. [15]: "Salmo 100." Dated in the end Monaco, 16 Dec. 1892. The settings of Lenau and Psalm 100 are in German.

FRKF 1200.03a–f

La Sulamite, op. 2

Holograph draft, in short score, of this "canto biblico" for soprano, tenor, chorus, and orchestra, 1898, 33 p. Notated in black ink, with additional pencil markings, on a combination of nested and separate bifolia as well as single sheets of 24-staff paper. At the top of p. [1] in Wolf-Ferrari's hand: "Cantico dei Cantici. EWF. 18 Agosto 1898 / Hindelang"; also dated Hindelang, 21 Aug. 1898 at the bottom of p. [5], 23 Aug. 1898 at the bottom of p. [9], and Hindelang, 27 Aug. [1898] at the bottom of p. [14].

Also, printed choral parts, Milan: Calcografia Musica Sacra [1898].

Ten copies of the soprano part, one incomplete, eight of the contralto part, seven of the tenor part, and three of the bass part, with an fragment of an additional bass part. They are generally housed in blank paper wrappers with the vocal category in manuscript. Several bear ownership signatures: Bellemo, Anna Rossetti, Tilde Rossetti (sopranos), Erminia Vianello, Duregati (contralto), Bellemo, Canaro, Giovanni Costantini (tenors), De Spirito, Pietro Giacompol (bass). The last named also wrote the date March 1899. A few scores bear manuscript markings, one of them a variant.

FRKF 1200.64, 1200.85

Talitha Kuni

Holograph manuscript, in full score, and short-score draft for this "sacred mystery" in two parts for soli, chorus, and orchestra, 1898, 94 p.

The full-score manuscript is written in black ink, with corrections and additions in red ink, on six gatherings, stitched together, of nested bifolia of oblong 14-staff paper; rehearsal numbers stamped in red ink. On title page, in Wolf-Ferrari's hand: "Herrn Unico Hensel / in Freundschaft gewidmet / (Ev. Marci caput V.) / 'Thalita-Cumi [sic]' / (Die Tochter des Jairus.) / Mistero sacro in due parti / per / Soli, Coro & Orchestra / di / Ermanno Wolf-Ferrari op. 3 / I Parte 9–12 Ott. 1898 / II Parte 16–18 Ott. 1898 / Milano." On the verso of the last page: "Instrumentato dal 23 al 26 Ottobre 1898 / EWolf-Ferrari."

The short-score manuscript is written in black ink on the first eleven pages of a gathering of ten nested bifolia of tall 24-staff paper, the pagination only 1–3. Signed and dated 9 Oct. 1898 at the top of p. 1, and dated 18 Oct. 1898 at the end.

Dated 1900 by Grove.

FRKF 1200.69

[Three songs]

Sonetto, Canto notturno, La Zingarella

Holograph manuscripts of three songs for voice and piano, the first on a text by Dante, the others on anonymous or unidentified texts, together with a second manuscript of the first song and additional manuscripts for the other two, 1896, 14 p.

The three songs are written in black ink on two nested bifolia of tall 12-staff paper (B & H. Nr. 5. C.), the second copy of *Sonetto* on a single bifolium of the same paper. The second manuscript of *Canto notturno* (vocal line only) is written in ink on the recto side of a single sheet of oblong 6-staff paper

(B. & H. Nr. 30. C.), marked #2 at the top; the draft of *La Zingarella*, in pencil and black ink, on both sides of a sheet of oblong 14-staff paper. At the top of p. [1] of the manuscript for the three songs, in Wolf-Ferrari's hand: "Ermanno Wolf-Ferrari / Sonetto / (Dante Alighieri)"; the song is dated Milan, Dec. 1896 at the end. At the top of p. [5], also in his hand: "E Wolf-Ferrari / Canto Notturno"; the song is dated Stuttgart, Sept. 1896 at the end. In the middle of p. [6], also in his hand: "La Zingarella / E Wolf-Ferrari"; this third song is dated Stuttgart, Sept. 1896 at the end. The second copy of *Sonetto* has a similar heading and is not dated.

FRKF 1200.60a–c

La vita nuova, op. 9

Holograph drafts, in short score, for this cantata for soprano, baritone, chorus, and orchestra, 1901, 32 p. Notated in black ink, red ink, and black pencil, on individual sheets of various types of paper, foliated 1–4, 4 [bis], 5–7, 7b, 8b, 9–11, and a gathering of two nested bifolia of tall 24-staff paper, numbered 12. At the top of fol. 1r, in Wolf-Ferrari's hand: "Vita Nuova / EWF. 24 Aprile 1901."

FRKF 1200.78

Vom Berge

Holograph draft, incomplete, of this song for voice and piano, on a text by Joseph von Eichendorff, with unidentified, apparently unrelated sketches, n.d, 2 p. Notated in black ink on the recto side of a sheet of tall 20-staff paper. At the top of the page, in Wolf-Ferrari's hand: "Vom Berge Eichendorff / EW." The sketches on the verso are written in black ink and pencil. Above the first staff: "Allegro moderato ma con passione."

FRKF 1200.79

C. CHORAL MUSIC

Due canti

Holograph manuscript of two choral songs, n.d., 19 p.

> Notated in black ink on various sizes of paper, stitched at the top for each song; a second copy of Canto no. 2 is written on a bifolium and a single leaf of tall 14-staff paper. The first two manuscripts are signed "Ermanno Wolf-Ferrari" in the upper right corner of the first page. Also on p. [1] of the first song, in Wolf-Ferrari's hand: "Due Canti / No. 1" and, at the bottom of the page, also in his hand, music publisher's number F 746 R and the note: "occore mandare un altro coro in posto del No. 2 il quale non è che un duplicato." The manuscript of the second song bears the manuscript heading "Due Canti / (No. 2)" and the manuscript note: "Fatta questa partitura inutilmente; perchè corrisponde al coro intitolato Un Canto; il quale è in sette righe e porta il Numero di catalogo 744." Also, note at the bottom: "Occore mandare un altro coro da supplire a questo; giacchè non è altro che un duplicato lo rileverà dalle unite bozze," and manuscript publisher's number F 747 R. On the second manuscript of Canto no. 2, note at the top of p. 1: "Questo è il giusto" and manuscript music publisher's number F 744 R at the bottom. Written for soprani (three parts), alti (three parts), tenors (two parts), and basses (four parts).

FRKF 1200.10

"Frottola"

Holograph manuscript of this choral song, n.d. [mid 1890s], 3 p. Notated in black ink on two sheets, stitched together at the top, of tall 12-staff paper. At the top of p. [1] in Wolf-Ferrari's hand: "Frottola"; at the bottom of the page, also in his hand, music publisher's number F 748 R. Written for two soprano, alto, tenor, and two bass parts.

FRKF 1200.21

La passione

Holograph manuscript of this four-part choral piece, 1906, 4 p. Notated in black ink on a bifolium of tall 12-staff paper. At the top of p. [1] in Wolf-Ferrari's hand: "La Passione / E. Wolf-Ferrari / Venezia 1906 / (?)." Scored for sopranos, altos, tenors, and basses.

FRKF 1200.36

Il riso

Holograph manuscript of this choral song with piano accompaniment, n.d., 3 p. Notated in black ink on a bifolium of tall 16-staff paper. At the top of p. [1] in Wolf-Ferrari's hand: "Canone del Padre G. B. Martini (1706–1784) Il Riso."

FRKF 1200.46

Totentanz

Holograph manuscript, in short score, incomplete, of this work for chorus and orchestra, n.d., 3 p. Notated in black ink on the first three pages of a gathering of two nested bifolia of tall 20-staff paper. At the top of p. [1] in Wolf-Ferrari's hand: "Totentanz."

FRKF 1200.72

[Two choral songs]

Stornello, Quartina

Holograph manuscript of these two unaccompanied choral songs, the first on an unidentified text, the second on a text by Goldoni, with an additional manuscript for the second song, n.d. [1890s?], 4 p.

> The two songs are written in blue and black ink, with additional markings in black and blue pencil, on both sides of a single sheet of oblong 14-staff paper; the second manuscript of *Quartina* is written in black ink on a single sheet of tall 10-staff paper. On the oblong sheet, in Wolf-Ferrari's hand, at the top of the recto side: "Stornello"; on the verso side: "2) Quartina / Goldoni." The second manuscript of *Quartina* has the heading: "Quartina / Parole di / Goldoni / Musica di / Ermanno Wolf=Ferrari" and is numbered 742 at the bottom. *Stornello* appears to be scored for tenors (two parts) and basses (two parts); "Quartina" is scored for sopranos, altos, tenors, and basses.

FRKF 1200.61a–b

D. ORCHESTRAL MUSIC

Le baruffe chiozzotte, overture

Holograph manuscript, in full score, of this concert overture after Goldoni, 1895, 42 p. Notated in black ink on a gathering of twelve nested, stitched bifolia, paginated 2–43 in Wolf-Ferrari's hand, of tall 20-staff paper. On p. [1] in his hand: "Ouverture / per / la commedia / 'Le barufe [sic] Chiozzotte. ['Zänkereien auf Chioggia'] / di / Carlo Goldoni. / Ermanno Wolf Ferrari." Dated Monaco, 7 March 1895 at the end.

FRKF 1200.07

Concerto for cello

Holograph draft, in short score, of the complete opening movement of a concerto for cello and orchestra, n.d., 4 p. Notated in black ink on the first four pages, only the first of which is paginated, of a gathering of two nested bifolia of tall 20-staff paper. At the top of p. 1, in Wolf-Ferrari's hand: "Concerto," and the tempo indication "Allegro molto moderato."

FRKF 1200.15

Fantasia for orchestra

Holograph manuscript, in full score, of this symphonic piece, 1895, 25 p. Notated in black ink, with a few additional markings in red pencil, on a gathering of seven nested, stitched bifolia of tall 20-staff paper (B. & H. Nr. 12. C), bound in brown cardboard wrappers; paginated 1–[25] by Wolf-Ferrari. On front wrapper, in his hand: "Fantasia / di / E. Wolf Ferrari"; on title page, also in his hand: "Fantasia / in / fa # minore / per / Grand' Orchestra / Ermanno Wolf Ferrari / in Maggio 1895 / Monaco."

FRKF 1200.20

Quattro pezzi per orchestra

Holograph manuscripts and drafts, in short score, for this otherwise unidentified, unfinished composition, n.d., 16 p.

> Written mostly in ink, with pencilled annotations on three single sheets and a bifolium of tall 14-staff paper (Zurich, Schutzmarke No. 6), paginated 1–3, 3b, and 4–5, housed in a bifolium of tall 16-staff paper (C.F. Zeller No. 17) serving as wrappers, and marked "I"; the second on two separate bifolia of tall 12-staff paper (Sünova Nr. 4), marked "II" at the top of the first page; the third on a single bifolium marked "III" at the top of the first page, all found inside a bifolium of tall 12-staff paper, marked in pencil, in Wolf-Ferrari's hand: "4 Pezzi / per orchestra." There are additional sketches in pencil facing the first page of the first piece. There is doubt as to whether the second and third pieces are part of this set.

FRKF 1200.38

Symphony in C major (fragment)

Holograph drafts for a fugue for the final movement, with unrelated sketches, n.d., 3 p. Notated in black ink on the recto side of a sheet of tall 18-staff paper. In the middle of this page, in Wolf-Ferrari's hand: "Per il Finale della / Sinfonia in Do. / Fuga a quattro temi." The four themes are labelled A–D. On the verso of the sheet and the recto of a similar sheet, sketches, in ink and in pencil, apparently relating to the *Passacaglia for organ*.

FRKF 1200.65

Symphony in E minor (fragment)

Holograph manuscript, in full and short score, of the first movement and sketches for the second movement, 1894, 12 p.

> The full-score manuscript is written in black ink on both sides of three individual sheets and the first two pages of a bifolium of tall 20-staff paper, paginated 1–8; pencil sketches for the second movement are on the last two pages of the bifolium.

> The short-score manuscript, incomplete, is written in black ink on the recto side of a single sheet of tall 12-staff paper. At the top of p. 1, in Wolf-Ferrari's hand: "Sinfonia / in / E Moll. Ermanno Wolf Ferrari." At the top of the short-score manuscript: "Sinfonia / 11 December 1894."

FRKF 1200.66

Symphony in F minor (fragment)

Holograph draft, in short score, of an opening "Andante un po' mosso" and the beginning of an "Allegro energico," n.d., 2 p. Notated in black ink on the first two pages of a bifolium of tall 20-staff paper. At the top of the first page, in Wolf-Ferrari's hand: "Sinfonia."

FRKF 1200.67

Symphony in F-sharp minor (fragment)

Holograph manuscript draft, with other possibly unrelated drafts, n.d., 4 p. Notated in black ink and pencil on a bifolium of tall 26-staff paper; only the first page is paginated. At the top of p. 1, in Wolf-Ferrari's hand: "Sinfonia in Fa♯ min / I Tempo."

FRKF 1200.68

[Theme and variations]

Holograph draft, in short score, for an unidentified orchestral work, n.p., 28 p. Notated in black ink on a gathering of six nested bifolia and a single sheet, laid in, of tall 12-staff paper. At the top of the first page, in Wolf-Ferrari's hand: "Tema."

FRKF 1200.71

E. CHAMBER MUSIC

Aria for violin and piano

Holograph manuscript, incomplete, and drafts of this composition, 1900, 7 p. The manuscript is written in black ink, with corrections in pencil, the drafts in black ink and pencil, on three separate bifolia of oblong 16-staff paper. At the top of the manuscript, in Wolf-Ferrari's hand: "Aria per Violino / con accompagnamento di Pianoforte di Ermanno Wolf-Ferrari / Monaco / Luglio 1900." The manuscript is incomplete, with only the violin part notated. The piano part is also absent from the two drafts, except for a brief sketch in the first one, which is also dated Monaco, July 1900.

FRKF 1200.04

Charfreitag

Holograph manuscript of this composition for string quartet, n.d., 6 p. Notated in black ink on a bifolium of oblong 14-staff paper and a single sheet, laid in, of oblong 16-staff paper (Litolff, Braunschweig). At the top of the first page, in Wolf-Ferrari's hand: "Charfreitag v. Wagner, Parsifal."

FRKF 1200.73

Fugue for string quartet

Holograph manuscript, incomplete, n.d. [mid-1890s], 2 p. Notated in black ink on both sides of a sheet of tall 20-staff paper. At the top of p. [1] in Wolf-Ferrari's hand: "Fuga a 4 Temi."

FRKF 1200.22

Idillio-concertino for oboe and strings

Holograph draft, in full score, n.d. [early 1930s], 47 p. Notated in pencil, with occasional corrections in black ink, on a gathering of five nested bifolia, paginated 1–20, a single bifolium, paginated 21–24, and a second gathering of three nested bifolia, paginated 25–43, with a single bifolium laid in, paginated "2," all of tall 16-staff paper, and housed in a blank bifolium serving as wrappers.

FRKF 1200.82

Invocazione, op. 31

Holograph manuscript, in full score, of this concert fantasy for cello and orchestra, n.d., 105 p. Notated in black ink, continuously, on 25 separate bifolia and two single sheets of tall 24-staff paper (J.E. & Co Nr. 8), paginated 1 to 105. On the title page, in Wolf-Ferrari's hand: "Prof. Paul Grümmer / gewidmet. / 'Invocation' / Konzert-Phantasie / Fantasia da Concerto / für Cello Solo / per Violoncello Solo / und / e / Orchester / Orchestra / Ermanno Wolf-Ferrari / op. 31." At the top of p. 1, also in Wolf-Ferrari's hand: "Fantasia da Concerto per Violoncello Solo / e Orchestra / 'Invocation' op. 32 / E. Wolf-Ferrari."

Dated 1954 by Grove.

FRKF 1200.29

Larghetto for piano trio

Holograph manuscript, n.d. [but after 1900?], 4 p. Notated in black ink, with additional markings in pencil, on a bifolium of oblong 8-staff paper. At the top of p. [1] in Wolf-Ferrari's hand: "Larghetto."

FRKF 1200.31

Quartet for strings (fragment)

Holograph draft of the second movement of a string quartet, with additional sketches, n.d., 2 p. Notated in black ink on one side of a sheet of oblong 9-staff paper, paginated 12 at the bottom, with drafts for a different movement, in pencil, on the verso. At the top of the page, roman numeral II and tempo indication "Largo assai ed espressivo."

FRKF 1200.62

Quintet for strings

Holograph draft, missing p. 1, of this quintet for two violins, two violas, and cello, n.d. [early 1930s?], 68 p. Notated in pencil, with occasional markings in red pencil, on the recto sides (and, once, on the verso) of individual sheets (for p. 1–16) and bifolia, written on all sides, of tall 12-staff paper (Sünova Nr. 4), paginated 2–67.

FRKF 1200.75

Septet for piano, woodwind, and strings

Holograph miscellaneous drafts, 5 p. Notated in black ink and pencil on a bifolium and a single sheet of tall 24-staff paper. At the top of the first page, in Wolf-Ferrari's hand: "Settimino per Pianoforte Violino Viola Cello, Clarinetto Fagotto e Corno."

FRKF 1200.52

Sextet for strings

Holograph manuscript, with an additional holograph draft of the fourth movement, 1894–95, 58 p. Written in black ink on separate bifolia, stitched and bound in brown cardboard, of oblong 14-staff paper, paginated 1–42 in Wolf-Ferrari's hand.

> The draft of the fourth movement is written in black ink, with corrections and additions in pencil, on one bifolium and single sheets of tall 20-staff paper, paginated 1 to 12 only. There are manuscript half-title and title pages in the bound volume. On the latter, in Wolf-Ferrari's hand: "Alla egregia Signorina Mathilde Schwarzenbach / Sestetto / in / do minore / per 2 Violini, 2 Viole e 2 Violoncelli / di / Ermanno Wolf-Ferrari / Monaco Marzo 1895."
>
> Blue paper label on the front cover of the volume, marked: "Sestetto / E Wolf Ferrari / Manuscript." The draft is preceded by a title page, labelled in Wolf-Ferrari's hand: "Sextett / c moll / Für / 2 Violin 2 Vodcen [?], 2 Celli / von / Ermanno Wolf-Ferrari / Monaco / Ottobre 1894," and a half-title marked "IV / Satz" in blue pencil. A short additional sketch in pencil is on a separate page.

FRKF 1200.53

Sextet for winds (fragments)

Holograph manuscript, in short score, 1900, 1 p. Notated in black ink on page [1] and in black ink and pencil on page [4] of a bifolium of tall 12-staff paper. At the top of page [1] in Wolf-Ferrari's hand: "Sestetto (Serenata) per Flauto, oboe, 2 Clarinetti, Corno e Fagotto / 29 Ott 1900 / EWF." On the top of p. [4] in Wolf-Ferrari's hand: "Serenata."

FRKF 1200.54

Sonata for violin and piano in A minor (fragment)

Holograph manuscript drafts, n.d., 10 p. Notated in black ink, with pencil corrections and additions, on three nested bifolia and a single sheet of tall 12-staff paper (B & H. Nr. 5. C.). At the top of p. [1] in Wolf-Ferrari's hand: "Sonata per Violino e Pf." The single sheet, written on both sides, is a new draft, in fair copy, of the beginning, with a different tempo indication (Allegro moderato instead of Allegro non troppo). The manuscript includes a draft of the first movement and the beginning of the second movement, marked "Allegro."

FRKF 1200.57

Sonata for violin and piano in G minor (fragment)

Holograph manuscript draft, 1895, 2 p. Notated in black ink on a single sheet of tall 20-staff paper. At the top of p. [1] in Wolf-Ferrari's hand: "Sonata / per violino e Piano / E Wolf Ferrari / Giugno 1895."

FRKF 1200.58

Sonata-concertino for english horn, strings, and two horns, op. 34

Holograph manuscripts, in full score and short score, and miscellaneous drafts, 1947, 57 p.

> The full-score manuscript is written in dark blue ink on four gatherings of nested bifolia of tall 16-staff paper (Schutzmarke Hug & Co.), placed within an additional bifolium serving as wrappers. On the front of the outer wrapper, in Wolf-Ferrari's hand: "Sonata-Concertino / per Corno Inglese, / orchestra d'archi e 2 Corni / op 34 / di / Ermanno Wolf-Ferrari / Zurigo, Gennaio 1947 / Partitura."
>
> The short score is written in pencil on single sheets of tall 12-staff paper (Schutzmarke Papier Carpentier No. 112 and Hug & Co.), paginated 1–9 (Preludio), 1–9 (Capriccio), 1–6 (Adagio), and 1–9 (Finale), with an additional folio 7 bis in the finale. Rehearsal numbers are indicated in blue ballpoint pen. This manuscript is housed in an additional bifolium serving as wrappers, labelled in pencil: "Sonata-Concertino in la♭ maggiore / per Corno Inglese / orchestra d'archi e 2 Corni / op. 34 / di / E. Wolf-Ferrari / Zurigo, Gennaio 1947."
>
> Both manuscripts were originally housed in a beige folder marked, in pencil: "Sonata-Concertino / in la♭ magg. / per Corno Inglese, / orch. d'archi e 2 Corni / op. 34 / [in another hand?:] Op. 35." There is also a rough draft, 17 p., written in pencil and blue ink on four separate bifolia and a single sheet of tall 12-staff paper.

FRKF 1200.83

String quartet in E minor, op. 23

Holograph manuscript draft and manuscript parts for the violins, 1940, 57 p. The draft is written in pencil, generally on the recto side of single sheets of tall 16-staff paper (Sünova No. 6), paginated 1–35, housed in a bifolium of the same paper, serving as wrappers. The violin parts are written in black ink, with additional markings in black and red pencil, on two separate bifolia of the same 16-staff paper, and the last two pages of an additional bifolium, in which they are placed. On the front of the outer bifolium in pencil, in Wolf-Ferrari's hand: "Quart / E moll / E. W-F / op. 23." Dated 18 Feb. 1940 on p. 10, at the end of the first movement, and 27 April to 7 May 1940 at the end of the fourth and last movement.

FRKF 1200.43

Suite for violin and string orchestra in F major, op. 16a

Holograph manuscript of the violin part for the composer's arrangement of the *Suite-concertino*, op. 16, n.d. [but ca. 1933], 10 p. Notated in black ink on a gathering of three nested bifolia of 12-staff paper, paginated 1–10; p. 9, laid in, is on a larger kind of 12-staff paper (Sünova Nr. 4). On the front of the outer bifolium, in Wolf-Ferrari's hand: "Suite / in fa maggiore / per Violino solo, orchestra d'archi / e due corni / di Ermanno Wolf-Ferrari op. 16 a / (Dalla Suite-Concertino per fagotto, / archi e due corni, / versione dell' autore)."

FRKF 1200.63A

Suite-concertino for bassoon and string orchestra in F major, op. 16

Holograph draft, in full score, of the second movement ("Strimpellata") and the end of the fourth movement, together with unidentified drafts, and a draft of the first and third movements, scored for piano and bassoon, n.d. 16 p. Notated in pencil on two separate bifolia of tall 16-staff paper, numbered [1] and 2, a bifolium of tall 18-staff paper, and a bifolium of 24-staff paper, numbered 3. Pages 4 of bifolium 2 and the unnumbered bifolium are paginated III 1 and III 2 respectively. At the top of the first page of bifolium 1, in Wolf-Ferrari's hand: "2a Strimpellata"; at the top of p. III 1, also in his hand: "III Canzone."

Dated 1933 by Grove.

FRKF 1200.63

F. PIANO MUSIC

Capriccio for piano

Holograph manuscript of this piano piece, 1895, 6 p. Notated in black ink on the first four pages, only the first of which is paginated, of a gathering of two nested bifolia of tall 20-staff paper. At the top of p. 1, in Wolf-Ferrari's hand: "Capriccio. / Ermanno Wolf Ferrari Novembre 1895." On the last three pages of the gathering, unrelated draft, in black ink, of a six-voice fugue.

FRKF 1200.12

Ghiribizzi quasi Ländler

Holograph manuscript of this piano piece, 1895, 3 p. Notated in black ink on the first three pages, only the first of which is paginated, of a bifolium of tall 20-staff paper. At the top of p. 1, in Wolf-Ferrari's hand: "Ghiribizzi / quasi / Ländler / E Wolf Ferrari Giugno 1895."

FRKF 1200.25

Phantasietanz

Holograph manuscript of this piano composition, n.d., 11 p. Notated in black ink on two single sheets and two nested bifolia, stiched together, of tall 10-staff paper. At the top of p. [1] in Wolf-Ferrari's hand: "Phantasietanz."

FRKF 1200.37

Prelude for piano

Holograph manuscript, n.d., 3 p. Notated in black ink on the first three pages of a gathering of two nested bifolia of tall 12-staff paper (B & H. Nr. 4 C.). At the top of p. [1] in Wolf-Ferrari's hand: "Preludio."

FRKF 1200.41

Sonatina for piano [with] Sonata for piano in C major [and] Sonata for piano in C minor

Holograph manuscripts, n.d., 20 p. Fair copies, in black ink with a few pencil annotations, on a gathering of five nested, stitched bifolia of tall 12-staff paper (B & H. Nr. 4. C.), paginated [1]–17, the last three pages unpaginated. At the top of p. [1], calligraphed, possibly not in Wolf-Ferrari's hand: "Sonatina"; at the top of p. 4, calligraphed in the same hand: "Sonata / Frl. Anny Baumann"; at the top of p. 10, calligraphed in the same hand: "Sonata / Frl. Mathilda Schwarzenbach."

FRKF 1200.59

Theme and variations for piano

Holograph draft, for an unidentified piano work, n.p., 2 p. Notated in black ink on the recto sides of two single sheets of tall 10-staff paper. At the top of the first page, in Wolf-Ferrari's hand: "Tema."

FRKF 1200.70

Unidentified piano composition in E minor

Three holograph drafts, all incomplete, n.d., 4 p. Notated in black ink on one or both sides of single sheets of tall 12-staff paper (B & H. Nr. 4. C.). Marked "Largo, agitato assai," "Agitato ma non troppo presto," and "Agitato ma con misura" at the top of each draft.

FRKF 1200.40

Unidentified piano composition in five movements

Holograph manuscript, n.d. [early 20th century?], 14 p. Notated in black ink on four separate bifolia, paginated in Wolf-Ferrari's hand, of tall 10-staff paper. The five movements are: "1. Capriccioso" (p. 1); "2. Poco meno mosso" (p. 3); "3. Delicato assai, tranquillo" (p. 6); "4. Non presto" (p. 10); "5. Moderato assai" (p. 13).

FRKF 1200.13

Unidentified piano composition in two movements

Holograph manuscript and sketches, n.d., 7 p., in black ink on the first three pages, only the first two of which are paginated, of a gathering of two nested bifolia of tall 12-staff paper (Litolff, Braunschweig); the sketches are in pencil on a bifolium of oblong 8-staff paper. The two movements are: "I. Larghetto" (p. 1) and "II. Moderato" (p. 2). Marked, possibly not in Wolf-Ferrari's hand: "Ermanno Wolf Fr." at the bottom of p. 1, preceded by an undeciphered inscription ("F.W. Alfiore [?] Rome").

FRKF 1200.32

Waltz for piano

Holograph draft, incomplete, of a piano waltz, n.d., 4 p. Notated in pencil on p. [5] to [8] of a gathering of two nested bifolia of oblong 8-staff paper.

FRKF 1200.80

Waltzes for piano

Holograph manuscript draft, probably incomplete, with an unrelated sketch, 6 p. Notated in pencil on the recto sides of five individual sheets of tall 10-staff paper. At the top of p. [1] in Wolf-Ferrari's hand: "Walzer." On verso of the last page, unidentified drafts in purple ink.

FRKF 1200.81

G. ORGAN MUSIC

Fugues for organ

Holograph sketches of fugues for organ, 1904, 11 p. Notated in ink on a gathering of three nested bifolia of tall 20-staff paper. At the top of p. [1]: "14 Luglio 1904." The manuscript comprises about 20 sketches, some for the same fugue.

FRKF 1200.24

Passacaglia for organ

Holograph manuscript, incomplete, n.d., 2 p. Notated in black ink on the first two pages of a bifolium of tall 12-staff paper. At the top of p. [1] in Wolf-Ferrari's hand: "Passacaglia." A second bifolium is evidently missing.

FRKF 1200.35

Prelude and fugue in C major for organ

Holograph manuscript, n.d., 4 p. Notated in black ink on a bifolium of tall 12-staff paper, housed in another similar bifolium serving as wrappers. At the top of p. [1] in Wolf-Ferrari's hand: "Preludio e fuga in do magg." On the front of the outer wrapper, the first four measures of a "Fughetta in Do."

FRKF 1200.42

Sonata for organ (fragment)

Three holograph drafts, n.d. [ca. 1900], 6 p. One draft is written in black ink on the first two pages of a bifolium of tall 12-staff paper; the other two are written, also in ink, with corrections and additions in black pencil, on single sheets of tall 18-staff paper. At the top of the bifolium, in Wolf-Ferrari's hand: "Organo / Sonata in Si min." The labelling on the other two manuscripts is similar.

FRKF 1200.56

Tre pezzi for organo

Holograph manuscript, in two copies, 1895, 11 p. Notated in black ink, the first manuscript on two nested bifolia of tall 18-staff paper, housed in a bifolium of tall 12-staff paper; the second written on a bifolium and an individual sheet of tall 24-staff paper. On the front of the folder housing the first manuscript, in Wolf-Ferrari's hand: "Alla Contessa / Lurani Cernuschi Greppi / Tre / Pezzi D'Organo / (Preludio, Canone, Labirinto armonico) / di / Ermanno Wolf-Ferrari / Milan, 14 Dicembre 1895"; on the front of the outer bifolium of the second manuscript: "Tre Pezzi per Organo / di / Seguito. - / (Preludio; Canone; Labirinto Armonico.) / composti da / Ermanno Wolf-Ferrari / Milano 14 Dicembre 1895."

FRKF 1200.39

Unidentified piece for organ

Holograph manuscript, n.d., 4 p. Notated in ink, with additional pencil notations, on a single bifolium of oblong 14-staff paper. At the top of the first page, in Wolf-Ferrari's hand: "Organo. / Cantata 104 Bach." Inscription at the end, possibly not in Wolf-Ferrari's hand: "Eg. Maestro / L. Cervi / Viale Monforte 7."

FRKF 1200.06

Unidentified compositions for organ

Holograph sketches, 1918, 56 p. Notated in black ink on three gatherings of five nested bifolia of tall 16-staff paper (Schutzmarke Nr. 6, Zurich), paginated 1–60 (but filled only up to p. 54), with an additional folio, unpaginated, laid in between p. 36 and 37, written in black ink and pencil. At the top of p. 1, in Wolf-Ferrari's hand: "März (1918) / I." Other dates found in the manuscript are: 1 April [1918?], p. 9; 5 April [1918?], p. 20; "Mai," p. 50; and "November," p. 52. About 90 works, many incomplete, several being drafts of a few measures only, one work present in two versions.

FRKF 1200.76

H. MISCELLANEOUS

Auflösungen aus dem Mollakkord

Holograph manuscript of harmonic exercises based on the Tristan-chord, 1928, 2 p. Notated in black ink on the recto sides of two sheets, paginated 1 and 2, of tall 14-staff paper (Zurich, Schutzmarke No. 6). At the top of p. 1, in Wolf-Ferrari's hand: "20 Nov 1928 / Auflosungen [sic] (oder sonstige Schritte) aus dem Mollakkord mit kleiner centroseptime." The manuscript proposes a large number of possible resolutions of the "Tristan chord," arranged in three categories.

FRKF 1200.05

"Bassschritte"

Holograph harmonic exercises, n.d., 5 p. Notated in black ink on two individual sheets and p. [3] and [4] of a bifolium, all of tall 14-staff paper (Zurich, Schutzmarke No. 6). Marked "Bassschritte!" in pencil on p. [1] of the bifolium. Five series of examples, notated on two systems, of chords built on bass lines, first ascending, then descending, arranged each time in seven categories, from half-tone to perfect fifths.

FRKF 1200.08

Contrapuntal exercises

Miscellaneous holograph contrapuntal exercises, written in black ink and pencil on six pages of oblong 12-staff paper, n.d. [early 1890s]. The first exercise, in three parts, is preceded by the heading "Contr. doppio all'ottava." It is followed by two drafts, both incomplete, of four-part fugues, the second written in pencil.

FRKF 1200.16

Embellishments for Rossini's *Semiramide*

Holograph manuscript, n.d., 1 p. Notated in black ink, with an annotation in red pencil, on the first page of a gathering of two nested, stapled bifolia of oblong 6-staff paper. At the top of the page, in Wolf-Ferrari's hand: "Cavatine Semiramide." The embellishments (for Semiramide's aria "Bel raggio lusinghier") are numbered 1 to 10.

FRKF 1200.49

Fugue in E minor

Holograph draft of a fugue, n.d., 1 p. Notated in ink on the first page of a bifolium of tall 16-staff paper. Above the first staff, in Wolf-Ferrari's hand: "Fuga."

FRKF 1200.23

[Gluck. *Paride ed Elena*. "O mio dolce ardor"]

Manuscript copy in Wolf-Ferrari's hand of the vocal line of this aria by Christoph Willibald Gluck, n.d., 1 p. Notated in black ink on the recto side of a sheet of tall 12-staff paper, with unrelated sketches in pencil on the verso. At the top of the page, in Wolf-Ferrari's hand: "Ch. Gluck / Aria."

FRKF 1200.73

Harmonic analyses of Rossini's *Il barbiere di Siviglia*

Holograph manuscript, n.d., 5 p. Notated in black ink on three nested bifolia of tall 24-staff paper (B. & H. Nr. 11. C.) At the top of the first page, in Wolf-Ferrari's hand: "Studi analitici sul Barbiere di Siviglia di Rossini / Atto I° Introduzione"; at the top of p. [3]: "Analisi Armonica / del Barbiere di Siviglia." The passages analyzed are: "Introduzione"; "Cavatina"; "Seguito e stretta dell'Introduzione"; "Cavatina Figaro"; "Duetto Figaro-Almaviva"; "Cavatina [di Rosina]"; "Aria di Basilio"; "Duetto Rosina-Figaro."

FRKF 1200.27

Scherzo

Holograph draft, n.d., 5 p. Notated in black ink, with pencil additions, on a bifolium of tall 12-staff paper (Sünova Nr. 4), and the recto side of one additional sheet, laid in. At the top of the first page, in Wolf-Ferrari's hand: "c) Scherzo [in pencil:] Burlesca?" Possibly for a symphony or an orchestral work.

FRKF 1200.73

Unidentified drafts and sketches

These comprise drafts for a variety of instrumental and vocal combinations: string quartet, piano, organ, orchestra, voice and piano, voice and orchestra, violin and orchestra, and unidentified mediums, as well as unidentified drafts of libretti and autograph notes, in German or Italian [ca. 234 p.]

> There is an operatic fragment, in full score, written in ink on two separate bifolia, paginated 77–84, and a single sheet, paginated 97–98, of tall 24-staff paper; the text is missing and the vocal part is labelled simply "Solo." Also, a two-page fragment, in full score, for an unidentified stage work (featuring a character identified as "Banditore"), with the rehearsal number 154 stamped in black ink.
>
> There is also an extented fragment of a symphonic work, written in pencil on five separate bifolia, numbered 2–6, and an additional sheet, laid in bifolium 4, of tall 24-staff paper (Sünova). An empty folder is marked: "Ballet-Suite / op 31 / E Wolf Ferrari / Alt Aussee März 1945."

FRKF 1200.73

WOLF-FERRARI MUSIC MANUSCRIPTS
London, Sotheby's, 28 May 1986, lot 630.

II. LITERARY MANUSCRIPT

Autograph manuscript on music, undated, in the form of a dialogue between a composer and an unidentified interlocutor, beginning with the question "So so, sie komponiren auch?" Written in black ink on p. [3]–[7] of two nested bifolia of tall ruled paper.

FRKF 1200.73

III. LETTERS

To Walter Backmeister

[1895 Feb. 2, Munich*] APCS

[1895 April 4, Munich*] ALS, 4 p. (env). Discusses a string quartet.

[1895 May 3, Munich*] ALS, 8 p. (env)

[1895*] Sept. 6, Venice, ALS, 4 p. (env)

[1896 Jan. 16, Milan*] APCS

[1896 July 27, Venice*] APCS

[1896 Oct. 7, Stuttgart*] APCS

1929 Oct. 17, Ottobrunn München 8 Land[S], ALS, 2 p. (env)

1931 Oct. 10, Planegg bei München, ALS, 2 p., on mourning stationery (env)

1935 May 23, Planneg[S], ALS, 2 p. (env)

1935 June 14, Planneg[S], ALS, 2 p. (env)

1935 June 28, Planneg[S], ALS, 2 p., with a musical notation.

1935 Aug. 12, Planneg[S], ALS, 2 p. (env)

[1935 Nov. 25*] Planegg bei München, APCS, both sides.

1935 Dec. 7, Planneg[S], ALS, 2 p. (env)

[1936 Feb. 13, Milan*] APCS. The postcard shows the Scala production of Wolf-Ferrari's *Il campiello*.

1936 Feb. 27, Planneg[S], ALS, 1 p. (env)

1940 Feb. 7, Plannegg, TLS, 1 p. (env)

[1940 April 14*] Plannegg, APCS, both sides.

1940 Oct. 7, Plannegg, ALS, 1 p. (env)

1941 Nov. 1, Planneg[S], ALS, 2 p. (env)

1941 Nov. 24, Planneg[S], ALS, 2 p. (env)

1944 Oct. 17, Alt-Aussee, ALS, 2 p. (env)

1945 March 21, Alt-Aussee, ALS, 2 p. (env)

1946 June 11, Alt-Aussee, ALS, 2 p. (env)

Additional materials:

> Front side of an envelope addressed in Wolf-Ferrari's hand, postmarked Munich, 8 March 1940.
>
> Letters from Wilhelmine Wolf-Ferrari to Walter Backmeister:
> 1948 May 11, Venice, ALS, 2 p., on mourning stationery (env)
> 1963 Oct. 24, Salsamaggiore, ALS, 2 p. (env)

[1964 Aug. 21, Würzburg*] APCS
1964 Aug. 31, Venice, ALS, 2 p. (env)

Photograph of Wolf-Ferrari, annotated on the verso by Wilhelmine Wolf-Ferrari, and a photograph of Wolf-Ferrari's tomb.

Annotations concerning the Wolf-Ferrari letters in an unidentified hand, 4 p., in black ink with red pencil markings.

The recipient, a law student at the beginning of the correspondence, became senior public prosecutor in Munich. The correspondence is mostly of a personal nature, while discussing aspects of Wolf-Ferrari's career.

Marburg, Stargardt, 5–6 March 1985, lot 932.
FRKF 829

IV. PRINTED MUSIC

Suite-concertino in fa maggiore per fagotto solo, orchestra d'archi e 2 corni. Op. 16. Riduzione di Ugo Solazzi per fagotto e pianoforte. Milan: G. Ricordi & C., 1933.

Folio, [2], 1–28. Music publisher's number: 122712. Laid in: the bassoon part, with the word bassoon crossed out in red pencil and replaced by "Violoncello," with red pencil markings throughout.

London, Sotheby's, 28 May 1986, lot 630.
FRKF 1200.84

RICARDO ZANDONAI (1883–1944)

Black-and-white photographic portrait of Zandonai (10.5 × 14.5 cm). Blind embossing of Veder [?], Bolzano. Inscribed by Zandonai, with a short musical quotation from his *Romeo e Giulietta*: "Da 'Giulietta' / [musical quotation] / alla gentile Sig.a Maria Vannata Mascagni / come cordialissimo omaggio / R. Zandonai / Pesaro, genn. 1942. [era fascista] XX."

London, Sotheby's, 26–27 Nov. 1987, lot 317.
FRKF 1342.1

ALEXANDER ZEMLINSKY (1871–1942)

Letter to an unidentified professor
    n.d., n.p., ALS, 3 p. Mentions Mahler.

FRKF 396

WORKS CITED

Abbiati, Franco. *Giuseppe Verdi*. 4 vols. Milan: Ricordi, 1959.

Arnaud, Claude. *Jean Cocteau*. Paris: Gallimard, 2003.

Baker, Evan, "Lettere di Giuseppe Verdi a Francesco Maria Piave 1843–1865." *Studi verdiani* 4 (1986–87), 136–66.

Baudelaire, Charles. *Correspondance*. Edited by Claude Pichois and Jean Ziegler. 2 vols. Paris: Gallimard, Bibliothèque de la Pléiade, 1973.

Bénézit, Emmanuel. *Dictionnaire critique et documentaire des peintres, sculpteurs, dessinateurs et graveurs de tous les temps et de tous les pays par un groupe d'écrivains spécialistes français et étrangers*. New, revised edition by Jacques Busse. 14 vols. Paris: Gründ, 1999. (Originally published 1911–23).

Berlioz, Hector. *Correspondance générale*. General editor: Pierre Citron. 8 vols. Paris: Flammarion, 1972–2003.

Burghauser, Jarmil. *Antonín Dvorák: Thematicky katalog*. Prague: Bärenreiter Editio Supraphon, 1996.

Burns, Robert. *The letters of Robert Burns*. Edited by John de Lancey Ferguson. 2 vols. Oxford: Clarendon Press, 1931.

Byron, George Gordon, Lord Byron. *Byron's letters and journals*. Edited by Leslie Marchand. 12 vols. Cambridge, Mass.: Belknap Press, 1973–82.

Chabrier, Emmanuel. *Correspondance*. Edited by Roger Delage, Frans Durif, and Thierry Bodin. [Paris]: Klincksieck, 1994.

Chopin, Frédéric. *Correspondance*. Edited by Bronislaw Édouard Sydow, Suzanne and Denise Chainaye, and Irène Sydow. 3 vols. Paris: Richard-Masse Éditeurs, n.d. [1953–60].

—. *Correspondance*. Edited by Bronislaw Édouard Sydow et al. 3 vols. Paris: La revue musicale, 1981.

Christie, Manson & Woods International Inc. *Manuscripts, drawings and printed books from the Frederick R. Koch Foundation*. Thursday, June 7, 1990, at 10:00 a.m. New York: Christie's, 1990.

Cocteau, Jean. *Oeuvres complètes*. 11 vols. Geneva: Marguerat, 1946–51.

—. *Oeuvres poétiques complètes*. Edited by Michel Décaudin et al. Paris: Gallimard, Bibliothèque de la Pléiade, 1999.

—. *Théâtre complet*. Edited by Michel Décaudin et al. Paris: Gallimard, Bibliothèque de la Pléiade, 2003.

Craggs, Stewart R. *Edward Elgar: A source book*. Aldershot: Scolar Press, 1995.

—. *John Ireland: A catalogue, discography, and bibliography*. Oxford: Clarendon Press; New York: Oxford University Press, 1993.

—. *William Walton: A catalogue*. Oxford and New York: Oxford University Press, 1990.

Crichton, Ronald. *Manuel de Falla: Descriptive catalogue of his works*. London: J. and W. Chester, 1976.

Debussy, Claude. *Correspondance (1872–1918)*. Edited by François Lesure and Denis Herlin. Paris: Gallimard, 2005.

—. *Correspondance de Claude Debussy et Pierre Louÿs (1893–1904)*. Edited by Henri Borgeaud. Paris: Librairie José Corti, 1945.

Dickens, Charles. *The letters of Charles Dickens. Pilgrim Edition*. Edited by Madeline House and Graham Storey. 12 vols. Oxford: Clarendon Press, 1965–2002.

Fauquet, Joël-Marie. *César Franck*. Paris: Fayard, 1999.

Flury, Roger. *Mascagni: A bio-bibliography*. Westport and London: Greenwood Press, 2001.

Gallego, Antonio. *Catálogo de obras de Manuel de Falla*. Madrid: Ministerio de Cultura, Dirección General de Bellas Artes y Archivios, 1987.

Gérard, Yves. *Thematic, biobliographical and critical catalogue of the works of Luigi Boccherini*. Translated by Andreas Mayor. Oxford: Oxford University Press, 1969.

Giroud, Vincent. *Heinrich Schütz to Henry Miller. Selections from the Frederick R. Koch Collection at Yale University*. New Haven: Beinecke Rare Book and Manuscript Library, 2001.

Grieg, Edvard. *Brev i utvalg 1862–1907*. Edited by Finn Benestad. 2 vols. Oslo: Aschehoug, 1998.

Halévy, Fromental. *Lettres*. Edited by Marthe Galland. Heilbronn: Musik-Edition Lucie Galland, 1999.

Harding, James. *Sacha Guitry: The last boulevardier*. New York: Scribner, 1968.

Holoman, D. Kern. *Catalogue of the works of Hector Berlioz*. Basel et al: Bärenreiter, 1987.

Irvine, Demar. *Massenet: A chronicle of his life and times*. Portland, Oregon: Amadeus Press, 1994.

Johnson, Cecil. *A bibliography of the writings of George Sterling*. San Francisco: The Windsor Press, 1931.

Kershaw, Alister. *A bibliography of the works of Richard Aldington from 1915 to 1948*. London: The Quadrant Press, 1950.

Kobylan´ska, Krystyna. *Frédéric Chopin: thematisch-bibliographisches Werkverzeichnis*. Munich: G. Henle, 1979.

Langfeld, William Robert. *Washington Irving, a bibliography*. Compiled ... with the assistance of Philip C. Blackburn. New York: The New York Public Library, 1933.

Latimore, Sarah Briggs, and Grace Clark Haskell. *Arthur Rackham, a bibliography*. Los Angeles: Suttonhouse, 1936.

Lesure, François. *Claude Debussy: biographie critique; suivie du catalogue de l'oeuvre*. Paris: Fayard, 2003.

Liszt, Franz. *Briefe*. Edited by La Mara. 8 vols. Leipzig: Breitkopf & Härtel, 1893–1905.

—. *Franz Liszts musikalische Werke*. Edited by the Franz Liszt Stiftung. 39 vols. Leipzig and New York: Breitkopf & Härtel, 1907–36.

Marcel Proust: l'écriture et les arts [Exhibition catalogue]. Edited by Jean-Yves Tadié and Florence Callu. Paris: Gallimard and Réunion des musées nationaux, 1999 (exhibition held at the Bibliothèque nationale de France, 9 November 1999 to 6 February 2000).

Marnat, Marcel. *Maurice Ravel*. Paris: Fayard, 1986.

Maugham, Robin. *Somerset and all the Maughams*. New York: The New American Library, 1966.

McCorkle, Margit L. *Johannes Brahms: thematisch-bibliographisches Werkverzeichnis*. In collaboration with Donald M. McCorkle. Munich: G. Henle, 1984.

Merrill, James. *Collected poems*. Edited by J.D. McClatchy and Stephen Yenser. New York: Knopf, 2001.

Meyerbeer, Giacomo. *Briefwechsel und Tagebücher*. Edited by Heinz Becker and Gudrun Becker. 7 vols. to date. Berlin: Walter de Guyter, 1960– .

Paymer, Marvin E. *Giovanni Battista Pergolesi, 1710–1736: A thematic catalogue of the opera omnia with an appendix listing omitted compositions*. New York: Pendragon Press, 1977.

Pedarra, Potito. "Catalogo delle composizioni di Ottorino Respighi." In *Ottorino Respighi*. Edited by Giancarlo Rostirolla. Turin: Edizioni dai Radiotelevisione italiana, 1985, p. 325–87.

Poulenc, Francis. *Correspondance 1910–1963*. Edited by Myriam Chimènes. Paris: Fayard, 1994.

Proust, Marcel. *A la recherche du temps perdu*. Edited by Jean-Yves Tadié et al. 4 vols. Paris: Gallimard, Bibliothèque de la Pléiade, 1987–89.

—. *Correspondance*. Edited by Philip Kolb. 21 vols. Paris: Plon, 1970–93.

—. *Écrits de jeunesse, 1887–1895*. Edited by Anne Borrel. [Combray]: Institut Marcel Proust international, [1991].

—. *Lettres à Reynaldo Hahn*. Edited by Philip Kolb. Paris: Gallimard, 1956; new ed. 1986.

—. *Les plaisirs et les jours*, Paris: Calmann Lévy, 1896.

Radiguet, Raymond. *Oeuvres complètes*. Edited by Chloé Radiguet and Julien Cendres. Paris: Stock, 1993.

Ratner, Sabina Teller. *Camille Saint-Saëns 1835–1921: A thematic catalogue of his complete works. Vol. 1: Instrumental music*. Oxford, New York: Oxford University Press, 2002.

Ravel, Maurice. *Lettres, écrits, entretiens*. Edited by Arbie Orenstein. Paris: Flammarion, 1989.

Rimbaud, Arthur. *Oeuvres completes*. Edited by Antoine Adam. Paris: Gallimard, Bibliothèque de la Pléiade, 1972.

Sand, George. *Correspondance*. Edited by Georges Lubin. 26 vols. Paris: Garnier frères, 1964–91 .

—. *Lettres retrouvées*. Edited by Thierry Bodin. Paris: Gallimard, 2004.

Satie, Erik. *Correspondance presque complète*. Edited by Ornella Volta. Paris: Fayard, IMEC, 2000.

Schickling, Dieter. *Giacomo Puccini: Catalogue of the works*. Kassel and New York: Bärenreiter, 2003.

Schiller, Justin. *Nonsensus: cross-referencing Edward Lear's original 116 limericks with eight holograph manuscripts and comparing them to printed texts from the 1846, 1855 and 1861 versions; together with a census of known copies of the genuine first edition*. Introductory remarks by Vivien Noakes. Stroud: Catalpa Press Ltd., 1988.

Schmidt, Carl B. *The music of Francis Poulenc (1899–1963): A catalogue*. Oxford: Clarendon Press; New York: Oxford University Press, 1995.

Schneider, Louis. *Les maîtres de l'opérette française: Hervé; Charles Lecocq*. Paris: Librairie académique Perrin, 1924.

Stendhal. *Correspondance générale*. Edited by V. del Litto, Elaine Williamson, Jacques Houbert, and Michel-E. Slatkine. 6 vols. Paris: H. Champion, 1997–99.

Stuckenschmidt, Hans Heinz. *Maurice Ravel: Variations on his life and work*. Translated by Samuel Rosenbaum. Philadelphia: Chilton Book Co., 1968.

Talvart, Hector, and Georges Place. *Bibliographie des auteurs modernes de langue française*. 22 vols. Paris: Éditions de la Chronique des lettres françaises, 1928–76.

Thieme, Ulrich, and Felix Becker. *Allgemeines Lexikon der bildenden Künstler von der Antike bis zur Gegenwart*. 37 vols. Leipzig: E.A. Seemann, 1907–50.

Verdi intimo: carteggio di Giuseppe Verdi con il conte Opprandino Arrivabene (1861–1886). Edited by Annibale Alberti. Verona: Mondadori, 1931.

Verlaine, Paul. *Correspondance générale, I : 1857–1885*, ed. Michael Pakenham. Paris: Fayard, 2005.

—. *Oeuvres en prose complètes*. Edited by Jacques Borel. Paris: Gallimard, Bibliothèque de la Pléiade, 1978.

—. *Oeuvres poétiques complètes*. Edited by Y.-G. Le Dantec, revised by Jacques Borel. Paris: Gallimard, Bibliothèque de la Pléiade, 1992.

Voltaire. *Correspondance*. Edited by Theodore Besterman. 13 vols. Paris: Gallimard, 1963–93.

Wagner, Richard. *Sämtliche Briefe*. Edited by Gertrud Strobel and Werner Wolf. 14 vols. to date. Leipzig: Deutscher Verlag für Musik VEB, 1967– .

Wagner Werk-Verzeichnis (WWV): Verzeichnis der musikalischen Werke Richard Wagners und ihrer Quellen. Edited by John Deathridge, Martin Geck, and Egon Voss. Mainz: Schott, 1986.

Waugh, Evelyn. *The letters of Evelyn Waugh*. Edited by Mark Amory. New Haven: Ticknor & Fields, 1980.

Wilde, Oscar. *The complete letters of Oscar Wilde*. Edited by Merlin Holland and Rupert Hart-Davis. London: Fourth Estate, 2000.

Woolf, Cecil. *A bibliography of Frederick Rolfe, Baron Corvo*. Second impression, revised and greatly enlarged. London: Rupert Hart-Davis, 1972.

Yon, Jean-Claude. *Jacques Offenbach*. Paris: Gallimard, 2000.

INDEX

Page numbers in *italics* refer to main entries.

A.E., *see* Russell, George William
Abbott, Berenice, 44
Abbott, George, 210
Abbott, John, 160
Abeniacar, Carlo, 232
Aberconway, Christabel, 314
Achard, Marcel, 44, 81
Adam, Adolphe, 189
Adami, Giuseppe, 234
Adelsward-Fersen, Jacques d', *see* Fersen
Adler, August, 161
Adlercron, Mrs. Rodolph (Hester Bancroft), 104
Aganoor-Pompili, Vittoria, 256
Ajalbert, Jean, 56
Albany, Leopold George Duncan Albert, Duke of, 287
Albaret, Céleste, 86
Albéniz, Isaac, 61, 67
Albéniz, Mme, 68
Albermarle, Elizabeth Southwell Keppel, Countess of, 111
Albermarle, George Thomas Keppel, 6th Earl of, 112
Albert, Eugen d', *3*, 287
Alboni, Marietta, 300
Aldington, Richard, *3*
Alexander, George, 277
Alexandra, Queen, consort of Edward VII, King of Great Britain, 239
Alexandrine, Duchess of Coburg, 163, 164
Alexis, Willibald, 127
Alfiore, F.W., 339
Allard, Mme, 107
Almeida, Antonio de, 200
Alophe (engraver), 97, 161
Amat, L., 189
Amato, Pasquale, 239
Ames, Winthrop, 288
Amfiteatroff, Anna, 255
Anarratone (prefect), 238
Anderson, Maxwell, 210
Andor, Octavie d', 70
André, Carl August, 177

André, Johann Anton, 325
Andrew, Emanuel, 158
Andrew, Lucy Eleanor (Maugham), 158
Anet, Claude, 41
Anfossi, Pasquale, 94
Angelini, Giuseppe Antonio, 92, 93, 94
Anouilh, Jean, 44
Anquetin, Louis, 302
Anson (barber), 98
Apollinaire, Guillaume, 37, 171, 213, 215
Aragon, Louis, 39
Arban, Jean-Baptiste, 152
Arbós, Enrique Fernández, 67
Arland, Marcel, 44
Arman-Jean, 302
Arnim, Elizabeth von, 278
Arnim, Ludwig Achim, Freiherr von, 141
Arnold, Malcolm, 323
Arnold, Matthew, 321
Arrivabene, Opprandino, conte, 293, 294, 295, 296
Ashton, Algernon, 8
Ashton, Sir Frederick, 309
Astruc, Gabriel, 28, 40, 41, 86, 264, 266
Atkins, J., 289
Aubry, *see* Jean-Aubry
Audel, Stéphane, 216
Auden, Wystan Hugh, *3*, 322
Audibran, François Adolphe Bruneau, 71
Audisio, Pietro, 239
Audran, Edmond, *3*, 264
Augé de Lassus, Lucien, 264, 265
Augener (publisher), 101
Augenstein, Johann Huldreich, Plate 1, *4*
August Ferdinand, prince of Prussia, 73
Aupick, Caroline, 9
Aurenche, Jean, 44
Auric, Georges, *4*, 33, 34, 36, 44, 77, 96, 214, 216, 240, 273
Auric, Nora, 36, 41, 216
Autant-Lara, Claude, 44
Aymé, Marcel, 44
Azevedo, Alexis, 295

Bach, Johann Sebastian, 251, 276, 340
Back, Barbara, 162
Backaus, Wilhelm, *5*
Backmeister, Walter, 341, 342

Bacon, Francis, Baron Verulam, Viscount St. Albans, 272
Badà, Angelo, 239
Badenhausen, Rolf, 36
Bagier, M., 296
Bai, Juyi, 7
Baillie, Matthew, 111
Bainbridge, G.F., 276
Baird, Edwin, 137
Balanchine, George, 15
Balestier, Wolcott, 108
Balfe, William Michael, *5*
Baltimore, Caecilius Calvert, 2nd Baron, 103
Bancroft, Hester, *see* Adlercron
Bancroft, Mrs., 104
Bantock, Sir Granville, *5–8*
Bantock, Helen, Lady, 8
Bantock, Raymond, 8
Banville, Théodore de, 55, 83
Baratel, Emmanuel, 97
Barbaja, Domenico, 208
Barbauld, Anna Letitia, 18
Barbette (pseudonym of Vander Clyde), 30–31
Barbier, Jules, 138, 268
Barbier, Pierre, 270
Barbot, Joseph, 263
Bardac, Emma, *see* Debussy, Emma
Bardare, Leone Emanuele, 296
Barezzi, Antonio, 294, 297, 300
Barillet, Pierre, 134, 135, 136
Barnes, Grace Edith, 104
Baron (engraver), 71
Baron, Émile, 56
Barraud, Henri, 274
Barrès, Maurice, 39
Barrett, William Alexander, 5
Barrie, James Matthew, 240
Barron, Jean, 182
Barron, Jeanne (Ladie), 182
Barry, Philip, 210
Bartier, Étienne, 114
Bartók, Béla, 218
Bassano, Napoléon Joseph Hugues Maret, duc de, 182
Bateman, Virginia, 107
Bathori, Jane, 218
Bathurst, Henry Bathurst, Earl, 130

[349]

Bathurst, Miss, 289
Battista, Ernesto, 235
Battut, Léon, 189
Baudelaire, Charles, *9*, 53, 58, 62, 84, 242
Baumann, Anny, 338
Baumer, Lewis Christopher Edward, *9*
Beardsley, Aubrey, *10*, 25, 277
Béarn, Arsias de, 71
Beaton, Cecil, 135, 309
Beaumarchais, Pierre Augustin Caron de, 196
Beaumont, Étienne, comte de, 34
Beaunier, André, 70, 223
Becker, Jean, 262
Beckford, William, *10–11*
Bédel (tapissier), 208
Beecham, Sir Thomas, 8
Beeching, Frank, *11–12*
Beethoven, Ludwig von, 306
Bégu, Bernard, 239
Behrman, S.N. (Samuel Nathaniel), 210
Belaieff (publisher), 78
Belasco, David, 239
Bell, Hugh, 105
Bell, Mrs. Hugh, 105
Bellaigue, Camille, 70
Bellanger, Pierre, 302
Bellemo (singer), 333
Bellini, Vincenzo, *12*, 141, 259, 303
Belvederi, Gualtiero, 124
Bemelmans, Ludwig, 134, 135, 136, 137
Bemmel, Eugene van, 96
Bender, J. Terry, 161
Bennett, Arnold, 210
Benoît, Camille, 62
Bentham, Jeremy, 290
Bentley, Eric, 172, 173
Béranger, Pierre-Jean de, 97
Bérard, Christian, 36, 37, 219, 280
Berberian, Cathy, 321
Berchut, S., 67
Bercioux, Eugène, 185
Berel, Paul, *see* Choudens
Bergé, Pierre, 39
Berger, Ludwig, 325
Bergman, Ingrid, 218
Berlioz, Harriet Smithson, 15
Berlioz, Hector, Plate 5, *12–15*, 58, 110, 172, 198, 288
Bernac, Pierre, 45, 179, 213, 214, 215, 216, 217, 218, 219, 274
Bernard, Tristan, 222

Bernardet, J.-C., O.S.B., 44
Berners, Gerald Hugh Tyrwhitt-Wilson, Baron, *15*, 248, 286
Bernhardt, Sarah, 62, 85, 86, 261, 272
Berrichon, Paterne, 36
Berry, Marie-Caroline de Bourbon-Sicile, duchesse de, 17, 97
Berry, Walter, 35, 230
Bertheau, Julien, 32
Berthelot, Daniel, 96
Berthelot, Philippe, 41, 42
Bertin, Armand, 13
Bertin, Marcelle, 37, 38
Bertin, Pierre, 37, 38, 273
Berton, Pierre, 127
Berton, Pierre-Montan, 208, 209
Bertrand, Eugène, 81
Bertrand, Pierre, 51
Berwick and Alba, Francisca Portocarrero y Palafox, Duchess of, 66
Biagini, Carlo, 238
Bibesco, Antoine, 41
Bibesco, Emmanuel, 41
Bibesco, Marthe, 41
Bickham, George, 158
Bigonnet, Roger, 214
Billy, Robert de, 224
Bineau, Jean-Martial, 181
Binet-Valmer, Gustave, 224
Birga, Arturo, 257
Birken, Sigmund von, 4
Bishop, T.H., 8
Bismark, Otto, Graf von Bismark-Schönhausen, 177
Bisset, T.H., 8
Bizet, Adolphe, 16
Bizet, Georges, *15–16*, 79, 80, 138, 139, 151
Bjørnson, Bjørnstjerne, 81
Blacker, Carlos, 326
Blake, William, 287, 322
Blanc, Louis, 77
Blanche, Jacques-Émile, 41, 88, 139, 230
Blarenberghe, Henri van, 222
Bloch, Ernest, 265
Bloede, G., 105
Blum, Ernest, 192
Blunden, Edmund, 272
Boccherini, Luigi, *16–17*
Bodenstedt, Friedrich von, 332
Boehm, H. Richard, 108
Boehm, J. (sculptor), 161

Boehm, Karl, 282
Boieldieu, François-Adrien, *17*
Boieldieu, Louis (Adrien), 17
Bois, Élie-Joseph, 222
Boisselot, Paul, 192
Boito, Arrigo, 295, 300, 333
Bolitho, Hector, 156
Bollante, abbate, 289
Bombelles, Karl Albert, Graf, 164, 165
Bondeville, Emmanuel, 86
Bonelli, Luigi, 125
Bonnet, Adolphine, 97
Bonnières, Robert de, 63
Bonniot, Edmond, 243
Boracchi, 299
Bordes, Charles, 62
Bornoff, Jack, 81
Borodin, Aleksandr Porfir'evich, *17*, 241, 252, 254
Borras, J., 290
Borrel, Eugène, 154
Botte (jeweller), 181
Bouffar, Zulma, 206
Boulanger, Lili, 244
Boulanger, Louis, 97, 100
Boulanger, Nadia, 216, 217
Boulenger, Jacques, 224
Boulez, Pierre, 217, 219
Boulton, Sir Harold, 5, 6, 7
Bourde, Paul, 257
Bourdet, Édouard, 210
Bourgeois, Georges, 239
Bourget, É., 195
Bourgoing, Anna Léonie de (Dollfus), 181
Bourgoing, Philippe de, 181, 182, 183
Bourgoing, Pierre de, 181, 182, 183
Bousquet, Marie-Louise, 41, 42, 60
Bovy, Berthe, 31
Bowring, Sir John, 289
Boyd, Hugh Stuart, 18
Boyd, Julian P., 170
Boyle, Mr., 112
Bracquemond, Félix, 9
Bracquemond, Pierre, 139
Bradley, W.A., 173
Brahms, Johannes, *17–18*, 85, 276
Brandenburg, Friedrich Wilhelm, Kurfürst von, *18*
Brander, Laurence, 159
Brandt, Caroline, 325
Braque, Georges, 41, 273
Brasseur, Jules, 75
Braunschweig, Karl, Herzog von, 73

Brecht, Bertold, 172, 173
Bréjean-Silver, Georgette, 153
Brendel, Franz, 306
Brentano, Clemens von, 141
Breton, André, 44
Bréval, Lucienne, 30
Bréville, Pierre de, 56
Brewer, Joseph, 324
Bridgetown, Mr., 27
Brisebarre, Bernard, *see* Joanny
Bristow, Anne, 3
Britten, Benjamin, 315
Brochmand, Jesper Rasmussen, bishop of Zeeland, 4
Broglio, Emilio, 294
Brohly, Suzanne, 59
Bronarski, Ludwig, 27
Brooke, Stopford, 19
Brooks, Romaine, 41
Brophy, John, 159
Brough, Lionel, 77
Brown, Al, 40
Brown, Eva Nellie, 94
Brown, Francis, 170
Brown, John E., 105
Brown, Martin, 210
Browning, Elizabeth Barrett, *18*, 120
Browning, Robert, *18*, 120
Brozick, M. de, 265
Bruce, Kate Mary, 161
Bruch, Max, *18*, 109
Bruneau, Alfred, 109, 139
Brunetière, Félix, 243
Brunet-Lafleur, Marie-Hélène (Mme Charles Lamoureux), 25
Brunswick-Wolfenbüttel, Philippine, Duchess of, 73
Brussel, Robert
Bryer & Bert (photographer), 52
Buckingham, J.S., 290
Buffet, Bernard, 29, 39
Bulkens, Dr., 165
Bülow, Hans von, 133, 140, 306
Burani, Paul, 25
Burgess, L.W., 108
Burghauser, Hugo, 275, 282, 283, 285
Burkitt, Mrs., 95
Burne-Jones, Sir Edward Coley, Plate 10, *19–24*
Burne-Jones, Georgiana, 19
Burne-Jones, Philip, 24
Burns, Robert, *24*
Bushby, Thomas, 105
Busoni, Ferruccio, 109

Busser, Henri, 59
Buxton, E., 167
Byron, Gordon Byron, Baron, *24*, 289, 290

Cahoon, Herbert, 278
Cairoli, Adelaide, 144
Calhoun, Eleanor, 107
Callot, Jacques, 316
Calvocoressi, Michel-Dimitri, 246, 286
Calzabigi, Ranieri de, 333
Cam, Mlle, 226
Cammarano, Salvatore, 296
Campbell, Brigadier General, 182
Campbell, Laura, 117
Campbell, Thomas, 289
Campion, Thomas, 171
Campra, André, 214
Canari (singer), 333
Canaris, Constantino, 289
Candidus, Karl, 17
Cangiullo, Francesco, 245
Canteloube, Joseph, 312
Canterbury, Charles Manners-Sutton, Viscount, 130
Cape, Jonathan (publisher), 178
Caplet, André, 59
Capoul, Victor, 130
Caraman-Chimay, princesse Alexandre de, 224
Carbone, Carmela, 18
Carbone, Grazia, 18
Cariben aîné, J., 182
Carignani, Carlo, 239
Carl Ludwig of Habsburg, Archduke, 163, 164
Carlyle, Thomas, 289
Carne, John, 290
Caroline, Princess of Wales, 111
Caron, Rose, 300
Carpenter, Edward Childs, 210
Carpenter, Edward, 8
Carpzov, Benedikt, 4
Carraud (singer), 206
Carraud, Gaston, 248
Carré, Albert, 68, 70, 86, 266, 270
Carré, Ambroise-Marie, 45
Carré, Marguerite, 51
Carré, Michel, 138
Carreras, Antoni, 81
Carteret, 181
Caruso, Enrico, *25*, 239

Carvalho, Mme Caroline Marie (Félix-Miolan), 15
Carvalho, Léon, 15, 16, 25, 263, 270, 294
Caryathis, *see* Jouhandeau, Élise
Casadesus, Robert, 248
Casa-Fuerte, Illan, marquis de, 224
Casals, Pablo, 109
Casella, Alfredo, 244
Casella, Hélène (Kahn), 243, 244
Caselli, Alfredo, 232, 235
Casey, J.J., 108
Caspers, M., 184
Castelnau, Henri-Pierre-Jean-Abdon, General, 26
Castelnuovo, Giacomo Barbo, conte di, 12
Castil-Blaze, 325
Castineau (photographer), 234
Castlereagh, Robert Stewart, Viscount, 130
Catalani, Alfredo, 145
Catelin, Adolphe, 13
Catusse, Mme Anatole, 224, 225
Cavacchioli, Enrico, 123, 127
Cavaillé-Coll, Aristide, 265
Cavé, Hygin-Auguste, 90
Cavendish, Caroline F., 166
Cazalis, Henri, 62, 63, 225
Cazals, F.-A. (Frédéric-Auguste), 302
Cebotari, Maria, 232
Ceccardi, Ceccardo Roccataglia, 234
Cecil, Lady, 105
Cendrars, Blaise, 34, 41
Cézanne, Paul, 326
Chabrier, Emmanuel, 3, *25*, 139, 177, 178, 219, 241, 272
Chabrier, Marie-Alice (Dejean), 25
Chabrillan, Céleste de, 200
Chadourne, Marc, 216
Chalmer, Edmund, 157
Chalupt, René, 243, 249
Chamberlain, Eva (Wagner), 305
Chamberlain, Joseph, 112
Chaminade, Cécile, *25*, 109
Champenois, J.J., 138
Champion, Édouard, 163, 230, 241
Champsaur, Félicien, 98
Chanel, Coco, 40
Chaplin, Charlie, 217
Chapman, Frederick, *25*
Chapman, R.W., 105
Chardin, Jean-Baptiste Siméon, 247
Chardonne, Jacques, 37
Charles VII, Holy Roman Emperor, 72

Charlotte Augusta, Princess of Great Britain, 111, 131
Charlotte of Belgium, Empress of Mexico, *26*, 164, 165
Charny, Mlle de, 271
Charpentier (gallery owner), 230
Charpentier, Claude, 26
Charpentier, Gustave, *26*, 58, 109
Chateaubriand, François-René, vicomte de, 61
Chateaubriant, M. de, 51
Chaumont-Quitry, Mme de, 67, 70
Chausson, Ernest, 63, 139
Chekhov, Anton Pavlovich, 308
Chenay (engraver), 97
Chérin, 76
Cherubini, Luigi, 17, 18
Chevalier, Louis, 216, 218
Chevigné, Laure-Marie-Charlotte (de Sade), comtesse de, 221
Chevillard, 76
Chirico, Giorgio de, 42
Chivot, Henri, 192
Chomel et Louis (firm), 62
Chopin, Frédéric, *26–27*, 252, 272, 303
Choudens (firm), 186, 192
Choudens, Paul de, 124
Christofle (firm), 98
Christofle, Marie P., 69
Cicéri, Pierre-Luc-Charles, 208, 209
Cilea, Francesco, 129
Cimarosa, Domenico, 94
"Cip" (translator), 125
Civinini, Guelfo, 239
Clabburn, W.H., 19
Clairambault (collector), 76
Clairville, *see* Jaime, Ernest
Claretie, Jules, 141, 146, 154
Clark, Charles Griffin, 180
Clark, Edward, 323, 324
Clark, Gordon Wyatt, 180
Clark, Mrs. Matthew (Squibb), 180
Clark, T.E., 8
Clarke, George, 10, 11
Claude, Camille, 147, 151
Claudel, Paul, *27*, 35
Claudius, Matthias, 276
Clemenceau, Georges, 265
Clemens, Cyril, 178
Clément, Edmond, 57
Clementi, Adriana, 255
Clémentine d'Orléans, Duchess of Coburg-Kohary, 163
Clergue, Lucien, 39

Cluytens, André, 217
Cobb, Irving S.
Coburn, Alvin Langdon, 8
Cochin, Henry, 63
Cochran, C.B. (Charles Blake), 309
Cocteau, Jean, Plate 22, *27–45*, 60, 76, 96, 178, 179, 180, 216, 229, 240, 241, 273, 286
Cocteau, Mme, 45
Coghlan, Rose, 326
Cohan, George M., 210
Coke, Miss, 112
Colbran, Isabella (Rossini), 260
Colefax, Sybil, Lady, 105
Coleridge, Hartley, 288
Colet, Louise, 71
Colette, 215
Coletti, Filippo, 299
Collaer, Paul, 44
Collins, Sewell, 108
Collins, Wilkie, 291
Collomb, Romain, 281
Colonne, Édouard, 85, 109, 151, 269
Columbus, Christopher, 102
Colvin, Frances Jane Sitwell, Lady, 105
Congreve, Arnold, 120
Constantin, Léon, 13
Coolidge, Elizabeth Sprague, 216
Coombe, Mrs. George, 117
Coppée, François, 63, 89
Coquelin, Constant, 261
Coralli, Jean, 90
Corbière, Tristan, 303
Cordell, Richard, 159
Cordier, Jules, 203
Corio, marchese, 163, 164
Cormon, Eugène, 194
Corneille, Pierre, 61
Cornelius, Peter, 133
Cornet, Julius, 306
Coronaro, Gellio Benvenuto, 129
Corradi, Edmondo, 123
Cortot, Alfred, *45*, 109
Cossmann, Bernhard, 303
Costallat, Georges, 25
Costantini, Giovanni, 333
Cotham, H.G., 8
Courbet, Gustave, 9, 15
Courcelles (collector), 76
Couvray, vicomte de, 163, 164
Couzinou, Robert, 87
Coward, Noel, *45–49*, 162, 210
Cox, Palmer, *50*
Cramer, Wood & Co. (firm), 206

Cranmer-Byng, L., 5, 6, 7
Cranmore, R.T., 290
Craven, Frank, 210
Crémieux, Adolphe, 92
Crémieux, Hector, 189, 191, 192, 194
Crenneville, Gräfin, 164
Crewe, Thomas, 158
Crips, Mary, 157
Crivelli, Gaetano, 208
Croisset, Francis de, *50–52*
Croisset, Germaine de, 51
Croisset, Marie-Thérèse de (Bischoffsheim), 52
Croisset, Philippe de, 51
Croiza, Claire, 244
Croly, George, 290, 291
Crosby, Harry, 35
Crosland, Alan, 259
Crothers, Rachel, 210
Cruikshank, George, 291
Cruppi, Mme Jean, 245
Crutchley, Brooke, 159
Cruvelli, Sophie, 299
Cuénod, Hugues, 217
Cui, César, 87, 109
Cumberland, Gerald, 8
Cummings, W.H., 94
Cunningham, Alan, 289
Cuny, Charles, General, 86
Cuny, Olivier Adolphe Amédée, General, 86
Curzon, Sir Clifford, 232
Custine, Astolphe de, 97
Cuyp, Albert, 89
Czinner, Paul, 310

Dallapiccola, Luigi, 215
D'Ambrosio, Paulina, 303
Damcke, Berthold, 13
Damcke, Louise, 13
Dami, Alphonse, 97
Dandelot, Arthur, 26, 265
Dane, Clemence, 288
Daniel-Lesur, *see* Lesur
D'Annunzio, Gabriele, *53*, 59, 256, 257
Dante Alighieri, 290, 332, 333, 334
Danzi, Franz, 325
Darclée, Hericlea, 234
Darwin, Charles, 102
Darzens, Rodolphe, 258
Daudet, Alphonse, *53*, 79, 88, 89, 107
Daudet, Julia, 53, 105, 107, 225
Daudet, Léon, 39, 105, 137, 229

Daudet, Lucien, 215, 225
Davaine, Dr., 62
Davenport, Homer, 108
Davies, Raymond Arthur, 90
Davies, Sir Thomas, 66
Debussy, Claude, Plate 14, *53–59*, 61, 67, 68, 109, 139, 140, 141, 177, 178, 179, 180, 219, 242, 243, 244, 247, 249, 303
Debussy, Emma, 57, 67, 273
Debussy, Lilly (Texier), 56, 57
De Clifford, Lady, 111
Deel, Basil L., 159
Defaure, 248
Degas, Edgar, 140
Dehmel, Richard, 283
Dehn, Paul, 308
De Just, Baron, 130
Delacroix, Eugène, 99, 272
Delage, Maurice, 244, 246, 247
Delahaye, Ernest, Plate 11, 301
Delahaye, Léon, 271
Delamain, Maurice, 37
De La Mare, Walter, 272
Delaroche, Paul, 90
Delarue-Mardrus, Lucie, 60
Delibes, Léo, *59*
Delle Donne, Marie, 37
Delle Donne, Robert, 37
Del Mar, Norman, 314
Del Monaco, Mario, 218
Delpech (engraver), 97
Delubac, Jacqueline (Guitry), 82
Delvincourt, Claude, 217, 219
Demetz, 86
Demombynes, Jean Gaudefroy, 154
Denis, Marie-Louise (Mignot), 202
Denoël, Robert, 76
Depoix, Julia, 70
Derain, André, 273, 274
Desbordes, Jean, 36, 40, 41, 43, *60*
Desbouchères, J., 51
Descartes, René, 102
Deschamps-Jéhin, Blanche, 147
De Segurola, Andrès de, 239
De Simone, R., 125
Desnoy, A., 16
De Spirito (singer), 333
Dessauer, Josef, 272, 277
Destinn, Emmy, 239, 283
Destouches, Raymond, 215
Detaille, Édouard, 86
Détroyat, Léonce, 271
De Valois, Ninette, 309
Deveria, Eugène, 97, 132

Diaghilev, Serge, 15, 28, 41, 42, 43, 54, 57, 67, 68, 218, 245, 250, 252, 253, 273, 274, 286
Dickens, Charles, 87, 106, 291
Diderot, Denis, 30
Didur, Adamo, 239
Diémer, Louis, 109
Dietrichstein, Moriz, Graf von, 275
Di Fiori, Domenico, 281
Dilke, Charles Wentworth, 106
Dingelstedt, Franz, 13
Disdéri, André-Adolphe-Eugène, 300
Di Stefano, Giuseppe, 218
Dixon, Richard Watson, 19
Dobrée, Bonamy, 159
Dörffel, Alfred, 13
Doernberg, Imma, Freifrau von, 317, 324
Doheny, Estelle, 282
Dongrie, Jean, 37
Donini, Agostino, 257
Donizetti, Gaetano, 12, 211, 298
Donnay, Maurice, *60*, 86, 88
"Dorémi" (pseudonym), 129
Dorfman, Adeline Smith, 315
Dortu, Willy, 37, 44
Doucet, Jacques, 39
Douglas, Alfred Bruce, Lord, *60*
Douin, Charles, 84
Douvry-Barbot, Caroline, 297
Doyle, Annette, 290
Doyle, Charles, 290
Doyle, Henry, 288
Doyle, James, 290
Doyle, John, 291
Doyle, Richard, 288, 289
Draeger frères, 35
Drake, William Henry, 102, 103
Draneht Bey, Paul, 297
Dreyfus, Alfred, 85, 139
Dreyfus, Mme Fernand, 245
Drieu La Rochelle, Pierre, 36
Drinkwater, A.E., 105
Droescher, Georg, 129
Dron, Marthe, 242
Drouet, Juliette, 98
Drummond, William, 322
Dubois, Théodore, 109
Dubufe, Édouard, 80, 99
Duc, J.-V., 300
Ducas, Adam, 289
Duché, Pierre, 302
Dudevant, Maurice, 27
Dufranne, Hector, 59

Dufy, Raoul, 31
Duglé, Angèle, 85
DuGuy (photographer), 52
Duhem, Jean, 248
Dukas, Paul, 57, *61–62*, 70, 109, 247
Dullin, Charles, 44
Du Locle, Camille, 191, 294, 296
Dumas, Alexandre (fils), *62*, 291
Dumas, Alexandre, 172, 299
Dunbar, William, 321
Duncan, Ada, 116
Duncan, Miss, 117
Dunkels, M., Miss, 308
Duparc, Henri, *62–63*, 109
Dupetit, Charles, 195
Duplay, Maurice, 225
Duplessis, Marie, 62
Dupont, Gabrielle, 56, 57
Duprez, Gilbert-Louis, 208
Durand (firm), 212
Durand, Jacques, 54, 249
Durandeau, É., 9
Duregati (singer), 333
Durey, Louis, 33, 34, 247, 273
Duru, Alfred, 192
Dusch, Alexander von, 324
Dussarp, Maurice, 230
Dussat, Jean, 182
Duval, Denise, 217, 219
Duvivier, Marthe, 147
Dvořák, Antonin, *64*, 109, *145*

Eames, Emma, 267
Edinburgh, Alfred, Duke of, *see* Saxe-Coburg and Gotha, 112, 276
Edmonson, Ann Jane, 158
Edward VII, King of Great Britain, *65*, 262
Edwards, D.L., 159
Edwards, Misia, *see* Sert, Misia
Egan, Pierce, *65*
Egerton, Daniel, *65*
Ehrlich, B.A., 274
Eichendorff, Joseph von, 334
Eisendecker, Wilhelm von, 177
Ekman, Ida, 279
Eldon, John Scott, Earl of, 130
Elgar, Sir Edward, *65–66*, 109
Élisabeth, Queen, consort of Albert I, King of the Belgians, 70
Ellice, Edward, 112
Elliott & Fry (photographer), 161
Elliott, Mr., 157

Ellis, Mr., 95
Éluard, Nusch, 214
Éluard, Paul, 214, 215, 216
Ely, Mathew, bishop of, 158
Ely, Thomas, bishop of, 158
Emanuel, G., 127
Emerson, Ralph Waldo, 101
Émie, Louis, 57
Enesco, Georges, 109
Enoch, Charles, 286
Érard (firm), 293
Érard, Sébastien, 272
Erckmann-Chatrian, 268
Erlanger, Camille, 109
Erlanger, Philippe, 216
Errazuriz, Eugenia, 285, 286
Escudier, Léon, 294, 296, 297
Escudier, Marie, 296, 297
Essington, Sir William, 180
Eugen von Habsburg, Archduke, 130
Eugène-Louis-Napoléon, prince impérial, *181–83*
Eugénie de Montijo, consort of Napoléon III, Emperor of the French, 62, 66, *181–83*
Evans, C.L., 159
Evans, Edwin, 57, 67, 245, 323
Evans, Frederick H., 277
Evans, Treyer, *66*
Evans, William, 121
Ewer & Co. (publisher), 167
Eyragues, Henriette de Montesquiou-Fésenzac, marquise d', 176

Faber, Johann Ludwig, 4
Faccio, Franco, 294, 295, 297
Faivre, Alfred-Louis, 13
Falconer, Edmond, 5
Falla, Manuel de, 61, *67–68*, 109, 292
Fantin-Latour, Henri, 14, 15
Farger, Jean, 146, 154
Fargue, Léon-Paul, 39, 41, 246
Farnie, Henry Brougham, 196
Farrelli, Francesco, 234
Fauchécourt, M. de, 181
Fauchey, Paul, 265
Fauré, Gabriel, 57, 62, 63, *69–70*, 85, 109, 178, 241, 247, 266, 270
Faure, Jean-Baptiste, 15, 114
Faure, Philippe, 97
Faure-Biguet, Jacques, 225
Favresse, P. (photographer), 234
Ferdinand IV, King of Naples, 72, 73

Ferdinand, August, Prince of Prussia, *see* August Ferdinand
Ferrand, Humbert, 14
Ferroud, Pierre-Octave, 216
Fersen, Jacques, 255
Février, Henry, 248
Feydeau, Ernest, 71
Feydeau, Georges, *70–71*
Fidès-Devriès, 147
Fino, Giuseppe, 253, 254, 255
Fino Savio, Chiarina, 250, 251, 252, 253, 254, 255, 256, 257
Fischer, Augustin, S.J., 163, 164
Fisher, John, Lord Bishop of Salisbury, 130
Fisher, William Arms, 8
Fitzgerald, P.D., Major, 107
Fitzwilliam, Charles William Wentworth, Earl, 112
Fizdale, Robert, 217
Flandres, Philippe de Belgique, comte de, 163, 164
Flaubert, Gustave, *71*, 85
Flechtlein, 37
Flecker, James Elroy, 250, 272
Flers, Robert de, 138, 221
Fletcher (binder), 112
Fletcher, Henry, 289
Fletcher, Phineas, 320
Florensa (engraver), 71
Fokine, Michel, 43
Fombertaux, Eugène, 97
Fontaine, Auguste Alfred, 147
Fonteyn, Margot, 309
Forain, Jean-Louis, 302
Fort, Paul, 43
Forzano, Giovacchino, 126, 232, 234, 328, 331
Foster & Bonner (firm), 158
Fougasse (pseudonym of Cyril Kenneth Bird), *71*
Fouquier-Tinville, Antoine Quentin, *71–72*
Fournier, Pierre, 217, 218
Franca, Tonio, 233
France, Anatole, 176
Frances, E.G., 158
Franchetti, Alberto, barone, 129
Franci, Arturo, 125, 142
Francis I, Emperor of Austria, 259
Francis, of Assisi, Saint, 319
Franck, César, 62, *72*
Franc-Nohain, 243
Frank, Alan, 312

Frank, Nino, 37
Franklin, Sir John, 291
Franz Joseph I, Emperor of Austria, 26
Fraser-Simson, Harold, 175
Fratellini brothers, 31
Frébault, Élie, 184
Frederick II, King of Prussia, *72–74*
Fredersdorf, Michael Gabriel, 73
Freeth, H.A., 159
French, Annie, *74*
Fresnay, Pierre, 216
Frezzolini, Emilia, 300
Friant, Louis Gilbert François Léon, comte, 26
Friedrich Wilhelm I, King of Prussia, 73, 74
Fritsch, Dr., 164
Fröding, Gustaf, 279
Fromont, Eugène, 57, 242
Frossoli, Alfonso, 234
Fuchs, Henriette, 70
Fürstner, Adolph, Plate 16, 129

Gabillon, Ludwig, *75*
Gabory, Georges, 43
Gänsbacher, Johann, 324
Galignani, Anthony, 15
Galipeaux, Félix, 71
Gallet, Louis, 15, 122
Gallimard (firm), 37
Gallimard, Gaston, 44, 220, 225
Gallo, Antonio, 299
Galsworthy, John, *75*, 210
Galt, John, 289
Gamba, Pietro, conte, 289
Garcia, Manuel, 268
Garden, Mary, 59, *75*
Gardoni, Italo, 300
Garibaldi, Giuseppe, 26
Garnier, Arsène (photographer), 97
Garnier, Mme H., 69
Garros, Roland, 28, 38
Garvan, Francis P., 108
Gaskell, Amy, 20
Gaskell, Elizabeth, 10
Gatti-Casazza, Giulio, 239, 247
Gaucher, Philippe, 180
Gaudier, René, 37, 38
Gauthier-Villars, Henry, *see* Willy
Gautier, Théophile, 63, 84, 180, 197
Genée, Richard, 190
Genet, Jean, 35, 40, 44, *75*

George IV, King of Great Britain, 111, 130
Gérard, Rosemonde, *76*
German, Edward, *76*
Gershwin, Ira, 112
Geslin, Gabriel, 265, 267, 268, 270
Gesvres, Bernard-François Potier, marquis, later duc de, 76
Gesvres, Léon Potier, duc de, *76*
Gevaert, François-Auguste, 109
Ghéon, Henri, 41, 225
Gheusi, Pierre-Barthélémy, 266
Ghil, René, 302
Ghisalberti, Mario, 329, 332
Ghislanzoni, Antonio, 211, 212, 296
Ghys, Mme Henry, 245
Giacompol, Pietro, 333
Gibbs, Frederick W., 119
Gide, André, 31, 32, 37, 39, 43, 57, *76–77*, 139
Gide, Casimir, 90
Gielgud, John, 310
Gigliucci, Porzia, 165
Gilbert, Achille Isidore, 15
Gilbert, C. Allan, 108
Gilbert, W.S., *77*
Gill, 98
Gille, Philippe, 59
Gills, 42
Gilly, Dinh, 239
Gilvarry, James, 225
Ginisty, Paul, 25
Giono, Jean, *77*
Giordano, Umberto, *77*, 129, 145
Giorgi, Maestro, 238
Girard, Mme, 70
Girardin, Delphine de, 100
Glatigny, Albert, *77*
Glazunov, Aleksandr Konstantinovich, 56, *78*, 109
Gleizes, Albert, 41
Glinka, Mikhail Ivanovich, 252
Gloucester, Mary, Duchess of, 111
Gluck, Christoph Willibald, 39, 94, 133, 303, 333, 340
Godard, Benjamin, 109
Goddard, Edward, 93, 94
Godebska, Misia, *see* Sert, Misia
Godebski, Ida, 243, 246, 247
Godebski, Jean, 243, 245
Godebski, Marie, 247
Godebski, Xavier Cyprian (Cipa), 243, 245, 246, 247, 273
Goethe, Johann Wolfgang von, 275, 327, 332

Goetze, Sigismund, 26, 166
Gold, Michael, 210
Goldmark, Carl, 109
Goldoni, Carlo, 328, 330, 331, 335
Goldsmith, Oliver, 159
Golisciani, Enrico, 77, 328, 329, 330, 331
Gomiecourt, Claire de, 69
Gondinet, Edmond, 59
Góngora y Argote, Luis de, 67
Gonzales, José Maria, 163
Good, Frank, 259
Goodman, Jules Eckert, 210
Goodwin & Tabb, Ltd, 44
Gottschalk, A.W., 131
Gounod, Anna (Zimmerman), 79
Gounod, Charles, Plate 12, 16, 64, 70, *78–80*, 85, 241, 265, 269, 294
Gramont, Antoine Alfred Agénor, duc de, 62
Gramont, Antoine Alfred Agénor, duc de [son of the preceding], 226
Granados, Enrique, 67, *81*, 178
Grandmougin, Charles, 150
Grangé, Eugène, 185
Granville-Barker, Harley, 210
Grasset (firm), 51, 60, 230, 240
Grasset, Bernard, 41, 42
Graux, Lucien, 168
Grechaninov, Aleksandr Tikhonovih, 109
Grécourt, 214
Grédy, Jean-Pierre, 135, 136
Green, Paul, 210
Greenaway, Kate, *81*
Gregh, Fernand, 222
Grégoire, Henri, 289
Gregory, Lady, 106
Gresse, Léon, 147
Gribble, Harry Wagstaff, 210
Grieg, Edvard, 56, *81*, 109
Grohe, Oskar, 328
Gross, Joseph, 275
Grote, George, 166
Groves, George, 259
Grümmer, Paul, 336
Grunne, Eugénie, comtesse de, 164
Gruyer, Hector, 16
Grzymala, Wojciech, 27
Guérin, Jacques, 271, 274
Guérin, Jean, 29, 38
Guggenthal, Victor von, 164
Guiche, Agénor, duc de, *see* Gramont
Guilbert, Yvette, *81*
Guilford, Lord, *see* North

Guillermy, Jean François César, baron de, 172
Guillot de Sainbris, Antonin, 72
Guiraud, Ernest, 185, 186, 187, 188
Guitry, Lucien, 292
Guitry, Sacha, 36, 42, 58, 72, *81–82*
Gunn, Archie, 108
Gunsbourg, Raoul, 188, 248, 265, 266
Gustl, 283
Guthrie, Anstey, 105
Guymond de la Touche, Claude, 404
Gwynn, Nell, 290

Hadow, W.H., 8
Hague, Elizabeth F., 209, 210, 211
Hahn, Reynaldo, 26, 53, 60, 82, *83–89*, 101, 137, 176, 221, 225, 226, 249, 265, 266
Hainl, Georges, 80
Halévy, Alexandrine (Lebas), 90
Halévy, Daniel, 27, 89, 220, 221, 222, 226, 231
Halévy, Élie, 14
Halévy, Flore, 90
Halévy, Fromental, 14, *90–92*, 132, 229, 263
Halévy, Léon, 14, 16, 17, 90, 91, *92*
Halévy, Léonie, 16, 80, 90, 172
Halévy, Ludovic, 14, 16, 17, 79, 80, 81, 90, 91, 92, 185, 189, 192, 195, 226
Halévy, Mélanie, 90
Hall, Glenn, 239
Hallowell, Anna, 105
Halperson, H., 239
Hamilton, Clayton, 210
Hammersley, Derek, 155
Hammersley, Violet, 155
Hammerstein, Oscar, 259
Han, Yu, 6
Handel, George Frideric, Plate 2, *92–94*, 133
Hanefeld, 74
Hanslick, Eduard, 276
Harburg, E.Y., 112
Harcourt, Eugène d', 59
Harden, Maximilian, 141
Hardy, Dudley, *94*
Hardy, Thomas, 272
Harland, Aline, 105
Harland, Henry, 25
Harrach, Graf von, 292
Harris, Augustus, 5
Harris, William, 8

Harrowby, Dudley Ryder, 1st Earl of, 130
Hart, Fritz, 8
Hart, Marvell, 8
Hart, Moss, 210
Hartmann, Georges, 57, 59, 152
Harty, Sir Hamilton, 8
Hassall, Christopher, 309, 322
Hatto, Jeanne, 51, 247
Hauff, Wilhelm, 330
Haussmann, Georges Eugène, baron, 294
Hauttecoeur, F., 58
Havet, Mireille, 41
Hawes, G.E., Colonel, 107
Hawkes, Ralph, 284
Haxton, Gerald, 162
Haydn, Joseph, *94*, 145, 259, 271, 281
Hayes, Alfred, 8
Hayet, Louis, 302
Hayman, Laura, 226, 227
Hayworth, Rita, 112
Heber, Richard, 10
Hébertot, Jacques, 273
Hecht, W., 75, 77, 291
Hedberg, Tor, 279
Heifetz, Jascha, 314
Heim, François-Joseph, 91
Hein, Carl, 232
Heine, Ferdinand, 306
Heine, Heinrich, 54, 138, 166, 305, 327, 328
Heinemann (firm), 155
Heinemann, William, 106
Hekking, Gérard, 244
Heller, Stephen, 222
Hellman, Lillian, 210
Helpmann, Robert, 309
Hemans, Felicia, 158
Hennevé, Louis, 86
Henriot (bookseller), 277
Henry, H. Wright, 8
Henry, Leigh, 44
Hensel, Ulrich, 333
Henseler, Anton, 332
Herbart, Pierre, 44
Herbert, George, 318
Heredia, José Maria de, 89, 139
Herleroy, Marguerite, 86, 87, 265, 266
Hermann-Léon, 72
Hertzka, Julius, 3
Hervey, T.K., 290
Hervieu, M.D., 288
Hervieu, Paul, 87
Hess, Julius, 108

Hesse, Hermann, 283
Hesse-Wartegg, Ernst von, 130
Heugel (publisher), 312
Heugel, Henri, 84, 153
Heyberger, Joseph, 79
Heyman, Sir Henry, 263, 266
Hikesios, 289
Hill, Mrs. F.H., 106
Hill, John T. (photographer), 162
Hiller, Ferdinand, 296
Hindemith, Gertrud, 318
Hindemith, Paul, 216, 318
Hinkel, Hans, 122
Hirt, Franz Josef, 247
Hitler, Adolf, 122
Hodge, William, 210
Hoeck, Mary, 38, 179
Hoffland, B., 290
Hoffmann, E.T.A. (Ernst Theodor Amadeus), 194, 325
Hofmannsthal, Hugo von, 43, *94–95*, 283
Hogg, James, 288
Holland, E.J., 160
Hollmann, Joseph, 153, 267
Holloway (binder), 291
Holmès, Augusta, 25
Holst, Gustav, 56, 67
Holstein, Count von, 140
Honegger, Arthur, 33, 34, 44, 56, 109, 214, 218, 219
Hopwood, Avery, 210
Hornby, Sir Phipps, 115
Hougham, Arthur, 8
Housman, Alfred Edward, *95*
Howard, F., 290
Howard, Leslie, 317
Howell, Miriam, 136
Howells, William Dean, 210
Hoyau (typesetter), 76
Hozier, d', 76
Hubay, Jenö, 109
Hudson, Henry, 102
Hüe, Georges, *95*, 109
Hugnet, Georges, 38
Hugo, Adèle (Foucher), 98, 99
Hugo, Adèle, 99, 100
Hugo, Alice, 98
Hugo, Charles, 97
Hugo, Georges, 98
Hugo, Jean, 4, 33, 35, 36, 38, 44, *96*
Hugo, Jeanne, 98, 137
Hugo, Léopoldine, 99, 100
Hugo, Valentine (Gross), Plate 20, 4, 28, 37, 38, 41, 44, *96*

Hugo, Victor, 69, 85, 89, *96–100*, 140, 267, 269, 299, 305
Hugo, Victor, known as François-Victor, 99, 100
Hugon, André, 302
Humières, Robert d', 227
Hummel, Johann Nepomuk, 27
Humperdinck, Engelbert, 109
Humphreys, W.K., 291
Hunt, Holman, 106
Hunt, Leigh, 290
Hüttenbrenner, Anselm, 275
Hüttenbrenner, Joseph, 275
Huxley, Aldus, 136
Hyman, G., 108

Ibert, Jacques, 216
Ibsen, Henrik, 324
Illica, Luigi, *101*, 123, 144
Imhauser, Fernand, 32
Indy, Vincent d', 25, 62, 63, *101*, 109, 139, 271
Inghelbrecht, D.-E. (Désiré-Émile), 55, 59
Ingres, Madame, 260
Ionides, Luke, 21
Ireland. John, *101*
Irving, Ernest, 323
Irving, Washington, *102–3*, 289
Isabey (photographer), 44
Isabey, Jean-Baptiste, 208, 209
Isherwood, Christopher, 3
Isola, Émile, 70
Isola, Vincent, 70

Jackson, David, 171
Jacob, Max, 37, *104*
Jaconet, Daniel, 241
Jaime, Adolphe, 191
Jaime, Adolphe (fils), 207
Jaime, Ernest, 200, 203
Jallot, Marcel, 38
James, Henry, *104–8*
James, William, 106
Jankowski, Andrzej, 178
Janssen, Ann Narding, 8
Janssen, Werner, 8
Jean-Aubry, G., 61, 67, 68, 218, 247, 248, 249, 292
Jellicoe, J.L., 290
Jellinek (gardener), 164
Jeritza, Maria, 283, 284, 285

Jerome, William Travers, *108*
Jilek, August, 163–65
Joachim, Joseph, 109, 276
Joanny, Jean-Baptiste, 97
Jobert, Jean, 249
Johnson, Nunnally, 136
Johnson, R.U., 106
Joinville, François Ferdinand Philippe d'Orléans, prince de, 137
Joly-Segalen, Annie, 180
Jommelli, Nicolò, 94
Joncières, Victorin, 109
Jones, Evelyn Howard, 326
Jones, J.E., 289
Jones, Mary Cadwalader, 106
Jordan, Eben D., 56
Joséphine, Queen, consort of Oscar I, King of Sweden and Norway, 183
Joubert, Joseph, abbé, 249
Jouhandeau, Élise, 273
Jourdan-Morhange, Hélène, 215, 249
Jousset, R., 79
Joyce, James, 180
Juarez, Benito, 26
Jullien, Adolphe, 14
Jullien, Louis, 302
Jusserand, Élise, 106
Jusserand, Jean-Jules, 106

Kahnt, C.F. (publisher), 131, 132
Kalerdji, Nikolai, 289
Karsten, Karl G., 174
Kastor, Robert, *109–11*
Kaufman, George, 210
Keats, John, 272
Kellermann, Berthold, 131, 133
Kelly, Gene, 112
Kelly, George, 210
Kelly, Sir Gerald, 161
Kennedy, Charles Rann, 210
Kennedy, J.M.C., *287*
Kennedy, Margaret, 311
Kennedy, Will, 290
Kennedy-Fraser, Marjory, 8
Kent, Mary Louisa Victoria, Duchess of, 112
Keppel family, *111–12*
Keppel, Anne, Lady, 112
Keppel, Frances, 112
Keppel, Sir Henry, 111
Keppel, Thomas, 111, 112
Keppel, William George, 112
Kern, Jerome, *112*

Kerner, Justinus Andreas Christian, 327
Kessel, Georges, 38, 43
Kessler, Harry, Graf, 43
Keynes, Geoffrey, 293
Khayyam, Omar, 272
Kihm, Jean-Jacques, 38
Kind, Friedrich, 325
Kindermann, August, 140
King, Jessie M., *112–13*
Kingsley, Charles, *113*
Kinloch-Cole, Kenneth, 106
Kipling, Rudyard, 76, 103, 113, 286
Kisling, Moïse, 273
Kistner (firm), 131
Kistner, Friedrich, 168, 276
Klein, Hermann, 263, 271
Klein, Hugo, 282
Klingemann, Karl, 167
Klingsor, Tristan, 87
Knight, J.C.B., *113*
Knobel, Betty, 283
Knockerbocker, Diedrich, 102
Knollys, Francis, 65
Knowles, James Sheridan, 290
Knox, William, 289
Kochno, Boris, 36, 280, 309, 323
Koechlin, Charles, *113*, 178, 179
Koechlin, Suzanne, 178, 179
Köhler (photographer), 285
Köhler, Christian Louis Heinrich, 132
Kogel, Gustav F., 284
Kolisch, Rudolf, 56
Koraes, Adamantios, 289
Korwalow, G., 8
Kostelanetz, André, 313
Koubetzky, A., 110
Kraus, Hans P., 115
Kreisler, Fritz, 110
Kriese, Antonio, 289
Krips, Josef, 315
Kubelík, Jan, 110
Kufferath, Maurice, 57
Kuhacsevich, Jacob, 164
Kuhacsevich, Mrs., 164

Laboye, Yobal (photographer), 179
Lacauchie, Alexandre François, 71
Lacombe, Georges, 44
Lacombe, Paul, 25
La Farge, John, 104, 106
La Fontaine, Jean de, 213
Lagarde, Joseph-Jean, baron, 16, 17

La Grua, Emma, 299
Lagut, Irène, 33
Lahor, Jean, *see* Cazalis
Laib, Paul (photographer), 161, 162
Lainé (collector), 76
Laing, Alexander Gordon, 289
Lalique, René, 261
Lalo, Édouard, 15, *114*
Lalo, Pierre, 245, 247
Laloy, Louis, 38, 57, 262
La Madelaine, Stephen de, 14
Lambert, Constant, 309, 314, 316, 320, 321
Lamoureux, Charles, 16, 85
Lander, Daniel, 39
Landon, Letitia Elizabeth, 290
Landowska, Wanda, 110, 179
Landskoff, H. (photographer), 179
Lane, John, 25
Langley, Robin, 318
Langner, Lawrence, 210
Langtry, Lilly, 326
Lannes, Jean, duc de Montebello, *114*
Lapauze, Mme Henry, 87
Lapointe, Armand, 192
Laroche, Ernest, 153
Laroche, Hermann (G.A. Larosh), 288
Larpent, Miss, 106
La Salle, Louis de, 222
Lassalle, Jean, 267
Latouche, Henri de, 281
Lauremberg, Johann, 4
Laurencin, Marie, 37, 96
Lauris, Georges de, 227
Lauriston, Alexandre Bernard Law, marquis de, 97
Laus, Emilia, 125
Lauzac, Marie, 81
Lauzières, Achille de, 271
Lavarello, Ernello, 252
Lawrence, Frieda von Richthofen, 136
Lawrence, Gertrude, 49
Léandre, Charles-Lucien, 51
Lear, Edward, Plate 6, *114–22*, 213
Léautaud, Paul, 42
Lebas, Hippolyte, 91
Le Borne, Fernand, 267
Lecocq, Charles, 110, *122*, 268
Leconte de Lisle, 54, 63, 148, 149, 301
Lee, Vernon, *see* Paget
Lefevre, Ernest, 100
Legouix, Robert, 54
Leguay (engraver), 97

Lehar, Franz, 110, *122*
Leicester, Anne Amelia Keppel Coke, Countess of, 111
Leicester, Thomas William Coke, 1st Earl of, 111
Leighton, Frederick, 65
Le Jeune (photographer), 161
Lely, Sir Peter, 290
Le Maire (painter), 209
Lemaire, Madeleine, 87, 89
Lemarchand, Jacques, 95
Lemarié, Berthe, 227
Le Masle, Pierre, 179
Lemcke, Carl, 17, 18
Léna, Maurice, 152
Lenau, Nicolaus, 333
Lenskii, Boris Vladimirovich, 8
Léo, Auguste, 27
Léon, Hermann, *see* Hermann-Léon
Léon, Paul, 70
Leoncavallo, Berthe, 129
Leoncavallo, Jeanne (Puel), 126
Leoncavallo, Ruggiero, Plate 16, 110, *123–30*, 145, 239
Leopold I, King of the Belgians, 111, *130–31*, 165
L'Épine, Ernest Louis Victor Jules, 184, 206
Le Play, Mme Frédéric, 17
Lerolle, Henry, 139
Leroux, Gaston, 41
Leroux, Xavier, 110
Lessmann, Otto, 285
Lesur, Daniel, 214
Lesure, François, 55
Leube, 199
Leupp, Miss, 106
Levadé, Charles, 88, 227
Levasseur, Nicolas, 260
Le Vavasseur, Gustave, 62
Levi, Hermann, 307
Levi, Samuele, 298
Levine, David, 231
Levy, Benn, 210
Lévy, Michel Maurice, *131*
Levy, Moses, 234
Lhérie, Paul, 212
L'Hoest, Lucien, 267
Lhote, André, 41
Li, Po, 5
Liddell, Robert, 159
Liebermann, Rolf, 39
Liebert, Herman W., 115
Liesse, 259

Lifar, Serge, 15, 54, 57, 67, 213, 214, 216, 218, 243, 245, 252, 253, 273, 286
Lignières, comte de, 76
Lind, Jenny, 296
Lindsay, Howard, 210
Linossier, Raymonde, 214
Lipsky, Captain von, 73
List und Francke (firm), 3
Liszt, Eduard, 133
Liszt, Franz, 62, 78, *131–33*, 268, 269, 306
Littleton, Alfred, 64
Liverpool, Robert Banks Jenkinson, 2nd Earl of, 130
Llewellyn Davies, Michael, 240
Llewellyn-Davies, Mrs. John, 240
Lloyd George, David, 265
Lockroy, Édouard, 98
Lockspeiser, Edward, 56
Loën, August, Baron von, 306
Logelain, Henri (photographer), 234
Lohf, Kenneth A., 20
Lombardo, Carlo, 142
Lonati, Mlle, 147
Long, Charles, 65
Long, Marguerite, 67, 243
Longmans (publisher), 155, 162
Loomis, N.H., 108
Loos, Anita, *133–37*
Loosey, Carl F., 164
Lorca, Federico Garcia, 68
Loring, Katharine Peabody, 106
Loring, Louisa, 106
Lortic (binder), 77
Lothar, Rudolph, 210
Loti, Pierre, 87, *137*, 258
Lottin de Laval, 132
Louis, Monsieur, 208
Louis-Philippe, King of the French, *137*, 138
Louise d'Orléans, consort of Leopold I, King of the Belgians, *137–38*
Louÿs, Pierre, 57, 58, 131, *138–40*, 239
Lucan, 95
Lucca, Francesco, 306
Luccardi, Vincenzo, 296, 297
Ludwig I, King of Bavaria, *140*
Ludwig II, King of Bavaria, *140*, 307
Lugné-Poë, Aurélien, 141
Lumley, Benjamin, 296
Luporini, 238
Lurani-Cernuschi Greppi, contessa, 340
Lushington, Franklin, 120
Lusignan, James, 289
Lutyens, Elizabeth, 323

Lynen, Marie, 17, 133, 288
Lyttleton, Sibylla, Lady, 120

Macaire et Cie (firm), 181
MacArthur, Charles, 134
MacCarthy, Desmond, 160
Macfaren, Natalie, 275
Machen, Arthur, 101
Machold, J., 164, 165
Mackenzie, Miss, 21
Maclaren, Archibald, 19
Macleod, Fiona, 7
Macmillan, Sir Frederick Orridge, 106
Macmillan, Giorgiana (Warrin), Lady, 106
MacNeice, Louis, 310
Macpherson, Miss, 21
Madoux-Frank, Mme Alfred, 249
Maes, J. (photographer), 97
Maeterlinck, Maurice, 59, 61, *141*, 256
Maffei, Andrea, 142, 297, 298, 299
Maggs Brothers Ltd, 26, 166, 287
Magnússon, Finnur, 289
Magrini, Angelo, Plate 21, 232, 233
Magrini, Erminia, 233, 234
Mahler, Alma, 249, 250, 284
Mahler, Gustav, 130, *141*, 284, 328, 343
Maigrot, Henri, 153
Maillard, M., 269
Malcolm, John, 289
Malibran, Maria, *141*
Malipiero, Gian Francesco, 218
Mallarmé, Stéphane, 8, 85, 243, 244, 291, 303
Mallet, Lady, 106
Mandeville, Miss, 120
Mann, Klaus, 284
Manoury, Adolphe Théophile, 147
Mantle, Burns, 210
Manuel, Eugène, 154
Manzoni, Alessandro, 294
Maquet, Auguste, 91
Marais, Jean, 36, 42, 96
Marbeau, L., 267
Marbury, Elizabeth, 326
Marcel (typesetter), 76
Marcello, Benedetto, 251
Marchand (singer), 196
Marchesi, Mathilde, 154
Marcoux (typesetter), 76
Marcus Aurelius, 289
Marcus, Edward and Betty, Foundation, 18

Maré, Rolf de, 33
Marenco, Romualdo, 295
Maria Adelaide, principessa di Savoia, 255
Maria Annunziata of Habsburg, Archduchess of Austria, 26
Mariani, Angelo, 295
Marie-Amélie, Queen, consort of Louis-Philippe, King of the French, 137, 208
Marie-Antoinette, Queen, consort of Louis XVI, King of France, 71
Marinetti, Filippo Tommaso, 270
Marini, Ignazio, 297
Mario, Giovanni Matteo, cavaliere di Candia, 300
Maritain, Jacques, 32, 35
Marotti, Guido, 234
Marquis, Don, 210
Mars, Victor de, 9
Marsh, Harvey, 65
Martin du Gard, Maurice, 39
Martin, Charles, 274
Martin, Gabriel, 153
Martin, H. Bradley, 11
Martin, Jean, 35
Martin, Jean-Marie, 54
Martínez Sierra, Gregorio, 67
Martinez, Angelo, 259
Martini, Giovanni Battista, 334
Mascagni, Lina, 101, 144
Mascagni, Maria, 144, 145, 211, 343
Mascagni, Mario, 142, 144, 145
Mascagni, Pietro, Plate 15, 110, 129, *142–45*, 239, 266
Massard (engraver), 71
Massenet, Jules, Plate 18, 50, 58, 84, 87, 88, 110, 139, *146–54*, 300
Massine, Leonide, 57, 67, 273
Masson, Alphonse Charles, 97
Masson, Paul-Marie, 154
Massoni, Piero, 234
Matarasso, Henri, Plate 22, 34, 39
Mater, André, 96
Mathers, Edward Powys, 6, 7
Mathews, Elkin, 25
Matisse, Henri, 174
Mattfeld, Mary, 239
Matthison, Friedrich von, 275
Matz, Mrs. Otto H., 106
Mauclair, Camille, 248
Maugham, Beldy, 156
Maugham, C.O., 159
Maugham, Charles, 162
Maugham, Cynthia, 155

Maugham, Diana, 155
Maugham, Elizabeth Mary Somerset, 159, 162
Maugham, Frederic Herbert, 1st Viscount, 156, 160, 161, 162
Maugham, George R., 158
Maugham, George, 158
Maugham, Helen Mary, Viscountess, 161, 162
Maugham, Henry Macdonald, 162
Maugham, Henry Neville, 156, 160, 162
Maugham, John, 156, 157
Maugham, Robert, 156, 158, 160, 161, 162
Maugham, Robert Ormond, 156, 161
Maugham, Robin, *155–62*
Maugham, Sophie (Barbara Sophia von Scheidlin), 162
Maugham, Syrie, 162
Maugham, Theophilus (Thomas Reid), 157, 158
Maugham, Thomas, 159
Maugham, W. Somerset, 155, 156, 159, 160, 161, *162*
Maugham, William, 155, 156, 157, 158, 162
Maugham, William Farringdon, 157
Maulnier, Thierry, 44
Maupassant, Guy de, *163*
Maurel, Victor, 147, 296
Maurois, André, 41, 42
Mautner, E., 190
Mavrocordato, prince, 289
Max, Adolphe, 30
Maximilian, Emperor of Mexico, 26, *163–65*
Mayer, Mr., 206
Mayer, Sir Robert, 318, 319
McClure, S.S., 106
McEwen, W.D.H., 290
McKenna, Rollie, 171
McLernon, Harold, 259
M'Crie, Thomas, 290
Mead, Philip J., 116
Mecklenburg-Strelitz, Karl, Duke of (formerly Prince of Miran), 73
Medini, Paolo, 300
Mee, Arthur, 160
Meegeren, Han van, 32
Meerti, Elise, 168
Meilhac (collector), 302
Meilhac, Henri, 16, 185, 195
Mendelssohn, Fanny (Hensel), 168
Mendelssohn, H.S. (photographer), 162

Mendelssohn-Bartholdy, Cécile, 168
Mendelssohn-Bartholdy, Felix, *165–68*
Mendès, Catulle, 25, 30, 31, 87, 88, 89
Menotti, Gian Carlo, *168*
Menuhin, Yehudi, 110
Mercereau, M., 261
Méreaux, Amédée, 98
Meredith, George, 105
Meredith, William, 169, 170, 171
Mérimée, Prosper, *172*, 281
Mérode, Cléo de, 83, 89
Merrill, Helen (Plummer), 170
Merrill, James, *169–71*
Merrrill, Charles E., 170
Méry, Joseph, 72, 189
Meser, C.F. (publisher), 307
Messager, André, 67, 87, 88, 89, 110, *172*, 221
Metastasio, Pietro, 281
Methuen & Co. Ltd, 174
Meunier, Charles, 261
Meurice, Paul, 98, 99, 100
Meurice, Mme Paul, 97, 98
Meyerbeer, Giacomo, 133, *172*, 277, 294, 298, 299, 303, 306, 324, 325
Meyer-Merian, Theodor, 131
Mezzaros, General, 98
Miaoulis, Antonio, 289
Michel, Marius, 176
Mignan, Édouard, 249
Mignano, Hortense Nunziante di, 257
Mignon, M., 208
Milford, Sir Humphrey, 160
Milhaud, Darius, 4, 31, 33, 43, 96, *172–73*, 216, 217, 218, 244, 249, 274
Millaud, Albert, 192
Millen, W.S., 291
Miller, Henry, *173–74*
Millerand, Alexandre, 265
Millevoye, Charles Hubert, 61
Milman, Henry Hart, 287
Milne, A.A. (Alan Alexander), *174–75*, 277, 278
Miran, Prince of, *see* Mecklenburg-Strelitz
Mirbeau, Octave, 85, 154
Missiano, Edoardo, 239
Mistral, Frédéric, 52
Mitterwurzer, Anton, 306
Mizner, Addison, 136
Mizner, Wilson, 136, 137
M'Lehose, Agnes, 24
Mocenigo, Nani, conte, 298
Moineaux, Jules, 191

Molière, 32, 78, 79, 208, 216, 329
Molstad, Perry, 95
Monneth, D., 289
Monod, M., 219
Montagu, Sir Charles Thomas Montagu-Douglas-Scott, 327
Montagu, Mary, 327
Montaigne, Michel de, 37
Montallegre, marquis de, 73
Montebello, marquise de, 137
Montebello, Napoléon Lannes, duc de, 137
Montebello, Roger, comte de, 52
Montesquiou-Fesenzac, Robert de, 70, 88, *176*, 221, 227, 229, 230
Monteux, Pierre, 267, 286
Monteverdi, Claudio, 216
Montijo, Maria Manuela Kirkpatrick, condesa de, *176*
Montt Torres, Manuel, 165
Moore, Thomas, 115
Morand, Paul, 4, 43
Morandi, Rodolfo, 234
Mordaunt, Elinor, 161
Moréas, Jean, 84, 85, 256, 302
Moreau, Gustave, 85
Moret, Ernest, 87, 88
Morgan, Ike, 108
Morgan, John, 290
Morgan, Louise, 159
Morgan, W., 108
Morice, Charles, 302
Morichini, 238
Morihien, Paul, 75
Mörike, Eduard Friedrich, 327
Morize, André, 56
Morlacchi, Francesco, *176*
Mornand, Louisa de, 227
Morny, Charles, duc de, 203
Morris, Charles, 322
Morris, William, 19, 23, 24
Morrow, George, *176*
Mortier, Pierre, 39
Mosattini, Guido, 234
Moscheles, Ignaz, 27, 167, *177*, 260
Moszkowski, Moritz, 252
Mottl, Felix, 110
Mouret, Gabriel, 58, 227
Mozart, Wolfgang Amadeus, Plate 3, 86, 88, 111, *177*, 269, 281, 306
Mugnone, Leopoldo, 235, 239
Müller & Pilgram (photographers), 288
Munch, Charles, 59

Munro, C.K. (Charles Kirkpatrick), 210
Muratore, Lucien, 51
Murray, Mae, 325
Musset, Alfred de, 54, 98, 123, 190
Musset, Paul de, 190
Mussorgsky, Modest Petrovich, 243, 248, 250
Mustel Père et Fils (firm), 138
Myers, Rollo, 113, *177–80*, 274

Nadar (photographic studio), 52, 98
Nahmias, Albert, 227, 228
Najac, Émile de, 3
Napoléon I, Emperor of the French, 208, 209, 289
Napoléon III, Emperor of the French, 77, 172, *181–83*
Natanson, Bolette, 33
Negri, Ada, 256
Neipperg, Leopold Johann Nepomuk, Graf von, 292
Nessi, Angelo, 124, 125
Neuburger, Pauline, 228
Neveux, Pol, 230
Newell, J.P., 159
Newmarsh, Rosa, 8
Nicholl, A., 289, 290, 291
Nichols, Grace, 106
Nicholson, Kenyon, 210
Nietzsche, Friedrich, 222
Nijinska, Bronislava, 213
Nijinsky, Vaslav, 43, 54
Nikisch, Arthur, 110
Niniteh, Mila, 40
Nino, 262
Niola, Emilia Tibaldi, 25
Niola, Raffaele, 25
Noailles, Anna Élisabeth de Brancovan, comtesse de, 33
Noailles, Marie-Laure de, 40
Noel, Georges, 32
Noël, Maurice, 51
Nomellini, Plinio, 235
Noriac, Jules, 185
North, Frederick, Earl of Guilford, 289
Northbrook, Thomas George Baring, Earl of, 120
Nouveau, Germain, 302
Novello and Co. (firm), 65
Novello, Clara, 165
Novello, J. Alfred, 168
Nowak, Leopold, 285

Nuitter, Charles, 184, 190, 194, 196, 298
Nussy-Saint-Saëns, Valentine, 266
Nyssen, Georg von, 177

Obouhov, Nicolas, 250
O'Connor, Arthur, 289
Odets, Clifford, 210
Odry, Jacques, 258, 291, 302
Offenbach, Herminie (d'Alcain), 197, 200, 207
Offenbach, Jacques, Plate 13, *184–207*, 332
Offenbach, Pepita, 206
Olczewska, Maria, 284
Olivier, Laurence, 312, 313
O'Marr, Elizabeth, 210
Omeis, Magnus Daniel, 4
O'Neill, Eugene, *207*, 210
O'Neill, Eugene Jr., 207
Opitz, Martin, 4
Orfer, Léo d', 301
Orléans, Pierre d', duc de Penthièvre, 228
Ors, Eugenio d', 42
Orsolini, Giuseppina, 296
O'Shaughnessy, Arthur, 66
Osmont, Charles Blanchot d', 26
Oswald, Marianne, 31

Pacini, Giovanni, *208*, 298
Paderewski, Ignace Jan, 110
Paër, Ferdinando, *208–9*
Paget, Violet, 105
Paisiello, Giovanni, 94, 252
Palestrina, Giovanni Pierluigi da, 58
Paley, Natalie, 41, 135
Palissot de Fontenoy, Charles, 404
Palma, Alerino, conte, 289
Panattoni, Carlo, 298
Pancrazi, Pietro, 235
Panichelli, Pietro, 234
Pantaleoni (singer), 212
Paradol, Lucinde, 91
Paravicini, Vincent Rudolph, 159
Paray, Paul, 249
Parker, Max, 259
Parny, Renée, *209*
Parrish, Maxfield, 102
Pasdeloup, Jules, 152
Pasquini, Bernardo, 251
Passerieu, François-Henri-Alexandre, 54

[360] INDEX

Passus, Mme Henri de, 63
Pastré, Céline (de Beaulaincourt), comtesse, 215
Pater, Walter, *209*
Patu, Claude-Pierre, 404
Paul (photographer), 179
Paulhan, Jean, 42
Pausinger, Joseph von, 262
Pauvert, Jean-Jacques, 75
Payn, Graham, 47
Payne, Mr. and Mrs., 106
Pea, Enrico, 235
Pecchio, Giuseppe, 289
Peel, Derek, 156
Peillard, Léonce, 40, *211*
Pellis, J.N. (photographer), 145
Penno, Gino, 218
Pepe, Gabriele, 289
Percy, Susan, Lady, 120
Péret, Benjamin, 44
Pergolesi, Giovanni Battista, *209*
Périer, Jean, 59, 86, *209*
Perlman, William J., *209–11*
Perosi, Lorenzo, 110
Perrault, Charles, 329, 330
Perrin, Émile, 263, 294
Perrin, Germaine, 280, 281
Perrocchi, Luigi, 126
Persse, Jocelyn Dudley, 106
Perucchini, Giovanni Battista, 259
Peruzzi, Edith Marion (Story), Countess, 106, 107
Peter, René, 139, 228
Petit, Alphonse, 97
Petit, Pierre, 97
Petrakis, Anargyros, 289
Petri, Herr, 78
Peyrefitte, Roger, 40, *211*
Pezzè-Pascolato, Maria, 329
Pforzheimer, Carl H., 174, 278
Piave, Francesco Maria, 208, 212, 213, 293, 296, 298, 299, 300
Picabia, Francis, 34
Picabia, Germaine Everling, 34, 40
Picasso, Jacqueline, 39
Picasso, Pablo, 37, 38, 39, 41, 67, 179, 273
Piccini, Niccolò, 94
Piccolo, Professor, 289
Pickering and Chatto (firm), 116
Pierattini, Achille, 126
Pierce, Hubbell, 171
Pierné, Gabriel, 110
Pillet, Léon, 296

Pindar, 289
Pinelli, Aldo von, 282
Pini, Argia, 256, 257
Pini-Corsi, Antonio, 239
Pinker, James B., 107, 108
Piper, John, 309
Piroli, I., 295
Pistolesi, P., 234
Pittaud-Deforges, Philippe Auguste, 206
Pius IX, Pope, 295
Pius X, Pope, 130
Pixis, Johann Peter, 27
Pizzetti, Ildebrando, *211*, 217, 255
Pizzolato, Giuseppe, 328, 331
Platen-Hallermund, Julius, Graf von, 307
Plato, 102
Plessis, Alphonsine, *see* Duplessis
Pleyel, Camille, 272
Plon, 97
Plummer, Peter, 94
Po-Chu-Yi, *see* Bai, Juyi
Poe, Edgar Allan, 272
Pohl, Richard, 14
Poliakovich, 165
Polignac, Marie-Blanche, comtesse de, 214
Polignac, Pierre, comte de, 229
Polignac, Winnaretta, princesse de, 39
Pollet (engraver), 97
Pollock, Channing, 210
Pollock, John, 108
Polo, Marco, 102
Ponchielli, Amilcare, *211–12*, 295, 296
Ponchon, Raoul, 301
Poniatowski, André, 58
Pont, baron du, 164
Poole, John, 290
Popesco, Elvire, 42
Porché, François, 37
Porel, Jacques, 228
Porro, Count, 289
Porter, Anna Maria, 290
Porter, Jane, 290, 291
Portman Christiaan Julius Lodewyck, 72
Potier, 91
Potpeschnigg, Heinrich, 328
Potter, Beatrix, *213*
Potter, Paul, 89
Poujaud, Paul, 53
Poulenc, Francis, Plate 20, 33, 38, 44, 96, 178, 179, *213–19*, 273, 274
Poulet-Malassis, Auguste, 9
Pourrat, Henri, 37

Pourtalès, Louise-Sophie-Mélanie (de Bussière), comtesse de, 221
Powers, T., 108
Poyser, Arthur T., 77
Praeger, Ferdinand, 14
Prassinou, Miss (singer), 173
Prévert, Jacques, 44
Prévost-Paradol, Anatole, 16, 91
Price, Cormell, Plate 10, 21–23
Prince impérial, *see* Eugène-Louis-Napoléon
Pringle, Thomas, 290
Printemps, Yvonne, 81, 216
Proctor, Bryan Waller, 290
Prodhomme, J.-G. (Jacques-Gabriel), 265
Prözl, Robert, 307
Prokofiev, Sergei, 8, 110
Proust, Jeanne (Mme Adrien), Plate 17, 59, 223, 229
Proust, Marcel, Plate 17, 4, 35, 37, 77, 86, 87, 88, 89, 171, *219–31*, 258, 271
Proust, Mme Robert, 271
Prunières, Henry, 62
Psalidas, Athanasios, 289
Puccini, Antonio, 234
Puccini, Elvira, 233, 234, 238
Puccini, Fosca, 234
Puccini, Giacomo, Plate 21, 110, 129, 130, 139, 144, 145, *231–39*, 295
Pugno, Raoul, 110
Pushkin, Aleksandr Sergeevich, 127

Quadren, Obristleutnant von, 73
Quaglia, Angelo, Cardinal, 140
Quaritch, Bernard (firm), 116
Quevedo, Francisco de, 272
Quinn, John, 10
Quittard, Henri, 272

Rabaud, Henri, 70, 250
Rabaut-Pomier, Jacques-Antoine, 71
Rachmaninoff, Sergei, 110
Racine, Jean, 98
Rackham, Arthur, *240*
Radiguet, Guy, 241
Radiguet, Raymond, 4, 35, 36, 38, 41, 42, 43, 44, 96, 215, 216, *240–41*, 273, 274
Radonetz, Eduard von, 164, 165
Raff, Joachim, 132
Raffet, Denis Auguste Marie, 71
Ramuz, C. F. (Charles Ferdinand), 286

Raphaelson, Samson, 210
Raunay, Jeanne, 70
Raveau, Alice, 270
Ravel, Maurice, 57, 62, 67, 68, 110, 178, 180, 216, 218, 219, *241–50*
Raven-Hill, Leonard, *250*
Raverat, Gwen, 293
Rawnsley, Willingham Franklin, 161
Ray, Man, 37
Raybould, Clarence, 8
Read, William, 290
Reber, Henri, 241, 303
Reed, William Henry, 66
Reggio, Eugénie Oudinot, duchesse de, 97
Régnier, Henri de, 139
Régnier, Marie de (Gérard d'Houville), 139
Régnier, Pierre de, 139
Rehberg, Willy, 70
Rehbinder, Wladimir, 52
Reichenbach, Franz, 184
Reid, Farringdon, 158
Reinboth, Johann, 4
Reinecke, Carl, 133, 276, 288
Reinhardt, Max, 210
Reiss, Albert, 239
Réjane, Gabrielle Charlotte Réju, called, 228
Rembrandt Harmenszoon van Rijn, 238
Renard, Jules, 180
Renaud, Émile, Plate 19, 267, 268
Renaudin, Pierre, 179
Rensellaer, Killian van, 102
Renshaw, Miss, 120
Reschiglian, Vincenzo, 239
Respighi, Elsa, 255
Respighi, Ottorino, *250–57*
Rességuier, Rudolf, Count, 26
Reszke, Édouard de, 147
Reszke, Jean de, 147, 300
Reyer, Ernest, 172, 300
Reynolds, R., 115
Rheineck, Freiherr von, 289
Ricci, Federico, 294, 298
Ricciotti Baccelli, G., 234
Rice, Elmer, 210
Richards, Grant, 95
Richardson, D.S., 290
Richardson, Samuel, 21
Richepin, Jean, 52
Richman, Arthur, 210
Richter, Hans, 307
Ricordi (firm), 129

Ricordi, Giulio, 212, 236, 300
Ricordi, Tito, 236, 295, 299, 300
Ridgewey, *257*
Riedel, Carl, 307
Riedel, Dr., 164, 165
Rimbaud, Arthur, 34, 36, *257–58*, 301, 302, 303
Rimsky-Korsakoff, Nikolay Andreyevich, 252, 253, 286, 288
Risler, Édouard, 88
Ristelhueber, Boulos, 37
Ritter, Alexander, 305
Ritter, Carl, 305
Rivas, Angel de Saavedra, duque de, 294
Rivollet, Georges, 149
Robecq, Anne-Marie de Luxembourg, princesse de, 404
Robert, Louis de, 230, 231, *258*
Roberts, David, 288
Roberts, Emma, 290
Robertson, A.M. (publisher), 282
Robertson, Graham, 5, 7
Robertson, Hugh S., 8
Robin, Louis, 50, 51, 52
Robins, Elizabeth, 105, 107
Robins, Raymond, 107
Rocchi, Francesco, 257
Roche, Emilie, 177
Roche, H., 289
Rodd, Francis James Rennell, Baron, 25, 130
Rodrigues, Mme Charles, 91
Roger-Ducasse, 70
Rogerson, Christina, 106
Roland-Manuel, 68, 214, 219, 241, 249, 273, 274
Rolfe, Frederick, Baron Corvo, *258–59*
Rolland, Romain, 113
Romani, Felice, 176
Romberg, Sigmund, *259*
Romieu, Émilie, 44
Romieu, Georges, 44
Ronsard, Pierre de, 305
Rooman, Fernand, 51
Rops, Félicien, 9, *259*, 291
Roqueplan, 277
Roques, A., 196
Roques, Léon, 58, 59
Roscoe, Thomas, 290
Roscoe, William, 290
Rosenbach, A.S.W. (Abraham Simon Wolf), 278
Rosenthal, Dr., 163
Roset, René, 98

Rosny, J.-H., 228
Ross, Robert Baldwin, 326
Rossato, Arturo, 145
Rossellini, Roberto, 218
Rossetti, Anna, 333
Rossetti, Christina Georgina, 272
Rossetti, Tilde, 333
Rossetti, William Michael, 325
Rossi, Giulio, 239
Rossi, Lorenzo, 145
Rossini, Gioachino, 145, *259–61*, 281, 294, 298, 340, 341
Rosslyn, Francis Robert St. Clair-Erskine, 4th Earl of, 107
Rostand, Claude, 217
Rostand, Edmond, 76, 139, 209, *261*
Rostand, Maurice, *261*
Rothschild (bank), 293
Rothschild, Baroness [James?] de, 141
Rouché, Jacques, 248, 266
Roujon, Henry, 268
Roulleau (typesetter), 76
Roussel, Albert, 110, 180, *261–62*
Rousset, David, 44
Rowlandson, Thomas, 316
Roy, Émile, 9
Royer, Alphonse, 298, 300
Rozières, Marie de, 221
Rubino, Antonio, 256
Rubinstein, Anton, 18, *262*
Rubinstein, Artur, 218
Rubinstein, Ida, 249
Rudolf, Crown Prince of Austria, *262*
Rückert, Friedrich, 276
Ruffo, Tita, 239
Ruolz-Fontenay, Henri de, 208
Ruskin, John, 222
Russell, George William ("A.E."), 8
Russell, J., & Sons (photographer), 161
Rydberg, Viktor, 279
Rysanek, Leonie, 218

Sachs, Augusta, 275
Sachs, Maurice, 37, 42, *263*
Saint-Allais (collector), 76
Saint-Aubin, Augustin de, 191
Saint-Chaffray, M. de, 269
Saint-Georges, Henri Vernoy de, 90, 91, 92, 189, 198, 202, *263*
Saint-Jean, Robert de, 40
Saint-Saëns, Camille, Plate 19, 80, 87, 88, 110, 114, 133, *263–72*
Sainte-Barbe, Édouard, 97

Salabert (publisher), 214, 242
Salacrou, Armand, 44, 216
Samaras, Spyros, 129
Samazeuilh, Gustave, 61, 62, 246, 249
Sampieri, Francesco, marchese, 133, 141, 260
Sand, George, 27, *272*, 303
Sanderson, Sybil, 154, 266
Santa Rosa, Santorre, 289
Sapelnikov, Vasilii, 288
Sarasate, Pablo de, 110, 114, 269
Sardou, Victorien, 81, 194, 207, 236, *272*
Sargent, Sir Malcolm, 314
Sarti, Giuseppe, 94
Sartre, Jean-Paul, 40, 44, 75
Sassoon, Siegfried, *272*
Satie, Erik, 4, 33, 36, 41, 44, 96, 177, 178, 179, 180, 216, 244, 247, *273–74*
Saubert, Johann, 4
Saudemont, André, 76
Sauer, Emil, 110
Sauguet, Henri, 214, 216, *274*
Saumoneau, M. (typesetter), 222
Sawyer, Lyddell, 161
Saxe, Maurice, comte de, 202
Saxe-Coburg and Gotha, Alfred, Duke of, 112
Sayn-Wittgenstein, Carolyne de, 307
Scanlon, Claude, 160
Scanlon, Lois, 160
"Scar" (artist), 108
Scheffel, Joseph Viktor von, 327
Scheffer, Ary, 303
Scheikévitch, Marie, 228
Scherbarth, Karl, 307
Scherchen, Hermann, 113
Schiller, Friedrich, 142, 333
Schiller, Justin, 116
Schillings, Max von, 110
Schjedelrup, Gerhard, 81
Schlesinger (publisher), 132
Schlesinger, Ernst, 284, 285
Schloss, Sophie, 207
Schmidt, Heinrich, 276
Schmitt, Florent, 110, 244, 247
Schmöll, Otto, 276
Schnabel, Artur, 56
Schneditz, Wolfgang, 284
Schnitzler, Arthur, 210
Schoenberg, Arnold, 244, 248
Schöpff, Friedrich Wilhelm, 276
Schott (publisher), 318
Schubert, Franz, Plate 4, *274–75*, 303
Schütz, Heinrich, Plate 1, 4

Schumann, Clara, *275*, 276
Schumann, Elisabeth, *275*, 283
Schumann, Ferdinand, 275
Schumann, Marie, *276*
Schumann, Robert, 133, 275, *276*, 306, 307
Schwartz, 92
Schwarzenbach, Mathilde, 337, 338
Scott, J.R.U., 8
Scott, Sir Walter, 24, 278, 289
Scotti, Antonio, 239
Scotti, Vittorio, 251
Scribe, Eugène, 91, 172, *277*
Scriggi, Tommaso, 289
Searle, Alan, 155, 162
Seery, Irving, 283
Segalen, Éliette, 180
Segalen, Victor, 180
Seligman, Sybil, 235
Sella, Quintino, 295
Selwyn, Edgar, 210
Sem, 51
Senard, Jean, 51
Senart (publisher), 131
Seneca, 289
Senterre, Mme, 272
Serres, Caroline de, 269
Sert, José Maria, 41, 286
Sert, Misia, 40, 68, 213, 218, 228, 250, 274, 286
Servais, Marcel, 41
Servières, J., *see* Halévy, Ludovic
Setzer (photographer), 285
Seurre, 92
Séverac, Déodat de, 178, 247
Sezzi, Carissio, 300
Sgambati, Giovanni, 296
Shakespeare, William, 13, 34, 211, 288, 290, 310, 311, 312, 313, 318, 331
Sharp, William, *see* Macleod, Fiona
Shaw, Geoffrey, 8
Shaw, George Bernard, *277*
Shaw, Irwin, 210
Shelley, Percy Bysshe, 255, 272
Shepard, Ernest H., 175, *277–78*
Shepperson, Claude Allin, *278–79*
Sherwood, Roy Edward, 210
Shields, 23
Shirley, Canon, 159
Shore, Mrs. (Robinson), 60
Sibelius, Jean, 8, 110, *279*
Sidmouth, Henry Addington, Viscount, 130
Sidner, Esther, 56

Siegel, Fritz, 283
Silas, Edouard, 14, 269
Silcher, Friedrich, 332
Silvain, Marcel, 71
Silvers, Louis, 259
Silvestre de Sacy, Antoine Isaac, 150
Silvestre, Armand, 63, 271
Simon and Schuster (firm), 137
Simon, Charles, 127
Simoni, Renato, 235
Simonson, Raoul, 291, 302
Simrock (firm), 168
Simrock, Nicolaus, 325
Sims, G.F., 95
Sinding, Christian, 81
Siraudin, Paul, 200
Sitwell, Dame Edith, *280*, 320, 321
Sitwell, Georgia, *280*
Sitwell, Sir Osbert, *280*, 323
Sitwell, Sacheverell, 15
Slezak, Leo, 284, 285
Slezak, Walter, 282, 288
Smalley, George, 107
Smithers, Leonard C., 327
Smyth, Miss, 288
Snell, Anna Alicia, 156, 159, 161, 162
Snell, Edith Mary, 156, 162
Snell, Rose Ellen, 162
Snow, Norman, 210
Soffredini, Alfredo, 143, 300
Solazzi, Ugo, 342
Solera, Temistocle, 297, 298
Sombasi, Giacomachi, 290
Somerset, Sir Henry, 162
Sonzogno (publisher), 77, 129, 144
Sophocles, 8, 44, 94, 166, 289
Sousa, John Philip, 110
Southey, Robert, 288
Souvestre, Marie, 107
Souzay, Gérard, 217
Speck, J., 239
Spendiaryan, Aleksandr Afanasy, 253
Spenser, Edmund, 309
Spezia, Maria, 299
Spohr, Louis, 307
Spontini, Gaspare, 14
Sprigge, Elizabeth, 38
Squibb, George, 180
Staël, Madame de (Anne-Louise-Germaine), 298
Stanfield, Clarkson, 288, 289, 290, 291
Stanhope, Leicester Fitzgerald Charles, 5th Earl of Harrington, 289
Stearn (photographer), 161

INDEX [363]

Stein, M., 108
Steinlen, Théophile Alexandre, 163, *280–81*
Stendhal (pseudonym of Henri Beyle), 24, 66, 176, *281*
Stephen, James Fitzjames, 107
Stephen, Lady, 107
Stephen, Thoby, 107
Sterling, George, *281–82*
Stewart, Donald Ogden, 211
Stignani, Ebe, 218
Stimson, Mrs., 107
Stock (publisher), 37
Stock, F.A., 316
Stoeckhardt, Kommissär, 73
Stolz, Robert, *282*
Stolz, Teresa, 101
Storchio, Rosina, 239
Story, William Wetmore, 107, 120
Story, Mrs. William, 120
Strachey, Lytton, 107
Straus, Geneviève, 228, 229, 230
Straus, Oscar, *282*
Strauss, Alice, *282–83*
Strauss, Franz, *282–83*, 284
Strauss, Johann, *283*
Strauss, Pauline, 283
Strauss, Richard, 43, 81, 95, 110, 138, 266, 275, 282, *283–85*
Stravinsky, Igor, 38, 41, 57, 67, 110, 216, 218, 219, 244, 247, 249, 254, 282, *285–86*, 323
Strong, Austin, 211
Strudwick, Ethel, 8
Stubbins, G.M., *159*
Sturgis, Julian, 287
Sturgis, Mrs. Julian, 107
Stuyvesant, Peter, 103
Sugana, Luigi, 328, 330, 331
Sullivan, Sir Arthur, *286–87*
Sully Prudhomme, 257
Sussex, Augustus Frederick, Duke of, 111, 160
Sutherland, Cromartie Sutherland-Leveson-Gower, 4th Duke of, 107
Sutherland, Millicent, 4th Duchess of, 107
Sutton, Mrs. Gurney, 120
Suzannet, Alain, comte de, 76, 261
Suzzo, Michel, 289
Svendsen, Johan Severin, 81
Sweet, S.W., 160
Swinburne, Algernon Charles, 320, 321, 322

Symons, Arthur, *287*
Szell, George, 316
Szymanowski, Karol, 244

Taeuntzien, General von, 73
Taglioni, Marie, 202
Tagore, Rabindranath, 251, 255
Tailhade, Laurent, 30
Tailleferre, Germaine, 33, 42, 214, 249
Tajan (singer), 196
Tamagno, Francesco, 235, 300
Tamagno, Margherita, 300
Tamberlick, Enrico, 299
Taras, John, 309
Targioni-Tozzetti, Antonio, 289
Targioni-Tozzetti, Giovanni, 142
Tattersall, E. Somerville, 65
Tausky, Vilem, 310
Taylor, A.E. (artist), 175
Taylor, Deems, *288*
Tchaikovsky, Peter Ilich, 18, 145, 222, 253, *288*
Tebaldi, Renata, 218
Tedeschi, A. (publisher), 129
Teleki, Sandor, 99
Télin, Robert, 35
Tennant, Stephen, 272, 316, 325, 326
Tennent, Eleanor Emerson, 291
Tennent, Sir James Emerson, *288–91*
Tennent, Lady, 288
Tennent, Robert James, 289
Tennyson, Alfred Tennyson, Baron, 65, 120
Tennyson, Emily, 120
Tennyson, Lionel, 120
Tessier, Valentine, 41
Testa, Silla Pierattini, 126
Thackeray, William Makepeace, 120, 290
Tharaud, Jérôme, 209
Thaw, Harry K., 108
Thibaud, Jacques, 110
Thomas, Albert, 96
Thomas, Ambroise, 57, 110
Thomas, Augustus, 211
Tichatschek, Joseph, 306, 307, 308
Tiénot, Yvonne, 178
Tighe, Mary, 289
Tinan, Jean de, 139, *291*
Torrese, Guido, 234
Toscanini, Arturo, 55, 110, 216, 239, 244, 255, 295, 296, 297, 298, 299, 300, 305
Toulet, Paul-Jean, 62
Tovey, Francis Donald, 8

Towne, Charles Hanson, 162
Tree, Sir Herbert Beerbohm, *291*
Tréfeu, Étienne, 190, 191, 196, 207
Trélat, Marie, 269
Tremelli, Mlle (singer), 147
Trikoupes, Spyridon, 289
Trinius, Wilhelm, 305
Trollope, Anthony, 108
Tronche, Gustave, 228
Tropmann, Jean-Baptiste, 182
Troutbeck, J., 80
Trower, Mrs., 107
Trubetskoi, Pavel Petrovich, 235
Trueba y Cosío, Joaquín Telesforo de, 290
Trulet, C., 125, 126
Tuckerman, Miss, 107
Turina, Giuditta, 12
Turina, Joaquín, 67, 68, *292*
Turpin, Alice, 41, 42, 60
Twain, Mark, 178
Tyrconell, William Talbot, 5th Baronet of Carton, "3rd Earl of," 74

Uhland, Ludwig, 333
Umberto I, King of Italy, 26
Underhill, F.T., 120
Unger, Georg, 307
Updike, Daniel B., 102
Urwin, Frank (photographer), 104

Vacquerie, Auguste, 98, 99, 100, 269
Vacquerie, Mme, 100
Valéry, Paul, 57, 140, 178
Vallas, Léon, 56
Vallette, Alfred, 42, 139
Vallin, Ninon, 244
Van de Welde, W., 289
Van Dyck, Sir Anthony, 89
Van Trees, James C., 259
Vander Poel, Halsted B., 312
Vandérem, Fernand, 228
Vandini, Alfredo, 235, 236, 237, 238, 239
Vanier, Léon, 302
Vansittart, Nicholas, 130
Varèse, Edgar, 41
Vaselli, 297
Vasnier, Marie-Blanche, 54, 55
Vaucaire, Maurice, 125, 239
Vaucaire, René, 55
Vaucorbeil, Auguste Emmanuel, 114
Vaudin, J.F., 13

Vaudoyer, Georges, 84
Vaudoyer, Jean-Louis, 228
Vaughan Williams, Ralph, *293*
Vederkop, 37
Vega, Lope de, 329
Ventura Rivera, Don, 163
Venturini, G. (publishers), 123, 125, 126
Venturini, V., 256
Verdi, Carlo, 294
Verdi, Giuseppe, Plate 7, 101, 110, 212, 239, 268, 272, *293–300*
Verdi, Giuseppina, 297, 299, 300
Vergnet, Edmond, 147
Verkenius, E.H.W., 166
Verlaine, Paul, Plate 11, 8, 53, 54, 55, 83, 84, 241, 242, 247, 258, 272, *301–3*
Vermeer, Jan, 32
Vianello, Erminia, 333
Viardot, Pauline, 87, 154, 272, *303*
Victoria, Tomás Luis de, 58
Vidal, Paul, 54, 110
Vidor, Charles, 112
Vieuille, Félix, 59, *303*
Villa-Lobos, Heitor, *303*
Villemessant, Jean Hippolyte Auguste Delaunay de, 77
Vilmorin, Louise de, 41
Vincent-Vallette, Mme Paul, 214
Vinès, Ricardo, 67, 219, 242
Vittoré, Mme, 228
Vivanti, Annie, 250
Vix, Geneviève, 51, 131
Vogel, Johannes, 4
Vollgruber, Aloïs, 132
Volta, Ornella, 179
Voltaire, 74, *304*
Vuillard, Édouard, 36
Vuillermoz, Émile, 57, 58, 249

Wachtl (photographer), 285
Wade, Allan, 108
Wade, Joseph Augustine, 290
Wagner, Cosima, 130, 308
Wagner, Franzisca, 305
Wagner, Johanna, 305
Wagner, Richard, Plate 9, 62, 81, 85, 110, 133, 140, 221, 222, 284, 294, *305–8*, 336, 340
Wagner, Siegfried, 110
Waléry (photographer), 62
Walford, Mrs., 108
Walker, Gertrude, 66
Wallington, E.W., 271

Walpole, Sir Hugh, 308
Walter, Bruno, 111
Walton, Elizabeth, 323
Walton, Michael, 323
Walton, Susana, 309
Walton, Sir William, 280, *308–24*
Ward, Mrs. Humphry, 106
Ward, Mrs. Richard, 121
Warden, David Baillie, 289
Warner, Philip Lee, 95
Warner, Sydney, 160
Wassermann, Jakob, 211
Watanabe, Kajiro, 8
Waterlow, Sydney, 108
Waters, Edward N., 90
Wateville, Mme de, 247
Watteau, Antoine, 89
Watts, Alaric Alexander, 290
Waugh, Evelyn, *324*
Webb, Clifton, 135
Webbe, John, 157
Weber, Carl Maria von, 14, 131, 133, 306, *324–25*
Weber, Gottfried
Weber, Johannès, 295
Wecker, Karl Friedrich, 276
Wehner, Rudolf, 305
Weidig, F., 141
Weil, Anne, 88
Weil, Mme Nathé, 228
Weiman, Rita, 211
Weingartner, Felix, 65, 111
Weiss, Fritz, 305
Welch, Henry, 180
Welch, Mrs. Henry (Thornton), 180
Weldon, Giorgina, 78
Wharton, Edith, 106
Whistler, James McNeill, *325*
Whistler, Rex, 317, *325–26*
White, Stanford, 108
Whiteside, J., 289
Wicard, Charles-Marie, 91
Widor, Charles-Marie, 111, *326*
Wiffen, Jeremiah Holmes, 290
Wigand, 73
Wilde, Oscar, 24, 48, 60, 76, 209, *326–27*
Wilde, Percival, 211
Wilder, Victor, 172
Wilhelm I, Emperor of Germany, *327*
Wilhelm II, Emperor of Germany, *327*
Willemetz, Albert, 42
Willett, Laura, 117
Williams, C.D., 108
Williams, Horace, 8

Williams, Jesse Lynch, 211
Willy, 250
Wilson, John (poet), 288
Wilson, John (printer), 102
Wilson, Mr., 95
Wilson, Ransom, 214
Winterfeld, Major General von, 73
Winters, Owen D., 174
Wister, Sarah Butler, 108
Wittgenstein, Ludwig, 323
Wobersnow, Commander von, 74
Wolf, Hugo, *327–28*
Wolf-Ferrari, Ermanno, 300, *328–42*
Wolf-Ferrari, Wilhelmine, 342
Wolff, Hermann, 271
Wolzogen, Alfred von, 193, 194, 206, 207
Wood, Sir Henry Joseph, 8
Wordsworth, William, 288, 290, 322
Woznicki, Casimir de, 163
Wright, Kenneth A., 101
Wright, Waller Rodwell, 289
Wyatt, Digby, 121
Wyatt, Susan, Lady, 121
Wyle, Thomas, 290

Yarde, Dorothy, 159
Yéméniz, N., 76
Young, Filson, 8
Ysaÿe, Eugène, 111, 267
Yturri, Gabriel de, 229

Zaehnsdorf, 287
Zandonai, Riccardo, 239, 254, *343*
Zandt, Marie van, 85
Zanetti, C.F., 256
Zangarini, Carlo, 239, 256, 257, 330
Zemlinsky, Alexander, *343*
Zenatello, Giovanni, 232
Zimmermann, Clemens von, 140
Zimmermann, Mme Pierre-Joseph-Guillaume, 303
Zola, Émile, 292

*This catalogue was composed in Fournier,
a typeface reproduced from a specimen of types originally
engraved before 1742 by Pierre Simon Fournier le jeune.
The digital version used here is based upon a recutting
produced in 1925 by The Monotype Corporation.*

❈

PRINTED BY THAMES PRINTING COMPANY,
NORWICH, CONNECTICUT

BOUND BY ACME BOOKBINDING COMPANY,
CHARLESTOWN, MASSACHUSETTS

DESIGN & TYPOGRAPHY BY HOWARD I. GRALLA